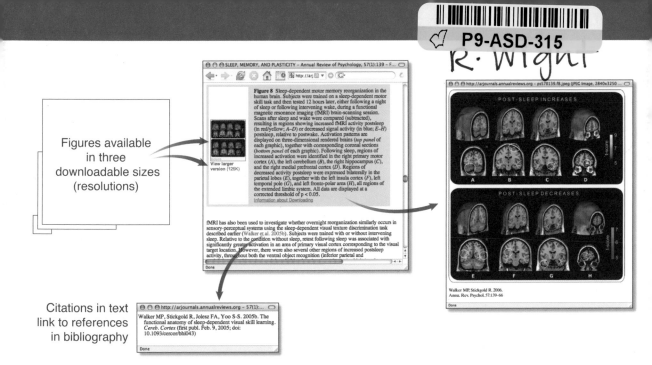

Figures available in three downloadable sizes (resolutions)

Citations in text link to references in bibliography

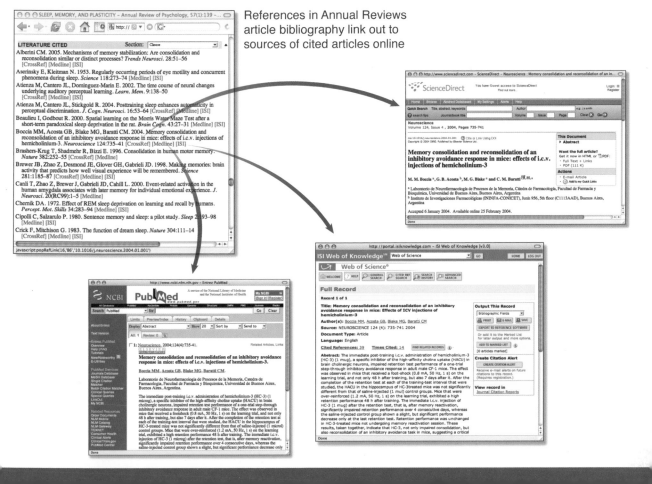

References in Annual Reviews article bibliography link out to sources of cited articles online

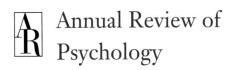

Annual Review of
Psychology

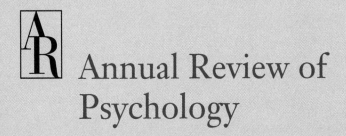

Annual Review of Psychology

Volume 60, 2009

Susan T. Fiske, *Editor*
Princeton University

Daniel L. Schacter, *Associate Editor*
Harvard University

Robert Sternberg, *Associate Editor*
Tufts University

www.annualreviews.org • science@annualreviews.org • 650-493-4400

Annual Reviews
4139 El Camino Way • P.O. Box 10139 • Palo Alto, California 94303-0139

Annual Reviews
Palo Alto, California, USA

International Standard Serial Number: 0066-4308
International Standard Book Number: 978-0-8243-0260-3
Library of Congress Catalog Card Number: 50-13143

TYPESET BY APTARA
PRINTED AND BOUND BY MALLOY INCORPORATED, ANN ARBOR, MICHIGAN

Preface

The Annual Reviews (AR) enterprise illustrates how our field can do well by doing good. The citation rate for *Annual Review of Psychology* chapters—and indeed for all AR series—places them at the top of their respective fields. This series consistently hovers between being the first or second most-cited publication in our field. Our authors rank among the tops in our field, and this publication reinforces their standing. Invitees often respond that they are honored to be asked by the editorial committee. Authors do well by publishing here. But more than that, AR authors do good. The chapter downloads and citations indicate that our colleagues, students, and public appreciate the wisdom, information, and convenience created by these integrative reviews. Most authors realize their colleagues will appreciate their heroic efforts. But the student and the public readers merit major recognition too.

This moment in our intellectual culture painfully pinpoints the critical need for intelligent, evidence-based analysis. This era apparently craves common-sense solutions and distrusts informed insight. Psychologists especially know that common sense is neither common—people disagree more than they think they do—nor sensible—people are not exactly rational. Yet our warnings about people's fallible decision-making, facile emotions, and dangerous responses increasingly influence public discourse. But hope is on the horizon: so too do our cautions capture the public imagination, learning about how to overcome these human frailties. The recent successes of popular books on neuroscience, decision-making, social influence, and mental health often build on integrative insights from AR chapters. Ultimately, we are getting through to the public.

To this end, the nonprofit publisher Annual Reviews promotes the public usage of our scientific efforts in several prescient initiatives. The AR Web page hosts a world-class search engine with live links to the larger literature. With the Web ever more replacing print media, AR offers all of the current conveniences, including video interviews with scientific luminaries, access to state-of-the-art special collections, social bookmarking, and (available soon) search results sorted by citedness. The cutting-edge AR enterprise is intellectually and economically healthy; it is doing well. More to the point, it is also measurably doing good.

Susan T. Fiske, Princeton

Daniel L. Schacter, Cambridge

Robert Sternberg, Medford

Annual Review of
Psychology

Contents

Volume 60, 2009

Psychobiological Mechanisms

Health and Social Systems

Research Methodology

Psychometrics: Analysis of Latent Variables and Hypothetical Constructs

Evaluation

Timely Topics

Indexes

Errata

An online log of corrections to *Annual Review of Psychology* articles may be found at
http://psych.annualreviews.org/errata.shtml

Related Articles

From the *Annual Review of Neuroscience*, Volume 31 (2008)

From the *Annual Review of Political Science*, Volume 11 (2008)

From the *Annual Review of Public Health*, Volume 29 (2008)

Emotion Theory and Research: Highlights, Unanswered Questions, and Emerging Issues

Carroll E. Izard

Psychology Department, University of Delaware, Newark, Delaware 19716-2577;
email: izard@psych.udel.edu

Annu. Rev. Psychol. 2009. 60:1–25

The *Annual Review of Psychology* is online at
psych.annualreviews.org

This article's doi:
10.1146/annurev.psych.60.110707.163539

Key Words

emotion schemas, emotion-cognition interactions, emotion
knowledge, emotion regulation, emotion utilization, meme,
development, consciousness, levels of awareness, emotion feelings

Abstract

Emotion feeling is a phase of neurobiological activity, the key component of emotions and emotion-cognition interactions. Emotion
schemas, the most frequently occurring emotion experiences, are dynamic emotion-cognition interactions that may consist of momentary/
situational responding or enduring traits of personality that emerge
over developmental time. Emotions play a critical role in the evolution
of consciousness and the operations of all mental processes. Types of
emotion relate differentially to types or levels of consciousness. Unbridled imagination and the ability for sympathetic regulation of empathy
may represent both potential gains and losses from the evolution and
ontogeny of emotion processes and consciousness. Unresolved issues
include psychology's neglect of levels of consciousness that are distinct
from access or reflective consciousness and use of the term "unconscious mind" as a dumpster for all mental processes that are considered
unreportable. The relation of memes and the mirror neuron system
to empathy, sympathy, and cultural influences on the development of
socioemotional skills are unresolved issues destined to attract future
research.

Contents

INTRODUCTION

This prefatory chapter, like every essay, review, or data-based article, is influenced by its author's feelings about the topics and issues under consideration as well as the author's personality and social and cultural experiences. To help counterbalance the effects of such influences on this article and provide some perspective on its contents, I present below the major theses that have emerged in my theorizing and research on emotions.

DET: differential emotions theory

THEORETICAL PRINCIPLES

The key principles of differential emotions theory (DET; Izard 2007a) have changed periodically. They change primarily because of advances in methodology and research. They may also change as a result of theoretical debates that highlight the need for some clarifications and distinctions among constructs. The current set of principles highlight distinctly different types of emotions and their roles in the evolution and development of different levels of consciousness/awareness and of mind, human mentality, and behavior. The ongoing reformulations of DET principles are facilitated by advances in emotion science, cognitive neuroscience, and developmental clinical science, as well as in social and personality psychology. For the present article, the seven principles below guided the choice of topics and the selective review of the literature on emotions and their relations to cognition, action, and consciousness. They led to a new perspective on emotion-related gains and losses from evolution and opened the door to theoretical development and research on emerging topics such as the role of the mirror neuron system in emotion experiences, empathy, and sympathy and memes and their relations to emotion schemas.

An overarching aspect of the theoretical perspective represented in the following principles and in this article is that emotion and cognition, though often treated correctly as having functionally separate features and influences (e.g., Bechara et al. 2000, Talmi & Frith 2007), are interactive and integrated or mingled in the brain (cf. Lewis 2005, Pessoa 2008, Phelps 2006). This thesis is consistent with the long-standing recognition of the high degree of connectivity among the brain's neural structures and systems. I hypothesize that emotion will have substantial and measurable effects on cognition and action when the stimulus or situation is a personally or socially significant one. The foregoing general thesis and the more specific hypothesis seem to run counter to extreme constructivist positions. Such positions (e.g., Barrett 2006) define or locate emotion at the level of perception and apparently have no place for the idea of interactions among distinct features of emotion (e.g., motivation/feeling) and cognition (e.g., higher-order conceptual processes). The present position may bear some similarity to componental–dynamic approaches, at least in terms of continuously changing aspects or configurations of mental processes (e.g., Ellsworth 1994, Scherer 2000). However, the present position may differ from the latter in viewing emotion and cognition as always interacting and

thus normally precluding pure cognitive and emotion states.

SEVEN PRINCIPLES

1. Emotion feeling (*a*) derives from evolution and neurobiological development, (*b*) is the key psychological component of emotions and consciousness, and (*c*) is more often inherently adaptive than maladaptive.

2. Emotions play a central role in the evolution of consciousness, influence the emergence of higher levels of awareness during ontogeny, and largely determine the contents and focus of consciousness throughout the life span.

3. Emotions are motivational and informational, primarily by virtue of their experiential or feeling component. Emotion feelings constitute the primary motivational component of mental operations and overt behavior.

4. Basic emotion feelings help organize and motivate rapid (and often more-or-less automatic though malleable) actions that are critical for adaptive responses to immediate challenges to survival or well-being. In emotion schemas, the neural systems and mental processes involved in emotion feelings, perception, and cognition interact continually and dynamically in generating and monitoring thought and action. These dynamic interactions (which range from momentary processes to traits or trait-like phenomena) can generate innumerable emotion-specific experiences (e.g., anger schemas) that have the same core feeling state but different perceptual tendencies (biases), thoughts, and action plans.

5. Emotion utilization, typically dependent on effective emotion-cognition interactions, is adaptive thought or action that stems, in part, directly from the experience of emotion feeling/motivation and in part from learned cognitive, social, and behavioral skills.

Mirror neuron system (MNS): is assumed to consist of neurons that fire both when one acts and when one observes the same action performed by another; neurons that "mirror" the behavior of another

Memes: behavioral (cognitive, emotional, action) units that can propagate (be readily copied) and become subject to natural selection

Emotion schemas: emotion-cognition interactions/structures that generate feeling-thought experiences and behavioral tendencies that range from momentary processes to trait-like phenomena (e.g., anger schemas, interest schemas)

Emotion feeling: a phase of neurobiological activity that is experienced as motivational and informational and that influences thought and action, a felt cognition, or action tendency

Levels of awareness: levels of consciousness, ranging from phenomenal consciousness to access (verbally reportable) and reflective consciousness, which support the processes in higher-order cognition-emotion schemas

6. Emotion schemas become maladaptive and may lead to psychopathology when learning results in the development of connections among emotion feelings and maladaptive cognition and action.

7. The emotion of interest is continually present in the normal mind under normal conditions, and it is the central motivation for engagement in creative and constructive endeavors and for the sense of well-being. Interest and its interaction with other emotions account for selective attention, which in turn influences all other mental processes.

Elaboration and empirical support for principles 1–6 can be found in the following sources and their reference lists (Ackerman et al. 1998; Izard 2002, 2007a; Izard et al. 2008a,b,c; Silvia 2006). Principles 1–3 apply to all emotions, and 4–6 primarily concern emotion schemas. Principle 7 consists of propositions about the most ubiquitous of all human emotions—interest-excitement. Specific empirical support does not exist for the hypothesis of continual interest in the normal mind.

In this article, I discuss the issues of defining the term "emotion" and types of emotion, emotion-cognition interactions, emotions and consciousness, relations among types of emotions and types of consciousness, and note some remarkable gains and losses from the evolution of emotions and multiple levels consciousness.

This article addresses a critical need for clear distinctions between basic positive and basic negative emotions and particularly between brief basic emotion episodes and emotion schemas. Unlike basic negative emotions that occur in brief episodes and involve very little cognition beyond minimal perceptual processes, emotion schemas involve emotion and cognition (frequently higher-order cognition) in dynamic interactions (Izard 1977, 1984; cf. emotional interpretation, Lewis 2005).

This article also contrasts phenomenal (primary) and access (reflective) consciousness, considers the construct of levels of consciousness, and questions the integrity of current conceptualizations of the unconscious mind. Typi-

cally, psychologists ignore the concepts of phenomenal consciousness and levels of consciousness and do not distinguish these constructs from the unconscious. I conclude by identifying some unanswered questions and briefly comment on a few emerging topics—continuous emotion-cognition interactions, memes and emotions, and the mirror neuron system and empathy—that seem destined to become more prominent in psychological science in the coming years.

ON THE ORIGINS AND NATURE OF EMOTIONS

None of the many efforts to make a widely acceptable definition of emotion has proved successful (Izard 2006, Panksepp 2003a). Yet, I dare once again to raise the 124-year-old storied question asked by James (1884): What is emotion? It happens that the answer James gave to his own question has a rather popular reprieve in the annals of contemporary neuroscience. Like James, Damasio (1999) argued that brain responses constitute emotion or the body expression of emotion and that emotion feeling is a consequence of the neurobiological (body) expression of emotion. In contrast, I propose that emotion feeling should be viewed as a phase (not a consequence) of the neurobiological activity or body expression of emotion (cf. Langer 1967/1982).

The Origins of Emotions

Russell (2003) proposed that core affect is continuous in the brain and provides information on the pleasure/displeasure and arousal value of stimuli. In contrast, I have maintained that a discrete emotion or pattern of interacting emotions are always present (though not necessarily labeled or articulated) in the conscious brain (Izard 1977, ch. 6; Izard 2007a,b). Barrett (2006) suggested that discrete emotions arise as a result of a conceptual act on core affect or as a function of "conceptual structure that is afforded by language" (Barrett et al. 2007, p. 304). In contrast, we have proposed that discrete emotion feelings cannot be created, taught, or learned via cognitive processes (Izard & Malatesta 1987; Izard 2007a,b). As Edelman & Tononi (2000) observed, "... emotions are fundamental both to the origins of and the appetite for conscious thought" (p. 218, cf. Izard 1977, ch. 6). So, perceptual and conceptual processes and consciousness itself are more like effects of emotions than sources of their origin. Discrete emotion experiences emerge in ontogeny well before children acquire language or the conceptual structures that adequately frame the qualia we know as discrete emotion feelings. Moreover, acquiring language does not guarantee that emotion experiences can always be identified and communicated verbally. Even adults have great difficulty articulating a precise description of their emotion feelings (cf. Langer 1967/1982).

Thus, emotion feelings can be activated and influenced by perceptual, appraisal, conceptual, and noncognitive processes (Izard 1993), but cannot be created by them. In describing the origins of qualia—conscious experiences that include emotion feelings—Edelman & Tononi (2000) wrote, "We can analyze them and give prescription for how they emerge, but obviously we cannot give rise to them without first giving rise to appropriate brain structures and their dynamics within the body of an individual organism" (p. 15). They maintained that such structures arise as a result of brain changes due to "developmental selection" (p. 79), an aspect of neural Darwinism. Eschewing the cognitive-constructivist approach advocated by Barrett (2006), Edelman & Tononi (2000) concluded that "the development of the earliest qualia occurs largely on the basis of multimodal, body-centered discriminations carried out by proprioceptive, kinesthetic, and autonomic systems that are present in the embryo and infant's brain, particularly in the brainstem" (p. 157).

Emotion Feeling as Neurobiological Activity

Apparently consistent with the position of Edelman (2006), Langer (1967/1982), and Panksepp (2003a,b), I propose that emotion feeling is a phase of neurobiological activity that is sensed by the organism. It is sensed and expressed even in children without a cerebral cortex (Merker 2007). This component of emotion is always experienced or felt, though not necessarily labeled or articulated or present in access consciousness.

Emotion feeling, like any other neurobiological activity, varies from low to high levels of intensity. The autonomic nervous system may modulate the emotion feeling but does not change its quality or valence (cf. Tomkins 1962, 1963). Neither a moderate nor a high level of autonomic nervous system activity is necessary for the emergence of emotion feelings. The conscious mind is capable of detecting and discriminating among slight changes in neurobiological activity and among the resultant qualia (Edelman 2006) that include emotion feelings. [Contrary to earlier formulations (Izard 1971, Tomkins 1962), neural processes in observable facial expressions may or may not be a part of the critical neurobiological activity involved in emotion feeling.]

Emotion feelings arise from the integration of concurrent activity in brain structures and circuits that may involve the brain stem, amygdale, insula, anterior cingulate, and orbitofrontal cortices (cf. Damasio 2003; Lane et al. 1997; Panksepp 2003a,b). Levels of emotion feelings, like other neurobiological activities, range from low and subtle to high and extreme. Current theory and evidence suggest that the feeling component of emotions contributed to the evolution of consciousness and to the affective, cognitive, and action processes involved in goal-oriented behavior.

Defining emotion feeling as a phase of a neurobiological process circumvents the argument that feeling is nonphysical and hence cannot be causal. A counterargument, though, is that at best, feelings are only the qualia of neurobiological processes and not neurobiological activity per se. However, even if this were true, Edelman (2006) maintains that qualia could still be described as causal because they are true representations of core thalamo-cortical activity. Thus, whether or not one accepts the present

Access consciousness: a level of awareness that includes verbally reportable content

Entrainment:
harmonious
synchronization of
neural processes

Individuation: those
processes through
which differentiated
components tend to
become a more unified
whole

Basic emotions:
emotions that organize
and motivate rapid
virtually automatic yet
malleable responses
that are critical in
meeting immediate
challenges to survival
or well-being

proposal that feelings are a phase of neurobiological activity, they can still be conceived as causal processes.

The present formulation of the origins and nature of emotion feelings differs from those that describe emotion feeling and emotion state (or emotion-related neurobiological activity) as separate and independent (e.g., Lambie & Marcel 2002). Moreover, the view of emotion feeling as a phase of the neurobiological activity or body expression of emotion differs from the idea that neurobiological or body expression must precede emotion feeling (Damasio 1999, p. 283). The current description of emotion feeling is tantamount to saying that it is evolved and unlearned neurobiological activity. For those who think that the idea of emotion feelings as evolved neurobiological processes is strange or unfounded, the tough questions are: Where else could emotion feelings come from? What else could they be?

Feeling is the Key Psychological Aspect of Emotion: Motivation and Information

Feeling is the dynamic component in emotion (cf. Panksepp 2003a,b) and in two related psychobiological processes—entrainment and individuation (cf. Langer 1967/1982). The motivational, cue-producing, and informational functions of feelings enable them to entrain, or simplify and organize, what might become (particularly in challenging situations) an overwhelming number of impulses into focused cognitive processes and a few adaptive actions (cf. Langer 1967/1982). Such feeling-mediated entrainment of impulses across situations and developmental time facilitates the formation of feeling-cognition-action patterns that constitute individuation—the organization of traits and their assembly into a unique personality. However, feeling an emotion does not guarantee that it will be labeled, articulated, or sensed in reflective consciousness or at a high level of awareness. The level of awareness of an emotion feeling depends in part on its intensity and expression, and after language acquisition, on

labeling, articulating, and acknowledging the emotion experience. These capacities, critical to personality and social development, depend on the neural activity and resultant processes involved in symbolization and language.

Through development, the conceptual self becomes important to the process of feeling and expressing an emotion, but a higher-order conceptual "self" is not essential for either. Infants experience and express basic emotions long before they can provide any evidence of a self-concept (Izard et al. 1995), and so do children without a cerebral cortex (Merker 2007).

Motivational and cue-producing emotion-feeling provides information relevant to cognition and action (Izard 1971, p. 185). Others have conceptualized emotion as information, and the topic has inspired a considerable body of related research (Clore et al. 2001, Schwarz & Clore 1983). Consistent with the idea that emotion feelings are cue-producing and informational phenomena, they may also afford a kind of prescience. Feelings may predict the effect of future stimulations by anticipating the link between future critical situations and subsequent emotion experiences and needs, e.g., danger→fear→safety or loss→sadness→social support (cf. Langer 1967/1982, Vol. 1, p. 101). Such anticipatory activities can facilitate the socialization processes associated with the learning of emotion-related social skills in an imagined or "as if" world.

Although an emotion feeling may begin to form reciprocal relations with perception or cognition by the time that it is fully sensed, there is no reason to assume that its quality is altered by perceptual and conceptual processes (Panksepp 2003a,b). Actually, the particular quality of each discrete emotion feeling evolved because its effects on other senses, cognition, and action are generally adaptive (cf. Edelman & Tononi 2000). For all basic emotions, motivational and action processes occur in similar fashion across situations. Among emotion schemas, however, there are wide differences in motivational, cognitive, and action processes across individuals. The determinants of which particular emotion feeling and what cognitive content occurs in a specific emotion schema include individual differences, learning, culture, and the conceptual processes influenced by them (Izard 2007a; cf. Shweder 1994).

Agreement on Components and Characteristics of Emotion

Though there is no consensus on a general definition of the term "emotion" (cf. Kleinginna & Kleinginna 1981), many experts do agree that emotions have a limited set of components and characteristics (Izard 2006). Although they do not agree in all details, they agree that emotions have an infrastructure that includes neural systems dedicated, at least in part, to emotion processes and that emotions motivate cognition and action and recruit response systems. We may also be reaching a consensus that there are different forms of emotions, e.g., basic emotions rooted and defined primarily in evolution and biology and emotion schemas that include cognitive components that differ across individuals and cultures (Izard 2007a, Panksepp 2007).

Emotions as Causal Processes

Although experts agree that emotions motivate or influence cognition and action, not all agree on precisely what mediates the effects of emotions. The answer may depend on whether it is a basic emotion or an emotion schema. It may also depend on whether and how a distinction is made in the roles of emotion neurophysiology and emotion feelings (cf. Panksepp 2003a,b).

Arguably, no one thing (even emotion) is ever the sole mediator of personally or socially significant behavior. Other person and contextual variables typically contribute to the causal processes. Yet, I propose that emotion feeling is virtually always one of the mediators of action in response to basic emotion and a mediator of thought and action in response to emotion schemas. Thus, the specific impact of emotion feeling in generating and altering behavior depends on the type of emotion involved in the causal process. Feeling in basic emotion affects action but not higher-order cognition, which

has little or no presence in basic emotion processes. Feeling in emotion schemas may frequently affect action and will surely affect cognition. Thinking is a key agent in regulating (sometimes suppressing; Gross 2002) and guiding behavior that stems from emotion schemas.

TYPES OF EMOTIONS

Emotions can be usefully divided into two broad types or kinds—basic emotion episodes and dynamic emotion-cognition interactions or emotion schemas. Failure to make and keep the distinction between these two kinds of emotion experiences may be the biggest source of misunderstandings and misconceptions in current emotion science (Izard 2007a, Gray et al. 2005). I included an update on the distinction between types of emotions here for two reasons. First, I see the fundamental nature of emotions and the closely connected issue of emotion-cognition-action processes as central to emotion science, now and for the foreseeable future. Second, I think researchers often look for the correlates and effects of basic emotions (labeled simply as emotions) when the variables in their experiments are actually emotion-cognition interactions or emotion schemas.

Basic Emotions

In the past, I have used the term "basic emotion" in referring to any emotion that is assumed to be fundamental to human mentality and adaptive behavior (Izard 1977). Recently, misunderstandings and debates about its meaning led me to draw a sharp distinction between basic emotions and affective-cognitive structures or emotion schemas (Izard 2007a). Here, consistent with that distinction, the term "basic emotion" refers to affective processes generated by evolutionarily old brain systems upon the sensing of an ecologically valid stimulus (Izard 2007a).

Basic positive emotions. The basic positive emotions of interest and joy (e.g., an infant's interest activated by the human face; Langsdorf et al. 1983) and joy activated by the familiar face of her mother (Izard et al. 1995) are equally essential to survival, evolution, and development. However, their structure and time course may differ significantly from each other. The infant's experiences of joy may be relatively brief by comparison with experiences of interest. The basic positive emotion of interest motivates play in early development and thus may have short or relatively long duration.

Basic positive emotions emerge in early ontogeny (Izard et al. 1995). Like the basic negative emotions, they are subject to developmental changes. The most critical of these changes is mediated by the acquisition of language and emotion labels and the ability to communicate (or share) emotion experiences through symbolic processes or language (Izard 1971, Izard et al. 2008).

Basic negative emotions. Basic negative emotions (sadness, anger, disgust, fear) typically run their course automatically and stereotypically in a brief time span. The basic emotion of fear (or a fear-action episode) was described rather precisely in the earliest human records: "A man who stumbles upon a viper will jump aside: as trembling takes his knees, pallor his cheeks; he backs and backs away ..." (Homer's *Iliad*, c. 7000 BCE, p. 68).

Research has repeatedly demonstrated that in mammals, the experience and expression of basic fear is mediated by the amygdala (LeDoux 1996, Mobbs et al. 2007). Typically, basic negative emotions are activated by subcortical sensory-discriminative processes in response to ecologically valid stimuli (Ekman 2003, LeDoux 1996, Öhman 2005). Perceptual processes and action usually follow and run their course rapidly and automatically to enhance the likelihood of gaining an adaptive advantage (cf. LeDoux 1996, Öhman 2002, Tomkins 1962). Because of their nature, some basic negative emotions (e.g., sadness, anger, fear) are difficult to study in the laboratory. Thus, most extant research on what are usually called emotions (most often negative emotions) actually concerns negative emotion schemas.

Basic or fundamental emotions? The discrete emotions of shame, guilt, and contempt (sometimes called the social or self-conscious emotions) and the pattern of emotions in love and attachment may be considered basic in the sense that they are fundamental to human evolution, normative development, human mentality, and effective adaptation. After language acquisition, the emotions related to the self-concept or self-consciousness are typically emotion schemas that involve higher-order cognition (e.g., about self and self-other relationships) and have culture-related cognitive components (Tangney et al. 2007).

Emotion Schemas: Dynamic Emotion-Cognition Interactions

The core idea of dynamic interaction between emotion and cognition has a long and venerable history dating back at least to the earliest written records: "... Peleus ... lashed out at him, letting his anger ride in execration ..." (Homer's *Iliad*, c. 7000 BCE). The idea was prominently displayed in seventeenth-century philosophy (Bacon 1620/1968, Spinoza 1677/1957) and was most eloquently elaborated by Langer (1967/1982).

In the vernacular, as well as in much of the literature of emotion science, the term "emotion" most frequently refers to what is described here as an emotion schema. An emotion schema is emotion interacting dynamically with perceptual and cognitive processes to influence mind and behavior. Emotion schemas are often elicited by appraisal processes but also by images, memories, and thoughts, and various noncognitive processes such as changes in neurotransmitters and periodic changes in levels of hormones (Izard 1993). Any one or all of these phenomena, as well as goals and values, may constitute their cognitive component. Appraisal processes, typically conceived as mechanisms of emotion activation (for a review, see Ellsworth & Scherer 2003), help provide the cognitive framework for the emotion component of emotion schemas. Their principal motivational component of emotion schemas consists of the processes involved in emotion feelings. Emotion schemas, particularly their cognitive aspects, are influenced by individual differences, learning, and social and cultural contexts. Nevertheless, the feeling component of a given emotion schema (e.g., a sadness schema) is qualitatively identical to the feeling in the basic emotion of sadness. Though there may be some differences in their underlying neural processes, the sadness feeling in each type of emotion shares a common set of brain circuits or neurobiological activities that determine its quality (cf. Edelman 2006, Edelman & Tononi 2000).

Positive and negative emotion schemas may have a relatively brief duration or continue over an indefinitely long time course. A principal reason why they can endure more or less indefinitely is because their continually interacting cognitive component provides a means to regulate and utilize them. Evidence indicates that experimentally facilitated formation of emotion schemas (simply learning to label and communicate about emotion feelings) generates adaptive advantages (Izard et al. 2008a; cf. Lieberman et al. 2007). Although we have very little data relating to their normative development, neuroscientists have begun to increase our knowledge of the substrates of emotion-cognition interactions (Fox et al. 2005, Gross 2002, Lewis 2005, Northoff et al. 2004, Phelps 2006).

Emotion schemas and traits of temperament/personality. Frequently recurring emotion schemas may stabilize as emotion traits or as motivational components of temperament/personality traits (Diener et al. 1995, Goldsmith & Campos 1982, Izard 1977, Magai & Hunziker 1993, Magai & McFadden 1995; cf. Mischel & Shoda 1995, Tomkins 1987). In normal development, the cognitive content of emotion schemas should enhance the regulatory, motivational, and functional capacities of their feeling components. However, in some gene X environment interactions, a cluster of interrelated emotion schemas may become a form of psychopathology (e.g., anxiety and de-

pressive disorders: Davidson 1994, 1998; J.A. Gray 1990; J.R. Gray et al. 2005; Izard 1972; Magai & McFadden 1995).

Early-emerging emotion schemas. Aside from the simple emotion-cognition connections that a prelinguistic infant forms (e.g., between her own feelings of interest and joy and a perception/image of her mother's face), the earliest emotion schemas probably consist of attaching labels to emotion expressions and feelings. Development of emotion labeling and the process of putting feelings into words begin toward the end of the second year of life and continue during the preschool and elementary school years (Izard 1971) and throughout the life span. Indeed, games and activities that promote the accurate labeling of emotion expressions and experiences have been a component of intervention processes for many years (see Domitrovich & Greenberg 2004 and Denham & Burton 2003 for reviews).

Emotion schemas or affective-cognitive units? The concept of affective-cognitive structure or emotion schema (Izard 1977, 2007a) seems quite similar to that of the affective-cognitive unit as described in the cognitive-affective personality system (CAPS) theory of personality (Mischel & Shoda 1995, 1998). One significant difference may be that in the CAPS approach, an affective-cognitive unit is conceived mainly as a stable or characteristic mediating process or part of the personality system. In DET, an emotion schema may be either a temporally stable trait-like phenomenon (affective-cognitive structure) or a brief emotion-cognition interaction that may mediate behavior in a specific situation. Compared to the CAPS approach, DET gives emotion a greater role in motivation and assumes that the emotion component of the emotion schema drives the behavior mapped or framed by perceptual-cognitive processes. DET also emphasizes that, as seen particularly clearly in early development and in emotion-based preventive interventions, connecting appropriate cognition to emotion feelings increases the individual's capacity for emotion modulation and self-regulation (Izard et al. 2008a). DET and CAPS agree in assigning a significant causal role to the dynamic interplay of emotion and cognition in determining human behavior. Both approaches also conceptualize the interplay of emotion and cognitive processes as sources of data on ideographic or within-subject differences in emotion-cognition-behavior relations.

In brief, emotion schemas are causal or mediating processes that consist of emotion and cognition continually interacting dynamically to influence mind and behavior. It is the dynamic interaction of these distinct features (emotion and cognition) that enables an emotion schema, acting in the form of a situation-specific factor or a trait of temperament/personality, to have its special and powerful effects on self-regulation and on perception, thought, and action (Izard et al. 2008a).

Transitions from Basic Emotions to Emotion Schemas

In early development, the first steps in the transition from basic positive emotions to positive emotion schemas consists simply of the infant using her increasing cognitive and emotion processing capacities to make connections between positive emotion feelings and positive thoughts, memories, and anticipations of people, events, and situations. Through learning and experience, the same stimuli that once elicited a basic positive emotion may become stimuli for positive emotion schemas and greater expectations (cf. Fredrickson 1998, 2007).

Basic negative emotions occur relatively more frequently in infancy than in later development. Moreover, the transition from basic negative emotions to basic negative emotion schemas and the regulatory advantage provided by their cognitive component may prove difficult and challenging. The transition from basic anger (protests) and sadness (withdrawal) of a toddler being separated from mom, to the interest-joy response of a four-year-old being dropped off at kindergarten, may involve several rather stressful times for many children.

For adults, transitions from a basic emotion to an emotion schema may start abruptly but finish smoothly and quickly. Simply sensing that the object in your path and just a step ahead of you is long, round, and moving may activate the basic emotion of fear and the accompanying high-intensity neurobiological reactions. However, if language, learning, and another 50 ms enable you to recognize and label the object as a harmless garden snake (i.e., construct an emotion schema), you might even take it gently into your hands rather than engage in extreme behavior. The concomitant change in neural and neuromotor circuits would constitute a paradigmatic transition across types and valences of emotion and emotion-related phenomena. In this case, one would make a transition from basic fear to interest-cognition-action sequences in a positive emotion schema.

EMOTIONS AND CONSCIOUSNESS

Whatever else it may be, emotion feeling is at bottom sensation. Thus emotion feelings, like other sensations, are by definition processes that are felt or at least accessible (in the broad sense of that term) in some level of consciousness. Level of cognitive development as well as top-down processes, such as attention shifting and focusing, may influence (or preclude) the registration of feeling in reflective or cognitively accessible consciousness (Buschman & Miller 2007). When that happens, emotion feelings/experiences occur in phenomenal consciousness (or at a low level of awareness). Phenomenal consciousness of an emotion feeling, the experience itself, generally co-occurs with some level of reflective/reportable consciousness (cf. Chalmers 1996). Thus, I propose that there are usually interactions among the neural systems that support these two types of consciousness (cf. Pessoa 2008). These interactions between the two sets of neural systems enable emotion feelings to retain their functionality in influencing thought and action, even in prelingual infants (Izard et al. 2008b).

Factors Affecting Emotion-Consciousness Relations

Another determinant of our level of awareness of emotion is the intensity of the neurobiological activity involved in emotion feeling. Low-intensity emotion feeling (e.g., interest arousal motivating learning skills related to aspects of one's work) would not ordinarily grab attention in the same way as a viper and might go unnoticed. In this case (and in other instances of low arousal), "unnoticed" does not mean that the feeling is "unconscious." It may register and be fully functional at some level of consciousness (cf. Lambie & Marcel 2002). The development of theory and techniques to examine the operations of emotion feelings in different levels of awareness should help reduce the number of psychological processes that are currently relegated to the ambiguous concept of the unconscious (Izard et al. 2008b; cf. Bargh & Morsella 2008).

Emotion Feelings and Consciousness

As the foregoing formulation suggests, the neurobiological processes involved in emotions generate conscious experiences of feelings (emotional sensations) just as in seeing green neurobiological activities in the visual brain create the experience/sensation of greenness (cf. Humphrey 2006). The sensory processes involved in emotion feelings like joy, sadness, anger, and fear may represent prototypical emotion experiences. Such emotion feelings are critical to the evolution of human mentality and reflective consciousness (cf. Edelman 2006, Langer 1967/1982).

Emotion experiences/sensations continue to be critical in the maintenance and functioning of consciousness. When trauma leads to damage or dysfunction of a sensory system, it affects the whole person, including the sense of self and of others as self-conscious. For example, when a dysfunctional visual cortex resulted

in blindsight, the blindsighted person could guess rather accurately the location of objects in the environment and learn to navigate around them. Yet, she experienced her sensation-less vision as emotionless and reported that "seeing without emotion is unbearable" (Humphrey 2006, p. 68–69). She may also think of herself as "less of a self" and one that could not feel "engaged in the 'hereness, nowness, and me-ness' of the experience of the moment" (Humphrey 2006, p. 70). In the social world, the blindsighted person lacks a basis for empathy and for understanding the mental states of others by simulation.

Taken together, these observations on the aftermath of the loss of the visual sensory system (which provides the bulk of our incoming information) suggest that having sensations may be the starting point of consciousness (Humphrey 2006, pp. 66–71). The emergence of the capacity to experience and respond to emotion feelings may have been the most critical step in its evolution (cf. Langer 1967/1982). Discrete emotion feelings play a central role in anticipating the effects of future stimulations and in organizing and integrating the associated information for envisioning strategies and entraining impulses for targeted goal-directed cognitive processes and actions. The coalescence of the emotion-driven anticipatory processes, entrainment (organizing and integrative processes), and the resultant individuation and sense of agency may have constituted the dawn of human consciousness (cf. Edelman 2006, Humphrey 2006, Langer 1967/1982).

TYPES OF EMOTION AND TYPES OF CONSCIOUSNESS

The concepts of consciousness and awareness have received very little attention in contemporary psychology. With a few exceptions, the contributors to a recently edited volume on emotion and consciousness dealt with many interesting issues other than some critical ones on the nature of consciousness and its relation to emotions (Barrett et al. 2005b). Most contributors explicitly or implicitly assumed that access or reflective consciousness was either the only kind of consciousness or the only one that mattered to psychologists (cf. Lambie & Marcel 2002, Merker 2007).

Basic Emotions and Phenomenal Consciousness

It is quite reasonable to assume that human infants (and all nonhuman mammals; Panksepp 2003a,b) have some form of consciousness (Izard et al. 2008b, Merker 2007). Wider acceptance of this notion should save young infants a lot of pain. Various invasive procedures (including circumcisions and needle pricks to draw blood for analyses) are still performed without analgesic. The facial expression of infants undergoing such procedures constitutes the prototypical expression of pain. With increasing age, the prototypical expression of pain in response to these procedures alternates with the prototypical expression of anger (Izard et al. 1987).

Developmental data suggest that young infants experience basic emotions (Izard et al. 1995). Their inability to report their emotion experiences via language rules out the idea that they experience emotions in access (verbally reportable) consciousness and suggests that their emotion feelings must occur in some other level of awareness or in phenomenal consciousness. Current conceptualizations of phenomenal consciousness, however, may not explain all emotion experiences in infancy (Izard et al. 2008b).

Developmental scientists have obtained evidence that shows that prelinguistic infants not only experience objects and events, but they also respond to and communicate nonverbally about objects and events in meaningful ways (Izard et al. 2008b). Moreover, their experience often involves emotion that is indexed by emotion-expressive behavior and other forms of action that influence the social and physical world (Claxton et al. 2003, Izard et al. 1995). Apparently, these behaviors reflect the development of different levels or complexities of awareness, and further studies of them may of-

fer possibilities of extending current conceptualizations of ways to access phenomenological experiences. These experiences do not fit precisely into the categories of "phenomenal" or "access" consciousness as traditionally defined. Yet these experiences are surely part of the infant's phenomenology, and the functionality of these experiential processes clearly demonstrates that they are accessible by noncognitive routes (Izard et al. 2008b, Merker 2007; cf. Block 2008).

Emotion Feelings and Phenomenal Consciousness

The conceptualization of emotion feeling as a phase of a neurobiological process is congruent with the idea that emotions can be sensed and registered in phenomenal consciousness and at low levels of awareness without being perceived. Such emotion feelings are often described erroneously, I think, as unconscious emotion (cf. Clore et al. 2005, Lambie & Marcel 2002). What may be unconscious is not the feeling but the perception of the feeling, and this lack of perception could account for the failure of the feeling to register in access consciousness. Insofar as emotion feeling is at bottom sensation, then generating a feeling ipso facto generates a state of consciousness. Thus, an emotion feeling always registers in phenomenal consciousness. Often, if not always, it also registers in some other level of consciousness that is accessible by various routes. After language acquisition, emotion feelings can often (but not always) be reported via symbolic processes. In prelingual infants, young children, and others with insufficient emotion vocabulary, it may be manifested in emotion-mediated behavior (cf. Izard et al. 2008b). Evidence suggests that emotion feelings are operative and expressible via facial and body movement and other behavior even when not reportable (cf. Lambie & Marcel 2002).

Happily, an enormous amount of information processing proceeds very well in the realm of the unconscious, but I propose that the functionality of emotion feelings (that are not in access or reflective consciousness) might be explained better in terms of phenomenal or other levels of consciousness. The term "unconscious" emotion implies nonfelt emotion. It seems very difficult if not impossible to identify and explain the mediators of the effects of nonfelt or nonconscious emotion (e.g., de Gelder 2005). Much of what has been called nonconscious emotion has not met the "requirement of deliberate probing by indirect measures" (Lambie & Marcel 2002, p. 16). Nor have data on unconscious emotions been examined in terms of the functional correlates of hypothesized emotion feelings. Such research might suggest replacing the concept of psychological unconscious with that of phenomenal consciousness or some other level of consciousness that cannot be verbally reported.

The concept of unlabeled, unarticulated, and linguistically inaccessible emotion feeling in phenomenal consciousness or some other cognitively inaccessible level of consciousness is compatible with the notion that this component of emotion is felt and functions as a mediator of behavior (cf. Clore et al. 2005, Izard et al. 2008b, Lambie & Marcel 2002). Because it is felt, the emotion feeling retains its characteristic motivational and informational qualities. To say that the feeling component of emotion can reside unfelt in phenomenal consciousness, any other level of consciousness, or the unconscious seems to be a pure non sequitur.

To acknowledge that the subjective component of emotion is felt and real in phenomenal and other cognitively inaccessible levels of consciousness may inspire theory and research on how an emotion feeling remains functional and motivational without being symbolized and made accessible in reflective consciousness via language. Evidence of the functionality of emotion feelings in prelingual infants and children without a cerebral cortex seems to support the argument for more research on the functionality of emotion feelings in phenomenal consciousness. So do the observations that patients who suffer blindsight report feelings without having corresponding visual experiences (Weiskrantz 2001). On the other hand,

subjects with blindsight can perceive objects and make accurate perceptual judgments without any corresponding sensation or feeling at all (Humphrey 2006). The extent to which these seemingly disparate observations on people with blindsight inform normative relations among perception, sensation, and emotion feelings is not yet clear. Neither are the effects and limits of top-down control of sensation in relation to perception and to emotion feelings and their registration at some level of consciousness (Buschman & Miller 2007).

Emotion Schemas and Access Consciousness

Emotion feelings can operate in phenomenal consciousness with little or no cognitive content. This fact is easy to appreciate while remembering that phenomenal experience is the modal variety in prelingual infants and nonhuman mammals. Although prelingual infants apparently demonstrate higher levels of awareness than phenomenal consciousness, they definitely cannot exhibit reflective consciousness as traditionally defined in terms of cognitive accessibility.

Once development enables emotion experiences to become connected to higher-order cognition, children begin to link emotion feelings and concepts and to form more and more complex emotion schemas. The language associated with a given emotion feeling in particular situations becomes a tool in emotion management, self-regulation, and other executive functions (Izard et al. 2008a).

Gains and Losses in the Evolution of Emotions and Consciousness

Darwin recognized many turns in evolution that pointed to the seeming cruelty of natural selection—life-threatening parasites, killer reptiles, and the bloody work of predators (Dawkins 1989). He also recognized the adaptive advantages in positive emotions and their expressions in social interactions: "...the mother smiles approval, and thus encourages her children on the right path, or frowns disapproval" (Darwin 1872/1965, p. 304). Gains related in some way to the emotions and their interactions with perception and cognition may represent the finest—and possibly most challenging—products of evolution.

Among the finest and most interesting products of evolution was gaining the capacity for language and eventually the learning of vocabulary for labeling emotions and describing and sharing emotion experiences. These gains also helped enable humans to anticipate future desirable and undesirable emotion feelings. Taken together, these newly emerged capacities represent enormous gains in executive functions, particularly for understanding and managing emotions and self-regulation (Izard 2002, Izard et al. 2008a). They have direct and indirect benefits for the cognitive and action processes involved in adaptive idiosyncratic and social functioning (Izard et al. 2008b, Lieberman et al. 2007). Some have argued that the enormous gains that resulted from brain evolution, the acquisition of language, and the accompanying increases in cognitive abilities did not come without some accompanying losses (Langer 1967/1982).

A possible loss: the evolutionary empathy-sympathy exchange. Basic empathy depends mainly on neurophysiological response systems that do not require or involve the higher-order cognitive processes involved in sympathy (Hoffman 2000). Thus, long before human evolution produced language and its accompanying cognitive prowess, a high-level of ability for empathy and empathic responding emerged in nonhuman animals (Langer 1967/1982). This great capacity for empathy apparently accounts for the lack of con-specific predation and cannibalism among nonhuman mammals. "Among the higher animals few, if any, of the carnivores—bears, wolves, lions and other great cats—habitually prey on their own kind" (Langer 1967/1982, Vol. 1, p. 141). They are restrained from predation, not by signals of appeasement or surrender, but by "a ready empathetic response, so common and effective that it takes no principle, moral or other, to

safeguard the members of a species against each other's appetites in ordinary conditions" (Langer 1967/1982, Vol. 1, p. 142).

The animal empathy that constitutes a safeguard against con-specific predation establishes a special kind of relationship that enables an essentially physiological transmission of the "feeling of one creature to another so it appears to the latter as its own" (Langer 1967/1982, Vol. 1, p. 140). In contrast, as the media are wont to remind us through blow-by-blow accounts of flagrantly aggressive and ethically and morally devious behavior, humans prey on each other with considerable frequency. And such predation often leads to death and destruction, even genocide. Furthermore, although cannibalism (a total breakdown in empathy) is generally absent among higher-order nonhuman animals, it has been observed in many human cultures.

Compared to instantaneous empathy, sympathy depends in important ways on conceptual processes (including the projected costs and benefits of helping) that are notably slower and less certain of occurrence. Sympathetic responses are also more subject to top-down control (e.g., mental manipulations stemming from biases and imagined consequences) than rapid, automatic, animal empathy. Thus, sympathetic responses may often be too little and too late for the victims of disasters, some of which result from only slightly disguised human predation exemplified in transactions between rich and poor and between high- and low-status ethnic groups. Thus, a potentially grave question remains: Does the evolutionary shift in capacities for empathy and sympathy represent a net loss or a net gain?

The pros and cons of unbridled imagination. There is also some question as to whether the evolutionary increases in the power of imagination should be judged a net gain or loss in weighing the emotion-related products of evolution. In some individuals and circumstances, unbridled imagination can facilitate tragedies on a personal as well as a national and global scale. Imagination can be fueled by either positive or negative emotion feelings or the interaction of both, and in turn, it can produce a cornucopia of both positive and negative emotion stimuli and behavioral responses (cf. Langer 1967/1982). Imagination doubtless played a role in the creation of nuclear weapons and still plays a role in planning their projected uses. It is also a factor in the development of factories, products, and policies that increase global warming and the pollution of the earth and the atmosphere at a dangerous rate.

In contrast, during early ontogeny the feeling-thought patterns of unbridled imagination facilitate cognitive and social development from the first moment that the young child engages in make-believe or pretend play. In these developmental processes and throughout the life span, imagination remains part emotion feeling and part cognition. It continues to add to individual and cultural accomplishments through the creative endeavors of artists and scientists.

Thus, "In the evolution of mind, imagination is as dangerous as it is essential" (Langer 1967/1982, Vol. 1, p. 137). Nurturing imagination through the life span with a good balance of emotion feelings and the encouragement of empathy, sympathy, and reason, and an appreciation of how these ingredients can interact and work together for the common good, ubiquitous peace, and the preservation and flourishing of the species seem equally essential.

Remarkable Gains from Linking Emotion Feelings and Language

The process of symbolizing emotion in awareness has the potential to add significantly to adaptive personality and social functioning. Language is by far the most common method of symbolization across individuals and cultures, and researchers have verified at the behavioral and neural levels the positive effects of linking words to discrete emotion expressions and feelings (L. Greenberg & Paivio 1997, Izard 1971, Izard et al. 2008a, Kennedy-Moore & Watson 1999, Lieberman et al. 2007). Major among the positive effects that accrue when we can use language to symbolize emotion feelings, especially

in early development but also throughout the life span, are those relating to increases in emotion knowledge, emotion regulation, and emotion utilization.

Emotion utilization is the harnessing of an emotion's inherently adaptive motivation/feeling component in constructive affective-cognitive processes and actions (Izard 1971, 2002, 2007a; Izard et al. 2008c; cf. Mayer & Salovey 1997). Emotion utilization involves spontaneous as well as planned actions, and it is conceptually different from direct attempts to regulate emotion or emotion-related behavior (cf. Eisenberg & Spinrad 2004). Although emotion regulation and emotion utilization are different constructs, they interact dynamically. Emotion utilization may be viewed as the optimal mode of emotion regulation, and various forms of the latter enhance the former.

It would be difficult to overestimate the significance of the civilizing and socializing effects of learning to recognize, articulate, and utilize emotion feelings constructively, not only in early development but also throughout the life span. A key process here is developing connections between feelings, words, and thoughts. Unfortunately, linking emotion feelings to maladaptive thoughts like those that characterize racism, sexism, ageism, unbridled profit motives, and plans for vengeance, revenge, or terrorism can wreak extensive havoc to individuals, ethnic groups, and all of human kind. For an abundance of evidence supporting the foregoing assertion, read history and watch or listen to any daily news program.

UNRESOLVED ISSUES AND TOPICS FOR FUTURE RESEARCH

Two unresolved issues seem to impede scientific advances in the study of consciousness and levels of awareness. The first concerns the role of phenomenal consciousness and various linguistically inaccessible levels of awareness in research on mind and behavior. The second concerns the relation of phenomenal consciousness and the psychological unconscious, their similarities and differences.

Psychologists' Neglect of Phenomenal Consciousness

Several factors may have contributed to the general neglect of phenomenal consciousness in psychological theory and research. The first is a long-standing reluctance to acknowledge the extent to which emotions drive cognition and action and the possibility that some of the driving emotions register only in phenomenal consciousness. The second is the strong tendency of mainstream psychology to neglect developmental perspectives on critical issues and thus to ignore evidence of the existence and functionality of phenomenal consciousness and other linguistically inaccessible levels of awareness in early development and probably in various forms of psychopathology. A third problem is that many psychologists think that most emotions are episodic, of limited duration, and in focal awareness. A related misconception is that once an emotion episode ends, the mind is free for purely rational processes. This notion persists despite eloquent arguments suggesting that there is no such thing as pure reason (Creighton 1921, Langer 1967/1982), especially in relation to personally or socially significant matters. Evidence suggests that in humans it may not be possible to study cognition and emotion separately (Lewis 2005, Phelps 2006). This conclusion is quite consistent with the present position, if the term "emotion" refers to emotion schemas.

A more appropriate goal would be to develop more effective ways to study emotion-cognition interactions and integration/mingling and consequent behavior change, particularly in research that involves constructs like emotion schemas (Izard 1977, 2007a), emotional interpretations (Lewis 2005), or affective-cognitive units (Mischel & Shoda 1995). This would include most emotion research that does not focus on basic negative emotion episodes.

A final and perhaps most worrisome reason why phenomenal consciousness is still not a major concern of psychologists is that it is conflated with the psychological "unconscious." Clearly, a vast amount of the processes of the brain and the rest of the body (blood circulation, digestion) often do occur without our awareness of them and, in normal circumstances, without direct effects on thought and action. When significant behavioral effects do occur without readily observable causes, they are often assigned to the psychological unconscious, where mechanisms are difficult to identify and explain (Kihlstrom 1999).

More parsimonious and accurate explanations of unconscious behavior might accrue if we looked for mediators of thought and action (e.g., emotions) that reside in phenomenal consciousness. An example is the phenomenological (feeling) component of an unlabeled and thus unarticulated emotion experience, a feeling that you know you are experiencing but cannot specifically identify or describe. Inability to put the feeling into words bars it from linguistic accessibility and thus from access consciousness as typically defined, but not from phenomenal consciousness and various levels of awareness. An emotion feeling in phenomenal and other nonlinguistic levels of consciousness retains its properties, including its power to motivate and regulate cognition and action. Thus, conceptualizing fully functional emotion feelings as processes in phenomenal consciousness (Panksepp 2005) provides an alternative way of explaining much of what has been attributed by others to the psychological unconscious (e.g., Kihlstrom 1999, Winkielman et al. 2005; cf. Clore et al. 2005, Lambie & Marcel 2002).

Concern about types of consciousness may stimulate further thought and research about which mental processes relate to phenomenal consciousness and which are truly unconscious. Such research could look for processes that reside at a level of awareness that is unavailable via cognitive or verbal access but not necessarily via other forms of access. Several types of nonverbal behaviors reflect the operations of mental processes that clearly are not in linguistically accessible consciousness and that may reside in phenomenal consciousness (Izard et al. 2008b; cf. Merker 2007). The lack of linguistic accessibility does not render an emotion or emotion feeling nonfunctional.

Phenomenal consciousness and other forms of linguistically inaccessible consciousness may be better concepts for psychology than is the concept of unconscious. The latter concept is notoriously vague and ill defined in the psychological literature. Dictionary definitions characterize it as not conscious as a state, without awareness, or sensation, virtually nonphysical, and thus make some uses of it very close to the domains of spookiness and Cartesian dualism.

The Psychological Unconscious: A Default Explanatory Construct?

Although there is considerable agreement on the qualities of thought processes in psychological or access (verbally reportable) consciousness, there is no consensus on the contents and processes of the unconscious (cf. Bargh & Morsella 2008). The behavior of prelingual infants suggests that it is not prudent to label all verbally unreportable processes as unconscious, a practice that may impede or misguide the search for causal processes. Better heuristics might come from the conceptualization of causal-process mechanisms operating at different levels of awareness and as accessible by multiple behaviors other than verbal report. Dividing the mind and all mental processes into two domains—conscious and unconscious—might be the greatest oversimplification in current psychological science. Moreover, misattribution of causal processes to the unconscious may open a Pandora's Box replete with blind alleys and dead ends.

Four things have contributed to psychologists' penchant for attributing causal processes to the unconscious rather than to emotion feelings, including emotion feelings in phenomenal consciousness. First, many psychologists have typically looked for nonemotion mediators to explain changes in cognition and action. Second, emotion feelings (and their roles in influencing cognitive processes) are notoriously difficult to identify and describe in words (Creighton 1921, Langer 1967/1982). However, infants and young children experience emotions and respond to them in meaningful ways long before they can label or describe emotions (Izard et al. 2008b). Such evidence points to the utility of assessing emotion feelings by measuring their functional correlates. Third, many psychologists remain reluctant to attribute to emotion a significant causal role in ordinary as well as critical thinking, decision making, and action despite a growing body of evidence to the contrary (e.g., Bechara et al. 2000, De Martino et al. 2006, Lerner & Tiedens 2006, Miller 2006, Naqvi et al. 2006). Fourth, many psychological scientists tend to think that emotions are typically brief and that emotion feelings are always sufficiently intense to grab and hold attention. Actually, plausible arguments suggest that emotion feelings are phenomena that vary on a very wide dimension of intensity while retaining their functional/causal properties (Izard 2007a).

Emerging Issues: Continuous Emotion, Memes, and the Mirror Neuron System

The topics of continuous emotion or continuous emotion-cognition interaction and integration, memes, and the mirror neuron system (MNS) may prove to be critical for emotion science and to psychology in general. The idea of continuous emotion in phenomenal consciousness or access consciousness will prove difficult to address in empirical research, but that may soon change with improved technology for studying brain-emotion-behavior relations. Already there is some convergence among theorists and researchers who argue that there is no such thing as a conscious mind without emotion or affect (Izard 2007a; cf. Lewis 2005, Phelps 2006, Russell 2003). The other two, memes and the MNS, relate to emotion and behavior in ways not completely understood. Yet, they have already become hot topics for those interested in new approaches to understanding within- and across-generations transmission of cognitive and action structures and the neurobiological bases for the transmission of emotion feelings in empathy and the processes in empathic and sympathetic responding.

Continuous Emotion-Cognition Interaction

The notion that some emotion or emotion-cognition interaction is continuous in phenomenal or access consciousness or some level of awareness is not new (e.g., Bacon 1620/1968). The hypothesis implicit in that idea may prove difficult to falsify. Yet, without the attribution of causal power to emotion (feeling) and the concept of continual emotion-cognition interaction, we may have no way to explain selective attention. And selective attention is a necessary factor in the simplest forms of exploration and learning as well as in higher-order cognition and sequences of organized behavior.

I have hypothesized that the brain automatically generates the emotion of interest to capture and sustain attention to particular objects, events, and goals. This mode of operation is standard when the brain is not responding to internal or external conditions that activate other emotions, emotion schemas, or emotion-cognition-environment interactions (Izard 2007a; cf. Panksepp 2003a,b).

A major challenge for future research is to understand how emotion and cognition behave in their continual interaction. One possibility is that they achieve complete integration and influence behavior as a unified force or single factor. However, I propose that although emotion and cognition continually interact, they do not lose their separate identities. They retain separate and distinct functional properties (cf. Pessoa 2008). Whereas emotion feeling undoubtedly contains a kind of information (Clore et al. 2001) or cues for behavior (Izard 1971, 2007a), emotion remains primarily about motivation. Cognition (particularly about goal concepts that typically have an emotion component) may be conceived as having a motivational aspect, but it remains primarily about knowledge.

Memes and Emotions

Memes are one of several epigenetic mechanisms that challenge the dominance of DNA as the central life force (cf. Noble 2006). Natural selection may operate on not only genes, DNA, or RNA. It can also act on "replicant" units (memes) that consist of cognition and action patterns, things other than biological structures that can be transmitted through imitative learning (Dawkins 1989). Apparently, memes emerged to serve unique adaptive functions in social interactions.

In the course of evolution, the brain continued to evolve and increase in complexity until learning via imitation became a major tool in the human repertoire and a way of acquiring memes. Imitation and make-believe play in early development should prove a fertile ground for studying the transmission of memes. Even newborn infants can imitate simple facial behavior (Meltzoff & Moore 1994) that may constitute part of the emotion expressions that they display later in infancy (Izard et al. 1995). By age three years, children show great imitative skills while enjoying the fantasyland of make-believe play and learning socioemotional skills by assuming the roles of persons far beyond them in age, knowledge, skills, and experience. Thus, it was both phylogenetic transmission and the highly creative processes of ontogenetic development (Noble 2006) that produced the capacity for imitative learning, which in turn essentially created a context where memes could replicate and compete (Jablonka & Lamb 2005).

Though memes were originally described in terms of cognition and action patterns (Dawkins 1989), the exclusion of emotion as a component may have been inadvertent. Indeed, emotion schemas seem perfect candidates for attaining status as memes. They not only have a cognitive component but also an emotion component and a kind of action component (the action tendencies in emotion states; Izard 2007a,b). Thus, emotion schemas are well suited to emerge and operate as memes. Their emotion feeling component is often expressed through facial, vocal, and body-movement signals that are easily imitated, even by young children. In addition, imitating the expressive behavior of another person may activate neural and sensory motor processes that increase the likelihood of experiencing the emotion (and action tendencies) of the other person (Izard 1990, Niedenthal 2007). Young children's imitation of their parents' positive emotion expressions and interactions may contribute to the development of memes that represent significant social skills. Thus, emotion-schema memes (ESMs) as replicant units with a feeling/motivational component seem to be an expectable (epigenetic) extension of biogenetic-evolutionary processes.

Because emotions are contagious (Hatfield et al. 1993, Tomkins 1962), memes that are essentially emotion schemas can propagate profusely. They can do so for two reasons. First, such schemas have the attention-grabbing and motivational power of an emotion (Youngstrom & Izard 2008). Second, they are highly functional phenomena independent of their relations to biological fitness and survival (cf. Aunger 2002, Blackmore 1999, Distin 2004). The idea that an emotion schema might form a replicant unit opens another door to investigations of the transfer of adaptive as well as maladaptive patterns of emotion, cognition, and action within and across generations.

Emotion schema memes begin to develop early in ontogeny, become plentiful, and may relate substantially to the MNS. There has been a surge of interest in the MNS, in part because it may be among the neural substrates of social perspective taking and empathy (e.g., Carr et al. 2003, Keysers & Perrett 2004, Rizzolatti & Craighero 2004).

Mirror Neuron Systems, Emotions, and Empathy

If the concept of memes becomes a staple in psychology, it may happen for two reasons. First, perhaps the most interesting and socially significant memes have an emotion component and are essentially emotion schemas whose behavioral manifestations (facial, vocal, gestural expressions of emotion) can be readily observed and analyzed. Second, they may depend in part on the MNS, which seems to mediate capabilities for perspective taking and empathy. The MNS may enable one to take the perspective of another and provide the shared emotion feeling that defines the essence of empathy (cf. Dapretto et al. 2006, Keysers & Perrett 2004). The MNS apparently translates one's sensory-perceptual experiences and accompanying conceptions of the expressions and movements of others into patterns of neural activity in the observer (cf. Langer 1967/1982). This neural activity and its products help the observer to understand and predict the thoughts and feelings of the observed person.

The MNS may relate to sympathy and altruism as well. The cognitive component of an emotion schema, in interaction with its feeling component, may transform empathy to sympathy. This transformation would entail a shift from a response governed primarily by neurophysiological or motor-system contagion to one that requires conceptual processes (cf. Langer 1967/1982). An MNS that facilitates sympathy, altruism, and mimetic processes would facilitate highly adaptive advantages (Miller 2008, Talmi & Frith 2007).

Empathy alone is not always sufficient to motivate helping behavior (Rosenthal 1964/1999). The cognition (particularly the action plans) in an ESM provides the context for its feeling component, and the interaction of the cognition and feeling in the meme can guide sympathetic actions. Dysfunction of the MNS may help account for the deficits in socialization that are observed in autism spectrum disorders (Oberman & Ramachandran 2007) and in antisocial personality or perhaps in any disorder involving deficits or dysfunction in social skills (Iacoboni 2007).

The possibility that the MNS and associated emotion systems mediate the generation and propagation of memes suggests the fruitfulness of studying memes that can be clearly identified as ESMs. ESMs should prove plentiful because they have an enormous appeal to forces that generate and propagate memes. The emotion component of an ESM has the motivational power to influence perception, grab attention, generate more emotion-cognition structures, and influence action. ESMs may constitute a

Emotion-schema memes (ESMs): epigenetic emotion-cognition processes derived from mimicry of emotion-expressive cognition and action and endowed with motivation for influencing development and behavior

major factor that shapes consciousness, personality and social functioning, and culture (Youngstrom & Izard 2008).

CONCLUDING REMARKS

Emotion research has increased exponentially since Tomkins's (1962, 1963) landmark volumes helped bring a nascent emotion science into an unevenly matched competition with the forces of the contemporaneous revolution that produced cognitive science. The two disciplines are becoming increasingly collaborative and progressing toward becoming one. As the realization of this exciting prospect proceeds, great challenges await scientists who will seek to understand how the brain assigns weights or significance to emotion and cognition (which assumedly retain distinct functions) as they are integrated or mingled in different periods of development, personalities, and contexts. They will find equally interesting challenges in research on ways to facilitate these processes to gain adaptive advantages, bolster constructive and creative endeavors, and prevent destructive and maladaptive behavior.

SUMMARY POINTS

1. Emotion feelings are a phase of neurobiological activity and the key psychological/motivational aspect of emotion. They constitute the primary motivational systems for human behavior.

2. Emotion feelings are prime factors in the evolution, organization, and operations of consciousness and the different levels of awareness.

3. The ability to symbolize feelings and put them into words provides a powerful tool for emotion regulation, influencing emotion-cognition relations, and developing high-level social skills.

4. The term "emotion" has defied definition mainly because it is multifaceted and not a unitary phenomenon or process. Use of the unqualified term "emotion" makes for misunderstandings, contradictions, and confusions in theory and research.

5. Basic emotions, emotion schemas, and emotion-schema memes are distinctly different in terms of their origin, content, causes, and effects.

6. Transitions from basic emotions to emotion schemas and emotion-schema memes are major milestones in development and in achieving social and emotion competence.

7. The psychological unconscious is an ill-defined and potentially misleading term. There is no consensus regarding its contents and functions. The concept of levels of awareness may provide a better bridge to understanding human mentality and brain/mind processes.

8. Emotion utilization is the harnessing of an emotion's inherently adaptive emotion motivation/feeling component in constructive affective-cognitive processes and actions. Symbolization and effective communication of emotion feelings play a key role in emotion utilization, particularly in real or simulated social interactions.

9. The concept of emotion-cognition interaction, well validated in neuroscience and behavioral research, suggests that the presence of functionally distinct features in the interactants would increase both the flexibility and generality of the resultant processes.

FUTURE ISSUES

1. Experimental validation of the hypothesis that the feeling component of some emotion or emotion schema is continuous at some level of awareness should prove an interesting challenge for future research. So should studies designed to verify the hypothesis that interest or an interest schema is the default emotion or emotion-cognition interaction.

2. Insights on the early development and life-span growth of emotion-schema memes should add substantially to our understanding of the contributions of social and cultural factors in mental processes and behavior.

3. Distinguishing between emotion regulation and emotion utilization may provide new insights on the independence and interdependence of these two constructs.

4. Determining how the emotion and cognitive components of emotion schemas and emotion-schema memes integrate or mingle in the brain should provide leads for translational research. The findings from such research should contribute to preventive interventions that facilitate the development of emotion and social competence and the prevention of psychopathology.

DISCLOSURE STATEMENT

The author is not aware of any biases that might be perceived as affecting the objectivity of this review.

ACKNOWLEDGMENT

Work on this article was supported by National Institute of Mental Health grants R21 MH068443 and R01 MH080909.

LITERATURE CITED

Ackerman BP, Abe JA, Izard CE. 1998. Differential emotions theory and emotional development: mindful of modularity. In *What Develops in Emotional Development? Emotions, Personality, and Psychotherapy*, ed. M Mascolo, S Griffin, pp. 85–106. New York: Plenum

Aunger R. 2002. *The Electric Meme: A New Theory of How We Think*. New York: Free Press. 392 pp.

Bacon F. 1620/1968. Novum Organum. In *The Works of Francis Bacon: Baron of Verulam, Viscount St. Alban, and Lord High Chancellor of England*, ed. J Spedding, RL Ellis, DD Heath, pp. 47–69. New York: Garrett Press

Bargh JA, Morsella E. 2008. The unconscious mind. *Perspect. Psychol. Sci.* 3:73–79

Barrett LF. 2006. Are emotions natural kinds? *Perspect. Psychol. Sci.* 1:28–58

Barrett LF, Lindquist KA, Bliss-Moreau E, Duncan S, Gendron M, et al. 2007. Of mice and men: natural kinds of emotions in the mammalian brain? A response to Panksepp and Izard. *Perspect. Psychol. Sci.* 2:297–312

Barrett LF, Niedenthal PM, Winkielman P. 2005a. *Emotion and Consciousness*. New York: Guilford

Barrett LF, Niedenthal PM, Winkielman P. 2005b. Introduction. See Barrett et al. 2005a, pp. 1–18

Bechara A, Damasio H, Damasio A. 2000. Emotion, decision making and the orbitofrontal cortex. *Cereb. Cortex* 10:295–307

Blackmore S. 1999. *The Meme Machine*. New York: Oxford Univ. Press

Block N. 2007. Consciousness, accessibility, and the mesh between psychology and neuroscience. *Behav. Brain Sci.* 30:481–99

Buschman TJ, Miller EK. 2007. Top-down versus bottom-up control of attention in the prefrontal and posterior parietal cortices. *Science* 315:1860–62

Carr L, Iacoboni M, Dubeau M-C, Mazziotta JC, Lenzi GL. 2003. Neural mechanisms of empathy in humans: a relay from neural systems for imitation to limbic areas. *Proc. Natl. Acad. Sci. USA* 100:5497–502

Chalmers DJ. 1996. *The Conscious Mind: In Search of a Fundamental Theory*. New York: Oxford Univ. Press

Claxton LJ, Keen R, McCarty ME. 2003. Evidence of motor planning in infant reaching behavior. *Psychol. Sci.* 14:354–56

Clore GL, Storbeck J, Robinson MD, Centerbar DB. 2005. Seven sins in the study of unconscious affect. See Barrett et al. 2005a, pp. 384–408

Clore GL, Wyer RS Jr, Dienes B, Gasper K, Gohm C, Isbell L. 2001. Affective feelings as feedback: some cognitive consequences. In *Theories of Mood and Cognition: A User's Guidebook*, ed. LL Martin, GL Clore, pp. 27–62. Mahwah, NJ: Erlbaum

Creighton JE. 1921. Reason and feeling. *Philos. Rev.* 30:465–81

Damasio AR. 1999. *The Feeling of What Happens: Body and Emotion in the Making of Consciousness*. New York: Harcourt Brace

Damasio A. 2003. The person within. *Nature* 423(6937):227

Dapretto M, Davies MS, Pfeifer JH, Scott AA, Sigman M, et al. 2006. Understanding emotions in others: mirror neuron dysfunction in children with autism spectrum disorders. *Nat. Neurosci.* 9:28–30

Darwin C. 1872/1965. *The Expression of the Emotions in Man and Animals*. New York: Oxford Univ. Press

Davidson RJ. 1994. Asymmetric brain function, affective style, and psychopathology: the role of early experience and plasticity. *Dev. Psychol.* 6:741–58

Davidson RJ. 1998. Affective style and affective disorders: perspectives from affective neuroscience. *Cogn. Emot.* 12:307–30

Dawkins R. 1989. *The Selfish Gene*. London: Oxford Univ. Press

de Gelder B. 2005. Nonconscious emotions: new findings and perspectives on nonconscious facial expression recognition and its voice and whole-body contexts. See Barrett et al. 2005a, pp. 123–49

De Martino B, Kumaran D, Seymour B, Dolan RJ. 2006. Frames, biases, and rational decision-making in the human brain. *Science* 313:684–87

Denham SA, Burton R. 2003. *Social and Emotional Prevention and Intervention Programming for Preschoolers*. New York: Kluwer Acad./Plenum

Diener E, Smith H, Fujita F. 1995. The personality structure of affect. *J. Personal. Soc. Psychol.* 69:130–41

Distin K. 2004. *The Selfish Meme: A Critical Reassessment*. New York: Cambridge Univ. Press

Domitrovich CE, Greenberg MT. 2004. Preventive interventions with young children: building on the foundation of early intervention programs. *Early Educ. Dev.* 15:365–70

Edelman GM. 2006. Second nature: the transformation of knowledge. In *Second Nature: Brain Science and Human Knowledge*, ed. GM Edelman, pp. 142–57. New Haven, CT: Yale Univ. Press

Edelman GM, Tononi G. 2000. *A Universe of Consciousness: How Matter Becomes Imagination*. New York: Basic Books. 274 pp.

Eisenberg N, Spinrad TL. 2004. Emotion-related regulation: sharpening the definition. *Child Dev.* 75:334–39

Ekman P. 2003. *Emotions Revealed*. New York: Times Books

Ellsworth PC. 1994. William James and emotion: Is a century of fame worth a century of misunderstanding? *Psychol. Rev.* 101:222–29

Ellsworth PC, Scherer KR. 2003. Appraisal processes in emotion. In *Handbook of Affective Sciences*, ed. RJ Davidson, KR Scherer, HH Goldsmith, pp. 572–95. New York: Oxford Univ. Press

Fox NA, Henderson HA, Marshall PJ, Nichols KE, Ghera MM. 2005. Behavioral inhibition: linking biology and behavior within a developmental framework. *Annu. Rev. Psychol.* 56:235–62

Fredrickson BL. 1998. What good are positive emotions? *Rev. Gen. Psychol.* 2:300–19

Fredrickson BL. 2007. Positive emotions. In *Handbook of Positive Psychology*, ed. CR Snyder, S Lopez, pp. 120–34. New York: Oxford Univ. Press

Goldsmith HH, Campos JJ. 1982. Toward a theory of infant temperament. In *The Development of Attachment and Affiliative Systems*, ed. RN Emde, RJ Harmon, pp. 231–83. Hillsdale, NJ: Erlbaum

Gray JA. 1990. Brain systems that mediate both emotion and cognition. *Cogn. Emot.* 4:269–88

Gray JR, Schaefer A, Braver TS, Most SB. 2005. Affect and the resolution of cognitive control dilemmas. See Barrett et al. 2005a, pp. 67–94

Greenberg LS, Paivio SC. 1997. *Working with Emotions in Psychotherapy*. New York: Guilford

Gross JJ. 2002. Emotion regulation: affective, cognitive, and social consequences. *Psychophysiology* 39:281–91

Hatfield E, Cacioppo JT, Rapson RL. 1993. Emotional contagion. *Curr. Dir. Psychol. Sci.* 2:96–99

Hoffman ML. 2000. *Empathy and Moral Development: Implications for Caring and Justice*. New York: Cambridge Univ. Press

Humphrey N. 2006. *Seeing Red*. Cambridge, MA: Harvard Univ. Press

Iacoboni M. 2007. Face to face: the neural basis of social mirroring and empathy. *Psychiatr. Ann.* 37:236–41

Izard CE. 1971. *The Face of Emotion*. New York: Appleton-Century-Crofts

Izard CE. 1972. *Patterns of Emotions: A New Analysis of Anxiety and Depression*. New York: Academic

Izard CE. 1977. *Human Emotions*. New York: Plenum

Izard CE. 1984. Emotion-cognition relationships and human development. In *Emotion, Cognition, and Behavior*, ed. CE Izard, J Kagan, RB Zajonc, pp. 17–37. New York: Cambridge Univ. Press

Izard CE. 1990. Facial expressions and the regulation of emotions. *J. Personal. Soc. Psychol.* 58:487–98

Izard CE. 1993. Four systems for emotion activation: cognitive and noncognitive processes. *Psychol. Rev.* 100:68–90

Izard CE. 2002. Translating emotion theory and research into preventive interventions. *Psychol. Bull.* 128:796–824

Izard CE. 2006. *Experts' Definitions of Emotion and Their Ratings of Its Components and Characteristics*. Unpubl. manuscr., Univ. Delaware, Newark

Izard CE. 2007a. Basic emotions, natural kinds, emotion schemas, and a new paradigm. *Personal. Psychol. Sci.* 2:260–80

Izard CE. 2007b. Levels of emotion and levels of consciousness. *Behav. Brain Sci.* 30:96–98

Izard CE, Fantauzzo CA, Castle JM, Haynes OM, Rayias MF, Putnam PH. 1995. The ontogeny and significance of infants' facial expressions in the first 9 months of life. *Dev. Psychol.* 31:997–1013

Izard CE, Hembree EA, Huebner RR. 1987. Infants' emotion expressions to acute pain: developmental change and stability of individual differences. *Dev. Psychol.* 23:105–13

Izard CE, King KA, Trentacosta CJ, Laurenceau JP, Morgan JK, et al. 2008a. Accelerating the development of emotion competence in Head Start children. *Dev. Psychol.* 20:369–97

Izard CE, Malatesta CZ. 1987. Perspectives on emotional development: differential emotions theory of early emotional development. In *Handbook of Infant Development*, ed. JD Osofsky, pp. 494–554. New York: Wiley Intersci. 2nd ed.

Izard CE, Quinn PC, Most SB. 2008b. Many ways to awareness: a developmental perspective on cognitive access. *Behav. Brain Sci.* 30:506–7

Izard C, Stark K, Trentacosta C, Schultz D. 2008c. Beyond emotion regulation: emotion utilization and adaptive functioning. *Child Dev. Perspect.* In press

Jablonka E, Lamb MJ. 2005. *Evolution in Four Dimensions: Genetic, Epigenetic, Behavioral, and Symbolic Variation in the History of Life*. Cambridge, MA: MIT Press. 462 pp.

James W. 1884. What is emotion? *Mind* 4:188–204

Kennedy-Moore E, Watson JC. 1999. *Expressing Emotion: Myths, Realities, and Therapeutic Strategies*. New York: Guilford

Keysers C, Perrett DI. 2004. Demystifying social cognition: a Hebbian perspective. *Trends Cogn. Sci.* 8:501–7

Kihlstrom JF. 1999. The psychological unconscious. In *Handbook of Personality: Theory and Research*, ed. LA Pervin, OP John, pp. 424–42. New York: Guilford

Kleinginna PR, Kleinginna AM. 1981. A categorized list of emotion definitions, with suggestions for a consensual definition. *Motiv. Emot.* 5:345–79

Lambie JA, Marcel AJ. 2002. Consciousness and the varieties of emotion experience: a theoretical framework. *Psychol. Rev.* 109:219–59

Lane RD, Ahern GL, Schwartz GE, Kaszniak AW. 1997. Is alexithymia the emotional equivalent of blindsight? *Biol. Psychiatry* 42:834–44

Langer SK. 1967/1982. *Mind: An Essay on Human Feeling*. Baltimore, MD: Johns Hopkins Univ. Press

Langsdorf P, Izard CE, Rayias M, Hembree E. 1983. Interest expression, visual fixation, and heart rate changes in 2- to 8-month-old infants. *Dev. Psychol.* 19:375–86

LeDoux JE. 1996. *The Emotional Brain: The Mysterious Underpinnings of Emotional Life*. New York: Simon & Schuster

Lerner JS, Tiedens LZ. 2006. Portrait of the angry decision maker: how appraisal tendencies shape anger's influence on cognition. *J. Behav. Decis. Mak.* 19:115–37

Lewis M. 2005. Bridging emotion theory and neurobiology through dynamic systems modeling. *Behav. Brain Sci.* 28:169–245

Lieberman MD, Eisenberger NI, Crockett MJ, Tom SM, Pfeifer JH, Way BM. 2007. Putting feelings into words. *Psychol. Sci.* 18:421–28

Magai C, Hunziker J. 1993. Tolstoy and the riddle of developmental transformation: a lifespan analysis of the role of emotions in personality development. In *Handbook of Emotions*, ed. MB Lewis, JM Haviland, pp. 247–59. New York: Guilford

Magai C, McFadden SH. 1995. *The Role of Emotions in Social and Personality Development: History, Theory, and Research*. New York: Plenum

Mayer JD, Salovey P. 1997. What is emotional intelligence? In *Emotional Development and Emotional Intelligence: Implications for Educators*, ed. P Salovey, D Sluyter, pp. 3–31. New York: Basic Books

Meltzoff AN, Moore MK. 1994. Imitation, memory, and the representation of persons. *Infant Behav. Dev.* 17:83–99

Merker B. 2007. Consciousness without a cerebral cortex: a challenge for neuroscience and medicine. *Behav. Brain Sci.* 30:63–134

Miller G. 2006. Neuroscience: The emotional brain weighs its options. *Science* 313:600–1

Miller G. 2008. Neuroscience: Mirror neurons may help songbirds stay in tune. *Science* 319:269

Mischel W, Shoda Y. 1995. A cognitive-affective system theory of personality: reconceptualizing situations, dispositions, dynamics, and invariance in personality structure. *Psychol. Rev.* 102:246–68

Mischel W, Shoda Y. 1998. Reconciling processing dynamics and personality dispositions. *Annu. Rev. Psychol.* 49:229–58

Mobbs D, Petrovic P, Marchant JL, Hassabis D, Weiskopf N, et al. 2007. When fear is near: Threat imminence elicits prefrontal-periaqueductal gray shifts in humans. *Science* 317(5841):1079–83

Naqvi N, Shiv B, Bechara A. 2006. The role of emotion in decision making: a cognitive neuroscience perspective. *Curr. Dir. Psychol. Sci.* 15:260–4

Niedenthal PM. 2007. Embodying emotion. *Science* 316:1002–5

Noble D. 2006. *The Music of Life*. New York: Oxford Univ. Press

Northoff G, Heinzel A, Bermpohl F, Niese R, Pfennig A, et al. 2004. Reciprocal modulation and attenuation in the prefrontal cortex: an fMRI study on emotional-cognitive interaction. *Hum. Brain Mapp.* 21:202–12

Oberman LM, Ramachandran VS. 2007. The simulating social mind: the role of the mirror neuron system and simulation in the social and communicative deficits of autism spectrum disorders. *Psychol. Bull.* 133:310–27

Öhman A. 2002. Automaticity and the amygdala: nonconscious responses to emotional faces. *Curr. Dir. Psychol. Sci.* 11:62–66

Öhman A. 2005. The role of the amygdala in human fear: automatic detection of threat. *Psychoneuroendocrinology* 30:953–58

Panksepp J. 2007. Neurologizing the psychology of affects: how appraisal-based constructivism and basic emotion theory can coexist. *Personal. Psychol. Sci.* 2:281–95

Panksepp J. 2003a. Damasio's error? *Conscious. Emot.* 4:111–34

Panksepp J. 2003b. At the interface of the affective, behavioral, and cognitive neurosciences: decoding the emotional feelings of the brain. *Brain Cogn.* 52:4–14

Panksepp J. 2005. Affective consciousness: core emotional feelings in animals and humans. *Conscious. Cogn.* 14:30–80

Pessoa L. 2008. On the relationship between emotion and cognition. *Nat. Rev. Neurosci.* 9:148–58

Phelps EA. 2006. Emotion and cognition: insights from studies of the human amygdala. *Annu. Rev. Psychol.* 57:27–53

Rizzolatti G, Craighero L. 2004. The mirror-neuron system. *Annu. Rev. Neurosci.* 27:169–92

Rosenthal AM. 1964/1999. *Thirty-Eight Witnesses: The Kitty Genovese Case*. Berkeley: Univ. Calif. Press

Russell JA. 2003. Core affect and the psychological construction of emotion. *Psychol. Rev.* 110:145–72

Scherer K. 2000. Emotion. In *Introduction to Social Psychology: A European Perspective*, ed. M Hewstone, W Stroebe, pp. 151–91. Oxford: Blackwell Sci.

Schwarz N, Clore GL. 1983. Mood, misattribution, and judgments of well-being: informative and directive functions of affective states. *J. Personal. Soc. Psychol.* 45:513–23

Shweder RA. 1994. "You're not sick, you're just in love": an attributional theory of motivation and emotion. In *The Nature of Emotion: Fundamental Questions*, ed. P Ekman, R Davidson, pp. 32–44. New York: Oxford Univ. Press

Silvia PJ. 2006. *Exploring the Psychology of Interest*. New York: Oxford Univ. Press

Spinoza B. 1677/1957. *The Ethics of Spinoza*. New York: Citadel

Talmi D, Frith C. 2007. Neurobiology: feeling right about doing right. *Nature* 446:865–66

Tangney JP, Stuewig J, Mashek DJ. 2007. Moral emotions and moral behavior. *Annu. Rev. Psychol.* 58:345–72

Tomkins SS. 1962. *Affect, Imagery, Consciousness: Vol. I. The Positive Affects*. New York: Springer

Tomkins SS. 1963. *Affect, Imagery, Consciousness: Vol. II. The Negative Affects*. New York: Springer

Tomkins SS. 1987. Script theory. In *The Emergence of Personality*, ed. J Aronoff, AI Rabin, RA Zucker, pp. 72–97. New York: Springer

Weiskrantz L. 2001. Blindsight–putting beta (β) on the back burner. In *Out of Mind: Varieties of Unconscious Processes*, ed. B De Gelder, EHF De Haan, CA Heywood, pp. 20–31. New York: Oxford Univ. Press

Winkielman P, Berridge KC, Wilbarger JL. 2005. Emotion, behavior, and conscious experience: once more without feeling. See Barrett et al. 2005a, pp. 335–62

Youngstrom EA, Izard CE. 2008. Functions of emotions and emotion-related dysfunction. In *Handbook of Approach and Avoidance Motivation*, ed. AJ Elliot, pp. 363–80. Mahwah, NJ: Erlbaum

Concepts and Categories: A Cognitive Neuropsychological Perspective

Bradford Z. Mahon[1,2] and Alfonso Caramazza[1,2]

[1]Department of Psychology, Harvard University, Cambridge, Massachusetts 02318;
[2]Center for Mind/Brain Sciences, CIMeC, University of Trento, Rovereto (TN),
Italy 38068; email: Mahon@fas.harvard.edu, Caram@wjh.harvard.edu

Annu. Rev. Psychol. 2009. 60:27–51

First published online as a Review in Advance on
September 3, 2008

The *Annual Review of Psychology* is online at
psych.annualreviews.org

This article's doi:
10.1146/annurev.psych.60.110707.163532

0066-4308/09/0110-0027$20.00

Key Words

category-specific semantic deficits, apraxia, semantic organization,
domain specific, sensory motor

Abstract

One of the most provocative and exciting issues in cognitive science is
how neural specificity for semantic categories of common objects arises
in the functional architecture of the brain. More than two decades of
research on the neuropsychological phenomenon of category-specific
semantic deficits has generated detailed claims about the organization
and representation of conceptual knowledge. More recently, researchers
have sought to test hypotheses developed on the basis of neuropsychological evidence with functional imaging. From those two fields,
the empirical generalization emerges that object domain and sensory
modality jointly constrain the organization of knowledge in the brain.
At the same time, research within the embodied cognition framework
has highlighted the need to articulate how information is communicated
between the sensory and motor systems, and processes that represent
and generalize abstract information. Those developments point toward
a new approach for understanding category specificity in terms of the
coordinated influences of diverse regions and cognitive systems.

Contents

INTRODUCTION

The scientific study of how concepts are represented in the mind/brain extends to all disciplines within cognitive science. Within the psychological and brain sciences, research has focused on studying how the perceptual, motor, and conceptual attributes of common objects are represented and organized in the brain. Theories of conceptual representation must therefore explain not only how conceptual content itself is represented and organized, but also the role played by conceptual content in orchestrating perceptual and motor processes.

Cognitive neuropsychological studies of brain-damaged patients provide strong evidence about the representation of conceptual knowledge and the relationship between conceptual knowledge and perceptual and motor processes. The cognitive neuropsychological approach ultimately seeks to evaluate models of cognitive processing through the proximate goal of explaining the profile of behavioral performance observed in brain-damaged patients. In the measure to which it is possible to establish the functional locus of impairment in a patient within a given model of cognitive functioning, then it is possible to test other assumptions of that model through further experiments with that patient. Dissociations of abilities in patients (and of processes in models) are central to the neuropsychological approach. This is because if a given behavior/process X can be impaired while another behavior/process Y is preserved, then one may conclude that the former process is not causally involved in the latter process. Another important source of evidence from neuropsychology are aspects of cognitive functioning that are observed to be systematically impaired or spared together (for discussion of methodological issues in cognitive neuropsychology, see Caramazza 1986, 1992; Shallice 1988).

Scope of the Review

The modern study of the representation of concepts in the brain was initiated by a series of papers by Elizabeth Warrington, Tim Shallice, and Rosaleen McCarthy. Those authors described patients with disproportionate semantic impairments for one, or several, categories of objects compared to other categories (see Hécaen & De Ajuriaguerra 1956 for earlier work). Since those initial investigations, a great deal has been learned about the causes of category-specific semantic deficits, and by extension, the organization of object knowledge in the brain.

The focus of this review is on neuropsychological research, and in particular, on the phenomenon of category-specific semantic deficits. Evidence from other fields within cognitive science and neuroscience and functional neuroimaging is reviewed as it bears on the theoretical positions that emerge from the study of category-specific semantic deficits. In particular, we highlight findings in functional neuroimaging related to the representation of different semantic categories in the brain. We also discuss the degree to which conceptual representations are grounded in sensory and motor processes, and the critical role that neuropsychological studies of patients with impairments to sensory and motor knowledge can play in constraining theories of semantic representation.

CATEGORY-SPECIFIC SEMANTIC DEFICITS: INTRODUCTION TO THE PHENOMENON

Patients with category-specific semantic deficits present with disproportionate or even selective impairments for one semantic category compared to other semantic categories. **Figure 1** (see color insert) illustrates cases of disproportionate impairment for animals (*upper left*; Blundo et al. 2006, Caramazza & Shelton 1998), fruit/vegetables (*upper right*; Hart et al. 1985, Samson & Pillon 2003), conspecifics (*lower left*; Miceli et al. 2000, Ellis et al. 1989), and nonliving things (*lower right*; Laiacona & Capitani 2001, Sacchett & Humphreys 1992). More than one hundred cases of category-specific semantic impairment have been reported (for review and discussion, see Capitani et al. 2003, Hart et al. 2007, Humphreys & Forde 2001, Tyler & Moss 2001). The majority of reported patients have

disproportionate impairments for living things compared to nonliving things (Capitani et al. 2003).

One important aspect of the performance profile of patients with category-specific semantic impairment is that the impairment is to conceptual knowledge and not (only) to modality-specific input or output representations. The evidence for locating the deficit at a conceptual level is that the category-specific deficit does not depend on stimuli being presented or that patients respond in only one modality of input or output. For instance, patients KC and EW (**Figure 1a**) were impaired for naming living animate things compared to nonliving things and fruit/vegetables. Both patients were also impaired for answering questions about living animate things, such as "Does a whale have legs" or "Are dogs domestic animals," but were unimpaired for the same types of questions about nonanimals (see **Figure 2a**, color insert, for data from EW and other representative patients).

Patients with category-specific semantic deficits may have additional, and also category-specific, deficits at presemantic levels of processing. For instance, patient EW was impaired for judging whether pictures depicted real or unreal animals but was unimpaired for the same task over nonanimal stimuli. The ability to make such decisions is assumed to index the integrity of the visual structural description system, a presemantic stage of object recognition (Humphreys et al. 1988). In contrast, patient KC was relatively unimpaired on an object decision task, even for the category of items (living animate) that the patient was unable to name. A similar pattern to that observed in patient KC was present in patient APA (Miceli et al. 2000). Patient APA was selectively impaired for conceptual knowledge of people (see **Figure 1c**). Despite a severe impairment for naming famous people, APA did not have a deficit at the level of face recognition (prosopagnosia).

Another important aspect of patients with category-specific semantic impairments is that they have difficulty distinguishing among basic-level items within the impaired category but do not necessarily have problems assigning items they cannot identify to the correct superordinate level category (e.g., they may know that a picture of a dog is an animal, but do not know which animal) (see Humphreys & Forde 2005 for discussion of a patient with greater difficulty at a superordinate than a basic level across all semantic categories).

A number of studies have now documented that variables such as lexical frequency, concept familiarity, and visual complexity may be unbalanced if items are sampled randomly from different semantic categories (Cree & McRae 2003, Funnell & Sheridan 1992, Stewart et al. 1992). In addition, Laiacona and colleagues (Barbarotto et al. 2002, Laiacona et al. 1998) have highlighted the need to control for gender-specific effects on variables such as concept familiarity (for discussion of differences between males and females in the incidence of category-specific semantic deficits for different categories, see Laiacona et al. 2006). However, the existence of category-specific semantic deficits is not an artifact of such stimulus-specific attributes. Clear cases have been reported for which stimulus-specific variables have been carefully controlled, and double dissociations have been reported using the same materials (e.g., Hillis & Caramazza 1991; see also the separate case reports in Barbarotto et al. 1995 and Laiacona & Capitani 2001).

OVERVIEW OF THEORETICAL EXPLANATIONS OF THE CAUSES OF CATEGORY-SPECIFIC SEMANTIC DEFICITS

Theories developed in order to explain category-specific semantic deficits fall into two broad groups (Caramazza 1998). Theories within the first group, based on the neural structure principle, assume dissociable neural substrates are differentially (or exclusively) involved in representing different semantic categories. Theories within the second group, based on the correlated structure principle, assume that conceptual knowledge of items

from different semantic categories is not represented in functionally dissociable regions of the brain.

According to theories based on the neural structure principle, category-specific semantic deficits are due to differential or selective damage to the neural substrate upon which the impaired category of items depends. Two broad classes of theories based on the neural structure principle are the sensory/functional theory (Warrington & McCarthy 1983, 1987; Warrington & Shallice 1984) and the domain-specific hypothesis (Caramazza & Shelton 1998).

The sensory/functional theory is composed of two assumptions. The first—the multiple semantics assumption—is that conceptual knowledge is organized into subsystems that parallel the sensory and motor modalities of input and output. The second assumption is that the critical semantic attributes of items from different categories of objects are represented in different modality-specific semantic subsystems.

The domain-specific hypothesis assumes that the first-order constraint on the organization of conceptual knowledge is object domain, with the possible domains restricted to those that could have had an evolutionarily relevant history—living animate, living inanimate, conspecifics, and tools.

Theories based on the correlated structure principle model semantic memory as a system that represents statistical regularities in the co-occurrence of object properties in the world (Caramazza et al. 1990, Devlin et al. 1998, McClelland & Rogers 2003, Tyler & Moss 2001). This class of models has been instrumental in motivating large-scale empirical investigations of how different types of features are distributed and correlated for different semantic categories. Several theories based on the correlated structure principle have been developed in order to explain the causes of category-specific semantic deficits (Caramazza et al. 1990, Devlin et al. 1998, Tyler & Moss 2001).

This review is organized to reflect the role that different theoretical assumptions have played in motivating empirical research. Initial hypotheses that were developed in order to explain category-specific semantic deficits appealed to a single principle of organization (modality specificity, domain specificity, or correlated structure). The current state of the field of category-specific semantic deficits is characterized by complex models that integrate assumptions from multiple theoretical frameworks (for discussion, see Caramazza & Mahon 2003).

THE NEURAL STRUCTURE PRINCIPLE

The Multiple Semantics Assumption

Beauvois initially proposed that the organization of the semantic system follows the organization of the various input and output modalities to and from the semantic system (Beauvois 1982, Beauvois et al. 1978). The original motivation for the assumption of multiple semantics was the phenomenon of optic aphasia (e.g., Lhermitte & Beavuois 1973; for review, see Plaut 2002). Patients with optic aphasia present with impaired naming of visually presented objects but relatively (or completely) spared naming of the same objects when presented through the tactile modality (e.g., Hillis & Caramazza 1995). The fact that optic aphasic patients can name objects presented through the tactile modality indicates that the naming impairment to visual presentation is not due to a deficit at the level of retrieving the correct names. In contrast to patients with visual agnosia (e.g., Milner et al. 1991), patients with optic aphasia can recognize, at a visual level of processing, the stimuli they cannot name. Evidence for this is provided by the fact that some optic aphasic patients can demonstrate the correct use of objects that they cannot name (e.g., Coslett & Saffran 1992, Lhermitte & Beauvois 1973; for discussion, see Plaut 2002). Beauvois (1982) explained the performance of optic aphasic patients by assuming that the conceptual system is functionally organized into visual and verbal semantics and that optic aphasia is due

to a disconnection between the two semantic systems.

Along with reporting the first cases of category-specific semantic deficit, Warrington and her collaborators (Warrington & McCarthy 1983, Warrington & Shallice 1984) developed an influential explanation of the phenomenon that built on the proposal of Beauvois (1982). Warrington and colleagues argued that category-specific semantic deficits are due to differential damage to a modality-specific semantic subsystem that is not itself organized by semantic category. Specifically, those authors noted that the patients they had reported with impairments for living things also had impairments for foods, plants, and precious stones (Warrington & Shallice 1984); in contrast, a patient with an impairment for nonliving things (Warrington & McCarthy 1983) was spared for living things, food, and plant life. Warrington and her collaborators reasoned that the association of impaired and spared categories was meaningfully related to the degree to which identification of items from those categories depends on sensory or functional knowledge. Specifically, they argued that the ability to identify living things differentially depends on sensory knowledge, whereas the ability to identify nonliving things differentially depends on functional knowledge.

Farah & McClelland (1991) implemented the theory of Warrington and colleagues in a connectionist framework. Three predictions follow from the computational model of Farah & McClelland (1991; for discussion, see Caramazza & Shelton 1998). All three of those predictions have now been tested. The first prediction is that the grain of category-specific semantic deficits should not be finer than living versus nonliving. This prediction follows from the assumption that all living things differentially depend on visual knowledge. However, as represented in **Figure 1**, patients have been reported with selective semantic impairments for fruit/vegetables (e.g., Hart et al. 1985, Laiacona et al. 2005, Samson & Pillon 2003) and animals (e.g., Blundo et al. 2006, Caramazza & Shelton

1998). The second prediction is that an impairment for a given category of knowledge will be associated with a disproportionate impairment for the modality of knowledge that is critical for that category. At variance with this prediction, it is now known that category-specific semantic deficits are associated with impairments for all types of knowledge (sensory and functional) about items from the impaired category (**Figure 2a**; e.g., Blundo et al. 2006, Caramazza & Shelton 1998, Laiacona & Capitani 2001, Laiacona et al. 1993, Lambon Ralph et al. 1998, Moss et al. 1998). The third prediction is that impairments for a type of knowledge will necessarily be associated with differential impairments for the category that depends on that knowledge type. Patients exhibiting patterns of impairment contrary to this prediction have been reported. For instance, **Figure 2b** shows the profile of a patient who was (a) more impaired for visual compared to functional knowledge, and (b) if anything, more impaired for nonliving things than living things (Lambon Ralph et al. 1998; see also **Figure 2c**, **Figure 4**, and discussion below).

Second Generation Sensory/Functional Theories

The original formulation of the sensory/functional theory was based on a simple division between visual/perceptual knowledge and functional/associative knowledge. Warrington & McCarthy (1987; see also Crutch & Warrington 2003) suggested, however, that knowledge of object color is differentially important for fruit/vegetables compared to animals. Since Warrington and McCarthy's proposal, further sensory- and motor-based dimensions that may be important for distinguishing between semantic categories have been articulated (e.g., Cree & McRae 2003, Vinson et al. 2003).

Cree & McRae (2003) used a feature-listing task to study the types of information that normal subjects spontaneously associate with different semantic categories. The semantic features were then classified into nine knowledge types: color, visual parts and surface properties, visual motion, smell, sound, tactile, taste, function, and encyclopedic (see Vinson et al. 2003 for a slightly different classification). Hierarchical cluster analyses were used to determine which semantic categories differentially loaded on which feature types. The results of those analyses indicated that (a) visual motion and function information were the two most important knowledge types for distinguishing living animate things (high on visual motion information) from nonliving things (high on function information), (b) living animate things were weighted lower on color information than fruit/vegetables, but higher on this knowledge type than nonliving things, and (c) fruit/vegetables were distinguished from living animate and nonliving things by being weighted the highest on both color and taste information.

Cree and McRae's analyses support the claim that the taxonomy of nine knowledge types is effective in distinguishing between the domains living animate, fruit/vegetables, and nonliving. Those analyses do not demonstrate, however, that the nine knowledge types are critical for distinguishing between items within the respective categories. As noted above, patients with category-specific semantic impairments do not necessarily have difficulty distinguishing between different domains (i.e., they might know it is an animal but cannot say which one). It is therefore not obvious that Cree and McRae's analyses support the claim that category-specific semantic deficits may be explained by assuming damage to one (or more) of the nine knowledge types.

At a more general level, the open empirical question is whether the additional knowledge types and the corresponding further functional divisions that are introduced into the semantic system can account for the neuropsychological evidence. Clearly, if fruit/vegetables and animals are assumed to differentially depend on different types of information (and by inference, different semantic subsystems), it is in principle possible to account for the tripartite distinction between animals, fruit/vegetables, and nonliving. As for the original formulation of the sensory/functional theory, the question is whether fine-grained category-specific semantic impairments are associated with impairments for the type of knowledge upon which items from the impaired category putatively depend. However, patients have been reported with category-specific semantic impairments for fruit/vegetables, without disproportionate impairments for color knowledge (e.g., Samson & Pillon 2003). Patients have also been reported with impairment for knowledge of object color without a disproportionate impairment for fruit/vegetables compared to other categories of objects (see **Figure 2c**; Luzzatti & Davidoff 1994, Miceli et al. 2001).

Another way in which investigators have sought to provide support for the sensory/functional theory is to study the semantic categories that are systematically impaired together. As noted above, one profile of the first reported cases that motivated the development of the sensory/functional theory (Warrington & Shallice 1984) was that the categories of animals, plants, and foods tended to be impaired or spared together. Those associations of impairing and sparing of categories made sense if all of those categories depended on the same modality-specific system for their identification. Following the same logic, it was argued that musical instruments patterned with living things (because of the importance of sensory attributes) (see Dixon et al. 2000 for relevant data), and that body parts patterned with nonliving things (because of the importance of functional attributes associated with object usage (e.g., Warrington & McCarthy 1987). However, as was the case for the dissociation between living animate things (animals) and living inanimate things (e.g., plants), it is now known that musical instruments dissociate from living things and that body parts dissociate from nonliving things (Caramazza & Shelton 1998, Laiacona & Capitani 2001, Shelton et al. 1998, Silveri et al. 1997, Turnbull & Laws 2000; for review and discussion, see Capitani et al. 2003).

More recently, Borgo & Shallice (2001, 2003) have argued that sensory-quality categories, such as materials, edible substances, and drinks are similar to animals in that they depend on sensory information for their identification. Those authors reported that impairment for living things was associated with impairments for sensory-quality categories. However, Laiacona and colleagues (2003) reported a patient who was impaired for living things but spared for sensory-quality categories (for further discussion, see Carroll & Garrard 2005).

Another dimension that has been argued to be instrumental in accounting for category-specific semantic deficits is differential similarity in the visual structure of items from different categories. Humphreys & Forde (2001; see also Tranel et al. 1997) argued that living things tend to be more structurally similar than nonliving things. If that were the case, then it could be argued that damage to a system not organized by object category will result in disproportionate disruption of items that are more "confusable" (see also Lambon Ralph et al. 2007, Rogers et al. 2004). Within Humphreys and Forde's framework, it is also assumed that activation dynamically cascades from visual object recognition processes through to lexical access. Thus, perturbation of visual recognition processes could trickle through the system to disrupt the normal functioning of subsequent processes, resulting in a naming deficit (see Humphreys et al. 1988). Laws and colleagues (Laws & Gale 2002, Laws & Neve 1999) also argued for the critical role of similarity in visual structure for explaining category-specific semantic deficits. However, in contrast to Humphreys and Forde (see also Tranel et al. 1997), Laws and colleagues argued that nonliving things tend to be more similar than living things.

Clearly, much work remains to be done in order to understand the role that visual similarity, and the consequent crowding (Humphreys & Forde 2001) of visual representations, has in explaining category-specific semantic deficits. On the one hand, there is no consensus regarding the relevant object properties over which similarity should be calculated or how such a similarity metric should be calculated. On the other hand, assuming an agreed-upon means for determining similarity in visual shape, the question remains open as to the role that such a factor might play in explaining the facts of category-specific semantic deficits.

The Domain-Specific Hypothesis

The domain-specific hypothesis of the organization of conceptual knowledge in the brain (Caramazza & Shelton 1998) assumes that the first-order constraint on the organization of information within the conceptual system is object domain. The semantic categories that may be organized by domain-specific constraints are limited to those that could have had an evolutionarily relevant history: living animate, living inanimate, conspecifics, and tools. On this proposal, the phenomenon of category-specific semantic deficit reflects differential or selective damage to the neural substrates that support one or another domain of knowledge. Research from developmental psychology converges with the assumption that conceptual knowledge is organized, in part, by innately specified constraints on object knowledge (e.g., Baillargeon 1998, Carey & Spelke 1994, Gallistel 1990, Gelman 1990, Keil 1981, Spelke et al. 1992, Wellman & Gelman 1992; for a review, see Santos & Caramazza 2002; see, e.g., Kiani et al. 2007 for convergent findings using neurophysiological methods with nonhuman primates). Research in developmental psychology has also highlighted other domains of knowledge beyond those motivated by neuropsychological research on patients with category-specific deficits, such as number and geometric/spatial reasoning (e.g., JF Cantlon, M Platt, & EM Brannon, manuscript under review; Feigenson et al. 2004; Hermer & Spelke 1994).

Unique predictions are generated by the original formulation of the domain-specific hypothesis as it was articulated in the context of category-specific semantic deficits. One prediction is that the grain of category-specific se-

mantic deficits will reflect the grain of those categories that could plausibly have had an evolutionarily relevant history (see **Figure 1**). Another prediction is that category-specific semantic impairments will be associated with impairments for all types of knowledge about the impaired category (see **Figure 2a**). A third prediction made by the domain-specific hypothesis is that it should be possible to observe category-specific impairments that result from early damage to the brain. Evidence in line with this expectation is provided by the case of Adam (Farah & Rabinowitz 2003). Patient Adam, who was 16 at the time of testing, suffered a stroke at one day of age. Adam failed to acquire knowledge of living things, despite normal levels of knowledge about nonliving things. As would be expected within the framework of the domain-specific hypothesis, Adam was impaired for both visual and nonvisual knowledge of living things (Farah & Rabinowitz 2003).

The Distributed Domain-Specific Hypothesis

The original formulation of the domain-specific hypothesis (Caramazza & Shelton 1998) anticipated the possibility of other dimensions of organization beyond object domain. It was proposed that correlational structure plays an important role in determining the organization of knowledge within domains. More important in the present context, it was also proposed that domain specificity would be found at both conceptual and perceptual levels of processing. We have since attempted to develop this account and have explored a model in which (*a*) object domain and sensory, motor, and emotional properties jointly constrain the organization of conceptual knowledge, and (*b*) object domain is a constraint on the organization of information at both a conceptual level as well as at the level of modality-specific visual input representations (Caramazza & Mahon 2003, 2006; Mahon & Caramazza 2003, 2008). We refer to this framework as the distributed domain-specific hypothesis in order to capture

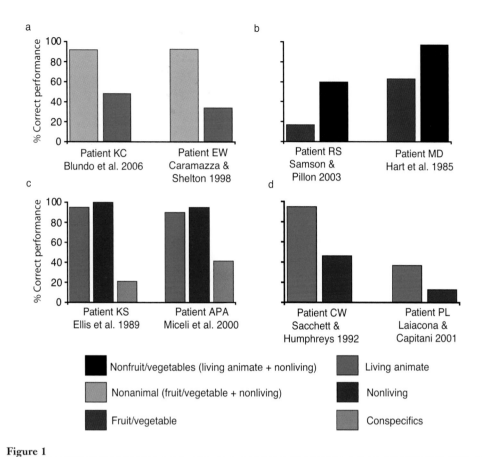

Figure 1

Representative picture naming performance of patients with category-specific semantic deficits for
(*a*) living animate things, (*b*) fruit/vegetables, (*c*) conspecifics, and (*d*) nonliving.

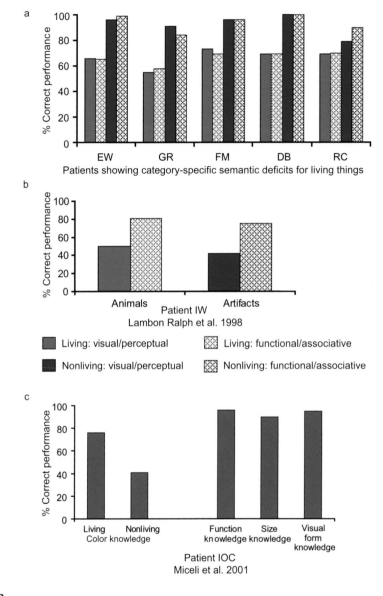

Figure 2

Relation between impairments for a type or modality of knowledge and category-specific semantic deficits. These data show that (*a*) category-specific semantic impairments are associated with impairments for all types of knowledge about the impaired category, (*b*) differential impairments for visual/perceptual knowledge can be associated with (if anything) a disproportionate impairment for nonliving things compared to living things, and (*c*) selective impairment for knowledge of object color is not associated with a corresponding disproportionate deficit for fruit/vegetables. Data for EW from Caramazza & Shelton 1998; GR and FM from Laiacona et al. 1993; DB from Lambon Ralph et al. 1998; and RC from Moss et al. 1998.

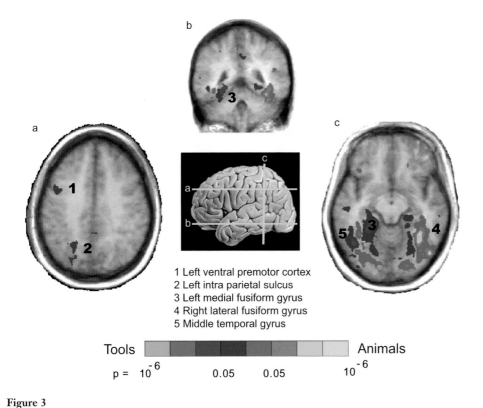

1 Left ventral premotor cortex
2 Left intra parietal sulcus
3 Left medial fusiform gyrus
4 Right lateral fusiform gyrus
5 Middle temporal gyrus

Tools | | Animals

p = 10⁻⁶   0.05   0.05   10⁻⁶

Figure 3

Category-specific patterns of blood oxygen–level dependent (BOLD) responses in the healthy brain. A network of regions that are differentially activated for living animate things is in red; a network of regions that are differentially activated for nonliving things is in blue. Data from Chao et al. (2002); graphics provided by Alex Martin.

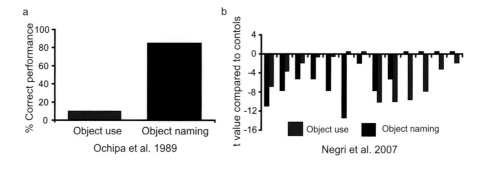

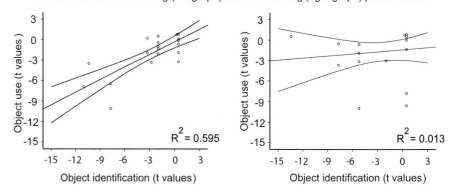

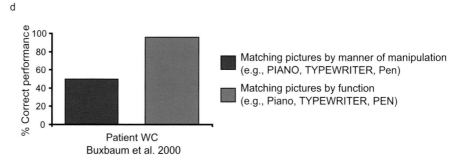

Figure 4

Relation between knowledge of how to manipulate tools and other knowledge of tools. (*a*) Ochipa and colleagues (1989) reported a patient with a severe impairment for manipulating objects but relatively preserved naming of the same objects. (*b*) A multiple single-case study of unselected unilateral stroke patients asked patients to use and identify the same set of objects (Negri et al. 2007). Performance of the patients is plotted as t values (Crawford & Garthwaite 2006) compared to control (n = 25) performance.

(*c*) Lesions to parietal cortex, in the context of lesions to lateral temporal and frontal regions, can be instrumental in modulating the relationship between performance in object identification and object use, at the group level (see Mahon et al. 2007, figure 7, for details and lesion overlap analyses). Each circle in the plots represents the performance of a single patient in object identification and object use. The 95% confidence intervals around the regression lines are shown. Reproduced with permission from Mahon and colleagues (2007). (*d*) Patient WC (Buxbaum et al. 2000) was impaired for matching pictures based on how objects are manipulated but was spared for matching pictures based on the function of the objects.

the idea that both object domain and a distributed network of modality-specific representations constrain the organization of conceptual knowledge of objects (we previously referred to this view as the domain-specific sensory-motor hypothesis; Mahon & Caramazza 2008). The central idea of this proposal is that domain-specific organization within a particular region is driven, in part, by the functional connectivity of the brain. That is, domain specificity is determined not only by the specific characteristics of processing within a given region, but also by how information in that region relates to information that is computed elsewhere and which is salient for the domain. The grain of that functional connectivity, according to the hypothesis, should reflect those object domains with evolutionarily important histories.

One expectation on the distributed domain-specific hypothesis is that impairments to abstract conceptual knowledge will dissociate from category-specific impairments at the level of object recognition. Consistent with this, and as noted above, impairments to conceptual knowledge are not necessarily associated with impairments at a modality-specific input level of visual processing. Some patients with conceptual-level impairments do have associated impairments for recognizing visually presented items (e.g., Caramazza & Shelton 1998), whereas other patients do not (e.g., Blundo et al. 2006; for a review, see Capitani et al. 2003).

Further convergent evidence is provided by the study of prosopagnosia. Patients with prosopagnosia have a deficit for recognizing visually presented faces but do not have difficulties retrieving other knowledge about the people they cannot recognize. For instance, such patients may be able to recognize the same people by the sound of their voice. The reverse dissociation—sparing of face recognition compared to recognition of other categories—has also been reported (Moscovitch et al. 1997).

Patients with prosopagnosia also constitute the other side of a double dissociation with patients such as APA, discussed above (see **Figure 1c**; Miceli et al. 2000). Patients

such as APA are impaired for conceptual knowledge of conspecifics but are not necessarily prosopagnosic. Thus, within the domain of conspecifics, category-specific deficits at a modality-specific level of visual recognition dissociate from impairments to more abstract knowledge of conspecifics. In addition, prosopagnosia can arise developmentally, suggesting that the constraints that drive neural specificity for face perception are, in part, innately specified (Duchaine et al. 2006, Nunn et al. 2001; for a comprehensive review of acquired and developmental prosopagnosia, see Duchaine & Yovel 2008).

THE CORRELATED STRUCTURE PRINCIPLE

Theories based on the correlated structure principle assume that the conceptual system has no structure that is specifically reflected in functional neuroanatomy. For instance, the organized unitary content hypothesis (OUCH) (Caramazza et al. 1990) was initially formulated as an explanation of optic aphasia that did not invoke the assumption of multiple semantics. Caramazza and colleagues (1990; see also Riddoch et al. 1988) argued that there are privileged relationships between certain types of input representations (e.g., visual form) and certain types of output representations (e.g., knowledge of object manipulation), thus explaining how optic aphasic patients might be spared for gesturing to objects while impaired for naming them.

Other researchers subsequently developed highly specified proposals based on the correlated structure principle, all of which build on the idea that different types of features are differentially correlated across different semantic categories (Devlin et al. 1998, Rogers et al. 2004, Tyler & Moss 2001). Those models of semantic memory have been implemented computationally, with simulated damage, in order to provide existence proofs that a system with no explicit functional organization may be damaged so as to produce category-specific semantic deficits. Because theories based on the correlated structure principle do not assume that the conceptual system has structure at the level of functional neuroanatomy, they are best suited to modeling the patterns of progressive loss of conceptual knowledge observed in neurodegenerative diseases, such as dementia of the Alzheimer type and semantic dementia. The type of damage in such patients is diffuse and widespread and can be modeled in connectionist architectures by removing, to varying degrees, randomly selected components of the network.

One important proposal is the conceptual-structure account of Tyler, Moss, and colleagues (Bright et al. 2005, Tyler & Moss 2001). That proposal assumes that living things have more shared features, whereas nonliving things have more distinctive features. The model further assumes that the shared features of living things are highly correlated (has eyes/can see), whereas for nonliving things, distinctive features are highly correlated (used for spearing/has tines). If distinctive features are critical for identification, and if greater correlation confers resilience to damage, then an interaction between the severity of overall impairment and the direction of category-specific semantic deficit is predicted. Mild levels of impairments should produce disproportionate impairments for living things compared to nonliving things. At more severe levels of impairments, the distinctive features of nonliving things will be lost and a disproportionate impairment for this category will be observed. The opposite prediction regarding the severity of overall impairment and the direction of category-specific impairment is predicted by the account of Devlin and colleagues (1998) because it is assumed that as damage becomes severe, whole sets of intercorrelated features will be lost, resulting in a disproportionate impairment for living things. However, it is now known that neither prediction finds clear empirical support (Garrard et al. 1998, Zannino et al. 2002; see also Laiacona & Capitani 2001 for discussion within the context of focal lesions; for further discussion and theoretical developments, see Cree & McRae 2003, Vinson et al. 2003).

One issue that is not resolved is whether correlations between different features should be calculated in a concept-dependent or concept-independent manner (Zannino et al. 2006). For instance, although the (distinctive) information "has tines" is highly correlated with the function "used for spearing" in the concept FORK (correlated as concept dependent), the co-occurrence of those properties in the world is relatively low (concept independent). Sartori, Lombardi, and colleagues (Sartori & Lombardi 2004, Sartori et al. 2005) have addressed a similar issue by developing the construct of "semantic relevance," which is computed through a nonlinear combination of the frequency with which particular features are produced for an item and the distinctiveness of that feature for all concepts in the database. Those authors have shown that living things tend to be lower, on average, than nonliving things in terms of their relevance, thus making living things on average "harder" than nonliving things. As is the case for other accounts of category-specific semantic deficits that are based on differences across categories along a single dimension, the existence of disproportionate deficits for the relatively "easy" category (nonliving things) is difficult to accommodate (see e.g., Hillis & Caramazza 1991, Laiacona & Capitani 2001; **Figure 1d**). Nevertheless, the theoretical proposal of Sartori and colleagues highlights the critical and unresolved issue of how to determine the psychologically relevant metric for determining feature correlations.

Another unresolved issue is whether high correlations between features will provide resilience to damage for those features, or will rather make damage contagious among them. It is often assumed that high correlation confers resilience to, or insulation from, damage; however, our understanding of how damage to one part of the brain affects other regions of the brain remains poorly developed. It is also not obvious that understanding the behavior of connectionist architectures constitutes the needed motivation for deciding whether greater correlation confers greater resilience to damage. In fact, theoretical differences about the role of correlations in conferring resilience to damage are in part responsible for the contrasting predictions that follow from the models of Tyler and colleagues (Tyler & Moss 2001) and Devlin and colleagues (1998) (for discussion, see Zannino et al. 2006).

Another example that illustrates our current lack of understanding of the role of feature correlation in determining patterns of impairment is provided by dissociations between sensory, motor, and conceptual knowledge. For instance, the visual structure of objects is highly correlated with more abstract knowledge of the conceptual features of objects. Even so, patients with impairments to abstract conceptual features of objects do not necessarily have corresponding impairments to object recognition processes (see above and Capitani et al. 2003 for review). Similarly, although manipulation knowledge ("how to" knowledge) is correlated with functional knowledge ("what for" knowledge), damage to the former does not imply damage to the latter (see Buxbaum et al. 2000, **Figure 4d**, and discussion below).

Theories based on the correlated structure principle are presented as alternatives to proposals that assume neural structure within the conceptual system. The implicit assumption in that argument is that the theoretical construct of a semantic feature offers a means for reducing different categories to a common set of elements (see Rogers et al. 2004 for an alternative proposal). However, no semantic features have been described that are shared across semantic categories, aside from very abstract features such as "has mass." In other words, in the measure to which semantic features are the substance of conceptual representations, different semantic categories would be represented by nonoverlapping sets of features. Thus, and as has been proposed on the basis of functional neuroimaging data (see, e.g., Haxby et al. 2001 and discussion below), it may be the case that regions of high feature correlation (e.g., within semantic category correlations in visual structure) are reflected in the functional neuroanatomy of the brain (see also Devlin et al. 1998 for a hybrid model in which both focal and diffuse le-

sions can produce category-specific effects and Caramazza et al. 1990 for an earlier proposal along those lines).

THE ANATOMY OF CATEGORY-SPECIFICITY

An important development in cognitive neuroscience that has paralleled the articulation of theories of semantic organization is the discovery of multiple channels of visual processing (Goodale & Milner 1992, Ungerleider & Miskin 1982). It is now known that visual processing bifurcates into two independent but interconnected streams (for discussion of how best to characterize the two streams, see Pisella et al. 2006). The ventral visual object–processing stream projects from V1 through ventral occipital and temporal cortices, terminating in anterior regions of the temporal lobe, and subserves visual object identification. The dorsal object–processing stream projects from V1 through dorsal occipital cortex to posterior parietal cortex and subserves object-directed action and spatial analysis for the purposes of object-directed grasping. The two-visual systems hypothesis has played a central role in understanding the neuroanatomy of category specificity.

Lesion Analyses

A natural issue to arise in neuropsychological research concerns which brain regions tend to be lesioned in association with category-specific deficits. The first study to address this issue systematically was by H. Damasio and colleagues (1996). Those authors found that name-retrieval deficits for pictures of famous people were associated with left temporal pole lesions, a result confirmed by other investigators (see Lyons et al. 2006 for an overview). Damasio and colleagues also found that deficits for naming animals were associated with (more posterior) lesions of anterior left ventral temporal cortex. Subsequent research has confirmed that deficits for naming animals are associated with lesions to anterior regions of temporal cortex (e.g., Brambati et al. 2006). Damasio and collaborators also found that deficits for naming tools were associated with lesions to posterior and lateral temporal areas, overlapping the left posterior middle gyrus. The critical role of the left posterior middle temporal gyrus for knowing about tools has also since been confirmed by other lesion studies (e.g., Brambati et al. 2006).

A subsequent report by Damasio and colleagues (2004) demonstrated that the same regions were also reliably damaged in patients with impairments for recognizing stimuli from those three categories. In addition, Damasio and colleagues (2004) found that deficits for naming tools, as well as fruit/vegetables, were associated with lesions to the inferior pre- and postcentral gyri as well as the insula. Consensus about the association of lesions to the regions discussed above with category-specific deficits is provided by Gainotti's analyses (e.g., Gainotti 2000) of published reports of patients with category-specific semantic deficits.

A number of investigators have interpreted the differential role of anterior mesial aspects of ventral temporal cortex in the processing of living things to reflect the fact that living things have more shared properties than nonliving things, such that more fine-grained discriminations are required to name them (Bright et al. 2005, Damasio et al. 2004, Simmons & Barsalou 2003; see also Humphreys & Forde 2001). Within this framework, the association of deficits to unique person knowledge and lesions to the most anterior aspects of the temporal lobe is assumed to reflect the greater discrimination that is required for distinguishing among conspecifics compared to animals (less) and nonliving things (even less).

Functional Imaging

Data from functional imaging, and in particular fMRI, have added in important ways to our understanding of how different semantic categories are processed in the healthy brain. In particular, although the lesion overlap approach is powerful in detecting brain regions that are critical for performing a given task, functional imaging has the advantage of detecting regions that are critical as well as regions that are automatically engaged by the mere presentation of a certain type of stimulus. Thus, in line with the lesion evidence described above, nonliving things, and in particular tools, differentially activate the left middle temporal gyrus (**Figure 3**, see color insert; e.g., Martin et al. 1996, Thompson-Schill et al. 1999; see Devlin et al. 2002 for a review). Other imaging data indicate that this region plays an important role in processing the semantics of actions (e.g., Kable et al. 2002, Kemmerer et al. 2008, Martin et al. 1995) as well as mechanical (i.e., unarticulated) motion (Beauchamp et al. 2002, 2003; Martin & Weisberg 2003).

In contrast, and not as apparent in lesion studies, tools differentially activate dorsal stream regions that mediate object-directed action. The activation of some of those regions is independent of whether action information is necessary in order to perform the task in which participants are engaged (e.g., picture naming). For instance, regions within dorsal occipital cortex, posterior parietal cortex, through to the anterior intraparietal sulcus, are automatically activated when participants observe manipulable objects (e.g., Chao & Martin 2000, Fang & He 2005). Those regions are important for determining volumetric and spatial information about objects as well as shaping and transporting the hand for object grasping (Binkofski et al. 1998, Culham et al. 2003, Frey et al. 2005). However, those dorsal occipital and posterior parietal regions are not thought to be critical for object identification or naming (e.g., Goodale & Milner 1992). Naming tools also differentially activates the left inferior parietal lobule (e.g., Mahon et al. 2007, Rumiati et al. 2004), a region that is important for representing complex object-associated manipulations (e.g., for review, see Johnson-Frey 2004, Lewis 2006).

One clear way in which functional imaging data have contributed beyond lesion evidence to our understanding of category specificity in the brain is the description of highly consistent topographic biases by semantic categories in the ventral object–processing stream (see **Figure 3b,c**; for reviews, see Bookheimer 2002, Gerlach 2007, Grill-Spector & Malach 2004, Op de Beeck et al. 2008, Thompson-Schill 2003). As opposed to the anterior-posterior mapping of semantic categories within the ventral stream described by the lesion evidence (e.g., Damasio et al. 1996), there is also a lateral-to-medial organization. The fusiform gyrus on the ventral surface of temporal-occipital cortex is critical for representing object color and form (e.g., Martin 2007, Miceli et al. 2001). Living animate things such as faces and animals elicit differential neural responses in the lateral fusiform gyrus, whereas nonliving things (tools, vehicles) elicit differential neural responses in the medial fusiform gyrus (e.g., Chao et al. 1999, Mahon et al. 2007, Noppeney et al. 2006). Stimuli that are highly definable in terms of their spatial context, such as houses and scenes, differentially activate regions anterior to these fusiform regions, in the vicinity of parahippocampal cortex (e.g., Bar & Aminoff 2003, Epstein & Kanwisher 1998). Other visual stimuli also elicit consistent topographical biases in the ventral stream, such as written words (see Dehaene et al. 2005 for discussion) and images of body parts (e.g., Downing et al. 2001).

HOW DOES THE ANATOMY OF CATEGORY SPECIFICITY INFORM COGNITIVE THEORY?

The existence of category specificity in the normal brain reduces confidence in theories that reject the neural structure principle. However, those functional imaging data are also relevant for adjudicating among theories based on the neural structure principle, in that different aspects of the functional imaging evidence sit more or less naturally with the distributed domain–specific hypothesis and the sensory/functional theory.

Tool Stimuli Differentially Activate Dorsal Stream Structures Involved in Object-Directed Action

The activation by tool stimuli of regions of the brain that mediate object-directed action has been argued to follow naturally from the sensory/functional theory. On that theory, the activation of dorsal structures by tool stimuli indexes the critical role of function knowledge in the recognition of nonliving things (e.g., Boronat et al. 2004, Kellenbach et al. 2003, Martin et al. 2000, Noppeney et al. 2006, Simmons & Barsalou 2003). That argument is weakened, however, in the measure to which it is demonstrated that the integrity of action knowledge is not necessary in order to have other types of knowledge about tools, such as knowledge of their function.

The neuropsychological phenomenon of apraxia offers a way of testing whether action knowledge is critical for supporting conceptual processing of tools. Apraxia refers to an impairment for using objects that cannot be explained by a deficit in visual object recognition or an impairment to low-level motor processes themselves. **Figure 4a** (see color insert) summarizes the performance profile of a patient (reported by Ochipa et al. 1989) who was impaired for using objects but was relatively preserved for naming the same objects [see **Figure 4b** for similar dissociations in a series of single case analyses (Negri et al. 2007); see also Rosci et al. (2003); for clear cases studies, see Moreaud et al. (1998), Rapcsak et al. (2005), Rumiati et al. (2001); see Rothi et al. (1991) for an influential cognitive model; for review, see Johnson-Frey (2004), Mahon & Caramazza (2005)]. Apraxic deficits for using objects are often observed subsequent to lesions in the regions of the dorsal stream (in particular, the left inferior parietal lobule), reviewed above, that are automatically activated when participants name tools. The fact that apraxic patients may be able to name objects that they cannot use indicates that the activation of those regions during naming tasks is not, in and of itself, necessary for successful completion of the task. At the same time, lesions to parietal cortex, in the context of lesions to the middle temporal gyrus and frontal regions, do modulate performance in object identification. In a recent analysis (Mahon et al. 2007), a group of unilateral stroke patients was separated into two groups according to the anatomical criterion of having lesions involving (**Figure 4c**, *middle left*) or not involving parietal cortex (**Figure 4c**, *middle right*). There was a relationship between performance in object identification and object use at the group level only in patients with lesions involving parietal cortex, a finding that suggests that action knowledge associated with objects is relevant for successful identification.

Other neuropsychological data indicate that the integrity of action knowledge is not necessary in order for patients to have accurate knowledge of object function. **Figure 4d** depicts the performance of patient WC (Buxbaum et al. 2000) on two picture-matching tasks. In a picture-matching task that required knowledge of object manipulation, performance was impaired; however, in a picture-matching task that required knowledge of object function, performance was spared. Functional imaging studies (Boronat et al. 2004, Canessa et al. 2008, Kellenbach et al. 2003) converge with those neuropsychological data in showing that manipulation but not function knowledge modulates neural responses in the inferior parietal lobule. There is also evidence, from both functional neuroimaging (e.g., Canessa et al. 2008) and neuropsychology (e.g., Sirigu et al. 1991), that temporal and not parietal cortex may be involved in the representation of function knowledge of objects.

The convergence between the neuropsychological evidence from apraxia and the functional-imaging evidence indicates that although a dedicated system exists for knowledge of object manipulation, that system is not critically involved in representing knowledge of object function. This suggests that the automatic engagement of action processing by manipulable objects, as observed in neuroimaging, may have consequences for a theory of pragmatics and/or action, but not necessarily for a theory of semantics (Goodale & Milner 1992, Jeannerod & Jacob 2005). This in turn weakens the claim that automatic activation of dorsal stream structures by manipulable objects is evidence for the sensory/functional theory.

Category Specificity Within the Ventral Stream

One finding from functional neuroimaging that sits more naturally with the distributed domain–specific hypothesis than the sensory/functional theory is the fact that ventral temporal cortex shows topographic biases by semantic category. In order to explain those data within the context of the sensory/functional theory, further assumptions are necessary about why there would be an organization by semantic category within the (putative) visual modality. In short, a hybrid model is required that combines the assumption of multiple semantics with some claim about how information would come to be topographically segregated by semantic category. A number of such proposals have been advanced, although not always in the context of the sensory/functional theory or more generally within the context of theories that emerge from category-specific semantic deficits (see, e.g., Gauthier et al. 2000, Haxby et al. 2001, Ishai et al. 1999, Levy et al. 2001, Mechelli et al. 2006, Rogers et al. 2005). All of those proposals share the view that dimensions defined over visual information generate the observed effects of category specificity in the ventral stream.

An alternative framework (see Mahon et al. 2007) is that category specificity in the ventral stream is not the result of only bottom-up processes operating locally over visual information. Rather, the organization of the ventral stream is just one manifestation of a network that includes many other regions. Such a connectivity-constrained account (Riesenhuber 2007) of category specificity is theoretically neutral regarding the issue of whether or not innately specified constraints determine such connectivity. For instance, although there is neural specificity for both written words and faces in regions of the ventral stream, face recognition—but not reading—could have a direct evolutionarily relevant history. Yet, it may be that neural specificity for written words in the ventral stream is driven by functional connectivity that relates visual processing to phonological processing (see Buchel et al. 1998 for relevant findings, and Dehaene et al. 2005 and Martin 2006 for discussion).

A connectivity-constrained account would offer a natural explanation for how category effects within ventral temporal cortex could be driven by nonvisual properties of the stimuli. For instance, Martin & Weisberg (2003) showed that different types of motion carried by the same geometrical shapes can drive responses in a category-specific manner in ventral temporal cortex. These findings are surprising because ventral temporal-occipital cortex is not itself motion sensitive (Beauchamp et al. 2003). In the same line, Mahon and colleagues (2007) found that neural responses for manipulable objects in the medial fusiform gyrus are driven by action-related properties of objects even though action knowledge is not itself represented in the fusiform gyrus. A connectivity constrained account also offers a natural account for why structures involved in affective processing and mental state attribution should be part of the network that is activated when information about living animate things is processed (for early discussion, see Caramazza & Shelton 1998; for findings from fMRI, see e.g. Martin & Weisberg 2003, Mitchell et al. 2002, Morris et al. 1999, Pasley et al. 2004).

It is unlikely that a single dimension will explain all aspects of the organization of the ventral object–processing stream. In particular, it may be the case that neural specificity for some stimulus types will be determined by qualitatively different types of constraints than neural specificity for other stimulus types. A recent study (Polk et al. 2007) investigated this issue by studying the similarity in neural responses to faces, houses, pseudowords, and chairs in monozygotic and dizygotic twins and in unrelated participants. The authors found that face- and place-related responses within face- and place-selective regions, respectively, were significantly more similar for monozygotic than for dizygotic twins. However, there was no difference between the two twin groups for written words in regions that responded selectively to written words. Those data demonstrate innate constraints on the patterns of neural responses to faces and places in regions of the ventral stream selective for those categories. Future research is required to address how innate factors influence neural specificity within the ventral object–processing stream and the organization of object knowledge in the brain more generally.

THE RELATION BETWEEN SENSORY, MOTOR, AND CONCEPTUAL KNOWLEDGE

Early formulations of the sensory/functional theory assumed that conceptual content, although tied in important ways to the sensory and motor systems, was more abstract than the token-based information contained within the sensory and motor systems (Warrington & McCarthy 1983, 1987; Warrington & Shallice 1984; see also Crutch & Warrington 2003). More recent formulations of the multiple-semantics approach have argued, within the embodied cognition framework, that conceptual content can be reductively grounded in sensory and motor processes (e.g., Barsalou 1999, 2008; H. Damasio et al. 2004; Gallese & Lakoff 2005; Prinz 2002; Pulvermüller 2005; Zwaan 2004; see also Patterson et al. 2007).

The first detailed articulation of the embodied cognition framework was by Allen Allport (1985), who proposed that conceptual knowledge is organized according to sensory and motor modalities and that the information represented within different modalities was format specific:

The essential idea is that the *same* neural elements that are involved in coding the sensory attributes of a (possibly unknown) object presented to eye or hand or ear also make up the elements of the auto-associated activity-patterns that represent familiar object-concepts in "semantic memory." This model is, of course, in radical opposition to the view, apparently held by many psychologists, that "semantic memory" is represented in some abstract, modality-independent, "conceptual" domain remote from the mechanisms of perception and motor organization. (Allport 1985, p. 53; emphasis in original)

One type of evidence, discussed above, that has been argued to support an embodied representation of object concepts is the observation that regions of the brain that directly mediate object-directed action are automatically activated when participants observe manipulable objects. However, the available neuropsychological evidence (**Figure 4**) reduces confidence in the claim that action knowledge plays a critical role in grounding the diverse types of knowledge that we have about tools. The strongest evidence for the relevance of motor and perceptual processes to conceptual processing is provided by demonstrations that the sensory and motor systems are automatically engaged by linguistic stimuli that imply action (e.g., Boulenger et al. 2006, Buccino et al. 2005, Glenberg & Kaschak 2002, Oliveri et al. 2004). It has also been demonstrated that activation of the motor system automatically spreads to conceptual and perceptual levels of processing (e.g., Pulvermüller et al. 2005).

The embodied cognition hypothesis makes strong predictions about the integrity of conceptual processes after damage to sensory and motor processes. It predicts, necessarily, and as Allport wrote, that "...the loss of particular attribute information in semantic memory should be accompanied by a corresponding *perceptual* (agnostic) deficit." (1985, p. 55; emphasis in original). Although there are long traditions within neuropsychology of studying patients with deficits for sensory and/or motor knowledge, only recently have those deficits been of

such clear theoretical relevance to hypotheses about the nature of semantic memory. Systematic and theoretically informed studies of such patients will play a pivotal role in evaluating the relation between sensory, motor, and conceptual knowledge. Central to that enterprise will be to specify how information is dynamically exchanged between systems in the context of specific task requirements. This will be important for determining the degree to which sensory and motor activation is in fact a critical component of conceptual processing (see Machery 2007, Mahon & Caramazza 2008 for discussion). It is theoretically possible (and in our view, likely) that although concepts are not exhausted by sensory and motor information, the organization of abstract concepts is nonetheless shaped in important ways by the structure of the sensory and motor systems. It is also likely, in our view, that processing of such abstract conceptual content is heavily interlaced with activation of the sensory and motor systems.

TOWARD A SYNTHESIS

We have organized this review around theoretical explanations of category specificity in the human brain. One theme that emerges is the historical progression from theories based on a single principle of organization to theories that integrate multiple dimensions of organization. This progression is due to the broad recognition in the field that a single dimension will not be sufficient to explain all aspects of the organization of object knowledge in the brain. However, not every dimension or principle of organization is of equal importance because not all dimensions have the same explanatory scope. A relative hierarchy of principles is therefore necessary to determine which of the many known facts are theoretically important and which are of only marginal significance.

Two broad findings emerge from cognitive neuropsychological research. First, patients have been reported with disproportionate impairments for a modality or type of knowledge (e.g., visual/perceptual knowledge, **Figure 2b**; manipulation knowledge, **Figure 4**). Second, category-specific semantic deficits are associated with impairments for all types of knowledge about the impaired category (**Figure 2a**). Analogues to those two facts are also found in functional neuroimaging. First, the attributes of some categories of objects (e.g., tools) are differentially represented in modality-specific systems (i.e., motor systems). Second, within a given modality-specific system (e.g., ventral visual pathway), there is functional organization by semantic category (e.g., living animate versus nonliving) (see **Figure 3** for an overview). Thus, across both neuropsychological studies and functional imaging studies, the broad empirical generalization emerges that there are two, orthogonal, constraints on the organization of object knowledge: object domain and sensory/motor modality. This empirical generalization is neutral with respect to how one explains the causes of category-specific effects in both functional neuroimaging and neuropsychology.

Many theoretical proposals of the causes of category specificity articulate dimensions along which semantic categories differ (e.g., Cree & McRae 2003, Devlin et al. 1998, Gauthier et al. 2000, Haxby et al. 2001, Humphreys & Forde 2001, Laws & Gale 2002, Levy et al. 2001, Mechelli et al. 2006, Op de Beeck et al. 2008, Rogers et al. 2004, Sartori & Lombardi 2004, Simmons & Barsalou 2003, Tranel et al. 1997, Tyler & Moss 2001, Warrington & Shallice 1984, Zannino et al. 2006). Understanding the role that such dimensions play in the genesis of category specificity in a particular part of the brain, or a particular component of a cognitive model, will be central to characterizing the functioning of that component of the system. However, progress in understanding the causes of category specificity in one region of the brain, or one functional component of a cognitive model, will require an understanding of how category specificity is realized throughout the whole brain and throughout the whole cognitive model.

All current theories of the organization of conceptual knowledge assume that a concept is composed of distinct types of information.

This shared assumption permits an explanation of how thinking about a single concept (e.g., hammer) can engage different regions of the brain that process distinct types of information (e.g., sensory versus motor). It also allows for an account of how patients may present with impairments for a type or modality of knowledge (e.g., know what a hammer looks like but not know how to use it). However, that assumption begs the question of how the different types of information that constitute a given concept are functionally unified. A central theoretical issue to be addressed by the field is to understand the nature of the mechanisms that unify different types of knowledge about the same entity in the world and that give rise to a functionally unitary concept of that entity.

Our own view—the distributed domain-specific hypothesis—assumes that the first-order principle of organization is object domain. Within any given domain of knowledge, there will be functional and neural specialization according to types or modalities of knowledge. For instance, visual motion properties of living animate things are represented in a different region/system than are visual form properties of living animate things. In addition, affective properties of living animate things may be represented by other, functionally and neuroanatomically, distinct systems. However, all of those types of information constitute the domain "living animate." For that reason, it is critical to specify the nature of the functional connectivity that relates processing across distinct subsystems specialized for different types of information. The basic expectation of the distributed domain-specific hypothesis is that the functional connectivity that relates processing across distinct types of information (e.g., emotional value versus visual form) will be concentrated around those domains that have had evolutionarily important histories. The strong prediction that follows from that view is that such neural circuits are the same circuits that are damaged in patients with category-specific semantic deficits.

Independently of whether the distributed domain-specific hypothesis is empirically confirmed, it serves to highlight two key aspects of human conceptual processing. First, humans do not have systems that support rich conceptual knowledge of objects in order to carry out only explicit knowledge tasks, such as object naming or similarity judgments. We have those systems because they serve action and ultimately have been in the service of survival. An understanding of the architecture of the conceptual system must therefore be situated in the context of the real-world computational problems that the conceptual system is structured to support. Second, human behavior arises due to the integration of multiple cognitive processes that individually operate over distinct types of knowledge. In contrast to the view that domain specificity implies modularity, we have emphasized the distributed nature of domain-specific neural circuits. On the distributed domain-specific hypothesis, the distinct (and potentially modular) processes within the sensory, motor, and affective systems are components of broader structures within the mind/brain. This framework thus emphasizes the need to understand how different types of cognitive processes, operating over different types of information, work in concert to orchestrate behavior.

In the more than 25 years since Warrington and colleagues' first detailed reports of patients with category-specific semantic deficits, new fields of investigation have emerged around the study of the organization and representation of conceptual knowledge. Despite that progress, the theoretical questions that currently occupy researchers are the same as those that were initially framed and debated two decades ago: What are the principles of neural organization that give rise to effects of category specificity? Are different types of information involved in processing different semantic categories and, if so, what distinguishes those different types of information? Future research will undoubtedly build upon the currently available theories as well as redeploy their individual assumptions within new theoretical frameworks.

FUTURE DIRECTIONS

1. To what degree do sensory and motor processes participate in higher cognitive function? The available evidence from neuropsychology places a clear upper limit on the degree to which conceptual knowledge can be assumed to be "embodied." However, equally compelling findings from functional neuroimaging demonstrate that the sensory and motor systems are automatically engaged during conceptual processing. It will be important to develop articulated models of the dynamics of activation flow among concepts and the sensory and motor systems in order to test hypotheses about the causes of sensory and motor activation during conceptual processing.

2. Are different domains of knowledge represented differently in males and females? Some researchers have highlighted the fact that patients with disproportionate semantic impairments for fruit/vegetables are male. This pattern remains even after controlling for gender-specific familiarity among items from different categories. Those data raise the question of whether early (and culturally influenced) differences in experience can qualitatively shape the functional architecture of the conceptual system.

3. How does damage to one region of the brain affect processing in other regions of the brain? Little is currently known about how damage to distinct regions within a network affects processing in other regions of the network. Detailed cognitive and anatomical studies of patients with semantic deficits will aide in understanding the dynamics of brain damage and the implications for cognitive models of conceptual processing.

DISCLOSURE STATEMENT

The authors are not aware of any biases that might be perceived as affecting the objectivity of this review.

ACKNOWLEDGMENTS

Preparation of this article was supported in part by a National Science Foundation Graduate Research Fellowship to BZM, National Institutes of Health grant DC04542 to AC, and by a grant from the Fondazione Cassa di Risparmio di Trento e Rovereto. The authors are grateful to Erminio Capitani, Marcella Laiacona, Alex Martin, and Daniel Schacter for their comments on an earlier draft.

LITERATURE CITED

Allport DA. 1985. Distributed memory, modular subsystems and dysphasia. In *Current Perspectives in Dysphasia*, ed. SK Newman, R Epstein, pp. 207–44. New York: Churchill Livingstone

Baillargeon R. 1998. Infants' understanding of the physical world. In *Advances in Psychological Science: 2. Biological and Cognitive Aspects*, ed. M Sabourin, F Craik, M Robert, pp. 503–29. London: Psychol. Press

Bar M, Aminoff E. 2003. Cortical analysis of visual context. *Neuron* 38:347–58

Barbarotto R, Capitani E, Spinnler H, Trivelli C. 1995. Slowly progressive semantic impairment with category specificity. *Neurocase* 1:107–19

Barbarotto R, Laiacona M, Macchi V, Capitani E. 2002. Picture reality decision, semantic categories, and gender: a new set of pictures, with norms and an experimental study. *Neuropsychologia* 40:1637–53

Barsalou LW. 1999. Perceptual symbol systems. *Behav. Brain Sci.* 22:637–60

Barsalou LW. 2008. Grounded cognition. *Annu. Rev. Psychol.* 59:617–45

Beauchamp MS, Lee KE, Haxby JV, Martin A. 2002. Parallel visual motion processing streams for manipulable objects and human movements. *Neuron* 24:149–59

Beauchamp MS, Lee KE, Haxby JV, Martin A. 2003. fMRI responses to video and point-light displays of moving humans and manipulable objects. *J. Cogn. Neurosci.* 15:991–1001

Beauvois M-F. 1982. Optic aphasia: a process of interaction between vision and language. *Philos. Trans. R. Soc. Lond. B* 298:35–47

Beauvois M-F, Saillant B, Mhninger V, Llermitte F. 1978. Bilateral tactile aphasia: a tacto-verbal dysfunction. *Brain* 101:381–401

Binkofski F, Dohle C, Posse S, Stephan KM, Hefter H, et al. 1998. Human anterior intraparietal area subserves prehension: a combined lesion and functional MRI activation study. *Neurology* 50:1253–59

Blundo C, Ricci M, Miller L. 2006. Category-specific knowledge deficit for animals in a patient with herpes simplex encephalitis. *Cogn. Neuropsychol.* 23:1248–68

Bookheimer S. 2002. Functional MRI of language: new approaches to understanding the cortical organization of semantic processing. *Annu. Rev. Neurosci.* 25:151–88

Borgo F, Shallice T. 2001. When living things and other "sensory-quality" categories behave in the same fashion: a novel category-specific effect. *Neurocase* 7:201–20

Borgo F, Shallice T. 2003. Category specificity and feature knowledge: evidence from new sensory-quality categories. *Cogn. Neuropsychol.* 20:327–53

Boronat CB, Buxbaum LJ, Coslett HB, Tang K, Saffran EM, et al. 2004. Distinctions between manipulation and function knowledge of objects: evidence from functional magnetic resonance imaging. *Cogn. Brain Res.* 23:361–73

Boulenger V, Roy AC, Paulignan Y, Deprez V, Jeannerod M, Nazir TA. 2006. Cross-talk between language processes and overt motor behavior in the first 200 msec of processing. *J. Cogn. Neurosci.* 18:1607–15

Brambati SM, Myers D, Wilson A, Rankin KP, Allison SC, et al. 2006. The anatomy of category-specific object naming in neurodegenerative diseases. *J. Cogn. Neurosci.* 18:1644–53

Bright P, Moss HE, Stamatakis EA, Tyler LK. 2005. The anatomy of object processing: the role of anteromedial temporal cortex. *Q. J. Exp. Psychol. B* 58:361–77

Buccino G, Riggio L, Melli G, Binkofski F, Gallese V, Rizzolatti G. 2005. Listening to action related sentences modulates the activity of the motor system: a combined TMS and behavioral study. *Cogn. Brain Res.* 24:355–63

Buchel C, Price C, Friston K. 1998. A multimodal language region in the ventral visual pathway. *Nature* 394:274–77

Buxbaum LJ, Veramonti T, Schwartz MF. 2000. Function and manipulation tool knowledge in apraxia: knowing "what for" but not "how." *Neurocase* 6:83–97

Canessa N, Borgo F, Cappa SF, Perani D, Falini A, et al. 2008. The different neural correlates of action and functional knowledge in semantic memory: an fMRI study. *Cereb. Cortex* 18:740–51

Cantlon JF, Platt M, Brannon EM. 2008. Beyond the number domain. *Trends Cogn. Sci.* Manuscr. under review

Capitani E, Laiacona M, Mahon B, Caramazza A. 2003. What are the facts of category-specific deficits? A critical review of the clinical evidence. *Cogn. Neuropsychol.* 20:213–62

Caramazza A. 1986. On drawing inferences about the structure of normal cognitive systems from the analysis of patterns of impaired performance: the case for single-patient studies. *Brain Cogn.* 5:41–66

Caramazza A. 1992. Is cognitive neuropsychology possible? *J. Cogn. Neurosci.* 4:80–95

Caramazza A. 1998. The interpretation of semantic category-specific deficits: What do they reveal about the organization of conceptual knowledge in the brain? *Neurocase* 4:265–72

Caramazza A, Hillis AE, Rapp BC, Romani C. 1990. The multiple semantics hypothesis: multiple confusions? *Cogn. Neuropsychol.* 7:161–89

Caramazza A, Mahon BZ. 2003. The organization of conceptual knowledge: the evidence from category-specific semantic deficits. *Trends Cogn. Sci.* 7:354–61

Caramazza A, Mahon BZ. 2006. The organisation of conceptual knowledge in the brain: the future's past and some future directions. *Cogn. Neuropsychol.* 23:13–38

Caramazza A, Shelton JR. 1998. Domain specific knowledge systems in the brain: the animate-inanimate distinction. *J. Cogn. Neurosci.* 10:1–34

Carey S, Spelke ES. 1994. Domain specific knowledge and conceptual change. In *Mapping the Mind: Domain Specificity in Cognition and Culture*, ed. L Hirschfeld, S Gelman, pp. 169–200. London: Cambridge Univ. Press

Carroll E, Garrard P. 2005. Knowledge of living, nonliving and "sensory quality" categories in semantic dementia. *Neurocase* 11:338–50

Chao LL, Haxby JV, Martin A. 1999. Attribute-based neural substrates in posterior temporal cortex for perceiving and knowing about objects. *Nat. Neurosci.* 2:913–19

Chao LL, Martin A. 2000. Representation of manipulable man-made objects in the dorsal stream. *Neuroimage* 12:478–84

Chao LL, Weisberg J, Martin A. 2002. Experience-dependent modulation of category related cortical activity. *Cereb. Cortex* 12:545–51

Coslett HB, Saffran EM. 1992. Optic aphasia and the right hemisphere: a replication and extension. *Brain. Lang.* 43:148–61

Crawford JR, Garthwaite PH. 2006. Methods of testing for a deficit in single case studies: evaluation of statistical power by Monte Carlo simulation. *Cogn. Neuropsychol.* 23:877–904

Cree GS, McRae K. 2003. Analyzing the factors underlying the structure and computation of the meaning of chipmunk, cherry, chisel, cheese, and cello and many other such concrete nouns. *J. Exp. Psychol. Gen.* 132:163–201

Crutch SJ, Warrington EK. 2003. The selective impairment of fruit and vegetable knowledge: a multiple processing channels account of fine-grain category specificity. *Cogn. Neuropsychol.* 20:355–72

Culham JC, Danckert SL, DeSourza JFX, Gati JS, Menon RS, Goodale MA. 2003. Visually guided grasping produces fMRI activation in dorsal but not ventral stream brain areas. *Exp. Brain Res.* 153:180–89

Damasio H, Grabowski TJ, Tranel D, Hichwa RD. 1996. A neural basis for lexical retrieval. *Nature* 380:499–505

Damasio H, Tranel D, Grabowski T, Adolphs R, Damasio A. 2004. Neural systems behind word and concept retrieval. *Cognition* 92:179–229

Dehaene S, Cohen L, Sigman M, Vinckier F. 2005. The neural code for written words: a proposal. *Trends Cogn. Sci.* 9:335–41

Devlin J, Gonnerman L, Andersen E, Seidenberg M. 1998. Category-specific semantic deficits in focal and widespread brain damage: a computational account. *J. Cogn. Neurosci.* 10:77–94

Devlin JT, Moore CJ, Mummery CJ, Gorno-Tempini ML, Phillips JA, et al. 2002. Anatomic constraints on cognitive theories of category-specificity. *Neuroimage* 15:675–85

Dixon MJ, Piskopos M, Schweizer TA. 2000. Musical instrument naming impairments: the crucial exception to the living/nonliving dichotomy in category-specific agnosia. *Brain Cogn.* 43:158–64

Downing PE, Jiang Y, Shuman M, Kanwisher N. 2001. A cortical area selective for visual processing of the human body. *Science* 293:2470–73

Duchaine B, Yovel G. 2008. Face recognition. In *The Senses: A Comprehensive Reference*, ed. A Basbaum, R Hoy, A Kaneko, G Shepherd, G Westheimer, pp. 329–58. Amsterdam: Elsevier

Duchaine BC, Yovel G, Butterworth EJ, Nakayama K. 2006. Prosopagnosia as an impairment to face-specific mechanisms: elimination of the alternative hypotheses in a developmental case. *Cogn. Neuropsychol.* 23:714–47

Ellis AW, Young AW, Critchley AMR. 1989. Loss of memory for people following temporal lobe damage. *Brain* 112:1469–83

Epstein R, Kanwisher N. 1998. A cortical representation of the local visual environment. *Nature* 392:598–601

Fang F, He S. 2005. Cortical responses to invisible objects in the human dorsal and ventral pathways. *Nat. Neurosci.* 8:1380–85

Farah M, McClelland J. 1991. A computational model of semantic memory impairment: modality specificity and emergent category specificity. *J. Exp. Psychol. Gen.* 120:339–57

Farah MJ, Rabinowitz C. 2003. Genetic and environmental influences on the organization of semantic memory in the brain: Is "living things" an innate category? *Cogn. Neuropsychol.* 20:401–8

Feigenson L, Dehaene S, Spelke ES. 2004. Core systems of number. *Trends Cogn. Sci.* 8:307–14

Frey SH, Vinton D, Norlund R, Grafton ST. 1995. Cortical topography of human anterior intraparietal cortex active during visually guided grasping. *Cogn. Brain Res.* 23:397–405

Funnell E, Sheridan J. 1992. Categories of knowledge: unfamiliar aspects of living and nonliving things. *Cogn. Neuropsychol.* 9:135–53

Gainotti G. 2000. What the locus of brain lesion tells us about the nature of the cognitive defect underlying category-specific disorders: a review. *Cortex* 36:539–59

Gallese V, Lakoff G. 2005. The brain's concepts: the role of the sensory motor system in reason and language. *Cogn. Neuropsychol.* 22:455–79

Gallistel CR. 1990. *The Organization of Learning*. Cambridge, MA: Bradford/MIT Press

Garrard P, Patterson K, Watson PC, Hodges JR. 1998. Category-specific semantic loss in dementia of Alzheimer's type: functional-anatomical correlations from cross-sectional analyses. *Brain* 121:633–46

Gauthier I, Skudlarski P, Gore JC, Anderson AW. 2000. Expertise for cars and birds recruits brain areas involved in face recognition. *Nat. Neurosci.* 3:191–97

Gelman R. 1990. First principles organize attention to and learning about relevant data: number and the animate-inanimate distinction as examples. *Cogn. Sci.* 14:79–106

Gerlach C. 2007. A review of functional imaging studies on category specificity. *J. Cogn. Neurosci.* 19:296–314

Glenberg AM, Kaschak MP. 2002. Grounding language in action. *Psychon. Bull. Rev.* 9:558–65

Goodale MA, Milner AD. 1992. Separate visual pathways for perception and action. *Trends Neurosci.* 15:20–25

Grill-Spector K, Malach R. 2004. The human visual cortex. *Annu. Rev. Neurosci.* 27:649–77

Hart J, Anand R, Zoccoli S, Maguire M, Gamino J, et al. 2007. Neural substrates of semantic memory. *J. Int. Neuropsychol. Soc.* 13:865–80

Hart J Jr, Berndt RS, Caramazza A. 1985. Category-specific naming deficit following cerebral infarction. *Nature* 316:439–40

Haxby JV, Gobbini MI, Furey ML, Ishai A, Schouten JL, Pietrini P. 2001. Distributed and overlapping representations of faces and objects in ventral temporal cortex. *Science* 293:2425–30

Hécaen H, De Ajuriaguerra J. 1956. Agnosie visuelle pour les objets inanimées par lésion unilatérale gauche. *Révue Neurol.* 94:222–33

Hermer L, Spelke ES. 1994. A geometric process for spatial reorientation in young children. *Nature* 370:57–59

Hillis AE, Caramazza A. 1991. Category-specific naming and comprehension impairment: a double dissociation. *Brain* 114:2081–94

Hillis AE, Caramazza A. 1995. Cognitive and neural mechanisms underlying visual and semantic processing: Implications from "optic aphasia." *J. Cogn. Neurosci.* 7:457–78

Humphreys GW, Forde EME. 2001. Hierarchies, similarity, and interactivity in object recognition: "category-specific" neuropsychological deficits. *Behav. Brain Sci.* 24:453–75

Humphreys GW, Forde EME. 2005. Naming a giraffe but not an animal: base-level but not superordinate naming in a patient with impaired semantics. *Cogn. Neuropsychol.* 22:539–58

Humphreys GW, Riddoch MJ, Quinlan PT. 1988. Cascade processes in picture identification. *Cogn. Neuropsychol.* 5:67–103

Ishai A, Ungerleider LG, Martin A, Schourten JL, Haxby JV. 1999. Distributed representation of objects in the human ventral visual pathway. *Proc. Natl. Acad. Sci. USA* 96:9379–84

Jeannerod M, Jacob P. 2005. Visual cognition: a new look at the two-visual systems model. *Neuropsychologia* 43:301–12

Johnson-Frey SH. 2004. The neural bases of complex tool use in humans. *Trends Cogn. Sci.* 8:71–78

Kable JW, Lease-Spellmeyer J, Chatterjee A. 2002. Neural substrates of action event knowledge. *J. Cogn. Neurosci.* 14:795–805

Keil FC. 1981. Constraints on knowledge and cognitive development. *Psychol. Rev.* 88:197–227

Kellenbach ML, Brett M, Patterson K. 2003. Actions speak louder than functions: the importance of manipulability and action in tool representation. *J. Cogn. Neurosci.* 15:20–46

Kemmerer D, Gonzalez Castillo J, Talavage T, Patterson S, Wiley C. 2008. Neuroanatomical distribution of five semantic components of verbs: evidence from fMRI. *Brain Lang.* In press

Kiani R, Esteky H, Mirpour K, Tanaka K. 2007. Object category structure in response patterns of neuronal population in monkey inferior temporal cortex. *J. Neurophysiol.* 97:4296–309

Laiacona M, Barbarotto R, Capitani E. 1993. Perceptual and associative knowledge in category specific impairment of semantic memory: a study of two cases. *Cortex* 29:727–40

Laiacona M, Barbarotto R, Capitani E. 1998. Semantic category dissociation in naming: Is there a gender effect in Alzheimer disease? *Neuropsychologia* 36:407–19

Laiacona M, Barbarotto R, Capitani E. 2005. Animals recover but plant life knowledge is still impaired 10 years after herpetic encephalitis: the long-term follow-up of a patient. *Cogn. Neuropsychol.* 22:78–94

Laiacona M, Barbarotto R, Capitani E. 2006. Human evolution and the brain representation of semantic knowledge: Is there a role for sex differences? *Evol. Hum. Behav.* 27:158–68

Laiacona M, Capitani E. 2001. A case of prevailing deficit on nonliving categories or a case of prevailing sparing of living categories? *Cogn. Neuropsychol.* 18:39–70

Laiacona M, Capitani E, Caramazza A. 2003. Category-specific semantic deficits do not reflect the sensory-functional organisation of the brain: a test of the "sensory-quality" hypothesis. *Neurocase* 9:3221–31

Lambon Ralph MA, Howard D, Nightingale G, Ellis AW. 1998. Are living and nonliving category-specific deficits causally linked to impaired perceptual or associative knowledge? Evidence from a category-specific double dissociation. *Neurocase* 4:311–38

Lambon Ralph MA, Lowe C, Rogers TT. 2007. Neural basis of category-specific semantic deficits for living things: evidence from semantic dementia, HSVE and a neural network model. *Brain* 130:1127–37

Laws KR, Gale TM. 2002. Category-specific naming and the "visual" characteristics of line drawn stimuli. *Cortex* 38:7–21

Laws KR, Neve C. 1999. A "normal" category-specific advantage for naming living things. *Neuropsychologia* 37:1263–69

Levy I, Hasson U, Avidan G, Hendler T, Malach R. 2001. Center-periphery organization of human object areas. *Nat. Neurosci.* 4:533–39

Lewis JW. 2006. Cortical networks related to human use of tools. *Neuroscientist* 12:211–31

Lhermitte F, Beauvois M-F. 1973. A visual speech disconnection syndrome: report of a case with optic aphasia, agnosic alexia and color agnosia. *Brain* 96:695–714

Luzzatti C, Davidoff J. 1994. Impaired retrieval of object-color knowledge with preserved color naming. *Neuropsychologia* 32:1–18

Lyons F, Kay J, Hanley JR, Haslam C. 2006. Selective preservation of memory for people in the context of semantic memory disorder: patterns of association and dissociation. *Neuropsychologia* 44:2887–98

Machery E. 2007. Concept empiricism: a methodological critique. *Cognition* 104:19–46

Mahon BZ, Caramazza A. 2003. Constraining questions about the organisation and representation of conceptual knowledge. *Cogn. Neuropsychol.* 20:433–50

Mahon BZ, Caramazza A. 2005. The orchestration of the sensory-motor systems: clues from neuropsychology. *Cogn. Neuropsychol.* 22:480–94

Mahon BZ, Caramazza A. 2008. A critical look at the embodied cognition hypothesis and a new proposal for grounding conceptual content. *J. Physiol. Paris* 102:59–70

Mahon BZ, Milleville S, Negri GAL, Rumiati RI, Martin A, Caramazza A. 2007. Action-related properties of objects shape object representations in the ventral stream. *Neuron* 55:507–20

Martin A. 2006. Shades of Déjerine—forging a causal link between the visual word form area and reading. *Neuron* 50:173–75

Martin A. 2007. The representation of object concepts in the brain. *Annu. Rev. Psychol.* 58:25–45

Martin A, Haxby JV, Lalonde FM, Wiggs CL, Ungerleider LG. 1995. Discrete cortical regions associated with knowledge of color and knowledge of action. *Science* 270:102–5

Martin A, Ungerleider LG, Haxby JV. 2000. Category specificity and the brain: the sensory/motor model of semantic representations of objects. In *Higher Cognitive Functions: The New Cognitive Neurosciences*, ed. MS Gazzaniga, pp. 1023–36. Cambridge, MA: MIT Press

Martin A, Weisberg J. 2003. Neural foundations for understanding social and mechanical concepts. *Cogn. Neuropsychol.* 20:575–87

Martin A, Wiggs CL, Ungerleider LG, Haxby JV. 1996. Neural correlates of category-specific knowledge. *Nature* 379:649–52

McClelland JL, Rogers TT. 2003. The parallel distributed processing approach to semantic cognition. *Nat. Rev. Neurosci.* 4:310–22

Mechelli A, Sartori G, Orlandi P, Price CJ. 2006. Semantic relevance explains category effects in medial fusiform gyri. *Neuroimage* 3:992–1002

Miceli G, Capasso R, Daniele A, Esposito T, Magarelli M, Tomaiuolo F. 2000. Selective deficit for people's names following left temporal damage: an impairment of domain-specific conceptual knowledge. *Cogn. Neuropsychol.* 17:489–516

Miceli G, Fouch E, Capasso R, Shelton JR, Tamaiuolo F, Caramazza A. 2001. The dissociation of color from form and function knowledge. *Nat. Neurosci.* 4:662–67

Milner AD, Perrett DI, Johnson RS, Benson OJ, Jordan TR, et al. 1991. Perception and action "visual form agnosia." *Brain* 114:405–28

Mitchell JP, Heatherton TF, Macrae CN. 2002. Distinct neural systems subserve person and object knowledge. *Proc. Natl. Acad. Sci. USA* 99:15238–43

Moreaud O, Charnallet A, Pellat J. 1998. Identification without manipulation: a study of the relations between object use and semantic memory. *Neuropsychologia* 36:1295–301

Morris JS, Öhman A, Dolan RJ. 1999. A subcortical pathway to the right amygdala mediating "unseen" fear. *Proc. Natl. Acad. Sci. USA* 96:1680–85

Moscovitch M, Winocur G, Behrmann M. 1997. What is special about face recognition? Nineteen experiments on a person with visual object agnosia and dyslexia but with normal face recognition. *J. Cogn. Neurosci.* 9:555–604

Moss HE, Tyler LK, Durrant-Peatfield M, Bunn EM. 1998. "Two eyes of a see-through": impaired and intact semantic knowledge in a case of selective deficit for living things. *Neurocase* 4:291–310

Negri GAL, Rumiati RI, Zadini A, Ukmar M, Mahon BZ, Caramazza A. 2007. What is the role of motor simulation in action and object recognition? Evidence from apraxia. *Cogn. Neuropsychol.* 24:795–816

Noppeney U, Price CJ, Penny WD, Friston KJ. 2006. Two distinct neural mechanisms for category-selective responses. *Cereb. Cortex* 16:437–45

Nunn JA, Postma P, Pearson R. 2001. Developmental prosopagnosia: Should it be taken at face value? *Neurocase* 7:15–27

Ochipa C, Rothi LJG, Heilman KM. 1989. Ideational apraxia: a deficit in tool selection and use. *Ann. Neurol.* 25:190–93

Oliveri M, Finocchiaro C, Shapiro K, Gangitano M, Caramazza A, Pascual-Leone A. 2004. All talk and no action: a transcranial magnetic stimulation study of motor cortex activation during action word production. *J. Cogn. Neurosci.* 16:374–81

Op de Beeck HP, Haushofer J, Kanwisher NG. 2008. Interpreting fMRI data: maps, modules, and dimensions. *Nat. Rev. Neurosci.* 9:123–35

Pasley BN, Mayes LC, Schultz RT. 2004. Subcortical discrimination of unperceived objects during binocular rivalry. *Neuron* 42:163–72

Patterson K, Nestor PJ, Rogers TT. 2007. Where do you know what you know? The representation of semantic knowledge in the human brain. *Nat. Rev. Neurosci.* 8:976–87

Pisella L, Binkofski BF, Lasek K, Toni I, Rossetti Y. 2006. No double-dissociation between optic ataxia and visual agnosia: multiple substreams for multiple visuo-manual integrations. *Neuropsychologia* 44:2734–48

Plaut DC. 2002. Graded modality-specific specialization in semantics: a computational account of optic aphasia. *Cogn. Neuropsychol.* 19:603–39

Polk TA, Park J, Smith MR, Park DC. 2007. Nature versus nurture in ventral visual cortex: a functional magnetic resonance imaging study of twins. *J. Neurosci.* 27:13921–25

Prinz JJ. 2002. *Furnishing the Mind. Concepts and Their Perceptual Basis.* Cambridge, MA: MIT Press

Pulvermüller F. 2005. Brain mechanisms linking language and action. *Nat. Rev. Neurosci.* 6:576–82

Pulvermüller F, Hauk O, Nikolin VV, Ilmoniemi RJ. 2005. Functional links between language and motor systems. *Eur. J. Neurosci.* 21:793–97

Rapcsak SZ, Ochipa C, Anderson KC, Poizner H. 1995. Progressive ideomotor apraxia: evidence for a selective impairment in the action production system. *Brain Cogn.* 27:213–36

Riddoch MJ, Humphreys GW, Coltheart M, Funnell E. 1988. Semantic systems or system? Neuropsychological evidence re-examined. *Cogn. Neuropsychol.* 5:3–25

Riesenhuber M. 2007. Appearance isn't everything: news on object representation in cortex. *Neuron* 55:341–44

Rogers TT, Hocking J, Mechelli A, Patterson K, Price CJ. 2005. Fusiform activation to animals is driven by the process, not the stimulus. *J. Cogn. Neurosci.* 17:434–45

Rogers TT, Lambon Ralph MA, Garrard P, Bozeat S, McClelland JL, et al. 2004. Structure and deterioration of semantic memory: a neuropsychological and computational investigation. *Psychol. Rev.* 111:205–35

Rosci C, Chiesa V, Laiacona M, Capitani E. 2003. Apraxia is not associated to a disproportionate naming impairment for manipulable objects. *Brain Cogn.* 53:412–15

Rothi LJ, Ochipa C, Heilman KM. 1991. A cognitive neuropsychological model of limb praxis. *Cogn. Neuropsychol.* 8:443–58

Rumiati Rl, Zanini S, Vorano L. 2001. A form of ideational apraxia as a selective deficit of contention scheduling. *Cogn. Neuropsychol.* 18:617–42

Rumiati RI, Weiss PH, Shallice T, Ottoboni G, Noth J, et al. 2004. The neural basis of pantomiming the use of visually presented objects. *Neuroimage* 21:1224–31

Sacchett C, Humphreys GW. 1992. Calling a squirrel a squirrel but a canoe a wigwam: a category-specific deficit for artifactual objects and body parts. *Cogn. Neuropsychol.* 9:73–86

Samson D, Pillon A. 2003. A case of impaired knowledge for fruit and vegetables. *Cogn. Neuropsychol.* 20:373–400

Santos LR, Caramazza A. 2002. The domain-specific hypothesis: a developmental and comparative perspective on category-specific deficits. In *Category-Specificity in the Brain and Mind*, ed. EME Forde, GW Humphreys, pp. 1–23. New York: Psychol. Press

Sartori G, Lombardi L. 2004. Semantic relevance and semantic disorders. *J. Cogn. Neurosci.* 16:439–52

Sartori G, Lombardi L, Mattiuzzi L. 2005. Semantic relevance best predicts normal and abnormal name retrieval. *Neuropsychologia* 43:754–70

Shallice T. 1988. *From Neuropsychology to Mental Structure.* London: Cambridge Univ. Press

Shelton JR, Fouch E, Caramazza A. 1998. The selective sparing of body part knowledge: a case study. *Neurocase* 4:339–51

Silveri MC, Gainotti G, Perani D, Cappelletti JY, Carbone G, Fazio F. 1997. Naming deficit for nonliving items: neuropsychological and PET study. *Neuropsychologia* 35:359–67

Simmons WK, Barsalou LW. 2003. The similarity-in-topography principle: reconciling theories of conceptual deficits. *Cogn. Neuropsychol.* 20:451–86

Sirigu A, Duhamel J, Poncet M. 1991. The role of sensorimotor experience in object recognition. *Brain* 114:2555–73

Spelke ES, Breinlinger K, Macomber J, Jacobson K. 1992. Origins of knowledge. *Psychol. Rev.* 99:605–32

Stewart F, Parkin AJ, Hunkin NM. 1992. Naming impairments following recovery from herpes simplex encephalitis. *Q. J. Exp. Psychol. A* 44:261–84

Thompson-Schill SL. 2003. Neuroimaging studies of semantic memory: inferring "how" from "where." *Neuropsychologia* 41:280–92

Thompson-Schill SL, Aguirre GK, D'Esposito M, Farah MJ. 1999. A neural basis for category and modality specificity of semantic knowledge. *Neuropsychologia* 37:671–76

Tranel D, Logan CG, Frank RJ, Damasio AR. 1997. Explaining category-related effects in the retrieval of conceptual and lexical knowledge of concrete entities: operationalization and analysis of factor. *Neuropsychologia* 35:1329–39

Turnbull OH, Laws KR. 2000. Loss of stored knowledge of object structure: implication for "category-specific" deficits. *Cogn. Neuropsychol.* 17:365–89

Tyler LK, Moss HE. 2001. Towards a distributed account of conceptual knowledge. *Trends Cogn. Sci.* 5:244–52

Ungerleider LG, Mishkin M. 1982. Two cortical visual systems. In *Analysis of Visual Behavior*, ed. DJ Ingle, MA Goodale, RJW Mansfield, pp. 549–86. Cambridge, MA: MIT Press

Vinson DP, Vigliocco G, Cappa S, Siri S. 2003. The breakdown of semantic knowledge: insights from a statistical model of meaning representation. *Brain Lang.* 86:347–65

Warrington EK, McCarthy RA. 1983. Category specific access dysphasia. *Brain* 106:859–78

Warrington EK, McCarthy RA. 1987. Categories of knowledge: further fractionations and an attempted integration. *Brain* 110:1273–96

Warrington EK, Shallice T. 1984. Category specific semantic impairment. *Brain* 107:829–54

Wellman HM, Gelman SA. 1992. Cognitive development: foundational theories of core domains. *Annu. Rev. Psychol.* 43:337–75

Zannino GD, Perri R, Carlesimo GA, Pasqualetti P, Caltagirone C. 2002. Category-specific impairment in patients with Alzheimer's disease as a function of disease severity: a cross-sectional investigation. *Neuropsychologia* 40:2268–79

Zannino GD, Perri R, Pasqualetti P, Caltagirone C, Carlesimo GA. 2006. Analysis of the semantic representations of living and nonliving concepts: a normative study. *Cogn. Neuropsychol.* 23:515–40

Zwaan RA. 2004. The immersed experiencer: toward an embodied theory of language comprehension. In *The Psychology of Learning and Motivation*, ed. BH Ross, pp. 35–62. New York: Academic

Mindful Judgment and Decision Making

Elke U. Weber and Eric J. Johnson

Center for the Decision Sciences (CDS), Columbia University, New York, New York 10027;
email: euw2@columbia.edu

Annu. Rev. Psychol. 2009. 60:53–85

First published online as a Review in Advance on
September 17, 2008

The *Annual Review of Psychology* is online at
psych.annualreviews.org

This article's doi:
10.1146/annurev.psych.60.110707.163633

Key Words

choice, preference, inference, cognition, emotion, attention, memory,
learning, process models

Abstract

A full range of psychological processes has been put into play to explain
judgment and choice phenomena. Complementing work on attention,
information integration, and learning, decision research over the past
10 years has also examined the effects of goals, mental representation,
and memory processes. In addition to deliberative processes, automatic
processes have gotten closer attention, and the emotions revolution
has put affective processes on a footing equal to cognitive ones. Psychological process models provide natural predictions about individual
differences and lifespan changes and integrate across judgment and decision making (JDM) phenomena. "Mindful" JDM research leverages our
knowledge about psychological processes into causal explanations for
important judgment and choice regularities, emphasizing the adaptive
use of an abundance of processing alternatives. Such explanations supplement and support existing mathematical descriptions of phenomena
such as loss aversion or hyperbolic discounting. Unlike such descriptions, they also provide entry points for interventions designed to help
people overcome judgments or choices considered undesirable.

Contents

INTRODUCTION

Since its origins in the 1950s, judgment and decision making (JDM) research has been dominated by mathematical functional relationship models that were its point of departure in the form of normative models. This focus on economics and statistics may have led JDM research to underutilize the insights and methods of psychology. Aided by the recent arrival

JDM: judgment and decision making

of neuroscience methodologies to complement behavioral research, the field has started to realize, however, that the brain that decides how to invest pension money and what car to buy is the same brain that also learns to recognize and categorize sounds and faces, resolves perceptual conflicts, acquires motor skills such as those used in playing tennis, and remembers (or fails to remember) episodic and semantic information. In this review, we make a strong case for the utility of this realization.

JDM reviews are often structured by task categories, with section headings such as "preferences," "beliefs," and "decisions under risk and uncertainty" (Payne et al. 1992), and "risky choice," "intertemporal choice," and "social decisions" (Loewenstein et al. 2007). In contrast, our review employs headings that might be found in a cognitive psychology textbook. It capitalizes on the 50 years of research on cognitive and motivational processes that have followed Simon's (1957) depiction of human decision makers as finite-capacity information processors and decision satisficers. Attentional (in particular, perceptual) and learning processes have a longer history of consideration, with phenomena such as "diminishing sensitivity of outcomes" or "reference point encoding" for perception and the "illusion of validity" for learning. Affective, memory, and prediction processes have only more recently emerged as explanations of judgment and choice phenomena.

We retain some task category distinctions to organize specific content where appropriate. Thus, we distinguish between preference and inference. Preferences involve value judgments and are therefore subjective, such as deciding how much to charge for an item on eBay. Inferences are about beliefs, such as the judged likelihood that a political candidate will win the next election, and typically have objectively verifiable answers. Although this distinction reflects tradition, it may not reflect psychological reality. Preferences and inferences seem to draw on the same cognitive processes.

Our ability to organize our review by psychological processes is a sign of the growing maturity of the field. JDM research no longer simply generates a growing list of phenomena that show deviations from the predictions of normative models. Instead, it has been developing and testing hypotheses about the psychological processes that give rise to judgments and choices and about the mental representations used by these processes. Although the number of JDM articles in major social psychology journals remained constant over the past 10 years, the number of JDM articles in major cognitive psychology journals increased by 50% over that period, reflecting the increased interest in integrating judgment and choice phenomena with the frameworks of hot and cold cognition.

New tools have undoubtedly contributed to this trend. This includes functional imaging and other neural and physiological recordings, process tracing tools (see sidebar Process Models and Process Tracing), and, increasingly, modeling tools such as mediation (Shrout & Bolger 2002) and multilevel analysis (Gelman & Hill 2007). A focus on psychological mechanisms has guided the decomposition of JDM task behavior into contributing cognitive processes and their variation across groups (Busemeyer & Diederich 2002, Stout et al. 2004, Wallsten et al. 2005, Yechiam et al. 2005). An increased focus on individual differences has been a noticeable feature of behavioral decision research over the past decade. Increased use of Web-based experimentation (Birnbaum & Bahra 2007) allows access to respondents with much broader and representative variation on demographic and cognitive variables, with new insights about individual, group, and life-span differences on JDM tasks, topics that are discussed in the second section of our review. More affordable genotyping has led to examinations of the heritability of economic traits like trust (Cesarini et al. 2007).

JDM research attracts public and media attention because it addresses real-world phenomena, from myopic dietary decisions to excessive stock market trading. Policy makers have increasingly utilized JDM theory and results when designing or changing institutions (Shafir 2008), the topic of our last major sec-

PROCESS MODELS AND PROCESS TRACING

Early models in decision research attempted to explain changes in judgments or decisions (the "output") as a result of changes in information considered (the "inputs") using tools such as regression and analysis of variance. This approach is problematic because it considers only a subset of observable behavior and because different models can predict one set of outputs from a given set of inputs. Process models help because they consider more variables and add multiple constraints. By virtue of hypothesizing a series of psychological processes that precede a judgment or choice, they make predictions about intermediate states of the decision maker, between the start and end of the decision ("What external information is sought out? What facts are recalled from memory?"). Process models also make predictions about the temporal order of these states ("What will a decision maker think about first, second, etc.?"). Process data are the data used to test hypotheses about these intervening processes and intermediate states. They include functional imaging and other measures of localized brain activation, response times, verbal protocols, eye-movement tracking, and other information-acquisition tools (see **www.mouselabweb.org**).

tion. The recognition that preferences are typically constructed rather than stored and retrieved (Lichtenstein & Slovic 2006) may be psychology's most successful export to behavioral economics and the policy community and illustrates the utility of psychological process explanations. We now know how, and increasingly why, characteristics of choice options and task guide attention, and how internal memory or external information search and option comparison affect choice in path-dependent ways. This not only explains apparent inconsistencies in choice, but also provides insights and recipes for decision aiding and interventions, including the design of decision environments that nudge people to construct their preferences in ways they will not regret after the fact (Thaler & Sunstein 2008).

Psychological process explanations cast light on areas obscured in the shadows of statistical decision-process approaches. For example, years of work with Egon Brunswik's lens model, which provided valuable insights into the

Preferences: in economics, inferred from choices and assumed to reflect utilities. In psychology, thought to be constructed in order to make a choice

Inferences: decision makers' judgments about the world using logic and often imperfect and uncertain information

performance of human decision makers, may have hidden the important distinction between automatic and deliberative (controlled) processes and their properties (Schneider & Chein 2003). Process explanations also serve an integrative function by explaining multiple phenomena, providing an organizing principle for a field criticized for being long on effects and short on unifying explanations. Judgments and choices typically engage multiple psychological processes, from attention-guided encoding and evaluation, to retrieval of task-relevant information from memory or external sources, prediction, response, and postdecision evaluation of consequences and resulting updating. Different tasks involve these processes to different degrees. For example, attention accounts for a larger proportion of response variance in decisions from description, where the decision maker is explicitly provided with all relevant information in numeric or graphic form. In contrast, memory and learning will be more important in decisions from experience, where information about outcomes and their likelihood is acquired by trial and error sampling of choice options over time (see Hertwig et al. 2004). Similarly, affective processes are more important in dynamic decisions under uncertainty, whereas analytic evaluations play a larger role in static risky decisions (Figner et al. 2008).

The last comprehensive Annual Review article on JDM was published more than 10 years ago (Mellers et al. 1998). Two reviews since then have addressed special topics, namely rationality (Shafir & LeBoeuf 2002) and unsolved problems in decision research (Hastie 2001). Given this time span between JDM articles, our review had to be extremely selective. Our mandate, to review research on cognitive processes in judgment and choice, necessitated the omission of papers that describe JDM phenomena without emphasizing psychological process interpretations. We also had to limit the scope of psychological processes covered. With a few exceptions, we omitted very basic perceptual processes (e.g., categorization) and processes that go beyond the individual (e.g., group judgments and decisions;

interdependent, competitive, and strategic decisions; advice giving; social judgments; information aggregations; and prediction markets). We were unable to go beyond judgment and choice processes, not covering problem solving, reasoning, or positive psychology. The burgeoning field of neuroeconomics recently received its own review (Loewenstein et al. 2007). When multiple papers could have been cited for a given point, we restricted ourselves to the most important, innovative, or comprehensive examples, and omitted citations for classic phenomena.

ATTENTION

Decision makers face a wealth of potentially relevant information in the external environment and memory. Given the processing limitations of *Homo sapiens*, selectivity is a central component of goal-directed behavior. Selective attention operates at very basic levels of perceptual identification (Lachter et al. 2004). It also operates at higher cognitive levels, including the initial perception of the situation and assessment of the task at hand (framing, goal elicitation), evidence accumulation (which can be external or internal, and usually is a combination of the two), and judgment or choice (determining cutoffs or decision rules).

A focus on attention as a finite resource, requiring selectivity, goes back to the beginnings of scientific psychology. William James in 1890 considered attention a necessary condition for subsequent memory, distinguished between voluntary and nonvoluntary attention, and suggested the use of eye movements to track attentional focus. More recently, Daniel Kahneman (1973) summarized what was known about attention during the postbehaviorist period when attention was used as a "label for some of the internal mechanisms that determine the significance of stimuli" (p. 2). Kahneman emphasized capacity limitations and the selective aspect of attention and distinguished between two determinants, momentary (voluntary) task intentions and more enduring dispositions such as the (involuntary) orienting response to novel stimuli. Herbert Simon (1978) identified conscious attention as a scarce resource for decision makers in the year of his Nobel prize; Kahneman's Nobel lecture (2003) reiterates that this scarce resource needs to be allocated wisely and points to automatic (orienting) processes and fast emotional reactions as means to that end.

Exogenous Influences

Orienting responses. Some features of the environment attract attention because responding to them has survival value. Changes in the environment, and especially the appearance of novel stimuli, introduce the possibility of opportunity and/or threat. Constant exposure to a stimulus leads to habituation, i.e., reduced responding, as things not previously responded to are likely to be neither dangerous nor promising. On the other hand, a change in the environment results in dishabituation and an orienting response (Posner & Rothbart 2007).

As a result of the orienting response to changes in the environment, things that vary automatically attract and maintain attention. A siren that wails will attract attention longer than a siren that operates at a constant frequency. This has implications for a wide range of issues, from research design to human factors and institutional design, with salient continuous changes in the level of key decision variables as a recipe for keeping people's attention on the task, a manipulation perfected by video games. Arguments by Birnbaum (1983) about the consequences of within- versus between-subject manipulations of base rates have recently been revived in the context of quantity (in)sensitivity in protected value tradeoffs. Bartels & Medin (2007) reconcile conflicting results by showing that between-subject designs lead to quantity insensitivity (e.g., the same willingness to pay to restore the pH level of one lake or of ten lakes) (Baron & Ritov 2004), whereas within-subject designs, which attract attention to variation in quantity, show sensitivity to the variable (Connolly & Reb 2003).

Task characteristics. In the same spirit of integrating across apparently contradictory research results, a range of JDM tasks and context characteristics have been examined for their effect of guiding attention and thus decision weight to different outcome dimensions. Violations of procedure invariance are one of the most vexing cases of deviation from normative models of preference. Selling prices typically exceed buying prices by a factor of two, even when strategic misrepresentation is eliminated, and discounting of future benefits is much steeper when people are asked to delay rather than accelerate consumption (Kahneman & Tversky 2000). Below, we review information-recruitment mechanisms that explain how the direction of an economic transactions (e.g., acquiring or giving up ownership; switching from immediate to delayed consumption or vice versa) can affect valuation. Relating such valuation asymmetries to attentional processes, Carmon & Ariely (2000) show that decision makers focus their attention on the foregone, i.e., the status quo and its characteristics attract more attention and thus importance and decision weight than do other choice options.

Judgment versus choice. It has long been known that judgment versus choice tasks can direct attention to different characteristics of choice options, from preference reversal studies of risky decisions in the 1970s to the theory of task-contingent weighting of multiattribute choice (see Lichtenstein & Slovic 2006). Editing operations cancel out common outcomes for choices but cannot do so for judgments, with resulting differences in attentional allocation and information use that translate into differences in preference. Consumer purchases are typically the result of choice from among multiple alternatives, where alignable features receive greater attention, whereas postpurchase consumer satisfaction is the result of judging the product in isolation, where features that are easily evaluated in an absolute sense receive greater attention (Hsee & Zhang 2004). Many task-detail-induced inconsistencies in judgment and choice can be explained by differences in attentional

PT: prospect theory

Beta-delta model:
explains greater
discounting of future
outcomes when
immediate rewards are
available than when all
rewards are in the
future by an
exponential delta
process that always
operates and an
additional exponential
beta process that only
operates when
immediate rewards are
present

focus, although the inconsistencies are not exclusively due to attentional mechanisms. Most stable JDM phenomena such as preference reversals are probably stable because they are multiply determined.

Description of choice options. The way in which information about choice options is communicated to decision makers influences preference construction through selective attention, even though variants may be informationally equivalent. One of these ways is the order in which options are presented. Candidate name order on ballots, for example, has been shown to influence preference and voting sufficiently to determine election results (Krosnick et al. 2004). Options encountered first capture attention, leading to reference-dependent subsequent evaluations and comparisons (Kahneman 2003). In decisions from description, some outcome dimension values (namely certainty on the probability dimension and immediacy on the delay dimension) are given special status, i.e., extra attention and decision weight of a more categorical than continuous nature, as captured by prospect theory's (PT) decision weight function and Laibson's (1997) beta-delta model of time discounting. Weber & Chapman (2005) show that certainty and immediacy are connected, in that adding delay "undoes" the special preference given to certainty, and adding uncertainty removes the special preference given to immediacy.

Process of knowledge provision. In decisions from description, attention is shared between outcome and probability information, which are both explicitly provided. In decisions from experience, the series of sequentially experienced outcomes focuses attention on this dimension, with more recent outcomes looming larger (Weber et al. 2004). The emergent evidence that rare events get underweighted in decisions from experience but overweighted in decisions from description, as captured by PT, can be explained by differences in attentional focus during information acquisition (Erev et al. 2008), because attention directed by both external and internal factors has been shown to translate into decision weight (Weber & Kirsner 1997).

Endogenous Influences

In addition to external influences, the internal state of the decision maker guides attention. Decision makers generally have more control over their internal states, thus allowing for more voluntary allocations of attention.

Goals. JDM research over the period of our review has started to interpret behavior in terms of goals and plans rather than (or in addition to) utilities (Krantz & Kunreuther 2007). Survival and economic well-being dictate that material goals play an important role in people's plans and decisions. Material goals are responsible for the effectiveness of financial incentives in shaping behavior. However, people harbor many other goals, some of which relate to nonmaterial dimensions of the choices made [e.g., being defensible (Lerner & Tetlock 1999)], whereas others relate to the nature of the decision process [e.g., wanting a procedurally just process (Tyler 2005) or a process that feels right (Higgins 2005)]. With multiple and often conflicting goals in play, selective attention to different subsets of goals has been shown to influence how a decision is made and what is selected (Krantz & Kunreuther 2007). A range of factors has been shown to situationally activate goals or chronically elevate their accessibility, including cultural values of the decision maker (Weber et al. 2005a), the content domain of the decision, e.g., risky choices about course grades versus stock investments (Rettinger & Hastie 2001), and task characteristics such as required accountability (Tetlock 2002). Activated goals determine whether the decision rules used are deontological ("What is right?") versus consequentialist ("What has the best outcomes?") versus affective ("What feels right?") (Bartels & Medin 2007). Ariely et al. (2000) point to the importance of goals in the context of choices between different streams of experience over time. Similar to the discussion above about quantity (in)sensitivity in the context of protected value tradeoffs, people are more or less duration sensitive when evaluating experiences over time as a function of how their attention is focused by how they report their experiences and why.

Affect as spotlight. Emotions experienced by the decision maker, in addition to the many cognitive factors mentioned above, focus attention on features of the environment that matter for emotion-appropriate action tendencies. Mood-congruent perception focuses attention on either upside opportunity or downside risk (Chou et al. 2007). Feelings of fear or worry focus attention on the source of the apparent threat and ready flight responses (Loewenstein et al. 2001). Feelings of anger focus attention on information about motives and responsibility and make decision makers eager to act and punish. Sadness elicits a desire to change one's state, resulting in reduced selling and inflated buying prices, whereas disgust triggers a desire to purge or acquire less, with the opposite effect on willingness to pay (Lerner et al. 2004).

ENCODING AND EVALUATION

One clear finding from behavioral decision research is that information is acquired by decision makers in ways not addressed by normative models. Goal-relevant and context-sensitive encoding of information is one of the ways in which people execute their task with minimal effort and, perhaps, maximal satisfaction. One important distinction to make is between information obtained from a search of external sources (external search; e.g., when choosing a cereal by studying product information in a supermarket aisle) versus information retrieved from memory (internal search; e.g., when retrieving options about which route to take on a drive home). Most decisions involve both kinds of search. The cereal choice probably involves recalling how much the previously purchased brand was enjoyed, and the choice of a route home uses external retrieval cues and information about traffic congestion. The distinction matters, however, because the properties of external search (reviewed in this section) are demonstrably different from the properties of retrieval from memory (reviewed in the next section on Memory Storage and Retrieval).

Evaluation is Relative

Outcomes. The humorist Thurber was once asked how he liked his new wife. His response "Compared to what?" reflects one of prospect theory's (Kahneman & Tversky 1979) major insights, namely that evaluation is relative. This insight continues to gather support, albeit in more complex ways than formalized by PT. Since neurons encode changes in stimulation (rather than absolute levels), absolute judgments on any dimension are much more difficult than relative judgments. The list of reference points used in relative evaluation continues to grow and includes other observed or counterfactual outcomes from the same or different choice alternatives, as well as expectations. For example, the range of options offered as potential certainty equivalents has been shown to affect people's valuation of gambles (Stewart et al. 2003). One important area for future research is to understand better the selection among reference points and how multiple reference points might be used.

Most discussions of relative evaluation have focused on the evaluation of a single outcome by comparing it to a reference point, typically by computing their difference in value. However, differences themselves may be in need of relative evaluation. If asked how good his $5000 salary increase was, Thurber probably would have also asked, "compared to what?" Gonzalez-Vallejo's (2002) proportional difference model is a stochastic model of choice that answers this question. Differences in attribute values of two choice options are normalized by dividing them by the best (for positive) or worst (for negative) possible outcome. These proportional differences are then integrated across attributes by a stochastic decision process, allowing the model to account for a broader range of choice patterns than other models (Gonzalez-Vallejo et al. 2003). Normalization

Variability or risk: the risk in risky choice options is introduced by not knowing what outcome will occur. In economics and finance, the variance of possible outcomes is used as a measure of risk

of outcome differences in ratio form also appears to hold for implicit evaluations of variability or risk. The coefficient of variation, defined as the standard deviation of possible choice outcomes divided by their expected value (i.e., risk per unit of return), predicts people's risky choices and risky foraging of animals far better than does the typical nonnormalized measures of variability or risk (standard deviation or variance) employed in finance (Weber et al. 2004).

The discriminability of differences is a central concern for relative evaluations. It lies at the root of Ernst Weber's 1834 basic law about the psychophysical coding of just-noticeable differences, which captures the observation that detectable increases in visual or auditory signal intensity are proportional to the starting value, i.e., need to be larger for larger starting values. Furlong & Opfer (2008) provide provocative evidence about the effect of outcome magnitude on the discriminability of differences. In their studies of humans and orangutans in the prisoners' dilemma game, changing the currency in which the usual payoffs for defection or cooperation are issued (for humans, dollar outcomes multiplied by 100 to produce outcomes in cents; for orangutans, grapes issued intact or cut into tiny pieces) increases the rate of cooperation, presumably because the difference in payoffs for defection over cooperation is less discriminable with the larger numeraires.

Probabilities. Traditionally, explicitly provided probability judgments of events were thought to reflect either a frequentist evaluation or an expression of a degree of belief. However, more recent formulations have posited transformations of explicitly provided outcome probabilities in choice into decision weights that are a function of the amount of attention paid to the different potential states of the world, which is affected by more than the states' likelihood of occurrence. Events may attract greater attention for perceptual and motivational reasons (Weber & Kirsner 1997). Thus, small-probability events may be overweighted by PT relative to their stated likelihood of occurrence because decision makers' attention

is regressive. In other words, decision makers pay more equal attention to all possible outcomes than is warranted by their (typically unequal) probabilities, and decision makers linger at extreme outcomes to assess best- and worse-case scenarios. Rank-dependent models of risky choice have provided such a reinterpretation of the way in which explicitly stated probabilities are evaluated in choice. They also provide an alternative way to think about risk-averse or risk-seeking behaviors. In cumulative PT (Tversky & Kahneman 1992), the subjective weight given to a given outcome no longer is simply a nonlinear transformation of its objective probability of occurring, but also reflects the relative rank of the outcome in the distribution of possible outcomes. Cumulative PT is only one way in which the evaluation of outcome probabilities can depend on the position of the outcome in the configuration of outcomes (Lopes & Oden 1999). More complex ways, such as those in Birnbaum's transfer of attention model (Birnbaum 2005), have been shown to account for a broader range of choice phenomena. These attentional effects become even more important when choice options contain more than two outcomes or when the gambles are mixed (Luce 2000, Payne 2005).

Choice from External Search

Heuristics for risky choice. Brandstätter et al.'s (2006) priority heuristic (PH) tries to account for many phenomena in risky choice in simpler ways than do models that involve tradeoffs, such as PT. The model is noteworthy for making not just choice predictions, but also predictions about response times and information acquisition. The PH has been criticized for its use of discrete measures of error (Rieger & Wang 2008) and for making choice predictions that are not observed (Birnbaum 2008). Johnson et al. (2008) found that although some implications of the PH were supported, the critical test, namely that decision makers do not integrate probabilities and payoffs, were not borne out by process measures. Despite the mixed empirical support surrounding the heuristic, the research exchange triggered by it demonstrates that process predictions and their tests can improve choice models.

Sampling and evaluation in external search. If we believe that decision makers often attend selectively to a subset of possible information, it is important to understand the properties of such samples, the processes used to produce them, and the consequences these samples have on decisions.

A class of what might be called middle-level sampling models ambitiously attempts to describe a large set of empirical regularities or stylized facts. Each model has its own set of assumptions about cognitive processes and representations and thus makes predictions not just for observed choices, but also for process measures such as response times (Ratcliff et al. 2006). Although these models share a concern with the accumulation of evidence via sampling, they emphasize different aspects of the decision process.

Prototypical of a class of models that could be characterized as stimulus sampling models are recent extensions of Busemeyer & Townsend's (1993) decision field theory (DFT) to multiattribute choice (Roe et al. 2001) and to models of value judgments as well as choice (Johnson & Busemeyer 2005). The key idea in DFT is that attributes of choice alternatives are repeatedly randomly sampled and that evidence accumulates over samples. This process of information retrieval, whether from the external environment or from memory, is assumed to be independent of the evaluation of the object, i.e., is not path dependent. When applied to choice, DFT posits a race between options, with each additional acquisition of evidence increasing or decreasing the valuation for an option, ending when the first option exceeds a preset threshold. In addition to having a closed-form mathematical formulation, DFT can also be expressed as a multilayer connectionist network and has been applied to explain context effects such as the similarity, attraction, and compromise effects (Roe et al. 2001). By adding a set of potential responses (in a comparison layer) to its

neural network version, DFT can generate predictions for several preference reversals (Busemeyer & Diederich 2002). DFT (and its decomposition) has also provided a useful framework to analyze group differences on the Bechara gambling task, as described below. Computational considerations have led to a modification of DFT that incorporates loss aversion into the accumulation of evidence (Usher & McClelland 2004), thus extending stimulus sampling models to explain the endowment effect and other JDM phenomena attributed to loss aversion.

Decision by sampling (Stewart et al. 2006), another mid-level model, is an interesting attempt to explain several stylized facts with two simple mechanisms: (*a*) value is constructed by simple ordinal comparisons between an object at hand and consecutive repeated samples of objects drawn from memory, and (*b*) the samples reflect the external ecological frequency of objects. Using archival data, these two assumptions are able to reproduce the PT value and probability weighting function and a time-discounting function that looks hyperbolic.

Decision by distortion. Stimulus sampling models typically assume samples that are unbiased reflections of the environment and are path-independent. In contrast, two streams of research suggest that choice involves a biased, and path-dependent, integration of information. Building on earlier ideas about constructed dominance by Montgomery and Svenson in the 1980s, Holyoak & Simon (1999) and Russo and colleagues (2000) posit that choices are speeded up and made with minimal regret by distorting the value of options to support early-emerging favorites. The existence of an early favorite leads to subsequent information being interpreted in a way that supports that favorite, bolstering its chances of being chosen (Simon et al. 2004), even for a single option (Bond et al. 2007). Simply being listed as the first option can cause this distortion of values and increase in choice (Russo et al. 2008), showing the influence of attentional focus on subsequent evaluation and choice.

Decision field theory (DFT): a mathematical and process model suggesting that decisions are made by aggregating samples randomly drawn from the information available about a set of alternatives

Inferences from External Search

In contrast to mechanisms such as availability, which posit that biases in inference result from biased representations produced by recall, several researchers have argued that such biases can result from biased sampling of external information, either as a function of how the information is presented by the environment or by biases in a search on the part of the decision maker (Fiedler 2000). For example, the observer of a conversation, which provides a sampling of the beliefs of the two conversing parties, may get a biased sample of what the participants believe because a range of Gricean conversational rules apply restrictions (e.g., not repeating what was just said). As a result, Fiedler argues, the observer may well conclude that the conversation is more hostile than it really is. By arguing that the observer is insensitive to the bias in the observed sample of beliefs, Fiedler (2000) moves the origins of observed bias from the decision maker's memory (as in availability) to the environment, aided by the decision maker's lack of understanding the biased origin of the sample. Juslin et al. (2007) have applied very similar ideas to confidence judgments.

Goal and Framing Effects

McKenzie & Nelson (2008) suggest that different semantic frames that might be seen as logically equivalent (e.g., a glass being half full or half empty) linguistically transmit different information because different frames elicit different semantic associates. Fischer et al. (1999) similarly suggest that different response modes have different goals and that evaluation differs to accommodate those goals. For example, prominent attributes receive more weight in tasks whose goal is to differentiate among options than in tasks whose goal is to equate options.

MEMORY PROCESSES

Making decisions without recourse to relevant prior memories is a difficult task and is a topic that has long fascinated writers and filmmakers. Memory is necessary for our ability to learn and to draw on past experience to predict future desires, events, or responses to outcomes. Yet the connection between properties of memory and judgment and choice has previously been underexplored. During the past decade, memory considerations have played a more prominent role in explanations of JDM phenomena, attempting to leverage what we know about memory to provide insight into the processes underlying known decision phenomena (Reyna et al. 2003, Schneider 2003), but this is still a relatively underdeveloped area of behavioral decision research.

Memory Storage and Retrieval

Memory accessibility and priming. Seeing a stimulus results in a transient increase in accessibility of the representation of that stimulus and related concepts, a phenomenon called priming, with effects on subsequent memory access, i.e., shorter reaction times and greater likelihood of retrieval. Priming is widely used in social cognition, where primed attitudes and values shape behavior. Extending this paradigm, Mandel & Johnson (2002) demonstrated priming effects in multiattribute choice. In a consumer choice task, their selective priming of product attributes with appropriate wallpaper on the initial page of an online shop affected not only choice but also information search and use.

Memory is reactive. Unlike computer memory, human memory is changed by attempts at retrieval. Accessing memory both increases short-term accessibility and changes the long-term content of memory.

Short-term effects. Studies of anchoring suggest that priming memory accessibility, and consequently preference, can be changed by asking a prior question, even if the answer to this question should be irrelevant to subsequent tasks, such as using the last four digits of a social security number as an anchor for pricing a gamble

(Chapman & Johnson 1999). This effect was replicated with fine wine by Ariely et al. (2003), who also show that such accessibility-mediated anchoring effects are strong and robust and persist in the presence of significant accuracy incentives, experience, and market feedback. The selective accessibility model provides similar mechanisms and provides evidence that anchors make some information more accessible as measured by reaction times (Mussweiler & Strack 2001), though accessibility may not be sufficient to explain all anchoring effects (Epley & Gilovich 2001).

Long-term effects. Accessing information about possible choice options not only generates short-term changes in the accessibility of related information but also changes memory in a more permanent fashion, a phenomenon long recognized in social cognition. In the context of consumer choice and a line of research that goes back to the work on the self-correcting nature of errors of prediction, measuring the longterm effects of purchase intentions on memory has been shown to change subsequent purchases (Chandon et al. 2004).

Retrieval and preference construction. A recent perspective on preference construction, query theory (QT; Johnson et al. 2007), suggests that decision makers consult their memory (or external sources) with queries about the choice alternatives, in particular their merits or liabilities. QT assumes that most tasks suggest a natural way to the order in which queries are posed. When one class of components of a memory structure is queried, the accessibility of other components that could be response competitors is temporarily suppressed to minimize intrusions, but with consequences for the success of subsequent queries for which these components are legitimate responses. Memory inhibition as the result of prior recall of related and competing material is one of the oldest and most developed memory phenomena (Anderson & Neely 1996). Johnson et al. (2007) show that QT accounts for the endowment effect, under the assumption that sellers and buyers have different query orders, and they demonstrate the causal involvement of query order and memory inhibition by making the endowment effect disappear by switching the natural order of queries. Extending this paradigm, Weber et al. (2007) show that queries about reasons supporting immediate versus delayed consumption are issued in reverse order for intertemporal decisions about accelerating or delaying consumption, explaining the well-known result that people are much more impatient when delaying than when accelerating consumption. Explicitly prompting queries in the order opposite to the naturally occurring one again eliminates the effect. The task- and goal-specific distortions in balance of support that is generated by QT-predicted and empirically observed memory retrieval interference presumably have the same function (i.e., faster decisions with less postdecision regret) in decisions based on internal search that predecisional distortions (discussed in the previous section) have in decisions based on external search. Both predecisional distortion of external information and QT-related biased memory retrieval suggest that the process of preference or inference construction is characterized by systematic path dependency, contrary to the assumptions of most mathematical models of judgment and choice.

Consistent with a memory interference account, Danner et al. (2007) show that three or more retrievals of a specific means towards a goal will succeed in inhibiting competing means for the same goal. It is worth noting that this "discovery" in social cognition in the context of habit formation and goals-means networks coincides with experimental practice in proactive interference studies (e.g., Dougherty & Sprenger 2006). Thus, memory retrieval is one more way in which goals have been tied more closely to decision making over the past decade.

Memory and Inference

Memory and support theory. Support theory (ST), proposed by Tversky & Koehler (1994), models probability judgments as a

Query theory (QT): a process model of valuation describing how the order of retrievals from memory ("queries") play a role in judging the value of objects, emphasizing output interference

comparison of support for focal hypothesis A (s(A)) with support for a set of alternative hypotheses B (s(B)), in the form of a ratio familiar from Luce's choice axiom: p(A,B) = s(A)/(s(A) + s(B)). Support theory is a rational model in the sense that it assumes that set B includes only relevant alternative hypotheses, i.e., hypotheses that have some probability of occurring. Since competing hypotheses are often generated by associative memory processes from long-term memory (Dougherty & Hunter 2003), irrelevant alternative hypotheses (that have no possibility of occurring in the context of interest) may well be generated and may affect probability judgments by occupying valuable slots in limited-capacity working memory [referred to as inhibition failure by Dougherty & Sprenger (2006)]. Irrelevant alternatives in working memory may not be identified as irrelevant, referred to as discrimination failure by Dougherty & Sprenger (2006), who provide evidence for such failures using a proactive interference paradigm. A negative correlation exists between individual differences in working-memory capacity and degree of subadditivity of probability judgments. The judged probability of a focal event (e.g., rain) is larger when compared to the implicit disjunction (not rain) than when it is compared to the explicit disjunctions (e.g., sunshine, snow, cloudy, all other), suggesting that people with greater working-memory capacity are able to include more alternative hypotheses in the implicit disjunction condition (Dougherty & Hunter 2003). In combination, these and related studies suggest that augmentation of support theory with realistic assumptions about the retrieval and evaluation of alternative hypotheses can significantly increase its predictive accuracy. Dougherty & Sprenger (2006) also illustrate how measures of individual differences can help distinguish among hypothesized judgmental processes.

Memory-based heuristics for inference. In 1996, Gigerenzer and Goldstein suggested the take-the-best (TTB) strategy as both an accurate and easy procedure for inferences based on memory retrieval. TTB mimics what is known as a lexicographic decision rule in choice, suggesting that good inferences can be made by using the most diagnostic cue(s) that distinguish between two alternatives. Knowledge about cue diagnosticity depends, of course, on metacognitive insight about past inferential accuracy. Initial simulations showed surprising levels of performance for a process that uses such limited information. TTB performs particularly well when the distribution of cue validities is highly skewed. However, TTB is not the only heuristic that does well. Simulations show that heuristics that are even simpler than TTB can do quite well in the same environments (Hogarth & Karelaia 2007). Other simple heuristics do as well or better (Chater et al. 2003) in other environments. Examinations of TTB as a descriptive model of memory-based inference suggest that it is not universally used, but also not infrequently employed, describing between 20% and 72% of inferences (Broder & Gaissmaier 2007). More importantly, use of the strategy appears to vary in a way that is adaptive given the environment, with more-intelligent decisions makers being more adaptive (Broder 2003). New developments are models that integrate TTB and full information use along a continuum, specified by the amount of weight given to the comparison of different attributes (Lee & Cummins 2004), and generalizations that relax the assumption that decision makers know the exact cue weights (Bergert & Nosofsky 2007).

A similar story surrounds the recognition heuristic (RH), posited as a powerful rule for inference in cases in which only one of two provided comparison alternatives is recognized, and applied in tasks such as deciding which of two cities is larger (Goldstein & Gigerenzer 2002). Initial demonstrations showed good performance over a wide range of domains, but subsequent studies have delineated boundary conditions. In a paradigm that teases apart recognition and cue validity, Newell & Shanks (2004) show that RH is abandoned when recognition is not the most reliable cue. Similarly, the recognition heuristic is not used when recognition can be attributed to other causes (Oppenheimer 2003). Although it is clear that recognition can be a useful tool in inference, the debate now seems to be whether recognition is always used as a first stage in inference (Pachur & Hertwig 2006) or whether recognition is simply one cue in inference that can be integrated (Richter & Spath 2006) but has no special status. In choice, recent work on decision modes (Weber et al. 2005a) identifies recognition as a decision mode that uses identification of a choice situation as a member of a class of situations for which a prescribed best action exists, following in the tradition of image theory by Lee Beach and work by James March in the early 1990s.

Work in inference seems to be reaching a conclusion similar to that of previous work in choice by Payne and colleagues (1992). The number of processes in the adaptive toolbox is large, and their use is adaptive to task characteristics. The interesting questions are how processing strategies are selected and when they succeed and fail. Answers to these questions will come from explicit models of strategy selection (Rieskamp & Otto 2006) and more formal and detailed models of the role of memory and forgetting in inference (Dougherty et al. 1999, Schooler & Hertwig 2005).

MULTIPLE INFORMATION PROCESSES

Normative JDM models have an appealing simplicity. With an axiomatic foundation, they employ a small number of primitives, abstract from content and context, and give rise to consistent judgments and decisions across situations. Initial attempts to make these models psychologically plausible and better able to describe observed judgment and choice patterns coincided with the cognitive revolution in psychology that used the digital computer as its metaphor for human information processing and contrasted algorithmic with heuristic solutions. Normative model modifications thus focused on cognitive shortcuts taken by limited-capacity information processors. This repertoire of alternative cognitive strategies was first investigated in the context of preference by Payne

et al. (1992) and subsequently extended to inference tasks (Goldstein & Gigerenzer 2002). In the context of preference, affective processes have recently been added to the list of potentially adaptive strategies (Finucane et al. 2000, Luce et al. 2000).

The Emotions Revolution

Though successful in many ways, the cognitive revolution may have been too focused on analytic and computational processes. The emotions revolution of the past decade or so has tried to correct this overemphasis by documenting the prevalence of affective processes, depicting them as automatic and essentially effort-free inputs that orient and motivate adaptive behavior. Review articles that describe the role of emotions in risky choice and their effort-reducing potential (Finucane et al. 2000, Loewenstein et al. 2001) incorporate prior work on emotional priming by Johnson and Tversky in 1983 and on psychological risk dimensions (Slovic 1999). Following Peters et al. (2006a), we describe research on four functions of affect: as spotlight (discussed under Attention), information, common currency, and motivator.

Affective Processes

Affect as information. Emotions experienced while making a decision are incorporated as information into choices (Schwarz 2002). Positive and negative past associations with available choice outcomes thus contribute to new decisions. Loewenstein et al. (2001) distinguish between immediate emotions and anticipated/expected emotions. Immediate emotions, aroused either by task-relevant characteristics or incidentally, and their effect on judgment and choice are the topics of this section.

Choice-option–elicited immediate emotions are at the base of traditional economic interpretations of utility as emotional carriers of value. Positive emotions increase value and result in approach, whereas negative values decrease value and result in avoidance (see Affect as Motivator below). The Iowa gambling task (Bechara et al. 1994) popularized the notion of a somatic marker that carries memories of the negative affect associated with losses in high-risk gambles; these memories prevent healthy respondents from choosing such gambles on subsequent trials. The absence of such affective information [initially demonstrated in frontal lobe patients and since then in other patient populations, including substance abusers (Stout et al. 2004)] is associated with performance deficits in the form of increased choices of disadvantageous risky gambles.

Incidental emotions (i.e., emotions unrelated to the judgment or decision at hand, typically elicited by a preceding event or activity) have also been shown to influence choice. Alice Isen's mood maintenance hypothesis from 1987 assumes that people in a good mood would like to maintain this pleasant state and thus try to avoid hard, analytic work and use cognitive shortcuts instead. Consistent with this hypothesis, Au et al. (2003) found that financial market traders traded differently when in a good or bad incidental mood (elicited by music). Good mood resulted in inferior performance and overconfidence, bad mood resulted in more accurate decisions and more conservative trading. Chou et al. (2007) compared mood maintenance to mood priming to explain patterns of risk taking in either a positive, negative, or neutral incidental mood, and found evidence mostly for mood priming (i.e., more risk taking in a happy mood and less in a sad mood) for both younger and older adults.

Incidental feelings influence judgments or choice also by being misattributed to having been elicited by the task at hand. Misattribution, an old experimental paradigm going back to Schwarz and Clore in 1983, is still in active use. Men were shown to misattribute their arousal after viewing photos of attractive females to arousal generated by the prospect of having to delay consumption in a subsequent intertemporal financial-choice task, and they therefore discounted future outcomes more strongly (Wilson & Daly 2004). Misattributions of the absence of fluency, the subjective feeling that forming a preference for a specific option is easy, as the result of incidental characteristics (a hard-to-read type font) have been shown to affects consumer decisions (Novemsky et al. 2007). We seem to have metacognitive awareness that these misattributions can occur, as evidenced by the fact that we use knowledge of other people's incidental mood states in strategically correct ways (Andrade & Ho 2007).

Affect as common currency. Interpretations of utility as the pleasure or pain associated with the experience of outcomes (experienced utility) go back to Bentham, predating the current economic interpretation of utility as inferred from choice (decision utility). Contextual effects on risky choice have been explained in decision affect theory as modifications of the emotional reactions to obtained outcomes as the result of pleasure or displeasure induced by relative comparisons between the obtained and counterfactual alternative outcomes (Mellers et al. 1999). In this sense, experienced emotions provide a common currency on which the effects of both different outcome dimensions and variations in decision context can be integrated. Decision affect theory provides a unifying framework that incorporates special cases of emotional reactions to counterfactual outcome comparisons such as regret or disappointment (Connolly & Zeelenberg 2002) or loss aversion in its interpretation as affective reaction (Lerner et al. 2004). To the extent that the output of multiple processing channels needs to be combined, an affective common currency seems to be a promising hypothesis.

Social psychological perspectives on JDM also rely on affect as a common currency. When people make a risky decision in a manner that fits their self-regulatory orientation (e.g., a promotion or prevention focus, which can be either chronic or situationally induced), they feel right about the process. This value from fit has been shown to transfer to their evaluation of the obtained outcome (Higgins 2005).

Affect as motivator. Just as preferences are constructed, so is affect. Affect construal theory

(Ellsworth & Scherer 2003) shows that the effect of affective reactions cannot be satisfactorily attributed to the emotions' valence and intensity, but rather is influenced by other situational appraisals. Emotions can be similar in valence and intensity (like fear versus anger) but result in very different judgments or choices because they are associated with different action tendencies. Thus, Lerner & Keltner (2001) show that fear increases risk estimates and risk-averse choices, whereas anger decreases risk estimates and increases risk-seeking choices. Similar results were found in a natural experiment, conducted after the 9/11 terrorist attack in the United States (Lerner et al. 2003). In a nationally representative sample of Americans, those who scored higher on an anxiety scale (fear) had greater perceptions of risk, and those who scored higher on a desire-for-vengeance scale (anger) had lower perceptions of risk up to 10 weeks after the attack. Gender differences in risk perception, with men perceiving fewer risks, were largely accounted for by gender differences in self-reported emotions. Emotions also affected endorsement of different terrorism policies.

Dual-Process Explanations

Dual-process models have a long history in the social sciences. Adam Smith argued that behavior was determined by the struggle between passions and an impartial spectator (Ashraf et al. 2005). More recent psychological models have distinguished between a rapid, automatic and effortless, associative, intuitive process (System 1), and a slower, rule-governed, analytic, deliberate and effortful process (System 2) (Kahneman 2003). Ferreira et al. (2006) provide experimental evidence for this dichotomy by varying processing goals, cognitive resources, priming, and formal training of respondents, and show that the automatic and controlled processes affected by these manipulations make independent contributions to judgments and choices under uncertainty. There is debate about the extent and way in which the two systems interact (Evans 2008, Keysers

et al. 2008). Serial interventionist models put System 2 into a supervisory role because System 2 knows the analytic rules that the intuitive System 1 is prone to violate and thus can intervene to correct erroneous intuitive judgments (Kahneman 2003), but other relationships, including parallel-competitive horse-race models (Sloman 1996), need to be considered.

Valuation of risky options. Both cognitive (Johnson et al. 2007) and affective processes (Lerner et al. 2004) have been shown to influence people's evaluative judgments. Hsee & Rottenstreich (2004) contrast valuation by feeling and valuation by calculation. Emotional reactions are assumed to be far more binary (i.e., elicited or not) than analytic assessments of either value or likelihood, with the result that, for more emotionally charged choice options, we observe both greater scope insensitivity and a more highly nonlinear probability-weighting function.

Risk taking. Behavioral researchers have provided psychological generalizations of the normative model of finance, which assumes that the prices of risky investment options reflect a tradeoff between risk and return that are more affect based. In finance (e.g., the capital asset pricing model), both risk and return are assumed to be immutable statistical properties of the risky option, captured by the variance and expected value of the outcome distribution. Psychophysical risk-return models assume that perceptions of risk and return are psychological constructs that can vary between individuals and as a result of past experiences and decision content and context. Perceived benefits are often well predicted by analytic considerations such as expected returns based on past returns (Weber et al. 2005b), but they also vary as a function of interests or expertise (Hanoch et al. 2006). However, perceived risk is less predicted by analytic considerations (such as expected volatility as a function of past volatility) and more by affective reactions related to familiarity with the choice option (a domestic stock with high name recognition) (Weber et al.

2005b) or decision domain (Weber et al. 2002). Observed risk taking is the result of a long list of cognitive and affective evaluation and integration processes. For example, payoff sensitivity as well as health and social risk taking as measured by a recent domain-specific risk-taking scale (Weber et al. 2002) uniquely predict recreational drug use by college students (Pleskac 2008). Although some affective reactions and their effect on risk taking are objectively justifiable [e.g., the cushioning effect of financially supportive networks found in more collectivist cultures (Weber & Hsee 1998)], others are not (Slovic 1999).

Perceptions of risk and ambiguity also seem to mediate the effect of narrow versus broad choice bracketing (Read et al. 1999) on risk taking (Venkatraman et al. 2006). Two studies presented choice options in a segregated way (narrow bracketing) or aggregated way (broad bracketing). These studies found that perceived riskiness [which loaded on affective variables, such as worry and loss, as also found by Weber et al. (2005b)] and perceived ambiguity (which loaded on cognitive variables, such as uncertainty, lack of understanding, and information needs) were distinct factors that independently mediated the effect of presentation format on preference.

Iowa gambling task. The Iowa gambling task, mentioned above, assumes that somatic markers that carry memories of the negative affect associated with losses in high-risk gambles prevent normal respondents from choosing such gambles on subsequent trials. Busemeyer and Stout (2002), however, show that both cognitive and affective evaluation and learning processes are needed to account for the choices made by normal and abnormal populations with the Iowa gambling task.

Dynamic risk-taking tasks. Much real-world risk taking (e.g., binge drinking) involves repeated decisions where risk levels escalate as the result of previous decisions. Estimates of risk taking assessed in static risky-choice tasks do not predict risk taking in dynamic environ-

ments very well (Wallsten et al. 2005). Several assessment instruments have attempted to fill this gap. The initial tool was devised by Slovic in 1966 for use with children, who face the repeated choice between continuing in the game by pulling one of a finite number of switches that have a high (but decreasing) probability of earning a gain, or stopping to claim the accumulated rewards. One of the switches (the "devil") terminates the game, with a loss of all accumulated rewards. Performance in this game predicts real-world risk taking of children when crossing a street (Hoffrage et al. 2003).

The Columbia Card Task (Figner et al. 2008) is like the devil task in its nonstationary riskiness, as an increasing number of cards (out of 32) are turned over, but in addition, the task varies the number of loss cards that terminate the game as well as the gain and loss per gain and loss card. In addition, the task allows for net losses, not just the elimination of previous gains. Thus, the Columbia Card Task allows for an assessment of the sensitivity of respondents' choices across conditions (i.e., the quality of their information use) as well as their risk taking. In the Balloon Analogue Risk Task (Lejuez et al. 2002), points are gained with each puff that incrementally inflates a balloon, with an increasing probability that the balloon may burst and all acquired gains will be lost. Although it is structurally equivalent to the devil task and Columbia Card Task in that the risk of bursting increases with previous puffs, the Balloon Analogue Risk Task does not explicitly inform decision makers of this nonstationarity, and Wallsten et al. (2005) find that participants misconstrue the task as stationary. Pleskac (2008) focuses attention on the nonstationarity of risk in his Angling Risk Task by specifying either sampling with or without replacement (catch and release versus catch and keep) and by varying the clarity of the water and thus knowledge of remaining odds. Respondents are found to use cognitive strategies in contingent and adaptive ways in this domain of dynamic risk taking, just as reported for choice task 25 years ago (Payne et al. 1992) and for inference tasks more recently.

Intertemporal choice. Both cognitive and affective mechanisms have been demonstrated to give rise to the discounting of future events. The cognitive processes specified by QT, which also explain the endowment effect and the status quo bias, account for both individual differences in discounting and for the observed asymmetry in discounting when people accelerate or delay consumption (Weber et al. 2007). An affect- or impulse-based process for choices that allow for immediate consumption is assumed to give rise to hyperbolic discounting in Laibson's (1997) beta-delta model, with some neuroscience evidence corroborating the involvement of immediate affect (beta regions) in only such decisions, with other more cognitive (delta) regions being activated by all intertemporal tradeoff decisions (McClure et al. 2004) but also some dissenting opinions (Glimcher et al. 2007).

More impatience for choices involving immediate consumption is not always found when controlling for length of delay. Read (2001) alternatively explains hyperbolic discounting as a form of subadditivity of discounting: People are less patient (per time unit) over shorter intervals regardless of when they occur. Zauberman et al. (2008) find that people's subjective perceptions of prospective duration lengths are nonlinear and concave in objective time and that intertemporal choices reflect a relatively constant rate of discounting relative to subjective time.

Self-other discrepancies. A dual-process model also explains differences in the risky decisions people make for themselves versus those they predict others will make. Although one's own emotional reactions to choice options are very accessible and salient, those of others are not. Analytic considerations such as differences in expected value, on the other hand, can be assumed to apply equally to oneself as well as to others. As a result, people's choices on the gain (Hsee & Weber 1997) and loss side (Faro & Rottenstreich 2006) are further away from risk neutrality than are the predictions they make about the choices of others. Evidence that this discrepancy (and

misprediction) is due to a different mix of affective and analytic considerations comes from the fact that the discrepancy is larger when predicting the decisions of abstract rather than concrete others (Hsee & Weber 1997) and is moderated by self-reported empathy (Faro & Rottenstreich 2006). Regardless of whether dual-process explanations will be supported by neuroscience evidence (see sidebar How Many Processes?), the distinction between affective and cognitive processes has been very fruitful at a conceptual level.

Dual-Representation Models

Knowledge representation is centrally connected to the psychological cognitive processes that make use of them. Fuzzy trace theory (Reyna 2004) accounts for apparent inconsistencies in inference and preference tasks by assuming that different cognitive processes can take advantage of different memory representations of choice options, i.e., encodings at different levels of precision, as a function of age and expertise (Reyna & Adam 2003). Dehaene et al. (2004) find evidence for an inbred rudimentary

---

HOW MANY PROCESSES?

Dual-process models have enjoyed great success and popularity, perhaps in part because we seem to be drawn to dualities, both biologically (with two eyes, ears, arms, and legs) and philosophically (with point and counterpoint). Our review documents how dual-process models have accounted for many judgment and decision-making phenomena. A more global perspective suggests, however, that ultimately a single system needs to integrate input from two or more subsystems to move from deliberation to action. In contrast, a more local perspective suggests a need for more than two systems since, in addition to the distinction between a reflective and reflexive system, reflexive processes engage multiple mechanisms, including automatic emotional reactions, semantic priming, or automated action sequences (Evans 2008, Keysers et al. 2008). Going into the future, computational modeling of these different subsystems and their reciprocal interconnections will likely build on and possibly supersede dual-process arguments.

number representation system, which presumably complements more sophisticated representations, in single-cell recordings that identify number-count cells in the monkey parietofrontal cortex.

Decision modes. Multiple-process assumptions underlie distinctions between qualitatively different modes of making decisions. Goals are chronic (personality-, gender-, and culture-based) and domain-specific, and they influence people's choice of affective, analytic, or rule-based processes because these decision modes differ in their effectiveness of satisfying material and nonmaterial goals (e.g., affiliation versus autonomy; Weber et al. 2005a). Social norms dictate the use of different decision principles in different domains (e.g., moral versus business decisions; Tetlock 2002). People seem to have metacognitive awareness that the mode in which a decision is made carries diagnostic information about the decision maker's motivation. Recipients of a requested favor evaluated the favor and favor granter differently depending on whether they thought that the favor granter had decided based on affect, cost-benefit calculation, or role-based obligation (Ames et al. 2004).

LEARNING

Homo sapiens needs to survive in stochastic and often nonstationary environments that require constant learning and updating. Although learning is often vicarious and transmitted to us in summarized form (similar to the prospectus of an investment option, providing a distribution of past returns), learning from experience still plays a powerful role in our judgments and decisions. Learning, as a topic of JDM research, may have been the proverbial baby that went out with the bathwater when the cognitive revolution replaced behaviorism. Most choice theories, including PT and DFT, do not include any learning processes (Pleskac 2008).

Elwin et al. (2007), in a historical summary of learning from feedback, go back to the argument made by Einhorn and Hogarth in 1978 that selective and incomplete feedback prevents us from accurate judgments and choices in many decision environments. Addressing the important and understudied topic of people's mental representation of feedback, they distinguish between positivist coding that represents what one sees and constructivist coding that represents what one believes, supplementing perception with knowledge and theory. They present evidence consistent with their constructivist representation that reinforces the view of attention as an active process.

Reinforcement-learning rules of the sort originally suggested by Bush and Mosteller in 1955 offer psychological process accounts for arriving at rational (Bayesian) learning as well as deviations. Reinforcement-learning rules have recently been investigated in a variety of JDM contexts. Fu & Anderson (2006) show that reinforcement learning provides an integrative explanation for a broad range of dependent measures in tasks from recurrent choice to complex skill acquisition.

Erev (1998) revisits signal detection theory and replaces its ideal observer cutoff with a cutoff reinforcement-learning process, allowing him to account for phenomena from conservatism to probability matching and the gambler's fallacy. Weber et al. (2004) show that reinforcement learning in risky decisions that are made from repeated personal experience predicts risk sensitivity to be proportional to the coefficient of variation of the risky options, rather than its variance, consistent with both animal and human data. Following March's 1996 simulations that demonstrate that reinforcement learning in risky choice in conjunction with adaptive sampling gives rise to PT's pattern of risk aversion for gains and risk seeking for losses, Denrell (2007) formalizes adaptive sampling in risky choice, i.e., option selection that utilizes the evaluations of choice options that are constantly being updated in the ongoing decision-by-experience process. The model predicts that apparent risk taking and risk avoidance can be the result of adaptive sampling, even when the decision maker has a risk-neutral value function and learning is optimal, reinforcing the realization that the relationship between risk attitudes and observed risk taking is more complex than envisaged by expected utility (Weber & Johnson 2008). Denrell's (2007) model also predicts that information about foregone payoffs will affect risk taking, consistent with other attempts to incorporate counterfactual outcomes or fictitious play into reinforcement-learning models (Camerer & Ho 1998). Finally, Erev & Barron (2005) operationalize implicit decision-mode selection as a reinforcement-learning process, where past success with different modes dictates their future use. They show that, in repeated risky decisions from experience, their model accounts for the observed effect of payoff variability, the underweighting of rare events, and loss aversion.

Practice ought to make perfect, and researchers have continued to look for evidence of optimal performance. Recently, such performance has been reported for human movement-planning tasks, where the tip of a finger needs to be placed on a computer touch screen so that gains will be incurred for hitting indicated target areas and losses are avoided for indicated penalty areas (Trommershauser et al. 2006). People learn to execute such pointing responses in ways that resemble expected-value maximization and are very accurate in selecting the higher expected-value option from a pair of possible responses. These tasks can be shown to be conceptually equivalent to choices between money gambles, where people often fail to achieve expected value or expected utility maximization (Erev & Barron 2005). More research on the precise differences between this paradigm and gambling choices is needed, but some differences are apparent. There is clear goal focus in the pointing task (hitting target area and avoiding penalty area), the appearance of a correct answer that can be found rather than a preference to be expressed, a continuous space of response alternatives, and a large amount of feedback.

Predictive Accuracy

Future states/experiences. Most decisions are forecasts of how options will make us feel in the future. This idea is captured by the distinction between decision utility (how we think options will make us feel) and experience utility (how experiencing those options actually feels). People tend to underestimate the ease of adapting to lifetime changes such as a move from California to Ohio, winning the lottery, or being turned down for tenure (Kahneman 2000). Other systematic mispredictions of subsequent experiences have recently been reported for regret (Sevdalis & Harvey 2007), loss (Kermer et al. 2006), and time slack and time savings (Zauberman & Lynch 2005).

Two mispredictions of time provide cognitive-process explanations for intertemporal inconsistencies (in contrast to the affective or dual-process explanation discussed above). Zauberman & Lynch (2005) show that time-money tradeoffs change over time because people have more (and overly) optimistic predictions about future time availability than about money availability. Greater discounting of costs in time than costs in money can lead to housing/commuting time decisions that do not maximize experienced well being. Trope & Liberman (2003) show that we often mispredict our preference among choice options that lie in the future because we construe events that lie in the future in more abstract and higher-level terms than events in the near future or present.

Anticipation of negative emotional reactions such as regret or negative reactions to loss after outcome feedback is received helps to motivate careful analysis of choice options and their possible outcomes (Connolly & Zeelenberg 2002). It is also adaptive to have mechanisms in place that minimize these negative feelings, ex-post, as they decrease outcome satisfaction and consume processing capacity. The fact that people experience fewer negative emotions as they get older (Mather & Carstensen 2003) suggests that negative emotion regulation is an acquired skill.

Expected utility: the average utility from some risky choice. Like expected value, except that outcomes are nonlinearly transformed into utilities, usually with decreasing marginal returns

Events. Predicting future events is a challenging task, as documented by Tetlock (2005) in a longitudinal study of expert political predictions. The accuracy of predictions of future key political events is generally not much better than chance. However, experts who acquire information broadly and on multiple topics, and who contingently apply different prediction strategies (foxes, in Isaiah Berlin's terms), are more successful in predicting future events than are experts who specialize in a small field and apply a smaller number of strategies more rigidly (hedgehogs).

CHARACTERISTICS OF THE DECISION MAKER

JDM research in psychology and economics has been mostly interested in average or typical behavior. Exceptions to this are risky and intertemporal choice, where individual differences in behavior have been examined and incorporated into normative models as parameters that capture the individuals' taste for risk and time delay. Risk attitude in particular (ranging from risk aversion to risk seeking) has sometimes been treated as a trait, despite a long literature showing that risk attitudes as measured by expected utility lack the cross-situational consistency required of traits. Personality theory's insight that individual traits exist but interact with situational variables explains existing results about the domain specificity of risk taking without giving up on stable traits (see Weber & Johnson 2008). Recent statistical advances such as hierarchical linear modeling and related Bayesian methods provide means to measure and explain individual differences in behavior in these more sophisticated ways.

Research over the past decade suggests that individual and cultural differences in decision making seem to be mediated by two classes of variables: (*a*) chronic differences in values and goals, presumably related to historical, geographic, or biological determinants, that focus attention on different features of the task environment and its opportunities and constraints; and (*b*) differences in reliance on differ-

ent automatic versus controlled processes, related to cognitive capacity, education, or experience. The review below is organized by predictor variable ("what individual difference dimension?"), describing for each which dependent measures ("what behavior?") this individual difference moderates. Dependent measures for which individual differences have been reported include (*a*) observed judgments or choices, in particular reported perceptions of risk, and risky and intertemporal choices; (*b*) model-based parameters inferred from observed behavior, including risk aversion and loss aversion; (*c*) the accuracy of judgments or inferences, as measured by their adherence to true values; and (*d*) the consistency of judgments or choices across situations/frames. In some instances, what we list as predictor variables are themselves shown to be predicted by other predictor variables.

Gender

Women appear to be more risk averse in many contexts and situations (Byrnes et al. 1999, Jianakopolos & Bernasek 1998). When the sources of this observed gender difference in risk taking are unpacked, women perceive the riskiness of choice options to be larger in most domains (all but social risk; see Weber et al. 2002) rather than having a more averse attitude toward risk as they perceive it. In those (and only those) domains where they perceive the risks to be larger, they appear to be more risk averse. Slovic (1999) summarizes evidence that observed gender differences in risk taking are not essentialist (i.e., biological), but rather the result of deep-seated affective comfort (or discomfort) with risk (feeling that it is controllable, or not) that comes with lower social status in a society. Emotional discomfort translates into larger perceptions of riskiness, an affective mechanism that connects these individual differences in risk taking to situational effects such as the home bias in investment decisions (Weber et al. 2005b) or gain/loss framing in medical informed-consent communications (Schwartz & Hasnain 2002). In contrast to these reliable gender differences in risk taking, no consistent gender differences have been reported on loss aversion or time discounting.

Age

Because psychological processes have developmental trajectories, JDM research has shown interest in comparing the decision processes and competencies of children, adolescents, younger, and older adults. Web-based experiments and field data have contributed to this interest with JDM data from a wider range of ages. Space limitations restrict us to a small subset of relevant studies and a focus on younger versus older adults. Gaechter et al. (2007) show that loss aversion measured in both risky choice and riskless consumer choice increases with age, with no significant gender effect. Older adults have also been found to be more risk averse (Jianakopolos & Bernasek 2006), though not every study finds this effect. Evidence on age effects on time discounting is also more mixed, with some studies showing no effect and others showing that both older and younger adults discount more than do middle-aged adults (Read & Read 2004). Age also affects what information is encoded and utilized. Consistent with evidence on life-span changes in emotion regulation, Carstensen & Mikels (2005) show greater effects of negative mood on the decisions of younger adults and greater effects of positive mood on the decisions of older adults.

Personality

Based on factor analyses in the 1960s and 1980s, personality theory has focused on five traits in recent years. Some JDM research has examined whether people's scores on the "big five" dimensions affects their decisions. Risk taking has again been the most common dependent measure examined. Thus, Nicholson et al. (2005) find that risk takers score high on extraversion and openness and low on neuroticism, agreeableness, and conscientiousness. Nicholson et al. (2005), as well as Zuckerman & Kuhlman (2000) and Weber et al. (2002), also identify

sensation seeking as associated with risk taking. Levin et al. (2002) examined the effects of personality traits on susceptibility to framing. Attribute-framing effects (e.g., meat 90% lean versus 10% fat) were larger for individuals low in conscientiousness and high in agreeableness. Risky framing effects (e.g., lives lost versus lives gained) were larger for individuals high in conscientiousness and neuroticism.

Cognitive Traits/Styles

Cognitive reflection test. The cognitive reflection test (CRT) is a three-item math-puzzle test designed to elicit an incorrect "intuitive" answer (generated by System 1) that needs to be overridden by System 2 intervention (Frederick 2005). Individual differences in people's ability to do so are found to be correlated with greater patience (less discounting) in intertemporal choices as well as risky choices closer to expected value maximization (less risk aversion for gains, less risk seeking for losses). This suggests that normative choice models may turn out to be descriptive for at least a subset of the general population, those who have a greater ability or inclination to use rational/analytic processing in their decisions. CRT scores correlate moderately with conventional IQ measures, some of which show higher correlations than the CRT with normative choices in specific domains. However, the CRT is the most consistent predictor across choice measures and by far the easiest test to administer.

Numeracy. Numeracy, defined as the ability to process basic mathematical and probabilistic concepts and measured by a scale created by Lipkus and colleagues in 2001, is uncorrelated with general IQ measures but has been shown to be reduce susceptibility to framing effects and improved judgment accuracy (Peters et al. 2006b). Somewhat counterintuitively, more-numerate individuals perform more accurately because they derive stronger and more accurate affective meaning from numbers and their comparisons.

Maximizing/satisficing/regret. Simon's 1957 distinction between maximization and satisficing as a choice objective has also been turned into an individual difference measure (Schwartz et al. 2002). Scoring higher on the maximization part of the scale has been found to be a net negative. Thus, maximizers find higher-paying jobs but are less satisfied with their job choice and experience, presumably because they are more susceptible to regret (Iyengar et al. 2006). de Bruin et al. (2007) also find the propensity to regret and tendency to maximize to be negatively related to the reported quality of decision outcomes and to decision-making competency, described next.

Decision-making competency. Fischhoff and colleagues have attempted to capture a common skill component in the judgments and choices made by adolescents (Parker & Fischhoff 2005) and adults (de Bruin et al. 2007). Combining performance on seven JDM tasks that can be scored for either accuracy or consistency into a decision-making competency measure, they find that this score is positively correlated with the reported quality of decision outcomes, even when controlling for IQ, age, and socioeconomic status. Older respondents showed greater competency in some of the seven tasks (recognition of social norms and resistance to sunk costs) but did worse on other tasks (applying decision rules and framing effects) (de Bruin et al. 2007), suggesting that there is more than a single underlying competency factor.

INCREASING POLICY RELEVANCE

One of the appeals of behavioral decision research has been that the questions that are at the forefront of the research agenda are also, at times, at the forefront of social concerns. Recently, we have seen an explosion of research that applies principles from behavioral decision research to address applications in policy and other areas (Thaler & Sunstein 2008). As we have argued, this increased translation from laboratory research on judgment and choice to the policy arena is facilitated by the increasing psychological process orientation of the field. Space constraints force us to be selective, focusing on health and wealth, and covering only a small subset of applications of JDM insights within those domains.

Health

Obesity is the result of thousands of small choices that have the outcome that caloric intake exceeds the decision maker's caloric expenditure. Wansink (2006) argues that these choices are often made with little awareness and shows in a series of clever experiments that making consumption decisions more mindful can change people's eating behavior. More importantly, changes in the decision environment that are cognizant of the simplifying evaluation and choice processes people apply (e.g., serving potato chips in small, single portions rather than a large bowl, because we evaluate consumption relative to bowl size) have the effect of reducing consumption.

Another important social issue addressed by JDM research has been the shortage of organs relative to demand for life-saving transplants. Johnson & Goldstein (2003) noticed that different European countries have different defaults for citizens who did not make an active decision concerning their status as an organ donor. They built upon prior work examining the effect of defaults and demonstrated—with a Web-based survey and archival records of organ-donation signups—that significantly more people are willing to be donors when the default is to be a donor (with the need to opt out in order not to be a donor) than when an active choice must be made to be a donor. They also demonstrated that the actual rate of organ transplants is significantly larger in opt-out than in opt-in countries (see also Gimbel et al. 2003). The observed effects are large, suggesting that the current shortage of some organs, such as hearts, could be overcome by a change in defaults.

Wealth

Similar to organ donation, participation rates in retirement savings plans are at levels judged too low. In the United States in particular, many employees are not saving toward their retirement even when their employers provide substantial financial incentives in the form of matching contributions. When Madrian & Shea (2001) changed the default action that was implemented when employees did not make an active decision to participate in a 401k plan from the usual one of no savings contribution to one of 3% of income contribution, participation of employees in the plan increased from 37% to 86%. Inspired by this and similar studies, the Department of Labor, with the help of enabling legislation, has allowed employers to change defaults. Thaler & Benartzi (2004) address the same problem with an intervention inspired by multiple behavioral-research insights. Their save-more-tomorrow plan capitalizes on discounting by asking people to commit to saving in the future, and it minimizes the impact of loss aversion by taking the contributions out of future raises rather than current income, as well as by making contributing the default. Initial applications have shown widespread adoption (by 78% of those who are offered participation, with 80% of them remaining in the program through four pay raises), and savings rates have increased from 3.5% to 13.6% of income. Retirement savings is one clear example of where behavioral decision research is having significant personal, business, and public policy effects.

Implications: The Behavioral Advantage

In each of these applications of JDM theory, the interventions suggested stand in contrast to interventions that might be suggested by standard economics. In the case of retirement savings, standard economic analysis suggests rather expensive government interventions (such as tax incentives) or effortful (for both provider and recipient) public education. The use of defaults is not only more effective but also much less costly. The same observation applies to organ donation, where the solutions suggested by economists (markets of some sort or other financial incentives) rightfully generate a lot of public controversy. Redesigns of the decision environment in ways described in our examples provide the same amount of choice flexibility and autonomy to the decision maker as do existing environments, but redirect, in a psychological jiu-jitsu, potentially harmful decision aversion to individually or socially desirable outcomes. Redesign of decision environments also follows directly from the psychological idea of constructed preferences, affects, and inferences.

CONCLUSIONS

Historically, JDM research has taken normative economic and statistical models as its starting point and adjusted them, one small step at a time, to keep the benefits of those models while giving them greater predictive accuracy. This incremental approach resulted in a proliferation of task-specific models that provide better predictions of observed behavior than do normative models, perhaps at the price of parsimony and impact on other social science disciplines. However, our review suggests that the small incremental adjustments to economic models, in their accumulation over the past 50 years, have added up to and converge on a more psychological theory of JDM. In addition to being integrative by reducing a large number of models and insights to a manageable list of underlying perceptual, cognitive, and emotional considerations, a psychological process framework also provides entry points for a better and possibly causal understanding of JDM phenomena and thus for intervention.

A recent review of our understanding of heuristics by Shah & Oppenheimer (2008) makes a very similar point. Arguing persuasively that the word "heuristic" has been used so indiscriminately as to have lost its meaning, the authors show that defining heuristics within an effort-reduction framework that is based in cognitive information processes reduces conceptual redundancy and allows domain-general principles to emerge. The integration and grounding of JDM theories and phenomena into psychological processes has been happening more at the cognitive end of psychology. It is also important to connect JDM research more firmly to theories and data about human motivation and emotion provided by other areas of psychology. Heath and colleagues (1999), for example, interpret goals as reference points, arguing that goals are motivating because of basic cognitive and perceptual processes, and thus illuminate the motivational properties of PT's value function. A focus on goals may provide a natural way of further integrating social and cognitive psychological insights. Goals play a central role in self-regulation (Higgins 2005) and have been shown to influence the way decisions are made, with the decision process in turn affecting the decision outcome (Weber et al. 2005a). Cognitive investigations of judgment and choice will benefit from addressing the focusing role of desires and goals. The impact of work in social cognition on behavioral decision research will be greatly enhanced by considering the cognitive processes that mediate reported behavior; we would encourage investigations that emphasize what the field knows about finite attention and implicit memory, a strategy that we believe contrasts with a focus on unconscious processing (Dijksterhuis 2004).

The debates of previous decades about rationality have abated, giving way to the realization that a given behavior is "rational" or not only within a specific definition of rationality and that there are several standards, each having merits within a (different) set of goals and constraints (Reyna et al. 2003, Tetlock & Mellers 2002). Emerging instead is a realization that broad-scale characterizations of human judgment or choice as flawed or rational are not particularly useful. The data often

speak with greater clarity and less dissent than polarized characterizations of them that are designed to buttress ideological positions. Consider, for example, the 1978 Lichtenstein, Fischhoff and Slovic study of estimates of perceived lethality and the 1996 Gigerenzer and Goldstein study of heuristics used in identifying the relative size of cities. The first study is cited as evidence that people are often biased in their heuristic judgments, the second as a demonstration of how good heuristic performance can be. In fact, judgment accuracy is very similar for both tasks, with mean correlations between estimated and actual lethality of around 0.7 and between estimated and actual city sizes of around 0.6. The types of errors made are also very similar in both data sets. People overestimate the frequencies of homicide relative to suicide, a result attributed to greater availability due to media biases in reporting. And German respondents choose Dallas as the larger city too often, relative to San Antonio, presumably due to greater availability as the result of the eponymous television show popular in Germany. A focus on understanding the causes of observed effects may be more productive than interpretations of data along ideological lines. Controversies of this sort are only partially addressed and resolved by adversarial collaborations (e.g., Mellers et al. 2001), which tend to focus on boundary conditions and relative effects sizes rather than the existence of shared or distinct mechanisms for the phenomenon under study.

The view of *Homo sapiens* as an adaptive decision maker has continued to receive support. Although we are restricted by finite attentional and processing capacity, we also are blessed by an abundance of ways in which we can focus and utilize this finite capacity that extends from goals to processes. We apply a wide repertoire of processing modes and strategies to our choices and inferences in a fashion that is cognizant of our goals, capacities, and internal and external constraints. In addition to strategies that differ in effort and accuracy (compensatory algorithms versus noncompensatory heuristic shortcuts), the past 10 years of research have also considered the information (material versus nonmaterial considerations) and processes (automatic versus controlled) used by different decision strategies. Whether identified decision strategies fall into two classes (Kahneman 2003) or along a continuum (Hammond 1996, Svenson 2003), some decision strategies are more automatic, associative, and affect laden, whereas others involve either implicit or explicit attempts to consider the pros and cons of different choice alternatives. Recent JDM research has also examined a broader set of goals/criteria assumed to underlie decision makers' implicit strategy selection, no longer restricted to effort and accuracy, but also including self-concept and self-regulation, social goals, and internal and external needs for justification. Content- and context-primed attention to subsets of goals (Krantz & Kunreuther 2007) and context- and path-dependent encoding, evaluation, and memory-retrieval processes have been shown to help us to come up with a satisfactory choice option in a short amount of time and without too much postdecisional regret. Predecisional distortions in the form of information-search or argument-generation processes that bias the balance of evidence in adaptive ways help us do so.

Functional-relationship explanations of deviations of behavior from normative models (e.g., PT for risky choice, hyperbolic discounting for intertemporal choice) can be further unpacked into psychological process explanations for observed regularities. Even though PT and hyperbolic discount models do not claim to be anything other than "as-if" models, people often take them as literal, interpreting both loss aversion and hyperbolic discounting as emotion-mediated effects. Our review has shown that, although affective processes play a role in both cases, cognitive (perceptual, attention, and memory) processes account for a large proportion of the variance in behavior (Johnson et al. 2007, Weber et al. 2007, Zauberman et al. 2008). A better understanding of the determinants of attention as a function of task, context, and characteristics of the decision maker is clearly a promising direction for future research (Payne et al. 2004).

To the extent that Annual Review articles provide a "state of the union" evaluation of a field, we declare that the JDM field, as it is entering early adulthood, is alive and well. It is a vibrant research enterprise, which young researchers are joining in record numbers; graduate student enrollment in the Society for Judgment and Decision Making grew by more than 40% over the past five years. It is also a global enterprise, with active research programs worldwide. Policy makers and institution builders in the private and public sector are applying its insights. The media report on its research, and popular books on the subject become bestsellers. With success comes responsibility. We encourage researchers to build on the successes and advances covered in this review, which means emphasizing common insights, processes, and results just as much as highlighting differences between models.

Incremental modifications of normative economic models have given shape to a psychological theory of JDM. This current theory shows the importance of understanding how decision makers attend to provided information, seek out additional information both by internal (memory) and external search, how information gets evaluated and integrated by both cognitive and affective processes, and how all of these stages are influenced by the decision environment (task, content, context) and the decision maker's internal state (beliefs, values, goals, prior experience). There is no question that this view of JDM is complex and not easy to translate into mathematically or otherwise tractable models. However, recent appeals to keep economics "mindless" (Gul & Pesendorfer 2005) to maintain the simplicity and coherence of its theoretical framework strike us as a self-imposed sentence of intellectual solipsism and policy irrelevance. The existing successes of a constructivist JDM research agenda that uses what we know about the mind of the decision maker to predict or modify consequential judgments and decisions hold future promises that clearly outweigh the drawbacks of its complexity.

DISCLOSURE STATEMENT

The authors are not aware of any biases that might be perceived as affecting the objectivity of this review.

ACKNOWLEDGMENTS

Preparation of this review was facilitated by fellowships of both authors at the Russell Sage Foundation and by grants from the National Science Foundation (SES-0352062) and the National Institute of Aging (R01AG027931-01A2). We thank Susan Fiske, Reid Hastie, David Krantz, Patricia Linville, Duncan Luce, and John Payne for helpful comments.

LITERATURE CITED

Ames DR, Flynn FJ, Weber EU. 2004. It's the thought that counts: on perceiving how helpers decide to lend a hand. *Personal. Soc. Psychol. Bull.* 30:461–74

Anderson MC, Neely JH. 1996. *Memory*. New York: Academic

Andrade EB, Ho TH. 2007. How is the boss's mood today? I want a raise. *Psychol. Sci.* 18:668–71

Ariely D, Kahneman D, Lowenstein G. 2000. Joint comment on "When does duration matter in judgment and decision making?" (Ariely & Loewenstein, 2000). *J. Exp. Psychol.: Gen.* 129:524–29

Ariely D, Loewenstein G, Prelec D. 2003. "Coherent arbitrariness": stable demand curves without stable preferences. *Q. J. Econ.* 118:73–105

Ashraf N, Camerer CF, Loewenstein G. 2005. Adam Smith, behavioral economist. *J. Econ. Perspect.* 19:131–45

Au K, Chan F, Wang D, Vertinsky I. 2003. Mood in foreign exchange trading: cognitive processes and performance. *Organ. Behav. Hum. Decis. Process.* 91:322–38

Baron J, Ritov I. 2004. Omission bias, individual differences, and normality. *Organ. Behav. Hum. Decis. Process.* 94:74–85

Bartels DM, Medin DL. 2007. Are morally motivated decision makers insensitive to the consequences of their choices? *Psychol. Sci.* 18:24–28

Bechara A, Damasio AR, Damasio H, Anderson SW. 1994. Insensitivity to future consequences following damage to human prefrontal cortex. *Cognition* 50:7–15

Bergert FB, Nosofsky RM. 2007. A response-time approach to comparing generalized rational and take-the-best models of decision making. *J. Exp. Psychol.: Learn. Mem. Cogn.* 33:107–29

Birnbaum MH. 1983. Base rates in Bayesian inference: signal detection analysis of the cab problem. *Am. J. Psychol.* 96:85–94

Birnbaum MH. 2005. A comparison of five models that predict violations of first-order stochastic dominance in risky decision making. *J. Risk Uncertain.* 31:263–87

Birnbaum MH. 2008. Evaluation of the priority heuristic as a descriptive model of risky decision making: comment on Brandstätter, Gigerenzer, and Hertwig 2006. *Psychol. Rev.* 115:253–60

Birnbaum MH, Bahra JP. 2007. Gain-loss separability and coalescing in risky decision making. *Manag. Sci.* 53:1016–28

Bond SD, Carlson KA, Meloy MG, Russo JE, Tanner RJ. 2007. Information distortion in the evaluation of a single option. *Organ. Behav. Hum. Decis. Process.* 102:240–54

Brandstätter E, Gigerenzer G, Hertwig R. 2006. The priority heuristic: making choices without trade-offs. *Psychol. Rev.* 113:409–32

Broder A. 2003. Decision making with the "adaptive toolbox": influence of environmental structure, intelligence, and working memory load. *J. Exp. Psychol.: Learn. Mem. Cogn.* 29:611–25

Broder A, Gaissmaier W. 2007. Sequential processing of cues in memory-based multiattribute decisions. *Psychon. Bull. Rev.* 14:895–900

Busemeyer JR, Diederich A. 2002. Survey of decision field theory. *Math. Soc. Sci.* 43:345–70

Busemeyer JR, Stout JC. 2002. A contribution of cognitive decision models to clinical assessment: decomposing performance on the Bechara gambling task. *Psychol. Assess.* 14:253–62

Busemeyer JR, Townsend JT. 1993. Decision field theory: a dynamic cognitive approach to decision-making in an uncertain environment. *Psychol. Rev.* 100:432–59

Byrnes JP, Miller DC, Schafer WD. 1999. Gender differences in risk taking: a meta-analysis. *Psychol. Bull.* 125:367–83

Camerer C, Ho TH. 1998. Experience-weighted attraction learning in coordination games: probability rules, heterogeneity, and time-variation. *J. Math. Psychol.* 42:305–26

Carmon Z, Ariely D. 2000. Focusing on the forgone: how value can appear so different to buyers and sellers. *J. Consum. Res.* 27:360–70

Carstensen LL, Mikels JA. 2005. At the intersection of emotion and cognition—aging and the positivity effect. *Curr. Dir. Psychol. Sci.* 14:117–21

Cesarini D, Dawes C, Johannesson M, Lichtenstein P, Wallace B. 2007. Genetic influences on economic preferences. *Work. Pap. Ser. Econ. Finance*, No. 679, Stockholm School Econ.

Chandon P, Morwitz VG, Reinartz WJ. 2004. The short- and long-term effects of measuring intent to repurchase. *J. Consum. Res.* 31:566–72

Chapman GB, Johnson EJ. 1999. Anchoring, activation, and the construction of values. *Organ. Behav. Hum. Decis. Process.* 79:115–53

Chater N, Oaksford M, Nakisa R, Redington M. 2003. Fast, frugal, and rational: how rational norms explain behavior. *Organ. Behav. Hum. Decis. Process.* 90:63–86

Chou KL, Lee TMC, Ho AHY. 2007. Does mood state change risk-taking tendency in older adults? *Psychol. Aging* 22:310–18

Connolly T, Reb J. 2003. Omission bias in vaccination decisions: Where's the "omission"? Where's the "bias"? *Organ. Behav. Hum. Decis. Process.* 91:186–202

Connolly T, Zeelenberg M. 2002. Regret in decision making. *Curr. Dir. Psychol. Sci.* 11:212–16

Danner UN, Aarts H, de Vries NK. 2007. Habit formation and multiple means to goal attainment: Repeated retrieval of target means causes inhibited access to competitors. *Personal. Soc. Psychol. Bull.* 33:1367–79

de Bruin WB, Parker AM, Fischhoff B. 2007. Individual differences in adult decision-making competence. *J. Personal. Soc. Psychol.* 92:938–56

Dehaene S, Molko N, Cohen L, Wilson AJ. 2004. Arithmetic and the brain. *Curr. Opin. Neurobiol.* 14:218–24

Denrell J. 2007. Adaptive learning and risk taking. *Psychol. Rev.* 114:177–87

Dijksterhuis A. 2004. Think different: the merits of unconscious thought in preference development and decision making. *J. Personal. Soc. Psychol.* 87:586–98

Dougherty MRP, Gettys CF, Ogden EE. 1999. MINERVA-DM: a memory processes model for judgments of likelihood. *Psychol. Rev.* 106:180–209

Dougherty MRP, Hunter J. 2003. Probability judgment and subadditivity: the role of working memory capacity and constraining retrieval. *Mem. Cogn.* 31:968–82

Dougherty MRP, Sprenger A. 2006. The influence of improper sets of information on judgment: how irrelevant information can bias judged probability. *J. Exp. Psychol.: Gen.* 135:262–81

Ellsworth P, Scherer KR. 2003. Appraisal processes in emotion. In *Handbook of Affective Sciences*, ed. RJ Davidson, KR Scherer, HH Goldsmith, pp. 572–618. New York: Oxford Univ. Press

Elwin E, Juslin P, Olsson H, Enkvist T. 2007. Constructivist coding: learning from selective feedback. *Psychol. Sci.* 18:105–10

Epley N, Gilovich T. 2001. Putting adjustment back in the anchoring and adjustment heuristic: differential processing of self-generated and experimenter-provided anchors. *Psychol. Sci.* 12:391–96

Erev I. 1998. Signal detection by human observers: a cutoff reinforcement learning model of categorization decisions under uncertainty. *Psychol. Rev.* 105:280–98

Erev I, Barron G. 2005. On adaptation, maximization, and reinforcement learning among cognitive strategies. *Psychol. Rev.* 112:912–31

Erev I, Glozman I, Hertwig R. 2008. What impacts the impact of rare events. *J. Risk Uncertain.* 36:153–77

Faro D, Rottenstreich Y. 2006. Affect, empathy, and regressive mispredictions of others' preferences under risk. *Manag. Sci.* 52:529–41

Ferreira MB, Garcia-Marques L, Sherman SJ, Sherman JW. 2006. Automatic and controlled components of judgment and decision making. *J. Personal. Soc. Psychol.* 91:797–813

Fiedler K. 2000. Beware of samples! A cognitive-ecological sampling approach to judgment biases. *Psychol. Rev.* 107:659–76

Figner B, Mackinlay RJ, Wilkening F, Weber EU. 2008. Affective and deliberative processes in risky choice: age differences in risk taking in the Columbia Card Task. *J. Exp. Psychol.: Learn. Mem. Cogn.* Under review

Finucane ML, Alhakami A, Slovic P, Johnson SM. 2000. The affect heuristic in judgments of risks and benefits. *J. Behav. Decis. Making* 13:1–17

Fischer GW, Carmon Z, Ariely D, Zauberman G. 1999. Goal-based construction of preferences: task goals and the prominence effect. *Manag. Sci.* 45:1057–75

Frederick S. 2005. Cognitive reflection and decision making. *J. Econ. Perspect.* 19:25–42

Fu WT, Anderson JR. 2006. From recurrent choice to skill learning: a reinforcement-learning model. *J. Exp. Psychol.: Gen.* 135:184–206

Furlong EE, Opfer JE. 2008. Cognitive constraints on how economic rewards affect cooperation. *Psychol. Sci.* In press

Gaechter S, Johnson EJ, Hermann A. 2007. Individual-level loss aversion in riskless and risky choices. *Inst. Study Labor Discuss. Pap. 2961*, Inst. Study Labor, Bonn, Germany

Gelman A, Hill J. 2007. *Data Analysis Using Regression and Multilevel/Hierarchical Models*. New York: Cambridge Univ. Press

Gimbel RW, Strosberg MA, Lehrman SE, Gefenas E, Taft F. 2003. Presumed consent and other predictors of cadaveric organ donation in Europe. *Prog. Transplant.* 13:17–23

Glimcher PG, Kable J, Louie K. 2007. Neuroeconomic studies of impulsivity: now or just as soon as possible? *Am. Econ. Rev.* 97:142–7

Goldstein DG, Gigerenzer G. 2002. Models of ecological rationality: the recognition heuristic. *Psychol. Rev.* 109:75–90

Describes a model of inference that proposes, counterintuitively, that less knowledge about a topic can lead to better performance.

Gonzalez-Vallejo C. 2002. Making trade-offs: a probabilistic and context-sensitive model of choice behavior. *Psychol. Rev.* 109:137–55

Gonzalez-Vallejo C, Reid A, Schiltz J. 2003. Context effects: the proportional difference model and the reflection of preference. *J. Exp. Psychol.: Learn. Mem. Cogn.* 29:942–53

Gul F, Pesendorfer W. 2005. *The Case for Mindless Economics*. Princeton, NJ: Princeton Univ. Press

Hammond KR. 1996. *Human Judgment and Social Policy: Irreducible Uncertainty, Inevitable Error, Unavoidable Injustice*. New York: Oxford Univ. Press

Hanoch Y, Johnson JG, Wilke A. 2006. Domain specificity in experimental measures and participant recruitment: an application to risk-taking behavior. *Psychol. Sci.* 17:300–4

Hastie R. 2001. Problems for judgment and decision making. *Annu. Rev. Psychol.* 52:653–83

Heath C, Larrick RP, Wu G. 1999. Goals as reference points. *Cogn. Psychol.* 38:79–109

Hertwig R, Barron G, Weber EU, Erev I. 2004. Decisions from experience and the effect of rare events in risky choice. *Psychol. Sci.* 15:534–39

Higgins ET. 2005. Value from regulatory fit. *Curr. Dir. Psychol. Sci.* 14:209–13

Hoffrage U, Weber A, Hertwig R, Chase VM. 2003. How to keep children safe in traffic: find the daredevils early. *J. Exp. Psychol.: Appl.* 9:249–60

Hogarth RM, Karelaia N. 2007. Heuristic and linear models of judgment: matching rules and environments. *Psychol. Rev.* 114:733–58

Holyoak KJ, Simon D. 1999. Bidirectional reasoning in decision making by constraint satisfaction. *J. Exp. Psychol.: Gen.* 128:3–31

Hsee CK, Rottenstreich Y. 2004. Music, pandas, and muggers: on the affective psychology of value. *J. Exp. Psychol.: Gen.* 133:23–30

Hsee CK, Weber EU. 1997. A fundamental prediction error: self-others discrepancies in risk preference. *J. Exp. Psychol.: Gen.* 126:45–53

Hsee CK, Zhang J. 2004. Distinction bias: misprediction and mischoice due to joint evaluation. *J. Personal. Soc. Psychol.* 86:680–95

Iyengar SS, Wells RE, Schwartz B. 2006. Doing better but feeling worse—looking for the "best" job undermines satisfaction. *Psychol. Sci.* 17:143–50

Jianakopolos NA, Bernasek A. 1998. Are women more risk adverse? *Econ. Inq.* 36:620–30

Jianakopolos NA, Bernasek A. 2006. Financial risk taking by age. *South. Econ. J.* 72:981–1001

Johnson EJ, Goldstein D. 2003. Do defaults save lives? *Science* 302:1338–39

Johnson EJ, Haubl G, Keinan A. 2007. Aspects of endowment: a query theory of value construction. *J. Exp. Psychol.: Learn. Mem. Cogn.* 33:461–74

Johnson EJ, Schulte-Mecklenbeck M, Willernsen MC. 2008. Process models deserve process data: comment on Brandstätter, Gigerenzer, and Hertwig 2006. *Psychol. Rev.* 115:263–72

Johnson JG, Busemeyer JR. 2005. A dynamic, stochastic, computational model of preference reversal phenomena. *Psychol. Rev.* 112:841–61

Juslin P, Winman A, Hansson P. 2007. The naïve intuitive statistician: a naïve sampling model of intuitive confidence intervals. *Psychol. Rev.* 114:678–703

Kahneman D. 1973. *Attention and Effort*. Englewood Cliffs, NJ: Prentice-Hall

Kahneman D. 2000. Experienced utility and objective happiness: a moment-based approach. In *Choices, Values, and Frames*, ed. D Kahneman, A Tversky, pp. 673–90. London: Cambridge Univ. Press

Kahneman D. 2003. Maps of bounded rationality: a perspective on intuitive judgment and choice. In *Les Prix Nobel: the Nobel Prizes 2002*, ed. T Frangsmyr, pp. 449–89. Stockholm: Nobel Found.

Kahneman D, Tversky A. 2000. *Choices, Values, and Frames*. New York: Cambridge Univ. Press

Kermer DA, Driver-Linn E, Wilson TD, Gilbert DT. 2006. Loss aversion is an affective forecasting error. *Psychol. Sci.* 17:649–53

Keysers C, Cohen J, Donald M, Guth W, Johnson EJ, et al. 2008. Explicit and implicit strategies in decision making. In *Better Than Conscious? Decision Making, the Human Mind, and Implications for Institutions*, ed. C Engel, W Singer, pp. 225–58. Cambridge, MA: MIT Press

Krantz DH, Kunreuther HC. 2007. Goals and plans in decision making. *Judgment Decis. Making* 2:137–68

Provides an example of how simple changes in choice architecture, in this case the default option, can produce large and consequential changes in choice.

Presents a recent update of decision field theory that accounts for new phenomena in both judgment and choice.

Provides a masterful overview of a dual-systems approach to decision-making.

Krosnick JA, Miller JM, Tichy MP. 2004. An unrecognized need for ballot reform: effects of candidate name order. In *Rethinking the Vote: The Politics and Prospects of American Election Reform*, ed. AN Crigler, MR Just, EJ McCaffery, pp. 51–74. New York: Oxford Univ. Press

Lachter J, Forster KI, Ruthruff E. 2004. Forty-five years after Broadbent 1958: still no identification without attention. *Psychol. Rev.* 111:880–913

Laibson D. 1997. Golden eggs and hyperbolic discounting. *Q. J. Econ.* 112:443–77

Lee MD, Cummins TDR. 2004. Evidence accumulation in decision making: unifying the "take the best" and the "rational" models. *Psychon. Bull. Rev.* 11:343–52

Lejuez CW, Read JP, Kahler CW, Richards JB, Ramsey SE, et al. 2002. Evaluation of a behavioral measure of risk taking: the Balloon Analogue Risk Task (BART). *J. Exp. Psychol.: Appl.* 8:75–84

Lerner JS, Gonzalez RM, Small DA, Fischhoff B. 2003. Effects of fear and anger on perceived risks of terrorism: a national field experiment. *Psychol. Sci.* 14:144–50

Lerner JS, Keltner D. 2001. Fear, anger, and risk. *J. Personal. Soc. Psychol.* 81:146–59

Lerner JS, Small DA, Loewenstein G. 2004. Heart strings and purse strings—carryover effects of emotions on economic decisions. *Psychol. Sci.* 15:337–41

Lerner JS, Tetlock PE. 1999. Accounting for the effects of accountability. *Psychol. Bull.* 125:255–75

Levin IP, Gaeth GG, Schreiber J. 2002. A new look at framing effects: distribution of effect sizes, individual differences, and independence of types of effects. *Organ. Behav. Hum. Decis. Process.* 88:411–29

Lichtenstein S, Slovic P. 2006. *The Construction of Preference*. London: Cambridge Univ. Press

Loewenstein GF, Rick S, Cohen J. 2007. Neuroeconomics. *Annu. Rev. Psychol.* 59:1–26

Loewenstein GF, Weber EU, Hsee CK, Welch N. 2001. Risk as feelings. *Psychol. Bull.* 127:267–86

Lopes LL, Oden GC. 1999. The role of aspiration level in risky choice: a comparison of cumulative prospect theory and SPA theory. *J. Math. Psychol.* 43:286–313

Luce MF, Payne JW, Bettman JR. 2000. Coping with unfavorable attribute values in choice. *Organ. Behav. Hum. Decis. Process.* 81:274–99

Luce RD. 2000. *Utility of Gains and Losses: Measurement-Theoretical and Experimental Approaches*. Mahwah, NJ: Erlbaum

Madrian BC, Shea DF. 2001. The power of suggestion: inertia in 401(k) participation and savings behavior. *Q. J. Econ.* 116:1149–87

Mandel N, Johnson EJ. 2002. When Web pages influence choice: effects of visual primes on experts and novices. *J. Consum. Res.* 29:235–45

Mather M, Carstensen LL. 2003. Aging and attentional biases for emotional faces. *Psychol. Sci.* 14:409–15

McClure S, Laibson D, Loewenstein G, Cohen J. 2004. Separate neural systems value immediate and delayed monetary rewards. *Science* 306:503–7

McKenzie CRM, Nelson JD. 2003. What a speaker's choice of frame reveals: reference points, frame selection, and framing effects. *Psychon. Bull. Rev.* 10:596–602

Mellers B, Hertwig R, Kahneman D. 2001. Do frequency representations eliminate conjunction effects? An exercise in adversarial collaboration. *Psychol. Sci.* 12:269–75

Mellers B, Schwartz A, Cooke ADJ. 1998. Judgment and decision making. *Annu. Rev. Psychol.* 49:447–77

Mellers B, Schwartz A, Ritov I. 1999. Emotion-based choice. *J. Exp. Psychol.: Gen.* 128:332–45

Mussweiler T, Strack F. 2001. The semantics of anchoring. *Organ. Behav. Hum. Decis. Process.* 86:234–55

Newell BR, Shanks DR. 2004. On the role of recognition in decision making. *J. Exp. Psychol.: Learn. Mem. Cogn.* 30:923–35

Nicholson N, Soane E, Fenton-O'Creevy M, Willman P. 2005. Personality and domain-specific risk taking. *J. Risk Res.* 8:157–76

Novemsky N, Dhar R, Schwarz N, Simonson I. 2007. Preference fluency in choice. *J. Mark. Res.* 44:347–56

Oppenheimer DM. 2003. Not so fast! (and not so frugal!): rethinking the recognition heuristic. *Cognition* 90:B1–9

Pachur T, Hertwig R. 2006. On the psychology of the recognition heuristic: retrieval primacy as a key determinant of its use. *J. Exp. Psychol.: Learn. Mem. Cogn.* 32:983–1002

Parker AM, Fischhoff B. 2005. Decision-making competence: external validation through an individual-differences approach. *J. Behav. Decis. Mak.* 18:1–27

Collects many classic and recent papers that document that preferences are often constructed while making a decision.

Presents an overview of the critical role of affect in decisions under risk.

Payne JW. 2005. It is whether you win or lose: the importance of the overall probabilities of winning or losing in risky choice. *J. Risk Uncertain.* 30:5–19

Payne JW, Bettman JR, Johnson EJ. 1992. Behavioral decision research: a constructive processing perspective. *Annu. Rev. Psychol.* 43:87–131

Payne JW, Bettman JR. 2004. Walking with the scarecrow: the information-processing approach to decision research. In *Blackwell Handbook of Judgment and Decision Making*, ed. DJ Koehler, N Harvey, pp. 110–32. Malden, MA: Blackwell

Peters E, Vastfjall D, Garling T, Slovic P. 2006a. Affect and decision making: a "hot" topic. *J. Behav. Decis. Making* 19:79–85

Peters E, Vastfjall D, Slovic P, Mertz CK, Mazzocco K, Dickert S. 2006b. Numeracy and decision making. *Psychol. Sci.* 17:407–13

Pleskac TJ. 2008. Decision making and learning while taking sequential risks. *J. Exp. Psychol.: Learn. Mem. Cogn.* 34:167–85

Posner MI, Rothbart MK. 2007. Research on attention networks as a model for the integration of psychological science. *Annu. Rev. Psychol.* 58:1–23

Ratcliff R, Thapar A, McKoon G. 2006. Aging and individual differences in rapid two-choice decisions. *Psychon. Bull. Rev.* 13:626–35

Read D. 2001. Is time-discounting hyperbolic or subadditive? *J. Risk Uncertain.* 23:5–32

Read D, Loewenstein G, Rabin M. 1999. Choice bracketing. *J. Risk Uncertain.* 19:171–97

Read D, Read NL. 2004. Time discounting over the lifespan. *Organ. Behav. Hum. Decis. Process.* 94:22–32

Rettinger DA, Hastie R. 2001. Content effects on decision making. *Organ. Behav. Hum. Decis. Process.* 85:336–59

Reyna VF. 2004. How people make decisions that involve risk—a dual-processes approach. *Curr. Dir. Psychol. Sci.* 13:60–66

Reyna VF, Adam MB. 2003. Fuzzy-trace theory, risk communication, and product labeling in sexually transmitted diseases. *Risk Anal.* 23:325–42

Reyna VF, Lloyd FJ, Brainerd CJ. 2003. Memory, development, and rationality: an integrative theory of judgment and decision making. In *Emerging Perspectives on Judgment and Decision Research*, ed. Schneider SL, Shanteau J, pp. 201–45. New York: Cambridge Univ. Press

Richter T, Spath P. 2006. Recognition is used as one cue among others in judgment and decision making. *J. Exp. Psychol.: Learn. Mem. Cogn.* 32:150–62

Rieger MO, Wang M. 2008. What is behind the priority heuristic? A mathematical analysis and comment on Brandstätter, Gigerenzer, and Hertwig 2006. *Psychol. Rev.* 115:274–80

Rieskamp JR, Otto PE. 2006. SSL: a theory of how people learn to select strategies. *J. Exp. Psychol.: Gen.* 135:207–36

Roe RM, Busemeyer JR, Townsend JT. 2001. Multialternative decision field theory: a dynamic connectionist model of decision making. *Psychol. Rev.* 108:370–92

Russo JE, Carlson KA, Meloy MG. 2008. Choose an inferior alternative. *Psychol. Sci.* In press

Russo JE, Meloy MG, Wilks TJ. 2000. Predecisional distortion of information by auditors and salespersons. *Manag. Sci.* 46:13–27

Schneider SL, Shanteau J. 2003. *Emerging Perspectives on Judgment and Decision Research*. London: Cambridge Univ. Press

Schneider W, Chein JM. 2003. Controlled and automatic processing: behavior, theory, and biological mechanisms. *Cogn. Sci.* 27:525–59

Schooler LJ, Hertwig R. 2005. How forgetting aids heuristic inference. *Psychol. Rev.* 112:610–28

Schwartz A, Hasnain M. 2002. Risk perception and risk attitude in informed consent. *Risk Decis. Policy* 7:121–30

Schwartz B, Ward A, Monterosso J, Lyubomirsky S, White K, Lehman DR. 2002. Maximizing versus satisficing: Happiness is a matter of choice. *Personal. Soc. Psychol.* 83:1178–97

Schwarz N. 2002. Emotion, cognition, and decision making. *Cogn. Emot.* 14:433–40

Sevdalis N, Harvey N. 2007. Biased forecasting of postdecisional affect. *Psychol. Sci.* 18:678–81

Shafir E, ed. 2008. *The Behavioral Foundations of Policy*. Princeton, NJ: Princeton Univ. Press

Shafir E, LeBoeuf RA. 2002. Rationality. *Annu. Rev. Psychol.* 53:491–517

Argues for a unifying conceptualization of heuristics in terms of effort reduction in cognitive information processes.

Shah AK, Oppenheimer DM. 2008. Heuristics made easy: an effort-reduction framework. *Psychol. Bull.* 134:207–22

Shrout PE, Bolger N. 2002. Mediation in experimental and nonexperimental studies: new procedures and recommendations. *Psychol. Methods* 7:422–45

Simon D, Krawczyk DC, Holyoak KJ. 2004. Construction of preferences by constraint satisfaction. *Psychol. Sci.* 15:331–36

Simon HA. 1957. *Models of Man: Social and Rational; Mathematical Essays on Rational Human Behavior in Society Setting.* New York: Wiley

Simon HA. 1978. Rationality as process and as product of thought. *Am. Econ. Rev.* 68:1–16

Sloman SA. 1996. The empirical case for two systems of reasoning. *Psychol. Bull.* 119:3–22

Slovic P. 1999. Trust, emotion, sex, politics, and science: surveying the risk-assessment battlefield. *Risk Anal.* 19:689–701

Stewart N, Chater N, Brown GDA. 2006. Decision by sampling. *Cogn. Psychol.* 53:1–26

Stewart N, Chater N, Stott HP, Reimers S. 2003. Prospect relativity: how choice options influence decision under risk. *J. Exp. Psychol.: Gen.* 132:23–46

Stout JC, Busemeyer JR, Lin AL, Grant SJ, Bonson KR. 2004. Cognitive modeling analysis of decision-making processes in cocaine abusers. *Psychon. Bull. Rev.* 11:742–47

Svenson O. 2003. Values, affect, and processes in human decision making: a differentiation and consolidation theory perspective. In *Emerging Perspectives on Judgment and Decision Research*, ed. SL Schneider, J Shanteau, pp. 287–326. London: Cambridge Univ. Press

Tetlock PE. 2002. Social functionalist frameworks for judgment and choice: intuitive politicians, theologians, and prosecutors. *Psychol. Rev.* 109:451–71

Tetlock PE. 2005. *Expert Political Judgment: How Good Is It? How Can We Know?* Princeton, NJ: Princeton Univ. Press

Tetlock PE, Mellers BA. 2002. The great rationality debate. *Psychol. Sci.* 13:94–99

Thaler RH, Benartzi S. 2004. Save More Tomorrow: using behavioral economics to increase employee saving. *J. Polit. Econ.* 112:S164–87

Thaler RH, Sunstein CR. 2008. *Nudge: Improving Decisions About Health, Wealth, and Happiness.* New Haven, CT: Yale Univ. Press

Trommershauser J, Landy MS, Maloney LT. 2006. Humans rapidly estimate expected gain in movement planning. *Psychol. Sci.* 17:981–88

Trope Y, Liberman N. 2003. Temporal construal. *Psychol. Rev.* 110:403–21

Tversky A, Kahneman D. 1992. Advances in prospect theory: cumulative representation of uncertainty. *J. Risk Uncertain.* 5:297–323

Tversky A, Koehler DJ. 1994. Support theory: a nonextensional representation of subjective-probability. *Psychol. Rev.* 101:547–67

Tyler TR. 2005. *Procedural Justice.* Hants, UK/Burlington, VT: Aldershot

Usher M, McClelland JL. 2004. Loss aversion and inhibition in dynamical models of multialternative choice. *Psychol. Rev.* 111:757–69

Venkatraman S, Aloysius JA, Davis FD. 2006. Multiple prospect framing and decision behavior: the mediational roles of perceived riskiness and perceived ambiguity. *Organ. Behav. Hum. Decis. Process.* 101:59–73

Wallsten TS, Pleskac TJ, Lejuez CW. 2005. Modeling behavior in a clinically diagnostic sequential risk-taking task. *Psychol. Rev.* 112:862–80

Wansink B. 2006. *Mindless Eating: Why We Eat More Than We Think.* New York: Bantam

Weber BJ, Chapman GB. 2005. The combined effects of risk and time on choice: Does uncertainty eliminate the immediacy effect? Does delay eliminate the certainty effect? *Organ. Behav. Hum. Decis. Process.* 96:104–18

Weber EU, Ames DR, Blais AR. 2005a. "How do I choose thee? Let me count the ways:" a textual analysis of similarities and differences in modes of decision making in China and the United States. *Manag. Organ. Rev.* 1:87–118

Weber EU, Blais AR, Betz NE. 2002. A domain-specific risk-attitude scale: measuring risk perceptions and risk behaviors. *J. Behav. Decis. Mak.* 15:263–90

Weber EU, Hsee C. 1998. Cross-cultural differences in risk perception, but cross-cultural similarities in attitudes towards perceived risk. *Manag. Sci.* 44:1205–17

Weber EU, Johnson EJ. 2008. Decisions under uncertainty: psychological, economic and neuroeconomic explanations of risk preference. In *Neuroeconomics: Decision Making and the Brain*, ed. P Glimcher, C Camerer, E Fehr, R Poldrack, pp. 127–44. New York: Elsevier

Weber EU, Johnson EJ, Milch KF, Chang H, Brodscholl JC, Goldstein DG. 2007. Asymmetric discounting in intertemporal choice—a query-theory account. *Psychol. Sci.* 18:516–23

Weber EU, Kirsner B. 1997. Reasons for rank-dependent utility evaluation. *J. Risk Uncertain.* 14:41–61

Weber EU, Shafir S, Blais A-Re. 2004. Predicting risk sensitivity in humans and lower animals: risk as variance or coefficient of variation. *Psychol. Rev.* 111:430–45

Weber EU, Siebenmorgen N, Weber M. 2005b. Communicating asset risk: how name recognition and the format of historic volatility information affect risk perception and investment decisions. *Risk Anal.* 25:597–609

Wilson M, Daly M. 2004. Do pretty women inspire men to discount the future? *Proc. R. Soc. Lond. Ser. B Biol. Sci.* 271:S177–79

Yechiam E, Busemeyer JR, Stout JC, Bechara A. 2005. Using cognitive models to map relations between neuropsychological disorders and human decision-making deficits. *Psychol. Sci.* 16:973–78

Zauberman G, Kim BK, Malkoc SA, Bettman J. 2008. Discounting time and time discounting: subjective time perception and intertemporal preferences. *J. Mark. Res.* In press

Zauberman G, Lynch JG. 2005. Resource slack and propensity to discount delayed investments of time versus money. *J. Exp. Psychol.: Gen.* 134:23–37

Zuckerman M, Kuhlman DM. 2000. Personality and risk-taking: common biosocial factors. *J. Personal.* 68:999–1029

Comparative Social Cognition

Nathan J. Emery[1] and Nicola S. Clayton[2]

[1]School of Biological & Chemical Sciences, Queen Mary, University of London, London E1 4NS, United Kingdom; email: n.j.emery@qmul.ac.uk

[2]Department of Experimental Psychology, University of Cambridge, Cambridge CB2 3EB, United Kingdom; email: nsc22@cam.ac.uk

Annu. Rev. Psychol. 2009. 60:87–113

First published online as a Review in Advance on October 2, 2008

The *Annual Review of Psychology* is online at psych.annualreviews.org

This article's doi: 10.1146/annurev.psych.60.110707.163526

0066-4308/09/0110-0087$20.00

Key Words

theory of mind, object-choice task, mental attribution, cooperation, competition, relationship intelligence

Abstract

Theory of mind is said to be uniquely human. Is this statement justified? Thirty years of research on a variety of species has produced differences in opinion, from unequivocal positive evidence to no evidence at all for mental attribution in animals. Our review concludes that animals are excellent ethologists, but on the whole, poor psychologists. Those studies that we believe present a good case for mental attribution all possess high ecological validity, including studies on food competition by chimpanzees and cache-protection strategies by corvids. Even though the current focus of research on prediction rather than explanation may be misplaced, we believe the field is now in a strong position to discover what animals really know about their fellow beings, be it based on simple associations, behavior reading, mind reading, or something else.

Contents

INTRODUCTION

In the 30 years since Premack & Woodruff (1978) asked the question, "Does the chimpanzee have a theory of mind?", are we any closer to finding the answer? Indeed, is this still an important question? Although comparative social cognition has become a prominent research area within comparative psychology, it is also perhaps one of the most controversial. This is not surprising, because theory of mind (ToM) is said to be uniquely human (Penn & Povinelli 2007, Saxe 2006). In this article, we do not intend to review all that is currently known about comparative social cognition. This might be interesting from a historical perspective, but we don't think it would get us any closer to an-

swering Premack & Woodruff's question, for an extensive review would produce an awful lot of smoke, but very little fire based on recent assertions that there is absolutely no evidence for ToM in animals (Penn & Povinelli 2007). We therefore adopt a slightly different approach. In order to say where we think the field is going, we have to briefly describe where it's been, discuss what the main problems and objections have been, and suggest possible ways to solve them. To do this, we agree with Penn & Povinelli (2007) that we need to think less about whether or not animals have a ToM and more about what form the underlying psychological mechanisms of social cognition take, whether they be associative, representational, symbolic, behavioral, or a mixture of different mechanisms. To this aim, we describe a number of new research paradigms based on ethological studies with high ecological validity. Thinking about why social cognition evolved and what it is used for may provide useful clues as to how we can begin to investigate the potential mechanisms of social cognition.

TRADITIONAL STUDIES OF THEORY OF MIND IN ANIMALS

Premack (1988) differentiated ToM into three classes: perceptual (the understanding of seeing and attention), motivational (the understanding of desires, goals, and intentions), and informational (the understanding of knowledge and beliefs).

Perceptual Theory of Mind

Many animals rapidly respond to eye-like shapes, which may be an antipredatory response (Burger et al. 1992, Coss 1978, Hampton 1994). However, eye gaze is also an important social signal, providing information about an individual's perception and, subsequently, knowledge of the external world as well as their emotions and mental states (Emery 2000). Observing another move their eyes results in reflexive gaze shifts to the same point in space or object (visual co-orienting) or tracking another's line of sight to interesting objects in the environment (gaze following). Many species follow gaze reflexively (Anderson & Mitchell 1999, Neiworth et al. 2002) and can also follow another's direction of gaze (either head and eyes or the eyes alone) to a specific object or location (Bugnyar et al. 2004; Burkart & Heschl 2006; Emery et al. 1997; Itakura 1996; Kaminski et al. 2005; Povinelli & Eddy 1996a; Tomasello et al. 1998, 1999). Tomasello et al. (1999) also found that chimpanzees would look behind barriers of different types that an experimenter had looked behind, rather than look directly at the barrier, the first object in the line of sight (see also Okamoto-Barth et al. 2007). A similar result was also found for the other great apes (Brauer et al. 2005) and for ravens (Bugnyar et al. 2004).

Gaze may also provide a clue to another's attentional state, particularly if someone is looking at them (Gomez 1996b). If an individual's eyes are open or not covered, this implies that the individual can see things, whereas if the eyes are closed or blocked, this implies that the individual cannot see. If the eyes are averted, this implies that the individual can see some things and not others. In a series of experiments, Povinelli & Eddy (1996b) examined whether young chimpanzees would beg toward one of two experimenters: one experimenter was facing the chimpanzees, whereas the other was looking away or his eyes were closed or covered (with blindfolds, buckets, or tinted goggles), or his back was turned. The chimpanzees were rewarded if they begged toward the experimenter who could see them. The chimpanzees did not differentiate between the two experimenters based on their ability to see, except at the level of discriminating between an experimenter who was facing forward and one whose back was turned. Follow-up studies on the same chimpanzees across different ages found the same results (Reaux et al. 1999).

In a similar paradigm, which used one experimenter instead of two and recorded a variety of spontaneous behaviors oriented toward a reward, Kaminski et al. (2004) found that chimpanzees, orangutans, and bonobos produced more communicative gestures (e.g., knocking, poking, begging, and giving) when the experimenter's face was oriented toward the subject compared to when the experimenter's back was turned, but there were no differences between the eyes-open and eyes-closed conditions. This finding suggests that apes are not responsive to the eyes (see also Tomasello et al. 2007), in contrast to capuchins in a similar task (Hattori et al. 2007).

A popular test for whether animals understand another's mental states from social cues (gaze, pointing) is the object-choice task. In this paradigm, animals are trained that food can be found under various containers, such as boxes or cups. An experimenter then baits one of two containers behind a screen, out of sight of the subject. When the screen is removed, an experimenter looks at (head and eyes or eye gaze alone) or points to the container concealing the food. The animal is then presented with a choice of the two containers to search for food. Perhaps surprisingly, primates have displayed a wide variety of responses and inconsistencies in performing this task, whereas other animals, especially domesticated animals, have had more success (Emery 2000, Miklosi & Soproni 2006).

Table 1 presents an overview of the results of these studies across a wide range of species. However, differences in experimental procedures and number of subjects and subtle differences in seemingly similar cue types do not allow for a real comparative analysis of species differences and so must be treated with some caution. For example, chimpanzees cannot use human head and eyes to locate food hidden in bowls, but they can use these cues to locate food hidden in tubes (Call et al. 1998). The addition of species-typical vocalizations to gaze cues also appeared to increase performance (Call et al. 2000), as did a simple methodological difference: the chimpanzee approaching an experimenter already providing a cue, making a choice, and then leaving the test room at the end of each trial (Barth et al. 2005). It is not clear why such subtle changes have such significant effects on performance in this task; however, it does suggest that chimpanzees' performance overall is quite poor and inflexible.

Table 1 Overview of all known object-choice tasks across a variety of mammalian and avian species

Species	TT	PP	PD	PG	HEP	HED	HT	EO	G
Ravens[1]	√	X	X		X	X			
Jackdaw[2]			√			X		X	√
Domestic goats[3]	√			√	X				
Domestic horses[4,5]	√	√	√						
Domestic dogs[6-12]		√		√	√		X	X	
Puppies[6,13]				√	√				
Wolves[14]	√	√	√						
Wolf cubs[13]	√	√	√						
Silver foxes[15]				√					
Domestic cats[8]		√	√						
Gray seals[16]			√				X		X
Fur seals[17]		√	X	√	√			X	
Dolphins[18,19]		√	√		√		√		√
Cotton top tamarins[20]	X	X			X			X	
Common marmosets[21]	X(√)	X(√)	X(√)		X(√)			X(√)	
Capuchins[22,23]	√	√		√	√(X)	√			X
Rhesus macaques[24,25]	√[24]	√[24]		√[24]	X				√[24]
Orangutans[26]	√			√	√	X		X	
Enculturated[27]	√			√	√	√		√	
Gorillas[28]	√	√			√	√		X	
Chimpanzees[29-31]		√	X		√			X	
Enculturated[27]	√			√	√	√		√	

TT, tap/touch; PP, point—proximal; PD, point—distal; PG, point + gaze; HEP, head + eyes—proximal; HED, head + eyes—distal; HT, head turning; EO, eyes only; G, glancing.

[1]Schloegl et al. 2008, 2007a; [2]von Bayern & Emery, manuscr. submitted; [3]Kaminski et al. 2005; [4]McKinley & Sambrook 2000; [5]Maros et al. 2008; [6]Hare et al. 2002; [7]Soproni et al. 2001; [8]Miklosi et al. 2005; [9]Hare & Tomasello 1999; [10]Miklosi et al. 1998; [11]Agnetta et al. 2000; [12]Soproni et al. 2002; [13]Viranyi et al. 2008; [14]Miklosi et al. 2003; [15]Hare et al. 2005; [16]Shapiro et al. 2003; [17]Schuemann & Call 2004; [18]Pack & Herman 2004; [19]Tschudin et al. 2001; [20]Neiworth et al. 2002; [21]Burkart & Heschl 2006; [22]Itakura & Anderson 1996; [23]Anderson et al. 1995; [24]Hauser et al. 2007; [25]Anderson et al. 1996; [26]Byrnit 2004; [27]Itakura & Tanaka 1998; [28]Peignot & Anderson 1999; [29]Call et al. 1998; [30]Call et al. 2000; [31]Barth et al. 2005.

The basic failure of most primates to use distal head and eye gaze cues and their general successes in using proximal head or pointing cues suggests that these species are probably using low-level, proximity-based social information, such as stimulus or local enhancement, to locate hidden food, rather than a high-level interpretation based on understanding mental states. However, this does not explain the superior performance of other animals (see below).

Motivational Theory of Mind

When Premack & Woodruff (1978) introduced the term "theory of mind," they were refer-ring to understanding another's intentions or goals, so-called motivational ToM. They examined whether a symbol-trained chimpanzee, Sarah, could select the appropriate response to a scenario concerning a human actor involved in a problem, such as being trapped in a locked cage or shivering next to an unlit heater. After each sequence, Sarah was shown a number of photographs of objects, one of which could be useful in solving the problem, such as a key or a lit match. Sarah accurately chose the photograph that was most appropriate for solving the problem (e.g., key for lock), which the authors proposed as evidence that she could understand the actor's intentions. However, she could also have paired these items based on previous associations learned in captivity (Savage-Rumbaugh et al. 1978).

One problem with interpreting goal-directed actions in terms of intentions is the distinction between external goals (e.g., food) and internal goals or action plans that will lead to goal objects (e.g., approaching and eating food; Tomasello et al. 2005). One way around this problem is to manipulate the actions of an agent so that the goal object is the same, but the means of interacting with the goal object are different. For example, Povinelli et al. (1998) tested chimpanzees' ability to discriminate between a human trainer who accidentally spilled juice on the floor, a second trainer who deliberately poured the juice on the floor in front of them, and a third trainer who aggressively threw juice onto the floor. The chimpanzees did not discriminate between any of the trainers, suggesting that they did not understand the difference between intentional and accidental acts. Call & Tomasello (1998) tested the ability of orangutans and chimpanzees to discriminate between an experimenter who intentionally placed a marker on the top of a box containing food and an experimenter who accidentally dropped the marker onto the box. All three species chose the box that had been intentionally marked. Chimpanzees were also more likely to request food, make a noise, or leave the test room when presented with an unwilling rather an unable experimenter (Call et al. 2004).

Gaze is a good proxy for another's interest and therefore should be a good predictor of another's future actions. Santos & Hauser (1999) tested whether cotton-top tamarins recognized the link between attention and intention using an expectancy violation paradigm. They presented the monkeys with short video sequences in which an experimenter looked at one of two objects (object A) and then reached for the same object (expected event); the experimenter then recorded the amount of time the monkeys looked at this sequence. The monkeys were then presented with an unexpected event in which the experimenter looked at object B but then reached for object A. If the experimenter's head and eyes (but not eyes alone) were oriented toward object B, but the experimenter then reached toward object A, the subjects looked longer at the screen than if the experimenter looked at and reached for the same object.

In an object choice task, cotton-top tamarins, rhesus macaques, and chimpanzees were presented with two food containers; an experimenter then performed one of two actions on one of the containers. The subjects could then choose one of the containers based on the experimenter's actions (Wood et al. 2007). One action was an intentional hand grasp (reaching toward one object with an open grip); the other action was an accidental hand flop (open hand with palm upward was flopped onto one of the containers). All three species choose the object targeted by the intentional action rather than the accidental action. In a separate experiment, the subjects observed an experimenter indicating one of the containers either with a hand-occupied or hand-empty elbow touch (i.e., held an object in both hands, and touched one of the containers with an elbow, or held an object in one hand and touched one of the containers with the elbow of the free arm). The difference between these two actions was that if the hand was occupied, the only way to indicate the location of the hidden food was to use the elbow, whereas if the hand was not occupied, perhaps the action was not intentional because the experimenter would have indicated this with the free hand. All three species did choose the container indicated by the hand-occupied elbow touch (Wood et al. 2007).

Informational Theory of Mind

The final category of mentalizing is informational ToM, which includes the mental states of knowledge and belief. Three different paradigms that have been developed to examine whether animals know that others have knowledge states that differ from their own: the Guesser-Knower, Competitive Conspecific, and Ignorant Helper paradigms. In the Guesser-Knower paradigm, a reward is hidden in one of several containers. The subject cannot see where the food is hidden, but can see that one experimenter can see (Knower) whereas a second cannot (Guesser). Once baiting was completed, the Guesser removed the occluder (a bucket, a bag, or a blindfold) or returned to the test room, and the subjects had to beg or point to one of the experimenters, the subjects' choice suggested to be based on whether they understood that the experimenters had different knowledge states.

This paradigm has been used with various species with mixed results. Povinelli et al. (1990) found that chimpanzees pointed toward the Knower (compared to the Guesser who left the room) on the majority of the trials, but only after many (200+) trials. During a transfer phase, the Guesser remained in the test room with a bag over his head. Again, the chimpanzees pointed significantly more often toward the Knower than the Guesser, but only after the first five trials (Povinelli 1994). In a replication of this study in younger chimpanzees, all subjects failed to distinguish between the Knower and Guesser (Povinelli et al. 1994).

One potential problem with this study is that chimpanzees do not understand that humans with bags, buckets, or blindfolds on their heads cannot see (Povinelli & Eddy 1996b). Therefore, the chimpanzees' inability to discriminate between the Knower and Guesser during the first five trials of the transfer phase could be attributed to a lack of understanding at this level rather than to a failure to relate seeing to knowing. Call et al. (2000) attempted to control for this possibility by replicating this basic design, but instead of the Guesser leaving the room or remaining in the room with a bag over his head during baiting, both the Knower and the Guesser remained in the room, and the Guesser had his back turned away from the subject while the Knower faced the subject. As an additional control, either the Knower or a third experimenter baited the container with food. Only two enculturated chimpanzees chose the correct cue provided by the Knower when the Knower baited the container, but not when a third experimenter baited the container.

An additional criticism of Povinelli et al. (1990) is the fact that the chimpanzee had to be taught to make begging gestures toward a human experimenter when they wanted food. Chimpanzees very rarely beg to others in the wild, and only infants beg to their parents; chimpanzees usually fight for access to food, so perhaps it is not surprising that competition is a better paradigm than cooperation for testing ToM in this species (see below). Similarly, rhesus monkeys did not appear to discriminate between trainers who were present during baiting and those that were not present, even after extensive opportunities for learning (Povinelli et al. 1991); however, capuchins were able to learn (Kuroshima et al. 2002).

In the Competitive Conspecific paradigm, two animals compete for food: only one subject knows the location of all the rewards, and the other subject knows whether its competitor had observed baiting in the past or its competitor was different from the individual that was present at the time of baiting. This paradigm was primarily developed by Menzel (1974) to examine whether chimpanzees could use others' behavior to locate hidden food or use their own behavior to deceive others into approaching locations that do not contain food (counterdeception). However, this task has been used recently to test what chimpanzees know about what others do or do not know (Hare et al. 2001, Hirata & Matsuzawa 2001).

The only other species to have been tested using this paradigm are domestic pigs (Held et al. 2001). The subjects were trained to locate food in one of four boxes baited by an experimenter. In nonrewarded probe tests, subjects were then tested for their ability to follow one of two pigs based on whether they had visual access to baiting (i.e., were knowledgeable or ignorant). All subjects except one failed to follow the knowledgeable conspecific. This may have been attributable to associations learned prior to the experiment. Uninformed pigs can also locate hidden food by utilizing the behavioral cues of an informed pig that had previously witnessed the food being hidden by an experimenter (Held et al. 2000); however, in this case

Figure 1

Mind reading and relationship intelligence. Cartoon © Randy Glasbergen. Reprinted with permission from **www.glasbergen.com**.

the pigs did not get to choose between a knowledgeable or an ignorant pig.

Finally, in the Informed Helper paradigm, a food item (or toy) is placed out of the subject's reach, and the subject has to indicate the location of hidden food to a human helper who is ignorant of its location. The helper also needs to use a tool to reach the food, which on some trials is also hidden from view. Whether the helper is knowledgeable or ignorant of the food, tool, or both is manipulated, and the subject's behavior differs based on how much information the experimenter possesses. This paradigm has been used with orangutans (Gomez 1996a), chimpanzees (Whiten 2000), and dogs (Viranyi et al. 2006), with differing results, suggesting that animals can signal the location of the item but not necessarily the location of the tool required to reach it.

False Belief Task

Commentators on Premack & Woodruff's (1978) paper stated that the most convincing evidence of ToM would be understanding that an agent's beliefs can differ from reality and so be counterfactual (i.e., false; Bennett 1978, Dennett 1978, Harman 1978). This form of mental attribution, so-called false belief, has been examined extensively in human children (Wimmer & Perner 1983). In the classic Sally-Anne task, a child witnesses a toy being placed into one of two containers in the presence of two dolls, Sally and Anne. An experimenter then takes Sally out of the room, and a second experimenter moves the toy from one box to the other, while Anne remains in the room. The experimenter then brings Sally back into the room, and asks the child where Sally will look for the toy. Typically, children over

3–4 years of age will say that Sally will look in the original box, because that's where she thinks the toy will be, because she didn't see the toy being moved. Children under 3–4 years, however will say Sally will look in the second box, because that's where they saw the toy last and cannot dissociate their knowledge of the toy's location from Sally's different knowledge or belief.

Language is often a fundamental feature of false belief tasks, so designing a nonverbal version has proved very challenging. However, human infants as young as 15 months old have been shown to solve a nonverbal version of the false belief task, using an expectancy violation paradigm (Onishi & Baillargeon 2005). For this and other reasons, the use of the false belief task as the standard task for determining whether an agent has a ToM has resulted in some controversy (Bloom & German 2000).

Call & Tomasello (1999) developed a nonverbal false belief task for chimpanzees, orangutans, and human children. In their design, an experimenter hid food out of the subject's view in one of two identical boxes. A second experimenter, the communicator (who had seen the baiting of the box) indicated which of the boxes contained food, and in control trials, the subjects learned to choose the box that was marked by the communicator. They also learned in additional control trials to choose the unmarked box if they saw the hider move the food from one box to another when the communicator was out of the room. Call & Tomasello (1999) suggested that if the subjects knew where the food was located (but the communicator did not), they should ignore the communicator's pointing because he had a false belief that the food remained in the box in which he had seen it placed. Only 5-year-old children passed the false belief component of this experiment, in which the hider swapped the boxes around, without showing the food, after the communicator had left the room and the communicator returned and pointed at the wrong box. The two species of apes were successful in all individual control components except false belief. This could have been because understanding false belief represents a case for third-order in-

tentionality (I <u>know</u> that you <u>believe</u> that you <u>know</u> X) and so may be beyond the cognitive capacities of any nonverbal creature, or because combining the individual components into one design may have been too challenging for the apes.

Problems with the Anthropocentric Approach

In her highly critical review of theory of mind research in primates, Heyes (1998) concluded that there was no evidence that chimpanzees or any other primates could represent another individual's behavior in terms of its causal structure, i.e., they lacked ToM. She provided alternative explanations for the results of the experiments, usually based on associative learning. For example, in the Guesser-Knower paradigm, the ability to choose the Knower as a means to get a reward could have been due solely to discrimination learning. The Knower was always present during baiting, and so choosing the Knower would always lead to a reward, whereas the Guesser was always absent during baiting (or their face was absent), and so choosing the Guesser would never lead to a reward. Therefore, the subject could quickly adopt a strategy based on presence or absence during baiting without recourse to explanation based on knowledge states.

An additional problem with many of the studies described in this section was their focus on proving (or disproving) whether animals have ToM. Although first tested on a chimpanzee, ToM was conceptualized as a human ability, and if by ToM we mean an all-encompassing human ToM, then surely this approach is doomed to failure. Dissociating ToM into its many constituents may be more promising; an animals' failure on a false belief task does not mean that that animal cannot reason about any mental states. We therefore advocate, along with others (Povinelli & Vonk 2003, Tomasello et al. 2003b), that the quest for ToM as a cognitive domain should be abandoned in favor of dissecting ToM into its constituent parts (i.e., mental states) and examining the conditions in which such parts may have evolved. This is the focus of the remainder of this review.

Advocating an Alternative

When Humphrey (1976) proposed the idea that primate intelligence had evolved to solve social problems, he provided a biological platform to explain why individuals with a theory of mind would be at an advantage over those who did not have a theory of mind. The natural lives of many primates and other social animals are filled with conflict over resources, in which being one step ahead of competitors should result in early procurement of those resources and in a manner less likely to result in personal injury. Such acts of deception may indeed involve the ability to recognize what others can see, what they intend to do, and what they know (Byrne & Whiten 1988). Likewise, if one does not have the "Machiavellian smarts" to outwit competitors subtly, the alternative is to use skills in the cooperative realm, such as making friends and forming alliances, so that less-subtle means can be used to procure resources instead. For example, forming a cooperative alliance may allow individuals to access resources previously unavailable to them.

In the previous section, we discussed some of the reasons for why studies on whether animals have a theory of mind may have failed to produce unambiguous results or results that are not prone to alternative interpretations (Heyes 1998). One additional reason not discussed by Heyes (1998), but raised by some commentators to her article (Matheson et al. 1998, Purdy & Domjan 1998), is the lack of any ecological validity in their design. Examples include using conspecifics as stimuli or protagonists, or basing studies on an animal's species-specific behavioral repertoire (Emery & Clayton 2004, Hare 2001). The following section reviews modern studies on comparative social cognition designed to approach the problem of understanding other minds from a biological and evolutionary perspective—what advantages does possessing a theory of mind have over not having a theory of mind, and why did the ability evolve?

THE BIOLOGY OF SOCIAL COGNITION

In this section, we discuss three programs of research into the biology of social cognition across a wide range of species: competition over food, cooperation and relationship intelligence, and domestication.

Food Competition in Chimpanzees

Chimpanzees tend to compete over food. Only in limited contexts does food sharing occur; either food is given from mother to infant, or close associates will share a bounty that cannot be monopolized by an individual, such as monkey prey killed during a cooperative hunt. Hare (2001) suggested that many of the earlier studies of chimpanzee social cognition, such as begging to request food from an experimenter that can see you, do not reflect the natural behavior of chimpanzees. Although they can be trained to beg to humans, it is not part of a wild chimp's behavioral repertoire. Hare and colleagues therefore designed a more naturalistic, ecologically valid test for visual perspective taking based on food competition rather than food sharing (Hare et al. 2000). In this paradigm, a subordinate and a dominant chimp were allowed access to an arena where food had previously been hidden. The subordinate chimp could see both pieces of food, whereas the dominant chimp could only see one. As dominant chimpanzees will monopolize all the food they can, the only way that the subordinate chimp could gain any of the food was to approach the hidden piece first. As the dominant could only see one piece, it was predicted that they should approach the visible piece first. Therefore, the subordinate's decision about which piece to approach first should have been dictated by their understanding of what the dominant could or could not see. When the chimps were released into the arena together, the subordinate chimp tended to get the hidden piece. To eliminate the possibility that the subordinate was only responding to the approach behavior or gaze direction of the dominant, the subordinate was released a few seconds before the dominant. As before, the subordinate tended to retrieve the hidden food. The same paradigm has also been used with capuchins and goats, which both act differently from chimpanzees. Capuchin subordinates will also approach the hidden piece first, but not when they are given a head start, a finding that suggests that they were using the dominant's behavior to guide their decision (Hare et al. 2003). Goats will also approach the hidden piece first, but only if they had received aggression from the dominant in the past. If they have received no aggression, they approached the visible piece first and so could maximize their return by getting both pieces (Kaminski et al. 2006).

Karin-D'Arcy & Povinelli (2002) suggested an alternative account of the chimpanzees' behavior, namely that because most animals prefer to feed at the periphery of a clearing to avoid potential predation, any preference for feeding behind a barrier may have been due solely to fear of eating in the open rather than an appreciation of another's line of sight (peripheral feeding hypothesis). Second, because dominants will always go for the piece of food that is in view, the subordinate must go for the food that only they can see, but to be successful the subordinate must also understand that it is only the food that is reached first that is important. In a replication of Hare's study, Karin-D'Arcy & Povinelli (2002) found that although the subordinate chimpanzees tended to retrieve the hidden food rather than the visible, they did not selectively reach or move toward the hidden piece of food first. Similarly, Brauer et al. (2007) found that subordinate chimps did not reach for the hidden food first unless the barriers, and thereby the food, were located closer to the dominants than the subordinates. It is far from clear that the chimpanzees do understand what others can and cannot see/know (Penn & Povinelli 2007, Povinelli & Vonk 2004).

Although controversial, this paradigm has been used with different levels of success in other species and often with modified designs. For example, subordinate capuchin monkeys prefer to approach the hidden piece of food, but not when they are given a head start. This suggests that their decision is based on the behavior of the dominant, not on their mental state (Hare et al. 2003). Similarly, domestic goats will also take the hidden piece of food, but only if they had received aggression from the dominant in the past (Kaminski et al. 2006). If they had never received aggression from this individual, they chose the visible piece. Again, these results suggest that the goats were basing their decisions on reading behavior (avoid approach of aggressive dominant) or conditional rules (if paired with aggressive X, go to the food by a barrier; if paired with nonaggressive Y, forage in the open).

Flombaum & Santos (2005) used humans as stimuli in a different competitive paradigm for semi-free-ranging macaques on Cayo Santiago. Here, a piece of food was located in front of each of two experimenters. The assumption was that the experimenter would be seen as a threat, and so food choice should have been dictated by understanding the attentional state of each experimenter, choosing the piece in front of the person with their attention directed away from the food. Flombaum & Santos (2005) found that more monkeys took the food placed in front of the experimenter whose attention was averted from the food than from the experimenter who was looking at the food. The monkeys appeared to make this discrimination when the person's back was turned, their face was in profile, their eyes were closed, they had a large card placed in front of their face and upper body, or they had a small card placed over their eyes. These results have been suggested as strong evidence for ToM in monkeys (Lyons & Santos 2006); however, a simpler explanation is that the monkeys avoided approaching the face with two eyes open and directed toward the food. These results are also slightly at odds with a recent study on the same population of rhesus macaques (described above), which suggested that they could use human gestural information (e.g., pointing, eye gaze) to locate hidden food (Hauser et al. 2007). It makes sense for the monkeys on this island to have become attuned to human social cues, especially communicative cues related to the presence of food, because this population of monkeys is food provisioned. Why the monkeys should also be wary of humans, when humans give them food, needs further investigation.

Santos et al. (2006), using the same competitive paradigm, extended their studies of what others can or cannot see to what they can or cannot hear. In this experiment, rhesus monkeys were confronted with one experimenter whose attention was directed elsewhere. Behind the experimenter were two containers, each holding a grape. One container made a noise when touched; the other container was silent. When the experimenter's back was turned, the subjects tended to take the food from the silent container, but when the experimenter was looking at the food, the monkeys did not discriminate between containers. This suggests that the monkeys discriminated between containers based on whether they would alert the experimenter that food was being taken. Perhaps the monkeys were displaying an aversive response to the container that made the sound; however, this does not explain why they did not discriminate between containers when the experimenter was looking at them. The experiments are intriguing, but difficult to interpret particularly because nothing is known about the monkeys' experimental history or background.

In some competitive situations, chimpanzees also seem to appreciate that others can perceive noise. If subjects could choose to steal food from an experimenter either by approaching via a tunnel that made a noise when opened or a tunnel that was silent when opened, they tended to choose the silent tunnel (Melis et al. 2006a). By contrast, chimpanzees competing with conspecifics in an arena did not appear to take into account whether the competitor had heard a container being baited noisily compared to one that they could not hear being baited. If the chimpanzees had understood that others can also hear some things and not hear others, they should have approached the silent container rather than the noisy container; however, they did not discriminate between them (Brauer et al. 2008). But, why were results from Melis et al. (2006a) so different? Brauer et al. (2008) suggested three potential reasons: The subjects experienced noise rather than caused the noise themselves, there was a delay between hearing the noise and the food competition (i.e., had to keep in mind that the competitor had also heard a noise), and other chimpanzees were used instead of humans. This final suggestion seems rather odd, as this paradigm has been touted as having high ecological validity. We would like to suggest an alternative explanation for the differences. In the visual domain, there are cues to whether another is attending to a visual stimulus, whereas there are no such cues to determine whether another is listening to an auditory stimulus, especially when that individual is out of view. Even if the subordinate could have watched the dominant during baiting, we do not believe that chimpanzees "prick up their ears" in order to orient toward the source of a sound.

A similar food competition paradigm has also been used to investigate what chimpanzees may know about what other chimpanzees know, particularly in their recent past (Hare et al. 2001). Again, a subordinate and dominant chimpanzee faced one another on opposite sides of an arena containing two cloth bags, one with a piece of food, the other empty. In competition tests, (a) the dominants were informed of the food's location, or their view was blocked during baiting (uninformed), or they had seen the food being hidden but it was subsequently moved out of sight (misinformed), or (b) the dominants had seen the food being hidden, but they were switched for a second dominant who had not seen the food being hidden. By contrast, the subordinate always saw where the food was hidden. As before, the subordinate was released first. However, rather than recording reaching behavior, investigators recorded only the number of pieces gained and the number of trials in which the subordinate failed to approach the food. In each case, the subordinate gained more pieces and failed to approach more often in the trials in which the dominant was ignorant of the food's location. In a final experiment, both bags contained food, but the dominant had only witnessed one bag being baited with food. In this case, the subordinate did not retrieve more food when the dominant was ignorant of the pieces' location.

Although these results have been proposed as evidence of ToM in chimpanzees (but not by the studies' authors, we might add), they must be handled carefully. Indeed, as we discussed above, we should cease treating ToM as a homologous collection of processes that are all intimately linked, and so if we find good evidence for one domain of ToM (e.g., seeing), we should not necessarily state that we have evidence for understanding in all domains of ToM (e.g., knowing, believing, or even hearing).

Cache Protection Strategies of Corvids

Chimpanzees and other primates are not the only species that compete over food. Many birds and mammals hide (cache) food for future consumption (Vander Wall 1990). The only benefit to caching food now is if it can be retrieved in the future. This not only requires a fully functioning memory to be able to recover those caches successfully and efficiently, but it also requires strategies to reduce the probability that caches are stolen by others (Dally et al. 2006a).

For most caching animals, cache loss through pilferage is an unavoidable problem unless the cachers are present at the time of theft to defend their caches aggressively. For corvids (crow family), the situation is different because thieves can use observational spatial memory to observe another's caches and then accurately locate those caches at a later time (Bednekoff & Balda 1996a,b; Bugnyar & Kotrschal 2002; Clayton et al. 2001), even if they were made from a completely different perspective (Watanabe & Clayton 2007). As such, cachers have to develop increasingly sophisticated cache-protection strategies not only

to hide their caches from view of an observer or reduce the amount and type of visual information available to an observer during caching, but also to move their caches from places observed by a potential thief to places they have not observed. These strategies, on the surface, would appear to require some understanding of another's behavior and possibly their mental states, from both the cacher's and thief's perspective, such as what another can or cannot see, what they have or haven't seen (knowledge), as well as installing false beliefs (that a cache remains in location A, when it has actually moved to location B). However, only experimental studies have the power to truly test whether caching animals process information about thieves' mental states rather than just their behavior.

Experiments on the social cognition of cache protection have been performed with two species of corvids, western scrub-jays (reviewed in Clayton et al. 2007) and ravens (reviewed in Bugnyar 2007). Corvids naturally cache in the laboratory and appear to make caching decisions based on the presence or absence of a conspecific competitor. If a competitor is not present, there is no need to protect caches in relation to what another can or cannot see. The only requirement is that caches are hidden completely from sight and can be recovered by the cache owner. If a conspecfic is watching during caching, it makes sense to try to reduce the amount of information available to observers so that they find it difficult to locate the caches once the caching bird has left the scene. Cachers appear to do this by caching in places that either are difficult for the observer to see or where the information of cache location is visually degraded.

For example, when scrub-jays in the laboratory were allowed to cache in trays either near to or far from an observing conspecific, they chose to cache in locations far from the conspecific; however, they did not discriminate between cache sites when they cached in private (Dally et al. 2005a). When the scrub-jays were presented with a choice of caching either behind a barrier or out in the open (distance was now no longer a relevant factor), the jays chose to cache in locations out of sight of the observer (Dally et al. 2005a). This was not the result of the jays being fearful of the presence of another jay and so ceasing to cache or eat in the open, because the jays did not discriminate between caching locations when they were given only powdered (i.e., noncacheable) food. If the scrub-jays were given the choice of caching in a tray that was in the shade (i.e., in a darkened corner of the cage) or a tray that was in the light (i.e., a well-lit corner of the cage), they chose to cache in the shaded tray, but only when they were observed caching. If they cached in private, they did not discriminate between the two trays (Dally et al. 2004). Similarly, ravens observed caching in a more naturalistic arena appeared to choose cache sites that were out of view and as far as possible from potential pilferers (Bugnyar & Kotrschal 2002). Other strategies employed during caching include making false caches (stones, small objects; Clayton et al. 1996, Heinrich 1999) as well as going through the actions of caching but not leaving a food item in the cache site (Heinrich 1999). Some caching animals will either scatter food so that pilferers will find only a small amount of their caches (Clarkson et al. 1986), whereas others will switch from scatter storing to storing their food in a larder, enabling them to aggressively defend their caches (Preston & Jacobs 2001).

Cache protection may also occur at the time of cache recovery. If the cacher was observed during caching, then any food that was not to be eaten should be rehidden, in which case it makes sense to move the cache to a new location unbeknown to the previous observer. However, if no other bird was present to see the original location of the cache site, then unless the cache was recovered to be eaten, the cacher should leave it in the original cache site. Emery & Clayton (2001) examined whether scrub-jays would treat their caches differently depending on whether they had cached in view of a conspecific or whether they had been cached when the observer's view was occluded (i.e., the cacher was in private). To distinguish between responses based on the observer's mental states,

rather than learning a simple behavioral cue, the birds always recovered their caches in private. If an observer had watched the cacher making caches, then the cacher recovered and rehid their caches in new places unbeknown to the observer. By contrast, they performed very little or no recaching when they had previously cached in private and recached indiscriminately. The jays also recached in new sites when the observed and in-private caching trials were interleaved, i.e., cached when observed in tray A and then cached in private in tray B and vice versa. This scenario produced exactly the same results (Emery & Clayton 2001), demonstrating that the jays were not just responding to the presence of another jay during the last caching event (as the last caching event may have been in private). These results suggest that the jays understood that the observer knew the location of their caches, and therefore when they return to the cache sites, they should protect them by moving them to new places, whereas if the bird could not observe them during caching because their view was blocked (in-private condition), they would be ignorant of the caches' location and so recaching would not be required.

Subsequent studies addressed the question of whether the jays could also appreciate the different knowledge states of particular observers. A cacher was allowed to hide food in tray A in the presence of observer A with a second tray (B) present, but covered so that caching in tray B was not possible. After a short delay, the same cacher was allowed to cache in tray B in front of observer B, with tray A now covered. After three hours, the cacher was given the opportunity to recover their caches from both trays in one of four conditions: to recover in the presence of observer A, or in the presence of observer B, or in front of a naïve bird (C) that had not witnessed caching in either tray, or to recover in private.

During the recovery period, the birds specifically recovered the caches that observers had seen them make. For example, cachers selectively recached items from tray A when recovering in the presence of observer A, but did not recache any items from tray B (which observer A had not witnessed being made and so would be ignorant of their location). Similarly, cachers selectively recached items from tray B when recovering in the presence of observer B but not from tray A. Observer B had not witnessed caches being made in tray A. By contrast, cachers did not recache items from either tray when recovering in the presence of the naïve bird, suggesting possible attribution of ignorance. Recaching in front of the naïve bird would have provided information they previously did not have. Finally, the cachers recached items from both trays when they recovered in private, as observers A and B had seen caches being made in these trays, so recaching them in private would move the caches to new places that potential pilferers had not seen. This replicates earlier studies of recaching in private when previously cached observed (Emery & Clayton 2001; Emery et al. 2004).

Recaching in front of another bird does not appear, on the surface, to be a particularly sensible strategy to protect caches. Indeed, dominant birds may not need to recache at all because they can defend caches aggressively (Dally et al. 2005b). However, lower-status birds should move their caches if they had been observed because of the threat provided by a pilferer with observational spatial memory. But, moving caches in front of another bird should provide new information of any new cache site. It appears that cachers did not just move their caches only one time if observed recaching, they moved them up to six times, whereas they only moved caches once if they recovered in private. Most surprisingly, when the cachers moved their caches around multiple times, they did not necessarily leave the food in the last location into which they made a bill probe. Many caches were left in earlier locations, but the scrub-jays continued to probe a few times afterward. These probes could be interpreted as pretending to cache (Dally et al. 2006b).

Ravens have also been tested for their ability to discriminate between competitors (human and conspecific) based on their knowledge states (Bugnyar & Heinrich 2005). Ravens were allowed to cache in a small arena, either in the presence of subordinate observers or in private. A third subordinate was located in an adjacent viewing area but its view of caching was blocked. The cacher was then given the opportunity to recover its caches either in private or in the presence of the subordinate that had witnessed caching (knowledgeable) or in the presence of the third (ignorant) subordinate. Cachers recovered more caches in the presence of the previous observer than the nonobserver, especially when they approached the caches within two minutes. Bugnyar & Heinrich (2005) suggest that their results provide evidence that the raven cachers were discriminating conspecifics on the basis of their state of knowledge; however, a simpler explanation, especially based on the fact that the "storers' response was exhibited only when the observers were moving toward the caches" (p. 1643), is that the cachers were using the competitor's approach as a predictive cue, despite the authors' paradoxical conclusion that "the present results provide little support for the hypothesis that approach patterns of potential pilferers allow storers to distinguish knowledgeable from ignorant competitors" (p. 1643). Bugnyar & Heinrich (2005) were careful to record various behaviors of the observer and nonobserver that may have been used to distinguish between them (in relation to the caches), such as latency to approach, time spent searching for caches, and number of places visited; however, the differences were only found in the in-private condition. This finding perhaps suggests that these behaviors were not appropriate indices of the competitor's intent to pilfer, or the differences were too subtle to differentiate.

In a similar experiment, humans hid food in the arena, with the focal observer either in the presence of a dominant nonobserver (whose view of caching was blocked) or a dominant or a subordinate observer (both whose view of caching was unfettered). Bugnyar & Heinrich (2005) predicted that if the focal was released into the arena with a dominant nonobserver, then the focal should delay retrieving the cache until the competitor was some distance from the cache site. However, if the focal was released with either a dominant or subordinate observer, the focal should move rapidly to the cache site in order to successfully pilfer the cache. Indeed, the focal subjects were often the first to the cache site when paired with an observer, but almost never when paired with a nonobserver. Unfortunately, it was impossible to control for a behavior-reading account, as both observers would have made a direct approach to the cache in order to reach the cache site before the focal subject.

In an extension of the previous experiment, ravens cached in the arena, observed by the focal subject and a nonstoring competitor (observer). The focal subject was then released into the arena, with the original storer, or with the observing nonstorer, or in private. The latency to the first pilfer attempt was significantly higher when the focal was released with the storer than with the nonstorer or in private. Surprisingly, there was no difference in the latency to pilfer between the storer and the nonstorer, suggesting that the storer was perhaps withholding information on the location of the caches (Bugnyar & Heinrich 2006).

There are three potential explanations for these results: a low-level explanation based on associative learning, a mid-level explanation based on sophisticated behavior-reading but with no understanding of mental states, and a high-level explanation based on the attribution of knowledge. The low-level interpretation suggests that the birds associated the action of specific caching events with the presence or absence of a specific individual (see also Heyes 1998). At recovery, the presence of that specific individual would trigger the recovery of caching. The mid-level explanation suggests that the storers read behavioral cues produced by the observers, such as spending more time attending to the tray they had cached in, compared to behavioral cues produced by nonobservers, such as lack of attention or interest in any cache site or failure to approach a cache site. By contrast, the high-level interpretation suggests that the storers remembered who was watching which specific caching event

and therefore attribute different mental states to these individuals based on their presence (knowledge) or absence (ignorance). For the Dally et al. (2006b) study, this level of interpretation would need to be quite sophisticated, as both individuals were both knowledgeable of some caching events and ignorant of others. For example, observer A had witnessed caching in tray A but not tray B, whereas observer B had witnessed caching in tray B but not tray A.

Is there any credence for the lower-level interpretations of these experiments? Heyes (1998), for example, stated that discrimination learning (presence versus absence) explained the results of earlier experiments on knowledge attribution in chimpanzees by Povinelli and colleagues (1990). This simpler explanation could also explain the ravens' and scrub-jays' behavior, but it would need to be more sophisticated and would need to be based on integrating information from the past (social context during caching) with planning for the future (potential pilfering by the observer). Note, however, that in these studies there was often only one caching and recovery trial for each condition, thereby minimizing the potential effects of learning.

We stated above that there is an alternative mid-level explanation, in which the storers' recaching behavior may have been controlled by the observer's behavior rather than their mental states. For the raven studies, Bugnyar & Heinrich (2005, 2006) attempted to control for this mid-level behavior-reading account by recording various approach and attention behaviors of the observers and nonobservers. Although the control is useful, unfortunately its success depends on recording the right behaviors, and important behaviors for the birds may not be important behaviors for humans. A less ambiguous approach is to design control procedures in an attempt to eliminate alternative behavior-reading explanations. Dally et al. (2006b) designed such a control experiment. The cacher was presented with two caching trays (A and B). Cachers could store in tray A only in the presence of observer A, and could store in tray B only in the presence of observer B, because in each case the other tray (A or B) was covered. The trays were then removed and presented to a second cacher (bird C), who was allowed to cache in either other original trays in the presence of an additional observer D. Then, at recovery, both trays were returned to the original cacher and they were allowed to recover caches, in the presence of either the two original observers (A or B) or the new cacher (D). If the cachers based their recaching decisions on the behavior of the observer bird, independent of whether they were present when caching in a particular tray, then the cacher should have recached items equally from both the observed tray and the other tray because observer D had witnessed caching in both trays (although by a different cacher, C). Observer D should therefore have attended to both trays equally, and so both trays would be equally at risk. By contrast, if the storers were attributing knowledge to the observer, they should have only recached items from the observed tray. Indeed, this is exactly what the cachers did (Dally et al. 2006b), suggesting that it is unlikely that the storers were using behavioral cues from observer D to influence their recaching decisions.

Bugnyar & Kotrschal (2002) suggested that cache-protection strategies and pilfering tactics may be an example of an arms race, leading to the development of increasingly complex strategies for hiding food from competitors from the perspective of the cacher and increasingly complex strategies for stealing caches without aggressive retaliation from the perspective of the pilferer (see also Emery et al. 2004). As individuals can simultaneously be both cachers and pilferers, even at the same point in time albeit with different caches, individuals not only have to keep track of their own caches but others' caches as well, also keeping in mind the social context during specific caching and pilfering events. It is therefore easy to envisage in such scenario the benefits to both caching and pilfering strategies of being able to read and predict another's behavior.

It has been suggested that because corvids cache inedible objects, such as twigs and stones, often in front of conspecifics, this form of social play may provide an opportunity to learn about others' pilfering intentions or pilfering techniques. Bugnyar et al. (2007), therefore, allowed ravens to cache small plastic objects and then to observe what either a pilfering (P) or an onlooker (O) human did with their caches. P always stole the caches, whereas O inspected the objects but never stole them. After this experience, the ravens were then allowed to cache food in front of either P or O. The ravens started caching food more quickly in the presence of P than O; ravens also tended to cache behind obstructions and took longer to cover caches with snow. This pattern was not repeated with objects. Bugnyar et al. (2007) suggested that the caching of objects might be a tool to learn about an individual's propensity to steal food.

How do such strategies develop? Western scrub-jays readily use cache-protection strategies in a rational manner, i.e., when the strategies are most likely to result in the maximum rate of cache return (Clayton et al. 2006). However, not all scrub-jays use cache-protection strategies; their implementation depends on experience, specifically experience of stealing another's caches. Whereas scrub-jays with previous experience of being a thief will recache food items to new sites when previously observed caching, scrub-jays with no previous experience of being a thief will not recache (Emery & Clayton 2001) and do not use distance as a caching strategy (Dally et al. 2006b). We have previously suggested that the fact that pilferers may use their past experience to guide their current caching and recaching decisions, in order to protect their caches from future cache theft, may be an example of experience projection, a form of simulation theory of mind or introspection (Clayton et al. 2007; Emery & Clayton 2004, 2008).

Cooperation and Relationship Intelligence

Although the competitive hypothesis explains some aspects of chimpanzee social cognition, several questions remain. For example, what of the sociocognitive abilities of dominants?

And although chimpanzees certainly compete, they do also cooperate—from hunting colobus monkeys (Boesch 1994) to developing short-term coalitions and long-term alliances with others (de Waal 1982). Chimpanzees have also recently been demonstrated to cooperate on artificial, instrumental tasks in the laboratory, either learning to cooperate with humans (Hirata & Fuwa 2007) or spontaneously cooperating with conspecifics (Melis et al. 2006c). This recent task requires the two subjects to pull simultaneously on either end of a rope looped through hoops attached to a weighted platform with food placed on top. If one subject does not pull at the same time as their partner, the rope will pass through the hoops and will no longer be of use in pulling in the platform. Chimpanzees have also been found to recognize the need for a partner and so release them from a locked compartment, as well as to choose the most appropriate partner, i.e., the one who has been the most successful with the task in the past (Melis et al. 2006b). Bonobos are more successful than chimpanzees at this task, possibly because bonobos are more tolerant of social partners and share food more frequently with a partner (Hare et al. 2007).

In contrast to these results, studies from the same lab (and others) have found that chimpanzees also fail to perform actions that would benefit a conspecific, even at no cost to themselves, with subjects taking into account only their own self-interests (Jensen et al. 2006, 2007; Silk et al. 2005). It is not yet clear why chimpanzees will cooperate in some prosocial situations but not in others. We certainly agree that the level of tolerance and intensity of the social relationship may be critical in this regard (Hare 2007).

Corvids also form alliances, which take the form of a close relationship between two birds based on high levels of affiliative behavior, such as preening, food sharing, and social support, including support after fights (Emery et al. 2007, Seed et al. 2007). When alliances are also mated pairs, cooperation takes the form of building nests, defending the nest from conspecifics and predators, and raising offspring (coordinating specific roles, such as foraging, feeding, and defending chicks). These joint actions could be construed as examples of shared intentionality, in which the focus of the pair is directed toward the same goal (nest, offspring, food, object, or conspecific). As with chimpanzees, rooks have been found to cooperate on a rope-pulling task requiring coordination within a pair (Seed et al. 2008). Like bonobos, rook pairs displayed great tolerance even between nonpartners, and the actions of both individuals were tightly coordinated in time. Such close coordination requires that the individuals within a pair attend to one another and to their actions. We suggest that being in a long-term relationship, such as a life-long pair bond, may afford the individuals within the pair enhanced sociocognitive skills in reading their partner's behavior and possibly their mental states. We have termed this "relationship intelligence" (Emery et al. 2007).

Domestication, Enculturation, and Socialization

We have already described the poor abilities of apes to use others' social cues to locate hidden food or to discriminate between the different attentional states of a human experimenter, except in a competitive context. Indeed, recent studies have perhaps surprisingly found that domestic dogs are superior to apes in these tasks. Dogs can use human social cues, such as head and eye direction and pointing (including cross-body pointing) to locate hidden food (Hare & Tomasello 1999; McKinley & Sambrook 2000; Miklosi et al. 1998; Soproni et al. 2001, 2002); use novel cues, such as markers, to find food (Agnetta et al. 2000); use conspecific cues (Hare & Tomasello 1999); and direct humans' searches for hidden food (Hare et al. 1998). In contrast to apes, dogs are also skilled in discriminating between different human attentional states (Call et al. 2003, Gacsi et al. 2004, Schwab & Huber 2006, Viranyi et al. 2004); however, the tests administered to dogs tend to be based on situations that often occur in the natural day-to-day lives of dogs living in human homes, such as obeying or disobeying commands given when the owner can or cannot see the dog, or forbidding the dog to take food when the owner can or cannot see it. Recently, Hare et al. (2002) found that when compared directly on the same object-choice task, dogs outperform chimpanzees, with 9 of 11 dogs choosing correctly compared with 2 of 11 chimpanzees.

Dogs have also demonstrated an understanding of the relationship between seeing and knowing in the Guesser-Knower paradigm (Cooper et al. 2003) and the Ignorant Helper paradigm (Viranyi et al. 2006); the performance of dogs is similar to that of apes. Hare & Tomasello (2005) have suggested that the long domestication of dogs by humans has selected for this skill in using human social cues (see also Miklosi 2008, Miklosi et al. 2004). Because these paradigms are dependent on reading cooperative signals produced by humans, we might predict that all animals that have been selected for their close relationship to humans should also show these skills, in direct contrast to primates, which have not been selected for these skills. Some findings suggest that working dogs that have been directly bred to understand human gestures or to produce gestures that are comprehensible to humans (for example, gestures used during sheep herding and pointing toward a kill during a shoot) perform better in social cognition experiments than do other dogs (Hare et al. 2002, McKinley & Sambrook 2000, Miklosi et al. 2003). In addition, other domesticated animals, such as horses, goats, and cats, can use a variety of human social cues in object choice tasks (Kaminski et al. 2005, McKinley & Sambrook 2000, Miklosi et al. 2005).

In a direct test of the domestication of social cognition hypothesis, Hare et al. (2002) compared domestic dogs and wolves on the same tasks. In the object-choice task, dogs located food correctly when provided with Gaze + Point + Tap, Gaze + Point, and Point cues, whereas wolves were correct only when using the Gaze + Point cue. On a nonsocial food-finding study that was not dependent on the use of human social cues, there was no difference

in the performance of dogs and wolves. Finally, dog puppies at different ages (9–12 weeks, 13–16 weeks, and 17–26 weeks old) and with different rearing histories (litter-reared or human-reared) were tested on the object-choice task using Gaze and Gaze + Point cues. There was no difference between the litter-reared and the human-reared puppies, and no difference between the three age groups in their use of human social cues. This final result suggests that there was no effect of age or experience of humans in the use of human attention cues, therefore reinforcing the premise that the process of domestication was the key to the enhancement of sociocognitive abilities in domestic dogs.

Some problems exist with this hypothesis. First, Miklosi et al. (2003) performed experiments similar to those of Hare and colleagues (although focusing only on comprehension of human pointing) in dogs and socialized wolves and found that some of the socialized wolves could learn to use some human gestures. In two further, nonsocial tasks used to gain access to food, a rope-pulling task and a bin-opening task, there were no differences in the ability of wolves and dogs to solve this task. When the tasks were then made insolvable, i.e., the bin was locked so the food could not be reached or the rope was tied to a post rather than to the food, the dogs, but not the wolves, looked back at their owner and spent more time gazing at their owner than did the wolves. Miklosi et al. (2003) suggested that the dogs were looking back at their owners either in an attempt to communicate with them that the food was not accessible or to derive information from their owners about how to solve the task (see also Gomez 1991).

A second issue is that general domesticity is often confounded with specific use as a working animal. Currently, the majority of dogs are kept as pets; however, throughout most of the period of domesticity, dogs were kept and trained as working animals (Miklosi 2008). Interestingly, another domestic working animal, the horse, has demonstrated some basic understanding of human-given social cues to locate food (McKinley & Sambrook 2000);

however, other domestic nonworking animals (cats, goats) and other nondomestic animals (seals, dolphins) have also demonstrated some proficiency in using human social cues.

A recent experiment on hand-raised jackdaws is interesting in this regard. Jackdaws were presented with a competitive attentional state test similar in design to the test of Flombaum & Santos (2005), in which a preferred wax worm was placed between an unknown human experimenter and the jackdaw, and the latency for the jackdaw to take the worm was recorded while the experimenter was either looking at the worm or looking away (e.g., back turned, head in profile, eyes averted, eyes closed, head in profile with eyes oriented toward the worm, and one eye open while the other was closed). The shortest latencies were recorded when the experimenter's attention was directed away from the worm, but only when the experimenter was unknown to the subject; with the caregiver, the jackdaws rapidly took the worm independent of the experimenter's attentional state (A.M.P. von Bayern & N.J. Emery, manuscript submitted). In a second experiment, the ability of hand-raised jackdaws to locate hidden food using human gestures was examined using an object-choice task. The experimenter either indicated the location of the food through communicative gestures (gaze alternation or cross-body distal pointing) or static attentional states (head and eye gaze or eyes only). The jackdaws could use the communicative gestures but not the attentional states to locate the food significantly above chance (A.M.P. von Bayern & N.J. Emery, manuscript submitted). These jackdaws were not domesticated or enculturated but were hand-fed by a human during their early socialization period until they became nutritionally independent. It is also worth noting that jackdaws have a very distinctive contrast between their light-colored iris and pupil, and they frequently focus on the eye region during social interactions. These factors probably provided these hand-raised jackdaws with the ability to attend to social information from the eyes and use it in functional ways. These experiments also suggest that interaction with humans during a critical socialization period may result in similar social skills in animals that have not been explicitly trained and have not been enculturated or selected to live with humans.

SO, WHAT DO ANIMALS KNOW (IF ANYTHING) ABOUT OTHER MINDS?

In this survey of comparative social cognition, what conclusions can we draw, if any, as to whether any nonhuman animal can think about another's mental states? Based on the evidence to date, whether one believes that animal's reason about others' behavior in terms of the underlying unobservable mental states may be a matter of faith. Some researchers believe that there is good evidence that some animals, specifically primates, do have a theory of mind (Santos et al. 2007); others suggest that some animals can read some mental states, such as seeing and knowing, but not others, such as false beliefs (Call 2001, Clayton et al. 2007, Tomasello et al. 2003a); and other investigators suggest that animals are restricted to thinking about another's behavior, but nothing more (Heyes 1998, Penn & Povinelli 2007, Povinelli & Vonk 2004). Povinelli, for example, has recently taken a position similar to that of Heyes (1998), suggesting that although chimpanzees and other animals are excellent readers of others' behavior, there is no evidence that they need to read others' mental states, and most current experiments do not allow for such an interpretation (Penn & Povinelli 2007, Povinelli & Vonk 2004).

Behavioral cues may be sufficient for predicting a novel individual's future actions but not for explaining their previous behavior, particularly when individuals have personality, past history, and experiences that contribute to their unique behavioral profile. Computing the statistical regularities of behavior when referred to patterns of behavior (e.g., behavior X leads to outcome Y) that are species-specific can act as simple heuristics, but it is less useful when taking into consideration the effects of context, personality, past history, etc. We suggest that compiling and updating a database on every individual that is encountered would be extremely inefficient, except in the case of tracking close relationships (see above). We are not implying that reasoning about mental states is more efficient, only that it may have greater flexibility when dealing with novel individuals or familiar individuals in novel situations.

Povinelli concedes that most of human social cognition probably does not involve recognizing unobservable mental states either, and perhaps our ToM may only be used for explaining "why" rather than predicting "what" (see also Andrews 2005). Indeed, the ability to predict another's future actions does not require the ability to attribute mental states; following the line of another's sight or the trajectory of the walk, especially in relation to a goal object, should be sufficient. By comparison, paradigms based on explaining why others did what they did may be better placed to produce evidence for reasoning about mental states rather than behavior alone (in human and nonhuman animals). One such paradigm could be to present subjects with an anomalous behavior and then to record their responses (Andrews 2005). For example, subjects may look longer at a sequence in which reaching to object B does not follow looking at object A (Santos & Hauser 1999), or subjects may look back to the face of the experimenter when the subjects follow the experimenter's gaze and do not find anything interesting in view (Tomasello & Call 2006; see also Povinelli & Dunphy-Lelii 2001).

Andrews (2005) suggested two additional heuristics that animals may use in social situations that are less dependent on reading behavior: trait attribution and inductive generalization. For trait attribution, one may respond to another individual in a particular way because the individual possesses a particular attribute that may be predictive of behavior. For example, dominant chimpanzees may be larger than subordinates and may adopt a particular posture. A subordinate that sees a dominant will respond in a species-specific manner—because dominants tend to be aggressive—so the subordinate should avoid competing for food in the presence of a dominant. In this scenario, a dominant does not need to act toward the food to initiate changes in the subordinate's behavior; its posture is sufficient.

For inductive generalization, one may respond to a particular individual in a specific way because the individual has always behaved in the same way in this context. Consider the following hypothetical scenario with food-caching scrub-jays: Public Enemy Number One is alpha and so always aggressively steals others' caches without any need to implement subtle pilfering techniques. Public Enemy Number One always looks intently at the caches being made and does not attempt to hide his looking behavior. By contrast, Jack the Lad is mid-ranking and will pilfer when given the opportunity, but only when the dominant cacher has left the scene; to do so he relies on having a good observational spatial memory. When Jack the Lad observes caching by another, his behavior is dependent on whether the cacher is dominant or subordinate to him. He always turns away from the cacher or hides if the cacher is dominant. But when caching in front of Sweetie-Pie, who is more subordinate to him, he behaves just as Public Enemy Number One behaved in front of him. The point is that the caching tactics are modulated by context (whether another is watching or not), and by prior knowledge of who is currently dominant over whom. Consequently, the cacher only needs to recognize these individuals to implement appropriate cache-protection strategies based on their previous interactions.

In view of these considerations, we believe the field is now in a strong position to discover what animals do really know about their fellow beings and the extent to which this knowledge is acquired through simple associations, behavior reading, mind reading, or something else.

SUMMARY AND FUTURE ISSUES

Research into animal ToM has focused on three different categories of mental states: perceptual (e.g., seeing or hearing), motivational (e.g., desires and intentions), and informational (e.g., knowledge and beliefs). As part of perceptual ToM, many animals can follow another's gaze or pointing cues, will look around a barrier to see what another is looking at, and will look back to the experimenter if they do not find anything interesting in their line of sight; however, only enculturated, domesticated, or human socialized (e.g., hand-reared) animals can use social cues to find hidden food. Studies with a high ecological validity, such as food competition in chimpanzees and cache-protection strategies in corvids, have provided good evidence for understanding both seeing and knowledge in others, whereas previous studies of comparative social cognition have been explained using simple associative mechanisms, such as discrimination learning. Although the false belief task has been suggested to be the benchmark test for ToM in humans, there is no evidence that any animal has passed this test. Experience projection (predicting or explaining another's behavior in relation to experiences a subject has had in the same situation) has been described for western scrubjays and may be a useful paradigm for testing what animals know about other minds. However, explaining why other individuals acted as they did, rather than predicting their intentions, may be the only unambiguous way to provide evidence for recognizing unobservable mental states.

We have several recommendations for the future of comparative social cognition. First, comparative social cognition needs to become more comparative. At present, most of the tests have been performed on chimpanzees, and occasionally the other great apes, monkeys, dogs and corvids, but there are few studies on other taxonomic groups. Where comparisons between species can be made—for example, with the object-choice task—care needs to be taken to standardize the methodology in order to be truly comparative. Second, paradigms with high ecological validity have been very productive in revealing what animals may know about conspecifics. As such, proposing why social cognition evolved may also perform a useful function in the design of experiments. Such theoretical considerations should focus not only on species' similarities but also on species' differences, for example, whether differences in mating system and other socioecological factors predict why corvids and apes have convergently evolved complex social networks, alliances, and postconflict tactics yet differ in whether they reconcile after a fight (Seed et al. 2007) and in the complexity of their cooperative understanding (Seed et al. 2008).

Third, future research needs to focus on determining whether animals represent individual mental states (or mental states in combination, such as seeing and knowing) rather than focus on investigating whether animals have a theory of mind. Furthermore, experiments need to be conducted to assess the relative contributions of the different psychological mechanisms that may contribute to social cognition (associative learning, behavior reading, concepts, or mental attribution). Fourth, the development of social cognition in human infants is an active and productive area of research. It will be equally important to determine how social cognition develops in nonhuman animals. To our knowledge, this question has so far been addressed only in young chimpanzees (Reaux et al. 1999, Tomasello & Carpenter 2005, Tomonaga et al. 2004) and ravens (Schloegl et al. 2007b). Finally, research needs to include other theoretical perspectives aside from the traditional theory-theory approach, such as introspection and simulation theory. The development of these perspectives will have important implications for how our sense of self develops with our sense of other agents.

DISCLOSURE STATEMENT

The authors are not aware of any biases that might be perceived as affecting the objectivity of this review.

ACKNOWLEDGMENTS

During the writing of this paper, Nathan Emery was primarily funded by a Royal Society University Research Fellowship, and our research was funded by grants from the BBSRC, Royal Society, and the University of Cambridge. We thank Randy Glasbergen for permission to reprint his wonderful cartoon.

LITERATURE CITED

Agnetta B, Hare B, Tomasello M. 2000. Cues to food location that domestic dogs (*Canis familiaris*) of different ages do and do not use. *Anim. Cogn.* 3:107–12

Anderson JR, Mitchell RW. 1999. Macaques but not lemurs co-orient visually with humans. *Folia Primatol.* 70:17–22

Anderson JR, Montant M, Schmidt D. 1996. Rhesus macaques fail to use gaze direction as an experimenter-given cue in an object-choice task. *Behav. Proc.* 37:47–55

Anderson JR, Sallaberry P, Barbier H. 1995. Use of experimenter-given cues during object-choice tasks by capuchin monkeys. *Anim. Behav.* 49:201–8

Andrews K. 2005. Chimpanzee theory of mind: looking in all the wrong places? *Mind Lang.* 20:521–36

Barth J, Reaux JE, Povinelli DJ. 2005. Chimpanzees (*Pan troglodytes*) use of gaze cues in object-choice tasks: different methods yield different results. *Anim. Cogn.* 8:84–92

Bednekoff PA, Balda RP. 1996a. Observational spatial memory in Clark's nutcrackers and Mexican jays. *Anim. Behav.* 52:833–39

Bednekoff PA, Balda RP. 1996b. Social caching and observational spatial memory in pinyon jays. *Behaviour* 133:807–26

Bennett J. 1978. Some remarks about concepts. *Behav. Brain Sci.* 4:557–60

Bloom P, German TP. 2000. Two reasons to abandon the false belief task as a test of theory mind. *Cognition* 77:B25–31

Boesch C. 1994. Cooperative hunting in wild chimpanzees. *Anim. Behav.* 48:653–67

Brauer J, Call J, Tomasello M. 2005. All great ape species follow gaze to distant locations and around barriers. *J. Comp. Psychol.* 119:145–54

Brauer J, Call J, Tomasello M. 2007. Chimpanzees really know what others can see in a competitive situation. *Anim. Cogn.* 10:439–48

Brauer J, Call J, Tomasello M. 2008. Chimpanzees do not take into account what others can hear in a competitive situation. *Anim. Cogn.* 11:175–78

Bugnyar T. 2007. An integrative approach to the study of "theory of mind"-like abilities in ravens. *Jap. J. Anim. Psychol.* 57:15–27

Bugnyar T, Heinrich B. 2005. Ravens, *Corvus corax*, differentiate between knowledgeable and ignorant conspecifics. *Proc. R. Soc. Lond. B Biol. Sci.* 272:1641–46

Bugnyar T, Heinrich B. 2006. Pilfering ravens, *Corvus corax*, adjust their behaviour to social context and identity of competitors. *Anim. Cogn.* 9:369–76

Bugnyar T, Kotrschal K. 2002. Observational learning and the raiding of food caches in ravens, *Corvus corax*: Is it "tactical" deception? *Anim. Behav.* 64:185–95

Bugnyar T, Schwab C, Schloegl C, Kotrschal K, Heinrich B. 2007. Ravens judge competitors through experience with play caching. *Curr. Biol.* 17:1804–8

Bugnyar T, Stowe M, Heinrich B. 2004. Ravens, *Corvus corax*, follow gaze direction of humans around obstacles. *Proc. R. Soc. Lond. B Biol. Sci.* 271:1351–36

Burger J, Gochfeld M, Murray B. 1992. Risk discrimination of eye contact and directedness of approach in black iguanas (*Ctenosaura similis*). *J. Comp. Psychol.* 106:97–101

Burkart J, Heschl A. 2006. Geometrical gaze following in common marmosets (*Callithrix jacchus*). *J. Comp. Psychol.* 120:120–30

Byrne RW, Whiten A, eds. 1988. *Machiavellian Intelligence: Social Expertise and the Evolution of Intellect in Monkeys, Apes and Humans.* Oxford: Clarendon

First to report the use of the object-choice task to test for perspective taking in animals.

Provides an adjunct to Povinelli's arguments by suggesting that experiments should focus on explanation rather than on prediction.

Byrnit JT. 2004. Nonenculturated orangutans' (*Pongo pygmaeus*) use of experimenter-given manual and facial cues in an object-choice task. *J. Comp. Psychol.* 118:309–15

Call J. 2001. Chimpanzee social cognition. *Trends Cogn. Sci.* 5:399–405

Call J, Agnetta B, Tomasello M. 2000. Social cues that chimpanzees do and do not use to find hidden objects. *Anim. Cogn.* 3:23–34

Call J, Brauer J, Kaminski J, Tomasello M. 2003. Domestic dogs are sensitive to the attentional state of humans. *J. Comp. Psychol.* 117:257–63

Call J, Hare B, Carpenter M, Tomasello M. 2004. "Unwilling" versus "unable": chimpanzees' understanding of human intentional action. *Dev. Sci.* 7:488–98

Call J, Hare B, Tomasello M. 1998. Chimpanzee gaze following in an object-choice task. *Anim. Cogn.* 1:89–99

Call J, Tomasello M. 1998. Distinguishing intentional from accidental actions in orangutans (*Pongo pygmaeus*), chimpanzees (*Pan troglodytes*) and human children (*Homo sapiens*). *J. Comp. Psychol.* 112:192–206

Call J, Tomasello M. 1999. A nonverbal false belief task: the performance of children and great apes. *Child Dev.* 70:381–95

Clarkson K, Eden SF, Sutherland WJ, Houston AI. 1986. Density dependence and magpie food hoarding. *J. Anim. Ecol.* 55:111–21

Clayton NS, Dally JM, Emery NJ. 2007. Social cognition by food-caching corvids: the western scrub-jay as a natural psychologist. *Philos. Trans. R. Soc. Lond. B* 362:507–22

Clayton NS, Emery NJ, Dickinson A. 2006. The rationality of animal memory. In *Rational Animals?*, ed. M Nudds, S Hurley, pp. 197–216. London: Oxford Univ. Press

Clayton NS, Griffiths DP, Bennett AD. 1996. Storage of stones by jays *Garrulus glandarious*. *Ibis* 136:331–34

Clayton NS, Griffiths DP, Emery NJ, Dickinson A. 2001. Elements of episodic-like memory in animals. *Philos. Trans. R. Soc. Lond. B Biol. Sci.* 356:1483–91

Cooper JJ, Ashton C, Bishop S, West R, Mills DS, Young RJ. 2003. Clever hounds: social cognition in the domestic dog (*Canis familiaris*). *Appl. Anim. Behav. Sci.* 81:229–44

Coss RG. 1978. Perceptual determinants of gaze aversion by the lesser mouse lemur (*Microcebus murinus*): the role of two facing eyes. *Behaviour* 64:248–67

Dally JM, Clayton NS, Emery NJ. 2006a. The behaviour and evolution of cache protection and pilferage. *Anim. Behav.* 72:13–23

Dally JM, Emery NJ, Clayton NS. 2004. Cache protection strategies in western scrub-jays (*Aphelocoma californica*): hiding food in the shade. *Proc. R. Soc. Lond. B* 271:S387–90

Dally JM, Emery NJ, Clayton NS. 2005a. Cache protection strategies in western scrub-jays: implications for social cognition. *Anim. Behav.* 70:1251–63

Dally JM, Emery NJ, Clayton NS. 2005b. The social suppression of caching by western scrub-jays (*Aphelocoma californica*). *Behaviour* 142:961–77

Dally JM, Emery NJ, Clayton NS. 2006b. Food-caching scrub-jays keep track of who was watching when. *Science* 312:1662–65

de Waal FBM. 1982. *Chimpanzee Politics*. Baltimore, MD: John Hopkins Univ. Press

Dennett DC. 1978. Beliefs about beliefs. *Behav. Brain Sci.* 4:568–70

Emery NJ. 2000. The eyes have it: the neuroethology, evolution and function of social gaze. *Neurosci. Biobehav. Rev.* 24:581–604

Emery NJ, Clayton NS. 2001. Effects of experience and social context on prospective caching strategies by scrub jays. *Nature* 414:443–46

Emery NJ, Clayton NS. 2004. Comparing the complex cognition of birds and primates. In *Comparative Vertebrate Cognition: Are Primates Superior to Nonprimates?*, ed. LJ Rogers, G Kaplan, pp. 3–55. New York: Kluwer Acad.

Emery NJ, Clayton NS. 2008. How to build a scrub-jay that reads minds. In *Origins of the Social Mind: Evolutionary and Developmental Views*, ed. S Itakura, K Fujita. Kyoto, Japan: Springer-Verlag. In press

Emery NJ, Dally JM, Clayton NS. 2004. Western scrub-jays (*Aphelocoma californica*) use cognitive strategies to protect their caches from thieving conspecifics. *Anim. Cogn.* 7:37–43

Emery NJ, Lorincz EN, Perrett DI, Oram MW, Baker CI. 1997. Gaze following and joint attention in rhesus monkeys (*Macaca mulatta*). *J. Comp. Psychol.* 111:286–93

Provided the first evidence for experience projection in animals, based on protecting caches.

Emery NJ, Seed AM, von Bayern AMP, Clayton NS. 2007. Cognitive adaptations of social bonding in birds. *Philos. Trans. R. Soc. Lond. B* 362:489–505

Flombaum JI, Santos LR. 2005. Rhesus monkeys attribute perceptions to others. *Curr. Biol.* 15:447–52

Gacsi M, Miklosi A, Varga O, Topal J, Csanyi V. 2004. Are readers of our face readers of our minds? Dogs (*Canis familaris*) show situation-dependent recognition of human's attention. *Anim. Cogn.* 7:144–53

Gomez JC. 1991. Visual behaviour as a window for reading the minds of others in primates. In *Natural Theories of Mind*, ed. A Whiten, pp. 195–207. Oxford: Blackwell Sci.

Gomez JC. 1996a. Nonhuman primate theories of (nonhuman primate) minds: some issues concerning the origins of mindreading. In *Theories of Theories of Mind*, ed. P Carruthers, PK Smith, pp. 330–43. London: Cambridge Univ. Press

Gomez JC. 1996b. Ostensive behavior in the great apes: the role of eye contact. In *Reaching Into Thought: The Minds of the Great Apes*, ed. A Russon, ST Parker, KA Bard, pp. 330–43. London: Cambridge Univ. Press

Hampton RR. 1994. Sensitivity to information specifying the line of gaze of humans in sparrows. *Behaviour* 130:41–51

Hare B. 2001. Can competitive paradigms increase the validity of experiments on primate social cognition? *Anim. Cogn.* 4:269–80

Hare B. 2007. From nonhuman to human mind: What changed and why? *Curr. Dir. Psychol. Sci.* 16:60–64

Hare B, Adessi E, Call J, Tomasello M, Visalberghi E. 2003. Do capuchin monkeys, *Cebus apella*, know what conspecifics do and do not see? *Anim. Behav.* 65:131–42

Hare B, Brown M, Williamson C, Tomasello M. 2002. The domestication of social cognition in dogs. *Science* 298:1634–36

Hare B, Call J, Agnetta B, Tomasello M. 2000. Chimpanzees know what conspecifics do and do not see. *Anim. Behav.* 59:771–85

Hare B, Call J, Tomasello M. 1998. Communication of food location between human and dog (*Canis familiaris*). *Evol. Comm.* 2:137–59

Hare B, Call J, Tomasello M. 2001. Do chimpanzees know what conspecifics know? *Anim. Behav.* 61:139–51

Hare B, Melis AP, Woods V, Hastings S, Wrangham RW. 2007. Tolerance allows bonobos to outperform chimpanzees on a cooperative task. *Curr. Biol.* 17:619–23

Hare B, Plyusnina I, Ignacio N, Schepina O, Stepika A, et al. 2005. Social cognitive evolution in captive foxes is a correlated by-product of experimental domestication. *Curr. Biol.* 15:228–30

Hare B, Tomasello M. 1999. Domestic dogs (*Canis familiaris*) use human and conspecific social cues to locate hidden food. *J. Comp. Psychol.* 113:173–77

Hare B, Tomasello M. 2005. Human-like social skills in dogs? *Trends Cogn. Sci.* 9:439–44

Harman G. 1978. Studying the chimpanzee's theory of mind. *Behav. Brain Sci.* 4:576–77

Hattori Y, Kuroshima H, Fujita K. 2007. I know you are not looking at me: capuchin monkeys' (*Cebus apella*) sensitivity to human attentional states. *Anim. Cogn.* 10:141–48

Hauser MD, Glynn DD, Wood JN. 2007. Rhesus monkeys correctly read the goal-relevant gestures of a human agent. *Proc. R. Soc. Lond. B* 274:1913–18

Heinrich B. 1999. *Mind of the Raven*. New York: Harper Collins

Held S, Mendl M, Devereux C, Byrne RW. 2000. Social tactics of pigs in a competitive foraging task: the "informed forager" paradigm. *Anim. Behav.* 59:569–76

Held S, Mendl M, Devereux C, Byrne RW. 2001. Behaviour of domestic pigs in a visual perspective taking task. *Behaviour* 138:1337–54

Heyes CM. 1998. Theory of mind in nonhuman primates. *Behav. Brain Sci.* 21:101–48

Hirata S, Fuwa K. 2007. Chimpanzees (*Pan troglodytes*) learn to act with other individuals in a cooperative task. *Primates* 48:13–21

Hirata S, Matsuzawa T. 2001. Tactics to obtain a hidden food item in chimpanzee pairs (*Pan troglodytes*). *Anim. Cogn.* 4:285–95

Humphrey NK. 1976. The social function of intellect. In *Growing Points in Ethology*, ed. PPG Bateson, RA Hinde, pp. 303–17. London: Cambridge Univ. Press

Itakura S. 1996. An exploratory study of gaze monitoring in nonhuman primates. *Jap. Psychol. Res.* 38:174–80

An influential study with high ecological validity investigating perspective taking in a food competition paradigm.

A second influential study with high ecological validity investigating perspective taking in a food competition paradigm.

An important review resulting in rethinking how comparative ToM experiments should be interpreted.

First paper to suggest social reasoning as the primary driving force for the evolution of intelligence.

Itakura S, Anderson JR. 1996. Learning to use experimenter-given cues during an object-choice task by a capuchin monkey. *Curr. Psychol. Cogn.* 15:103–12

Itakura S, Tanaka M. 1998. Use of experimenter-given cues during object choice tasks by chimpanzees (*Pan troglodytes*), an orangutan (*Pongo pygmaeus*) and human infants (*Homo sapiens*). *J. Comp. Psychol.* 112:119–26

Jensen K, Call J, Tomasello M. 2007. Chimpanzees are vengeful but not spiteful. *Proc. Natl. Acad. Sci. USA* 104:13046–50

Jensen K, Hare B, Call J, Tomasello M. 2006. What's in it for me? Self-regard precludes altruism and spite in chimpanzees. *Proc. R. Soc. Lond. B* 273:1013–21

Kaminski J, Call J, Tomasello M. 2004. Body orientation and face orientation: two factors controlling apes' begging behavior from humans. *Anim. Cogn.* 7:216–23

Kaminski J, Call J, Tomasello M. 2006. Goats' behaviour in a competitive food paradigm: evidence for perspective taking? *Behaviour* 143:1341–56

Kaminski J, Riedel J, Call J, Tomasello M. 2005. Domestic goats, *Capra hircus*, follow gaze direction and use social cues in an object choice task. *Anim. Behav.* 69:11–18

Karin-D'Arcy MR, Povinelli DJ. 2002. Do chimpanzees know what each other see? A closer look. *Int. J. Comp. Psychol.* 15:21–54

Kuroshima H, Fujita K, Fuyuki A, Masuda T. 2002. Understanding of the relationship between seeing and knowing by tufted capuchin monkeys (*Cebus apella*). *Anim. Cogn.* 5:41–48

Lyons DE, Santos LR. 2006. Ecology, domain specificity and the origins of theory of mind: Is competition the catalyst? *Philos. Compass* 1:481–92

Maros K, Gacsi M, Miklosi A. 2008. Comprehension of human pointing gestures in horses (*Equus caballus*). *Anim. Cogn.* 11:457–66

Matheson M, Cooper M, Weeks J, Thompson R, Fragaszy DM. 1998. Attribution is more likely demonstrated in more natural contexts. *Behav. Brain Sci.* 21:124–26

McKinley J, Sambrook TD. 2000. Use of human-given cues by domestic dogs (*Canis familiaris*) and horses (*Equus caballus*). *Anim. Cogn.* 3:13–22

Melis AP, Call J, Tomasello M. 2006a. Chimpanzees (*Pan troglodytes*) conceal visual and auditory information from others. *J. Comp. Psychol.* 120:154–62

Melis AP, Hare B, Tomasello M. 2006b. Chimpanzees recruit the best collaborators. *Science* 311:1297–300

Melis AP, Hare B, Tomasello M. 2006c. Engineering cooperation in chimpanzees: tolerance constraints on cooperation. *Anim. Behav.* 72:275–86

Menzel EW. 1974. A group of young chimpanzees in a one-acre field. In *Behavior of Non-Human Primates: Modern Research Trends*, ed. A Schrier, F Stollnitz, pp. 83–153. New York: Academic

Miklosi A. 2008. *Dog Behaviour, Evolution and Cognition*. London: Oxford Univ. Press

Miklosi A, Kubinyi E, Topal J, Gacsi M, Viranyi Z, Csanyi V. 2003. A simple reason for a big difference: Wolves do not look back at humans, but dogs do. *Curr. Biol.* 13:763–66

Miklosi A, Polgardi R, Topal J, Csanyi V. 1998. Use of experimenter-given cues in dogs. *Anim. Cogn.* 1:113–21

Miklosi A, Pongracz P, Lakatos G, Topal J, Csanyi V. 2005. A comparative study of the use of visual communicative signals in interactions between dogs (*Canis familiaris*) and humans, and cats (*Felis catus*) and humans. *J. Comp. Psychol.* 119:179–86

Miklosi A, Soproni K. 2006. A comparative analysis of animals' understanding of the human pointing gesture. *Anim. Cogn.* 9:81–93

Miklosi A, Topal J, Csanyi V. 2004. Comparative social cognition: What can dogs teach us? *Anim. Behav.* 67:995–1004

Neiworth JJ, Burman MA, Basile BM, Lickteig MT. 2002. Use of experimenter-given cues in visual co-orienting and in an object-choice task by a New World monkey species, cotton-top tamarins (*Saguinus oedipus*). *J. Comp. Psychol.* 116:3–11

Okamoto-Barth S, Call J, Tomasello M. 2007. Great apes' understanding of other individuals' line of sight. *Psychol. Sci.* 18:462–68

Onishi KH, Baillargeon R. 2005. Do 15-month-old infants understand false beliefs? *Science* 308:255–58

Pack AA, Herman LM. 2004. Bottlenosed dolphins (*Tursiops truncatus*) comprehend the referent of both static and dynamic human gazing and pointing in an object-choice task. *J. Comp. Psychol.* 118:160–71

A classic study on whether chimpanzees can infer intentions and knowledge in a foraging paradigm.

Peignot P, Anderson JR. 1999. Use of experimenter-given manual and facial cues by gorillas (*Gorilla gorilla*) in an object-choice task. *J. Comp. Psychol.* 113:253–60

Penn DC, Povinelli DJ. 2007. On the lack of evidence that nonhuman animals possess anything remotely resembling a "theory of mind." *Philos. Trans. R. Soc. Lond. B* 362:731–44

Povinelli DJ. 1994. Comparative studies of animal mental state attribution: a reply to Heyes. *Anim. Behav.* 48:239–41

Povinelli DJ, Dunphy-Lelii S. 2001. Do chimpanzees seek explanations? Preliminary comparative investigations. *Can. J. Psychol.* 55:93–101

Povinelli DJ, Eddy TJ. 1996a. Chimpanzees: joint visual attention. *Psychol. Sci.* 7:129–35

Povinelli DJ, Eddy TJ. 1996b. What young chimpanzees know about seeing. *Monogr. Soc. Res. Child Dev.* 61(3):1–189

Povinelli DJ, Nelson K, Boysen S. 1990. Inferences about guessing and knowing by chimpanzees. *J. Comp. Psychol.* 104:203–10

Povinelli DJ, Parks KA, Novak MA. 1991. Do rhesus monkeys (*Macaca mulatta*) attribute knowledge and ignorance to others? *J. Comp. Psychol.* 105:318–25

Povinelli DJ, Perilloux HK, Reaux JE, Bierschwale DT. 1998. Young and juvenile chimpanzees' (*Pan troglodytes*) reactions to intentional versus accidental and inadvertent actions. *Behav. Proc.* 42:205–18

Povinelli DJ, Rulf AB, Bierschwale DT. 1994. Absence of knowledge attribution and self-recognition in young chimpanzees (*Pan troglodytes*). *J. Comp. Psychol.* 180:74–80

Povinelli DJ, Vonk J. 2003. Chimpanzee minds: suspiciously human? *Trends Cogn. Sci.* 7:157–60

Povinelli DJ, Vonk J. 2004. We don't need a microscope to explore the chimpanzee's mind. *Mind Lang.* 19:1–28

Premack D. 1988. "Does the chimpanzee have a theory of mind?" revisited. In *Machiavellian Intelligence*, ed. RW Byrne, A Whiten, pp. 160–78. Oxford: Oxford Univ. Press

Premack D, Woodruff G. 1978. Does the chimpanzee have a theory of mind? *Behav. Brain Sci.* 4:515–26

Preston SD, Jacobs LF. 2001. Conspecific pilferage but not presence affects Merriam's kangaroo rat cache strategy. *Behav. Ecol.* 12:517–23

Purdy JE, Domjan M. 1998. Tactics in theory of mind research. *Behav. Brain Sci.* 21:129–30

Reaux JE, Theall LA, Povinelli DJ. 1999. A longitudinal investigation of chimpanzees' understanding of visual perception. *Child Dev.* 70:275–90

Santos LR, Flombaum JI, Phillips W. 2007. The evolution of human mindreading: how nonhuman primates can inform social cognitive neuroscience. In *Evolutionary Cognitive Neuroscience*, ed. SM Platek, JP Keenan, TK Shackelford, pp. 433–56. Cambridge, MA: MIT Press

Santos LR, Hauser MD. 1999. How monkeys see the eyes: cotton-top tamarins' reactions to changes in visual attention and action. *Anim. Cogn.* 2:131–39

Santos LR, Nissen AG, Ferrugia JA. 2006. Rhesus monkeys, *Macaca mulatta*, know what others can and cannot hear. *Anim. Behav.* 71:1175–81

Savage-Rumbaugh S, Rumbaugh DM, Boysen S. 1978. Sarah's problems of comprehension. *Behav. Brain Sci.* 4:555

Saxe R. 2006. Uniquely human social cognition. *Curr. Opin. Neurobiol.* 16:235–39

Schloegl C, Kotrschal K, Bugnyar T. 2007a. Do common ravens (*Corvus corax*) rely on human or conspecific gaze cues to detect hidden food? *Anim. Cogn.* 11:231–41

Schloegl C, Kotrschal K, Bugnyar T. 2007b. Gaze following in common ravens, *Corvus corax*: ontogeny and habituation. *Anim. Behav.* 74:769–78

Schloegl C, Kotrschal K, Bugnyar T. 2008. Modifying the object-choice task. Is the way you look important for ravens? *Behav. Proc.* 77:61–65

Schuemann M, Call J. 2004. The use of experimenter-given cues by South African fur seals (*Arctocephalus pusillus*). *Anim. Cogn.* 7:224–30

Schwab C, Huber L. 2006. Obey or not obey? Dogs (*Canis familiaris*) behave differently in response to attentional states of their owners. *J. Comp. Psychol.* 120:169–75

Seed AM, Clayton NS, Emery NJ. 2007. Postconflict third-party affiliation in rooks, *Corvus frugilegus*. *Curr. Biol.* 17:152–58

Seed AM, Clayton NS, Emery NJ. 2008. Cooperative problem solving in rooks (*Corvus frugilegus*). *Proc. R. Soc. Lond. B* 275:1421–29

Presents a convincing argument that animals only represent behavior, not mental, states.

The original study of ToM in chimpanzees, which started the field of comparative social cognition.

Shapiro AD, Janik V, Slater P. 2003. A gray seal's (*Halichoerus grypus*) responses to experimenter-given pointing and directional cues. *J. Comp. Psychol.* 117:355–62

Silk JB, Brosnan SF, Vonk J, Heinrich B, Povinelli DJ, et al. 2005. Chimpanzees are indifferent to the welfare of other group members. *Nature* 435:1357–59

Soproni K, Miklosi A, Topal J, Csanyi V. 2001. Comprehension of human communicative signs in pet dogs (*Canis familiaris*). *J. Comp. Psychol.* 115:122–26

Soproni K, Miklosi A, Topal J, Csanyi V. 2002. Dogs' (*Canis familiaris*) responsiveness to human pointing gestures. *J. Comp. Psychol.* 116:27–34

Tomasello M, Call J. 2006. Do chimpanzees know what others see—or only what they are looking at? In *Rational Animals?*, ed. S Hurley, M Nudds, pp. 371–84. London: Oxford Univ. Press

Tomasello M, Call J, Hare B. 1998. Five primate species follow the visual gaze of conspecifics. *Anim. Behav.* 55:1063–69

Tomasello M, Call J, Hare B. 2003a. Chimpanzees understand psychological states—the question is which ones and to what extent. *Trends Cogn. Sci.* 7:153–56

Tomasello M, Call J, Hare B. 2003b. Chimpanzees versus humans: It's not that simple. *Trends Cogn. Sci.* 7:239–40

Tomasello M, Carpenter M. 2005. The emergence of social cognition in three young chimpanzees. *Monogr. Soc. Res. Child Dev.* 70(1):1–122

Tomasello M, Carpenter M, Call J, Behne T, Moll H. 2005. Understanding and sharing intentions: the origin of cultural cognition. *Behav. Brain Sci.* 28:675–735

Tomasello M, Hare B, Agnetta B. 1999. Chimpanzees, *Pan troglodytes*, follow gaze direction geometrically. *Anim. Behav.* 58:769–77

Tomasello M, Hare B, Lehmann H, Call J. 2007. Reliance on head versus eyes in the gaze following of great apes and human infants: the cooperative eye hypothesis. *J. Hum. Evol.* 52:314–20

Tomonaga M, Tanaka M, Matsuzawa T, Myowa-Yamakoshi M, Kosugi D, et al. 2004. Development of social cognition in infant chimpanzees (*Pan troglodytes*): face recognition, smiling, gaze and the lack of triadic interactions. *Jap. Psychol. Res.* 46:227–35

Tschudin A, Call J, Dunbar RIM, Harris G, Van Der Elst C. 2001. Comprehension of signs by dolphins (*Tursiops truncatus*). *J. Comp. Psychol.* 115:100–5

Vander Wall SB. 1990. *Food Hoarding in Animals*. Chicago: Univ. Chicago Press

Viranyi Z, Gacsi M, Kubinyi E, Topal J, Belenyi B, et al. 2008. Comprehension of human pointing gestures in young human-reared wolves (*Canis lupis*) and dogs (*Canis familiaris*). *Anim. Cogn.* 11:373–87

Viranyi Z, Topal J, Gacsi M, Miklosi A, Csanyi V. 2004. Dogs respond appropriately to cues of humans' attentional focus. *Behav. Proc.* 66:161–72

Viranyi Z, Topal J, Miklosi A, Csanyi V. 2006. A nonverbal test of knowledge attribution: a comparative study on dogs and children. *Anim. Cogn.* 9:13–26

Watanabe S, Clayton NS. 2007. Observational visuospatial encoding of the cache locations of others by western scrub-jays (*Aphelocoma californica*). *J. Ethol.* 25:271–79

Whiten A. 2000. Chimpanzee cognition and the question of mental rerepresentation. In *Metarepresentation: A Multidisciplinary Approach*, ed. D Sperber, pp. 139–67. London: Oxford Univ. Press

Wimmer H, Perner J. 1983. Beliefs about beliefs: representation and constraining function of wrong beliefs in young children's understanding of deception. *Cognition* 13:103–28

Wood JN, Glynn DD, Phillips BC, Hauser MD. 2007. The perception of rational goal-directed action in nonhuman primates. *Science* 317:1402–5

Learning from Others: Children's Construction of Concepts

Susan A. Gelman

Department of Psychology, University of Michigan, Ann Arbor, Michigan 48109-1109;
email: gelman@umich.edu

Annu. Rev. Psychol. 2009. 60:115–40

First published online as a Review in Advance on
July 16, 2008

The *Annual Review of Psychology* is online at
psych.annualreviews.org

This article's doi:
10.1146/annurev.psych.59.103006.093659

Key Words

language, developmental psychology, parental input

Abstract

Much of children's knowledge is derived not from their direct experiences with the environment but rather from the input of others. However, until recently, the focus in studies of concept development was primarily on children's knowledge, with relatively little attention paid to the nature of the input. The past 10 years have seen an important shift in focus. This article reviews this approach, by examining the nature of the input and the nature of the learner, to shed light on early conceptual learning. These findings argue against the simple notion that conceptual development is either supplied by the environment or innately specified, and instead demonstrate how the two work together. The implications for how children reconcile competing belief systems are also discussed.

Contents

INTRODUCTION

In a classic passage, Jean Piaget described a young child playing with pebbles and in so doing, discovering principles of mathematics:

> [H]e lined them up in a row, counted them from left to right, and got ten. Then, just for fun, he counted them from right to left to see what number he would get, and was astonished that he got ten again. He put the pebbles in a circle and counted them, and once again there were ten. He went around the circle in the other way and got ten again. And no matter how he put the pebbles down, when he counted them, the number came to ten. He discovered here what is known in math-

ematics as commutativity, that is, the sum is independent of the order (Piaget 1970).

By reorganizing, counting, and exploring—all self-directed, all derived from his own actions—the child apparently discerned basic mathematical laws. This humble yet remarkable example illustrates the power of self-directed discovery and learning. Just as Plato's *Meno* argued for an intuitive grasp of the principles of geometry in the absence of any mathematical instruction, so too Piaget's compelling example illustrates the intuitive logic and structure of the child's untutored mind, attempting to organize experience into a coherent system.

Many years of research following on Piaget's original insights confirm the active, self-directed nature of childhood cognition (Bruner 1973, Gopnik & Meltzoff 1997, Wellman & Gelman 1998). Moreover, having an opportunity to explore the world actively seems to have direct benefits on interactions and learning. For example, Needham et al. (2002) find that 3-month-old infants who receive special experience picking up toys with "sticky mittens" (mittens with Velcro, enabling infants to pick up objects at any earlier age than they could do otherwise) show more sophisticated engagement with and exploration of objects than infants without the extra experience. Similarly, 3-month-olds with firsthand experience with reaching learn more rapidly than infants who only observe reaching without actively engaging in this behavior (Sommerville et al. 2005).

Much research on cognitive development focuses exclusively on children's knowledge, without asking where such knowledge comes from (Maratsos 2007). This focus reflects an implicit model of the child as a lone scientist, forming and testing hypotheses on her own. It also reflects a threefold assumption that (*a*) development concerns structural change, (*b*) input from others concerns content, and (*c*) structure is more interesting (i.e., consequential, noncontingent) than content. Certainly, much of the content that children learn from others is relatively contingent or inconsequential (e.g., one's phone number, the color of barns).

Yet even the most self-directed learning has a hidden level of cultural input, often invisible because it is so pervasive and thus taken for granted. In the example of pebble counting above, this input includes a previously learned, culturally sanctioned symbolic system that permits counting (1, 2, 3...) as well as a conventional language system that may have encouraged treating the objects as interchangeable (as all are classified as pebbles). Moreover, recent studies of the domain specificity of children's theories (e.g., theory of mind, theory of physics) make apparent that content knowledge is integral to structure and development (Carey 1985, 2008; Wellman & Gelman 1998).

Clearly, then, children learn a tremendous amount about the world from the people around them. Moreover, this simple observation sheds light on concept development more broadly when we consider the following questions: What is the nature of that input, and what is the nature of the human mind that allows it to take advantage of that input? How do biases in the child and cues in the environment work together to enable learning?

In this review, I focus on how children's concept learning entails learning from others. By "concepts," I mean mental representations that organize experience. Even infants use concepts—when smiling at a human face, pointing to the family pet and saying "Kitty!", or reaching eagerly for a spoonful of applesauce. Although some theorists equate concepts and categories, and consider concepts to be the mental representations that correspond to categories of things in the world, such as dogs or chairs (Margolis 1994), I would broaden the set to include properties (green, happy), events or states (jumping, wet), individuals (Daddy, Lassie), and abstract ideas (goodness, liberty) (see also Medin et al. 2000 regarding the diversity of human concepts). Although concepts are generally understood to be the building blocks of ideas (e.g., the thought "Lassie is a happy dog" requires possession of the constituent concepts), concepts are also embedded in larger knowledge structures (Gelman 1996). Concepts therefore cannot be understood wholly as isolated components.

Importantly, the view that children learn from those around them does not mean that children simply, passively take in what they are exposed to (Callanan 2006, Harris & Koenig 2006). Any account that presumes children's concepts are simply the by-product of what they are exposed to—without active processing or constraints—is problematic in failing to explain how concepts are so similar over individuals and contexts. It also fails to explain how adults (those providing the input) come to have the knowledge they do. One could propose that adults learned their concepts from the input of their own parents, who learned them from the input of their parents, etc., but this simply pushes back the problem to an infinite regress.

Treating children as passively taking in input also would not predict the well-demonstrated phenomenon that children resist counterevidence. A classic example comes from Piagetian training studies, in which children persist in supplying incorrect answers to seemingly simple questions, even following instruction (Ginsburg & Opper 1969). In the realm of stereotyping, children and adults distort recall to conform to prior assumptions and expectations (Liben & Signorella 1987). Similar memory and processing biases are found in children's folk theories of physics, biology, and psychology (Schulz et al. 2007). Clearly, then, young children actively process the information around them and are not passive conduits into which information pours.

Thus, I take as a starting assumption that child biases and environmental input are both critical and that it is important not to characterize concept acquisition processes as exclusively learned or innate (Callanan 2006). Marler (1991) provides clear evidence from the development of birdsong that innate skeletal frameworks do not preclude learning from experience (see also R. Gelman & Williams 1998). Parental input and child biases are argued to work together toward a common goal (Markman 1992), with children's interpretive biases and parents' input acting in consistent and mutually reinforcing ways.

I begin this review by sketching out the scope of the problem, arguing that a wide array of concepts require social input beyond the information children can acquire directly from their senses. I then review several ways that language serves a particularly important role in conveying conceptual information to children: through testimony, through naming, and through covert categories. Childhood essentialism is reviewed as a belief system that is informed by explicit and implicit language input. Next I discuss the critical issue of children's credulity and skepticism, where research evidence indicates that children have a mixture of sensitivity and selectivity to the social information that surrounds them. I address the question of how children come to distinguish between reliable and unreliable information, how and when children distinguish fiction and pretense from fact, and the extent to which different, seemingly competing explanatory systems coexist in early childhood. Finally, I consider a number of open questions, before summarizing and concluding.

THE SCOPE OF THE PROBLEM

According to empiricism, knowledge derives from our senses. Concepts are therefore either direct representations of perceptual/sensory experience or combinations of such experiences. This is an old idea, but one with a lot of tread still on it. Many find an empiricist approach to learning attractive because it offers the possibility that one can understand mental processes by building up from simple building blocks. Current-day examples of this would include the argument that high-level cognition results from low-level associations among sensory cues, built up gradually and over many lived examples: "[D]umb forces on selective attention—that is, associative connections and direct stimulus pulls—underlie the seeming smartness of children's novel word interpretations" (Smith et al. 1996, pp. 145–146).

Empiricist approaches have had a resurgence in recent years, in part due to the demonstration that infants can track low-level statistical cues with much greater accuracy than had been previously realized (e.g., Gopnik et al. 2004, Saffran et al. 1996, Xu & Tenenbaum 2007), and in part due to new empiricist models that provide a more detailed and realistic appreciation of children's concepts (Sloutsky & Fisher 2004, Yoshida & Smith 2003).

Yet knowledge is not just derived from sensory input. Harris & Koenig (2006) note that testimony not only augments knowledge acquired through firsthand experience, but that testimony also may be the only plausible source of information for concepts that are not readily accessible by direct observation, such as how the brain works (Gottfried et al. 1999), the shape of the earth (Vosniadou 1994), and the life cycle of animals (Gimenez & Harris 2002). Children develop rich, extended beliefs about all of these concepts during the preschool and early elementary school years.

Generally, concepts for which cultural input is vital include at least scientific concepts (germs, hearts, and oxygen; Harris et al. 2006); classification of the natural world (whales, eels, and other organisms that don't look at all like typical species members; Gelman 2003); social concepts (race, caste, ethnicity, and personality traits, for which one often cannot determine membership based wholly on appearances; Dunham et al. 2006, Hirschfeld 1996); and supernatural concepts (God, witchcraft; Boyer 2003). In reflecting on this list, one is likely to agree that "[p]robably most of what we believe or know past the level of rather basic cognition is a result of social transmissions from our superiors in status and knowledge" (Maratsos 2007, p. 122).

Moreover, three recent approaches in the field of psychology emphasize that learning is not a solitary act, but rather is one that is embedded in social and cultural understandings: theory of mind, cultural psychology, and comparative research. Studies of theory of mind tell us that certain kinds of fundamental learning require attending to others as a crucial source of information (Baldwin 2000). The typically developing child interprets, assesses, and evaluates the surrounding social input (Wellman 1990); disruptions to these capacities can be devastating (Baron-Cohen et al. 1993). In a long tradition influenced by Vygotsky (1978), cultural psychologists from a broad range of areas within psychology have come to the conclusion that cultural contexts play a significant role in the nature of concepts (Medin & Atran 2004, Nisbett et al. 2001, Rogoff 2003). Finally, comparative studies with humans and nonhuman species suggest that certain forms of social learning—imitative learning, instructed learning, and collaborative learning—may be unique to humans (or if not unique, then at least particularly well developed) (Tomasello et al. 1993; but see Whiten et al. 2005). The work I review regarding children draws on findings and concepts from all these fields.

LANGUAGE AS A MEANS OF MODIFYING CHILDREN'S (AND ADULTS') CONCEPTS

Children use several distinct kinds of informational sources when constructing concepts, in addition to their own observations and actions. These include perceptual cues (which things look most alike; Quinn & Eimas 1997, Rakison & Oakes 2003), others' actions on the world (how others group objects in the environment or how they use objects functionally; Bigler et al. 2001, Brand et al. 2002, Meltzoff 2007), explicit assertions (Harris & Koenig 2006), and implicit cues from language (Gelman et al. 1998). Importantly, adult input need not be didactic or explicitly instructional—and indeed typically is not (Callanan 2006, Harris & Koenig 2006).

I focus here on cues transmitted via language—both explicit assertions and implicit cues—as language is acquired early and is one of the most powerful means of expressing and imparting cultural beliefs, knowledge, and values in humans. Certainly, I do not claim that concepts require a conventional language system; note the impressive conceptual abilities of preverbal infants, nonhuman primates, and deaf children with no language input (Cohen & Cashon 2006, Goldin-Meadow 2003, Hauser 2000). I also sidestep the so-called Whorfian question regarding whether language shapes the pattern and structure of thought (e.g., Gleitman & Papafragou 2005). Instead, my focus is on what kinds of information are conveyed to children by means of language. I divide this section into testimony, lexicalization, and covert and implicit categories.

Testimony

Language enables one to express assertions that provide new information, either explicit (e.g., "The earth is round") or implicit [e.g., objects can be divided into animate ("he," "she") and inanimate ("it")] (Harris & Koenig 2006). The assertions of others can thus provide important conceptual information. This notion was articulated by Vygotsky (1934/1962), who distinguished between spontaneous and scientific concepts, and observed that scientific concepts require information beyond firsthand experience. Harris et al. (2006, p. 94) more generally noted the pervasive influence of testimony on all aspects of everyday thought and beliefs: "... we are obliged to swim in a veritable ocean of testimony.... We are dependent on testimony for information about the historical past, our current whereabouts and potential threats to our well-being in the future."

Sperber (1996) provided a hypothetical example of a girl learning about plant reproduction who hears from a reliable authority (such as a teacher) that there are both male and female plants. The relation of gender to plants may at first make little sense to the child. Yet she can understand certain implications of this statement (that plants come in different types and that reproduction is somehow relevant). Furthermore, the initial, fragile connections encourage the child to further theory development and ultimately more elaborated concepts. The testimony thus provides a placeholder for more learning to come.

Empirical studies bear out the reality of this proposal. Ganea et al. (2007) note that one important function of testimony via language is to enable one to update knowledge and beliefs in the absence of any direct contact with an object. For example, if someone tells me that my favorite coffee cup fell to the floor and broke, I can readily alter my representation of the cup. Although this may seem like a simple and straightforward step, it takes time to develop. Ganea et al. (2007) provided young children with a name for a toy, then later told each child that the toy became wet (when it was out of view). Could the child then identify the toy, when given its name? Although 22-month-olds succeeded on the task, 19-month-olds did not—even though they did fine when the same information was given to describe an object that was present. This capacity to revise a mental representation of an absent object develops over this period. Interestingly, young children have even more difficulty using other symbolic media (e.g., pictures, three-dimensional replicas) on the same sort of task (Harris et al. 1997), which suggests that verbal testimony (i.e., language) is particularly informative for young children.

Harris and Koenig point out, as evidence of this trust, children's acceptance of unobservable facts (e.g., round shape of earth) and incorporation of such facts into a coherent new understanding (Gottfried & Jow 2003, Vosniadou 1994), children's acceptance of religious and supernatural claims that in fact have no observable basis whatsoever (Bering 2006), and children's persistent questioning of adults when encountering anomalous events in need of explanation (e.g., Frazier et al. 2008).

Paradoxically, the pervasive, ubiquitous nature of testimony can at times make it difficult to assess its effects. If all children are bathed in testimonial language about mental states, for example, then how is one to determine whether this language influences development? On rare occasion, however, access to ordinary kinds of testimony is blocked, permitting a glimpse into its effects. Studies with deaf children suggest that experience with rich home conversations,

including discussion of needs, desires, beliefs, and other mental states, may have a profound influence on children's theory-of-mind development (Peterson & Siegal 2000). Children who are born deaf into a hearing family and have no opportunity to converse with a fluent speaker perform consistently worse on theory-of-mind tasks than do children who are born deaf but have a parent or other family member who signs fluently. It would be valuable to conduct more detailed analyses of the input to determine the extent to which explicit testimony plays a role.

Although testimony can be direct and highly revealing, often it is incomplete and fragmentary (Gelman et al. 1998, Jipson & Callanan 2003, Keil 2003). It is unlikely to be a full road map for children as they construct complex understandings. It need not be didactic, and the messages need not be literally stated. Instead, testimony can be quite subtle in its implications. For example, in a study of how parents talk to children during a visit to a science museum, parents provided more explanations of science concepts to boys than to girls, even controlling for amount of overall talk (Crowley et al. 2001). This differential focus on explanatory talk could subtly suggest that an in-depth and probing curiosity about science is more appropriate in boys than in girls. Another example of subtle implications is suggested by Harris's (2007) idea that the manner in which testimony is provided may suggest an "implicit epistemology" (p. 118) to children. For example, a child who tends to hear confident, full responses to her questions may come to believe that knowledge is more certain and complete, as compared to a child who hears tentative, incomplete responses.

Lexicalization

A rich empirical literature shows that children's initial, nonlinguistic concepts are affected by the labels they hear (e.g., "a bird," "a wug"). Labels can be considered a form of testimony, but I consider them separately because there is a large literature on lexicalization effects, and they raise a distinct set of issues.

First, what do I mean by lexicalization? Lexicalized concepts are those that correspond to a word in a person's language (e.g., "cup"), as contrasted to those concepts that do not (e.g., "objects that are smaller than a breadbox"). Lexicalized concepts generally have cultural significance: They are shared within a community, are relatively stable, and are passed down from one generation to the next. Nonlexicalized concepts may also have these features; for example, there typically is no single word for "living thing" in the world's languages, despite the significance of the concept (Waxman 2005). However, lexicalized concepts have special significance, particularly for children.

From their earliest use, words—especially count nouns—seem to serve as "placeholders" for children (Waxman 2004). Studies conducted with children ranging from 13 months through the preschool years demonstrate that children treat objects that receive the same noun label as if they have common, nonobvious properties (Gelman & Coley 1990, Gelman & Markman 1986, Graham et al. 2004, Jaswal & Markman 2007). They do so in two respects: First, labels enable dissimilar objects to be treated alike, as having properties in common [e.g., upon learning that a blackbird feeds its young mashed-up food, children are more likely to extend that property to another bird (e.g., a flamingo) than to a superficially more similar nonbird (e.g., bat)], and second, labels promote inferences regarding nonobvious features, such as internal parts, functions, and other nonvisible behaviors (see Gelman 2003 for review). Waxman & Markow (1995) propose that count nouns are "invitations" to children to form categories and look for deeper correlates: Common labels lead even infants to search for commonalities; distinct labels lead children to search for differences. Even 9-month-olds (who are not yet producing speech) are more likely to attend to relevant within-category similarities when they hear two different items labeled with the same word (Balaban & Waxman 1997). Relatedly, Xu (2002) found that 9-month-old infants were more likely to treat two objects as the same kind of thing when they received identical labels and to treat them as two different kinds of things when they received two different labels (see Plunkett et al. 2008 for related findings). Thus, for young children, lexicalization implies that the items named have common properties that extend well beyond those that were previously known.

Lexicalization exerts especially powerful effects with atypical or anomalous category instances (e.g., learning that a penguin is a bird) for which perceptual features might be misleading. By 12 months of age (i.e., when they are first starting to talk), infants use category labels to redirect their attention (Graham et al. 2004). By 20 months of age, infants can use naming as a cue to categorize objects (Nazzi & Gopnik 2001). By 24 months of age, children can use label information to reclassify an atypical instance (e.g., learning that an object that looks like a cat is actually a dog and making appropriate novel inferences accordingly; Jaswal & Markman 2007).

Lexicalization also implies a more stable, enduring, unchanging construal, as compared to other form of expression (Markman & Smith, cited in Markman 1989). For example, children 2–6 years of age are more likely to invent a single lexical item (e.g., "pencil-tree") to express an intrinsic object-property relation (e.g., a tree with pencils growing on the branches) than a momentary object-property relation (e.g., a tree with pencils next to it; Gelman et al. 1989). By 5 years of age, when children hear a person referred to with a novel lexical item (e.g., "carrot-eater"), they judge that this property being expressed is especially stable (e.g., the person eats eat carrots more persistently than does someone who "eats carrots whenever she can"; Gelman & Heyman 1999). Similar naming effects have been found with adults (Reynaert & Gelman 2007, Yamauchi 2005) and even when making judgments about one's own traits or characteristics (Walton & Banaji 2004).

In the realm of social categories, lexicalization has broad implications, in part due to the relevance of such labels to identity and to in- versus out-groups. Labels have powerful effects for children's social categories, both familiar and novel (Diesendruck & haLevi 2006, Patterson & Bigler 2006). Negative labels (e.g., learning disabled) can result in children being stigmatized by peers and to behave in a way that maintains negative peer interactions (Milich et al. 1992). Labeling does not exert a simple, automatic associative effect, but instead interacts with the child's prior causal beliefs. A negative label can have not only negative implications, but also positive ones as well (e.g., someone labeled as hyperactive is viewed as less likely to change but also as correspondingly less likely to be blamed for their behavior; Heyman & Legare 2007). Conversely, a positive label can have negative effects (e.g., someone labeled as gifted may have decreased motivation to persist in the face of failure; see Mueller & Dweck 1998). Similarly, Heyman & Legare (2007) found that when characters were described with labels such as math whiz, children tended to view the character's ability as more innately determined and less likely to change with a change in effort. Furthermore, Cimpian et al. (2007) found that 4-year-old children who were praised with a label (e.g., "You are a good drawer") versus a descriptive phrase (e.g., "You did a good job drawing") showed lower self-evaluations, more sad feelings, and less persistence after making an unsuccessful drawing. Cimpian et al. (2007) report, "When asked what he would do after the teacher's criticism, one child said, 'Cry. I would do it for both of them [both drawings with mistakes]'" (p. 315).

Lexicalization effects are not limited to nouns and extend to other parts of speech. One well-studied example concerns a comparison of English and Korean spatial terms. Whereas English expresses a distinction between containment and support (with the preposition "in" versus "on"), Korean expresses a distinction between loose- and tight-fitting containment (with the verb "nehta" versus "kkita"). Children's earliest language use reflects these distinctions, with English- and Korean-speaking children using spatial terms in crosscutting ways (Bowerman & Choi 2003). A key question is whether these different language patterns have conceptual consequences. It is possible, for ex-

ample, that speakers in both languages have access to both ways of conceptualizing spatial relations, but choose to use only the conventional ones when talking because language is a conventional system (a weaker claim, according to which language influences "thinking for speaking"; Slobin 1996). Contrary to this view, however, English-speaking adults have difficulty solving a task that requires grouping spatial relations in the Korean way (i.e., loose fitting versus tight fitting; McDonough et al. 2003). Interestingly, 5-month-old infants exposed to English successfully categorized both contrasts (Hespos & Spelke 2004). Thus, it appears that children are initially more open to a wider range of conceptual possibilities, which become narrowed as a function of language experience. This finding also suggests that the lexicalization effect is not one of words creating concepts where none had belonged, but rather involves words serving as tools to emphasize particular ways of thinking that were already available (Gelman 2003).

Covert and Implicit Categories

Whorf (1956) introduced the notion of "covert categories" in language—categories that are not explicitly marked but rather inferred based on the contexts of language use. For example, the female proper names in a language (e.g., Sally, Elizabeth, Rachel) form a covert category, because each individually is co-referential with the pronoun "she," even though nothing overtly marks them all as alike. (This is in contrast to the explicit marking of gender in French, for example.) Similarly, verbs that cannot take "un" in English form a covert category (e.g., break, separate, spill) because they are treated as alike and have certain semantic features that bind them together.

In this section, I include not only covert categories in Whorf's sense, but also what I call implicit categories—those cases in which a meaningful category is implied by speakers' language use (including overt morphological markers) but does not receive a common label. For example, I consider gender in French to be an implicit category because items that receive the same gendered pronoun (e.g., table, soup, bank) are not explicitly labeled as instances of a common category (e.g., they are not overtly considered female). Instead, a link among these kinds is implied by means of their participation in a common linguistic frame ("la + X", "une + X"). My interest is whether and how the use of such devices communicates meaningful information to children.

A number of researchers have demonstrated attention to covert or implicit categories among adult speakers of a language (Hill & Mannheim 1992). For example, Boroditsky et al. (2003) found that speakers of a language with grammatical gender (e.g., German, Spanish) implicitly group together same-gendered instances, as assessed by memory tasks, object descriptions, and picture similarity ratings. One thorny question with this work concerns the broader issue of the nature of linguistic influence in these studies. Does language influence thought or instead just direct speakers' attention? For example, can language create concepts that weren't there to begin with? Or does language serve to draw attention and highlight available concepts? An illustration of the issue involves the finding that adult speakers of Chinese and English seem to conceptualize time concepts differently from one another, in ways that correspond to differences in how English and Chinese speakers talk about time (either horizontally or vertically, respectively; Boroditsky 2001). However, these differences can be readily reversed with a simple priming task, thus suggesting that the language effects are not deeply entrenched.

Of interest in the current context is whether covert or implicit categories guide children's reasoning. Lucy & Gaskins (2003) have studied how speakers of different languages notice different aspects of experience and categorize the world differently. Specifically, speakers of Yucatec Mayan use a classifier system in which different-shaped things can receive the same name but with a different classifier attached. In Yucatec, the word for banana, banana leaf, and banana tree are all the same root word,

varying only according to which classifier is used. This pattern contrasts with the English system of naming, for which shape is a fairly good predictor of how a count noun is used (e.g., bananas are all crescent-shaped, trees are all roughly a certain shape, and so on). Interestingly, when asked to group objects on the basis of either shape or substance in a nonlinguistic sorting task (i.e., none of the items are labeled), English speakers are more likely to sort on the basis of shape whereas Yucatec Mayan speakers are more likely to sort on the basis of substance. Surprisingly, however, this differentiation does not appear until somewhere between 7 and 9 years of age, suggesting that meta-linguistic awareness of the language patterns may be required for the effect.

Covert and implicit categorizations in language often are language specific, with some languages including distinctions that are unavailable (or not readily available) in other languages (Danziger 2005, Slobin 2006). One such example is the distinction between the verbs *ser* and *estar* ("to be") in Spanish, which roughly corresponds to a distinction between inherent and accidental properties (Sera 1992). Heyman & Diesendruck (2002) studied how the use of *ser* and *estar* influences judgments of human traits and characteristics (such as "shy") using a task that assessed children's interpretations of story characters. For bilingual children ranging in age from 6 to 10 years, describing a person's psychological characteristics with *ser* led children to treat the traits as relatively more stable than when the same characteristics were described with *estar*. For example, after hearing that Maria is shy (*Maria es/está penosa*), the *estar* form led children to rate the characteristic as less stable, as compared to both the *ser* form (in Spanish) and the "to be" form (in English). One important question is whether children first honor the conceptual distinction between inherent and accidental properties before learning its formal linguistic expression or whether the language distinction precedes and encourages the conceptual distinction. Future studies examining the *ser/estar* distinction in younger children may help address this question.

Another example of language-specific covert categories is found in English, which honors a distinction between count nouns (roughly corresponding to object shape; e.g., a ball, a duck) and mass nouns (roughly corresponding to object substance; e.g., water, rice). English consistently distinguishes these two kinds grammatically, throughout the lexicon, whereas Japanese treats all inanimate nouns as alike. Consistent with these structural differences between English and Japanese, young Japanese-speaking children (2 to 4 years of age) draw the boundary between objects and substances differently from English-speaking children (Imai & Gentner 1997, Yoshida & Smith 2003). Whereas both English-speaking and Japanese-speaking children agree that a complex object (such as a clock) is an individual, and a continuous boundless mass (such as milk) is a substance, they differ in their assessment of simple objects. A molded piece of plastic, for example, would be an object for the English speaker but would be a substance for the Japanese speaker. These findings do not suggest radically different ontologies for speakers of English and Japanese, but rather subtle effects at the margins.

CHILDHOOD ESSENTIALISM AS A CASE STUDY

I turn now to a specific conceptual understanding that develops in childhood, psychological essentialism, to work through in more extended detail how a combination of explicit testimony, implicit cues in language, and child expectations and capacities work together to guide conceptual learning.

I focus on essentialism for two reasons. First, it is a pervasive bias and thus of central interest to understanding concepts (Gelman 2003). Second, competing theoretical accounts regarding the origins of essentialism vary widely. One suggestion is that essentialism is an innate, domain-specific modular capacity (e.g., Atran 1998); another is that particular explicit cultural inputs, especially detailed knowledge of modern science, is required (e.g., Fodor 1998). Still

others have suggested that essentialism derives from assumptions about naming. For example, hearing the word "fish" for a range of distinct animals (clown fish, eels, sharks, minnows) may imply that these varied instances share something other than their outward appearances (Mayr 1991), thereby motivating children to look for underlying shared similarities. Given the nature of these debates, investigation of the input is central.

What is Psychological Essentialism?

Before turning to the issue of input, I first briefly review what is meant by "psychological essentialism." Essentialism is a doctrine that has been discussed by scholars for thousands of years, in fields as diverse as biology, philosophy, linguistics, literary criticism, and psychology (Gelman 2003). It is important to note that there are serious problems with essentialism as a metaphysical doctrine and that the characterization below applies to implicit beliefs about the world, rather than the world itself. It is thus most aptly considered a reasoning heuristic.

Psychological essentialism is the idea that members of certain categories have an underlying, unchanging property or attribute (essence) that determines identity and observable features. Despite outward changes in appearances over the lifetime of an individual (e.g., from infant to adult) and despite outward variation in appearance across members of a category (e.g., from typical to atypical instances), people believe that category members share an immutable feature or substance (essence) that causes category members to be what they are and have the properties that they do. For example, "birds" are outwardly very variable (hummingbird, eagle, toucan . . .) and undergo enormous changes over the life cycle (egg to chick to mature bird), yet many believe that all birds have a bird essence that makes them what they are and directs their development. Although some adults may have specific ideas of what the category essence is (perhaps DNA in the case of birds, for example), in many cases there is only a placeholder—the idea that there is some causal essence without knowing what that might be (Medin & Ortony 1989).

In brief, certain categories are treated as if they have the following: nonobvious properties, inductive potential, stability over transformations, sharp boundaries, innate potential, and causal features (Gelman 2003). Prentice & Miller (2006, p. 129) review some of the extensive evidence for essentialism in children and adults as follows:

> ...a wolf remains a wolf even if it is wearing sheep's clothing (Gelman & Markman 1986, 1987), even if a doctor performs an operation that makes it look like a sheep (Keil 1989), and even if it eats something that turns it into an object resembling a sheep (Rips 1989). Moreover, a wolf will develop wolflike characteristics even if it grows up in a community of sheep (Gelman & Wellman 1991).

Essentialist beliefs have implications for a broad range of concepts, including social categories (Haslam et al. 2000), evolutionary theory (Evans 2000, Kelemen 2004, Mayr 1991, Shtulman 2006), and causal reasoning (Ahn 1998, Rehder 2007). See also Malt (1994), Braisby et al. (1996), and Strevens (2000) for arguments against essentialism, as well as Gelman (2003) and Ahn et al. (2001) for discussion.

Language Cues to Essentialism

The question of developmental origins is complex, but it seems that both biases in the child and cues in the environment are important influences on essentialist reasoning. Children and adults from widely different environments show essentialist effects, including children in impoverished neighborhoods in Brazil (Diesendruck 2001, Sousa et al. 2002), Torguud adults in Western Mongolia (Gil-White 2001), Vezo children in Madagascar (Astuti et al. 2004), Yucatec Mayan children in Mexico (Atran et al. 2001), a Native American community in the United States (Waxman et al. 2007), and middle-class children and adults in the United States (Gelman 2003). The variability in cultural contexts suggests that children have some sort of predisposition to look for essences.

However, environmental cues also undoubtedly convey important information. Cultures vary from one another in the degree to which individuals essentialize, which categories are essentialized (e.g., ethnicity, caste, and occupation are essentialized in some cultures but not in others), and how essentialism is instantiated (e.g., whether essence is believed to be in the DNA, in the blood, or ingested in mother's milk, for example) (Waxman et al. 2007). In Madagascar, for example, the Zafimaniry rarely essentialized human groups (though they did essentialize nonhuman animal kinds; Bloch et al. 2001). They judged, for example, that a person of one ethnic/racial group adopted by members of another group would take on the identity of the adoptive parents—not the birth parents. Even within a culture, degree of essentializing varies. For example, in the Indian caste system, mode of reasoning depends on one's own position in the hierarchy (Mahalingam 1998): Higher-caste individuals in India are more likely to endorse essentialism than are lower-caste individuals, which suggests that essentialism is more often employed when to do so has political benefits. Individual variation also exists, with some individuals more than others consistently endorsing essentialist beliefs (Bastian & Haslam 2006, Gelman et al. 2007).

Recent studies have begun to look at the kinds of testimony and implicit cues in language that parents may use to express essentialism to children. Detailed examination of parent-child conversations during picturebook-reading sessions reveals that parents provide little direct essentialist talk to young children (e.g., rarely if ever discussing internal commonalities, innate properties, or defining characteristics; Gelman et al. 1998). In contrast, however, implicit essentialist talk about categories is pervasive in parents' child-directed speech. Parents frequently use several indirect strategies that imply that categories are stable and have a nonobvious basis. These include labeling (e.g., this is a bird; "That is a lady sewing a dress, right?"), appearance-reality statements (e.g., "Well, that looks like a kangaroo but it's called an aardvark"), contrasting distinct categories (e.g., "Do you think that's more of a girl job or a boy job?"), and responding approvingly to essentialist statements that children produce. For example, in one study of gender-related talk in a book-reading context (Gelman et al. 2004), 64% of mothers contrasted distinct gender categories (male and female) at least once, and 89% of mothers engaged in gender labeling at least once, in conversations with children 2 to 6 years of age.

Furthermore, one of the most interesting and pervasive implicit strategies that parents use is to make a broad statement about the category as a whole (e.g., "Bats live in caves"; "Girls play with dolls"), thereby implying that the category (e.g., bats, girls) can be considered as a group. These general statements are known as generics (Carlson & Pelletier 1995). Whereas nongeneric utterances refer to particular members of a kind (e.g., one bird, some birds), generics refer to a kind construed more broadly (birds in general). Generic noun phrases are expressed in English with multiple formal devices, including bare plurals (e.g., "Bats live in caves"), indefinite singulars (e.g., "A hammer is a tool"), and definite singulars (e.g., "The elephant is found in Africa and Asia"). All these expressions have in common a conceptual basis: They refer to a kind as a whole.

Generics embody several essentialist assumptions. Bohan (1993), discussing essentialist views of gender, noted that essentialism characterizes a category (such as "women") as natural, timeless, and universal, thereby failing to acknowledge social, historical, or political contexts that might lead to variation within the category. Generics likewise characterize a category as universal and abstract away from any particular or situated context. Whereas specific nouns can refer to particular points in time or space ("My cat caught a mouse"; "Those ballet dancers are graceful"), generics cannot. Cats catch mice; ballet dancers are girls—these statements characterize a category as timeless, universal, and devoid of context.

In order for generic noun phrases to be a plausible mechanism for transmitting essentialism, they must be available in the input to young children, they must be used in ways that map onto relevant conceptual distinctions (distinguishing essentialized kinds from other categories), and they must be appropriately understood by young children. In addition to being frequent in parental speech to children in diverse cultural and linguistic contexts (United States, China, Peru; Gelman & Tardif 1998), generic noun phrases are produced by children exposed to minimal linguistic input (deaf children not exposed to sign language; Goldin-Meadow et al. 2005), understood appropriately by children (Hollander et al. 2002), and stored by children in long-term memory (Gelman & Raman 2007). Children understand the semantic implications of generics as kind-referring (Cimpian & Markman 2008, Gelman & Raman 2003) and as extending beyond current context (Gelman & Bloom 2007). These component pieces all suggest that generics are available in the input, semantically important and early acquired, and have the potential to influence children's conceptual representations.

At times, explicit and implicit messages about categories conflict with one another, perhaps because speakers are more consciously aware of the messages they present explicitly than those they present implicitly. For example, in a study of parental input regarding gender categories (Gelman et al. 2004), mothers were more forthcoming in implicit essentializing messages (e.g., generics, labeling, gender contrasts) than in their explicit stereotyping and essentializing statements. Similarly, contexts that provoked explicit expressions of gender equality (e.g., a picture of a female firefighter elicited more egalitarian talk than a picture of a male firefighter) were also more likely to result in an upsurge in implicit focus on gender (e.g., the female firefighter elicited more generics, labeling, and contrasts involving gender than the male firefighter). It is ironic that attempts to counter children's stereotypes by means of egalitarian examples have the unintended consequence of heightening parents' attention to gender as a dimension on which to classify people.

This distinction between implicit and explicit expressive devices in language is consistent with other research demonstrating a distinction between explicit and implicit attitudes, in both adults (Lemm & Banaji 1999) and children (Baron & Banaji 2006). Explicit stereotypes and attitudes are typically assessed by verbal self-report measures (e.g., "Do you agree that men and women ought to have equal opportunities for employment?"), whereas implicit stereotypes and attitudes can be assessed by means of response speed on a simple judgment task (e.g., Greenwald & Banaji 1995). Implicit attitudes can differ from explicit attitudes in magnitude and valence (Lemm & Banaji 1999). For example, participants' explicit attitudes toward women in leadership roles (e.g., managers, politicians) were generally unrelated to their implicit attitudes. Lemm & Banaji (1999) suggest that implicit attitudes and beliefs are endorsed at an unconscious level and are only tangentially related to conscious judgments. An important question for the future is the extent to which explicit and implicit essentialist language influences children's judgments and inferences.

EVIDENCE FOR EARLY AND SELECTIVE SENSITIVITY TO INPUT FROM OTHERS

Although I have emphasized that knowledgeable others provide important information to children, a crucial point is that this information by itself does not provide all the answers. First, children need to be able to take in and interpret the evidence and information that others supply. Meltzoff (1995) outlines how young children (even babies) are exquisitely prepared to imitate other humans (though not to imitate machines) and thereby to gain new information. Similarly, Tomasello et al. (1993) have demonstrated a uniquely human capacity, present in early childhood, to learn by imitation (i.e., precisely copying the means by which an action is carried out) rather than emulation (i.e., achiev-

ing the same ends, but by different means). These important lines of research make clear that learning by observation requires special capacities on the part of the learner.

Furthermore, children must be able to evaluate the cues they receive—to believe some of the information provided, but to show appropriate skepticism as well (Harris & Koenig 2006). Both credulity and skepticism are adaptive. Credulity is adaptive in that it allows children to learn new things. Children constantly face new technology (airplanes fly, despite what common sense tells us), new cultural belief systems (religious, historical), etc. Credulity can also be considered having an open mind. As the bumper sticker goes, "Minds are like parachutes: They only function when open." On the other hand, skepticism is adaptive, given the many ways in which adult input misleads, intentionally or not, by means of deception, fiction, metaphor, and just plain old mistakes (more on fiction in the next section). A capacity for skepticism shields children from misleading input (Koenig et al. 2004). The trick is to get the right balance, to deploy both credulity and skepticism in the right contexts. I illustrate this point first in the realm of word learning, and I then extend it to conceptual input more broadly.

Word Learning and the Division of Linguistic Labor

A seemingly straightforward, paradigmatic example of children learning from parental input is the process of word learning: A child requires input from others in order to acquire a conventional label, such as "dog." As noted above, children have an early openness to the labels of others, even when the labels compete with children's perceptual groupings. This deference to cultural experts reflects a "division of linguistic labor" (Putnam 1975). An intriguing extension of the idea that children seek adult authority in naming is that concepts need not be wholly stored in the mind of an individual child, but can be placeholders with pointers to others in the community. Recently, several researchers have proposed that children may be quite sensitive to a division of labor—both linguistic and cognitive—such that some concepts are merely placeholders that point to knowledge that is accessible only to experts (Lutz & Keil 2002, Markman & Jaswal 2003). Putnam (1975) illustrates by noting that he does not know anything about how elms and beeches differ—he only knows that they do differ, and the knowledge of precisely how they differ (i.e., the meanings of "elm" and "beech") is stored in the minds of experts. This fundamental principle seems in place at the start of word learning (Graham et al. 2004).

An example of this distinction between possessing conceptual knowledge and having a conceptual placeholder can be found in a study by Coley et al. (1999), who examined biological categories in U.S. college students and the Itzaj Maya of Guatemala. U.S. college students showed a discrepancy between their knowledge and expectations: They had strong expectations that a middle taxonomic level [which Coley et al. (1999) call the generic-species level, not to be confused with the use of the word generic in the previous section; here, generic is used in the biological Linnaean sense of genus] would be most informative when making inductive inferences about novel properties—yet had surprisingly little knowledge about the biological categories at this level. (Interestingly, the Itzaj Maya had a much more detailed knowledge base about these categories and correspondingly no evidence for a distinction between knowledge and expectations.) At first this result may seem mysterious: How could people know that the generic-species level is especially informative, without knowing much about these categories? However, this pattern of results makes sense when one considers the naming system in these taxonomies: Generic-species categories are named with a single label (e.g., squirrel, trout, oak). Levels below that (in English and universally) are typically labeled as subtypes, with compound names (e.g., "gray squirrel," "rainbow trout," "red oak"; Berlin et al. 1973). Adults (and young children; Gelman et al. 1989) interpret compound nouns as reflecting subor-

dination in a hierarchy. The category level that is lexicalized receives privileged status:

> [L]abels may "stake out" a category, despite lack of specific knowledge about members of that category.... This may include the assumptions that the category will be coherent, category members will share many underlying properties beyond what meets the eye, and that in effect, there is "where the conceptual action is." In other words, labels may signal categories that are believed to embody an essence ... (Coley et al. 1999, p. 214).

We can therefore think of labels as embodying expert knowledge, which experts then transmit to novices. This whole system works only if the novices are willing to accept the wisdom of the experts.

Both adults and children defer to experts on experimental tasks involving naming (Kalish 1998, Malt 1990). Children seem to accept even surprising or counterintuitive labels (Gelman & Coley 1990, Gelman & Markman 1986, Graham et al. 2004, Jaswal & Markman 2007). Mervis et al. (2003) refer to this as the authority principle. By 20 months of age, the child in their study (Ari) accepted new labels even for items that already had a name. For example, when Ari's father said, "That birdie's a cardinal," Ari accepted that it was a type of bird (p. 265).

Some have proposed that the learning that goes on in such cases is merely a passive incorporation of the input: automatic, associative, and unreflective (Smith et al. 1996). For example, Sloutsky & Fisher (2004) proposed that words are at first associated with perceptual features in the input. On this view, the lexicalization effects reviewed above are automatic consequences of the fact that the label per se serves as an automatic cue (to attention or to judgments of similarity) that directly influences children's judgments. The word becomes in effect just another feature of the object.

Yet even the case of mapping a word to a referent is incomplete without considering children's evaluation and judgment of the situation. Notably, there are key contexts in which the child hears a word in the direct presence of its referent but fails to learn it: when the speaker is looking elsewhere from where the child is looking (Baldwin 1991); when the speaker has proven to be unreliable in prior naming instances (Koenig et al. 2004) or uncertain during the naming act (Sabbagh & Baldwin 2001); or when the speaker has an unreliable naming history and is distracted (Jaswal & Malone 2007).

Tomasello & Akhtar (2000, p. 181) list several ways in which children's word learning reflects their assumptions about the intentions of the speaker and not simply automatic, associative linking of a auditory input with a visual percept. By 24 months of age, children override spatiotemporal contiguity and perceptual salience in several respects when learning words: (*a*) They assume that words refer to intentional actions even if the target novel word is immediately followed by an accidental action and only later followed by an intentional action (see also Diesendruck et al. 2004 for related findings). (*b*) They determine which aspect of the context is novel for the (adult) speaker, and use that information to determine the referent of a word—even when what is novel for the speaker differs from what is novel for the child. (*c*) They learn new action words for actions that they anticipate an adult will do, even when the adult has not actually performed the action. (*d*) They use adult gaze direction rather than perceptual salience to determine reference.

Jaswal (2004) conducted a compelling series of studies that demonstrates this point. In this work, 3- and 4-year-old children were shown anomalous category instances (a cat that looked like a dog) and were asked to make inferences about various properties (e.g., would it drink milk or eat bones?). When the pictures were unlabeled, the children nearly always based their inferences on perceptual similarity (e.g., the cat-like dog would drink milk), whereas when the pictures were labeled, children were less likely to base their inferences on perceptual similarity (e.g., they less often judged that the cat-like dog would drink milk). Importantly, however, children were even less likely to use similarity when the experimenter prefaced the label with an additional phrase that clarified that the label was intentional and not merely a slip of the tongue ("You're not going to believe this, but this is actually a dog"). Even a more subtle indicator that the label was intended (modifying the label) was sufficient to encourage children to use the label the majority of the time. As Jaswal (2004) notes, children used their assessment of the speaker's communicative intent in order to decide whether to use the label. The power of labels comes from their intentional use, not from simple association with an object.

The evidence thus argues that labels yield their effects by activating other assumptions, such as a belief that items sharing a label belong to a common natural kind (Gelman 2003). When children have reasons to doubt the sincerity, attention, or capability of the speaker, then labels no longer have their effect.

Skepticism and Credulity Regarding Adult Testimony

The evaluative stance we see on the part of children occurs not just with word learning, but also with learning from testimony more generally. Studies show that children are highly sensitive to the intentions of an adult speaker in deciding whether to trust his or her assertions. Koenig & Harris (2005) review a developmental sequence, starting at about 16–18 months, when infants first show evidence of distinguishing between true and false statements and rejecting false claims, and gradually displaying more sophisticated selective mistrust of others, with developmental changes through the preschool years.

Harris & Koenig (2006) emphasize the "constructive role" children play in "reworking and organizing the various pieces of testimony that they receive." In other words, children show healthy skepticism of expert input. By 4 years of age, children are skeptical of statements made by a speaker who previously said untrue things (Clément et al. 2004)—an ability all the more remarkable when one considers how difficult it is for children and adults to monitor the source of a piece of information (Lindsay et al. 1991). They are less likely to accept functional information provided by a speaker who was inaccurate at labeling in the past (Koenig & Harris 2005a). Kushner et al. (2008) find that 3- and 4-year-old children also use information about a speaker's knowledge and expertise in a causal learning task. They discriminate between informative and uninformative sources of information and further they distinguish between knowledge possession and knowledge use (in other words, it is not enough for a person to be knowledgeable; he or she must also take effective steps to use that knowledge). Thus, when choosing among causal factors, preschool children know that a knowledgeable but blind-folded person will be no more informative than an unknowledgeable person. Preschool children (4–5 years) also use a speaker's motive to decide whether their self-descriptions are truthful (Gee & Heyman 2007).

Another important way in which children play an active role in this process is by eliciting testimony by means of questions (Chouinard 2007). Chouinard posits that children are more receptive to testimony that they themselves elicit and that children's questions serve as a mechanism to further cognitive development. In natural language conversations as well as in more controlled laboratory contexts, Chouinard (2007) finds that preschool children ask many information-seeking questions from others (more than one per minute), that even preverbal infants seek such information nonverbally by one year of age, that they typically obtain the information they seek, that they are persistent in seeking the information they are looking for, and that they use the responses they get in order to solve problems at hand (e.g., to figure out what toy is hidden in a closed box). Altogether, then, these studies demonstrate that children use an information-requesting mechanism to learn about the world (Chouinard 2007). This mechanism includes a variety of information-recruiting methods, particularly including verbal questions, but also gestures, vocalizations, etc., that elicit information from others. Frazier et al. (2008) furthermore find that children expect informative responses to their questions. Thus, when asking a causal question, children 2 to 4 years of age expect causal answers and are more likely to repeat their question or provide their own explanation when they do not receive a causal response from the adult.

CONCLUSIONS

It is a truism that children learn from those around them. Yet what does this mean? On the one hand, children are not solitary learners, independently figuring out the world from first principles, reinventing the proverbial wheel with each new generation. But on the other hand, neither are children passive sponges, absorbing whatever they see and hear. Along with the importance of the words and testimony of others is the importance of an evaluative child, judging and assessing the nature and relevance of the information coming in. Children's early sensitivity to this information is a testament to the importance of the child's social/psychological understandings, pragmatic and linguistic skills, and theory-building capacities (Carey et al. 2008, Gergely et al. 2007, Gopnik & Meltzoff 1997). The observation that children are richly informed by the testimony and evidence of others also does not mean that there are no innate constraints. Innate capacities and environmental evidence work together in development.

Cashing out these rather broad generalizations requires a serious engagement with the evidence at hand, in terms of both the cues available to the child and the child's capacity to make sense of those cues. At this point, much is still unknown. One open question is the relative power of social information (testimony) versus evidence from children's own observations. Although one might expect children to be deep-down empiricists, believing most powerfully in what they can see, this is not the case. Testimony at times effectively overrides children's own perceptions (Jaswal & Markman 2007, Lee et al. 2002). Another question concerns the developmental patterns. Although some find that skepticism about the testimony of others increases with age (children from ages 6 to 11 years become increasingly skeptical of another's self-report claims; Heyman et al. 2007), others find increasing credulity with age (e.g., Bering & Parker 2006, Shtulman & Carey 2007). In any case, there is unlikely to be a stage-like progression, as children as young as 3 years of age show some skepticism (reviewed above), whereas children 7 years of age and older show some credulity. Even adults come to believe in things formerly deemed impossible [such as the four-minute mile or the possibility of a human voice emerging from a small box (my grandfather's description of his first encounter with a radio)].

These findings also pose a challenge regarding the nature of children's naïve theories (of physics, biology, and psychology). Wellman & Gelman (1998) proposed that these theories entail deep ontological commitments. Yet children can show surprising credulity. Examples of nonskeptical endorsement of testimony include children's acceptance of a flying, candy-eating witch (Woolley et al. 2004), a glass-breaking ghost (Lee et al. 2002), an invisible princess (Bering & Parker 2006), magical transformations (deLoache et al. 1997, Subbotsky 2001), instant duplications (Hood & Bloom 2008), and monsters (Harris et al. 1991). Why don't such inconsistencies bother children? How far can their theoretical commitments be pushed? Schulz et al. (2007) provide evidence that by preschool age, children's beliefs are malleable but not infinitely flexible.

Finally, perhaps the most challenging question of all is how children know what to believe when. Simple strategies are ruled out: As reviewed above, children neither simply incorporate all input nor simply ignore anything they can't see with their own eyes. I turn to this below by considering (a) how children reason about fiction, deception, and pretense, and (b) the coexistence of competing conceptual systems.

Fiction, Deception, and Pretense: Challenges for Learning

The vast puzzle of what counts as evidence to children's developing theories is compli-cated by the fact that even children encounter fiction, lies, and pretense. Stories, TV, and movies are particularly messy, seamlessly weaving together fictional and real components (Gerrig 1993, Skolnick & Bloom 2006). Pretense likewise is ubiquitous in adults' interactions with children, and is potentially confusing (e.g., when a parent talks into a banana, treating it as a telephone; Lillard & Witherinton 2004). Natural language, too, can be misleading to young children as they learn about fundamental ontological distinctions (e.g., living versus nonliving, psychological versus nonpsychological). Metaphors—including unintended metaphors—are rampant in everyday talk (Lakoff 1987). We say that computers, cars, and telephones "think" or "want"; that deficits, crystals, and feelings "grow"; etc. We personify computers, ships, and cars with proper names or animate pronouns (Hall et al. 2004).

Nonetheless, children are not deeply confused about the ontological status of unclear items. By at least 3 years of age, children readily distinguish reality from fantasy (Taylor 1999, Woolley & Wellman 1990), as well as living things from highly similar yet distinct contrast cases (R. Gelman et al. 1995, Gelman & Opfer 2002, Jipson & Gelman 2007). They are not confused about pretense items (Kavanaugh & Harris 1994, Nishida & Lillard 2007). Clearly, children are grappling with the information provided in fictional contexts and are doing the hard work of attempting to sort the real wheat from the fictional chaff.

In tackling this problem, children seem to use all the interpretive tools at their disposal. This likely includes (though is not limited to) theory-of-mind reasoning (Wellman 1990), pragmatic inferences (Siegal & Surian 2004), sensitivity to linguistic cues regarding certainty (Matsui et al. 2006), attention to modality (face-to-face interactions versus videos; Kuhl 2007, Troseth & DeLoache 1998), narrative cues to reality (Woolley & Cox 2007), discourse cues (Harris et al. 2006), and naïve theories that enable children to distinguish plausible from implausible causal processes (Jipson & Callanan 2003, Schulz et al. 2007, Wellman & Gelman

1998). These results suggest that children's current belief systems place constraints on how they incorporate new concepts. The nature of these constraints is currently largely unknown and will be fruitful to address in future research.

Coexistence of Conceptual Systems

How does development proceed when the child is exposed to seemingly incompatible conceptual systems? At the same time that children construct commonsense theories of the natural world that correspond, roughly, to scientific principles in the biological, physical, and psychological domains (Wellman & Gelman 1998), they are also encountering nonrational beliefs concerning the supernatural world, including religion and magic. In part, this is because adults encourage beliefs that they themselves don't share (e.g., Tooth Fairy, Santa Claus), but it is also because nonrational beliefs (astrology luck, God's will, ghosts) are abundant in adult thought (Hood 2008).

There is now growing evidence that rational and irrational modes of thought coexist in human reasoning: An individual can possess both rational (scientific) and nonrational modes of explanation without viewing them as competing or contradictory (Nemeroff & Rozin 1989, Raman & Winer 2002, Rosengren et al. 2000). One controversial issue is whether children truly believe in supernatural events or instead only seem to endorse such beliefs (Subbotsky 2001, Taylor 1999, Woolley 1997). For example, children may adopt a play mode when answering questions about fantasy elements, or they may enjoy acting as if a fantastical event were possible. On the other hand, both children and adults seem genuinely convinced by fantasies or seemingly magical spells (e.g., in which an inanimate entity is made to come alive), making real-life approach or avoidance decisions on the basis of these nonrational modes of thought (Edman & Kameoka 1997, Harris et al. 1991, Phelps & Woolley 1994). Important questions for the future include how genuine such convictions are and in what contexts they emerge.

Illness is a realm that may be especially susceptible to nonrational explanations, given the often-obscure (or even unknown) causes of illnesses, the highly charged emotional contexts in which people reason about illness, the lack of personal control over many illness outcomes, and the multiple belief systems corresponding to historical and cultural variability in the knowledge base (Siegal & Peterson 1999). For example, in a study of illness concepts in South Africa, where HIV infection rates are very high, both children and adults endorse both biological and supernatural explanations for AIDS and other illness (Legare & Gelman 2008). In this set of studies, although biological causes were favored overall and endorsed uniformly in all age groups, more than half of the participants provided both biological and supernatural explanations at least once. Furthermore, increases with age in understanding the hidden nature of disease did not correspond to decreases in the endorsement of supernatural explanations. Thus, endorsement of witchcraft does not reflect an absence of accurate biological explanations.

Another example of the integrated nature of potentially competing belief systems can be found in religious and scientific beliefs regarding species origins (e.g., creationism; evolution). An important point here is that the persistence of creationist beliefs and rejection or misinterpretation of evolutionary theory derives not just from competing forms of testimony or socialization, but also from cognitive biases on the part of children and adults that compete with the information they are hearing from others (Evans 2000, Gelman 2003, Kelemen 2004, Mayr 1991, Shtulman 2006).

Some Open Questions

I end by sketching out a few of the many issues that remain open for future research. Fuller characterizations of the input are certainly needed. For example, children's own word productions have been used as indirect evidence regarding what words children hear (Smith 2000), but in future research it will be important to discover how tightly children's productions correspond to the input. Studies of testimony as well at times make assumptions about the input language (Harris et al. 2006) and would be enriched by a closer examination of what children actually hear. The level of analysis may at time require a powerful microscope, including close analysis of linguistic cues (Gelman et al. 1998) and of perceptual cues (Yoshida & Smith 2008). Microgenetic methods also offer great potential for examining how input from others influences conceptual change (Amsterlaw & Wellman 2006, Opfer & Siegler 2004, Siegler & Crowley 1991). Furthermore, just because a modification is found in the input, this does not necessarily mean that it is used by the child. So, studies of input need to be paired with studies of uptake.

This approach raises many new questions. To what extent are social or cultural cues available to other species? When in development do children first show sensitivity to the various social cues outlined in this review? How does the relationship of children to expertise change with age and, especially, as they enter and proceed in formal schooling? What counts as a reliable source at different points in development? To what extent do those interacting with children modify their language and interactional style to emphasize or support conceptual learning? And to the extent that such modifications are made, to what extent do they influence the learning process? Although there is a broad literature on the effects or noneffects of child-directed speech on language learning, much less is known about the nature and effects of child-directed speech on concepts or child-directed modifications in action (Brand et al. 2002).

Finally, what are the implications of this research for a portrait of human concepts? The research reviewed in this article argues strongly against the idea that children's concepts can be characterized as wholly mechanistic or as wholly perceptually based. Much of what children learn comes from others, and in order to make sense of this information, a complex array of psychological, theory-based, linguistic, and interpretive understandings are required (Bloom 2000).

DISCLOSURE STATEMENT

The author is not aware of any biases that might be perceived as affecting the objectivity of this review.

ACKNOWLEDGMENTS

Preparation of this review was supported by NICHD grant HD36043 and a James McKeen Cattell Fellowship.

LITERATURE CITED

Ahn W. 1998. The role of causal status in determining feature centrality. *Cognition* 69:135–78

Ahn W, Kalish C, Gelman SA, Medin DL, Luhmann C, et al. 2001. Why essences are essential in the psychology of concepts. *Cognition* 82:59–69

Amsterlaw J, Wellman HM. 2006. Theories of mind in transition: a microgenetic study of the development of false belief understanding. *J. Cogn. Dev.* 7:139–72

Astuti R, Solomon GEA, Carey S. 2004. Constraints on conceptual development. *Monogr. Soc. Res. Child Dev.* Ser. 277, Vol. 69, No. 3

Atran S. 1998. Folk biology and the anthropology of science: cognitive universals and cultural particulars. *Behav. Brain Sci.* 21:547–609

Atran S, Medin D, Lynch E, Vapnarsky V, Ucan Ek' U, Sousa P. 2001. Folkbiology doesn't come from folkpsychology: evidence from Yukatek Maya in cross-cultural perspective. *J. Cogn. Cult.* 1:3–42

Balaban MT, Waxman SR. 1997. Do words facilitate object categorization in 9-month-old infants? *J. Exp. Child Psychol.* 64:3–26

Baldwin DA. 1991. Infants' contribution to the achievement of joint reference. *Child Dev.* 62:875–90

Baldwin DA. 2000. Interpersonal understanding fuels knowledge acquisition. *Curr. Dir. Psychol. Sci.* 9:40–45

Baron AS, Banaji MR. 2006. The development of implicit attitudes: evidence of race evaluations from ages 6 and 10 and adulthood. *Psychol. Sci.* 17:53–58

Baron-Cohen S, Tager-Flusberg H, Cohen DJ, eds. 1993. *Understanding Other Minds: Perspectives from Autism.* New York: Oxford Univ. Press

Bastian B, Haslam N. 2006. Psychological essentialism and stereotype endorsement. *J. Exp. Soc. Psychol.* 42:228–35

Bering JM. 2006. The folk psychology of souls. *Behav. Brain Sci.* 29:453–62

Bering JM, Parker BD. 2006. Children's attributions of intentions to an invisible agent. *Dev. Psychol.* 42:253–62

Berlin B, Breedlove D, Raven P. 1973. General principles of classification and nomenclature in folk biology. *Am. Anthropol.* 74:214–42

Bigler RS, Spears Brown C, Markell M. 2001. When groups are not created equal: effects of group status on the formation of intergroup attitudes in children. *Child Dev.* 72:1151–62

Bloch M, Solomon GEA, Carey S. 2001. Zafimaniry: an understanding of what is passed on from parents to children. A cross-cultural investigation. *J. Cogn. Cult.* 1:43–68

Bloom P. 2000. *How Children Learn the Meanings of Words.* Cambridge, MA: MIT Press

Bohan JS. 1993. Regarding gender: essentialism, constructionism, and feminist psychology. *Psychol. Women Q.* 17:5–21

Boroditsky L. 2001. Does language shape thought? Mandarin and English speakers' conceptions of time. *Cogn. Psychol.* 43:1–22

Boroditsky L, Schmidt LA, Phillips W. 2003. Sex, syntax and semantics. In *Language in Mind: Advances in the Study of Language and Thought*, ed. D Gentner, S Goldin-Meadow, pp. 61–79. Cambridge, MA: MIT Press

Bowerman M, Choi S. 2003. Space under construction: language-specific spatial categorization in first language acquisition. In *Language in Mind: Advances in the Study of Language and Thought*, ed. D Gentner, S Goldin-Meadow, pp. 389–427. Cambridge, MA: MIT Press

Boyer P. 2003. Religious thought and behaviour as by-products of brain function. *Trends Cogn. Sci.* 7:119–24

Braisby N, Franks B, Hampton J. 1996. Essentialism, word use, and concepts. *Cognition* 59:247–74

Brand RJ, Baldwin DA, Ashburn LA. 2002. Evidence for "motionese": modifications in mothers' infant-directed action. *Dev. Sci.* 5:72–83

Bruner JS. 1973. *Beyond the Information Given.* New York: Norton

Callanan MA. 2006. Cognitive development, culture, and conversation: comments on Harris and Koenig's "Truth in Testimony: How Children Learn about Science and Religion." *Child Dev.* 77:525–30

Carey S. 1985. *Conceptual Change in Childhood.* Cambridge, MA: MIT Press

Carey S. 2008. *The Origin of Concepts.* New York: Oxford Univ. Press. In press

Carlson GN, Pelletier FJ, eds. 1995. *The Generic Book.* Chicago: Univ. Chicago Press

Chouinard MM. 2007. Children's questions: a mechanism for cognitive development. *Monogr. Soc. Res. Child Dev.* 72(1):vii–ix, 1–112; discussion 113–26

Cimpian A, Arce HC, Markman EM, Dweck CS. 2007. Subtle linguistic cues affect children's motivation. *Psychol. Sci.* 18:314–16

Cimpian A, Markman EM. 2008. Preschool children's use of cues to generic meaning. *Cognition* 107:19–53

Clément F, Koenig M, Harris P. 2004. The ontogenesis of trust. *Mind Language* 19:360–79

Cohen LB, Cashon Cara H. 2006. Infant cognition. In *Handbook of Child Psychology: Volume 2, Cognition, Perception, and Language*, ed. D Kuhn, RS Siegler, W Damon, RM Lerner, pp. 214–51. Hoboken, NJ: Wiley. 6th ed.

Coley JD, Medin DL, Proffitt JB, Lynch E, Atran S. 1999. Inductive reasoning in folkbiological thought. In *Folkbiology*, ed. DL Medin, S Atran, pp. 205–32. Cambridge, MA: MIT Press

Crowley K, Callanan MA, Tenenbaum HR, Allen E. 2001. Parents explain more often to boys than to girls during shared scientific thinking. *Psychol. Sci.* 12:258–61

Danziger E. 2005. The eye of the beholder: how linguistic categorization affects "natural" experience. In *Complexities: Beyond Nature and Nurture*, ed. S McKinnon, S Silverman, pp. 64–80. Chicago: Univ. Chicago Press

DeLoache JS, Miller KF, Rosengren KS. 1997. The credible shrinking room: very young children's performance with symbolic and nonsymbolic relations. *Psychol. Sci.* 8:308–13

Diesendruck G. 2001. Essentialism in Brazilian children's extensions of animal names. *Dev. Psychol.* 37:49–60

Diesendruck G, haLevi H. 2006. The role of language, appearance, and culture in children's social category-based induction. *Child Dev.* 77:539–53

Diesendruck G, Markson L, Akhtar N, Reudor A. 2004. Two-year-olds' sensitivity to speakers' intent: an alternative account of Samuelson and Smith. *Dev. Sci.* 7:33–41

Dunham Y, Baron AS, Banaji MR. 2006. From American city to Japanese village: a cross-cultural investigation of implicit race attitudes. *Child Dev.* 77:1268–81

Edman JL, Kameoka VA. 1997. Cultural differences in illness schemas: an analysis of Filipino and American illness attributions. *J. Cross-Cult. Psychol.* 28:252–65

Evans EM. 2000. Beyond Scopes: why creationism is here to stay. In *Imagining the Impossible*, ed. KS Rosengren, CN Johnson, PL Harris, pp. 305–33. New York: Cambridge Univ. Press

Fodor J. 1998. *Concepts: Where Cognitive Science Went Wrong*. London: Oxford Univ. Press

Frazier B, Gelman SA, Wellman HM. 2008. Preschoolers' search for explanatory information within adult-child conversation. Unpubl. manuscr.

Ganea PA, Shutts K, Spelke ES, DeLoache JS. 2007. Thinking of things unseen: infants' use of language to update mental representations. *Psychol. Sci.* 18:734–39

Gee CL, Heyman GD. 2007. Children's evaluation of other people's self-descriptions. *Soc. Dev.* 16:800–18

Gelman R, Durgin F, Kaufman L. 1995. Distinguishing between animates and inanimates: not by motion alone. In *Causal Cognition: A Multidisciplinary Debate*, ed. D Sperber, D Premack, AJ Premack, pp. 150–84. Oxford, UK: Clarendon

Gelman R, Williams EM. 1998. Enabling constraints for cognitive development and learning: domain specificity and epigenesis. In *Handbook of Child Psychology: Volume 2. Cognition, Perception, and Language*, ed. W Damon, pp. 575–630. Hoboken, NJ: Wiley

Gelman SA. 1996. Concepts and theories. In *Perceptual and Cognitive Development*, ed. R Gelman, TK Au, pp. 117–50. San Diego, CA: Academic

Gelman SA. 2003. *The Essential Child: Origins of Essentialism in Everyday Thought*. New York: Oxford Univ. Press

Gelman SA, Bloom P. 2007. Developmental changes in the understanding of generics. *Cognition* 105:166–83

Gelman SA, Coley JD. 1990. The importance of knowing a dodo is a bird: categories and inferences in 2-year-old children. *Dev. Psychol.* 26:796–804

Gelman SA, Coley JD, Rosengren K, Hartman E, Pappas T. 1998. Beyond labeling: the role of parental input in the acquisition of richly-structured categories. *Monogr. Soc. Res. Child Dev.* Ser. 253, No. 1

Gelman SA, Heyman GD. 1999. Carrot-eaters and creature-believers: the effects of lexicalization on children's inferences about social categories. *Psychol. Sci.* 10:489–93

Gelman SA, Heyman GD, Legare CH. 2007. Developmental changes in the coherence of essentialist beliefs about psychological characteristics. *Child Dev.* 78:757–74

Gelman SA, Markman EM. 1986. Categories and induction in young children. *Cognition* 23:183–209

Gelman SA, Markman EM. 1987. Young children's inductions from natural kinds: the role of categories and appearances. *Child Dev.* 58:1532–41

Gelman SA, Opfer JE. 2002. Development of the animate-inanimate distinction. In *Blackwell Handbook of Childhood Cognitive Development*, ed. U Goswami, pp. 151–66. Malden, MA: Blackwell

Gelman SA, Raman L. 2003. Preschool children use linguistic form class and pragmatic cues to interpret generics. *Child Dev.* 74:308–25

Gelman SA, Raman L. 2007. This cat has nine lives? Children's memory for genericity in language. *Dev. Psychol.* 43:1256–68

Gelman SA, Tardif TZ. 1998. Generic noun phrases in English and Mandarin: an examination of child-directed speech. *Cognition* 66:215–48

Gelman SA, Taylor MG, Nguyen SP. 2004. Mother-child conversations about gender. *Monogr. Soc. Res. Child Dev.* Ser. 275, Vol. 69, No. 1

Gelman SA, Wellman HM. 1991. Insides and essences: early understandings of the nonobvious. *Cognition* 38:213–44

Gelman SA, Wilcox SA, Clark EV. 1989. Conceptual and linguistic hierarchies in young children. *Cogn. Dev.* 4:309–26

Gergely G, Egyed K, Király I. 2007. On pedagogy. *Dev. Sci.* 10:139–46

Gerrig RJ. 1993. *Experiencing Narrative Worlds: On the Psychological Activities of Reading*. New Haven, CT: Yale Univ. Press

Gil-White FJ. 2001. Are ethnic groups biological "species" to the human brain? *Curr. Anthropol.* 42:515–54

Giménez M, Harris PL. 2002. Understanding constraints on inheritance: evidence for biological thinking in early childhood. *Br. J. Dev. Psychol.* 20:307–24

Ginsburg HP, Opper S. 1969. *Piaget's Theory of Intellectual Development*. Englewood Cliffs, NJ: Prentice-Hall

Gleitman L, Papafragou A. 2005. Language and thought. In *The Cambridge Handbook of Thinking and Reasoning*, ed. KJ Holyoak, RG Morrison, pp. 633–61. New York: Cambridge Univ. Press

Goldin-Meadow A. 2003. *The Resilience of Language: What Gesture Creation in Deaf Children Can Tell Us About How All Children Learn Language*. New York: Psychol. Press

Goldin-Meadow S, Gelman SA, Mylander C. 2005. Expressing generic concepts with and without a language model. *Cognition* 96:109–26

Gopnik A, Meltzoff N. 1997. *Words, Thoughts, and Theories*. Cambridge, MA: MIT Press

Gopnik A, Glymour C, Sobel DM, Schulz LE, Kushnir T, Danks DA. 2004. Theory of causal learning in children: causal maps and Bayes nets. *Psychol. Rev.* 111:3–32

Gottfried GM, Gelman SA, Schultz J. 1999. Children's understanding of the brain: from early essentialism to biological theory. *Cogn. Dev.* 14:147–74

Gottfried GM, Jow EE. 2003. "I just talk with my heart": the mind-body problem, linguistic input, and the acquisition of folk psychological beliefs. *Cogn. Dev.* 18:79–90

Graham SA, Kilbreath CS, Welder AN. 2004. Thirteen-month-olds rely on shared labels and shape similarity for inductive inferences. *Child Dev.* 75:409–42

Greenwald AG, Banaji MR. 1995. Implicit social cognition: attitudes, self-esteem, and stereotypes. *Psychol. Rev.* 102:4–27

Hall DG, Veltkamp BC, Turkel WJ. 2004. Children's and adults' understanding of proper namable things. *First Lang.* 24:5–32

Harris P. 2007. Commentary. *Monogr. Soc. Res. Child Dev.* 72:113–20

Harris PL, Brown E, Marriott C, Whittall S, et al. 1991. Monsters, ghosts and witches: testing the limits of the fantasy-reality distinction in young children. *Br. J. Dev. Psychol.* 9:105–23

Harris PL, Kavanaugh RD, Dowson L. 1997. The depiction of imaginary transformations: early comprehension of a symbolic function. *Cogn. Dev.* 12:1–19

Harris PL, Koenig MA. 2006. Trust in testimony: how children learn about science and religion. *Child Dev.* 77:505–24

Harris PL, Pasquini ES, Duke S. 2006. Germs and angels: the role of testimony in young children's ontology. *Dev. Sci.* 9:76–96

Haslam N, Rothschild L, Ernst D. 2000. Essentialist beliefs about social categories. *Br. J. Soc. Psychol.* 39:113–27

Hauser MD. 2000. *Wild Minds: What Animals Really Think*. New York: Holt

Hespos SJ, Spelke ES. 2004. Conceptual precursors to language. *Nature* 430:453–56

Heyman GD, Diesendruck G. 2002. The Spanish ser/estar distinction in bilingual children's reasoning about human psychological characteristics. *Dev. Psychol.* 38:407–17

Heyman GD, Fu G, Lee K. 2007. Evaluating claims people make about themselves: the development of skepticism. *Child Dev.* 78:367–375

Heyman G, Legare C. 2007. *Noun labels and social categories*. Presented at Cogn. Dev. Society Meet., Santa Fe, New Mexico

Hill JH, Mannheim B. 1992. Language and world view. *Annu. Rev. Anthropol.* 21:381–406

Hirschfeld LS. 1996. *Race in the Making: Cognition, Culture, and the Child's Construction of Human Kinds*. Cambridge, MA: MIT Press

Hollander MA, Gelman SA, Star J. 2002. Children's interpretation of generic noun phrases. *Dev. Psychol.* 38:883–89

Hood BM. 2008. *The Supernatural Sense.* San Francisco, CA: HarperOne. In press

Hood BM, Bloom P. 2008. Children prefer certain individuals over perfect duplicates. *Cognition* 106:455–62

Imai M, Gentner D. 1997. A cross-linguistic study of early word meaning: universal ontology and linguistic influence. *Cognition* 62:169–200

Jaswal VK. 2004. Don't believe everything you hear: preschoolers' sensitivity to speaker intent in category induction. *Child Dev.* 75:1871–85

Jaswal VK, Malone LS. 2007. Turning believers into skeptics: 3-year-olds' sensitivity to cues to speaker credibility. *J. Cogn. Dev.* 8:263–83

Jaswal VK, Markman EM. 2007. Looks aren't everything: 24-month-olds' willingness to accept unexpected labels. *J. Cogn. Dev.* 8:93–111

Jipson JL, Callanan MA. 2003. Mother-child conversation and children's understanding of biological and nonbiological changes in size. *Child Dev.* 74:629–44

Jipson JL, Gelman SA. 2007. Robots and rodents: children's inferences about living and nonliving kinds. *Child Dev.* 78:1675–88

Kalish CW. 1998. Natural and artificial kinds: Are children realists or relativists about categories? *Dev. Psychol.* 34:376–91

Kavanaugh RD, Harris PL. 1994. Imagining the outcome of pretend transformations: assessing the competence of normal children and children with autism. *Dev. Psychol.* 30:847–54

Keil FC. 1989. *Concepts, Kinds, and Cognitive Development.* Cambridge, MA: MIT Press

Keil FC. 2003. Categorisation, causation, and the limits of understanding. *Lang. Cogn. Processes* 18:663–92

Kelemen D. 2004. Are children "intuitive theists"? Reasoning about purpose and design in nature. *Psychol. Sci.* 15:295–301

Koenig MA, Clément F, Harris PL. 2004. Trust in testimony: children's use of true and false statements. *Psychol. Sci.* 15:694–98

Koenig MA, Harris PL. 2005. The role of social cognition in early trust. *Trends Cogn. Sci.* 9:457–59

Koenig MA, Harris PL. 2005a. Preschoolers mistrust ignorant and inaccurate speakers. *Child Dev.* 76:1261–77

Kuhl PK. 2007. Is speech learning "gated" by the social brain? *Dev. Sci.* 10:110–20

Kushnir T, Wellman HM, Gelman SA. 2008. The role of preschoolers' social understanding in evaluating the informativeness of causal interventions. *Cognition.* In press

Lakoff G. 1987. *Women, Fire, and Dangerous Things.* Chicago: Univ. Chicago Press

Lee K, Cameron CA, Doucette J, Talwar V. 2002. Phantoms and fabrications: young children's detection of implausible lies. *Child Dev.* 73:1688–702

Legare CH, Gelman SA. 2008. Bewitchment, biology, or both: the coexistence of natural and supernatural explanatory frameworks across development. *Cogn. Sci.* In press

Lemm K, Banaji MR. 1999. Unconscious attitudes and beliefs about women and men. In *Wahrnehmung und Herstellung von Geschlecht (Perceiving and Performing Gender)*, ed. U Pasero F Braun, pp. 215–33. Opladen: Westdutscher Verlag

Liben LS, Signorella ML. 1987. *New Directions for Child Development, No. 38: Children's Gender Schemata.* San Francisco, CA: Jossey-Bass

Lillard AS, Witherington DC. 2004. Mothers' behavior modifications during pretense and their possible signal value for toddlers. *Dev. Psychol.* 40:95–113

Lindsay DS, Johnson MK, Kwon P. 1991. Developmental changes in memory source monitoring. *J. Exp. Child Psychol.* 52:297–318

Lucy JA, Gaskins S. 2003. Interaction of language type and referent type in the development of nonverbal classification preferences. In *Language in Mind: Advances in the Study of Language and Thought*, ed. D Gentner, S Goldin-Meadow, pp. 465–92. Cambridge, MA: MIT Press

Lutz DJ, Keil FC. 2002. Early understanding of the division of cognitive labor. *Child Dev.* 73:1073–84

Mahalingam R. 1998. *Essentialism, Power, and Representation of Caste: A Developmental Study.* Ph.D. dissert., Univ. Pittsburgh

Malt BC. 1990. Features and beliefs in the mental representation of categories. *J. Mem. Lang.* 29:289–315

Malt BC. 1994. Water is not H_2O. *Cogn. Psychol.* 27:41–70

Maratsos MP. 2007. Commentary. *Monogr. Soc. Res. Child Dev.* 72:121–26

Margolis E. 1994. A reassessment of the shift from the classical theory of concepts to prototype theory. *Cognition* 51:73–89

Markman EM. 1989. *Categorization and Naming in Children: Problems of Induction.* Cambridge, MA: MIT Press

Markman EM. 1992. Constraints on word learning: speculations about their nature, origins, and domain specificity. In *Modularity and Constraints in Language and Cognition*, ed. MA Gunnar, M Maratsos, pp. 59–101. Hillsdale, NJ: Erlbaum

Markman EM, Jaswal VK. 2003. Commentary on Part II: abilities and assumptions underlying conceptual development. See Rakison & Oakes 2003, pp. 384–402

Marler P. 1991. The instinct to learn. In *The Epigenesis of Mind: Essays on Biology and Cognition*, ed. S Carey, R Gelman, pp. 37–66. Hillsdale, NJ: Erlbaum

Matsui T, Yamamoto T, McCagg P. 2006. On the role of language in children's early understanding of others as epistemic beings. *Cogn. Dev.* 21:158–73

Mayr E. 1991. *One Long Argument: Charles Darwin and the Genesis of Modern Evolutionary Thought.* Cambridge, MA: Harvard Univ. Press

McDonough L, Choi S, Mandler JM. 2003. Understanding spatial relations: flexible infants, lexical adults. *Cogn. Psychol.* 46:229–59

Medin DL, Atran S. 2004. The native mind: biological categorization and reasoning in development and across cultures. *Psychol. Rev.* 111:960–83

Medin DL, Lynch EB, Solomon KO. 2000. Are there kinds of concepts? *Annu. Rev. Psychol.* 51:121–47

Medin DL, Ortony A. 1989. Psychological essentialism. In *Similarity and Analogical Reasoning*, ed. S Vosniadou, A Ortony, pp. 179–95. New York: Cambridge Univ. Press

Meltzoff AN. 1995. Understanding the intentions of others: re-enactment of intended acts by 18-month-old children. *Dev. Psychol.* 31:838–50

Meltzoff AN. 2007. The "like me" framework for recognizing and becoming an intentional agent. *Acta Psychol.* 124:26–43

Mervis CB, Pani JR, Pani AM. 2003. Transaction of child cognitive-linguistic abilities and adult input in the acquisition of lexical categories at the basic and subordinate levels. See Rakison & Oakes 2003, pp. 242–74

Milich R, McAninch CB, Harris MJ. 1992. Effects of stigmatizing information on children's peer relations: Believing is seeing. *School Psychol. Rev.* 21:400–9

Mueller C, Dweck CS. 1998. Praise for intelligence can undermine children's motivation and performance. *J. Personal. Soc. Psychol.* 75:33–52

Nazzi T, Gopnik A. 2001. Linguistic and cognitive abilities in infancy: When does language become a tool for categorization? *Cognition* 80:B11–20

Needham A, Barrett T, Peterman K. 2002. A pick me up for infants' exploratory skills: Early simulated experiences reaching for objects using "sticky" mittens enhances young infants' object exploration skills. *Infant Behav. Dev.* 25:279–95

Nemeroff C, Rozin P. 1989. "You are what you eat": applying the demand-free "impressions" technique to an unacknowledged belief. *Ethos* 17:50–69

Nisbett RE, Peng K, Choi I, Norenzayan A. 2001. Culture and systems of thought: holistic versus analytic cognition. *Psychol. Rev.* 108:291–310

Nishida TK, Lillard AS. 2007. The informative value of emotional expressions: "social referencing" in mother-child pretense. *Dev. Sci.* 10:205–12

Opfer JE, Siegler RS. 2004. Revisiting preschoolers' living things concept: a microgenetic analysis of conceptual change in basic biology. *Cogn. Psychol.* 59:301–32

Patterson MM, Bigler RS. 2006. Preschool children's attention to environmental messages about groups: social categorization and the origins of intergroup bias. *Child Dev.* 77:847–60

Peterson CC, Siegal M. 2000. Insights into theory of mind from deafness and autism. *Mind Lang.* 15:123–45

Phelps KE, Woolley JD. 1994. The form and function of young children's magical beliefs. *Dev. Psychol.* 30:385–94

Piaget J. 1970. *Genetic Epistemology.* Trans. E. Duckworth. New York: Columbia Univ. Press

Plunkett K, Hu J, Cohen LB. 2008. Labels can override perceptual categories in early infancy. *Cognition* 106:665–81

Prentice DA, Miller DT. 2006. Essentializing differences between women and men. *Psychol. Sci.* 17:129–35

Putnam H. 1975. The meaning of "meaning." In *Mind, Language, and Reality*, ed. H Putnam, pp. 215–71. New York: Cambridge Univ. Press

Quinn PC, Eimas PD. 1997. A reexamination of the perceptual-to-conceptual shift in mental representations. *Rev. Gen. Psychol.* 1:271–87

Rakison DH, Oakes LM, eds. 2003. *Early Category and Concept Development: Making Sense of the Blooming Buzzing Confusion*. New York: Oxford Univ. Press

Raman L, Winer GA. 2002. Children's and adults' understanding of illness: evidence in support of a coexistence model. *Genetic, Social, Gen. Psychol. Monogr.* 128:325–55

Rehder B. 2007. Essentialism as a generative theory of classification. In *Causal Learning: Psychology, Philosophy, and Computation*, ed. A Gopnik, L Schultz, pp. 190–207. New York: Oxford Univ. Press

Reynaert CC, Gelman SA. 2007. The influence of language form and conventional wording on judgments of illness. *J. Psycholing. Res.* 36:273–95

Rips LJ. 1989. Similarity, typicality, and categorization. In *Similarity and Analogical Reasoning*, ed. S Vosniadou, A Ortony, pp. 21–59. New York: Cambridge Univ. Press

Rogoff B. 2003. *The Cultural Nature of Human Development*. New York: Oxford Univ. Press

Rosengren KS, Johnson CN, Harris PL. 2000. *Imagining the Impossible: Magical, Scientific, and Religious Thinking in Children*. New York: Cambridge Univ. Press

Sabbagh MA, Baldwin DA. 2001. Learning words from knowledgeable versus ignorant speakers: links between preschoolers' theory of mind and semantic development. *Child Dev.* 72:1054–70

Saffran JR, Aslin RN, Newport EL. 1996. Statistical learning by 8-month-old infants. *Science* 274:1926–28

Schulz LE, Bonawitz EB, Griffiths TL. 2007. Can being scared cause tummy aches? Naive theories, ambiguous evidence, and preschoolers' causal inferences. *Dev. Psychol.* 43:1124–39

Sera MD. 1992. To be or to be: use and acquisition of the Spanish copulas. *J. Mem. Lang.* 31:408–27

Shtulman A. 2006. Qualitative differences between naïve and scientific theories of evolution. *Cogn. Psychol.* 52:170–94

Shtulman A, Carey S. 2007. Improbable or impossible? How children reason about the possibility of extraordinary events. *Child Dev.* 78:1015–32

Siegal M, Peterson CC, eds. 1999. *Children's Understanding of Biology and Health*. New York: Cambridge Univ. Press

Siegal M, Surian L. 2004. Conceptual development and conversational understanding. *Trends Cogn. Sci.* 8:534–38

Siegler RS, Crowley K. 1991. The microgenetic method: a direct means for studying cognitive development. *Am. Psychol.* 46:606–20

Skolnick D, Bloom P. 2006. The intuitive cosmology of fictional worlds. In *The Architecture of the Imagination: New Essays on Pretense, Possibility, and Fiction*, ed. S Nichols, pp. 73–86. New York: Oxford Univ. Press

Slobin DI. 1996. From "thought and language" to "thinking for speaking." In *Rethinking Linguistic Relativity*, ed. JJ Gumperz, SC Levinson, pp. 70–96. New York: Cambridge Univ. Press

Slobin DI. 2006. What makes manner of motion salient? Explorations in linguistic typology, discourse, and cognition. In *Space in Languages: Linguistic Systems and Cognitive Categories*, ed. M Hickmann, S Robert, pp. 59–81. Amsterdam: Benjamins

Sloutsky VM, Fisher AV. 2004. Induction and categorization in young children: a similarity-based model. *J. Exp. Psychol.: Gen.* 133:166–88

Smith LB. 2000. Learning how to learn words: an associative crane. In *Becoming a Word Learner: A Debate on Lexical Acquisition*, pp. 51–80. New York: Oxford Univ. Press

Smith LB, Jones SS, Landau B. 1996. Naming in young children: a dumb attentional mechanism? *Cognition* 60:143–71

Sommerville JA, Woodward AL, Needham A. 2005. Action experience alters 3-month-old infants' perception of others' actions. *Cognition* 96:B1–11

Sousa P, Atran S, Medin D. 2002. Essentialism and folkbiology: evidence from Brazil. *J. Cogn. Culture* 2:195–223

Sperber D. 1996. *Explaining Culture: A Naturalistic Approach*. Oxford, UK: Blackwell

Strevens M. 2000. The essentialist aspect of naive theories. *Cognition* 74:149–75

Subbotsky E. 2001. Causal explanations of events by children and adults: Can alternative causal modes coexist in one mind? *Br. J. Dev. Psychol.* 19:23–45

Taylor M. 1999. *Imaginary Companions and the Children Who Create Them*. New York: Oxford Univ. Press

Tomasello M, Akhtar N. 2000. Five questions for any theory of word learning. In *Becoming a Word Learner: A Debate on Lexical Acquisition*, pp. 179–86. New York: Oxford Univ. Press

Tomasello M, Kruger AC, Ratner HH. 1993. Cultural learning. *Behav. Brain Sci.* 16:495–552

Troseth GL, DeLoache JS. 1998. The medium can obscure the message: young children's understanding of video. *Child Dev.* 69:950–65

Vosniadou S. 1994. Universal and culture-specific properties of children's mental models of the earth. In *Mapping the Mind: Domain Specificity in Cognition and Culture*, ed. LA Hirschfeld, SA Gelman, pp. 412–30. New York: Cambridge Univ. Press

Vygotsky LS. 1934/1962. *Thought and Language*. Cambridge, MA: MIT Press

Vygotsky LS. 1978. *Mind in Society: The Development of Higher Psychological Processes*. Cambridge, MA: Harvard Univ. Press

Walton GM, Banaji MR. 2004. Being what you say: the effect of essentialist linguistic labels on preferences. *Social Cogn.* 22:193–213

Waxman SR. 2004. Everything had a name, and each name gave birth to a new thought: links between early word learning and conceptual organization. In *Weaving a Lexicon*, ed. DG Hall, SR Waxman, pp. 295–335. Cambridge, MA: MIT Press

Waxman SR. 2005. Why is the concept "living thing" so elusive? Concepts, languages, and the development of folkbiology. In *Categorization Inside and Outside the Laboratory: Essays in Honor of Douglas L. Medin*, ed. W Ahn, RL Goldstone, BC Love, AB Markman, P Wolff, pp. 49–67. Washington, DC: Am. Psychol. Assoc.

Waxman SR, Markow DB. 1995. Words as invitations to form categories: evidence from 12- to 13-month-old infants. *Cogn. Psychol.* 29:257–302

Waxman SR, Medin D, Ross N. 2007. Folkbiological reasoning from a cross-cultural developmental perspective: early essentialist notions are shaped by cultural beliefs. *Dev. Psychol.* 43:294–308

Wellman HM. 1990. *The Child's Theory of Mind*. Cambridge, MA: MIT Press

Wellman HM, Gelman SA. 1998. Knowledge acquisition in foundational domains. In *Handbook of Child Psychology: Volume 2, Cognition, Perception, and Language*, ed. D Kuhn, RS Siegler, pp. 523–73. Hoboken, NJ: Wiley. 6th ed.

Whiten A, Horner V, de Waal FBM. 2005. Conformity to cultural norms of tool use in chimpanzees. *Nature* 437:737–40

Whorf BL. 1956. *Language, Thought, and Reality*. Cambridge, MA: MIT Press

Woolley JD. 1997. Thinking about fantasy: Are children fundamentally different thinkers and believers from adults? *Child Dev.* 68:991–1011

Woolley JD, Boerger EA, Markman AB. 2004. A visit from the Candy Witch: factors influencing young children's belief in a novel fantastical being. *Dev. Sci.* 7:456–68

Woolley JD, Cox V. 2007. Development of beliefs about storybook reality. *Dev. Sci.* 10:681–93

Woolley JD, Wellman HM. 1990. Young children's understanding of realities, nonrealities, and appearances. *Child Dev.* 61:946–61

Xu F. 2002. The role of language in acquiring object kind concepts in infancy. *Cognition* 85:223–50

Xu F, Tenenbaum JB. 2007. Word learning as Bayesian inference. *Psychol. Rev.* 114:245–72

Yamauchi T. 2005. Labeling bias and categorical induction: generative aspects of category information. *J. Exp. Psychol.: Learn. Mem. Cogn.* 31:538–53

Yoshida H, Smith LB. 2003. Shifting ontological boundaries: how Japanese- and English-speaking children generalize names for animals and artifacts. *Dev. Sci.* 6:1–34

Yoshida H, Smith LB. 2008. What's in view for toddlers? Using a head-camera to study visual experience. *Infancy*. In press

Social Withdrawal in Childhood

Kenneth H. Rubin,[1] Robert J. Coplan,[2] and Julie C. Bowker[3]

[1] Department of Human Development, University of Maryland, College Park, Maryland 20742-1131; email: krubin@umd.edu

[2] Department of Psychology, Carleton University, Ottawa, Ontario K1S 5B6 Canada; email: robert_coplan@carleton.ca

[3] Department of Psychology, University at Buffalo, Buffalo, New York 14260; email: jcbowker@buffalo.edu

Annu. Rev. Psychol. 2009. 60:141–71

First published online as a Review in Advance on October 13, 2008

The *Annual Review of Psychology* is online at psych.annualreviews.org

This article's doi: 10.1146/annurev.psych.60.110707.163642

Key Words

shyness, behavioral inhibition, peer rejection, victimization, friendship, parenting

Abstract

Socially withdrawn children frequently refrain from social activities in the presence of peers. The lack of social interaction in childhood may result from a variety of causes, including social fear and anxiety or a preference for solitude. From early childhood through to adolescence, socially withdrawn children are concurrently and predictively at risk for a wide range of negative adjustment outcomes, including socio-emotional difficulties (e.g., anxiety, low self-esteem, depressive symptoms, and internalizing problems), peer difficulties (e.g., rejection, victimization, poor friendship quality), and school difficulties (e.g., poor-quality teacher-child relationships, academic difficulties, school avoidance). The goals of the current review are to (*a*) provide some definitional, theoretical, and methodological clarity to the complex array of terms and constructs previously employed in the study of social withdrawal; (*b*) examine the predictors, correlates, and consequences of child and early-adolescent social withdrawal; and (*c*) present a developmental framework describing pathways to and from social withdrawal in childhood.

Contents

INTRODUCTION

Social withdrawal is not a clinically defined behavioral, social, or emotional disorder in childhood. Indeed, some individuals appear content to spend most of their hours and days removed from others. These individuals include those who spend significant time alone, working, playing, and otherwise acting on their computers. Others may design homes, automobiles, space modules, or may spend their time writing scripts, poems, lyrics, book chapters, and so forth. Often these individuals have a distinct need for solitude. Conversely, there are those individuals who, while in social company, avoid their confreres, or who actively choose lives of solitude to escape the initiation and maintenance of interpersonal relationships. And finally, there are individuals who have little choice in the matter of solitude because they are isolated or rejected by others in their social communities. In the cases of the avoidance of social company and the isolation from social company, solitude could hardly be construed as psychologically or socially adaptive. It is not the display of solitude per se that may pose a problem; rather, the central issue is that social withdrawal may reflect underlying difficulties of a social or emotional nature.

To some researchers, the expression of social withdrawal represents the developmental outcome of particular temperamental dispositions (e.g., Fox et al. 2005). To others, withdrawal is viewed as a behavioral index of the child's isolation, exclusion, or rejection by the peer group (e.g., Boivin et al. 1995, Gazelle & Ladd 2003). Still others believe that social withdrawal in childhood, depending upon the age at which it is observed, reflects the lack of a social approach motive and a preference for object manipulation and construction over interpersonal exchange (e.g., Coplan et al. 2004). Finally, there are those who believe that social withdrawal is linked to psychological maladaptation as it represents a behavioral expression of internalized thoughts and feelings of social anxiety or depression (Vasa & Pine 2006). As the reader may deduce, social withdrawal is a somewhat fuzzy construct that has defied precise meaning and understanding. In this regard, it becomes immediately apparent why there has not been general agreement among traditionally trained clinical psychologists concerning the relevance and significance of social withdrawal vis-à-vis the development and expression of psychologically abnormal emotions, thoughts, and behaviors in childhood and adolescence.

Given the slippery nature of the phenomenon, one purpose of this review is to provide some definitional clarity for the construct of social withdrawal. Such clarity is particularly important because social withdrawal appears to have many "faces" (e.g., Rubin & Mills 1988), and the multiple forms of social solitude typically expressed in childhood carry with them different psychological functions and meanings (e.g., Asendorpf 1990, Coplan et al. 1994, Harrist et al. 1997). To make matters more con-

fusing, the expression of different forms of solitude appears to have different meanings, not only at different points in childhood, but also within different social contexts (Rubin et al. 2002) and cultures (e.g., Chen et al. 2005). Before defining social withdrawal and associated constructs, we briefly describe the relatively recent history of the study of social withdrawal and relevant developmental and clinical theory. We also review the various ways in which social withdrawal, in its many forms, has been assessed.

A second purpose of this review is to examine factors that may predict social withdrawal during childhood. Third, we consider the correlates and consequences of child and early-adolescent social withdrawal. These latter two goals are accomplished by referring to a developmental framework within which pathways to and from social withdrawal are described (see **Figure 1**). We conclude this review with a discussion of future research directions.

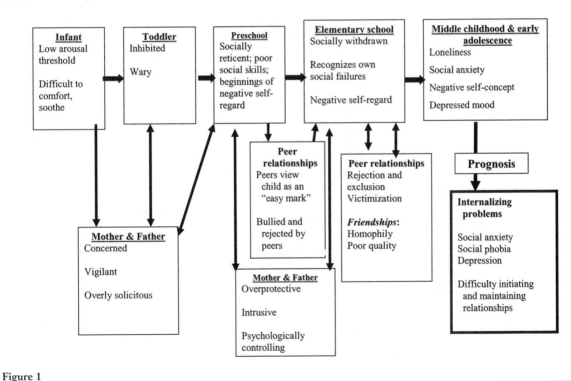

Figure 1

Social withdrawal: a transactional model.

The Significance of Peer Interaction and the Lack Thereof: Relevant History and Theory

Historically, social withdrawal has been considered by clinical psychologists to have limited developmental significance. For example, up until the late 1960s, it was argued that childhood social withdrawal was relatively unstable and not significantly predictive of maladjustment during the adolescent and adult periods (e.g., Kohlberg et al. 1972, Robins 1966). The studies from which these early conclusions were drawn, however, were methodologically and conceptually flawed (Rubin & Coplan 2004). For instance, the samples comprised the exclusive use of clinic or high-risk participants. There was an overreliance on teacher assessments of social withdrawal with unknown validity. And the central focus was on outcomes related to externalizing rather than internalizing disorders. Nevertheless, this view was prevalent until relatively recently despite the fact that developmental scientists have stressed the importance of peer interaction since the turn of the twentieth century.

Cooley (1902) was among the first to suggest that peer interaction made a significant contribution to children's socialization. And in his early writings, Piaget (e.g., 1932) argued that exposure to instances of peer conflict and opportunities for social negotiation aided children in the acquisition and development of perspective-taking skills, cause-and-effect social reasoning, and an understanding of morality.

Mead (1934) proposed that the ability to self-reflect, to consider the self in relation to others, and to understand the perspectives of others was largely a function of participation in organized, rule-governed activities with peers. He suggested that exchanges among peers, whether experienced in the arenas of cooperation or competition, conflict or friendly discussion, allowed the child to gain an understanding of the self as both a subject and an object. Sullivan (1953) proposed that the experience of peer relationships was essential for the child's development of the concepts of mutual respect, equality, and reciprocity. He emphasized the importance of "chumships," or special best-friendships, for the emergence of these concepts and also for psychological well-being. Theorists in the social learning camp have long suggested (and found) that children learn social behaviors and social norms directly through peer tutelage, reinforcement, and punishment, and indirectly by observing peers "in action" (Bandura & Walters 1963).

Current research on social withdrawal is also guided by the writings of Hinde (1987). From Hinde, social withdrawal can be considered an individual characteristic that influences the quality of a person's social relationships (e.g., friendship) and the individual's reputation and standing in the peer group (e.g., peer rejection). Hinde's conceptual model serves as a useful heuristic to present central lines of inquiry and major research findings regarding children who avoid and withdraw from the peer group.

Building upon the extant theoretical work, strong empirical support has developed for the notion that peer interactions (and the lack thereof) and the relationships that derive from children's interactions or solitude can serve to promote both adaptive and maladaptive social, emotional, and social-cognitive functioning (see Rubin et al. 2006a for a recent review).

Defining Social Withdrawal in Childhood

The study of children's and adolescents' solitary and withdrawn behavior has been associated with such constructs as shyness, behavioral inhibition, isolation and rejection, social reticence, passivity, and peer neglect. Oft-times, these referents have been used interchangeably, and inconsistencies in definitions and assessments have been pervasive. Recently, however, there has been an attempt to organize these varied constructs in a psychologically meaningful manner (e.g., Rubin & Asendorpf 1993, Rubin & Coplan 2004).

Rubin (1982) originally proposed a distinction between two causal processes that may underlie children's lack of social interaction. "Active isolation" denotes the process whereby some children spend time alone in social company because their peers actively reject and isolate them. Putative causes of active isolation are varied and include the display of such nonnormative, unacceptable behavior as aggression, undercontrolled impulsivity, and social immaturity, as well as such factors as minority group membership and interests and inclinations that vary from those of the majority of peer group members (e.g., Rubin & Mills 1988, Rubin et al. 2006a). In contrast, "social withdrawal" refers to the child's isolating himself/herself from the peer group. In this latter regard, social withdrawal is viewed as emanating from such internal factors as anxiety, negative self-esteem, and self-perceived difficulties in social skills and social relationships (Rubin & Asendorpf 1993). The roots of this conceptualization are founded in some of the earliest relevant research, with socially withdrawn children described as "those who are bothering themselves rather than others" (Morris et al. 1954, p. 743). Of course, it may be the case that although some socially withdrawn children initially remove themselves from social interaction, they may also come to be excluded by peers. Thus, over time, it may become increasingly difficult to distinguish between withdrawal and active isolation. Indeed, social withdrawal in childhood may be a catalyst in a transactional model that describes the development of such negative outcomes as negative self-regard, loneliness, peer rejection, victimization, anxiety, and depression (see **Figure 1**).

In the end, social withdrawal may be best construed as an umbrella term describing a given behavioral prototype (solitude in one form or another) derived from a variety of underlying causes (Rubin & Coplan 2004). Thus, for example, many researchers have focused on fear, wariness, and anxiety as underlying affective contributors to children's withdrawal from their peers. In this regard, several related constructs have emerged.

Kagan, Fox, and colleagues (e.g., Fox et al. 2005, Kagan et al. 2007) have used the term "behavioral inhibition" (BI) to describe biologically based wariness during exposure to novel people, things, and places. Similarly, "shyness" has been conceptualized as wariness in the face of social novelty and/or self-conscious behavior in situations of perceived social evaluation (Asendorpf 1991, Cheek & Buss 1981, Crozier 1995, Zimbardo 1977). "Social reticence" represents a behavioral construct comprising the watching of others from afar, remaining unoccupied in social company, and hovering near but not engaging others in interaction (Coplan et al. 1994). This behavioral construct putatively reflects internalized feelings of social anxiety as well as conflicted motivations of approach and avoidance. "Anxious-solitude" has been used to denote wariness in familiar peer contexts (e.g., Gazelle & Ladd 2003, Gazelle & Rudolph 2004). These terms share the implication that solitude may result from conflicting emotions and motivations. That is, some children may be motivated to approach others to engage in social interaction; however, their social approach motivation is attenuated by social fear and anxiety, resulting in the simultaneous motivation to avoid others (e.g., Asendorpf 1990, Coplan et al. 2004).

Clearly, there is a conceptual similarity here with social phobia, an internalizing disorder characterized by "a marked and persistent fear of social or performance situations in which embarrassment may occur" (Am. Psychiatr. Assoc. 1994, p. 411). There has been some debate in the literature as to the conceptual nature of the relation between shyness and social phobia (i.e., Does social phobia refer to extreme shyness; Chavira et al. 2002). Indeed, Rapee and colleagues (2005) reported that 90% of "extremely shy" preschool-age children met criteria for an anxiety disorder. Results from a growing number of both retrospective and longitudinal studies have demonstrated empirical links between inhibition in early childhood and the development of anxiety disorders (particularly social phobia) in later childhood, adolescence, and adulthood (e.g., Schwartz et al. 1999, Van Ameringen et al. 1998).

Our review is centered on the broader construct of social withdrawal, with a particular focus on inhibition, shyness, and solitude. However, it is also the case that some children may engage in less social interaction because they are socially disinterested (or unsociable) and may simply prefer to play alone (Asendorpf 1990, Coplan et al. 2004). We review the extant literature on this understudied topic in a later section.

Clinical Perspectives

The construct of social withdrawal is found in almost every textbook or review chapter on abnormal or clinical child psychology (e.g., McClure & Pine 2006, Parker et al. 2006). It is also found on most standardized assessments of abnormal socio-emotional functioning (e.g., Achenbach & Edelbrock 1981). The phenomenon is consistently cited as evidence for an "overcontrolled disorder" (e.g., Lewis & Miller 1990) or an internalizing problem (Achenbach & Edelbrock 1981). In source after source, social withdrawal is contrasted with aggression as one of the two most frequently identified major dimensions of dysfunctional behavior in childhood.

Social withdrawal is subsumed under several categories of disturbance in the *Diagnostic and Statistical Manual of Mental Disorders* (DSM IV, American Psychiatric Association 1994) and the *Classification of Mental and Behavioral Disorders* (ICD-10; World Health Org. 1993). In these systems, social withdrawal is viewed as a symptom rather than as a syndrome with its own etiology and prognoses; as such, it has been associated with such clinical disorders of childhood and adolescence as autism, anxiety and phobic disorders, major depression, personality disorders, and schizophrenia. In this review, we provide links between social withdrawal and anxiety and depression. A more detailed description of links between social withdrawal and diagnostic classifications may be found in Rubin et al. (2003).

Anxiety disorders represent one of the most common disorders of childhood (Achenbach 1982, Rapee & Sweeney 2001). Whatever it is that causes children's social fears and anxieties, their social interactions and relationships with peers are inevitably impaired. Clearly, the avoidance of social interaction may serve to reduce visceral arousal. If avoidant behavior does decrease anxiety, then social withdrawal or avoidance will be reinforced, and the probability of recurrence is increased (see Crozier & Alden 2005 for relevant reviews). Not surprisingly, therefore, anxiety-disordered children often withdraw from social company. However, the relation between withdrawal and anxiety is likely transactional and cyclical in nature. Social withdrawal and avoidance interfere with the normal development of social skills. Such deficiencies in social skills will then serve to reinforce social anxiety and to foster negative self-appraisals and negative self-esteem (e.g., Nelson et al. 2005).

In contrast, social withdrawal accompanying depression may have different social consequences. Whereas social withdrawal induced by social anxiety may yield sympathy, interest, and social overtures from others, depressed-withdrawn individuals may attempt to elicit support in a way that actually causes others to withdraw from them or even ignore or reject them (e.g., Mullins et al. 1986). In support, Harrist and colleagues found that sad/depressed young withdrawn children were rejected by their peers at the start of elementary school, whereas anxious-withdrawn children were not (Harrist et al. 1997). A partial understanding of why such interpersonal consequences ensue derives from the DSM-IV and ICD-10 descriptions of children who have major depression or dysthymia. These children experience depressed mood, social withdrawal, feelings of hopelessness, low self-esteem, and poor concentration, as well as appetite and sleep disturbances; hence, they are not particularly pleasant confreres. Moreover, others may view depressive behaviors as being within a person's realm of control, in contrast to being a victim of a nervous or anxious disposition.

Social withdrawal appears to be not only a concomitant but also a predictor of depression (Bell-Dolan et al. 1993, Rubin et al. 1995). Recently, Gullone et al. (2006) found that social withdrawal predicted depressive symptoms for those children who had insecure attachment relationships with their parents.

In summary, social withdrawal surfaces in numerous diagnostic categories of the two major classification systems, DSM-IV and ICD-10. Specifically, social withdrawal is listed as a symptom, or marker, of anxiety and phobic disorders and major depression. It may be that the forms of solitude and the motivations underlying these behavioral expressions vary from one disturbance to another.

THE ASSESSMENT OF SOCIAL WITHDRAWAL

A wide variety of measures has been used to assess childhood social withdrawal and its associated constructs, including behavioral observations, parent and teacher ratings, and peer and self-reports. The extant battery of measures captures the various forms and meanings of social withdrawal.

Some measures assess the broader construct of social withdrawal. For example, the Revised Class Play (RCP; Masten et al. 1985) is a widely used peer-rating procedure wherein classmates (or grade-mates) nominate peers who fit various behavioral descriptors. Rubin & Mills (1988) suggested separating the items that loaded on the original RCP Sensitivity/Isolation factor (Masten et al. 1985) to create two conceptually distinct constructs—shyness/social wariness (e.g., items such as "someone who is shy," "someone whose feelings get hurt easily") and social isolation/exclusion (e.g., "a person who is often left out"; "a person who can't get others to listen"). These two constructs have been found to be differentially correlated with such constructs as aggression and disruptive behavior (e.g., Zeller et al. 2003), results which nicely demonstrate that children can distinguish between their shy/withdrawn and rejected/

isolated peers, at least during late childhood and early adolescence when peer nomination measures are most commonly used. More recently, Rubin and colleagues have added items to this measure to create an *Extended Class Play*; this measure further distinguishes between peer rejection/isolation/victimization (e.g., "someone who is hit or kicked by others") and shyness/social withdrawal (e.g., "someone who gets nervous about participating in class discussions"; see Rubin et al. 2006d).

Researchers have also used items from the Child Behavior Checklist and Teacher Report Form (Achenbach & Rescorla 2006) to obtain parents' and teachers' perceptions of social withdrawal. The items from these measures provide a broader-based assessment of several aspects of children's socially withdrawn behaviors. As well, behavioral observations have been employed (e.g., the Play Observation Scale; Rubin 2001) to assess different forms of solitude in the presence of both unfamiliar peers and classmates at school. A more detailed discussion of the different types of children's nonsocial behaviors is presented below.

Several additional taxonomies have been developed to assess such constructs as behavioral inhibition, shyness, and anxious-solitude. For example, BI is typically assessed in an observational paradigm developed by Kagan and colleagues (e.g., Kagan et al. 1988). Young children are presented with a series of novel events involving adult strangers. Inhibition is indicated by such measures as latency to approach the adult stranger, latency to offer the first spontaneous utterance, and proximity to mother. In a move away from assessing inhibition in the company of unfamiliar adults who behave in unfamiliar ways (e.g., dressed in a clown costume; not referencing the child when entering the room), Rubin and colleagues (e.g., Rubin et al. 1997) developed a procedure to assess BI in the company of unfamiliar toddler peers. Measures included the toddler's maintenance of contact with his/her mother and the frequency of anxious behaviors. Interestingly, there was little overlap between inhibition as assessed by the adult and peer paradigms (Rubin et al. 1997). Bishop and colleagues (2003) recently developed a parent and teacher rating scale (Behavioral Inhibition Questionnaire) designed to assess behavioral inhibition in peer situations and in response to behavioral challenges, separation, performance situations, unfamiliar adults, and other novel situations. They reported that both maternal and teacher reports of BI were strongly associated with observed BI in the Kagan paradigm.

Several parent-rating measures exist to assess shyness in childhood, including the Colorado Child Temperament Inventory (Rowe & Plomin 1977) and the Child Social Preference Scale (Coplan et al. 2004). The latter also indexes social disinterest. For older children and adolescents, self-report measures of shyness include the Revised Cheek and Buss Shyness Scale (Cheek & Buss 1981) and the Children's Shyness Questionnaire (CSQ; Crozier 1995).

Finally, a number of different teacher rating scales have been employed to assess children's shy and socially anxious behaviors at daycare, preschool, and elementary school. For example, the "anxious with peers" subscale of the Child Behavior Scale (Ladd & Profilet 1996) and items from the previously noted Teacher Report Form (Achenbach 1991) measure the construct of anxious-solitude (Gazelle & Ladd 2003). The anxiety and withdrawal items from the Social Behavior Questionnaire (Tremblay et al. 1991) have been used to assess childhood anxiety-social withdrawal (Pedersen et al. 2007).

There is moderate to high agreement between sources of assessment with regard to measures of BI, shyness, and social withdrawal (Bishop et al. 2003, Coplan et al. 2008, Ladd & Profilet 1996). However, some researchers have suggested that discrepancies between such ratings may be meaningful. For example, Spooner et al. (2005) reported that a group of self-reported shy children whose shyness was "undetected" at school (i.e., they were not rated as shy by teachers) had low self-esteem.

THE DEVELOPMENTAL COURSE OF CHILDHOOD SOCIAL WITHDRAWAL

Biological Foundations

Many researchers and theorists contend that the expression of solitary behavior that reflects internalized feelings of social anxiety is rooted in differences in the excitability of the amygdala and its projections to the cortex, hypothalamus, sympathetic nervous system, corpus striatum, and central gray (Kagan et al. 1993). Thus, it is argued that that enhanced amygdala activation to novelty and activation of "fear" circuitry may underlie not only infant negative reactivity to novelty, but also BI and preschool social reticence (Degnan & Fox 2007, Fox et al. 2001, Kagan et al. 1988). In support of these conjectures, McManis and colleagues (2002) have reported that children who were emotionally reactive at 4 months and who displayed high levels of BI at ages 14 and 21 months were likely to demonstrate right frontal electroencephalogram (EEG) asymmetries in late childhood. Similar concurrent and predictive associations have been revealed between right frontal EEG asymmetry and BI in infancy and reticence in early childhood (see Fox et al. 2005 for an extensive review). And recently, Henderson and colleagues (2004) found that two types of solitude (social reticence and solitary-constructive and exploratory behavior) were associated with a pattern of greater relative right frontal EEG asymmetry. However, reticent children were rated by their mothers to be more socially fearful and displayed lower cardiac vagal tone than those children who were observed to spend time exploring and constructing on their own while in social company.

Further support of an underlying biological constitution of socially inhibited and reticent behavior is drawn from studies indicating that lower cardiac vagal tone is concurrently and predictively associated with BI, a precursor of socially reticent behavior (Fox et al. 2001, Rubin et al. 2002) and social reticence itself during early childhood (Rubin et al. 1997).

Furthermore, Hastings et al. (2005) reported that observed BI, maternal reports of social fearfulness, and cardiac vagal tone loaded on a single factor (with cardiac vagal tone loading negatively) at two years of age. And finally, the hypothalamic-pituitary-adrenocortical axis is thought to be activated during stressful or novel situations. Finally, researchers have demonstrated that elevated cortisol (a stress hormone) is associated with the demonstration of behavioral inhibition (Spangler & Schieche 1998) and social reticence (Schmidt et al. 1997) in early childhood. Additional work on the associations between event-related potentials, functional magnetic resonance imaging, and the demonstration of BI and social solitude has been recently thoroughly reviewed in Fox et al. (2005).

Taken together, the relations between biology and behavior in the study of social withdrawal may be best thought of as transactional in nature. We contend that biological factors may underlie the display of BI and reticence. In turn, behavioral indicators of underlying biologically based fearfulness and anxiety may evoke social responses from parents and peers (see **Figure 1** and discussion below). These responses may affect inhibited and fearful children in such a way that physiologically based dispositions and those behaviors reflective of them are maintained or modified (see also Degnan & Fox 2007).

The Stability of Social Withdrawal

Given that biological factors may provide a constitutional basis for the expression of inhibited, shy, and withdrawn behavior, one might expect that the behavioral tendency to withdraw from and avoid peers would be relatively stable. Beginning in early childhood, observations of BI at two years are significant predictors of social wariness and reticence at four years and beyond (e.g., Kagan et al. 1988, Rubin et al. 2002). Moreover, BI, shyness, social reticence, and social withdrawal appear to be moderately stable from the preschool period through adolescence and early adulthood (Caspi et al. 2003, Degnan et al. 2008, Denissen et al. 2008, Hart et al. 1997, Sanson et al. 1996). Typically, across all developmental periods, children at the extremes of social withdrawal show the greatest stability in their behavior over time (e.g., Asendorpf & van Aken 1994, Schneider et al. 1988, Schwartz et al. 1999). Rubin et al. (1995), for example, found that approximately two-thirds of children identified as extreme in social withdrawal maintained their status across any two-year period from five to eleven years.

In addition to temporal stability, several investigators have examined the cross-contextual consistency of social withdrawal (e.g., Coplan & Rubin 1998; Rubin 1993; Schneider et al. 1998, 2000). For example, Schneider and colleagues have shown that socially withdrawn children and young adolescents avoid their peers consistently across a variety of different social settings, including in the school, home, and the larger community (Schneider et al. 1998, 2000).

In summary, these findings nicely illustrate that many children who withdraw from their peers do so consistently across time and context. And it may be that biological factors play a contributing role in this stability. However, human physiology is hardly immutable. Thankfully, not all behaviorally inhibited infants and toddlers go on to become withdrawn and socially anxious children (Degnan & Fox 2007). In recent years, researchers have implicated such factors as parenting style, the quality of the parent-child relationship, and the quality of children's and adolescents' peer relationships in the development, maintenance, and moderation of socially withdrawn behavioral patterns. We review this work below.

Parenting

Attachment relationships. Attachment theorists have long maintained that the primary attachment relationship develops during the first year of life, usually between the mother and the infant. Maternal sensitivity and responsiveness influence whether the relationship will be secure or insecure (Ainsworth et al. 1978). Researchers have shown that secure attachment predicts social competence, whereas insecurity predicts both externalizing (aggression) and internalizing (withdrawal) forms of behavior (Shamir-Essakow et al. 2005, van Brakel et al. 2006). In the case of the latter, it is suggested that insecure "ambivalent" infants ("C" babies) are guided by a fear of rejection; consequently, in their extrafamilial peer relationships they are postulated to attempt to avoid rejection through passive, adult-dependent behavior and withdrawal. This posited connection between C status (ambivalent attachment) and inhibited, dependent, withdrawn behaviors has been supported in several studies (e.g., Calkins & Fox 1992, Erickson et al. 1985, Renken et al. 1989, Shulman et al. 1994).

Parenting and parenting beliefs. It bears noting, however, that insecure attachment relationships are also predicted by maternal behavior. For example, mothers of insecurely attached C babies are overinvolved and overcontrolling when compared with mothers of securely attached babies (Erickson et al. 1985). It is this overcontrolling, intrusive, and overly protective parenting style that is strongly associated, contemporaneously and predictively, with BI and socially withdrawn and reticent behavior. The association between overcontrolling, intrusive, and overly protective parenting and socially withdrawn and anxious behavior may be best expressed as follows. Parents who are overly protective and directive tend to overmanage situations for their children, restrict their children's behaviors, discourage independence, and control their children's activities. As a result, it has been posited that dispositionally inhibited children who are raised by overly restrictive, protective, and controlling parents may not develop necessary coping and problem-solving strategies in their interpersonal milieus.

Contemporaneous and predictive links between parental overprotectiveness, overcontrol, and intrusion and children's socially wary and withdrawn behavior have been reported in several studies (e.g., Barber et al. 1994; Coplan et al. 2004; Lieb et al. 2000; Mills & Rubin 1998; Rubin et al. 1997, 2001). Taken together, these findings support earlier, classic writings pertaining to the role of parental overprotectiveness in the development of anxiety and social withdrawal (Levy 1943, Winder & Rau 1962). Moreover, the data also support the growing clinical literature linking overprotective, intrusive parenting to the development of social anxiety, of which social withdrawal is a behavioral indicator (Hudson & Rapee 2001, Manassis & Bradley 1994).

Of course, children's social reticence and withdrawal may also cause parental overprotection and overcontrol. Indeed, Rubin and colleagues have consistently reported that toddler BI and preschool reticence predict subsequent parental directiveness and overcontrol (e.g., Hastings & Rubin 1999, Rubin et al. 1999). In this sense, it has been suggested that when some parents perceive their children to be socially anxious and vulnerable, they attempt to be supportive by manipulating their children's social behaviors in a power-assertive, highly directive fashion (that is, they direct their children's behavior). Thus, for parents of socially withdrawn children, simply anticipating or viewing their children's withdrawal in the company of peers may evoke parental feelings of concern and sympathy (Mills & Rubin 1990, Rubin & Mills 1992). These anticipations or experiences may be triggered by parental beliefs that their child's withdrawal from social company is dispositionally based (Mills & Rubin 1990), that it is associated with strong and debilitating child feelings of social anxiety (e.g., Fox et al. 1996, Hastings et al. 2005), and that it is accompanied by child behaviors that evoke, in peers, attempts to be socially dominant. In turn, these beliefs may evoke parental behavior of a quick fix variety. That is, to release the child from social discomfort, the parent may simply take over by telling the child what to do and how to do it (Rubin et al. 1999). In transactional models of the development of social withdrawal and anxiety (see **Figure 1**), these parenting behaviors are thought to reinforce the child's feelings of insecurity, resulting in the maintenance of a cycle of child hopelessness/helplessness and parent overcontrol/overprotection (Barrett et al. 1996, Rapee 1997, Wood et al. 2003). Moreover, allowing the child to avoid feared social behaviors, over time, may prevent the child from attaining developmentally appropriate social competencies.

These findings suggest that the developmental course of social withdrawal may emanate from parental reactions to their young children's biologically based characteristics. For example, Rubin and colleagues (2002) found that for toddlers whose mothers were overly solicitous and controlling, BI among peers predicted subsequent reticent behavior in the preschool peer group; however, for toddlers whose mothers were not intrusively controlling, the relation between toddler BI and preschool reticence was nonsignificant.

Coplan et al. (2008) recently reported a moderating role of parental characteristics in the relations between temperamental shyness and socio-emotional adjustment in kindergarten. Results indicated that relations between shyness (as assessed at the start of the school year) and indices of maladjustment (at the end of the school year) were significantly stronger among children with mothers characterized by higher neuroticism, threat sensitivity, and an overprotective parenting style, and the relations were significantly weaker for children with mothers characterized by high agreeableness and an authoritative parenting style.

Researchers have also examined the role of parenting in the stability of socially inhibited and withdrawn behaviors beyond early childhood. For example, Hane and colleagues (2008) reported that 4-year shyness predicted 7-year observed social withdrawal among peers when mothers engaged them with low degrees of positivity. The relation between 4-year shyness and 7-year withdrawal was nonsignificant when mothers engaged in high degrees of positivity. Relatedly, observed preschool reticence

among peers predicted observed 7-year social withdrawal only when mothers were observed to be highly negative during observed interactions at 7 years of age. Similarly, Degnan et al. (2008) found that when mothers were highly negative (high control and intrusiveness), their negatively reactive infants exhibited greater social wariness at 7 years than was the case for positively reactive infants. Also, maternal solicitous behavior, as assessed during mothers' free play with their preschoolers, moderated the continuity between preschool reticence and 7-year social wariness and withdrawal. Thus, for children with mothers observed to be low on solicitousness, 4-year reticence was not significantly related to 7-year social wariness and withdrawal; however, for children with mothers observed to be highly solicitous, 4-year reticence was positively related to 7-year social wariness and withdrawal.

In summary, we have painted a portrait of mothers (and in one study, fathers; Rubin et al. 1999) of socially reticent and anxiously withdrawn children as endorsing and practicing intrusive, controlling, and overprotective parenting strategies that are likely detrimental to the child's developing senses of autonomy and social efficacy (see also Wood et al. 2003). Significantly, almost identical results have derived from retrospective studies of socially anxious and shy adults. In these latter cases, it has been found that among the parenting characteristics described by this group of adults, overprotection, control, and insensitivity stand out (e.g., Schlette et al. 1998). Such parenting beliefs and behaviors are not conducive to the development of social competence or positive self-regard. Indeed, research has shown that an overprotective, overly concerned parenting style is associated with submissiveness, dependency, and timidity in early childhood. These characteristics are typical of socially withdrawn children and may increase the likelihood of problematic peer relations (Olweus 1993). We expand on this point in the sections below wherein we focus on the peer relationships of socially withdrawn children.

CORRELATES AND CONSEQUENCES OF CHILDHOOD SOCIAL WITHDRAWAL

Peer Interactions

In social milieus, shy-withdrawn children rarely initiate contact with peers, take longer than typical children to initiate conversation, and speak less frequently than their nonwithdrawn counterparts (e.g., Asendorpf & Meier 1993, Coplan et al. 2008, Crozier & Perkins 2002, Evans 2001). This description not only describes the social initiations and interactions of socially withdrawn children, it partially defines the construct of withdrawal.

When socially withdrawn children do interact with peers, they appear to be less socially competent than typical children (e.g., Bohlin et al. 2005, Chen et al. 2006, Nelson et al. 2005, Rubin & Krasnor 1986). For example, in an observational study, Stewart & Rubin (1995) found that socially withdrawn children pursued more lower-cost social goals (e.g., "Could you look at this?") and fewer high-cost social goals ("Can I play with you?"), and that their attempts to meet their social goals were less likely to succeed than those of their nonwithdrawn age-mates.

In recent years, researchers have also begun to explore the underlying meanings and consequences of different subtypes of observed socially withdrawn (i.e., solitary) behaviors. As noted above, reticent behavior is considered a behavioral expression of a social approach-avoidance conflict (Asendorpf 1990) and includes the prolonged watching of other children without accompanying play (onlooking) and being unoccupied (Coplan et al. 1994). Strong empirical support links right frontal EEG asymmetries, low vagal tone, adult-rated shyness, and observed BI with observed reticence with both unfamiliar and familiar peers in the laboratory and at school (Degnan et al. 2008, Fox et al. 2005). Importantly, however, much of this work has been limited to samples of 4- to 7-year-olds.

Early studies of solitary-passive play, which includes quiet exploration and solitary, constructive activities (Rubin 1982), indicated that it was a relatively benign form of nonsocial play, at least in early childhood (Coplan et al. 1994, Rubin 1982). In this regard, it was speculated that solitary-passive play may be a behavioral marker of social disinterest (e.g., Rubin & Asendorpf 1993). Intuitively, this assumption makes sense; children who are socially disinterested would be expected to spend more time alone than engaging in social interaction.

However, recent results have called this assumption into question. To begin with, Coplan and colleagues (2004) reported that parent-rated social disinterest was not associated with observed solitude of any form. Henderson et al. (2004) speculated that for some shy children, solitary-passive behavior may serve as a strategy for coping with feelings of social unease. That is, having learned early that the expression of socially reticent behavior elicits peer rejection and victimization (see below), some socially anxious children may mask their social qualms by expressing quiet constructive and exploratory activity among peers. Furthermore, results from several recent studies have suggested that solitary-passive behavior in early childhood may, like reticence, be a liability (Spinrad et al. 2004), especially for boys (Coplan et al. 2001, Nelson et al. 2005). At this time, it would be prudent to assume that children may display solitary-passive play for different reasons. But again, it is important to note that there does not exist a literature on solitary-passive behavior beyond the mid-elementary school years.

Peer Relationships

Rejection, victimization, and submissiveness. As noted above, when socially withdrawn children attempt to meet their social goals in the company of their peers, they are more likely to directly experience peer neglect and rejection than their more sociable age-mates (e.g., Chen et al. 2006, Nelson et al. 2005,

Rubin & Krasnor 1986, Stewart & Rubin 1995). Relatedly, it is also well known that socially withdrawn children are actively disliked by their peers (Boivin et al. 1995, Gazelle & Ladd 2003, Hart et al. 2000, Ladd 2006, Oh et al. 2008, Ollendick et al. 1990, Rubin et al. 1993). In fact, social withdrawal is one of the strongest correlates and consequences of peer rejection during middle childhood and adolescence (e.g., Deater-Deckard 2001, Newcomb et al. 1993). It is argued that peers reject socially withdrawn children because their demeanor runs contrary to age-specific norms and expectations for social interaction and relationship- and group-involvement (Rubin et al. 2006d). Furthermore, researchers have argued that atypical behavior becomes more salient to the peer group with increased age; this may explain why the association between social withdrawal and peer rejection steadily increases with age (Ladd 2006).

Approximately 10% of the school population experiences victimization by peers (Natl. Inst. Child Health Human Dev. 2001, Olweus 1984). Children who are victimized experience repeated and consistent physical and verbal abuse from their peers and classmates. Given the reserved and quiescent demeanor of many socially withdrawn children and given that they often attempt to avoid social company to begin with, one might expect that they would be protected from a bullying experience. After all, why would bullies bother to victimize those who are socially restrained and unremarkable? And yet, researchers have consistently reported that this group of children and young adolescents is at high risk for peer victimization (e.g., Hanish & Guerra 2004, Kochenderfer-Ladd 2003). Significant associations have also been revealed between social anxiety and victimization during later childhood and early adolescence (e.g., Grills & Ollendick 2002).

Aggressive children may "invite" or encourage peer victimization through peer provocation (e.g., upsetting other children, initiating fights). In contrast, the shy, timid nature of socially withdrawn children may elicit the social perception of being easy targets. They may evoke victimization precisely be-cause they present themselves as physically and emotionally weak and unlikely to retaliate (e.g., Rubin et al. 2006d). This view is consistent with Olweus's (1993) characterization of socially withdrawn boys as "whipping boys" and with Perry and colleagues' research on "passive victims" (e.g., Perry et al. 1988). Because social withdrawal and avoidance are strategies often used to cope with peer victimization (Eisenberg et al. 1998, Gazelle & Rudolph 2004), a transactional cycle may exist whereby the initially withdrawn child is victimized, which in turn increases his/her withdrawal from social company and subsequent victimization.

Friendships. Although socially withdrawn children may have difficulties forming large numbers of friendships (Pedersen et al. 2007), it is nevertheless the case that withdrawn children and young adolescents are as likely as their typical age-mates to have at least one mutual and stable best friend (e.g., Ladd & Burgess 1999, Rubin et al. 2006d, Schneider 1999). Rubin and colleagues (2006d), for example, found that approximately 65% of socially withdrawn 10-year-olds had a mutual best friendship, and approximately 70% of these best friendships were maintained across the academic year; these friendship-involvement and -stability percentages were nearly identical to those of nonwithdrawn 10-year-olds. Thus, despite their difficulties in the larger peer group, withdrawn children do appear able to form and maintain close dyadic relationships within the school milieu.

Prevalence aside, it is nevertheless the case that socially withdrawn children do differ from their peers on other dimensions of friendship. To begin with, investigators have found greater similarities between friends than between non-friends in terms of shared internalized distress (Hogue & Steinberg 1995) and social withdrawal and shyness (Haselager et al. 1998). Moreover, the best friends of extremely withdrawn children and young adolescents are more likely to be socially withdrawn and victimized than are the mutual best friends of nonwithdrawn children (Rubin et al. 2006d). Thus, many socially withdrawn children and young adolescents appear to be involved in friendships with other children who are experiencing similar psychosocial difficulties.

The friendships of socially withdrawn children and young adolescents also tend to be relatively poor in relationship quality. Schneider (1999) reported that eight- and nine-year-old friendship dyads comprising one or two socially withdrawn children were rated by observers as relatively restricted in their verbal communication. And Rubin et al. (2006d) found that withdrawn young adolescents rated their best friendships as lacking in helpfulness, guidance, and intimate disclosure; the best friends of these withdrawn young adolescents rated their friendships as involving less fun and help and guidance than did the best friends of nonwithdrawn young adolescents.

Importantly, the extent to which group and dyadic relationship factors conspire to maintain or alter the developmental trajectories of social withdrawal in early adolescence has been examined by Oh et al. (2008). These researchers found three distinct growth trajectory classes for social withdrawal from the final year of elementary school (fifth grade), across the transition to middle school (sixth grade), and then to the final year of middle school (eighth grade): a low stable, an increasing, and a decreasing class. Friendlessness, friendship instability, and exclusion and victimization by peers were significant predictors of the trajectory of increased social withdrawal over the four-year period. Decreases in social withdrawal were evident for those young adolescents who experienced decreases in rejection and victimization as they made the transition from elementary to middle school. In many ways, this finding is consistent with those of Gazelle & Rudolph (2004), who reported that when anxious-solitary youth experienced less peer exclusion they displayed an increase in social approach. Taken together, these findings may suggest that withdrawn children and young adolescents experience increased motivation to engage others in social interaction when the social landscape becomes "kinder" and "gentler."

Self and Social Cognitions

Given that socially withdrawn children and young adolescents often experience peer rejection and victimization, it should not be surprising that they feel and think poorly of themselves. Moreover, as noted above, the social initiations of socially withdrawn children often result in peer noncompliance despite the fact that these initiations and requests are less likely than are those of nonwithdrawn children to require carrying out action that involves both effort and mobility (Rubin & Krasnor 1986, Stewart & Rubin 1995). This in vivo failure to obtain peer compliance and collegiality with peers has been found to predict negative self-perceptions of social skills and peer relationships (e.g., Nelson et al. 2005). That is, real-life peer rejection (e.g., noncompliance) predicts negative thoughts and feelings about the self. Importantly, socially withdrawn children's self-perceptions are quite accurate; that is, they are well aware of their social difficulties (e.g., Asendorpf 1994).

Thus, it should not be surprising that social withdrawal is also associated with loneliness and depressed affect from the earliest years of childhood through early adolescence (e.g., Coplan et al. 2007, Eisenberg et al. 1998, Hymel et al. 1990, Prior et al. 2000). Moreover, the combination of withdrawal and peer rejection, exclusion, and/or victimization appears to be the strongest predictor of these negative outcomes (e.g., Bell-Dolan et al. 1995, Boivin & Hymel 1997, Gazelle & Ladd 2003, Gazelle & Rudolph 2004), supporting the premise that it is the negative response of the peer group that results in withdrawn children's internalized negative thoughts and feelings.

Rubin and colleagues (e.g., Rubin et al. 2003, 2008) have further posited that the consistent and stable experience of rejection and victimization experienced by withdrawn children may lead to the development of an attributional schema in which social failures are blamed on internal rather than external or situational causes. Consistent with this supposition is the earlier finding that extremely withdrawn children blamed their social failures on personal, dispositional characteristics rather than on external events or circumstances (Rubin & Krasnor 1986). Indeed, these findings were expanded upon by Wichmann et al. (2004), who reported that when 9- to-13-year-old withdrawn children were presented with hypothetical social situations in which they experienced ambiguously caused negative events, they attributed the causes of these events to internal and stable "self-defeating" causes. Moreover, when asked how they go about resolving the experienced dilemma, withdrawn children indicated a preferred strategy of withdrawal and escape (see also Burgess et al. 2006). Taken together, these results are reminiscent of Graham & Juvonen's (2001) findings that youngsters who identified themselves as victimized by peers blamed themselves for their peer relationship problems. Given that self-blame and avoidant coping can lead to a variety of negative outcomes of an internalizing nature, such as depression, low self-esteem, and increased withdrawal (e.g., Garnefski et al. 2005, Reijntjes et al. 2006), the aforementioned findings suggest a self-reinforcing cycle of negative socioemotional and social-cognitive functioning for socially withdrawn children.

LONG-TERM CONSEQUENCES OF SOCIAL WITHDRAWAL AND RELATED CONSTRUCTS

Over the past two decades, it has become increasingly clear that there are long-term costs associated with childhood inhibition, shyness, and withdrawal. It is known that internalizing problems (e.g., loneliness, anxiety, and depression) are contemporaneous correlates of childhood and early adolescent social withdrawal (e.g., Boivin et al. 1995, Morison & Masten 1991, Ollendick et al. 1990). In the Waterloo Longitudinal Project, Rubin and colleagues reported that observed and peer-rated social withdrawal at seven years of age predicted self-reported negative self-regard and loneliness at nine and ten years of age (Hymel et al. 1990, Rubin et al. 1989). Moreover, so-cial withdrawal at seven years predicted loneliness, depression, and negative self-regard at 14 years (e.g., Rubin et al. 1995). Other researchers have reported similar longitudinal relations between social withdrawal and later problems of the internalizing ilk (e.g., Boivin et al. 1995, Ollendick et al. 1990).

Similarly, in reports deriving from the Australian Temperament Project, it has been found that children rated as consistently shy from early childhood onward were at high risk for the development of anxiety; indeed, 42% of children rated as highly shy in early childhood had anxiety problems in adolescence; those never rated as shy had an 11% incidence of anxiety difficulties (Prior et al. 2000). Relatedly, there exists evidence that extremely inhibited children are at increased risk for developing anxiety disorders (particularly social phobia) in later childhood and adolescence (e.g., Hayward et al. 1998, Schwartz et al. 1999).

Asendorpf and colleagues (e.g., Asendorpf & van Aken 1999, Denissen et al. 2008) have reported that shy-inhibited children are viewed by both teachers and parents as having an over-controlled personality. These are children who are simultaneously high in ego-control and low in ego-resiliency (Block & Block 1980). In their longitudinal follow-ups of such children, Asendorpf and colleagues have found that, over a 19-year period, overcontrolled children remained consistently shyer as young adults than resilient-competent children (Asendorpf & Denissen 2006). For children who viewed themselves as shy, Asendorpf found an association with perceived lack of support from peers. Moreover, over the long run, shy males (but not females) entered romantic relationships later than nonshy males, a finding in keeping with that of Caspi and colleagues (Caspi et al. 1988).

ACADEMICS AND SCHOOL ADJUSTMENT

Going to school appears to be particularly stressful for shy-withdrawn children. Coplan & Arbeau (2008) cite the presence of a large group of (initially unfamiliar) peers, increased demands for verbal participation, and a high child-to-staff ratio as factors that may exacerbate shy-withdrawn feelings of social fear and self-consciousness. Indeed, there is increasing empirical support for the notion that the transition to school is particularly problematic for shy-withdrawn children (Coplan et al. 2008, Evans 2001, Rimm-Kaufman & Kagan 2005).

Language skills. Along with refraining from interaction with peers, speech restraint is central to most operational definitions of shyness and social withdrawal (e.g., Rezendes et al. 1993). It has been well documented that shy-withdrawn children speak less frequently than do their peers to both children and adults in the classroom environment (Asendorpf & Meier 1993, Evans 2001, Evans & Bienert 1992, Rimm-Kaufman et al. 2002, Rimm-Kaufman & Kagan 2005).

Shy-withdrawn children tend to perform more poorly than nonshy-withdrawn children on standardized tests of expressive language (e.g., Crozier & Perkins 2002, Evans 1996, Spere et al. 2004). And yet, findings regarding indices of receptive language skills have been less consistent, with some researchers reporting poorer performance by shy-withdrawn children (e.g., Crozier & Perkins 2002, Spere et al. 2004), and others failing to find such associations (e.g., Evans 1996). This has led to some debate as to whether shy children might suffer from a performance deficit (as a result of the social stresses of the testing environment) as opposed to a competence deficit (e.g., Crozier & Hostettler 2003).

Notwithstanding the "actual" language abilities of shy-withdrawn children, it has been suggested that individual differences in language abilities may serve as an important moderator of the relations between withdrawal and adjustment (Asendorpf 1994). Coplan & Armer (2005) found that the relation between shyness and indices of school maladjustment were significantly reduced at higher levels of expressive language. Similar results were also recently reported in terms of pragmatic language skills (Coplan & Weeks 2008). Perhaps then, the in-

ability or reticence to be verbally expressive in the classroom may be considered atypical and unacceptable to classmates. This may result in rejection by peers, and peer rejection is known to predict poor school performance even in the earliest school years (Buhs & Ladd 2001, Ladd et al. 1999). Consequently, if expressive language skills facilitate the social and school adjustment of shy-withdrawn children, then these findings should be incorporated into the design of intervention programs.

Academic achievement. There is preliminary evidence linking shyness-withdrawal with a lack of displayed academic competence both in early (e.g., Coplan et al. 2001, Lloyd & Howe 2003) and later childhood (Masten et al. 1985). Student participation and social interaction are viewed as important contributors to the attainment of learning objectives (Daly & Korinek 1980). In this regard, teachers may perceive withdrawn children's quietness as a lack of interest or understanding of a topic (Crozier & Perkins 2002). Indeed, teachers and peers perceive "quiet" children as being less intelligent (e.g., McCroskey & Daly 1976, Richmond et al. 1985). In addition, anxiety, self-consciousness, and worries about being called upon may interfere with shy-withdrawn children's classroom earning (Evans 2001). This may contribute to a lack of academic confidence, which is evidenced in withdrawn children's tendency to rate themselves more poorly on self-report measures of scholastic and academic competence (e.g., Crozier 1995).

Finally, when given the opportunity to demonstrate their academic competence, shy children may evidence performance deficits because of stress associated with test performance. Crozier & Hostettler (2003) recently explored the academic achievement (vocabulary and math) of shy children in three different testing environments: (*a*) individually administered oral assessments; (*b*) individually administered written assessments; and (*c*) group-administered written assessment. Results indicated that shy children scored significantly lower than nonshy children in both individually administered conditions, but there were no significant differences between groups in the group-administered condition. These researchers suggested that in a group setting, shy children did not feel the same performance pressure that is experienced in individual administration settings. These findings have potentially important implications for assessing the academic performance of shy-withdrawn children.

Teacher-child relationships and classroom climate. Some researchers have suggested that withdrawn children may either go unnoticed by teachers or that teachers may encourage shy behaviors because reserved, quiescent, compliant behavior helps to maintain classroom order (e.g., Keogh 2003, Rimm-Kaufman et al. 2002). However, recent findings suggest that shy-withdrawn children do not go unnoticed by teachers. For example, researchers have reported that that socially withdrawn children require more attention from teachers (e.g., Coplan & Prakash 2003) and develop less close and more highly dependent relationships with them (e.g., Ladd & Burgess 1999, Rudasill et al. 2006). Moreover, children whose relationships with teachers are characterized by less closeness and greater dependency are at increased concurrent and predictive risk for a number of school adjustment difficulties (e.g., Hamre & Pianta 2006).

Importantly, moderating effects may derive from classroom climate. Gazelle (2006) found that anxiously withdrawn first graders were more rejected (boys) and victimized (girls) by peers and demonstrated more depressive symptoms (girls) in classrooms with negative emotional climates (i.e., frequent disruptive child behaviors, conflictual relationships between students and teacher, infrequent prosocial peer interactions).

Sex Differences

There is little evidence to suggest that sex differences exist in the prevalence or frequency of inhibition, shyness, and social withdrawal in childhood and early adolescence. This lack of sex differences has been reported for observed behavioral inhibition (e.g., Mullen et al. 1993); parent-reported child shyness (e.g., Coplan et al. 2004, Rowe & Plomin 1977); observed social withdrawal in the peer group (e.g., Coplan et al. 2001); peer-nominated social withdrawal (e.g., Lemerise 1997, Rubin et al. 1993); and teacher-rated social anxiety and withdrawal (e.g., Ladd & Profilet 1996, Thijs et al. 2004). The one exception derives from self-reports; young adolescent girls tend to self-report greater shyness than boys (e.g., Crozier 1995).

Notwithstanding, strong evidence suggests that shyness-withdrawal carries a greater cost for boys than girls. Henderson et al. (2001) found that negative reactivity at 9 months predicted displays of social wariness at age 4 years for boys but not for girls. And Dettling et al. (1999) noted that shyness in preschool-aged boys but not girls was associated with increased cortisol levels over the day at childcare. Put another way, shy boys appear to experience greater stress as the day progresses in a social setting. As well, beginning in early childhood, shy-withdrawn boys are more likely to be excluded and rejected by peers than are shy-withdrawn girls (e.g., Coplan et al. 2004, Coplan & Arbeau 2008, Gazelle & Ladd 2003).

Across the lifespan, shyness-withdrawal appears to be more strongly associated with socioemotional difficulties for boys than for girls. Thus, socially withdrawn boys but not girls describe themselves as more lonely, as having poorer social skills, and as having lower self-esteem than their typical peers (Morison & Masten 1991, Nelson et al. 2005, Rubin et al. 1993). Caspi and colleagues (1988) found that males who were shy in childhood married, became fathers, and established careers at a later age than their nonshy peers. In contrast, females who were shy in childhood did not marry or start families later than other women in the same cohort.

The different outcomes associated with social withdrawal for boys may be partly attributable to societal or cultural expectations;

in Western societies, shyness-withdrawal appears to be less acceptable for boys than for girls (Sadker & Sadker 1994). Findings can also be explained, in part, by the ways in which parents think about shyness and social withdrawal and how they respond to or interact with their shy or socially withdrawn sons and daughters. For example, the mothers of inhibited-withdrawn toddler and preschool age girls are reported to be warm, responsive, and sensitive; mothers of young withdrawn boys are reportedly more power assertive, less affectionate, and less responsive than parents of typical children (e.g., Stevenson-Hinde 1989). Although it is difficult to ascertain whether dispositional factors lead to different parental responses or whether different parenting behavior leads to different social behavioral profiles for boys versus girls, the bottom line is that passive, inhibited, withdrawn boys experience socialization and social relationship histories that differ from their female counterparts.

Culture

A thorough review of cultural differences in the prevalence, correlates, and consequences of BI, reticence, shyness, and social withdrawal appeared in the *Annual Review of Psychology* in 2008 (Chen & French 2008). Consequently, the review presented here is rather abbreviated. The psychological meaning attributed to any given social behavior is, in large part, a function of the ecological niche within which it is produced. If a given behavior is viewed as acceptable, then parents (and significant others) will attempt to encourage its development; if the behavior is perceived as maladaptive or abnormal, then parents (and significant others) will attempt to discourage its growth and development. Of course, the very means by which people go about encouraging or discouraging the given behavior may be culturally determined and defined.

Initial work on the prevalence, correlates, and consequences of BI, shyness, and social withdrawal began with the suggestion that within collectivistic cultures a strong emphasis was placed on group cohesion; consequently,

shy-reserved behavior may be more greatly appreciated than in Western cultures that espouse individualistic beliefs and norms. In an extensive series of studies, Chen and colleagues demonstrated that shy, reticent, reserved behavior in the People's Republic of China is encouraged and accepted by mothers, teachers, and peers, and is positively associated with social competence, peer acceptance, and academic success (e.g., Chen et al. 1995). In contrast, in cultural contexts within which such individual characteristics as assertiveness, expressiveness, and competitiveness are valued and encouraged, social withdrawal has been linked to peer rejection. Thus, in such countries as Argentina, Canada, Greece, Italy, the Netherlands, and the United States (Casiglia et al. 1998, Cillessen et al. 1992, Rubin et al. 1993, Schaughency et al. 1992), socially wary and withdrawn children are largely rejected by their peers.

And yet, these findings do not represent the last word. Hart and colleagues (2000) have found that social reticence is associated with a lack of peer acceptance not only in young American children, but also among Russian and Chinese youngsters. Relatedly, Chen et al. (2005) found that over the years, since the early 1990s, shy, reserved behavior among urban Chinese elementary school children has increasingly become associated with negative peer reputations. Chen has argued that the changing economic and political climate in China is being accompanied by preferences for more assertive, yet competent, social behavior.

Interestingly, beginning as early as 2 years of age, the prevalence of behavioral inhibition varies across culture (Rubin et al. 2006b,c). Chinese and South Korean toddlers are observed and rated by parents to be more inhibited than their Australian, Italian, and Canadian age-mates. Importantly, the association between toddler shy/inhibited behavior and parental acceptance is significantly negative among Canadian and Italian parents (Rubin et al. 2006b,c) but positive among Chinese parents (Chen et al. 1998). It would appear as if the expression of inhibited behavior may be interpreted as reservedness and respectfulness (and compliant) among Chinese parents and as expressions of fearfulness among Western parents.

And yet, cross-cultural research on BI and social withdrawal may well be fraught with methodological and conceptual difficulty. To begin with, one shortcoming in all of this work is that investigators have taken measures originally developed for use specifically within a Western cultural context and have employed them within other cultural milieus. When conducting cross-cultural research, the emic-etic problem represents a major methodological challenge. Cross-cultural studies are especially susceptible to measurement artifacts and bias (van de Vijver & Leung 1997). The emic perspective refers to conceptual schemes and categories that are viewed as meaningful by members of the culture under study. In contrast, the etic perspective refers to extrinsic concepts and categories that have meaning for scientific observers. That is, etic constructs are consistent across different cultures and are therefore universal or pan-cultural truths or principles (Bornstein 1991). Importantly, researchers can sometimes inappropriately impose etics on other cultures when, in fact, the construct in question is emic in nature. The etic approach has dominated in the cross-cultural study of phenomena having to do with social withdrawal.

Another shortcoming derives from the interchanging of different social withdrawal-related constructs in the extant cross-cultural work (with the implicit assumption being that all forms of solitude may carry with them the same meaning). The danger of so doing may best be summarized in the findings of a recent study on maternal beliefs about socially withdrawn behavior. Cheah & Rubin (2004) presented mothers with a series of vignettes in which they were asked how they would react if they consistently viewed their preschoolers playing alone when in a preschool setting. Chinese mothers responded with greater anger than American mothers; they also suggested that they would teach their children how to play with others, whereas American

mothers indicated a tendency toward over-protectiveness. Taking these findings together with those noted above on *BI* and shyness, it would appear as if shyness and social withdrawal are viewed as rather different constructs by Chinese parents. Thus, reserved, shy behavior (as studied by Chen and colleagues) may eventually be conducive to harmonious group interactions, whereas socially withdrawn behavior (e.g., Cheah & Rubin 2004) that removes the child from familiar others could undermine such goals. In this regard, socially withdrawn behavior could be perceived by Chinese mothers as "nonsocial" behavior that undermines the predominant collectivistic teachings of preschool caregivers, as well as the societal goals of group harmony and close interaction.

All of this suggests that cross-cultural research on the topic of social withdrawal, in its many forms, has a long way to go. Researchers have interpreted their data as suggesting cultural differences in the meanings of inhibition, shyness, reticence, and so on. It thus follows that the next step is to examine whether the displays of these behaviors are linked cross-culturally in similar or different ways, not only with such social factors as parenting and peer relationships, but also with biological assessments including EEG, electrocardiogram, and the production of cortisol.

DEVELOPMENTAL PATHWAYS TO AND FROM SOCIAL WITHDRAWAL

In this review, we have referred to a developmental model concerning the etiology, correlates, and outcomes of social withdrawal during childhood and adolescence (see **Figure 1**). Our suggested pathway derives from the data reviewed above as well as extant theoretical perspectives linking conceptually related dispositional, interactional, and relationship constructs. From our perspective, the ontogeny of a socially withdrawn profile begins with newborns who are biologically predisposed to have a low threshold for arousal when confronted with social (or nonsocial) stimulation and novelty. This hyperarousal may make these babies extremely difficult for their parents to soothe and comfort. We propose that some parents may find these dispositional characteristics aversive and difficult to handle. Parents may react to easily aroused and wary babies with the belief that the child is vulnerable and requires protection. Such overprotective and oversolicitous parenting, in concert with the child's disposition of a low threshold for arousal and an inability to be easily soothed, is posited to predict the development of an insecure parent-infant attachment relationship. Thus, it is suggested that the interplay of endogenous, socialization, and early relationship factors leads to a sense of felt insecurity.

We also propose that the infant's temperament along with feelings of insecurity may guide him or her onto a trajectory toward behavioral inhibition. The consistent expression of inhibition precludes these children from experiencing the positive outcomes associated with social exploration and peer play. Thus, we predict a developmental sequence in which an inhibited, fearful, insecure child withdraws from her/his social world of peers, fails to develop those skills derived from peer interaction, and consequently, becomes increasingly anxious and isolated from the peer group.

Social withdrawal becomes increasingly salient to the peer group with age. This deviation from age-appropriate social norms is associated with the establishment of peer rejection; for example, as noted above, even by the early years of childhood, social withdrawal and anxiety are associated with peer rejection and unpopularity.

Reticence to explore and play cooperatively in the peer environment is associated with, and predictive of, the development of an impoverished style of interpersonal negotiation skills. We have indicated that socially wary and withdrawn children make relatively few attempts to direct the behaviors of their peers and that when they do, their efforts are likely to be met by peer rebuff. And we have reviewed literature suggesting that an outcome of social interactive failure and peer rejection is the de-velopment of negative self-esteem and negative self-perceptions of social skills and peer relations. Sensing the child's difficulties and perceived helplessness, his/her parents might attempt to direct their child's social behaviors in a power-assertive fashion by telling the child how to act or what to do, or by actually solving the child's interpersonal dilemmas for him/her. As we have described above, an overcontrolled or overinvolved parenting style maintains and exacerbates the socially withdrawn child's inter- and intrapersonal difficulties.

Drawing from the extant literature, we believe that when socially withdrawn children present themselves as wary and anxious in the peer group, not only might they become increasingly rejected, but they also may be victimized by the peer group at large. This does not mean to suggest that they will be friendless; however, given the literature reviewed above, it may be that their friendships will be with children or adolescents much like themselves.

In summary, we propose that social incompetence of an overcontrolled, withdrawn nature may be the product of an inhibited temperament, an insecure parent-child relationship, shared genetic vulnerabilities or traits with the parents, overly directive and protective parenting, and peer rejection and victimization, and the interactions among "all of the above." The posited consequences of this constellation of factors are the development of (*a*) negative thoughts and feelings about the self, (*b*) social anxiety, and (*c*) loneliness. If the establishment and maintenance of close interpersonal relationships is considered a significant objective that has not been met, another outcome may be depression.

It is very important to note that we do not consider infant dispositional characteristics to necessarily lead to the pathway described above. A wary, fearful/inhibited temperament may be deflected toward the development of social competence by responsive and sensitive caregiving (Degnan & Fox 2007). An inhibited, emotionally dysregulated temperament does not necessarily produce an incompetent, internalized, or overcontrolled behavioral style. On the other hand, it may well be that parental overcontrol and overinvolvement may deflect the temperamentally easy-going infant toward a pathway of internalizing difficulties.

Additionally, the ability to cope with one's fearful and shy dispositions by displaying socially and emotionally competent behaviors may move the child off the pathway to peer rejection and victimization. And having close friendships with others who are socially and emotionally competent may be protective. These latter suggestions are merely testable suggestions. Data remain to be gathered to address these positions.

The developmental pathway we have offered above represents a useful heuristic for studying the etiology of social withdrawal. We speculate that there are direct and indirect ways in which dispositional characteristics, parent-child relationships, parenting styles, and peer relationships may influence the development and maintenance of social withdrawal, its concomitants, and its outcomes.

FUTURE DIRECTIONS

Other Forms of Social Withdrawal

Most research on social withdrawal has focused on children who are, or who become, socially fearful and anxious (i.e., inhibited/shy). As noted above, however, some children may refrain from social interaction because although not strongly averse to peer interaction (i.e., low social-avoidance motivation), they also lack a strong motivation to engage others in interaction (i.e., low social-approach motivation). This nonfearful preference for solitude has been labeled unsociability (Asendorpf 1990) or social disinterest (Coplan et al. 2004) in children, and solitropic orientation in adults (Leary et al. 2003).

Results from recent research indicate that parents (Coplan et al. 2004), teachers (Arbeau & Coplan 2007, Thijs et al. 2004), and even young children (Coplan et al. 2007) distinguish between social disinterest and other forms of social withdrawal (e.g., shyness). In early childhood, there is evidence to suggest that social disinterest is comparably benign (e.g., Asendorpf & Meier 1993, Coplan et al. 2004, Harrist et al. 1997). However, the longer-term outcomes of unsociability remain largely unexplored. Some researchers have suggested that unsociability may become increasingly maladaptive in middle childhood, as those who rarely interact socially (for whatever reason) may lag behind in important social and social-cognitive skills (Rubin & Asendorpf 1993).

In contrast, others have stressed the potential positive benefits of solitude in adolescence and adulthood (e.g., Larson 1997). For example, it has been argued that adults' ability to enjoy solitary activities is a positive indication of well-being (e.g., Burke 1991, Maslow 1970). Solitude may also offer practical benefits if unsociable adolescents or adults spend their solitary time constructively, developing independent thinking, reading, writing, or other skills. Indeed, adults who express a nonfearful preference for solitude can be as happy as their more extroverted counterparts (Hills & Argyle 2000). To address these questions, longitudinal studies are needed to assess the distinctiveness, stability, and outcomes of social disinterest beyond early childhood.

Asendorpf (1990) has also proposed that some socially withdrawn children may be characterized by the combination of low social-approach and high social-avoidance motivations. These avoidant children would not only desire solitude, but also would avoid social interaction. In the only empirical study of social avoidance to date, Coplan et al. (2006) used a more general assessment of approach to reward (the behavioral activation system) and high avoidance of punishment (the behavioral inhibition system) to identify a group of children who had both a low behavioral activation system and a high behavioral inhibition system (conceptually similar to avoidance). Compared with their age-mates, avoidant children reported the highest levels of negative affect and depressive symptoms and the lowest levels of positive affect and overall well-being. The development of new methodologies for identifying social avoidance (and to distinguish it from shyness and social disinterest) will be necessary in order to allow future researchers to explore this phenomenon further.

Protective Factors

Although being excluded and having a withdrawn friend appear to represent significant risk factors in the lives of socially withdrawn children (e.g., Gazelle & Ladd 2003, Oh et al. 2008), it is important for future researchers to explore the significance of protective factors in studies of social withdrawal and associated adjustment outcomes. Drawing from recent theory and research on risk and resilience (e.g., Luthar 2006), such characteristics as emotional regulation and expressiveness may alter withdrawn children's risk and adjustment difficulties (Pope & Bierman 1999). Indeed, Bowker et al. (2008) recently reported that withdrawn children and young adolescents who expressed little negative internalizing emotion in the peer group (sadness, anxiety, fearfulness) did not experience increased peer rejection and victimization throughout the school year (both in elementary school and middle school). In contrast, withdrawn children and young adolescents who were highly emotionally expressive became significantly more victimized and excluded by the end of the school year. These data suggest the significance of coping actively with felt anxiety or fearfulness in the peer group. Regulating emotional expressiveness appeared to be a protective factor for withdrawn children and young adolescents.

Talents or special skills that are valued by the child and the community have also been offered as possible protective factors for high-risk children (Werner 1995). In this regard, researchers would do well to consider whether scholastic achievement or participation in extracurricular activities and clubs improves the ways in which socially withdrawn children think and feel about themselves and their social worlds. For example, Findlay & Coplan (2008) recently reported evidence suggesting that participation in organized sports appears to play a unique protective role for shy-withdrawn children.

Little is known about school-based risk and protective factors for socially withdrawn children, particularly beyond the early childhood years. Such school-based factors as the warm-supportive classroom environment have been shown to be beneficial for shy and wary children (Gazelle 2006). It would appear important for researchers to consider the significance of additional features of schooling, such as the experience of transitions. In the United States, for example, many students make multiple transitions—from elementary school to middle school, from middle school to high school, and from high school to college. These transitions may be particularly difficult for socially withdrawn youngsters because of the stress associated with meeting unfamiliar peers (Barber & Olsen 2004); at the same time, such transitions may prove to be a protective turning point, in that it may provide an opportunity to break free of previously negative peer reputations (Seidman & French 2004).

Finally, researchers have shown that parents who are sensitive to their behaviorally inhibited children's characteristics and needs, who encourage independence, and who provide opportunities for peer interaction (e.g., by arranging play dates) help their children to become less inhibited and more socially skilled during early childhood (e.g., Rubin 2002; Rubin et al. 2001, 2002). Certainly, parent-child relationships continue to be important and influential relationships for older children and young adolescents, and yet there have been no studies examining the possible protective "power" of parents for withdrawn children in these older developmental periods.

Early Intervention and Prevention

Despite the extant empirical research demonstrating the concurrent and predictive "risk" associated with social withdrawal in childhood, comparatively little research has been devoted to intervention and prevention. Early attempts employed a range of intervention strategies and demonstrated rather mixed results (see Greco & Morris 2001 for a detailed review). Perhaps the most popular intervention strategy has been social skills training (SST), which involves training in verbal and nonverbal communication skills and incorporates components of coaching, modeling, and training for solving social problems. Some SST programs have demonstrated moderate short-term success in enhancing the social skills of withdrawn children and adolescents (e.g., Bienert & Schneider 1995, Jupp & Griffiths 1990, Sheridan et al. 1990). However, other SST programs have produced inconsistent findings and treatment effects that fail to generalize from one setting to the next (see Schneider 1992). Moreover, the children identified as socially withdrawn in many of these previous studies may have represented a fairly heterogeneous treatment group.

Early-intervention research clearly has a lot of catching up to do. Larger-scale studies with longer follow-up periods and careful designs are clearly needed. Social skills programs must be developed that are specifically designed for the particular needs of shy and withdrawn children. Moreover, other forms of peer-mediated interactions, such as peer-pairing and facilitated play (e.g., Furman et al. 1979), should be incorporated. As well, given what is known of the parents of socially withdrawn children, interventions would do well to involve parents. Recent evidence suggests that education and training programs for parents can reduce social anxiety in shy-withdrawn young children (e.g., Rapee et al. 2005) and improve treatment outcomes for school-aged anxious children (e.g., Spence et al. 2000). Beyond reductions in symptoms and improvements in treatment outcomes, it would be important to determine whether such interventions can modify socially withdrawn children's biology (e.g., EEG; Fox et al. 2001). Finally, it may also be possible to increase the effectiveness and generalizability of early intervention by employing a school-based approach. School-based programs reduce barriers to treatment (e.g., transportation), reach a broader range of children, and tend to reduce participant attrition (Barrett et al. 2005).

DISCLOSURE STATEMENT

The authors are not aware of any biases that might be perceived as affecting the objectivity of this review.

LITERATURE CITED

Achenbach TM. 1982. *Developmental Psychopathology*. New York: Wiley. 2nd ed.

Achenbach TM. 1991. *Manual for the Child Behavior Checklist/4–18 and 1991 Profile*. Burlington: Univ. Vermont, Dept. Psychiatry

Achenbach TM, Edelbrock C. 1981. Behavioral problems and competencies reported by parents of normal and disturbed children aged 4–16. *Monogr. Soc. Res. Child Dev.* 46:1–82

Achenbach TM, Rescorla LA. 2006. *Multicultural Understanding of Child and Adolescent Psychopathology: Implications for Mental Health Assessment*. New York: Guilford

Ainsworth MS, Blehar MC, Waters E, Wall S. 1978. *Patterns of Attachment: A Psychological Study of the Strange Situation*. Hillsdale, NJ: Erlbaum

Am. Psychiatr. Assoc. 1994. *Diagnostic and Statistical Manual of Mental Disorders*. Washington, DC: Am. Psychiatr. Assoc. 4th ed.

Arbeau KA, Coplan RJ. 2007. Kindergarten teachers' beliefs and responses to hypothetical prosocial, asocial, and antisocial children. *Merrill-Palmer Q.* 53:291–318

Asendorpf JB. 1990. Development of inhibition during childhood: evidence for situational specificity and two-factor model. *Dev. Psychol.* 26:721–30

Asendorpf JB. 1991. Development of inhibited children's coping with unfamiliarity. *Child Dev.* 62:1460–74

Asendorpf JB. 1994. The malleability of behavioral inhibition: a study of individual developmental functions. *Dev. Psychol.* 30:912–19

Asendorpf JB, Denissen J. 2006. Predictive validity of personality types versus personality dimensions from early childhood to adulthood: implications for the distinction between core and surface traits. *Merrill-Palmer Q.* 52:486–513

Asendorpf JB, Meier GH. 1993. Personality effects on children's speech in everyday life: sociability-mediated exposure and shyness-mediated reactivity to social situations. *J. Personal. Soc. Psychol.* 65:1072–83

Asendorpf JB, van Aken MAG. 1994. Traits and relationship status: stranger versus peer group inhibition and test intelligence versus peer group competence as early predictors of later self-esteem. *Child Dev.* 65:1786–98

Asendorpf JB, van Aken MAG. 1999. Resilient, overcontrolled, and undercontrolled personality prototypes in childhood: replicability, predictive power, and the trait-type issue. *J. Personal. Soc. Psychol.* 77:815–32

Bandura A, Walters RH. 1963. *Social Learning and Personality Development*. New York: Holt, Rinehart & Winston

Barber BK, Olsen J. 2004. Assessing the transitions to middle and high school. *J. Adolesc. Res.* 19:3–30

Barber BK, Olsen JE, Shagle SC. 1994. Associations between parental psychological and behavioral control and youth internalized and externalized behaviors. *Child Dev.* 65:1120–36

Barrett PM, Dadds MR, Rapee RM. 1996. Family treatment of childhood anxiety disorders: a controlled trial. *J. Consult. Clin. Psychol.* 64:333–42

Barrett PM, Lock S, Farrell L. 2005. Developmental differences in universal preventive intervention for child anxiety. *Clin. Child Psychol. Psychiatry* 10:539–55

Bell-Dolan DJ, Foster SL, Christopher JS. 1995. Girls' peer relations and internalizing problems: Are socially neglected, rejected, and withdrawn girls at risk? *J. Clin. Child Psychol.* 24:463–73

Bell-Dolan DJ, Reaven N, Peterson L. 1993. Child depression and social functioning: a multidimensional study of the linkages. *J. Clin. Child Psychol.* 22:306–15

Bienert H, Schneider BH. 1995. Deficit-specific social skills training with peer-nominated aggressive-disruptive and sensitive-isolated preadolescents. *J. Clin. Child Psychol.* 24:287–99

Bishop G, Spence SH, McDonald C. 2003. Can parents and teachers provide a reliable and valid report of behavioral inhibition? *Child Dev.* 74:1899–917

Block JH, Block J. 1980. The role of ego-control and ego-resiliency in the organization of behavior. In *Minnesota Symposium on Child Psychology*, vol. 13, ed. WA Collins, pp. 39–101. Hillsdale, NJ: Erlbaum

Bohlin G, Hagekull B, Andersson K. 2005. Behavioral inhibition as a precursor of peer social competence in early school age: the interplay with attachment and nonparental care. *Merrill-Palmer Q.* 51:1–19

Boivin M, Hymel S. 1997. Peer experiences and social self-perceptions: a sequential model. *Dev. Psychol.* 33:135–45

Boivin M, Hymel S, Bukowski WM. 1995. The roles of social withdrawal, peer rejection, and victimization by peers in predicting loneliness and depressed mood in childhood. *Dev. Psychopathol.* 7:765–85

Bornstein MH. 1991. Approaches to parenting in culture. In *Cultural Approaches to Parenting*, ed. MH Bornstein, pp. 3–19. Hillsdale, NJ: Erlbaum

Bowker JC, Rubin KH, Rose-Krasnor L, Booth-LaForce C. 2008. Social withdrawal, negative emotion, and peer difficulties during late childhood. Manuscr. under review

Buhs ES, Ladd GW. 2001. Peer rejection as an antecedent of young children's school adjustment: an examination of mediating processes. *Dev. Psychol.* 37:550–60

Burgess KB, Wojslawowicz JC, Rubin KH, Rose-Krasnor L, Booth-LaForce C. 2006. Social information processing and coping styles of shy/withdrawn and aggressive children: Does friendship matter? *Child Dev.* 77:371–83

Burke N. 1991. College psychotherapy and the development of a capacity for solitude. *J. Coll. Stud. Psychother.* 6:59–86

Calkins SD, Fox NA. 1992. The relations among infant temperament, security of attachment, and behavioral inhibition at twenty-four months. *Child Dev.* 63:1456–72

Casiglia AC, Lo Coco A, Zappulla C. 1998. Aspects of social reputation and peer relationships in Italian children: a cross-cultural perspective. *Dev. Psychol.* 34(4):723–30

Caspi A, Elder GH, Bem DJ. 1988. Moving away from the world: life-course patterns of shy children. *Dev. Psychol.* 24:824–31

Caspi A, Harrington H, Milne B, Amell JW, Theodore RF, Moffitt TE. 2003. Children's behavioral styles at age 3 are linked to their adult personality traits at age 26. *J. Personal.* 71:495–513

Chavira DA, Stein MB, Malcarne VL. 2002. Scrutinizing the relationship between shyness and social phobia. *J. Anxiety Disord.* 16:585–98

Cheah CSL, Rubin KH. 2004. A cross-cultural examination of maternal beliefs regarding maladaptive behaviors in preschoolers. *Int. J. Behav. Dev.* 28:83–94

Cheek JM, Buss AH. 1981. Shyness and sociability. *J. Personal. Soc. Psychol.* 41:330–39

Chen X, Cen G, Li D, He Y. 2005. Social functioning and adjustment in Chinese children: the imprint of historical time. *Child Dev.* 76:182–95

Chen X, DeSouza A, Chen H, Wang L. 2006. Reticent behavior and experiences in peer interactions in Canadian and Chinese children. *Dev. Psychol.* 42:656–65

Chen X, French D. 2008. Children's social competence in cultural context. *Annu. Rev. Psychol.* 59:591–616

Chen X, Hastings PD, Rubin KH, Chen H, Cen G, Stewart SL. 1998. Child-rearing practices and behavioral inhibition in Chinese and Canadian toddlers: a cross-cultural study. *Dev. Psychol.* 34:677–86

Chen X, Rubin KH, Li Z. 1995. Social functioning and adjustment in Chinese children: a longitudinal study. *Dev. Psychol.* 31:531–39

Cillessen A, van Ijzendoorn H, van Lieshout C, Hartup WW. 1992. Heterogeneity among peer-rejected boys: subtypes and stabilities. *Child Dev.* 63:893–905

Cooley CH. 1902. *Human Nature and the Social Order.* New York: Scribner

Coplan RJ, Arbeau KA. 2008. The stresses of a brave new world: shyness and adjustment in kindergarten. *J. Res. Childhood Educ.* 22:377–89

Coplan RJ, Arbeau KA, Armer M. 2008. Don't fret, be supportive! Maternal characteristics linking child shyness to psychosocial and school adjustment in kindergarten. *J. Abnorm. Child Psychol.* 36:359–71

Coplan RJ, Armer M. 2005. 'Talking yourself out of being shy': Shyness, expressive vocabulary, and adjustment in preschool. *Merrill-Palmer Q.* 51:20–41

Coplan RJ, Gavinski-Molina MH, Lagace-Seguin D, Wichmann C. 2001. When girls versus boys play alone: gender differences in the associates of nonsocial play in kindergarten. *Dev. Psychol.* 37:464–74

Coplan RJ, Girardi A, Findlay LC, Frohlick SL. 2007. Understanding solitude: young children's attitudes and responses towards hypothetical socially-withdrawn peers. *Soc. Dev.* 16:390–409

Coplan RJ, Prakash K. 2003. Spending time with teacher: characteristics of preschoolers who frequently elicit versus initiate interactions with teachers. *Early Childhood Res. Q.* 18:143–58

Coplan RJ, Prakash K, O'Neil K, Armer M. 2004. Do you "want" to play? Distinguishing between conflicted-shyness and social disinterest in early childhood. *Dev. Psychol.* 40:244–58

Coplan RJ, Rubin KH. 1998. Exploring and assessing nonsocial play in the preschool: the development and validation of the Preschool Play Behavior Scale. *Soc. Dev.* 7:71–91

Coplan RJ, Rubin KH, Fox NA, Calkins SD, Stewart SL. 1994. Being alone, playing alone, and acting alone: distinguishing among reticence, and passive-, and active-solitude in young children. *Child Dev.* 65:129–38

Coplan RJ, Weeks M. 2008. Shy and soft-spoken? Shyness, pragmatic language, and socio-emotional adjustment in early childhood. *J. Inf. Child Dev.* In press

Coplan RJ, Wilson J, Frohlick SL, Zelenski J. 2006. A person-oriented analysis of behavioral inhibition and behavioral activation in childhood. *Personal. Individ. Differ.* 917–27

Crozier R, Alden LE, eds. 2005. *Essentials of Social Anxiety for Clinicians.* New York: Wiley

Crozier WR. 1995. Shyness and self-esteem in middle childhood. *Br. J. Educ. Psychol.* 65:85–95

Crozier WR, Hostettler K. 2003. The influence of shyness on children's test performance. *Br. J. Educ. Psychol.* 73:317–28

Crozier WR, Perkins P. 2002. Shyness as a factor when assessing children. *Educ. Psychol. Pract.* 18:239–44

Daly JA, Korinek J. 1980. Interaction in the classroom: an overview. In *Communication Yearbook IV*, ed. D Nimmo, pp. 515–32. New Brunswick, NJ: Transaction Books

Deater-Deckard K. 2001. Annotation: recent research examining the role of peer relationships in the development of psychopathology. *J. Child Psychol. Psychiatry* 425:565–79

Degnan KA, Fox NA. 2007. Behavioral inhibition and anxiety disorders: multiple levels of a resilience process. *Dev. Psychopathol.* 19:729–46

Degnan KA, Henderson HA, Fox NA, Rubin KH. 2008. Predicting social wariness in middle childhood: The moderating roles of child care history, maternal personality, and maternal behavior. *Soc. Dev.* 17:471–87

Denissen JJA, Asendorpf JB, van Aken MAG. 2008. Childhood personality predicts long-term trajectories of shyness and aggressiveness in the context of demographic transitions in emerging adulthood. *J. Personal.* 76:67–100

Dettling AC, Gunnar MR, Donzella B. 1999. Cortisol levels of young children in full-day childcare centers: relations with age and temperament. *Psychoneuroendocrinology* 24:519–36

Eisenberg N, Shepard SA, Fabes RA, Murphy BC, Guthrie IK. 1998. Shyness and children's emotionality, regulation, and coping: contemporaneous, longitudinal, and across-context relations. *Child Dev.* 69:767–90

Erickson MF, Sroufe LA, Egeland B. 1985. The relationship between quality of attachment and behavior problems in preschool in a high-risk sample. *Monogr. Soc. Res. Child Dev.* 50(1–2):147–66

Evans MA. 1996. Reticent primary grade children and their more talkative peers: verbal, nonverbal, and self-concept characteristics. *J. Educ. Psychol.* 88:739–49

Evans MA. 2001. Shyness in the classroom and home. In *International Handbook of Social Anxiety: Concepts, Research and Interventions Relating to the Self and Shyness*, ed. WR Crozier, LE Alden, pp. 159–83. Westport, CT: Wiley

Evans MA, Bienert H. 1992. Control and paradox in teacher conversations with shy children. *Can. J. Behav. Sci.* 24:502–16

Findlay LC, Coplan RJ. 2008. Come out and play: shyness in childhood and the benefits of organized sports participation. *Can. J. Behav. Sci.* In press

Fox NA, Henderson HA, Marshall PJ, Nichols KE, Ghera MM. 2005. Behavioral inhibition: linking biology and behavior within a developmental framework. *Annu. Rev. Psychol.* 56:235–62

Fox NA, Henderson HA, Rubin K, Calkins SD, Schmidt LA. 2001. Continuity and discontinuity of behavioral inhibition and exuberance: psychophysiological and behavioral influences across the first 4 years of life. *Child Dev.* 72:1–21

Fox NA, Schmidt LA, Calkins SD, Rubin KH, Coplan RJ. 1996. The role of frontal activation in the regulation and dysregulation of social behavior during the preschool years. *Dev. Psychopathol.* 8:89–102

Furman W, Rahe DF, Hartup WW. 1979. Rehabilitation of socially withdrawn preschool children through mixed-age and same-age socialization. *Child Dev.* 50:915–22

Garnefski N, Kraaij V, van Etten M. 2005. Specificity of relations between adolescents' cognitive emotion regulation strategies and internalizing and externalizing psychopathology. *J. Adolesc.* 28:619–31

Gazelle H. 2006. Class climate moderates peer relations and emotional adjustment in children with an early history of anxious solitude: a child x environment model. *Dev. Psychol.* 42:1179–92

Gazelle H, Ladd GW. 2003. Anxious solitude and peer exclusion: a diathesis-stress model of internalizing trajectories in childhood. *Child Dev.* 74:257–78

Gazelle H, Rudolph KD. 2004. Moving toward and away from the world: social approach and avoidance trajectories in anxious solitary youth. *Child Dev.* 75:829–49

Graham S, Juvonen J. 2001. An attributional approach to peer victimization. In *Peer Harassment in School: The Plight of the Vulnerable and Victimized*, ed. J Juvonen, S Graham, pp. 49–72. New York: Guilford

Greco LA, Morris TL. 2001. Treating childhood shyness and related behavior: empirically investigated approaches used to promote positive social interactions. *Clin. Child Fam. Psychol. Rev.* 4:299–318

Grills A, Ollendick T. 2002. Peer victimization, global self-worth, and anxiety in middle school children. *J. Clin. Child Adolesc. Psychol.* 311:59–68

Gullone E, King NJ, Ollendick TH. 2006. The role of attachment representation in the relationship between depressive symptomatology and social withdrawal in middle childhood. *J. Child Fam. Stud.* 15(3):271–85

Hamre BK, Pianta RC. 2006. Student-teacher relationships. In *Children's Needs III: Development, Prevention, and Intervention*, ed. GG Bear, KM Minke, pp. 59–71. Washington, DC: Natl. Assoc. School Psychol.

Hane AA, Cheah CSL, Rubin KH, Fox NA. 2008. The role of maternal behavior in the relation between shyness and social withdrawal in early childhood and social withdrawal in middle childhood. *Soc. Dev.* In press

Hanish LD, Guerra NG. 2004. Aggressive victims, passive victims, and bullies: developmental continuity or developmental change. *Merrill-Palmer Q.* 50:17–38

Harrist AW, Zaia AF, Bates JE, Dodge KA, Pettit GS. 1997. Subtypes of social withdrawal in early childhood: sociometric status and social-cognitive differences across four years. *Child Dev.* 682:278–94

Hart CH, Yang C, Nelson LJ, Robinson CC, Olsen JA, et al. 2000. Peer acceptance in early childhood and subtypes of socially withdrawn behaviour in China, Russia and the United States. *Int. J. Behav. Dev.* 241:73–81

Haselager GJT, Hartup WH, van Lieshout CFM, Riksen-Walraven JMA. 1998. Similarities between friends and nonfriends in middle childhood. *Child Dev.* 694:1198–208

Hastings PD, Rubin KH. 1999. Predicting mothers' beliefs about preschool-aged children's social behavior: evidence for maternal attitudes moderating child effects. *Child Dev.* 703:722–41

Hastings PD, Rubin KH, Mielcarek L. 2005. Helping anxious boys and girls to be good: the links between inhibition, parental socialization, and the development of concern for others. *Merrill-Palmer Q.* 51:501–27

Hayward C, Killen JD, Kraemer HC, Taylor CB. 1998. Linking self-reported childhood behavioral inhibition to adolescent social phobia. *J. Am. Acad. Child Adolesc. Psychiatry* 37:1308–16

Henderson HA, Fox NA, Rubin KH. 2001. Temperamental contributions to social behavior: the moderating roles of frontal EEG asymmetry and gender. *J. Am. Acad. Child Adolesc. Psychiatry* 40:68–74

Henderson HA, Marshall PJ, Fox NA, Rubin KH. 2004. Psychophysiological and behavioral evidence for varying forms and functions of nonsocial behaviors in preschoolers. *Child Dev.* 75(1):251–63

Hills P, Argyle M. 2000. Happiness, introversion-extroversion and happy introverts. *Personal. Individ. Differ.* 30:595–608

Hinde RA. 1987. *Individuals, Relationships and Culture: Links Between Ethology and the Social Sciences.* New York: Cambridge Univ. Press

Hogue A, Steinberg L. 1995. Homophily of internalized distress in adolescent peer groups. *Dev. Psychol.* 31:897–906

Hudson JL, Rapee RM. 2001. Parent-child interactions and anxiety disorders: an observational study. *Behav. Res. Therapy* 39:1411–27

Hymel S, Rubin K, Rowden L, LeMare L. 1990. Children's peer relationships: longitudinal prediction of internalizing and externalizing problems from middle to late childhood. *Child Dev.* 61(6):2004–21

Jupp JJ, Griffiths MD. 1990. Self-concept changes in shy, socially isolated adolescents following social skills training emphasizing role plays. *Aust. Psychol.* 25:165–77

Kagan J, Reznick JS, Snidman N. 1988. Biological bases of childhood shyness. *Science* 240:167–71

Kagan J, Snidman N, Arcus D. 1993. On the temperamental categories of inhibited and uninhibited children. In *Social Withdrawal, Inhibition, and Shyness in Childhood,* ed. KH Rubin, JB Asendorpf, pp. 19–28. Hillsdale, NJ: Erlbaum

Kagan J, Snidman N, Kahn V, Towsley S. 2007. The preservation of two infant temperaments into adolescence. *Monogr. Soc. Res. Child Dev.* 72:1–75

Keogh B. 2003. *Temperament in the Classroom: Understanding Individual Differences.* Baltimore, MD: Brookes

Kochenderfer-Ladd B. 2003. Identification of aggressive and asocial victims and the stability of their peer victimization. *Merrill-Palmer Q.* 49(4):401–25

Kohlberg L, LaCrosse J, Ricks D. 1972. The predictability of adult mental health from childhood behavior. In *Manual of Child Psychopathology,* ed. BB Wolman, pp. 1217–84. New York: McGraw-Hill

Ladd GW. 2006. Peer rejection, aggressive or withdrawn behavior, and psychological maladjustment from ages 5 to 12: an examination of four predictive models. *Child Dev.* 77:822–46

Ladd GW, Birch SH, Buhs E. 1999. Children's social and scholastic lives in kindergarten: related spheres of influence? *Child Dev.* 70:1373–400

Ladd GW, Burgess KB. 1999. Charting the relationship trajectories of aggressive, withdrawn, and aggressive/withdrawn children during early grade school. *Child Dev.* 70:910–29

Ladd GW, Profilet SM. 1996. The Child Behavior Scale: a teacher-report measure of young children's aggressive, withdrawn, and prosocial behaviors. *Dev. Psychol.* 32:1008–24

Larson R. 1997. The emergence of solitude as a constructive domain of experience in early adolescence. *Child Dev.* 68:80–93

Leary MR, Herbst KC, McCrary F. 2003. Finding pleasure in solitary activities: desire for aloneness or disinterest in social contact? *Personal. Individ. Differ.* 35:59–68

Lemerise EA. 1997. Patterns of peer acceptance, social status, and social reputation in mixed-age preschool and primary classrooms. *Merrill-Palmer Q.* 43:199–218

Levy DM. 1943. *Maternal Overprotection.* New York: Columbia Univ. Press

Lewis M, Miller SM. 1990. *Handbook of Developmental Psychopathology.* New York: Plenum

Lieb R, Wittchen HU, Hofler M, Fuetsch M, Stein MB, Merikangas KR. 2000. Parental psychopathology, parenting styles, and the risk of social phobia in offspring: a prospective-longitudinal community study. *Arch. Gen. Psychiatry* 57:859–66

Lloyd B, Howe N. 2003. Solitary play and convergent and divergent thinking skills in preschool children. *Early Childhood Res. Q.* 18:22–41

Luthar SS. 2006. Resilience in development: a synthesis of research across five decades. In *Developmental Psychopathology: Risk, Disorder, and Adaptation,* ed. D Cicchetti, DJ Cohen, pp. 740–95. New York: Wiley

Manassis K, Bradley SJ. 1994. The development of childhood anxiety disorders: toward an integrated model. *J. Appl. Dev. Psychol.* 15:345–66

Maslow AH. 1970. *Motivation and Personality.* New York: Harper & Row. 2nd ed.

Masten AS, Morrison P, Pellegrini DS. 1985. A revised class play method of peer assessment. *Dev. Psychol.* 3:523–33

McClure E, Pine D. 2006. Social anxiety and emotion regulation: a model for developmental psychopathology perspectives on anxiety disorders. In *Developmental Psychopathology: Vol. 3: Risk, Disorder, and Adaptation,* ed. D Cicchetti, pp. 470–502. New York: Wiley

McCroskey JC, Daly JA. 1976. Teacher expectations of the communication apprehensive child in the elementary school. *Hum. Commun. Res.* 3:67–72

McManis MH, Kagan J, Snidman NC, Woodward SA. 2002. EEG asymmetry, power, and temperament in children. *Dev. Psychobiol.* 41:169–77

Mead GH. 1934. *Mind, Self, and Society: From the Standpoint of a Social Behaviorist.* Oxford, UK: Univ. Chicago Press

Mills RSL, Rubin KH. 1990. Parental beliefs about problematic social behaviors in early childhood. *Child Dev.* 61:138–51

Mills RSL, Rubin KH. 1998. Are behavioural and psychological control both differentially associated with childhood aggression and social withdrawal? *Can. J. Behav. Sci.* 30(2):132–36

Morison P, Masten AS. 1991. Peer reputation in middle childhood as a predictor of adaptation in adolescence: a seven-year follow-up. *Child Dev.* 62:991–1007

Morris DP, Soroker E, Buruss G. 1954. Follow-up studies of shy, withdrawn children—I. Evaluation of later adjustment. *Am. J. Orthopsychiatry* 24:743–54

Mullen M, Snidman N, Kagan J. 1993. Free-play behavior in inhibited and uninhibited children. *Inf. Behav. Dev.* 16:383–89

Mullins LL, Peterson L, Wonderlich SA, Reaven NM. 1986. The influence of depressive symptomatology in children on the social responses and perceptions of adults. *J. Child Clin. Psychol.* 15:233–40

Natl. Inst. Child Health Human Dev. Early Child Care Res. Netw. 2001. Child care and children's peer interaction at 24 and 36 months: the National Institute of Child Health and Human Development Study of Early Child Care. *Child Dev.* 72:1478–500

Nelson LJ, Rubin KH, Fox NA. 2005. Social and nonsocial behaviors and peer acceptance: a longitudinal model of the development of self-perceptions in children ages 4 to 7 years. *Early Educ. Dev.* 20:185–200

Newcomb AF, Bukowski WM, Pattee L. 1993. Children's peer relations: a meta-analyic review of popular, rejected, neglected, controversial, and average sociometric status. *Psychol. Bull.* 113:99–128

Oh W, Rubin KH, Bowker JC, Booth-LaForce CL, Rose-Krasnor L, Laursen B. 2008. Trajectories of social withdrawal from middle childhood to early adolescence. *J. Abnorm. Child Psychol.* 36(4):553–66

Ollendick TH, Greene RW, Weist MD, Oswald DP. 1990. The predictive validity of teacher nominations: a five-year follow up of at-risk youth. *J. Abnorm. Child Psychol.* 18(6):699–713

Olweus D. 1984. Stability in aggressive and withdrawn, inhibited behavior patterns. In *Aggression in Children and Youth,* ed. RM Kaplan, VJ Konecni, RW Novaco, pp. 104–36. The Hague: Nijhoff

Olweus D. 1993. Victimization by peers: antecedents and long-term outcomes. In *Social Withdrawal, Inhibition and Shyness in Childhood,* ed. KH Rubin, JB Asendorpf, pp. 315–41. Hillsdale, NJ: Erlbaum

Parker JG, Rubin KH, Erath S, Wojslawowicz JC, Buskirk A. 2006. Peer relationships, child development, and adjustment: a developmental psychopathology perspective. In *Developmental Psychopathology, Vol. 2: Risk, Disorder, and Adaptation*, ed. D Cicchetti, pp. 419–93. New York: Wiley

Pedersen S, Vitaro F, Barker E, Borge A. 2007. The timing of middle-childhood peer rejection and friendship: linking early behavior to early-adolescent adjustment. *Child Dev.* 78(4):1037–51

Perry DG, Kusel SJ, Perry LC. 1988. Victims of peer aggression. *Dev. Psychol.* 24(6):807–14

Piaget J. 1932. *The Moral Judgment of the Child*. Glencoe, IL: Free Press

Pope A, Bierman K. 1999. Predicting adolescent peer problems and antisocial activities: the relative roles of aggression and dysregulation. *Dev. Psychol.* 35:335–46

Prior M, Smart D, Sanson A, Oberklaid F. 2000. Does shy-inhibited temperament in childhood lead to anxiety problems in adolescence? *J. Am. Acad. Child Adolesc. Psychiatry* 39:461–68

Rapee R. 1997. Potential role of child rearing practices in the development of anxiety and depression. *Clin. Psychol. Rev.* 17:47–67

Rapee R, Kennedy S, Ingram M, Edwards S, Sweeney L. 2005. Prevention and early intervention of anxiety disorders in inhibited preschool children. *J. Consult. Clin. Psychol.* 73:488–97

Rapee R, Sweeney L. 2001. Social phobia in children and adolescents: nature and assessment. In *International Handbook of Social Anxiety: Concepts, Research and Interventions Relating to the Self and Shyness*, ed. W Crozier, L Alden, pp. 505–23. West Sussex, UK: Wiley

Reijntjes AHA, Stegge H, Meerum Terwogt M, Kamphuis JH, Telch MJ. 2006. Emotion regulation and its effects on mood improvement in response to in vivo peer rejection challenge. *Emotion* 6:543–52

Renken B, Egeland B, Marvinney D, Sroufe LA, Mangelsdorf S. 1989. Early childhood antecedents of aggression and passive-withdrawal in early elementary school. *J. Personal.* 57:257–81

Rezendes M, Snidman N, Kagan J, Gibbons J. 1993. Features of speech in inhibited and uninhibited children. In *Social Withdrawal, Inhibition, and Shyness*, ed. KH Rubin, JB Asendorpf, pp. 177–87. Hillsdale, NJ: Erlbaum

Richmond VP, Beatty MJ, Dyba P. 1985. Shyness and popularity: children's views. *West. J. Speech Commun.* 49:116–25

Rimm-Kaufman SE, Early D, Cox M, Saluja G, Pianta R, Bradley R, et al. 2002. Early behavioral attributes and teachers' sensitivity as predictors of competent behavior in the kindergarten classroom. *J. Appl. Dev. Psychol.* 23:451–70

Rimm-Kaufman SE, Kagan J. 2005. Infant predictors of kindergarten behavior: the contribution of inhibited and uninhibited temperament types. *Behav. Disord.* 30:329–46

Robins LN. 1966. *Deviant Children Grown Up*. Baltimore, MD: Williams & Wilkins

Rowe D, Plomin R. 1977. Temperament in early childhood. *Personal. Assess.* 41:150–56

Rubin KH. 1982. Nonsocial play in preschoolers: necessarily evil? *Child Dev.* 533:651–57

Rubin KH. 1993. The Waterloo Longitudinal Project: correlates and consequences of social withdrawal from childhood to adolescence. In *Social Withdrawal, Inhibition, Shyness in Childhood*, ed. KH Rubin, JB Asendorpf, pp. 291–314. Hillsdale, NJ: Erlbaum

Rubin KH. 2001. *The Play Observation Scale (POS)*. College Park: Univ. Maryland

Rubin KH. 2002. *The Friendship Factor*. New York: Viking

Rubin KH, Asendorpf J, eds. 1993. *Social Withdrawal, Inhibition and Shyness in Childhood*. Hillsdale, NJ: Erlbaum

Rubin KH, Bowker J, Kennedy A. 2008. Avoiding and withdrawing from the peer group in middle childhood and early adolescence. In *Handbook of Peer Interactions, Relationships, and Groups*, ed. KH Rubin, W Bukowski, B Laursen. New York: Guilford. In press

Rubin KH, Bukowski W, Parker JG. 2006a. Peer interactions, relationships, and groups. In *Handbook of Child Psychology: Vol 3. Social, Emotional, and Personality Development*, ed. N Eisenberg, pp. 571–645. New York: Wiley

Rubin KH, Burgess KB, Hastings PD. 2002. Stability and social-behavioral consequences of toddlers' inhibited temperament and parenting. *Child Dev.* 73:483–95

Rubin KH, Burgess K, Kennedy AE, Stewart S. 2003. Social withdrawal and inhibition in childhood. In *Child Psychopathology*, ed. E Mash, R Barkley, pp. 372–406. New York: Guilford

Rubin KH, Cheah CSL, Fox NA. 2001. Emotion regulation, parenting and display of social reticence in preschoolers. *Early Educ. Dev.* 121:97–115

Rubin KH, Chen X, Hymel S. 1993. The socio-emotional characteristics of extremely aggressive and extremely withdrawn children. *Merrill-Palmer Q.* 39:518–34

Rubin KH, Chen X, McDougall P, Bowker A, McKinnon J. 1995. The Waterloo Longitudinal Project: predicting adolescent internalizing and externalizing problems from early and mid-childhood. *Dev. Psychopathol.* 7:751–64

Rubin KH, Coplan RJ. 2004. Paying attention to and not neglecting social withdrawal and social isolation. *Merrill-Palmer Q.* 50:506–34

Rubin KH, Hastings PD, Stewart SL, Henderson HA, Chen X. 1997. The consistency and concomitants of inhibition: some of the children all of the time. *Child Dev.* 68(3):467–83

Rubin KH, Hemphill SA, Chen X, Hastings P, Sanson A, et al. 2006b. Parenting beliefs and behaviors: initial findings from the International Consortium for the Study of Social and Emotional Development (ICSSED). In *Parental Beliefs, Parenting, and Child Development in Cross-Cultural Perspective*, ed. KH Rubin, OB Chung, pp. 81–103. London: Psychol. Press

Rubin KH, Hemphill SA, Chen X, Hastings P, Sanson A, et al. 2006c. A cross-cultural study of behavioral inhibition in toddlers: east-west-north-south. *Int. J. Behav. Dev.* 30:219–26

Rubin KH, Hymel S, Mills RSL. 1989. Sociability and social withdrawal in childhood: stability and outcomes. *J. Personal.* 57:237–55

Rubin KH, Krasnor LR. 1986. Social-cognitive and social behavioral perspectives on problem solving. In *Cognitive Perspectives on Children's Social and Behavioral Development. The Minnesota Symposia on Child Psychology, Vol. 18*, ed. M. Perlmutter, pp. 1–68. Hillsdale, NJ: Erlbaum

Rubin KH, Mills RSL. 1988. The many faces of social isolation in childhood. *J. Consult. Clin. Psychol.* 56(6):916–24

Rubin KH, Mills RSL. 1992. Parents' ideas about the development of aggression and withdrawal. In *Parental Belief Systems*, ed. I Sigel, J Goodnow, A McGillicuddy-deLisi, pp. 41–68. Hillsdale, NJ: Erlbaum

Rubin KH, Nelson LJ, Hastings PD, Asendorpf J. 1999. The transaction between parents' perceptions of their children's shyness and their parenting styles. *Int. J. Behav. Dev.* 23:937–58

Rubin KH, Wojslawowicz JC, Rose-Krasnor L, Booth-LaForce CL, Burgess KB. 2006d. The best friendships of shy/withdrawn children: prevalence, stability, and relationship quality. *J. Abnorm. Child Psychol.* 34:139–53

Rudasill KM, Rimm-Kaufman SE, Justice LM, Pernce K. 2006. Temperament and language skills as predictors of teacher-child relationship quality in preschool. *Early Educ. Dev.* 17:271–91

Sadker M, Sadker D. 1994. *Failing at Fairness: How Americans' Schools Cheat Girls*. New York: Scribner's

Sanson A, Pedlow R, Cann W, Prior M, Oberklaid F. 1996. Shyness ratings: stability and correlates in early childhood. *Int. J. Behav. Dev.* 19:705–24

Schaughency EA, Vannatta K, Langhinrichsen J, Lally CM, Seely J. 1992. Correlates of sociometric status in school children in Buenos Aires. *J. Abnorm. Child Psychol.* 20:317–26

Schlette P, Brandstrom S, Eisemann M, Sigvardsson S, Nylander PO, et al. 1998. Perceived parental rearing behaviours and temperament and character in healthy adults. *Personal. Individ. Differ.* 24:661–68

Schmidt LA, Fox NA, Rubin KH, Sternberg EM, Gold PW, et al. 1997. Behavioral and neuroendocrine responses in shy children. *Dev. Psychobiol.* 30:127–40

Schneider BH. 1992. Didactic methods for enhancing children's peer relations: a quantitative review. *Clin. Psychol. Rev.* 12:363–82

Schneider BH. 1999. A multi-method exploration of the friendships of children considered socially withdrawn by their peers. *J. Abnorm. Psychol.* 27:115–23

Schneider BH, Richard JF, Younger AJ, Freeman P. 2000. A longitudinal exploration of the continuity of children's social participation and social withdrawal across socioeconomic status levels and social settings. *Eur. J. Soc. Psychol.* 30:497–519

Schneider BH, Younger AJ, Smith T, Freeman P. 1998. A longitudinal exploration of the cross-context stability of social withdrawal in early adolescence. *J. Early Adolesc.* 18:374–96

Schwartz CE, Snidman N, Kagan J. 1999. Adolescent social anxiety as an outcome of inhibited temperament in childhood. *J. Am. Acad. Child Adolesc. Psychiatry* 38:1008–15

Seidman E, French SE. 2004. Developmental trajectories and ecological transitions: a two-step procedure to aid in the choice of prevention and promotion interventions. *Dev. Psychopathol.* 16:1141–59

Shamir-Essakow G, Ungerer JA, Rapee RM. 2005. Attachment, behavioral inhibition, and anxiety in preschool children. *J. Abnorm. Child Psychol.* 33:131–43

Sheridan SM, Kratochwill TR, Elliott SN. 1990. Behavioral consultation with parents and teachers: delivering treatment for socially withdrawn children at home and school. *School Psychol. Rev.* 19:33–52

Shulman S, Elicker J, Sroufe LA. 1994. Stages of friendship growth in preadolescence as related to attachment history. *J. Soc. Personal. Relat.* 11:341–61

Spangler G, Schieche M. 1998. Emotional and adrenocortical responses of infants to the strange situation: the differential function of emotional expression. *Int. J. Behav. Dev.* 22:681–706

Spence S, Donovan C, Brechman-Toussaint M. 2000. The treatment of childhood social phobia: the effectiveness of a social skills training-based, cognitive-behavioural intervention, with and without parental involvement. *J. Child Psychol. Psychiatry* 41:713–26

Spere KA, Schmidt LA, Theall-Honey LA, Martin-Chang S. 2004. Expressive and receptive language skills of temperamentally shy preschoolers. *Inf. Child Dev.* 13:123–33

Spinrad TL, Eisenberg N, Harris E, Hanish L, Fabes RA, et al. 2004. The relation of children's everyday nonsocial peer play behavior to their emotionality, regulation, and social functioning. *Dev. Psychol.* 40:67–80

Spooner A, Evans MA, Santos R. 2005. Hidden shyness in children: discrepancies between self-perceptions and the perceptions of parents and teachers. *Merrill-Palmer Q.* 51(4):437–93

Stevenson-Hinde J. 1989. Behavioral inhibition: issues of context. In *Perspectives on Behavioral Inhibition*, ed. JS Reznick, pp. 125–38. Chicago: Univ. Chicago Press

Stewart SL, Rubin KH. 1995. The social problem solving skills of anxious-withdrawn children. *Dev. Psychopathol.* 7:323–36

Sullivan HS. 1953. *The Interpersonal Theory of Psychiatry*. New York: Norton

Thijs JT, Koomen HM, de Jong PF, Van Der Leij, van Leeuwen MG. 2004. Internalizing behaviors among kindergarten children: measuring dimensions of social withdrawal with a checklist. *J. Clin. Child Adolesc. Psychol.* 33:802–12

Tremblay RE, Loeber R, Gagnon C, Charlebois P, Larive'e S, LeBlanc M. 1991. Disruptive boys with stable and unstable high fighting behavior patterns during junior elementary school. *J. Abnorm. Child Psychol.* 19:285–300

Van Ameringen MV, Mancini C, Oakman JM. 1998. The relationship of behavioral inhibition and shyness to anxiety disorder. *J. Nerv. Ment. Dis.* 186:425–31

van Brakel AML, Muris P, Bogels SM, Thomassen C. 2006. A multifactorial model for the etiology of anxiety in nonclinical adolescents: main and interactive effects of behavioral inhibition, attachment, and parental rearing. *J. Child Fam. Stud.* 15:569–79

van de Vijver FJR, Leung K. 1997. Methods and data analysis for cross-cultural research. Newbury Park, CA: Sage

Vasa RA, Pine DS. 2006. Anxiety disorders. In *Child and Adolescent Psychopathology: Theoretical and Clinical Implications*, ed. C Essau, pp. 78–112. New York: Routledge/Taylor & Francis

Werner E. 1995. Resilience in development. *Curr. Direct. Psychol. Sci.* 4(3):81–85

Wichmann C, Coplan RJ, Daniels T. 2004. The social cognitions of socially withdrawn children. *Soc. Dev.* 13:377–92

Winder CL, Rau L. 1962. Parental attitudes associated with social deviance in preadolescent boys. *J. Abnorm. Soc. Psychol.* 64:418–24

Wood JJ, McLeod BD, Sigman M, Hwang WC, Chu BC. 2003. Parenting and childhood anxiety: theory, empirical findings, and future directions. *J. Child Psychol. Psychiatry* 44:134–51

World Health Org. 1993. *The ICD Classification of Mental and Behavioral Disorders: Diagnostic Criteria for Research*. Geneva: World Health Org.

World Health Org. 1994. *Pocket Guide to the ICD-10 Classification of Mental and Behavioural Disorders*. Washington, DC: Am. Psychiatr. Press

Zeller M, Vannatta K, Schafer J, Noll R. 2003. Behavioral reputation: a cross-age perspective. *Dev. Psychol.* 39:129–39

Zimbardo PG. 1977. *Shyness: What It Is, What to Do About It*. Reading, MA: Addison-Wesley

The Adaptive Brain: Aging and Neurocognitive Scaffolding

Denise C. Park[1] and Patricia Reuter-Lorenz[2]

[1]The Center for Brain Health, University of Texas at Dallas, Dallas, Texas 75235, email: denise@utdallas.edu

[2]Department of Psychology, University of Michigan, Ann Arbor, Michigan 48109, email: parl@umich.edu

Annu. Rev. Psychol. 2009. 60:173–96

The *Annual Review of Psychology* is online at psych.annualreviews.org

This article's doi:
10.1146/annurev.psych.59.103006.093656

0066-4308/09/0110-0173$20.00

Key Words

default network, dedifferentiation, hippocampus, compensation, cognitive reserve, frontal activation

Abstract

There are declines with age in speed of processing, working memory, inhibitory function, and long-term memory, as well as decreases in brain structure size and white matter integrity. In the face of these decreases, functional imaging studies have demonstrated, somewhat surprisingly, reliable increases in prefrontal activation. To account for these joint phenomena, we propose the scaffolding theory of aging and cognition (STAC). STAC provides an integrative view of the aging mind, suggesting that pervasive increased frontal activation with age is a marker of an adaptive brain that engages in compensatory scaffolding in response to the challenges posed by declining neural structures and function. Scaffolding is a normal process present across the lifespan that involves use and development of complementary, alternative neural circuits to achieve a particular cognitive goal. Scaffolding is protective of cognitive function in the aging brain, and available evidence suggests that the ability to use this mechanism is strengthened by cognitive engagement, exercise, and low levels of default network engagement.

Contents

---

fMRI: functional
magnetic resonance
imaging

PET: positron
emission tomography

INTRODUCTION

All highly developed nations in the world are experiencing substantial increases in the proportion of elderly adults in the population due to falling birth rates combined with increased longevity. By 2050, there will be many more older adults in wealthy, developed countries (26%) than children under 15 (about 16% of total population) (J. E. Cohen 2003). The aging of the population represents both an opportunity and threat for society. The opportunity comes from the tremendous reserve of human capital and experience represented by older citizens; the threat emerges from the disconcerting fact that at this time, adults aged 85 and older have a dementia rate (typically in the form of Alzheimer's disease) of nearly 50% (Hebert et al. 2003), with a very high cost to affected individuals and families, as well as to limited medical resources. At present, it is fair to say that neurocognitive frailty is the biggest threat to successful aging in our society.

Fortunately, as our aging population has grown, so has our knowledge about the aging mind. For the past 25 years, our understanding of the behavioral changes that occur in cognition with age has increased tremendously, and in the past 10 years, the advent of neuroimaging tools has ushered a truly stunning increase in what we know about the aging mind. Neuroimaging techniques such as structural and functional magnetic resonance imaging (fMRI) and positron emission tomography (PET) allow us to see how both brain structure and function change with age. In the present review, we integrate the vast body of behavioral research in cognitive aging with recent data revealed by imaging techniques. We argue that the unprecedented opportunity to look into the operation of the mind afforded by neuroimaging indicates the brain and cognitive system to be more dynamic and adaptive then was ever previously suspected. We propose that the extant behavioral and brain data can best be understood within a new model: the scaffolding theory of aging and cognition (STAC).

After reviewing the range of data examining brain and behavioral function with age, we believe that the corpus of these data suggests that the brain is a dynamic organism seeking to maintain homeostatic cognitive function. With age, the number of dopaminergic receptors declines; many brain structures show volumetric shrinkage; white matter becomes less dense; and brains of even very highly functioning individuals are frequently characterized by destructive neurofibrillary plaques and tangles. We argue that the brain responds to these neural insults by engaging in continuous functional reorganization and functional repairs that result in self-generated support of cognitive function. We term this homeostatic, adaptive model of aging the scaffolding theory of aging and cognition. Encarta defines scaffolding as "a supporting framework." In the context we are using this term, scaffolding is a process that results in changes in brain function through strengthening of existing connections, formation of new connections, and disuse of connections that have become weak or faulty.

We begin our review with a brief and broad overview of major behavioral theories of cognitive aging and then discuss what has been learned about the structure of the aging brain. Because our notion of scaffolding has developed largely from the results of functional imaging studies of aging, we then review the findings regarding frontal, mediotemporal, and ventral visual function from the neuroimaging and aging literature. In the next section, we present the STAC model and critical assumptions that describe how the brain continues to change and reorganize with age, along with key predictions of the model. We close with a summary of what issues associated with STAC are speculative or unresolved, and we propose directions for new research.

BEHAVIORAL MECHANISMS OF COGNITIVE AGING

We have an extensive amount of knowledge about how cognition changes with age (Park & Schwarz 2000). As individuals age, many aspects of information processing become less efficient, including speed of processing, working memory capacity, inhibitory function, and long-term memory. At the same time, other aspects of cognitive function such as implicit memory and knowledge storage, are protected and relatively resistant to cognitive aging. A summary of typi-

cal findings from many different studies of cognitive aging appears in **Figure 1** (see color insert), which depicts results from a lifespan sample of adults aged 20–89 who were tested extensively (Park et al. 2002). Park et al. (2002) collected three measures of perceptual speed, two measures of visuospatial working memory, and two measures of verbal working memory. In addition, subjects completed recall tests of both verbal and visuospatial recall, as well as three different vocabulary tests. The results clearly show that there are gradual age-related declines in the cognitive mechanisms of speed, working memory, and long-term memory, beginning in young adulthood. Only verbal ability, which is an estimate of accrued knowledge rather than a cognitive mechanism, is protected from age differences. Because these data are cross-sectional, it is possible that the observed differences are due to cohort effects or some other confound. However, data from the Victoria Longitudinal Study (Hultsch et al. 1999) show strikingly similar findings for speed of processing, working memory, list recall, and vocabulary, suggesting that the results are also found in longitudinal data and are not primarily due to cohort effects.

A major challenge for cognitive aging researchers has been to understand the causes of age-related declines in cognitive function. The general approach has been to isolate specific mechanisms and then determine whether the mechanism can account for the vast majority of age-related variance on a diverse set of cognitive measures. One dominant construct in the cognitive aging literature has been that of speed of processing. Salthouse (1991, 1996) has cogently argued that perceptual speed (measured by the rate at which individuals can make "same/difference" judgments about simple shapes, dot matrices, or strings of letters or digits) is a fundamental, cognitive primitive that accounts for nearly all of the age-related variance on a broad range of cognitive tasks. Salthouse (1991, 1996) has marshaled considerable evidence for this argument in an impressive research program that spans thousands of subjects and many different and creative methodological approaches.

STAC: scaffolding theory of aging and Ccognition

A second important approach to understanding cognitive aging comes from evidence that working memory function decreases with age and, along with speed, mediates age-related variance on a broad array of cognitive behaviors (Park et al. 1996, 2002; Wingfield et al. 1988). Indeed, working memory, which encompasses both the short-term maintenance and active manipulative processing of information, figures prominently in a third view of cognitive aging that emphasize declines in executive control processes, namely inhibitory function (Hasher & Zacks 1988, Hasher et al. 2007). According to this view, age-related deficits in cognition stem from the inefficiency of inhibitory processes that normally control the contents of consciousness (i.e., working memory). Older adults show working memory deficiencies and slowing due to selection of irrelevant information into the contents of working memory, along with inefficient deletion of working memory contents that are no longer relevant to task performance. Inhibitory dysfunction with age is a source of general attentional dysregulation and accounts for age-related deficits in other cognitive domains such as task switching, response competition, and response suppression.

Further theorizing about aging has emphasized the distinction between automatic and effortful/controlled processing (Hasher & Zacks 1979), especially in reference to age-related changes in mechanisms specific to memory. Jacoby and colleagues (Jennings & Jacoby 1993) have demonstrated that some memory differences with age are due to declines in controlled, but not automatic, processes resulting in poor explicit memory but relatively good memory for gist or versions of stimuli that feel familiar. Indeed, there is considerable support for the idea that in the absence of environmental support or explicit instruction, older adults engage less in controlled processes such as binding operations and elaborative processing that facilitates explicit recollective memory (Daniels et al. 2006). Congruent with this position, Johnson and colleagues (Chalfonte & Johnson 1996, Hashtroudi et al. 1989) have shown that age-related memory declines are characterized by poor memory for source and other contextual details associated with target information. Consequently, aging memory relies heavily on gist, making it highly susceptible to distortions and misremembering, as demonstrated by the impressive research program of Schacter and colleagues (Dodson & Schacter 2002, Koutstaal & Schachter 1997, Norman & Schacter 1997).

The effortful-automatic distinction dovetails nicely with other recent ideas about cognitive control processes and their decline with age (Braver & Barch 2002). Cognitive control operations guide thought and action in accord with task goals, especially when bottom-up, automatic, or prepotent stimulus-response associations must be overridden. Age-related declines in cognitive control make older adults more susceptible to the influence of automatic, bottom-up processes.

A different and increasingly influential idea about the sources of cognitive decline was put forward by Baltes & Lindenberger (1997, Lindenberger & Baltes 1994). Lindenberger & Baltes (1994) presented compelling evidence demonstrating that measures of audition and visual acuity are important predictors of performance on a broad array of cognitive tasks in an older adult sample. In a later study, Baltes & Lindenberger (1997) found that for younger adults (age 60 or less), there was no relationship between sensory function and measures of cognition, indicating that abilities that are independent in young adults become interrelated in old age. Baltes & Lindenberger (1997) argued, "the age-associated link between sensory and intellectual functioning may reflect brain aging" and further suggested, "visual and auditory systems evolve as powerful regulators of intellectual performance in old and very old age... [due to] a common process of aging-induced dedifferentiation." Whereas young adults selectively engage specific mechanisms for different tasks, dedifferentiation in older adults leads to declining specialization with age. Dedifferentiation can be thought of mechanistically as a decrease in neural specificity and thus a broadening of neural tuning curves such that a given region that responds selectively in young adults will respond to a wider array of inputs in old adults. The concept of dedifferentiation is particularly important because it makes relatively specific predictions about neural function based on behavioral data and provides a strong link between behavioral-based and brain-based theories of cognitive aging.

In summary, age-related cognitive declines may be best understood in terms of a range of mechanisms including speed, working memory, inhibition, and cognitive control (Moscovitch & Winocur 1992, West 1996) that show varying degrees of vulnerability in different individuals. Although these mechanisms can all be categorized as executive processes, other sources of decline, such as dedifferentiation of cognitive function, must also be considered. Given the broad spectrum of cognitive changes with age, it is unlikely that any single process or unitary mechanism can fully explain age-related deficits across all individuals. As we argue below with respect to the STAC model, behavioral performance in older adults must ultimately be understood in terms of combined influence of age-related neurocognitive declines and age-related compensatory processes, many of which are also executive in nature. In the next section, we consider neurological evidence that provides additional constraints and new directions for theorizing about cognitive aging.

AGING AND THE STRUCTURE OF THE BRAIN

Volumetric Data

When neuroimaging tools became available to researchers, one of the first approaches to studying aging involved using structural MRI to determine age differences in the size of brain structures, typically measured by the volume of the structure. There is a surprising amount of convergence between the behavioral data on aging and cognition and the structural data from the brain. **Figure 2** presents volumetric measures of a number of brain structures across the lifespan in a cross-sectional study (Raz et al. 2005). A particularly unique aspect of this study

is that subjects were measured both initially and five years later, so the "spaghetti graph" shows individual measurements for each subject at both of these intervals. **Figure 2** indicates that the greatest shrinkage across the lifespan occurs in the caudate, cerebellum, hippocampus, and prefrontal areas. There is minimal shrinkage in the entorhinal cortex, and the visual cortex volume remains stable across the lifespan (Raz 2000, Raz et al. 2004). Resnick and colleagues (2003) reported evidence for decline in gray and white matter over a period as short as two years in very healthy older adults over age 59, with frontal and parietal cortex showing greater decreases than temporal and occipital (see also Good et al. 2001).

Other measures relating brain structure to aging tell a similar story. Salat et al. (2004) examined measures of thinning in the cortical mantle in a lifespan sample of adults and reported that global thinning was apparent by middle age, with regionally specific thinning occurring in areas similar to those reported above. A particularly intriguing finding was their report of significant age-related atrophy in the calcarine cortex, an area near primary visual cortex, as other studies have suggested that visual cortex is largely preserved with age. The Salat et al. (2004) finding of both frontal and visual cortical thinning with age may provide the neurobiological link for the evidence reported by Baltes & Lindenberger (1997) that declining visual function in old age is closely linked to declining performance on cognitive tasks with significant frontal components.

White Matter

Besides thinning and volumetric shrinkage, studies also have measured the characteristics of white matter, which is composed of axonal bundles beneath the cortical structures of the brain. Diffusion tensor imaging measures the rate and direction at which water diffuses through white matter and provides an index of the density or structural integrity of the white matter. Head et al. (2004) note an anterior-to-posterior gradient across the brain for white matter integrity

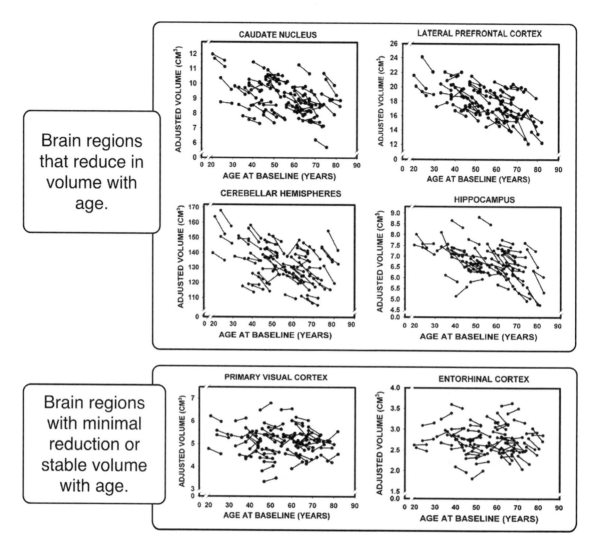

Figure 2

Cross-sectional and longitudinal aging brain volumes across various brain regions (adapted from Raz et al. 2005). Each pair of line-connected dots represents an individual subject's first and second measurement. The caudate, hippocampal, cerebellar, and frontal regions all show both cross-sectional and longitudinal reduction in volume with age. The entorhinal, parietal, temporal, and occipital regions are relatively preserved with age.

WMHs: white matter hyperintensities

with age, such that the greatest structural deficiency in white matter is observed in anterior (frontal) regions of the brain. Another measure of white matter health is the number of white matter hyperintensities (WMHs) present in a structural scan. The hyperintensities represent an abnormality of signal from white matter, which likely results from demyelination, trauma, inflammatory disease, or other neural insults. Wen & Sachdev (2004) measured the number of WMHs in a large sample of adults 60–64 years of age. Subjects had an average of 19.1 WMHs, with the largest proportion of tissue affected in frontal and occipital areas. The WMH data suggest, as did the Salat et al. (2004) data on cortical thinning, that visual areas do show negative age-associated effects in structural measures. All subjects in the Wen &

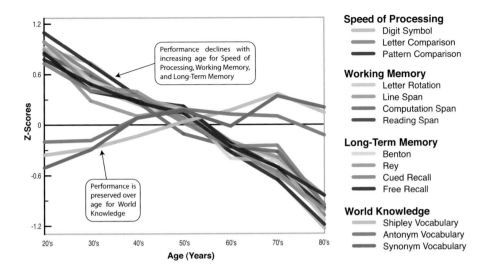

Figure 1

Cross-sectional aging data adapted from Park et al. (2002) showing behavioral performance on measures of speed of processing, working memory, long-term memory, and world knowledge. Almost all measures of cognitive function show decline with age, except world knowledge, which may even show some improvement.

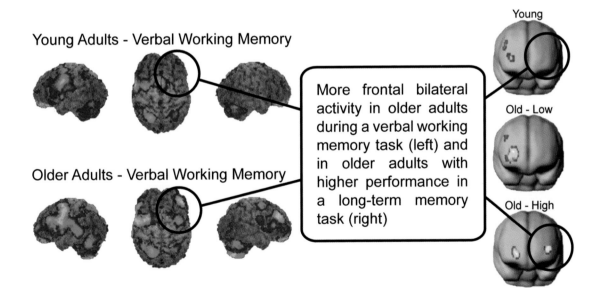

Figure 3

Frontal bilaterality is increased with age. (*Left side*) Left lateralized frontal engagement in young adults during a verbal working memory task; in older adults, an additional right frontal engagement is observed (adapted from Reuter-Lorenz et al. 2000). (*Right side*) Right lateralized engagement in young adults and low-performing older adults during a long-term memory task, and bilateral frontal engagement in high-performing older adults (adapted from Cabeza et al. 2002).

Sachdev (2004) study had some small WMHs, and at least half had severe WMHs. Overall, the white matter data, in agreement with volumetric data, present a clear picture of age-related decrease, with particular susceptibility in the frontal areas. The white matter changes are often considered a likely candidate to be the basis for age-related slowing of behavior, as the decreased integrity of the white matter tracts points to a less efficient system for information transmission with age.

Relationship of Structural Measures to Cognition

There is some evidence that age-related changes in volume of specific brain structures have direct consequences for cognitive function. Rodrigue & Raz (2004) reported that shrinkage of entorhinal cortex over a five-year period in an older adult sample predicted poor memory performance. Rosen et al. (2003) found evidence that both hippocampal and entorhinal volume were related to memory performance, although Tisserand et al. (2000) failed to find relationships between hippocampal volume and cognitive performance after controlling for age. The role of frontal volume in predicting cognitive function is not as straightforward as one might expect. Curiously, Salat et al. (2002) noted that increased orbital frontal volume correlated with declining working memory in older adults, and Gunning-Dixon & Raz (2003) found no relationship between prefrontal volume and working memory performance in a lifespan sample. Gunning-Dixon & Raz (2003) did find the expected relationship between prefrontal volume, age, and performance on the Wisconsin Card-Sorting Task—that is, that greater volume predicted better performance, but they failed to find a relationship between prefrontal volume and working memory. Gunning-Dixon & Raz (2003) also found that WMHs predicted performance on the Wisconsin-Card-Sorting Task but did not predict working memory performance. Wolfson et al. (2005) reported that mobility-impaired older subjects, over a 20-month period, showed a fivefold increase in WMHs relative to an unimpaired control group. The magnitude of the increase predicted some changes in mobility, outlining the importance of the accrual of these lesions for everyday functional abilities.

Dopaminergic Receptors

In addition to the structural measures described, techniques also exist for measuring the number of dopamine receptors in the brain. Dopaminergic receptors are integral to cognition because they play an important role in regulating attention and in modulating response to contextual stimuli. Li et al. (2001) suggest that the loss of such dopaminergic receptors is responsible for many of the cognitive aging effects described in this review. Support for this argument comes from computational modeling (Li et al. 2001) as well as imaging work. Wong et al. (1997) and Yang et al. (2003) used radioligands (a radioactive substance that, when injected, binds to dopamine and allows imaging of areas where receptors are located) to measure dopaminergic receptors, and found strong relationships among age, the number of receptors, and cognition. Backman et al. (2000) reported that literally all age-related variance on perceptual speed and episodic memory tasks was attenuated when dopamine receptor binding was statistically controlled. All of these data suggest that dopaminergic receptors play an important role in at least some aspects of cognitive aging. Whether the receptors are the major, or even sole, factor accounting for normal cognitive aging awaits further research.

At this point, we have painted a clear and relatively consistent picture of cognitive function and neural structures across the lifespan. Generally, cognitive function declines in parallel across the lifespan with decreasing brain volume, dopamine receptors, and white matter integrity. At the same time, direct relationships between declining structural measures of the brain and cognitive function are not always observed (Salat et al. 2002, Tisserand et al. 2000), and when they are observed, they are of a modest magnitude. White matter hyperintensities appear to have more significance than total brain volume, but knowledge about brain structure does not fully explain age-related variance in cognitive function.

FUNCTIONAL IMAGING AND VIEWS OF THE AGING MIND

Prefrontal Bilaterality

Functional imaging techniques (fMRI or PET, with most recent studies involving fMRI) allow cognitive neuroscientists to see the brain in action by measuring increases in blood flow and oxygenation in specific brain structures. The changes in blood flow are time-locked to the mental activities in which individuals are engaging so that one can see how brain activity changes as task demands change, with a resolution of about two seconds. Although this is much slower than the rates of many mental and neural processes, it is still the case that functional imaging research has been hugely informative in developing a more complex view of the aging mind than existed prior to the advent of this technique.

One of the most noteworthy features of functional data is the startling discontinuity that exists between patterns of neural activation in young and old adults. The behavioral and structural data suggest that one might expect to see declining neural activity with age, congruent with the declines in neural structures and cognitive behaviors. Quite surprisingly, initial studies, which focused on verbal working memory (Reuter-Lorenz et al. 2000) and verbal long-term memory (Cabeza et al. 1997, Grady et al. 1999), showed evidence for focal, left prefrontal activity in young adults, whereas older adults showed activation in both left and right prefrontal areas, as shown in **Figure 3** (see color insert). This bilateral activation seemed to suggest that the old brain was working harder and engaging in more distributed, compensatory processing to perform a task that was focal (unilateral) in young adults. A great deal of discussion immediately followed as to whether this appealing explanation was actually correct

(Cabeza 2002, Park et al. 2001, Reuter-Lorenz 2002). Perhaps the additional activation in the contralateral hemisphere reflected inefficient operation of inhibitory mechanisms, and this activation was actually interference and a major cause of some of the behavioral deficits observed in cognitive aging.

Since these initial observations and discussions occurred, much more has been learned about the role of additional bilateral, and in many instances, prefrontal, activity in the aging brain. There is now a corpus of evidence suggesting that additional contralateral recruitment is indeed functional and supportive of cognition in older adults. The first finding is the tendency for older adults to engage both the left and right hemispheres, which has been associated with higher performance in older adults in comparison with younger adults (Cabeza et al. 2002, Reuter-Lorenz et al. 2001, Rypma & D'Esposito 2001). Likewise, in a category-learning task, older adults showed greater parietal activation bilaterally than did young adults, and this bilateral activity was associated with higher performance (Fera et al. 2005). Divided visual field experiments manipulating unilateral versus bilateral hemispheric engagement in task performance provided converging evidence that older adults showed unique benefits from engaging both hemispheres (Cherry et al. 2005, Reuter-Lorenz et al. 1999).

A second key finding is that overactivation of prefrontal regions has been specifically linked to improved memory in older adults. In particular, a study of subsequent memory effects of picture encoding in young and older adults (Gutchess et al. 2005) showed heightened parahippocampal activation in young compared to old for pictures that were later correctly remembered. In contrast, older adults showed heightened middle frontal activation for items that were remembered. Thus, increased frontal activation in older adults was uniquely associated with remembering. Moreover, for older adults, high levels of inferior frontal activation were associated with low levels of parahippocampal activation, suggesting that higher frontal activity may be compensatory for decreased mediotemporal activations. Morcom et al. (2003) also showed evidence for more frontal bilaterality in older adults compared to young when encoding subsequently remembered words. In a later study, Cabeza et al. (2004) confirmed a pattern of increased frontal bilaterality and decreased hippocampal activation in older adults that was shared across tasks of attention, working memory, and long-term memory, demonstrating the global nature of this pattern.

A third line of evidence favoring a compensatory interpretation of bilaterality with age comes from a longitudinal study by Persson et al. (2006). They demonstrated that older individuals who showed the most shrinkage in hippocampal volume over a ten-year period had poorer memories but also showed the greatest additional activation in right prefrontal cortex (Persson et al. 2006). Hence, individuals who endured the greatest neural insults and memory decline also showed the greatest extra prefrontal activation.

Studies that used repetitive transcranial magnetic stimulation (rTMS) in young and older adults have provided especially compelling evidence in favor of contralateral activity enhancing cognitive function in older adults. rTMS is a technique that transiently disrupts neural function by applying repetitive magnetic stimulation to a specific area of the brain, creating highly focal and temporary "lesions." In a seminal study conducted by Rossi et al. (2004), young and older adults studied pictures while rTMS was applied to the subjects' left or right dorsolateral prefrontal cortex (DLPFC); the subjects then made recognition judgments while rTMS was again applied to the left or right DLPFC. One of the most interesting finding from this work was that young adults' memory retrieval accuracy was more significantly affected when the rTMS was applied to the left compared to the right hemisphere. In contrast, older adults' retrieval was equally affected by the rTMS, whether it was applied to left or right, suggesting that the activations in both hemispheres were useful for performing the recognition task in older adults.

In another line of work, memory improvement was demonstrated in older adults using rTMS in a "stimulating mode" to prime or increase the activation of the underlying prefrontal circuitry (Sole-Padulles et al. 2006). fMRI confirmed that older adults who showed greater increases in prefrontal activation post-rTMS also showed the greatest memory improvement. In summary, converging evidence from a range of studies using different approaches suggests that the additional age-associated neural activation, especially in prefrontal areas, appears to be functional and to enhance task performance. Many researchers and models have described these activation increases as "compensatory" and suggestive of an adaptive brain that functionally reorganizes and responds to neural aging, a view of aging that would have been highly unlikely from the behavioral data alone.

Compensation for What?

If one wishes to make the argument that the additional activation in prefrontal areas evidenced by older adults is functional and adaptive, it becomes important to specify for what aspects of neural aging the prefrontal activations are compensating.

Deficient hippocampal activations. One obvious possibility, based on the discussion thus far, is that the compensation is for the structural changes that occur in the brain in terms of both volumetric decrease and white matter integrity. Indeed, Persson et al. (2006) demonstrate important functional increases in prefrontal activations associated with hippocampal shrinkage and memory loss. There are other candidates, however, for the cause of functional compensation besides structural changes and age-associated neural insults. Park & Gutchess (2005) reviewed functional activations associated with long-term memory and noted the frequency with which decreased hippocampal/parahippocampal activations are observed in older adults in the same context that the increased frontal activations are observed. They argued that enhanced prefrontal activity is due

rTMS: repetitive transcranial magnetic stimulation

DLPFC: dorsolateral prefrontal cortex

to a declining activation in mediotemporal areas, an argument confirmed by Gutchess et al. (2005) in a study that contrasted remembered pictures with forgotten pictures in old and young adult subjects. The Persson et al. (2006) findings are also congruent with such an interpretation, and a wealth of evidence suggests that both hippocampal structure (Driscoll et al. 2003) and function (Daselaar et al. 2003, Johnson et al. 2004, Park et al. 2003) are deficient with age (although see Dickerson et al. 2004 for evidence that mild cognitive impairment is associated with greater activation in hippocampal/parahippocampal structures—a finding somewhat at odds with the present argument).

A different view of the role of hippocampal function has been suggested by Buckner (2004). He proposes that age-associated frontal shrinkage along with increases in frontal activation are typical of normal aging, whereas declining hippocampal/entorhinal volume and activation is associated with pathological aging and is a marker for subclinical dementia. Both the Buckner (2004) proposition and the frontal compensation for hippocampal deficits argument could be correct, if one considers the possibility that both bilaterality and hippocampal function exist on a continuum. Perhaps within the realm of healthy elderly, one sees a compensatory relationship between the two structures, but shrinkage and dysfunction may reach a critical point as pathology increases, and at that point, the reciprocity no longer exists.

Dedifferentiation as an impetus for compensation. In addition to decreased hippocampal activation, there is growing evidence that ventral visual and sensory cortex may show less activation and neural specificity with age. On the surface, this is a surprising pattern of findings because the volume of these structures is largely preserved with aging. However, clear evidence exists for alterations in these structures with age when one examines the neural specificity of activations to categories of perceptual input. It is well known that young adults show activations that are highly specific

to faces in left and right fusiform areas of ventral visual cortex (Kanwisher et al. 1997). They also show category-specific activations to pictures of places, houses, and outdoor scenes in the parahippocampus (Epstein & Kanwisher 1998) and to words and numbers in the left fusiform gyrus and collateral sulcus (Polk et al. 2002, Puce et al. 1996). Based on the Baltes & Lindenberger (1997) evidence that sensory and cognitive function is dedifferentiated with age relative to young adults, one might expect these areas to be less specific in older adults. Park et al. (2004) investigated this hypothesis and discovered that in comparison with young adults, older adults show markedly less neural specificity in the fusiform face area, parahippocampal place area, and the lateral occipital area specialized for letters. The notion that neural tissue that is highly specialized in young adults dedifferentiates or becomes less specific in old was reinforced by the work of Chee et al. (2006), who utilized an adaptation paradigm (Malach et al. 1995) to study neural response in ventral visual cortex. In this paradigm, neural response becomes increasingly less pronounced as a visual stimulus is repeated and one can map which areas are specialized for which functions by varying elements of the stimuli. Chee et al. (2006) demonstrated decreased specificity in older adults for object recognition in the lateral occipital cortex and decreased binding of target to context in the hippocampus, but also showed relatively intact processing of background information in the parahippocampal place area. Payer et al. (2006) also reported evidence for decreased specificity of face and place areas on a working memory task. Given these alterations in ventral visual processing, perhaps some of the increased activation of frontal cortex provides additional compensatory processing to recognize and differentiate categories as we age.

A different approach to the frontal/sensory issue was taken by Cabeza et al. (2004), who noted a preponderance of increased frontal and decreased sensory activation in old compared to young subjects across attentional, working memory, and long-term memory tasks. In a later study, Davis et al. (2007) further confirmed this shift from posterior brain activations to anterior activations, and suggested that the increased frontal activation that occurs with age is in response to deficient ventral visual and sensory activations. Overall, there is growing evidence that the additional work of the frontal sites may be a broad response to decreased efficiency of neural processes in perceptual areas of the brain.

Compensation and the default network.
Functional imaging measures changes in blood flow relative to some baseline. During baseline, subjects typically lay quietly in the magnet and fixate on a plus sign against an otherwise blank screen. The default network refers to the sites that are activated during the baseline interval when the brain is supposedly at rest and includes sites across frontal, parietal, mediotemporal, and visual areas such as the posterior cingulate, middle frontal cortex, the lateral parietal region, and the lingual gyrus (Raichle et al. 2001). Perhaps the most notable aspect of the default network is that it is suppressed when the brain shifts to a demanding cognitive task (Greicius et al. 2003). However, a number of authors have found that older adults show significantly less suppression of the default network than young adults (Grady et al. 2006, Persson et al. 2007), and that the failure to suppress is actively related to lower performance on some cognitive tasks (Damoiseaux et al. 2007, Persson et al. 2007). It seems plausible that another cause of increased frontal activity in older adults is a failure to shift out of this relaxation or default state into more active modes of cognitive processing (Reuter-Lorenz & Cappell 2008, Reuter-Lorenz & Lustig 2005).

THE SCAFFOLDING THEORY OF COGNITIVE AGING

In the previous sections, a broad range of behavioral and neural data from the cognitive aging literature has been discussed. Little doubt exists that the extent of cognitive and structural decline is substantial. Nevertheless, people generally function remarkably well even into advanced old age, and do so even in the presence of a great deal of pathology as discovered at autopsy (T. W. Mitchell et al. 2002). The puzzle for cognitive neuroscientists is not so much in explaining age-related decline, but rather in understanding the high level of cognitive success that can be maintained by older adults in the face of such significant neurobiological change.

We propose the scaffolding theory of cognitive aging as a testable model for resolving this puzzle (see **Figure 4**). STAC posits that behavior is maintained at a relatively high level with age, despite neural challenges and functional deterioration, due to the continuous engagement of compensatory scaffolding—the recruitment of additional circuitry that shores up declining structures whose functioning has become noisy, inefficient, or both. The pervasive evidence in the functional brain-imaging literature of greater bilateral activation and overactivation of frontal areas in older adults reflects the engagement of "compensatory scaffolding"—the patterns of brain activation that include both declining networks and the associated compensatory circuitry recruited to meet the task demands. STAC also provides for mechanisms that can bolster compensatory scaffolding. The joint operation of these declining and compensatory forces, as shown in **Figure 4**, determines cognitive function in late adulthood. Below, we summarize major tenets of STAC, detail predictions from the STAC model, and describe how the STAC model can be distinguished from other views of cognitive aging.

Scaffolding is a Dynamic, On going Property of an Adaptive Brain

Scaffolding is a process that characterizes neural dynamics across the lifespan. It is not merely the brain's response to normal aging; it is the brain's normal response to challenge. The concept of scaffolding has been used to explain the brain's response to novel skill acquisition in young adults. To acquire a novel skill, an initial set of neural circuits must be engaged and developed that provides the structure for task performance in the early skill-acquisition stages

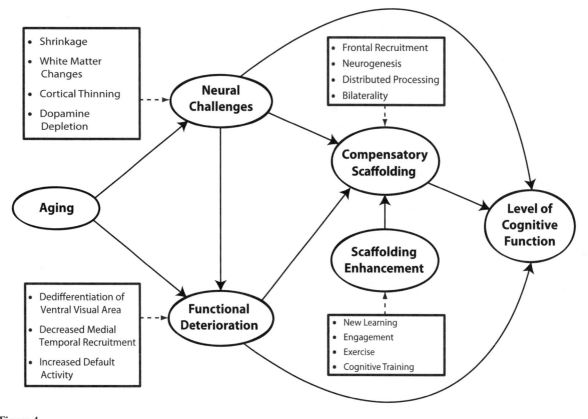

Figure 4

A conceptual model of the scaffolding theory of aging and cognition (STAC).

(Petersen et al. 1998; see also Church et al. 2008 for an example of scaffolding in early development). As learning proceeds, performance becomes less effortful and with enough practice, becomes overlearned. By this stage of overlearning (some would call this skilled performance), the circuitry has shifted from a broader, dispersed network to a specific, honed, and optimal circuit of neural regions that are functionally interconnected to mediate efficient processing and storage. Petersen et al. (1998) noted that the regions that provided scaffolding at the early stages of practice continue to be minimally active even as more-specific regions assume task control. This suggests that the initial scaffolding may remain available as secondary or functionally ready circuitry that can be recruited when performance takes place under challenge.

Extending Petersen et al.'s (1998) argument, we suggest that reliance on such secondary networks or scaffolds may be an important aspect of healthy cognitive aging and provide considerable support toward the maintenance of cognitive function as age-associated structural deterioration increases. We presume that scaffolding processes operate with more efficiency in youth, when scaffolding is typically and frequently engaged to meet novel situations and to achieve new learning. With age, scaffolding processes may be invoked to perform familiar tasks and basic cognitive operations as these processes become increasingly challenging with the degradation of existing neural circuitry. We speculate that perhaps the maintenance of language in old age results from the continuous use of language throughout life and a particularly elaborate scaffolding network for this behavior that is both critical and overlearned. We view the recruitment of neural scaffolds as a normal adaptive response of the brain that takes place throughout the lifespan. In response to the challenge neurobiological challenges of aging, new scaffolds can be established, or previously established scaffolds acquired in early development or during new learning can be recruited.

Prefrontal Cortex is a Primary Locus for Scaffolding

Scaffolding can be understood as circuits that provide supplementary, complementary, and, in some cases, alternative ways to achieve a particular behavioral output or cognitive goal. Once it is fully developed, the prefrontal cortex is the most versatile structure in the brain. In the aging brain, scaffolding processes largely reside in this structure. There may be flexibility in other areas as well, and this is an important area for exploration. Not surprisingly, as reviewed above, prefrontal circuits figure prominently in age-related overactivation. In fact, the initial evidence that led to compensatory models of frontal activation (Cabeza 2002) was centered in regions of inferior, lateral, and rostral regions of the prefrontal cortex.

It is important to recognize that some parts of the brain are dedicated to the performance of specific tasks and may not easily play a role in scaffolding, and we hypothesize that scaffolding is frequently erected and engaged to compensate for deficits in these areas. The ventral visual cortex is an example of dedicated circuitry focused on computing the form-based properties of visual input. Such dedicated areas are functionally altered with age, as the dedifferentiation of ventral visual cortex research suggests (Chee et al. 2006, Park et al. 2004, Payer et al. 2006), and it is the poor function of such areas which require the utilization of scaffolding. The hippocampus is another dedicated structure that performs specific functions such as binding and relational processing (N. J. Cohen et al. 1999); both its structure and function decline with age (K. J. Mitchell et al. 2000, Small et al. 2000). Hence, it is likely another neu-

ral structure for which scaffolding is required if cognitive performance is to be optimized in the older adult (Park & Gutchess 2005). Accordingly, the pervasive tendency for age-related overactivation of prefrontal sites coupled with underactivation in more-posterior cortices of the occipital and temporal lobes (Davis et al. 2007) is consistent with the notion that prefrontal circuitry provides scaffolding for age-related inefficiencies of dedicated, hard-wired cortical circuits.

Scaffolding is a Neurocognitive Response to Challenge

Challenges to the neural system can be extrinsic, such as when the brain is confronted with novel, unanticipated, or increased levels of task demand. But challenge can also be intrinsic, such as when the neural circuitry is altered metabolically or structurally. Intrinsic alterations can be transient, as in states of sleep deprivation (Drummond et al. 2004), or continuous, as in the case of biological aging. Because the circuits engaged for scaffolding are not entirely arbitrary, there are similarities in the brain's response to different forms of challenge. Consider the challenge posed by increasing levels of task demand. Banich (1998) demonstrated that younger adults engage in processing that becomes increasingly bilateral as task complexity increases. Older adults also show patterns of bilateral neurocognitive engagement, but at lower levels of task demand (Reuter-Lorenz et al. 1999). In this way, the brain's response to extrinsic challenge (higher task demand in young adults) resembles its response to intrinsic challenge (aging). Similarly, in verbal working memory, neurocognitive operations that are sufficient for small loads are inadequate for larger memory loads. Younger adults respond to this challenge by increasing recruitment of right dorsolateral prefrontal cortex (Hillary et al. 2006, Reuter-Lorenz & Cappell 2008). Thus, right DLPFC provides the scaffolding to meet the extrinsically imposed challenge. Likewise, in older adults, right DLPFC activation is evident even at low levels of task demand because biological aging of the brain has resulted in intrinsic conditions that require compensatory scaffolding.

Consistent with the notion that scaffolding occurs in response to challenge are data demonstrating right frontal overactivation in response to other forms of intrinsic challenge posed by disease states such as multiple sclerosis (Hillary et al. 2006) and possibly such interventions as chemotherapy. Scaffolding is not unique to the intrinsic challenge posed by aging. Aging constitutes ongoing and increasing levels of challenges that persist at lower levels of intensity throughout adulthood—continually activating the brain's adaptive response to its own aging (Reuter-Lorenz & Mikels 2007).

Scaffolded Networks are Less Efficient than Honed Cognitive Networks

As new skills are acquired, performance becomes more efficient and less error prone. At the neural level, this increased efficiency can be explained by the establishment of efficient circuitry that is highly functionally interconnected, which includes honing the neural circuitry through practice and decreasing reliance on the rudimentary, scaffolded stages of skill acquisition. In contrast, with aging, declining neurobiological efficiency of such honed networks leads to increasing reliance on scaffolding, the erection of new scaffolds, or some combination of these compensatory processes. Consequently, performance is less efficient than when it is mediated by the finely honed network in the younger brain. Note, however, that without the compensatory engagement of scaffolded circuits, the older brain would have to rely exclusively on honed networks that are in decline, resulting in poorer performance overall.

The Aged Brain is Less Efficient at Generating Scaffolding, and Pathology May Entirely Limit Scaffolding Operations

Although plasticity is evident throughout the lifespan, age-related declines in neurobiological regeneration will necessarily limit the scaffolding capacity of the aging brain (Burke & Barnes 2006). At the same time, the need for scaffolding is substantial because of reduced efficiency of dedicated circuits. As aging proceeds, the need for compensatory scaffolding exceeds the capacity for plasticity and reorganization, leading to the more frank expression of cognitive loss in the oldest old (Baltes & Mayer 1999). Buckner et al. (2005) utilized five imaging techniques that included visualization of amyloid deposition (a plaque deposited on neurons that is associated with Alzheimer's disease), and interestingly, high deposits were also associated with high levels of default activity as well as with decreased activation in posterior cortex. Buckner et al. (2005) speculate that increased default activity with aging may enhance amyloid deposition and the promotion of Alzheimer's disease. Lustig et al. (2003) have shown an association between Alzheimer's disease and default activity. In our view, Alzheimer's disease represents the conjoint influence of severe pathological challenge and sustained disintegration of the reparative process due to an attack on cellular health that limits the ability to engage in scaffolding. Ultimately, neural pathology penetrates the scaffolding, leading to selective and eventually total collapse of the scaffolding and the structure it is protecting.

Individual Variability and the Factors that Promote Scaffolding

The causes of cognitive aging are multifactorial, and individuals will vary in both the magnitude of decline and the amount of protective scaffolding that can be engaged. Greater degrees of structural or functional aging could occur due to genetic susceptibility (e.g., hetero- or homozygosity for APOE4) to some diseases (e.g., hypertension), adverse experiences (e.g., chemotherapy), or advanced age. Individual differences could also result from the readiness and efficiency of scaffolding. More effective scaffolding could be the result of higher levels of physical fitness, cognitive stimulation, or other factors that promote scaffolding activity (see next section). Preservation of cognitive function with age could thus occur due to a slow rate of cognitive aging or particularly efficient scaffolding mechanisms. Presumably, individuals who have exceptionally high cognitive ability in old age would be those with low genetic susceptibility to biological aging and with highly effective scaffolding.

Scaffolding is Promoted by Training and Cognitive Activity

A wealth of evidence from experimental studies with nonhuman animals suggests that changes in cortical structures can result from external challenge. In a seminal study, Zhou & Merzenich (2007) demonstrated that adult rats that had degraded auditory cortices early in life were able, with intensive discrimination training in adulthood, to develop normal auditory function. The training resulted in remapping of the auditory cortex through top-down neuromodulation rather than from revitalization of auditory neurons degraded early in life. The STAC model is reminiscent of this finding, as it suggests that top-down frontal function may modulate age-related losses in perceptual function occurring at the level of ventral visual cortex. There is also evidence that the enhancement of brain-derived neurotrophic factor and serotonin increases cognitive performance in older animals (Mattson et al. 2004), and we propose that these substances could play an important role in maintenance of the ability to scaffold or develop mechanisms for an aging brain. Similar to the findings evidenced by the Zhou & Merzenich (2007) data, the mechanism for enhancement of brain-derived neurotrophic factor appears to be external challenge, either in the form of exercise (Cotman & Berchtold 2002, Kramer et al. 2004) or, more speculatively, cognitive challenge. There is also evidence that depression down-regulates these substances (Tsai 2003), which could impair scaffolding abilities and provide some of the basis for decreased cognition with depression.

Studies of aged animals also reveal increased neural volume as a result of cognitive challenge.

Kempermann et al. (1998) demonstrated that old rats that had been maintained in complex visual and play environments showed birth of new neurons in the hippocampus in old age, unlike control subjects. Kobayashi et al. (2002) reported improved learning ability in rats exposed to an enriched environment, even in old age, and concluded, "These results show that aged animals still have appreciable plasticity in cognitive function and suggest that environmental stimulation could benefit aging humans as well." Kempermann et al. (2002) reported a similar effect and demonstrated that short-term exposure of rats to an enriched environment, even in old age, led to a fivefold increase in hippocampal neurogenesis as well as a decrease in age-related atrophy in the dentate gyrus.

Although no direct experimental studies have manipulated the relationship of sustained cognitive challenge to enhanced neural structure in humans, a wealth of studies link sustained cognitive engagement across the lifespan to higher levels of cognitive function as well as to delayed age of onset for dementia. Schooler et al. (1999) reported that individuals who engaged in complex work into late adulthood showed increased intellectual functioning, and in another study, Bosma et al. (2003) reported a similar finding. Other data indicate that high levels of education and occupational attainment protect against the risk of Alzheimer's disease (Stern et al. 1994). Finally, a number of studies have reported that highly educated people who tend to be involved in more cognitively stimulating activities are more cognitively resilient in the early stages of Alzheimer's disease (Bennett et al. 2003, Wilson & Bennett 2003, Wilson et al. 2000), even after controlling for other related variables. The scaffolding model not only predicts these effects, it delineates a specific mechanism—the creation of additional neural connections and possibly neural tissue—that controls the observed effects. It is also possible, if not probable, that cognitive training promotes scaffolding and could be an important mechanism for understanding broadly facilitative training effects as opposed to narrow and specific effects.

It should be noted here that the scaffolding model bears some relationship to ideas of cognitive reserve advanced by Stern (2002), who suggests cognitive reserve is "using brain networks that are less susceptible to disruption." He also discusses compensation and describes it as "using brain structures or networks not normally used by individuals with intact brains in order to compensate for brain damage." In the Stern (2002) model, cognitive reserve (the use of pathways resistant to disruption) is invoked when the brain is under challenge, with high-ability individuals having more of these pathways. We suggest that individual differences in cognitive reserve may determine the quality, quantity, and/or effectiveness of scaffolding, and in this respect, the two models may be complementary. Therefore, STAC is related to cognitive reserve but differs in some critical ways. The particular strength of STAC is that it considers the engagement and erection of scaffolding a normal and adaptive neural response that is utilized in the face of challenge across the entire lifespan, rather than a process specific to old age. Rudimentary processes provide scaffolding for the establishment and, later on in life, the preservation of more complex processes. In this respect, the engagement of scaffolding need not be a sign of pathology or abnormality. Moreover, according to STAC, the engagement of scaffolding is inherently a compensatory response; the net result may be that performance is less efficient than it would be with intact, finely honed circuitry, but presumably less impaired than if the scaffolds were not engaged. The compensatory function of scaffolding, similar to compensation in the Stern model (use of non-normal pathways), occurs when existing circuitry can no longer meet the task requirements and the brain develops new pathways.

Greenwood (2007) provides a detailed review of relevant biological processes and a nuanced analysis of some imaging results in a paper that proposes a functional plasticity account of aging, wherein cortical thinning initiates reorganization and age-related recruitment changes. The Greenwood perspective on plasticity is in striking agreement with many of the ideas expressed here. However, a key difference is STAC's conception of scaffolding as a lifelong and continuously adaptive process that utilizes prior and newly formed scaffolds in response to ongoing age-related neurobiological declines.

By its treatment of scaffolding as a lifelong neural response to challenge, STAC provides an explicit model that integrates structural, functional, and experiential data to understand cognitive function with age.

PREDICTIONS OF THE SCAFFOLDING THEORY OF COGNITIVE AGING

We have presented a broad model that integrates a disparate array of findings across many domains of cognitive neuroscience and aging. Below, we consider some testable hypotheses that are logical extensions of STAC.

Scaffolding is a direct response to the magnitude of neural insults that occur with age. Thus, decreases in dopamine receptors, degree of white matter health, and magnitude of shrinkage of neural structures should all predict an increase in scaffolding. It is important to recognize that a curvilinear relationship may exist between degree of scaffolding and neural insults, as a brain can be sufficiently damaged such that scaffolding will no longer be possible.

Scaffolding is not arbitrary. This essentially suggests that brain structures are not interchangeable. For example, Reuter-Lorenz et al. (2001) hypothesized that storage deficits can be compensated for by heightened executive processing, but that the opposite is unlikely. The most likely sites for scaffolding to occur is in contralateral, homologous structures [see recent evidence by Putnam et al. (2008) relating white matter anisotropy to homologous frontal recruitment] or in penumbral areas directly surrounding focal areas for activation (as in stroke patients; Saur et al. 2006, Ward & Cohen 2004). It is important to assess which type of scaffolding is most effective. We hypothesize that subjects who show enhanced bilaterality or enhanced activation in penumbral areas are showing evidence of scaffolding that may be particularly efficient. Scaffolding may also occur by activating areas that are responses to higher levels of challenge in younger adults (Reuter-Lorenz et al. 1999).

Scaffolds, although not arbitrary, may show more site variability with age than does the primary site of activation. As the brain ages, the most efficient site for a scaffolded response may vary depending on which areas of the brain are most healthy within a given subject. For example, a given subject might compensate for diminished function in the fusiform face area by recruiting from the penumbra (see an interesting paper by Baker et al. 2005 on function reorganization of visual cortex with macular degeneration), from a homologous area, or by deployment of additional frontal resources. To the extent that different subjects compensate from different sites, group analyses may be misleading. Specific analytic tools and procedures that allow for the study of individual differences, including functional connectivity and pattern analysis, will be helpful in understanding and identifying functional scaffolding.

Younger brains that use scaffolding characteristic of older adults are at risk for poorer performance and accelerated aging. Reliance on scaffolding is less efficient than using a finely honed network. Middle-aged adults who show extensive scaffolding may be at risk for later pathology and more pronounced age deficits. This pattern of findings is congruent with those reported by Persson et al. (2006) who found a relationship between hippocampal shrinkage and increased right frontal recruitment over 10 years in a longitudinal study. Younger brains that need to rely on scaffolding presumably do so in response to some inefficiency or underlying vulnerability that may be subclinical and potentially measurable behaviorally given sufficient challenge. For example, Smith et al. (2001), using PET and operation span, found that poorly performing young adults showed the same extended activation pattern as that of older adults.

Although we think of scaffolding as primarily functional recruitment, scaffolding can also be instantiated as structural changes in neural sites. For example, the well-known London taxicab driver study (Maguire et al. 2000) demonstrated that cab drivers had larger hippocampi than did controls, suggesting that perhaps the sustained engagement of the structure for wayfinding increased its volume. This argument's credibility was enhanced by the finding that the more experienced (and older) the driver was, the larger the difference relative to controls. This finding, along with others in the animal literature, suggests that scaffolding could also take the form of structural changes (including neurogenesis) in the brain.

Compensatory scaffolding can both be created and dissipated by training. Scaffolding is created as an individual acquires a new task or strategy, but paradoxically, training may also result in a decrease in reliance on scaffolding and more reliance on the primary, honed network. We tentatively hypothesize that when older adults are already relying on overactivation relative to young adults for task performance, the target for training should be to decrease activation in these secondary scaffolded areas and improve the efficiency of honed networks. This will lead to a more efficient use of neural resources. Similarly, if older adults show significant underactivation or deterioration of a network (e.g., dedifferentiated ventral visual function), the focus of training should be to establish new scaffolds in penumbral areas to perform a task that is being done inefficiently or not at all.

Creating novel scaffolds through training for task performance is possible but particularly effortful. The rehabilitation literature illustrates the possibility that entirely new neural circuitry can be developed from thousands of repetitions. Are there areas of the brain that are particularly amenable to novel scaffolds, and if so, what types of scaffolding tasks are they best suited to perform (e.g., sensory, motor, or cognitive)? Cognitive neuroscientists should begin to map areas that are particularly amenable to scaffolding of different types. This would yield huge gains in developing tools and techniques for maintaining maximum function of the human mind in late adulthood.

CONCLUSION

The STAC model integrates the impact of biological aging and experience to account for the neural reorganization of function that occurs in late adulthood. STAC invokes a scaffolding mechanism as a basis for understanding neurocognitive aging—a mechanism that has been used in educational, developmental, and rehabilitative contexts to describe how existing strengths can be harnessed to build new skills or recover and sustain capabilities that have been threatened by challenge. STAC therefore places neurocognitive aging within the context of both plasticity and challenge, and by so doing draws potentially informative parallels between the brain's response to aging, early development, new skill acquisition, and both transient and chronic states of disorder, including sleep deprivation, neurological lesions, and other pathological stressors.

According to STAC, the performance of older adults must be understood in terms of multiple determining factors: those that influence decline and those that influence compensatory scaffolding. The speculations we offer about what these factors may be point to guidelines for successful aging and for the development of interventions that may not only forestall declines, but also promote the potential for effective scaffolding. STAC embraces the brain's lifelong potential for plasticity and its ability to adapt to its own aging. We recognize that many questions remain unanswered by STAC and that some aspects of the model are quite speculative. Nevertheless, STAC provides a broad integrative framework for understanding the relationship of structural and functional changes in the brain in combination with life experiences to understand levels of cognitive function in late adulthood.

The need to understand how to preserve or enhance cognitive function in late adulthood could not be more urgent. We believe some of the most significant scientific breakthroughs of the twenty-first century will involve behavioral and pharmacological interventions to preserve cognitive function and forestall the onset of dementing disorders. Theoretical models such as STAC that provide a blueprint for investigation of mechanisms associated with preservation and positive change provide clear direction for important questions. Happily, increasingly sophisticated behavioral and imaging techniques for understanding the mind provide methodologies to find answers.

SUMMARY POINTS

1. The basic hardware of cognition significantly declines with advanced age, although knowledge and expertise are relatively protected from age-related decline. Neural structure also shows changes. Many brain structures show significant shrinkage, the integrity of the white matter decreases, and dopamine depletion occurs.

2. In contrast to the age-related declines in cognitive function and brain structure, functional brain activity increases with age, particularly in the frontal cortex. The proposed scaffolding theory of aging and cognition suggests that this increased functional activity is due to compensatory scaffolding—the recruitment of additional circuitry with age that shores up declining structures whose function has become noisy, inefficient, or both.

3. Prefrontal cortex is the most flexible structure in the brain, and brain scaffolding processes in the aging brain largely reside in this structure.

4. Scaffolding is the brain's response to cognitive challenge and is not unique to aging. Aging simply results in more frequent cognitive challenges at lower levels of intensity.

5. Scaffolded networks that develop with age may be less efficient than the original, direct, and finely honed networks developed at younger ages.

6. The aged brain is less efficient at generating scaffolding, and significant pathology (as occurs in advanced Alzheimer's disease) may entirely limit scaffolding operations.

7. The causes of cognitive aging are multifactorial, and individuals will vary in both the magnitude of decline and the amount of protective scaffolding that can be activated. Presumably, individuals who have exceptionally high cognitive ability in old age would be those with low genetic susceptibility to biological aging and a high level of scaffolding generation.

8. Scaffolding is promoted by cognitive activity. A wealth of evidence in the animal literature suggests that changes in cortical structures can occur as a result of external challenge, and growing evidence suggests that humans develop scaffolds as a result of stimulating experiences.

FUTURE ISSUES

1. If scaffolding is a response to neural insults with age, is there a direct relationship between brain degradation and degree of scaffolding?

2. Does the occurrence of compensatory scaffolding at a younger age (say in middle age) predict cognitive frailty in later adulthood?

3. What activities promote brain health? Can we develop a set of lifestyle changes that would be protective of the brain in late adulthood?

4. How much do specific types of cognitive training change the brain? What type of training is most effective in sustaining cognitive health?

5. Are certain types or sites for neural scaffolding particularly effective (e.g., bilateral recruitment of frontal areas versus penumbral activation)?

DISCLOSURE STATEMENT

The authors are not aware of any biases that might be perceived as affecting the objectivity of this review.

ACKNOWLEDGMENTS

This work was supported by a grant from the National Institute on Aging (5R37AG006265–24), whose support is gratefully acknowledged. Additionally, the authors thank Andy Hebrank and Blair Flicker, who provided a great deal of support in manuscript preparation.

LITERATURE CITED

Backman L, Ginovart N, Dixon RA, Wahlin TB, Wahlin A, et al. 2000. Age-related cognitive deficits mediated by changes in the striatal dopamine system. *Am. J. Psychiatry* 157(4):635–37

Baker CI, Peli E, Knouf N, Kanwisher NG. 2005. Reorganization of visual processing in macular degeneration. *J. Neurosci.* 25(3):614–18

Baltes PB, Lindenberger U. 1997. Emergence of a powerful connection between sensory and cognitive functions across the adult life span: a new window to the study of cognitive aging? *Psychol. Aging* **12(1):12–21**

Baltes PB, Mayer KU. 1999. *The Berlin Aging Study: Aging from 70 to 100.* New York: Cambridge Univ. Press

Banich MT. 1998. The missing link: the role of interhemispheric interaction in attentional processing. *Brain Cogn.* 36(2):128–57

Bennett DA, Wilson RS, Schneider JA, Evans DA, Mendes de Leon CF, et al. 2003. Education modifies the relation of AD pathology to level of cognitive function in older persons. *Neurology* 60(12):1909–15

Bosma H, van Boxtel MP, Ponds RW, Houx PJ, Burdorf A, Jolles J. 2003. Mental work demands protect against cognitive impairment: MAAS prospective cohort study. *Exp. Aging Res.* 29(1):33–45

Braver TS, Barch DM. 2002. A theory of cognitive control, aging cognition, and neuromodulation. *Neurosci. Biobehav. Rev.* 26(7):809–17

Buckner RL. 2004. Memory and executive function in aging and AD: multiple factors that cause decline and reserve factors that compensate. *Neuron* **44(1):195–208**

Buckner RL, Snyder AZ, Shannon BJ, LaRossa G, Sachs R, et al. 2005. Molecular, structural, and functional characterization of Alzheimer's disease: evidence for a relationship between default activity, amyloid, and memory. *J. Neurosci.* 25(34):7709–17

Burke SN, Barnes CA. 2006. Neural plasticity in the ageing brain. *Nat. Rev. Neurosci.* 7(1):30–40

Cabeza R. 2002. Hemispheric asymmetry reduction in older adults: the HAROLD model. *Psychol. Aging* 17(1):85–100

Cabeza R, Anderson ND, Locantore JK, McIntosh AR. 2002. Aging gracefully: compensatory brain activity in high-performing older adults. *Neuroimage* 17(3):1394–402

Cabeza R, Daselaar SM, Dolcos F, Prince SE, Budde M, Nyberg L. 2004. Task-independent and task-specific age effects on brain activity during working memory, visual attention and episodic retrieval. *Cereb. Cortex* 14(4):364–75

Cabeza R, Grady CL, Nyberg L, McIntosh AR, Tulving E, et al. 1997. Age-related differences in neural activity during memory encoding and retrieval: a positron emission tomography study. *J. Neurosci.* 17(1):391–400

Cabeza R, Nyberg L, Park DC, eds. 2005. *Cognitive Neuroscience of Aging: Linking Cognitive and Cerebral Aging.* **New York: Oxford Univ. Press**

Chalfonte BL, Johnson MK. 1996. Feature memory and binding in young and older adults. *Mem. Cogn.* 24(4):403–16

Chee MW, Goh JO, Venkatraman V, Tan JC, Gutchess A, et al. 2006. Age-related changes in object processing and contextual binding revealed using fMR adaptation. *J. Cogn. Neurosci.* 18(4):495–507

Cherry BJ, Adamson M, Duclos A, Hellige JB. 2005. Aging and individual variation in interhemispheric collaboration and hemispheric asymmetry. *Aging Neuropsychol. Cogn.* 12(4):316–39

Church JA, Coalson RS, Lugar HM, Petersen SE, Schlaggar BL. 2008. A developmental fMRI study of reading and repetition reveals changes in phonological and visual mechanisms over age. *Cereb. Cortex.* doi:10.1093/cercor/bhm228

Cohen JE. 2003. Human population: the next half century. *Science* 302(5648):1172–75

Cohen NJ, Ryan J, Hunt C, Romine L, Wszalek T, Nash C. 1999. Hippocampal system and declarative (relational) memory: summarizing the data from functional neuroimaging studies. *Hippocampus* 9(1):83–98

Cotman CW, Berchtold NC. 2002. Exercise: a behavioral intervention to enhance brain health and plasticity. *Trends Neurosci.* 25(6):295–301

Damoiseaux JS, Beckmann CF, Arigita EJ, Barkhof F, Scheltens P, et al. 2007. Reduced resting-state brain activity in the "default network" in normal aging. *Cereb. Cortex.* doi:10.1093/cercor/bhm207

Daniels K, Toth J, Jacoby L. 2006. The aging of executive functions. In *Lifespan Cognition: Mechanisms of Change*, ed. E Bialystok, FIM Craik, pp. 96–111. New York: Oxford Univ. Press

Daselaar SM, Veltman DJ, Rombouts SA, Raaijmakers JG, Jonker C. 2003. Deep processing activates the medial temporal lobe in young but not in old adults. *Neurobiol. Aging* 24(7):1005–11

Davis SW, Dennis NA, Daselaar SM, Fleck MS, Cabeza R. 2007. Que PASA? The posterior anterior shift in aging. *Cereb. Cortex.* **doi:10.1093/cercor/bhm155**

Dickerson BC, Salat DH, Bates JF, Atiya M, Killiany RJ, et al. 2004. Medial temporal lobe function and structure in mild cognitive impairment. *Ann. Neurol.* 56(1):27–35

Dodson CS, Schacter DL. 2002. Aging and strategic retrieval processes: reducing false memories with a distinctiveness heuristic. *Psychol. Aging* 17(3):405–15

Driscoll I, Hamilton DA, Petropoulos H, Yeo RA, Brooks WM, et al. 2003. The aging hippocampus: cognitive, biochemical and structural findings. *Cereb. Cortex* 13(12):1344–51

Drummond SP, Brown GG, Salamat JS, Gillin JC. 2004. Increasing task difficulty facilitates the cerebral compensatory response to total sleep deprivation. *Sleep* 27(3):445–51

Epstein R, Kanwisher N. 1998. A cortical representation of the local visual environment. *Nature* 392(6676):598–601

Fera F, Weickert TW, Goldberg TE, Tessitore A, Hariri A, et al. 2005. Neural mechanisms underlying probabilistic category learning in normal aging. *J. Neurosci.* 25(49):11340–48

Good CD, Johnsrude IS, Ashburner J, Henson RN, Friston KJ, Frackowiak RS. 2001. A voxel-based morphometric study of ageing in 465 normal adult human brains. *Neuroimage* 14(1 Pt. 1):21–36

Grady CL, McIntosh AR, Rajah MN, Beig S, Craik FI. 1999. The effects of age on the neural correlates of episodic encoding. *Cereb. Cortex* 9(8):805–14

Grady CL, Springer MV, Hongwanishkul D, McIntosh AR, Winocur G. 2006. Age-related changes in brain activity across the adult lifespan. *J. Cogn. Neurosci.* 18(2):227–41

Greenwood PM. 2007. Functional plasticity in cognitive aging: review and hypothesis. *Neuropsychology* 21(6):657–73

Greicius MD, Krasnow B, Reiss AL, Menon V. 2003. Functional connectivity in the resting brain: a network analysis of the default mode hypothesis. *Proc. Natl. Acad. Sci. USA* 100(1):253–58

Gunning-Dixon FM, Raz N. 2003. Neuroanatomical correlates of selected executive functions in middle-aged and older adults: a prospective MRI study. *Neuropsychologia* 41(14):1929–41

Gutchess AH, Welsh RC, Hedden T, Bangert A, Minear M, et al. 2005. Aging and the neural correlates of successful picture encoding: frontal activations compensate for decreased medial-temporal activity. *J. Cogn. Neurosci.* 17(1):84–96

Hasher L, Lustig C, Zacks RT. 2007. Inhibitory mechanisms and the control of attention. In *Variation in Working Memory*, ed. A Conway, C Jarrold, M Kane, J Towse, pp. 227–49. New York: Oxford Univ. Press

Hasher L, Zacks RT. 1979. Automatic and effortful processes in memory. *J. Exp. Psychol. Gen.* 108(3):356–88

Hasher L, Zacks RT. 1988. Working memory, comprehension, and aging: a review and a new view. In *The Psychology of Learning and Motivation*, ed. GH Bower, pp. 193–225. New York: Academic

Hashtroudi S, Johnson MK, Chrosniak LD. 1989. Aging and source monitoring. *Psychol. Aging* 4(1):106–12

Head D, Buckner RL, Shimony JS, Williams LE, Akbudak E, et al. 2004. Differential vulnerability of anterior white matter in nondemented aging with minimal acceleration in dementia of the Alzheimer type: evidence from diffusion tensor imaging. *Cereb. Cortex* 14(4):410–23

Hebert LE, Scherr PA, Bienias JL, Bennett DA, Evans DA. 2003. Alzheimer disease in the US population: prevalence estimates using the 2000 census. *Arch. Neurol.* 60(8):1119–22

Hillary FG, Genova HM, Chiaravalloti ND, Rypma B, DeLuca J. 2006. Prefrontal modulation of working memory performance in brain injury and disease. *Hum. Brain Mapp.* 27(11):837–47

Hultsch DF, Hertzog C, Dixon RA, Small BJ. 1999. *Memory Changes in the Aged*. London: Cambridge Univ. Press

Jennings JM, Jacoby LL. 1993. Automatic versus intentional uses of memory: aging, attention, and control. *Psychol. Aging* 8(2):283–93

Johnson SC, Baxter LC, Susskind-Wilder L, Connor DJ, Sabbagh MN, Caselli RJ. 2004. Hippocampal adaptation to face repetition in healthy elderly and mild cognitive impairment. *Neuropsychologia* 42(7):980–89

Kanwisher N, McDermott J, Chun MM. 1997. The fusiform face area: a module in human extrastriate cortex specialized for face perception. *J. Neurosci.* 17(11):4302–11

Kempermann G, Gast D, Gage FH. 2002. Neuroplasticity in old age: sustained fivefold induction of hippocampal neurogenesis by long-term environmental enrichment. *Ann. Neurol.* 52(2):135–43

Kempermann G, Kuhn HG, Gage FH. 1998. Experience-induced neurogenesis in the senescent dentate gyrus. *J. Neurosci.* 18(9):3206–12

A nice presentation on age differences in white matter integrity with differences in demented and nondemented individuals.

Kobayashi S, Ohashi Y, Ando S. 2002. Effects of enriched environments with different durations and starting times on learning capacity during aging in rats assessed by a refined procedure of the Hebb-Williams maze task. *J. Neurosci. Res.* 70(3):340–46

Koutstaal W, Schachter DL. 1997. Gist-based false recognition of pictures in older and younger adults. *J. Mem. Lang.* 37(4):555–83

Kramer AF, Bherer L, Colcombe SJ, Dong W, Greenough WT. 2004. Environmental influences on cognitive and brain plasticity during aging. *J. Gerontol. A Biol. Sci. Med. Sci.* 59(9):M940–57

Li SC, Lindenberger U, Sikstrom S. 2001. Aging cognition: from neuromodulation to representation. *Trends Cogn. Sci.* 5(11):479–86

Lindenberger U, Baltes PB. 1994. Sensory functioning and intelligence in old age: a strong connection. *Psychol. Aging* 9(3):339–55

Lustig C, Snyder AZ, Bhakta M, O'Brien KC, McAvoy M, et al. 2003. Functional deactivations: change with age and dementia of the Alzheimer type. *Proc. Natl. Acad. Sci. USA* 100(24):14504–9

Maguire EA, Gadian DG, Johnsrude IS, Good CD, Ashburner J, et al. 2000. Navigation-related structural change in the hippocampi of taxi drivers. *Proc. Natl. Acad. Sci. USA* 97(8):4398–403

Malach R, Reppas JB, Benson RR, Kwong KK, Jiang H, et al. 1995. Object-related activity revealed by functional magnetic resonance imaging in human occipital cortex. *Proc. Natl. Acad. Sci. USA* 92(18):8135–39

Mattson MP, Maudsley S, Martin B. 2004. BDNF and 5-HT: a dynamic duo in age-related neuronal plasticity and neurodegenerative disorders. *Trends Neurosci.* 27(10):589–94

Mitchell KJ, Johnson MK, Raye CL, D'Esposito M. 2000. fMRI evidence of age-related hippocampal dysfunction in feature binding in working memory. *Brain Res. Cogn. Brain Res.* 10(1–2):197–206

Mitchell TW, Mufson EJ, Schneider JA, Cochran EJ, Nissanov J, et al. 2002. Parahippocampal tau pathology in healthy aging, mild cognitive impairment, and early Alzheimer's disease. *Ann. Neurol.* 51(2):182–89

Morcom AM, Good CD, Frackowiak RS, Rugg MD. 2003. Age effects on the neural correlates of successful memory encoding. *Brain* 126(Pt. 1):213–29

Moscovitch M, Winocur G. 1992. The neuropsychology of memory and aging. In *The Handbook of Aging and Cognition*, ed. TA Salthouse, FIM Craik, pp. 315–72. Hillsdale, NJ: Erlbaum

Norman KA, Schacter DL. 1997. False recognition in younger and older adults: exploring the characteristics of illusory memories. *Mem. Cogn.* 25(6):838–48

Park DC, Gutchess AH. 2005. Long-term memory and aging: a cognitive neuroscience perspective. See Cabeza et al. 2005, pp. 218–45

Park DC, Lautenschlager G, Hedden T, Davidson NS, Smith AD, Smith PK. 2002. Models of visuospatial and verbal memory across the adult life span. *Psychol. Aging* 17(2):299–320

Park DC, Polk TA, Mikels J, Taylor SF, Marshuetz C. 2001. Cerebral aging: integration of brain and behavioral models of cognitive function. *Dialogues Clin. Neurosci.* 3:151–65

Park DC, Polk TA, Park R, Minear M, Savage A, Smith MR. 2004. Aging reduces neural specialization in ventral visual cortex. *Proc. Natl. Acad. Sci. USA* 101(35):13091–95

Park DC, Schwarz N, eds. 2000. *Cognitive Aging: A Primer*. Philadelphia, PA: Psychol. Press

Park DC, Smith AD, Lautenschlager G, Earles JL, Frieske D, et al. 1996. Mediators of long-term memory performance across the life span. *Psychol. Aging* 11(4):621–37

Park DC, Welsh RC, Marshuetz C, Gutchess AH, Mikels J, et al. 2003. Working memory for complex scenes: age differences in frontal and hippocampal activations. *J. Cogn. Neurosci.* 15(8):1122–34

Payer D, Marshuetz C, Sutton B, Hebrank A, Welsh RC, Park DC. 2006. Decreased neural specialization in old adults on a working memory task. *Neuroreport* 17(5):487–91

Persson J, Lustig C, Nelson JK, Reuter-Lorenz PA. 2007. Age differences in deactivation: a link to cognitive control? *J. Cogn. Neurosci.* 19(6):1021–32

Persson J, Nyberg L, Lind J, Larsson A, Nilsson LG, et al. 2006. Structure-function correlates of cognitive decline in aging. *Cereb. Cortex* 16(7):907–15

Petersen SE, van Mier H, Fiez JA, Raichle ME. 1998. The effects of practice on the functional anatomy of task performance. *Proc. Natl. Acad. Sci. USA* 95(3):853–60

Polk TA, Stallcup M, Aguirre GK, Alsop DC, D'Esposito M, et al. 2002. Neural specialization for letter recognition. *J. Cogn. Neurosci.* 14(2):145–59

Details clear evidence for decreased neural specificity in the aging brain.

Puce A, Allison T, Asgari M, Gore JC, McCarthy G. 1996. Differential sensitivity of human visual cortex to faces, letterstrings, and textures: a functional magnetic resonance imaging study. *J. Neurosci.* 16(16):5205–15

Putnam MC, Wig GS, Grafton ST, Kelley WM, Gazzaniga MS. 2008. Structural organization of the corpus callosum predicts the extent and impact of cortical activity in the nondominant hemisphere. *J. Neurosci.* 28(11):2912–18

Raichle ME, MacLeod AM, Snyder AZ, Powers WJ, Gusnard DA, Shulman GL. 2001. A default mode of brain function. *Proc. Natl. Acad. Sci. USA* 98(2):676–82

Raz N. 2000. Aging of the brain and its impact on cognitive performance: integration of structural and functional findings. In *The Handbook of Aging and Cognition*, ed. F Craik, TA Salthouse, pp. 1–90. Hillsdale, NJ: Erlbaum

Raz N, Lindenberger U, Rodrigue KM, Kennedy KM, Head D, et al. 2005. Regional brain changes in aging healthy adults: general trends, individual differences and modifiers. *Cereb. Cortex* 15(11):1676–89

Raz N, Rodrigue KM, Head D, Kennedy KM, Acker JD. 2004. Differential aging of the medial temporal lobe: a study of a five-year change. *Neurology* 62(3):433–38

Resnick SM, Pham DL, Kraut MA, Zonderman AB, Davatzikos C. 2003. Longitudinal magnetic resonance imaging studies of older adults: a shrinking brain. *J. Neurosci.* 23(8):3295–301

Reuter-Lorenz PA. 2002. New visions of the aging mind and brain. *Trends Cogn. Sci.* 6(9):394–400

Reuter-Lorenz PA, Cappell K. 2008. Neurocognitive aging and the compensation hypothesis. *Curr. Dir. Psychol. Sci.* 17(3):177–82

Reuter-Lorenz PA, Jonides J, Smith EE, Hartley A, Miller A, et al. 2000. Age differences in the frontal lateralization of verbal and spatial working memory revealed by PET. *J. Cogn. Neurosci.* 12(1):174–87

Reuter-Lorenz PA, Lustig C. 2005. Brain aging: reorganizing discoveries about the aging mind. *Curr. Opin. Neurobiol.* 15(2):245–51

Reuter-Lorenz PA, Marshuetz C, Jonides J, Smith EE, Hartley A, Koeppe R. 2001. Neurocognitive ageing of storage and executive processes. *Eur. J. Cogn. Psychol.* 13(1–2):257–78

Reuter-Lorenz PA, Mikels J. 2008. Affective working memory: converging evidence for a new construct. In *Emotional Mind: New Directions in Affective Science*, ed. S Yoshikawa. In press

Reuter-Lorenz PA, Stanczak L, Miller A. 1999. Neural recruitment and cognitive aging: two hemispheres are better than one especially as you age. *Psychol. Sci.* 10:494–500

Rodrigue KM, Raz N. 2004. Shrinkage of the entorhinal cortex over five years predicts memory performance in healthy adults. *J. Neurosci.* 24(4):956–63

Rosen AC, Prull MW, Gabrieli JD, Stoub T, O'Hara R, et al. 2003. Differential associations between entorhinal and hippocampal volumes and memory performance in older adults. *Behav. Neurosci.* 117(6):1150–60

Rossi S, Miniussi C, Pasqualetti P, Babiloni C, Rossini PM, Cappa SF. 2004. Age-related functional changes of prefrontal cortex in long-term memory: a repetitive transcranial magnetic stimulation study. *J. Neurosci.* 24(36):7939–44

Rypma B, D'Esposito M. 2001. Age-related changes in brain-behaviour relationships: evidence from event-related functional MRI studies. *Eur. J. Cogn. Psychol.* 13(1–2):235–56

Salat DH, Buckner RL, Snyder AZ, Greve DN, Desikan RS, et al. 2004. Thinning of the cerebral cortex in aging. *Cereb. Cortex* 14(7):721–30

Salat DH, Kaye JA, Janowsky JS. 2002. Greater orbital prefrontal volume selectively predicts worse working memory performance in older adults. *Cereb. Cortex* 12(5):494–505

Salthouse TA. 1991. *Theoretical Perspectives on Cognitive Aging*. Hillsdale, NJ: Erlbaum

Salthouse TA. 1996. The processing-speed theory of adult age differences in cognition. *Psychol. Rev.* 103(3):403–28

Saur D, Lange R, Baumgaertner A, Schraknepper V, Willmes K, et al. 2006. Dynamics of language reorganization after stroke. *Brain* 129(Pt. 6):1371–84

Schooler C, Mulatu MS, Oates G. 1999. The continuing effects of substantively complex work on the intellectual functioning of older workers. *Psychol. Aging* 14(3):483–506

Small SA, Nava AS, Perera GM, Delapaz R, Stern Y. 2000. Evaluating the function of hippocampal subregions with high-resolution MRI in Alzheimer's disease and aging. *Microsc. Res. Tech.* 51(1):101–8

Summarizes structural changes in the aging brain and variables that modify changes in structure.

A very accessible review of the compensatory role played by age-related increases in brain activation.

An overview of how neuroimaging work has changed scientific thinking about the aging mind.

Smith EE, Geva A, Jonides J, Miller A, Reuter-Lorenz P, Koeppe RA. 2001. The neural basis of task-switching in working memory: effects of performance and aging. *Proc. Natl. Acad. Sci. USA* 98(4):2095–100

Sole-Padulles C, Bartres-Faz D, Junque C, Clemente IC, Molinuevo JL, et al. 2006. Repetitive transcranial magnetic stimulation effects on brain function and cognition among elders with memory dysfunction. A randomized sham-controlled study. *Cereb. Cortex* 16(10):1487–93

Stern Y. 2002. What is cognitive reserve? Theory and research application of the reserve concept. *J. Int. Neuropsychol. Soc.* 8(3):448–60

Stern Y, Gurland B, Tatemichi TK, Tang MX, Wilder D, Mayeux R. 1994. Influence of education and occupation on the incidence of Alzheimer's disease. *JAMA* 271(13):1004–10

Tisserand DJ, Visser PJ, van Boxtel MP, Jolles J. 2000. The relation between global and limbic brain volumes on MRI and cognitive performance in healthy individuals across the age range. *Neurobiol. Aging* 21(4):569–76

Tsai SJ. 2003. Brain-derived neurotrophic factor: a bridge between major depression and Alzheimer's disease? *Med. Hypotheses* 61(1):110–13

Ward NS, Cohen LG. 2004. Mechanisms underlying recovery of motor function after stroke. *Arch. Neurol.* 61(12):1844–48

Wen W, Sachdev P. 2004. The topography of white matter hyperintensities on brain MRI in healthy 60- to 64-year-old individuals. *Neuroimage* 22(1):144–54

West RL. 1996. An application of prefrontal cortex function theory to cognitive aging. *Psychol. Bull.* 120(2):272–92

Wilson RS, Bennett DA. 2003. Cognitive activity and risk of Alzheimer's disease. *Curr. Dir. Psychol. Sci.* 12(3):87–91

Wilson RS, Gilley DW, Bennett DA, Beckett LA, Evans DA. 2000. Person-specific paths of cognitive decline in Alzheimer's disease and their relation to age. *Psychol. Aging* 15(1):18–28

Wingfield A, Stine EA, Lahar CJ, Aberdeen JS. 1988. Does the capacity of working memory change with age? *Exp. Aging Res.* 14(2–3):103–7

Wolfson L, Wei X, Hall CB, Panzer V, Wakefield D, et al. 2005. Accrual of MRI white matter abnormalities in elderly with normal and impaired mobility. *J. Neurol. Sci.* 232(1–2):23–27

Wong DF, Young D, Wilson PD, Meltzer CC, Gjedde A. 1997. Quantification of neuroreceptors in the living human brain: III. D2-like dopamine receptors. Theory, validation, and changes during normal aging. *J. Cereb. Blood Flow Metab.* 17(3):316–30

Yang YK, Chiu NT, Chen CC, Chen M, Yeh TL, Lee IH. 2003. Correlation between fine motor activity and striatal dopamine D2 receptor density in patients with schizophrenia and healthy controls. *Psychiatry Res.* 123(3):191–97

Zhou X, Merzenich MM. 2007. Intensive training in adults refines A1 representations degraded in an early postnatal critical period. *Proc. Natl. Acad. Sci. USA* 104(40):15935–40

Comprehensively reviews how various cognitive activity and lifestyle factors affect the risk of being diagnosed with Alzheimer's disease.

A Tale of Two Systems: Co-Occurring Mental Health and Substance Abuse Disorders Treatment for Adolescents

Elizabeth H. Hawkins

Addictive Behaviors Research Center, University of Washington, Seattle, Washington 98195; email: elizbeth@u.washington.edu

Annu. Rev. Psychol. 2009. 60:197–227

The *Annual Review of Psychology* is online at psych.annualreviews.org

This article's doi: 10.1146/annurev.psych.60.110707.163456

Key Words

behavioral health services, evidence-based practices, integrated treatment, therapeutic interventions

Abstract

Co-occurring disorders present serious challenges to traditional mental health and substance abuse treatment systems. Among adolescents in need of behavioral health services, co-occurring disorders are highly prevalent and difficult to treat. Without effective intervention, youth with co-occurring disorders are at increased risk of serious medical and legal problems, incarceration, suicide, school difficulties and dropout, unemployment, and poor interpersonal relationships. In general, current service systems are inadequately prepared to meet this need due to a variety of clinical, administrative, financial, and policy barriers. This article presents an overview of co-occurring disorders among adolescents, highlights general considerations for co-occurring disorders treatment, reviews selected treatment models and outcomes, and discusses recommendations and best practice strategies.

Contents

INTRODUCTION

Adolescence is a time of dramatic physical, developmental, social, and emotional change. It is also a time when both mental health and substance abuse problems commonly first emerge. Symptoms are often mistaken for the normative angst and emotional volatility that can accompany youth. This, in addition to multiple systemic and organizational barriers, leads co-occurring disorders to be frequently underdiagnosed (King et al. 2000). In recent years, however, attention has increasingly focused on the issue of co-occurring mental health and

Co-occurring disorders: refers to an individual who meets DSM-IV criteria for at least one mental health and one substance abuse disorder

substance use disorders among young people (President's New Freedom Commission Ment. Health 2003, U.S. Dep. Health Human Serv. 2002). Clinicians, researchers, and policymakers are now recognizing that individuals with co-occurring disorders are less likely to receive treatment and tend to have poor outcomes in traditional treatment settings when they do receive care. This can result in disastrous consequences, both individual and societal, because the presence of co-occurring disorders increases the risk for serious medical and legal problems, incarceration, suicide, school difficulties and dropout, unemployment, homelessness, and poor peer and parental relationships (U.S. Dep. Health Human Serv. 2002). Co-occurring disorders present significant challenges to traditional mental health and substance abuse service sectors, and critical changes are needed in order to provide effective and competent treatment for adolescents.

The goal of this article is to provide a better understanding of these issues by offering a background overview of co-occurring disorders, a discussion of general treatment considerations, a review of selected treatment models and outcomes, and a presentation of recommendations and best practice strategies. Sources were primarily drawn from the published peer-review literature found in the MEDLINE and PsycINFO databases.

CO-OCCURRING DISORDERS AMONG ADOLESCENTS

Definitions

Co-occurring disorder, also known as dual diagnosis, commonly refers to a person who meets *Diagnostic and Statistical Manual of Mental Disorders* (DSM-IV-TR; Am. Psychiatr. Assoc. 2000) criteria for at least one mental health and one substance use disorder. These disorders must be independent of each other, not merely a cluster of symptoms resulting from a single disorder (Cent. Subst. Abuse Treat. 2005). This is often difficult to determine because the effects of substance use can resemble mental health symptomatology and vice versa. In addition, substance abuse can lead to mental illness and mental illness can lead to substance abuse.

The term "substance use disorders" encompasses both abuse and dependence. Substance abuse is characterized by a maladaptive pattern of use that results in significant and recurrent negative consequences, such as failure to fulfill major role obligations, use in situations that are physically dangerous, legal problems, and social or interpersonal difficulties. Substance dependence, often commonly referred to as "addiction," is more severe and is additionally marked by the development of compulsive drug-seeking behavior, tolerance, and withdrawal symptomatology (Am. Psychiatr. Assoc. 2000). The term "substance abuse," although referring to a distinct clinical diagnosis, is often informally used to describe substance use disorders in general (Cent. Subst. Abuse Treat. 2007a).

Among adolescents, diagnostic criteria are less standardized due to developmental, psychological, and social differences between adult and adolescent substance use and misuse (Hawkins et al. 2004). For example, youth often use less frequently but in greater amounts, and use occurs more often within the context of partying (Oetting & Beauvais 1989, White & LaBouvie 1989). This binge-style pattern of drinking and drug use increases risk for immediate adverse consequences but decreases the likelihood that substance-abusing adolescents will experience tolerance or withdrawal symptoms.

Serious emotional disturbance (SED) refers to youth under the age of 18 who currently or at any time during the past year have had a DSM-IV diagnosable mental, behavioral, or emotional disorder (Cent. Subst. Abuse Treat. 1998). This disorder must result in a functional impairment that significantly interferes or limits a child's family, school, or community activities (Cent. Subst. Abuse Treat. 1998). The determination of SED includes any mental disorder listed in the DSM-IV with the exception of substance-related disorders, developmental disorders, dementia, and mental disorders due to a general medical condition.

Although it is commonly understood that co-occurring disorders refer to individuals with both mental health and substance use disorders, there is little agreement about the precise definition. The label co-occurring disorders has been used to categorize everything from currently meeting diagnostic criteria for both classes of disorders to both being present at some point during the lifetime of the individual, whether concurrent or not (Angold et al. 1999). The Substance Abuse and Mental Health Services Administration's (SAMHSA) Co-Occurring Center for Excellence recommends using a broad service definition of co-occurring disorder that includes individuals who (a) are prediagnosis, in which there is one established and one evolving disorder; (b) are postdiagnosis, in which one or more of the disorders have resolved for a substantial period of time; or (c) have a single disorder and acute symptoms of a co-occurring condition, such as substance-related suicidal ideation (Cent. Subst. Abuse Treat. 2007a).

SAMHSA: Substance Abuse and Mental Health Services Administration

Epidemiology

Determining the true prevalence of co-occurring disorders among youth is very difficult for a number of reasons. Many people underreport behavioral health symptoms in survey research (Turner et al. 1998), the diagnostic precision and definition of comorbidity are often very different from one study to another, and there are usually biases in epidemiological estimates based on sample differences. Prevalence data generally come from either population-based community or clinical studies. Although gathering community data is the preferable method, it often underestimates rates for adolescents because of selection bias. For example, studies of youth often capitalize on school-based surveys, but youth with co-occurring disorders are less likely to attend school on a regular basis and so may be missed. And clinical samples, although useful for many purposes, tend to overestimate the prevalence of co-occurring disorders (Costello et al. 2000).

Despite these methodological difficulties, there does seem to be agreement that co-occurring disorders among adolescents are the norm rather than the exception (Riggs 2003, Roberts & Corcoran 2005). Among representative community samples, 12-month estimates from both the Epidemiologic Catchment Area Survey (Regier et al. 1990) and the U.S. National Comorbidity Study (Kessler 2004, Kessler et al. 1996) show that about 22%–23% of the adult population has a diagnosable psychiatric disorder. About 15% of these are believed to have a co-occurring substance abuse disorder. Data from the National Comorbidity Study further indicate that about half of respondents with a lifetime substance abuse disorder (51.4%) also met criteria for at least one lifetime mental health disorder. Likewise, half of those with a lifetime mental disorder (50.9%) also had history of a substance abuse disorder. The National Household Survey on Drug Abuse (Subst. Abuse Ment. Health Serv. Admin. 2002) estimates that about 7% of adults surveyed qualified as having serious mental illness, a more severe designation than merely having a diagnosable mental disorder. Of these, approximately 20% also had a substance abuse disorder.

Although these large-scale epidemiological studies often do not give specific prevalence rates for adolescents, it is believed that the rates are comparable to or higher than those for adults (Rohde et al. 1991). Kandel and colleagues (1999) looked at this issue using data from the Methods for the Epidemiology of Child and Adolescent Mental Disorders Study, which included a community sample of 401 adolescents from four geographic regions in the United States (Lahey et al. 1996). They found that 6.2% of 14- to 18-year-olds had a current substance use disorder, with the prevalence increasing with age to a high of 9.9% among 17-year-olds. On the mental health side, 27.8% of youth had a current anxiety, mood, or disruptive behaviors disorder diagnosis. Among youth with a current substance use disorder, 76% had a comorbid psychiatric disorder. When looking at lifetime comorbidity, the Oregon Adolescent Depression Project (Lewinsohn et al. 1993) reports a similar finding. In their study of 1710 Oregon high school students ages 14 to 18, they found psychiatric comorbidity among 66.2% of youth with a substance use disorder.

Further evidence of the high rate of co-occurring disorders among adolescents comes from research utilizing clinical samples. In one study of youth seeking mental health treatment, approximately 43% had been diagnosed with a co-occurring disorder (Cent. Mental Health Serv. 2001). Research on adolescents entering substance abuse treatment found that 72% of marijuana users reported two or more psychiatric symptoms (Diamond et al. 2006). The Center for Substance Abuse Treatment reports that among adolescents entering substance abuse treatment, 62% of males and 83% of females also had one or more emotional or behavioral disorders (U.S. Dep. Health Human Serv. 2002). A study of Latino and African American adolescents who were referred to outpatient substance abuse treatment indicates that 87% reported symptoms of at least one co-occurring disorder, with about 54% reporting symptoms of three or more disorders (Robbins et al. 2002). Finally, data pooled from 77 substance abuse treatment studies funded by the Center for Substance Abuse Treatment, the National Institute on Alcohol Abuse and Alcoholism, the National Institute on Drug Abuse, the Robert Wood Johnson Foundation, and the Interventions Foundation found that 90% of adolescents under the age of 15 with substance dependence had at least one co-occurring mental health problem in the past year (Chan et al. 2008). Approximately 81% were identified as having at least one externalizing problem, 69% as having one or more internalizing problems, and 61% as having both externalizing and internalizing problems.

Characteristics

General rates of comorbidity are high among adolescents, but certain diagnostic combinations are more likely than others. Study after study has found the highest rate of co-occurring substance use disorders among youth with disruptive behavior disorders and the lowest among those with anxiety disorders (Boyle & Offord 1991, Brown et al. 1990, Cohen et al. 1993, DeMilio 1989, Greenbaum et al. 1991, Kaminer 1991, Kandel et al. 1999, Lewinsohn et al. 1993, Roehrich & Gold 1986). In a meta-analysis, Costello and colleagues (2000) found that youth with a substance use disorder had a five to seven times increased risk of also having a disruptive behavior disorder, such as attention deficit hyperactivity disorder (ADHD), conduct disorder, or oppositional defiant disorder. Youth who abused substances were approximately four times more likely to have comorbid depression and were two times more likely to have an anxiety disorder.

Although the research literature is small, there does seem to be evidence of gender differences in patterns among adolescents with co-occurring disorders. Males tend to have higher rates of illicit drug use, particularly frequent use (Johnston et al. 2007), and are more likely to develop polysubstance abuse or dependence. As well, they are more likely to be diagnosed with externalizing disorders, such as conduct disorder and ADHD, whereas girls are more likely to have internalizing mood or anxiety disorders (Latimer et al. 2002, Loeber & Keenan 1994). Consequently, males tend to have higher rates of co-occurring disorders because disruptive behavior disorders are highly linked to comorbidity, and males have higher rates of both substance abuse and externalizing disorders.

However, even though males have higher absolute rates of co-occurring disorders, the risk for comorbidity is higher for females. It has been reported by the National Household Survey on Drug Abuse (Subst. Abuse Ment. Health Serv. Admin. 1996) that females with high rates of psychological problems are as likely as males to smoke cigarettes, binge drink, and use illicit drugs. Similarly, although females are less likely to have a disruptive behavior disorder, when they do they are more likely to have a co-occurring substance abuse problem than are males (Boyle & Offord 1991). In their meta-analysis, Costello and colleagues (2000) found

that females who used alcohol or drugs were at greater risk for comorbidity than were males. This relationship held for every disorder category except for depression. Finally, in a study of adolescents referred to drug treatment (Rowe et al. 2004), it was found that females had higher rates of co-occurring substance abuse, internalizing, and externalizing disorders than did males (83% versus 44%). These findings all point to the conclusion that the pattern and severity of co-occurring disorders may be different in males and females.

Etiology

It is clear that mental health and substance use disorders often co-occur. Both can be considered developmental disorders, in the sense that they generally begin in childhood or adolescence while the brain is still developing. Inevitably, the question arises as to which type of disorder tends to emerge first. According to Mueser and colleagues (1998), there are four general models for the development of co-occurring disorders: (a) common factor models, in which shared risk factors predispose individuals to both mental health and substance abuse disorders; (b) secondary substance abuse disorder models, which posit that mental illness increases risk for developing a substance use disorder; (c) secondary mental/psychiatric disorder models, in which substance abuse precipitates a mental disorder in individuals who might not otherwise develop problems; and (d) bidirectional models, which state that the presence of either a mental health or substance abuse disorder increases vulnerability for developing the other disorder. Based on their review of the literature, these researchers found modest support for the common factor model and the secondary substance abuse disorder model.

Common factor model. According to the common factor model, high rates of comorbidity are the result of shared risk factors. Indeed, research shows that both mental health and substance abuse disorders among adolescents are associated with similar risk factors, including family history, individual personality variables, environmental factors, and traumatic events. It is important to note that various risk factors may be more or less salient depending on the developmental stage of the child (Kandel 1982). For example, parental influences may be particularly critical with younger youth, whereas peer influences gain more relevancy as the child grows older.

Family history includes genetic factors, parental psychopathology, and parental substance use. Individual personality variables associated specifically with disruptive behavior disorders and the development of co-occurring disorders include sensation seeking, risk taking, and impulsive behavior. Shared environmental risks include poverty and lower socioeconomic status (Hawkins et al. 1992, Holzer et al. 1986, Reinherz et al. 1992), the availability of alcohol and drugs within the home, poor parental support, poor parental supervision or neglect (Clark et al. 2005), parental separation or divorce (Libby et al. 2005), and affiliation with deviant peers (Cornelius et al. 2007, Moss et al. 2003). Traumatic events associated with the development of mental health and substance abuse problems include physical or sexual abuse and significant early loss (Libby et al. 2005). The onset of sexual behavior at an early age has also been found to predict subsequent substance use disorders among youth (Cornelius et al. 2007, McGue & Iacono 2005).

Secondary substance abuse disorder model. Although consensus is far from clear on this issue, and individual cases differ, research suggests that mental health problems most often precede substance abuse among youth. Data from the National Comorbidity Study found that among adults surveyed, the median age of onset for a mental disorder was 11, whereas the substance abuse disorder developed between 5 to 10 years later (Kessler 2004, Kessler et al. 1996). Approximately 83% of those with lifetime co-occurring disorders reported having at least one mental health disorder prior to the onset of a substance abuse disorder, with about 13% reporting that a substance use disorder preceded the mental health disorder and 4% reporting that they first occurred in the same year. (Kessler et al. 1996). When looking at 12-month co-occurrence rates, approximately 89% of respondents reported having a mental health disorder prior to onset of a substance abuse disorder, 10% reported the substance abuse disorder as occurring first, and 1% reported that they first occurred in the same year (Kessler et al. 1996). Similarly, Libby and colleagues (2005) found that almost 70% of their adolescent sample had onset of major depression prior to the onset of a substance use disorder. Finally, one longitudinal study found that signs of emotional and behavioral problems at young ages (e.g., not getting along with others, low self-esteem, showing physical signs of stress, inattentiveness) distinguished those who were later to become heavy marijuana users (Shedler & Block 1990).

It is commonly assumed that older children and adolescents with mental health problems often begin using substances as a means of self-medication, to forget unpleasant experiences, or to fill an emotional void (Mainous et al. 1996, Weiss & Mirin 1987). The social stress model posits that adolescents may begin using alcohol and drugs as a method of coping with stressors that occur within the family, school environment, peer relationships, or the community (Rhodes & Jason 1990). Older siblings, parents, or other adults who use substances in these ways may model this behavior. Youth not only learn the substance use behavior, but they may also internalize a positive expectancy that alcohol or drugs are a helpful way of escape or a useful method of coping with stress, tension, or overwhelming emotional states. This expectancy, in turn, predicts alcohol and drug use (Rather et al. 1992, Simons-Morton et al. 1999, Stacy et al. 1991).

Course

Adolescence is a critical period for the development and acquisition of major social, emotional, and occupational life skills. The presence of either a mental health or substance use disorder can disrupt this period and have long-term effects. It has been noted that prevalence rates of depression and substance abuse are increasing for younger generations as compared to what older research has shown (Burke et al. 1990, Kessler et al. 1994). This indicates that the developmental impact and associated negative sequelae may be more pronounced for youth with co-occurring disorders, as comorbidity is often associated with an earlier age of onset of symptoms and a more chronic and persistent course.

In general, psychopathology in adolescence may be associated with lower social competence (McGee et al. 1990) and continued or long-term impairment in young adulthood (Fleming et al. 1993, Kandel & Davies 1986). One study found that early onset of psychiatric disorders (by age 14) was strongly related to impaired psychological functioning at age 18 (Giaconia et al. 1994), even among youth who were not actively symptomatic at that age.

Compared to adolescents with substance use disorders alone, those with psychiatric comorbidity are more likely to have an earlier onset of substance use and to use more frequently and chronically (Cent. Subst. Abuse Treat. 2007b, Chan et al. 2008, Greenbaum et al. 1991, Grella et al. 2001, Rohde et al. 1996, Rowe et al. 2004). Adolescents who have early onset of substance use tend to continue using as they age and are at greater risk of developing substance dependence as adults (Brown et al. 1994, Crowley et al. 1998, Giaconia et al. 1994, Robins & Pryzbeck 1985). Youth with co-occurring substance abuse and behavioral disorders tend to have higher rates of polysubstance use, engage in more delinquent and criminal activity, and are at higher risk for out-of-home placements (Randall et al. 1999). They are also more likely to drop out of treatment and have poorer outcomes (Crowley et al. 1998, Kaminer et al. 1992, Wise et al. 2001).

GENERAL CONSIDERATIONS IN THE TREATMENT OF CO-OCCURRING DISORDERS

Barriers to Treatment

Adolescents with co-occurring disorders often fail to receive effective treatment, if any at all. Although both mental health and substance use disorders are considered psychiatric conditions, and both are delineated in the DSM-IV (Am. Psychiatr. Assoc. 2000), in practice, there has been a divergence in how they are assessed and treated. What follows is a brief discussion of some of the major barriers to receiving treatment, including youth and family issues, a fragmented service delivery system, clinical and administrative barriers, and funding gaps and policy barriers.

Youth and family issues. A great stigma is associated with both mental health and substance abuse problems. This stigma affects help-seeking behavior at all levels. The youth often believes s/he is fine, perhaps no different or even better off than peers, and may be highly resistant to any form of intervention. Parents, while concerned about their child's behavior, might fear the social or economic repercussions of treatment. They might believe they can handle it alone or that the adolescent will outgrow the behavior. In addition, parental psychopathology or substance use, both of which are more common among families with co-occurring disordered youth (Rowe et al. 2001), may foster resistance to treatment.

In a study examining reasons for early termination among youth attending outpatient substance abuse treatment, it was found that therapist-client racial match, practical obstacles such as transportation or other responsibilities, and treatment readiness were related to whether a youth attended sessions (Mensinger et al. 2006). In another study, poor therapeutic alliance and parental money concerns were main reasons cited for ending mental health treatment early (Garcia & Weisz 2002). Stigma, resistance, and family stressors, coupled with lack of education about co-occurring disorders and available resources, often results in an underutilization of adolescent treatment services.

Fragmented service delivery system. Traditional behavioral health treatment in this country revolves around separate and often disconnected systems. In general, conceptualizations of illness and corresponding treatment philosophies are strikingly different, and required educational backgrounds, training experiences, and licensing requirements vary widely between mental health and substance abuse sectors. Few significant cross-training opportunities are present in training programs (Drake et al. 2001), and incentives and resources for seeking them out are limited once students have become practitioners. There are no widely accepted models for co-occurring disorders specialist certifications, and becoming dually certified or licensed is an onerous burden that most do not undertake. As a result, few providers at the local level are knowledgeable and capable of treating co-occurring disorders.

Historically, some degree of animosity has existed between mental health and substance abuse treatment systems. Each side is justifiably invested in its own system and feels strongly about the education and training it promotes. Substance abuse treatment providers commonly believe in the medical or disease model of addictions, whereas mental health providers are more likely to believe in a biopsychosocial model. Both sets of providers are highly specialized, and often there is disdain for the idea that the other can adequately assess or treat both disorders. These conflicts often make it difficult to coordinate and collaborate across systems.

Further, there is generally poor communication and coordination between behavioral health care systems and other child-serving agencies, such as education, child welfare, juvenile justice, and medical health care. This is especially problematic for youth with co-occurring disorders because juvenile justice is often the gateway through which these adoles-

cents are first referred to mental health and substance abuse services (Libby & Riggs 2005), and they are much more likely than their peers to be involved in multiple systems.

Clinical and administrative barriers. Clinically, there is a lack of comprehensive, developmentally appropriate treatment services for co-occurring youth. The vast majority of research has tested adult interventions, but these are generally not suitable for adolescents. Age and developmental stage must be taken into account, as well as the differing emotional pressures and needs faced by adolescents. For example, youth are highly vulnerable to influences from peers and family, both of which need to be considered in a treatment setting (Lysaught & Wodarski 1996).

As a result, treatment agencies and programs tend to be unprepared to serve youth with co-occurring disorders. They most often lack provider capacity, appropriate treatment models, administrative guidelines, and quality assurance procedures. In addition, comprehensive screening, assessment, treatment planning, and outcome measures are not commonly used.

Funding gaps and policy barriers. Funding for both mental health and substance abuse services comes from a patchwork of separate federal, state, local, and private funding sources (U.S. Dep. Health Human Serv. 2002). Coverage is limited and does not cover the need in either system, thus creating competition. It is estimated that only about one-third of people in need of mental health treatment receive services (U.S. Dep. Health Human Serv. 1999), and only 20% of those in need of substance abuse treatment receive care (Subst. Abuse Ment. Health Serv. Admin. 2000). Co-occurring disorders are often not covered by either system, and many providers are reluctant to assess and diagnose a problem for which treatment or reimbursement is unavailable.

Another factor influencing financing for co-occurring disorders is that mental health services are generally covered under Medicaid, whereas substance abuse benefits are optional (Libby & Riggs 2005). As a result, mental health services have developed a Medicaid billing system to supplement other funding sources, and substance abuse centers tend to rely on block funds and grants. Having different funding streams and administrative requirements hinders cross-system collaboration and the development of integrated treatment services.

Which System is Primary?

There is often debate surrounding which disorder to treat first with adolescents with co-occurring disorders. Mental health systems may be unwilling to provide services until substance use has stopped and associated symptoms are under control. Likewise, the substance abuse system may be leery of treating clients with active mental illness symptoms or those who are on psychotropic medications. Frequently, there is the belief that any drug use, even that which is prescribed psychiatrically, is harmful. Traditionally, neither system has the knowledge, experience, or capacity to provide integrated treatment.

To address this issue of where and how to treat people with co-occurring disorders, SAMHSA worked in collaboration with the National Association of State Mental Health Program Directors (NASMHPD) and the National Association of State Alcohol and Drug Abuse Directors (NASADAD). Together, NASMHPD and NASADAD (1998) developed a conceptual framework to aid in understanding co-occurring conditions and the level of coordination needed between service systems to address them. It is based on relative symptom severity, not diagnosis, and comprises four quadrants: (*a*) low addiction, low mental illness severity; (*b*) low addiction, high mental illness severity; (*c*) high addiction, low mental illness severity; and (*d*) high addiction, high mental illness severity.

The model recommends moving toward integration as the severity of the co-occurring disorder increases, and it delineates a continuum of care based on provider behavior that spans minimal coordination consultation, collaboration, and integration (Cent. Subst. Abuse Treat. 2007a, Nat. Assoc. State Ment. Health Prog. Directors, Nat. Assoc. State Alcohol Drug Abuse Directors 1998). Minimal coordination occurs when one service provider is aware of a co-occurring condition but has little to no contact with other providers. Consultation is relatively informal and includes the occasional exchange of clinical information. Collaboration is more structured and involves regular and planned communication between providers. It is marked by the existence of formal agreements or expectations regarding contact between providers. And last, integration refers to the development of a single treatment plan that addresses both mental health and substance abuse conditions. Integrated treatment can be provided by two individuals in separate systems that have entered into a formal arrangement to develop and implement a treatment plan that addresses the co-occurring disorders. It can also be provided by two individuals in the same system or by one individual who is qualified to treat both conditions.

The utility of this framework has been questioned by a panel of experts (Pincus et al. 2006), and an argument could be made that it is less developmentally appropriate for adolescents than adults. For youth with co-occurring disorders, it is necessary to provide integrated services, including prevention and early intervention, regardless of which quadrant they fall into. Both disorders should be considered primary and treated as such (Drake et al. 1991, Minkoff 1991). Since many adolescents with co-occurring disorders do not recognize their substance use as a problem, integrated services may offer an opportunity to engage and motivate youth in treatment while offering additional supportive services (Drake et al. 1998). To ensure optimal outcomes, it is critical to provide comprehensive assessment and treatment planning that includes the family, school, and other systems with which the child is involved (e.g., child welfare, juvenile justice, medical).

Integrated services: any process in which mental health and substance abuse services are combined at the individual-client level to include at a minimum integrated screening, assessment, treatment planning, services delivery, and continuing care

Program Readiness for Integrated Services

Traditionally, if adolescents with co-occurring disorders were to receive dual treatment, it would be either serial or parallel. Serial treatment refers to individuals receiving treatment for one kind of disorder followed sequentially by treatment for the other. Parallel treatment refers to individuals who receive both kinds of treatment at the same time, but the providers either have little or no coordination with one another. Currently it is recognized that serial and parallel treatment models are not effective and that integration is necessary for optimal outcomes. Services integration includes any process in which mental health and substance abuse services are combined at the individual-client level (Cent. Subst. Abuse Treat. 2007c).

The American Society of Addiction Medicine has developed a patient placement system that categorizes three types of substance abuse programs for people with co-occurring disorders. These are addiction-only, dual-diagnosis-capable, and dual-diagnosis-enhanced services (Am. Soc. Addict. Med. 2001). Dual-diagnosis-capable programs address co-occurring issues throughout their assessment and treatment planning and delivery, whereas dual-diagnosis-enhanced programs provide integrated treatment services for those who are more symptomatic or functionally impaired. SAMHSA (2005) employs a system that classifies both mental health and substance abuse programs as basic, intermediate, or advanced in terms of their abilities to provide integrated care. According to SAMHSA (Cent. Subst. Abuse Treat 2007c), integrated care includes at a minimum providing integrated screening, assessment, treatment planning, treatment delivery, and continuing care. Integrated services can be offered by a single provider in one setting, by two or more providers in the same setting, or by multiple providers in multiple settings. Systems integration can facilitate this by offering infrastructure support and sustainability.

Unmet Treatment Needs and Consequences

Youth with co-occurring disorders are challenging to serve. Symptoms are often more severe than in individuals with just one disorder, and adolescents with co-occurring disorders tend to have multiple psychosocial and family issues that further complicate their care. Treatment engagement and retention are difficult, and intervention outcomes tend to be poor. In one study of adolescents in substance abuse treatment, it was found that youth without co-occurring disorders showed the best long-term outcomes. Those with co-occurring externalizing disorders recovered more slowly, and those with both co-occurring externalizing and internalizing disorders had the worst outcomes (Rowe et al. 2004). Youth with co-occurring disorders are more likely to relapse after treatment (Grella et al. 2001), and relapse usually occurs more quickly than for youth with substance use disorders only (Tomlinson et al. 2004). Youth experiencing psychiatric symptoms and limited feelings of self-efficacy appear most vulnerable to relapse following periods of conflict, life stress, or negative emotional states (Ramo et al. 2005).

It is estimated that the majority of people with co-occurring disorders do not receive treatment (Subst. Abuse Ment. Health Serv. Admin. 2000, U.S. Dep. Health Human Serv. 1999). Many never get identified or referred for services or they fail to attend their intake appointment. Of those who do enter outpatient therapy, between 40% and 60% terminate early (Kazdin 1996, Wierzbicki & Pekarik 1993). The cost of failing to effectively treat these youth is high. Youth with co-occurring disorders have higher rates of impaired functioning, suicide attempts, and academic difficulties (Lewinsohn et al. 1996). Left untreated, their problems are likely to continue into adulthood with a chronic and persistent course. This sets the stage for increased risk as adults of unemployment, homelessness, victimization, legal difficulties, serious medical problems, emergency room care, and institutionalization (U.S. Dep. Health Human Serv. 1999).

TREATMENT MODELS AND OUTCOMES

As the need for integrated treatment for adolescents with co-occurring disorders has become increasingly clear, it has intersected with a separate but related movement concerning best practices. Over the past decade, there have been increased demands from consumers, family members, and policymakers for accountability for behavioral health interventions and improved outcomes. Although the idea of evidence-based practice is not new (Mechanic 1998), there is no commonly accepted definition, and organizations have responded in various ways.

The Institute of Medicine (2001, p. 147) defines evidence-based practice as "the integration of best research evidence with clinical expertise and patient values." The Presidential Task Force on Evidence-Based Practice (2006) of the American Psychological Association (APA) expanded this definition for the field of psychology to "the integration of the best available research with clinical expertise in the context of patient characteristics, culture, and preferences." In addition, APA has published a variety of resources that delineate criteria for evaluating the efficacy of clinical interventions (Am. Psychol. Assoc. 1995, 2002) as well as specify those treatments they consider to be empirically validated (Chambless & Ollendick 2001).

Rather than advancing a concrete definition of evidence-based practice, the National Institute on Drug Abuse (1999) outlined 13 principles of effective treatment plus developed a clinical toolbox of science-based materials for drug abuse treatment providers. Likewise, SAMHSA does not offer a single definition of evidence-based practice. Instead, under the auspices of the National Registry of Evidence-Based Programs and Practices (NREPP), mental health and substance abuse interventions are evaluated and rated by independent reviewers on the qual-

ity of their research and their readiness for dissemination.

An examination of these various evidence-based practice lists and registries reveals a paucity of interventions developed to concurrently treat mental health and substance abuse disorders in adolescents. Those that do emerge tend to fall into one of two general approaches. The first is treatment planning and care coordination, which helps create a system of care in which individual services are provided to best meet the needs of each adolescent and his/her family. The second approach includes a handful of research-supported integrated interventions that simultaneously address both mental health and substance abuse disorders. Major findings of the treatment models reviewed here are summarized in **Table 1**.

Treatment Planning and Care Coordination

With the traditional separation of mental health and substance abuse fields, integrated service systems have been hard to achieve. Although successful efforts are being made, numerous clinical, administrative, financial, and policy barriers stand in the way of mainstream adoption of these models. However, there are treatment planning and support services that help facilitate a more coordinated treatment approach without the necessity of integrated programs. Two such services, intensive case management and wraparound, are described here.

In intensive case management, specially trained professionals assess and coordinate the supports and services necessary to help individuals with serious mental illness live in the community. For adolescents with co-occurring disorders, this may include developing and monitoring a comprehensive service plan, providing support services to the client and his/her family, and providing crisis intervention and advocacy services as needed. A case manager generally has a small caseload to allow for the frequency and intensity of services needed. One model, New York's Child and Youth Intensive Case Management, was developed to maintain

Evidence-based practice (APA definition): the integration of the best available research with clinical expertise in the context of patient characteristics, culture, and preferences

APA: American Psychological Association

NREPP: National Registry of Evidence-Based Programs and Practices

Table 1 Major findings of co-occurring disorder treatment models

	Major findings	Supporting research studies	Model cited by
Treatment planning and care coordination			
Child and Youth Intensive Case Management	• Reduction in hospitalization rates and duration • Increase in days spent in the community • Decrease in symptoms • Higher functioning levels	• Evans et al. 1994 • Evans et al. 1996	• U.S. Department of Health and Human Services
Wraparound	• Decrease in at-risk and delinquent behavior • Increase in less restrictive environment placements • Increase in school attendance and grade point average • Decrease in school disciplinary actions	• Bruns et al. 2006 • Carney & Buttell 2003	• National Alliance on Mental Illness • National Mental Health Association • Substance Abuse and Mental Health Services Administration • U.S. Surgeon General
Cognitive behavioral and motivational enhancement interventions			
MET/CBT 5	• Reduction in substance use • Higher number of youth in recovery at the end of the study • Low cost of intervention per day of abstinence achieved	• Compton & Pringle 2004 • Dennis et al. 2004	• U.S. Department of Health and Human Services
Seeking Safety	• Decrease in substance use and associated problems • Decrease in some trauma-related and psychopathology symptoms • Decrease in cognitions related to substance abuse and post-traumatic stress disorder	• Hien et al. 2004 • Najavits et al. 1998 • Najavits et al. 2006 • Zlotnick et al. 2003	• Addiction Technology Transfer Center • National Registry of Evidence-Based Programs and Practices
Dialectical behavior therapy	• Increase in treatment retention • Reduction in suicidal behavior • Decrease in psychiatric hospitalizations • Decrease in substance abuse, anger, and serious problem behaviors • Reduction in interpersonal difficulties	• Grove Street 2004 • Rathus & Miller 2002 • Trupin et al. 2002	• American Psychological Association • National Registry of Evidence-Based Programs and Practices
Family Therapies			
Family behavior therapy	• Reduction in frequency of alcohol and drug use • Decrease in problem behaviors and depression • Improved family relationships • Increase in school attendance	• Azrin et al. 1994 • Azrin et al. 2001	• National Institute on Drug Abuse • National Registry of Evidence-Based Programs and Practices
Multidimensional family therapy	• Reduction in substance use • Decrease in internalizing and externalizing psychiatric symptoms • Improvement in school performance • Increase in family functioning	• Dennis et al. 2004 • Liddle 2001 • Liddle et al. 2004 • Rowe et al. 2004	• National Institute on Drug Abuse • Office of Juvenile Justice and Delinquency Prevention • Substance Abuse and Mental Health Services Administration • U.S. Department of Health and Human Services

(Continued)

Table 1 (*Continued*)

	Major findings	Supporting research studies	Model cited by
Multisystemic therapy	• Reduction in alcohol and drug use • Decrease in psychiatric symptomatology • Improvement in family and peer relations • Decrease in out-of-home placements • Decrease in criminal activity, rearrests, and days incarcerated	• Borduin et al. 1995 • Henggeler et al. 1992 • Henggeler et al. 1999 • Schaeffer & Borduin 2005	• National Alliance on Mental Illness • National Institute on Drug Abuse • National Registry of Evidence-Based Programs and Practices • Office of Juvenile Justice and Delinquency Prevention • President's New Freedom Commission • U.S. Surgeon General

children with serious emotional disturbance in the least restrictive environment possible. Findings from two controlled studies suggest that this program is associated with fewer hospitalizations, fewer hospital days, more days spent in the community, a decrease in symptoms, and better functioning (Evans et al. 1994, 1996). Intensive case management was cited as an effective intervention for youth with co-occurring disorders by the U.S. Department of Health and Human Services (2002).

Wraparound is a family-driven model of care coordination for children and youth with mental health problems who are also involved with one or more other systems (e.g., child welfare, juvenile justice, special education). As the name implies, comprehensive services and supports are "wrapped" around the child in order to meet all of his/her complex needs. Wraparound requires a team-based planning process through which families, formal supports, and natural supports develop, monitor, and evaluate an individualized plan. The essential values of wraparound are that the planning process, as well as the services and supports provided, are individualized, family driven, strengths based, culturally competent, and community oriented (Burchard et al. 2002).

Wraparound does not endorse any specific therapeutic interventions. Instead it helps facilitate a system of care that increases engagement, accessibility, and acceptability of treatment thus allowing the individual services involved to be maximally effective. Wraparound

has been evaluated in nine controlled outcome studies that consistently show positive findings. Results include a decrease in at-risk and delinquent behavior (Carney & Buttell 2003) and an increase in positive outcomes in less-restrictive environment placements, school attendance, school disciplinary actions, and grade-point average (Bruns et al. 2006). Wraparound has been cited as a promising practice in the Surgeon General's reports on youth violence (U.S. Dep. Health Human Serv. 2001) and mental health (U.S. Dep. Health Human Serv. 1999) and is endorsed by the National Alliance on Mental Illness (2007), the National Mental Health Association, and SAMHSA's Center for Mental Health Services.

Integrated Treatment Models

Despite the current focus on evidence-based practices (see sidebar Evidence-Based Practice Resources), very few interventions have been developed and evaluated specifically for adolescents with co-occurring disorders. Clinical trials often suffer from difficulties engaging youth in treatment, poor attendance and compliance with treatment, and high rates of early termination (Donohue et al. 1998, Wise et al. 2001). Despite these difficulties, a few effective and promising outpatient treatment models have emerged. It should be noted that although these treatments are distinct, there is much overlap between them in terms of conceptual framework, clinical strategies, and techniques.

Cognitive-behavioral and motivational enhancement interventions. Cognitive-behavioral therapy (CBT) is not a single, unified treatment but rather an umbrella term that incorporates a variety of interventions aimed at present-focused, goal-directed behavior change. Core strategies include identifying and challenging irrational and maladaptive thoughts and patterns, cognitive restructuring, and learning more functional skills through modeling and role-play exercises.

From a cognitive-behavioral point of view, substance use is a learned behavior that is initiated and maintained by an interplay of cognitive processes, environmental factors, and behavioral reinforcement. Treatment often involves a focus on self-monitoring, identifying and changing reinforcement contingencies, coping skills training, and relapse prevention. Cognitive-behavioral interventions are well supported in the treatment of both adolescent mental health (Barrett et al. 2001, Kazdin 1995, Kendall et al. 1997, Rohde et al. 1994) and substance use disorders (Kaminer et al. 1998, Kaminer & Burleson 1999, Liddle et al. 2001). Although few studies have examined the effectiveness of CBT for the treatment of adolescent co-occurring disorders, it is believed that they would likely be helpful, especially for youth with comorbid depression and substance abuse (Waldron & Kaminer 2004).

Motivational enhancement interventions are often coupled with CBT. Motivational in-

terviewing (MI, Miller & Rollnick 2002) is a nonconfrontational, client-directed intervention that emphasizes an empathetic nonjudgmental stance, developing discrepancy, avoiding argumentation, rolling with resistance, and supporting self-efficacy for change. Motivational enhancement treatment (MET) is a four-session adaptation of MI developed for Project MATCH (Proj. MATCH Res. Group 1993), a clinical multisite trial of treatments for alcohol use disorders. MI-based interventions have been found to be effective in reducing substance use among adolescents presenting to an emergency department (Monti et al. 1999, 2001), among first-year college students (Baer et al. 1992, 2001; Marlatt et al. 1998, Roberts et al. 2000), and among college students in the high-risk Greek system (Larimer et al. 2001). For youth with co-occurring disorders, MI/MET alone is likely insufficient to effect change (Tevyaw & Monti 2004). However, it has been suggested that motivational enhancement interventions may be helpful with this population in increasing treatment engagement and retention, motivation to change, and goal setting (Myers et al. 2001). The nonlecturing stance of MI and its ability to be used with individuals in a wide range of readiness-to-change states may make MI particularly attractive to adolescents (Tevyaw & Monti 2004).

Motivational Enhancement Treatment/ Cognitive Behavioral Therapy 5. One specific model that has received considerable interest of late is the five-session motivational enhancement treatment/cognitive behavioral therapy (MET/CBT5) developed for use in the Cannabis Youth Treatment Study. MET/CBT5 consists of two individual MET sessions followed by three sessions of group CBT. The MET component focuses on moving the adolescent through the stages of change (Prochaska & DiClemente 1984) and developing motivation to change, whereas the CBT component emphasizes learning and practicing coping skills to handle high-risk substance use situations (Diamond et al. 2002). In the Cannabis Youth Treatment Study, five short-term outpatient treatment models were

CBT: cognitive-behavioral therapy

MI: motivational interviewing

MET: motivational enhancement therapy

compared: (*a*) MET/CBT5; (*b*) 12-session MET/CBT (MET/CBT12), which supplemented MET/CBT5 with seven additional group CBT sessions; (*c*) a family support network intervention, which used MET/CBT12 plus six parent education group meetings; (*d*) the adolescent community reinforcement approach, which consisted of 10 individual sessions with the adolescent, four sessions with caregivers, and a limited amount of case management provided by the therapist; and (*e*) multidimensional family therapy, which was typically composed of six sessions with the adolescent, three sessions with the parents, and six sessions with the entire family.

The main target of this study was the treatment of marijuana abuse. However, unlike many clinical trials, youth with co-occurring disorders were not excluded. As a result, more than 95% of the 600 adolescents reported one or more other problems, including 53% with conduct disorder, 38% with ADHD, 23% with generalized anxiety, 18% with major depression, and 14% with traumatic stress disorders. Overall, 83% had had justice system involvement, and 23% had received mental health treatment (Dennis et al. 2004). Results showed that all five treatment models were effective at reducing substance use at the 3-, 6-, 9-, and 12-month follow-up periods. There was little difference in clinical outcomes based on treatment condition, and relapse rates were high (Dennis et al. 2004). Two-thirds of the adolescents were still reporting substance use or related problems at the 12-month follow-up, underscoring that substance use among many youth, especially those with co-occurring disorders, is best conceptualized as a chronic condition (Kazdin 1987). However, when treatment costs were combined with clinical outcomes, MET/CBT5 was found to be one of the most cost-effective interventions studied (Compton & Pringle 2004, Dennis et al. 2004).

The findings from the Cannabis Youth Treatment Study highlight the potential for cognitive-behavioral and motivational enhancement interventions in the treatment of adolescent co-occurring disorders, and MET/CBT 5 has been cited as an effective intervention for this population (U.S. Dep. Health Human Serv. 2002). However, comparing the effectiveness of CBT or MET with other treatments is difficult because CBT and MET strategies and techniques are widely incorporated into other intervention models. Future research may yield subgroups of youth with co-occurring disorders for whom such an intervention is most effective.

Seeking Safety. Seeking Safety (Najavits 2007) was developed in the 1990s for individuals diagnosed with both a substance use disorder and post-traumatic stress disorder (PTSD). Although the treatment originally was designed as a cognitive-behavioral intervention, it was expanded to also include interpersonal and case management topics. Treatment is present-focused and revolves around teaching clients how to attain safety by identifying and eliminating self-destructive behaviors and learning new coping skills. The treatment has five principles (Najavits et al. 2006): (*a*) safety as a priority; (*b*) integrated treatment of both disorders; (*c*) a focus on ideals to counteract the loss of ideals in both PTSD and substance abuse; (*d*) four content areas: cognitive, behavioral, interpersonal, and case management; and (*e*) attention to therapist processes.

Seeking Safety was developed to be highly flexible. It can be conducted in individual or group sessions, with single or mixed gender, and with varying session lengths and pacing. The treatment consists of 25 topics that are independent of one another; all 25 can be implemented or a subset can be chosen. Individual topics can be further customized to be implemented in a single session or over multiple sessions, depending on clinical needs. Although Seeking Safety can be used as a stand-alone intervention, it was designed to be integrated with other treatments. In fact, the model includes an intensive case management component to help engage clients in additional treatments (Najavits 2007).

Seeking Safety has been evaluated with adults, both women and men, in a variety of therapeutic settings including residential treatment centers, prisons, community mental

DBT: dialectical behavior therapy

health programs, and Veterans Affairs. Results indicate positive outcomes in terms of reductions in substance use, trauma-related symptoms, suicide risk, and depression, along with improvements in social adjustment, family functioning, and problem-solving skills (Hien et al. 2004, Najavits et al. 1998, Zlotnick et al. 2003).

Seeking Safety has also been tested in a randomized clinical trial with adolescent females meeting DSM-IV criteria for both PTSD and a substance use disorder (Najavits et al. 2006). The original treatment model was followed as closely as possible, with implementation modifications made as appropriate to match the developmental level of the youth. In comparison to adolescents receiving treatment as usual, those who participated in the Seeking Safety condition had decreases in substance use and associated problems, some trauma-related and psychopathology symptoms, and cognitions related to substance abuse and PTSD.

The body of research supporting Seeking Safety meets APA's criteria for an empirically supported treatment (Najavits 2007). Seeking Safety has also been recognized by NREPP as an evidence-based program for co-occurring disorders among adolescents, young adults, and adults and as a best practice by the Addiction Technology Transfer Center Network.

Dialectical Behavior Therapy. Although little research has explicitly tested dialectical behavior therapy (DBT) as an intervention for adolescent co-occurring disorders, it is an approach that holds much promise for this population. It was originally developed as a treatment for suicidal and parasuicidal adults with borderline personality disorder and blends standard elements of cognitive-behavioral therapy with mindfulness and meditation practices. DBT is recognized as an effective treatment for borderline personality disorder by APA and as an evidence-based practice for the treatment of co-occurring disorders among young adults by NREPP.

According to Linehan (1993), the central problem in borderline personality disorder is an emotional dysregulation that contributes to in-terpersonal, self, cognitive, and behavioral dysregulation. This dysregulation is caused and maintained by a transactional process between an emotionally vulnerable person and an invalidating environment (Woodberry et al. 2002). Consequences include engagement in impulsive, high-risk behaviors such as substance abuse, high-risk sexual encounters, and self-injurious behaviors. At the core of DBT is a focus on dialectics or the synthesis of two seemingly opposite positions. For example, a primary dialectical challenge is to accept people as they are while at the same time helping them to change.

DBT has been formally adapted for multiproblem, suicidal adolescents to make the treatment more developmentally and culturally appropriate (Miller et al. 2007). Modifications include shortening the first phase of treatment from one year to 16 weeks, including parents in the skills training group, including parents and other family members in individual therapy sessions as needed, reducing the number of skills to teach, simplifying and adapting materials to better address the needs of adolescents and their families, and developing a new skills training module called "Walking the Middle Path." Miller and colleagues (2002) discuss detailed methods to further synthesize DBT with family therapy principles and goals. By working with the family and adolescent together, the family is recognized as a partner rather than a target in treatment.

DBT has been adapted and used with a variety of adolescent treatment populations including inpatient (Katz et al. 2002, 2004; Sunseri 2004) and outpatient (Katz et al. 2002) suicidal youth, adolescents with serious emotional disturbance in a residential facility (Grove St. Adolesc. Resid. Bridge Central Mass. 2004), young adolescents with oppositional defiant disorder (Nelson-Gray et al. 2006), adolescent binge eating disorder (Safer et al. 2007), and incarcerated juvenile offenders (Trupin et al. 2002). Research has shown that the use of DBT among adolescents leads to increases in treatment retention and reductions in suicidal behavior, psychiatric hospitalization, substance abuse, anger, serious problem behaviors, and interpersonal difficulties (Grove St. Adolesc. Resid. Bridge Central Mass. 2004, Rathus & Miller 2002, Trupin et al. 2002).

DBT's focus on emotional validation and acceptance coupled with skills training makes it an attractive treatment option for adolescents with co-occurring conditions. The many successful adaptations of DBT to various treatment settings and populations demonstrate that it may be an effective intervention for youth with complicated and severe diagnostic profiles (Trupin et al. 2002). Adolescents in these studies tended to have a high level of comorbidity and to exhibit a wide variety of extreme problem behaviors. In fact, DBT research often deliberately seeks the type of participants that are excluded from other clinical studies. Although outcomes are preliminary, DBT appears to be a very promising treatment model that merits future consideration for the treatment of adolescent co-occurring disorders.

Family therapies. Although various family-based therapies for adolescent co-occurring disorders may differ in terms of strategies and techniques, they share certain common elements. All utilize basic research on developmental psychology and psychopathology, emphasize the systemic and contextual nature of adolescent problem behavior, and focus on the important role parents and caregivers play in youth treatment and outcomes (Liddle et al. 2004). Research shows that, compared to control conditions, family-based therapies often have better success engaging and retaining families in treatment, reducing youth substance use, increasing school attendance and performance, and improving family functioning (Azrin et al. 1994, Donohue et al. 1998, Friedman 1989, Henggeler et al. 1991, Liddle & Dakof 2002, Szapocznik et al. 1983, Waldron et al. 2001). Three family-based therapy models that have shown positive outcomes for the integrated treatment of adolescent co-occurring disorders are highlighted here.

Family Behavior Therapy. Family behavior therapy (FBT) is an intervention that targets

adolescent substance use and associated behavioral problems (Donohue & Azrin 2001). It is recognized as an evidence-based practice for the treatment of adolescent co-occurring disorders by NREPP and as a scientifically based approach to drug treatment by the National Institute on Drug Abuse (1999).

The theory underlying FBT draws heavily on the community reinforcement approach, and the model employs multiple evidence-based techniques such as behavioral contracting, stimulus control, urge control, and communication skills training (Azrin et al. 2001). FBT is designed to be highly flexible and to accommodate a wide variety of adolescents in an office-based setting, although home-based sessions can be conducted when the target population is particularly hard to reach. FBT emphasizes treatment engagement and retention strategies including frequent early phone communication with youth and caregivers, enlisting the family in choosing its own treatment plan from a menu of alternatives, and the provision of food and beverages at sessions.

In a clinical trial, FBT was compared with supportive group counseling treatment (Azrin et al. 1994). Youth in the FBT condition showed better outcomes in terms of substance use, problem behaviors, depression, family relationships, and school attendance. However, the sample size in this study was very small. In another study comparing FBT to individual-cognitive problem-solving therapy, both interventions were equally effective at reducing the frequency of alcohol and drug use and improving conduct problems (Azrin et al. 2001).

Multidimensional Family Therapy. Multidimensional family therapy (MDFT) was developed as a family-based treatment for adolescents with substance use and related emotional and behavioral problems (Liddle 1999). It is a comprehensive approach that targets multiple domains of risk, protection, and functioning within the youth, his/her family, and community. Interventions concentrate on the individual problems, strengths, and goals of the adolescent, as well as focusing on parent issues, parenting and family relationships, and

FBT: family behavior therapy

MDFT: multidimensional family therapy

MST: multisystemic therapy

extrafamilial influences (Hogue et al. 2006). In contrast to other family-based therapies, MDFT targets youth and parents individually as well as interactively. In addition to parenting behavior, parental and caregiver well-being and substance use are also a program focus. In order to increase treatment accessibility and relevancy, MDFT can be delivered in both home and community settings. Further, the format, components, and timing can be adjusted to best meet the needs of different clinical populations.

MDFT was one of the five interventions tested in the Cannabis Youth Treatment study. It, like the other study interventions, demonstrated significant posttreatment reductions in substance use that were sustained at the 12-month follow-up (Dennis et al. 2004). In another randomized clinical trial of MDFT (Liddle et al. 2001), participants in the MDFT condition showed a sharp reduction in drug use that was maintained at the 6- and 12-month follow-ups. In addition, youth who received MDFT had improved school performance and family functioning. MDFT was tested with a sample of adolescents referred to an inner-city drug treatment program (Rowe et al. 2004). The youth showed an extremely high rate of psychiatric comorbidity, with only 12% of the sample meeting criteria for substance abuse or dependence alone. In addition to having a substance use disorder, 20% had one mental health disorder, 24% had two, 17% had three, and 26% had four or more. Youth in the MDFT condition showed reductions in marijuana use and drug involvement as well as both internalizing and externalizing symptoms (Liddle 2001). These treatment effects were retained after termination. MDFT has also shown positive results as a brief early intervention for young high-risk adolescent substance users (Liddle et al. 2004).

The strong research base demonstrating the effects of MDFT in both indicated prevention and treatment settings has led it to be recognized as a best practice by the Office of Juvenile Justice and Delinquency Prevention, the National Institute on Drug Abuse (1999), the U.S. Department of Health and Human Services (2002), and SAMHSA (2005).

Multisystemic Therapy. Multisystemic therapy (MST) was developed as a family- and community-based treatment approach for youth with co-occurring substance abuse and antisocial behavior (Henggeler & Borduin 1990, Henggeler et al. 1998). It is based on Bronfenbrenner's (1979) social ecology theory and posits that adolescent antisocial behavior is multidetermined and linked to variables of the individual and his or her family, peer group, school, and community. Interventions are developed in conjunction with the family with the explicit goal of structuring the youth's environment to promote healthier, less risky behavior. MST services are usually intense, short term (average of four to six months), and offered in the youth's natural environment, such as at home or school. MST draws heavily on strategies and techniques found in cognitive behavioral, behavioral, and family therapies. However, it differs by offering more intensive and direct interactions with the youth and his environment and by providing services outside of traditional care settings (Henggeler & Borduin 1990).

To date, MST has been tested in 15 published outcome studies. In two of the early efficacy trials, MST was related to posttreatment reductions in self-report of alcohol and drug use (Henggeler et al. 1992), one-year follow-up improvements in family and peer relations and a decrease in out-of-home placements (Henggeler et al. 1992), a decrease in psychiatric symptomatology and substance-related arrests at four-year follow-up (Borduin et al. 1995), and a decrease in rearrests and days incarcerated at the 14-year follow-up (Schaeffer & Borduin 2005). In a subsequent randomized trial of MST with substance-abusing and delinquent youth, adolescents in the MST condition had decreased alcohol and drug use, criminal activity, and number of out-of-home placement days posttreatment (Henggeler et al. 1999). However, these results were not maintained at the six-month or four-year follow-up, and outcomes regarding criminal activity, substance use, and mental health functioning were not as good as earlier studies (Henggeler et al. 1991). Finally, in a 2004 meta-analysis of MST outcome studies (Curtis et al. 2004), it was found that youth who had received MST were functioning better and offending less than 70% of those in the control conditions. MST outcomes tended to show reductions in emotional and behavioral problems in individual family members, improvements in parent-youth and family relations, and decreases in youth criminality, involvement with deviant peers, and youth aggression toward peers. Similar to past studies (Huey et al. 2000, Mann et al. 1990), this meta-analysis found that improvements in family relations predicted decreases in youth problems and delinquent peer affiliation.

Based on these findings, MST has been cited as an effective treatment for youth with co-occurring disorders by the National Institute on Drug Abuse (1999), the U.S. Surgeon General's report of youth violence (2001), NREPP, the Office of Juvenile Justice and Delinquency Prevention, the President's New Freedom Commission on Mental Health (2003), and the National Alliance on Mental Illness (2007).

RECOMMENDATIONS

Although the literature review presented here is comprehensive, it is by no means exhaustive. A handful of existing treatment approaches has shown positive outcomes, and additional research is currently under way. However, virtually all of the models share modest reductions in symptoms, difficulties maintaining treatment gains, and high relapse rates. Although the field is far from having a definitive list of best-practice strategies or programs for the treatment of adolescent co-occurring disorders, certain themes have emerged that can help provide guidance.

Principles to Guide Clinical Practice

Rethinking co-occurring disorders. Traditionally, mental health and substance abuse treatment has been conducted in very separate and disconnected systems. Neither side habitually assessed for or treated co-occurring conditions. Now, epidemiologic research overwhelmingly shows that co-occurring disorders are the norm rather than the exception. Among adolescents, the presence of co-occurring disorders is related to more severe symptomatology, greater treatment challenges, and poorer outcomes. We cannot continue to perpetuate the historical separation of the mental health and substance abuse fields. Both mental health and substance abuse disorders must be conceptualized as psychiatric conditions, with common developmental etiologies and trajectories. In an adolescent with co-occurring disorders, both conditions must be considered primary and treated as such.

In addition, it is essential to redefine ideals of treatment success. Although it is appealing to consider that pairing a certain disorder with an evidence-based practice will result in remission of symptoms and recovery, this is unlikely to occur in individuals with complex diagnostic profiles. Co-occurring disorders can be thought of as chronically relapsing conditions, with treatment as a necessary component of care and maintenance. According to Kazdin (1994, p. 585), "it may be useful to conceive of treatment as a routine and ongoing part of everyday life." Relapse prevention skills (Marlatt & Gordon 1985) can be targeted to both substance abuse and mental health conditions and can help identify relapse warning signs and triggers and strengthen coping strategies to either prevent a relapse or lessen its consequences.

Greater emphasis on prevention and early intervention. Research showing that mental health problems often precede substance abuse in adolescents indicates that there is a critical period for the prevention of co-occurring disorders. Early identification and intervention for mental health conditions, coupled with substance abuse prevention, may help prevent or lessen the severity of co-occurring disorders.

However, regardless of which disorder emerges first, effective early treatment is likely to reduce risk of future problems. Moving toward a public health model that emphasizes health promotion and disease prevention through a full continuum of prevention, intervention, and aftercare services is essential.

In order to accomplish early identification and referrals for comprehensive assessment and treatment, though, behavioral health screening needs to become commonplace in all child-serving agencies. Early identification and intervention by gatekeepers (e.g., primary care doctors, school counselors and psychologists, child-welfare workers, probation officers) can lead to better access to services for children and youth with problems and may help prevent the need for more intensive and expensive treatment later on (King et al. 2000). When indicated, these front-line professionals should be able to refer identified youth for further assessment and treatment. In addition, they should be an active component of care teams if the child receives services.

Integrated behavioral health assessment and treatment. A comprehensive evaluation for behavioral health disorders and psychosocial problems should be the standard of care for anyone entering either the mental health or substance abuse treatment system. Behavioral health symptomatology must be assessed as well as a wide variety of life domains impacted by co-occurring disorders (Sacks et al. 2008). In addition to developing an integrated care plan for both mental health and substance abuse disorders, when life problems and deficits are identified they should be incorporated into the treatment planning process.

There is strong support for the need to develop effective interventions that treat both mental health and substance abuse disorders simultaneously. Although treatment does not necessarily need to be provided by a single individual, service systems must be integrated to allow for coordinated assessment, treatment planning, intervention delivery, and outcome monitoring. Integrated treatment should be in-dividualized and flexible, allowing the treatment and care coordination plan to include a wide variety of needed services and supports. This is especially true for adolescents with co-occurring disorders, as they are likely to be involved in multiple systems such as juvenile justice, child welfare, and specialized educational services. Multidisciplinary care teams developing and implementing a single unified treatment plan are ideal.

Effective systems of care for adolescents with co-occurring disorders include several critical components of integrated treatment programs identified by Drake and colleagues (2001). These include integrated services that incorporate motivational and social support interventions; a comprehensive, multisystem approach; the availability of multiple therapeutic modalities; a long-term perspective that includes transition, aftercare, and support services; and a focus on risk reduction. In addition, extensive family involvement is critical. Research consistently shows that when families are involved in adolescent treatment, outcomes are better (Copello & Orford 2002, Kazdin et al. 1990, Liddle 2004, Waldron 1997). Within the family context, it is vital to address issues of cultural sensitivity and competence to ensure that services are appropriate for each individual adolescent and family.

No wrong door. One of the philosophies underlying the recommendation for comprehensive screening and assessment in a wide variety of social and health services agencies is that of "no wrong door." This policy acknowledges that individuals with co-occurring conditions might not understand the differences between various social service and treatment systems and may present to any one of them. Rather than placing the burden for finding appropriate services on the individual, agencies accept responsibility for responding to the person's needs either through direct service provision or linkages to other programs. Extensive referral networks and lines of communication and coordination are required for a no wrong door policy to be effective.

Research Considerations

Your comorbidity is not my comorbidity. All mental health and substance use disorders are not equally likely to co-occur among adolescents. For example, disruptive behavior disorders and mood disorders have higher rates of comorbidity with substance abuse than do anxiety disorders. Research shows that patterns of comorbidity are also likely to vary based on population characteristics such as age and gender. Younger adolescents tend to have a different diagnostic pattern and course than do older adolescents. Females, too, are likely to present with different clusters of symptoms and treatment needs than will males.

These varied patterns clearly have implications for the development and implementation of therapeutic interventions. Greater specificity of the various subtypes of co-occurring disorders, along with prevention and treatment implications, is needed in the research literature. Future directions include examining the differential impact that individual variables such as age, gender, race, ethnicity, and sexual preference have on the development and treatment of co-occurring disorders.

Need for additional process and translational research. Research on adolescent co-occurring disorders is still in its infancy. Although certain treatment models have shown positive outcomes, by and large it is unclear what are the underlying mechanisms of change. This is seen clearly in large controlled trials of multiple forms of evidence-based or promising treatments. Results often show support for the effectiveness of all forms of intervention, with little differential impact to be found between conditions. Although there is much theoretical and strategic overlap between current best practice approaches, it would be helpful for research to begin delineating which components of these treatments are the most effective in achieving favorable therapeutic change.

In addition to aiding in the development of effective interventions, identifying which process components are linked to positive outcomes will also support the transport of evidence-based treatment models into standard clinical practice (Hogue et al. 2006, Weisz & Kazdin 2003). This sort of translational research can identify which are the critical elements and conditions to be included in community settings, while allowing other aspects of the treatment to be adapted to best meet the needs of a specific population.

Systemic Recommendations

Develop and expand professional resources. A significant barrier to the provision of integrated services is a lack of cross-training in both mental health and substance abuse fields. Educational and training programs can begin to address this by offering courses on co-occurring disorders and by providing clinical opportunities to work with this population. With the high prevalence of co-occurring disorders in both adults and adolescents, such experiences should be required rather than optional. Furthermore, it is essential to expand the cross-training opportunities available to current service providers through workforce development and continuing education efforts. This includes providing and promoting training for gatekeepers (primary care physicians, nurses, school counselors, child welfare workers, etc.) so that they can adequately screen and assess for mental health, substance abuse, and co-occurring disorders.

In addition to these training and retraining measures, it is essential to reform the certification and licensure process. There are currently few incentives for either individual clinicians or programs to seek out cross-training. The development of certification programs for co-occurring disorders specialists, with corresponding reimbursement schedules, may provide the leverage needed to change this dynamic. Developing and expanding cross-training opportunities, and updating and revising current certification and licensure requirements, may increase appropriate treatment provider capacity for youth with co-occurring disorders.

Eliminate gaps in coverage. Lack of adequate funding is a fundamental problem facing treatment systems. There currently is simply not enough money available to address the needs of individuals with mental health, substance abuse, and co-occurring disorders. Research shows that the average cost of treating youth with co-occurring disorders is more than twice that of serving an adolescent with either a mental health or a substance abuse disorder alone, $29,057 versus $13,067 (King et al. 2000). Although this may seem like a steep price to pay, failing to serve these youth results in dire individual consequences and high costs to society through increased rates of institutionalization, incarceration, homelessness, and comorbid medical costs. In addition, untreated co-occurring disorders are likely to persist and worsen over time, leading to the need for more intensive treatment services in the future.

Political solutions for eliminating gaps in coverage include promoting parity for mental health and substance abuse services and advocating for the government to fund behavioral health services at the level of need. Although we can remain hopeful that in future years such political gains will be achieved, alternative solutions are necessary until then.

One strategy is to reprogram current funds from higher- to lower-cost services, such as through jail diversion or deinstitutionalization programs. Related to this is expanding the current crisis- and treatment-based model of health care to include a wider array of prevention and early-intervention services. Another method that may offer cost savings in the long term is the added use of ancillary support services, such as intensive case management, wraparound, employment and education training, housing services, and transportation. Although these programs require an upfront cost with few options for reimbursement, such services can increase the effectiveness of the interventions offered and reduce future treatment and societal costs. Finally, linking funding to outcomes to ensure that programs that receive public support are providing the most effective services available has been proposed as a strategy for reducing the funding gap (U.S. Dep. Health Human Serv. 2002).

Flexible funding. The myriad of administrative, policy, and financial barriers outlined above pose a major impediment to the delivery of effective co-occurring disorders treatment. Creative and flexible financing strategies are needed to overcome these obstacles and support the development of integrated treatment systems. Within the financing realm, categorical funding refers to money that is provided to an agency or organization to be used exclusively for a certain type of services or a certain population. Flexible funding provides recipients with some level of discretion in how it is used (Cent. Subst. Abuse Treat. 2007d).

The availability of flexible funding from multiple sources that can be combined or pooled at the local level in less-restrictive ways is essential. One form of pooling is blended funding, in which mental health and substance abuse service dollars are combined and made indistinguishable from one another. Many believe, however, that blended funding may hinder the timely development of integrated services and will negatively impact treatment for individuals with solely mental health or substance abuse problems (U.S. Dep. Health Human Serv. 2002). Another option for flexible financing is the use of braided funds. With braiding, the funding sources remain visible and can be tracked and monitored separately. Although it is evident that flexible funding strategies are needed in order to sustain the multidisciplinary care teams and support services indicated in the effective treatment of adolescent co-occurring disorders, there is no clear consensus on the best method for achieving this.

CONCLUSION

The co-occurrence of mental health and substance use disorders among adolescents are of great concern. Clinical, research, and policy distinctions traditionally separate their treatment, despite the fact that both are psychiatric conditions. Throughout this review, certain themes have resonated. First, co-occurring disorders are highly prevalent and are to be expected in every adolescent service setting. Second, there is wide variability in the subtypes, severity, and treatment needs of adolescents with co-occurring mental health and substance abuse conditions. Third, a comprehensive integrated service system is the most promising method of effectively treating this population. And last, critical clinical, administrative, and systemic changes must be made in order to adequately provide services for adolescent co-occurring disorders.

Great progress has been made in recent years in shifting the way in which co-occurring disorders are conceptualized and treated. It is clear that additional work is necessary, however. Although the needs of these youth are great, and the barriers are daunting, many promising avenues of care are currently available. By continuing to address the salient clinical, research, and policy issues, we can persist in making practice improvements that substantially enhance the quality of services provided to these youth and improve their outcomes.

SUMMARY POINTS

1. Co-occurring disorders are highly prevalent and are to be expected in every adolescent service setting.

2. Youth with co-occurring disorders tend to have severe symptoms, multiple psychosocial and family issues, and are often engaged in numerous systems such as specialized education services, child welfare, or juvenile justice.

3. Co-occurring disorders among adolescents are associated with difficulties in treatment engagement and retention, poor treatment outcomes, high relapse rates, and a chronic and persistent course that often continues into adulthood.

4. Comprehensive integrated treatment programs appear to be the most effective method of treating co-occurring disorders in adolescents.

5. Critical clinical, administrative, financial, and policy changes are necessary to support effective systems of care for youth with co-occurring disorders and improve their outcomes.

DISCLOSURE STATEMENT

The author is not aware of any biases that might be perceived as affecting the objectivity of this review.

ACKNOWLEDGMENTS

The author is grateful to Alan Marlatt, Neha Bahadur, Jason Schuman, and Katherine Thornton for the important roles they played during the preparation of this review.

LITERATURE CITED

Am. Psychiatr. Assoc. 2000. *Diagnostic and Statistical Manual of Mental Disorders.* Washington, DC: Am. Psychiatr. Assoc. 4th ed., text rev.

Am. Psychol. Assoc. 1995. *Template for Developing Guidelines: Interventions for Mental Disorders and Psychosocial Aspects of Physical Disorders.* Washington, DC: Am. Psychol. Assoc.

Am. Psychol. Assoc. 2002. Criteria for evaluating treatment guidelines. *Am. Psychol.* 57:1052–59

Am. Psychol. Assoc. Pres. Task Force on Evidence-Based Pract. 2006. Evidence-based practice in psychology. *Am. Psychol.* 61(4):271–85

Am. Soc. Addict. Med. 2001. Patient placement criteria for the treatment of substance-related disorders: ASAM PPC-2R. Chevy Chase, MD: Am. Soc. Addict. Med. 2nd rev. ed.

Angold A, Costello E, Erkanli A. 1999. Comorbidity. *J. Child Psychol. Psychiatry* 40(1):57–87

Azrin NH, Donohue B, Besalel VA, Kogan ES, Acierno R. 1994. Youth drug abuse treatment: a controlled outcome study. *J. Child Adolesc. Subst. Abuse* 3:1–16

Azrin NH, Donohue B, Teichner GA, Crum T, Howell J, DeCato LA. 2001. A controlled evaluation and description of individual-cognitive problem solving and family-behavior therapies in dually-diagnosed conduct-disordered and substance-dependent youth. *J. Child Adolesc. Subst. Abuse* 11(1):1–43

Baer JS, Kivlahan DR, Blume AW, McKnight P, Marlatt GA. 2001. Brief intervention for heavy-drinking college students: 4-year follow-up and natural history. *Am. J. Public Health* 91:1310–16

Baer JS, Marlatt GA, Kivlahan DR, Fromme K, Larimer M, Williams E. 1992. An experimental test of three methods of alcohol risk reduction with young adults. *J. Consult. Clin. Psychol.* 60:974–79

Barrett PM, Shortt AL, Wescombe K. 2001. Examining the social validity of the FRIENDS treatment program for anxious children. *Behav. Change* 18:63–77

Borduin CM, Mann BJ, Cone LT, Henggeler SW, Fucci BR, et al. 1995. Multisystemic treatment of serious juvenile offenders: long-term prevention of criminality and violence. *J. Consult Clin. Psychol.* 63:569–78

Boyle MH, Offord DR. 1991. Psychiatric disorder and substance use in adolescence. *Can. J. Psychiatry* 36:699–705

Bronfenbrenner U. 1979. *The Ecology of Human Development.* Cambridge, MA: Harvard Univ. Press

Brown SA, Mott MA, Meyers MG. 1990. Adolescent alcohol and drug treatment outcome. In *Drug and Alcohol Abuse Prevention,* ed. RR Watson, pp. 373–403. Clifton, NJ: Humana

Brown SA, Myers MG, Mott MA, Vik PW. 1994. Correlates of success following treatment for adolescent substance abuse. *Appl. Prev. Psychol.* 3:61–73

Bruns EJ, Rast J, Walker JS, Peterson CR, Bosworth J. 2006. Spreadsheets, service providers, and the statehouse: using data and the wraparound process to reform systems for children and families. *Am. J. Commun. Psychol.* 38:201–12

Burchard JD, Bruns EJ, Burchard SN. 2002. The wraparound approach. In *Community Treatment for Youth: Evidence-Based Interventions for Severe Emotional and Behavioral Disorders,* ed. BJ Burns, K Hoagwood, pp. 69–90. New York: Oxford Univ. Press

Burke KC, Burke JD, Regier DA, Rae DS. 1990. Age at onset of selected mental disorders in five community populations. *Arch. Gen. Psychiatry* 47:511–18

Carney MM, Buttell F. 2003. Reducing juvenile recidivism: evaluating the wraparound services model. *Res. Soc. Work Pract.* 13:551–68

Cent. Ment. Health Services. 2001. *Mental health care for youth: a national assessment, annual/final progress report, January 2001-December 2001.* Rockville, MD: Subst. Abuse Ment. Health Serv. Admin.

Cent. Subst. Abuse Treat. 1998. *Contracting for managed substance abuse and mental health services: a guide for public purchasers.* Tech. Assist. Publ. Ser. No. 22. DHHS Publ. No. (SMA) 98–3173. Rockville, MD: Subst. Abuse Ment. Health Serv. Admin.

Cent. Subst. Abuse Treat. 2005. *Substance abuse treatment for persons with co-occurring disorders.* Treatment Improvement Protocol (TIP) Ser., No. 42. DHHS Publ. No. (SMA) 05–3992. Rockville, MD: Subst. Abuse Ment. Health Serv. Admin.

Cent. Subst. Abuse Treat. 2007a. *Definitions and terms relating to co-occurring disorders.* COCE overview paper 1. DHHS Publ. No. (SMA) 07–4163. Rockville, MD: Subst. Abuse Ment. Health Serv. Admin.

Cent. Subst. Abuse Treat. 2007b. *The epidemiology of co-occurring substance use and mental disorders.* COCE overview paper 8. DHHS Publ. No. (SMA) 07–4308. Rockville, MD: Subst. Abuse Ment. Health Serv. Admin.

Cent. Subst. Abuse Treat. 2007c. *Services integration.* COCE overview paper 6. DHHS Publ. No. (SMA) 07–4294. Rockville, MD: Subst. Abuse Ment. Health Serv. Admin.

Cent. Subst. Abuse Treat. 2007d. *Systems integration.* COCE overview paper 7. DHHS Publ. No. (SMA) 07–4295. Rockville, MD: Subst. Abuse Ment. Health Serv. Admin.

Chambless DL, Ollendick TH. 2001. Empirically supported psychological interventions: controversies and evidence. *Annu. Rev. Psychol.* 52:685–716

Chan YF, Dennis ML, Funk RR. 2008. Prevalence and comorbidity of major internalizing and externalizing problems among adolescents and adults presenting to substance abuse treatment. *J. Subst. Abuse Treat.* 34:14–24

Clark DB, Thatcher DL, Maisto SA. 2005. Supervisory neglect and adolescent alcohol use disorders: effects on AUD onset and treatment outcome. *Addict. Behav.* 30(9):1737–50

Cohen P, Cohen J, Brook J. 1993. An epidemiological study of disorders in late childhood and adolescence: 2. Persistence of disorders. *J. Child Psychol. Psychiatry* 34:869–77

Compton WM, Pringle B. 2004. Services research on adolescent drug treatment. Commentary on "The Cannabis Youth Treatment (CYT) Study: main finding from two randomized trials." *J. Subst. Abuse Treat.* 27:195–96

Copello A, Orford J. 2002. Addiction and the family: Is it time for services to take notice of the evidence? *Addiction* 97:1361–63

Cornelius JR, Clark DB, Reynolds M, Kirisci L, Tarter R. 2007. Early age of first sexual intercourse and affiliation with deviant peers predict development of SUD: a prospective longitudinal study. *Addict. Behav.* 32(4):850–54

Costello EJ, Armstrong TD, Erkanli A. 2000. *Report on the developmental epidemiology of comorbid psychiatric and substance use disorders.* Paper presented to Nat. Inst. Drug Abuse. Durham, NC: Duke Univ. Med. Cent., Cent. Dev. Epidemiol.

Crowley TJ, Mikulich SK, MacDonald M, Young SE, Zerbe GO. 1998. Substance-dependent, conduct-disordered adolescent males: severity of diagnosis predicts 2-year outcome. *Drug Alcohol Depend.* 49:225–37

Curtis NM, Ronan KR, Borduin CM. 2004. Multisystemic treatment: a meta-analysis of outcome studies. *J. Fam. Psychol.* 18:411–19

DeMilio L. 1989. Psychiatric syndromes in adolescent substance abusers. *Am. J. Psychiatry* 146:1212–14

Dennis ML, Godley SH, Diamond GS, Tims FM, Babor T, et al. 2004. The Cannabis Youth Treatment (CYT) study: main findings from two randomized trials. *J. Subst. Abuse Treat.* 27:197–213

Diamond G, Godfrey SH, Liddle HA, Sampl S, Webb C, et al. 2002. Five outpatient treatment models for adolescent marijuana use: a description of the Cannabis Youth Treatment interventions. *Addiction* 97(Suppl. 1):70–83

Diamond G, Panichelli-Mindel SM, Shera D, Dennis ML, Tims F, Ungemack J. 2006. Psychiatric syndromes in adolescents seeking outpatient treatment for marijuana with abuse and dependency in outpatient treatment. *J. Child Adolesc. Subst. Abuse* 15:37–54

Donohue B, Azrin NH. 2001. Family behavior therapy. In *Innovations in Adolescent Substance Abuse Interventions*, ed. EF Wagner, HB Waldron, pp. 205–27. New York: Pergamon

Donohue B, Azrin N, Lawson H, Friedlander J, Teicher G, Rindsberg J. 1998. Improving initial session attendance of substance abusing and conduct disordered adolescents: a controlled study. *J. Child Adolesc. Subst. Abuse* 8:1–13

Drake RE, Essock SM, Shaner A, Carey KB, Minkhoff K, et al. 2001. Implementing dual diagnosis services for clients with severe mental illness. *Psychiatr. Serv.* 52(4):469–76

Drake RE, McLaughlin P, Pepper B, Minkoff K. 1991. Dual diagnosis of major mental illness and substance disorder: an overview. *New Dir. Ment. Health Serv.* 50:3–12

Drake RE, Mercer-McFadden C, Mueser K, McHugo G, Bond G. 1998. Review of integrated mental health and substance abuse treatment for patients with dual disorders. *Schizophr. Bull.* 24(4):589–608

Evans ME, Armstrong MI, Kuppinger AD. 1996. Family-centered intensive case management: a step toward understanding individualized care. *J. Child Fam. Stud.* 5:55–65

Evans ME, Banks SM, Huz S, McNulty TL. 1994. Initial hospitalization and community tenure outcomes of intensive case management for children and youth with serious emotional disturbance. *J. Child Fam. Stud.* 3(2):225–34

Fleming JE, Boyle MH, Offord DR. 1993. The outcome of adolescent depression in the Ontario Child Health Study follow-up. *J. Am. Acad. Child Adolesc. Psychiatry* 32:28–33

Friedman AS. 1989. Family therapy vs. parent groups: effects on adolescent drug abusers. *Am. J. Fam. Ther.* 17:335–47

Garcia JA, Weisz JR. 2002. When youth mental health care stops: therapeutic relationship problems and other reasons for ending youth outpatient treatment. *J. Consult. Clin. Psychol.* 70:439–43

Giaconia RM, Reinherz HZ, Silverman AB, Pakiz B, Frost AK, Cohen E. 1994. Ages of onset of psychiatric disorders in a community population of older adolescents. *J. Am. Acad. Child Adolesc. Psychiatry* 33:706–17

Greenbaum PE, Prange ME, Friedman RM, Silver SE. 1991. Substance abuse prevalence and comorbidity with other psychiatric disorders among adolescents with severe emotional disturbances. *J. Am. Acad. Child Adolesc. Psychiatry* 30:575–83

Grella CE, Hser Y, Joshi V, Rounds-Bryant J. 2001. Drug treatment outcomes for adolescents with comorbid mental and substance use disorders. *J. Nerv. Ment. Dis.* 189:384–92

Grove St. Adolesc. Resid. Bridge Central MA. 2004 (Oct.). Using dialectical behavior therapy to help troubled adolescents return safely to their families and communities. *Psychiatr. Serv.* 55(10):1168–70

Hawkins EH, Marlatt GA, Cummins LH. 2004. Preventing substance abuse in American Indian and Alaska Native youth: promising strategies for healthier communities. *Psychol. Bull.* 130(2):304–23

Hawkins JD, Catalano RF, Miller JY. 1992. Risk and protective factors for alcohol and other drug problems in adolescence and early adulthood: implications for substance abuse prevention. *Psychol. Bull.* 112(1):64–105

Henggeler SW, Bourdin CM. 1990. *Family Therapy and Beyond: A Multisystemic Approach to Treating the Behavior Problems of Children and Adolescents*. Pacific Grove, CA: Brooks/Cole Publ.

Henggeler SW, Borduin CM, Melton GB, Mann BJ, Smith L, et al. 1991. Effects of multisystemic therapy on drug use and abuse in serious juvenile offenders: a progress report from two outcome studies. *Fam. Dyn. Addict. Q.* 1:40–51

Henggeler SW, Melton GB, Smith LA. 1992. Family preservation using multisystemic therapy: an effective alternative to incarcerating serious juvenile offenders. *J. Consult. Clin. Psychol.* 60:953–61

Henggeler SW, Pickrel SG, Brondino MJ. 1999. Multisystemic treatment of substance abusing and dependent delinquents: outcomes, treatment fidelity, and transportability. *Ment. Health Serv. Res.* 1:171–84

Henggeler SW, Schoenwald SK, Borduin CM, Rowland MD, Cunningham PB. 1998. *Multisystemic Treatment of Antisocial Behavior in Children and Adolescents*. New York: Guilford

Hien DA, Cohen LR, Litt LC, Miele GM, Capstick C. 2004. Promising empirically supported treatments for women with comorbid PTSD and substance use disorders. *Am. J. Psychiatry* 161:1426–32

Hogue A, Dauber S, Samuolis J, Liddle HA. 2006. Treatment techniques and outcomes in multidimensional family therapy for adolescent behavior problems. *J. Fam. Psychol.* 20(4):535–43

Holzer CE III, Shea BM, Swanson JW, Leaf PJ, Myers JK, et al. 1986. The increased risk for specific psychiatric disorders among persons of low socioeconomic status: evidence from the Epidemiologic Catchment Area Surveys. *Am. J. Soc. Psychiatry* 6:259–71

Huey SJ, Henggeler SW, Brondino MJ, Pickrel SG. 2000. Mechanisms of change in multisystemic therapy: reducing delinquent behavior through therapist adherence and improved family and peer functioning. *J. Consult. Clin. Psychol.* 68:451–67

Inst. Med. 2001. *Crossing the Quality Chasm: A New Health System for the 21st Century*. Washington, DC: Nat. Acad. Press

Johnston LD, O'Malley PM, Bachman JG, Schulenberg JE. 2007. *Monitoring the Future National Survey Results on Drug Use, 1975–2006: Volume I, Secondary School Students 2006*. NIH Publ. No. 07–6205. Bethesda, MD: Nat. Inst. Drug Abuse

Kaminer Y. 1991. The magnitude of concurrent psychiatric disorders in hospitalized substance abusing adolescents. *Child Psychiatry Hum. Dev.* 22(2):89–95

Kaminer Y, Blitz C, Burleson JA, Sussman J, Rounsaville BJ. 1998. Psychotherapies for adolescent substance abusers: treatment outcome. *J. Nerv. Ment. Dis.* 186:684–90

Kaminer Y, Burleson JA. 1999. Psychotherapies for adolescent substance abusers: 15-month follow-up. *Am. J. Addict.* 8:114–19

Kaminer Y, Tarter RE, Bukstein O, Kabene M. 1992. Comparison between treatment completers and non-completers among dually diagnosed substance abusing adolescents. *J. Am. Acad. Child Adolesc. Psychiatry* 31:1046–49

Kandel DB. 1982. Epidemiological and psychological perspectives on adolescent drug use. *J. Am. Acad. Child Psychiatry* 21:328–47

Kandel DB, Davies M. 1986. Adult sequelae of adolescent depressive symptoms. *Arch. Gen. Psychiatry* 43:255–62

Kandel DB, Johnson JG, Bird HR, Weissman MM, Goodman SH, et al. 1999. Psychiatric comorbidity among adolescents with substance use disorders: findings from the MECA study. *J. Am. Acad. Child Adolesc. Psychiatry* 38:693–99

Katz LY, Cox BJ, Gunasekara S, Miller AL. 2004. Feasibility of dialectical behavior therapy for suicidal adolescent inpatients. *J. Am. Acad. Child Adolesc. Psychiatry* 43(3):276–82

Katz LY, Gunasekara S, Miller AL. 2002. Dialectical behavior therapy for inpatient and outpatient parasuicidal adolescents. In *Adolescent Psychiatry: Developmental and Clinical Studies*, Vol. 26, ed. LT Flaherty, pp. 161–78. Hillsdale, NJ: Analytic

Kazdin AE. 1987. Treatment of antisocial behavior in children: current status and future directions. *Psychol. Bull.* 102:187–202

Kazdin AE. 1994. *Behavior Modification in Applied Settings*. Pacific Grove, CA: Brooks/Cole Publ.

Kazdin AE. 1995. *Conduct Disorder*. Newbury Park, CA: Sage

Kazdin AE. 1996. Dropping out of child psychotherapy: issues for research and implications for practice. *Clin. Child Psychol. Psychiatry* 1:133–56

Kazdin AE, Siegel TC, Bass D. 1990. Drawing on clinical practice to inform research on child and adolescent psychotherapy: survey of practitioners. *Prof. Psychol. Res. Pract.* 21:189–98

Kendall PC, Flannery-Schroeder E, Panichelli-Mindel SM, Southam-Gerow M, Henin A, et al. 1997. Therapy for youths with anxiety disorders: a second randomized clinical trial. *J. Consult. Clin. Psychol.* 65(3):366–80

Kessler RC. 2004. The epidemiology of dual diagnosis. *Biol. Psychiatry* 56:730–37

Kessler RC, McGonagle KA, Zhao S, Nelson CB, Hughes M, et al. 1994. Lifetime and 12-month prevalence of DSM-III-R psychiatric disorders in the United States: results from the National Comorbidity Study. *Arch. Gen. Psychiatry* 51:8–19

Kessler RC, Nelson CB, McGonagle KA, Edlund MJ, Frank RG, Leaf PJ. 1996. The epidemiology of co-occurring addictive and mental disorders: implications for prevention and service utilization. *Am. J. Orthopsychiatry* 66(1):17–31

King RD, Gaines LS, Lambert EW, Summerfelt WT, Bickman L. 2000. The co-occurrence of psychiatric and substance abuse diagnoses in adolescents in different service systems: frequency, recognition, cost, and outcomes. *J. Behav. Health Serv. Res.* 27:417–30

Lahey BB, Flagg EW, Bird HR, Schwab-Stone ME, Canino G, et al. 1996. The NIMH Methods for the Epidemiology of Child and Adolescent Mental Disorders (MECA) study: background and methodology. *J. Am. Acad. Child Adolesc. Psychiatry* 35:855–64

Larimer ME, Turner AP, Anderson BK, Fader JS, Kilmer JR, et al. 2001. Evaluating a brief alcohol intervention with fraternities. *J. Stud. Alcohol* 62:370–80

Latimer WW, Stone AL, Voight A, Winters KC, August GJ. 2002. Gender differences in psychiatric comorbidity among adolescents with substance use disorders. *Exp. Clin. Psychopharmacol.* 10(3):310–15

Lewinsohn PM, Hops H, Roberts RE, Seeley JR, Andrews JA. 1993. Adolescent psychopathology, I: prevalence and incidence of depression and other DSM-III-R disorders in high school students. *J. Abnorm. Psychol.* 102:133–44

Lewinsohn PM, Rohde P, Seeley JR. 1996. Adolescent psychopathology: III. The clinical consequences of comorbidity. *J. Am. Acad. Child Adolesc. Psychiatry* 34(4): 510–19

Libby AM, Orton HD, Stover SK, Riggs PD. 2005. What came first, major depression or substance use disorder? Clinical characteristics and substance use comparing teens in a treatment cohort. *Addict. Behav.* 30:1649–62

Libby AM, Riggs PD. 2005. Integrated substance use and mental health treatment for adolescents: aligning organizational and financial incentives. *J. Child Adolesc. Psychopharmacol.* 15(5):826–34

Liddle HA. 1999. Theory development in a family-based therapy for adolescent drug abuse. *J. Clin. Child Psychol.* 28:521–32

Liddle HA. 2001. Advances in family-based therapy for adolescent substance abuse: findings from the Multi-dimensional Family Therapy research program. In *Problems of Drug Dependence 2001: Proceedings from the 63rd Annual Scientific Meeting of the College on Problems of Drug Dependence, Inc.*, ed. LS Harris, pp. 113–15. NIDA Res. Monog. No. 182. NIH Publ. No. 02–5097. Bethesda, MD: Nat. Inst. Drug Abuse

Liddle HA. 2004. Family-based therapies for adolescent alcohol and drug use: research contributions and future research needs. *Addiction* 99(Suppl. 2):76–92

Liddle HA, Dakof GA. 2002. A randomized controlled trial of intensive outpatient, family-based therapy vs residential drug treatment for comorbid adolescent drug abusers. *Drug Alcohol Depend.* 66:S2–202

Liddle HA, Dakof GA, Parker K, Diamond GS, Barrett K, Tejada M. 2001. Multidimensional family therapy for adolescent substance abuse: results of a randomized clinical trial. *Am. J. Drug Alcohol Abuse* 27:651–87

Liddle HA, Rowe CL, Dakof GA, Ungaro RA, Henderson C. 2004. Early intervention for adolescent substance abuse: Pretreatment to posttreatment outcomes of a randomized controlled trial comparing multidimensional family therapy and peer group treatment. *J. Psychoactive Drugs* 36:49–63

Linehan MM. 1993. *Cognitive-Behavioral Treatment of Borderline Personality Disorder*. New York: Guilford

Loeber R, Keenan K. 1994. Interaction between conduct disorder and its comorbid conditions: effects of age and gender. *Clin. Psychol. Rev.* 14:497–523

Lysaught E, Wodarski JS. 1996. Model: a dual focused intervention for depression and addiction. *J. Child Adolesc. Subst. Abuse* 5(1):55–71

Mainous AG, Martin CA, Oler MJ, Richardson ET, Haney AS. 1996. Substance use among adolescents: fulfilling a need state. *Adolescence* 31:807–15

Mann BJ, Borduin CM, Henggeler SW, Blaske DM. 1990. An investigation of systemic conceptualizations of parent-child coalitions and symptom change. *J. Consult. Clin. Psychol.* 58:336–44

Marlatt GA, Baer JS, Kivlahan DR, Dimeff LA, Larimer ME, et al. 1998. Screening and brief intervention for high-risk college student drinkers: results from a 2-year follow-up assessment. *J. Consult. Clin. Psychol.* 66:604–15

Marlatt GA, Gordon JR, eds. 1985. *Relapse Prevention: Maintenance Strategies in the Treatment of Addictive Behaviors*. New York: Guilford

McGee R, Feehan M, Williams S, Partridge F, Silva PA, Kelly J. 1990. DSM-III disorders in a large sample of adolescents. *J. Am. Acad. Child Adolesc. Psychiatry* 29:611–19

McGue M, Iacono WG. 2005. The association of early adolescent problem behavior with adult psychopathology. *Am. J. Psychiatry* 162:1118–24

Mechanic D. 1998. Bringing science to medicine: the origins of evidence-based practice. *Health Affairs* 17(6):250–51

Mensinger JL, Diamond GS, Kaminer Y, Wintersteen MB. 2006. Adolescent and therapist perception of barriers to outpatient substance abuse treatment. *Am. J. Addict.* 15:16–25

Miller AL, Glinski J, Woodberry KA, Mitchell AG, Indik J. 2002. Family therapy and dialectical behavior therapy with adolescents. Part I: proposing a clinical synthesis. *Am. J. Psychother.* 56(4):568–84

Miller AL, Rathus JH, Linehan MM. 2007. *Dialectical Behavior Therapy with Suicidal Adolescents*. New York: Guilford

Miller WR, Rollnick S. 2002. *Motivational Interviewing: Preparing People for Change*. New York: Guilford. 2nd ed.

Minkoff K. 1991. Program components of a comprehensive integrated care system for serious mentally ill patients with substance disorders. In *New Directions for Mental Health Services: Dual Diagnosis of Major Mental Illness and Substance Disorder*, ed. K Minkoff, RE Drake, 50:13–27. San Francisco, CA: Jossey-Bass

Monti PM, Barnett NP, O'Leary TA, Colby SM. 2001. Motivational enhancement for alcohol-involved adolescents. In *Adolescents, Alcohol, and Substance Abuse: Reaching Teens Through Brief Interventions*, ed. PM Monti, SM Colby, TA O'Leary, pp. 145–82. New York: Guilford

Monti PM, Colby SM, Barnett NP, Spirito A, Rohsenow DJ, et al. 1999. Brief intervention for harm reduction with alcohol-positive older adolescents in a hospital emergency department. *J. Consult. Clin. Psychol.* 67:989–94

Moss HB, Lynch KG, Hardie TL. 2003. Affiliation with deviant peers among children of substance dependent fathers from preadolescence into adolescence: associations with problem behaviors. *Drug Alcohol Depend.* 71:117–25

Mueser KT, Drake RE, Wallach MA. 1998. Dual diagnosis: a review of etiological theories. *Addict. Behav.* 23(6):717–34

Myers MG, Brown SA, Tate S, Abrantes A, Tomlinson K. 2001. Toward brief interventions for adolescents with substance abuse and comorbid psychiatric problems. In *Adolescents, Alcohol, and Substance Abuse: Reaching Teens Through Brief Interventions*, ed. PM Monti, SM Colby, TA O'Leary, pp. 275–96. New York: Guilford

Najavits LM. 2007. Seeking Safety: an evidence-based model for substance abuse and trauma/PTSD. In *Therapist's Guide to Evidence-Based Relapse Prevention: Practical Resources for the Mental Health Professional*, ed. KA Witkiewitz, GA Marlatt, pp. 141–67. San Diego, CA: Elsevier

Najavits LM, Gallop RJ, Weiss RD. 2006. Seeking Safety therapy for adolescent girls with PTSD and substance use disorder: a randomized controlled trial. *J. Behav. Health Serv. Res.* 33(4):453–63

Najavits LM, Weiss RD, Shaw SR, Muenz L. 1998. "Seeking Safety": outcome of a new cognitive-behavioral psychotherapy for women with posttraumatic stress disorder and substance dependence. *J. Trauma. Stress* 11:437–56

Nat. Alliance Ment. Illness. 2007. *Choosing the Right Treatment: What Families Need to Know About Evidence-Based Practices*. Arlington, VA: Nat. Alliance Ment. Illness

Nat. Assoc. State Ment. Health Prog. Directors, Nat. Assoc. State Alcohol Drug Abuse Directors. 1998. *National dialogue on co-occurring mental health and substance abuse disorders*. Washington, DC: Nat. Assoc. State Alcohol Drug Abuse Directors. **http://www.nasadad.org/index.php?doc_id=101**

Nat. Inst. Drug Abuse. 1999. *Principles of drug addiction treatment: a research-based guide*. NIH Publ. No. 99–4180. Bethesda, MD: Nat. Inst. Health

Nelson-Gray RO, Keane SP, Hurst RM, Mitchell JT, Warburton JB, et al. 2006. A modified DBT skills training program for oppositional defiant adolescents: promising preliminary findings. *Behav. Res. Ther.* 44(12):1811–20

Oetting ER, Beauvais F. 1989. Epidemiology and correlates of alcohol use among Indian adolescents living on reservations. In *Alcohol Use Among U.S. Ethnic Minorities*, ed. D Spiegler, D Tate, S Aitken, C Christian, pp. 239–67. NIAAA Res. Monogr. 18. Rockville, MD: Nat. Inst. Alcohol Abuse Alcoholism

Pincus HA, Watkins K, Vilamovska AM, Keyser D. 2006. *Models of care for co-occurring disorders: final report*. RAND Corp. final rep. Cent. Subst. Abuse Treat. Rockville, MD: Subst. Abuse Ment. Health Serv. Admin.

President's New Freedom Commission Ment. Health. 2003. *Achieving the promise: transforming mental health care in America. Final report*. DHHS Publ. No. SMA 03–3832. Rockville, MD: Dep. Health Human Serv.

Prochaska JO, DiClemente CC. 1984. *The Trans Theoretical Approach: Crossing Traditional Boundaries of Therapy*. Homewood, IL: Dow Jones/Irwin

Proj. MATCH Res. Group. 1993. Project MATCH: rationale and methods for a multisite clinical trial matching patients to alcoholism treatment. *Alcohol. Clin. Exp. Res.* 17:1130–45

Ramo DE, Anderson KG, Tate SR, Brown SA. 2005. Characteristics of relapse to substance use in comorbid adolescents. *Addict. Behav.* 30(9):1811–23

Randall J, Henggeler SW, Pickrel S, Brondino MJ. 1999. Psychiatric comorbidity and the 16-month trajectory of substance-abusing and substance-dependent juvenile offenders. *J. Am. Acad. Child Adolesc. Psychiatry* 38:1118–25

Rather BC, Goldman MS, Roehrich L, Brannick M. 1992. Empirical modeling of an alcohol expectancy network using multidimensional scaling. *J. Abnorm. Psychol.* 101:174–83

Rathus JH, Miller AL. 2002. Dialectical behavior therapy adapted for suicidal adolescents. *Suicide Life Threat. Behav.* 32(2):146–57

Regier D, Farmer M, Rea D, Locke BZ, Keith SJ, et al. 1990. Comorbidity of mental disorders with alcohol and other drug abuse: results from the epidemiologic catchment area study. *J. Am. Med. Assoc.* 264(19):2511–18

Reinherz HZ, Giaconia RM, Pakiz B, Silverman AB, Frost AK, et al. 1993. Psychosocial risks for major depression in late adolescence: a longitudinal community study. *J. Am. Acad. Child Adolesc. Psychiatry* 32(6):1155–63

Rhodes JE, Jason LA. 1990. The social stress model of substance abuse. *J. Consult. Clin. Psychol.* 58:395–401

Riggs P. 2003. Treating adolescents for substance use and comorbid psychiatric disorders. *NIDA Sci. Pract. Perspect.* 2(1):18–29

Robbins MS, Kumar S, Walker-Barnes C, Feaster DJ, Briones E, Szapocznik J. 2002. Ethnic differences in comorbidity among substance-abusing adolescents referred to outpatient therapy. *J. Am. Acad. Child Adolesc. Psychiatry* 41(4):394–401

Roberts AR, Corcoran K. 2005. Adolescents growing up in stressful environments, dual diagnosis, and sources of success. *Brief Treat. Crisis Interv.* 5:1–8

Roberts LJ, Neal DJ, Kivlahan DR, Baer JS, Marlatt GA. 2000. Individual drinking changes following a brief intervention among college students: clinical significance in an indicated preventive context. *J. Consult. Clin. Psychol.* 68:500–5

Robins LN, Pryzbeck TR. 1985. Age of onset of drug use as a factor in drug and other disorders. In *NIDA Research Monograph 56. Etiology of Drug Abuse: Implications for Prevention*, ed. CL Jones, RJ Battjes, pp. 178–92. Rockville, MD: Nat. Inst. Drug Abuse

Roehrich H, Gold MS. 1986. Diagnosis of substance abuse in an adolescent psychiatric population. *Int. J. Psychiatry Med.* 18:137–43

Rohde P, Lewinsohn PM, Seeley JR. 1991. Comorbidity of unipolar depression: II. Comorbidity with other mental disorders in adolescents and adults. *J. Abnorm. Psychol.* 100:214–22

Rohde P, Lewinsohn PM, Seeley JR. 1994. Response of depressed adolescents to cognitive-behavioral treatment: Do differences in initial severity clarify the comparison of treatments? *J. Consult. Clin. Psychol.* 62:851–54

Rohde P, Lewinsohn PM, Seeley JR. 1996. Psychiatric comorbidity with problematic alcohol use in high school students. *J. Am. Acad. Child Adolesc. Psychiatry* 35(1):101–9

Rowe CL, Liddle HA, Dakof GA. 2001. Classifying clinically referred adolescent substance abusers by level of externalizing and internalizing symptoms. *J. Child Adolesc. Subst. Abuse* 11(2):41–65

Rowe CL, Liddle HL, Greenbaum PE, Henderson CE. 2004. Impact of psychiatric comorbidity on treatment of adolescent drug abusers. *J. Subst. Abuse Treat.* 26(2):129–40

Sacks S, Chandler R, Gonzales J. 2008. Responding to the challenge of co-occurring disorders: suggestions for future research. *J. Subst. Abuse Treat.* 34:139–46

Safer DL, Lock J, Couturier JL. 2007. Dialectical behavior therapy modified for adolescent binge eating disorder: a case report. *Cogn. Behav. Pract.* 14(2):157–67

Schaeffer CM, Borduin CM. 2005. Long-term follow-up to a randomized clinical trial of multisystemic therapy with serious and violent juvenile offenders. *J. Consult. Clin. Psychol.* 73(3):445–53

Shedler J, Block J. 1990. Adolescent drug use and psychological health: a longitudinal inquiry. *Am. Psychol.* 45:612–30

Simons-Morton B, Haynie DL, Crump AD, Saylor KE, Eitel P, Yu K. 1999. Expectancies and other psychosocial factors associated with alcohol use among early adolescents boys and girls. *Addict. Behav.* 24:229–38

Stacy AW, Newcomb MD, Bentler PM. 1991. Cognitive motivation and drug use: a 9-year longitudinal study. *J. Abnorm. Psychol.* 100:502–15

Subst. Abuse Ment. Health Serv. Admin. 1996. *Mental health estimates from the 1994 National Household Survey on Drug Abuse.* Rockville, MD: Subst. Abuse Ment. Health Serv. Admin.

Subst. Abuse Ment. Health Serv. Admin. 2000. *Prevention of comorbidity in children and adolescents: the nexus of mental health and substance abuse.* Background paper. Silver Spring, MD: Johnson, Bassin & Shaw

Subst. Abuse Ment. Health Serv. Admin. 2002. *Results from the 2001 National Household Survey on Drug Abuse: volume I. Summary of national findings.* DHHS Publ. No. SMA 02–3758. Rockville, MD: Subst. Abuse Ment. Health Serv. Admin.

Subst. Abuse Ment. Health Serv. Admin. 2005. *Transforming mental health care in America. Federal action agenda: first steps.* DHHS Publ. No. SMA 05–4060. Rockville, MD: Subst. Abuse Ment. Health Serv. Admin.

Subst. Abuse Ment. Health Serv. Admin. 2007. *The DASIS report: male admissions with co-occurring psychiatric and substance use disorders: 2005.* Rockville, MD: Subst. Abuse Ment. Health Serv. Admin.

Sunseri PA. 2004. Preliminary outcomes on the use of dialectical behavior therapy to reduce hospitalization among adolescents in residential care. *Residential Treat. Child. Youth* 21:59–76

Szapocznik J, Kurtines WM, Foote FH, Perez-Vidal A, Hervis O. 1983. Conjoint versus one-person family therapy: some evidence for the effectiveness of conducting family therapy through one person. *J. Consult. Clin. Psychol.* 51:889–99

Tevyaw TO, Monti PM. 2004. Motivational enhancement and other brief interventions for adolescent substance abuse: foundations, applications and evaluations. *Addiction* 99(Suppl. 2):63–75

Tomlinson KL, Brown SA, Abrantes A. 2004. Psychiatric comorbidity and substance use treatment outcomes of adolescents. *Psychol. Addict. Behav.* 18:160–69

Trupin EW, Stewart DG, Beach B, Boesky L. 2002. Effectiveness of a dialectical behaviour therapy program for incarcerated female juvenile offenders. *Child Adolesc. Mental Health* 7(3):121–27

Turner CF, Ku L, Rogers SM, Lindberg LD, Pleck JH, Sonenstein FL. 1998. Adolescent sexual behavior, drug use, and violence: increased reporting with computer survey technology. *Science* 280:867–73

U.S. Dep. Health Human Serv. 1999. *Mental Health: A Report of the Surgeon General*. Rockville, MD: U.S. Dep. Health Human Serv.

U.S. Dep. Health Human Serv. 2001. *Youth Violence: A Report of the Surgeon General*. Rockville, MD: U.S. Dep. Health Human Serv.

U.S. Dep. Health Human Serv. 2002. *Report to Congress on the Prevention and Treatment of Co-occurring Substance Abuse and Mental Disorders*. Rockville, MD: Subst. Abuse Ment. Health Serv. Admin.

Waldron HB. 1997. Adolescent substance abuse and family therapy outcome: a review of randomized trials. In *Advances in Clinical Child Psychology*, ed. TH Ollendick, RJ Prinz, pp. 199–234. New York: Plenum

Waldron HB, Kaminer Y. 2004. On the learning curve: the emerging evidence supporting cognitive-behavioral therapies for adolescent substance abuse. *Addiction* 99(Suppl. 2):93–105

Waldron HB, Slesnick N, Brody JL, Turner CW, Peterson JR. 2001. Treatment outcomes for adolescent substance abuse at 4- and 7-month assessments. *J. Consult. Clin. Psychol.* 69:802–13

Weiss RD, Mirin SM. 1987. Substance abuse as an attempt at self-medication. *Psychiatr. Med.* 3:357–67

Weisz JR, Kazdin AE. 2003. Concluding thoughts: present and future of evidence-based psychotherapies for children and adolescents. In *Evidence-Based Psychotherapies for Children and Adolescents*, ed. AE Kazdin, JR Weisz, pp. 439–51. New York: Guilford

White HR, LaBouvie EW. 1989. Towards the assessment of adolescent problem drinking. *J. Stud. Alcohol* 50:30–37

Wierzbicki M, Pekarik G. 1993. A meta-analysis of psychotherapy dropout. *Prof. Psychol. Res. Pract.* 24:190–95

Wise BK, Cuffe SP, Fischer T. 2001. Dual diagnosis and successful participation of adolescents in substance abuse treatment. *J. Subst. Abuse Treat.* 21(3):161–65

Woodberry KA, Miller AL, Glinski J, Indik J, Mitchell AG. 2002. Family therapy and dialectical behavior therapy with adolescents. Part II: a theoretical review. *Am. J. Psychother.* 56(4):585–602

Zlotnick C, Najavits LM, Rohsenow DJ. 2003. A cognitive-behavioral treatment for incarcerated women with substance use disorder and posttraumatic stress disorder: findings from a pilot study. *J. Subst. Abuse Treat.* 25:99–105

Therapy for Specific Problems: Youth Tobacco Cessation

Susan J. Curry, Robin J. Mermelstein, and Amy K. Sporer

Institute for Health Research and Policy, University of Illinois at Chicago, Chicago, Illinois 60608; email: suecurry@uic.edu, robinm@uic.edu, aksporer@uic.edu

Annu. Rev. Psychol. 2009. 60:229–55

The *Annual Review of Psychology* is online at psych.annualreviews.org

This article's doi:
10.1146/annurev.psych.60.110707.163659

0066-4308/09/0110-0229$20.00

Key Words

adolescents, smoking, prevalence, treatment, dependence, intervention

Abstract

Cigarette smoking is the leading cause of premature morbidity and mortality in the United States. The majority of children smoke their first cigarette in early adolescence, and many older teens have well-established dependence on nicotine. Efforts to promote and support smoking cessation among these youth smokers are critical. The available experimental studies of youth cessation interventions find that behavioral interventions increase the chances of youth smokers achieving successful cessation. Currently there is insufficient evidence for the effectiveness of pharmacological treatments with youth smokers. Many innovative studies have been compromised by challenges in recruiting sufficient numbers of youth, obtaining approval for waivers of parental consent, and high attrition in longitudinal studies. Key areas for future work include bridging the fields of adolescent development and treatment design, matching treatments to developmental trajectories of smoking behavior, better understanding treatment processes and treatment moderators, and building demand for evidence-based cessation treatments.

Contents

INTRODUCTION

Why Is Youth Tobacco-Use Cessation an Important Problem for Psychology?

Nicotine-related disorders are among the deadliest diagnoses in the *Diagnostic and Statistical Manual of Mental Disorders, Fourth Edition* (Am. Psychiatr. Assoc. 2000). Cigarette smoking, the most common form of nicotine use, is the leading cause of premature morbidity and mortality in the United States (Cent. Dis. Control Prev. 2007). Smoking kills more people than AIDS, alcohol, car accidents, illegal drugs, murders, and suicides combined (Lindblom 2008). The Centers for Disease Control and Prevention (CDC) estimates that cigarette smoking is responsible for approximately one of every five deaths annually (Cent. Dis. Control Prev. 2005), and about one-third of youth smokers

will die prematurely from smoking-related diseases (Cent. Dis. Control Prev. 1996). More than six million adolescents alive today will ultimately die from smoking unless smoking rates decline. With national data indicating that almost 90% of adult smokers begin while in their adolescent years (Campaign for Tobacco Free Kids 2008), understanding patterns and prevalence of youth smoking and quitting behaviors is critical.

From a psychological perspective, tobacco use and dependence is a chronic, relapsing disease that begins early in life. Adolescence is a time of heightened vulnerability for both the initiation of tobacco use (U.S. Dep. Health Hum. Serv. 1994) and the development of nicotine dependence (Jamner et al. 2003). Dr. David Kessler, former Food and Drug Administration (FDA) Commissioner, aptly stated, "It is

AIDS: acquired immune deficiency syndrome

CDC: Centers for Disease Control and Prevention

FDA: Food and Drug Administration (United States)

easy to think of smoking as an adult problem. It is adults who die from tobacco-related diseases..." However, "a person who hasn't started smoking by age 19 is unlikely to ever become a smoker. Nicotine addiction begins when most tobacco users are teen-agers, so let's call this what it really is: a pediatric disease" (Hilts 1995).

With the majority of children smoking their first cigarette in early adolescence, many older teens have well-established dependence on nicotine. Efforts to promote and support smoking cessation among these new generations of smokers are critical. The present review represents the first comprehensive summary of research in adolescent tobacco-cessation treatment in the *Annual Review of Psychology*. This review builds on previous syntheses of the field (Backinger et al. 2003, Mermelstein 2003, Pbert et al. 2006, Prokhorov et al. 2003), systematic reviews (Garrison et al. 2003, McDonald et al. 2003, Sussman 2002), and meta-analyses (Grimshaw & Stanton 2006, Sussman et al. 2006). We address youth cessation from several perspectives. First, we examine the question, "who are youth tobacco users?" with respect to their prevalence and patterns of smoking and tobacco use, neurocognitive development, psychosocial development, and nicotine addiction. The second section reviews the state of the art in youth tobacco cessation, drawing on expert summaries and meta-analyses along with recently published results from treatment outcome studies. Our review is limited to treatments delivered to individual smokers, although we acknowledge that policy-level interventions, including product taxes, clean indoor air legislation, and purchase, use, and possession laws, also influence youth tobacco use (e.g., DiFranza et al. 2006, Jason et al. 2007, Pierce 2007). Following the evidence review, we examine the inherent challenges in building the evidence base for youth cessation treatment, including recruitment and retention in studies and human subjects' protections. The article concludes with a view to future directions in youth cessation treatment research.

WHO ARE YOUTH TOBACCO USERS?

Prevalence and Patterns of Youth Smoking

Cigarette use by youth in the United States has been measured through national surveys since the early 1970s. Two primary sources of information on youth substance use are the Monitoring the Future study (1975–2007), a school-based survey of adolescents in the United States, and the National Survey on Drug Use and Health (formerly the National Household Surveys on Drug Abuse), a household-based survey of the civilian, noninstitutionalized population of the United States aged 12 years old or older. The two surveys have some key methodological differences, such as interview setting (school versus home), sampling methods, and assessing school dropouts. The Monitoring the Future survey, with its school-based administration format, may underrepresent smoking, given the well-documented association between smoking and school drop-out (U.S. Dep. Health Hum. Serv. 1994). Both surveys are reliable sources of substance-use prevalence for youth in the United States (Gfroerer et al. 1997) and, importantly, both show similar historical trends in prevalence rates. Two additional biennial school-based surveys began measuring national- and state-level youth health risk behaviors and tobacco-use behaviors in the 1990s: the Youth Risk Behavior Surveillance System and the National Youth Tobacco Survey. Smoking-cessation measures that complement data from Monitoring the Future study and the National Survey on Drug Use and Health are reported here.

Trends in cigarette smoking. Prevalence rates of cigarette smoking among twelfth-grade students peaked in the mid-1970s, with current smoking (use in the past 30 days) reaching 39% in 1976. Through 1977, the rate of daily smoking was maintained at 29%, with 19% of twelfth graders smoking half of a pack or more per day. During the years that followed, prevalence rates declined substantially, with current and daily smoking among high school seniors dropping almost 10 percentage points by 1981 (29% and 20%, respectively; Johnston et al. 2007a). After remaining relatively flat throughout the 1980s, the smoking prevalence among all youth in the United States began to rise through the late 1990s. Many economic and social factors are likely responsible for this increase in youth smoking prevalence throughout the 1990s, including the decrease in cigarette prices and the use of youth-targeted advertising and marketing by tobacco companies (Nelson et al. 1995).

In the wake of the 1998 Master Settlement Agreement between the Attorneys General and the major tobacco companies, and the resulting efforts and influx of monies from the settlement to fund research and community programs to address the health effects of smoking (e.g., American Legacy Foundation), the prevalence of youth smoking began again to decline steadily through 2006 (Johnston et al. 2007a). In 2007, however, only eighth-grade students showed continued change from the previous year in current and daily smoking (from 8.7% in 2006 to 7.1% in 2007, and 4.0% to 3.0%, respectively). Although prevalence rates are lower than ever, more than one-fifth of high school seniors in the United States were current smokers in 2007, with more than half of them reporting daily smoking (Monitoring the Future 2007).

Smoking patterns among subgroups of youth. Based on 2006 national estimates, 2.6 million (10.4%) youth aged 12 to 17 were current smokers (Substance Abuse and Mental Health Services Admin. 2007). Among high school seniors who reported smoking in the past month (21.6%), 56% were daily smokers and 27% smoked half of a pack or more every day (Johnston et al. 2007a). The rates of daily smoking were similar for males and females in twelfth grade (12.0% and 11.8%, respectively; Johnston et al. 2007a). There are, however, substantial differences in smoking prevalence among racial/ethnic groups. In comparison with black and Hispanic high school seniors, white youth have two to three times the rates of daily smoking (5.7% black, 7.0% Hispanic, 15.3% white; Johnston et al. 2007a), and nearly double the rates of current smoking among 12- to 17-year-olds (6.0% black, 8.2% Hispanic, 12.4% white; Substance Abuse and Mental Health Services Admin. 2007). Educational aspirations also remain one of the strongest discriminators of smoking among adolescents. Smoking prevalence among twelfth graders who had no plans to either attend or complete four years of college was 32.4% in 2007, compared to 19.0% for twelfth graders who planned to complete four years of college (Monitoring the Future 2007).

As the prevalence of smoking among adolescents has declined over time, its social meaning may have changed, and current adolescent smokers may be more "hard core" than were adolescents who smoked in previous decades (Chassin et al. 2007a). Chassin et al. (2007a) tested this "hardening" hypothesis among two cohorts of adolescents, one from 1980, and the other from 2001, and found that middle school adolescents who smoked in 2001 showed more "deviance proneness" than their counterparts in 1980. In addition, Chassin and colleagues (2007a) found that youth who smoked in 2001 reported smoking more cigarettes per day than did adolescent smokers in 1980, providing further support for the notion of the hardening of the adolescent smoking population. These findings also bolster the suggestion that today's youth who smoke may be more dependent on nicotine than were previous cohorts and, as a result of both increased dependence and a combination of deviant-prone risk factors, may have more difficulty stopping smoking.

Despite this potential hardening of adolescent smokers, the majority of adolescents who smoke cigarettes want to quit. Available national data indicate that half of the current smokers in middle school reported wanting to stop smoking, and 55% had tried to quit in the past 12 months (Cent. Dis. Control

Prev. 2006b,c). Almost two-thirds (62.1%) of the high school students who reported current smoking wanted to quit, and more than half reported having tried to quit smoking at least once in the previous year (Cent. Dis. Control Prev. 2006c). Although cessation attempts were reported similarly across all subgroups (i.e., gender, race/ethnicity) of current smokers, Hispanic high school students were significantly less likely to want to quit, as compared to white and black students (Cent. Dis. Control Prev. 2006c).

Although cigarette smoking accounts for the vast majority of youth tobacco use and has been the primary focus of the limited treatment development and research that exists, the use of smokeless tobacco is also problematic among youth, especially among certain subgroups. In 2006, the prevalence rate of current smokeless tobacco use (used in the past 30 days) among high school seniors was 6.1%, a reduction by almost half from when it was first reported at 11.5% in 1986 (Johnston et al. 2007a). Smokeless tobacco is used predominantly by males (11.0% versus 1.5% females) who are white (8.8% versus 3.8% Hispanic and 0.5% black) and live in nonmetropolitan statistical areas (MSAs) (24.7% versus large MSA 11.6% and other MSA 13.1%) communities in the North Central or South regions of the United States (19.3% and 17.0%, respectively, versus 11.9% Northeast and 10.3% West; Johnston et al. 2007a). An MSA is a geographic entity defined by the U.S. Office of Management and Budget as one or more contiguous counties containing a core urban area with a population of 50,000 or more. Smokeless tobacco use has a range of negative health consequences, both similar to and different from those of cigarette smoking, but also has some unique determinants to its use and implications for interventions. Our review focuses primarily on interventions for cigarette smoking, not to diminish the importance of the smokeless tobacco-use problem among adolescents, but rather as a reflection of the difference between the behavioral patterns of use and resulting interventions.

BEYOND EXPERIMENTATION: THE DEVELOPMENT OF SMOKING BEHAVIOR

Smoking among adolescents is not an "all or nothing" or unitary phenomenon. Rather, adolescents progress through stages of smoking, ranging from initial trials of smoking to more frequent but irregular use, to more regular use and dependence (Mayhew et al. 2000). As newer data analytic techniques have come into use (e.g., latent variable growth mixture modeling), researchers have started to identify trajectories of smoking behavior among adolescents that might help to describe better the heterogeneity of longitudinal patterns of use, with an eye toward identifying factors that discriminate among these trajectories (e.g., Chassin et al. 2000, Colder et al. 2001, Stanton et al. 2004). Of particular importance is identifying factors that distinguish between youth who experiment with smoking and desist after relatively few trials from youth who experiment, rapidly escalate, and become dependent smokers. Cessation interventions may become more powerful if researchers could better tailor interventions to the unique characteristics of youth in each of these distinct trajectories of use, or intervene in the window of opportunity between early trials and dependence. Early intervention is important not only for preventing the numerous, significant health problems that result from cigarette smoking and occur even in adolescence (U.S. Dep. Health Hum. Serv. 1994), but also to help reduce the risk that cigarette smoking conveys for the development of future substance use (Lewinsohn et al. 1999) and other psychological disorders (e.g., depression) as adolescents move into young adulthood (Brown et al. 1996, Kandel et al. 1986).

Nicotine Dependence in Youth

Although adolescent smokers are interested in stopping smoking, they have difficulty in achieving and maintaining abstinence (Choi et al. 2002), one of the key indicators of

MSAs: metropolitan statistical areas

nicotine dependence (Am. Psychiatr. Assoc. 2000). Evidence is increasing that adolescent smokers exhibit physiological, psychological, and behavioral features of nicotine dependence (e.g., Colby et al. 2000, Prokhorov et al. 2005), yet there is still much debate in the literature about the dimensionality of nicotine dependence in adolescents and how dependence develops and progresses (Shadel et al. 2000). Current conceptualizations of nicotine dependence in adults suggest that dependence is a syndrome consisting of several core features, including craving, compulsion to smoke, and withdrawal (Shadel et al. 2000, Shiffman et al. 2004). This syndrome conceptualization has been adopted for youth as well (Shadel et al. 2000). Measures of nicotine dependence for adolescents have frequently assessed only limited aspects of dependence, however. For example, the modified version of the Fagerstrom Tolerance Questionnaire (Prokhorov et al. 1996, 1998) is a seven-item scale that assesses primarily behavioral features of dependence, such as how soon after waking the adolescent smokes a cigarette or whether one has difficulty refraining from smoking in places where smoking is forbidden. Other scales, such as the Hooked on Nicotine Checklist (DiFranza et al. 2002; O'Loughlin et al. 2002a, 2003), may capture more features of dependence, with items that tap into feelings of cravings, feeling like one is addicted to tobacco, or withdrawal symptoms, although the scale is still conceptualized as unidimensional. A multidimensional measure of nicotine dependence, the Nicotine Dependence Syndrome Scale (Shiffman et al. 2004), has also been modified for adolescents (Clark et al. 2005, Nichter et al. 2002), with good psychometric properties. Factors assessed by this scale include tolerance, drive, priority, and continuity of smoking. However, whether these measures predict cessation has been less well studied, and particularly whether they predict cessation above and beyond smoking rate. More frequent and higher amounts of smoking is one of the more consistent and stronger factors associated with a failure to quit among adolescents (e.g., Sargent et al. 1998, Sussman

et al. 1998, Tucker et al. 2002, Zhu et al. 1999).

Biological, Behavioral, and Psychological Determinants of Youth Initiation and Cessation

That nicotine addiction can begin in adolescence has long been apparent to the tobacco industry, as reflected in their aggressive marketing to youth (Pierce 2007). With a lifetime prevalence of cigarette use at nearly 50% by twelfth grade, one could view tobacco use as a manifestation of adolescent development (Monitoring the Future 2007). However, there is good consensus among researchers that cigarette smoking among adolescents is an addictive behavior and not just one of several "problem behaviors" that might appear during adolescence. The tobacco industry, through pricing and marketing strategies, has been remarkably successful at positioning tobacco use at the intersection of adolescent psychosocial development such that youth may see tobacco use as a perfect antidote to the normal emotional and social challenges of adolescence. Cigarettes are available in homes, in local stores, have the least amount of stigma attached to their use in comparison with other illegal substances, and are a means of social bonding. In addition, the harmful effects of tobacco use are far enough into the future that youth can rationalize their current use by assuming they will stop before experiencing any serious health problems. Importantly, too, the physiological effects of nicotine can mitigate negative affect and some of the stress and storm of adolescence.

Cigarette smoking among adolescents is a complex and multidetermined behavior, controlled by a combination of interacting biological, psychosocial, and environmental influences. Numerous age-related processes come into play during adolescence that increase the risk for the development of smoking and dependence, including neuronal sensitivity to nicotine (Belluzzi et al. 2004, 2005; Cao et al. 2007), the effects of nicotine on continuing brain development (Leslie et al. 2004), cognitive-emotional responses to smoking cues and tobacco advertisements (Tercyak et al. 2002), affective and physiological stress reactivity, and an increase in emotionality, risk-taking, and impulsivity (Steinberg 2004). Along with these biobehavioral, normative changes, adolescents also experience multiple transitional events and developmental challenges, placing youth at increased risk for emotional and behavioral problems (Steinberg 2004, Steinberg & Morris 2001). This confluence of interacting and often competing factors comes into play in important ways in understanding not only the development of nicotine dependence in youth, but also the difficulties adolescents have in stopping smoking and the challenges that researchers face in designing interventions that match the developmental stage and unique characteristics of adolescents.

Smoking cessation interventions for adolescents need to consider the range of behavioral and psychological determinants of smoking among adolescents, with special consideration given to factors that maintain smoking or that might promote or hinder cessation. A great deal is known about factors that predict the early stages of cigarette use among adolescents (e.g., Conrad et al. 1992, U.S. Dep. Health Hum. Serv. 1994), but much less is known about predicting progression from early use to nicotine dependence (Turner et al. 2004) or about predictors of cessation. Tobacco use among adolescents does not occur in a vacuum, and a variety of individual and situational factors influence adolescents' initial tobacco use, continued use, and eventual dependence. Three primary streams of influence affect adolescent tobacco use: individual or person-level variables, immediate social or normative influences, and broader environmental and cultural influences (Turner et al. 2004). We highlight here only a few of the key factors that may be important to consider in developing cessation interventions for adolescents.

Individual psychosocial and behavioral influences on smoking. Individual influence variables include demographic factors such as gender and ethnicity, with substantial race/ethnic differences in both prevalence rates, as noted above (Johnston et al. 2007a), and reasons for smoking or not smoking (Mermelstein 1999). Genetics also account for a substantial portion of smoking behavior, with some researchers estimating that genetic effects account for 56% of the variance in smoking initiation and 70% of the variance in nicotine dependence (Sullivan & Kendler 1999). Adolescents' physiological responses to smoking and nicotine are yet another potentially important predictor of escalation (Eissenberg & Balster 2000). Subjective affective and physiological responses to early trials of smoking may be associated with progression from initial use to more regular smoking (Mermelstein et al. 2007).

Cigarette smoking among adolescents is also strongly associated with a variety of comorbidities and problem behaviors, including a well-documented link with externalizing disorders (McMahon 1999). Although cigarette smoking among adolescents is also associated with attention deficit hyperactivity disorder (ADHD), it is not clear whether this association is independent of the frequently co-occurring link with conduct disorder (Baker et al. 2004). Whalen and colleagues (2003) have hypothesized that smoking among adolescents with ADHD may serve an important function by improving attentional and self-regulatory competence and helping to modulate affect. The presence of ADHD may present notable challenges to cessation interventions both in terms of skills training and in terms of addressing the potential behavioral and cognitive problems that may arise for adolescents as they try to stop smoking.

Perhaps one of the most commonly reported relationships with adolescent smoking is the one with negative affect or depressive symptoms. Theoretical, empirical, and anecdotal evidence suggest a compelling link between mood and smoking among adolescents. Like adults, adolescent smokers report smoking in response to stress and as a way to boost their moods or to control anger (Chassin et al. 2007b, Kassel et al. 2003, Mermelstein 1999). Indeed, one of the most commonly proposed hypotheses

ADHD: attention deficit hyperactive disorder

about the mood-smoking relationship, for both adults and adolescents, is that individuals smoke as a form of self-medication, hoping to relieve their negative affect (Carmody 1989, Khantzian 1997, Lerman et al. 1996, Wills & Cleary 1995). Thus, negative affect or depressive symptoms may prospectively predict smoking or increases in smoking level, and persistently high levels of smoking may also predict increases in depressive symptoms among adolescents (Windle & Windle 2001). Negative affect, such as perceived stress (Sussman et al. 1998) and depressive symptoms (Zhu et al. 1999), have also predicted failure to quit smoking for adolescents.

Nicotine is well accepted as a potentially powerful mood regulator in terms of its effects on the brain's neural circuits (Brody 2006, Lerman et al. 1996, Pomerleau & Pomerleau 1984, Pontieri et al. 1996). For adolescents, who are in a critical phase of brain development and refinement of emotional regulation, the effects of nicotine on mood regulation and brain circuitry may be especially potent (Jamner et al. 2003).

There is also growing evidence for an association between affect dysregulation and cigarette use in adolescence. Wills and colleagues (2006) found that poor emotional control was positively related to the frequency of cigarette use in adolescents as well as to other substance use. Deficient emotional regulation has also predicted progression from experimentation to regular cigarette smoking (Novak & Clayton 2001). These relationships between smoking and affect regulation among adolescents are compelling when one considers the challenges of stopping smoking on top of the normative mood fluctuations in adolescence (Arnett 1999).

Interpersonal influences on smoking. Social influences also remain one of the more powerful predictors of adolescent smoking, for both initiation and progression (Kobus 2003). Adolescents are more likely to smoke if their close friends smoke (Chassin et al. 1984, Kobus 2003). Parents also exert substantial influence

on adolescents' smoking behavior, with much evidence supporting a link between parent smoking and progression to regular smoking among adolescents (Chassin et al. 1998a,b). Interpersonal influences may be particularly important for adolescents in stopping smoking. Having parents who smoke may hinder cessation among adolescents (Chassin et al. 1996, Zhu et al. 1999), as does having peers who smoke (Tucker et al. 2002). Stanton et al. (2006) found that one of the strongest predictors of cessation among a large sample of Australian high school students was whether adolescents had actively engaged other students in trying to quit as well, which suggests one strategy for future interventions to help counter the negative influence of smoking peers.

Environmental influences on smoking. The broad social and cultural environments play a substantial role in adolescents' smoking progression and include such factors as tobacco advertising, marketing, and media influences, as well as no-smoking policies, restrictions on youth access to cigarettes, and prices of cigarette products. There is consistent evidence that higher cigarette prices discourage smoking initiation, decrease smoking rate, and encourage cessation (Liang et al. 2003), and that adolescents are more responsive to price than are adults (Chaloupka 1999). Compared with experimenters and lower-rate smokers, adolescents who are more frequent smokers appear particularly sensitive to price (Emery et al. 2001, Liang & Chaloupka 2002). Price effects may occur through a number of mediating mechanisms (Liang et al. 2003), but they may create an impetus for adolescents to consider cessation as well as create a broader social environment more supportive of cessation attempts.

Tobacco Use and Cessation in the Context of Neurocognitive Development

Cigarette smoking and smoking cessation among adolescents also need to be considered in the context of normative neurocognitive development in adolescence. Adolescence is a time of neurodevelopmental plasticity and change (Steinberg 2004, 2007), and changes in the structure and function of the brain during adolescence are likely to significantly affect behavior and psychological functioning (Spear 2000). The prefrontal regions of the brain (home of executive functions) show gradual change in structure and function during adolescence (Casey et al. 2000) and are not fully developed until later in young adulthood (Steinberg 2007). However, the more socioemotional neural network matures closer to puberty and may well drive much of adolescent decision making (Steinberg 2007). Thus, self-regulatory skills do not mature as quickly as those that regulate reward mechanisms. Bechara (2005) has proposed a neurocognitive model for drug addiction that posits competition between an impulsive and a reflective neural system. This imbalance is normative in adolescents, and Steinberg (2007) summarizes multiple lines of evidence for the relative lack of an effective cognitive control system in adolescence based on these competing, but interactive, neural systems.

Are adolescents developmentally competent to engage in the complex array of coping skills (including planning, anticipating high-risk situations, and problem solving) that are required to sustain abstinence from smoking? Steinberg (2007) maintains that although logical reasoning abilities are mostly developed by age 15, the immature psychosocial capacities of adolescents (including delay of gratification, impulse control, emotional regulation, and resistance to peer influence) may undermine efforts or plans that are needed to resist risky behaviors. Steinberg (2007) further suggests that when adolescents are emotionally aroused, the cognitive control network is not yet strong enough to exert control. Thus, when one considers the emotional overlay of withdrawal symptoms following smoking cessation (which include increases in anger, irritability, difficulties concentrating, and increases in dysphoria) combined with this relatively weak cognitive control capacity, the risk for relapse or failure to quit smoking becomes great. Considering these neurocognitive developmental factors in adolescents, competent engagement in coping skills and appropriate decision making is possible, but only when conditions are optimal (Steinberg 2007). Optimal conditions include low peer and other social influences, for example. Challenges for cessation interventions for adolescents thus include helping adolescents to maintain emotional control and reducing deleterious social influences.

Understanding Nicotine Addiction in Youth: Challenges for Cessation

Biological, behavioral, and social factors converge during adolescence to promote smoking and the development of dependence and, potentially, to work against effective self-regulation and smoking cessation. A variety of liabilities, including both normative neurobiological developmental factors (e.g., immature frontal-limbic connections, immature frontal lobe development) and social influences, in combination with both normative and nonnormative patterns of emotional dysregulation in adolescence, present challenges for researchers to consider in developing interventions. These developmental considerations suggest that interventions need to take into account the appropriate cognitive and emotional level of the adolescent and adjust coping skill recommendations to match these abilities. In addition, many of the challenges faced by adults when trying to stop smoking, including withdrawal distress and social adjustments that need to be made in dealing with friends and families who smoke, are heightened for adolescents because of their relative lack of control over their environments compared to adults, their increased emotional lability, and the relative importance of social and interpersonal adjustments during this developmental period. Thus, interventions for adolescent smokers may need to be both more comprehensive in their consideration of factors that influence successful cessation as well as presented in an appealing, understandable, and accessible manner for youth.

OPPORTUNITIES AND CHALLENGES FOR YOUTH TOBACCO-CESSATION INTERVENTIONS

As described in previous sections, a sizeable proportion of youth smokers, even infrequent smokers, exhibit signs of nicotine addiction, and most are likely to continue smoking into adulthood. That youth smoking persists into adulthood does not reflect a lack of motivation to quit; the majority of youth smokers want to quit and make serious attempts to do so (Marshall et al. 2006). Similar to adults, most young smokers attempt to quit without using available behavioral and pharmacological treatments (Cent. Dis. Control Prev. 2006a, Curry et al. 2007b). A vast and robust evidence base for the effectiveness of behavioral and pharmacological interventions for adult smokers drives an imperative to encourage adults to utilize evidence-based treatments when attempting to quit (Fiore et al. 2000). Is there a sufficient evidence base to take the same approach with youth smokers?

Although meager in comparison with the adult cessation treatment literature, there is a growing evidence base for youth cessation treatments. Published treatment outcome studies evaluating interventions for youth cessation date back to the mid-1970s (Thompson 1978), but the cumulative evidence base still includes fewer than 50 experimental studies and even fewer randomized controlled trials. However, there are now two published meta-analyses of youth cessation interventions that cover studies conducted through mid-2006 (Grimshaw & Stanton 2006, Sussman et al. 2006) as well as several systematic reviews (Garrison et al. 2003, McDonald et al. 2003, Sussman 2002). Also encouraging are 12 publications of experimental studies since the meta-analyses. This emergent research provides an appropriate base from which to inform youth cessation treatment theory, research, and practice.

Conceptual Underpinnings of Youth Cessation Interventions

With the exception of three published trials of pharmacotherapy, youth cessation treatments comprise behavioral programs most often offered in group formats in school settings. Most publications do not explicate a specific overarching conceptual framework, but that does not mean that the interventions lack conceptual guidance, and it is possible to classify conceptually the program components utilized in the behavioral treatments. The Cochrane Collaborative Review distinguished among studies that used the transtheoretical model of change, psychosocial interventions focused on motivational enhancement and behavioral management, and pharmacological interventions (Grimshaw & Stanton 2006). The review notes that several studies included aspects of all three intervention models. The transtheoretical ("stages-of-change") model describes a series of five stages of readiness for cessation, ranging from not even thinking about quitting to initiating cessation and achieving long-term abstinence. Each stage of change is associated with different cognitive and behavioral process (Prochaska et al. 1992). Sussman et al's (2006) meta-analysis articulated three nonoverlapping treatment theories: social influence, cognitive-behavioral, and motivational enhancement. Social influence models emphasize social interactions and peer relationships that can facilitate or undermine cessation efforts and ways to counter tobacco industry strategies that influence youth tobacco use. Motivational enhancement focuses on increasing salient reasons for youth to quit smoking and addresses youth concerns and ambivalence about tobacco-use cessation. Cognitive-behavioral treatment focuses primarily on learning coping skills and problem-solving strategies for understanding and disrupting patterns of tobacco use, dealing with tobacco-use cravings, resisting social pressures to use tobacco, and managing stressful situations.

Regardless of how the conceptual underpinnings are categorized, it is clear that the content of behavioral interventions targeting youth cessation mirrors the content of programs for adults (Curry et al. 2007a). A comprehensive review of theories underlying evidence-based behavioral treatment for tobacco-use cessation is beyond the scope of this review. The most commonly applied theoretical models in tobacco-cessation research include value expectancy theories, social cognitive theory, and the transtheoretical model (Curry et al. 2003, Glanz et al. 2002). It is not uncommon to draw on concepts from several theoretical perspectives when creating an overarching intervention model (Curry et al. 2008). In general, theoretical models informing behavioral interventions for tobacco-use cessation share two common themes: (a) individuals must be sufficiently motivated to attempt cessation; and (b) they must have, and perceive that they have, the requisite skills and supports to initiate and maintain cessation. Thus, behavioral interventions typically target smokers' motivation, self-efficacy, skills, and social support.

Two of the most common intervention paradigms that derive from these conceptual underpinnings are motivational interviewing (Miller & Rollnick 2002) and skills training (Elder et al. 1999). Together, they offer a range of strategies targeting perceptions of personal risk from tobacco use, outcome expectations for quitting or remaining a smoker, self-efficacy, coping and problem-solving abilities, and enlisting social support. Motivational interviewing offers concrete strategies for working with smokers to enhance motivation for quitting and resolve ambivalence. This is accomplished by helping individuals articulate both their concerns about and their reasons for quitting. According to Miller & Rollnick (2002), the active ingredients of motivational interviewing are providing feedback, enhancing personal responsibility, giving advice along with a menu of options, supporting self-efficacy, and providing a nonconfrontational and supportive context. Skills training is a commonly used cognitive-behavioral treatment approach. Unlike motivational interviewing, which is used to increase individuals' motivation or desire to quit, skills training is used with individuals who are actively working on cessation. The core components of skills training include (a) training to identify and cope with high-risk situations associated with tobacco use, (b) modifying cognitive expectancies and attributions associated with smoking, (c) teaching stress management skills, and (d) modifying general lifestyle activities (Elder et al. 1999).

Although these skills-training components are likely critical ingredients for cessation interventions, they need to consider the background self-regulation abilities of adolescents, given the youth's stage of neurocognitive development and social context. The cognitive skills required for successful behavior change include the ability to identify and self-monitor behavioral patterns, anticipate problem situations, develop and prepare plans for handling high-risk situations, and remember both the plan and the need to take action in the future (Mermelstein 2003). Consider as well the overlap of youth who smoke and have ADHD or other comorbidities, and the challenge becomes one for intervention developers to modify more traditional coping-skills training to meet the unique characteristics of adolescent smokers.

Promising Intervention Models and Channels

Overall treatment effectiveness. Meta-analysis of high-quality experimental studies provides the optimal synthesis of treatment effectiveness. The recently published Cochrane Collaborative Review, "Tobacco cessation interventions for young people" (Grimshaw & Stanton 2006), applied stringent eligibility criteria to identify 15 studies for review. A separate meta-analysis published by Sussman and colleagues (2006) used more lenient selection criteria and included 48 studies. Because of different inclusion and exclusion criteria and different categorizations of interventions, direct comparison of the two meta-analyses is not possible.

In the aggregate, compared with control conditions (randomized and nonrandomized), youth tobacco-cessation treatment significantly increased the likelihood of cessation. The Sussman et al. (2006) analysis reported a 2.9% absolute advantage in quitting and a 46% increase in the probability of quitting with treatment in comparison with no treatment. When analyzed separately, treatment approaches that were described as cognitive-behavioral, motivation enhancing, social influence, and the stages-of-change or transtheoretical model all had relatively higher quit rates in comparison with control conditions. Moreover, the review concluded that behavioral programs consisting of at least five sessions had relatively higher quit rates than did less-intensive programs.

With regard to medication, there was insufficient evidence for the effectiveness of pharmacological treatments with youth smokers. It is interesting to compare these general conclusions to those meta-analyses of adult cessation programming (e.g., Fiore et al. 2000). Findings are consistent in favor of cognitive-behavioral elements (e.g., problem solving, coping skills training) and multisession programs. Perplexing is the lack of support for the effectiveness of pharmacotherapy among youth smokers compared with the overwhelming findings of effectiveness among adult smokers. This relatively lower effectiveness of pharmacotherapy for adolescents may be the result of differences between adolescents and adults in the pharmacokinetics of cessation medications, patterns of dependence, behavioral patterns of smoking, and the relative importance of social influence factors, compared to physical dependence factors and withdrawal, for adolescents. In comparison with adults, adolescents report much greater variability in smoking patterns (Mermelstein et al. 2002), a factor that might work against the more stable state of nicotine that is achieved by adult smokers and that is often better addressed by some pharmacotherapies (e.g., nicotine patch). Factors that typically predict success with pharmacotherapy for adults (e.g., number of cigarettes per day) also are not consistently predictive of success with nicotine-replacement therapy for youth (Franken et al. 2006). These contrasting findings point to the need for research that is more focused on the pharmacokinetics of therapies and comparison with behavioral smoking patterns for youth. Equally important, though, may be the overwhelming contribution of social influence factors in the ability of youths to quit. Pharmacotherapies fail to address the contextual reasons for smoking and relapse, and these factors may have greater relevance for youth cessation than for adult cessation.

Our search of the literature revealed 12 experimental studies published between 2003 and 2007 that were not included in either of the meta-analyses (Helstrom & Hutchison 2007, Horn et al. 2007, Joffe et al. 2005, Mermelstein & Turner 2006, Muramoto et al. 2007, Patten et al. 2007, Pbert et al. 2006, Rodgers et al. 2005, Stotts et al. 2003, Sun et al. 2007, Walsh et al. 2003, Woodruff et al. 2007). Two studies evaluated pharmacotherapy, either bupropion (Muramoto et al. 2007) or nicotine replacement (Stotts et al. 2003). Findings in the bupropion study were mildly encouraging, but the advantages of pharmacotherapy in this population are yet to be established. Muramoto and colleagues (2007) found significant increases in biochemically confirmed short-term abstinence (seven-day point prevalence) among youth taking 300 mg of bupropion daily compared to both 150-mg and placebo conditions throughout a 26-week follow-up period. However, there were no drug effects on long-term abstinence (confirmed 30-day prolonged abstinence). Stotts et al. (2003) recruited long-term smokeless tobacco users to evaluate nicotine patches. Over a one-year follow-up, there were no significant differences in rates of abstinence from smokeless tobacco between active and placebo patch conditions. However, when the active and placebo patch conditions were combined, they outperformed a usual-care control group with regard to smokeless tobacco use. Neither patch condition resulted in significantly higher abstinence from all forms of tobacco; quitting smokeless tobacco did not result in less use of tobacco overall. A nonrandomized open-label trial came to the same conclusion regarding the lack of efficacy of nicotine patch treatment for adolescent smokers (Hurt et al. 2000).

Five recent studies evaluated behavioral programs in general populations of adolescents using two-group designs comparing individually delivered treatment to no treatment or very brief intervention (Pbert et al. 2006, Rodgers et al. 2005, Sun et al. 2007, Walsh et al. 2003, Woodruff et al. 2007). Each of these studies reported significant treatment effects, lending support to the conclusion from the Sussman et al. (2006) meta-analysis that youth tobacco-cessation treatment significantly increases the likelihood of quitting. Of the remaining five studies, three were essentially "horse-race" studies comparing two different interventions and did not include a no-treatment control group. Joffe et al. (2005) compared two different nationally distributed behavioral programs (NoT on Tobacco versus Kickin' Butts). Patten et al. (2007) compared a home-based Internet-delivered treatment to a four-session health clinic–based intervention. Neither study reported significant treatment effects. In contrast, Mermelstein & Turner (2006) compared a group treatment (NoT on Tobacco) with and without a Web- and telephone-based adjunct. Results at a three-month follow-up showed significantly higher quit rates in the group-plus-adjunct condition.

Two other studies evaluated motivational enhancement interventions in teens who did not present voluntarily for cessation treatment. In one study, teens who had been arrested or required to appear in court for a variety of offenses were given the option to participate in a diversionary program (Helstrom & Hutchison 2007). The other study recruited participants for treatment who presented for care for any reason in an emergency room in a suburban, university-affiliated hospital (Horn et al. 2007). Neither study reported significant treatment effects.

Treatment settings. The impact of youth cessation interventions depends not only on the effectiveness of treatment but also on the potential reach of interventions to the target population (Glasgow et al. 2006). Given that the vast majority of adolescent smokers attend school, it is not surprising that most youth cessation interventions have been evaluated in school-based settings (either classroom or school clinics). Other settings include outreach at shopping malls and amusement parks (Lipkus et al. 2004) and worksites that have large youth employee populations, such as grocery stores (Stoddard et al. 2005). The Sussman et al. (2006) review calculated the net treatment effect for program settings that included the classroom as well as school and medical clinics. Results showed significant treatment effects for both the classroom and school clinics but not for the medical clinics.

It would be unwise to dismiss the health-care setting as important to expanding the reach and impact of youth cessation efforts. According to the 2006 National Health Interview Survey, more than 86% of youth aged 11 to 17 years had at least one contact with a health care professional in the previous year (Bloom & Cohen 2007). There is wide consensus, including American Academy of Pediatrics preventive care guidelines, that providers of healthcare to youth and adolescents are uniquely poised to facilitate youth cessation and so should routinely screen for tobacco use and provide advice and assistance based on the Public Health Service clinical practice guideline for treating tobacco use and dependence (Friend & Colby 2006, Klein & Camenga 2004, Pbert et al. 2003, Prokhorov et al. 2003). Two recent studies are encouraging in their findings that multisession behavioral interventions delivered to youth smokers in either school-based (Pbert et al. 2006) or community-based (Hollis et al. 2005) health care settings can significantly increase rates of smoking cessation. School nurses delivered a behavioral intervention one-on-one in the school health clinic, demonstrating the feasibility of using front-line youth health care providers to facilitate smoking cessation. In the community-based intervention, youths' health care providers provided brief advice to quit smoking; the behavioral support comprised an interactive computer program accessed at the health clinic and brief telephone follow-up counseling. Disseminating these encouraging findings to youth health care settings is important because recent summaries of current practices regarding tobacco cessation indicate that although pediatricians and family physicians routinely screen for tobacco use, they seldom provide assistance and follow-up to identified smokers (Friend & Colby 2006, Pbert et al. 2003).

Innovative intervention channels. Several innovative channels for delivering cessation support to youth smokers warrant further investigation, preferably using sufficiently powered randomized trials with long-term outcome assessment. Outreach telephone counseling, particularly through national and state quitline portals, has very high potential reach to youth smokers (Tedeschi et al. 2005). Although outreach telephone counseling has been included as a treatment component in some studies (e.g., Lipkus et al. 2004), and 44% of state quitlines in the United States report specialized teen cessation protocols (Cummins et al. 2006), there are no published randomized trials of the effectiveness of quitlines for youth callers.

Not surprising, there are several technology-based platforms, including PC-based expert systems (Hollis et al. 2005), Internet programs (Dallery et al. 2007, Mermelstein & Turner 2006, Patten et al. 2007, Woodruff 2001, Woodruff et al. 2007), and cell-phone text messaging (Rodgers et al. 2005). The potential reach of these interventions to youth smokers is also extraordinarily high. According to the Pew Internet and American Life Project, in 2004, 87% percent of U.S. teens age 12–17 reported using the Internet, with 51% reporting daily use. Prevalence of Internet use increased with age from 60% of sixth graders to 94% of eleventh and twelfth graders (Lenhart et al. 2005). Cell phone ownership was reported by 45% of teens in 2004, and 33% reported text messaging with a cell phone (Lenhart et al. 2005). A 2007 updated survey found that 63% of teens had their own cell phone (Macgill 2007).

To date, one study (conducted in New Zealand) has evaluated cell phone text messaging as a cessation program modality (Rodgers et al. 2005). Participants received regular personalized messages centered on a planned quit date. Messages were personalized to participant characteristics as assessed at baseline. The program sent five messages per day during the week before the quit date and the four weeks following. Outgoing free text messaging capability began on their quit date so that participants could text message others for social support. Other text message platforms included matching with quit buddies, phone-based opinion polls, and outreach messages to generate tips for coping with cravings.

Computer- and Internet-based programs permit real-time assessment of constructs such as sociodemographic characteristics, motivation to quit, and smoking patterns that can be used to provide tailored interventions (Curry 2007). Video technology allows attention-grabbing graphics and movies of teen testimonials to enhance the appeal and relevance of the interventions (Hollis et al. 2005). In one recently evaluated program, the Internet-based intervention was provided through a "virtual world." As described by the investigators, "...participants can see each other as 3-dimensional figures (i.e., avatars) on their computer screens, move around in the 'world', and have real-time discussions with each other" (Woodruff et al. 2007, p. 1773). The program, entitled "The Breathing Room," was set in a mall-like location with virtual storefronts that supported the counseling components (e.g., an art gallery to introduce tobacco advertising effects and a pharmacy for discussion of pharmacotherapy). Up to four youth together participated with an online counselor so there were opportunities for peer-to-peer interaction during treatment. Short-term results from a randomized evaluation with 136 adolescent smokers recruited from high schools are mildly encouraging. Prevalent abstinence rates at the postintervention follow-up favored the intervention group (35% versus 22%, p < 0.01), but there were no differences in abstinence rates at the 12-month follow-up (37% and 38%, respectively). Note that lack of long-term effects was due to increases in prevalent abstinence in the control group; the prevalent abstinence rate in the intervention group was virtually unchanged over time. Given the episodic nature of much youth smoking, the similarity in prevalent abstinence rates at end of treatment and 12 months should not be interpreted as sustained abstinence. The outcome paper did not report long-term abstinence rates. It is important to note that the ultimate dissemination of Internet cessation programs for youth is not yet reliable. Several years ago, one research group conducted an Internet search for online teen cessation programs and found that the key words "teen quit smoking" led to a number of teen pornography sites (7 out of the top 20) in one search engine (Elliott et al. 2001). Two years later, a study found only one pornographic site in the top 30 hits (Koo & Skinner 2003). This study also reported, however, that fewer than half of the sites identified through an Internet search were relevant to youth cessation.

E-technology can also extend the reach of traditional behavioral approaches to tobacco-cessation treatment. Contingency management based on biomarkers of tobacco use abstinence has shown some promise for youth smoking cessation in small-scale trials (Krishnan-Sarin et al. 2006, Roll 2005), although its effectiveness has not yet been established in a large-scale randomized trial with long-term outcome. Recently, investigators have completed a successful pilot test of the implementation of a voucher reinforcement system for youth cessation in which youth make twice-daily Web-camera video recordings of themselves providing a breath carbon monoxide sample and send the video and electronic breath sample readings to a centralized smoking cessation clinic. Abstinent participants then receive vouchers that can be used for purchases at various Internet vendors (Dallery et al. 2007, Glenn & Dallery 2007).

Mandatory treatment. We are unaware of circumstances under which adult smokers can be mandated to attend tobacco-cessation treatment programs. In contrast, youth tobacco users can be mandated to participate in treatment, usually as a consequence of violating school rules or community ordinances against purchase, use, or possession (i.e., purchase, use, and possession laws). Often treatment is offered to youth violators as an alternative to paying a monetary fine (Jason et al. 2007); these are called tobacco diversion programs. A national survey of nearly 600 community-based youth cessation programs found that for 9% of the programs, all participants were youth who were mandated to treatment, and an additional 35% of programs had both mandatory and voluntary participants (Curry et al. 2007a). Among the latter programs, 58% of participants on average were mandated.

There are no randomized studies of the impact of mandated treatment on youth cessation. One pilot study evaluation of a tobacco-diversion program in Minnesota surveyed 73 youth who opted to pay a fine and 39 youth who elected to participate in the diversion program (Lazovich et al. 2001). As the numbers indicate, the majority (65%) of youth elected to pay fines. Interviews conducted within 30 days of their initial citation found higher self-reported abstinence from smoking among those who paid the fines (23%) compared with those who attended the tobacco-diversion program (5.1%). Notably, youth who elected to participate in the tobacco-cessation program were more likely to report longer smoking histories and higher nicotine addiction scores, both of which are associated with greater difficulty quitting. As we have noted elsewhere (Curry et al. 2007a), motivation theory suggests that mandated treatment participation would undermine intrinsic motivation to quit and therefore diminish treatment effectiveness. Given the prevalence of mandated cessation treatment, further studies are warranted to ensure that mandated treatment does not have unintended negative consequences for youth cessation.

Challenges for Building the Evidence Base

IRB: Institutional Review Board

A review of the youth cessation literature reveals the significant challenges in conducting treatment trials with youth smokers. These hurdles relate to study design, assessment and validation of smoking status, recruitment, retention, and human subjects' requirements. There are several excellent analyses of these issues with regard both to youth cessation and prevention research (Backinger et al. 2003, Flay & Collins 2005, Grimshaw & Stanton 2006, Mercer et al. 2007, Mermelstein et al. 2002). Here we touch briefly on three key issues: recruitment of sufficient numbers of youth for adequate statistical power, institutional review board (IRB) requirements, and retention of youth cohorts for longitudinal follow-up.

When conducted in defined settings where rates of recruitment can be estimated (e.g., schools), between 2% and 10% of youth smokers will sign up for treatment (Backinger et al. 2003). With the average high school enrollment at 800 students (U.S. Dept. Education 2003) and estimating an overall smoking prevalence across grades at 15%, this translates to recruiting between 2 and 12 smokers per school. Similar challenges apply to recruiting youth smokers for treatment in medical settings, although health care providers may be stronger motivators for treatment than are school personnel. Nonetheless, one sees quickly that cluster-randomized trials with multiple sites are necessary for adequate rigor and statistical power, designs that are expensive and logistically complex. Community-based recruitment is no less challenging, even in settings where large numbers of youth naturally congregate. For example, Lipkus and colleagues (2004) recruited in 11 shopping malls spread across four states and screened more than 13,000 youth aged 15–18 years to enroll 402 smokers in their treatment study.

Clearly, we need creative approaches to enroll youth in cessation treatment studies. One approach to enhancing treatment demand is to implement pretreatment interventions aimed at increasing youth motivation for cessation prior to enrolling them in formal cessation programs. For example, a recent study explored the feasibility of using a "vanity and oral health issues" approach to motivate youth attending a continuation high school in rural California to join a tobacco-cessation group (Semer et al. 2005). In this innovative study, youth smokers attending a school-based health fair could have their picture digitally modified to simulate facial wrinkling or oral cancer disfigurement. Students received a hard copy color photograph. In addition, each participant received an oral cancer screening by a county school nurse. Among health fair participants, 57% of regular smokers signed up for treatment, and 65% of those who signed up participated in the full treatment program. This combined yield of 37% of youth smokers engaging in treatment is considerably higher than the 2% to 10% average participation rate.

Many researchers report that difficulties with recruitment stem primarily from IRB's requirements that they obtain active parental consent for youth to participate in their studies. Active parental consent obviously requires contacting youths' parents, explaining the research aims and requirements, and obtaining written or oral consent for their child to participate. The term "passive consent," which is often referred to when active consent is not obtained, is not a formal IRB option. Rather, researchers need to obtain a waiver of parental consent from their IRBs. The strategy of sending advance mailings to parents informing them about the research and providing the opportunity for them to request exclusion of their child from the study can allay IRB concerns that the waiver of consent would leave parents uninformed and unable to decide whether their child can be a research participant. This strategy describes passive consent.

Tigges (2003) reviewed methodological issues associated with use of active parental consent in research related to adolescents' risky behaviors and documented its effect on participation rates, costs, and selection bias. There is evidence that active consent excludes up to 70% of eligible youth, and these youth are more likely to be minority or to have the highest rates of risky and problem behaviors. Aggressive strategies for obtaining active consent typically cost $20 to $25 per youth and still can exclude more than half of a target population. Although federal regulations allow for waivers of parental consent, half of the respondents to a national survey of IRB administrators indicated that they never granted parental waivers (Wagener et al. 2004). The Institute of Medicine released a report in 2004, entitled "The ethical conduct of clinical research involving children," (Field & Behrman 2004) that recommended that IRBs consider waivers of parental permission under three conditions: the research is important to the health and well-being of adolescents, the research cannot be conducted reasonably without a waiver, and the research involves a treatment that an adolescent can consent to receive under state laws. In a survey of researchers conducting studies of tobacco-cessation interventions with adolescents, 62% reported requesting a waiver of parental consent, and 62% of the requests were granted (Diviak et al. 2004). The reasons cited in their waiver applications were consistent with the Institute of Medicine recommendations: teen participation in the study involved minimal risk, it would be difficult to recruit sufficient numbers of teens if parental permission was required, recruiting with active parental consent would result in a less representative sample, and the responses of teens needed to be confidential from parents and school administrators. Parental waivers of consent appear to be possible, but certainly are not easy to obtain or consistently granted across different IRBs.

Even with recruitment of sufficient numbers of participants into their research, investigators are further challenged by high attrition. Of the 13 studies included in the Cochrane Collaborative Review (Grimshaw & Stanton 2006) that reported loss to follow-up information, eight lost at least 33% of their participants by six months. Loss to follow-up rates are no better among the 12 experimental studies published after the Cochrane review; six of nine studies for which follow-up rates could be de-termined lost at least one-third of their participants. The best follow-up rates are reported for studies conducted in health care settings (Brown et al. 2003, Hollis et al. 2005), where investigators presumably can take advantage of the health care organization's patient-tracking efforts. It is both disappointing and surprising that the vast majority of treatment outcome papers describe little about the efforts made to retain their cohorts (or in some cases do not even describe retention rates). Thus, it is difficult to ascertain the extent to which high rates of loss to follow-up are inherent in youth studies or avoidable with effective retention strategies. One of the best examples of cohort retention is described by Peterson and colleagues, who conducted a smoking prevention project that had more than 90% cohort retention during a 15-year follow-up period (Peterson et al. 2000). They had the advantage of enrolling youth in their cohort when they were in the third grade and obtained multiple tracking contacts from the youths' parents. However, they describe approaches that could be adapted as best practices in research with older youth, including collecting addresses of parents or other adults who could be contacted for tracing purposes; using U.S. postal service forwarding and address correction services to find youth and later young adults who have moved; and using publicly available databases and online people search engines.

To summarize, a sufficient number of good quality youth cessation intervention studies now exist to provide evidence-based recommendations based on rigorous meta-analyses. We can say confidently that behavioral interventions increase the chances of youth smokers achieving successful cessation. With regard to intervention components, it appears that motivational enhancement and cognitive-behavioral approaches are efficacious with youth as well as adult smokers. Currently, there is no evidence that nicotine-replacement treatment aids youth cessation. Results from one study of bupropion are mildly encouraging, at least with regard to short-term outcomes. Overall, however, the evidence base for youth cessation treatment is quite modest. Many innovative studies have been compromised by challenges in recruiting sufficient numbers of youth, obtaining approval for waivers of parental consent, and high attrition in longitudinal data collection. As we note below, these challenges provide important insights for future directions in youth cessation interventions.

FUTURE DIRECTIONS

Youth tobacco cessation is a dynamic and growing area for treatment research. We are heartened by the progress in developing and evaluating effective behavioral interventions for youth tobacco cessation and, at the same time, humbled by the need to accelerate this progress. There are clearly many opportunities to move the field forward. We highlight four possible areas for future work: (*a*) bridging the fields of adolescent development and treatment design, (*b*) matching treatments to optimal intervention points based on knowledge gained from identifying developmental trajectories of smoking behavior, (*c*) gaining a greater understanding of effective treatment processes and treatment moderators, and (*d*) building demand for evidence-based cessation treatments.

Bridging Research on Adolescent Development and Cessation Treatment

Interventions for youth tobacco cessation are largely modifications of successful approaches used with adults. Although treatment developers often note that the interventions are "tailored" to adolescents, this tailoring usually reflects modifications to the formatting or surface appeal of intervention elements (e.g., use of age-appropriate graphics, designs, marketing) rather than tailoring to match the cognitive-developmental stage of the youth. A striking disconnect exists between what we know about social and cognitive development and challenges from the adolescent development literature and youth smoking-cessation intervention design. Clearly, there are more op-

portunities here for cross-fertilization between these fields. For example, youth cessation interventions may want to address more directly some of the self-regulation challenges and cognitive skills of adolescence. To date, most interventions have remained highly focused on specific strategies for not smoking, with relatively little attention to some of the key determinants of smoking, such as management of negative affect, impulsivity, or decision-making skills. More intensive consideration of some of these more general self-regulatory skills may be needed for improving cessation rates and preventing relapse. Modifying intervention materials and techniques to better match the developmental stages of youth is also important. Adolescents are also a developmentally heterogeneous group, and better tailoring to age or developmental level may be useful. Older adolescents, particularly those moving toward emerging adulthood (18–21 years of age), may have unique challenges for cessation that arise with their numerous life transitions, and may require even different approaches and vehicles for intervention.

Optimizing Intervention Points Based on Trajectories of Youth Tobacco Use

Thus far, most interventions for adolescents have focused on the ends of the smoking continuum—either prevention of initiation or cessation with youth who are already likely addicted smokers with difficulty quitting. As researchers are better able to identify key subgroups of youth who are most vulnerable to rapidly escalate in their smoking, then researchers can aim to interrupt progression from experimentation to dependence. Some of these interventions may involve more innovative approaches to changing both the social context and meaning of smoking to youth. For example, the use of peer leaders or key influential peers as a way to reach out informally and discourage smoking among adolescents may show some promise (Stanton et al. 2006, Starkey et al. 2005). In addition, as researchers gain a better understanding of the time course for the development of dependence, it may be possible to target interventions better to the window of opportunity between initial trials and nicotine dependence.

Focus on Treatment Processes and Treatment Moderators

Researchers have paid relatively little attention to understanding the mechanisms or processes within youth cessation interventions, an understanding that may help improve the next generation of interventions. What elements result in greater change? For example, although most youth cessation interventions incorporate self-management strategies, we know little about whether adolescents actually use these approaches or whether they are related to outcome. Identifying treatment moderators is also an important next step for the field. Potential moderators include not only youth participant characteristics (e.g., gender, ethnicity, socioeconomic status, educational aspirations, comorbidities), but social context as well (e.g., parental smoking, peer smoking, environmental policy characteristics). Beyond identifying possible moderators, it would also be helpful to know how a moderator works.

Building Demand for Cessation Interventions

Across all ages, use of tobacco-cessation interventions remains low (Cent. Dis. Control Prev. 2006a, Curry et al. 2007b). Recent efforts have focused on applying market research principles and methods to foster demand for treatment. For example, the National Tobacco Cessation Collaborative (2007) outlined several core strategies for increasing the use of evidence-based tobacco-cessation treatments. These strategies highlight the importance of viewing young smokers as consumers and taking a fresh look at quitting from their perspective; of marketing and promoting cessation products and services in ways that reach young smokers where they are; and of systematically measuring, tracking, reporting, and studying quitting and treatment use to identify opportunities and successes. Qualitative studies of youth beliefs and preferences for tobacco-cessation treatment provide some insight into their low rates of interest in treatment, such as erroneous beliefs that nicotine replacement causes cancer, lack of self-identity as a smoker, and the belief that treatments are for older, addicted smokers (Amos et al. 2006, MacDonald et al. 2007, Molyneux et al. 2006, O'Loughlin et al. 2002b). Unfortunately, these studies provide little in the way of concrete suggestions for alternative approaches, as most youth say that the only thing that would help them is willpower. We encourage future research to examine the effectiveness of marketing strategies to promote high-reach channels for smoking-cessation treatment, such as cell phone text messaging, Internet programs, and telephone quitlines.

In many ways, research on youth tobacco cessation is in its own adolescence; the field has moved beyond the first-generation studies and evaluation of initial trials of cessation approaches to a second generation of more rigorously designed randomized controlled trials. It is important that we ensure continued investment in this area because it is one of our best hopes for our children's future.

SUMMARY POINTS

1. Tobacco use and dependence is a chronic, relapsing disease that begins early in life. More than one-fifth of high school seniors in the United States were current smokers in 2007, with more than half of them reporting daily smoking.

2. A variety of liabilities, including both normative neurobiological developmental factors (e.g., immature frontal limbic connections, immature frontal lobe development) and social influences controlled by a combination of interacting biological, psychosocial, and environmental influences, in combination with both normative and nonnormative patterns of emotional dysregulation in adolescence, present challenges for researchers to consider in developing interventions.

3. The majority of youth smokers want to quit and make serious attempts to do so, but most youth attempt to quit without using available treatments.

4. The content of behavioral interventions targeting youth cessation mirrors the content of programs for adults and includes motivational enhancement and cognitive behavioral strategies.

5. The number of good-quality youth cessation intervention studies is sufficient to say confidently that behavioral interventions increase the chances of youth smokers achieving cessation and that motivational enhancement and cognitive behavioral approaches are efficacious with youth.

6. There is no evidence that nicotine-replacement treatment aids youth smoking cessation, and only one study of bupropion has been conducted, with mildly encouraging results.

7. Overall, the evidence base for youth cessation treatment is quite modest, in part because many studies have been compromised by challenges in recruiting sufficient numbers of youth, obtaining approval for waivers of parental consent, and high attrition in longitudinal data collection.

FUTURE ISSUES

1. How can we better connect research on adolescent social and cognitive development research to youth cessation intervention design?

2. How can we harness youth engagement with technology to extend the reach and impact of youth cessation interventions?

3. Is it possible to target youth cessation interventions at transition points in their trajectories of tobacco use initiation, for example by targeting the window of opportunity between initial experimentation and nicotine dependence?

4. What are the effective mechanisms or processes within youth cessation interventions, including treatment moderators, such as sociodemographic characteristics and aspects of the social context, and treatment mediators, such as changes in expectancies, motivation, and skills?

5. Can we effectively apply market research principles and methods to foster greater youth demand for treatment?

DISCLOSURE STATEMENT

The authors are not aware of any biases that might be perceived as affecting the objectivity of this review. Prior to 2006, Dr. Curry consulted on outcomes research and health education for

Pfizer, Inc., and consulted on an international study of smokers for Sanofi-Aventis. In 2006, Dr. Mermelstein consulted on approaches to evaluating smoking cessation outcomes with adolesecents for Pfizer, Inc.

ACKNOWLEDGMENTS

Work on this manuscript was supported by awards P01 CA098262 (SJC, RJM), Robert Wood Johnson Foundation Grant 61337 (SJC, RJM, AKS), and U48-DP-00048 (SJC). We gratefully acknowledge the assistance of Jill Lindsay with literature searching, database management, and manuscript preparation.

LITERATURE CITED

Am. Psychiatr. Assoc. 2000. *Diagnostic and Statistical Manual of Mental Disorders, Fourth Edition (DSM-IV)*. Washington, DC: Am. Psychiatr. Assoc.

Amos A, Wiltshire S, Haw S, McNeill A. 2006. Ambivalence and uncertainty: experiences of and attitudes towards addiction and smoking cessation in the mid-to-late teens. *Health Educ. Res.* 21(2):181–91

Arnett JJ. 1999. Adolescent storm and stress, reconsidered. *Am. Psychol.* 54(5):317–26

Backinger CL, McDonald P, Ossip-Klein DJ, Colby SM, Maule CO, et al. 2003. Improving the future of youth smoking cessation. *Am. J. Health Beh.* 27(Suppl. 2):170–84

Baker TB, Brandon TH, Chassin L. 2004. Motivational influences on cigarette smoking. *Annu. Rev. Psychol.* 55:463–91

Bechara A. 2005. Decision making, impulse control and loss of willpower to resist drugs: a neurocognitive perspective. *Nat. Neurosci.* 8(11):1458–63

Belluzzi J, Lee A, Oliff H, Leslie FM. 2004. Age-dependent effects of nicotine on locomotor activity and conditioned place preference in rats. *Psychopharmacology* 174(3):389–95

Belluzzi J, Wang R, Leslie FM. 2005. Acetaldehyde enhances acquisition of nicotine self-administration in adolescent rats. *Neuropsychopharmacology* 30:705–12

Bloom B, Cohen RA. 2007. Summary health statistics for U.S. children: National Health Interview Survey, 2006. *Vital Health Stat.* 10(234):36–37

Brody AL. 2006. Functional brain imaging of tobacco use and dependence. *J. Psychiatr. Res.* 40(5):404–18

Brown RA, Lewinsohn PM, Seeley JR, Wagner EF. 1996. Cigarette smoking, major depression, and other psychiatric disorders among adolescents. *J. Am. Acad. Child Adolesc. Psychiatry* 35(12):1602–10

Brown RA, Ramsey SE, Strong DR, Myers MG, Kahler CW, et al. 2003. Effects of motivational interviewing on smoking cessation in adolescents with psychiatric disorders. *Tob. Control* 12(Suppl. 4):3–10

Campaign for Tobacco Free Kids. 2008. *Smoking and Kids* (fact sheet). **www.tobaccofreekids.org/ research/factsheets/pdf/0001.pdf**

Cao J, Belluzzi J, Loughlin SE, Keyler DE, Pentel PR, Leslie FM. 2007. Acetaldehyde, a major constituent of tobacco smoke, enhances behavioral, endocrine, and neuronal responses to nicotine in adolescent and adult rats. *Neuropsychopharmacology* 32:2025–35

Carmody TP. 1989. Affect regulation, nicotine addiction, and smoking cessation. *J. Psychoactive Drugs* 21(3):331–42

Casey BJ, Giedd JN, Thomas KM. 2000. Structural and functional brain development and its relation to cognitive development. *Biol. Psychol.* 54(1–3):241–57

Cent. Dis. Control Prev. 1996. Projected Smoking-Related Deaths Among Young—United States. *MMWR Morb. Mortal. Wkly. Rep.* 45(44):971–74

Cent. Dis. Control Prev. 2005. Annual Smoking-Attributable Mortality, Years of Potential Life Lost, and Productivity Losses—United States, 1997–2001. *MMWR Morb. Mortal. Wkly. Rep.* 54(25):625–28

Cent. Dis. Control Prev. 2006a. Use of Cessation Methods among Smokers Aged 16–24 Years—United States, 2003. *MMWR Morb. Mortal. Wkly. Rep.* 55(50):1351–4

Cent. Dis. Control Prev. 2006b. Youth Risk Behavior Surveillance—United States, 2005. *MMWR CDC Surveill. Summ.* 55(SS-5):1–112

Cent. Dis. Control Prev. 2006c. Youth Tobacco Surveillance—United States, 2001–2002. *MMWR CDC Surveill. Summ.* 55(SS-3):1–56

Cent. Dis. Control Prev. 2007. Cigarette Smoking Among Adults—United States, 2006. *MMWR Morb. Mortal. Wkly. Rep.* 56(44):1157–61

Chaloupka F. 1999. Macro-social influences: the effects of prices and tobacco-control policies on the demand for tobacco products. *Nicotine Tob. Res.* 1(Suppl. 1):105–9

Chassin L, Presson CC, Morgan-Lopez A, Sherman SJ. 2007a. "Deviance proneness" and adolescent smoking 1980 versus 2001: Has there been a "hardening" of adolescent smoking? *J. Appl. Dev. Psychol.* 28(3):264–76

Chassin L, Presson CC, Pitts S, Sherman SJ. 2000. The natural history of cigarette smoking from adolescence to adulthood in a midwestern community sample: multiple trajectories and their psychosocial correlates. *Health Psychol.* 19(3):223–31

Chassin L, Presson CC, Rose JS, Sherman SJ. 1996. The natural history of cigarette smoking from adolescence to adulthood: demographic predictors of continuity and change. *Health Psychol.* 15(6):478–84

Chassin L, Presson CC, Rose JS, Sherman SJ. 1998a. Maternal socialization of adolescent smoking: intergenerational transmission of smoking-related beliefs. *Psychol. Addict. Behav.* 12(3):206–16

Chassin L, Presson CC, Rose JS, Sherman SJ. 2007b. What is addiction? Age-related differences in the meaning of addiction. *Drug Alcohol. Depend.* 87(1):30–38

Chassin L, Presson CC, Sherman SJ. 1984. Cigarette smoking and adolescent psychosocial development. *Basic Appl. Soc. Psychol.* 5(4):295–315

Chassin L, Presson CC, Todd M, Rose JS, Sherman SJ. 1998b. Maternal socialization of adolescent smoking: the intergenerational transmission of parenting and smoking. *Dev. Psychol.* 34(6):1189–201

Choi WS, Ahluwalia JS, Nazir N. 2002. Adolescent smoking cessation: implications for relapse-sensitive interventions. *Arch. Pediatr. Adolesc. Med.* 156(6):625–26

Clark DB, Wood DS, Martina CS, Corneliusa JR, Lynch KG, Shiffman S. 2005. Multidimensional assessment of nicotine dependence in adolescents. *Drug Alcohol. Depend.* 77(3):235–42

Colby SM, Tiffany ST, Shiffman S, Niaura R. 2000. Measuring nicotine dependence among youth: a review of available approaches and instruments. *Drug Alcohol. Depend.* 59(Suppl. 1):23–39

Colder CR, Mehta P, Blanada K, Campbell R, Meyhew K, et al. 2001. Identifying trajectories of adolescent smoking: an application of latent growth mixture modeling. *Health Psychol.* 20(2):127–35

Conrad K, Flay BR, Hill D. 1992. Why children start smoking cigarettes: predictors of onset. *Br. J. Addict.* 87(12):1711–24

Cummins S, Zhu SH, Van de Meer R, Campbell S. 2006. *Range of quitline practice in North American and Europe.* Presented at Annu. Meet. World Conf. Tobacco or Health, 13th, Washington, DC

Curry SJ. 2007. eHealth research and healthcare delivery beyond intervention effectiveness (commentary). *Am. J. Prev. Med.* 32(Suppl. 5):127–30

Curry SJ, Byers T, Hewitt M, ed. 2003. *Fulfilling the Potential for Cancer Prevention and Early Detection.* Washington, DC: Nat. Acad. 136 pp.

Curry SJ, Emery S, Sporer AK, Mermelstein R, Flay BR, et al. 2007a. A national survey of tobacco cessation programs for youths. *Am. J. Public Health* 97(1):171–77

Curry SJ, Sporer AK, Pugach O, Campbell RT, Emery S. 2007b. Use of tobacco cessation treatments among young adult smokers: 2005 National Health Interview Survey. *Am. J. Public Health* 97(8):1464–69

Curry SJ, Wetter DW, Grothaus LC, McClure JB, Taplin SH. 2008. Designing and evaluating individual-level interventions for cancer prevention and control. In *Handbook of Behavioral Science and Cancer*, ed. SM Miller, DJ Bowen, RT Croyle, J Rowland, pp. 61–84. Washington, DC: Am. Psychol. Assoc.

Dallery J, Glenn IM, Raiff BR. 2007. An Internet-based abstinence reinforcement treatment for cigarette smoking. *Drug Alcohol Depend.* 86(2–3):230–38

DiFranza J, Savageau JA, Fletcher KE, Ockene JK, Rigotti NA, et al. 2002. Measuring the loss of autonomy over nicotine use in adolescents: the DANDY (Development and Assessment of Nicotine Dependence in Youths) study. *Arch. Pediatr. Adolesc. Med.* 156:397–403

DiFranza J, Wellman RJ, Sargent JD, Weitzman M, Hipple BJ, Winickoff JP. 2006. Tobacco promotion and the initiation of tobacco use: assessing the evidence for causality. *Pediatrics* 117(6):e1237–48

Diviak KR, Curry SJ, Emery SL, Mermelstein RJ. 2004. Human participants challenges in youth tobacco cessation research: researchers' perspectives. *Ethics Behav.* 14(4):321–34

Eissenberg T, Balster RL. 2000. Initial tobacco use episodes in children and adolescents: current knowledge, future directions. *Drug Alcohol. Depend.* 59(Suppl. 1):41–60

Elder JP, Ayala GX, Harris S. 1999. Theories and intervention approaches to health-behavior change in primary care. *Am. J. Prev. Med.* 17(4):321–34

Elliott SP, Edwards CC, Woodruff SI, Conway TL. 2001. On-line teen smoking cessation: What's porn got to do with it? *Tob. Control* 10(4):397

Emery S, White MM, Pierce JP. 2001. Does cigarette price influence adolescent experimentation? *J. Health Econ.* 20(2):261–70

Field MJ, Behrman RE, ed. 2004. *Ethical Conduct of Clinical Research Involving Children.* Washington, DC: The National Academic. 425 pp.

Fiore MC, Bailey W, Cohen S, Dorfman SF, Goldstein MG, et al. 2000. *Treating Tobacco Use and Dependence: Clinical Practice Guideline.* Rockville, MD: US Dept. Health Human Serv., US Public Health Serv.

Flay BR, Collins LM. 2005. Historical review of school-based randomized trials for evaluating problem behavior prevention programs. *Ann. Am. Acad. Polit. Soc. Sci.* 599:115–46

Franken FH, Pickworth WB, Epstein DH, Moolchan ET. 2006. Smoking rates and topography predict adolescent smoking cessation following treatment with nicotine replacement therapy. *Cancer Epidemiol. Biomarkers Prev.* 15(1):154–57

Friend BK, Colby S. 2006. Healthcare providers' use of brief clinical interventions for adolescent smokers. *Drugs: Educ. Prev. Policy* 13(3):263–80

Garrison MM, Christakis DA, Ebel BE, Wiehe SE, Rivara FP. 2003. Smoking cessation interventions for adolescents—a systematic review. *Am. J. Prev. Med.* 25(4):363–67

Gfroerer J, Wright D, Kopstein A. 1997. Prevalence of youth substance use: the impact of methodological differences between two national surveys. *Drug Alcohol Depend.* 47(1):19–30

Glanz K, Rimer BK, Lewis FM, ed. 2002. *Health Behavior and Health Education: Theory, Research, and Practice.* San Francisco, CA: Jossey-Bass. 3rd ed. 558 pp.

Glasgow RE, Klesges LM, Dzewaltowski DA, Estabrooks PA, Vogt TM. 2006. Evaluating the impact of health promotion programs: using the RE-AIM framework to form summary measures for decision making involving complex issues. *Health Educ. Res.* 21(5):688–94

Glenn IM, Dallery J. 2007. Effects of Internet-based voucher reinforcement and a transdermal nicotine patch on cigarette smoking. *J. Appl. Behav. Anal.* 40(1):1–13

Grimshaw GM, Stanton A. 2006. Tobacco cessation interventions for young people. *Cochrane Database Syst. Rev.* No. CD003289

Helstrom A, Hutchison KB. 2007. Motivational enhancement therapy for high-risk adolescent smokers. *Addict. Behav.* 32(10):2404–10

Hilts PJ. 1995. F.D.A. head calls smoking a pediatric disease. *New York Times*, Mar. 9. **http://query.nytimes. com/gst/fullpage.html?res=990CE1D81F3AF93AA35750C0A963958260**

Hollis JF, Polen MR, Whitlock EP, Lichtenstein E, Mullooly JP, et al. 2005. Teen Reach: outcomes from a randomized, controlled trial of a tobacco reduction program for teens seen in primary medical care. *Pediatrics* 115(4):981–89

Horn K, Dino G, Hamilton C, Noerachmanto N. 2007. Efficacy of an emergency department-based motivational teenage smoking intervention. *Prev. Chronic Dis.* 4(1):1–12

Hurt RD, Croghan GA, Beede SD, Wolter TD, Croghan IT, Patten CA. 2000. Nicotine patch therapy in 101 adolescent smokers: efficacy, withdrawal symptom relief, and carbon monoxide and plasma cotinine levels. *Arch. Pediatr. Adolesc. Med.* 154(1):31–37

Jamner LD, Whalen CK, Loughlin SE, Mermelstein R, Audrain-McGovern J, et al. 2003. Tobacco use across the formative years: a road map to developmental vulnerabilities. *Nicotine Tob. Res.* 5(Suppl. 1):71–87

Jason LA, Pokorny SB, Adams M, Hunt Y, Gadiraju P, Schoeny M. 2007. Do fines for violating possession-use-purchase laws reduce youth tobacco use? *J. Drug Educ.* 37(4):393–400

Joffe A, Ash S, Sheng P. 2005. Randomized trial of single versus multi-session group smoking cessation intervention for adolescents. *J. Adolesc. Health.* 36(2):118

Johnston LD, O'Malley PM, Bachman JG, Schulenberg JE. 2007a. *Monitoring the Future: National Survey Results on Drug Use, 1975–2006. Volume I: Secondary School Students.* No. 07–6205, Nat. Inst. Drug Abuse, Bethesda, MD

Kandel DB, Davies M, Karus D, Yamaguchi K. 1986. The consequences in young adulthood of adolescent drug involvement. an overview. *Arch. Gen. Psychiatry* 43(8):746–54

Kassel JD, Stroud LR, Paronis CA. 2003. Smoking, stress, and negative affect: correlation, causation, and context across stages of smoking. *Psychol. Bull.* 129(2):270–304

Khantzian EJ. 1997. The self-medication hypothesis of substance use disorders: a reconsideration and recent applications. *Harv. Rev. Psychiatry* 4(5):231–44

Klein JD, Camenga DR. 2004. Tobacco prevention and cessation in pediatric patients. *Pediatr. Rev.* 25(1):17–26

Kobus K. 2003. Peers and adolescent smoking. *Addiction* 98(1):37–55

Koo M, Skinner H. 2003. Improving Web searches: case study of quit-smoking Web sites for teenagers. *J. Med. Educ. Res.* 5(4):e28

Krishnan-Sarin S, Duhig AM, McKee SA, McMahon TJ, Liss T, et al. 2006. Contingency management for smoking cessation in adolescent smokers. *Exp. Clin. Psychopharmacol.* 14(3):306–10

Lazovich D, Ford J, Forster J, Riley B. 2001. A pilot study to evaluate a tobacco diversion program. *Am. J. Public Health* 91(11):1790–91

Lenhart A, Madden M, Hitlin P. 2005. *Teens and technology.* **www.pewinternet.org/pdfs/PIP_Teens_Tech_July2005web.pdf**

Lerman C, Audrain J, Orleans CT, Boyd R, Gold K, et al. 1996. Investigation of mechanisms linking depressed mood to nicotine dependence. *Addict. Behav.* 21(1):9–19

Leslie FM, Loughlin SE, Wang R, Perez L, Lotfipour S, Belluzzia JD. 2004. Adolescent development of forebrain stimulant responsiveness: insights from animal studies. *Ann. NY Acad. Sci.* 1021:148–59

Lewinsohn PM, Rohde P, Brown RA. 1999. Level of current and past adolescent cigarette smoking as predictors of future substance use disorders in young adulthood. *Addiction* 94(6):913–21

Liang L, Chaloupka FJ. 2002. Differential effects of cigarette price on youth smoking intensity. *Nicotine Tob. Res.* 4(1):109–14

Liang L, Chaloupka FJ, Nichter M, Clayton R. 2003. Prices, policies and youth smoking, May 2001. *Addiction* 98(Suppl. 1):105–22

Lindblom E. 2008. *Toll of Tobacco in the United States* (fact sheet). **www.tobaccofreekids.org/research/factsheets/**

Lipkus IM, McBride CM, Pollak KI, Schwartz-Bloom RD, Tilson E, Bloom PN. 2004. A randomized trial comparing the effects of self-help materials and proactive telephone counseling on teen smoking cessation. *Health Psychol.* 23(4):397–406

MacDonald S, Rothwell H, Moore L. 2007. Getting it right: designing adolescent-centered smoking cessation services. *Addiction* 102(7):1147–50

Macgill AR. 2007. *Parent and Teenager Internet Use.* **www.pewinternet.org/pdfs/PIP_Teen_Parents_data_memo_Oct2007.pdf**

Marshall L, Schooley M, Ryan H, Cox P, Easton A, et al. 2006. Youth Tobacco Surveillance—United States, 2001–2002. *CDC Surveill. Summ.* 55(SS03):1–56

Mayhew KP, Flay BR, Mott JA. 2000. Stages in the development of adolescent smoking. *Drug Alcohol. Depend.* 59(Suppl. 1):61–81

McDonald P, Colwell B, Backinger CL, Husten C, Maule CO. 2003. Better practices for youth tobacco cessation: evidence of review panel. *Am. J. Health Behav.* 27(Suppl. 2):144–58

McMahon RJ. 1999. Child and adolescent psychopathology as risk factors for subsequent tobacco use. *Nicotine Tob. Res.* 1(1–2):S45–50

Mercer SL, DeVinney BJ, Fine LJ, Green LW, Dougherty D. 2007. Study designs for effectiveness and translation research: identifying trade-offs. *Am. J. Prev. Med.* 33(2):139–54

Mermelstein R. 1999. Explanations of ethnic and gender differences in youth smoking: a multi-site, qualitative investigation. *Nicotine Tob. Res.* 1(Suppl. 1):91–98

Mermelstein R. 2003. Teen smoking cessation. *Tob. Control* 12(Suppl. 1):25–34

Mermelstein R, Colby S, Patten C, Prokhorov A, Brown R, et al. 2002. Methodological issues in measuring treatment outcome in adolescent smoking cessation studies. *Nicotine Tob. Res.* 4(4):395–403

Mermelstein R, Hedeker D, Flay B, Shiffman S. 2007. Real-time data capture and adolescent cigarette smoking. In *The Science of Real-Time Data Capture: Self-Reports in Health Research*, ed. A Stone, S Shiffman, A Atienza, pp. 117–35. New York: Oxford Univ. Press

Mermelstein R, Turner L. 2006. Web-based support as an adjunct to group-based smoking cessation for adolescents. *Nicotine Tob. Res.* 8(Suppl. 1):69–76

Miller WR, Rollnick S. 2002. *Motivational Interviewing: Preparing People for Change.* New York: Guilford. 342 pp.

Molyneux A, Lewis S, Coleman T, McNeill T, Godfrey C, et al. 2006. Designing smoking cessation services for school-age smokers: a survey and qualitative study. *Nicotine Tob. Res.* 8(4):539–46

Monitoring the Future. 2007. *Trends in cigarette smoking and smokeless tobacco.* Tables 1, 8. Univ. Mich. News Serv.: Ann Arbor. **www.monitoringthefuture.org**

Muramoto ML, Leischow SJ, Sherrill D, Matthews E, Strayer LJ. 2007. Randomized, double-blind, placebo-controlled trial of 2 dosages of sustained-release bupropion for adolescent smoking cessation. *Arch. Pediatr. Adolesc. Med.* 161(11):1068–74

National Tobacco Cessation Collaborative. 2007. *Innovations in Building Consumer Demand for Tobacco-Cessation Products and Services: 6 Core Strategies for Increasing the Use of Evidence-Based Tobacco Cessation Treatment.* Washington, DC: Nat. Tob. Cessation Collab.

Nelson DE, Giovino GA, Shopland DR, Mowery PD, Mills SL, Eriksen MP. 1995. Trends in cigarette smoking among U.S. adolescents, 1974 through 1991. *Am. J. Public Health* 85(1):34–40

Nichter M, Nichter M, Thompson PJ, Shiffman S, Moscicki AB. 2002. Using qualitative research to inform survey development on nicotine dependence among adolescents. *Drug Alcohol. Depend.* 68(Suppl. 1):41–56

Novak SP, Clayton RR. 2001. The influence of school environment and self-regulation on transitions between stages of cigarette smoking: a multilevel analysis. *Health Psychol.* 20(3):196–207

O'Loughlin J, DiFranza J, Tarasuk J, Meshefedjian G, McMillan-Davey E, et al. 2002a. Assessment of nicotine dependence symptoms in adolescents: a comparison of five indicators. *Tob. Control* 11:354–60

O'Loughlin J, DiFranza J, Tyndale RF, Meshefedjian G, McMillan-Davey E, et al. 2003. Nicotine-dependence symptoms are associated with smoking frequency in adolescents. *Am. J. Prev. Med.* 25(3):219–25

O'Loughlin J, Kishchuk N, DiFranza J, Tremblay M, Paradis G. 2002b. The hardest thing is the habit: a qualitative investigation of adolescent smokers' experience of nicotine dependence. *Nicotine Tob. Res.* 4(2):201–9

Patten CA, Croghan IT, Meis TM, Decker PA, Pingree S, et al. 2007. Randomized clinical trial of an Internet-based versus brief office intervention for adolescent smoking cessation. *Patient Educ. Couns.* 64(1–3):249–58

Pbert L, Moolchan ET, Muramoto M, Winickoff JP, Curry S, et al. 2003. The state of office-based interventions for youth tobacco use. *Pediatrics* 111(6):e650–60

Pbert L, Osganian SK, Gorak D, Druker S, Reed G, et al. 2006. A school nurse-delivered adolescent smoking cessation intervention: a randomized controlled trial. *Prev. Med.* 43(4):312–20

Peterson AV, Mann SL, Kealey KA, Marek PM. 2000. Experimental design and methods for school-based randomized trials—experience from the Hutchinson Smoking Prevention Project (HSPP). *Control. Clin. Trials* 21(2):144–65

Pierce JP. 2007. Tobacco industry marketing, population-based tobacco control, and smoking behavior. *Am. J. Prev. Med.* 33(Suppl. 6):327–34

Pomerleau OF, Pomerleau CS. 1984. Neuroregulators and the reinforcement of smoking: towards a biobehavioral explanation. *Neurosci. Biobehav. Rev.* 8(4):503–13

Pontieri FE, Tanda G, Orzi F, Di Chiara G. 1996. Effects of nicotine on the nucleus accumbens and similarity to those of addictive drugs. *Nature* 382:255–57

Prochaska JO, DiClemente CC, Norcross J. 1992. In search of how people change. *Am. Psychol.* 47:1102–14

Prokhorov AV, Hudmon KS, Cinciripini PM, Marani S. 2005. "Withdrawal symptoms" in adolescents: a comparison of former smokers and never-smokers. *Nicotine Tob. Res.* 7(6):909–13

Prokhorov AV, Hudmon KS, Stancic N. 2003. Adolescent smoking: epidemiology and approaches for achieving cessation. *Pediatr. Drugs* 5(1):1–10

Prokhorov AV, Koehly LM, Pallonen UE, Hudmon KS. 1998. Adolescent nicotine dependence measured by the Modified Fagerstrom Tolerance Questionnaire at two time points. *J. Child Adolesc. Subst. Abuse* 7:35–47

Prokhorov AV, Pallonen UE, Fava JL, Ding L, Niaura R. 1996. Measuring nicotine dependence among high-risk adolescent smokers. *Addict. Behav.* 21(1):117–27

Rodgers A, Corbett T, Bramley D, Riddell T, Wills M, et al. 2005. Do u smoke after txt? Results of a randomised trial of smoking cessation using mobile phone text messaging. *Tob. Control* 14(4):255–61

Roll J. 2005. Assessing the feasibility of using contingency management to modify cigarette smoking by adolescents. *J. Appl. Behav. Anal.* 38(4):463–67

Sargent JD, Mott LA, Stevens M. 1998. Predictors of smoking cessation in adolescents. *Arch. Pediatr. Adolesc. Med.* 152(4):388–93

Semer N, Ellison J, Mansellm C, Hoika L, MacDougall W, et al. 2005. Development and evaluation of a tobacco cessation motivational program for adolescents based on physical attractiveness and oral health. *Int. J. Dent. Hyg.* 79(4):1–17

Shadel WG, Shiffman S, Niaura R, Nichter M, Abrams DB. 2000. Current models of nicotine dependence: what is known and what is needed to advance understanding of tobacco etiology among youth. *Drug Alcohol. Depend.* 59(Suppl. 1):9–22

Shiffman S, Waters A, Hickcox M. 2004. The nicotine dependence syndrome scale: a multidimensional measure of nicotine dependence. *Nicotine Tob. Res.* 6(2):327–48

Spear LP. 2000. The adolescent brain and age-related behavioral manifestations. *Neurosci. Biobehav. Rev.* 24(4):417–63

Stanton W, Baade P, Moffatt J. 2006. Predictors of smoking cessation processes among secondary school students. *Subst. Use Misuse* 41(13):1683–94

Stanton W, Flay B, Colder C, Mehta P. 2004. Identifying and predicting adolescent smokers' developmental trajectories. *Nicotine Tob. Res.* 6(5):843–52

Starkey F, Moore L, Campbell R, Sidaway M, Bloor M, ASSIST. 2005. Rationale, design and conduct of a comprehensive evaluation of a school-based peer-led antismoking intervention in the UK: the ASSIST cluster randomised trial. *BMC Public Health* 7:301

Steinberg L. 2004. Risk taking in adolescence: What changes, and why? *Ann. NY Acad. Sci.* 1021:51–58

Steinberg L. 2007. Risk taking in adolescence: new perspectives from brain and behavioral science. *Curr. Dir. Psychol. Sci.* 16(2):55–59

Steinberg L, Morris AS. 2001. Adolescent development. *Annu. Rev. Psychol.* 52:83–110

Stoddard AM, Fagan P, Sorensen G, Hunt M, Frazier L, Girod K. 2005. Reducing cigarette smoking among working adolescents: results from the SMART study. *Cancer Causes Control* 16(10):1159–64

Stotts RC, Roberson PK, Hanna EY, Jones SK, Smith CK. 2003. A randomised clinical trial of nicotine patches for treatment of spit tobacco addiction among adolescents. *Tob. Control* 12(Suppl. 4):11–15

Substance Abuse and Mental Health Services Admin. 2007. *Results From the 2006 National Survey on Drug Use and Health: National Findings.* No. SMA 07–4293, Off. Appl. Stud., NSDUH Series H-32, Rockville, MD

Sullivan PF, Kendler KS. 1999. The genetic epidemiology of smoking. *Nicotine Tob. Res.* 1(Suppl. 2):51–57

Sun P, Miyano J, Rohrbach LA, Dent CW, Sussman S. 2007. Short-term effects of Project EX-4: a classroom-based smoking prevention and cessation intervention program. *Addict. Behav.* 32(2):342–50

Sussman S. 2002. Effects of sixty-six adolescent tobacco use cessation trials and seventeen prospective studies of self-initiated quitting. *Tob. Induced Dis.* 1(1):35–81

Sussman S, Dent CW, Severson H, Burton D, Flay BR. 1998. Self-initiated quitting among adolescent smokers. *Prev. Med.* 27(5, Pt. 3):A19–28

Sussman S, Ping S, Dent C. 2006. A meta-analysis of teen cigarette smoking cessation. *Health Psychol.* 25(5):549–57

Tedeschi GJ, Zhu SH, Anderson CM, Cummins S, Ribner NG. 2005. Putting it on the line: telephone counseling for adolescent smokers. *J. Couns. Dev.* 83(4):416–24

Tercyak KP, Goldman P, Smith A, Audrain J. 2002. Interacting effects of depression and tobacco advertising receptivity on adolescent smoking. *J. Pediatr. Psychol.* 27(2):145–54

Thompson EL. 1978. Smoking education programs 1960–1976. *Am. J. Public Health* 68(3):250–57

Tigges BB. 2003. Parental consent and adolescent risk behavior research. *J. Nurs. Scholarsh.* 35(3):283–89

Tucker JS, Ellickson PL, Klein DJ. 2002. Smoking cessation during the transition from adolescence to young adulthood. *Nicotine Tob. Res.* 4(3):321–32

Turner L, Mermelstein R, Flay B. 2004. Individual and contextual influences on adolescent smoking. *Ann. NY Acad. Sci.* 1021:175–97

U.S. Dep. Education NCES. 2003. *Overview of Public Elementary and Secondary Schools and Districts: School Year 2001–02*. Rep. NCES 2003–411, by Lee McGraw Hoffman, U.S. Dep. Educ., Nat. Cent. Educ. Stat., Washington, DC

U.S. Dep. Health Hum. Serv. (USDHHS). 1994. *Preventing Tobacco Use Among Young People. A Report of the Surgeon General (Executive Summary)*. U.S. Dep. Health Human Serv., Cent. Disease Control Prev., Nat. Cent. Chronic Disease Prev. Health Promotion, Off. Smoking Health, 1997, Atlanta, GA

Wagener DK, Sporer AK, Simmerling M, Flome JL, An LC, Curry SJ. 2004. Human participants challenges in youth-focused research: perspectives and practices of IRB administrators. *Ethics Behav.* 14(4):335–49

Walsh MM, Hilton JF, Ellison JA, Gee L, Chesney MA, et al. 2003. Spit (smokeless) tobacco intervention for high school athletes: results after 1 year. *Addict. Behav.* 28(6):1095–113

Whalen CK, Jamner LD, Henker B, Gehricke JG, King PS. 2003. Is there a link between adolescent cigarette smoking and pharmacotherapy for ADHD? *Psychol. Addict. Behav.* 17(4):332–35

Wills TA, Cleary S. 1995. *Stress coping model for alcohol-tobacco interactions in adolescence*. Alcohol and Tobacco From Basic Science to Clinical Practice, No. 95–3931, Nat. Inst. Alcohol Abuse Alcoholism, Bethesda, MD

Wills TA, Walker C, Mendoza D, Ainette MG. 2006. Behavioral and emotional self-control: relations to substance use in samples of middle and high school students. *Psychol. Addict. Behav.* 20(3):265–78

Windle M, Windle RC. 2001. Depressive symptoms and cigarette smoking among middle adolescents: prospective associations and intrapersonal and interpersonal influences. *J. Consult. Clin. Psychol.* 69(2):215–26

Woodruff SI. 2001. Pilot test of an Internet virtual world chat room for rural teen smokers. *J. Adolesc. Health* 29:239–43

Woodruff SI, Conway TL, Edwards CC, Elliott SP, Crittenden J. 2007. Evaluation of an Internet virtual world chat room for adolescent smoking cessation. *Addict. Behav.* 32(9):1769–86

Zhu SH, Sun J, Billings SC, Choi WS, Malarcher A. 1999. Predictors of smoking cessation in U.S. adolescents. *Am. J. Prev. Med.* 16(3):202–7

Neuropsychological Assessment of Dementia*

David P. Salmon[1] and Mark W. Bondi[2,3]

[1]Department of Neurosciences, [2]Department of Psychiatry, University of California, San Diego, California 92093; [3]Veterans Affairs San Diego Healthcare System, San Diego, California 92161; email: dsalmon@ucsd.edu

Annu. Rev. Psychol. 2009. 60:257–82

First published online as a Review in Advance on July 9, 2008

The *Annual Review of Psychology* is online at psych.annualreviews.org

This article's doi: 10.1146/annurev.psych.57.102904.190024

Key Words

cognition, memory, Alzheimer's disease

Abstract

Neuropsychological studies show that cognitive deficits associated with Alzheimer's disease (AD) are distinct from age-associated cognitive decline. Quantitative and qualitative differences are apparent across many cognitive domains, but are especially obvious in episodic memory (particularly delayed recall), semantic knowledge, and some aspects of executive functions. The qualitatively distinct pattern of deficits is less salient in very old AD patients than in younger AD patients. Although decline in episodic memory is usually the earliest cognitive change that occurs prior to the development of the AD dementia syndrome, asymmetry in cognitive abilities may also occur in this "preclinical" phase of the disease and predict imminent dementia. Discrete patterns of cognitive deficits occur in AD and several neuropathologically distinct age-associated neurodegenerative disorders. Knowledge of these differences helps to clinically distinguish among various causes of dementia and provides useful models for understanding brain-behavior relationships that mediate cognitive abilities affected in various neurodegenerative diseases.

Contents

INTRODUCTION

The detection and characterization of cognitive deficits associated with age-related neurodegenerative diseases such as Alzheimer's disease (AD) is the focus of growing clinical research interest as increasing numbers of people survive into older age. This interest is fueled by the need to accurately detect the onset of cognitive changes that signal the beginning of a progressive dementia syndrome and to differentiate among disorders with distinct etiologies and sites of pathology. This can be a particularly difficult task given the insidious onset and slow progression of most neurodegenerative diseases, but it is critically important given the lack of a reliable biological marker

Dementia: syndrome of acquired intellectual impairment of sufficient severity to interfere with social or occupational functioning caused by brain dysfunction

that can distinguish AD from normal aging or other neurodegenerative disorders that lead to dementia. Accurate clinical diagnosis of dementia and its underlying cause is crucial for prognosis and the early and appropriate application of disease-specific treatments that are currently available or in development.

Neuropsychological research on dementia has focused on AD because it is the most common cause of dementia and is primarily defined by its impact on cognition. This research has led to increased knowledge about the particular cognitive deficits that occur in the earliest stages of AD, and this has enhanced the ability to clinically diagnosis the disease early in its course. The impact of aging on the ability to detect AD has been described, and subtle cognitive changes that might foreshadow the development of dementia in those with "preclinical" AD have been identified. The cognitive manifestations of AD have been compared and contrasted to those of other age-related neurodegenerative disorders in order to improve differential diagnosis and provide information about the neurological basis of various cognitive abilities that are affected. The contributions of this research to the neuropsychological assessment of dementia are reviewed below.

NEUROPSYCHOLOGICAL DETECTION OF ALZHEIMER'S DISEASE

Alzheimer's disease is an age-related degenerative brain disorder characterized by neuronal atrophy, synapse loss, and the abnormal accumulation of amyloidogenic plaques and neurofibrillary tangles in medial temporal lobe limbic structures (e.g., entorhinal cortex, hippocampus) and the association cortices of the frontal, temporal, and parietal lobes (Braak & Braak 1991). Consistent with these widespread neuropathological changes, the primary clinical manifestation of AD is a progressive global dementia syndrome that usually begins in later life (i.e., ages 60–70). In the usual case, the dementia syndrome is characterized by prominent amnesia with additional deficits in language and semantic knowledge, abstract reasoning, executive functions, attention, and visuospatial abilities (Salmon & Bondi 1999). These cognitive deficits and the decline in everyday function they produce are the core features of the AD dementia syndrome and are the focus of clinical assessment of the disease.

Although the pattern of progression of AD pathology is not fully known, evidence suggests that the earliest changes occur in medial temporal lobe structures (e.g., hippocampus, entorhinal cortex) that are critical for episodic memory (Braak & Braak 1991). This is consistent with a wealth of neuropsychological evidence showing that episodic memory impairment (i.e., amnesia) is usually the earliest and most salient aspect of the AD dementia syndrome (for review, see Salmon 2000). Studies of the clinical utility of episodic memory measures for the early detection of AD have identified a number of characteristics that are quite effective in differentiating between mildly demented AD patients and normal older adults. First, patients with very early AD are particularly impaired on measures of delayed recall (i.e., have abnormally rapid forgetting), with several studies showing that absolute delayed recall scores or "savings" scores (i.e., amount recalled after the delay divided by the amount recalled on the immediate learning trial) can differentiate mildly demented AD patients from healthy elderly controls with approximately 85% to 90% accuracy (for review, see Salmon 2000). Second, to-be-remembered information is not accessible after a delay even if retrieval demands are reduced by the use of recognition testing (e.g., Delis et al. 1991). Third, AD patients exhibit an abnormal serial position effect characterized by an attenuation of the primacy effect (i.e., recall of words from the beginning of a list), suggesting that they cannot effectively transfer information from primary memory to secondary memory (e.g., Bayley et al. 2000). Fourth, semantic encoding is less effective in improving the episodic memory performance of patients with AD than normal elderly individuals (for review, see Bäckman & Small 1998). Fifth, patients with AD have an enhanced tendency to produce intrusion errors (i.e., when previously learned information is produced during the attempt to recall new material) on both verbal and nonverbal memory tests, presumably due to increased sensitivity to interference and/or decreased inhibitory processes (Butters et al. 1987, Jacobs et al. 1990). Evaluation of these characteristics of the memory deficit associated with AD is incorporated into several memory tests that are effective for early detection of the disease (e.g., Buschke 1973, Buschke et al. 1997, Knopman & Ryberg 1989) and in clinical algorithms developed to differentiate AD from other types of dementia (e.g., Delis et al. 1991).

As the neuropathology of AD spreads beyond medial temporal lobe structures to the association cortices of the temporal, frontal, and parietal lobes (Braak & Braak 1991), a number of higher-order cognitive abilities are affected. Patients with AD develop a semantic memory deficit that manifests itself as a loss of general knowledge and impairment of language abilities (i.e., aphasia). Patients with AD are often impaired on tests of confrontation naming, verbal fluency, and semantic categorization, and have a reduced ability to recall overlearned facts (e.g., the number of days in a year) (for reviews, see Chan et al. 1998, Hodges & Patterson 1995, Nebes 1989). Interestingly, patients are highly consistent in the individual items they miss across different semantic memory tests that employ unique modes of access and output (e.g., fluency versus confrontation naming; Chertkow & Bub 1990, Hodges et al. 1992) or within the same test across unique evaluations (Norton et al. 1997). This suggests that AD results in a true loss of semantic knowledge rather than only an impaired ability to retrieve information from intact semantic memory stores (also see Salmon et al. 1999). A similar loss of knowledge is thought to contribute to the severe deficit that patients with AD exhibit in the ability to remember past events that were successfully remembered prior to the onset of the disease (i.e., retrograde amnesia) (for review, see Salmon 2000).

Deficits in executive functions responsible for concurrent mental manipulation of

Executive functions: higher-order cognitive processes involved in planning, concept formation, problem solving, cue-directed behavior, and the concurrent manipulation and retention of information

Episodic memory: memory for autobiographical events and episodes that depend upon temporal and/or spatial contextual cues for their retrieval

Semantic memory: general fund of knowledge that consists of overlearned facts and concepts that are not dependent upon contextual cues for retrieval (e.g., meanings of words and well-known geographical, historical, and arithmetical facts)

information, concept formation, problem solving, and cue-directed behavior occur early in the course of AD (Perry & Hodges 1999). The ability to perform concurrent manipulation of information appears to be particularly vulnerable. Lefleche & Albert (1995) demonstrated that very mildly demented patients with AD were significantly impaired relative to elderly normal control subjects on tests that required set shifting, self-monitoring, or sequencing, but not on tests that required cue-directed attention or verbal problem solving. Patients with AD have also been shown to be impaired on (*a*) difficult problem-solving tests such as the Tower of London puzzle (Lange et al. 1995) and the modified Wisconsin Card Sorting Task (Bondi et al. 1993), (*b*) tests of relational integration (Waltz et al. 2004), and (*c*) various other clinical neuropsychological tests that assess executive functions such as the Porteus Maze Task, Part B of the Trail-Making Test, and the Raven Progressive Matrices Task (e.g., Grady et al. 1988).

Deficits in attention and visuospatial abilities develop during the course of AD, but are usually less salient than other cognitive deficits in the early stages of disease (Butters et al. 1988, Storandt et al. 1984). When attention deficits do occur, they are usually evident on dual-processing tasks, tasks that require the disengagement and shifting of attention, and working memory tasks that are dependent upon the control of attentional resources (for reviews, see Parasuraman & Haxby 1993, Perry & Hodges 1999). Visuospatial deficits associated with AD usually affect visuoconstructional abilities assessed by the Block Design Test, the Clock Drawing Test, and complex figure copying (i.e., apraxia), and visuoperceptual abilities tapped by tests such as Judgment of Line Orientation or the Money Road Map Test (for reviews, see Cronin-Golomb & Amick 2001, Freedman et al. 1994).

The neuropsychological research reviewed above suggests that in the usual case, AD is associated with a specific pattern of cognitive deficits that can effectively differentiate the disease from normal aging. This was confirmed in a study by Salmon and colleagues (2002) that compared the performances of 98 patients with early AD (i.e., scored ≥24 on the Mini-Mental State Exam) and 98 gender-, age-, and education-matched normal control subjects on sensitive measures of learning and memory, executive abilities, language, and visuospatial abilities. The diagnosis of AD was verified in each of the AD patients by subsequent autopsy or longitudinal clinical evaluations that showed a typical course for the disease. Receiver Operating Characteristic curve analyses showed excellent sensitivity and specificity for the detection of very mild AD for learning and delayed recall measures from the California Verbal Learning Test (sensitivity: 95%–98%, specificity: 88%–89%), the category fluency test (sensitivity: 96%, specificity: 88%), and Part B of the Trail-Making Test (sensitivity: 85%, specificity: 83%) (see **Figure 1**). A diagnostic model obtained using a nonparametric recursive partitioning procedure (classification tree analysis) showed that a combination of performance on the category fluency test (a measure of semantic memory and executive function) and the delayed recall measure of the Visual Reproduction Test accurately classified 96% of the patients with AD and 93% of the elderly normal control subjects, a level of accuracy higher than achieved with any individual cognitive measure. These results support the view that deficits in episodic memory (e.g., rapid forgetting), certain executive functions (e.g., cognitive set shifting), and semantic knowledge are particularly characteristic of early AD.

The Impact of Aging on the Neuropsychological Detection of Alzheimer's Disease

Although much progress has been made in identifying the typical pattern of cognitive deficits associated with early AD, the boundaries between normal age-related cognitive change and early signs of AD remain especially difficult to delineate in very elderly individuals (i.e., over the age of 80). This is because many of the early structural and functional brain

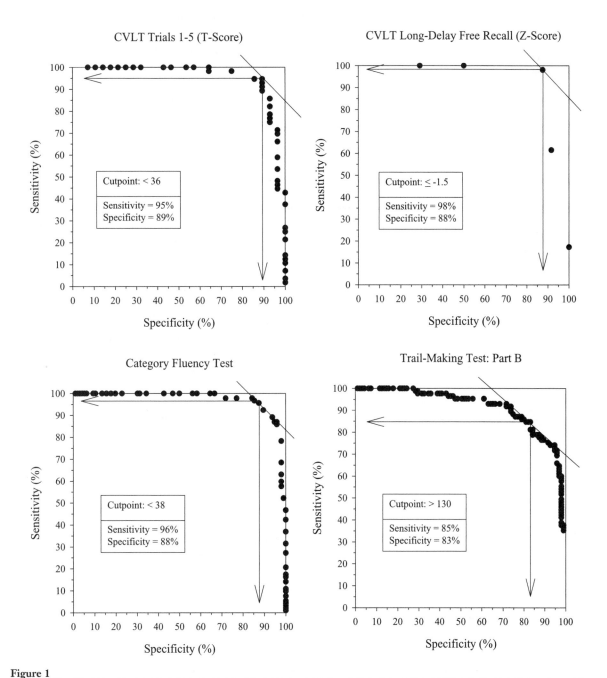

Figure 1

Receiver Operating Characteristic curves comparing sensitivity and specificity for the accurate diagnosis of early Alzheimer's disease (AD) achieved with the Trial 1–5 Learning measure from the California Verbal Learning Test (CVLT), the Long-Delay Free Recall measure from the CVLT, the Category Fluency Test (a semantic memory and executive function measure), and Part B of the Trail-Making Test (an executive function measure). The maximally effective cut-point for memory and executive function measures showed excellent sensitivity and specificity in distinguishing between very mild AD and normal aging. (Adapted from Salmon et al. 2002.)

MRI: magnetic resonance imaging

changes of AD overlap with changes observed in normal aging. Normal aging is associated with mild brain atrophy and increased white matter abnormality seen on magnetic resonance imaging (MRI) scans (e.g., Jack et al. 1998, Jernigan et al. 2001, Pfefferbaum et al. 1994), decreased hemodynamic response seen on functional MRI scans (D'Esposito et al. 1999), and reduced synaptic density evident upon histopathological examination of brain tissue (Masliah et al. 1993). These brain changes are thought to mediate age-related decline in information processing speed, executive function, learning efficiency, and effortful retrieval (for review, see Hedden & Gabrieli 2004). Because normal aging can detrimentally affect many of the same cognitive abilities affected by AD, the prominence of specific deficits related to AD may be much less evident in the Very-Old (over the age of 80) than in the Young-Old (below the age of 70), especially after performance is standardized to that of the age-appropriate normal cohort. As a result, a less distinct and somewhat atypical cognitive deficit profile is associated with AD in the Very-Old compared to the Young-Old.

This difference in profiles was illustrated in a study that directly compared the neuropsychological test performance of AD patients who were Very-Old or Young-Old (Bondi et al. 2003). Despite achieving similar raw scores on all neuropsychological measures, the Young-Old and Very-Old AD patients differed in the severity and pattern of the cognitive deficits they exhibited in relation to their age-appropriate controls (see **Figure 2**). The Young-Old AD patients were generally more impaired than the Very-Old patients and showed a typical AD profile. That is, they exhibited worse deficits in episodic memory (i.e., savings scores) and executive functions than in other cognitive domains. The Very-Old AD patients, in contrast, exhibited a similar level of impairment across all cognitive domains so that their deficit profile lacked the disproportionate saliency of memory and executive function deficits typical of the disease. Because the raw scores of the Young-Old and Very-Old AD patients were similar, the driving force behind their unique deficit profiles was the age-related differences in the performance of the normal control cohorts. Thus, normal aging can

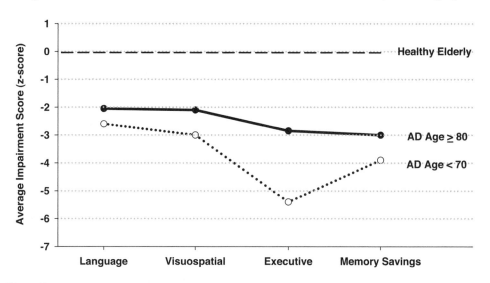

Figure 2

The average composite impairment score achieved by Alzheimer's disease (AD) patients older than age 80 or younger than age 70 in the cognitive domains of language, visuospatial abilities, executive functions, and memory (savings scores). The presented scores are z-scores referenced to the patient groups' respective age-appropriate healthy elderly control cohort. (Adapted from Bondi et al. 2003.)

significantly affect the severity and pattern of neuropsychological deficits associated with early AD and reduce the saliency of the deficit profile as a diagnostic marker of the disease. This finding has important clinical implications because it identifies the significant risk of false negative diagnostic errors in very elderly AD patients if the clinician expects to see the typical deficit pattern characteristic of younger AD patients. Accurate detection of AD in the very elderly patient may require a multifaceted approach to diagnosis that integrates neuropsychological assessment, neuroimaging, and genetic factors.

Neuropsychological Detection of "Preclinical" Alzheimer's Disease

It is commonly accepted that the neurodegenerative changes of AD begin well before clinical manifestations of the disease become apparent (e.g., Katzman 1994). As the pathologic changes of AD gradually accumulate, a threshold for the initiation of the clinical symptoms of the disease is eventually reached. Once this threshold is crossed, cognitive deficits become evident and gradually worsen in parallel with continued neurodegeneration. When the cognitive deficits become global and severe enough to interfere with normal social and occupational functioning, established criteria for dementia and a clinical diagnosis of AD are met. It is clear from this sequence of events that subtle cognitive decline is likely to occur in a patient with AD well before the clinical diagnosis can be made with any certainty. Identification of the cognitive changes that occur during this "preclinical" phase of the disease might provide a reliable way to detect AD in its earliest stages, when potential disease-modifying treatments might be most effective (Thal 1999). Because of the importance of this goal, the attempt to identify preclinical cognitive changes of AD is one of the most active areas of neuropsychological research.

In light of neuropathological evidence that the earliest changes of AD usually occur in the medial temporal lobe structures that are known

to be critical for episodic memory (Braak & Braak 1991), it is not surprising that the search for preclinical cognitive markers of the disease has focused largely on this aspect of cognition. Indeed, a number of prospective longitudinal studies of cognitive function in nondemented older adults have shown that a subtle decline in episodic memory often occurs prior to the emergence of the obvious cognitive and behavioral changes required for a clinical diagnosis of AD (for review, see Twamley et al. 2006). These findings led to the development of formal criteria for mild cognitive impairment (MCI), a predementia condition in elderly individuals that is characterized by both subjective and objective memory impairment that occurs in the face of relatively preserved general cognition and functional abilities (for reviews, see Albert & Blacker 2006, Collie & Maruff 2000, Petersen et al. 2001).

The course of episodic memory change during the preclinical phase of AD has been the focus of a number of studies (Bäckman et al. 2001, Chen et al. 2001, Rubin et al. 1998, Small et al. 2000, Storandt et al. 2002). These studies suggest that memory performance may be poor but stable a number of years prior to the development of the dementia syndrome in those with AD, and then decline rapidly in the period immediately preceding the dementia diagnosis. Small et al. (2000) and Bäckman et al. (2001), for example, found that episodic memory was mildly impaired six years prior to dementia onset, but changed little over the next three years. In contrast, Chen et al. (2001) and Lange et al. (2002) showed a significant and steady decline in episodic memory beginning about three years prior to the dementia diagnosis in individuals with preclinical AD. These results indicate that an abrupt decline in memory in an elderly individual might better predict the imminent onset of dementia than poor but stable memory ability.

Although the search for cognitive changes in preclinical AD has largely focused on episodic memory, several recent reviews and meta-analyses suggest that largely nonspecific cognitive decline occurs in the two to three years preceding a dementia diagnosis (Bäckman et al. 2004, 2005; Twamley et al. 2006). Although these studies consistently find a decline in episodic memory, they also often reveal additional deficits in executive functions, perceptual speed, verbal ability, visuospatial skill, and attention during the preclinical phase of AD. This widespread decline in cognitive abilities mirrors evidence that multiple brain regions (e.g., medial temporal lobes, frontal lobes, anterior cingulate cortex) are impaired in preclinical AD (Albert et al. 2001, Small et al. 2003).

Consistent with this broader view, Jacobson and colleagues (2002) found that asymmetry in cognitive performance can be a marker of preclinical AD. Based upon prior research documenting lateralized cognitive deficits (e.g., greater verbal than visuospatial deficits, or vice versa) in subgroups of mildly demented AD patients, these investigators compared cognitively normal elderly adults with preclinical AD (i.e., they were diagnosed with AD approximately one year later) and age- and education-matched normal control subjects on a derived neuropsychological test measure that reflected the absolute difference between verbal and visuospatial ability (i.e., a measure of cognitive asymmetry). Although the groups performed similarly on individual cognitive tests of memory, language, and visuospatial ability, a greater proportion of the preclinical AD patients than the controls had asymmetric cognitive changes in either the verbal or visuospatial direction that were obscured when cognitive scores are averaged over the entire group. Thus, the consideration of both cognitive asymmetry and subtle declines in memory may improve the ability to detect AD in its earliest, preclinical stages.

ALZHEIMER'S DISEASE AS A DISCONNECTION SYNDROME

A growing body of evidence indicates that an important early consequence of AD is the loss of effective interaction between various regions of the cortex (e.g., De Lacoste & White 1993). From an anatomical perspective, neurofibrillary tangles have been shown to have a strong predilection for cortical layers (e.g., layer-III and layer-V) and cell types (e.g., midsize pyramidal neurons) that support connections between functionally related cortical association areas. This is most clearly seen in the limbic system, where neurofibrillary tangle pathology in midsize pyramidal neurons of the entorhinal cortex disconnects the hippocampus from neocortex (e.g., Hyman et al. 1984). Although less obvious, this disconnection also occurs in the neocortex, where AD pathology in layer-III and layer-V pyramidal neurons selectively disrupts corticocortical pathways that connect functionally related cortical association areas (for review of the corticocortical disconnection, see Hof & Morrison 1999).

Neurophysiologically, cortical disconnection appears to lead to marked abnormalities in the interregional pattern of blood-flow activation elicited during the performance of cognitive tasks (for review, see Delbeuck et al. 2003). It also appears to underlie reduced coherence (i.e., synchronization) between electroencephalography signals measured at different scalp surface electrode sites that correspond to neocortical association areas that must work in concert during integrative cognitive tasks (e.g., cross-modal stimulus processing) (e.g., Dunkin et al. 1995, Hogan et al. 2003, Jelic et al. 1996, Knott et al. 2000, Stevens et al. 2001). Evoked potential refractory effects related to presentation of intermodal stimuli (i.e., auditory and visual) are also abnormally reduced in patients with AD, consistent with impaired interaction between visual and auditory cortical systems (Golob et al. 2001).

Few studies have directly examined the behavioral consequences of functional disconnectivity in patients with AD, but those that have tend to find a selective impairment in information integration (Della Sala et al. 2000, Freedman & Oscar-Berman 1997, Kurylo et al. 1996, Lakmache et al. 1998, Tippett et al. 2003). This was illustrated in a study by Foster and colleagues (1999) that examined the impact of AD on "feature binding" (Treisman 1996), the moment-by-moment ability to combine discrete sensory inputs analyzed in distinct cortical regions (e.g., color, shape, location) into a coherent representation of a single object. Feature binding was hypothesized to be particularly sensitive to cortical disconnection in AD because defective interaction among neocortical areas should produce a specific deficit in effectively integrating distinct stimulus features despite an intact ability to process each feature separately. Consistent with this notion, Foster and colleagues (1999) found that patients with AD exhibited disproportionately greater response times (compared to normal controls) when required to identify targets on the basis of a conjunction of two or more features (i.e., a conjunction search) than when required to identify targets solely on the basis of a single feature (i.e., a feature search). Tales et al. (2002) recently extended this finding by demonstrating that the selective impairment of patients with AD on conjunction search tasks could not be attributed to different attentional demands inherent in conjunction versus single-feature tasks.

Building upon these previous findings, Festa and colleagues (2005) examined the impact of corticocortical disconnectivity in AD on the ability to integrate motion and color information that is processed in distinct visual processing "streams." These streams are functionally segregated parallel cortical circuits that analyze different aspects of the visual scene (e.g., Ungerleider & Mishkin 1982). The dorsal stream projecting from striate cortex to parietal cortex selectively analyzes motion and luminance contrast information, while the ventral stream projecting from striate cortex to temporal cortex selectively analyzes form and color information. Previous research has shown that neurologically intact individuals can integrate (i.e., bind) either type of surface feature (color or luminance) with motion information in order to substantially reduce thresholds for motion detection (e.g., Croner & Albright 1997). Color or luminance information is equally effective in this regard even though enhancement of motion detection from color cues places relatively greater demand on cross-cortical interaction since it requires the integration of information across ventral (motion) and dorsal

(color) cortical streams (Dobkins & Albright 1998). Enhancement of motion detection from luminance cues only requires the integration of information within the ventral stream.

Festa and colleagues (2005) showed that AD patients had normal enhancement of motion detection with luminance cues, but enhancement was significantly less than normal with color cues (see **Figure 3**). That is, patients could effectively bind information processed within one visual stream, but could not crosscortically bind information processed in separate cortical streams. This deficit could not be easily attributed to general cognitive dysfunction because both luminance-motion and colormotion integration were normal in demented patients with Huntington's disease who do not have prominent cortical dysfunction. Rather, these results provide psychophysical evidence for cortical disconnectivity in AD and suggest that AD might serve as a model system for investigating the neurocognitive substrates of sensory integration. The specificity of cortical

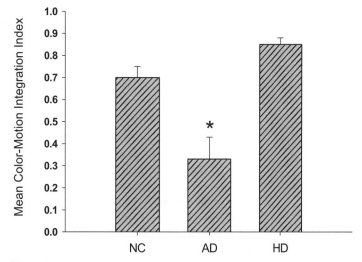

Figure 3

The mean color-motion integration index scores achieved by normal control (NC) subjects, Alzheimer's disease (AD) patients, and Huntington's disease (HD) patients on a visual sensory integration task. The color-motion integration index reflects the gain in motion direction detection derived from using color information that segments coherently moving targets from distracters. Patients with AD, but not those with HD, were significantly (*) impaired in integrating motion and color information. (Adapted from Festa et al. 2005.)

HD: Huntington's
disease

DLB: dementia with
Lewy bodies

FTD: frontotemporal
dementia

disconnectivity in AD suggests that it may have potential as a cognitive marker for detecting and tracking progression of the disease.

DISTINGUISHING ALZHEIMER'S DISEASE FROM OTHER AGE-RELATED CAUSES OF DEMENTIA

Although AD is the leading cause of dementia in the elderly, it has been known for some time that dementia can arise from a wide variety of etiologically and neuropathologically distinct disorders that give rise to different patterns of relatively spared and impaired cognitive abilities. Knowledge of these differences may lead to better understanding of the neurobiological basis of specific cognitive deficits (and normal cognition) and improve differential diagnosis of various neurodegenerative disorders. The remaining sections review similarities and differences in the cognitive deficits of AD and those of other age-related causes of dementia including Huntington's disease (HD), dementia with Lewy bodies (DLB), frontotemporal dementia (FTD), and vascular dementia.

Alzheimer's Disease versus Huntington's Disease

HD is an inherited, autosomal dominant disease that results in the midlife (i.e., ages 30–40) development of movement disorder (e.g., chorea, dysarthria, gait disturbance, oculomotor dysfunction), behavioral changes (e.g., depression, irritability, anxiety) and dementia. These deficits arise primarily from a progressive deterioration of the neostriatum (caudate nucleus and putamen) (Vonsattel & Di Figlia 1998) that disrupts frontostriatal loops that consist of projections from the frontal neocortex to the striatum, striatum to the globus pallidus, globus pallidus to thalamus, and thalamus back to specific regions of frontal cortex (e.g., dorsolateral prefrontal, orbitofrontal, and anterior cingulate cortex) (Alexander et al. 1986). These circuits are believed to provide a subcortical influence on both motor control

and higher cognitive functions (Alexander et al. 1986). The cognitive and behavioral deficits associated with HD have been described as a "subcortical dementia" syndrome that is broadly characterized by slowness of thought, impaired attention, executive dysfunction, poor learning, visuoperceptual and constructional deficits, and personality changes such as apathy and depression (McHugh & Folstein 1975). This syndrome differs from the "cortical dementia" syndrome of AD (described above), and the two disorders are often used as a model to study the cortical-subcortical dementia distinction.

Qualitative differences between AD and HD exist in many aspects of cognition, and they may aid in differentiating between subcortical and cortical dementia syndromes. As mentioned above, a severe deficit in episodic memory is characteristic of AD and has been attributed to ineffective consolidation (i.e., storage) of new information (Salmon 2000). Patients with HD, in contrast, exhibit a mild-to-moderate memory impairment that appears to result from a general deficit in the ability to initiate and carry out systematic retrieval of successfully stored information (Butters et al. 1985, 1986). This distinction was illustrated in a study by Delis and colleagues (1991) that directly compared AD and HD patients on a rigorous test of verbal learning and memory, the California Verbal Learning Test. Although the HD and AD patients had comparable immediate and delayed free-recall deficits (based on age-corrected normative data), they differed in several important ways. First, patients with AD exhibited equivalent deficits when memory was assessed using free recall or recognition procedures, whereas patients with HD were less impaired with recognition testing than free recall testing. The significant improvement with recognition testing suggests that HD patients' memory impairment is attenuated when the need for effortful, strategic retrieval is reduced (Butters et al. 1985, 1986). A similar improvement with recognition testing is observed in the remote memory test performance of patients with HD (but not AD patients), presumably a reflection of ineffective retrieval during free recall (Sadek et al. 2004). Second, patients with AD exhibited significantly faster forgetting over a delay interval than did patients with HD. Whereas HD patients retained approximately 70% of the initially acquired information over a 20-minute delay, AD patients retained less than 20%. The qualitative difference in the performances of AD and HD patients is consistent with the notion that information is not effectively consolidated and rapidly dissipates in patients with AD, whereas information can be successfully stored but not effectively retrieved by patients with HD. This is not to say, however, that impaired retrieval is the only cause of the episodic memory deficit in HD. Some residual memory deficit is apparent even when retrieval demands are reduced (Brandt et al. 1992; for review, see Montoya et al. 2006).

Qualitative differences in the language and semantic knowledge deficits exhibited by patients with AD and HD are evident on tests of naming, verbal fluency, and semantic categorization. Patients with AD exhibit a significant confrontation naming deficit (e.g., Bayles & Tomoeda 1983) that is not shared by patients with HD (Hodges et al. 1991), and the two groups produce distinct patterns of naming errors wherein a greater proportion of AD errors are semantically based (e.g., superordinate errors such as calling a "camel" an "animal") and a greater proportion of HD errors are perceptually based (e.g., calling a "pretzel" a "snake") (Hodges et al. 1991). On tests of verbal fluency, patients with HD are severely and equivalently impaired on both letter-fluency (i.e., generate words that begin with the letters F, A, or S) and category-fluency (i.e., generate exemplars of animals, fruits, or vegetables) tasks, whereas patients with AD are more impaired on category-fluency than on letter-fluency tasks (for reviews, see Henry et al. 2004, 2005). In addition, the temporal dynamics of retrieval from semantic memory during the letter- and category-fluency tasks indicate that patients with AD have a lower-than-normal mean latency consistent with the notion that they effectively draw exemplars from a semantic set that is abnormally small due to a loss of semantic knowledge,

whereas patients with HD have a higher-than-normal mean response latency, consistent with the view that they have a normal-size semantic set but draw exemplars abnormally slowly due to a disruption of retrieval processes (Rohrer et al. 1999). Studies using multidimensional modeling techniques indicate that the network of semantic associations for patients with HD is virtually identical to that of control subjects, whereas that of patients with AD is characterized by weaker and more conceptually concrete associations (for review, see Chan et al. 1998). Thus, AD appears to be characterized by a decline in the structure and organization of semantic knowledge that does not occur in HD.

Deficits in attention, working memory, and executive functions occur in both AD and HD, but specific aspects of these cognitive processes are differentially affected in the two disorders. A general deficit in attention is usually more salient in patients with HD than in those with AD (e.g., Butters et al. 1988). A deficit in shifting or allocating attention is often quite apparent in HD (Hanes et al. 1995, Lange et al. 1995, Lawrence et al. 1996) and appears to be particularly evident when attentional shifts must be internally regulated (Sprengelmeyer et al. 1995). The ability to effectively shift attention between stimulus dimensions in a visual discrimination task in which first one stimulus dimension (e.g., color) and then another (e.g., shape) was reinforced as correct was impaired in moderately to severely demented patients with HD, but not in patients with AD or in mildly demented patients with HD (Lange et al. 1995, Lawrence et al. 1996). All aspects of working memory are affected relatively early in HD, including the maintenance of information in the temporary memory buffers (e.g., as evidenced by poor digit-span performance), inhibition of irrelevant information, and the use of strategic aspects of memory (e.g., planning, organization) to enhance free recall (for review, see Salmon et al. 2001). In contrast, AD is initially characterized by relatively mild working-memory deficits that primarily involve disruption of the central executive with sparing of the phonological loop and visuospatial scratchpad

(Baddeley et al. 1991, Collette et al. 1999). It is not until later stages of AD that all aspects of the working memory system become compromised (Baddeley et al. 1991, Collette et al. 1999).

The prominent deficits in attention and working memory that occur in HD are accompanied by impairment of various executive functions involved in planning and problem solving such as goal-directed behavior, the ability to generate multiple response alternatives, the capacity to resist distraction and maintain response set, and the cognitive flexibility to evaluate and modify behavior (for review, see Brandt & Bylsma 1993). Deficits in these abilities are apparent on a variety of tests that require executive functions such as the Wisconsin Card Sorting Test (Paulsen et al. 1995, Peinemann et al. 2005, Pillon et al. 1991, Ward et al. 2006), the Stroop Test (Peinemann et al. 2005, Ward et al. 2006), the Tower of London Test (Lange et al. 1995), the Gambling Decision Making task (Stout et al. 2001), and tests of verbal concept formation (Hanes et al. 1995). These deficits progress throughout the course of disease (Ho et al. 2003, Ward et al. 2006) but are not unique to HD. A number of studies have shown that extensive executive dysfunction also occurs in AD (for review, see Perry & Hodges 1999). Specific aspects of executive dysfunction may be more common in one dementia syndrome than in another, but few studies have directly compared this aspect of cognition in the two disorders.

Although visuospatial deficits are characteristic of both AD (for review, see Cronin-Golomb & Amick 2001) and HD (Ward et al. 2006; for review, see Brandt & Butters 1986), relatively little is known about the specific components of visuospatial processing that might be differentially affected in the two disorders. In one of the few studies to directly address this issue, Brouwers and colleagues (1984) found that patients with AD, but not those with HD, were impaired on tests of visuoconstructional ability that required extrapersonal orientation (e.g., copying a complex figure), whereas patients with HD, but not those with AD, were impaired on visuospatial tasks that required personal orientation (e.g., the Money Road Map Test). This dissociation was supported by the results of another study that examined the ability to mentally rotate representations of objects (Lineweaver et al. 2005). Patients with HD were significantly slower than normal control subjects in performing mental rotation (perhaps due to general bradyphrenia) but were as accurate as controls in making the rotation and reporting the correct side of the target. Patients with AD, in contrast, performed the mental rotation as quickly as controls but were significantly impaired in making an accurate rotation and reporting the correct side of the target. This may reflect a deficit in extrapersonal visual orientation in AD secondary to neocortical damage in brain regions thought to be involved in processing visual motion (e.g., the middle temporal gyrus).

Alzheimer's Disease versus Dementia with Lewy Bodies

DLB is a clinico-pathologic condition characterized by a dementia syndrome that occurs in the presence of cell loss and the deposition of Lewy bodies (abnormal intracytoplasmic eosinophilic neuronal inclusion bodies) in a subcortical pattern similar to that of Parkinson's disease (e.g., in brain stem nuclei including the substantia nigra, locus ceruleus, dorsal motor nucleus of the vagus, and substantia innominata), the presence of Lewy bodies diffusely distributed throughout the limbic system (e.g., cingulate, insula, amygdala, hippocampus, entorhinal cortex, and transentorhinal cortex) and neocortex (e.g., temporal, parietal, and frontal lobes), and in many cases AD pathology (i.e., neuritic plaques, neurofibrillary tangles) that occurs in the same general distribution throughout the brain as in "pure" AD (for review, see Ince & Perry 2005). There is widespread depletion of cortical choline acetyltransferase in the neocortex and striatum in DLB (e.g., Tiraboschi et al. 2002) and a disruption of dopaminergic input to the striatum due to the loss of pigmented substantia nigra neurons (Ince & Perry 2005). DLB is not rare and may occur in approximately 20% of all elderly demented patients (McKeith et al. 1996).

The distribution of neuropathologic changes in DLB and AD is quite similar, so it is not surprising that the two disorders result in similar dementia syndromes. Both disorders are initially characterized by the insidious onset of cognitive decline with no other prominent neurological abnormalities (Hansen et al. 1990, McKeith et al. 1996). Memory impairment is often the earliest feature of both disorders, but with time, cognitive deficits become widespread and inexorably progress to severe dementia. Because of these similarities, patients with DLB are often clinically diagnosed as having probable or possible AD during life (e.g., Merdes et al. 2003). However, several clinical features occur with a higher prevalence in patients with DLB than in those with pure AD. These features include mild spontaneous motor features of Parkinsonism (e.g., bradykinesia, rigidity, and masked facies, but without a resting tremor), recurrent and well-formed visual hallucinations, and fluctuating cognition with pronounced variations in attention or alertness (for review, see McKeith et al. 2005). These clinical distinctions form the basis for consensus criteria adopted by the International Consortium on DLB to clinically diagnose DLB and distinguish it from AD (McKeith et al. 1996, 2005).

Given the difficulty in clinically differentiating DLB from AD, a number of studies of autopsy-confirmed or clinically diagnosed patients have attempted to delineate the two disorders further based on patterns of neuropsychological deficits. These studies have consistently shown that the most salient neuropsychological difference between the two disorders is a disproportionately severe visuospatial and visuoconstructive deficit in patients with DLB. This has been shown using tests of visual perception (e.g., segregation of overlapping figures), tests of visual search (e.g., parallel search tasks that usually elicit the pop-out phenomenon), and tests that require drawing simple and complex two-dimensional figures or the construction of three-dimensional objects (for review, see Salmon & Hamilton 2006). These particularly severe deficits in visuospatial and visuoperceptual abilities are often apparent even when DLB patients perform better than do AD patients on tests of verbal memory (e.g., Lambon Ralph et al. 2001).

The prominence of visuoperceptual, visuospatial, and visuoconstructional deficits in patients with DLB may be related to occipital cortex dysfunction that does not usually occur in patients with AD. Studies using positron emission tomography (PET) or single-photon emission computerized tomography (SPECT) neuroimaging have shown that relatively early DLB is characterized by hypometabolism and decreased blood flow in primary visual and visual-association cortex that is not evident in AD (e.g., Minoshima et al. 2001). These metabolic changes are paralleled by pathologic changes in occipital cortex of patients with DLB that include white matter spongiform change with coexisting gliosis (Higuchi et al. 2000) and, in some cases, deposition of Lewy bodies (e.g., Gomez-Tortosa et al. 1999). Because occipital cortex pathology is rare in pure AD, it is not surprising that the visuoperceptual and visuospatial abilities that may be dependent upon these cortices are disproportionately impaired in patients with DLB.

Patients with DLB often also have disproportionately severe deficits in executive functions and attention in comparison to equally demented patients with pure AD. This difference is evident on tests of attention such as the Wechsler Adult Intelligence Scale-Revised Digit Span subtest or the Cancellation Test, tests of initiation and systematic retrieval from semantic memory such as the Initiation/Perseveration subscale of the Mattis Dementia Rating Scale or the phonemic verbal fluency test, and tests of abstract reasoning such as the Raven Colored Progressive Matrices or the Wechsler Adult Intelligence Scale-Revised Similarities subtest (for review, see Salmon & Hamilton 2006). A series of studies using a computer-based testing paradigm (i.e., the Cambridge Neuropsychological Test Automated Battery)

PET: positron emission tomography

demonstrated that patients with DLB were more impaired than patients with AD on a conditional pattern-location paired-associates learning task (Galloway et al. 1992), a delayed matching-to-sample task (Sahgal et al. 1992a), a visual search task that assessed the ability to fo-

cus attention (Sahgal et al. 1992b), and a spatial working-memory task that assessed both spatial memory and the ability to use an efficient search strategy (Sahgal et al. 1995). These prominent attention and executive function deficits are similar to those that occur in patients with basal ganglia dysfunction that interrupts fronto-striatal circuits (e.g., HD). These circuits may be affected in two ways in patients with DLB: by direct neocortical Lewy body pathology in the association areas of the frontal lobes and by substantia nigra pathology that interrupts dopaminergic projections to the striatum. When superimposed upon the AD pathology that is also often present in the frontal cortex of patients with DLB, these pathological changes may result in disproportionately severe deficits in executive function and attention.

In contrast to DLB patients' disproportionately severe deficits in visuospatial abilities, executive functions, and attention, their memory deficit is generally less severe than that of AD patients and may reflect a qualitative difference in the processes affected. This was illustrated in a study that directly compared the performances of patients with autopsy-confirmed DLB (all with concomitant AD pathology) or pure AD on the California Verbal Learning Test and the Wechsler Memory Scale-Revised Logical Memory Test (Hamilton et al. 2004). Although the two groups were equally impaired in their ability to learn new verbal information on these tests, DLB patients exhibited better retention and better recognition memory than did patients with pure AD. These results suggest that a deficit in retrieval plays a greater role in the memory impairment of patients with DLB than in that of patients with AD. Although the pattern of deficits does not rule out the possibility that poor encoding contributes to memory impairment in both disorders, it appears that DLB patients have better retention than do patients with AD when retrieval demands are reduced through the use of the recognition format (see **Figure 4**). The observed differences are consistent with neuropathologic (Lippa et al. 1998) and MRI (Barber et al. 2001, Hashimoto et al. 1998) evidence that medial

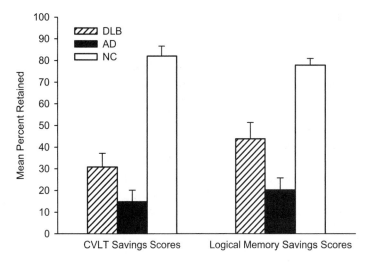

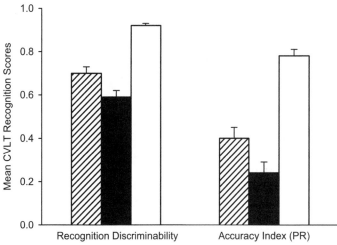

Figure 4

The average scores achieved by normal control (NC) subjects, patients with Alzheimer's disease (AD), and patients with dementia with Lewy bodies (DLB) on various learning and memory measures from the California Verbal Learning Test (CVLT) and the Wechsler Adult Intelligence Scale-Revised Logical Memory Test. Despite similar levels of global cognitive impairment, the DLB patients were less impaired than the AD patients on measures of retention (memory savings score) and recognition memory (recognition discriminability and recognition accuracy index). PR, percent retained. (Adapted from Hamilton et al. 2004.)

temporal lobe structures important for memory (e.g., hippocampus, entorhinal cortex, parahippocampal gyrus) are less severely affected in DLB than in AD. A combination of only moderate medial temporal lobe damage and frontostriatal dysfunction might explain the less severe retention deficit and greater impact of deficient retrieval processes in DLB than in AD.

The general pattern of greater visuospatial, attention, and executive function impairment in DLB than AD, and greater memory impairment in AD than DLB, has been confirmed in a number of recent studies that compared clinically diagnosed or autopsy-diagnosed patient groups on batteries of neuropsychological tests (Ferman et al. 2006, Guidi et al. 2006, Johnson et al. 2005, Kraybill et al. 2005, Stavitsky et al. 2006). Consideration of these patterns of deficits (particularly those of visuospatial abilities) may have important clinical utility in distinguishing between AD and DLB in mildly demented patients (Tiraboschi et al. 2006).

Alzheimer's Disease versus Frontotemporal Dementia

Frontotemporal dementia (FTD) is a clinicopathologic condition characterized by deterioration of personality and cognition associated with prominent frontal and temporal lobar atrophy. A number of conditions fall under the rubric of FTD including Pick's disease, familial chromosome 17-linked frontal lobe dementia, dementia lacking distinctive histopathology, semantic dementia, and primary progressive aphasia (for review, see Kertesz 2006). Although each of these variants has a unique clinical presentation, the most common variant of FTD typically begins with the insidious onset of personality and behavioral changes (e.g., inappropriate social conduct, apathy, disinhibition, perseverative behavior, loss of insight, hyperorality, decreased speech output) that are accompanied or soon followed by cognitive deficits that include alterations in executive functions, attention, and/or language, often with relative sparing of visuospatial abilities and memory (for reviews, see Boxer

& Miller 2006, Grossman 2002, Neary 2005). FTD accounts for approximately 6%–12% of all cases of dementia (Kertesz 2006).

Recent attempts to differentiate FTD and AD based on the nature and severity of behavioral symptoms have met with some success (see Kertesz 2006). However, the disorders are clinically similar and remain difficult to distinguish during life (Mendez et al. 1993, Varma et al. 1999). This has led some investigators to propose that consideration of the patterns of cognitive deficits associated with FTD and AD might aid in clinically distinguishing between the two disorders. A number of studies suggest that patients with FTD are more impaired than those with AD on tests of verbal fluency (Frisoni et al. 1995, Lindau et al. 1998, Mathuranath et al. 2000) or less impaired on tests of memory (Binetti et al. 2000, Frisoni et al. 1995, Lindau et al. 1998, Pachana et al. 1996, Thomas-Anterion et al. 2000) and visuospatial abilities (Elfgren et al. 1994, Mendez et al. 1996). Unfortunately, these findings are often based on relatively small, clinically defined (not autopsy-confirmed) patient samples that are susceptible to cross-contamination, and on studies that compared FTD and AD patients who were at different stages of illness. In addition, the ability to detect differences was attenuated by the choice of neuropsychological test in some studies, such as those that may have failed to find a significant difference in the visuospatial-constructional abilities of FTD and AD patients because they used a Rey-Osterrieth Complex Figure task that is known to require attention and organizational abilities dependent on the frontal lobes (Frisoni et al. 1995, Lindau et al. 1998, Pachana et al. 1996, Varma et al. 1999).

Several studies that examined profiles of cognitive deficits associated with FTD and AD suggest that FTD patients have a greater deficit in executive functions than in other cognitive abilities, whereas AD patients have executive dysfunction that is proportional to their deficits in language and visuospatial abilities and less prominent than their episodic memory deficit (Forstl et al. 1996, Rascovsky et al.

2002, Starkstein et al. 1994). In a study that retrospectively compared the cognitive profiles of patients with autopsy-confirmed FTD or AD who were matched for education and level of dementia at the time of testing, Rascovsky and colleagues (2002) found that FTD patients performed significantly worse than AD patients on word-generation tasks that are sensitive to frontal lobe dysfunction (i.e., letter and category fluency tests), but significantly better on tests of memory (i.e., Mattis Dementia Rating Scale Memory subscale) and visuospatial abilities (i.e., Block Design and Clock Drawing tests) that are sensitive to dysfunction of medial temporal and parietal association cortices. A logistic regression model using letter fluency, memory subscale, and Block Design test scores provided good discriminability between the groups, correctly classifying 91% of AD patients and 77% of FTD patients. Similar levels of diagnostic accuracy were observed in studies comparing clinically diagnosed patients on executive function, visuospatial, and memory tests (Elfgren et al. 1994, Gregory et al. 1997, Libon et al. 2007, Lipton et al. 2005).

In a related study, Rascovsky and colleagues (2007) compared the performances of autopsy-confirmed FTD and AD patients on letter and semantic category fluency tests to determine if distinct patterns of deficits might be evident on these relatively simple tasks. Although both verbal fluency tasks utilize frontal lobe–mediated executive processes, distinct patterns were hypothesized because semantic category fluency requires a search through semantic or conceptual memory and is critically dependent upon knowledge of the physical and/or functional attributes that define a particular semantic category, whereas letter fluency requires the use of phonemic cues to guide retrieval and may thus require greater effort and more active strategic search than semantic category fluency. Results showed that despite similar age, education, and dementia severity, FTD patients performed worse than AD did patients overall, and letter fluency was worse than semantic fluency for the FTD patients, whereas semantic fluency was worse than letter fluency for the AD patients (see **Figure 5**). A derived measure of the disparity between letter and semantic fluency (the Semantic Index) correctly classified 92% of AD patients and 85% of FTD patients for an overall correct classification of nearly 90%. The unique patterns of fluency deficits in FTD and AD may be indicative of differences in the relative contribution of frontal lobe–mediated retrieval deficits (most prominent in FTD) and temporal lobe–mediated semantic deficits (most prominent in AD) in the two disorders.

Alzheimer's Disease versus Vascular Dementia

Vascular dementia (VaD) refers to a cumulative decline in cognitive functioning secondary to multiple or strategically placed infarctions, ischemic injury, or hemorrhagic lesions. The clinical and neuropathologic presentation of VaD is quite heterogeneous, and a variety of conditions fall under the general rubric of VaD. As Hodges & Graham (2001) pointed out, these conditions generally fall into three large categories: multi-infarct dementia associated with

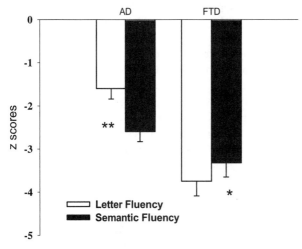

Figure 5

Mean z-scores achieved by patients with Alzheimer's disease (AD) and patients with frontotemporal dementia (FTD; excluding semantic dementia) on the letter fluency and semantic category fluency tests. FTD patients were more impaired on the letter fluency than semantic fluency task, whereas AD patients were more impaired on the semantic fluency than letter fluency task. *$p < 0.05$, **$p < 0.01$. (Adapted from Rascovsky et al. 2007.)

multiple large cortical infarctions (usually affecting 10cc or more of brain tissue), dementia due to strategically placed infarction (e.g., left angular gyrus damage related to infarction of the posterior branch of the medial cerebral artery), and subcortical ischemic vascular dementia due to subcortical small vessel disease that results in multiple lacunar strokes, leukoaraiosis (Binswanger's disease), or diffuse white matter pathology.

Specific research criteria for the broadly defined diagnosis of VaD have been proposed (e.g., Chui et al. 1992, Roman et al. 1993). In general, these guidelines require that multiple cognitive deficits (i.e., dementia) occur in the presence of focal neurological signs and symptoms and/or laboratory (e.g., computerized tomography or MRI scan) evidence of cerebrovascular disease that is thought to be etiologically related to the cognitive impairment. A relationship between dementia and cerebrovascular disease is often indicated if the onset of dementia occurs within several months of a recognized stroke, cognitive functioning abruptly deteriorates, or the course of cognitive deterioration is fluctuating or stepwise. In one set of diagnostic criteria (Roman et al. 1993), VaD can be subcategorized on the basis of the suspected type of vascular pathology (as determined by clinical, radiologic, and neuropathologic features), and possible or probable VaD may be assigned depending on the certainty of the contribution of cerebrovascular disease to the dementia syndrome. Definite VaD is diagnosed only on the basis of histopathologic evidence of cerebrovascular disease that occurs in the absence of neurofibrillary tangles and neuritic plaques exceeding those expected for age (i.e., AD) and without clinical evidence of any other disorder capable of producing dementia (e.g., Pick's disease, diffuse Lewy body disease).

Recent studies of the neuropsychological deficits associated with VaD have primarily focused on differentiating between subcortical VaD and AD. These studies largely show that patients with subcortical VaD are more impaired than those with AD on tests of executive functions, whereas patients with AD are more impaired than those with subcortical VaD on tests of episodic memory (particularly delayed recall) (Desmond 2004, Graham et al. 2004, Kertesz & Clydesdale 1994, Lafosse et al. 1997, Lamar et al. 1997). In addition, these studies suggest that the executive dysfunction associated with subcortical VaD is its most prominent deficit, perhaps because subcortical pathology interrupts frontosubcortical circuits that mediate this aspect of cognition. Indeed, a study by Price and colleagues (2005) showed that VaD patients with a significant volume of white matter abnormality on imaging exhibited a profile of greater executive/visuoconstructional impairment than impairment of memory and language abilities.

Although neuropsychological studies provide consistent evidence for distinct cognitive profiles in subcortical VaD and AD, most of these studies employed clinically diagnosed patients without autopsy confirmation of diagnosis. This may have led to some degree of misclassification of patients across groups because AD and VaD are quite heterogeneous and can overlap in their clinical presentations. To avoid this potential confound, Reed and colleagues (2007) recently compared the profiles of neuropsychological deficits exhibited by patients with autopsy-confirmed subcortical VaD or AD. Consistent with previous studies of clinically diagnosed patients, patients with AD had a deficit in episodic memory (both verbal and nonverbal) that was significantly greater than their executive function deficit. In contrast, patients with subcortical VaD had a deficit in executive functions that was greater than their deficit in verbal (but not nonverbal) episodic memory, but this difference was not significant. An analysis of individual patient profiles was carried out to explore these differences further. This analysis showed that 71% of AD patients exhibited a profile with memory impairment more prominent than executive dysfunction, whereas only 45% of patients with subcortical VaD exhibited a profile with more prominent executive dysfunction than memory impairment. Interestingly, relatively severe cerebrovascular disease at autopsy was often not associated with clinically significant cognitive decline. When the profile analysis was restricted to those patients who exhibited significant cognitive impairment at their clinical assessment, the distinction between subcortical VaD and AD patients was more pronounced, with 79% of AD patients exhibiting a low memory profile (5% with a low executive profile) and 67% of subcortical VaD patients exhibiting a low executive profile (0% with a low memory profile). The results of this study suggest that relatively distinct cognitive deficit profiles might be clinically useful in differentiating between subcortical VaD and AD, but additional research with autopsy-diagnosed patients is needed to further define the deficit profile that will be most useful in this regard.

CONCLUSIONS

Considerable progress has been made in differentiating between the cognitive changes that occur as a normal consequence of aging and those that signal the onset of a dementia syndrome caused by AD or another neurodegenerative disease. Clinical and experimental neuropsychological research has identified many of the basic cognitive processes that are adversely affected by AD and is beginning to uncover the earliest preclinical cognitive changes that might predict the subsequent development of dementia and AD in nondemented individuals. Neuropsychological research has also made considerable progress in delineating different patterns of relatively preserved and impaired cognitive abilities that distinguish between AD and other age-associated neurodegenerative disorders. Greater understanding of the cognitive distinctions between these disorders can aid in the development of better differential diagnosis and has important implications for the nature of brain-behavior relationships underlying memory, language, executive functions, and other cognitive abilities.

SUMMARY POINTS

1. Cognitive deficits associated with AD can be differentiated from age-associated cognitive decline by quantitative and qualitative differences in episodic memory, semantic knowledge, and some aspects of executive functions. However, the qualitatively distinct pattern of deficits is less salient in very old AD patients than in younger AD patients.

2. Decline in episodic memory (particularly delayed recall) is usually the earliest cognitive change that occurs prior to the development of the AD dementia syndrome and may predict imminent dementia. Recent evidence suggests that asymmetry in cognitive abilities may also occur in this preclinical phase of AD.

3. The cortical neuropathology of AD appears to result in a loss of functional connectivity that allows effective interaction between distinct and relatively intact cortical information-processing systems. This loss has been demonstrated in AD patients' impaired ability to bind distinct visual stimulus features that are effectively processed in different cortical streams (i.e., motion and color). This behavioral manifestation of cortical disconnectivity has potential as a cognitive marker for detecting and tracking progression of AD.

4. Distinct patterns of cognitive deficits occur in AD and other age-associated neurodegenerative disorders such as Huntington's disease, dementia with Lewy bodies, frontotemporal dementia, and vascular dementia. Differences in the cognitive profiles associated with these various disorders can aid in differential diagnosis and provide a useful model for understanding brain-behavior relationships that mediate the affected cognitive abilities.

FUTURE ISSUES

1. The early diagnosis of AD in a preclinical stage that might be most amenable to treatments that halt or slow disease progression remains an extremely important goal. It is essential to recognize and verify the accuracy of subtle cognitive abnormalities (e.g., poor delayed recall performance, cognitive asymmetry) that might identify those nondemented elderly individuals who are destined to develop dementia.

2. The role of cortical disconnectivity in producing the specific pattern of cognitive deficits that occurs in early AD needs to be determined. Furthermore, the identification of cognitive processes that are particularly vulnerable to the effects of cortical disconnectivity in early AD might provide a cognitive marker that could be used to assess the effects of medications that specifically target cortical function (e.g., the N-methyl-D-aspartate receptor antagonist memantine).

3. It remains difficult to estimate rate of cognitive decline in AD and other age-related neurodegenerative diseases, but emerging evidence suggests that certain aspects of current cognitive performance can predict subsequent rate of global cognitive decline in patients with AD (e.g., Chan et al. 1995). Further research is needed to confirm this possibility and to generalize it to other neurodegenerative disorders such as DLB and FTD.

4. There is a continuing need to identify differences in the profiles of cognitive deficits associated with AD and other age-related neurodegenerative diseases (e.g., DLB, FTD) and to determine how these profiles can be incorporated with other clinical features to improve the accuracy of differential diagnosis in very mildly demented individuals. Accurate early diagnosis is a particularly important goal since the various neurodegenerative disorders are likely to respond differently to the potential treatments for dementia that are in development.

DISCLOSURE STATEMENT

The authors are not aware of any biases that might be perceived as affecting the objectivity of this review.

ACKNOWLEDGMENTS

The preparation of this review was supported by funds from NIA grants AG-05131, AG-12963, and AG-12674 to the University of California, San Diego.

LITERATURE CITED

Albert MS, Blacker D. 2006. Mild cognitive impairment and dementia. *Annu. Rev. Clin. Psychol.* 2:379–88

Albert MS, Moss MB, Tanzi R, Jones K. 2001. Preclinical prediction of AD using neuropsychological tests. *J. Int. Neuropsychol. Soc.* 7:631–39

Alexander GE, DeLong MR, Strick PL. 1986. Parallel organization of functionally segregated circuits linking basal ganglia and cortex. *Annu. Rev. Neurosci.* 9:357–81

Bäckman L, Jones S, Berger AK, Laukka EJ, Small BJ. 2004. Multiple cognitive deficits during the transition to Alzheimer's disease. *J. Intern. Med.* 256:195–204

Bäckman L, Jones S, Berger AK, Laukka EJ, Small BJ. 2005. Cognitive impairment in preclinical Alzheimer's disease: a meta-analysis. *Neuropsychology* 19:520–31

Measures of episodic memory and executive function predicted the development of dementia within three years in patients with mild memory difficulty.

A review showing that multiple cognitive domains (i.e., episodic memory, executive function, and perceptual speed) are adversely affected several years before a clinical diagnosis of AD.

Bäckman L, Small BJ. 1998. Influences of cognitive support on episodic remembering: tracing the process of loss from normal aging to Alzheimer's disease. *Psychol. Aging* 13:267–76

Bäckman L, Small BJ, Fratiglioni L. 2001. Stability of the preclinical episodic memory deficit in Alzheimer's disease. *Brain* 124:96–102

Baddeley AD, Bressi S, Della Sala S, Logie R, Spinnler H. 1991. The decline of working memory in Alzheimer's disease: a longitudinal study. *Brain* 114:2521–42

Barber R, McKeith IG, Ballard C, Gholkar A, O'Brien JT. 2001. A comparison of medial and lateral temporal lobe atrophy in dementia with Lewy bodies and Alzheimer's disease: magnetic resonance imaging volumetric study. *Dement. Geriatr. Cogn. Disord.* 12:198–205

Bayles KA, Tomoeda CK. 1983. Confrontation naming impairment in dementia. *Brain Lang.* 19:98–114

Bayley PJ, Salmon DP, Bondi MW, Bui BK, Olichney J, et al. 2000. Comparison of the serial position effect in very mild Alzheimer's disease, mild Alzheimer's disease, and amnesia associated with electroconvulsive therapy. *J. Int. Neuropsychol. Soc.* 6:290–98

Binetti G, Locascio JJ, Corkin S, Vonsattel JP, Growdon JH. 2000. Differences between Pick disease and Alzheimer disease in the clinical appearance and rate of cognitive decline. *Arch. Neurol.* 57:225–32

Bondi MW, Houston WS, Salmon DP, Corey-Bloom J, Katzman R, et al. 2003. Neuropsychological deficits associated with Alzheimer's disease in the very old: discrepancies in raw vs standardized scores. *J. Int. Neuropsychol. Soc.* 9:783–95

Bondi MW, Monsch AU, Butters N, Salmon DP, Paulsen JS. 1993. Utility of a modified version of the Wisconsin Card Sorting Test in the detection of dementia of the Alzheimer type. *Clin. Neuropsychol.* 7:161–70

Boxer AL, Miller BL. 2006. Clinical features of frontotemporal dementia. *Alzheimer Dis. Assoc. Disord.* 19:S3–6

Braak H, Braak E. 1991. Neuropathological staging of Alzheimer-related changes. *Acta Neuropathol.* 82:239–59

Brandt J, Butters N. 1986. The neuropsychology of Huntington's disease. *Trends Neurosci.* 9:118–20

Brandt J, Bylsma FW. 1993. The dementia of Huntington's disease. In *Neuropsychology of Alzheimer's Disease and Other Dementias*, ed. RW Parks, RF Zec, RS Wilson, pp. 265–82. New York: Oxford Univ. Press

Brandt J, Corwin J, Krafft L. 1992. Is verbal recognition memory really different in Huntington's and Alzheimer's disease? *J. Clin. Exp. Neuropsychol.* 14:773–84

Brouwers P, Cox C, Martin A, Chase T, Fedio P. 1984. Differential perceptual-spatial impairment in Huntington's and Alzheimer's dementias. *Arch. Neurol.* 41:1073–76

Buschke H. 1973. Selective reminding for analysis of memory and learning. *J. Verb. Learn. Verb. Behav.* 12:543–50

Buschke H, Sliwinski MJ, Kuslansky G, Lipton RB. 1997. Diagnosis of early dementia by the double memory test. *Neurology* 48:989–97

Butters N, Granholm E, Salmon DP, Grant I, Wolfe J. 1987. Episodic and semantic memory: a comparison of amnesic and demented patients. *J. Clin. Exp. Neuropsychol.* 9:479–97

Butters N, Salmon DP, Cullum CM, Cairns P, Troster AI, et al. 1988. Differentiation of amnesic and demented patients with the Wechsler Memory Scale-Revised. *Clin. Neuropsychol.* 2:133–48

Butters N, Wolfe J, Granholm E, Martone M. 1986. An assessment of verbal recall, recognition and fluency abilities in patients with Huntington's disease. *Cortex* 22:11–32

Butters N, Wolfe J, Martone M, Granholm E, Cermak LS. 1985. Memory disorders associated with Huntington's disease: verbal recall, verbal recognition and procedural memory. *Neuropsychologia* 23:729–43

Chan AS, Salmon DP, Butters N. 1998. Semantic network abnormalities in patients with Alzheimer's disease. In *Fundamentals of Neural Network Modeling*, ed. RW Parks, DS Levine, DL Long, pp. 381–93. Cambridge, MA: MIT Press

Chan AS, Salmon DP, Butters N, Johnson S. 1995. Semantic network abnormality predicts rate of cognitive decline in patients with Alzheimer's disease. *J. Int. Neuropsychol. Soc.* 1:297–303

Chen P, Ratcliff G, Belle SH, Cauley JA, DeKosky ST, Ganguli M. 2001. Patterns of cognitive decline in presymptomatic Alzheimer disease: a prospective community study. *Arch. Gen. Psychiatry* 58:853–58

Chertkow H, Bub D. 1990. Semantic memory loss in dementia of Alzheimer's type. *Brain* 113:397–417

Chui H, Victoroff J, Margolin D, Jagust W, Shankle R, Katzman R. 1992. Criteria for the diagnosis of ischemic vascular dementia proposed by the State of California Alzheimer's Disease Diagnostic Treatment Centers. *Neurology* 42:473–80

Collette F, Van Der Linden M, Bechet S, Salmon E. 1999. Phonological loop and central executive functioning in Alzheimer's disease. *Neuropsychologia* 37:905–18

Collie A, Maruff P. 2000. The neuropsychology of preclinical Alzheimer's disease and mild cognitive impairment. *Neurosci. Biobehav. Rev.* 24:365–74

Croner LJ, Albright TD. 1997. Image segmentation enhances discrimination of motion in visual noise. *Vision Res.* 37:1415–27

Cronin-Golomb A, Amick M. 2001. Spatial abilities in aging, Alzheimer's disease, and Parkinson's disease. In *Handbook of Neuropsychology, Vol. 6: Aging and Dementia*, ed. F Boller, SF Cappa, pp. 119–43. Amsterdam: Elsevier. 2nd ed.

De Lacoste M, White CL. 1993. The role of cortical connectivity in Alzheimer's disease pathogenesis: a review and model system. *Neurobiol. Aging* 14:1–16

Delbeuck X, Van Der Linden M, Collette F. 2003. Alzheimer's disease as a disconnection syndrome? *Neuropsychol. Rev.* 13:79–92

Delis DC, Massman PJ, Butters N, Salmon DP, Cermak LS, Kramer JH. 1991. Profiles of demented and amnesic patients on the California Verbal Learning Test: implications for the assessment of memory disorders. *Psychol. Assess.* 3:19–26

Della Sala S, Kinnear P, Spinnler H, Stangalino C. 2000. Color-to-figure matching in Alzheimer's disease. *Arch. Clin. Neuropsychol.* 15:571–85

Desmond DW. 2004. The neuropsychology of vascular cognitive impairment: Is there a specific cognitive impairment? *J. Neurol. Sci.* 226:3–7

D'Esposito M, Zarahn E, Aguirre GK, Rypma B. 1999. The effect of normal aging on the coupling of neural activity to the BOLD hemodynamic response. *NeuroImage* 10:6–14

Dobkins KR, Albright TD. 1998. The influence of chromatic information on visual motion processing in the primate visual system. In *High-Level Motion Processing—Computational, Neurobiological and Psychophysical Perspectives*, ed. T Watanabe, pp. 53–94. Cambridge, MA: MIT Press

Dunkin JJ, Osato S, Leuchter AF. 1995. Relationships between EEG coherence and neuropsychological tests in dementia. *Clin. Electroencephal.* 26:47–59

Elfgren C, Brun A, Gustafson L, Johanson A, Minton L, et al. 1994. Neuropsychological tests as discriminators between dementia of Alzheimer's type and frontotemporal dementia. *Int. Geriatr. Psychiatry* 9:635–42

Ferman TJ, Smith GE, Boeve BF, Graff-Radford NR, Lucas JA, et al. 2006. Neuropsychological differentiation of dementia with Lewy bodies from normal aging and Alzheimer's disease. *Clin. Neuropsychol.* 20:623–36

Festa E, Insler RZ, Salmon DP, Paxton J, Hamilton JM, Heindel WC. 2005. Neocortical disconnectivity disrupts sensory integration in Alzheimer's disease. *Neuropsychology* 19:728–38

Förstl H, Besthorn C, Geiger-Kabisch C, Sattel H, Schreitter-Gasser U. 1996. Frontal lobe degeneration and Alzheimer's disease: a controlled study on clinical findings, volumetric brain changes and quantitative electroencephalography data. *Dementia* 7:27–34

Foster JK, Behrmann M, Stuss DT. 1999. Visual attention deficits in Alzheimer's disease: simple versus conjoined feature search. *Neuropsychology* 13:223–45

Freedman M, Leach L, Kaplan E, Winocur G, Shulman KI, Delis DC. 1994. *Clock Drawing: A Neuropsychological Analysis*. New York: Oxford Univ. Press

Freedman M, Oscar-Berman M. 1997. Breakdown of cross-modal function in dementia. *Neuropsychiatry Neuropsychol. Behav. Neurol.* 10:102–6

Frisoni GB, Pizzolato G, Geroldi C, Rossato A, Bianchetti A, Trabucchi M. 1995. Dementia of the frontal type: neuropsychological and 99[TC-HMPAO] SPECT features. *J. Geriatr. Psychiatry Neurol.* 8:42–48

Galloway PH, Sahgal A, McKeith IG, Lloyd S, Cook JH, et al. 1992. Visual pattern recognition memory and learning deficits in senile dementias of Alzheimer and Lewy body types. *Dementia* 3:101–7

Golob EJ, Miranda GG, Johnson JK, Starr A. 2001. Sensory cortical interactions in aging, mild cognitive impairment, and Alzheimer's disease. *Neurobiol. Aging* 22:755–63

Gómez-Tortosa E, Newell K, Irizarry MC, Albert M, Growdon JH, Hyman BT. 1999. Clinical and quantitative pathologic correlates of dementia with Lewy bodies. *Neurology* 53:1284–91

Grady CL, Haxby JV, Horwitz B, Sundaram M, Berg G, et al. 1988. Longitudinal study of the early neuropsychological and cerebral metabolic changes in dementia of the Alzheimer type. *J. Clin. Exp. Neuropsychol.* 10:576–96

AD patients exhibited specific deficits in binding visual features when cross-cortical integration was required (e.g., motion-color versus motion-luminance).

AD patients had abnormal increase in reaction time with increasing array size during conjoined feature search suggesting impaired perceptual integration.

Graham NL, Emery T, Hodges JR. 2004. Distinct cognitive profiles in Alzheimer's disease and subcortical vascular dementia. *J. Neurol. Neurosurg. Psychiatry* 75:61–71

Gregory CA, Orrell M, Sahkian B, Hodges J. 1997. Can frontotemporal dementia and Alzheimer's disease be differentiated using a brief battery of tests? *Int. Geriatr. Psychiatry* 12:357–83

Grossman M. 2002. Frontotemporal dementia: a review. *J. Int. Neuropsychol. Soc.* 8:566–83

Guidi M, Paciaroni L, Paolini S, DePadova S, Scarpino O. 2006. Differences and similarities in the neuropsychological profile of dementia with Lewy bodies and Alzheimer's disease in the early stage. *J. Neurol. Sci.* 248:120–23

Hamilton JM, Salmon DP, Galasko D, Delis DC, Hansen LA, et al. 2004. A comparison of episodic memory deficits in neuropathologically-confirmed dementia with Lewy bodies and Alzheimer's disease. *J. Int. Neuropsychol. Soc.* 10:689–97

Hanes KR, Andrewes DG, Pantelis C. 1995. Cognitive flexibility and complex integration in Parkinson's disease, Huntington's disease, and schizophrenia. *J. Int. Neuropsychol. Soc.* 1:545–53

Hansen L, Salmon D, Galasko D, Masliah E, Katzman R, et al. 1990. The Lewy body variant of Alzheimer's disease: a clinical and pathologic entity. *Neurology* 40:1–8

Hashimoto M, Kitagaki H, Imamura T, Hirono N, Shimomura T, et al. 1998. Medial temporal and whole-brain atrophy in dementia with Lewy bodies. *Neurology* 51:357–62

Hedden T, Gabrieli JDE. 2004. Insights into the ageing mind: a view from cognitive neuroscience. *Nat. Rev.* 5:87–97

Henry JD, Crawford JR, Phillips LH. 2004. Verbal fluency performance in dementia of the Alzheimer's type: a meta-analysis. *Neuropsychologia* 42:1212–22

Henry JD, Crawford JR, Phillips LH. 2005. A meta-analytic review of verbal fluency deficits in Huntington's disease. *Neuropsychology* 19:243–52

Higuchi M, Tashiro M, Arai H, Okamura N, Hara S, et al. 2000. Glucose hypometabolism and neuropathological correlates in brains of dementia with Lewy bodies. *Exp. Neurol.* 162:247–56

Ho AK, Sahakian BJ, Brown RG, Barker RA, Hodges JR, et al. 2003. Profile of cognitive progression in early Huntington's disease. *Neurology* 61:1702–6

Hodges JR, Graham NL. 2001. Vascular dementias. In *Early Onset Dementia: A Multidisciplinary Approach*, ed. JR Hodges, pp. 319–37. Oxford: Oxford Univ. Press

Hodges JR, Patterson K. 1995. Is semantic memory consistently impaired early in the course of Alzheimer's disease? Neuroanatomical and diagnostic implications. *Neuropsychologia* 33:441–59

Hodges JR, Salmon DP, Butters N. 1991. The nature of the naming deficit in Alzheimer's and Huntington's disease. *Brain* 114:1547–58

Hodges JR, Salmon DP, Butters N. 1992. Semantic memory impairment in Alzheimer's disease: failure of access or degraded knowledge? *Neuropsychologia* 30:301–14

Hof PR, Morrison JH. 1999. The cellular basis of cortical disconnection in Alzheimer's disease and related dementing conditions. In *Alzheimer Disease*, ed. RD Terry, R Katzman, KL Bick, SS Sisodia, pp. 207–32. New York: Raven

Hogan MJ, Swanwick GRJ, Kaiser J, Rowan M, Lawlor S. 2003. Memory-related EEG power and coherence reductions in mild Alzheimer's disease. *Int. J. Psychophysiol.* 49:147–63

Hyman BT, Damasio AR, Van Hoesen GW, Barnes CL. 1984. Alzheimer's disease: cell specific pathology isolates the hippocampal formation. *Science* 225:1168–70

Ince PG, Perry EK. 2005. Pathology of dementia with Lewy bodies. In *Dementia*, ed. A Burns, J O'Brien, D Ames, pp. 615–33. London: Hodder Arnold. 3rd ed.

Jacobs D, Salmon DP, Tröster AI, Butters N. 1990. Intrusion errors in the figural memory of patients with Alzheimer's and Huntington's disease. *Arch. Clin. Neuropsychol.* 5:49–57

Jacobson MW, Delis DC, Bondi MW, Salmon DP. 2002. Do neuropsychological tests detect preclinical Alzheimer's disease? Individual-test versus cognitive discrepancy analyses. *Neuropsychology* 16:132–39

Jack CR, Petersen RC, Xu YC, Waring SC, O'Brien PC, et al. 1998. Medial temporal atrophy on MRI in normal aging and very mild Alzheimer's disease. *Neurology* 49:786–94

Jelic V, Shigeta M, Julin P, Almkvist O, Winblad B, Wahlund LO. 1996. Quantitative electroencephalography power and coherence in Alzheimer's disease and mild cognitive impairment. *Dementia* 7:314–23

Jernigan TJ, Archibald SL, Fennema-Notestine C, Gamst AC, Stout JC, et al. 2001. Effects of age on tissues and regions of the cerebrum and cerebellum. *Neurobiol. Aging* 22:581–94

Johnson DK, Morris JC, Galvin JE. 2005. Verbal and visuospatial deficits in dementia with Lewy bodies. *Neurology* 65:1232–38

Katzman R. 1994. Apolipoprotein E and Alzheimer's disease. *Curr. Opin. Neurobiol.* 4:703–7

Kertesz A. 2006. Progress in clinical neurosciences: frontotemporal dementia–Pick's disease. *Can. J. Neurol. Sci.* 33:141–48

Kertesz A, Clydesdale S. 1994. Neuropsychological deficits in vascular dementia vs Alzheimer's disease: frontal lobe deficits prominent in vascular dementia. *Arch. Neurol.* 51:1226–31

Knopman DS, Ryberg S. 1989. A verbal memory test with high predictive accuracy for dementia of the Alzheimer type. *Arch. Neurol.* 46:141–45

Knott V, Mohr E, Mahoney C, Ilivitsky V. 2000. Electroencephalographic coherence in Alzheimer's disease: comparisons with a control group and population norms. *J. Geriatr. Psychiatry Neurol.* 13:1–8

Kraybill ML, Larson EB, Tsuang DW, Teri L, McCormick WC, et al. 2005. Cognitive differences in dementia patients with autopsy-verified AD, Lewy body pathology, or both. *Neurology* 64:2069–73

Kurylo DD, Corkin S, Rizzo JF, Growdon JH. 1996. Greater relative impairment of object recognition than of visuospatial abilities in Alzheimer's disease. *Neuropsychology* 10:74–81

Lafosse JM, Reed BR, Mungas D, Sterling SB, Wahbeh H, Jagust WJ. 1997. Fluency and memory differences between ischemic vascular dementia and Alzheimer's disease. *Neuropsychology* 11:514–22

Lakmache Y, Lassonde M, Gauthier S, Frigon J-Y, Lepore F. 1998. Interhemispheric disconnection syndrome in Alzheimer's disease. *Proc. Natl. Acad. Sci. USA* 95:9042–46

Lamar M, Podell K, Carew TG, Cloud BS, Resh R, et al. 1997. Perseverative behavior in Alzheimer's disease and subcortical ischemic vascular dementia. *Neuropsychology* 11:523–34

Lambon Ralph MA, Powell J, Howard D, Whitworth AB, Garrard P, Hodges JR. 2001. Semantic memory is impaired in both dementia with Lewy bodies and dementia of Alzheimer's type: a comparative neuropsychological study and literature review. *J. Neurol. Neurosurg. Psychiatry* 70:149–56

Lange KL, Bondi MW, Salmon DP, Galasko D, Delis DC, et al. 2002. Decline in verbal memory during preclinical Alzheimer's disease: examination of the effect of APOE genotype. *J. Int. Neuropsychol. Soc.* 8:943–55

Lange KW, Sahakian BJ, Quinn NP, Marsden CD, Robbins TW. 1995. Comparison of executive and visuospatial memory function in Huntington's disease and dementia of Alzheimer type matched for degree of dementia. *J. Neurol. Neurosurg. Psychiatry* 58:598–606

Lawrence AD, Sahakian BJ, Hodges JR, Rosser AE, Lange KW, Robbins TW. 1996. Executive and mnemonic functions in early Huntington's disease. *Brain* 119:1633–45

Lefleche G, Albert MS. 1995. Executive function deficits in mild Alzheimer's disease. *Neuropsychology* **9:313–20**

Libon DJ, Xie SX, Moore P, Farmer J, Antani S, et al. 2007. Patterns of neuropsychological impairment in frontotemporal dementia. *Neurology* 68:369–75

Lindau M, Almkvist O, Johansson SE, Wahlund LO. 1998. Cognitive and behavioral differentiation of frontal lobe degeneration of the non-Alzheimer's type and Alzheimer's disease. *Dementia Geriatr. Cogn. Disord.* 9:205–13

Lineweaver TT, Salmon DP, Bondi MW, Corey-Bloom J. 2005. Distinct effects of Alzheimer's disease and Huntington's disease on performance of mental rotation. *J. Int. Neuropsychol. Soc.* 11:30–39

Lippa CF, Johnson R, Smith TW. 1998. The medial temporal lobe in dementia with Lewy bodies: a comparative study with Alzheimer's disease. *Ann. Neurol.* 43:102–6

Lipton AM, Ohman KA, Womack KB, Hynan LS, Ninman ET, Lacritz LH. 2005. Subscores of the FAB differentiate frontotemporal lobar degeneration from AD. *Neurology* 65:726–31

Masliah E, Mallory M, Hansen LA, DeTeresa R, Terry RD. 1993. Quantitative synaptic alterations in the human neocortex during normal aging. *Neurology* 43:192–97

Mathuranath PS, Nestor PJ, Berrios GE, Rakowicz W, Hodges JR. 2000. A brief cognitive test battery to differentiate Alzheimer's disease and frontotemporal dementia. *Neurology* 55:1613–20

McHugh PR, Folstein MF. 1975. Psychiatric symptoms of Huntington's chorea: a clinical and phenomenologic study. In *Psychiatric Aspects of Neurological Disease*, ed. DF Benson, D Blumer, pp. 267–85. New York: Raven

Executive function deficits in early AD involve concurrent manipulation of information (e.g., set-shifting, sequencing) rather than cued-directed attention or problem solving.

McKeith IG, Dickson DW, Lowe J, Emre M, O'Brien JT, et al. 2005. Diagnosis and management of dementia with Lewy bodies: third report of the DLB consortium. *Neurology* 65:1863–72

McKeith IG, Galasko D, Kosaka K, Perry E, Dickson D, et al. 1996. Clinical and pathological diagnosis of dementia with Lewy bodies (DLB): Report of the Consortium on Dementia with Lewy Bodies (CDLB) International Workgroup. *Neurology* 47:1113–24

Mendez MF, Cherrier M, Perryman K, Pachana N, Miller B, Cummings JL. 1996. Frontotemporal dementias versus Alzheimer's disease: differential cognitive features. *Neurology* 47:1189–94

Mendez MF, Selwood A, Mastri AR, Frey WH. 1993. Pick's disease versus Alzheimer's disease: a comparison of clinical characteristics. *Neurology* 43:289–92

Merdes AR, Hansen LA, Jeste DV, Galasko D, Hofstetter CR, et al. 2003. Influence of Alzheimer pathology on clinical diagnostic accuracy in dementia with Lewy bodies. *Neurology* 60:1586–90

Minoshima S, Foster NL, Sima A, Frey KA, Albin RL, Kuhl DE. 2001. Alzheimer's disease versus dementia with Lewy bodies: cerebral metabolic distinction with autopsy confirmation. *Ann. Neurol.* 50:358–65

Montoya A, Pelletier M, Menear M, Duplessis, Richer F, Lepage M. 2006. Episodic memory impairment in Huntington's disease: a meta-analysis. *Neuropsychologia* 44:1984–94

Neary D. 2005. Frontotemporal dementia. In *Dementia*, ed. A Burns, J O'Brien, D Ames, pp. 667–77. London: Hodder Arnold. 3rd ed.

Nebes R. 1989. Semantic memory in Alzheimer's disease. *Psychol. Bull.* 106:377–94

Norton LE, Bondi MW, Salmon DP, Goodglass H. 1997. Deterioration of generic knowledge in patients with Alzheimer's disease: evidence from the Number Information Test. *J. Clin. Exp. Neuropsychol.* 19:857–66

Pachana NA, Boone KB, Miller BL, Cummings JL, Berman N. 1996. Comparison of neuropsychological functioning in Alzheimer's disease and frontotemporal dementia. *J. Int. Neuropsychol. Soc.* 2:505–10

Parasuraman R, Haxby JV. 1993. Attention and brain function in Alzheimer's disease. *Neuropsychology* 7:242–72

Paulsen JS, Salmon DP, Monsch AU, Butters N, Swenson M, Bondi MW. 1995. Discrimination of cortical from subcortical dementias on the basis of memory and problem-solving tests. *J. Clin. Psychol.* 51:48–58

Peinemann A, Schuller S, Pohl C, Jahn T, Weindl A, Kassubek J. 2005. Executive dysfunction in early stages of Huntington's disease is associated with striatal and insular atrophy: a neuropsychological and voxel-based morphometric study. *J. Neurol. Sci.* 239:11–19

Perry RJ, Hodges JR. 1999. Attention and executive deficits in Alzheimer's disease: a critical review. *Brain* 122:383–404

Petersen RC, Doody R, Kurz A, Mohs RC, Morris JC, et al. 2001. Current concepts in mild cognitive impairment. *Arch. Neurol.* 58:1985–92

Pfefferbaum A, Mathalon DH, Sullivan EV, Rawles JM, Zipursky RB, Lim KO. 1994. A quantitative magnetic resonance imaging study of changes in brain morphology from infancy to late adulthood. *Arch. Neurol.* 51:874–87

Pillon B, Dubois B, Ploska A, Agid Y. 1991. Severity and specificity of cognitive impairment in Alzheimer's, Huntington's, and Parkinson's diseases and progressive supranuclear palsy. *Neurology* 41:634–43

Price CC, Jefferson AL, Merino JG, Heilman KM, Libon DJ. 2005. Subcortical vascular dementia: integrating neuropsychological and neuroradiologic data. *Neurology* 65:376–82

Rascovsky K, Salmon DP, Hansen LA, Thal LJ, Galasko D. 2007. Disparate phonemic and semantic fluency deficits in autopsy-confirmed frontotemporal dementia and Alzheimer's disease. *Neuropsychology* 21:20–30

Rascovsky K, Salmon DP, Ho GJ, Galasko D, Peavy GM, et al. 2002. Cognitive profiles differ in autopsy-confirmed fronto-temporal dementia and Alzheimer's disease. *Neurology* 58:1801–8

Reed BR, Mungas DM, Kramer JH, Ellis W, Vinters HV, et al. 2007. Profiles of neuropsychological impairment in autopsy-defined Alzheimer's disease and cerebrovascular disease. *Brain* 130:731–39

Rohrer D, Salmon DP, Wixted JT, Paulsen JS. 1999. The disparate effects of Alzheimer's disease and Huntington's disease on semantic memory. *Neuropsychology* 13:381–88

Román GC, Tatemichi TK, Erkinjuntti T, Cummings JL, Masdeu JC, et al. 1993. Vascular dementia: diagnostic criteria for research studies. *Neurology* 43:250–60

Rubin EH, Storandt M, Miller JP, Kinscherf DA, Grant EA, et al. 1998. A prospective study of cognitive function and onset of dementia in cognitively healthy elders. *Arch. Neurol.* 55:395–401

DLB patients had significant metabolic reductions in the occipital cortex that distinguished them from AD patients (90% sensitivity, 80% specificity).

Neuropsychological deficit patterns differentiated between patients with autopsy-confirmed FTD (prominent word-generation deficits) and AD (prominent memory and visuospatial deficits).

Neuropsychological deficit profiles distinguished between AD (memory worse than executive dysfunction) and small vessel cerebrovascular disease (memory equal to executive dysfunction).

Sadek JR, Johnson SA, White DA, Salmon DP, Taylor KI, et al. 2004. Retrograde amnesia in dementia: comparison of HIV-associated dementia, Alzheimer's disease and Huntington's disease. *Neuropsychology* 18:692–99

Sahgal A, Galloway PH, McKeith IG, Edwardson JA, Lloyd S. 1992b. A comparative study of attentional deficits in senile dementias of Alzheimer and Lewy body types. *Dementia* 3:350–54

Sahgal A, Galloway PH, McKeith IG, Lloyd S, Cook JH, et al. 1992a. Matching-to-sample deficits in patients with senile dementias of the Alzheimer and Lewy body types. *Arch. Neurol.* 49:1043–46

Sahgal A, McKeith IG, Galloway PH, Tasker N, Steckler T. 1995. Do differences in visuospatial ability between senile dementias of the Alzheimer and Lewy body types reflect differences solely in mnemonic function? *J. Clin. Exp. Neuropsychol.* 17:35–43

Salmon DP. 2000. Disorders of memory in Alzheimer's disease. In *Handbook of Neuropsychology, Vol. 2: Memory and Its Disorders*, ed. LS Cermak, pp. 155–95. Amsterdam: Elsevier. 2nd ed.

Salmon DP, Bondi MW. 1999. Neuropsychology of Alzheimer's disease. In *Alzheimer Disease*, ed. RD Terry, R Katzman, KL Bick, SS Sisodia, pp. 39–56. Philadelphia, PA: Lippincott Williams & Wilkens. 2nd ed.

Salmon DP, Hamilton JM. 2006. Neuropsychological features of dementia with Lewy bodies. In *Dementia with Lewy Bodies*, ed. J O'Brien, I McKeith, D Ames, E Chiu, pp. 49–72. London: Taylor & Francis

Salmon DP, Hamilton JM, Peavy GM. 2001. Neuropsychological deficits in Huntington's disease: implications for striatal function in cognition. In *Handbook of Neuropsychology, Vol. 6: Aging and Dementia*, ed. F Boller, SF Cappa, pp. 373–402. Amsterdam: Elsevier. 2nd ed.

Salmon DP, Heindel WC, Lange KL. 1999. Differential decline in word generation from phonemic and semantic categories during the course of Alzheimer's disease: implications for the integrity of semantic memory. *J. Int. Neuropsychol. Soc.* 5:692–703

Salmon DP, Thomas RG, Pay MM, Booth A, Hofstetter CR, et al. 2002. Alzheimer's disease can be accurately diagnosed in very mildly impaired individuals. *Neurology* 59:1022–28

Small BJ, Fratiglioni L, Viitanen M, Winblad B, Bäckman L. 2000. The course of cognitive impairment in preclinical Alzheimer disease: three- and six-year follow-up of a population-based sample. *Arch. Neurol.* 57:839–44

Small BJ, Mobly JL, Laukka EJ, Jones S, Bäckman L. 2003. Cognitive deficits in preclinical Alzheimer's disease. *Acta Neurol. Scand. Suppl.* 179:29–33

Sprengelmeyer R, Lange H, Homberg V. 1995. The pattern of attentional deficits in Huntington's disease. *Brain* 118:145–52

Starkstein SE, Migliorelli R, Teson A, Sabe L, Vazquez S, et al. 1994. Specificity of changes in cerebral blood flow in patients with frontal lobe dementia. *J. Neurol. Neurosurg. Psychiatry* 57:790–96

Stavitsky K, Brickman AM, Scarmeas N, Torgan RL, Tang M-X, et al. 2006. The progression of cognition, psychiatric symptoms, and functional abilities in dementia with Lewy bodies and Alzheimer's disease. *Arch. Neurol.* 63:1450–56

Stevens A, Kircher T, Nickola M, Bartels M, Rosellen N, Wormstall H. 2001. Dynamic regulation of EEG power and coherence is lost early and globally in probable DAT. *Eur. Arch. Psychiatry Clin. Neurosci.* 251:199–204

Storandt M, Botwinick J, Danziger WL, Berg L, Hughes CP. 1984. Psychometric differentiation of mild senile dementia of the Alzheimer type. *Arch. Neurol.* 41:497–99

Storandt M, Grant EA, Miller JP, Morris JC. 2002. Rates of progression in mild cognitive impairment and early Alzheimer's disease. *Neurology* 59:1034–41

Stout JC, Rodawalt WC, Siemers ER. 2001. Risky decision making in Huntington's disease. *J. Int. Neuropsychol. Soc.* 7:92–101

Tales A, Butler SR, Fossey J, Gilchrist ID, Jones RW, Troscianko T. 2002. Visual search in Alzheimer's disease: a deficiency in processing conjunctions of features. *Neuropsychologia* 40:1849–57

Thal LJ. 1999. Clinical trials in Alzheimer disease. In *Alzheimer Disease*, ed. RD Terry, R Katzman, KL Bick, SS Sisodia, pp. 423–39. Philadelphia, PA: William & Wilkens. 2nd ed.

Thomas-Anterion C, Jacquin K, Laurent B. 2000. Differential mechanisms of impairment of remote memory in Alzheimer's and frontotemporal dementia. *Dement. Geriatr. Cogn. Disord.* 11:100–6

Tippett LJ, Blackwood K, Farah MJ. 2003. Visual object and face processing in mild-to-moderate Alzheimer's disease: from segmentation to imagination. *Neuropsychologia* 41:453–68

Delayed recall, category fluency, and global cognitive status provided excellent discriminability between very mildly impaired AD patients and NC subjects.

Tiraboschi P, Hansen LA, Alford M, Merdes A, Masliah E, et al. 2002. Early and widespread cholinergic losses differentiate dementia with Lewy bodies from Alzheimer disease. *Arch. Gen. Psychiatry* 59:946–51

Tiraboschi P, Salmon DP, Hansen LA, Hofstetter CR, Thal LJ, Corey-Bloom J. 2006. What best differentiates Lewy body from Alzheimer's disease in early-stage dementia? *Brain* 129:729–35

Treisman A. 1996. The binding problem. *Curr. Opin. Neurobiol.* 6:171–78

Twamley EW, Ropacki SAL, Bondi MW. 2006. Neuropsychological and neuroimaging changes in preclinical Alzheimer's disease. *J. Int. Neuropsychol. Soc.* 12:707–35

Ungerleider LG, Mishkin M. 1982. Two cortical visual systems. In *The Analysis of Visual Behavior*, ed. DJ Ingle, RJW Mansfield, MS Goodale, pp. 549–86. Cambridge, MA: MIT Press

Varma AR, Snowden JS, Lloyd JJ, Talbot PR, Mann DMA, Neary D. 1999. Evaluation of the NINCDS-ADRDA criteria in the differentiation of Alzheimer's disease and frontotemporal dementia. *J. Neurol. Neurosurg. Psychiatry* 66:184–88

Vonsattel JP, Di Figlia M. 1998. Huntington disease. *J. Neuropathol. Exp. Neurol.* 57:369–84

Waltz JA, Knowlton BJ, Holyoak KJ, Boone KB, Back-Madruga C, et al. 2004. Relational integration and executive function in Alzheimer's disease. *Neuropsychology* 18:296–305

Ward J, Sheppard JM, Shpritz B, Margolis RL, Rosenblatt A, Brandt J. 2006. A four-year study of cognitive functioning in Huntington's disease. *J. Int. Neuropsychol. Soc.* 12:445–54

Relations Among Speech, Language, and Reading Disorders

Bruce F. Pennington[1] and Dorothy V.M. Bishop[2]

[1]Department of Psychology, University of Denver, Colorado 80208;
email: bpenning@du.edu

[2]Department of Experimental Psychology, University of Oxford, OX1 3UD,
United Kingdom; email: dorothy.bishop@psy.ox.ac.uk

Annu. Rev. Psychol. 2009. 60:283–306

First published online as a Review in Advance on
July 24, 2008

The *Annual Review of Psychology* is online at
psych.annualreviews.org

This article's doi:
10.1146/annurev.psych.60.110707.163548

Key Words

comorbidity, speech sound disorder, specific language impairment,
developmental dyslexia, genetics

Abstract

In this article, we critically review the evidence for overlap among three
developmental disorders, namely speech sound disorder (SSD), language impairment (LI), and reading disability (RD), at three levels of
analysis: diagnostic, cognitive, and etiological. We find that while overlap exists at all three levels, it varies by comorbidity subtype, and the
relations among these three disorders are complex and not fully understood. We evaluate which comorbidity models can be rejected or
supported as explanations for why and how these three disorders overlap and what new data are needed to better define their relations.

Contents

INTRODUCTION

A fundamental question to be addressed by psychologists is how atypical development relates to typical development. An adequate theory must account for both human universals and individual differences, preferably with the same underlying mechanisms. Every example of atypical development poses both a challenge and an opportunity for developmental theory. In this review, we focus on a pervasive characteristic of atypical development, co-occurrence or comorbidity among behavioral disorders, specifically speech, language, and literacy disorders. Understanding this comorbidity has implications for the genetics, neuropsychology, prevention, and treatment of these disorders as well as for our understanding of the development of language. Historically, theorists have focused on explaining individual disorders (e.g., Morton & Frith 1995) and have viewed their co-occurrence as a peripheral issue. However, in recent years theorists have increasingly recognized that comorbidity is of interest in its own right. We argue that placing comorbidity at the

center of inquiry leads to a new perspective on theoretical models of disorders.

In this review, we first define speech, language, and reading disorders and critically review the evidence for their overlap at three levels of analysis: (*a*) diagnostic, (*b*) cognitive or neuropsychological, and (*c*) etiological. Because overlap exists at all three levels of analysis, we consider and evaluate which models of comorbidity can be rejected by current evidence, which are supported, and what new data are needed to distinguish among currently supported models. We conclude with a discussion of broader implications and future directions for research.

DIAGNOSTIC DEFINITIONS AND EPIDEMIOLOGY

The essential defining characteristics of the three disorders are summarized in **Table 1**. In each case, the disorder involves an unexpected difficulty in one aspect of development that cannot be readily explained by such factors as low intelligence or sensorimotor impairment. All three disorders lack a sharp dividing line between impairment and normality; thus, diagnosis involves setting an arbitrary threshold on what are essentially continua.

It has been customary in language impairment (LI) and reading disability (RD) to focus on specific developmental disorders, i.e., those where a significant discrepancy exists between language or literacy and general intelligence. However, such definitions have been criticized on both logical and practical grounds. In the field of reading disability, it is now broadly accepted that it is not valid to distinguish between children who have a large discrepancy between poor reading and IQ, and those who do not. Both types of poor reader have similar underlying deficits in phonological processing and both respond to similar kinds of treatment (see review in Fletcher et al. 1999). Analogous arguments have been advanced for LI (e.g., Bishop & Snowling 2004). Although the focus here is on children of broadly normal nonverbal ability, we use the terms RD

Table 1 Basic characteristics of language impairment, reading disability, and speech sound disorder

	Language impairment (LI)	Reading disability (RD)	Speech sound disorder (SSD)
Synonyms	Developmental dysphasia Developmental language disorder	Developmental dyslexia	Phonological disorder Articulation disorder
Defining characteristics	Expressive and/or receptive language development is impaired in the context of otherwise normal development (i.e., nonverbal IQ and self-help skills) Language impairment interferes with activities of daily living and/or academic achievement	Child has significant difficulty learning to read accurately and fluently despite intelligence within normal limits and adequate opportunity to learn	Child substitutes or omits sounds from words more than do same-aged peers; speech production errors interfere with intelligibility of speech
Exclusionary criteria	Severe neglect Acquired brain damage Significant hearing impairment Known syndrome, such as autistic disorder	Inadequate educational opportunity Acquired brain damage Significant hearing impairment Known syndrome, such as autistic disorder	Structural or neurological abnormality of articulators Significant hearing impairment IQ < 70
Prevalence	Depends on cutoff used Epidemiological study (Tomblin et al. 1997): 7.4% (CI 6.3–8.5%) of 6-year-olds met psychometric criterion	Depends on cutoff used; typical value is around 9%	2%–13% (mean = 8.2%) (Shriberg et al. 1999)
Odds ratio M:F	3 in referred sample (Broomfield & Dodd 2004); 1.5 in epidemiological sample (Tomblin et al. 1997)	1.9 to 3.3 in 4 epidemiological studies (reviewed by Rutter et al. 2004)	1.5 to 2.4 (mean = 1.8) (Shriberg et al. 1999)
Risk factors	Family history has significant effect No effect of parental education; slight effect of birth order (later-born at more risk) (Tomblin et al. 1991)	Parental education Home literacy environment Bioenvironmental risk factors, such as lead poisoning and head injuries	No effect of race, SES, or otitis media history, but significant effects of gender, family history, and low maternal education (Campbell et al. 2003)

and LI without the "specific" prefix rather than adopt a discrepancy-based definition of these disorders.

When dealing in particular with LI, the question arises as to whether the child's sociocultural background might affect performance on language measures and hence liability to be diagnosed with disorder. In general, that should not be the case, provided one is sensitive to the possibility that some nonstandard dialects may have grammatical and vocabulary differences from the standard. Tests of language processing, rather than linguistic knowledge, are largely immune to cultural influence and are sensitive indicators of LI (Campbell et al. 1997).

EVIDENCE FOR COMORBIDITY

Any attempt to summarize the evidence for comorbidity between speech sound disorder (SSD), LI, and RD will be tentative, not least because the prevalence of these disorders is age dependent. Clearly, RD cannot be identified until children have been exposed to reading instruction. On the other hand, SSD is typically most apparent in the preschool years, and it often resolves by the time the child starts to learn to read. LI also declines in prevalence with age, with many children having an early delay in language development that subsequently resolves (Bishop & Edmundson 1986). Another problem for this field is that no study has evaluated prevalence of SSD, LI, and RD in the same children; most comorbidity studies examine only two disorders. A third point is that sampling bias in clinical samples may artifactually inflate comorbidity. Berkson (1946) showed that apparent comorbidities between otherwise independent disorders will arise in referred samples if the probability for referral of either or both disorders is less than one. In this case, comorbid individuals will be overrepresented because their probability of being referred is a combined function of the referral rates of each of their disorders. Berkson's bias does not imply any overt bias to select comorbid cases; the bias is simply the result of the compounding of independent probabilities. The effect would be magnified if the concerns of parents or teachers resulted in an additional bias to refer comorbid cases. Epidemiological data are needed for unbiased estimates of comorbidity rates. However, few investigators have published epidemiological studies of the comorbidity among pairs of these disorders, and their three-way morbidity is touched upon only in unpublished epidemiological data.

Table 2 summarizes existing data on comorbidity among SSD, LI, and RD expressed as relative risks (i.e., rate in the group with the risk diagnosis/rate in the group without the risk diagnosis; for studies that did not have a control group, we used the population rate as denominator). So a relative risk of 2.0 means that those in the risk group (e.g., with SSD) are twice as likely to have a comorbid diagnosis (e.g., LI) as those without the risk diagnosis (e.g., non-SSD controls or the general population). For a common multifactorial disorder, these two methods of calculating relative risk should yield roughly similar estimates. The table is divided into data from epidemiological versus referred samples, and it illustrates that more variation exists among individual studies within each type of sample than across sample types. Thus, Berkson's and other referral biases do not appear to play a major role. Genuine comorbidity exists among these conditions because the pairwise comorbidities are significantly greater than chance in both types of sam-

ples. However, except for the Iowa sample (1*d*), the risk for later RD in SSD and LI is almost entirely restricted to SSD+LI (RR = 4.6–8.9), whereas the rate of later RD in SSD without LI is negligible (RR = 0.9–1.6, all ns). More data are needed to specify the risk for later RD in LI without SSD because the two values in the table (3.2–3.6 for Iowa and 0.5 for the Longitudinal Twin Study) do not agree.

The convergent results for elevated rates of later RD in SSD+LI could reflect that SSD+LI is an etiological and/or cognitive subtype, or that etiological and/or cognitive risk factors in SSD and LI interact synergistically to greatly increase risk for later RD. If the latter is true, it implies that the developing reader may compensate for the cognitive risk factors posed by SSD or even LI alone by using alternative strategies, but the combination of their cognitive risk factors makes compensation much more difficult.

In studies specifically concerned with SSD and LI, comorbidity varies with age. Broomfield & Dodd (2004) categorized all new referrals to pediatric speech and language therapy services in a British Primary Care Trust and found robust bidirectional comorbidity between SSD and LI (entry 6 in **Table 2**). In contrast, Shriberg et al. (1999) found a lower comorbidity rate in an epidemiological study of 6-year-olds in the United States (entry 1*a* in **Table 2**). Although different modes of sampling may have caused the differences in the two studies (clinical sample in the U.K. study and an epidemiological sample in the U.S. study), it is also likely that the degree of comorbidity varies with age: Only 15% of children in the study by Broomfield & Dodd (2004) were over age 6. Bishop & Edmundson (1987) noted that although preschool children appeared to be more vulnerable to speech than language problems, speech problems resolved more readily. In their clinically identified sample, many children who presented with both speech and language problems at age 4 had only residual language difficulties when seen 18 months later.

The best evidence for the comorbidity of LI and RD comes from the same Iowa

Table 2 Comorbidity rates among speech sound disorder (SSD), language impairment (LI), and reading disability (RD) (relative risks)

	Sample sizes		SSD in LI	LI in SSD	RD in LI	RD in SSD	RD in SSD+LI	RD in SSD–LI	RD in LI–SSD
Epidemiological	1328	1a[r]	3.3	2.3	–	–	–	–	–
	570*	1b[r]	–	–	6.2 (second), 6.9 (fourth)	–	–	–	–
	527	1c[p]	–	–	1.9–2.2 (second, fourth, eighth)	–	–	–	–
	604	1d[r]	–	–	2.8 (second), 3.1 (eighth)	–	3.9 (second), 4.9 (eighth)	2.2 (second), 2.3 (eighth)	3.2 (second), 3.6 (eighth)
	453	2[r]	2.2	2.3	1.9	2.6	6.0	1.6+	0.5+
	925–955	3[r]	–	–	4.4 (7y), 4.9 (9y), 5.1(11y)	–	–	–	–
	1655	4[r]	6.1	6.1	–	–	–	–	–
Referred	277	5[p]	–	9.1	–	1.6	8.1	1.6+	–
	936	6[p]	5.7	6.9	–	–	–	–	–
	123	7[p]	–	4.0	–	2.5	7.4	1.1+	–
	110	8[p]	–	–	5.7	–	–	–	–
	82	9[p]	–	–	2.3	–	–	–	–

+ = NS.

* = defined RD as 1 SD below weighted mean on reading comprehension composite.

Key: relative risk = rate in risk group/population rate (p) or rate in risk + group/rate in risk – group (r).

1: Iowa sample. 1a, Shriberg et al. (1999); 1b, Catts et al. (2002); 1c, Catts et al. (2005); 1d, Tomblin (unpublished).

2: Colorado Longitudinal Twin Sample, R.L. Peterson, B.F. Pennington, L.D. Shriberg, & R. Boada (manuscript under review).

3: Silva et al. (1987).

4: Beitchman et al. (1986).

5: Cleveland SSD sample, B.A. Lewis & L.A. Freebairn (unpublished).

6: Broomfield & Dodd (2004).

7: Denver SSD sample, Raitano et al. (2004), R.L. Peterson, B.F. Pennington, L.D. Shriberg, & R. Boada (manuscript under review).

8: McArthur et al. (2000).

9: Bishop & Adams (1990).

epidemiological sample that was studied by Shriberg et al. (1999). Catts et al. (2002) followed up children who had been identified with specific language impairment (SLI) at 6 years of age and found a relative risk of about 3. In a later follow-up of the Iowa sample to eighth grade (Catts et al. 2005), the comorbidity rates between LI and RD were lower but still significant (**Table 2**). Interestingly, this study also found that the LI without RD group performed significantly better than either the RD or the comorbid groups on both phonological awareness and nonword repetition. Of these two phono-logical measures, the LI without RD group was worse than controls only on nonword repetition, not on phonological awareness. Whether a similar cognitive profile would be found in LI without SSD is not known.

However, because LI and SSD are commonly comorbid, it can be difficult to establish whether associations with RD are specific to one of these disorders. Several prospective studies of smaller referred samples of children with SSD have found an increased rate of later RD (Bishop & Adams 1990, Catts 1993, Nathan et al. 2004, Snowling et al. 2000), although

Connectionist Model

<u>Speech Development</u>

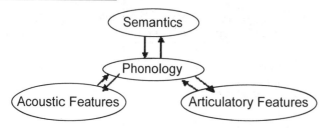

Figure 1

Connectionist models of speech development. Adapted from Guenther (1995), Joanisse (2000), Westerman & Miranda (2004).

several studies have found that the association is most robust for children with SSD+LI and is not found for children with isolated SSD (Bird et al. 1995, Larrivee & Catts 1999, Leitao & Fletcher 2004, Lewis & Freebairn 1992). New unpublished data from three prospective studies with large samples of children with SSD have resolved this issue. As mentioned above, in all three studies the risk for later RD in SSD is mediated by comorbid LI and this risk is substantial (4.3–8.9). In contrast, the risk is negligible for later RD in SSD without LI or, in one case, LI without SSD. This pattern for RD risk in SSS+/–LI was found across referred and epidemiological samples; thus, it is not due to a referral artifact. But more research is needed to understand the conflicting findings for RD risk in LI without SSD.

In summary, population samples have established that SSD and LI are comorbid, although the rates vary with age, and that LI and later RD are comorbid, but we lack published population

Connectionist Model

<u>Reading Development</u>

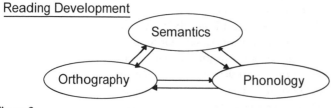

Figure 2

Connectionist model of reading development. From Harm & Seidenberg (1999).

data on the comorbidity between SSD and later RD. However, SSD+LI carries most of the risk for later RD, and the risk posed by SSD only, or sometimes LI only, appears to be negligible. Overlap among pairs of these three disorders sometimes varies as a function of comorbidity with the third disorder. This complex pattern of comorbidity makes it unlikely that all three disorders are pleiotropic manifestations of the same underlying cognitive or genetic liability (e.g., generalist genes for a general verbal trait; Plomin & Kovas 2005). This raises the question of whether the cognitive overlap of the three disorders mirrors the diagnostic overlap. That is, is the cognitive profile in SSD+LI (and later RD) distinct from that in either SSD without LI or LI without SSD?

COGNITIVE MODELS OF LANGUAGE IMPAIRMENT, READING DISABILITY, AND SPEECH SOUND DISORDER

It is useful to consider cognitive models of LI, RD, and SSD in the context of typical development and in relation to each other. **Figures 1** and **2** depict typical development of speech, language, and literacy, with written language skills building on earlier developing oral language skills. In developing an oral language, one of the first tasks an infant must master is the perception and production of the speech sounds specific to the native language (Kuhl 2004). Although innate constraints influence some aspects of human language acquisition (e.g., Pinker 1991), mastering a particular oral, and especially written, language requires extensive learning, much of it implicit statistical learning (Saffran et al. 1996). Consequently, connectionist models, which implement statistical learning of speech, language, and reading, provide a useful framework for thinking about relations among LI, RD, and SSD at the cognitive level.

Figure 1 depicts a simplified connectionist model of speech development (adapted from Guenther 1995, Joanisse 2000, Westermann & Miranda 2004) and **Figure 2** depicts a connectionist model of single-word reading development (Harm & Seidenberg 1999). Two key components are shared by both models: phonology and semantics. These models illustrate that a problem in developing phonological representations could affect speech, language, and reading development, and indeed, as reviewed below, evidence does exist for phonological impairment in SSD, LI, and RD. However, these models also illustrate that development in each of these three domains is affected in multiple ways, and some of these ways have not been considered in cognitive models of these disorders.

The development of speech production has been depicted in several computational models (Guenther 1995; Joanisse 2000, 2004, 2007; Joanisse & Seidenberg 2003; Markey 1994; Menn et al. 1993; Plaut & Kello 1999; Westermann & Miranda 2004). The difficult developmental task these models address is how young children learn the complex mapping between acoustic features and articulatory gestures, particularly when important aspects of the articulatory gestures made by adult models are not observable. Babbling almost certainly supplements imitation in learning these mappings. In these models, hidden units learn the particular abstract mapping between acoustic features and articulatory gestures that signal meaning differences for that child, and the representations of these abstract mappings are phonological representations. However, these models do not explain clinical cases where phonological representations develop without speech (e.g., anarthric children with oral reading skills; Bishop 1985).

Lexical semantics is intimately involved in the determination of which acoustic and articulatory features are counted as relevant for a young child's particular lexicon in a particular language. As the child's vocabulary increases, the nature of her phonological representations also changes. Consequently, the development of phonological representations is protracted, and the weighting given to different acoustic features in speech perception changes with development (Nittrouer 1999).

These computational models demonstrate that a problem in speech production such as that found in SSD could have several causes, including a bottom-up problem in processing acoustic features, a motor problem in planning and producing articulatory gestures, a problem learning the mapping between the two, a problem identifying which phonetic differences signal differences in meaning and which are equivalent (i.e., in learning phonological representations, a top-down problem in learning semantic representations that impedes the differentiation of phonological representations), or some combination of these problems. Similarly, these models suggest that there could be bottom-up auditory, representational (phonology in RD and syntax in LI), top-down semantic, learning, and multiple deficit theories of RD and LI. As we discuss below, existing cognitive models of these disorders have focused on single cognitive deficits and have tended to be static rather than developmental. That is, they have posited a congenital deficit in either a bottom-up auditory skill or a particular kind of representation (phonology or syntax) and have not considered the possibilities of how deficits might emerge from a developmental process or how deficient learning of new mappings between representations could cause disorders.

Language Impairment

A broad distinction can be drawn between two classes of LI model: those that regard the language difficulties as secondary to more general nonlinguistic deficits, and those that postulate a specifically linguistic deficit. The best-known example of the first type of model is the rapid temporal processing (RTP) theory of Tallal and colleagues, which maintains that language learning is handicapped because of poor temporal resolution of perceptual systems. This bottom-up auditory model of LI has also been applied to RD and SSD.

The first evidence for the RTP theory came from a study where children were required to match the order of two tones (Tallal & Piercy

1973). When tones were rapid or brief, children with LI had problems in correctly identifying them, even though they were readily discriminable at slow presentation rates. The theory has continued to develop over the years, and Tallal (2004) proposed a neural basis in the form of spike-timing-dependent learning. Tallal argued that although the underlying mechanism affected all auditory stimuli, its effects were particularly detrimental to language learning because development of neural representations of phonemes depends on fine-grained temporal analysis. Children who have poor temporal resolution will chunk incoming speech in blocks of hundreds of milliseconds rather than tens of milliseconds, and this will affect speech perception and hence on aspects of language learning.

Another theoretical account that stresses nonlinguistic temporal processing has been proposed by Miller et al. (2001), who showed that children with LI had slower reaction times than did control children matched on nonverbal IQ on a range of cognitive tasks, including some, such as mental rotation, that involved no language. Unlike the RTP theory, this account focuses on slowing of cognition rather than perception.

A more specialized theory is the phonological short-term memory deficit account of SLI by Gathercole & Baddeley (1990a). These authors noted that many children with SLI are poor at repeating polysyllabic nonwords, a deficit that has been confirmed in many subsequent studies (Graf Estes et al. 2007). This deficit has been interpreted as indicating a limitation in a phonological short-term memory system that is important for learning new vocabulary (Gathercole & Baddeley 1990b) and syntax. This theory, like the more specifically linguistic theories, places the core deficit in a system that is specialized for language processing, but the system is for memory and learning rather than for linguistic representations per se.

More recently, Ullman & Pierpont (2005) proposed a theory that encompasses both short-term memory and syntactic deficits under the umbrella of "procedural learning," which is

contrasted with a declarative learning system that is involved in learning new verbal information. They argue that LI is not a specifically linguistic disorder but is rather the consequence of an impaired system that will also affect learning of other procedural operations, such as motor skills.

Many authors, such as Bates (2004), have argued that domain-general deficits in cognitive and perceptual systems are sufficient to account for LI. This position differs radically from linguistic accounts of LI, which maintain that humans have evolved specialized language-learning mechanisms and that LI results when these fail to develop on the normal schedule. Thus, language-specific representational theories of LI coexist with similar linguistic theories of RD and SSD that focus on phonological representations. A range of theories of this type for LI focus on the syntactic difficulties that are a core feature of many children with LI. Children with LI tend to have problems in using verb inflections that mark tense, so they might say "yesterday I walk to school" rather than "yesterday I walked to school." Different linguistic accounts of the specific nature of such problems all maintain that the deficit is located in a domain-specific system that handles syntactic operations and is not a secondary consequence of a more general cognitive processing deficit (see, e.g., Rice & Wexler 1996, van der Lely 1994).

Although these theories focus on different perceptual, cognitive, and linguistic deficits, they are nonetheless hard to choose between for several reasons. First, the theories do not necessarily predict pure deficits in just one area—for instance, the RTP theory predicts that children with SLI will have phonological and syntactic problems, but the theory regards these as secondary to the basic perceptual deficit. Even where a domain-specific linguistic deficit is postulated, it could be argued that other more general deficits may coexist, perhaps because of pleiotropic effects of genes. Second, it is often easy to explain away a failure to find a predicted deficit on the grounds that the child has grown out of the deficit (which nevertheless has affected language acquisition) or that the deficit applies only to a subgroup of children with SLI.

Studies that examine deficits predicted by different theories in the same children aid in disentangling different theoretical accounts. The results of such studies can be illuminating. Bishop et al. (1999) studied a sample of twin children, many of whom met criteria for LI. These children were given a battery of tests, including a measure of auditory processing, derived from the RTP theory, and a measure of phonological short-term memory, nonword repetition. Children with LI did worse than controls did on both measures, but some children have normal language despite poor scores on the tests of RTP or nonword repetition. The intercorrelation between the measures, though significant, was low (around 0.3). Furthermore, genetic analysis suggested different etiologies for the auditory deficit, which appeared environmental in origin, and the nonword repetition deficit, which was heritable. One might wonder whether these deficits identify different subgroups of children with LI, but the results indicated rather that the two deficits interacted and that children with a double deficit were the most severely affected. A similar pattern of results was obtained in a later twin study in which children were assessed on a test of nonword repetition and on a test of productive verb morphology (Bishop et al. 2006). Both measures revealed deficits in children with LI, and in this case, both were heritable, yet the intercorrelation between these measures was low (though significant) and there was no evidence that common genes were implicated. Once again, children with both deficits had the most severe problems, and some children with normal language scored in the impaired range on one of the measures of underlying deficit.

These two studies raise some general points that also apply to other developmental disorders:

a) Any theory that postulates a single underlying deficit is inadequate to account for the disorder: several distinct deficits seem implicated, none of which is necessary or sufficient on its own for causing LI.

b) Although the different deficits can be dissociated and appear to have distinct etiologies, they tend to co-occur at above-chance levels.

c) It is possible to have a single deficit—e.g., in auditory processing or phonological short-term memory—without necessarily showing LI.

d) Children with LI typically show more than one deficit.

Reading Disability

A cognitive model of RD has greater consensus than does a model of LI. **Figure 3** depicts the processes involved in extracting meaning from written text. This figure shows that reading comprehension can be first broken down into cognitive components and then into developmental precursors of these cognitive components. One key component is fluent printed word recognition, which is highly predictive of reading comprehension, especially in the early years of reading instruction (Curtis 1980). The other key component is listening comprehension, that is, oral language comprehension (Hoover & Gough 1990).

The terms "developmental dyslexia" or "reading disability" have traditionally been reserved for children who have difficulties with basic printed word recognition. It is possible for a child to have reading comprehension problems despite adequate printed word recognition, but this is not counted as dyslexia. Instead, individuals with such problems are described as poor comprehenders, and the cognitive causes of their reading comprehension problems are distinct from those that interfere with word recognition (Nation 2005).

Printed word recognition can be broken into two component written language skills, phonological and orthographic coding (**Figure 3**). Phonological coding refers to the ability to use knowledge of rule-like letter-sound correspondences to pronounce words that have never

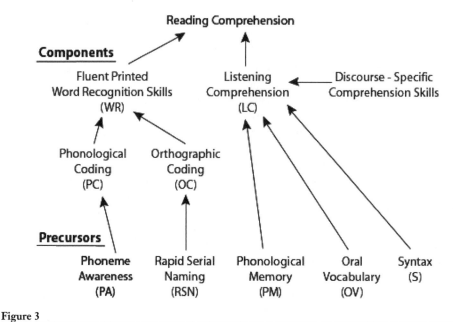

Figure 3

The processes involved in extracting meaning from written text.

been seen before (usually measured by pseudoword reading); orthographic coding refers to the use of word-specific patterns to aid in word recognition and pronunciation. Words that do not follow typical letter-sound correspondences (e.g., have or yacht) must rely, at least in part, on orthographic coding to be recognized, as do homophones (e.g., rows versus rose).

A large body of work has shown that most children with RD have disproportionate problems with pseudoword reading and that this deficit in phonological coding is related to poor phonological awareness. Phonological awareness is measured by tasks that require manipulation of the sound structure of spoken words (e.g., "what is cat without the /k/?"). Despite agreement about the importance of phoneme awareness deficits in RD, there is disagreement about whether these difficulties are themselves caused by lower-level processing deficits. Phoneme awareness is a complex metalinguistic skill that clearly involves multiple components. One argument is that phoneme awareness deficits arise from impaired phonological representations (Fowler 1991a, Swan & Goswami 1997a). Another argument postu-

lates that the central deficit is not specific to language, but rather is a consequence of the same RTP deficit proposed as an explanation for SLI (Tallal 1980). However, evidence for the RTP hypothesis for RD is patchy at best (see McArthur & Bishop 2001 for a review).

A parsimonious explanation for current data is that deficits in phonological representations lead to both phoneme awareness and phonological coding difficulties in RD. The phonological representations hypothesis is appealing because it helps explain why RD is associated not only with deficits in phoneme awareness, but also with impairments on a wide variety of phonological tasks, including phonological memory (Byrne & Shea 1979, Shankweiler et al. 1979) and picture naming (Fowler & Swainson 2004, Swan & Goswami 1997b).

An important caveat is that the relationship between phoneme awareness and reading is bidirectional, so that over time, poor reading also causes poor phoneme awareness (Morais et al. 1979, Perfetti et al. 1987, Wagner et al. 1994). Another caveat is that the evidence for the emergence of phoneme awareness being a necessary precursor for reading development is not airtight (Castles & Coltheart 2004) because longitudinal studies supporting this claim have not completely eliminated the confound of preschoolers already having some reading skill at time one. A recent study found that children with chance-level performance on phoneme awareness tasks could nonetheless use letter names to learn letter sounds and thus begin to decode printed words (Treiman et al. 2008). So explicit phoneme awareness may not be necessary for learning to read, but it seems clear that appropriately structured phonological representations are needed. The exact meaning of "appropriately structured" is still unclear in the context of reading development. As discussed above, phonological representations develop and can develop atypically in a variety of ways. The nature of the underlying phonological deficit in RD is the subject of several hypotheses, including that children with RD (*a*) lack segmental phonological representations (Boada & Pennington 2006, Fowler 1991), (*b*) have problems detecting suprasegmental information in phonological representations (Goswami et al. 2002), (*c*) retain allophonic representations (Serniclaes et al. 2004), or (*d*) have less-distinct phonological representations (Elbro et al. 1998). More research is needed to test these hypotheses not only in RD, but also across all three disorders considered here (e.g., Corriveau et al. 2007 have recently extended Goswami's suprasegmented theory to LI). These three disorders possibly share deficits on broad phonological measures, such as phonological awareness or nonword repetition, but they differ in how their phonological representations are deficient.

Because RD is often comorbid with LI, the question is raised as to the extent to which RD is associated with broader language deficits, e.g., as measured by tests of vocabulary and syntax. Although the phonological deficit hypothesis stresses children's difficulties in learning letter-sound mappings, poor general language skills could also handicap reading acquisition because one can use linguistic context to infer meaning of a novel word (e.g., Cain et al. 2004). On IQ tests, children with RD tend to underperform relative to their typically developing counterparts not only on phonological tasks, such as digit span, but also on all verbal subtests (D'Angiulli & Siegel 2003). Some of this performance deficit likely resulted from RD, since children with reading difficulties have impoverished opportunities to learn from print (e.g., Stanovich 1986; cf. Scarborough & Parker 2003), but some may well reflect subtle, wide-ranging language impairments. The evidence on this point from predyslexic children is particularly compelling, because deficits on a wide range of language skills are evident before they learn to read (Pennington & Lefly 2001, Scarborough 1990).

The presence of comorbid language problems in RD raises doubts that a phonological deficit is sufficient to cause RD. Moreover, as is discussed below, children with SSD have phonological deficits similar to those found in RD, but they usually do not develop RD unless they have comorbid LI. It appears that normal performance on rapid serial naming (RSN) tasks is a protective factor (R.L. Peterson, B.F. Pennington, L.D. Shriberg, & R. Boada, manuscript under review; Raitano et al. 2004). RSN is impaired in both RD and attention deficit/hyperactivity disorder (ADHD) (Shanahan et al. 2008), so RSN appears to be a cognitive risk factor shared by RD and ADHD. Moreover, because nonlinguistic processing-speed measures such as perceptual speed tasks (Wechsler Symbol Search) played a role similar to that of RSN as a cognitive risk factor for both RD and ADHD, it does not appear that the RSN problem is just a by-product of phonological or name-retrieval problems. We recently tested the hypothesis that processing or perceptual speed is a shared risk factor for RD and ADHD using structural equation modeling (L. McGrath, B.K. Pennington, R.K. Olson, & E.G. Willcutt, manuscript under review). We found that processing speed (i.e., latent traits composed of RSN and nonlinguistic perceptual speed tasks) was a unique predictor of both RD and ADHD symptoms and reduced the correlation between them to a nonsignificant value. Phoneme awareness and language skill were unique predictors of RD symptoms, and inhibition was a unique predictor of ADHD symptoms. These results support a multiple-deficit model of both RD and ADHD. The total variance explained in RD symptoms by phoneme awareness, language skill, and processing speed was more than 80%. Thus, the best current understanding of the neuropsychology of RD indicates that at least three cognitive risk factors are involved, which is consistent with a multiple-deficit model.

At least one of these underlying deficits, deficient phonological representations, overlaps with deficits that are found in studies of LI. However, rather surprisingly, a deficit in RSN is not characteristic of children with LI unless they also have reading impairment (D.V.M. Bishop, D. McDonald, & S. Bird, manuscript under review). Furthermore, although children with RD tend to have lower scores on language tests, they typically do not show the kinds of grammatical limitation seen in LI (Bishop & Snowling 2004). Overall, multiple underlying deficits appear to exist in RD, as in LI, with the most serious problems being found in children who have two or more of the disorders. Of particular interest is the indication that at least one underlying deficit, poor phonological processing, is common to both RD and LI.

The procedural learning account of LI is relatively new, and few studies have tested its predictions. Nevertheless, it is noteworthy that it overlaps with the automatization deficit account of dyslexia (Nicolson & Fawcett 1990). Both theories maintain that specific brain circuitry involving the cerebellum is involved in the poor learning of reading or rule-governed aspects of language, especially phonology and syntax, and in both cases it is argued that associated motor impairments are another symptom of this neurobiological deficit (Nicolson et al. 2001, Ullman & Pierpont 2005). The automatization deficit account of dyslexia has been challenged as a general account of this disorder by findings that motor impairments are seen in only a subset of cases (e.g., Ramus 2003). Nevertheless, as we have argued for LI, this does not necessarily mean that these deficits are irrelevant to the causation of the disorder; they may have their effect only when in combination with other deficits.

Speech Sound Disorder

SSD was originally considered a disorder of generating oral-motor programs, and children with speech sound impairments were said to have functional articulation disorder (Bishop 1997). However, a careful analysis of error patterns has rendered a pure motor deficit unlikely as a full explanation for the disorder. For example, children with SSD sometimes produce a sound correctly in one context but incorrectly in another. If children were unable to execute particular motor programs, then we might expect that most of their errors would take the form of phonetic distortions arising from an approximation of that motor program. However, the most common errors in children with SSD are substitutions of phonemes, not distortions (Leonard 1995). Moreover, a growing body of research demonstrates that individuals with SSD often show deficits on a range of phonological tasks, including speech perception, phoneme awareness, and phonological memory (Bird & Bishop 1992, Kenney et al. 2006, Leitao et al. 1997, Raitano et al. 2004). Though it remains possible that a subgroup of children have SSD primarily because of motor impairments, it now seems likely that the majority of children with SSD have a type of language disorder that primarily affects phonological development. Interestingly, RSN is not impaired in SSD (Raitano et al. 2004), and SSD children can have persisting phoneme awareness problems but normal reading development (R.L. Peterson, B.F. Pennington, L.D. Shriberg, & R. Boada, manuscript under review). Thus, intact RSN appears to be a protective factor in these children.

EVIDENCE FOR COGNITIVE OVERLAP

This brief review of cognitive models of disorders indicates that some close similarities exist in the theories that have been advanced to account for LI, RD, and SSD. For all three disorders, phonological deficits, possibly due to auditory perceptual problems, have been proposed as a core underlying cause. Although this overlap may help explain why the disorders are often comorbid, it leaves us with the puzzle of phenotypic variation between disorders. In short, if the same theoretical account applies to all disorders, why do they involve different behavioral deficits? And why, for instance, do we find children with SSD who have poor phonological skills yet do not have reading problems? An answer is suggested by our analysis of RD and LI as disorders that involve multiple cognitive deficits. A phonological deficit may be a key feature of all three disorders, yet its specific manifestation will depend on the presence of other deficits. This kind of model is implicit in the analysis by Bishop & Snowling (2004), who argue that LI is not just a more severe form of RD—rather, RD and LI both usually involve poor phonological processing, but LI is seen when this deficit is accompanied by broader difficulties affecting aspects of language such as syntax. The finding (by R.L. Peterson, B.F. Pennington, L.D. Shriberg, & R. Boada, manuscript under review) that children with SSD often read well despite poor phonological skills indicates that phonological deficit alone will not usually lead to later reading problems—it does so when it is accompanied by poor RSN. A closely similar conclusion was reached (by D.V.M. Bishop, D. McDonald, & S. Bird, manuscript under review) in a study of comorbidity between RD and LI. The study found that children who had LI without RD performed normally on tests of RSN. Both these studies suggest that although phonological deficit is a risk factor for RD, good RSN can act as a protective factor. This evidence for interaction between deficits has implications for how we model comorbidity between disorders (discussed below).

In summary, although cognitive overlap exists among these three disorders (i.e., phonological deficits), the cognitive profile varies as a function of comorbidity. Moreover, these cognitive profile differences appear to map onto the comorbidity patterns reviewed above. That is, the presence or absence of RSN deficits in SSD and LI relates to their comorbidity with later RD. But more systematic research is needed to test how cognitive profiles vary by comorbidity subtypes. This research will require large samples that have been followed longitudinally.

EVIDENCE FOR ETIOLOGICAL OVERLAP

Strong evidence demonstrates that LI, RD, and SSD are genetically influenced. That evidence is summarized in **Table 3**, which shows that each disorder is familial, moderately heritable, and has several replicated linkages to specific chromosome locations (for reviews, see Fisher & Francks 2006, Lewis et al. 2000, McGrath et al. 2006, Paracchini et al. 2007). **Table 3** also contains a footnote that explains the nomenclature for chromosome locations and loci associated with disorders. The RD loci have replicated across languages and cultures, including Swahili-speaking children in Tanzania (Grigorenko et al. 2007). For both RD and SSD, several candidate genes have been identified, and several of these are candidates for both disorders.

Twin studies have also been used to examine relations among these disorders. Most twin studies have found high h^2_g (0.6 or above)[1] for LI. However, a recent analysis by Bishop & Hayiou-Thomas (2008) found that this depended on whether children with SSD were included in the sample. For 4-year-olds who had LI without SSD, genes did not seem implicated in the etiology. Few twin studies have looked at both LI and RD in the same children, although in two separate samples Bishop and colleagues reported that RD was heritable only when

---

[1]The term h^2_g refers to the heritability of the extreme group's deficit. Unlike h^2, which estimates what proportion of the phenotypic variance across the whole distribution is attributable to genetic influence, h^2_g estimates the magnitude of genetic influences on the low (or high) tail of the distribution. Unless they are completely categorical, h^2_g is the appropriate heritability for disorders.

Table 3 Summary of genetic studies of speech sound disorder (SSD), language impairment (LI), and reading disability (RD)

	SSD	LI	RD
Familiality (relative risk)	~6[a]	2–4[a]	4–8[d]
Heritability*	~0.80–1.00[a,b]	0.36–0.96[b,c]	0.58
Chromosome regions[e,g]	1p34-36 (DYX8) 3p12-q13 (DYX5) 6p22 (DYX2) 15q21 (DYX1)	13q21 (SLI3) 16q24 (SLI1) 19q13 (SLI2)	1p34-36 (DYX8)** 2p15-16 (DYX3) 3p12-q13 (DYX5) 6p22 (DYX2) 15q21 (DYX1) 18p11 (DYX6) Xq27.3 (DYX9)
Candidate genes[e,f]	FOXP2 ROBO1 DCDC2 KIAA0319 DYXC1		ROBO1 DCDC2 KIAA0319 DYX1C1 MRPL19 C20RF3

*Estimates based on twin concordance data (double difference between monozygotic and dizygotic) or from group heritability computed using DeFries-Fulker method (DeFries & Fulker 1985).

**Nonsex chromosomes are numbered according to their size, so chromosome 1 is the largest and chromosome 22 (or possibly 21) is the smallest. Each chromosome has two arms, one short (p) and one long (q). Morphologically defined regions within each arm are denoted by a number, counting outward from the centromere that lies between the two arms (e.g., p1, p2, p3, and q1, q2, q3), and these regions are subdivided into bands (p11) and subbands (p11.1) and sub-subbands (p11.11). So the term "1p34-p36" means a location on the short arm of chromosome 1 including regions 34, 35, and 36. The names of loci associated with a disorder are capitalized and numbered according to order of discovery (DYX1 means the first dyslexia locus discovered, DYX2 means the second, and so on).

[a]Lewis et al. (2006).

[b]Viding et al. (2004).

[c]Bishop & Hayiou-Thomas (2008).

[d]Pennington & Olson (2005).

[e]McGrath et al. (2006).

[f]Anthoni et al. (2007).

[g]Newbury & Monaco (2008).

accompanied by poor nonword repetition (Bishop 2001, Bishop et al. 2004).

A multivariate analysis of reading skill in twins (Tiu et al. 2004) supported the multiple-deficit model (L. McGrath, B.K. Pennington, R.K. Olson, & E.G. Willcutt, manuscript under review) discussed above, in which phoneme awareness, RSN, and language skill independently contributed to predicting reading skill. Tiu et al. (2004) found that phoneme awareness, RSN, and full-scale IQ each made independent phenotypic contributions to reading skill and, in the etiological model based on the twin design, each construct had both shared and independent genetic relations to reading skills. More work of this kind is needed to test multiple-deficit models of each disorder and how both familiality and heritability vary by co-morbidity subtypes.

Family and twin studies can provide evidence for genetic influences on disorders and their relations, but to identify the genes involved we need to use methods of molecular genetic analysis. Linkage analysis identifies chromosomal regions that are likely to harbor genes involved in etiology of disorder. This method capitalizes on the fact that genes close together on a chromosome tend to be inherited together.

Thus, the method involves looking for chromosomal regions that are co-inherited at above-chance levels in affected family members. It is important to recognize that discovering linkage is not the same as finding a gene—there may be many genes in the linkage region, and it can be a painstaking task to identify which are implicated. Furthermore, it is unusual to find genetic variants that are perfectly associated with disorder; the famous case of a mutation in the FOXP2 gene that was found in all affected members and no unaffected members of a family with LI and SSD is the exception rather than the rule. In general, where a disorder has a complex, multifactorial etiology, the genes involved will have only a probabilistic influence on disorder—i.e., they act as quantitative trait loci (QTLs) rather than as major genes that cause disorder. Furthermore, any one linkage analysis is likely to turn up some spurious linkages that arise by chance, purely because many statistical comparisons are conducted. Molecular geneticists in this field are rightly cautious about interpreting linkages until they have been replicated in an independent sample (Newbury & Monaco 2008).

Initially, there was surprise that RD and LI linkages did not overlap, but it has become clear that the most powerful way to demonstrate common linkage is to study two disorders together; when this is done, there is evidence that some linkage regions affect more than one disorder (Monaco 2007). As shown in **Table 3**, SSD shows linkage to known RD risk loci (Smith et al. 2005, Stein et al. 2004). Recent attempts to replicate the 6p22 and 15q21 loci in an independent SSD sample have been partially successful (Stein et al. 2006).

Once linkage has been established, the next step is to identify a specific gene and understand its mode of action. So far, the greatest success for this approach in speech and language disorders, or even behaviorally defined disorders generally, has been with the FOXP2 gene, whose effects in brain and whose roles in the evolution of vocal communication across species have been studied extensively (Fisher 2007).

As shown in **Table 3**, the linkage studies of RD have been followed by the initial identification of six candidate genes in four of these linkage regions. The names of genes can be acronyms for the gene product (DCDC2 means "doublecortin doublecortin 2") but can also refer to the disorder they help cause (in the name DYX1C1, C1 means the first candidate for the first dyslexia risk locus, DYX1) or to other things. All these candidate genes for RD are involved in brain development, either in neuronal migration or in axon guidance. Their role in neuronal migration is consistent with that found in the pioneering work of Galaburda et al. (1985), who discovered ectopias (i.e., neurons that end up in the wrong location, such as in white instead of gray matter, because of migrational errors) in the brains of deceased dyslexics (most of whom had comorbid LI).

Although considerable progress has been made in specifying the genetic causes of these disorders, we should not forget that the heritability of these disorders is generally significantly less than 100%, so environmental variables must play a role in their development (see risk factors in **Table 1**). Even when heritabilities are higher, as they are for SSD, the environment can affect the phenotype. Such environmental variables are likely to include the home language environment and instructional quality (especially for RD), as well as environmental events that have a more direct effect on biology (e.g., maternal health during pregnancy, lead poisoning, or head injury). Unfortunately, few studies investigating main effects of such environmental variables on language development have used genetically sensitive designs.

In addition to main effects of environment, it is likely that the disorders considered here are influenced by gene-by-environment (G × E) interactions. A G × E interaction is identified when the impact of a given environment depends on the genotype of the individual. G × E interaction has been clearly demonstrated in selective breeding experiments with animals and plants, but is much harder to demonstrate in humans, where control over genotype is not possible. If candidate genes are identified, one can then see whether a measured environmental factor interacts with genotype in determining the phenotype (Rutter 2006).

A recent study investigated $G \times E$ interaction using SSD/RD linkage peaks with the strongest evidence of linkage to speech phenotypes, 6p22 and 15q21, and measures of the home language/literacy environment in a sample of children with SSD and their siblings. Results showed four significant and trend-level $G \times E$ interactions at both the 6p22 and 15q21 locations across several phenotypes and home environmental measures (McGrath et al. 2007). The direction of the interactions was such that, in relatively enriched environments, genetic risk factors substantially influenced the phenotype, whereas in less-optimal environments, genetic risk factors had less influence on phenotype. This directionality of the interactions is consistent with the bioecological model of $G \times E$ (Bronfenbrenner & Ceci 1994). This work is preliminary because these linkage-based methods are a step away from the ideal of using identified risk alleles to test for $G \times E$ (Rutter 2006).

In summary, evidence indicates that LI, RD, and SSD are familial, heritable, and linked to QTLs in certain chromosomal regions. One genetic mutation in FOXP2 has been shown to have a clear role in causing a rare form of speech dyspraxia associated with LI, and several candidate genes have been identified that act as QTLs for RD. Preliminary evidence suggests that some of these QTLs are pleiotropic and affect both RD and SSD, whereas less evidence exists for QTLs shared by LI and RD. Since the heritability of these disorders is less than 100%, environmental factors also play a role in their etiology, and it is likely that G-E correlations and $G \times E$ interactions also exist in their etiology.

WHICH COMORBIDITY MODELS ARE SUPPORTED?

Models of comorbidity have been proposed by Klein & Riso (1993), quantified by Neale & Kendler (1995), and applied to the disor-

ders considered here by D.V.M. Bishop, D. McDonald, & S. Bird (manuscript under review) and Pennington et al. (2005). Space does not permit a full description of these comorbidity models; instead, we focus on which comorbidity models can be rejected as explanations for the comorbidity among SSD, LI, and RD based on the data reviewed in the previous sections. Summarizing these data briefly, we found robust comorbidity among pairs of the three disorders (**Table 2**) but not perfect overlap. Cognitive and genetic risk factors (**Table 3**) are also shared by LI, RD, and SSD.

First, we can conclude that the comorbidity between SSD and LI and LI and RD is not an artifact of selection, population stratification, definitional overlap, or rater biases. These comorbidities have been found in population samples (**Table 2**). Their diagnostic definitions do not overlap (**Table 1**) and depend on objective tests, not raters.

Turning to nonartifactual explanations, Neale & Kendler (1995) differentiated three broad types: alternate forms, multiformity, and correlated liabilities. All three types of comorbidity models are versions of the continuous liability threshold model, which assumes that there is a continuous liability distribution of multifactorial causes (genetic and/or environmental causes) for a disorder, and that the sum total of their influences can be represented as a continuous liability distribution; a disorder occurs if an individual crosses a particular threshold on that liability distribution (see **Figure 4**).

The simplest kind of model proposes a single underlying liability distribution—in effect, the risk factors for all three comorbid disorders are seen as identical, but the manifestation of that risk can vary. This kind of model is suggested by research by Lewis and colleagues, who in a series of studies have noted that relatives of children with SSD are at increased risk of LI and RD as well as SSD (Lewis et al. 2007). This finding is compatible with the notion that the same heritable liability increases risk for all three disorders, although these authors hypothesized disorder-specific genes as well. So the single-liability model suggests that "generalist

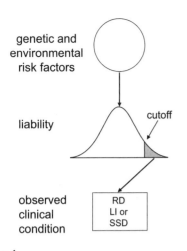

genetic and
environmental
risk factors

liability   cutoff

observed
clinical
condition

| RD |
| LI or |
| SSD |

Figure 4

Continuous liability distribution. RD, reading
disability; LI, language impairment; SSD, speech
sound disorder.

genes" (Plomin & Kovas 2005) may exist for a
general verbal trait, the low extreme of which
underlies these disorders. In its simplest form,
this corresponds to Neale & Kendler's (1995)
alternate forms model, which hypothesized that
individuals who cross a particular threshold on a
liability distribution have the probability of p of
having a disorder A and the probability r of having a disorder B. This means that both disorders
share a single liability, yet whether the person
manifests disorder A or B depends on chance
or risk factors that vary across individuals. This
model raises the question of why the same liability should manifest differently in different
people: It seems unlikely that this would be entirely due to chance; rather, it seems plausible
that different environmental or genetic risks in
the individual child interact with the underlying
liability to determine the outcome.

Age is one systematic factor that has been
proposed as influencing outcome. Scarborough
& Dobrich (1990) suggested that the same risk
factors that led to LI in a preschool child could
lead to RD in a school-aged child. They talked
of "illusory recovery," in which the problems of
a child with LI appeared to resolve only to be
replaced later by literacy problems. Subsequent
research, however, suggests that LI does not
disappear in children with LI who then develop

RD, although LI may become less overt (Bishop
& Adams 1990, Catts et al. 1999). A variant of
this model treats RD as a condition that is both
later in onset and less severe than SSD or LI;
according to such a severity model, a child with
a moderate liability may present only with RD
in middle childhood, whereas one with a higher
liability will be identified with SSD and/or LI
in preschool and with RD a few years later.

Although a model with a single-liability dimension is parsimonious, most experts in this
field would regard it as unlikely on the grounds
that all three disorders—SSD, LI, and RD—
appear heterogeneous. Although agreement is
lacking about the best way of subtyping these
disorders, quite marked phenotypic and etio-
logic differences can exist within each category,
as we have shown. Furthermore, some children
with severe LI do not have RD, which is inconsistent with a model that treats LI as indicative of a more severe liability. In addition, some
children with SSD do not have RD, which also
rejects this severity hypothesis for the relation
between SSD and RD.

These results suggest that a better kind of
model may be one that allows for separate liabilities for the different disorders, but where at
least one of the liabilities can lead to a comorbid form. This corresponds to a multiformity
model (Neal & Kendler 1995). Pennington
et al. (1993) considered this kind of model
when investigating comorbidity between RD
and ADHD, and suggested that RD might lead
to the phenotypic manifestation of ADHD in
the absence of etiological influences typically
associate with ADHD in isolation. One can
readily imagine that a child might appear to be
inattentive or hyperactive in the classroom because of the frustration elicited by difficulties
with reading rather than as a consequence of
the neurocognitive difficulties that are typically
associated with ADHD in the absence of RD.
The multiformity model usually describes each
disorder as having its own distinct etiology, but
there are cases where the etiology for disorder A
can lead to comorbid A+B. However, if rates of
comorbidity are high, the multiformity model
can also be seen as an extension of the alternate

forms model, whereby A and B usually have the same underlying cause (but with different liability thresholds), but subtypes of either A or B exist with separate etiological pathways.

A more extreme view of subtypes is to treat the comorbid disorder as etiologically distinct from either disorder occurring alone. This model of three independent disorders might postulate, for instance, that SSD with LI is etiologically distinct from pure SSD or pure LI, requiring three separate liability distributions to account for the patterns of co-occurrence between these two disorders. The comorbidity and genetic results presented here are consistent with this model, but the cognitive results are not consistent because SSD+LI overlaps cognitively with both SD and LI.

Neale & Kendler (1995) also postulated correlated liabilities models. In these models, each disorder has its own liability, a continuous relation exists between the liability to one disorder and the liability to the second disorder. An increase in liability for one disorder is correlated with the increase in liability for the second disorder. The relationship between the liability of the two disorders occurs via a significant correlation between the risk factors (correlated liabilities) or a direct causal relationship between the manifest phenotypes of the two disorders (A causes B, B causes A, or reciprocal causation). If the relationship is between manifest phenotypes, this actually becomes the multiformity model. In contrast, if the liabilities themselves are correlated, even at subthreshold levels, then subclinical comorbidity will occur even if one diagnostic phenotype is not expressed.

Our review of the etiology of LI, RD, and SSD indicates that some support exists for the correlated liabilities model of the relation between SSD and RD because both disorders are linked to some of the same QTLs. But this finding is also somewhat puzzling because SSD without LI does not pose much risk for later RD. So this finding needs to be tested in larger samples to determine whether the linkage of SSD to RD loci is mainly due to SSD+LI. Another puzzle is the robust comorbidity between SSD and LI and between LI (even without SSD) and RD in some studies, but so far, no QTLs have been discovered that are shared in either case. Clearly, more work is needed to test how well the correlated liabilities model (i.e., shared genetic and possibly environmental risk factors) accounts for the comorbidity among SSD, LI, and RD.

Although the Neale & Kendler (1995) models are a major contribution to the comorbidity literature because they are the most complete set of models yet proposed and because they are specified quantitatively, they nonetheless have some limitations. Specifically, they do not include either a neural or a cognitive level, they are not explicitly developmental, and they only deal with pairwise comorbidities. The main way of testing between them involves considering family or twin data to see how far a given disorder, or a comorbid form, breeds true, but even with ideal (simulated) data sets, some of the models can be difficult to distinguish empirically (Rhee et al. 2004).

The specific developmental disorders that we consider here, however, provide an alternative route to testing between models, provided one is willing to make the assumption that disorders caused by different liabilities might have different cognitive profiles. For instance, to test the three independent disorders model to explain comorbidity between RD and LI, we might predict that the cognitive profile in comorbid RD+LI would differ from that in pure RD or pure LI. Because the phenotype of each of the disorders considered here can be quite variable, and well-articulated models elucidate the underlying cognitive deficits associated with these disorders, this seems a promising approach. Contrary to the three independent disorders model, cognitive deficits characteristic of SSD, LI, and RD overlap to some extent.

In summary, the comorbidity observed among LI, RD, and SSD in not readily explained by any of the Neale and Kendler models but rather may require a model in which multiple cognitive deficits interact. Models of this type have been proposed by Bishop & Snowling (2004), Bishop (2006), and Pennington (2006), and a specific version to account for comorbidity between LI and RD was formally specified and tested by D.V.M. Bishop, D. Mc-Donald, & S. Bird (manuscript under review).

The multiple overlapping risk factors model of developmental disorders proposed by D.V.M. Bishop, D. McDonald, & S. Bird (manuscript under review) differs from the Neale and Kendler models in that it does not have a separate liability for each disorder, nor does it attempt to account for two disorders in terms of a single liability. Rather, it postulates several independent liability distributions, each of which determines a specific underlying deficit, and the disorder that is observed depends on the combination of liabilities that are suprathreshold. Some liabilities, such as that for phonological processing deficit, are implicated in SSD, LI, and RD. Others, such as liability for RSN deficit, appear to be specific to RD (although they might turn out to be implicated in other neurodevelopmental disorders such as ADHD; see Shanahan et al. 2008).

The multiple overlapping risk factors model can account for several features of the data reviewed here. In particular, it predicts that we should find some risk factors that are general to the three disorders of SSD, LI, and RD, and others that are specific. Furthermore, it predicts that a deficit in one underlying cognitive skill will not lead to overt disorder unless other deficits are also present.

CONCLUDING COMMENTS

LI, RD, and SSD are conditions that have traditionally been viewed as separate, and indeed, they can occur in pure form. This has led researchers to look for a single underlying cause for each disorder, both at the cognitive level and at the etiological level. Insofar as single cause explanations do not work, the alternative approach has been to look for subtypes that have a single cause. The research reviewed here suggests that such an approach is doomed to failure. LI, RD, and SSD are complex multifactorial disorders, not only in terms of their genetic and environmental etiology, but also in terms of their cognitive underpinnings. Each disorder appears to arise as the consequence of a specific constellation of underlying deficits. Each individual deficit may be common in the general population and may only assume clinical significance when combined with another deficit. Some deficits, especially those affecting phonological processing, appear to play a part in all three disorders; others are specific to one of the disorders.

We have shown that some evidence exists for similar patterns of relations among the three disorders at the three levels of analysis considered here: diagnostic, cognitive, and etiological. But more systematic research is needed to test these patterns and define the relations among these three communication disorders.

In the past, researchers often either ignored comorbidity or strenuously attempted to avoid it by studying "pure" groups. We argue that this is the wrong approach, and that to understand these disorders fully, we need to consider the relationships between them, both cognitive and etiological.

ACKNOWLEDGMENTS

The preparation of this article was supported by NIH grants HD27802 and HD049027 (to BFP) and a Wellcome Trust Principal Research Fellowship (to DVMB). Barbara Lewis, Richard Olson, and Bruce Tomblin very generously provided unpublished data from their longitudinal samples for Table 2. Irina Kaminer and Jenni Rosenberg helped prepare this table and Suzanne Miller helped prepare the manuscript.

LITERATURE CITED

Anthoni H, Zucchelli M, Matsson H, Muller-Myhsok B, Fransson I, et al. 2007. A locus on 2p12 containing the coregulated MRPL19 and C2ORF3 genes is associated to dyslexia. *Hum. Mol. Genet.* 16:667–77

Bates EA. 2004. Explaining and interpreting deficits in language development across clinical groups: Where do we go from here? *Brain Lang.* 88:248–53

Beitchman JH, Nair R, Clegg M, Ferguson B, Patel PG. 1986. Prevalence of psychiatric disorders in children with speech and language disorders. *J. Am. Acad. Child Psychiatry* 25(4):528–35

Berkson J. 1946. Limitations of the application of fourfold table analysis to hospital data. *Biometrics* 2:47–51

Bird J, Bishop DV. 1992. Perception and awareness of phonemes in phonologically impaired children. *Eur. J. Disord. Commun.* 27:289–311

Bird J, Bishop DV, Freeman NH. 1995. Phonological awareness and literacy development in children with expressive phonological impairments. *J. Speech Hear. Res.* 38:446–62

Bishop DV. 1997. *Uncommon Understanding: Development and Disorders of Language Comprehension in Children.* Hove, UK: Psychol. Press

Bishop DV. 2001. Genetic influences on language impairment and literacy problems in children: same or different? *J. Child Psychol. Psychiatry* 42:189–98

Bishop DV. 2006. Developmental cognitive genetics: how psychology can inform genetics and vice versa. *Q. J. Exp. Psychol.* 59:1153–68

Bishop DV, Adams C. 1990. A prospective study of the relationship between specific language impairment, phonological disorders and reading retardation. *J. Child Psychol. Psychiatry* 31:1027–50

Bishop DV, Adams CV, Norbury CF. 2004. Using nonword repetition to distinguish genetic and environmental influences on early literacy development: a study of 6-year-old twins. *Genes Brain Behav.* 5:158–69

Bishop DV, Adams CV, Norbury CF. 2006. Distinct genetic influences on grammar and phonological short-term memory deficits: evidence from 6-year-old twins. *Genes Brain Behav.* 5:158–69

Bishop DV, Bishop SJ, Bright P, James C, Delaney T, Tallal P. 1999. Different origin of auditory and phonological processing problems in children with language impairment: evidence from a twin study. *J. Speech Lang. Hear. Res.* 42:155–68

Bishop DV, Edmundson A. 1986. Is otitis media a major cause of specific developmental language disorders? *Br. J. Disord. Commun.* 21:321–38

Bishop DV, Edmundson A. 1987. Language-impaired 4-year-olds: distinguishing transient from persistent impairment. *J. Speech Hear. Dis.* 52:156–73

Bishop DV, Haylou-Thomas ME. 2008. Heritability of specific language impairment depends on diagnostic criteria. *Genes Brain Behav.* In press

Bishop DV, Snowling MJ. 2004. Developmental dyslexia and specific language impairment: same or different? *Psychol. Bull.* 130:858–86

Bishop DVM. 1985. Spelling ability in congenital dysarthria: evidence against articulatory coding in translating between graphemes and phonemes. *Cogn. Neuropsychol.* 2:229–51

Bishop DVM, Hayiou-Thomas ME. 2008. Heritability of specific language impairment depends on diagnostic criteria. *Genes Brain Behav.* 7(3):365–72

Boada R, Pennington BF. 2006. Deficient implicit phonological representations in children with dyslexia. *J. Exp. Child Psychol.* 95:153–93

Bronfenbrenner U, Ceci SJ. 1994. Nature-nurture reconceptualized in developmental perspective: a bioecological model. *Psychol. Rev.* 101:568–86

Broomfield J, Dodd B. 2004. Children with speech and language disability: caseload characteristics. *Int. J. Lang. Comm. Dis.* 39(3):303–24

Byrne B, Shea P. 1979. Semantic and phonetic memory codes in beginning readers. *Mem. Cogn.* 7:333–38

Cain K, Oakhill J, Lemmon K. 2004. Individual differences in the inference of word meanings from context. *J. Educ. Psychol.* 96:671–81

Campbell T, Dollaghan C, Needleman H, Janosky J. 1997. Reducing bias in language assessment: processing-dependent measures. *J. Speech Lang. Hear. Res.* 40:519–25

Campbell T, Dollaghan C, Rockette H, Paradise JL, Feldman HM, et al. 2003. Risk factors for speech delay of unknown origin in 3-year-old children. *Child. Dev.* 74(2):346–57

Castles A, Coltheart M. 2004. Is there a causal link from phonological awareness to success in learning to read? *Cognition* 91:77–111

Catts HW. 1993. The relationship between speech-language impairments and reading disabilities. *J. Speech Hear. Res.* 36:948–58

Catts HW, Adlof SM, Hogan TP, Weismer SE. 2005. Are specific language impairment and dyslexia distinct disorders? *J. Speech Lang. Hear. Res.* 48:1378–96

Catts HW, Fey ME, Tomblin JB, Zhang X. 1999. Language basis of reading and reading disabilities. *Sci. Stud. Reading* 3:331–61

Catts HW, Fey ME, Tomblin JB, Zhang X. 2002. A longitudinal investigation of reading outcomes in children with language impairments. *J. Speech Lang. Hear. Res.* 45:1142–57

Corriveau K, Pasquini E, Goswami U. 2007. Basic auditory processing skills and specific language impairment: a new look at an old hypothesis. *J. Speech Lang. Hear. Res.* 50:647–66

Curtis ME. 1980. Development of components of reading skill. *J. Educ. Psychol.* 72:656–69

D'Angiulli A, Siegel LS. 2003. Cognitive functioning as measured by the WISC-R: Do children with learning disabilities have distinctive patterns of performance? *J. Learn. Disabil.* 36:48–58

DeFries JC, Fulker DW. 1985. Multiple regression analysis of twin data. *Behav. Genet.* 15:467–73

Elbro C, Borstrom I, Petersen D. 1998. Predicting dyslexia from kindergarten: the importance of distinctness of phonological representations of lexical items. *Read. Res. Q.* 33:36–60

Fisher SE. 2007. Molecular windows into speech and language disorders. *Folia Phoniatrica et Logopaedica* 59:130–40

Fisher SE, Francks C. 2006. Genes, cognition and dyslexia: learning to read the genome. *Trends Cogn. Sci.* 10:250–57

Fletcher JM, Foorman BR, Shaywitz SE, Shaywitz BA. 1999. Conceptual and methodological issues in dyslexia research: a lesson for developmental disorders. In *Neurodevelopmental Disorders*, ed. H Tager-Flusberg, pp. 271–305. Cambridge, MA: MIT Press

Fowler A. 1991. How early phonological development might set the stage for phoneme awareness. In *Phonological Processes in Literacy: A Tribute to Isabelle Y. Liberman*, ed. SA Brady, DP Shankweiler, pp. 97–117. Hillsdale, NJ: Erlbaum

Fowler AE, Swainson B. 2004. Relationships of naming skills to reading, memory, and receptive vocabulary: evidence for imprecise phonological representations of words by poor readers. *Ann. Dyslexia* 54:247–80

Galaburda AM, Sherman GF, Rosen GD, Aboitiz F, Geschwind N. 1985. Developmental dyslexia: four consecutive cases with cortical anomalies. *Ann. Neurol.* 18:222–33

Gathercole SE, Baddeley AD. 1990a. Phonological memory deficits in language disordered children: Is there a causal connection? *J. Mem. Lang.* 29(3):336

Gathercole SE, Baddeley AD. 1990b. The role of phonological memory in vocabulary acquisition: a study of young children learning new names. *Br. J. Dev. Psychol.* 81:439–54

Goswami U, Thomson J, Richardson U, Stainthorp R, Hughes D, et al. 2002. Amplitude envelope onsets and developmental dyslexia: a new hypothesis. *Proc. Natl. Acad. Sci. USA* 99:10911–16

Graf Estes K, Evans JL, Else-Quest NM. 2007. Differences in the nonword repetition performance of children with and without specific language impairment: a meta-analysis. *J. Speech Lang. Hear. Res.* 50:177–95

Grigorenko EL, Naples A, Chang J, Romano C, Ngorosho D, et al. 2007. Back to Africa: tracing dyslexia genes in east Africa. *Read. Writ.* 20:27–49

Guenther FH. 1995. Speech sound acquisition, coarticulation, and rate effects in a neural network model of speech production. *Psychol. Rev.* 102:594–621

Harm MW, Seidenberg MS. 1999. Phonology, reading acquisition, and dyslexia: insights from connectionist models. *Psychol. Rev.* 106:491–528

Hoover WA, Gough PB. 1990. The simple view of reading. *Read. Writ.* 2:127–60

Joanisse MF. 2000. *Connectionist phonology*. Ph.D. thesis. Univ. South. Calif., Los Angeles

Joanisse MF. 2004. Specific language impairments in children: phonology, semantics, and the English past tense. *Curr. Dir. Psychol. Sci.* 13:156–60

Joanisse MF. 2007. Phonological deficits and developmental language impairments: evidence from connectionist models. In *Neuroconstructivism: Perspectives and Prospects*, ed. D Mareschal, S Sirois, G Westermann, MH Johnson, pp. 205–29. Oxford, UK: Oxford Univ. Press

Joanisse MF, Seidenberg MS. 2003. Phonology and syntax in specific language impairment: evidence from a connectionist model. *Brain Lang.* 86:40–56

Kenney MK, Barac-Cikoja D, Finnegan K, Jeffries N, Ludlow CL. 2006. Speech perception and short-term memory deficits in persistent developmental speech disorder. *Brain Lang.* 96:178–90

Klein DN, Riso LP. 1993. Psychiatric disorders: problems of boundaries and comorbidity. In *Basic Issues in Psychopathology*, ed. CG Costello, pp. 19–66. New York: Guilford

Kuhl PK. 2004. Early language acquisition: cracking the speech code. *Nat. Rev. Neurosci.* 5:831–43

Larrivee LS, Catts HW. 1999. Early reading achievement in children with expressive phonological disorders. *Am. J. Speech Lang. Pathol.* 8:118–28

Leitao S, Fletcher J. 2004. Literacy outcomes for students with speech impairment: long-term follow-up. *Int. J. Lang. Commun. Dis.* 39:245

Leitao S, Hogben J, Fletcher J. 1997. Phonological processing skills in speech and language impaired children. *Eur. J. Disord. Commun.* 32:91–111

Leonard LB. 1995. Phonological impairment. In *The Handbook of Child Language*, ed. P Fletcher, B MacWhinney, pp. 573–602. Oxford, UK: Blackwell

Lewis BA, Freebairn LA. 1992. Residual effects of preschool phonology disorders in grade school, adolescence, and adulthood. *J. Speech Hear. Res.* 35:819–31

Lewis BA, Freebairn LA, Hansen AJ, Miscimarra L, Iyengar SK, Taylor HG. 2007. Speech and language skills of parents of children with speech sound disorders. *Am. J. Speech Lang. Pathol.* 16:108–18

Lewis BA, Freebairn LA, Hansen AJ, Stein CM, Shriberg LD, et al. 2006. Dimensions of early speech sound disorders: a factor analytic study. *J. Commun. Dis.* 39:139–57

Lewis BA, Freebairn LA, Taylor HG. 2000. Follow-up of children with early expressive phonology disorders. *J. Learn. Disabil.* 33:433

Markey KL. 1994. *The sensorimotor foundations of phonology: a computational model of early childhood articulatory and phonetic development.* Ph.D. thesis. Univ. Colorado, Boulder

McArthur GM, Bishop DV. 2001. Auditory perceptual processing in people with reading and oral language impairments: current issues and recommendations. *Dyslexia* 7(3):150–70

McArthur GM, Hogben JH, Edwards VT, Heath SM, Mengler ED. 2000. On the "specifics" of specific reading disability and specific language impairment. *J. Child Psychol. Psychiatry* 41:869–74

McGrath LM, Hutaff-Lee C, Scott A, Boada R, Shriberg LD, Pennington BF. 2007. Children with co-morbid speech sound disorder and specific language impairment have increased rates of attention deficit/hyperactivity disorder. *J. Abnorm. Child Psychol.* 36:151–63

McGrath LM, Pennington BF, Willcutt EG, Boada R, Shriberg LD, Smith SD. 2007. Gene × environment interactions in speech sound disorder predict language and preliteracy outcomes. *Dev. Psychopathol.* 19:1047–72

McGrath LM, Smith SD, Pennington BF. 2006. Breakthroughs in the search for dyslexia candidate genes. *Trends Mol. Med.* 12:333–41

Menn L, Markey KL, Mozer M, Lewis C. 1993. Connectionist modeling and the microstructure of phonological development: a progress report. In *Developmental Neurocognition: Speech and Face Processing in the First Year of Life*, ed. B. de Boysson-Bardies, pp. 421–33. Dordrecht, The Netherlands: Kluwer Acad.

Miller CA, Kail R, Leonard LB, Tomblin JB. 2001. Speed of processing in children with specific language impairment. *J. Speech Lang. Hear. Res.* 44(2):416–33

Monaco AP. 2007. Multivariate linkage analysis of specific language impairment (SLI). *Ann. Hum. Genet.* 71:660–73

Morais J, Cary L, Alegria J, Bertelson P. 1979. Does awareness of speech as a sequence of phones arise spontaneously? *Cognition* 7:323–31

Morton J, Frith U. 1995. Causal modeling: structural approach to developmental psychopathology. In *Developmental Psychopathology*, ed. D Cicchetti, DJ Cohen, pp. 357–90. New York: Wiley

Nathan L, Stackhouse J, Goulandris N, Snowling MJ. 2004. The development of early literacy skills among children with speech difficulties: a test of the "Critical Age Hypothesis." *J. Speech Lang. Hear. Res.* 47:377–91

Nation K. 2005. Children's reading comprehension difficulties. In *The Science of Reading*, ed. MJ Snowling, C Hulme, pp. 248–65. Oxford, UK: Blackwell Sci.

Neale MC, Kendler KS. 1995. Models of comorbidity for multifactorial disorders. *Am. J. Hum. Genet.* 57:935–53

Newbury DF, Monaco AP. 2008. The application of molecular genetics to the study of language impairments. In *Understanding Developmental Language Disorders*, ed. CF Norbury, JB Tomblin, DVM Bishop. Hove, UK: Psychol. Press

Nicolson RI, Fawcett AJ. 1990. Automaticity: a new framework for dyslexia research? *Cognition* 35:159–82

Nicolson RI, Fawcett AJ, Dean P. 2001. Developmental dyslexia: the cerebellar deficit hypothesis. *Trends Neurosci.* 24:508–11

Nittrouer S. 1999. Do temporal processing deficits cause phonological processing problems? *J. Speech Lang. Hear. Res.* 42:925–42

Paracchini S, Scerri T, Monaco AP. 2007. The genetic lexicon of dyslexia. *Annu. Rev. Genom. Hum. Genet.* 8:57–79

Pennington BF. 2006. From single to multiple deficit models of developmental disorders. *Cognition* 101:385–413

Pennington BF, Groisser D, Welsh MC. 1993. Contrasting cognitive deficits in attention deficit hyperactivity disorder versus reading disability. *Dev. Psychol.* 29:511–23

Pennington BF, Lefly DL. 2001. Early reading development in children at family risk for dyslexia. *Child Dev.* 72:816–33

Pennington BF, Olson RK. 2005. Genetics of dyslexia. In *The Science of Reading: A Handbook*, ed. M Snowling, C Hulme, pp. 453–72. Oxford, UK: Blackwell Sci.

Pennington BF, Willcutt EG, Rhee SH. 2005. Analyzing comorbidity. In *Advances in Child Development and Behavior*, ed. RV Kail, pp. 263–304. Oxford, UK: Elsevier

Perfetti CA, Beck I, Bell LC, Hughes C. 1987. Phonemic knowledge and learning to read are reciprocal: a longitudinal study of first grade children. *Merrill-Palmer Q.* 33:283–319

Pinker S. 1991. Rules of language. *Science* 253:530–35

Plaut DC, Kello CT. 1999. The emergence of phonology from the interplay of speech comprehension and production: a distributed connectionist approach. In *The Emergence of Language*, ed. B MacWhinney, pp. 381–415. Hillsdale, NJ: Erlbaum

Plomin R, Kovas Y. 2005. Generalist genes and learning disabilities. *Psychol. Bull.* 131:592–617

Raitano NA, Pennington BF, Tunick RA, Boada R, Shriberg LD. 2004. Pre-literacy skills of subgroups of children with speech sound disorders. *J. Child Psychol. Psychiatry* 45:821–35

Ramus F. 2003. Developmental dyslexia: specific phonological deficit or general sensorimotor dysfunction? *Curr. Opin. Neurobiol.* 13(2):212–18

Rhee SH, Hewitt JK, Lessem JM, Stallings MC, Corley RP, Neale MC. 2004. The validity of the Neale and Kendler model-fitting approach in examining the etiology of comorbidity. *Behav. Genet.* 34:251–65

Rice ML, Wexler K. 1996. Toward tense as a clinical marker of specific language impairment in English-speaking children. *J. Speech Hear. Res.* 39:1239–57

Rutter M. 2006. *Genes and Behavior: Nature-Nurture Interplay Explained*. Oxford, UK: Blackwell Sci.

Rutter M, Caspi A, Fergusson DM, Horwood LJ, Goodman R, et al. 2004. Gender differences in reading difficulties: findings from four epidemiological studies. *JAMA* 291:2007–12

Saffran JR, Aslin RN, Newport EL. 1996. Statistical learning by 8-month-old infants. *Science* 274:1926–28

Scarborough HS. 1990. Very early language deficits in dyslexic children. *Child Dev.* 61:1728–43

Scarborough HS, Dobrich W. 1990. Development of children with early language delay. *J. Speech Hear. Res.* 33(1):70–83

Scarborough HS, Parker JD. 2003. Matthew effects in children with learning disabilities: development of reading, IQ, and psychosocial problems from grade 2 to grade 8. *Ann. Dyslexia* 53:47–71

Serniclaes W, Van Heghe S, Mousty P, Carre R, Sprenger-Charolles L. 2004. Allophonic mode of speech perception in dyslexia. *J. Exp. Child Psychol.* 87:336–61

Shanahan M, Yerys B, Scott A, Willcutt E, DeFries JC, et al. 2006. Processing speed deficits in attention deficit hyperactivity disorder and reading disability. *J. Abnorm. Child Psychol.* 34(5):585–602

Shankweiler DP, Liberman IY, Mark LS, Fowler CA, Fischer FW. 1979. The speech code and learning to read. *J. Exp. Psychol.: Hum. Learn. Memory* 5:531–45

Shriberg LD, Tomblin JB, McSweeny JL. 1999. Prevalence of speech delay in 6-year-old children and comorbidity with language impairment. *J. Speech Lang. Hear. Res.* 42:1461–81

Silva PA, Williams S, McGee R. 1987. A longitudinal study of children with developmental language delay at age three: later intelligence, reading and behaviour problems. *Dev. Med. Child Neurol.* 29(5):630–40

Smith SD, Pennington BF, Boada R, Shriberg LD. 2005. Linkage of speech sound disorder to reading disability loci. *J. Child Psychol. Psychiatry* 46:1045–56

Snowling M, Bishop DV, Stothard SE. 2000. Is preschool language impairment a risk factor for dyslexia in adolescence? *J. Child Psychol. Psychiatry* 41:587–600

Stanovich KE. 1986. Matthew effects in reading: some consequences of individual differences in the acquisition of literacy. *Read. Res. Q.* 21:360–406

Stein CM, Millard C, Kluge A, Miscimarra LE, Cartier KC, et al. 2006. Speech sound disorder influenced by a locus in 15q14 region. *Behav. Genet.* 36:858–68

Stein CM, Schick JH, Taylor H, Shriberg LD, Millard C, et al. 2004. Pleiotropic effects of a chromosome 3 locus on speech-sound disorder and reading. *Am. J. Hum. Genet.* 74:283–97

Swan D, Goswami U. 1997a. Phonological awareness deficits in developmental dyslexia and the phonological representations hypothesis. *J. Exp. Child Psychol.* 66:18–41

Swan D, Goswami U. 1997b. Picture naming deficits in developmental dyslexia: the phonological representations hypothesis. *Brain Lang.* 56:334–53

Tallal P. 1980. Auditory temporal perception, phonics, and reading disabilities in children. *Brain Lang.* 9:182–98

Tallal P. 2004. Improving language and literacy is a matter of time. *Nat. Rev. Neurosci.* 5:721–28

Tallal P, Piercy M. 1973. Developmental aphasia: impaired rate of nonverbal processing as a function of sensory modality. *Neuropsychologia* 11:389–98

Tiu RD Jr, Wadsworth SJ, Olson RK, DeFries JC. 2004. Causal models of reading disability: a twin study. *Twin Res.* 7:275–83

Tomblin JB, Hardy JC, Hein HA. 1991. Predicting poor-communication status in preschool children using risk factors present at birth. *J. Speech Hear. Res.* 34(5):1096–105

Tomblin JB, Records NL, Buckwalter P, Zhang X, Smith E, O'Brien M. 1997. Prevalence of specific language impairment in kindergarten children. *J. Speech Lang. Hear. Res.* 40(6):1245–60

Treiman R, Pennington BF, Shriberg LD, Boada R. 2008. Which children benefit from letter names in learning letter sounds? *Cognition* 106(3):1322–38

Ullman MT, Pierpont EI. 2005. Specific language impairment is not specific to language: the procedural deficit hypothesis. *Cortex* 41:399–433

van der Lely HK. 1994. Canonical linking rules: forward versus reverse linking in normally developing and specifically language-impaired children. *Cognition* 51:29–72

Viding E, Spinath FM, Price TS, Bishop DV, Dale PS, Plomin R. 2004. Genetic and environmental influence on language impairment in 4-year-old same-sex and opposite-sex twins. *J. Child Psychol. Psychiatry* 45:315–25

Wagner RK, Torgesen JK, Rashotte CA. 1994. Development of reading-related phonological processing abilities: new evidence of bidirectional causality from a latent variable longitudinal study. *Dev. Psychol.* 30:73–87

Westermann G, Miranda ER. 2004. A new model of sensorimotor coupling in the development of speech. *Brain Lang.* 89:393–400

Political Ideology: Its Structure, Functions, and Elective Affinities

John T. Jost,[1] Christopher M. Federico,[2] and Jaime L. Napier[1]

[1]Department of Psychology, New York University, New York, New York 10003;
[2]Departments of Psychology and Political Science, University of Minnesota, Minneapolis, Minnesota 55455; email: john.jost@nyu.edu, federico@umn.edu, jnapier@nyu.edu

Annu. Rev. Psychol. 2009. 60:307–37

The *Annual Review of Psychology* is online at psych.annualreviews.org

This article's doi:
10.1146/annurev.psych.60.110707.163600

0066-4308/09/0110-0307$20.00

Key Words

political orientation, motivated social cognition, system justification, authoritarianism

Abstract

Ideology has re-emerged as an important topic of inquiry among social, personality, and political psychologists. In this review, we examine recent theory and research concerning the structure, contents, and functions of ideological belief systems. We begin by defining the construct and placing it in historical and philosophical context. We then examine different perspectives on how many (and what types of) dimensions individuals use to organize their political opinions. We investigate (*a*) how and to what extent individuals acquire the discursive contents associated with various ideologies, and (*b*) the social-psychological functions that these ideologies serve for those who adopt them. Our review highlights "elective affinities" between situational and dispositional needs of individuals and groups and the structure and contents of specific ideologies. Finally, we consider the consequences of ideology, especially with respect to attitudes, evaluations, and processes of system justification.

Contents

INTRODUCTION

Goethe's (1809/1966) Enlightenment-era novel, *Elective Affinities*, invites the reader to consider parallels between the law-governed manner in which chemical elements combine and separate and the forces of attraction and repulsion in human social relationships. In an early passage foreshadowing clandestine affairs, one of the major characters, who has been boning up on chemistry textbooks, explains his fascination with the chemical reaction (pp. 39–44): "[I]t really looks as though one relation had been deliberately chosen in preference to another," so much so that "we believe these elements capable of exercising some sort of willpower and selection, and feel perfectly justified using the term 'elective affinities'!" Sociologist Max Weber later picked Goethe's concept of elective affinity (*Wahlverwandtschaft*) to characterize the link between ideas (or belief systems) and interests (or needs), that is, the "selective process" by which "ideas and their publics... find their affinities" (Gerth & Mills 1948/1970, p. 63; see also Lewins 1989). From this perspective, people can be said to choose ideas, but there is also an important and reciprocal sense in which ideas choose people.

We think that the metaphor of elective affinities remains a promising one for conceiving of the forces of mutual attraction that exist between the structure and contents of belief systems and the underlying needs and motives of individuals and groups who subscribe to them. These forces of attraction—or, in the language of Tomkins (1963), "ideo-affective resonances"—are the focus of our review. In rendering a social psychological analysis of this subject matter, we identify a set of relational motives, epistemic motives, and existential motives that help to explain why certain people—once they are exposed to certain political ideas—stick with those ideas (and the ideas stick with them). In doing so, we assume that ideological outcomes result from a combination of top-down socialization processes and bottom-up psychological predispositions.

WHAT IS AN IDEOLOGY?

Ideology has been dubbed "the most elusive concept in the whole of social science"

(McLellan 1986, p. 1). Its practitioners have been accused, with more than a little justice, of "semantic promiscuity" (Gerring 1997, p. 957; see also Converse 1964, p. 207). Many scholars address the definitional challenge by listing the plethora of definitions that exist in the literature, in the hope that the target can be discerned from the pattern of firing (e.g., Gerring 1997, pp. 958–959; Jost 2006, p. 653; Lane 1962, pp. 13–14). Because space is precious, we eschew this strategy, tempting though it is.

Basic Definitions

We are inclined to begin instead with a simple, general, and hopefully uncontroversial textbook definition of political ideology, such as that offered by Erikson & Tedin (2003), namely a "set of beliefs about the proper order of society and how it can be achieved" (p. 64; see also Adorno et al. 1950, Campbell et al. 1960/1965, Kerlinger 1984). Denzau & North (1994/2000) suggest something similar, except that they also highlight the role of social groups or collectivities (see also Parsons 1951): "ideologies are the shared framework of mental models that groups of individuals possess that provide both an interpretation of the environment and a prescription as to how that environment should be structured" (p. 24). If one accepts that ideology is shared, that it helps to interpret the social world, and that it normatively specifies (or requires) good and proper ways of addressing life's problems, then it is easy to see how ideology reflects and reinforces what psychologists might refer to as relational, epistemic, and existential needs or motives (Jost et al. 2008a). These are the major sources of elective affinities that we focus on in this review.

Specific ideologies crystallize and communicate the widely (but not unanimously) shared beliefs, opinions, and values of an identifiable group, class, constituency, or society (Freeden 2001, Knight 2006). Ideologies also endeavor to describe or interpret the world as it is—by making assertions or assumptions about human nature, historical events, present realities, and future possibilities—and to envision the world

as it should be, specifying acceptable means of attaining social, economic, and political ideals. To the extent that different ideologies represent socially shared but competing philosophies of life and how it should be lived (and how society should be governed), it stands to reason that different ideologies should both elicit and express at least somewhat different social, cognitive, and motivational styles or tendencies on the part of their adherents (see also Jost 2006).

Overcoming the Historical Tension Between Critical and Value-Neutral Approaches

Philosophers and social scientists have long disagreed about whether to embrace a critical, even judgmental tone in describing and analyzing ideologies or, alternatively, to adopt a more value-neutral posture (Jost et al. 2008b, Knight 2006). The former, more critical tradition descends from the writings of Marx & Engels (1846/1970), who regarded ideology (in contrast to science) as a potentially dangerous form of illusion and mystification that typically serves to conceal and maintain exploitative social relations. Along these lines, Mannheim (1936) depicted certain ideologies as "more or less conscious disguises of the real nature of a situation" (p. 55). Habermas (1989), too, treated ideology as a form of "systematically distorted communication," and this characterization remains common in certain circles of social theorists. The pejorative cast of ideology survives to some extent in social psychological theories of social dominance and system justification (Jost et al. 2004a, Sidanius & Pratto 1999).

However, most empirical research in sociology, psychology, and political science reflects an ostensibly value-neutral conception, according to which "ideology" refers indiscriminately to any belief system, that is, to any "configuration of ideas and attitudes in which the elements are bound together by some form of constraint or functional interdependence" (Converse 1964, p. 206). In this tradition of scholarship, ideology is treated as a "relatively benign organizing device" (Knight 2006, p. 622), and its

Elective affinity: force of mutual attraction involving the structure and contents of belief systems and the motives of their adherents

Relational motives: the desire to affiliate and establish interpersonal relationships; a need for personal or social identification, solidarity with others, and shared reality

Epistemic motives: the drive to reduce uncertainty, complexity, or ambiguity; cognitive preference for certainty, structure, order, and/or closure

Existential motives: the drive to manage threatening circumstances; a personal search for security, self-esteem, and meaning in life

System justification: motivation to defend, bolster, and justify the status quo; tendency to view current social arrangements as fair, legitimate, and desirable

cognitive function of structuring political knowledge and expertise is emphasized. Researchers tend to conclude that members of the public are ideological only to the extent that they hold attitudes that are stable, logical, coherent, consistent, and relatively sophisticated or knowledgeable (e.g., Converse 2000; Feldman 1988, 2003; Kinder 1998; but see Gerring 1997 and Jost 2006, p. 657, for accounts that put more conceptual space between constructs of ideology and sophistication).

Insights that emerge from critical and value-neutral inquiries have frequently been juxtaposed and assumed to be incompatible with one another, and scholars from the two traditions seem rarely (if ever) to communicate with one another. However, we propose that these two approaches are not mutually exclusive insofar as the same belief systems can simultaneously serve multiple (i.e., epistemic, existential, and relational) functions. That is, we propose that a given ideology can reflect both genuine (and even highly accurate) attempts to understand, interpret, and organize information about the political world as well as conscious or unconscious tendencies to rationalize the way things are or, alternatively, the desire for them to be different (e.g., Jost et al. 2003b,c). In this review, we summarize theory and research bearing on a host of social psychological variables, some of which would be expected to increase (or decrease) ideological coherence, stability, and sophistication, whereas others would be expected to increase (or decrease) ideological distortion, rationalization, and obfuscation.

THE DIMENSIONAL STRUCTURE OF POLITICAL ATTITUDES

One of the perennial questions asked by social and political psychologists concerns the structure of ideology, that is, the manner and extent to which political attitudes are cognitively organized according to one or more dimensions of preference or judgment (e.g., Converse 2006, Duckitt 2001, Eagly & Chaiken 1998, Eysenck 1954/1999, Feldman 2003, Kerlinger 1984). Most researchers assume that ideology is represented in memory as a kind of schema—i.e., a learned knowledge structure consisting of an interrelated network of beliefs, opinions, and values (Fiske et al. 1990, Hamill et al. 1985, Judd & Krosnick 1989, Lau & Redlawsk 2001; see also Erikson & Tedin 2003, Kinder 1998). However, disagreement persists concerning the number of dimensions that are employed (or required) to organize the contents of the ideological schema of the ordinary citizen. In this section of the review, we summarize the highlights of this debate.

The Traditional Notion of a Single Left-Right Dimension

Since the time of the French Revolution, ideological opinions have been classified most often in terms of a single left-right dimension. This usage derives from the fact that late-eighteenth-century supporters of the status quo sat on the right side of the French Assembly hall and its opponents sat on the left. In the United States and elsewhere, it is becoming increasingly common to substitute "liberal" and "conservative" for "left" and "right," respectively, and this equation expresses well the long-lasting ideological divide concerning preferences for change versus stability, which goes back at least as far as 1789. Much of the ideological conflict over change versus the status quo, therefore, pertains to age-old disputes concerning the proper role of hierarchy, authority, and inequality (Bobbio 1996, Burke 1790/1987).

This formulation of the left-right distinction and many others contain two interrelated aspects, namely (a) advocating versus resisting social change (as opposed to tradition), and (b) rejecting versus accepting inequality (Jost et al. 2003b,c). This bipartite definition should be relatively noncontroversial (but see Greenberg & Jonas 2003), and it accords with numerous characterizations of the left and right offered by political scientists (e.g., Erikson & Tedin 2003, p. 65; Lipset & Raab 1978, p. 19; McClosky & Zaller 1984, p. 189; Rathbun 2007, pp. 382–383). Left-wing and right-wing respondents alike in the United

States, Germany, and the Netherlands associated the right with such terms as "conservative," "system maintenance," "order," "individualism," "capitalism," "nationalism," and "fascism," and they associated the left with "progressive," "system change," "equality," "solidarity," "protest," "opposition," "radical," "socialism," and "communism" (Fuchs & Klingemann 1990, pp. 213–214). The two core aspects of the left-right dimension (attitudes concerning change versus stability and equality versus inequality) are correlated for historical reasons owing to the fact that over the past several centuries, Western societies have become more egalitarian in terms of human rights and liberties, economic distribution, and the dispersion of political power. In some cases, social and economic equality increased gradually, and in other cases it occurred because of revolutionary events, which were often resisted or opposed by conservatives and those identified with the right (e.g., Burke 1790/1987, Hirschman 1991, Lipset & Raab 1978; see also Nosek et al. 2009).

Scholars typically agree on the historical and philosophical significance of the left-right distinction, and it is clear that "political elites" in government, party and activist organizations, the media, and academia make relatively easy and frequent use of this dimension in political discourse and decision-making (e.g., Jennings 1992, McCarty et al. 2006, McClosky & Zaller 1984, Poole & Rosenthal 1997). Nevertheless, the work of Converse (1964) generated considerable skepticism about whether ordinary citizens actually use the specific ideological contents associated with left and right to organize their political attitudes (e.g., Bishop 2005; Converse 2000; Feldman 1988, 2003; Fiorina 2005; Kinder 1998). A related concern is whether a single survey item that asks participants to place themselves on a left-right continuum is theoretically and methodologically useful (Knight 1999). To address these perennially tricky questions, Jost (2006) revisited the strong claim that ordinary citizens are truly "innocent of ideology" and found, among other things, that ideological self-placement was an extremely strong predictor of voting intentions

in the American National Election Studies between 1972 and 2004. This comports with other evidence that ideology affects even modestly informed citizens' political attitudes (Abramowitz & Saunders 2008, Barker & Tinnick 2006, Erikson & Tedin 2003, Feldman 2003, Jacoby 1991, Knutsen 1995, Layman & Carsey 2002). Although it is clear that people are far from perfect in their use of abstract ideological concepts, most citizens can and do use a subset of core values or principles that, for all intents and purposes, may be considered ideological in the sense of being broad postures that explain and justify different states of social and political affairs (e.g., Feldman 1988; Feldman & Steenbergen 2001; Goren 2004; Jost et al. 2003b,c; Lavine et al. 1997; McCann 2008; Peffley & Hurwitz 1985; Rathbun 2007).

Jost et al. (2003b,c) proposed that these two core aspects of the left-right ideological dimension are rooted in a set of interrelated epistemic, existential, and relational needs or motives. That is, the dimensional structure and attitudinal contents of liberalism and conservatism were theorized to stem, at least in part, from basic social psychological orientations concerning uncertainty and threat (see also Jost 2006, Jost et al. 2007). This argument is derived from the work of Adorno et al. (1950), Allport (1954), Rokeach (1960), Tomkins (1963), Wilson (1973), and others. Consistent with an integrated theoretical framework, a meta-analytic review of 88 studies (Jost et al. 2003b,c) conducted in 12 countries between 1958 and 2002 confirmed that both situational and dispositional variables associated with the management of threat and uncertainty were empirically related to political orientation. Specifically, death anxiety, system instability, fear of threat and loss, dogmatism, intolerance of ambiguity, and personal needs for order, structure, and closure were all positively associated with conservatism. Conversely, openness to new experiences, cognitive complexity, tolerance of uncertainty, and (to a small extent) self-esteem were all positively associated with liberalism. Subsequent research has shown that—at both implicit and explicit levels of

resistance to change and acceptance of inequality, on the other, insofar as preserving the [inegalitarian] status quo allows one to maintain what is familiar and known while rejecting the risky, uncertain prospect of social change" (Jost et al. 2007, p. 990; see also Jost et al. 2004b, pp. 271–272).

Multidimensional Models of Ideology

The left-right model of ideological structure has parsimony on its side and has fared surprisingly well in terms of theoretical utility and empirical validity (Benoit & Laver 2006, Bobbio 1996, Campbell et al. 1960/1965, Carney et al. 2008, Fuchs & Klingemann 1990, Jacoby 1991, Jost 2006, Knight 1999, Knutsen 1995, Tomkins 1963). Nevertheless, a number of authors have argued that more than one dimension is needed to illuminate the structure of most citizens' political attitudes (e.g., Conover & Feldman 1981, Kerlinger 1984, Kinder 1998, Peffley & Hurwitz 1985; see also sidebar Symbolic and Operational Aspects of Political Ideology). We review some of the most influential multidimensional models here.

Are liberalism and conservatism orthogonal dimensions? A prominent challenge to the unidimensional approach comes from those who argue that left and right represent two independent, unipolar dimensions rather than opposite ends of a single bipolar dimension (e.g., Conover & Feldman 1981, Kerlinger 1984). Exploratory and confirmatory factor analyses suggest that evaluations of "liberal" and "conservative" attitude objects often load onto different latent variables and that these variables are at least somewhat independent of one another. However, it should be noted that measures of liberalism and conservatism are seldom if ever truly uncorrelated. For instance, after many years of attempting to develop scales that would measure liberalism and conservatism as orthogonal dimensions, Kerlinger (1984, pp. 224–226) found that respondents' scores on his liberalism scale (which combined a motley set of items concerning civil rights, racial equality, socialized medicine, labor

analysis—liberals do exhibit stronger preferences for social change and equality (as well as progress and flexibility over tradition and stability, respectively) when compared with conservatives (e.g., Anderson & Singer 2008; Jost et al. 2004a, 2008b; Nosek et al. 2009). These results and others are best interpreted in light of elective affinities: "The idea is that there is an especially good fit between needs to reduce uncertainty and threat, on the one hand, and

unions, equality of women, birth control, love, and human warmth) remained stubbornly correlated at –0.20 with scores on his conservatism scale (which combined sundry items pertaining to religion, church, business, profits, authority, law and order, moral standards, and manners). Even more decisively, subsequent factor-analytic studies revealed that latent variables corresponding to evaluations of liberals and conservatives do indeed exhibit a strong negative relationship after accounting for nonrandom measurement error attributable to response format (Federico 2007, Green 1988, Sidanius & Duffy 1988).

Social and economic dimensions of political ideology. A number of studies suggest that attitudes concerning social or cultural issues are factorially distinct from attitudes concerning economic issues (Duckitt et al. 2002, Evans et al. 1996, Layman & Carsey 2002, Lipset 1960, Saucier 2000, Shafer & Claggett 1995, Stenner 2005). Some researchers have gone further and suggested that these "social" and "economic" dimensions are basically orthogonal. For instance, it is possible for people to be socially liberal and economically conservative (i.e., "libertarian") or to be socially conservative and economically liberal (i.e., "populist"), although neither of these groups are large (e.g., Zaller 1992, p. 27). Recent work by Napier & Jost (2008b) on "working class authoritarianism" suggests that people who are low in socioeconomic status are more likely to be drawn to right-wing ideology because of largely social or cultural issues, whereas people who are high in socioeconomic status are more likely to be drawn to right-wing ideology because of economic reasons (see also Lipset 1960). Nonetheless, both social and economic forms of conservatism were positively associated with right-wing orientation in the 19 countries investigated. Benoit & Laver (2006, pp. 134–135), too, found that social and economic dimensions of ideology were positively intercorrelated in 41 of the 44 nations they examined. Thus, although the social and economic dimensions of political ideology may be distinct in conceptual

and factor-analytic terms, it is rare for them to be completely orthogonal.

Drawing in part on the distinction between social and economic dimensions of ideology, Duckitt et al. (2002) articulated a dual-process model of ideology that posits two different motivational foundations. Specifically, they argued that an individual's social dominance orientation (SDO; Sidanius & Pratto 1999) is connected to a view of the world as a ruthless competitive jungle in which power struggles are endemic, whereas an individual's degree of right-wing authoritarianism (RWA; Altemeyer 1998) reflects a view of the world as dangerous and threatening and therefore necessitating a sense of security and social order in society (see also Schwartz & Boehnke 2004). Consistent with Duckitt's formulation, research indicates that SDO scores tend to predict economic conservatism better than social conservatism, whereas RWA scores tend to predict social conservatism better than economic conservatism (Duckitt 2006, Duriez et al. 2005, Sibley et al. 2007). Nevertheless, it is important to bear in mind that SDO and RWA scores are positively correlated, even if they are not so highly intercorrelated as to be redundant variables (Altemeyer 1998, Jost et al. 2003b, Sidanius & Pratto 1999, Weber & Federico 2007, Whitley 1999).

Reconciling Unidimensional and Multidimensional Approaches

At this point in our review, we would do well to ask why evaluations of liberalism and conservatism are in fact negatively intercorrelated and why social and economic forms of political ideology are positively intercorrelated (see also sidebar Is "Tough-Mindedness" Orthogonal to Political Orientation?). The answers, clearly, pertain to the structure of left-right ideology, that is, its role in organizing a wide range of individual attitudes and opinions (Converse 1964, 2000, 2006; Federico & Schneider 2007). But where does ideological structure come from (when it comes)? The disciplines differ, at least in terms of emphasis, in how they approach this

Authoritarianism: personality characteristics indicating latent antidemocratic tendencies, including xenophobia, racism, and ethnocentrism; such tendencies are exacerbated under threat

IS "TOUGH-MINDEDNESS" ORTHOGONAL TO POLITICAL ORIENTATION?

Based on historical observations that left-wing and right-wing extremists have at times adopted equivalently intolerant methods and orientations in attempting to realize their political goals, some scholars have proposed that in addition to the left-right dimension of ideological content there exists a second, content-free dimension of psychological style (e.g., Greenberg & Jonas 2003, Shils 1954). For example, Eysenck (1954/1999) argued for a tough-mindedness versus tender-mindedness dimension that was allegedly independent of the left-right dimension. Rokeach (1960, 1973) similarly suggested that dogmatism, which he linked to the devaluation of freedom, was in principle distinguishable from the left-right dimension, which was yoked to the value of equality. However, both of these efforts failed to produce convincing evidence that the two proposed dimensions were orthogonal. That is, scales of tough-mindedness and dogmatism may be distinguishable from left-right measures in factor analyses, but scores on the psychological variables are nonetheless correlated with political attitudes, so that those on the right are indeed more tough-minded and dogmatic than those on the left, at least in Western nations (Jost et al. 2003b,c; Stone & Smith 1993). For example, Jost (2006, p. 664) reported a correlation of 0.27 between political liberalism and scores on the tender-mindedness facet of the agreeableness subscale of the Big Five personality instrument. Similarly, a meta-analysis by Jost et al. (2003b,c) revealed that the correlation between liberalism-conservatism and measures of dogmatism and intolerance of ambiguity was substantial (weighted mean $r = 0.34$).

Top-down processes: acquisition of political attitudes through exposure to ideological bundles that are socially constructed by political elites

Bottom-up processes: underlying psychological needs and motives that influence an individual's receptiveness to specific ideological positions

issue. Political scientists generally focus on top-down processes such as political leadership and party politics (Fiorina 2005, Poole & Rosenthal 1997, Sniderman & Bullock 2004, Zaller 1992), that is, the ways in which attitudes are "organized into coherent structures by political elites for consumption by the public" (Feldman 1988, p. 417). Psychologists, by contrast, are more likely to consider bottom-up cognitive and motivational processes that lead citizens to develop ideological belief systems that possess at least some degree of dimensional structure (Adorno et al. 1950, Jost 2006, Judd & Krosnick 1989, Lavine et al. 1997, Tomkins 1963). We propose that by integrating complementary

insights concerning these top-down and bottom-up processes, it may be possible to reconcile seemingly contradictory positions and findings concerning the dimensionality of political ideology.

Given the assumed interaction between top-down and bottom-up processes, it seems reasonable to suggest that specific elements (or dimensions) of political ideology are more likely to be collapsed into a single left-right dimension for those who are most highly engaged in political activity, that is, those who are high in both ability and motivation. This is consistent with formal theories of electoral competition and decision-making, which imply that an unconstrained issue space—one in which positions on different issues and value priorities are not organized or bundled together—imposes excessive informational demands on voters (Federico 2007, Hinich & Munger 1994, Lau & Redlawsk 2001). That is, relying on left-right ideological cues should make it easier for those political actors who are sufficiently motivated and cognitively sophisticated to deduce candidates' positions on various issues, to simplify the process of matching their own preferences up with optimal candidates (by reducing the number of dimensions on which matching must occur), and to increase confidence about how candidates will behave once elected (e.g., see Lavine & Gschwend 2006).

Consistent with this argument, research shows that symbolic and operational forms of ideology are more likely to be congruent for those who are highly informed about and/or engaged in politics (Bennett 2006, Converse 1964, McClosky & Zaller 1984, Sniderman et al. 1991, Zaller 1992). Similarly, evaluations of liberal and conservative attitude objects are more likely to reflect unidimensionality for those who are high in education and political expertise (Sidanius & Duffy 1988) and the motivation to evaluate political objects (Federico & Schneider 2007). Furthermore, attitudes on both social and economic issues are more stable, intercorrelated, and dimensionally structured for elected officials in comparison with ordinary citizens (Jennings 1992, Poole & Rosenthal

1997) and for those members of the public who are high in political knowledge and involvement (Converse 2000, 2006; Erikson & Tedin 2003; Federico & Schneider 2007; Layman & Carsey 2002).

There is also evidence that heightened political competition increases the pressure to structure political attitudes according to a single left-right dimension. For example, cross-national comparisons reveal that the basic motivational dimensions linked by Duckitt and colleagues (2002) to SDO and RWA are more strongly correlated in countries with established systems of political competition between left-wing and right-wing parties (Duriez et al. 2005). Similarly, periods of elevated partisan conflict seem to produce more tightly constrained issue agendas (Bennett 2006, Fiorina 2005, Hetherington 2001, McCarty et al. 2006), and over time, cross-cutting ideological agendas are assimilated to the single left-right dimension (Layman & Carsey 2002, Stimson 2004). Thus, while it may be possible to distinguish multiple ideological dimensions, there are social, cognitive, and motivational needs to effectively coordinate party activities, reduce informational demands on citizens, and tap into basic differences in value orientations; all of these factors would be expected to pull for a simpler, more parsimonious dimensional structure, especially for those who are both knowledgeable about and engaged in political matters. In other words, by incorporating both top-down and bottom-up processes, it is possible to understand why ideological attitudes are at least sometimes structured according to a left-right dimension as well as when (and why) they are not.

CONTENTS OF IDEOLOGIES AND THEIR SOCIAL PSYCHOLOGICAL FUNCTIONS

Treating ideology as an interrelated set of attitudes, values, and beliefs with cognitive, affective, and motivational properties implies that ideologies can (and should) be analyzed both in terms of their contents and their functions (Abelson 1988; Adorno et al. 1950; Ball &

Dagger 1991; Campbell et al. 1960/1965; Jost 2006; Jost et al. 2003b,c; Lewins 1989). That is, ideology can be thought of as having both a discursive (socially constructed) superstructure and a functional (or motivational) substructure. The discursive superstructure refers to the network of socially constructed attitudes, values, and beliefs bound up with a particular ideological position at a particular time and place (Jost et al. 2003c). Defined in this way, the discursive superstructure can be thought of as a "social representation" (Moscovici 1988) that guides political judgment in a top-down schematic fashion and is typically transmitted from political elites to the public at large (Zaller 1992). The functional substructure refers to the ensemble of social and psychological needs, goals, and motives that drive the political interests of ordinary citizens in a bottom-up fashion and are served by the discursive contents of ideology (Jost 2006, Jost et al. 2003b). We propose that the nature of the relationship between top-down and bottom-up processes is characterized by elective affinities: "Ideas, selected and reinterpreted from the original doctrine, do gain an affinity with the interests of certain members of special strata; if they do not gain such an affinity, they are abandoned" (Gerth & Mills 1948/1970, p. 63).

From the Top Down: Elite Construction and Dissemination of the Discursive Superstructure

Just as political elites such as elected officials, party leaders, and media representatives can help to impose structure by simplifying the political environment, they can also strongly influence the specific contents of a political ideology, that is, its discursive superstructure (e.g., Converse 2000, Layman & Carsey 2002, McClosky & Zaller 1984, Sniderman et al. 1991). Prominent examples include the leadership role of Lyndon Johnson and his successors in urging supporters of the Democratic party to embrace liberal civil rights legislation to assist racial and ethnic minorities (e.g., Sears et al. 2000) as well as the relatively strong influences that politicians, journalists, and other intellectuals have over the public's degree of acceptance of their nation's involvement in war (Berinsky 2007, Zaller 1992). In these cases and others, Zaller (1992) concludes that "exposure to elite discourse appears to promote support for the ideas carried in it" (p. 11).

The communication process. The socially shared content of a discursive superstructure, that is, its specific bundling of attitudes, values, and beliefs, presumably results from both communicative and strategic forms of interaction between partisan elites and their followers (Graber 2004, Habermas 1989, Hinich & Munger 1994, Zaller 1992). This is the sense in which, as Sniderman & Bullock (2004) put it, "political institutions do the heavy lifting" (p. 351). Most likely, this allows a relatively small and unrepresentative group of political operatives to wield a disproportionate amount of influence, as commentators both within and without the Marxist tradition have long noted (e.g., Eagleton 1991, Habermas 1989, Mannheim 1936, McLellan 1986, Weber 1922/1946, Zaller 1992, Zelditch 2001). The worry persists, in other words, that the "ideas of the ruling class are in every epoch the ruling ideas" (Marx & Engels 1846/1970). As we shall see below, a number of contemporary social psychological approaches have updated and expanded this focus on the system-justifying nature of ideological content, taking into account bottom-up as well as top-down processes (e.g., Jost & Hunyady 2002, Sidanius & Pratto 1999).

However, in most contemporary societies, there are political elites on the left as well as the right, and they, too, are capable of shaping the discursive superstructure (e.g., Hinich & Munger 1994). That is, the ideological bundles or packages that are socially constructed by political elites can be seen as "anchoring" both ends of the left-right spectrum, thereby arraying the options on an ideological "menu" from which members of the mass public select their voting and other preferences (Sniderman & Bullock 2004). More specifically, the content associated with different ideological positions is absorbed by members of the mass public who take cues from those elites who share their basic partisan or ideological orientations (Converse 1964, 2000, 2006; Sniderman et al. 1991; Sniderman & Bullock 2004; Zaller 1992). This raises the question of how successful elites are in spreading their ideological messages to the public at large.

The moderating role of citizens' cognitive abilities and motivation. Following Campbell et al. (1960/1965) and Converse (1964), evidence suggests that some citizens are more able and/or willing than others to learn the contents of the discursive superstructure as defined by political elites (e.g., Bennett 2006, Delli Carpini & Keeter 1996, Federico & Schneider 2007, Federico & Sidanius 2002, Judd & Krosnick 1989, Sniderman et al. 1991, Zaller 1992). Decades of research suggest that the majority of the population exhibits a relatively low level of knowledge about the specific discursive contents of liberal and conservative ideologies, a relative inability and/or unwillingness to understand political conflict in strictly liberal-conservative terms, and a relatively low level of ideological consistency (or constraint) in their attitudes toward many different issues (e.g., Converse 2000, Dalton 2003, Stimson 2004). Even at the level of broad moral postures, value conflict seems to be more common than a high degree of consistency among potentially competing values (Feldman 2003, Jacoby 2006, Kuklinski et al. 2001, Tetlock 1986).

These findings suggest that most citizens do not learn the contents of various ideologies in all their glorious detail, but the findings should not be taken as a sign that people in general are utterly devoid of ideological commitment or understanding (e.g., Billig 2003, Gamson 1992, Lane 1962). As Lane (1962) put it, "the common man has a set of emotionally charged political beliefs" that "embrace central values and institutions" and are "rationalizations of interests (sometimes not his own)" that "serve as moral justifications for daily acts and beliefs" (pp. 15–16). In this sense, most people possess "latent" if not "forensic" ideologies (see also Jost 2006). More specifically, even those who are relatively uninterested or uninformed about politics do exhibit at least some understanding of the core aspects of liberal-conservative differences (Federico & Schneider 2007; Feldman 1988, 2003; Goren 2001; Knutsen 1995; Peffley & Hurwitz 1985). Evidence of ideological reasoning—or perhaps a better word is commitment—is substantially clearer concerning core attitudes pertaining to social change and egalitarianism as compared with more peripheral attitudes (Anderson & Singer 2008, Carmines & Layman 1997, Conover & Feldman 1981, Eagly et al. 2004, Goren 2004, Jost 2006, Jost et al. 2008b, McClosky & Zaller 1984, Rathbun 2007).[1] Moreover, familiarity with the discursive superstructure is easier to detect in the general public once survey-based measurement error is taken into account (e.g., Achen 1975, Zaller 1992; but see Converse 2000, 2006).

The main factor governing the mass acquisition of ideological content seems to be attention to and comprehension of information flowing from political elites (Bennett 2006; Converse 2000, 2006; Kuklinski et al. 2001; Lau & Redlawsk 2001; Lupia et al. 2000). Highly engaged political experts—those possessing relatively well-developed political schemas that can be used to assimilate new information—are most likely to receive, process, and use such information (e.g., Erikson & Tedin 2003, Fiske et al. 1990, Hamill et al. 1985, Lavine et al. 1997, Luskin 1990, Zaller 1992). There is evidence that motivation matters in addition to cognitive abilities. Studies show that individuals with a high need to evaluate, that is, a chronic tendency to form opinions and judge things as either good or bad (Bizer et al. 2004), are also more likely to acquire and use discursive ideological content (Federico 2004, 2007; Federico & Schneider 2007). This last line of work suggests that researchers would do well to consider a wider range of motives that affect citizens' receptiveness to ideological messages.

From the Bottom Up: Psychological Origins of the Motivational Substructure

Political scientists tend to acknowledge that dispositional characteristics of ordinary citizens should affect their ability and motivation to absorb ideological messages conveyed by political elites, but the focus, as discussed above, is generally on variables such as political involvement, sophistication, and expertise (e.g., Zaller 1992). Psychologists have proposed a wider variety of personality and individual difference variables that should affect not only one's degree of exposure to mass media but also one's ideological proclivities (see Jost et al. 2003b). Thus, Adorno et al. (1950) pointed out that an individual's belief system "reflects his personality and is not merely an aggregate of opinions picked up helter-skelter from the ideological environment" (p. 176; see also McClosky 1958, Tomkins 1963, Wilson 1973). Although research on personality and political orientation fell out of favor for many years, there are clear indications that interest has revived in bottom-up psychological processes contributing to ideological outcomes (e.g., Barker & Tinnick 2006, Block & Block 2006, Caprara 2007, Carney et al. 2008, Jost et al. 2008b, Kemmelmeier 2007, Leone & Chirumbolo 2008, Ozer & Benet-Martinez 2006, Sidanius & Pratto 1999, Stenner 2005, Thornhill & Fincher 2007, Van Hiel & Mervielde 2004, Weber & Federico 2007). Ultimately, a psychological perspective is needed to address the pesky question raised by Sniderman & Bullock (2004, p. 353), namely "why are some disposed to a liberal or broadly left political outlook while others are disposed to a conservative or broadly right orientation?"

A growing body of evidence suggests that left-right ideological stances reflect, among other things, the influences of heredity, childhood temperament or personality, and both situational and dispositional variability in social, cognitive, and motivational needs to reduce

---

[1]Rathbun (2007, p. 397), for instance, reported extraordinarily high correlations between support for hierarchy and right-wing orientation (0.70) and between support for community and left-wing orientation (0.61).

uncertainty and threat. For instance, Alford and colleagues (2005) compared samples of identical and fraternal twins in the United States and Australia and estimated that as much as 40% to 50% of the statistical variability in ideological opinions (but not political partisanship) was attributable to genetic factors (see also Bouchard et al. 2003, Carmen 2007). Jost (2006) proposed that the heritability of a set of basic cognitive, motivational, and personality orientations could account for the heritability of political attitudes (see Olson et al. 2001 for evidence of this kind). Alford & Hibbing (2007) downplayed this possibility on the basis of a study that turned up relatively weak correlations between Big Five measures of personality and political attitudes (but see Carney et al. 2008).

A longitudinal study by Block & Block (2006) is noteworthy because it suggests that childhood personality characteristics predict political attitudes 20 years later. Specifically, these researchers found that preschool children who were rated independently by their teachers as more self-reliant, energetic, resilient, relatively undercontrolled and dominating, and more likely to develop close relationships were more liberal than their peers at age 23. By contrast, preschool children who were characterized as feeling easily victimized and offended, indecisive, fearful, rigid, inhibited, vulnerable, and relatively overcontrolled were more conservative at age 23. Although it is not possible to rule out certain confounding factors associated with the location of the study (Berkeley, California), these results should not be dismissed, in part because they are very consistent with the results of a meta-analytic review that summarized data from 12 countries over a 44-year period (Jost et al. 2003b,c). The findings from that review and from subsequent research suggest that at least three major classes of psychological variables comprise the motivational substructure of political ideology: epistemic, existential, and relational motives (see **Figure 1**).

Epistemic motives: ideology offers certainty. It has been suggested that ideology "serves as a guide and compass through the thicket of political life," that is, it addresses a number of epistemic needs, such as explanation, evaluation, and orientation (Ball & Dagger 1991, pp. 1–2). We should not be surprised to learn, then, that psychological variables pertaining to the management of uncertainty predict both reliance on ideology in general and endorsement of specific policy positions, such as support for the Iraq War (e.g., Federico et al. 2005; Golec & Federico 2004; Jost et al. 2003b,c, 2007). For example, studies conducted in several countries demonstrate consistently that individuals who score higher on the Need for Cognitive Closure scale, which measures the motivation to "seize and freeze" on beliefs that offer simplicity, certainty, and clarity, are significantly more likely to hold conservative or right-wing attitudes (Jost et al. 2003b, pp. 358–359; see also Chirumbolo et al. 2004, Leone & Chirumbolo 2008, Van Hiel et al. 2004). Moreover, some evidence suggests that people who score high on the need to evaluate (i.e., to render a good/bad judgment) are more likely to gravitate toward conservative ideology (Bizer et al. 2004), whereas those who score high on the Need for Cognition scale, which measures enjoyment of thinking, are more likely to gravitate toward liberal ideology (Sargent 2004). These findings and others support the notion that an elective affinity exists between epistemic motives to reduce uncertainty and political conservatism (Jost et al. 2007).

Consistent with the idea that some people are more aware of the discursively constructed menu of political options than others and that such awareness allows people to select the ideology that is right for them, the relationship between epistemic motives (e.g., need for cognitive closure) and ideological self-placement is stronger among political experts and those who are more interested in politics (e.g., Federico & Goren 2009, Kemmelmeier 2007). The fact that ideologies exhibit, at least for some citizens, properties of cognitive schemata—such as hierarchical organization and spreading activation of construct

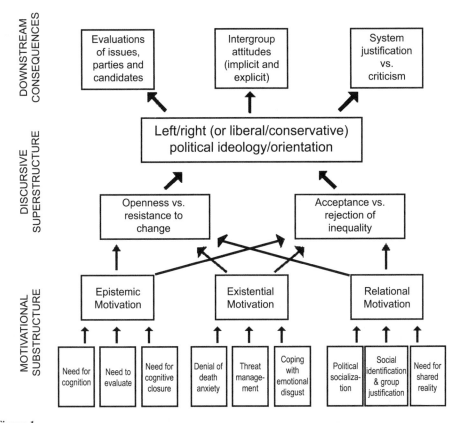

Figure 1

The motivational substructure, discursive superstructure, and downstream consequences of political ideology.

accessibility—provides yet another kind of evidence that they are serving epistemic functions associated with comprehension, explanation, and prediction (Fiske et al. 1990, Hamill et al. 1985).

Given that nearly everyone wants to achieve at least some degree of certainty, is it possible that conservatism possesses a natural psychological advantage over liberalism? Although answering this question is obviously fraught with challenges, several lines of research suggest that this might be the case. First, a series of experiments by Skitka et al. (2002) demonstrated that "the default attributional position is a conservative response," insofar as both liberals and conservatives are quick to draw individualistic (rather than system-level) conclusions about the causes of poverty,

unemployment, disease, and other negative outcomes, but only liberals correct their initial response, taking into account extenuating circumstances. When a distraction (or cognitive load) is introduced, making it difficult for liberals to engage in correction processes, they tend to blame individuals for their fate to the same degree that conservatives do. Skitka et al. (2002) therefore concluded, "It is much easier to get a liberal to behave like a conservative than it is to get a conservative to behave like a liberal" (p. 484; see also Kluegel & Smith 1986, Skitka 1999). Research by Crandall & Eidelman (2007) takes this general line of reasoning even further, showing that a host of everyday variables associated with increased cognitive load and/or increased need for cognitive closure, such as drinking alcohol, lead people to become more politically conservative. Both of these lines of research are consistent with the notion that conservative styles and opinions are generally simpler, more internally consistent, and less subject to ambiguity, in comparison with liberal styles and opinions (e.g., Jost et al. 2003b,c; Rokeach 1960; Tetlock 1983, 2007). A third reason to suggest that conservatism enjoys a psychological advantage over liberalism comes from research on system justification, which suggests that most people (including liberals) are motivated to adapt to and even rationalize aspects of the status quo, that is, to develop and maintain relatively favorable opinions about existing institutions and authorities and to dismiss or reject the possibility of change, especially in its more radical forms (Jost et al. 2004a). Studies show that justifying the status quo serves the palliative function of increasing positive affect, decreasing negative affect, and making people happier in general, but it also undermines support for social change and the redistribution of resources (Jost & Hunyady 2002, Napier & Jost 2008a, Wakslak et al. 2007).

Nevertheless, some people are motivated by sensation-seeking, novelty, curiosity, and openness to new experiences, and they are significantly more likely than others to embrace politically liberal and leftist opinions and causes (for a review, see Jost et al. 2003b, pp. 356–357; see also Jost et al. 2007). Of the Big Five personality dimensions, openness is most strongly predictive of political orientation, with liberals scoring consistently higher than conservatives (Carney et al. 2008, Jost 2006, Stenner 2005). The only other Big Five dimension that consistently correlates with political orientation (in U.S. and other samples) seems to be conscientiousness. Conservatives generally score higher than others do on conscientiousness-related motives and themes, especially needs for order, structure, and discipline. These personality differences emerge even in nonpolitical contexts. For instance, the bedrooms and offices of conservatives contain more items relating to conscientiousness, such as postage stamps and cleaning supplies, whereas liberals' rooms contain more items relating to openness, such as travel books, music, and art supplies (Carney et al. 2008).

Work summarized by Caprara & Zimbardo (2004) focuses on the importance of perceived similarities between the personality characteristics of voters and would-be political leaders (see also McCaul et al. 1995). For instance, they find that Italian citizens are more likely to support politicians and parties whose images are consistent with citizens' own self-images, so that center-right voters prefer candidates who are seen as conscientious and energetic, whereas center-left voters prefer candidates who are seen as open and friendly (Caprara & Zimbardo 2004, p. 586). Although more research is needed to investigate interactions between psychological and other characteristics of leaders and followers, insights derived from the "congruency model" suggest new ways of identifying the occurrence of elective affinities in the area of political psychology.

Existential motives: ideology offers security. According to terror management theory (TMT), ideologies—or "cultural worldviews," in the argot of TMT—serve the existential function of allowing people to symbolically transcend the threat induced by the uniquely human awareness of one's own mortality (Greenberg et al. 1997, Pyszczynski et al. 1999, Solomon et al. 2004). That is, political and other belief systems are seen as assisting people in the motivated belief that they are persons of value in a meaningful universe that transcends the finite self, thereby providing a sense of existential security. Consistent with this claim, a vast experimental literature demonstrates that making research participants aware of their own mortality leads them to hew more closely to established belief systems and identities. For example, mortality salience appears to produce greater patriotism and hostility toward critics of one's nation, a stronger endorsement of the unique validity of one's own religion, stronger support for traditional gender norms, greater attention to established norms of procedural fairness, increased levels of stereotyping, and a generally stronger preference for aggressive responses to individuals and groups who are perceived as threatening to the cultural worldview (for a review, see Pyszczynski et al. 1999; see also Arndt et al. 2002, Schimel et al. 1999, van den Bos et al. 2005).

Jost et al. (2004b) proposed that an elective affinity exists between psychological needs to minimize threat—including threat arising from death anxiety—and conservative ideology. Accordingly, they found that priming liberals, moderates, and conservatives with thoughts of death produced an across-the-board increase in issue-based conservatism. Such a result is consistent with the meta-analysis of Jost et al. (2003b), which showed that fear of death, system threat, and perceptions of a dangerous world were all positively associated with the holding of conservative attitudes (see also Weber & Federico 2007; but see Greenberg & Jonas 2003 for a different position). Jost et al. (2007) replicated an earlier finding that conservatives score higher than liberals do on a dispositional measure of death anxiety; in three studies they also ruled out the possibility that needs to manage uncertainty and threat are associated with ideological extremity in general rather than with political conservatism in particular.

In fact, a barrage of recent studies suggests that existential motives to cope with anxiety and threat lead disproportionately to conservative outcomes. Experimental studies conducted shortly before the 2004 presidential election revealed that although college students favored Democratic challenger John Kerry in the control condition, they showed a preference reversal following exposure to mortality salience primes, supporting Republican President George W. Bush instead (Cohen et al. 2005, Landau et al. 2004). Ullrich & Cohrs (2007) showed in several experiments that increasing the salience of terrorism led participants to score more highly on a measure of system justification, further strengthening the case that conservatism serves system-justifying ends (see also Jost et al. 2008b). Finally, a study of high-exposure survivors of the September 11, 2001 terrorist attacks found that Democrats as well as Republicans reported "conservative shifts" in the 18 months following the attacks (Bonanno & Jost 2006).

Consistent with all of these findings, the research literature on right-wing authoritarianism shows that highly threatening situations are frequently (but not always) associated with ideological shifts to the right. For example, archival research suggests that the appeal of conservative and right-wing leaders and policies is enhanced during periods of high social, economic, or political threat (Davis & Silver 2004, Doty et al. 1991, McCann 2008, Willer 2004). Presumably, this is because threat encourages people to embrace social and political attitudes that offer "relatively simple yet cognitively rigid solutions" to questions of security (Bonanno & Jost 2006, p. 311), and these types of solutions are more likely to resonate with the cognitive and rhetorical styles of those on the political right than the left (Jost et al. 2003b,c; Tetlock 2007; see also sidebar Mortality Salience, Authoritarianism, and Selective Exposure to Political Information). Along these lines, a doctoral dissertation by Thorisdottir (2007) demonstrated in several experiments that threatening stimuli (such as frightening movie clips) elicit a temporary increase in closed-mindedness (measured as one facet of the Need for Cognitive Closure scale) and that increased closed-mindedness was associated with an affinity for conservative (and certainty-oriented) policies and opinions.

Another psychological variable suggesting that existential concerns about safety, security, and threat management underlie left-right ideological differences is that of emotional disgust.[2] Recent studies show, for instance, that conservatives score higher than do liberals on dispositional measures of disgust sensitivity and

---

[2]To date, more research has been conducted on cognitive differences between liberals and conservatives (e.g., Jost et al. 2003b,c; Skitka et al. 2002; Tetlock 1983, 2007) than on emotional differences, but it seems likely that emotional differences also exist (e.g., Tomkins 1963). A recent study by Leone & Chirumbolo (2008) suggests, for instance, that leftists are more likely to exhibit emotional approach, whereas rightists are more likely to exhibit emotional avoidance.

MORTALITY SALIENCE, AUTHORITARIANISM, AND SELECTIVE EXPOSURE TO POLITICAL INFORMATION

An experiment by Lavine et al. (2005) revealed that a mortality salience manipulation led high (but not low) authoritarians to selectively expose themselves to information in a manner that was consistent with their position on capital punishment. This finding suggests that not everyone responds to threatening stimuli in the same manner (see also Davis & Silver 2004, Stenner 2005). It is important to point out, however, that low authoritarians did not show greater open-mindedness (or a decrease in selective exposure) following mortality salience priming (Lavine et al. 2005, p. 232). Lavine et al. (2005) concluded their article by emphasizing elective affinities, that is, "interactions between dispositional motivational needs and cognitive styles on one hand, and exigencies of the social and political environment on the other" (p. 240). Specifically, they suggested that those who tune into "the now ubiquitous format of one-sided (generally right-wing) talk radio (e.g., Rush Limbaugh, Sean Hannity, Michael Savage, Bill O'Reilly)" are motivated not merely by chronic anger and resentment but that "viewers' preferences for one-sided vs 'fair and balanced' formats are at least partly a function of perceived environmental threat" (p. 240).

that disgust sensitivity predicts specific policy opinions on issues such as abortion as well as prejudicial intergroup attitudes (Hodson & Costello 2007, Inbar et al. 2008). Given the apparent link between disgust and moral judgment (Haidt 2001), these differences could help to explain why conservatives tend to value purity and to be more moralistic than liberals in sexual and other cultural domains (Haidt & Graham 2007, Jarudi et al. 2008, Skitka et al. 2002). If this reasoning is correct, political and other messages that elicit disgust reactions should benefit conservatives disproportionately, much as threat-related messages seem to help conservatives and hurt liberals.

Relational motives: ideology offers solidarity. A vast research literature on political socialization, reviewed by Sears & Levy (2003), indicates that ideological beliefs are likely to be transmitted from parents to children, especially if both parents have similar beliefs and discuss politics frequently (Jennings & Niemi 1981) and if bonds within the family are close (Davies 1965). Similarly, peer and reference groups also exert a reasonably strong influence on left-right self-placement (Alwin et al. 1991; see Jost et al. 2008a for a brief review). These relational influences on ideological outcomes are strongest in late adolescence and early adulthood, that is, while personal identity is still in the process of development (Alwin 1993, Sears & Levy 2003). Moreover, consistent with other work on social influence, the resulting identifications tend to persist as long as one's relational context does not change markedly (e.g., Alwin et al. 1991).

It seems likely that some passive forms of learning and social influence are involved in the transmission of social and political attitudes from parents to offspring and from peer to peer, but the possibility also arises that more active forms of influence occur, and these are likely to involve relational motives for social identification, affiliation, and/or the attainment of shared reality (e.g., Baumeister & Leary 1995, Fiske 2004, Hardin & Higgins 1996, Tajfel & Turner 1986). For instance, Jost et al. (2008a) found that students whose parents were ideologically divergent scored higher on a measure of system justification after writing about either a positive or a negative interaction with their more conservative parent, suggesting that an implicitly activated desire to bond with close others can have ideological consequences. Thus, loyalty, friendship, social comparison, and perceived social support are central to developing and sustaining political conviction (Abelson 1988, p. 269). Furthermore, Gerber et al. (2008) found that exerting social pressure (by informing registered voters that their neighbors would know whether or not they voted) increased turnout substantially.

The study of relational motives has the capacity to shed light on the factors that affect whether or not the discursive superstructure developed by partisan elites becomes a shared social representation (or stereotype) that penetrates public consciousness (e.g., Billig 2003, Denzau & North 1994/2000,

Hardin & Higgins 1996, Marx & Engels 1846/1970, Moscovici 1988, Parsons 1951). At present, very little solid research exists in this area. However, we do know that important reference groups—including those based on race, ethnicity, gender, social class, political party, and religious affiliation—are used as cues for political judgment and behavior by citizens at nearly every level of political sophistication (e.g., Bartels 2000, Campbell et al. 1960/1965, Conover & Feldman 1981, Eagly et al. 2004, Hamill et al. 1985, Lau & Redlawsk 2001, Rahn 1993, Sniderman et al. 1991). A number of studies suggest that party leaders are capable of instigating political polarization and bringing about "conflict extension" in the electorate (Hetherington 2001, Layman & Carsey 2002). Cohen (2003) demonstrated that people are more likely to endorse a given policy position when they believe that it was proposed by their own political party than when the same policy was seen as part of the opposing party's agenda.

There is also some evidence that ideological affinities flow from group identification and realistic group interest (Bobo 1999, Campbell et al. 1960/1965, Sniderman et al. 2004). In general, the perception of collective self-interest does influence ideological preferences when group identification is relatively salient, with members of low-status and low-power groups tacking slightly to the left, especially on economic issues (Bobo 1999, Kluegel & Smith 1986, Lipset 1960, Napier & Jost 2008b).[3] However, this effect is not a simple or reflexive one: Not everyone adopts group-interested (or group-justifying) ideological positions. In fact, for some members of disadvantaged groups, relational needs to express solidarity with one's own kind may be countered (or trumped) by system-justifying tendencies that serve epistemic or existential needs—or perhaps relational needs tied to other social relationships (e.g., see Henry & Saul 2006, Jost et al. 2003d,

Lane 1962). Thus, the effect of group interest, while present, is rarely total (see also Sears & Funk 1991).

Although it is abundantly clear that processes associated with social identification, partisanship, and group interest can exert political influence in both liberal and conservative directions (e.g., Bartels 2000, Cohen 2003, Green et al. 2002), Jost et al. (2008a) speculated that—as with epistemic and existential motives—some relational motives could favor conservative outcomes in general. This is broadly consistent with the commonly held notion that conservatives are especially likely to value tradition, conformity, social order, and consensual adherence to rules, norms, and conventions (e.g., Altemeyer 1998, Conover & Feldman 1981, Feldman 2003, Haidt & Graham 2007, Jost 2006). It is also consistent with the assumption that it is generally easier to establish common ground with respect to the status quo than with respect to its many possible alternatives and to communicate effectively by transmitting messages that are relatively simple and unambiguous rather than reflecting the kind of complex, nuanced, and perhaps ambivalent cognitive and rhetorical styles that seem to be more common on the political left than the right (see Jost et al. 2008a). On the other hand, Caprara & Zimbardo (2004) observed that leftists were more concerned about friendliness and agreeableness than were rightists in Italy, and Carney et al. (2008) found in a study of nonverbal interaction styles that liberals were more expressive and smiled more frequently than did conservatives, suggesting that under these circumstances liberals possessed a higher degree of relational motivation.

SOCIAL AND POLITICAL CONSEQUENCES OF IDEOLOGY

Thus far, our review has focused on the dimensional structure and discursive contents of left-right ideology as well as its motivational antecedents or functional substructure. However, much evidence suggests that acquisition of the

---

[3] Eagly et al. (2004) found that women, in comparison with men, are generally more liberal with respect to one core value, namely egalitarianism, but they are more conservative when it comes to issues bearing on moral traditions.

discursive superstructure—which requires both exposure to the ideological menu communicated by institutional elites as well as the ability and motivation to absorb the messages—has important downstream social and political consequences (see **Figure 1**). We review some of these below.

Effects on the Evaluations of Issues, Parties, Candidates, and Other Attitude Objects

Perhaps the most obvious consequence of ideological orientation is its influence on political attitudes and behaviors such as voting. Many studies have shown that those who identify as liberal tend to adopt issue positions that are conventionally recognized as left-of-center, evaluate liberal political figures more favorably, and vote for candidates of the left, whereas those who identify as conservative tend to adopt positions that are right-of-center, evaluate conservative political figures more favorably, and vote for candidates on the right (e.g., Conover & Feldman 1981, Evans et al. 1996, Federico & Schneider 2007, Jacoby 1991, Kerlinger 1984, Knutsen 1995, Lavine & Gschwend 2006, Zaller 1992). In fact, ideology and partisanship (which typically has an ideological thrust) are among the strongest and most consistent predictors of political preferences (e.g., see Erikson & Tedin 2003, Jacoby 1991, Jost 2006).

Moreover, left-right differences in evaluative preferences emerge in many areas outside the realm of formal politics. For instance, Jost et al. (2008b) found that self-identified liberals were significantly more favorable concerning foreign films, big cities, poetry, tattoos, and foreign travel, whereas conservatives were more favorable concerning fraternities and sororities, sport utility vehicles, drinking alcohol, and watching television (see also Carney et al. 2008, Jost 2006). Findings such as these strengthen the case that ideological divides are, among other things, personality divides, but the direction of causality is still unknown. We sus-

pect that ideological identifications both reflect and reinforce social and personal preferences, styles, and activities, but this is speculative and requires empirical confrontation using experimental and longitudinal research designs.

At a higher level of abstraction, ideology also predicts citizens' general value orientations, with leftists exhibiting greater egalitarianism and openness to change than rightists (Evans et al. 1996; Federico & Sidanius 2002; Feldman 1988, 2003; Jost 2006; Kerlinger 1984; Peffley & Hurwitz 1985; Rokeach 1973; Sidanius & Pratto 1999). Interestingly, many of these patterns are observable at the level of automatic or implicit attitudes as well. For example, in studies employing the Implicit Association Test, liberals on average displayed implicit (as well as explicit) preferences for words such as "flexible," "progress," and "feminism," whereas conservatives preferred their opposites, namely "stable," "tradition," and "traditional values" (Jost et al. 2008b). Ideological self-placement also has important effects on justice judgments and attributions for social stratification, with conservatives emphasizing principles of equity, ability, effort, and meritocracy as well as adopting a more punitive stance and being more likely to make internal attributions for others' outcomes in life in comparison with liberals (e.g., Altemeyer 1998, Kluegel & Smith 1986, Skitka 1999, Skitka et al. 2002, Sniderman et al. 1991). Haidt & Graham (2007) have suggested that the values of liberals and conservatives are rooted in distinct moral foundations, such that conservatives are more likely to incorporate ingroup, authority, and purity concerns in rendering moral (or perhaps moralistic) judgments.

Thus, heterogeneous research programs yield the common conclusion that ideological commitments are robust predictors of a wide range of attitudes, preferences, judgments, and behaviors. Nevertheless, it should be noted that—as with respect to the structure and contents of ideological beliefs—the downstream consequences of ideology are not readily observable at all levels of political sophistication (e.g., Converse 2000, 2006). Once again, factors concerning the ability and motivation to use the discursive contents of ideology moderate its effects on other social and political outcomes (e.g., Erikson & Tedin 2003, Kemmelmeier 2007, Kinder 1998, Zaller 1992). At the same time, one tenet of the psychological perspective on ideology that we take in this review is that people may behave in ideologically meaningful ways (or be affected by their own ideological proclivities) without necessarily being consciously or fully aware of the role of ideology in their lives, much as native speakers are generally capable of following grammatical or syntactical rules without being able to fully articulate them (see Jost 2006).

Effects on Implicit and Explicit Intergroup Attitudes

Ideological self-placement is strongly predictive of intergroup attitudes. More specifically, conservative and right-wing orientations are generally associated with stereotyping, prejudice, intolerance, and hostility toward a wide variety of outgroups, especially low-status or stigmatized outgroups (e.g., Altemeyer 1998, Duckitt et al. 2002, Federico & Sidanius 2002, Lambert & Chasteen 1997, Napier & Jost 2008b, Sidanius & Pratto 1999, Sidanius et al. 1996, Whitley 1999, Wilson 1973). The fact that conservatives express less-favorable attitudes than liberals express toward disadvantaged or stigmatized groups is not seriously disputed in social science research, although there is some debate about whether the differences are motivated by intergroup bias or a differential degree of commitment to individualism, traditionalism, meritocracy, and other conservative values (e.g., Sears et al. 1997, Sidanius et al. 1996, Sniderman et al. 2000).

It is important to note that differences between liberals and conservatives with respect to intergroup attitudes emerge even on implicit or nonconscious measures, suggesting that they are not attributable to differences in socially desirable responding (e.g., Cunningham et al.

2004; Jost et al. 2004a; Nosek et al. 2007, 2009). Some research suggests that conservatives are more likely to endorse traditional forms of racism, whereas liberals are more likely to show signs of subtle or aversive racism, indicating the presence of conflict between egalitarian ideals and biased impulses (Feldman & Huddy 2005, Nail et al. 2003). It is also worth noting that such affinities have likely been surmised already by political elites who are responsible for the contents of political advertisements. Research on political communication suggests that (*a*) conservative campaigns are more likely than liberal campaigns to play the "race card" (Mendelberg 2001), and (*b*) subtle (but nefarious) racial primes that visually or verbally link African Americans to crime or welfare tend to benefit conservative candidates and hurt liberal candidates (Valentino 1999, Valentino et al. 2002).

It is seldom pointed out explicitly that the effects of political orientation on ingroup-outgroup evaluations depend upon the status of the participant's own group. That is, conservatism is typically correlated with ingroup favoritism for members of high-status groups, but it is frequently correlated with outgroup favoritism for members of low-status groups (e.g., Jost et al. 2004a, Levin et al. 2002). Thus, increasing political conservatism is associated with a stronger prostraight/antigay preference on implicit and explicit measures for heterosexuals and homosexuals alike (Jost et al. 2004a). These findings suggest again that conservatism is a system-justifying ideology, insofar as it leads even members of disadvantaged groups to perpetuate the unequal status quo at the level of both implicit and explicit intergroup attitudes (Jost et al. 2008b).

The differences between liberals and conservatives with respect to intergroup attitudes are readily interpretable in light of our analysis of the functional substructure of ideology (i.e., in terms of epistemic, existential, and relational motives). For instance, research in social cognition demonstrates that people adopt stereotypes at least in part to conserve mental resources and to impose order and structure on the social world (e.g., Macrae et al. 1996, Moskowitz 2005). We know that conservatives exhibit heightened needs to avoid ambiguity, novelty, uncertainty, and complexity and to achieve order, structure, and closure (Jost et al. 2003b,c), and this (in conjunction with a relative acceptance of inequality) may help to explain why stereotypes and prejudicial attitudes are more appealing to them than they are to liberals. The connection between rigid or dogmatic thinking styles and prejudice has long been noted (e.g., Rokeach 1960), as has the connection between intolerance of ambiguity and prejudice (e.g., Adorno et al. 1950, Allport 1954). The personal need for structure has also been associated with right-wing authoritarianism (Altemeyer 1998), negative attitudes toward gays and lesbians (Smith & Gordon 1998), and the formation of erroneous system-justifying stereotypes (Schaller et al. 1995). Similarly, the need for cognitive closure predicts stereotyping, prejudice, and right-wing authoritarianism (Kruglanski 2004), conservatism (Jost et al. 2003b), and racism (Van Hiel et al. 2004). Although it is impossible to establish directions of causality among these variables based upon the existing research literature, it seems clear that they are empirically linked.

Existential motives to avoid threat may also play a part in the relatively higher levels of prejudice and intergroup hostility observed among conservatives, as evidenced by terror management research showing that mortality salience increases stereotyping and prejudice (Schimel at al. 1999). Some studies suggest that mortality salience increases prejudice, but only in people who are already predisposed toward the holding of prejudicial attitudes (Greenberg et al. 1992). There is also evidence that threats to self-esteem increase stereotyping and prejudice (Allport 1954, Fein & Spencer 1997) and may be linked to political orientation (see Jost et al. 2003b for a review). Furthermore, the emotion of disgust is predictive of intergroup hostility and prejudice as well as political conservatism (Hodson & Costello 2007, Inbar

et al. 2008, Talaska et al. 2008). Finally, it is relatively easy to see how relational needs to maintain solidarity with one's ingroup could facilitate prejudice and discrimination against outgroup members (Tajfel & Turner 1986) as well as the sharing of ideologies that justify unequal treatment (Jost et al. 2008a).

Ideology as a System-Justifying Device

It should be clear by now that we regard ideology as not merely an organizing device or a shortcut for making heuristic judgments about various political objects; it is also a device for explaining and even rationalizing the way things are or, alternatively, how things should be different than they are. Thus, political ideologies typically make at least tacit reference to some social system, either as an affirmation or a rejection of it (Anderson & Singer 2008, Ball & Dagger 1991, Freeden 2001, Jost 2006, Knight 2006, Lipset & Raab 1978, Marx & Engels 1846/1970, Parsons 1951). As we have mentioned above, research on system justification theory suggests that most people—to varying degrees depending on epistemic, existential, and relational needs—engage in both conscious and nonconscious rationalization of the status quo through the use of spontaneous social judgments (e.g., stereotypes) and by latching onto pre-existing ideologies such as conservatism (Jost et al. 2004a, Lane 1962). These and other system-justifying mechanisms imbue social, economic, and political arrangements with fairness and legitimacy (Jost et al. 2003a,d; Kay et al. 2007; Major et al. 2002; Sidanius & Pratto 1999). From the point of view of political elites, system justification is beneficial insofar as it contributes to the stability of the social system and increases voluntary deference on the part of ordinary citizens (Tyler 2006).

The power of ideology to explain and justify discrepancies between the current social order and some alternative not only maintains support for the status quo, but also serves for its adherents the palliative function of alleviating dissonance or discomfort associated with the awareness of systemic injustice or inequality (e.g., Jost & Hunyady 2002, Napier & Jost 2008a). The endorsement of system-justifying beliefs is associated with increased positive affect, decreased negative affect, and high personal satisfaction or contentment (Jost et al. 2003d, Kluegel & Smith 1986, Lerner 1980, Wakslak et al. 2007). In attempting to understand why conservatives report being happier than liberals, Napier & Jost (2008a) found that the association between political ideology and subjective well-being was explained to a significant degree by respondents' differential tendencies to rationalize economic inequality in society. Furthermore, the happiness gap between conservatives and liberals in the United States was tied to the nation's level of income inequality, so that as inequality has increased over the last 30 years, the subjective well-being of liberals has dropped more precipitously than has that of conservatives. Thus, it appears that system-justifying ideologies such as conservatism can "provide a kind of ideological buffer against the negative hedonic consequences of social and economic inequality" (Napier & Jost 2008a; see also Anderson & Singer 2008).

In sum, ideology can play an important role as a system-serving bundle of attitudes, values, and beliefs. However, as with respect to the organizing role of ideology, it is best to conclude with a few caveats about the reach of ideology as a system-justification device. Although system-justifying attitudes, values, and beliefs are widespread, they rarely diffuse or "work" completely, especially in large, highly complex societies and among those who are suspicious of and/or geographically distant from centers of power (e.g., Abercrombie et al. 1980; see also Sidanius & Pratto 1999). This opens the door to at least some degree of change and flux in social relations. Nevertheless, we think that it would be a mistake to underestimate the ideological significance of the human tendency to make a "virtue of necessity" by accepting and even celebrating features of the status quo; from this perspective, system-justification motivation appears to give conservatism a psychological head start over its more critical rivals.

CONCLUDING REMARKS

Our purpose in this article has been to review recent scholarship on political ideology as a social psychological phenomenon. We have endeavored to integrate insights derived from a variety of research programs addressing different levels of analysis and therefore distinctive facets of political ideology (see **Figure 1**). Given the resurgence of ideologically inspired conflict and polarization in the current era (e.g., Abramowitz & Saunders 2008, Jost 2006, Layman & Carsey 2002, Stimson 2004), it is our hope that this summary of existing research will not only help us to better understand the present but also point the way to a more constructive future. To succeed, we will need the continued engagement of the social scientific research community as a whole. For our own part, we have taken seriously the possibility first suggested by Adorno et al. (1950) that a "structural unity" exists between underlying psychological needs and ideological manifestations of those needs. Although contemporary researchers are much closer than were the members of the Frankfurt School to understanding the connections between the discursive superstructure of ideology and its motivational substructure, it is plain to see that we still do not know as much about these elective affinities as one would like. We take some solace in the possibility, however uncertain, that this review will inspire other researchers to join in the challenging task of identifying sound scientific principles that explain why certain individuals and groups choose particular constellations of ideas or, similarly, why some ideologies find deep resonance in the minds of some political actors but not others. Psychologically oriented investigations of ideological phenomena carry with them an inescapable limitation but also take on what many would regard as a societal obligation of the highest order. As the authors of *The Authoritarian Personality* pointed out many years ago, "Knowledge of the psychological determinants of ideology cannot tell us what is the *truest* ideology; it can only remove some of the barriers in the way of its pursuit" (Adorno et al. 1950, p. 11). If there is a nobler or more difficult task than this for a political psychologist, we know not what it is.

FUTURE ISSUES

1. It is commonly assumed that political elites are the architects of ideology, but little research has examined the motivational processes involved in elite construction of the discursive superstructure. The range of epistemic, existential, and relational motives we have examined in this chapter are assumed to affect elites as well as mass publics, but existing research has been limited to purely strategic motives (e.g., the assembly of a winning party coalition; see Hinich & Munger 1994). Future research would do well to investigate the role of substructural motives (or functions) in the elite context, where actors are not only consumers of ideology but are also capable of bundling or packaging its contents in the first place (see Tetlock 1983 for an example).

2. Political scientists have generally assumed that the assembly of ideological packages by elites is at least somewhat arbitrary, so that ideologies are socially constructed by the repeated bundling of certain contents in order to gain electoral advantage (e.g., Sniderman & Bullock 2004). Our analysis in terms of elective affinities suggests that there are clear social psychological constraints on the types of attitudes, values, and beliefs that can be bundled together. This possibility was raised in early discussions of mass belief systems (e.g., Converse 1964, Rokeach 1960), but it has been largely ignored since then in favor of perspectives that focus almost exclusively on the role of elites in establishing conventional (but essentially arbitrary) discursive superstructures (e.g., Zaller 1992). Future work should address motivational (as well as cognitive) sources of constraint to explain how and why specific constellations of attitudes, values, and beliefs coalesce into relatively coherent (and sometimes incoherent, at least with respect to logical sophistication) ideological packages.

3. We have suggested that the metaphor of elective affinities, which is taken from the writings of Goethe (1809/1966), Weber (1922/1946), and Gerth & Mills (1948/1970), is an especially useful one because it aptly characterizes the forces of mutual attraction that bring people and ideas together. In other words, it highlights the fact that every ideological outcome arises from an interaction between top-down processes of socialization (or exposure) and bottom-up processes of need fulfillment. However, the concept is openly agnostic about (and therefore willfully imprecise concerning) directions of causality between top-down and bottom-up factors. We, like many others (e.g., Adorno et al. 1950, Alford et al. 2005, Lane 1962, Sniderman & Bullock 2004, Zaller 1992), assume that the contents of the discursive superstructure and the motives driving the functional substructure of ideology meet somewhere in the middle, but how this occurs has yet to be clearly and carefully documented. It would be particularly useful to identify interactions between top-down and bottom-up processes.

4. The metaphor of ideological menu dependence is consistent with our analysis of elective affinities, insofar as people must be exposed to a more-or-less complete range of options in order to be able to select an ideology that matches their psychological and other dispositions. This could also explain why the effects of personality on political orientation in the general population would be stronger in Western democratic nations (that offer at least some variability in the ideological menu) than in authoritarian and totalitarian regimes that restrict ideological alternatives (see Greenberg & Jonas 2003, Jost et al. 2003b). A related issue is whether there are important differences between Eastern and Western nations in the psychological underpinnings of political orientation (e.g., see Thorisdottir et al. 2007). In this review, we have taken a largely Western perspective, but it would be illuminating to conduct parallel investigations in Asian, African, and other cultural contexts.

5. We have said relatively little about rational choice models of political preferences, except to note that some (albeit modest) evidence supports the notion that individual and collective self-interest does influence ideological outcomes. It would be useful in future work to determine whether the kinds of epistemic, existential, and relational motives we have identified in this chapter are compatible or incompatible with rational actor models. For instance, to what extent is it rational (or congruent with self-interest) for people to embrace certain ideologies because they appear to satisfy their personal needs for cognition, evaluation, structure, or closure?

6. In this review and elsewhere, we have generally assumed that system justification motivation increases one's affinity for conservative (versus liberal) ideology. This may be contingent upon one's societal context, however. It is unclear whether system-justification motivation in Scandinavia, for instance, would be associated with increased or decreased support for high rates of taxation, universal health care coverage, state-sponsored childcare, tuition, and so on. Furthermore, it is at least conceivable that the two core aspects of left-right ideology (resistance to change and acceptance of inequality) are decoupled or even negatively correlated in socialist or communist regimes and that this could be due to the marshaling of system justification tendencies in support of egalitarian rather than hierarchical ideals.

DISCLOSURE STATEMENT

The authors are not aware of any biases that might be perceived as affecting the objectivity of this review.

ACKNOWLEDGMENTS

The writing of this chapter was supported in part by research awards to the first author by the New York University Center for Catastrophe Preparedness and Response (CCPR) and the National Science Foundation (Grant #BCS-0617558). We are grateful to Cara Jolly and Briehan Truesdell for administrative and other assistance with respect to this project as well as to the members of the Jost Lab at NYU for their input and inspiration. Finally, we thank Susan T. Fiske, György Hunyady, Lawrence J. Jost, Howard Lavine, and Tom R. Tyler for helpful suggestions and advice concerning prior drafts.

LITERATURE CITED

Abelson RP. 1988. Conviction. *Am. Psychol.* 43:267–75

Abercrombie N, Hill S, Turner B, eds. 1980. *The Dominant Ideology Thesis.* London: Allen & Unwin

Abramowitz AI, Saunders KL. 2008. Is polarization really a myth? *J. Polit.* 70:542–55

Achen CH. 1975. Mass political attitudes and the survey response. *Am. Polit. Sci. Rev.* 69:1218–23

Adorno TW, Frenkel-Brunswik E, Levinson DJ, Sanford RN. 1950. *The Authoritarian Personality.* New York: Harper

Alford JR, Funk CL, Hibbing JR. 2005. Are political orientations genetically transmitted? *Am. Polit. Sci. Rev.* 99:153–67

Alford JR, Hibbing JR. 2007. Personal, interpersonal, and political temperaments. *Ann. Am. Acad. Polit. Soc. Sci.* 614:196–212

Allport GW. 1954. *The Nature of Prejudice.* Reading, MA: Addison-Wesley

Altemeyer RA. 1998. The other "authoritarian personality." *Adv. Exp. Soc. Psychol.* 30:47–91

Alwin DF. 1993. Personality and social structure. *Contemp. Sociol.* 22:58–61

Alwin DF, Cohen RL, Newcomb TM. 1991. *Political Attitudes Over the Life Span.* Madison: Univ. Wisc. Press

Anderson CJ, Singer MM. 2008. The sensitive left and the impervious right: multilevel models and the politics of inequality, ideology, and legitimacy in Europe. *Comp. Polit. Stud.* 41:564–99

Arndt J, Greenberg J, Cook A. 2002. Mortality salience and the spreading activation of worldview-relevant constructs: exploring the cognitive architecture of terror management. *J. Exp. Psychol.* 131:307–24

Ball T, Dagger R, eds. 1991. *Ideals and Ideologies: A Reader.* New York: HarperCollins

Barker DC, Tinnick JD. 2006. Competing visions of parental roles and ideological constraint. *Am. Polit. Sci. Rev.* 100:249–63

Bartels LM. 2000. Partisanship and voting behavior, 1952–1996. *Am. J. Polit. Sci.* 44:35–50

Baumeister RF, Leary MR. 1995. The need to belong: desire for interpersonal attachments as a fundamental human motivation. *Psychol. Bull.* 117:497–529

Bennett S. 2006. Democratic competence, before Converse and after. *Crit. Rev.* 18:105–42

Benoit K, Laver M. 2006. *Party Policy in Modern Democracies.* London: Routledge

Berinsky AJ. 2007. Assuming the costs of war: events, elites, and American public support for military conflict. *J. Polit.* 69:975–97

Billig M. 2003. Political rhetoric. In *Oxford Handbook of Political Psychology*, ed. DO Sears, L Huddy, R Jervis, pp. 222–50. New York: Oxford Univ. Press

Bishop GF. 2005. *The Illusion of Public Opinion: Fact and Artifact in American Public Opinion Polls.* Lanham, MD: Rowman & Littlefield

Bizer GY, Krosnick JA, Holbrook AL, Petty RE, Wheeler SC, Rucker DD. 2004. The impact of personality on cognitive, behavioral, and affective political processes: the effects of need to evaluate. *J. Personal.* 72:995–1027

Block J, Block JH. 2006. Nursery school personality and political orientation two decades later. *J. Res. Personal.* 40:734–49

Bobbio N. 1996. *Left and Right.* Cambridge, UK: Polity

Bobo L. 1999. Prejudice as group position: microfoundations of a sociological approach to racism and race relations. *J. Soc. Issues* 55:445–72

Bonanno GA, Jost JT. 2006. Conservative shift among high-exposure survivors of the September 11th terrorist attacks. *Basic Appl. Soc. Psychol.* 28:311–23

Bouchard T, Segal N, Tellegen A, McGue M, Keyes M, Krueger R. 2003. Evidence for the construct validity and heritability of the Wilson-Patterson conservatism scale: a reared-apart twins study of social attitudes. *Personal. Individ. Differ.* 34:959–69

Burke E. 1790/1987. *Reflections on the Revolution in France, and on the Proceedings in Certain Societies in London Relative to that Event*, ed. JGA Pocock. Indianapolis, IN: Hackett Publ.

Campbell A, Converse PE, Miller WE, Stokes DE. 1960/1965. *The American Voter.* Oxford, UK: Wiley

Caprara GV. 2007. The personalization of modern politics. *Euro. Rev.* 15:151–64

Caprara GV, Zimbardo P. 2004. Personalizing politics: a congruency model of political preference. *Am. Psychol.* 59:581–94

Carmen I. 2007. Genetic configurations of political phenomena. *Ann. Am. Acad. Polit. Soc. Sci.* 614:34–55

Carmines EG, Layman GC. 1997. Value priorities, partisanship, and electoral choice: the neglected case of the United States. *Polit. Behav.* 19:283–316

Carney DR, Jost JT, Gosling SD, Potter J. 2008. The secret lives of liberals and conservatives: personality profiles, interaction styles, and the things they leave behind. *Polit. Psychol.* In press

Chirumbolo A, Areni A, Sensales G. 2004. Need for cognitive closure and politics: voting, political attitudes and attributional style. *Int. J. Psychol.* 39:245–53

Cohen F, Ogilvie DM, Solomon S, Greenberg J, Pyszczynski T. 2005. American roulette: the effect of reminders of death on support for George W. Bush in the 2004 presidential election. *Anal. Soc. Issues Public Policy* 5:177–87

Cohen GL. 2003. Party over policy: The dominating impact of group influence on political beliefs. *J. Personal. Soc. Psychol.* 85:808–22

Conover PJ, Feldman S. 1981. The origins and meaning of liberal-conservative self-identifications. *Am. J. Polit. Sci.* 25:617–45

Converse PE. 1964. The nature of belief systems in mass publics. In *Ideology and Discontent*, ed. D Apter, pp. 206–61. New York: Free Press

Converse PE. 2000. Assessing the capacity of mass electorates. *Annu. Rev. Pol. Sci.* 3:331–53

Converse PE. 2006. Democratic theory and electoral reality. *Crit. Rev.* 18:75–104

Crandall CS, Eidelman S. 2007. *The psychological advantage of the status quo*. Presented at Annu. Meet. Int. Soc. Polit. Sci., 30th, Portland, OR

Cunningham WA, Nezlek JB, Banaji MR. 2004. Implicit and explicit ethnocentrism: revisiting the ideologies of prejudice. *Personal. Soc. Psychol. Bull.* 30:1332–46

Dalton RJ. 2003. *Citizen Politics*. Chatham, NJ: Chatham House

Davies JC. 1965. The family's role in political socialization. *Ann. Am. Acad. Polit. Soc. Sci.* 361:10–19

Davis DW, Silver BD. 2004. Civil liberties vs. security: public opinion in the context of the terrorist attacks on America. *Am. J. Polit. Sci.* 48:28–46

Delli Carpini MX, Keeter S. 1996. *What Americans Know About Politics and Why It Matters*. New Haven, CT: Yale Univ. Press

Denzau AD, North DC. 1994/2000. Shared mental models: ideologies and institutions. In *Elements of Reason: Cognition, Choice, and the Bounds of Rationality*, ed. A Lupia, MC McCubbins, SL Popkin, pp. 23–46. New York: Cambridge Univ. Press

Doty RM, Peterson BE, Winter DG. 1991. Threat and authoritarianism in the United States, 1978–1987. *J. Personal. Soc. Psychol.* 61:629–40

Duckitt J. 2001. A cognitive-motivational theory of ideology and prejudice. In *Advances in Experimental Social Psychology*, ed. MP Zanna, pp. 41–113. San Diego, CA: Academic

Duckitt J. 2006. Differential effects of Right Wing Authoritarianism and Social Dominance Orientation on outgroup attitudes and their mediation by threat from competitiveness to outgroups. *Personal. Soc. Psychol. Bull.* 32:684–96

Duckitt J, Wagner C, du Plessis I, Birum I. 2002. The psychological bases of ideology and prejudice: testing a dual-process model. *J. Personal. Soc. Psychol.* 83:75–93

Duriez B, Van Hiel A, Kossowska M. 2005. Authoritarianism and social dominance in Western and Eastern Europe: the importance of the socio-political context and of political interest and involvement. *Polit. Psychol.* 26:299–320

Eagleton T. 1991. *Ideology: An Introduction*. London: Verso

Eagly AH, Chaiken S. 1998. Attitude structure and function. In *The Handbook of Social Psychology*, ed. DT Gilbert, ST Fiske, G Lindzey, 3:269–322. Boston, MA: McGraw-Hill

Eagly AH, Diekman AB, Johannesen-Schmidt MC, Koenig AM. 2004. Gender gaps in sociopolitical attitudes: a social psychological analysis. *J. Personal. Soc. Psychol.* 87:796–816

Erikson RS, Tedin KL. 2003. *American Public Opinion*. New York: Longman. 6th ed.

Evans G, Heath A, Lalljee M. 1996. Measuring left-right and libertarian-conservative attitudes in the British electorate. *Br. J. Sociol.* 47:93–112

Eysenck HJ. 1954/1999. *The Psychology of Politics*. New York: Routledge

Federico CM. 2004. Predicting attitude extremity: the interactive effects of expertise and the need to evaluate—and their mediation by evaluative integration. *Personal. Soc. Psychol. Bull.* 30:1281–94

Federico CM. 2007. Expertise, evaluative motivation, and the structure of citizens' ideological commitments. *Polit. Psychol.* 28:535–62

Federico CM, Golec A, Dial JL. 2005. The relationship between the need for closure and support for military action against Iraq: moderating effects of national attachment. *Personal. Soc. Psychol. Bull.* 31:621–32

Federico CM, Goren P. 2009. Motivated social cognition and ideology: Is attention to elite discourse a prerequisite for epistemically motivated political affinities? In *Social and Psychological Bases of Ideology and System Justification*, ed. JT Jost, AC Kay, H Thorisdottir. In press

Federico CM, Schneider M. 2007. Political expertise and the use of ideology: moderating effects of evaluative motivation. *Public Opin. Q.* 71:221–52

Federico CM, Sidanius J. 2002. Sophistication and the antecedents of whites' racial policy attitudes: racism, ideology, and affirmative action in America. *Public Opin. Q.* 66:145–76

Fein S, Spencer SJ. 1997. Prejudice as self-image maintenance: affirming the self through derogating others. *J. Personal. Soc. Psychol.* 73:31–44

Feldman S. 1988. Structure and consistency in public opinion: the role of core beliefs and values. *Am. J. Polit. Sci.* 32:416–40

Feldman S. 2003. Values, ideology, and structure of political attitudes. In *Oxford Handbook of Political Psychology*, ed. DO Sears, L Huddy, R Jervis, pp. 477–508. New York: Oxford Univ. Press

Feldman S, Huddy L. 2005. Racial resentment and white opposition to race-conscious programs: principles or prejudice? *Am. J. Polit. Sci.* 49:168–83

Feldman S, Steenbergen MR. 2001. The humanitarian foundation of public support for social welfare. *Am. J. Polit. Sci.* 45:658–77

Fiorina MP. 2005. *Culture War? The Myth of a Polarized America*. New York: Pearson Longman

Fiske ST. 2004. *Social Beings*. New York: Wiley

Fiske ST, Lau RR, Smith RA. 1990. On the varieties and utilities of political expertise. *Soc. Cogn.* 8:31–48

Free LA, Cantril H. 1967. *The Political Beliefs of Americans*. New Brunswick, NJ: Rutgers Univ. Press

Freeden M, ed. 2001. *Reassessing Political Ideologies*. London: Routledge

Fuchs D, Klingemann HD. 1990. The left-right schema. In *Continuities in Political Action: A Longitudinal Study of Political Orientations in Three Western Democracies*, ed. MK Jennings, JW van Deth, pp. 203–34. Berlin: Walter de Gruyter

Gamson WA. 1992. *Talking Politics*. London: Cambridge Univ. Press

Gerber AS, Green DP, Larimer CW. 2008. Social pressure and voter turnout: evidence from a large-scale field experiment. *Am. Pol. Sci. Rev.* 102:33–48

Gerring J. 1997. Ideology: a definitional analysis. *Polit. Res. Q.* 50:957–94

Gerth HH, Mills CW. 1948/1970. *Essays from Max Weber*. London: Routledge & Kegan Paul

Goethe JW. 1809/1966. *Elective Affinities*. Chicago, IL: Gateway Edition

Golec A, Federico CM. 2004. Understanding political conflict and its resolution: interactive effects of the need for closure and salient conflict schemas. *J. Personal. Soc. Psychol.* 87:750–62

Goren P. 2001. Core principles and policy-reasoning in mass publics: a test of two theories. *Br. J. Polit. Sci.* 31:159–77

Goren P. 2004. Political sophistication and policy reasoning: a reconsideration. *Am. J. Polit. Sci.* 48:462–78

Graber DA. 2004. Mediated politics and citizenship in the twenty-first century. *Annu. Rev. Psychol.* 55:545–71

Green DP. 1988. On the dimensionality of public sentiment toward partisan and ideological groups. *Am. J. Pol. Sci.* 32:758–80

Green DP, Palmquist B, Schickler E. 2002. *Partisan Hearts and Minds*. New Haven, CT: Yale Univ. Press

Greenberg J, Jonas E. 2003. Psychological motives and political orientation—the left, the right, and the rigid: comment on Jost et al. 2003. *Psychol. Bull.* 129:376–82

Greenberg J, Simon L, Pyszczynski T, Solomon S, Chatel D. 1992. Terror management and tolerance: Does mortality salience always intensify negative reactions to others who threaten one's worldview? *J. Personal. Soc. Psychol.* 63:212–20

Greenberg J, Solomon S, Pyszczynski T. 1997. Terror management theory of self-esteem and cultural worldviews: empirical assessments and conceptual refinements. *Adv. Exp. Soc. Psychol.* 29:61–139

Habermas J. 1989. *The Theory of Communicative Action, Volume Two*. Boston, MA: Beacon

Haidt J. 2001. The emotional and its rational tail: a social intuitionist approach to moral judgment. *Psychol. Rev.* 108:814–34

Haidt J, Graham J. 2007. When morality opposes justice: conservatives have moral intuitions that liberals may not recognize. *Soc. Justice Res.* 20:98–116

Hamill R, Lodge M, Blake F. 1985. The breadth, depth, and utility of partisan, class, and ideological schemas. *Am. J. Polit. Sci.* 29:850–70

Hardin CD, Higgins ET. 1996. Shared reality: how social verification makes the subjective objective. In *Handbook of Motivation and Cognition*, ed. RM Sorrentino, ET Higgins, 3:28–84. New York: Guilford

Henry PJ, Saul A. 2006. The development of system justification in the developing world. *Soc. Justice Res.* 19:365–78

Hetherington MJ. 2001. Resurgent mass partisanship: the role of elite polarization. *Am. Polit. Sci. Rev.* 95:619–31

Hinich MJ, Munger MC. 1994. *Ideology and the Theory of Political Choice*. Ann Arbor: Univ. Mich. Press

Hirschman AO. 1991. *The Rhetoric of Reaction: Perversity, Futility, Jeopardy*. Cambridge, MA: Belknap

Hodson G, Costello K. 2007. Interpersonal disgust, ideological orientation, and dehumanization as predictors of intergroup attitudes. *Psychol. Sci.* 18:691–98

Inbar Y, Pizarro DA, Bloom P. 2008. Conservatives are more easily disgusted than liberals. *Cogn. Emot.* In press

Jacoby W. 1991. Ideological identification and issue attitudes. *Am. J. Polit. Sci.* 35:178–205

Jacoby W. 2006. Value choices and American public opinion. *Am. J. Polit. Sci.* 50:706–23

Jarudi I, Kreps T, Bloom P. 2008. Is a refrigerator good or evil? The moral evaluation of everyday objects. *Soc. Justice Res.* In press

Jennings MK. 1992. Ideological thinking among mass publics and political elites. *Public Opin. Q.* 56:419–41

Jennings MK, Niemi RG. 1981. *Generations and Politics: A Panel Study of Young Adults and their Parents*. Princeton, NJ: Princeton Univ. Press

Jost JT. 2006. The end of the end of ideology. *Am. Psychol.* 61:651–70

Jost JT, Banaji MR, Nosek BA. 2004a. A decade of system justification theory: accumulated evidence of conscious and unconscious bolstering of the status quo. *Polit. Psychol.* 25:881–920

Jost JT, Blount S, Pfeffer J, Hunyady G. 2003a. Fair market ideology: its cognitive-motivational underpinnings. *Res. Org. Behav.* 25:53–91

Jost JT, Fitzsimons G, Kay AC. 2004b. The ideological animal: a system justification view. In *Handbook of Experimental Existential Psychology*, ed. J Greenberg, SL Koole, T Pyszczynski, p. 263–82. New York: Guilford

Jost JT, Glaser J, Kruglanski AW, Sulloway F. 2003b. Political conservatism as motivated social cognition. *Psychol. Bull.* 129:339–75

Jost JT, Glaser J, Kruglanski AW, Sulloway F. 2003c. Exceptions that prove the rule: using a theory of motivated social cognition to account for ideological incongruities and political anomalies. *Psychol. Bull.* 129:383–93

Jost JT, Hunyady O. 2002. The psychology of system justification and the palliative function of ideology. *Euro. Rev. Soc. Psychol.* 13:111–53

Jost JT, Ledgerwood A, Hardin CD. 2008a. Shared reality, system justification, and the relational basis of ideological beliefs. *Soc. Personal. Psychol. Compass* 2:171–86

Jost JT, Napier JL, Thorisdottir H, Gosling SD, Palfai TP, Ostafin B. 2007. Are needs to manage uncertainty and threat associated with political conservatism or ideological extremity? *Personal. Soc. Psychol. Bull.* 33:989–1007

Jost JT, Nosek BA, Gosling SD. 2008b. Ideology: its resurgence in social, personality, and political psychology. *Perspect. Psychol. Sci.* 3:126–36

Jost JT, Pelham BW, Sheldon O, Sullivan BN. 2003d. Social inequality and the reduction of ideological dissonance on behalf of the system: evidence of enhanced system justification among the disadvantaged. *Euro. J. Soc. Psychol.* 33:13–36

Judd CM, Krosnick JA. 1989. The structural bases of consistency among political attitudes: effects of expertise and attitude importance. In *Attitude Structure and Function*, ed. AR Pratkanis, SJ Breckler, AG Greenwald, pp. 99–128. Hillsdale, NJ: Erlbaum

Kay AC, Jost JT, Mandisodza AN, Sherman SJ, Petrocelli JV, Johnson AL. 2007. Panglossian ideology in the service of system justification: how complementary stereotypes help us to rationalize inequality. In *Advances in Experimental Social Psychology*, Vol. 39, ed. M Zanna, p. 305–58. San Diego, CA: Elsevier

Kemmelmeier. 2007. Political conservatism, rigidity, and dogmatism in American foreign policy officials: the 1966 Mennis data. *J. Psychol.* 141:77–90

Kerlinger FN. 1984. *Liberalism and Conservatism: The Nature and Structure of Social Attitudes*. Hillsdale, NJ: Erlbaum

Kinder DR. 1998. Opinion and action in the realm of politics. In *The Handbook of Social Psychology*, ed. DT Gilbert, ST Fiske, G Lindzey, 2:778–867. Boston, MA: McGraw-Hill

Kluegel JR, Smith ER. 1986. *Beliefs About Inequality*. New York: Walter de Gruyter

Knight K. 1999. Liberalism and conservatism. In *Measures of Social Psychological Attitudes*, ed. JP Robinson, PR Shaver, LS Wrightsman, 2:59–158. San Diego, CA: Academic

Knight K. 2006. Transformations of the concept of ideology in the twentieth century. *Am. Polit. Sci. Rev.* 100:619–26

Knutsen O. 1995. Left-right materialist value orientations. In *The Impact of Values*, ed. JW van Deth, E Scarbrough, pp. 160–96. New York: Oxford Univ. Press

Kruglanski AW. 2004. *The Psychology of Closed Mindedness*. East Essex, UK: Taylor & Francis

Kuklinski JH, Quirk P, Jerit J, Rich R. 2001. The political environment and decision-making: information, motivation, and policy tradeoffs. *Am. J. Polit. Sci.* 45:410–25

Lambert AJ, Chasteen AL. 1997. Perceptions of disadvantage versus conventionality: political values and attitudes toward the elderly versus blacks. *Personal. Soc. Psychol. Bull.* 23:469–81

Landau MJ, Solomon S, Greenberg J, Cohen F, Pyszczynski T, Arndt J. 2004. Deliver us from evil: the effects of mortality salience and reminders of 9/11 on support for President George W. Bush. *Personal. Soc. Psychol. Bull.* 30:1136–50

Lane RE. 1962. *Political Ideology*. Oxford, UK: Free Press

Lau RR, Redlawsk D. 2001. Advantages and disadvantages of cognitive heuristics in political decision-making. *Am. J. Polit. Sci.* 45:951–71

Lavine H, Gschwend T. 2006. Issues, party and character: the moderating role of ideological thinking on candidate evaluation. *Br. J. Polit. Sci.* 37:139–63

Lavine H, Lodge M, Freitas K. 2005. Threat, authoritarianism, and selective exposure to information. *Polit. Psychol.* 26:219–44

Lavine H, Thomsen CJ, Gonzales MH. 1997. The development of interattitudinal consistency: the shared consequences model. *J. Personal. Soc. Psychol.* 72:735–49

Layman GC, Carsey TM. 2002. Party polarization and "conflict extension" in the American electorate. *Am. J. Polit. Sci.* 46:786–802

Leone L, Chirumbolo A. 2008. Conservatism as motivated avoidance of affect: need for affect scales predict conservatism measures. *J. Res. Personal.* 42:755–62

Lerner M. 1980. *The Belief in a Just World: A Fundamental Delusion*. New York: Plenum

Levin S, Federico CM, Sidanius J, Rabinowitz J. 2002. Social dominance orientation and intergroup bias: the legitimation of favoritism for high-status groups. *Personal. Soc. Psychol. Bull.* 28:144–57

Lewins F. 1989. Recasting the concept of ideology: a content approach. *Br. J. Sociol.* 40:678–93

Lipset SM. 1960. *Political Man*. Garden City, NY: Doubleday

Lipset SM, Raab. 1978. *The Politics of Unreason*. Chicago, IL: Univ. Chicago Press

Lupia A, McCubbins MD, Popkin SL. 2000. Incorporating reason into the study of politics. In *Elements of Reason: Cognition, Choice, and the Bounds of Rationality*, ed. A Lupia, MD McCubbins, SL Popkin, pp. 1–20. New York: Cambridge Univ. Press

Luskin R. 1990. Explaining political sophistication. *Polit. Behav.* 12:331–61

Macrae CN, Stangor C, Hewstone M. 1996. *Stereotypes and Stereotyping*. New York: Guilford

Major B, Quinton W, McCoy S. 2002. Antecedents and consequences of attributions to discrimination: theoretical and empirical advances. In *Advances in Experimental Social Psychology*, ed. MP Zanna, 34:251–329. San Diego, CA: Academic

Mannheim K. 1936. *Ideology and Utopia*. New York: Harvest Books

Marx K, Engels F. 1846/1970. *The German Ideology*. Transl. CJ Arthur. New York: Int. Publ.

McCann SJH. 2008. Societal threat, authoritarianism, conservatism, and U.S. state death penalty sentencing (1977–2004). *J. Personal. Soc. Psychol.* 94:913–23

McCarty N, Poole KT, Rosenthal H. 2006. *Polarized America*. Cambridge, MA: MIT Press

McCaul KD, Ployhart RE, Hinsz VB, McCaul HS. 1995. Appraisals of a consistent versus a similar politician: voter preferences and intuitive judgments. *J. Personal. Soc. Psychol.* 68:292–99

McClosky H. 1958. Conservatism and personality. *Am. Polit. Sci. Rev.* 53:27–45

McClosky H, Zaller J. 1984. *The American Ethos*. Cambridge, MA: Harvard Univ. Press

McLellan D. 1986. *Ideology*. Minneapolis: Univ. Minn. Press

Mendelberg T. 2001. *The Race Card: Campaign Strategy, Implicit Messages, and the Norm of Equality*. Princeton, NJ: Princeton Univ. Press

Moscovici S. 1988. Some notes on social representations. *Euro. J. Soc. Psychol.* 18:211–50

Moskowitz GB. 2005. *Social Cognition: Understanding Self and Others*. New York: Guilford

Nail PR, Harton HC, Decker BP. 2003. Political orientation and modern versus aversive racism: tests of Dovidio and Gaertner's integrated model. *J. Personal. Soc. Psychol.* 84:754–70

Napier JL, Jost JT. 2008a. Why are conservatives happier than liberals? *Psychol. Sci.* 19:565–72

Napier JL, Jost JT. 2008b. The "antidemocratic personality" revisited: a cross-national investigation of working class authoritarianism. *J. Soc. Issues*. 64:595–617

Nosek BA, Banaji MR, Jost JT. 2009. The politics of intergroup attitudes. In *Social and Psychological Bases of Ideology and System Justification*, ed. JT Jost, AC Kay, H Thorisdottir. In press

Nosek BA, Smyth FL, Hansen JJ, Devos T, Lindner NM, et al. 2007. Pervasiveness and correlates of implicit attitudes and stereotypes. *Euro. Rev. Soc. Psychol.* 18:36–88

Olson J, Vernon P, Harris J. 2001. The heritability of attitudes: a study of twins. *J. Personal. Soc. Psychol.* 80:845–60

Ozer DJ, Benet-Martinez V. 2006. Personality and the prediction of consequential outcomes. *Annu. Rev. Psychol.* 57:400–21

Page BI, Shapiro RY. 1992. *The Rational Public*. Chicago, IL: Univ. Chicago Press

Parsons T. 1951. *The Social System*. New York: Free Press

Peffley MA, Hurwitz J. 1985. A hierarchical model of attitude constraint. *Am. J. Polit. Sci.* 29:871–90

Poole KT, Rosenthal H. 1997. *Congress: A Political-Economic History of Roll-Call Voting*. New York: Oxford Univ. Press

Pyszczynski T, Greenberg J, Solomon S. 1999. A dual process model of defense against conscious and unconscious death-related thoughts: an extension of terror management theory. *Psychol. Rev.* 106:835–45

Rahn W. 1993. The role of partisan stereotypes in information processing about political candidates. *Am. J. Polit. Sci.* 37:472–96

Rathbun BC. 2007. Hierarchy and community at home and abroad: evidence of a common structure of domestic and foreign policy beliefs in American elites. *J. Confl. Resolution* 51:379–407

Rokeach M. 1960. *The Open and Closed Mind*. Oxford, UK: Basic Books

Rokeach M. 1973. *The Nature of Human Values*. New York: Free Press

Sargent M. 2004. Less thought, more punishment: need for cognition predicts support for punitive responses to crime. *Personal. Soc. Psychol. Bull.* 30:1485–93

Saucier G. 2000. Isms and the structure of social attitudes. *J. Personal. Soc. Psychol.* 78:366–85

Schaller M, Boyd C, Yohannes J, O'Brien M. 1995. The prejudiced personality revisited: personal need for structure and formation of erroneous group stereotypes. *J. Personal. Soc. Psychol.* 68:544–55

Schimel J, Simon L, Greenberg J, Pyszczynski T, Solomon S, et al. 1999. Support for a functional perspective on stereotypes: evidence that mortality salience enhances stereotypic thinking and preferences. *J. Personal. Soc. Psychol.* 77:905–26

Schwartz SH, Boehnke K. 2004. Evaluating the structure of human values with confirmatory factor analysis. *J. Res. Personal.* 38:230–55

Sears DO, Funk CL. 1991. The role of self-interest in social and political attitudes. *Adv. Exp. Soc. Psychol.* 24:1–91

Sears DO, Hetts JJ, Sidanius J, Bobo L. 2000. Race in American politics: framing the debates. In *Racialized Politics: The Debate about Racism in America*, ed. DO Sears, J Sidanius, L Bobo, pp. 1–43. Chicago, IL: Univ. Chicago Press

Sears DO, Levy S. 2003. Childhood and adult political development. In *Oxford Handbook of Political Psychology*, ed. DO Sears, L Huddy, R Jervis, pp. 60–109. Oxford: Oxford Univ. Press

Sears DO, van Laar C, Carrillo M, Kosterman R. 1997. Is it really racism? The origins of white American opposition to race-targeted policies. *Public Opin. Q.* 61:16–53

Shafer BE, Claggett WJM. 1995. *The Two Majorities: The Issue Context of American Politics.* Baltimore, MD: Johns Hopkins Univ. Press

Shils EA. 1954. Authoritarianism: "right" and "left." In *Studies in the Scope and Method of "The Authoritarian Personality,"* ed. R Christie, M Jahoda, pp. 24–49. Glencoe, IL: Free Press

Sibley CG, Wilson MS, Duckitt J. 2007. Effects of dangerous and competitive worldviews on right-wing authoritarianism and social dominance orientation over a five-month period. *Polit. Psychol.* 28:357–71

Sidanius J, Duffy G. 1988. The duality of attitude structure: a test of Kerlinger's critical referents theory within samples of Swedish and American youth. *Polit. Psychol.* 9:649–70

Sidanius J, Pratto F. 1999. *Social Dominance: An Intergroup Theory of Social Hierarchy and Oppression.* New York: Cambridge Univ. Press

Sidanius J, Pratto F, Bobo L. 1996. Racism, conservatism, affirmative action, and intellectual sophistication: a matter of principled conservatism or group dominance? *J. Personal. Soc. Psychol.* 70:476–90

Skitka LJ. 1999. Ideological and attributional boundaries on public compassion: reactions to individuals and communities affected by a natural disaster. *Personal. Soc. Psychol. Bull.* 25:793–92

Skitka LJ, Mullen E, Griffin T, Hutchinson S, Chamberlin B. 2002. Dispositions, ideological scripts, or motivated correction? Understanding ideological differences in attributions for social problems. *J. Personal. Soc. Psychol.* 83:470–87

Smith MR, Gordon RA. 1998. Personal need for structure and attitudes toward homosexuality. *J. Soc. Psychol.* 138:83–87

Sniderman PM, Brody RA, Tetlock PE. 1991. *Reasoning and Choice.* New York: Cambridge Univ. Press

Sniderman PM, Bullock J. 2004. A consistency theory of public opinion and political choice: the hypothesis of menu dependence. In *Studies in Public Opinion: Attitudes, Nonattitudes, Measurement Error, and Change*, ed. WE Saris, PM Sniderman, pp. 337–57. Princeton, NJ: Princeton Univ. Press

Sniderman PM, Crosby GC, Howell WG. 2000. The politics of race. In *Racialized Politics: The Debate About Racism in America*, ed. DO Sears, J Sidanius, L Bobo, pp. 236–79. Chicago, IL: Univ. Chicago Press

Sniderman PM, Hagendoorn L, Prior M. 2004. Predisposing factors and situational triggers: exclusionary reactions to immigrant minorities. *Am. Polit. Sci. Rev.* 98:35–49

Solomon S, Greenberg J, Pyszczynski T. 2004. The cultural animal: twenty years of terror management theory and research. In *Handbook of Experimental Existential Psychology*, ed. J Greenberg, SL Koole, T Pyszczynski, pp. 13–34. New York: Guilford

Stenner K. 2005. *The Authoritarian Dynamic.* London: Cambridge Univ. Press

Stimson JA. 2004. *Tides of Consent.* New York: Cambridge Univ. Press

Stone WF, Smith LD. 1993. Authoritarianism: left and right. In *Strength and Weakness: The Authoritarian Personality Today*, ed. WF Stone, G Lederer, R Christie, pp. 144–56. New York: Springer-Verlag

Tajfel H, Turner JC. 1986. The social identity theory of intergroup behavior. In *The Psychology of Intergroup Relations*, ed. S Worchel, W Austin, pp. 7–24. Chicago, IL: Nelson-Hall

Talaska CA, Fiske ST, Chaiken S. 2008. Legitimating racial discrimination: a meta-analysis of the racial attitude-behavior literature shows that emotions, not beliefs, best predict discrimination. *Soc. Justice Res.* In press

Tetlock PE. 1983. Cognitive style and political ideology. *J. Personal. Soc. Psychol.* 45:118–26

Tetlock PE. 1986. A value pluralism model of ideological reasoning. *J. Personal. Soc. Psychol.* 50:819–27

Tetlock PE. 2007. Psychology and politics: the challenges of integrating levels of analysis in social science. In *Social Psychology: Handbook of Basic Principles*, ed. AW Kruglanski, ET Higgins, pp. 888–912. New York: Guilford. 2nd ed.

Thorisdottir H. 2007. *The effects of perceived threat on political attitudes: uncertainty, lack of control and closed mindedness.* PhD thesis. New York Univ.

Thorisdottir H, Jost JT, Liviatan I, Shrout PE. 2007. Psychological needs and values underlying left-right political orientation: cross-national evidence from Eastern and Western Europe. *Public Opin. Q.* 71:175–203

Thornhill R, Fincher CL. 2007. What is the relevance of attachment and life history to political values? *Evol. Hum. Behav.* 28:215–22

Tomkins SS. 1963. Left and right: a basic dimension of ideology and personality. In *The Study of Lives*, ed. RW White, pp. 388–411. New York: Atherton

Tyler TR. 2006. Psychological perspectives on legitimacy and legitimation. *Annu. Rev. Psychol.* 57:375–400

Ullrich J, Cohrs JC. 2007. Terrorism salience increases system justification: experimental evidence. *Soc. Justice Res.* 20:117–39

Valentino NA. 1999. Crime news and the priming of racial attitudes during evaluations of the President. *Public Opin. Q.* 63:293–320

Valentino NA, Hutchings VL, White IK. 2002. Cues that matter: how political ads prime racial attitudes during campaigns. *Am. Polit. Sci. Rev.* 96:75–90

Van Den Bos K, Poortvliet PM, Maas M, Miedema J, Van Den Ham EJ. 2005. An enquiry concerning the principles of cultural norms and values: the impact of uncertainty and mortality salience on reactions to violations and bolstering of cultural worldviews. *J. Exp. Soc. Psychol.* 41:91–113

Van Hiel A, Mervielde I. 2004. Openness to experience and boundaries in the mind: relationships with cultural and economic conservative beliefs. *J. Personal.* 72:659–86

Van Hiel A, Pandelaere M, Duriez B. 2004. The impact of need for closure on conservative beliefs and racism: differential mediation by authoritarian submission and authoritarian dominance. *Personal. Soc. Psychol. Bull.* 30:824–37

Wakslak CJ, Jost JT, Tyler TR, Chen ES. 2007. Moral outrage mediates the dampening effect of system justification on support for redistributive social policies. *Psychol. Sci.* 18:267–74

Weber CW, Federico CM. 2007. Interpersonal attachment and patterns of ideological belief. *Polit. Psychol.* 28:389–416

Weber M. 1922/1946. *From Max Weber: Essays in Sociology.* New York: Oxford Univ. Press

Whitley BE. 1999. Right-wing authoritarianism, social dominance orientation, and prejudice. *J. Personal. Soc. Psychol.* 77:126–34

Willer R. 2004. The effects of government-issued terror warnings on presidential approval ratings. *Curr. Res. Soc. Psychol.* 10:1–12

Wilson GD. 1973. *The Psychology of Conservatism.* New York: Academic

Zaller J. 1992. *The Nature and Origins of Mass Opinion.* New York: Cambridge Univ. Press

Zelditch M. 2001. Theories of legitimacy. In *The Psychology of Legitimacy*, ed. JT Jost, B Major, pp. 33–53. London: Cambridge Univ. Press

Prejudice Reduction: What Works? A Review and Assessment of Research and Practice

Elizabeth Levy Paluck[1] and Donald P. Green[2]

[1]Harvard Academy for International and Area Studies, Weatherhead Center for International Affairs, Harvard University, Cambridge, Massachusetts 02138; email: epaluck@wcfia.harvard.edu

[2]Institution for Social and Policy Studies, Yale University, New Haven, Connecticut 06520-8209; email: donald.green@yale.edu

Annu. Rev. Psychol. 2009. 60:339–67

First published online as a Review in Advance on October 13, 2008

The *Annual Review of Psychology* is online at psych.annualreviews.org

This article's doi:
10.1146/annurev.psych.60.110707.163607

Key Words

field experiments, evaluation, stereotype reduction, cooperative learning, contact hypothesis, peace education, media and reading interventions, diversity training, cultural competence, multicultural education, antibias education, sensitivity training, cognitive training

Abstract

This article reviews the observational, laboratory, and field experimental literatures on interventions for reducing prejudice. Our review places special emphasis on assessing the methodological rigor of existing research, calling attention to problems of design and measurement that threaten both internal and external validity. Of the hundreds of studies we examine, a small fraction speak convincingly to the questions of whether, why, and under what conditions a given type of intervention works. We conclude that the causal effects of many widespread prejudice-reduction interventions, such as workplace diversity training and media campaigns, remain unknown. Although some intergroup contact and cooperation interventions appear promising, a much more rigorous and broad-ranging empirical assessment of prejudice-reduction strategies is needed to determine what works.

Contents

INTRODUCTION

Prejudice: a negative bias toward a social category of people, with cognitive, affective, and behavioral components

By many standards, the psychological literature on prejudice ranks among the most impressive in all of social science. The sheer volume of scholarship is remarkable, reflecting decades of active scholarly investigation of the meaning, measurement, etiology, and consequences of prejudice. Few topics have attracted a greater

range of theoretical perspectives. Theorizing has been accompanied by lively debates about the appropriate way to conceptualize and measure prejudice. The result is a rich array of measurement strategies and assessment tools.

The theoretical nuance and methodological sophistication of the prejudice literature are undeniable. Less clear is the stature of this literature when assessed in terms of the practical knowledge that it has generated. The study of prejudice attracts special attention because scholars seek to understand and remedy the social problems associated with prejudice, such as discrimination, inequality, and violence. Their aims are shared by policymakers, who spend billions of dollars annually on interventions aimed at prejudice reduction in schools, workplaces, neighborhoods, and regions beset by intergroup conflict. Given these practical objectives, it is natural to ask what has been learned about the most effective ways to reduce prejudice.

This review is not the first to pose this question. Previous reviews have summarized evidence within particular contexts (e.g., the laboratory: Wilder 1986; schools: Stephan 1999; cross-nationally: Pedersen et al. 2005), age groups (e.g., children: Aboud & Levy 2000), or for specific programs or theories (e.g., cooperative learning: Johnson & Johnson 1989; intergroup contact: Pettigrew & Tropp 2006; cultural competence training: Price et al. 2005). Other reviews cover a broad range of prejudice-reduction programs and the theories that underlie them (e.g., Oskamp 2000, Stephan & Stephan 2001).

Our review differs from prior reviews in three respects. First, the scope of our review is as broad as possible, encompassing both academic and nonacademic research. We augment the literature reviews of Oskamp (2000) and Stephan & Stephan (2001) with hundreds of additional studies. Second, our assessment of the prejudice literature has a decidedly methodological focus. Our aim is not simply to canvass existing hypotheses and findings but to assess the internal and external validity of the evidence. To what extent have studies established that interventions reduce prejudice? To what extent do these findings generalize to other settings? Third, building on prior reviews that present methodological assessments of cultural competence (Kiselica & Maben 1999) and antihomophobia (Stevenson 1988) program evaluations, our methodological assessment provides specific recommendations for enhancing the practical and theoretical value of prejudice reduction research.

Scope of the Review

We review interventions aimed at reducing prejudice, broadly defined. Our purview includes the reduction of negative attitudes toward one group (one academic definition of prejudice) and also the reduction of related phenomena like stereotyping, discrimination, intolerance, and negative emotions toward another group. For the sake of simplicity, we refer to all of these phenomena as "prejudice," but in our descriptions of individual interventions we use the same terms as the investigator.

By "prejudice reduction," we mean a causal pathway from some intervention to a reduced level of prejudice. Excluded, therefore, are studies that describe individual differences in prejudice, as these studies do not speak directly to the efficacy of specific interventions. Our concern with causality naturally leads us to place special emphasis on studies that use random assignment to evaluate programs, but our review also encompasses the large literature that uses nonexperimental methods.

Method

Over a five-year period ending in spring 2008, we searched for published and unpublished reports of interventions conducted with a stated intention of reducing prejudice or prejudice-related phenomena. We combed online databases of research literatures in psychology, sociology, education, medicine, policy studies, and organizational behavior, pairing primary search words "prejudice," "stereo-type," "discrimination," "bias," "racism," "homophobia," "hate," "tolerance," "reconciliation," "cultural competence/sensitivity," and "multicultural" with operative terms like "reduce," "program," "intervention," "modify," "education," "diversity training," "sensitize," and "cooperat*." To locate unpublished academic work, we posted requests on several organizations' email listservs, including the Society for Personality and Social Psychology and the American Evaluation Association, and we reviewed relevant conference proceedings. Lexis-Nexis and Google were used to locate nonacademic reports by nonprofit groups, government and nongovernmental agencies, and consulting firms that evaluate prejudice. We examined catalogues that advertise diversity programs to see if evaluations were mentioned or cited. Several evaluation consultants sent us material or spoke with us about their evaluation techniques.

Our search produced an immense database of 985 published and unpublished reports written by academics and nonacademics involved in research, practice, or both. The assembled body of work includes multicultural education, antibias instruction more generally, workplace diversity initiatives, dialogue groups, cooperative learning, moral and values education, intergroup contact, peace education, media interventions, reading interventions, intercultural and sensitivity training, cognitive training, and a host of miscellaneous techniques and interventions. The targets of these programs are racism, homophobia, ageism; antipathy toward ethnic, religious, national, and fictitious (experimental) groups; prejudice toward persons who are overweight, poor, or disabled; and attitudes toward diversity, reconciliation, and multiculturalism more generally. We excluded from our purview programs that addressed sex-based prejudice (the literature dealing with beliefs, attitudes, and behaviors toward women and men in general, as distinguished from gender-identity prejudices like homophobia). Sex-based inequality intersects with and reinforces other group-based prejudice (Jackman 1994, Pratto & Walker 2004),

Prejudice reduction: a causal pathway from an intervention (e.g., a peer conversation, a media program, an organizational policy, a law) to a reduced level of prejudice

but given the qualitatively different nature and the distinctive theoretical explanations for sex-based prejudice and inequality (Eagly & Mlednic 1994, Jackman 1994, Sidanius & Pratto 1999), we believe relevant interventions deserve their own review. The resulting database (available at **www.betsylevypaluck.com**) constitutes the most extensive list of published and unpublished prejudice-reduction reports assembled to date.

This sprawling body of research could be organized in many different ways. In order to focus attention on what kinds of valid conclusions may be drawn from this literature, we divide studies according to research design. This categorization scheme generates three groups: nonexperimental studies in the field, experimental studies in the laboratory, and experimental studies in the field. **Supplemental Table 1** (follow the **Supplemental Material link** from the Annual Reviews home page at **http://www.annualreviews.org**) provides a descriptive overview of the database according to this scheme. The database comprises 985 studies, of which 72% are published. Nearly two-thirds of all studies (60%) are nonexperimental, of which only 227 (38%) use a control group. The preponderance of nonexperimental studies is smaller when we look at published work; nevertheless, 55% of published studies of prejudice reduction use nonexperimental de-

signs. Of the remaining studies, 284 (29%) are laboratory experiments and 107 (11%) are field experiments (see sidebar Field Versus Laboratory Experiments). A disproportionate percentage of field experiments are devoted to school-based interventions (88%).

Within each category, we group studies according to their theoretical approach or intervention technique, assessing findings in light of the research setting, participants, and outcome measurement. A narrative rather than a meta-analytic review suits this purpose, in the interest of presenting a richer description of the prejudice-reduction literature. Moreover, the methods, interventions, and dependent variables are so diverse that meta-analysis is potentially meaningless (Baumeister & Leary 1997; see also Hafer & Bègue 2005), especially given that many of the research designs used in this literature are prone to bias, rendering their findings unsuitable for meta-analysis.

Our review follows the classification structure of our database. We begin with an overview of nonexperimental prejudice-reduction field research. This literature illustrates not only the breadth of prejudice-reduction interventions, but also the methodological deficiencies that prevent studies from speaking authoritatively to the question of what causes reductions in prejudice. Next we turn to prejudice reduction in the scientific laboratory, where well-developed theories about prejudice reduction are tested with carefully controlled experiments. We examine the theories, intervention conditions, participants, and outcome measures to ask whether the findings support reliable causal inferences about prejudice reduction in nonlaboratory settings. We follow with a review of field experiments in order to assess the correspondence between these two bodies of research. Because field experiments have not previously been the focus of a research review, we describe these studies in detail and argue that field experimentation remains a promising but underutilized approach. We conclude with a summary of which theoretically driven interventions seem most promising in light of current evidence, and we provide recommendations for future

FIELD VERSUS LABORATORY EXPERIMENTS

In an experimental design, units of observation (e.g., individuals, classrooms) are assigned at random to a treatment and to placebo or no-treatment conditions. Field experiments are randomized experiments that test the effects of real-world interventions in naturalistic settings, but the distinction between field and lab is often unclear. The laboratory can be the site of very realistic interventions, and conversely, artificial interventions may be tested in a nonlaboratory setting. When assessing the degree to which experiments qualify as field experiments, one must consider four aspects of the study: (*a*) participants, (*b*) the intervention and its target, (*c*) the obtrusiveness of intervention delivery, and (*d*) the assessed response to the intervention.

research (see sidebar Public Opinion Research and Prejudice Reduction).

NONEXPERIMENTAL RESEARCH IN THE FIELD

Random assignment ensures that participants who are "treated" with a prejudice-reduction intervention have the same expected background traits and levels of exposure to outside influences as participants in the control group. Outcomes in a randomized experiment are thus explained by a quantifiable combination of the intervention and random chance. By contrast, in nonexperimental research the outcomes can be explained by a combination of the intervention, random chance, and unmeasured pre-existing differences between comparison groups. So long as researchers remain uncertain about the nature and extent of these biases, nonexperimental research eventually ceases to be informative and experimental methodology becomes necessary to uncover the unbiased effect (Gerber et al. 2004). For these reasons, randomized experiments are the preferred method of evaluation when stakes are high (e.g., medical interventions).

Prejudice is cited as a cause of health, economic, and educational disparities (e.g., American Psychological Association 2001), as well as terrorism and mass murder (Sternberg 2003). For scientists who understand prejudice as a pandemic of the same magnitude as that of AIDS or cancer, a reliance on nonexperimental methods seems justifiable only as a short-run approach en route to experimental testing. Nevertheless, in schools, communities, organizations, government offices, media outlets, and health care settings, the overwhelming majority of prejudice-reduction interventions (77%, or 367 out of the 474 total field studies in our database) are evaluated solely with nonexperimental methods, when they are evaluated at all.

Studies with No Control Group

The majority of nonexperimental field studies do not use a control group to which an inter-

PUBLIC OPINION RESEARCH AND PREJUDICE REDUCTION

It is ironic but not coincidental that the largest empirical literature on the subject of prejudice—namely, public opinion research on the subject of race and politics—has little, if any, connection to the subject of prejudice reduction. Many of the most important and influential theories about prejudiced beliefs, attitudes, and actions have grown out of public opinion research. These theories examine the role of preadult socialization experiences (Sears 1988), group interests and identities (Bobo 1988), political culture and ideology (Sniderman & Piazza 1993), and mass media portrayals of issues and groups (Gilliam & Iyengar 2000, Mendelberg 2001). They diagnose the origins of prejudice, often tracing it to large-scale social forces such as intergroup competition for status and resources, but rarely do they propose or test interventions designed to ameliorate prejudice. Taking prejudice as a fixed personal attribute, this literature instead tends to offer suggestions about how to frame issues (e.g., public spending on welfare) in ways that mitigate the expression of prejudice (e.g., by reminding respondents that most welfare recipients are white).

vention group may be compared; most evaluations of sensitivity and cultural-competence programming, mass media campaigns, and diversity trainings are included in this category. Many no-control evaluations use a postintervention feedback questionnaire. For example, Dutch medical students described their experiences visiting patients of different ethnicities (van Wieringen et al. 2001), and Canadian citizens reported how much they noticed and liked the "We All Belong" television and newspaper campaign (Environics Research Group Limited 2001). Other feedback questionnaires ask participants to assess their own change: Diversity-training participants graded themselves on their knowledge about barriers to success for minorities and the effects of stereotypes and prejudice (Morris et al. 1996). Other no-control group studies use repeated measurement before and after the intervention: We were unable to locate a sensitivity- or diversity-training program for police that used more than a prepost survey of participating officers. Such strategies may reflect a lack of resources for, understanding of, or commitment to rigorous evaluation.

Notwithstanding the frequency with which this repeated measures design is used, its defects are well known and potentially severe (Shadish et al. 2002). Change over time may be due to other events; self-reported change may reflect participants' greater familiarity with the questionnaire or the evaluation goals rather than a change in prejudice. Although such methodological points may be familiar to the point of cliché, these basic flaws cast doubt on studies of a majority of prejudice-reduction interventions, particularly those gauging prejudice reduction in medical, corporate, and law enforcement settings.

Qualitative Studies

A number of purely qualitative studies have recorded detailed observations of an intervention group over time with no nonintervention comparison (e.g., Roberts 2000). These studies are important for generating hypotheses and highlighting social psychological processes involved in program take-up, experience, and change processes, but they cannot reliably demonstrate the impact of a program. Qualitative measurement has no inherent connection to nonexperimental design, though the two are often conflated (e.g., Nagda & Zúñiga 2003, p. 112). Qualitative investigation can and should be used to develop research hypotheses and to augment experimental measurement of outcomes.

Cross-Sectional Studies

Diversity programs and community desegregation policies are often evaluated with a cross-sectional study. For example, one study reported that volunteer participants in a company's "Valuing Diversity" seminar were more culturally tolerant and positive about corporate diversity than were "control" employees—those who chose not to attend the seminar (Ellis & Sonnenfield 1994). Even defenders of diversity training would concede that peo-

ple with positive attitudes toward diversity are more likely to voluntarily attend a diversity seminar. Such evaluations conflate participants' predispositions with program impact. Although many cross-sectional studies report encouraging results, post hoc controls for participant predispositions cannot establish causality, even with advanced statistical techniques (Powers & Ellison 1995), due to the threat of unmeasured differences between treatment and control groups.

Quasi-Experimental Panel Studies

Prejudice-reduction interventions in educational settings, and some in counseling and diversity training, are more likely to receive attention from academically trained researchers who employ control groups and repeated measurement (e.g., Rudman et al. 2001). But with the exception of a few studies that use near-random assignment, most of these studies' findings have questionable internal validity.

For one, many quasi-experimental evaluations choose comparison groups that are substantially different from the intervention participants—such as younger students or students in a different school. Others choose comparison groups and assess preintervention differences more exactly. To evaluate a social justice educational program focused on dialogue and hands-on experience, investigators administered a pretest to all University of Michigan freshmen, some of whom had already signed up for the program (Gurin et al. 1999). Using this pretest, investigators selected a control group that was similar to program volunteers in gender, race/ethnicity, precollege and college residence, perspective taking, and complex thinking. After four years and four post-tests, results demonstrated that white students in the program were, among other things, more disposed to see commonality in interests and values with various groups of color than were white control students. This impressive study demonstrates the great lengths to which researchers must go to minimize concerns about selection bias, and yet no amount of preintervention measurement can guarantee that the nonrandom treatment and control groups are equivalent when subjects self-select into the treatment group. Studies such as this one provide encouraging results that merit further testing using randomized designs (see also Rudman et al. 2001).

Near-Random Assignment

Fewer than a dozen studies have used comparison groups that were composed in an arbitrary, near-random fashion. Near-random assignment bolsters claims of causal impact insofar as exposure to the intervention is unlikely to be related to any characteristic of the intervention group. A good example is a waiting list design. In one of the few studies of corporate diversity training able to speak to causal impact (Hanover & Cellar 1998), a company's human resources department took advantage of a phased-in mandatory training policy and assigned white managers to diversity training or waiting list according to company scheduling demands. After participating in a series of sessions involving videos, role-plays, discussions, and anonymous feedback from employees in their charge, trainees were more likely than untrained managers to rate diversity practices as important and to report that they discourage prejudiced comments among employees. Unfortunately, all outcomes were self-reported, and managers may have exaggerated the influence of the training as a way to please company administration. Putting this important limitation aside, this research design represents a promising approach when policy dictates that all members of the target population must be treated.

Conclusion: Nonexperimental Research

That we find the nonexperimental literature to be less informative than others who have reviewed this literature (e.g., Stephan & Stephan 2001) does not mean this research is uninformative with respect to descriptive questions. These studies yield a wealth of information about what kinds of programs are used with various populations, how they are implemented, which aspects engage participants, and the like. However, the nonexperimental literature cannot answer the question of "what works" to reduce prejudice in these real-world settings. Out of 207 quasi-experimental studies, fewer than twelve can be considered strongly suggestive of causal impact (or lack thereof). Unfortunately, the vast majority of real-world interventions—in schools, businesses, communities, hospitals, police stations, and media markets—have been studied with nonexperimental methods. We must therefore turn to experiments conducted in academic laboratories and in the field to learn about the causal impact of prejudice reduction interventions.

EXPERIMENTAL RESEARCH CONDUCTED IN THE LABORATORY

Academics studying prejudice reduction in the laboratory employ random assignment and base their interventions on theories of prejudice. Laboratory interventions using intergroup approaches aim at changing group interactions and group boundaries. Interventions using individual approaches target an individual's feelings, cognitions, and behaviors. Building on prior reviews (Crisp & Hewstone 2007, Hewstone 2000, Monteith et al. 1994, Wilder 1986), we describe an array of laboratory interventions and assess the extent to which these studies inform real-world prejudice-reduction efforts.

Intergroup Approaches

Prejudice-reduction strategies that take an intergroup approach are based on the general idea that peoples' perceptions and behaviors favor their own groups relative to others. Two major lines of thought have inspired techniques to address this in-group/out-group bias: the contact hypothesis (Allport 1954), which recommends exposure to members of the out-group under

Quasi-experimental studies: experiments with treatment and placebo or no-treatment conditions in which the units are not randomly assigned to conditions

Contact hypothesis: under positive conditions of equal status, shared goals, cooperation, and sanction by authority, interaction between two groups should lead to reduced prejudice

Minimal group paradigm (MGP): randomly assigned groups of research participants engage in activities to observe the power of "mere categorization" on the development and expression of in-group favoritism, out-group derogation, and other group phenomena

certain optimal conditions, and social identity and categorization theories (Miller & Brewer 1986, Tajfel 1970), which recommend interventions that break down or rearrange social boundaries.

Contact hypothesis. The contact hypothesis states that under optimal conditions of equal status, shared goals, authority sanction, and the absence of competition, interaction between two groups should lead to reduced prejudice (Pettigrew & Tropp 2006). Although there have been dozens of laboratory studies since Allport's original formulation of the hypothesis, among the most compelling are Cook's (1971, 1978) railroad studies. Cook simulated interracial workplace contact by hiring racially prejudiced white young adults to work on a railroad company management task with two "coworkers," a black and a white research confederate. Participants believed that they were working a real part-time job. Over the course of a month, the two confederates worked with participants under the optimal conditions of the contact hypothesis. At the end of the study, participants rated their black coworkers highly in attractiveness, likeability, and competence, a significant finding considering the study took place in 1960s in the American South. Several months later, participants also expressed less racial prejudice than controls expressed in an ostensibly unrelated questionnaire about race relations and race-relevant social policies. This exemplary piece of laboratory research employed a realistic intervention and tested its effects extensively and unobtrusively.

Social identity and categorization theories. Laboratory interventions guided by social identity and categorization theories address a variety of group prejudices, but often experimenters create new groups to study using the well-known minimal group paradigm (MGP; Tajfel 1970). Participants are sorted into two groups based on an irrelevant characteristic, such as the tendency to overestimate the number of dots on a screen (in actuality, assignment to the groups is random). Simple classification is of-

ten enough to create prejudice between these newly formed groups, but some researchers enhance in-group preference by having participants play group games or read positive information about their own group. In non-MGP studies, participants are reminded of a preexisting group identity, such as academic or political party affiliation. Once battle lines are drawn, these interventions use one of four kinds of strategies for reducing prejudice between the two groups: decategorization, recategorization, crossed categorization, and integration—each of which has generated a subsidiary theoretical literature (Crisp & Hewstone 2007).

In a decategorization approach, individual identity is emphasized over group identity through instruction or encouragement from the researcher. For example, participants in one study were less likely to favor their own (randomly assembled) group over the other group when the two groups worked cooperatively under instructions to focus on individuals (Bettencourt et al. 1992).

In recategorization research, participants are encouraged to think of people from different groups as part of one superordinate group using cues such as integrated seating, shirts of the same color (e.g., Gaertner & Dovidio 2000), or shared prizes (Gaertner et al. 1999). These studies have succeeded in encouraging members of minimal groups and political affiliation-based groups to favor their in-group less in terms of evaluation and rewards and to cooperate more with the out-group (Gaertner & Dovidio 2000).

Crossed categorization techniques (Crisp & Hewstone 1999) are based on the idea that prejudice is diminished when people in two opposing groups become aware that they share membership in a third group. Most commonly, prejudice against a novel group is diminished when it is crossed with another novel group category using the MGP (e.g., Brown & Turner 1979, Marcus-Newhall et al. 1993).

Integrative models (Gaertner & Dovidio 2000, Hornsey & Hogg 2000b) follow crossed categorization techniques with their strategy of preserving recognition of group differences within a common group identity. In laboratory experiments, the common group identity is created by highlighting a superordinate identity (e.g., a university) without diminishing the value of identities constituting it (e.g., science and humanities students; Hornsey & Hogg 2000a) or by having two groups use their distinct areas of expertise to solve a task under equal status conditions (Dovidio et al. 1997).

All of these approaches achieve a measure of success in reducing prejudice as defined by preference for one's own group. Few laboratory interventions, especially those that use the MGP, target out-group derogation. The decategorization model has been criticized for its failure to extend this bias reduction toward the entire group (Rothbart & John 1985) and for submerging meaningful subgroup identities (Berry 1984). The integrative and crossed categorization models claim the most empirical and normative support, and have been used to bolster arguments for multicultural policies such as appreciating ethnic diversity under a common national identity (e.g., Brewer & Gaertner 2001, Hornsey & Hogg 2000b). Mixed findings from crossed categorization techniques may reflect varying definitions of in-group bias (Mullen et al. 2001), or the fact that these interventions change the perception of group boundaries but do not reduce out-group bias (Vescio et al. 2004).

Individual Approaches

Prejudice-reduction techniques aimed at individual phenomena such as feelings and cognitions are guided by a diverse set of theories that recommend a wide range of strategies, including instruction, expert opinion and norm information, manipulating accountability, consciousness-raising, and targeting personal identity, self-worth, or emotion.

Instruction. Ignorance has long been blamed as one of the roots of prejudice (Stephan & Stephan 1984), and the laboratory has been used to test different instructional solutions. Applied didactic techniques have been devel-

oped by researchers working with the U.S. military and with corporations sending employees overseas, teaching people how to interpret behaviors of different cultural and/or racial groups (e.g., Landis et al. 1976).

Other instruction techniques focus on ways to think, such as training in complex thinking and in statistical logic, with the hypothesis that this will help individuals avoid faulty group generalizations. These approaches claim modest success: After training, students are more likely to write positive stories about a picture depicting an interracial encounter, to report friendliness toward racial and ethnic out-groups (Gardiner 1972), and to avoid stereotyping fictitious characters presented in a vignette (Schaller et al. 1996).

Expert opinion and norm information. A body of social psychological research shows that prejudiced attitudes and behaviors are powerfully influenced by social norms (Crandall & Stangor 2005) and that under certain conditions people are persuaded by expert opinion (Kuklinski & Hurley 1996). Telling participants that experts believe personality is malleable (a position that undermines stereotyping; Levy et al. 1998) or that racial stereotyping is not normative for their peer group (Stangor et al. 2001; see also Monteith et al. 1996) reduces stereotyping against stigmatized groups in the laboratory. More subtle manipulations designed to convey a tolerant social norm (e.g., an antiracism advertisement; GR Maio, SE Watt, M Hewstone, & KJ Rees, unpubl. manuscr.) seem to produce weaker effects.

Manipulating accountability. Theories emphasizing the irrationality of prejudice predict that asking people to provide concrete reasons for their prejudices should reduce them. Accountability interventions have succeeded in MGP studies, in which participants allocated more points to a fictitious out-group when they were required to justify their allocation amounts (Dobbs & Crano 2001). Students who believed they would be held accountable to peers for their evaluations of a Hispanic

Social norms: perceptions that are descriptive of what people are doing or prescriptive of what people should do (as a member of a group, an organization, or a society)

Implicit Attitudes Test (IAT): a test involving classification tasks; measures strengths of automatic associations computed from performance speeds

student involved in a school disciplinary case were also less likely to stereotype this student (Bodenhausen et al. 1994).

Consciousness-raising. Research on implicit prejudice proliferated following striking demonstrations that prejudiced attitudes and beliefs can operate without a person's awareness or endorsement (Devine 1989). A number of "(un)consciousness-raising" strategies (Banaji 2001, p. 136) aim to combat implicit prejudice through thought suppression, awareness, reconditioning, and control (see Blair 2002 for a review).

Instructions to suppress stereotypes (i.e., push them out of awareness) have had the opposite intended effect by increasing the accessibility of such stereotypes (Galinsky & Moskowitz 2000). For example, business students who watched diversity training videos instructing them to suppress negative thoughts about the elderly evaluated older job candidates less favorably than did students who did not receive suppression instructions (Kulik et al. 2000). Some evidence suggests that stereotype suppression does not lead inexorably to higher rates of stereotyping or prejudiced behavior (Monteith et al. 1998), particularly when suppression is coupled with mental retraining exercises (Kawakami et al. 2000a,b), but the overall pattern of findings suggests suppression is not an effective prejudice-reduction strategy.

Laboratory experiments have also tested the opposite strategy: encouraging awareness of memories, attitudes, or beliefs that relate to prejudice. For example, one intervention required students to remember a time when they treated an Asian person in a prejudiced manner (Son Hing et al. 2002). As predicted, students who previously scored high on an implicit prejudice test—by solving word fragments with the negative stereotypical Asian words "sly" and "short"—were more likely to feel guilt over this memory and to encourage funding for an Asian student association on a subsequent questionnaire.

Other laboratory interventions aim to recondition implicit attitudes and beliefs. Some

use classical conditioning techniques—pairing stigmatized groups with positive images and words—to improve college students' implicit stereotypes about the elderly, black Americans, and skinheads (Karpinski & Hilton 2001; Kawakami et al. 2000a,b; Olson & Fazio 2008). Presenting positive images of famous black people (e.g., Martin Luther King) and negative images of famous whites (e.g., Charles Manson) reduced implicit prejudice as measured by the Implicit Attitudes Test (IAT; Greenwald et al. 1998), but conscious attitudes remained unchanged (Dasgupta & Greenwald 2001, Wittenbrink et al. 2001). Other studies alter implicit attitudes and social distancing behaviors through approach-avoidance conditioning—i.e., by asking subjects to pull forward on a joystick when presented with words or faces representing a stigmatized group (Kawakami et al. 2007).

Targeting emotions. Psychologists contend that emotional states can influence the expressions of prejudice (e.g., E. Smith 1993), and some perspective-taking interventions encourage the perceiver to experience the target's emotions (Batson 1991). Writing an essay from the perspective of an elderly person decreased subsequent stereotypes about the elderly; writing an essay from the perspective of the opposite MGP group led to more positive ratings of the out-group's personality characteristics (Galinsky & Moskowitz 2000, Vescio et al. 2003). Instructions to be empathic when reading about everyday discrimination against blacks eliminated the difference between participants' evaluations of white and black Americans (Stephan & Finlay 1999). Similarly, instructions to "focus on your feelings" as opposed to thoughts when watching a video portraying anti-black discrimination increased desire to interact with blacks, an effect that was explained by a change in emotions toward blacks as a group (Esses & Dovidio 2002). This particular intervention did not change participants' beliefs or policy endorsements concerning blacks.

Targeting value consistency and self-worth.
Two related social psychological theories of motivation explain how the need to maintain consistency among valued cognitions or behaviors or to protect their self-worth might move people to express or repress prejudice. Festinger's cognitive dissonance theory (1957) has been used in several laboratory interventions that encourage participants to see prejudice as inconsistent with some valued attitude or trait. For example, college students were also more likely to soften pre-existing anti-black positions on social policies and to report more egalitarian attitudes and beliefs after agreeing to write public statements in favor of pro-black policies (Eisenstadt et al. 2003).

Steele's self-affirmation theory (1998) predicts that people will resist derogating others when their own self-worth is affirmed. Laboratory results are supportive: Individuals who affirmed their self-image by writing about their values or who received positive feedback about their intelligence were more likely to rate a Jewish job candidate positively in terms of her personality and her suitability for the job (Fein & Spencer 1997). Receiving positive feedback from a black manager of the laboratory experiment also decreased the amount of negative black stereotypes on a word-completion task (Sinclair & Kunda 1999).

Lessons for the Real World from Laboratory Experiments

Laboratory experiments test a wide range of prejudice reduction theories with a high degree of creativity and precision. Computers, video cameras, and even physiological measurements track manifestations of prejudice change. The laboratory environment and the experimental method lead to tight, internally valid conclusions about the causal impact of the intervention.

But do laboratory experiments yield reliable strategies for prejudice reduction in the world? Specifically, in the drive for simplification and abstraction, do laboratory experiments eliminate elements of their interventions, environ-

ments, and theories that are critical to the external validity of their lessons for real-world prejudice reduction?

Interventions. Laboratory studies typically test quick fixes. Consider a typical minimal group paradigm experiment, in which prejudice is created, modified, and reassessed over the course of one hour. Brief manipulations can have powerful effects (e.g., Bargh et al. 1996), but studies rarely test to see if the change lasts longer than the study period.

Many laboratory prejudice interventions are also subtle; above we reviewed techniques based on slight changes in instructions, t-shirt color, and seating assignments. By contrast, real-world institutions are much more heavy-handed: They impose speech codes, citizenship requirements, immigration quotas, and economic sanctions that shape intergroup perceptions and relationships. Lessons on the power of authority and conformity handed down by Milgram, Asch, and Zimbardo have not been fully exploited in laboratory prejudice-reduction research. Two exceptions are research on conformity to perceived norms of prejudice (e.g., Stangor et al. 2001) and on orders to suppress stereotyping (e.g., Galinsky & Moskowitz 2000). Subtle manipulations undoubtedly have many advantages and applications, yet an exclusive focus on subtle techniques means that the laboratory is not approximating the full range of situational interventions.

A broader point is that laboratory interventions are often separated and abstracted from their real-world modalities. For example, in laboratory studies of empathy and prejudice reduction, participants receive instructions from the experimenter to imagine others' feelings. In the world, this message would be evoked within a moving speech, by a movie, or by the example of a peer. People interpret messages differently depending on who delivers the message and in what manner (Kuklinski & Hurley 1996). Laboratory studies eliminate larger institutions and social processes in which interventions are embedded—which may fundamentally change

Self-affirmation theory: predicts that when the self is under threat, people derogate others to affirm their self-identity; they refrain from other-derogation when their identity is affirmed

the impact and intervening psychological processes of the intervention.

Environment. Laboratory experiments themselves supply evidence challenging the external validity of the laboratory environment—to name a few, the presence of others affects emotional reactions (Ruiz-Belda et al. 2003), and a brief discussion with a peer can eliminate the influence of an authority's opinion (Druckman & Nelson 2003). The lack of correspondence between mundane living conditions and laboratory environments may be particularly damning for prejudice research, given some theoretical views that prejudice is a social norm set by peers and by the structure of the immediate situation (Crandall & Stangor 2005). Laboratory experiments like Cook's railroad job experiments address this concern by making the laboratory both an experimentally controlled and a realistic environment.

Populations. Warnings that North American college students differ from the general population (Sears 1986) are often acknowledged but disregarded by laboratory researchers. These students, who comprise the overwhelming majority of laboratory participants, are particularly exceptional when it comes to expressions of prejudice. At least in the United States, college students report less prejudice than does the average individual (Judd et al. 1995) and are more aware of social proscriptions against the expression of prejudice (Crandall et al. 2002). College subjects come to the lab having had more exposure to some form of diversity or antibias training (McCauley et al. 2000).

Prejudices. If prejudice were likened to a sickness, many laboratory interventions would be walk-in clinics, built to handle low-grade prejudices. Many studies get around the problem of college students' politically correct response patterns by studying socially acceptable prejudices against skinheads, political parties, or the elderly (e.g., Karpinski & Hilton 2001). Moreover, prejudices created with the minimal group paradigm for maximum experimental control

lack the historical, political, and economic forces that animate and sustain real-world prejudice, and "...a fundamental challenge remains to discover ways of changing 'hard-core' prejudiced beliefs" (Monteith et al. 1994).

Outcome measures. Measuring prejudice is a formidable challenge for all types of research, including laboratory studies. Behaviors measured in the laboratory are often low-stakes abstractions of real-world behaviors, such as giving up tokens to another group or brief interactions with a stranger. Laboratory investigators also rely on indirect measures to measure racial and ethnic prejudice. The linguistic bias index is an indirect measure in which verbs and nouns from participants' writing samples are classified according to their implication that out-group failings are dispositional while in-group failings are situation-specific (Maass 1999). Other measures gauge subtle forms of unease or reticence more than antipathy. One example is "immediacy behaviors," such as physical posture toward and distance from another person (Kawakami et al. 2007).

Controversy surrounds the interpretation of a "prejudiced score" on tests of implicit prejudice such as the IAT. Some studies find implicit prejudice to be correlated with the disintegration of real-world interracial friendships (Towles-Schwen & Fazio 2006), but a recent meta-analysis found that across 32 studies the IAT's ability to predict discriminatory behavior varies widely and sometimes inexplicably (AG Greenwald, TA Poehlman, E Uhlmann, & MR Banaji, unpubl. manuscr.). Other measures of implicit prejudice, such as word fragment completion (e.g., "short" versus "smart" in the case of Asians; Son Hing et al. 2002), are not empirically linked to behavior. Most importantly, few studies have connected the reduction of implicit prejudice with a reduction in prejudiced behavior.

Theories. A thorough review of theories developed in the laboratory goes beyond the scope of this essay, but we note that theory development in the laboratory mostly takes its lead from other laboratory experiments. We worry this creates a theoretical echo chamber in which ideas are not cross-fertilized by research conducted in real-world settings. Additionally, most theory developed in laboratories addresses one or two dimensions of prejudice, (e.g., cognition and behavior); one may question whether these theories are sufficiently multifaceted to predict how and when prejudice is expressed or changed in real-world settings (Paluck 2008).

The ultimate arbiters of the debate about the external validity of prejudice-reduction laboratory studies are research programs that straddle the two settings. Currently, such programs are extremely rare. An exception is the cooperative learning research program (e.g., Johnson & Johnson 1989, Roseth et al. 2008), in which field studies are sometimes inconsistent with laboratory results (e.g., Rich et al. 1995). One research program hardly settles the issue, and the correspondence between findings in the lab and field merits active investigation.

Conclusion: Experimental Research in the Laboratory

Reviewers of the psychological prejudice-reduction literature regularly comment that "... promising laboratory studies always need to be tested in field settings" (Miller & Harrington 1990, p. 218), but translation is rarely attempted, and psychologists frequently offer their laboratory findings as guidance for policymakers (e.g., Crisp & Hewstone 2007, p. 239). Those interested in creating effective prejudice-reduction programs must remain skeptical of the recommendations of laboratory experiments until they are supported by research of the same degree of rigor outside of the laboratory.

EXPERIMENTAL RESEARCH CONDUCTED IN THE FIELD

Over a half-century ago, psychologist Stuart Cook endeavored to make his research "... both socially useful and scientifically meaningful" (Selltiz & Cook 1948) by using lab and survey methods to develop the theoretical models he then tested using "true experiments" in the field (Cook 1985, p. 452). To what extent have prejudice-reduction researchers followed this example?

Of the hundreds of reports culled from our literature search, we identified 107 randomized field experiments. Thirty-six of these were studies of cooperative learning, which means that 71 experiments speak to the efficacy of all other types of prejudice interventions. To put this number into perspective, a PsychInfo database search for studies of one type of prejudice—implicit—retrieves 116 empirical articles. Our review's database contains four times as many laboratory experiments and five times as many nonexperimental field studies as noncooperative learning field experiments; this group of 71 studies is further dwarfed by the hundreds and perhaps thousands of unevaluated antiprejudice interventions implemented yearly in schools, businesses, and governments. Because the cooperative learning experiments have been summarized elsewhere (Roseth et al. 2008), **Supplemental Table 1** is confined to the 71 remaining studies.

Supplemental Table 1 describes these 71 field experiments, from the earliest in 1958 to present. Eighty percent of the studies are from North America. Almost one-third of these studies address prejudice against African Americans, 20% address multiple prejudices or are more generally "antibias" treatments; 13% of the studies address a non-African American group prejudice, including Mexican and Native Americans; 11% of the studies address "cultural competence"—comfort and ability to interact with people of different cultures. Of the remaining 18% of studies, 6 address prejudice against the disabled, 3 address prejudices against immigrants or refugees, 3 address religious prejudice, and 1 addresses prejudice against gay men.

Fifty-six percent of the interventions lasted one day or less. Excluding the cooperative learning studies, 84% of intervention studies took place with students or school personnel. This means antiprejudice education has developed a research literature, whereas the rest of the prejudice-reduction enterprise lacks randomized controlled evaluations.

Evaluations also focus on volunteers (e.g., Haring 1987, Pagtolun-an & Clair 1986, Stewart et al. 2003). It is easy to understand why, for practical reasons, interventions would tend to be directed toward people who are open to their messages. Unfortunately, field research on prejudice reduction does not have much to say about influencing those who do not sign up for antiprejudice interventions. Four studies took place in settings of extreme intergroup conflict, measuring reactions to peace education, a media program, and diversity training in Israel, Rwanda, and South Africa, respectively. The literature provides little empirical guidance to policymakers seeking to intervene with populations living in conflict or postconflict environments.

The breadth of answers to the question "What reduces prejudice in the world?" narrows further when we probe these studies' designs. Several suffer from weak outcome measurement. Most rely solely on self-report questionnaires; only 11 studies involve directly observed measures of behavior (two gather third-party reports). We would expect behavioral measurement to be the strength of field studies, which take place in environments where the behaviors of interest actually occur. Many clever unobtrusive measures of real-world behavior have been developed (Crosby et al. 1980), but these measurement techniques are rarely used in this literature. One of the few exceptions is a study of a disability awareness program that used audit study methods, sending disabled and nondisabled confederates to ask for help from employees who had attended the program (Wikfors 1998).

Inadequate power is another frequent problem; approximately half of the studies have sample sizes of below 100 individuals. Thirteen of the studies with larger sample sizes assign groups (e.g., classrooms, schools) to treatment and control groups but fail to make the necessary corrections for intracluster correlations within groups when calculating significance levels.

We now review the best of prejudice-reduction interventions and theories tested with field experiments. The most frequently studied interventions are cooperative learning (34% of all field experiments), entertainment (reading and media: 28%), discussion and peer influence (16%), and instruction (15%). We also review interventions that receive a great deal of attention in the lab but seldom in field settings: contact (10% of field experimental studies), cognitive training (5%), value consistency and self-worth interventions (4%), and social categorization (2%).

Cooperative Learning

Derived from Deutsch's (1949) theory of social interdependence and best known through Eliot Aronson's "Jigsaw classroom" technique (Aronson et al. 1978), cooperative learning lessons are engineered so that students must teach and learn from one another. For example, teachers in Jigsaw classrooms give each student one piece of the lesson plan, so that good lesson comprehension requires students to put together the pieces of the "puzzle" collectively. Approximately eight variants on this basic cooperative learning model exist (Slavin et al. 1984). Expected outcomes include interpersonal attraction, perspective taking, social support, and constructive management of conflict.

Meta-analyses of the effects of cooperative techniques (which included nonexperimental results) on relationships crossing ethnic, racial, and ability boundaries have consistently confirmed a positive impact of cooperation on outcomes such as positive peer relationships and helpfulness (Johnson & Johnson 1989, Roseth et al. 2008). The few studies that investigate generalization of cross-group friendships to individuals outside of the immediate classroom find weaker effects (cf., Warring et al. 1985). Fewer studies measure generalization to the entire racial or ethnic group or track long-term effects. Nevertheless, the cooperative learning literature sets the standard for programmatic field research on causal mechanisms. That 79% of all U.S. elementary schools by the early 1990s used cooperative learning (Puma et al. 1993) attests to the influence a well-documented causal effect can have on policy implementation.

Entertainment

Books, radio, television, and film are vivid and popular couriers of many kinds of social and political messages. *Uncle Tom's Cabin*, published by Harriet Beecher Stowe in 1852, was heralded as the turning point in American abolitionist opinion—not only for the information it provided about the brutality of slavery, but also for its ability to "go to the heart" (cited in Strange 2002, p. 263).

Reading and media interventions, most of them using an engaging narrative rather than an informational style, comprise 42% of all non-cooperative learning prejudice-reduction field experiments. We analyze the reading interventions separately because they share the specific modality of a book, but all of these interventions potentially draw from many of the same change processes via narrative persuasion or extended contact, which we describe below.

Reading. All 17 field experiments on the impact of reading on prejudice were conducted in schools—studies have yet to examine the effect of literature on prejudice among general audiences. One clear advantage of these reading experiments is that they evaluate substantially longer interventions compared to other field interventions. Whereas half of all field experiments focused on an intervention lasting one day or less, reading interventions lasted five weeks on average. Children in pre-K through high school were randomly assigned to read stories from or about other cultures (Gwinn 1998; Wham et al. 1996) about African, Native American, or disabled people (Clunies-Ross & O'Meara 1989, Fisher 1968, Hughes 2007, Yawkey 1973), or about contact between children from different groups (Cameron & Rutland 2006, Cameron et al. 2006, Liebkind & McAlister 1999, Slone et al. 2000).

Eleven of the 17 field experiments on reading report positive results, mostly for self-reported attitudinal outcomes; none measured behavior. The evidence is mixed or null for multicultural literature, more positive for portrayals of people of another culture or race, and wholly positive for books that portray contact between children who are similar to the audience and children of different cultures or races. For example, Cameron & Rutland (2006) randomly assigned 253 five- to eleven-year-old English schoolchildren to listen to stories about a nondisabled child's close friendship with a disabled child. The books described the two children's adventures, such as exploring in the woods. Across the three randomized conditions, the books emphasized characters' individual characteristics versus their group membership, versus a different unrelated story. Like eight other reading field experiments, this intervention included a group discussion led by the experimenter at the end of the story. Story hours took place once per week for six weeks.

The positive attitudinal effects found in this study and in four others that examined stories about intergroup friendship are consistent with the positive impact of vicarious experiences of cross-group friendship that is predicted by the extended contact hypothesis (Wright et al. 1997). Theories of narrative persuasion suggest additional processes that could explain prejudice reduction findings from reading field experiments that were not as theoretically motivated. For example, stories are channels for communicating social norms—descriptions of what peers are doing (and therefore what the reader or listener should do; Bandura 1986, 2006). Narratives encourage perspective taking (Strange 2002) and empathy (Zillmann 1991); texts can "transport" us into an imaginative world where we inhabit other characters, learn new things, and in general remove filters that might otherwise screen out different perspectives (Gerrig 1993, Green & Brock 2002).

Media. We found 13 media studies, 7 of which were one-time viewing experiences, such as a documentary or an educational movie. Because few programs were based on theory, it is difficult to draw broad lessons from the pattern of their findings, but like many of the reading studies, their results are suggestive for those interested in narrative persuasion, empathy, perspective taking, social norms, and the like. Most media experiments were conducted in schools, on media-driven multicultural or antibias education. Few have gauged the impact of media on large audiences or the impact of large-scale media campaigns (which span long periods of time or multiple theatres, cable networks, or airwaves). Two exceptions are a study of a children's multicultural television series (Mays et al. 1973) and of a "reconciliation" radio soap opera.

A year-long field experiment in Rwanda (Paluck 2008, Paluck & Green 2008) tested the impact of a radio soap opera featuring a fictional story of two Rwandan communities and their struggles with prejudice and violence. The program aimed to change beliefs using didactic messages and to influence perceived norms through realistic radio characters who could speak to audience experiences. Nearly 600 Rwandan citizens, prisoners, and genocide survivors listened to the program or to a health radio soap opera. The investigators found the radio program affected listeners' perceptions of social norms and their behaviors with respect to intermarriage, open dissent, cooperation, and trauma healing, but did little to change listeners' personal beliefs. The program also encouraged greater empathy. The results pointed to an integrated model of behavioral prejudice reduction in which intergroup behaviors are linked more closely to social norms than to personal beliefs.

Discussion is featured in many studies of entertainment, because storytelling and media consumption are inherently social practices, and also because an implicit theory in much intervention design is that peer discussion amplifies message impact. We now turn to consider discussion and peer influence as interventions in their own right and how they have fared in field experimental research.

Discussion and Peer Influence

Although psychologists examine group discussion for processes related to polarization of attitudes and minority influence, they seldom focus on communication for prejudice reduction. One of the few exceptions is Fisher (1968), which found that the addition of discussion strengthened the positive attitudinal effects of a reading intervention.

Evidence of the benefits (and potential pitfalls) of discussing opinions about intergroup relations is also found in peer influence studies. For example, Blanchard and colleagues (1991, 1994) find that white university females' opinions about a racial incident on campus conformed to the publicly expressed opinions of confederates who were randomly assigned to condone, condemn, or remain neutral in their reactions. Another study of norms, a field experiment assessing the Anti-Defamation League Peer Training program (Paluck 2006b), showed that students were able to influence close friends and casual acquaintances in their school with public behaviors such as speaking out against biased jokes. Although few field experiments have experimentally isolated the effects of normative communication and discussion in field interventions of prejudice reduction, these findings indicate that theories of social norms and mechanisms of small group or peer discussion are promising avenues for research and intervention.

Instruction

Under the umbrella category of "instruction" we find myriad interventions: multicultural education, "ethnic studies," stand-alone lectures, awareness workshops, and peace education. Few instructional techniques are guided by theoretical models of learning or prejudice reduction (see Bigler 1999 critiquing multicultural education in particular). The lack of theory may explain in part the lack of impressive findings. One notable exception is Lustig's (2003) investigation of a peace education program in Israel that aimed to increase perspective taking and empathy using instruction about foreign conflicts. Twelfth-grade Israeli Jewish students were randomly assigned to a "permanent peace" curriculum (versus no curriculum) about conflicts in ancient Greece and modern-day Ireland. Questionnaire-based opinions about the Israeli-Palestinian conflict revealed no effect of the curriculum, but there were striking differences between essays students were asked to write from the Palestinian point of view. Curriculum student essays were more likely to be written in the first as opposed to the third person, and they were more sympathetic to damages and to the symmetry of Israeli-Palestinian conflict. This study is an excellent example of the benefits of multiple and non-traditional outcome measurement, and of interventions informed by theories of prejudice reduction.

Less-Frequently Studied Approaches in the Field

Given the academic focus on the contact hypothesis, social identity theory and related social categorization strategies, cognitive forms of prejudice, and motivational theories of identity and dissonance, the field experimental literature on these areas is surprisingly thin.

Contact hypothesis. What is most notable about field experiments categorized as "contact" experiments is their general lack of resemblance to the conditions of contact specified by Allport (1954). Within the small body of field experiments on contact, there is also a tendency to address prejudices that may be more related to unfamiliarity (e.g., disability) than to antipathy.

Among more recent studies, we find two of note. One study capitalized on random assignment of minority and white students to college dorm rooms (Duncan et al. 2003). The experiment's findings from a subsequent Internet-based survey are important for their suggestion that cross-race contact affects more general attitudes such as support for affirmative action, although weak effects on other attitudinal and behavioral outcomes suggest this finding requires more study. The second study, conducted with the Outward Bound camping expedition organization, randomly assigned 54 white teenagers to racially homogeneous (all white) or heterogeneous expedition groups (Green & Wong 2008). In these expeditions, an experienced leader teaches campers group survival techniques under most of Allport's (1954) conditions for ideal intergroup contact: equal status, a common (survival) goal, authority sanction, and intimate contact. One month after the two- to three-week trip, in an ostensibly unrelated phone survey, white teens from the heterogeneous groups reported significantly less aversion to blacks and gays and described themselves as less "prejudiced" compared to the homogeneous group teens. The intensity and naturalistic quality of the intervention recall the seminal field study of contact, the Sherif et al. (1961) Robbers Cave experiment. The study's limitations—small sample size, the lack of behavioral outcome measures, and short-term follow-up—invite replication and extension.

Social identity and categorization. Although principles of social identity and categorization theory broadly inform some field interventions (e.g., Cameron & Rutland 2006), very few field experiments have been designed to test crossed, integrated, re- and decategorization strategies developed in the laboratory. Two exceptions are studies by Nier et al. (2001) and Houlette et al. (2004) testing the Common Ingroup Identity model.

Over the course of 12 hour-long sessions, instructors in 61 randomly assigned first- and second-grade classrooms led discussions about sex, race, and body size exclusion from the "green circle of community" (Houlette et al. 2004), versus an enhanced program, versus no program. In the enhanced program, the perimeter of the classroom was circled with green tape and all students wore the same green vests. Mixed, modest results showed that children in the program classrooms were slightly more likely to favor drawings of cross-sex or -race children. Weight remained a powerful

Social identity and categorization theory: describes how social group classification produces perceptions of multiple, crossed, and hierarchically arranged social identities, and how group identities give rise to phenomena such as in-group favoritism and out-group derogation

predictor of children's hypothetical choices of playmates. The enhanced program did not amplify these effects (which speaks to our previous question about the real-world effects of subtle laboratory interventions such as seating arrangements and similar clothing).

Value consistency and self-worth. Compared to their importance in the laboratory literature, studies of the motivating forces of consistency and self-worth are scarce in the field experimental literature. A notable exception is the Rokeach value confrontation technique (Gray & Ashmore 1975, Rokeach 1971). Rokeach (1971, 1973) lectured college students about (fictitious) research findings on values revealing people who value equality are more likely to be sympathetic toward black Americans' civil rights (during this historical period, most North American students favored equality but not black civil rights). In postintervention questionnaires that stretched as far as 17 months later, students from the lecture and the no-lecture classes increased their support of black civil rights, perhaps in part through exposure to the more liberal college atmosphere, but treatment students eventually outpaced others in their support (Rokeach never corrected for intraclass correlations, which should lead to more caution about the statistical significance of his findings). Twenty-one months later, twice as many experimental as control subjects were enrolled in an ethnic core course, and three to five months after the intervention, 51 treatment versus 18 control participants responded to solicitations sent by the NAACP (although a comparable number of control students responded the following year). Although the strength of these results is at times mixed, this series of studies is notable for its behavioral measures and longitudinal design.

Cognitive training. Excellent laboratory and quasi-field experimental research has examined stereotype retraining with young children (Levy 1999, Levy et al. 2004), but there are very few studies of cognitive retraining in the field experimental literature. Five field experiments, all conducted on North American students, show weak results in both the short- and long-term (e.g., Katz 1978, 2000).

Lessons of Field Experimental Research

The strongest conclusion to be drawn from the field experimental literature on prejudice reduction concerns the dearth of evidence for most prejudice-reduction programs. Few programs originating in scientific laboratories, nonprofit or educational organizations, government bureaus, and consulting firms have been evaluated rigorously. Theories with the strongest support from the laboratory sometimes receive scant attention in the field. Entire genres of prejudice-reduction interventions, including moral education, organizational diversity training, advertising, and cultural competence in the health and law enforcement professions, have never been tested, as well as countless individual programs within the broad genre of educational interventions.

Nonetheless, the field experimental literature on prejudice reduction suggests some tentative conclusions and promising avenues for reducing prejudice. Cooperative learning emerges as an important tool for breaking down boundaries between students. This research program should be emulated and extended. More research is needed on the behavioral and longitudinal impact of cooperative learning and its impact on out-group dislike as well as in-group preference.

Media and reading interventions bear out assorted predictions of the extended contact hypothesis and of narrative persuasion, specifically that extended contact can reduce out-group hostility, and narratives can communicate norms and inspire empathy and perspective taking. Theoretically driven programs of research on entertainment and narrative interventions would systematize what is at present a rather disjointed set of studies and findings. Extended contact and narrative persuasion might also provide frameworks for other strategies associated with empathy or perspective taking such as role playing (e.g., the Jane Elliot Blue Eyes/Brown Eyes intervention; Stewart et al. 2003), which have met with mixed success, perhaps in part because of a lack of theoretical grounding.

Given the importance of social psychological processes such as obedience and conformity, experimental evaluations of peer influence and discussion should become a priority for future field research. Isolating the influence of discussion from the impact of the intervention itself is an important future step (Kelman & Fisher 2003, p. 335).

Recommendations

Few rigorous field studies to date have addressed psychology's most important theories of interpersonal and intrapersonal prejudice change: contact, social identity and categorization, identity and value-motivated techniques, and social cognitive (stereotype and implicit prejudice) interventions. We recommend more field experimentation on social psychology's principal theories of prejudice.

The strength of field experimentation rests not only in its ability to assess causal relationships but also in its ability to assess whether an intervention's effects emerge and endure among the cacophony of real-world influences including larger political and economic changes and proximal social pressures and distractions. We recommend that more field experiments assess the strength and persistence of effects with outcome measurement that moves beyond the site of the intervention. Types of outcome measures should be increased to capture prejudice from different angles, especially with unobtrusive and behavioral measures, and the settings should be expanded so as to augment our knowledge about changing prejudice outside of the classroom and with older populations.

Although laboratory studies concentrate on interventions targeted at specific forms of prejudice (e.g., stereotyping), the complexities of real-world contexts often force the field experimentalist to design and parse the impact of multidimensional interventions aimed at several forms of prejudiced speech, behavior, and attitudes. Studying prejudice reduction in the field opens our eyes to the utility of more multidimensional theories of prejudice reduction. Field experimentation can be productive for assessing the functional interdependence of cognitive, affective, normative, and other forms of prejudice, and thus for building prejudice-reduction theories based on this recognition of the interrelationships and on the sequencing and long-term effects of change in one part of the system (e.g., an intervention that changes social norms, which then affect behaviors and finally beliefs; see Paluck 2008 for one such attempt). Field experimentation is not only a method for testing theoretical ideas developed in the laboratory—the field itself should be used as a laboratory for generating richer, more multidimensioned theory.

DISCUSSION

In terms of size, breadth, and vitality, the prejudice literature has few rivals. Thousands of researchers from an array of disciplines have addressed the meaning, measurement, and expression of prejudice. The result is a literature teeming with ideas about the causes of prejudice. In quantitative terms, the literature on prejudice reduction is vast, but a survey of this literature reveals a paucity of research that supports internally valid inferences and externally valid generalization.

In order to formulate policies about how to reduce prejudice, one currently must extrapolate well beyond the data, using theoretical presuppositions to fill in the empirical blanks. One can argue that diversity training workshops succeed because they break down stereotypes and encourage empathy. Alternatively, one can argue that such workshops reinforce stereotypes and elicit reactance among the most prejudiced participants. Neither of these conflicting arguments is backed by the type of evidence that would convince a skeptic. We currently do not know whether a wide range of programs and policies tend to work on average, and we are quite far from having an empirically grounded

Table 1   Summary of prejudice-reduction approaches, theories, and future directions for research

Intervention approach	Theoretical frameworks	Evidence needed
Supported by experimental evidence from field and laboratory		
Cooperative learning	Social Interdependence Theory	Longitudinal, generalization to wider groups, reduction of negative out-group attitudes
Entertainment	Extended contact, narrative persuasion (empathy, perspective taking, transport-imagery), social norm theory, social cognitive theory	Theory-driven programmatic research; studies of longer duration and with adults
Peer influence, discussion/dialogue	Social norm theory, small group influence, social impact theory, contact hypothesis	Field experimental evidence; isolation of effects of discussion from other aspects of intervention
Contact	Contact and extended contact hypothesis	Field experimental evidence for differing contact conditions and more antagonistic groups
Value consistency and self-worth	Cognitive dissonance, self-affirmation and self-perception theory	Field experimental evidence; evidence with "unmotivated" populations
Cross-cultural/intercultural training	Acculturation theory, Bhawuk/Landis model	Field experimental evidence; behavioral, longitudinal effects
Supported mostly by laboratory evidence		
Social categorization	Social identity theory, crossed-categorization, common in-group identity, de- and recategorization	Field experimental evidence; evidence with antagonistic groups and longitudinal effects
Cognitive training	Implicit prejudice, classical conditioning	Field experimental evidence; longitudinal effects
In need of theoretical and research support		
Diversity training	Dependent on technique/modality used	Theory-driven intervention design and field experimentation
Multicultural, antibias, moral education	Socialization theories of prejudice, cognitive, moral development and learning theories	Field experimental evaluations with longitudinal outcome measurement
Sensitivity, cultural competence for health and law	Dependent on technique/modality used	Theory-driven intervention design and field experimentation
Conflict resolution	Interactive conflict resolution models	Theory-driven field experimentation

understanding of the conditions under which these programs work best.

Looking across all of the settings, populations, and methodologies used to study the reduction of prejudice, we classify the main approaches to prejudice reduction according to the evidence accumulated thus far for their impact in the real world, and we list theories and methods that could point the way forward (see **Table 1**).

Cooperative learning is the most outstanding example of theoretically driven, programmatic laboratory and field research; we hope future research will address questions about the longevity and generality of cooperative learning's effects. Although media, reading, and other forms of narrative and normative communication are not currently considered cutting-edge approaches, we point to the apparent success of this technique in the real world and to its potential for reducing prejudice through narrative persuasion, social norms, empathy, perspective taking, and extended contact. The persuasive and positive influence of peers (indirectly via observation or directly via discussion) is a promising area of prejudice reduction supported by laboratory research (Stangor et al. 2001) and by creative real-world interventions (Aboud & Doyle 1996; Blanchard et al. 1991, 1994; McAlister et al. 2000; Nagda et al. 2004; Paluck 2006b) highlighting the communicative and normative nature of prejudice change.

The contact hypothesis, which benefited from early and innovative field and laboratory studies, remains unproven in the real world due to the limited number of randomized studies conducted in field settings and the narrow range of prejudices tested in those studies. Researchers should aspire to extend real-world experimental tests to domains such as summer camps, multinational peacekeeping units, and refugee settlements. Other approaches that require more field experimental tests are consistency and self-worth interventions based on balance and self-affirmation theories, as well as cross-cultural training approaches. Given that motivation is a critical lever of change for these interventions, field tests would illuminate whether these techniques are successful with participants who are unmotivated to change, and what adjustments are needed in order to reach this population. Interventions aimed at changing cognitions (e.g., stereotypes or automatic associations) or cognitive abilities (e.g., complex thinking or statistical reasoning) have successfully reduced prejudice in the laboratory, but the magnitude and persistence of these effects also await testing in real-world settings.

Several areas of prejudice reduction are in need of research and theory. Although antibias, multicultural, and moral education are popular approaches, they have not been examined with a great deal of rigor, and many applications are theoretically ungrounded. Spending on corporate diversity training in the United States alone costs an estimated $8 billion annually (cited in Hansen 2003), and yet the impact of diversity training remains largely unknown (Paluck 2006a). Despite research showing that medical practitioners' negative bias can affect their administration of care (Flores et al. 2000) and reports of sharply increased demand within the law enforcement field following September 2001 (*New York Times*, Jan. 23, 2005), sensitivity trainings administered to medical personnel and police are rarely based on theory or subjected to rigorous evaluation. Finally, although there is a distinguished tradition of psychological research on conflict resolution for elite negotiators (Kelman & Fisher 2003), there is lit-tle sustained experimental evaluation of conflict negotiation and reduction for the many millions of ordinary citizens living in conflict or postconflict settings (G Salomon & B Nevo, unpubl. manuscr.; cf., Bargal & Bar 1992).

Final Thoughts

Field experiments present a range of practical challenges, but we believe that the failure to implement field experimental designs is in part a failure of creativity. Random assignment to waiting lists solves the problem of control groups who wish to undergo treatment and represents a low-cost opportunity for randomized field experimentation. Randomly phasing in a program to different parts of a target population solves the problem of the "saturation model" intervention. For interventions where it is absolutely impossible to leave out a control group, researchers can use rigorous and underappreciated quasi-experimental techniques such as regression discontinuity (Shadish et al. 2002). A lack of field experimental training among practitioners who evaluate prejudice-reduction programs, doubts about the feasibility of randomized field methodology, and insufficient incentives for academics to conduct "applied" research all contribute to the scarcity of randomized field experiments in prejudice reduction. We believe that each of these limitations can be overcome through partnerships between academics and practitioners (which is how we have conducted our prejudice-reduction work to date; e.g., Green & Wong 2008; Paluck 2006b, 2008; Paluck & Green 2008).

Laboratory research plays an important role in the process of developing and testing interventions, but too often this process stops short of real-world tests. The result is a dearth of rigorously tested interventions and also of rigorously tested theoretical ideas. We urge more research programs in the spirit of psychologists such as Stuart Cook, Kurt Lewin, and Donald Campbell: hypothesis generation through field observation, and intervention testing with parallel laboratory and field experiments. The imperative to test ideas in the field will keep theories appropriately complex and attuned to real-world conditions, and continually revisiting the laboratory will help to refine understandings of the causal mechanisms at work, which in turn helps inspire new interventions.

In addition to becoming more methodologically rigorous, the study of prejudice reduction must branch out substantively. As our review of the literature demonstrates, the kinds of interventions that have been evaluated do not pit prejudice against its strongest potential adversaries. Studies to date have largely relied on passive and indirect interventions such as cooperative contact. What if interventions were instead to harness forces such as obedience and conformity, the very forces that have been implicated in some of the most notorious expressions of prejudice in world history? If people can be induced to express prejudice at the behest of political leaders, can they also be induced to repudiate prejudice if instructed to do so? If social cues induce conformity to prejudiced norms, can social cues also induce conformity to tolerant norms? The prejudice-reduction literature should be regarded as an opportunity to assess the power and generality of basic psychological theory.

SUMMARY POINTS

1. Notwithstanding the enormous literature on prejudice, psychologists are a long way from demonstrating the most effective ways to reduce prejudice. Due to weaknesses in the internal and external validity of existing research, the literature does not reveal whether, when, and why interventions reduce prejudice in the world.

2. Entire genres of prejudice-reduction interventions, including diversity training, educational programs, and sensitivity training in health and law enforcement professions, have never been evaluated with experimental methods.

3. Nonexperimental research in the field has yielded information about prejudice-reduction program implementation, but it cannot answer the question of what works to reduce prejudice in these real-world settings.

4. Laboratory experiments test a wide range of prejudice-reduction theories and mechanisms with precision. However, researchers should remain skeptical of recommendations based upon environments, interventions, participants, and theories created in laboratory settings until they are supported by research of the same degree of rigor outside of the laboratory.

5. Laboratory research and field research are rarely coordinated; in particular, many prejudice-reduction theories with the strongest support from the laboratory receive scant attention in the field.

6. Field experimentation remains a promising but underutilized approach. Promising avenues for prejudice reduction based on existing field experimentation include cooperative learning, media, and reading interventions.

FUTURE ISSUES

1. More field experimentation can provide evidence that is missing, particularly for the contact hypothesis, peer influence and discussion/dialogue interventions, values and self-worth interventions, social categorization theory, and cognitive training.

2. Theoretical perspectives and more rigorous evaluation methods should be brought to bear on common prejudice interventions such as diversity training; multicultural, antibias, and moral education; sensitivity and cultural competence training; and conflict resolution.

3. Psychologists should look to historical exemplars of theoretically and methodologically rigorous applied prejudice-reduction studies, such as those conducted by Stuart Cook. The hallmark of Cook's work was theoretically grounded randomized field interventions and highly realistic experimental laboratory interventions.

4. In addition to becoming more methodologically rigorous, the study of prejudice reduction must branch out substantively to include more direct interventions based on classic psychological findings (e.g., those that leverage the power of conformity and authority). Researchers should also strive to reduce deeply held prejudices rather than the more transitory prejudices associated with "minimal" groups.

DISCLOSURE STATEMENT

The authors are not aware of any biases that might be perceived as affecting the objectivity of this review.

LITERATURE CITED

Aboud FE, Doyle AB. 1996. Does talk of race foster prejudice or tolerance in children? *Can. J. Behav. Sci.* 28:161–70

Aboud FE, Levy SR. 2000. Interventions to reduce prejudice and discrimination in children and adolescents. In *Reducing Prejudice and Discrimination*, ed. S Oskamp, pp. 269–93. Mahwah, NJ: Erlbaum

Allport G. 1954. *The Nature of Prejudice*. Reading, MA: Addison-Wesley. 537 pp.

Am. Psychol. Assoc. 2001. *Declaration for the UN World Conference Against Racism, Racial Discrimination, Xenophobia, and Related Intolerance*. **http://wwwapaorg/pi/oema/racismdeclarationpdf**

Aronson E, Blaney N, Stephan W, Sikes J, Snapp M. 1978. *The Jigsaw Classroom*. Thousand Oaks, CA: Sage

Banaji MR. 2001. Implicit attitudes can be measured. In *The Nature of Remembering: Essays in Honor of Robert G. Crowder*, ed. HL Roediger, JS Nairne, I Neath, AM Surprenant, pp. 117–50. Washington, DC: Am. Psychol. Assoc.

Bandura A. 1986. *Social Foundations of Thought and Action*. Englewood Cliffs, NJ: Prentice Hall

Bandura A. 2006. Toward a psychology of human agency. *Perspect. Psychol. Sci.* 1:164–80

Bargal D, Bar H. 1992. A Lewinian approach to intergroup workshops for Arab-Palestinian and Jewish youth. *J. Soc. Issues* 48:139–54

Bargh JA, Chen M, Burrows L. 1996. Automaticity of social behavior: direct effect of trait construct and stereotype activation on action. *J. Personal. Soc. Psychol.* 71:230–44

Batson CD. 1991. *The Altruism Question: Toward a Social-Psychological Answer*. Hillsdale, NJ: Erlbaum. 272 pp.

Baumeister R, Leary M. 1997. Writing narrative literature reviews. *Rev. Gen. Psychol.* 13:311–20

Berry JW. 1984. Multicultural policy in Canada: a social psychological analysis. *Can. J. Behav. Sci.* 16:353–70

Bettencourt A, Brewer M, Croak M, Miller N. 1992. Cooperation and the reduction of intergroup bias: the role of reward structure and social orientation. *J. Exp. Soc. Psychol.* 284:301–19

Bigler RS. 1999. The use of multicultural curricula and materials to counter racism in children. *J. Soc. Issues* 55:687–705

Blair I. 2002. The malleability of automatic stereotypes and prejudice. *Personal. Soc.Psychol. Rev.* 63:242–61

Blanchard FA, Crandall CS, Brigham JC, Vaughn LA. 1994. Condemning and condoning racism: a social context approach to interracial settings. *J. Appl. Psychol.* 79:993–97

Blanchard FA, Lilly T, Vaughn LA. 1991. Reducing the expression of racial prejudice. *Psychol. Sci.* 2:101–5

Bodenhausen GV, Kramer GP, Süsser K. 1994. Happiness and stereotypic thinking in social judgment. *J. Personal. Soc. Psychol.* 66:621–32

Brewer MB, Gaertner SL. 2001. Strategies for reducing intergroup bias. In *Handbook of Social Psychology: Intergroup Processes*, ed. RJ Brown, SL Gaertner, pp. 451–513. Oxford: Blackwell Sci.

Brown RJ, Turner JC. 1979. The criss-cross categorization effect in intergroup discrimination. *Br. J. Soc. Clinical Psychol.* 18:371–83

Cameron L, Rutland A. 2006. Extended contact through story reading in school: reducing children's prejudice towards the disabled. *J. Soc. Issues* 62:469–88

Cameron L, Rutland A, Brown RJ, Douch R. 2006. Changing children's intergroup attitudes towards refugees: testing different models of extended contact. *Child Dev.* 77:1208–19

Clunies-Ross G, O'Meara K. 1989. Changing the attitudes of students towards peers with disabilities. *Aust. Psychol.* 24:273–84

Cook SW. 1971. *The effect of unintended interracial contact upon racial interaction and attitude change.* Proj. No. 5–1320, Final Rep. Washington, DC: U.S. Dep. Health Educ. Welfare

Cook SW. 1978. Interpersonal and attitudinal outcomes in cooperating interracial groups. *J. Res. Dev. Educ.* 12:97–113

Cook SW. 1985. Experimenting on social issues: the case of school desegregation. *Am. Psychol.* 40:452–60

Crandall CS, Eshleman A, O'Brien LT. 2002. Social norms and the expression and suppression of prejudice: the struggle for internalization. *J. Personal. Soc. Psychol.* 82:359–78

Crandall CS, Stangor C. 2005. Conformity and prejudice. In *On the Nature of Prejudice: Fifty Years After Allport*, ed. JF Dovidio, P Glick, LA Rudman, pp. 295–309. Malden, MA: Blackwell Sci.

Crisp RJ, Hewstone M. 1999. Differential evaluation of crossed category groups: patterns processes and reducing intergroup bias. *Group Proc. Intergroup Relat.* 2:303–33

Crisp RJ, Hewstone M. 2007. Multiple social categorization. *Adv. Exp. Soc. Psychol.* 39:163–254

Crosby F, Bromley S, Saxe L. 1980. Recent unobtrusive studies of Black and White discrimination and prejudice: a literature review. *Psychol. Bull.* 87:546–63

Dasgupta N, Greenwald AG. 2001. On the malleability of automatic attitudes: combating automatic prejudice with images of admired and disliked individuals. *J. Personal. Soc. Psychol.* 81:800–14

Deutsch M. 1949. A theory of co-operation and competition. *Hum. Relat.* 2:129–52

Devine PG. 1989. Stereotypes and prejudice: their automatic and controlled components. *J. Personal. Soc. Psychol.* 56:5–18

Dobbs M, Crano WD. 2001. Outgroup accountability in the minimal group paradigm: implications for aversive discrimination and social identity theory. *Personal. Soc. Psychol. Bull.* 27:355–64

Dovidio JF, Gaertner SL, Validzic A, Matoka K, Johnson B, Frazier S. 1997. Extending the benefits of recategorization: evaluations, self-disclosure, and helping. *J. Exp. Soc. Psychol.* 33:401–20

Druckman JN, Nelson KR. 2003. Framing and deliberation: how citizens' conversations limit elite influence. *Am. J. Pol. Sci.* 474:729–45

Duncan JG, Boisjoly J, Levy DM, Kremer M, Eccles J. 2003. *Empathy or Antipathy? The Consequences of Racially and Socially Diverse Peers on Attitudes and Behaviors.* Work. Pap., Inst. Policy Res., Northwestern Univ., Chicago, IL

Eagly A, Mladinic A. 1994. Are people prejudiced against women? Some answers from research on attitudes, gender stereotypes, and judgments of competence. In *European Review of Social Psychology*, ed. W Stroebe, M Hewstone, 5:1–35. New York: Wiley

Eisenstadt D, Leippe MR, Rivers JA, Stambush MA. 2003. Counterattitudinal advocacy on a matter of prejudice: effects of distraction commitment and personal importance. *J. Appl. Soc. Psychol.* 33(10):2123–52

Ellis C, Sonnenfield JA. 1994. Diverse approaches to managing diversity. *Hum. Res. Manag.* 33:79–109

Environics Res. Group Ltd. 2001. *Citizenship Advertising Campaign "Canada: We All Belong." PN5048 contract 6C501-010874/001/CB.* Communication Canada

Esses VM, Dovidio JF. 2002. The role of emotions in determining willingness to engage in intergroup contact. *Personal. Soc. Psychol. Bull.* 289:1202–14

Fein S, Spencer SJ. 1997. Prejudice as self-image maintenance: affirming the self through derogating others. *J. Personal. Soc. Psychol.* 73:31–44

Festinger LA. 1957. *A Theory of Cognitive Dissonance*. Stanford, CA: Stanford Univ. Press. 291 pp.

Fisher FL. 1968. Influences of reading and discussion on the attitudes of fifth graders toward American Indians. *J. Educ. Res.* 623:130–34

Flores G, Gee D, Kastner B. 2000. The teaching of cultural issues in US and Canadian medical schools. *Acad. Med.* 75:451–55

Gaertner SL, Dovidio JF. 2000. *Reducing Intergroup Bias: The Common Ingroup Identity Model*. Philadelphia, PA: Psychol. Press. 212 pp.

Gaertner SL, Dovidio JF, Rust MC, Nier J, Banker B, Ward CM. 1999. Reducing intergroup bias: elements of intergroup cooperation. *J. Personal. Soc. Psychol.* 76:388–402

Galinsky AD, Moskowitz GB. 2000. Perspective taking: decreasing stereotype expression, stereotype accessibility, and in-group favoritism. *J. Personal. Soc. Psychol.* 784:708–24

Gardiner GS. 1972. Complexity training and prejudice reduction. *J. Appl. Soc. Psychol.* 2:326–42

Gerber AS, Green DP, Kaplan EH. 2004. The illusion of learning from observational research. In *Problems and Methods in the Study of Politics*, ed. I Shapiro, R Smith, T Massoud, pp. 251–73. New York: Cambridge Univ. Press

Gerrig RJ. 1993. *Experiencing Narrative Worlds*. New Haven, CT: Yale Univ. Press. 294 pp.

Gilliam FD Jr, Iyengar S. 2000. Prime suspects: the impact of local television news on the viewing public. *Am. J. Polit. Sci.* 44:560–73

Gray DB, Ashmore RD. 1975. Comparing the effects of informational role-playing and value-discrepant treatments of racial attitudes. *J. Appl. Soc. Psychol.* 5:262–81

Green DP, Wong JS. 2008. Tolerance and the contact hypothesis: a field experiment. In *The Political Psychology of Democratic Citizenship*, ed. E Borgida. London: Oxford Univ. Press. In press

Greenwald AG, McGhee DE, Schwartz JKL. 1998. Measuring individual differences in implicit cognition: the implicit association test. *J. Personal. Soc. Psychol.* 74:1464–80

Gurin P, Peng T, Lopez G, Nagda BR. 1999. Context identity and intergroup relations. In *Cultural Divides: The Social Psychology of Intergroup Contact*, ed. D Prentice, D Miller, pp. 133–70. New York: Sage

Gwinn CB. 1998. The effect of multicultural literature on the attitudes of second-grade students. Unpubl. PhD dissert., Univ. Minn.

Green MC, Brock TC. 2002. In the mind's eye: transportation-imagery model of narrative persuasion. In *Narrative Impact*, ed. MC Green, JJ Strange, TC Brock, pp. 315–41. Mahwah, NJ: Erlbaum

Hafer C, Begue L. 2005. Experimental research on just-world theory: problems, developments, and future challenges. *Psychol. Bull.* 1311:128–67

Hanover JMB, Cellar DF. 1998. Environmental factors and the effectiveness of workforce diversity training. *Hum. Resour. Dev. Q.* 9:105–24

Hansen F. 2003. Diversity's business case: doesn't add up. *Workforce* 824:28–32

Haring TG, Breen C, Pitts-Conway V, Lee M. 1987. Adolescent peer tutoring and special friend experiences. *J. Assoc. Persons Severe Handicaps* 12:280–86

Hewstone M. 2000. Contact and categorization: social psychological interventions to change intergroup relations. In *Stereotypes and Prejudice: Essential Readings*, ed. C Stangor, pp. 394–418. New York: Psychol. Press

Hornsey M, Hogg M. 2000a. Intergroup similarity and subgroup relations: some implications for assimilation. *Personal. Soc. Psychol. Bull.* 268:948–58

Hornsey M, Hogg M. 2000b. Assimilation and diversity: an integrative model of subgroup relations. *Personal. Soc. Psychol. Rev.* 42:143–56

Houlette M, Gaertner SL, Johnson KS, Banker BS, Riek BM, Dovidio JM. 2004. Developing a more inclusive social identity: an elementary school intervention. *J. Soc. Issues* 601:35–55

Hughes JM, Bigler RS, Levy SR. 2007. Consequences of learning about historical racism among European American and African American children. *Child Dev.* 78:1689–705

Jackman MR. 1994. *The Velvet Glove: Paternalism and Conflict in Gender Class and Race Relations*. Berkeley, CA: Univ. Calif. Press. 425 pp.

Johnson DW, Johnson RT. 1989. *Cooperation and Competition: Theory and Research*. Edina, MN: Interaction Book Co. 265 pp.

Judd CM, Park B, Ryan CS, Brauer M, Kraus S. 1995. Stereotypes and ethnocentrism: diverging interethnic perceptions of African American and White American youth. *J. Personal. Soc. Psychol.* 69:460–81

Karpinski A, Hilton JL. 2001. Attitudes and the Implicit Association Test. *J. Personal. Soc. Psychol.* 81:774–78

Katz P. 2000. Research summary. *Intergroup Relations Among Youth: Summary of a Research Workshop.* New York: Carnegie Corp.

Katz PA, Zalk SR. 1978. Modification of children's racial attitudes. *Dev. Psychol.* 145:447–61

Kawakami K, Dovidio JF, Moll J, Hermsen S, Russin A. 2000a. Just say no to stereotyping: effects of training in trait negation on stereotype activation. *J. Personal. Soc. Psychol.* 78:871–88

Kawakami K, Phills CE, Steele JR, Dovidio JF. 2000b. Close distance makes the heart grow fonder: improving implicit racial attitudes and interracial interactions through approach behaviors. *J. Personal. Soc. Psychol.* 926:957–71

Kelman HC, Fisher RJ. 2003. Conflict analysis and resolution. In *Political Psychology*, ed. DO Sears, L Huddy, R Jervis, pp. 315–56. London: Oxford Univ. Press

Kiselica MS, Maben P. 1999. Do multicultural education and diversity training appreciation training reduce prejudice among counseling trainees? *J. Ment. Health Couns.* 213–40

Kuklinski JH, Hurley NL. 1996. It's a matter of interpretation. In *Political Persuasion and Attitude Change*, ed. D Mutz, P Sniderman, R Brody, pp. 125–44. Ann Arbor: Mich. Univ. Press

Kulik CT, Perry EL, Bourhis AC. 2000. Ironic evaluation processes: effects of thought suppression on evaluations of older job applicants. *J. Org. Behav.* 21:689–711

Landis D, Day HR, McGrew PL, Thomas JA, Miller AB. 1976. Can a black "culture assimilator" increase racial understanding? *J. Soc. Issues* 32:169–83

Levy SR. 1999. Reducing prejudice: lessons from social-cognitive factors underlying perceiver differences in prejudice. *J. Soc. Issues* 55:745–65

Levy SR, Stroessner S, Dweck CS. 1998. Stereotype formation and endorsement: the role of implicit theories. *J. Personal. Soc. Psychol.* 74:421–36

Levy SR, West TL, Ramirez LF, Pachankis JE. 2004. Racial and ethnic prejudice among children. In *The Psychology of Prejudice and Discrimination: Racism in America*, Vol. 1, ed. J Chin, pp. 37–60. Westport, CT: Praeger Publ.

Liebkind K, McAlister AL. 1999. Extended contact through peer modelling to promote tolerance in Finland. *Eur. J. Soc. Psychol.* 295–6:765–80

Lustig I. 2003. *The influence of studying foreign conflicts on students' perceptions of the Israeli Palestinian conflict.* Unpubl. master's thesis: Univ. Haifa, Israel

Maass A. 1999. Linguistic intergroup bias: stereotype perpetuation through language. *Adv. Exp. Soc. Psychol.* 31:79–121

Marcus-Newhall A, Miller N, Holtz R, Brewer MB. 1993. Cross-cutting category membership with role assignment: a means of reducing intergroup bias. *Br. J. Soc. Psychol.* 32:125–46

Mays L, Henderson EH, Seidman SK, Steiner VJ. 1975. *An Evaluation Report on Vegetable Soup: The Effects of a Multi-Ethnic Children's Television Series on Intergroup Attitudes of Children.* Dept. Educ., Albany, NY

McAlister A, Ama E, Barroso C, Peters RJ, Kelder S. 2000. Promoting tolerance and moral engagement through peer modeling. *Cultur. Divers. Ethnic Minor. Psychol.* 64:363–73

McCauley C, Wright M, Harris M. 2000. Diversity workshops on campus: a survey of current practice at U.S. colleges and universities. *Coll. Student J.* 34:100–14

Mendelberg T. 2001. *The Race Card.* Princeton, NJ: Princeton Univ. Press

Miller N, Brewer MB. 1986. Categorization effects on ingroup and outgroup perception. In *Prejudice Discrimination and Racism*, ed. JF Dovidio, SL Gaertner, pp. 209–230. Orlando, FL: Academic

Miller N, Harrington HJ. 1990. A model of social category salience for intergroup relations: empirical tests of relevant variables. In *European Perspectives in Psychology*, ed. R Takens, pp 205–20. New York: Wiley

Monteith MJ, Deneen NE, Tooman G. 1996. The effect of social norm activation on the expression on opinions concerning gay men and blacks. *Basic Appl. Soc. Psychol.* 18:267–88

Monteith MJ, Sherman J, Devine PG. 1998. Suppression as a stereotype control strategy. *Personal. Soc. Psychol. Rev.* 2:3–82

Monteith MJ, Zuwerink JR, Devine PG. 1994. Prejudice and prejudice reduction: classic challenges contemporary approaches. In *Social Cognition: Impact on Social Psychology*, ed. PG Devine, DL Hamilton, pp. 323–46. San Diego, CA: Academic

Morris L, Romero J, Tan DL. 1996. Changes in attitude after diversity training. *Training Dev.* 509:54–55

Mullen B, Migdal M, Hewstone M. 2001. Crossed categorization versus simple categorization and intergroup evaluations: a meta-analysis. *Eur. J. Soc. Psychol.* 31:721–36

Nagda B, Kim C, Truelove Y. 2004. Learning about difference: learning with others, learning to transgress. *J. Soc. Issues* 60:195–214

Nagda B, Zúñiga X. 2003. Fostering meaningful racial engagement through intergroup dialogues. *Group Process Intergr.* 6:111–28

Nier JA, Gaertner SL, Dovidio JF, Banker BS, Ward CM, Rust MC. 2001. Changing interracial evaluations and behavior: the effects of a common group identity. *Group Process Interg.* 44:299–316

Olson MA, Fazio RH. 2008. Reducing automatically activated racial prejudice through implicit evaluative conditioning. *Personal. Soc. Psychol. Bull.* 32:421–33

Oskamp S. 2000. *Reducing Prejudice and Discrimination*. Mahwah, NJ: Erlbaum. 370 pp.

Pagtolun-An IM, Clair JM. 1986. An experimental study of attitudes toward homosexuality. *Dev. Behav.* 7:121–35

Paluck EL. 2006a. Diversity training and intergroup contact: a call to action research. *J. Soc. Issues* 623:439–51

Paluck EL. 2006b. *Peer pressure against prejudice: a field experimental test of a national high school prejudice reduction program*. Work. Pap., Harvard Univ., Cambridge, MA

Paluck EL. 2008. Reducing intergroup prejudice and conflict using the media: a field experiment in Rwanda. *J. Personal. Soc. Psychol.* In press

Paluck EL, Green DP. 2008. *Deference dissent and dispute resolution: a field experiment on a mass media intervention in Rwanda*. Work. Pap., Harvard Univ., Cambridge, MA

Pedersen A, Walker I, Wise M. 2005. "Talk does not cook rice": beyond antiracism rhetoric to strategies for social action. *Aust. Psychol.* 401:20–30

Pettigrew TF, Tropp LR. 2006. A meta-analytic test of intergroup contact theory. *J. Personal. Soc. Psychol.* 90:751–83

Powers DA, Ellison CG. 1995. Interracial contact and black racial attitudes: the contact hypothesis and selectivity bias. *Soc. Forces* 74:205–26

Price EG, Beach MC, Gary TL, Robinson KA, Gozu A, Palacio A. 2005. A systematic review of the methodological rigor of studies evaluating cultural competence training of health professionals. *Acad. Med.* 806:579–86

Puma MJ, Jones CC, Rock D, Fernandez R. 1993. Prospects: The congressionally mandated study of educational growth and opportunity. *Interim rep.*, Bethesda, MD: Abt Assoc.

Rich Y, Kedem P, Shlesinger A. 1995. Enhancing intergroup relations among children: a field test of the Miller-Brewer model. *Int. J. Intercult. Relat.* 194:539–53

Roberts K. 2000. *Toward Competent Communities: Best Practices for Producing Community-Wide Study Circles*. Lexington, KY: Topsfield Found.

Rokeach M. 1971. Long-range experimental modification of values attitudes and behavior. *Am. Psychol.* 26:453–59

Rokeach M. 1973. *The Nature of Human Values*. New York: Free Press

Roseth C, Johnson D, Johnson R. 2008. Promoting early adolescents' achievement and peer relationships: the effects of cooperative competitive and individualistic goal structures. *Psychol. Bull.* 1342:223–46

Rothbart M, John OP. 1985. Social categorization and behavioral episodes: a cognitive analysis of the effects of intergroup contact. *J. Soc. Issues* 413:81–104

Rudman LA, Ashmore RD, Gary ML. 2001. "Unlearning" automatic biases: the malleability of implicit prejudice and stereotypes. *J. Personal. Soc. Psychol.* 815:856–68

Ruiz-Belda MA, Fernandez-Dols JM, Carrera P, Barchard K. 2003. Spontaneous facial expressions of happy bowlers and soccer fans. *Cogn. Emot.* 17:315–26

Schaller M, Asp CH, Rosell MC, Heim SJ. 1996. Training in statistical reasoning inhibits the formation of erroneous group stereotypes. *Personal. Soc. Psychol. Bull.* 22:829–44

Sears DO. 1986. College sophomores in the laboratory: influences of a narrow data-base on social psychology's view of human nature. *J. Personal. Soc. Psychol.* 51:515–30

Sears DO. 1988. Symbolic racism. In *Handbook of Social Psychology*, ed. G. Lindzey, E Aronson, 5:315–458. Reading, MA: Addison-Wesley. Rev. ed.

Selltiz C, Cook S. 1948. Can research in social science be both socially meaningful and scientifically useful? *Am. Soc. Rev.* 13:454–59

Shadish WR, Cook TD, Campbell DT. 2002. *Experimental and Quasi-Experimental Designs for Generalized Causal Inference*. Boston: Houghton-Mifflin. 623 pp.

Sherif M, Harvey OJ, White BJ, Hood WR, Sherif CW. 1961. *Intergroup Conflict and Cooperation: The Robbers Cave Experiment*. Norman: Univ. Oklahoma Book Exchange. 263 pp.

Sidanius J, Pratto F. 1999. *Social Dominance: An Intergroup Theory of Social Hierarchy and Oppression*. New York: Cambridge Univ. Press. 416 pp.

Sinclair L, Kunda Z. 1999. Reactions to a Black professional: motivated inhibition and activation of conflicting stereotypes. *J. Personal. Soc. Psychol.* 77:885–904

Slavin RE, Leavey MB, Madden NA. 1984. Combining cooperative learning and individualized instruction: effects on student mathematics achievement, attitudes, and behaviors. *Element. Sch. J.* 84:409–22

Slone M, Tarrasch R, Hallis D. 2000. Ethnic stereotypic attitudes among Israeli children: two intervention programs. *Merrill-Palmer Q.* 46:370–89

Smith E. 1993. Social identity and social emotions: towards new conceptualizations of prejudice. In *Affect, Cognition, and Stereotyping*, ed. D Mackie, D Hamilton, pp. 297–315. New York: Academic

Sniderman PM, Piazza T. 1993. *The Scar of Race*. Cambridge, MA: Harvard Univ. Press

Son Hing LS, Li W, Zanna MP. 2002. Inducing hypocrisy to reduce prejudicial responses among aversive racists. *J. Exp. Soc. Psychol.* 381:71–78

Stangor C, Sechrist GB, Jost JT. 2001. Changing racial beliefs by providing consensus information. *Personal. Soc. Psychol. Bull.* 27:484–94

Steele CM. 1998. The psychology of self-affirmation: sustaining the integrity of the self. In *Advances in Experimental Social Psychology, Vol. 21: Social Psychological Studies of the Self: Perspectives and Programs*, ed L Berkowitz, pp. 261–302. San Diego, CA: Academic

Stephan WG. 1999. *Reducing Prejudice and Stereotyping in Schools*. New York: Teachers Coll. Press. 142 pp.

Stephan WG, Finlay K. 1999. The role of empathy in improving intergroup relations. *J. Soc. Issues* 554:729–44

Stephan WG, Stephan CW. 1984. The role of ignorance in intergroup relations. In *Groups in Contact: The Psychology of Desegregation*, ed. N Miller, MB Brewer, pp. 229–57. Orlando, FL: Academic

Stephan WG, Stephan CW. 2001. *Improving Intergroup Relations*. Thousand Oaks, CA: Sage. 360 pp.

Sternberg RJ. 2003. A duplex theory of hate: development and application to terrorism massacres and genocide. *Rev. Gen. Psychol.* 73:299–328

Stevenson MR. 1988. Promoting tolerance for homosexuality: an evaluation of intervention strategies. *J. Sex Res.* 254:500–11

Stewart TL, LaDuke JR, Bracht C, Sweet BAM, Gamarel KE. 2003. Do the "eyes" have it? A program evaluation of Jane Elliot's "Blue Eyes/Brown Eyes" diversity training exercise. *J. Appl. Soc. Psychol.* 339:1898–921

Strange JL. 2002. How fictional tales wag real-world beliefs. In *Narrative Impact: Social and Cognitive Foundations*, ed. MC Green, J Strange, T Brock, pp. 263–86. Mahwah, NJ: Erlbaum

Tajfel H. 1970. Experiments in intergroup discrimination. *Sci. Am.* 223:96–102

Towles-Schwen T, Fazio RH. 2006. Automatically activated racial attitudes as predictors of the success of interracial roommate relationships. *J. Exp. Soc. Psychol.* 42:698–705

van Wieringen JCM, Schulpen TWJ, Kuyvenhoven MM. 2001. Intercultural training of medical students. *Med. Teach.* 23:80–82

Vescio TK, Judd CM, Kwan VSY. 2004. Categorization and intergroup bias in crossed contexts: evidence of reductions in the strength of categorization but not intergroup bias. *J. Exp. Soc. Psychol.* 40:478–96

Vescio TK, Sechrist GB, Paolucci MP. 2003. Perspective taking and prejudice reduction: the mediational role of empathy arousal and situational attributions European. *J. Soc. Psychol.* 33 455–72

Warring DW, Johnson D, Maruyama G, Johnson R. 1985. Impact of different types of cooperative learning on cross-ethnic and cross-sex relationships. *J. Educ. Psychol.* 77:53–59

Wham MA, Barnhart J, Cook G. 1996. Enhancing multicultural awareness through the storybook reading experience. *J. Res. Dev. Educ.* 301:1–9

Wikfors EL. 1998. Effects of a disabilities awareness workshop: employees' knowledge attitude and interaction. PhD dissert., Univ. Florida. *Dissert. Abstracts Int.* 58:2495

Wilder DA. 1986. Social categorization: implications for creation and reduction of intergroup bias. In *Advances in Experimental Social Psychology, Vol. 19*, ed. L Berkowitz, pp. 239–355. New York: Academic

Wittenbrink B, Judd CM, Park B. 2001. Spontaneous prejudice in context: variability in automatically activated attitudes. *J. Personal. Soc. Psychol.* 81:815–27

Wright SC, Aron A, McLaughlin-Volpe T, Ropp SA. 1997. The extended contact effect: knowledge of cross-group friendships and prejudice. *J. Personal. Soc. Psychol.* 73:73–90

Yawkey TD. 1973. Attitudes toward Black Americans held by rural and urban white early childhood subjects based upon multi-ethnic social studies materials. *J. Negro Educ.* 42:164–69

Zillmann D. 1991. Empathy: affect from bearing witness to the emotions of others. In *Responding to the Screen: Reception and Reaction Processes*, ed. J Bryant, D Zillmann, pp. 335–67. Hillsdale, NJ: Erlbaum

RELATED RESOURCE

Readers can find the database of studies included in this review (full citation, abstract, and methodological categorization) posted at **www.betsylevypaluck.com.** On the same Web site, we have posted an alternative version of this review that includes more historical references and study details.

Personality: The Universal and the Culturally Specific

Steven J. Heine and Emma E. Buchtel

Department of Psychology, University of British Columbia, Vancouver, British Columbia, V6T 1Z4 Canada; email: heine@psych.ubc.ca, ebuchtel@interchange.ubc.ca

Annu. Rev. Psychol. 2009. 60:369–94

The *Annual Review of Psychology* is online at psych.annualreviews.org

This article's doi: 10.1146/annurev.psych.60.110707.163655

Key Words

self-enhancement, cultural equilibria, Big 5, personality utility

Abstract

There appears to be a universal desire to understand individual differences. This common desire exhibits both universal and culturally specific features. Motivations to view oneself positively differ substantially across cultural contexts, as do a number of other variables that covary with this motivation (i.e., approach-avoidance motivations, internal-external frames of reference, independent-interdependent views of self, incremental-entity theories of abilities, dialectical self-views, and relational mobility). The structure of personality traits, particularly the five-factor model of personality, emerges quite consistently across cultures, with some key variations noted when the structure is drawn from indigenous traits in other languages. The extent to which each of the Big 5 traits is endorsed in each culture varies considerably, although we note some methodological challenges with comparing personality traits across cultures. Finally, although people everywhere can conceive of each other in terms of personality traits, people in collectivistic cultures appear to rely on traits to a lesser degree when understanding themselves and others, compared with those from individualistic cultures.

Contents

INTRODUCTION

In previous decades, the study of culture was largely limited to the work of anthropologists, who mainly sought evidence for culture in people's social environments. More recently, the study of culture has also been taken up by psychologists, who primarily look for evidence of culture in the person. These two complementary efforts to understand the nature of cultural beings have been fused in the field of cultural psychology, which hinges on the assumption that personality and culture are mutually constituted (see Heine 2008, Shweder 1990). That is, one cannot fully understand the nature of people without considering the cultural context within which they exist; nor can one fully understand a cultural context without considering the values and beliefs of the people who inhabit it. Cultural psychologists seek to understand people as they are embedded within their cultures.

Over the past two decades, much cultural psychological research has revealed pronounced cultural variation in many psychological processes that were hitherto assumed to be universal, such as the fundamental attribution error (Choi et al. 1999) and preferences for choice (Iyengar & Lepper 1999). This cultural variation has important implications for studying psychology across cultures. The study of psychology in general and of personality in particular has largely been guided by Western research. For example, 92% of publications in the *Journal of Personality and Social Psychology* are from authors at North American institutions, and 99% are from authors at Western schools (Quinones-Vidal et al. 2004). The narrowness of the sample upon which most personality research has been conducted raises important questions about the generalizability of this research (see Arnett 2008, Henrich et al. 2008). Much cross-cultural personality research has been conducted to address these questions (for recent reviews, see Benet-Martinez 2007, Diener et al. 2003, Triandis & Suh 2002).

Personality psychology has been conceptualized by some as the study of human nature (e.g., Buss 1984). In this respect there is no better topic in psychology in which to investigate the role of culture, as the nature of humans is very much that of a cultural species (Heine & Norenzayan 2006, Tomasello 1999). A key question to consider is how cultural learning comes to shape the ways that people understand themselves and others. In this article, we explore the relation between culture and personality by reviewing cross-cultural research in (*a*) how people evaluate themselves, (*b*) the structure and content of personality across cultures, and (*c*) the utility of personality information across cultures. There appears to be a universal desire to understand individual differences—that is, personality (Funder 2007). But culture has a large role to play in how we use and understand information about individual differences. In this review, we pay particular attention to evidence suggesting universality or cultural variability of these different aspects of personality and to describing how culture influences individual differences.

THE EVALUATION OF THE SELF ACROSS CULTURES

The mutual constitution of person and culture becomes especially evident in the exploration of how people evaluate themselves across cultures, such as by considering trait-level self-esteem. That people are motivated to view themselves positively is one of the most deeply held assumptions about the self (Maslow 1943, Tesser 1988). However, much research reveals strong variation in the strength of this motivation across cultures. For example, studies of Mexican-Americans (Tropp & Wright 2003), Native Americans (Fryberg & Markus 2003), and Bangladeshis (Schmitt & Allik 2005) reveal significantly less positive self-views than those found in studies conducted with Westerners.

In particular, cross-cultural research finds that East Asians evince far less motivation for self-enhancement than do Westerners. In a recently published meta-analysis, across 91 cross-cultural comparisons using 30 different methods, the Western samples self-enhanced more than the East Asian samples by an average effect size of $d = 0.84$ (Heine & Hamamura 2007). Analyses within cultures of self-enhancement biases (another indicator of motivation for self-esteem) also reveal striking differences. Among Western samples, the average effect size of self-enhancing biases was $d = 0.87$, a strong effect that was evident in all 14 of the methods that were used; in contrast, for East Asians, the average effect was $d = -0.01$ (Heine & Hamamura 2007). Moreover, the methods that did yield a positive self-enhancing effect for East Asians (i.e., those where people compare themselves to the average other) appear to have been largely driven by a methodological artifact: the "everyone is better than their group's average effect" (Klar & Giladi 1997; see Hamamura et al. 2007). Cultural differences in self-enhancement between East Asians and

Westerners are thus large and consistently found across diverse methods.

These cultural differences in motivations for self-enhancement are not easily accounted for by alternative explanations such as (*a*) East Asians being motivated to esteem their groups rather than their individual selves (much research finds that Westerners also evaluate their groups more positively than do East Asians; Crocker et al. 1994, Heine & Lehman 1997, Snibbe et al. 2003); (*b*) East Asians enhance themselves in domains that are of most importance to them [the most extensive meta-analysis on this topic finds no correlation between self-enhancement and importance for East Asians, $r = -0.01$, in contrast to a positive correlation for Westerners, $r = 0.18$ (Heine et al. 2007a), but see discussion regarding whether studies should be excluded from this meta-analysis (Heine et al. 2007b; Sedikides et al. 2007a,b)]; and (*c*) East Asians are presenting themselves self-critically, but are privately evaluating themselves in a self-enhancing manner [the cultural differences are similarly pronounced with studies using hidden behavioral measures (Heine et al. 2000, 2001), although the cultural differences are largely absent for measures of implicit self-esteem (Kitayama & Uchida 2003, Kobayashi & Greenwald 2003)]. These findings have led some to conclude that motivations for high self-esteem are far weaker, if not largely absent, among East Asians than among Westerners (e.g., Heine et al. 1999).

In support of this conclusion, some research finds that positive assessments of one's self appear to be of less utility for East Asians than for Westerners. A number of studies find that positive self-views are less correlated with subjective well-being (Diener & Diener 1995, Kwan et al. 1997), self-concept clarity (Campbell et al. 1996), and depression (Heine & Lehman 1999) in East Asia than they are in North America. Moreover, whereas experimentally manipulated positive self-views lead to enhanced persistence among North Americans, such manipulations lead to less persistence among East Asians (Heine et al. 2001). In summary, positive self-views appear to be associated

Self-enhancement biases: the tendency to evaluate the self more positively than others

with fewer positive consequences among East Asians than among Westerners.

What Processes Are Implicated in Cultural Variation in Self-Enhancement Motivations?

Why are self-enhancement motivations such a salient and important feature of Western personalities, but not of East Asians? That pronounced cultural differences between Westerners and East Asians in self-enhancing motivations emerge so consistently across diverse methods raises the question of why these cultural differences exist. One way to assess this kind of question is to consider the psychological processes that relate to the cultural differences. Thus far, in an effort to make sense of the observed cultural variation in self-enhancing motivations, several different processes have been explored and assessed.

Approach-avoidance motivation. One relevant process contributing to the cultural differences in self-enhancing motivations is approach-avoidance motivation. Approach motivation focuses on advancement, accomplishments, and aspirations; it involves a concern with the presence or absence of positive outcomes. In contrast, avoidance motivation focuses on safety, responsibilities, and obligations; it is concerned with the presence or absence of negative outcomes (Higgins 1996).

There is much evidence that East Asians differ from Westerners in the extent to which they show approach and avoidance motivations. In general, various studies find that in comparison with Westerners, East Asians show relatively more evidence for avoidance motivation and relatively less evidence for approach motivation. For example, in comparison with North Americans, East Asians embrace more personal avoidance goals (Elliot et al. 2001), rate opportunities to lose as more important than opportunities to win (Lee et al. 2000), persist more on a task after failure and less after success (Heine et al. 2001), and are motivated more by negative role models—someone that people want to

ensure they do not become like (Lockwood et al. 2005). Furthermore, this cultural difference is evident in the ways that people process information: East Asians have been shown to have better memory for details regarding opportunities for losses than for opportunities for gains (Aaker & Lee 2001), they recall events better if they contain prevention information, and they view book reviews to be more helpful if those reviews contain prevention information (Hamamura et al. 2008b). These reliably observed cultural differences in approach-avoidance motivation have been proposed to be the result of the different kinds of positive self-views (i.e., self-esteem and face) that are prioritized by Westerners and East Asians, respectively (see Hamamura & Heine 2008, Heine 2005).

Internal versus external frame of reference. Another mechanism that is implicated in cultural variation in self-enhancing motivations is the perspective of the evaluator. In evaluating themselves, people can attend to whether they are meeting their own internal standards of competence (i.e., I think I'm doing well), or they can attend to whether they are meeting other people's standards of competence (i.e., others think I'm doing well). Although these two orientations are not independent, as people's evaluations of themselves are influenced by their assessments of how they are meeting others' standards (Leary & Baumeister 2000), people can vary in the extent to which they more closely attend to their own or to others' standards. Elsewhere, we propose that a concern with maintaining "face" leads East Asians to attend more to the standards of others when evaluating themselves, whereas a concern with enhancing self-esteem leads Westerners to attend more to their own internal standards (see Heine 2005, Heine et al. 2008b). This reasoning suggests that East Asians should pay closer attention to the perspective of others than do Westerners.

There is much recent evidence for this cultural difference in perspective taking (for a review, see Cohen et al. 2007). For example,

Cohen & Gunz (2002) demonstrated that in comparison with Westerners, East Asians are more likely to recall memories of themselves when they were at the center of attention from a third-person perspective. Apparently, East Asians' attention to an audience leaked into and distorted their memories of themselves. Similarly, East Asians outperformed Westerners on a visual perspective-taking task, making fewer visual fixations on objects that were not visible to a person who was giving instructions to them (Wu & Keysar 2007).

Cross-cultural research on self-awareness also identifies cultural divergences in frames of reference. When individuals are aware of how they appear to others, they are said to be in the state of objective self-awareness (Duval & Wicklund 1972), and this leads to a number of predictable responses (e.g., people become more self-critical and are less likely to engage in counter-normative behaviors; Diener & Wallbom 1976, Fejfar & Hoyle 2000). In a state of objective self-awareness, people are aware of how they appear as an object (a "me") in contrast to the experience of being a subject (an "I"). To the extent that East Asians are aware of an audience and adjust their behaviors to that audience, they would more likely be in a habitual state of objective self-awareness than would North Americans. If this is the case, then stimuli that enhance objective self-awareness (for example, seeing oneself in front of a mirror) should have little effect on East Asians. Even without a mirror present, East Asians should be considering themselves in terms of how they appear to others. Some recent cross-cultural research corroborates this hypothesis: whereas North Americans were more self-critical and were less likely to cheat on a test when a mirror was present compared to when it was absent, the presence of a mirror had no effect on Japanese for either dependent variable (Heine et al. 2008b). Moreover, although North American self-evaluations were much more positive than Japanese when the mirror was not present, they were at relatively similar levels to Japanese when they were in front of the mirror. One reason that self-evaluations tend to be so much more positive for North Americans than for Japanese may be that North Americans are less likely to consider how they appear to others. Objectivity constrains the ability to maintain a positive self-view.

Independent versus interdependent views of self. Cultural variation in self-enhancement can also be better understood when considering the kinds of self-concepts that are most common in various cultures. One way of considering the self is to see it as a relatively autonomous, self-sustaining collection of attributes that is largely independent from others. This independent view of self is more common in Western cultures and has been the working model for many of the theories of self that have been developed by a Western-dominated social psychology. In contrast, a second way of construing selves is to see them as being fundamentally interconnected, situationally variable, and grounded in roles and relationships with significant ingroup others. This interdependent view of self is more common in non-Western cultures and has been linked to a wide array of distinct phenomena (for reviews, see Heine 2001, Markus & Kitayama 1991, Triandis 1989).

Measures of self-esteem and self-enhancing biases tend to be positively associated with independence and negatively associated with interdependence (although these latter correlations tend to be weaker), regardless of the culture that has been investigated (Heine et al. 1999, Heine & Renshaw 2002, Oyserman et al. 2002). One way to account for these correlations is to consider the consequences of elaborating a positive self-view. Self-enhancement is associated with both costs and benefits to the individual. Paulhus (1998) makes the case that these benefits and costs are realized in two different domains. First, benefits of self-enhancement tend to be intrapsychic in nature. That is, focusing on what is good about the self tends to be associated with subjective well-being and self-efficacy and is negatively associated with dysphoria and depression (Taylor & Armor 1996, Taylor & Brown 1988). One clear benefit of self-enhancing, then, is that it feels good.

However, the intrapsychic benefits that derive from self-enhancement come at the expense of one's relationships. A number of researchers have highlighted how self-enhancers risk attracting the scorn of those around them (Colvin et al. 1995, Paulhus 1998, Vohs & Heatherton 2001; for a contrary view, see Taylor et al. 2003). To put it simply, most people do not particularly like self-enhancers. These interpersonal costs are especially evident in long-term relationships (Robins & Beer 2001), the kinds of relationships that are particularly implicated in interdependent selves (Adams 2005).

The costs and benefits of self-enhancement in these two domains suggest that to the extent an individual's culture prioritizes intrapsychic over interpersonal concerns, self-enhancement would be a beneficial strategy. The positive feelings that arise from self-enhancement will be seen as worth the price of the alienation of those around one. In contrast, to the extent that an individual's culture emphasizes interpersonal relationships over intrapsychic rewards, self-improvement and face maintenance should be a more beneficial strategy. The benefits of deepening relations with others outweigh the costs of the negative feelings associated with self-improvement. There is much evidence that people in Western cultures are more concerned with positive feelings than are people in East Asian cultures (Diener et al. 1995, Kitayama et al. 2000, Mesquita & Karasawa 2002), and that people in East Asian cultures are more concerned with maintaining interpersonal harmony than are people in Western cultures (Morling et al. 2002, Suh et al. 1998). This evidence suggests that the cost-benefit ratio of self-enhancing is not as favorable for East Asians as it is for North Americans.

Incremental versus entity theories of abilities. The value of self-enhancement also depends on the lay theories that people hold about the nature of abilities. One way to conceive of abilities is to view them as arising from a set of relatively fixed and innate attributes. This kind of "entity theory" (Dweck & Leggett 1988) of abilities reflects beliefs in an underlying essence

that is tied to abilities. Within such a worldview, an individual's successes and failures directly reflect upon his or her perceived capabilities and self-worth. To the extent that abilities are perceived to be largely immutable and reflecting essential aspects of the individual, having a positive assessment of one's abilities would be accompanied by subjective well-being and would provide the individual with the requisite confidence to perform at his or her best on a task. Viewing one's abilities negatively, on the other hand, would seem to be tied closely to depression and would decrease any motivation to improve. There would be little reason to try harder if one's failures were perceived to be immutable (Dweck 1999).

A second way of conceiving of abilities is to view them as being malleable and ultimately improvable. This kind of incremental theory of abilities reflects a belief in the key role of effort in abilities. Within this worldview, rather than successes and failures being diagnostic of one's capabilities and self-worth, they are instead perceived as revealing the extent of one's efforts. Doing poorly on a task does not indicate that one is lacking the potential, but rather that one needs to direct additional effort to improvement. This suggests that those with incremental views of abilities should not find failures as painful, or successes as pleasant, as those with entity theories, and hence performance on tasks should be less tied to their self-esteem.

Cultural differences in entity and incremental theories of abilities parallel those of self-enhancement motivations. For example, a number of studies have identified greater tendencies for East Asians compared with North Americans to attribute school achievement to effort and not to abilities (e.g., Holloway 1988, Stevenson & Stigler 1992; but see mixed evidence on cultural comparisons of Likert scale measures of malleability, e.g., Heine et al. 2001, Hong et al. 1999, Norenzayan et al. 2002). Likewise, experimental manipulations of incremental theories of abilities corroborate the cultural differences. Japanese come to respond to failure in a way similar to Americans when entity-theories are primed, whereas

Americans come to respond to failure in the ways Japanese do when incremental theories are primed (Heine et al. 2001). It appears that another reason cultures differ in the positivity of their self-views is the cultural variation in lay theories of abilities.

Dialectical reasoning about the self. Cultural variation in self-enhancing motivations can be understood in yet another way: East Asian and Western cultures differ in their tolerance for contradiction (Peng & Nisbett 1999). That is, whereas Westerners typically respond to contradictory statements by trying to dismiss or transcend the contradiction, East Asians are more content to accept the contradictions as they are. The tendency to perceive and tolerate psychological contradiction has been termed "naïve dialecticism" (Peng & Nisbett 1999). This cultural difference in attitudes toward contradiction is not limited to how people perceive contradictory logical arguments about the world; the difference also generalizes to how people view themselves. When describing themselves, East Asians maintain more contradictory self-views than do Westerners. For example, compared with Westerners, East Asians are more likely to endorse opposing statements about their personalities (e.g., they accept statements regarding being both introverted and extraverted; Choi & Choi 2002, Hamamura et al. 2008a), they acknowledge experiencing positive and negative affective states more simultaneously (Bagozzi et al. 1999), they view themselves as acting less consistently across different situations (Kanagawa et al. 2001, Suh 2002), they have more contradictory knowledge about themselves that is simultaneously accessible (Spencer-Rodgers et al. 2008), and they are more likely to endorse both positive and negative statements about their own self-esteem (Hamamura et al. 2008a, Spencer-Rodgers et al. 2004).

One reason, then, why East Asians might show self-views that are less self-positive than those of Westerners is that they hold dialectical views of themselves (e.g., I am a good person, but I am also a bad person). A dialectical view of the self would lead to moderately positive views of the self rather than overwhelmingly positive self-views, which is precisely the way that East Asian self-enhancement scores differ from those of North Americans (Heine et al. 1999). Importantly, Spencer-Rodgers et al. (2004) find that people's scores on a measure of dialecticism mediate the differences in self-esteem between East Asians and North Americans. Cultural differences in self-enhancement thus also stem from cultural differences in attitudes toward self-consistency.

Relational mobility. Another more recent effort to understand the mechanisms underlying cultural variation in self-enhancing motivations comes from the study of relational mobility (see Oishi et al. 2007, Yuki et al. 2007b; cf., Adams 2005). Relational mobility refers to the perceived amount of opportunity that an individual has for forming new relationships. In many individualistic contexts, such as those of American undergraduates, for example, individuals live in a high-relational-mobility context, in which they are frequently meeting new people and have the potential to forge new relationships on a day-to-day basis. In contrast, in many collectivistic contexts, for example, much of Japanese society, there is little relational mobility in that people tend to belong to nonoverlapping groups (such as a school club or an office) where there is little movement between social groups and the membership is largely stable (also see Adams 2005 for similar arguments in West African communities). Because self-esteem is influenced by the degree to which one feels socially accepted (Leary & Baumeister 2000), it has been proposed that people will rely on their self-esteem to predict when they will be accepted by others (Sato et al. 2007). In contexts where people have many opportunities for forming new relationships, then, having high self-esteem will serve to aid them in functioning well. Indeed, the perceived availability of opportunities for forming new relationships has been shown to significantly mediate East-West cultural differences in both self-esteem (Sato et al. 2007) and in the relation between self-esteem and well-being (Yuki et al. 2007a). Relational mobility thus is another compelling candidate for a mechanism that can explain cultural variation in self-enhancement motivations.

Summary of mechanisms related to self-enhancement. The above review reveals six different mechanisms that underlie the observed cultural difference in self-enhancement, and it is possible that additional mechanisms will prove to be relevant in the future. This hardly provides a parsimonious account for cultural variation in positive self-views—the tendency for North Americans to self-enhance more than East Asians thus appears to be overdetermined. Why might there be so many different mechanisms related to this cultural difference?

We suggest that the similar pattern across cultures for each of the six phenomena reviewed above indicates that it is not productive to think of these as independent mechanisms underlying self-enhancement. Rather, we propose that we can understand the cultural variation in each of these phenomena as indicating a stable equilibrium point in a dynamical system (Cohen 2001, Kitayama 2002). That is, the elements of a culture are not independent from each other. One feature of a culture (such as having a norm where extended families live in the same household) will influence another feature (such as the likelihood that other family members get involved in decisions regarding who one will marry; Lee & Stone 1980). This interdependence among different features of cultures reduces the variability of possible cultural arrangements. Each aspect of a culture is influenced by, and in turn influences, other aspects of the culture. This interdependence results in a relatively small number of stable equilibria within a system. If an individual deviates from an equilibrium point, the interrelations among the various parts of the system will constrain her options, and she will likely gravitate back toward the cultural norm (Boyd et al. 1997).

In present East Asian cultural contexts, a dynamical system exists such that people tend to view themselves as interdependent with significant others, have few opportunities to forge new relationships, tolerate contradictions, have more incremental theories of abilities, are especially attentive to others' perspectives, are vigilant of potential losses, and exhibit self-critical motivations. Each of these psychological variables is sustained by the other variables, and they represent a fairly stable system. It is unlikely, say, that just one of these variables could be changed without influencing the other variables as well. The mutual interdependence of these variables suggests that there are few opportunities for much change in any single variable because the presence of the other variables would act to constrain and stabilize the system (Boyd et al. 1997). We submit that cultural change in these variables is only likely to occur when the pressures for change are great enough that the system reaches a tipping point and then gravitates toward a new equilibrium (Cohen 2001). For example, another equilibrium point is found in present North American contexts, where people tend to view themselves as independent from others, have many opportunities to develop new relationships, eschew contradictions, have entity theories of abilities, primarily consider their own perspective, are attentive to opportunities for gain, and evince self-enhancing motivations. The dynamic systems of the cultures of East Asia and North America are not best described as different from each other on a single variable, such as their self-construals, but rather they represent different systems that gravitate toward divergent equilibria. Cultural change in these cultures is likely to be noticed across the entire system when a tipping point is reached, rather than being restricted to any transformation of a single variable. This systems view of culture calls into question the value of efforts to identify mediational variables that are theorized to underlie cultural differences (Heine & Norenzayan 2006).

In summary, a cluster of interrelated variables correlates with self-enhancement and distinguishes East Asians from Westerners. We submit that these variables mutually influence each other and manifest in at least two different stable equilibria within East Asian and Western cultural contexts. It is possible that other cultural contexts possess different equilibria points among these same variables.

STRUCTURE AND CONTENT OF PERSONALITY ACROSS CULTURES

In the above section, we outlined cultural differences in one aspect of individual difference, namely self-enhancement. The degree to which self-enhancement is a salient and important trait depends on an intertwined set of cultural variables. Self-enhancement, however, is only one type of individual difference. Are other individual differences in fact equally important in all societies?

People tend to be curious and reflective about the ways that individuals differ from each other. This curiosity may well be universal across cultures, at least to a certain degree. Various different personality typologies have been proposed over time and around the world that serve to classify people into different types. For example, Hippocrates proposed that there were four basic types of human temperaments, which depended upon the balance of the four fluids, or humors, that were present in the body: blood, yellow bile, phlegm, and black bile. Ayurvedic medicine from India proposes that there are three metabolic body-types (vata, pita, and kapha), thus maintaining that one's metabolism rate provides the foundation of individual temperaments. Popular Japanese folklore views the four blood types as underlying reliable differences in personality. In short, across cultures and history, people have come up with a remarkably diverse array of ways for carving up personalities.

Western psychologists have also made many targeted research efforts toward developing personality typologies to classify the variety of ways to be a person. Several different schemes have been proposed (e.g., Ashton et al. 2004, Cattell 1957, Eysenck 1975), each varying in the number of core traits and the content of

those traits. However, the typology that is by far the most widely accepted and researched is the Five-Factor Model (McCrae & Costa 1987; for criticisms of this model, see Block 1995, McAdams 1992). According to this model [first derived by Fiske (1949)], there are five core personality traits: openness to experience, conscientiousness, extraversion, agreeableness, and neuroticism. The "Big 5" are said to underlie the nearly 18,000 traits that exist in the English language (Allport & Odbert 1936). Several hundreds of studies have explored these traits and their relation to other constructs. This research raises some interesting and important questions regarding personality across cultures: Is the five-factor structure something basic about human nature that we should find in the personalities of people in all cultures that we look? Or, alternatively, does the five-factor model reflect ideas about personhood that are limited to the West, where the vast majority of this research has been conducted?

Apparent Near Universality of Personality Structure

A number of evolutionary psychological perspectives on personality maintain that the five-factor model reflects universal kinds of individual variation. Some have argued that the Big 5 are fundamental responses to core challenges faced by humans (e.g., Ellis et al. 2002, Goldberg 1981). For example, it would be adaptive for people to be able to identify who was likely to rise in the social hierarchy (extraversion), who could be reliable and dependable (conscientiousness), who would have difficulty coping with adversity (neuroticism), who could be a good friend (agreeableness), and whom one could turn to for wise advice (openness; Buss 1991)—that is, the accurate perception of the Big 5 in others could enhance one's fitness. However, arguments for why it is adaptive for individuals themselves to vary in the Big 5 are currently incomplete, as the heritability of personality traits (typically around 0.40; Plomin et al. 2001) makes it appear that between-individual variability should be drastically reduced, as long as personality traits uniformly afforded fitness across all environments. Compelling evolutionary accounts for why individuals differ in the degree to which they possess adaptive personality traits may be developed if we consider individuals' responses to their different environmental niches (Penke et al. 2007). Regardless of the particular evolutionary theory that is applied, to the extent that the Big 5 evolved in response to core challenges from the ancestral environment, it follows that the model should be cross-culturally universal in its application.

Some evidence supporting the biological universality of the Five-Factor model can be found in comparative research, which has identified markers of the Big 5 traits in a number of animal species (Gosling & John 1999). For example, behavioral patterns consistent with each of the Big 5 traits have been identified in chimpanzees (King & Figueredo 1997), and some traits, for example neuroticism, have been identified in species as diverse as hyenas (Gosling 1998), guppies (Budaev 1997), and octopuses (Mather & Anderson 1993). It is possible that the Big 5 (or at least some of the dimensions) represent fundamental responses to biological challenges encountered by many, if not most, species. However, the vast majority of animal studies have been conducted by Western researchers, and the similarity of the traits that are observed between animals and humans might be due to people interpreting animal behavior through the lens of their most familiar ways of categorizing people—an account that is addressed to a degree by noting that evidence for traits in animals is clearer for some traits and in some species than in others (Gosling 2001). Nonetheless, the best evidence for the universality of a psychological construct requires the consideration of data from multiple cultures (Norenzayan & Heine 2005). The study of the cross-cultural generalizability of the Big 5 is one of the most ambitiously researched attempts to address the question of universality for any psychological phenomenon, and several large-scale multicultural studies have been conducted.

Various measures of the Big 5 [e.g., Neuroticism-Extroversion-Openness Personality Inventory-Revised (NEO-PI-R); Costa & McCrae 1992] have been translated into a number of languages and have been distributed to thousands of people in dozens of cultures around the world. Early cross-cultural comparisons of the factor structure of the Big 5 were promising: Four out of five factors (all except Openness) emerged in Hong Kong (Bond 1979), Japan (Bond et al. 1975), and the Philippines (Guthrie & Bennett 1971), revealing considerable similarity in the structure of personality across these diverse cultures. More recent studies with some other cultures have fared even better—all five factors emerged in cultures from countries as diverse as Israel (Montag & Levin 1994), Korea (Piedmont & Chae 1997), and Turkey (Somer & Goldberg 1999). One large-scale study investigated people from 50 different cultures from all continents except Antarctica and had participants evaluate someone they knew well on trait adjectives that assessed the Big 5 (McCrae et al. 2005). In most of the 50 cultures, the factor structure of the Big 5 was replicated. In a number of developing cultures (in countries including Botswana, Ethiopia, Lebanon, Malaysia, Puerto Rico, and Uganda), the factor structure was not so evident. However, in these latter cultures, the quality of data was rather poor, which suggests that people may not have fully understood the questions or were unfamiliar with answering questions in that format (McCrae et al. 2005). If unfamiliarity with Western measures can account for the poor data fit found in some cultures, then there is good evidence that the Big 5 reflect the universal structure of personality (also see Allik & McCrae 2004, Yik et al. 2002). Still, support for universality would be stronger if convergent evidence emerged from studies of developing and small-scale societies (cf., Henrich et al. 2005).

It is important to note that the measures of the Big 5 (such as the NEO-PI-R) were initially developed through the exploration of English personality terms, and largely with Americans. The challenge with factor analyses is that they only speak to the structure that emerges from the universe of items that were considered. It is possible that a different set of items, particularly those that were more meaningful in other cultural contexts, might reveal a different underlying personality structure. An important question to consider, then, is whether the Big 5 personality dimensions emerge regardless of what traits one considers, or whether they reflect the underlying structure of the kinds of personality traits that are discussed in English.

A number of investigations have explored this question. For example, Cheung et al. (1996) sought to identify what kinds of personality dimensions would emerge if they factor-analyzed indigenous Chinese personality traits rather than relied on translations of English traits. The researchers first explored the kinds of personality traits that were common in Chinese by examining Chinese novels, Chinese proverbs, people's personality descriptions, and the Chinese psychology literature. These efforts revealed 26 unique personality constructs (as well as another 12 clinical constructs). The constructs were then put into a personality questionnaire (the Chinese Personality Assessment Inventory), which was completed by Chinese participants. The resultant factor structure was not the same as the Big 5; rather, four factors emerged that were captured by the following labels: dependability (reflecting responsibility, optimism, and trustworthiness), interpersonal relatedness (reflecting harmony, thrift, relational orientation, and tradition), social potency (reflecting leadership, adventurousness, and extraversion), and individualism (reflecting logical orientation, defensiveness, and self-orientation). Further analyses included the Chinese Personality Assessment Inventory together with a measure of the Big 5 (Cheung et al. 2003). That analysis revealed that there was substantial overlap between three of the factors; namely, neuroticism correlated with dependability, extraversion correlated with social potency, and individualism correlated with agreeableness. Openness to experience did not correlate with any of the Chinese factors, and

interpersonal relatedness was not correlated with any of the Big 5 factors. Perhaps, then, interpersonal relatedness may be a sixth personality factor that is especially salient in Chinese culture. Whether interpersonal relatedness is a reliable sixth factor in Western samples has yet to be demonstrated.

Similar approaches have been taken with other cultures. For example, Church et al. (1997; also see Church et al. 1998) developed an indigenous list of Filipino personality traits and explored their underlying factors through factor analysis. This analysis revealed five traits that were highly similar to the Big 5; however, they also revealed two additional factors: temperamentalness and a negative valence dimension, which did not correlate strongly with any of the Big 5. Likewise, Benet-Martinez & Waller (1995, 1997) found that an investigation of Spanish personality constructs revealed seven underlying personality factors, although these did not map on so well to the Big 5. Similarly, Saucier et al. (2005) found that a six-factor solution emerged from indigenous Greek terms and was somewhat at odds with the Big 5. In general, investigations with indigenous traits reveal that although the Big 5 personality traits appear to be cross-culturally robust, they may not be an exhaustive list of the ways that personality can emerge in other cultures. Some alternative dimensions have emerged from explorations of personality structures using indigenous personality terms, and future research is necessary to determine the robustness and universality of these other factors.

Cross-Cultural Variability in Levels of Personality Traits

Given the evidence that the Five-Factor model of personality appears to adequately capture the structure of personality traits in many cultures, researchers have recently begun to compare mean levels of personality traits across large samples of cultures (e.g., McCrae 2002, McCrae et al. 2005, Schmitt et al. 2007). This burgeoning research program has resulted in debate about the meaning and validity of such cross-cultural comparisons. Below, we outline some of the findings of these large cross-cultural comparisons and discuss the debate about their validity.

Some of the most thorough multinational comparisons that have been conducted in psychology have compared Big 5 traits across cultures. As of this writing, aggregate personality means from the NEO-PI-R (Costa & McCrae 1992) have been reported for self-ratings from 36 cultures (McCrae 2002) and for peer-ratings from 51 cultures (McCrae et al. 2005), and a modified Big 5 measure was used to collect people's perceptions of their compatriots in 49 cultures (Terracciano et al. 2005). Another popular measure, the Big Five Inventory (BFI; Benet-Martínez & John 1998), has been used to collect self-ratings in 56 nations (Schmitt et al. 2007). This hard-won wealth of data has attracted much interest and sparked further research (e.g., McCrae & Allik 2002). It has shown, for example, that according to the self-report means, the most neurotic people on the planet are Spaniards, the most extraverted are Norwegians, the least conscientious are Japanese, the most open to new experiences are Austrian, and the most agreeable are Malaysian (McCrae 2002).

Part of the promise of these kinds of multinational comparisons of mean levels of personality traits is that they stand to map out the "personality profiles" of cultures across the globe. The value of this research enterprise would be especially noteworthy to the extent that it offered cultural profiles that were of greater validity than those profiles formed on the basis of inferior or biased methods, such as those formed on the basis of people's stereotypes. To demonstrate this point, Terracciano, McCrae, and colleagues investigated how well people's perceptions of the national character of their country correlated with the means from self-reports and peer reports on the NEO-PI-R discussed above (McCrae & Terracciano 2006, Terracciano et al. 2005). The results indicated that there were essentially no correlations between the national character profiles—what people believe their average compatriot is like—and the actual na-

tional average self-ratings or peer ratings on the NEO-PI-R. The investigators argued that the findings provided strong evidence that common perceptions of national character in fact have little to no connection with reality; people's views of their compatriots do not appear to contain "even a kernel of truth" (McCrae & Terracciano 2006, p. 160).

The assertion that aggregate self-reports or peer reports are appropriate validity criteria in themselves, and that perceptions of national character are therefore illusory, has been met with some resistance (Ashton 2007, Heine et al. 2008a, McGrath & Goldberg 2006, Perugini & Richetin 2007). Indeed, the literature on cross-cultural methodology raises a number of caveats that should make one cautious in drawing conclusions from direct comparisons of mean levels of personality traits across cultures. For example, there are questions of whether items are interpreted in the same way by people from all cultures (e.g., Church & Katigbak 2002, Grimm & Church 1999, Poortinga et al. 2002), whether people respond to items in the same way (Chen et al. 1995, Greenfield 1997, Hamamura et al. 2008a, Poortinga et al. 2002), and whether individuals in different cultures compare themselves to different standards when making ratings (e.g., Heine et al. 2002, 2008a; Peng et al. 1997). Nevertheless, some personality researchers have optimistically maintained that most of these potential biases can be controlled for (e.g., the acquiescence bias; McCrae 2001, McCrae et al. 2005) or that these differences still yield largely interpretable results (McCrae et al. 2005, Schmitt et al. 2007). The difficulties in comparing mean scores on subjective Likert scales across cultures means that researchers must seriously consider what kinds of data could actually validate such cross-cultural comparisons.

What are the sources of evidence for and against the validity of such cross-national personality comparisons? Though evidence from data clustering of national personality profiles and some correlations with other national-level variables have been put forth as validating mean nation-level scores, other evidence suggests that this kind of national profiling may be inaccurate, such as the low reliability between different measures of the Big 5, disagreement with expert ratings, and bizarre correlations with behavioral measures. We discuss this evidence below.

Cluster analyses indicate some reasonable relationships emerging from the cross-cultural comparisons of the traits. For example, analyses of profile similarity reveal that cultures of similar geographical or historical backgrounds tend to cluster together (Allik & McCrae 2004, McCrae et al. 2005, Schmitt et al. 2007). Though suggestive of validity, we note that cluster analyses are difficult to examine as validity evidence. For example, Schmitt et al. (2007) find that although most of the closest pairings on BFI personality profiles are predictable (e.g., Botswana and South Africa, Cyprus and Greece), some others are not explainable by geographic or historical similarity (e.g., Estonia and Mexico, Israel and Finland). More problematic, similar personality profiles could reflect either actual personality similarities or simply similar cultural standards for comparison and are therefore not necessarily good evidence of validity (Heine et al. 2008a).

Researchers have also calculated correlations of mean trait levels with other country-level data to establish validity of the cross-cultural comparisons. For example, Schmitt et al. (2007) found that extraversion correlated with liberal views toward sexuality both within and between cultures. McCrae (2002) found that Hofstede's (2001) cultural dimensions correlated with some of the Big 5 measures. This convergence with other criteria would appear to be a good demonstration of the validity of the country scores. However, we note a few points about using other kinds of country scores to validate the personality data. First, it is crucial that any validity criteria be theoretically relevant a priori. For example, noting that neuroticism and masculinity are correlated (McCrae 2002) does not provide validity unless there are clear theoretical reasons to anticipate such correlations beforehand. Second, validity correlations should be reliable across different measurements of the Big 5. We note that no significant correlations exist between any of the Big 5 and Hofstede's (2001) five dimensions that replicate across three independent measures of the Big 5 (McCrae 2002, McCrae et al. 2005, Schmitt et al. 2007). Third, we emphasize that the strongest kind of criteria that one could seek to validate country mean scores would be those that utilized different methods. Finding significant correlations between two sets of self-report measures could reflect the fact that both measures are compromised by the same kinds of culturally specific reference-group effects and response biases.

Many sources of evidence call into question the validity of these cross-cultural comparisons. One first step to demonstrating validity is to establish the reliability of the findings—it is difficult to make the case that one rank ordering of means is valid if it is not reproduced through other methods. However, the rank orderings that have emerged from the above endeavors to compare personality traits across cultures do not correlate particularly strongly. For example, correlations between the country scores for the self-report measures of the Big 5 with the NEO-PI-R and the BFI ranged from 0.22 to 0.45 (Schmitt et al. 2007), which are quite modest given that these are measures of the same constructs. Perhaps more disturbing is that the correlations between the country scores from the BFI and NEO-PI-R measures correlate more weakly for the corresponding traits than they do for their noncorresponding traits in four of the Big 5 traits (e.g., the BFI measure of openness correlates 0.73 with the NEO-PI-R measure of extraversion, but only 0.27 with the NEO-PI-R measure of openness; Schmitt et al. 2007). This is in direct violation of the multitrait-multimethod matrix approach to validating personality traits (Campbell & Fiske 1959). Furthermore, as described above, the country scores from the perceptions of national character showed no significant positive correlations with the country scores from the NEO-PI-R for any of the Big 5 traits (Terracciano et al. 2005). In sum, there is little convergence among the country scores

Reference-group effects: implicit comparison to the average, or ideal, amount of a construct within your group when making self-ratings across different assessments of the same personality traits.

One method of validating conflicting cross-cultural data has been to utilize expert ratings (e.g., Heine et al. 2002, John & Robins 1994). The relative rankings of cultures on mean self-ratings of traits has been shown to disagree with the judgments of cultural experts (Church & Katigbak 2002, McCrae 2001), whereas the national character profiles are closer to expert ratings (Terracciano et al. 2005, footnote #26). However, a weakness of this validation strategy is that the expert ratings, such as the National Character ratings, may draw on the same invalid cultural stereotypes (McCrae & Terracciano 2006, Terracciano et al. 2005).

We submit that the strongest evidence for validity would come from actual observations of personality-related behavior frequency in the different cultures, but such data are difficult to find or produce (e.g., Ashton 2007). A recent example of using behavioral data to validate the country scores of conscientiousness (the trait with the clearest behavioral markers; also see Roberts et al. 2007), and the only one for which we could find cross-national data, found that National Character ratings correlated highly with national rankings on conscientious-related behaviors such as clock accuracy and efficiency of postal clerks (average $r = 0.61$), whereas the NEO-PI-R and BFI self- and peer-report aggregate means correlated negatively or not at all with these behaviors (average rs ranged from -0.43 to 0.06; Heine et al. 2008a). These findings indicate that the National Character ratings are more accurate than average self-reports or peer reports at predicting the conscientious behaviors of average citizens. These findings dovetail with other evidence that comparisons of self-report measures across cultures suffer from some serious methodological confounds (Cohen 2007; Heine 2008; Heine et al. 2001, 2002; Kitayama 2002). We suggest that in the absence of convergent evidence from other designs, any cultural differences in means on subjective Likert scales should be taken with a grain of salt. At the least, future cross-cultural comparisons of personality need to more seriously consider validity criteria and the development of improved methods.

Although methodological artifacts such as the reference-group effect make it problematic to compare means across cultures, it is important to underscore that those same problems do not typically emerge when using self-report scales within cultures. Within a culture, people tend to evaluate themselves in contrast to similar referents, a method that preserves the validity of the rank order of individuals within a culture as well as with correlations both within and between self-report scales. In fact, as discussed above, cross-cultural studies of the structure of personality have revealed much evidence for universality. Arguably, it is part of the human condition to perceive personality in terms of universal traits. However, another question to consider is the extent to which people attend to and rely on personality information in their efforts to understand themselves and others. Are personality traits of equal utility across cultures?

THE UTILITY OF PERSONALITY ACROSS CULTURES

Markus & Kitayama (1991) played a key role in relaunching the field of cultural psychology when they posited that the self-concept varied in significant ways across cultures. Although in the West the self tends to be identified more as an independent entity, importantly grounded in internal traits, the interdependent self-concept that is more common in the rest of the world is largely based on its relationships and roles with others. This difference in self-definition across cultures raises the possibility that in societies more characterized by interdependent selves, personality traits might be of less utility for understanding oneself or in predicting the behavior of others than are more relationally defined aspects of the self—such as social roles (see Markus & Kitayama 1998). Below we consider evidence that speaks to the question of whether personality is of comparable utility between individualistic and collectivistic societies.

Content of the Self-Concept

One source of information germane to the question of the utility of personality is the kind of information that people spontaneously consider when describing themselves. Open-ended descriptions of the self-concept measured using the Twenty Statements Test (Kuhn & McPartland 1954) have consistently revealed evidence for a weaker tendency to list pure psychological attributes (largely personality traits) among people from various collectivistic cultures (e.g., Native Americans, Cook Islanders, Masai, Samburu, Malaysians, and East Asians) than among those from individualistic cultures (e.g., Australians, Americans, Canadians, and Swedes) when describing themselves. Instead, people from various non-Western cultures are more likely to describe themselves in terms of their social roles (Ip & Bond 1995, Ma & Schoeneman 1997) or specific descriptors that are not abstract trait terms (Rhee et al. 1995). Evidence from these studies suggests that the self-concepts of people in collectivistic cultures may not emphasize abstract personality traits in the same way that self-concepts common in individualistic societies do. Personality traits may not be useful to the same degree everywhere for describing the self.

Incremental Versus Entity Theories of Self

Another phenomenon related to the perceived utility of personality trait knowledge is the lay theory that people tend to embrace regarding the nature of their selves. As discussed above, people tend to view the self as being either a rather stable and immutable entity or as more fluid and changing. Dweck and colleagues (Dweck & Leggett 1988, Hong et al. 1999) have described these views as entity and incremental theories of self, respectively. Typical views of personality in individualistic cultures are grounded in the notion that personality traits are inherited and somewhat stable across the lifespan—ideas that are conceptually consistent with an entity theory of self.

The notion of an ever-changing and incremental theory of the self would seem to be at odds with the notion of trait theories (Levy et al. 1998, Molden & Dweck 2006). As described above, past cross-cultural research on theories of self finds that in comparison with Westerners, East Asians are less likely to conceptualize their selves in entity terms (Heine et al. 2001, Norenzayan et al. 2002). The incremental nature of the self-views of East Asians is inconsistent with Western views of stable and innate personality traits. It remains to be seen whether people from collectivistic cultures outside of East Asia also demonstrate incremental views of themselves. In summary, lay theories of the self, at least in East Asia, are at odds with the prevailing view of personality as consisting of stable traits, and such a view may be utilized less in such cultures for the understanding of self and others.

Perceived Consistency of Traits

Another perspective on the utility of personality traits is the consistency that those traits manifest across situations. To the extent that people's perceptions about their personality vary considerably across situations, this would render personality traits to be less useful for understanding the person (Mischel 1968; though see Fleeson 2004 for new interpretations of the person-situation debate). Indeed, the lay theories of personality and personhood in collectivistic contexts may in fact be closer to that proposed by Mischel & Shoda (1995), in which a person's traits shift across situations in an individually characteristic pattern. The power of the situation over behavior is acknowledged more in collectivistic cultures than it is within individualistic cultures. Much cross-cultural research has explored the extent to which personality is consistent across situations.

For example, Kanagawa et al. (2001) examined how much the testing situation—filling out a questionnaire in front of a professor versus in front of one peer, a group of peers, or alone—influenced self-descriptions. They found that Japanese self-descriptions (on

Twenty Statements Test: a method of measuring the content of the self-concept by asking participants to complete twenty "I am . . ." statements the Twenty Statements Test) varied significantly more depending on the testing situation than did Americans' self-descriptions. Likewise, in an experience-sampling study, Oishi et al. (2004) asked participants in India, Japan, Korea, and the United States to record their mood and who they were with (i.e., their situation) at random moments during the day. Cultural differences emerged in the effect of situations on mood. For example, whereas Japanese participants felt much happier when with a romantic partner than otherwise, Americans did not experience as much of a mood change. Mood was more influenced by situation in collectivistic cultures than in individualistic cultures. Similarly, Suh (2002) asked Korean and American participants to report what they believed their personality to be like with five different people (e.g., parents, close friend, or stranger) as well as in general. The results indicated that Korean participants reported much less consistency among these six ratings than did American participants; moreover, consistent selves were more strongly correlated with positive outcomes for Americans than they were for Koreans. Relatedly, a number of studies have found that East Asians tolerate more contradiction in their thoughts of self, including variation across contexts, than do Westerners (Choi & Choi 2002; Hamamura et al. 2008a; Spencer-Rodgers et al. 2004, 2008).

These studies suggest that the East Asian self is not as consistent across situations in comparison with the Western self. This raises the question of how the East Asian self might maintain enough coherence to be even considered a self. One possibility is that despite being unstable across situations, one might display a stable personality within situations across time. One's global traits might not be a good way to define one's self, but one's traits within a certain social role—around a certain relationship—might be. To investigate this question, English & Chen (2007) asked Asian American and Euro-American participants to rate their personality traits within certain relationship contexts. As found by Suh (2002), the correlation of traits between relationship contexts

was smaller for Asian Americans than it was for Euro-Americans. Importantly, however, Asian Americans showed as much consistency within that relationship situation over time as Euro-Americans did. In other words, their self-ratings of traits within a certain relationship context were quite stable over time; that is, who one is with one's mother does not change, even if this is quite different from who one is with one's roommate. Likewise, in other research, when East Asians were asked if they had a "true self," they considered a context-sensitive self. In contrast, Westerners responded to this question by considering their feelings of self that were invariant across situations (Kashima et al. 2004; also see Tafarodi et al. 2004). This research highlights how the self-concept in East Asian contexts appears to be grounded in one's roles and relationships rather than something that primarily derives from component traits. Future research is necessary to see whether the Western and East Asian patterns generalize to other cultural contexts.

Attributions for Behavior

The above review has considered how people in collectivistic cultures appear to rely on personality traits less than do those from individualistic cultures in understanding themselves. Other research indicates that people from collectivistic cultures might rely on personality traits less than Westerners do for understanding others as well. This research on how people explain the behavior of others reveals another way that utility of personality varies across cultures. A number of classic studies have found that when asked to explain the behavior of others, people tend to largely attend to the person's disposition as a means for explaining the behavior, even when there are compelling situational constraints available (Jones & Harris 1967, Ross et al. 1977). This tendency to ignore situational information in favor of personality information when explaining the behaviors of others is so commonly observed that it has been termed the "fundamental attribution error." However, as with so many other psychological phenomena, this original research had been conducted almost exclusively with Western participants. Observations with a number of collectivistic cultures have painted a different picture regarding people's preferred ways of making sense of the behavior of others. Geertz (1975) described how Balinese do not tend to conceive of people's behavior in terms of underlying dispositions, but instead see it as emerging out of the roles that they have. Shweder & Bourne (1982) found that Indians tended to eschew trait descriptions of others' behaviors but rather would explain their behaviors in descriptive terms. Building upon this idea, Miller (1984) found that Indians showed evidence for a reverse fundamental attribution error in that Indian adults tended to favor situational information over personality accounts. More recently, several studies conducted with East Asians and Americans reveal that whereas Americans attend to dispositions first, regardless of how compelling the situational information may be (Gilbert & Malone 1995), East Asians are more likely than are Americans to infer that behaviors are strongly controlled by the situation (Norenzayan et al. 2002) and are more likely to attend to situational information (Miyamoto & Kitayama 2002, Morris & Peng 1994, Van Boven et al. 1999), particularly when that information is especially salient (Choi & Nisbett 1998). They may even automatically consider the situational information prior to the personality information (Knowles et al. 2001; but for contrary findings, see Lieberman et al. 2005). Furthermore, in an investigation of people's lay beliefs about personality across eight cultures, Church et al. (2006) found that people from individualistic cultural backgrounds (i.e., American and Euro-Australian) strongly endorsed implicit-trait beliefs, such as the notions that traits remain stable over time and predict behavior over many situations. In contrast, they found that those from collectivistic cultural backgrounds (i.e., Asian Australian, Chinese Malaysian, Filipino, Japanese, Mexican, and Malay) more strongly endorsed contextual beliefs about personality, such as ideas that traits do not fully describe a

person as well as roles or duties and that trait-related behavior will change from situation to situation. In summary, people in collectivistic cultures appear to be less likely than are people from individualistic cultures to utilize personality information in explaining the behavior of others.

Spontaneous Trait Inferences

Do these cultural differences also exhibit themselves at an automatic, cognitive level? Much research has revealed that people spontaneously encode observed behaviors in terms of underlying traits: For example, learning of one person giving money to another person in need may be encoded as "generous" (Uleman 1987). However, until recently, the majority of this research had been conducted in Western cultures, thus failing to shed light on the question of the universality of this tendency. More recent cross-cultural studies suggest that such spontaneous trait inferences might not be so common elsewhere. For example, Maass et al. (2006) found that whereas Italians inferred traits from behaviors and viewed trait adjectives to be predictive of future behaviors, Japanese did this significantly less so. Rather, Japanese tended to rely more on behavior-descriptive verbs in their person descriptions and memories of target events. Likewise, Zarate et al. (2001) found that Latinos showed evidence of fewer spontaneous trait inferences compared with North Americans. Similarly, tendencies to make spontaneous trait inferences have been shown to correlate with trait measures of independence (Duff & Newman 1997), which are more common in individualistic cultures. In a study that explored how well people encoded trait versus role information about themselves, Wagar & Cohen (2003) utilized the self-reference effect, in which words encoded in relation to elaborated areas of self-concept are remembered better, to determine whether social or personality traits were more cognitively elaborated areas of the self-concept. This study revealed that Asian Canadians, compared to Euro-Canadians, remembered social-role words better than they remembered trait words when they were encoded in relation to the self, a finding that suggests that the social role aspect of identity was more cognitively elaborated than were personality traits. These studies converge to suggest that people from collectivistic cultures are less likely to spontaneously encode trait information either about others or about themselves.

Personality Traits and Behavior

The above review is consistent with our thesis that personality, defined as situation-consistent traits, is of less importance in collectivistic cultures than it is in individualistic ones. Ultimately, however, the most compelling kind of evidence in support of this claim would be evidence that personality traits are less predictive of behavior in collectivistic cultures. Among the many forces that prompt and guide behavior, such as norms, role obligations, peer pressure, and situational influences, we should expect that personality traits play a less central role among collectivists than they do among individualists. Is there any evidence for a greater decoupling of personality and behavior among people from collectivistic cultures?

This question is challenging to address because evidence for the relationship between behaviors and personality is relatively rare even in Western contexts owing to the practical difficulties of assessing behaviors. Some evidence for the predictive validity of personality traits in behaviors among Westerners includes behavioral residue, such as how one decorates one's dorm room (Gosling et al. 2002), life outcomes, such as health and occupational success (Roberts et al. 2007), and discreetly observed behaviors, such as whether one cheats on an exam (e.g., Nathanson et al. 2006). Thus far, however, such direct behavioral evidence has been limited to studies with Westerners.

Some indirect evidence speaks to the question of the predictive validity of personality traits across cultures. For example, consider one cross-cultural difference that was reviewed above: When explaining other people's behaviors, those from collectivistic cultures rely on personality information less than do those from individualistic cultures, and they are less likely to communicate that information (e.g., East Asian newspapers tend not to report on information about people's personalities as much as do Western newspapers; Morris & Peng 1994). Although it is possible that people are wrong in their theories about what are the actual causes for others' behaviors, it is informative that in comparison with individualists, collectivists believe that personality is a less compelling explanation for people's behavior; collectivists may indeed perceive a weaker correlation between observed personalities and behaviors.

A second indirect source of evidence comes from studies that compare people's self-reported personality with peer ratings. Peer ratings are often used as an index for behaviors because peers are in the position to form personality assessments on the basis of observed behaviors (e.g., Gosling et al. 1998, John & Robins 1994). For example, a study by Suh (2002) compared self-reported personality traits with ratings made by friends and parents of Korean and American participants. Results indicated that the self-peer correlations were lower among Koreans than they were among Americans. Moreover, correlations between parent ratings and friend ratings were also lower among Koreans than among Americans. These findings are consistent with the notion that personality traits, as perceived by the self, are less predictive of behavior (as witnessed by the observers) among East Asians and Americans. East Asians act more differently across contexts than do Americans, suggesting that contextual factors are guiding their behavior relatively more so than are traits. Before we can draw any firm conclusions on any cultural differences in the predictive validity of traits, it will be necessary to utilize more direct measures of behavior and to consider a wider array of cultural samples. Indeed, thus far almost all of the literature relevant to the question of the cross-cultural utility of personality has focused only on North American and East Asian samples.

CONCLUSION

Personality research has been greatly informed by investigations outside of Western culture, and such data provide new perspectives to address important questions. Personality research has taken an important step in advancing the field from what was largely the study of American undergraduates to the study of human nature. We applaud this move, and we urge the field to consider a much broader spectrum of samples, including those from other social classes and other age groups, and to target nonliterate subsistence populations as well. Such kinds of investigations have the potential to identify what appear to be human universals (e.g., the structure of personality) and what is culturally variable (e.g., the positivity of evaluations of personality, the distribution of personality traits, and the utility of personality).

An understanding of what is universal and what is variable about human personality is not some tangential question, but rather stands to illuminate fundamental concerns of the field (for more discussion, see Norenzayan & Heine 2005). Evidence for universality is particularly informative for guiding evolutionary theories regarding the adaptiveness of certain facets of personality, whereas evidence for variability provides important information regarding boundary conditions, mechanisms, and the role of contextual variables in influencing aspects of personality. The fact that so little work on personality has been conducted outside of Western samples (Quinones-Vidal et al. 2004) or has employed methods other than self-report [more than 95% of papers in the *Journal of Personality* rely on self-report methods (Kagan 2007), which are particularly problematic for cross-cultural comparisons; Heine et al. 2002, 2008a; Peng et al. 1997)] means that there are still vast lacunae in our understanding of human personality.

DISCLOSURE STATEMENT

The authors are not aware of any biases that might be perceived as affecting the objectivity of this review.

LITERATURE CITED

Aaker JL, Lee AY. 2001. "I" seek pleasures and "We" avoid pains: the role of self-regulatory goals in information processing and persuasion. *J. Consum. Res.* 28:33–49

Adams G. 2005. The cultural grounding of personal relationship: enemyship in West African worlds. *J. Personal. Soc. Psychol.* 88:948–68

Allik J, McCrae RR. 2004. Toward a geography of personality traits: patterns of profiles across 36 cultures. *J. Cross-Cult. Psychol.* 35:13–28

Allport GW, Odbert HS. 1936. Trait-names: a psycho-lexical study. *Psychol. Monogr.* 47:171–220

Arnett JJ. 2008. The neglected 95%: why American psychology needs to become less American. Work. pap., Clark Univ., Worcester, MA

Ashton MC. 2007. Self-reports and stereotypes: a comment on McCrae et al. *Eur. J. Personal.* 21:983–86

Ashton MC, Lee K, Perugini M, Szarota P, de Vries RE, et al. 2004. A six-factor structure of personality-descriptive adjectives: solutions from psycholexical studies in seven languages. *J. Personal. Soc. Psychol.* 86:356–66

Bagozzi R, Wong N, Yi Y. 1999. The role of culture and gender in the relationship between positive and negative affect. *Cogn. Emot.* 13:641–72

Benet-Martínez V. 2007. Cross-cultural personality research: conceptual and methodological issues. In *Handbook of Research Methods in Personality Psychology*, ed. RW Robins, CR Fraley, RF Krueger, pp. 170–89. New York: Guilford

Benet-Martínez V, John OP. 1998. Los cinco grandes across cultures and ethnic groups: multitrait multimethod analysis of the Big Five in Spanish and English. *J. Personal. Soc. Psychol.* 75:729–50

Benet-Martinez V, Waller NG. 1995. The Big Seven factor model of personality description: evidence for its cross-cultural generality in a Spanish sample. *J. Personal. Soc. Psychol.* 69:701–18

Benet-Martinez V, Waller NG. 1997. Further evidence for the cross-cultural generality of the Big Seven factor model: indigenous and imported Spanish personality constructs. *J. Personal.* 65:567–98

Block J. 1995. A contrarian view of the five-factor approach to personality description. *Psychol. Bull.* 117:187–215

Bond MH. 1979. Dimensions of personality used in perceiving peers: cross-cultural comparisons of Hong Kong, Japanese, American, and Filipino university students. *Int. J. Psychol.* 14:47–56

Bond MH, Nakazato H, Shiraishi D. 1975. Universality and distinctiveness in dimensions of Japanese person perception. *J. Cross-Cult. Psychol.* 6:346–57

Boyd R, Borgerhoff-Mulder M, Durham WH, Richerson PJ. 1997. Are cultural phylogenies possible? In *Human by Nature: Between Biology and the Social Sciences*, ed. P Weingart, pp. 355–86. Mahwah, NJ: Erlbaum

Budaev SV. 1997. "Personality" in the guppy (*Poecilia reticulata*): a correlational study of exploratory behavior and social tendency. *J. Comp. Psychol.* 111:399–411

Buss DM. 1984. Evolutionary biology and personality psychology: toward a conception of human nature and individual differences. *Am. Psychol.* 39:1135–47

Buss DM. 1991. Evolutionary personality psychology. *Annu. Rev. Psychol.* 42:459–91

Campbell DT, Fiske DW. 1959. Convergent and discrimination validation by the multi-trait multimethod matrix. *Psychol. Bull.* 56:81–105

Campbell JD, Trapnell PD, Heine SJ, Katz IM, Lavallee LF, Lehman DR. 1996. Self-concept clarity: measurement, personality correlates, and cultural boundaries. *J. Personal. Soc. Psychol.* 70:141–56

Cattell RB. 1957. *Personality and Motivation Structure and Measurement.* New York: World Book Co.

Chen C, Lee S-Y, Stevenson HW. 1995. Response style and cross-cultural comparisons of rating scales among East Asian and North American students. *Psychol. Sci.* 6:170–75

Cheung FM, Cheung SF, Leung K, Ward C, Leong F. 2003. The English version of the Chinese Personality Assessment Inventory. *J. Cross-Cult. Psychol.* 34:433–52

Cheung FM, Leung K, Fan RM, Song W, Zhang J-X, Zhang J-P. 1996. Development of the Chinese Personality Assessment Inventory. *J. Cross-Cult. Psychol.* 27:181–99

Choi I, Choi Y. 2002. Culture and self-concept flexibility. *Personal. Soc. Psychol. Bull.* 28:1508–17

Choi I, Nisbett RE. 1998. Situational salience and cultural differences in the correspondence bias and in the actor-observer bias. *Personal. Soc. Psychol. Bull.* 24:949–60

Choi I, Nisbett RE, Norenzayan A. 1999. Causal attribution across cultures: variation and universality. *Psychol. Bull.* 125:47–63

Church AT, Katigbak MS. 2002. The five-factor model in the Philippines: investigating trait structure and levels across cultures. In *Five-Factor Model of Personality Across Cultures*, ed. RR McCrae, J Allik, pp. 129–54. New York: Kluwer Acad./Plenum

Church AT, Katigbak MS, Del Prado AM, Ortiz FA, Mastor KA, et al. 2006. Implicit theories and self-perceptions of traitedness across cultures: toward integration of cultural and trait psychology perspectives. *J. Cross-Cult. Psychol.* 37:694–716

Church AT, Katigbak MS, Miramontes LG, del Prado AM, Cabrera HF. 2007. Culture and the behavioural manifestations of traits: an application of the act frequency approach. *Eur. J. Personal.* 21:389–417

Church AT, Katigbak MS, Reyes JAS. 1998. Further exploration of Filipino personality structure using the lexical approach: Do the Big-Five or Big-Seven dimensions emerge? *Eur. J. Personal.* 12:249–69

Church AT, Reyes JAS, Katigbak MS, Grimm SD. 1997. Filipino personality structure and the Big Five Model: a lexical approach. *J. Personal.* 65:477–528

Cohen D. 2001. Cultural variation: considerations and implications. *Psychol. Bull.* 127:451–71

Cohen D. 2007. Methods in cultural psychology. In *Handbook of Cultural Psychology*, ed. S Kitayama, D Cohen, pp. 196–236. New York: Guilford

Cohen D, Gunz A. 2002. As seen by the other...: perspectives on the self in the memories and emotional perceptions of Easterners and Westerners. *Psychol. Sci.* 13:55–59

Cohen D, Hoshino-Browne E, Leung AK-Y. 2007. Culture and the structure of personal experience: insider and outsider phenomenologies of the self and social world. In *Advances in Experimental Social Psychology*, Vol. 39, ed. MP Zanna, pp. 1–67. San Diego, CA: Elsevier Acad.

Colvin CR, Block J, Funder DC. 1995. Overly positive evaluations and personality: negative implications for mental health. *J. Personal. Soc. Psychol.* 68:1152–62

Costa PT Jr, McCrae RR. 1992. *Revised NEO Personality Inventory (NEO-PI-R) and NEO Five Factor Inventory (NEO-FFI) Professional Manual.* Odessa, FL: Psychol. Assess. Resourc.

Crocker J, Luhtanen R, Blaine B, Broadnax S. 1994. Collective self-esteem and psychological well-being among white, black, and Asian college students. *Personal. Soc. Psychol. Bull.* 20:503–13

Diener E, Diener M. 1995. Cross-cultural correlates of life satisfaction and self-esteem. *J. Personal. Soc. Psychol.* 68:653–63

Diener E, Diener M, Diener C. 1995. Factors predicting the subjective well-being of nations. *J. Personal. Soc. Psychol.* 69:851–64

Diener E, Oishi S, Lucas RE. 2003. Personality, culture, and subjective well-being: emotional and cognitive evaluations of life. *Annu. Rev. Psychol.* 54:403–25

Diener E, Wallbom M. 1976. Effects of self-awareness on antinormative behavior. *J. Res. Personal.* 10:107–11

Duff KJ, Newman LS. 1997. Individual differences in the spontaneous construal of behavior: idiocentrism and the automatization of the trait inference process. *Soc. Cogn.* 15:217–41

Duval TS, Wicklund R. 1972. *A Theory of Objective Self-Awareness.* New York: Academic

Dweck CS. 1999. *Self-Theories: Their Role in Motivation, Personality, and Development.* New York: Psychol. Press

Dweck CS, Leggett EL. 1988. A social-cognitive approach to motivation and personality. *Psychol. Rev.* 95:256–73

Elliot AJ, Chirkov VI, Kim Y, Sheldon KM. 2001. A cross-cultural analysis of avoidance (relative to approach) personal goals. *Psychol. Sci.* 12:505–10

Ellis BJ, Simpson JA, Campbell L. 2002. Trait-specific dependence in romantic relationships. *J. Personal.* 70:611–60

English T, Chen S. 2007. Culture and self-concept stability: consistency across and within contexts among Asian Americans and European Americans. *J. Personal. Soc. Psychol.* 93:478–90

Eysenck HJ. 1975. *Manual of the Eysenck Personality Questionnaire.* London: Hodder & Stoughton

Fejfar MC, Hoyle RH. 2000. Effect of private self-awareness on negative affect and self-referent attribution: a quantitative review. *Personal. Soc. Psychol. Rev.* 4:132–42

Fiske DS. 1949. Consistency of the factorial structures of personality ratings from different sources. *J. Abnorm. Soc. Psychol.* 44:329–44

Fleeson W. 2004. Moving personality beyond the person-situation debate: the challenge and the opportunity of within-person variability. *Curr. Dir. Psychol. Sci.* 13:83–87

Fryberg SA, Markus HR. 2003. On being American Indian: current and possible selves. *Self Identity* 2:325–44

Funder DC. 2007. *The Personality Puzzle.* New York: Norton

Geertz C. 1975. On the nature of anthropological understanding. *Am. Sci.* 63:4–53

Gilbert DT, Malone PS. 1995. The correspondence bias. *Psychol. Bull.* 117:21–38

Goldberg LR. 1981. Language and individual differences: the search for universals in personality lexicons. In *Review of Personality and Social Psychology*, ed. L Wheeler, pp. 141–65. Beverly Hills, CA: Sage

Gosling SD. 1998. Personality dimensions in spotted hyenas (*Crocuta crocuta*). *J. Comp. Psychol.* 112:107–18

Gosling SD. 2001. From mice to men: What can we learn about personality from animal research? *Psychol. Bull.* 127:45–86

Gosling SD, John OP. 1999. Personality dimensions in nonhuman animals: a cross-species review. *Curr. Dir. Psychol. Sci.* 8:69–75

Gosling SD, John OP, Craik KH, Robins RW. 1998. Do people know how they behave? Self-reported act frequencies compared with online codings of observers. *J. Personal. Soc. Psychol.* 74:1337–49

Gosling SD, Ko SJ, Mannarelli T, Morris ME. 2002. A room with a cue: personality judgments based on offices and bedrooms. *J. Personal. Soc. Psychol.* 82:379–98

Greenfield PM. 1997. Culture as process: empirical methods for cultural psychology. In *Handbook of Cross-Cultural Psychology*, ed. JW Berry, YH Poortinga, J Pandey, pp. 301–46. Boston, MA: Allyn & Bacon

Grimm SD, Church AT. 1999. A cross-cultural study of response biases in personality measures. *J. Res. Personal.* 33:415–41

Guthrie GM, Bennett AB. 1971. Cultural differences in implicit personality theory. *Int. J. Psychol.* 6:305–12

Hamamura T, Heine SJ. 2008. Approach and avoidance motivations across cultures. In *Handbook of Approach and Avoidance Motivations*, ed. AJ Elliot, pp. 549–62. Mahwah, NJ: Erlbaum

Hamamura T, Heine SJ, Paulhus DL. 2008a. Cultural differences in response styles: the role of dialectical thinking. *Personal. Individ. Differ.* 44:932–42

Hamamura T, Heine SJ, Takemoto T. 2007. Why the better-than-average effect is a worse-than-average measure of self-enhancement: an investigation of conflicting findings from studies of East Asian self-evaluations. *Motiv. Emot.* 31:247–59

Hamamura T, Meijer Z, Heine SJ, Kamayo K, Hori I. 2008b. Approach-avoidance motivations and information processing: a cross-cultural analysis. *Unpubl. manuscr., Univ. Br. Columbia*

Heine SJ. 2001. Self as cultural product: an examination of East Asian and North American selves. *J. Personal.* 69:881–906

Heine SJ. 2005. Constructing good selves in Japan and North America. In *Culture and Social Behavior: The Tenth Ontario Symposium*, ed. D Cohen, JM Olson, MP Zanna, pp. 95–116. Hillsdale, NJ: Erlbaum

Heine SJ. 2008. *Cultural Psychology*. New York: Norton

Heine SJ, Buchtel EE, Norenzayan A. 2008a. What do cross-national comparisons of personality traits tell us? The case of conscientiousness. *Psychol. Sci.* 19:309–13

Heine SJ, Hamamura T. 2007. In search of East Asian self-enhancement. *Personal. Soc. Psychol. Rev.* 11:4–27

Heine SJ, Kitayama S, Hamamura T. 2007a. The inclusion of additional studies yields different conclusions: a reply to Sedikides, Gaertner, & Vevea 2005, JPSP. *Asian J. Soc. Psychol.* 10:49–58

Heine SJ, Kitayama S, Hamamura T. 2007b. Which studies test the question of pancultural self-enhancement? A reply to Sedikides, Gaertner, & Vevea, 2007. *Asian J. Soc. Psychol.* 10:198–200

Heine SJ, Kitayama S, Lehman DR, Takata T, Ide E, et al. 2001. Divergent consequences of success and failure in Japan and North America: an investigation of self-improving motivations and malleable selves. *J. Personal. Soc. Psychol.* 81:599–615

Heine SJ, Lehman DR. 1997. The cultural construction of self-enhancement: an examination of group-serving biases. *J. Personal. Soc. Psychol.* 72:1268–83

Heine SJ, Lehman DR. 1999. Culture, self-discrepancies, and self-satisfaction. *Personal. Soc. Psychol. Bull.* 25:915–25

Heine SJ, Lehman DR, Markus HR, Kitayama S. 1999. Is there a universal need for positive self-regard? *Psychol. Rev.* 106:766–94

Heine SJ, Lehman DR, Peng K, Greenholtz J. 2002. What's wrong with cross-cultural comparisons of subjective Likert scales? The reference-group effect. *J. Personal. Soc. Psychol.* 82:903–18

Heine SJ, Norenzayan A. 2006. Towards a psychological science for a cultural species. *Perspect. Psychol. Sci.* 1:251–69

Heine SJ, Renshaw K. 2002. Interjudge agreement, self-enhancement, and liking: cross-cultural divergences. *Personal. Soc. Psychol. Bull.* 28:578–87

Heine SJ, Takata T, Lehman DR. 2000. Beyond self-presentation: evidence for self-criticism among Japanese. *Personal. Soc. Psychol. Bull.* 26:71–78

Heine SJ, Takemoto T, Moskalenko S, Lasaleta J, Henrich J. 2008b. Mirrors in the head: cultural variation in objective self-awareness. *Personal. Soc. Psychol. Bull.* 34:879–87

Henrich J, Boyd R, Bowles S, Camerer C, Fehr E, et al. 2005. "Economic man" in cross-cultural perspective: behavioral experiments in 15 small-scale societies. *Behav. Brain Sci.* 28:795–855

Henrich J, Heine SJ, Norenzayan A. 2008. Are college-educated Americans the weirdest people in the world? Work. Pap., Univ. Brit. Columbia

Higgins ET. 1996. The "self-digest": self-knowledge serving self-regulatory functions. *J. Personal. Soc. Psychol.* 71:1062–83

Hofstede G. 2001. *Culture's Consequences: Comparing Values, Behaviors, Institutions, and Organizations Across Nations*. Thousand Oaks, CA: Sage

Holloway SD. 1988. Concepts of ability and effort in Japan and the United States. *Rev. Educ. Res.* 58:327–45

Hong Y, Chiu C, Dweck CS, Lin DM, Wan W. 1999. Implicit theories, attributions, and coping: a meaning system approach. *J. Personal. Soc. Psychol.* 77:588–99

Ip GWM, Bond MH. 1995. Culture, values, and the spontaneous self-concept. *Asian J. Psychol.* 1:30–36

Iyengar SS, Lepper MR. 1999. Rethinking the value of choice: a cultural perspective on intrinsic motivation. *J. Personal. Soc. Psychol.* 76:349–66

John OP, Robins RW. 1994. Accuracy and bias in self-perception: individual differences in self-enhancement and the role of narcissism. *J. Personal. Soc. Psychol.* 66:206–19

Jones EE, Harris VA. 1967. The attribution of attitudes. *J. Exp. Soc. Psychol.* 3:1–24

Kagan J. 2007. A trio of concerns. *Perspect. Psychol. Sci.* 2:361–76

Kanagawa C, Cross SE, Markus HR. 2001. "Who am I?" The cultural psychology of the conceptual self. *Personal. Soc. Psychol. Bull.* 27:90–103

Kashima Y, Kashima E, Farsides T, Kim U, Strack F, et al. 2004. Culture and context-sensitive self: the amount and meaning of context-sensitivity of phenomenal self differ across cultures. *Self Identity* 3:125–41

King JE, Figueredo AJ. 1997. The Five-Factor Model plus dominance in chimpanzee personality. *J. Res. Personal.* 31:257–71

Kitayama S. 2002. Culture and basic psychological processes—toward a system view of culture: comment on Oyserman et al. 2002. *Psychol. Bull.* 128:89–96

Kitayama S, Markus HR, Kurokawa M. 2000. Culture, emotion, and well-being: good feelings in Japan and the United States. *Cogn. Emot.* 14:93–124

Kitayama S, Uchida Y. 2003. Explicit self-criticism and implicit self-regard: evaluating self and friend in two cultures. *J. Exp. Soc. Psychol.* 39:476–82

Klar Y, Giladi EE. 1997. No one in my group can be below the group's average: a robust positivity bias in favor of anonymous peers. *J. Personal. Soc. Psychol.* 73:885–901

Knowles ED, Morris MW, Chiu C, Hong Y. 2001. Culture and the process of person perception: evidence for automaticity among East Asians in correcting for situational influences on behavior. *Personal. Soc. Psychol. Bull.* 27:1344–56

Kobayashi C, Greenwald A. 2003. Implicit-explicit differences in self-enhancement for Americans and Japanese. *J. Cross-Cult. Psychol.* 34:522–41

Kuhn MH, McPartland TS. 1954. An empirical investigation of self-attitudes. *Am. Sociol. Rev.* 19:68–76

Kwan VSY, Bond MH, Singelis TM. 1997. Pancultural explanations for life satisfaction: adding relationship harmony to self-esteem. *J. Personal. Soc. Psychol.* 73:1038–51

Leary MR, Baumeister RF. 2000. The nature and function of self-esteem: sociometer theory. In *Advances in Experimental Social Psychology*, ed. MP Zanna, pp. 1–62. San Diego, CA: Academic

Lee AY, Aaker JL, Gardner WL. 2000. The pleasures and pains of distinct self-construals: the role of interdependence in regulatory focus. *J. Personal. Soc. Psychol.* 78:1122–34

Lee GR, Stone LH. 1980. Mate-selection systems and criteria: variation according to family structure. *J. Marr. Fam.* 42:319–26

Levy SR, Stroessner SJ, Dweck CS. 1998. Stereotype formation and endorsement: the role of implicit theories. *J. Personal. Soc. Psychol.* 74:1421–36

Lieberman MD, Jarcho JM, Obayashi J. 2005. Attributional inference across cultures: similar automatic attributions and different controlled corrections. *Personal. Soc. Psychol. Bull.* 31:889–901

Lockwood P, Marshall TC, Sadler P. 2005. Promoting success or preventing failure: cultural differences in motivation by positive and negative role models. *Personal. Soc. Psychol. Bull.* 31:379–92

Ma V, Schoeneman TJ. 1997. Individualism versus collectivism: a comparison of Kenyan and American self-concepts. *Basic Appl. Soc. Psychol.* 19:261–73

Maass A, Karasawa M, Politi F, Suga S. 2006. Do verbs and adjectives play different roles in different cultures? A cross-linguistic analysis of person representation. *J. Personal. Soc. Psychol.* 90:734–50

Markus HR, Kitayama S. 1991. Culture and the self: implications for cognition, emotion, and motivation. *Psychol. Rev.* 98:224–53

Markus HR, Kitayama S. 1998. The cultural psychology of personality. *J. Cross-Cult. Psychol.* 29:63–87

Maslow A. 1943. A theory of human motivation. *Psychol. Rev.* 50:370–96

Mather JA, Anderson RC. 1993. Personalities of octopuses (*Octopus rubescens*). *J. Comp. Psychol.* 107:336–40

McAdams DP. 1992. The five-factor model of personality: a critical appraisal. *J. Personal.* 60:329–61

McCrae RR. 2001. Trait psychology and culture: exploring intercultural comparisons. *J. Personal.* 69:819–46

McCrae RR. 2002. NEO-PI-R data from 36 cultures: further intercultural comparisons. In *The Five-Factor Model of Personality Across Cultures*, ed. RR McCrae, J Allik, pp. 105–25. New York: Kluwer Acad./Plenum

McCrae RR, Allik J, eds. 2002. *The Five-Factor Model of Personality Across Cultures*. New York: Kluwer Acad./Plenum

McCrae RR, Costa PT Jr. 1987. Validation of the five-factor model of personality across instruments and observers. *J. Personal. Soc. Psychol.* 52:82–90

McCrae RR, Terracciano A. 2006. National character and personality. *Curr. Dir. Psychol. Sci.* 15:156–61

McCrae RR, Terracciano A, 79 members Personal. Profiles Cultures Proj. 2005. Personality profiles of cultures: aggregate personality traits. *J. Personal. Soc. Psychol.* 89:407–25

McGrath RE, Goldberg LR. 2006. How to measure national stereotypes? *Science* 311:776–77

Mesquita B, Karasawa M. 2002. Different emotional lives. *Cogn. Emot.* 17:127–41

Miller JG. 1984. Culture and the development of everyday social explanation. *J. Personal. Soc. Psychol.* 46:961–78

Mischel W. 1968. *Personality and Assessment*. New York: Wiley

Mischel W, Shoda Y. 1995. A cognitive-affective system theory of personality: reconceptualizing the invariances in personality and the role of situations. *Psychol. Rev.* 102:246–68

Miyamoto Y, Kitayama S. 2002. Cultural variation in correspondence bias: the critical role of attitude diagnosticity of socially constrained behavior. *J. Personal. Soc. Psychol.* 83:1239–48

Molden DC, Dweck CS. 2006. Finding "meaning" in psychology: a lay theories approach to self-regulation, social perception, and social development. *Am. Psychol.* 61:192–203

Montag L, Levin J. 1994. The five-factor personality model in applied settings. *Eur. J. Personal.* 8:1–11

Morling B, Kitayama S, Miyamoto Y. 2002. Cultural practices emphasize influence in the United States and adjustment in Japan. *Personal. Soc. Psychol. Bull.* 28:311–23

Morris MW, Peng K. 1994. Culture and cause: American and Chinese attributions for social and physical events. *J. Personal. Soc. Psychol.* 67:949–71

Nathanson C, Paulhus DL, Williams KM. 2006. Predictors of a behavioral measure of scholastic cheating: personality and competence but not demographics. *Contemp. Educ. Psychol.* 31:97–122

Norenzayan A, Choi I, Nisbett RE. 2002. Cultural similarities and differences in social inference: evidence from behavioral predictions and lay theories of behavior. *Personal. Soc. Psychol. Bull.* 28:109–20

Norenzayan A, Heine SJ. 2005. Psychological universals: What are they and how can we know? *Psychol. Bull.* 131:763–84

Oishi S, Diener E, Napa Scollon C, Biswas-Diener R. 2004. Cross-situational consistency of affective experiences across cultures. *J. Personal. Soc. Psychol.* 86:460–72

Oishi S, Lun J, Sherman GD. 2007. Residential mobility, self-concept, and positve affect in social interactions. *J. Personal. Soc. Psychol.* 93:131–41

Oyserman D, Coon HM, Kemmelmeier M. 2002. Rethinking individualism and collectivism: evaluation of theoretical assumptions and meta-analyses. *Psychol. Bull.* 128:3–72

Paulhus DL. 1998. Interpersonal and intrapsychic adaptiveness of trait self-enhancement: a mixed blessing? *J. Personal. Soc. Psychol.* 74:1197–208

Peng K, Nisbett RE. 1999. Culture, dialectics, and reasoning about contradiction. *Am. Psychol.* 54:741–54

Peng K, Nisbett RE, Wong NYC. 1997. Validity problems comparing values across cultures and possible solutions. *Psychol. Meth.* 2:329–44

Penke L, Denissen JJA, Miller GF. 2007. The evolutionary genetics of personality. *Eur. J. Personal.* 21:549–87

Perugini M, Richetin J. 2007. In the land of the blind, the one-eyed man is king. *Eur. J. Personal.* 21: 977–81

Piedmont RL, Chae JH. 1997. Cross-cultural generalizability of the five-factor model of personality. *J. Cross-Cult. Psychol.* 28:131–55

Plomin R, DeFries JC, McClearn GE, McGuffin P. 2001. *Behavioral Genetics*. New York: Worth Publ.

Poortinga YH, Van de Vijver FJR, Van Hemert DA. 2002. Cross-cultural equivalence of the Big Five: a tentative interpretation of the evidence. In *The Five-Factor Model of Personality Across Cultures*, ed. RR McCrae, J Allik, pp. 281–302. New York: Kluwer Acad./Plenum

Quinones-Vidal E, Lopez-Garcia JJ, Penaranda-Ortega M, Tortosa-Gil F. 2004. The nature of social and personality psychology as reflected in *JPSP*, 1965–2000. *J. Personal. Soc. Psychol.* 86:435–52

Rhee E, Uleman JS, Lee HK, Roman RJ. 1995. Spontaneous self-descriptions and ethnic identities in individualistic and collectivistic cultures. *J. Personal. Soc. Psychol.* 69:142–52

Roberts BW, Kuncel NR, Shiner R, Caspi A, Goldberg LR. 2007. The power of personality: the comparative validity of personality traits, socio-economic status, and cognitive ability for predicting important life outcomes. *Perspect. Psychol. Sci.* 2:313–45

Robins RW, Beer JS. 2001. Positive illusions about the self: short-term benefits and long-term costs. *J. Personal. Soc. Psychol.* 80:340–52

Ross LD, Amabile TM, Steinmetz JL. 1977. Social roles, social control, and biases in social-perception processes. *J. Personal. Soc. Psychol.* 35:485–94

Sato K, Yuki M, Oishi S. 2007. *The influence of relational mobility on self-esteem.* Presented at Conf. Asian Assoc. Soc. Psychol., 7th, Kota Kinabalu, Malaysia

Saucier G, Georgiades S, Tsaousis I, Goldberg LR. 2005. The factor structure of Greek personality adjectives. *J. Personal. Soc. Psychol.* 88:856–75

Schmitt DP, Allik J. 2005. Simultaneous administration of the Rosenberg self-esteem scale in 53 nations: exploring the universal and culture-specific features of global self-esteem. *J. Personal. Soc. Psychol.* 89:623–42

Schmitt DP, Allik J, McCrae RR, Benet-Martinez V. 2007. The geographic distribution of Big Five personality traits: patterns and profiles of human self-description across 56 nations. *J. Cross-Cult. Psychol.* 38:173–212

Sedikides C, Gaertner L, Vevea J. 2007a. Evaluating the evidence for pancultural self-enhancement. *Asian J. Psychol.* 10:201–3

Sedikides C, Gaertner L, Vevea J. 2007b. Inclusion of theory-relevant moderators yield the same conclusions as Sedikides, Gaertner, and Vevea 2005: a meta-analytical reply to Heine, Kitayama, and Hamamura 2007. *Asian J. Soc. Psychol.* 10:59–67

Shweder RA. 1990. Cultural psychology: What is it? In *Cultural Psychology: Essays on Comparative Human Development*, ed. JW Stigler, RA Shweder, G Herdt, pp. 1–43. London: Cambridge Univ. Press

Shweder RA, Bourne EJ. 1982. Does the concept of the person vary cross-culturally? In *Cultural Conceptions of Mental Health and Therapy*, ed. AJ Marsella, GM White, pp. 158–99. New York: Kluwer Acad.

Snibbe AC, Markus HR, Kitayama S, Suzuki T. 2003. "They saw a game": self and group enhancement in Japan and the U.S. *J. Cross-Cult. Psychol.* 34:581–95

Somer O, Goldberg LR. 1999. The structure of Turkish trait-descriptive adjectives. *J. Personal. Soc. Psychol.* 76:431–50

Spencer-Rodgers J, Boucher HC, Mori SC, Wang L, Peng K. 2008. The dialectical self-concept: contradiction, change, and holism in East Asian cultures. *Personal. Soc. Psychol. Bull.* In press

Spencer-Rodgers J, Peng K, Wang L, Hou Y. 2004. Dialectical self-esteem and East-West differences in psychological well-being. *Personal. Soc. Psychol. Bull.* 30:1416–32

Stevenson HW, Stigler JW. 1992. *The Learning Gap.* New York: Summit

Suh EM. 2002. Culture, identity consistency, and subjective well-being. *J. Personal. Soc. Psychol.* 83:1378–91

Suh EM, Diener E, Oishi S, Triandis HC. 1998. The shifting basis of life satisfaction judgments across cultures: emotions versus norms. *J. Personal. Soc. Psychol.* 74:482–93

Tafarodi RW, Lo C, Yamaguchi S, Lee WW, Katsura H. 2004. The inner self in three countries. *J. Cross-Cult. Psychol.* 35:97–117

Taylor SE, Armor DA. 1996. Positive illusions and coping with adversity. *J. Personal.* 64:873–98

Taylor SE, Brown JD. 1988. Illusion and well-being: a social psychological perspective on mental health. *Psychol. Bull.* 103:193–210

Taylor SE, Lerner JS, Sherman DK, Sage RM, McDowell NK. 2003. Portrait of the self-enhancer: well adjusted and well liked or maladjusted and friendless? *J. Personal. Soc. Psychol.* 84:165–76

Terracciano A, Abdel-Khalek AM, Ádám N, Adamovová L, Ahn C-K, et al. 2005. National character does not reflect mean personality trait levels in 49 cultures. *Science* 310:96–100

Tesser A. 1988. Toward a self-evaluation maintenance model of social behavior. In *Advances in Experimental Social Psychology*, ed. L Berkowitz, pp. 181–227. San Diego, CA: Academic

Tomasello M. 1999. *The Cultural Origins of Human Cognition.* Cambridge, MA: Harvard Univ. Press

Triandis HC. 1989. The self and social behavior in differing cultural contexts. *Psychol. Rev.* 96:506–20

Triandis HC, Suh EM. 2002. Cultural influences on personality. *Annu. Rev. Psychol.* 53:133–60

Tropp LR, Wright SC. 2003. Evaluations and perceptions of self, ingroup, and outgroup: comparisons between Mexican-American and European-American children. *Self Identity* 2:203–21

Uleman JS. 1987. Consciousness and control: the case of spontaneous trait inferences. *Personal. Soc. Psychol. Bull.* 13:337–54

Van Boven L, Kamada A, Gilovich T. 1999. The perceiver as perceived: everyday intuitions about the correspondence bias. *J. Personal. Soc. Psychol.* 77:1188–99

Vohs KD, Heatherton TF. 2001. Self-esteem and threats to self: implications for self-construals and interpersonal perceptions. *J. Personal. Soc. Psychol.* 81:1103–18

Wagar BM, Cohen D. 2003. Culture, memory, and the self: an analysis of the personal and collective self in long-term memory. *J. Exp. Soc. Psychol.* 39:468–75

Wu S, Keysar B. 2007. The effect of culture on perspective taking. *Psychol. Sci.* 18:600–6

Yik MSM, Russell JA, Ahn C, Fernandez-Dols JM, Suzuki N. 2002. Relating the five-factor model of personality to a circumplex model of affect: a five language study. In *The Five-Factor Model of Personality Across Cultures*, ed. RR McCrae, J Allik, pp. 79–104. New York: Kluwer Acad.

Yuki M, Sato K, Schug JR, Horikawa H, Takemura K, Kaneko M. 2007a. *The "openness" of a society and the relationship between self-esteem and subjective well-being.* Presented at Conf. Asian Assoc. Soc. Psychol., 7th, Kota Kinabalu, Malaysia

Yuki M, Schug JR, Horikawa H, Takemura K, Sato K, et al. 2007b. Development of a scale to measure perceptions of relational mobility in society. Work. pap., Hokkaido Univ., Sapporo, Japan

Zarate MA, Uleman JS, Voils CI. 2001. Effects of culture and processing goals on the activation and binding of trait concepts. *Soc. Cogn.* 19:295–323

Community Psychology: Individuals and Interventions in Community Context

Edison J. Trickett

Community & Prevention Research Division, Department of Psychology, University of Illinois at Chicago, Chicago, Illinois 60607; email: trickett@uic.edu

Annu. Rev. Psychol. 2009. 60:395–419

The *Annual Review of Psychology* is online at psych.annualreviews.org

This article's doi:
10.1146/annurev.psych.60.110707.163517

0066-4308/09/0110-0395$20.00

Key Words

ecology, culture, neighborhood, diversity, research relationship

Abstract

Community psychology has historically focused on understanding individual behavior in sociocultural context, assessing high-impact contexts, and working in and with communities to improve their resources and influence over their futures. This review adopts an ecological perspective on recent developments in the field, beginning with philosophy of science and progressing through a series of substantive research and intervention domains that characterize current work. These domains include research on the ecology of lives, the assessment of social settings and their impact on behavior, culture and diversity as expressed in the community research process, and community intervention.

Contents

INTRODUCTION

From its "official" origin in 1965 (Bennett et al. 1966), community psychology has been guided by the dual objectives of understanding people in context and attempting to change those aspects of the community that pollute the possibilities for local citizens to control their own lives and improve their community. An ecological perspective, directing attention to the social and cultural contexts of communities and the community life of individuals, has been central to both the research and action arms of this agenda (Kelly 1968).

Conceptually, the ecological perspective provides a framework for understanding people in community context and the community context itself. It adopts a coping and adaptation perspective on individual behavior in community context and assumes that people are agentic and not passive responders to their environments. As such, attention is directed to the transactions between individuals with varied cultural histories, skills, resources, and personal predicaments and the opportunities, resources, and constraints of the social contexts of relevance to them. The ecological perspective also explicitly asserts the adaptive value of diversity in the kinds of behaviors individuals select in their efforts to survive and indeed thrive. The adaptive value of individual behavior is thus assessed only in the context in which it arises as a means of coping. No one kind of adaptive behavior fits all.

With respect to the community context, an ecological perspective focuses attention on how to describe high-impact social settings, communities, and their effects on individuals. In so doing, it draws attention to how the community context may be viewed and assessed across multiple ecological levels, how culture is expressed across varied segments of the community, and the role of community traditions, resources, social structures, and norms in affecting individual and group life. It adopts an historical perspective (Kelly 1968) on the community context, emphasizing the formative role of cultural and community history in understanding current community functioning. Incorporating the traditional psychological concern with individual differences, an ecological perspective directs specific attention not only to main effects but also to the interactive effects of social contexts and individuals representing different cultural identifications, coping styles, genders, and social roles in those contexts.

The action agenda flows from an appreciation of knowledge about the ecology of the community and the lives of individuals in it. From an ecological perspective, knowledge about the local community is prerequisite and prelude to decisions about what kinds of actions serve community goals and interests, and what individuals, groups, and social settings are most central to the action goal. Further, action is predicated on the importance of developing collaborative and empowering relationships with community groups and organizations in the intervention process. Identifying local resources, definitions of problems or issues, and hopes for community change are central to this quest. The goal is to increase local resources in the service of increasing community capacity to improve community life. The specifics of such efforts may range widely, from the creation and sustained presence of a locally valued social program to the development of local skills and interorganizational networks to the creation of citizen participation mechanisms to advocate for needed community resources.

In both the research and action domains, an ecological perspective in community psychology places the notion of context front and center in its work. As Hess (2005) notes, while "the importance of context, of course, is hardly a novel idea to community psychology; it is arguably the dominant insight of the field" (p. 245).

The historical context of social turmoil and protest underlying the creation of the field in the 1960s is currently reflected in ongoing work and represents a continuity of commitment over time. Scholars such as Prilleltensky (e.g., Prilleltensky & Prilleltensky 2006) and Watts (e.g., Watts & Flanagan 2007) provide a sociopolitical perspective on local ecology and guidelines for community interventions aimed at the elimination of oppression and promotion of social justice. The ongoing salience of such concepts as empowerment

(Rappaport 2005) as a value, process, and intended outcome of much community research and intervention further reflects this sociopolitical tradition. The historical concern with marginalized groups and diversity is reflected in the wide variety of community settings and populations with which community psychologists currently work, including domestic violence organizations (Townsend & Campbell 2007), refugee resettlement settings (Birman et al. 2008), organizations providing services related to HIV/AIDS (Miller 2008), Native American communities (Mohatt et al. 2006), lesbian, gay, bisexual, transgender (LGBT) organizations and populations (D'Augelli 2006), rural African American families (Kohn-Wood & Wilson 2005), and individuals with disabilities (McDonald et al. 2007). In addition, the increasing international visibility of community psychology (Reich et al. 2007) is furthering an appreciation of community research and intervention across a wide range of cultural ecologies.

Previous reviews have addressed both the action-oriented commitments of the field and its concern with assessing high-impact social contexts and their effects on individuals. Reppucci et al. (1999) continued the long-standing tradition of reviewing social, community, and preventive interventions, emphasizing violence prevention and the promotion of competence across the life span. More recently, Shinn & Toohey (2003) reviewed research on the "community contexts of human welfare," suggesting that psychologists have traditionally committed "context minimization error" by ignoring the enduring important influences of neighborhood and community contexts on human behavior.

The present review builds on these prior articles by providing a current portrait of the field that includes both community interventions and research on community contexts and people embedded in them. The review elaborates on the context minimization issue raised by Shinn & Toohey (2003) by adopting an ecological perspective that makes context a central organizing concept for both community research and intervention (Kelly 2006, Trickett 2005). Specific implications of an ecological perspective are illustrated in subsequent sections, beginning with recent discussions of philosophy of science and methods central to understanding people in context. Next, the review outlines work that portrays the ecology of lives lived in differing community contexts, followed by work on the assessment of contexts themselves and their effects on individuals. The role of culture in community research is then discussed, followed by the implications of an ecological perspective for community intervention, including a section on community response to such traumatic community events as natural disasters and terrorist attacks. A conclusion then provides a review and recommendations for future developments in the field. Each of these topics reflects the infusion of an ecological perspective throughout the field of community psychology.

PHILOSOPHY OF SCIENCE AND METHODOLOGICAL CONTRIBUTIONS

Philosophy of Science

Consistent with an ecological perspective is the notion that theories of behavior and research findings are themselves reflections of culture and context. This underscores the possibility that much social science knowledge may be particular, not universal, and "that many psychological theories may not hold across the range of environments in which ordinary Americans live their lives" (Shinn & Toohey 2003, p. 428). From an ecological perspective, the research task is to ascertain the range of applicability of any specific set of findings and to frame the issue of generalization through the question, "in what contexts would one not expect this finding to be replicated?"

Underlying this perspective is a contextualist worldview and epistemology. Tebes' (2005) paper on philosophy of science and the practice of community research provides an important recent statement refining earlier contextualist positions in the field (e.g., Kingry-Westergaard & Kelly 1990). Tebes asserts that although logical empiricism is no longer an appropriate framework for community psychology, it still dominates social and behavioral science. He suggests that contextualism is a potential advance over logical positivism, but one that runs the risk of devolving into utter relativism. Tebes recommends a modified contextualist perspective, which, after McGuire (1986), he calls "perspectivism." He summarizes its assumptions: "(a) since knowledge is situated and contextual, community science should be grounded in a perspectivist epistemology; (b) since all knowledge is imperfect and yields only an approximation of the 'truth', community science should emphasize hypothesis generation along with hypothesis-testing as a means to advance knowledge; (c) since different methods yield different approximations of the 'truth', community science should adopt a methodology based on critical multiplism, in which multiple methods are used to obtain the best approximation of the 'truth'; and (d) since it is essential for knowledge in community science to be applicable to a diverse array of people and settings, community science should balance its focus on internal validity with one that emphasizes external and ecological validity" (Tebes 2005, p. 214). Tebes' portrayal of knowledge as a context-dependent and multimethod search for theory that attempts to account for diversity across settings and people represents a quintessential articulation of an ecological perspective in the field.

Rappaport (2005) applies this contextualist/perspectivist philosophy to the development of science itself and how the social context in which it operates affects its methods, topics, and value assumptions. Asserting that "community psychology is (thank God) more than science," Rappaport cautions that the increasing interdependence between science and state, as exemplified by the role of external funding for university-based research, represents a cause for concern about the topics studied and the independence of knowledge gained. His concern is less with the conventional methods of science than about the degree to which such methods are typically devoid of any social critique. He cites the community psychology concern about social justice as an example of what is too often missing as a criterion for assessing the value of community research, and suggests that "our unique contribution is a self conscious social and professional analysis and critique that is both added to and changes our conventional science" (Rappaport 2005, p. 236). Here, the community psychology goal of social transformation informs the spirit and content of the work conducted within a contextualist/perspectivist philosophy of science.

Hess (2005) affirms that Rappaport's (2005) critique of science represents not a rejection of science per se but rather a sharpening of the question, "what kind of science should we be?" In support of the integration of ideology and research practice, Hess (2005) advocates the value of researcher openness to revising assumptions as one gets to know the world of the other; research that both embraces and examines ideology rather than research unilaterally driven by ideology; and, "by emphasizing the rich learning potential of any single encounter, a clearer epistemological justification for idiographic, narrative, and case-based research" (p. 247). Taken together, these papers suggest that community psychology is fully engaged in developing its epistemological perspectives and the ongoing task of making self-conscious the values underlying community research and practice. In this integration of epistemology and social values, the papers reinforce both the value of a contextualist/perspectivist philosophy of science and the assertion that the practice of community research and intervention is based on values reflected in method, content, and process.

Methodological Contributions

Complementing a contextualist/perspectivist philosophy of science are methodological advances that sharpen our ability to assess contexts and people in them. Luke (2005) suggests that the emphasis on traditional statis-

tical methods, such as regression, may have contributed to "context minimization error" by masking or distorting the diversity in and contextual embeddedness of data. As testament to the longevity of this issue, he quotes John Dewey: "I should venture to assert that the most pervasive fallacy of philosophic thinking goes back to neglect of context" (Luke 2005, p. 188).

Luke highlights four methods that promote an ability to capture context: multilevel modeling, geographic information systems, social network analysis, and cluster analysis. Multilevel modeling addresses the levels of context in which individuals are embedded, whereas geographic information systems provide a quantitative information base from which to assess community assets and health assessments. Network analysis involves relational rather than individual attribute data and can be institutional as well as individual, and cluster analysis involves cases rather than variables and can be used to describe heterogeneity in the data relating contextual variation to diverse outcomes. Each provides a way of capturing community context and, in so doing, helps address such basic community psychology questions as how "groups have been affected in specific ways by the economic, social, cultural, and physical situations in which they are embedded" (Luke 2005, p. 185).

Various recent research examples illustrate the value of such methods in assessing contextual influences. Allen (2005) conducted a multilevel analysis of community coordinating councils to disaggregate individual and council-level contributors to the perception of achieving council goals. She found that the setting climate, including the presence of shared mission, shared decision-making, and efficient and inclusive leadership, accounted for 20% of the perceived effectiveness of the council. Reflecting on the potential value of clustering cases rather than selecting out specific variables in research on intimate partner violence (IPV), Bogat et al. (2005) suggest that "the main tenet of this agenda is that causes, processes, and effects of IPV are person and context specific: therefore, results that relate variables to each other are of limited value if it can be shown that the processes that take place, the meaning of the variables, the profiles of the transgressors, and the women who experience IPV depend on time, environment and research design" (p. 49).

Although the approaches described above provide opportunities for advancing our knowledge about how to take context into account, they rest on a linear conception of cause-and-effect relationships. Such a conception is countered by a systems theory perspective described by Hirsh et al. (2007). Defining a system as "a functional whole, composed of a set of components, coupled together to function in a way that might not be apparent from the functioning of the separate component parts" (p. 240), Hirsh et al. (2007) starkly contrast the implicit linear world view underlying much psychological research with the assumptions necessitated by a systems perspective. "We continue to rely on methods that assume a very different kind of world than the one that is reflected in the settings in which we work. The unidirectional models we use to try to draw links between a set of variables and an outcome are not consistent with what we know about the complexity of the phenomena we hope to study. Rather than develop small scale models of what we believe actually happens over time, we willingly suspend our disbelief that an uncomplicated, linear, and unidirectional snapshot fairly represents those processes of interest as they actually seem to unfold" (Hirsh et al. 2007, p. 239). Developing such complex models and their appropriate analytic techniques represents a significant conceptual and methodological challenge.

An additional methodological advance involves an increasing appreciation that methods themselves are part of the ecology that influences the impact of community research. A graphic example is found in Foster-Fishman et al.'s (2005) use of Photovoice in a community development project. Photovoice is a participatory method whereby cameras and training are provided to individuals often neglected in decision-making processes who generate local photographs and dialogue about their significance. Semi-structured interviews with participants in a community-building project in Michigan found that the Photovoice process increased self-confidence, emergent critical awareness of their environment, cultivation of resources for social and political action such as enhanced relational networks and increased commitment to community, and emergent involvement as change agents.

Thus, on both quantitative and qualitative fronts, community psychology is furthering an appreciation of how to develop methods that respect and indeed illuminate the ways in which the ecological context affects the lives of individuals. Recent research provides evidence that methods themselves create phenomena in community research and intervention that need to be accounted for conceptually and pragmatically. However, recent work in this area also suggests that competing world views underlie the varied methodological contributions and that a critical next step involves the further elaboration of such perspectives as systems theory for research methods in the field.

ECOLOGY OF LIVES

The philosophy of science and method advances discussed above frame an ecological perspective on individuals in social context. Applied to individual lives, an ecological perspective draws attention to how individuals with diverse skills, resources, and worldviews cope with and adapt to their local community contexts. These contexts, in turn, consist of adaptive requirements for survival, local norms, cultural history, and environmental risk and protective factors such as poverty and accessible social supports.

To understand the ecology of lives, recent work in community psychology has followed at least two related paths. The first has been to embrace the descriptive value of qualitative research methods as ways of understanding how individuals in diverse ecologies make sense of their life circumstances. The second is to view the lives of individuals as composed of varied domain-specific contexts (Swindle & Moos 1992) and to assess the consistency and variability of behavior across life domains that call for different kinds of adaptive behavior. An ecological perspective draws attention to the interdependence of life domains, such that behavior in any one domain, such as "acting white" in school (Fordham & Ogbu 1986), may both reflect and affect behavior in other life domains of importance to the individual.

Qualitative Understanding

A rich example of the coping and adaptation perspective on individual lives is provided by Kidd & Davidson's (2007) qualitative study of the street lives of more than 200 multiracial homeless youth in urban centers. A moving portrait of strength and resilience is provided through the stories told by these youth, who tested, refined, adopted, or rejected the meaning systems made available to them in the challenges of life on the street. These systems, in turn, were dependent on the youths' particular background, street context, and learning process. As a consequence, the street experience varied widely across respondents. For example, the change to street life was viewed positively by some but not others; for many, it affected their sense of identity and their view of world, yet in differing ways. The authors stress the power of context in asserting that these youth are "rewriting. . . . the life narrative" (Kidd & Davidson 2007, p. 234) and that these adaptations reflect far more than surface adjustments to transitory situations.

The implications of this perspective for community intervention are richly described by De Jesus (2007) in addressing the role of community advocates working on HIV/AIDS among immigrant Cape Verdean women in the Northeastern United States. Her interviews with these women provide a multilayered ecological perspective on contextual barriers "limiting the effectiveness of individual-level HIV/AIDS prevention and intervention models" (De Jesus 2007, p. 121). For example, community stigma attached to AIDS and religious prohibitions against condom use affected willingness to disclose HIV status and seek help, and traditional gender identities suggested that, for these women, use of condoms, or requesting men to use condoms, "signals distrust, disrespect, or infidelity" (De Jesus 2007, p. 128). This perspectivist approach, and the potential lack of ecological congruence or fit between program models and the ecology of lives, was echoed earlier by Riger (2001). Citing feminist standpoint theory as a frame for understanding lives from the inside out, she states, "We may find that our interventions are a small part of people's lives and that multiple factors cause them to resist change. . . or that the program does not address people's current needs or that people experience our programs in ways that are different than what we intend" (Riger 2001, p. 71).

Life Domains Approach

In addition to qualitative work describing the lives in context of varied groups, community psychology research has contributed to an appreciation of how individual lives are composed of different life domains that have different demand characteristics. An elegant example of this approach to the ecology of lives is Pederson et al.'s (2005) study of more than 560 urban adolescents representing multiple racial and cultural groups. These authors assessed patterns of involvement and performance in six adolescent "contexts of competence" and subsequently determined the relationship of these patterns to the developmental outcomes of self-esteem, depression, and self-reported delinquency seriousness. Pederson et al.'s (2005) "contexts of competence" included the peer, academic, athletic, employment, religious, and cultural contexts. Findings emphasize the setting dependence of competence and suggest three overarching conclusions: "First, we conclude that it is viable and fruitful to conceptualize adolescent competence as holistic, multidimensional, and contextually based. Second, our results demonstrate the existence of multiple profiles of contextual competence among low income urban adolescents, contrary to dominant stereotypes about these youth. Third, high engagement in multiple contexts of adolescent development is associated with more adaptive psychological outcomes than engagement in one or fewer domains" (Pederson et al. 2005, p. 78). Their intervention recommendations include the value of engaging adolescents in multiple settings and fostering connections among those settings.

A life-domains perspective was also applied by Birman et al. (2002) and Coatsworth et al. (2005) to the acculturative tasks of immigrant adolescents. Birman et al. (2002) assessed the adaptive value of linguistic, behavioral, and identity acculturation of former Soviet adolescents' self-reported adaptive functioning in varied life domains such as peer and family relationships and school performance. Differing acculturative styles were adaptive in different adolescent life domains. For example, American identity and behavioral acculturation were related to several school outcomes, including higher overall grade-point average and increased sense of involvement in school, whereas a greater sense of Russian identity was related to greater parental support but increased psychological distress overall. A similar set of domain-specific findings for Hispanic immigrant youth was reported by Coatsworth et al. (2005): Different acculturative styles were related to adaptation across individual, peer, family, and school domains. Importantly, no single style predicted poor adaptation across all domains involved.

The ecology of lives perspective, then, provides a window into the coping and adaptation process of individuals occupying varied ecological niches. In addition, it suggests that an appreciation of everyday lives is a conceptual precondition for designing interventions relevant to the circumstances faced by individuals in their community context. It further promotes an exploration of how both qualitative and quantitative methods can contribute to an appreciation of local ecology expressed in multiple ecological levels of the community context. The relative paucity of this work at present needs to be remedied in future research on diverse populations living in varied community contexts.

ASSESSMENT OF CONTEXTS AND THEIR EFFECTS ON INDIVIDUALS

In addition to the ecology of lives, an ecological perspective in community psychology draws attention to the community context itself and high-impact social settings within the community. Focal questions here involve how to characterize such contexts, as well as what effects, both main and interactive, they have on individuals. Three themes predominate in recent community psychology literature: (*a*) measures to assess social/community settings, (*b*) within-setting processes that both describe the setting environment and affect individual behavior in the setting, and (*c*) research linking varied aspects of communities, such as extent of social disorganization or resident fear of crime, to individual outcomes.

Shinn & Yoshikawa (2008) provide a useful ecological template for each of these topics in their edited book on the power of social settings to influence youth development. The book is organized to reflect multiple levels of ecological influence on community life, with descriptions of efforts to assess and change settings ranging across levels of analysis from the classroom to the school to the community. For example, Russell & McGuire (2008) discuss ways of assessing school social climate and its effects on sense of school connection for LGBT high school students. At a community level, Fagan et al. (2008) describe the use of local epidemiological data gathered by community organizations to make decisions about where to locate intervention efforts.

Measurement of Social/Community Contexts

Recent work reflects multiple levels of analyses ranging from classroom to neighborhood. At the school classroom level, Pianta & Allen (2008) report on an observational scheme for assessing three aspects of school classrooms that are theoretically related to important student outcomes: relationship supports, competence supports, and relevance. Henry (2008) describes a comprehensive methodology for measuring classroom peer norms that includes both actual norms, defined as what participants think, and perceived norms, or what they think others think. In addition, it includes methods for assessing the level of approval and disapproval for certain behaviors and the degree to which these behaviors are regulated in class through approval or disapproval processes. Each of these advances in classroom-level measurement provides a framework for understanding and intervention at the classroom level.

At the school level, Mattison & Aber (2007) report the development of a high school racial climate measure. Racial climate is seen as a critical aspect of the school environment because racial stratification and racial discrimination affect perception of the opportunity structure of school and subsequent school investment by students. In two high schools with African American and white students, African American students viewed their schools as being less fair in their treatment of African American students and more in need of change as an institution. In addition, different dimensions of racial climate predicted different school outcomes, underscoring the value of viewing racial climate as a multidimensional construct. Also at the school level, Vieno et al. (2005) developed a self-report measure of democratic school climate, defined as a "social climate of fairness, participation, and expression" (p. 330). Using a sample of more than 4000 10- to 18-year-old students in 134 schools in northern Italy, Vieno et al. (2005) found a significant relationship of perceived democratic climate to sense of community at each level of data aggregation: individual, classroom, and school. These school-level studies provide support for viewing schools as multilevel settings not adequately captured by classroom-level assessments only.

Although it is relatively straightforward to define a classroom and a school, definitions of neighborhood are still contested. Nicotera (2007) provides an overview of the multiple ways neighborhoods have been defined, including census and other administrative data, windshield surveys, rating scales, structured/unstructured interviews and ethnographies, residents' written descriptions, photographs, drawings, and mixed-method constructions. Nicotera (2007) suggests that neighborhoods have been conceptualized as complex, multidimensional entities that encompass both objective and subjective elements as well as being subject to both proximal and distal influences. She nominates four general definitional categories—social composition, economic composition, social processes, and physical composition/resources—and argues that different methods are best suited for assessing different aspects of neighborhoods, with quantitative methods particularly useful for measuring structural features and qualitative methods stronger in terms of capturing process dynamics.

The multiplicity of definitions and means of assessing neighborhoods are fully borne out in recent community psychology literature. McWayne et al. (2007) used city-level administrative data to define neighborhoods. "Common factor analyses and multistage hierarchical cluster analyses (of 1801 block groups) yielded two dimensions (i.e., Social Stress, Structural Danger) and two typologies (i.e., Racial Composition, Property Structure Composition) of neighborhood context" (McWayne et al. 2007, p. 47). They conclude that their work supports the perspective of "ecological researchers [who] have posited that information on multiple dimensions of both the physical and social aspects of neighborhood could prove useful for understanding underlying processes of neighborhood effects on child development" (McWayne et al. 2007, pp. 47–48). Alternatively, Dupere & Perkins (2007) gathered data from adults in 50 neighborhoods defined empirically in terms of resident definitions and associations rather than administrative or census data. Kruger et al. (2007, p. 269) suggested a fluidity in defining neighborhoods, asserting that "it may also be appropriate to consider different neighborhood boundaries for different constructs" of interest to the researcher.

Thus, efforts at environmental assessment have recently been reported at the classroom, school, and community or neighborhood levels of the ecological context. The contested nature of how to define key ecological levels, such as neighborhood, and the multiple ways in which neighborhood is currently being defined reinforce prior issues raised by Shinn & Toohey (2003) about the importance of defining boundaries in neighborhood research. Kruger's (2007) assertion that neighborhood boundaries may be defined differently for different constructs further complicates this issue and makes it a prime conceptual target for future work.

Within-Setting Processes

Processes within key social settings in the community represent an important set of proximal ecological influences on individual behavior (Weinstein 2006). A general framework for assessing social settings and their processes is provided by Tseng & Seidman (2007). Viewing settings through the lens of systems theory, they identify three aspects that both define setting ecology and provide targets for subsequent setting-level change: social processes (transaction between two or more groups of people), resources (human, economic, physical, temporal), and organization of resources (how they are arranged and allocated). Tseng & Seidman (2007) propose that the nature and degree of resources and how resources are organized structure the social processes in settings, which in turn affects setting outcomes. Consistent with a systems framework, they view social processes as ongoing transactions between two or more people, shaped by individual roles in the setting, which have a temporal quality wherein behaviors, recalibrated based on feedback, become patterned or regularized over time. Such social processes include norms, relationships, and participation in activities.

An alternative theoretical framework, behavior setting theory, was employed by Brown et al. (2007) to assess setting dynamics in consumer-run organizations such as drop-in centers, support groups, advocacy groups, and other nonprofits. They found that increased organizational size negatively affected member participation and involvement in organizational decision making, thus decreasing the empowerment possibilities of the setting for members. They emphasize the importance of organizational roles as an aspect of setting dynamics underplayed in behavior setting theory, and suggest that within the same organization some roles may be overpopulated and others underpopulated.

Felton (2005) used narrative theory to describe the tone and spirit of an agency staffed and run entirely by mental health system consumers. Their agency narrative represents "a collective identity shared by members ... that embodies the group's core beliefs and values ... and affects the functioning of the community ... by defining community membership, securing commitment to community goals, and creating group cohesion" (Felton 2005, p. 374). Narrative themes, such as "mental illness can happen to anyone," and "recovery is possible," help staff define a coherent sense of mission, affect agency social climate, and provide a framework for clients' understanding of their situation (e.g., "I'm in recovery from my treatment") (Felton 2005, p. 383).

Ozer et al. (2008) and Way et al. (2007) described research on school processes. Ozer et al. (2008) assessed processes, events, and experiences that affected perceived sense of school connection among a group of ethnically diverse immigrant adolescents in high school. Overall, interactions indicating that students were cared about as people rather than only learners positively influenced their sense of school connection. This was manifested in teacher behaviors large and small, ranging from a clear and ongoing commitment to student learning to such seemingly simple acts as knowing students' names and following up on promises made at an earlier time. Temporal changes in middle school processes were documented by Way et al. (2007), who found that the perceived social climate of middle school became less positive over time for the same cohort of students, and that positive peer relationships declined more for boys than girls.

Within-setting processes related to race have also been recently addressed. Griffith et al. (2007) describe a "Dismantling Racism" project in a Southern public health department. Their framework focuses on institutional racism, expressed in such processes as hiring and promotion, organizational climate, and harmful individual acts by administrators who are unaware of how their behavior affects others. In his description of "race talk," Pollock (2008) found that the everyday inadvertent acts of educators can harm students of color in a public school. Pollock (2008) invokes the concept of "color-muteness," or inability to talk about race, as one that can negatively affect teachers and students alike, and he outlines various school processes that reflect it and that can be confronted to address race in more authentic and respectful ways.

Thus, community psychology has directed explicit attention to specific processes in high-impact social settings that are relevant to both individual well-being and organizational mission. The wide variety of processes outlined in recent research suggests that setting processes may be variable both across different types of settings and within the same settings over time. They may involve not only local issues but also larger national topics such as race. The assessment of such processes has been approached from multiple theoretical perspectives, such as systems theory and narrative theory. Together, they suggest that future work may benefit from multimethod and longitudinal assessments of how diverse types of settings in diverse communities function and change over time as a function of internal and external forces.

The Relationship of Community Contexts to Outcomes

In addition to describing important processes within social settings, community psychology has devoted considerable attention to assessing the effects of community contexts on individuals. Recent research adds to Shinn & Toohey's (2003) earlier integrative review of this literature.

Dupere & Perkins (2007), for example, reported neighborhood differences in how patterns of environmental stressors and social resources combined to affect the mental health of adults. Employing multilevel models for nested data (residents within blocks), they found that "in environments facing average levels of environmental stressors, higher levels of formal citizen participation are associated with better mental health outcomes, whereas in environments facing relatively high levels of stressors, low informal ties with neighbors are associated with better mental health outcomes" (Dupere & Perkins 2007, p. 117). Furthermore, the influence of neighborhood social ties differed across community settings such that "the positive impact of informal social ties found in advantaged predominantly white communities is not necessarily found in minority communities, and the protective effects of informal ties may even be reversed in those communities" (Dupere & Perkins 2007, p. 117).

Birman et al. (2005) studied the effects of community ethnic density on adolescent acculturation in a sample of demographically comparable former Soviet adolescents living in two communities: one ethnically dense, the other more multicultural and ethnically dispersed. Adolescents in the ethnically diverse community became more American over time than did those in the ethnically dense community, who were more likely to retain aspects of their Russian culture. In addition, a community-by-discrimination interaction showed that perceived discrimination at school was related to heightened Russian identity and lowered American identity only in the ethnically dense community, where the adolescents constituted 15% of the high school population. In the community where the adolescents were dispersed across several culturally diverse schools, there was no relationship between perceived discrimination and either Russian or American identity. The pattern of findings in the ethnically dense community is consistent with the "reactive identity" hypothesis, suggesting that identity is heightened as a reaction to discrimination that threatens identity. However, this pattern is community specific.

Two other studies provide complex and rich accounts of the effects of neighborhood ethnic composition on black and white adolescents. Wickrama (2005) conducted secondary analyses of approximately 16,000 adolescents participating in the National Study of Adolescent Health to assess the differential effects of family and community variables on black and white adolescent distress. Although being black was related to increased distress over and above family and community characteristics and their interactions, the role of the community ethnic composition was race specific. "Community composition (percentage of minorities) had a meager detrimental influence on the mental health of white adolescents, but it had a significant beneficial influence on the mental health of black adolescents after controlling for community poverty. In general, living in white-dominant neighborhoods is an important risk factor for depressive symptoms among black youth" (Wickrama 2005, p. 276).

One possible interpretation of the meager ethnic community effects for whites in Wickrama's study is the likelihood that few if any whites lived in black-dominated neighborhoods. However, Bolland et al. (2007) assessed the relationship of hopelessness to multiple adolescent risk behaviors in their study of African American, Caucasian, and mixed-race adolescents living in 13 high-poverty neighborhoods in Mobile, Alabama. In neighborhoods with a minority Caucasian population, African Americans had the lowest level of risk behaviors, with Caucasians reporting the highest substance use and mixed-race participants reporting the highest levels of violence. Furthermore, hopelessness was not a moderator of risk for African Americans but was a strong moderator for Caucasian youth for alcohol use and sexual intercourse, and with mixed-race youth for weapon carrying, weapon use, and sexual intercourse. Bolland et al. (2007) suggest that minority status per se in specific community contexts may create a negative person-environment fit,

and that Caucasians living in these contexts do not experience much protection by being part of a larger majority in general. Taken together, these two studies suggest the value of separating minority status as a contextual characteristic from minority status as an identity.

Finally, two studies (McWayne et al. 2007, Szapocznik et al. 2006) addressed the role of the physical environment of neighborhoods on child school outcomes. McWayne et al. (2007) found that kindergarten children living in neighborhoods composed primarily of semidetached or single-family homes had higher performance ratings in mathematics and language arts than did children from neighborhoods composed primarily of row homes. Szapocznik et al. (2006), assessing the diversity of use of city blocks in Little Havana, Miami, found that children, particularly males, from mixed-use blocks (blocks whose buildings serve multiple purposes, such as businesses located in proximity to residential housing), had the most optimal outcomes in school.

The emerging community psychology literature on the relationship of community contexts to outcomes thus continues to advance our understanding of how person-environment transactions in diverse communities have both main effects and interactive effects on a wide variety of outcomes. Effects on both children and adults have been found with respect to community physical characteristics, overall level of disadvantage, ethnic density, and level of community violence. Communities range from urban to rural and populations include multiple races and ethnicities, including immigrants. Outcomes range from mental health to acculturation processes to school performance. In particular, Bolland et al.'s (2007) finding that minority status in the local community predicts outcomes is of particular importance in affirming the power of local context to affect behavior.

CULTURE AND COMMUNITY PSYCHOLOGY

The issue of culture and cultural diversity is so deeply embedded in the spirit and history of community psychology that O'Donnell (2006) recently advocated the adoption of a cultural community psychology focusing explicitly on cultural diversity in community context. An ecological perspective on cultural diversity includes its expression across multiple levels of the community context, ranging from individuals to social settings to community norms and tradition. Snowden (2005) underscores the importance of understanding culture in local community context: "We need to further develop theoretically informed, empirically grounded bodies of knowledge on how community structures, norms, and processes operate in local communities and how they affect human well-being, especially in culturally diverse and ethnic minority communities" (p. 1).

Bond & Harrell (2006) outline three diversity principles that reflect the main themes recently reported in the broader community psychology literature: (*a*) that every community has multilayered cultural characteristics and diversity dynamics whose composition, characteristics, functioning, and interactions need to be understood; (*b*) that such understanding is contextualized understanding, reflecting historical events, patterns of change over time, the sociopolitical context, and the local setting; and (*c*) that in community research and intervention in varied sociocultural contexts, what we do has to reflect who we are culturally as well as professionally.

Community Psychology in Cross-Cultural Context

Although community psychology shares with other disciplines, such as cross-cultural psychology, a concern with how culture affects behavior, the cross-cultural work of community psychologists tends to represent the field's distinctive emphasis on social problems and issues. Shinn (2007), for example, provides a broad perspective on international homelessness, showing how the definition and rates of homelessness vary across countries, with homeless families much more prevalent in the United States than in Europe. She links these differen-

tial rates to European social policies that provide more generous resources and reflect a more empathic attitude toward social responsibility for homelessness than is present in the United States.

The broad international perspective outlined by Shinn (2007) provides a road map for investigating more specific cross-cultural comparisons that illuminate both consistency and variability in the expression of social problems across cultural contexts. For example, Munoz et al. (2005) identified three groups of homeless people in Madrid characterized by (*a*) economic problems, (*b*) health problems, abuse problems, and death of parent, and (*c*) accumulation of stressful life events in childhood and alcohol abuse. They found these subgroups similar to subgroups of homeless identified in the United States, suggesting both cross-cultural consistency and the need for differentiated interventions depending on subgroup. Milburn et al. (2006), on the other hand, reported different behavioral profiles of homeless youth in Australia and the United States, "reflecting differences in the effectiveness of service systems in the two countries in keeping youth with fewer problems out of homelessness" (p. 63). Although such a cross-cultural emphasis is only now emerging in community psychology literature, it signals an opportunity to learn about how culture is reflected not only in the identification of social issues but also in social policies present in varied countries. How these issues and policies at the country level are reflected in diverse communities in these varied countries represents an important emerging research agenda for the field.

Cultural History and Community Research

One aspect of ecological theory involves the ecological principle of succession (Kelly 1968), or how historical changes in the community context over time shape the current context and provide a trajectory for future community change. The specific implications of cultural history for community research and intervention are underscored by several recent papers. Messinger (2006) finds "history at the table" in a case study of problems that emerged during the planning of an antipoverty program in a rural Southern community and argues that understanding "local history is a vital component in planning and implementing social programs" (p. 283). Gone (2007) describes the current upsurge in Native American commitment to cultural preservation and revitalization as a response to the "shattering legacy of Euro-American colonialism. . . . on the cultural practices of indigenous societies" (p. 291). He outlines multiple implications of this history for both the creation and resolution of health disparities in Native American communities and suggests that "underutilization" of health clinics by Native Americans cannot be understood or altered in the absence of an appreciation of this history.

Mohatt et al. (2006) provide a rich example of the implications of Gone's perspective in research among Alaskan Native communities. Their emic investigation of factors that offer Alaskan Native youth protection from substance abuse in remote, rural, face-to-face kinship communities yielded a model that includes local cultural factors at multiple levels of the ecological context: community, family, and individual. Central to the model is the role of communal and historical trauma in disrupting cultural meaning systems and its intergenerational transmission. They emphasize that this broad cultural history has affected different Native American communities in different ways, calling for community-specific knowledge of how it is manifested in everyday life.

Another specific example of the power of cultural history is found in Rivera & Tharp's (2006) description of a Zuni Pueblo community's involvement in restructuring their children's school setting to better reflect culturally meaningful educational practices. The school focus is culturally compelling because of the historical role of government schools as a mechanism for obliterating Native American culture. Community surveys and focus groups were part of a community empowerment process designed to build consensus about the importance of meaningful instructional practices in Zuni pedagogy and Zuni culture. In a very different cultural context, Goodkind (2006) describes the development of a Learning Circles and Advocacy program for Hmong refugees founded on ecological and empowerment principles that provided a setting to validate Hmong identity and cultural knowledge as well as mutual learning between Hmong participants and college students. Each of the research projects outlined above reinforces the importance not only of understanding the role of cultural history as part of community ecology but the value of supporting its retention as an intervention objective.

Diversity Challenges and the Process of Community Research

Within an ecological perspective, the nature of the research relationship between researcher and community is part of the ecology. Because of this, attention is paid to such process issues as the development of trust, selection of relevant community collaborators, and discussions about how varied stakeholders should be included across varied aspects of the research process. This process emphasis is nowhere more prominent than in projects involving interactions between cultural groups and researchers from diverse cultural backgrounds. Many of these "diversity challenges" are found in Bond & Harrell's (2006) edited group of papers designed to redress the "scarcity of work that explores the subtleties, contradictions, and dilemmas that emerge as professionals attempt to put the valuing of diversity into action" (p. 157).

The stories in the papers range widely across groups, topics, and diversity issues. D'Augelli (2006) provides a moving description of the personal and professional challenges involved in being a gay community psychologist working in rural areas. Indeed, the very issue of how open to be about one's sexual orientation provides a diversity challenge to LGBT professionals. D'Augelli's (2006) description of his many efforts to develop a supportive community for LGBT students and faculty at his university clarifies the intimate connection between the personal and the professional, particularly when sociopolitical diversity issues are at stake. Furthermore, it underscores the role of courage and risk taking in such professional work.

Another predominant theme involves insider-outsider dynamics that arise when the researchers are themselves from the cultural community where the work is occurring. For example, Gone (2006) reports on the complexities of conducting work in an American Indian community of which he was a tribal member. The agenda was to develop a culturally appropriate intervention involving mental health services, work that required considerable cultural knowledge of such concepts as the cultural construal of self, wellness, healing, and spirituality. Even as a cultural insider who understood the importance of such concepts, Gone had to deal with his "outside" intervention role as one that fed into a history of colonization. Here, mental health services were seen as another effort to inflict assimilationist assumptions, this time of mental health and well-being, on Native Americans. In this complex insider-outsider situation, he was asked by an elder, "How does it feel to be an Apple Indian?" (red outside, white inside). Many other intercultural intricacies of community research and intervention are found in this compelling account of the complexities and communicative blunders of working across insider-outsider roles, even within a presumably shared cultural background.

The different twist to the insider-outsider issue was addressed by Brodsky & Faryal (2006) in their account of "qualitative, community-based research carried out by a U.S. researcher in Pakistan and Afghanistan with an underground Afghan women's humanitarian and political organization" (p. 311). Here, one author was an organization and cultural insider and the other an outside researcher from another culture. Both the underground nature of the organization and Afghan culture more gener-

ally promoted a norm of secrecy around organizational or personal information, severely constraining the outside researcher's ability to gather triangulated qualitative data and necessitating the development of clear need-to-know guidelines around the disclosing of information to the researcher. The joint but differential contributions of both authors to the project led them to conclude that "collaboration does not imply equal contribution to each component of a project, but rather recognition that diverse skills of both parties are necessary to the final product" (Brodsky & Faryal 2006, p. 318).

The telling of such diversity stories serves as a heuristic for theory development about the role of culture in community research and intervention. Stories such as those reported above portray a complex set of issues for community researchers of varied cultural backgrounds and serve as reminders that community research and intervention are affected by who the researchers are culturally as well as professionally. The stories further emphasize the importance of studying the process issues in community research as it is conducted in contrasting ecological contexts and by researchers from varied sociocultural backgrounds.

More generally, community psychology has paid particular attention not only to the role of culture as a deep and enduring worldview that shapes the meaning of events, interpersonal interactions, and relationships, but also to the complex and nuanced dynamics of intercultural contact between outside researchers/interventionists and the cultural practices of varied communities. The illustrative topics of cross-cultural community work, the shaping role of cultural history, and insider-outsider dynamics all move us toward a richer understanding of how cultural diversity is infused throughout all aspects of community research and intervention. Gathering additional stories from previously unheard sources represents an important next step in amplifying the experiential database on which community psychology can contribute to an understanding of cultural diversity.

COMMUNITY INTERVENTION: SYSTEMS THEORY, COMMUNITY CAPACITY, AND CONTEXT

One of the characteristics of community psychology is its dual emphasis on community research and community intervention. Prior Annual Review chapters written by community psychologists have summarized social, community, and preventive interventions (e.g., Reppucci et al. 1999). The ecological perspective of the field, however, focuses less on specific programs and more sharply on how interventions are coupled with community contexts. Here, attention is drawn to such questions as how the social and cultural context can affect the definition and implementation of community interventions, how community organizations assess the relevance of outside evidence-based interventions for their particular setting and organizational mission, and how community organizations might be mobilized and coordinated to achieve a communitywide goal. In short, emphasis here is placed on contextual issues related to developing, implementing, and assessing community interventions that (*a*) emphasize intervention-community interdependence and/or (*b*) emphasize community-level outcomes and processes related to achieving those outcomes. Each of these contextual issues is well represented in recent community psychology literature.

The Ecological Context as a System: Systems Theory and Community Intervention

Because the intervention goal in community psychology addresses changes in the community contexts of individual behavior (Shinn & Toohey 2003), attention has recently been drawn to systems theory as a conceptual framework guiding community change. The rationale for this perspective is outlined by Foster-Fishman (2007b), who defines systems change as "an intentional process designed to alter the status quo by shifting and realigning the form and function of a targeted system" (p. 197). Foster-Fishman (2007) nominates several definitional properties of systems, including systems norms (attitudes, values, and beliefs), systems resources (human, social, economic, opportunity, and programmatic/organizational resources), systems regulations (policies, procedures, and routines), and systems operations (power and decision making). System assessment is viewed as a prelude to system intervention because it is necessary to understand how systemic conditions affect both intervention processes and goals.

Parsons (2007) provides an example of how system conditions affect both the possible and the desirable in terms of systemic change efforts. Where internal agreement and certainty are high among system components, the system is stable, organized, and predictable. Here, the change process is likely to be slow and incremental. At the other end, however, the system is operating at a state of "far from equilibrium." In this ecological context, small occurrences may have large and unanticipated consequences, and "if a system is to make a significant change from its status quo, the changes are likely to come from creative self-organizing rather than from planned change" (Parsons 2007, p. 407). Thus, system conditions suggest not only what needs intervention but also from where the impetus for change should come.

Several recent studies apply a systems perspective to the development of community collaboratives "hypothesized to effect systems change through their ability to simultaneously engage and mobilize multiple constituents and sectors of the system to work in a coordinated and value-added manner" (Kreger et al. 2007, p. 306). For example, Emshoff et al. (2007) employ systems thinking to describe community collaboratives working to improve health and reduce health disparities. Systems thinking was also used to capture systems-level activities and impacts of mental health consumer organizations (Jansen et al. 2007) as well as promoting systems change in the response of health care organizations to domestic violence (Allen et al. 2007).

A compelling example of how systems theory can be integrated with the empowerment agenda of the field is found in Hirsh et al.'s (2007) work in the area of school reform. After describing key systems theory concepts, they outline a participatory process to develop a model of the system in which reform will occur. The model building includes both scientists and local stakeholders who occupy different roles and thus bring local as well as scientific knowledge to the model-building process. Both the process of model development and the model itself promote collaborative anticipatory thinking about the systemic consequences of varied potential social change efforts while simultaneously identifying underlying causal structures amenable to intervention.

The emergence of systems thinking applied to community collaborations and setting level change represents a promising conceptual direction in illuminating how interventions may be designed as events in systems (Hawe et al. 2008). Such an emphasis reinforces the importance of understanding the community as prelude to any effort to affect it.

Building Community Capacity/Resources

From an ecological perspective, community capacity building is defined in terms of efforts to increase local resources for current and future problem solving or community betterment. Capacity may be expressed in multiple ways and at varied ecological levels of the community context. Illustrative examples in recent community psychology literature include (*a*) efforts to increase the capacity of community organizations, and (*b*) increasing capacity at the community level.

Organizational capacity. At the organizational level, recent research has addressed both local indigenous efforts undertaken by organizations to improve their functioning as well as efforts to improve capacity through the introduction of externally developed programs.

Indigenous efforts to increase capacity. Several specific strategies to enhance capacity of local service organizations and universities have been recently reported. With respect to changes in organizational mission and climate, Uttal (2006) describes how a social service agency serving a large number of Latino immigrants engaged in an action research project to transform its organizational culture from a philosophy of individual treatment to one emphasizing community involvement and attitude change about local responsibility for child rearing. This philosophy was operationalized not only in the development of culturally appropriate training for community members but also in addressing structural issues such as local racism and a critical analysis of how cultural values and traditions could be reflected in the new mission of community involvement. Cauce (2007) describes an action research initiative at the University of Washington to build capacity in the work environment through a collaborative process addressing four aspects of campus ecology: leadership and empowerment, support and resources, climate for diversity, and senses of community and satisfaction. Diverse task forces gathered, analyzed, and fed back information to the University community, and subsequent data-driven action steps were taken. Each of these efforts reflects a definition of capacity that includes an appreciation of organizational mission and improving the quality of life through change at multiple organization levels.

Capacity building through the implementation of externally developed programs. An additional series of papers reflect on the notion that capacity building can be fostered through the introduction of externally developed programs into existing community organizations. The evidence-based practice movement represents one example of this approach. As previously described, an ecological perspective views interventions as events in systems (Hawe et al. 2008). How organizations as systems respond to the introduction of externally developed interventions is a question that has received considerable recent attention in the field. For example,

Gregory et al. (2007) show how school climate affected the level and rate of change in implementation of a multisite violence-prevention program. They found that teacher-reported support between staff and among teachers and students predicted higher average levels of implementation, whereas teacher-reported administrative leadership predicted greater growth in implementation. These differentiated findings lead Gregory et al. (2007) to call for "an ecological perspective on program implementation in school settings—a perspective that can be missed by interventionists who stay within the classroom walls" (p. 258).

Townsend & Campbell (2007) adopt an alternative perspective on organizational forces affecting program implementation. Their qualitative study of 16 organizations offering rape prevention programs assessed why these programs tended to adopt homogeneous practices over time regardless of their effectiveness. They suggest that the push for organizational homogeneity reflects a survival response to the uncertainty of the organizational field. When there is uncertainty over whether organizations can get the resources they need to survive, the tendency is to adopt practices that provide legitimacy without necessarily improving performance.

These specific examples are complemented by Miller & Shinn's (2005) broad perspective on why the program development–program dissemination model of increasing organizational capacity has had, thus far, limited success. They note that the development–dissemination model often leads to a mismatch of what scientists develop and what organizations can implement and that, ecologically speaking, it ignores the degree of congruence among community, organizational, and program values that can facilitate or undermine program success. Furthermore, they suggest that a "pro-innovation bias" minimizes the potential value of ongoing indigenous practices that may already be working, and that the development–dissemination model assumes a naïve and simplistic model of organizational decision making that lacks appreciation of organizational ecology. In their paper, Miller & Shinn (2005) highlight the costs to

capacity building of not adopting an "events in systems" perspective on the introduction of externally developed programs into ongoing organizations.

As one alternative, Miller & Shinn (2005) propose that community psychologists should learn from communities by locating and studying successful indigenous programs. This call is reflected in a recent study by Birman et al. (2008). Rather than beginning with evidence-based practice, Birman et al. (2008) gathered "practice-based evidence" from an existing comprehensive, community-based mental health program for refugees. Through a collaborative assessment process of program structure and philosophy, measures of client progress were developed to assess the effectiveness of services provided to 97 children who spoke 26 different primary languages. The extensive description of the flexible service model titrated to specific client situations and the evidence on overall client improvement serve as an example of studying indigenous practices that have some demonstrated effects and are, by definition, sustainable.

Community capacity. At the community level, the meaning of capacity building has taken multiple forms. Two recent examples include efforts to understand conditions affecting community mobilization and the creation of supportive community contexts that enable successful behavior change.

Community capacity as community mobilization potential. Foster-Fishman et al. (2007a) assess the conditions under which local residents become involved in individual activism and neighborhood collective action in a community-building initiative in Battle Creek, Michigan. They define community capacity as the degree to which a context has structures and processes in place to help mobilize residents for action—the interaction of human, organization, and social capital. Results from a random-digit-dial phone survey suggest that "resident perceptions of neighborhood readiness (i.e., hope for the future and collective efficacy) and capacity for change (i.e., social ties and neighborhood leadership), and the level of neighborhood problems were strongly related to whether and how much residents were involved. Moreover, different elements of these neighborhood conditions were more or less important depending on the type and level of resident involvement" (Forster-Fishman et al. 2007, p. 91). Their data suggest that the definition and level of community capacity shift depending on the community intervention goals for which capacity development is needed.

Community capacity building as creating a supportive community context. Another pathway to community capacity building is through mobilizing varied sectors of the community relevant to specific community issues. Campbell et al. (2007) provide an elegant example of this approach in their report of an HIV/AIDS community building project in South Africa. The work is predicated on the "growing recognition that the implementation of discrete programs aimed at delivering services to vulnerable groupings is likely either to fail, or not be sustained in the long run, if the surrounding context and supporting systems do not shift in ways that support the goals of program efforts" (p. 348). This project focuses on promoting collaborative and supportive relationships among community members to achieve sexual behavior change, reducing stigma associated with HIV/AIDS, supporting those living with AIDS and their caregivers, enlisting the cooperation of local agencies and volunteers, and increasing access to health services and welfare grants. Capacity is reflected in how these targeted change efforts affect the development of six psychosocial resources needed to develop an AIDS-competent community: (*a*) knowledge and skills, (*b*) safe social spaces, (*c*) ownership of and responsibility for dealing with the problem, (*d*) confidence in local strengths and identifying them, (*e*) solidarity or "bonding social capital," viewing social capital as shaped by economic political factors such as poverty and gender, and (*f*) bridging partnerships with networks and agencies outside the community. These

measurable goals are approached through an empowerment and community-based participatory research perspective. In both studies community capacity is reflected in the creation or development of structures, processes, and networks of relationships that promote organized action with respect to community issues.

An ecological community psychology perspective on community intervention, then, focuses on how interventions are coupled with the host settings, how factors in the community or setting context affect the relevance, fidelity, and impact of such interventions, and how, through collaborative relationships, local practices can be better understood and built upon as a community resource. In so doing, the concept of intervention is broadened from a focus on specific programs or activities to a more systemic perspective that views any specific intervention as an "event in system" inclusive of both the requirements of the intervention and the culture, resources, and hopes of the organizations or communities involved.

COMMUNITY INTERVENTION AND DISASTERS

A particularly salient community psychology concern involves a community-level perspective on understanding and responding to the multiple effects of both natural and human-made disasters. One sweeping multilevel framework is provided by Hobfoll et al. (2007), whose communitywide response framework is designed to address five essential intervention goals: sense of safety, calming, sense of self- and community-efficacy, connectedness, and hope. The intent is not to promote specific intervention models because of the heterogeneity of traumatic events and their effects in varied community contexts; rather, the authors provide principles to be flexibly applied depending on the particular ecology of the disaster. Across ecological levels of the community context, interventions are designed to counter the predictable loss of personal, social, and economic resources related both to the immediate reaction to traumatic events as well as recovery in the aftermath. As Hobfoll et al. (2007) state, "The advantage of a community model over the individual. . . . is that the group (e.g., mosque, school, business organization, chamber of commerce, Rotary Club) can develop hope-building interventions such as helping others clean up and rebuild, making home visits, organizing blood drives, and involving members of the community who feel that they cannot act individually because of the magnitude of the problem" (p. 300).

Norris et al. (2005) provide a vivid example of the relevance of a community-level analysis in their report on the effects of a natural disaster, Mexico's 1999 flood, on social support and social embeddedness (quantity and types of relationships with others). Following these processes through repeated assessments of flood victims across a 24-month period in two Mexican communities, they test the hypothesis that although the typical post-trauma coping strategy involves the mobilization of supports, over time support deterioration occurs because need exceeds supply. Although support mobilization and deterioration patterns differed depending on the degree of personal and community-wide collective trauma, deterioration of support was far greater in one community than the other and the difference increased over time. Norris et al. (2005) suggest the concept of "community resilience" in assessing community capacity to mobilize local resources that can affect individual response to traumatic events. The careful approach to developing culturally relevant instruments, the large sample size, and the thorough analytic strategy make this study an exemplar of a community-level approach to the study of natural disasters.

Other studies report on community factors influencing response to terrorism. Hausman et al. (2007) employed a random-digit-dialing procedure to assess neighborhood social capital as a mediating factor in individual preparedness and concerns about terrorism. Social capital was measured in terms of community participation and involvement, extent of local social networks, and trust and reciprocity in the neighborhood. Here, the greater the perceived neighborhood social capital, the greater the preparedness and the greater the concerns about terrorism. Evan-Chen et al. (2007), drawing on Hobfoll's (1998) conservation-of-resources theory, found that although adolescent exposure to terrorism in Israel increased violent behavior, these effects were buffered in the presence of environmental resources.

Thus, community-level factors have become increasingly prominent in work on responses to natural and human disasters. This work supports the value of adopting a communitywide and community-specific perspective in both an assessment of factors influencing individual and community-level responses to disasters and in designing community interventions that assess, draw on, and, where necessary, augment community resources to ameliorate individual difficulties.

CONCLUSION

Community psychology has historically represented one effort to move from a psychology of the individual to a psychology of the individual in community context. The present review examines recent developments within this broad agenda. The evolution of contextualist/perspectivist philosophies of science represents one aspect of the broader movement in the field. The commitment to viewing science and practice as value laden has been represented in its assessment of community psychology as "more than science" and in its efforts to promote social justice and citizen empowerment in varied sociocultural community contexts. Throughout the literature is the repeated affirmation of the interdependence of research and practice, with each informing the other.

The ecological perspective underlying the present review represents one conceptual framework for directing and organizing this community psychology agenda. The shift to an ecological perspective has, over time, led to investigations illuminating the ecology of lives; it is reflected in efforts to characterize both the community context and the high-impact settings it includes, such as schools; it has led to an appreciation of how deeply cultural history and current traditions are reflected in community life, and it has been reflected in activities designed to increase the quality and quantity of community resources through such activities as capacity building and other collaborative approaches to working with rather than in communities. As such, it represents an integration of social values, appreciation of levels of analysis of local ecology on behavior, and a commitment to process and relationship building as prelude to and participation in community change efforts across multiple cultural communities.

Future Directions

The work reviewed above represents not only significant intellectual progress in furthering work in community psychology; it also provides a framework for much-needed future developments. Advances in multilevel statistical and methodological approaches to studying the complexities of community life need to be complemented with additional efforts to unravel methods for studying social systems that reflect a nonlinear understanding of behavior. Designs for conducting research and intervention with small samples such as specific refugee groups (Birman et al. 2008) and Alaska Native communities (Mohatt et al. 2006), or under circumstances such as natural disasters that preclude the possibility of highly controlled intervention trials (Hobfoll et al. 2007), need further exploration. The various definitions of key concepts such as collaboration (Trickett & Espino 2004) and neighborhood (Dupere & Perkins 2007, Kruger et al. 2007) have sharpened the need to deconstruct such commonly used, though not consensually defined, terms. Reports of conducing community research and interventions in varied sociocultural communities has brought to the fore the need to develop better process models for approaching and documenting the relationship between outsiders and insiders in community research (Brodsky et al. 2006) as well as the effects of that relationship on the validity of knowledge gained and the social impact of the work itself. Finally, though only modestly represented in the current review, there is an increasing international movement in community psychology (Reich et al. 2007). The emergence of research from other countries can only increase the field's appreciation for how culture, context, and community shape our behavior and provide the reference point for our efforts to learn about and be useful to communities. Together, these areas of future work provide a road map for furthering an ecological understanding of individuals and intervention in community context.

DISCLOSURE STATEMENT

The author is not aware of any biases that might be perceived as affecting the objectivity of this review.

ACKNOWLEDGMENTS

The author thanks Susan Fiske, Dina Birman, Robin Lin Miller, and James Kelly for their helpful comments on earlier drafts of this review.

LITERATURE CITED

Allen N. 2005. A multi-level analysis of community coordinating councils. *Am. J. Community Psychol.* 35(1/2):49–64

Allen N, Lehrer A, Mattison E, Miles T, Russell A. 2007. Promoting systems change in the health care response to domestic violence. *J. Community Psychol.* 35(1):103–20

Bennett C, Andreson L, Cooper S, Hasol L, Klein D, Rosenblum G. 1966. *Community Psychology: A Report of the Boston Conference on the Education of Psychologists for Community Mental Health*. Boston, MA: Boston Univ. Press

Birman D, Beehler S, Harris E, Everson ML, Batia K, et al. 2008. International Family, Adult, and Child Enhancement Services (FACES): a community-based comprehensive services model for refugee children in resettlement. *Am. J. Orthopsychiatry* 78:121–32

Birman D, Trickett EJ, Buchanan R. 2005. A tale of two cities: replication of a study on the acculturation and adaptation of immigrant adolescents from the former Soviet Union in a different community context. *Am. J. Community Psychol.* 35(1–2):87–101

Birman D, Trickett EJ, Vinokurov A. 2002. Acculturation and adaptation of Soviet Jewish refugee adolescents: predictors of adjustment across life domains. *Am. J. Community Psychol.* 30(5):585–607

Bogat G, Levendosky A, von Eye A. 2005. The future of research on intimate partner violence: person-oriented and variable-oriented perspectives. *Am. J. Community Psychol.* 36(1–2):49–70

Bolland J, Bryant C, Lian B, McCallum D, Vazsonyi A, et al. 2007. Development and risk behavior among African-American, Caucasian, and mixed-race adolescents living in high-poverty inner-city neighborhoods. *Am. J. Community Psychol.* 40(3/4):230–49

Bond M, Harrell S. 2006. Listening to diversity stories: principles for practice in community research and action. *Am. J. Community Psychol.* 37(3–4):365–76

Brodsky A, Faryal T. 2006. No matter how hard you try, your feet still get wet: insider and outsider perspectives on bridging diversity. *Am. J. Community Psychol.* 37(3–4):311–20

Brown L, Shepherd M, Wiruk S, Meissen G. 2007. How settings change people: applying behavior setting theory to consumer-run organizations. *J. Community Psychol.* 35(3):399–416

Campbell C, Nair Y, Maimane S. 2007. Building contexts that support effective community responses to HIV/AIDS: a South African case study. *Am. J. Community Psychol.* 39(3/4):347–64

Cauce A. 2007. Bringing community psychology home: the leadership, community, and values initiative. *Am. J. Community Psychol.* 39(1/2):1–12

Coatsworth JD, Maldonado-Molina M, Pantin H, Szapocznik J. 2005. A person-centered and ecological investigation of acculturation strategies in Hispanic immigrant youth. *J. Community Psychol.* 33(2):157–74

D'Augelli AR. 2006. Coming out, visibility, and creating change: empowering lesbian, gay, and bisexual people in a rural university community. *Am. J. Community Psychol.* 37(3/4):203–10

De Jesus M. 2007. HIV/AIDS and immigrant Cape Verdean women: contextualized perspectives of Cape Verdean community advocates. *Am. J. Community Psychol.* 39(1/2):121–32

Dupere V, Perkins D. 2007. Community types and mental health: a multilevel study of local environmental stress and coping. *Am. J. Community Psychol.* 39(1/2):107–20

Emshoff J, Darnell A, Darnell D, Erickson S, Schneider S. 2007. Systems change as an outcome and a process in the work of community collaboratives for health. *Am. J. Community Psychol.* 39(3/4):255–68

Evan-Chen M, Irzhaky H. 2007. Exposure to terrorism and violent behavior among adolescents in Israel. *J. Community Psychol.* 35(1):43–55

Fagan A, Hawkins JD, Catalano R. 2008. Using community epidemiologic data to improve social settings: the Communities that Care prevention system. See Shinn & Yoshikawa 2008, pp. 292–312

Felton B. 2005. Defining location in the mental health system: a case study of consumer-run agency. *Am. J. Community Psychol.* 35(1/2):373–86

Fordham S, Ogbu J. 1986. Black students' school success: coping with the "burden of acting white." *Urban Rev.* 18(3):176–206

Foster-Fishman P, Cantillon D, Pierce S, Van Egeren L. 2007a. Building an active citizenry: the role of neighborhood problems, readiness, and capacity for change. *Am. J. Community Psychol.* 39(1/2):91–106

Foster-Fishman P, Nowell B, Deacon Z, Nievar A, McCann P. 2005. Using methods that matter: the impact of reflection, dialogue, and voice. *Am. J. Community Psychol.* 36(3–4):275–91

Foster-Fishman P, Nowell B, Yang H. 2007b. Putting the system back into systems change: a framework for understanding and changing organizational and community systems. *Am. J. Community Psychol.* 39(3/4):197–216

Gone J. 2006. Research reservations: response and responsibility in an American Indian community. *Am. J. Community Psychol.* 37(3/4):333–40

Gone J. 2007. "We never was happy living like a whiteman": mental health disparities and the postcolonial predicament of American Indian communities. *Am. J. Community Psychol.* 40(3/4):290–300

Goodkind J. 2006. Promoting Hmong refugees' well-being through mutual learning: valuing knowledge, culture, and experience. *Am. J. Community Psychol.* 37(1–2):77–93

Gregory A, Henry D, Schoeny M. 2007. School climate and implementation of a preventive intervention. *Am. J. Community Psychol.* 40(3–4):250–60

Griffith D, Mason M, Yonas M, Eng E, Jeffries V, et al. 2007. Dismantling institutional racism: theory and action. *Am. J. Community Psychol.* 39(3/4):381–92

Hausman A, Becker J, Brawer R. 2007. Identifying value indicators and social capital in community health partnerships. *J. Community Psychol.* 33(6):691–703

Hawe P, Shiell A, Riley T, Pattison P. 2008. Theorizing interventions as events in systems. *Am. J. Community Psychol.* In press

Henry D. 2008 Changing classroom social settings through attention to norms. See Shinn & Yoshikawa 2008, pp. 40–57

Hess J. 2005. Scientists in the swamp: narrowing the language-practice gap in community psychology. *Am. J. Community Psychol.* 35(3–4):239–52

Hirsh G, Levine R, Miller R. 2007. Using systems dynamics modeling to understand the impact of social change initiatives. *Am. J. Community Psychol.* 39(3/4):239–54

Hobfoll S. 1998. *Stress, Culture, and Community: The Psychology and Philosophy of Stress.* New York: Plenum

Hobfoll S, Watson P, Bell C, Bryant R, Brymer M, et al. 2007. Five essential elements of immediate and mid-term mass trauma intervention: empirical evidence. *Psychiatry* 70(4):283–315

Janzen R, Nelson G, Hausfather N, Ochacka J. 2007. Capturing systems level activities and impacts of mental health consumer-run organizations. *Am. J. Community Psychol.* 39(3/4):287–300

Kelly JG. 1968. Toward an ecological conception of preventive interventions. In *Research Contributions from Psychology to Community Mental Health*, ed. J Carter Jr, pp. 77–99. New York: Behav. Publ.

Kelly JG. 2006. *On Becoming Ecological: An Expedition into Community Psychology.* New York: Oxford Univ. Press

Kidd SA, Davidson L. 2007. "You have to adapt because you have no other choice": stories of strength and resilience of 208 homeless youth in New York City and Toronto. *J. Community Psychol.* 35(2):219–38

Kingry-Westergaard C, Kelly J. 1990. A contextualist epistemology for ecological research. In *Researching Community Psychology*, ed. P Tolan, C Keys, F Chertok, L Jason, pp. 23–32. Washington, DC: Am. Psychol. Assoc.

Kohn-Wood L, Wilson M. 2005. The context of caretaking in rural areas: family factors influencing the level of functioning of seriously mentally ill patients living at home. *Am. J. Community Psychol.* 36(1–2):1–13

Kreger M, Brindis C, Manuel D, Sassoubre L. 2007. Lessons learned in systems change initiatives: benchmarks and indicators. *Am. J. Community Psychol.* 39(3/4):301–20

Kruger D, Hutchison P, Monroe M, Reischl T, Morrel-Samuels S. 2007. Assault injury rates, social capital, and fear of neighborhood crime. *J. Community Psychol.* 35(4):483–98

Luke D. 2005. Getting the big picture in community science: methods that capture context. *Am. J. Community Psychol.* 35(1/2):185–200

Mattison E, Aber M. 2007. Closing the achievement gap: the association of racial climate with achievement and behavioral outcomes. *Am. J. Community Psychol.* 40:1–12

McDonald K, Keys C, Balcazar F. 2007. Disability, race/ethnicity and gender: themes of cultural oppression, acts of individual resistance. *Am. J. Community Psychol.* 39(1/2):145–62

McGuire W. 1986. A perspectivist looks at contextualism and the future of behavioral science. In *Contextualism and Understanding in Behavioral Science*, ed. R Rosnow, M Georgundi, pp. 271–303. New York: Pergamon

McWayne C, McDermott P, Fantuzzo J, Culhane D. 2007. Employing community data to investigate social and structural dimensions of urban neighborhoods: an early childhood education example. *Am. J. Community Psychol.* 39(1/2):47–60

Messinger L. 2006. History at the table: conflict in planning in a community in the rural American South. *Am. J. Community Psychol.* 37(3–4):283–91

Milburn N, Rotheram-Borus MJ, Rice E, Mallet S, Rosenthal D. 2006. Cross-national variations in behavioral profiles among homeless youth. *Am. J. Community Psychol.* 37(1–2):63–76

Miller RL, Kobes S, Forney J. 2008. Building the capacity of small community-based organizations to better serve youth. See Shinn & Yoshikawa 2008, pp. 173–91

Miller RL, Shinn M. 2005. Learning from communities: overcoming difficulties in dissemination of prevention and promotion efforts. *Am. J. Community Psychol.* 35:169–83

Mohatt G, Trimble J, Dickson R. 2006. Psychosocial foundations of academic performance in culturally based education programs for American Indian and Alaska native youth: reflections on a multidisciplinary perspective. *J. Am. Indian Educ.* 45(3):38–59

Munoz M, Panadero S, Santos EP, Quiroga MA. 2005. Role of stressful life events in homelessness: an intragroup analysis. *Am. J. Community Psychol.* 35(1–2):35–47

Nicotera N. 2007. Measuring neighborhood: a conundrum for human service researchers and practitioners. *Am. J. Community Psychol.* 40(1/2):26–51

Norris F, Baker C, Murphy A, Kaniasty K. 2005. Social support mobilization and deterioration after Mexico's 1999 flood: effects of context, gender, and time. *Am. J. Community Psychol.* 36(102):15–28

O'Donnell CR. 2006. Beyond diversity: toward a cultural community psychology. *Am. J. Community Psychol.* 37:1–7

Ozer E, Wolf J, Kong C. 2008. Sources of perceived school connection among ethnically diverse urban adolescents. *J. Adolesc. Res.* 23:438–70

Parsons B. 2007. The state of methods and tools for social systems change. *Am. J. Community Psychol.* 39(3–4):405–9

Pederson S, Seidman E, Yoshikawa H, Rivera A, Allen L, et al. 2005. Contextual competence: multiple manifestations among urban adolescents. *Am. J. Community Psychol.* 35(1/2):65–82

Pianta R, Allen J. 2008. Building capacity for positive youth development in secondary school classrooms: changing teachers' interactions with students. See Shinn & Yoshikawa 2008, pp. 21–39

Pollock M. 2008. An intervention in progress: pursuing precision in school race talk. See Shinn & Yoshikawa 2008, pp. 102–14

Prilleltensky I, Prilleltensky O. 2006. Promoting well-being: linking personal, organizational, and community change. New York: Wiley

Rappaport J. 2005. Community psychology is (thank God) more than science. *Am. J. Community Psychol.* 35(1/2):231–39

Reich S, Reimer M, Prilleltensky I, Montero M, eds. 2007. *International Community Psychology: History and Theories.* New York: Springer

Reppucci N, Wollard J, Fried C. 1999. Social, community, and preventive interventions. *Annu. Rev. Psychol.* 50:387–418

Riger S. 2001. Transforming community psychology. *Am. J. Community Psychol.* 29(1):69–81

Rivera H, Tharp R. 2006. A Native American community's involvement and empowerment to guide their children's development in the school setting. *J. Community Psychol.* 34(4):435–51

Russell S, McGuire J. 2008. The school climate for lesbian, gay, bisexual and trans-gender (LGBT) students. See Shinn & Yoshikawa 2008, pp. 133–49

Shinn M. 2007. International homelessness: policy, socio-cultural, and individual perspectives. *J. Soc. Issues* 63(3):657–77

Shinn M, Toohey S. 2003. Community contexts of human welfare. *Annu. Rev. Psychol.* 54:427–59

Shinn M, Yoshikawa H. 2008. *Toward Positive Youth Development: Transforming Schools and Community Programs.* New York: Oxford Univ. Press

Snowden L. 2005. Racial, cultural, and ethnic disparities in health and mental health: toward theory and research at community levels. *Am. J. Community Psychol.* 35(1/2):1–8

Swindle R, Moos R. 1992. Life domains in stressors, coping, and adjustment. In *Person-Environment Psychology,* ed. WB Walsh, K Craik, R Price, pp. 1–34. Hillsdale, NJ: Erlbaum

Szapocznik J, Lombard J, Martinez F, Mason C, Gorman-Smith D, et al. 2006. The impact of the built environment on children's school conduct grades: the role of diversity of use in a Hispanic neighborhood. *Am. J. Community Psychol.* 38(3–4):299–310

Tebes J. 2005. Community science, philosophy of science, and the practice of research. *Am. J. Community Psychol.* 35:213–30

Townsend S, Campbell R. 2007. Homogeneity in community-based rape prevention programs: empirical evidence of institutional isomorphism. *J. Community Psychol.* 35(3):367–82

Trickett EJ. 2005. Community interventions and HIV/AIDS: affecting the community context. In *Community Interventions and AIDS*, ed. E Trickett, W Pequegnat, pp. 3–27. New York: Oxford Univ. Press

Trickett EJ, Espino SR. 2004. Collaboration and social inquiry: multiple meanings of a construct and its role in creating useful and valid knowledge. *Am. J. Community Psychol.* 34(1–2):1–69

Tseng V, Seidman E. 2007. A systems framework for understanding social settings. *Am. J. Community Psychol.* 39(3–4):217–28

Uttal L. 2006. Organizational cultural competency: shifting programs for Latino immigrants from a client-centered to a community-based orientation. *Am. J. Community Psychol.* 38(3–4):251–62

Vieno A, Perkins D, Smith T, Santinello M. 2005. Democratic school climate and sense of community in school: a multilevel analysis. *Am. J. Community Psychol.* 36:327–41

Watts R, Flanagan C. 2007. Pushing the envelope on youth civic engagement: a developmental and liberation psychology perspective. *J. Community Psychol.* 35(6):779–92

Way N, Reddy R, Rhodes J. 2007. Students' perceptions of school climate during the middle school years: associations with trajectories of psychological and behavioral adjustment. *Am. J. Community Psychol.* 40(3/4):194–213

Weinstein R. 2006. Reaching higher in community psychology: social problems, social settings, and social change. *Am. J. Community Psychol.* 37(1/2):9–20

Wickrama K, Noh S, Bryant C. 2005. Racial differences in adolescent distress: differential effects of the family and community for blacks and whites. *J. Community Psychol.* 33(3):261–82

Leadership: Current Theories, Research, and Future Directions

Bruce J. Avolio,[1] Fred O. Walumbwa,[2] and Todd J. Weber[3]

[1] Department of Management, University of Nebraska, Lincoln, Nebraska 68588-0491; email: bavolio2@unl.edu

[2] Department of Management, The Arizona State University, Glendale, Arizona 85306-4908; email: fred.walumbwa@asu.edu

[3] Department of Management, University of Nebraska, Lincoln, Nebraska 68588-0491; email: tweber2@unl.edu

Annu. Rev. Psychol. 2009. 60:421–49

First published online as a Review in Advance on July 23, 2008

The *Annual Review of Psychology* is online at psych.annualreviews.org

This article's doi: 10.1146/annurev.psych.60.110707.163621

Key Words

authentic leadership, cognitive leadership, complexity leadership, cross-cultural leadership, new-genre leadership, shared leadership

Abstract

This review examines recent theoretical and empirical developments in the leadership literature, beginning with topics that are currently receiving attention in terms of research, theory, and practice. We begin by examining authentic leadership and its development, followed by work that takes a cognitive science approach. We then examine new-genre leadership theories, complexity leadership, and leadership that is shared, collective, or distributed. We examine the role of relationships through our review of leader member exchange and the emerging work on followership. Finally, we examine work that has been done on substitutes for leadership, servant leadership, spirituality and leadership, cross-cultural leadership, and e-leadership. This structure has the benefit of creating a future focus as well as providing an interesting way to examine the development of the field. Each section ends with an identification of issues to be addressed in the future, in addition to the overall integration of the literature we provide at the end of the article.

Contents

INTRODUCTION

One of our goals for this integrative review is to examine the ways in which the field of leadership is evolving and the consequences of its evolutionary path for the models, methods, and populations examined. For example, at the outset of the field of leadership, the primary focus was on studying an individual leader, who was most likely a male working in some large private-sector organization in the United States. Today, the field of leadership focuses not only on the leader, but also on followers, peers, supervisors, work setting/context, and culture, including a much broader array of individuals representing the entire spectrum of diversity, public, private, and not-for-profit organizations, and increasingly over the past 20 years, samples of populations from nations around the globe. Leadership is no longer simply described as an individual characteristic or difference, but rather is depicted in various models as dyadic, shared, relational, strategic, global, and a complex social dynamic (Avolio 2007, Yukl 2006).

We organize our examination of how leadership is evolving by discussing significant areas of inquiry that represent current pillars in leadership research, some understandably taller than others. We highlight the current state of each particular area of inquiry, and discuss what we know, what we don't know, and what remains interesting possibilities to pursue in future research. Given our space limitations, we focus more on the current state of these respective areas in terms of advances in theory, research, and practice, including the criticisms and boundaries of theories, models, and methods wherever appropriate. From this analysis, we offer some recommendations for future directions that the science of leadership could pursue, and we discuss the potential implications for leadership practice.

Looking back over the past 100 years, we cannot imagine a more opportune time for the field of leadership studies. Never before has so much attention been paid to leadership, and the fundamental question we must ask is, what do we know and what should we know about leaders and leadership? We begin addressing these questions not by going back to the earliest work in leadership, but rather by focusing on what is most current in the field. We then examine other areas from which the current work has emerged, rather than examining leadership material covered in recent reviews (Gelfand et al. 2007, Goethals 2005) or providing a comprehensive historical review of the field that is better left to the *Handbook of Leadership* (Bass & Bass 2008; see also Yukl & Van Fleet 1992).

OVERVIEW OF AUTHENTIC LEADERSHIP

One of the emerging pillars of interest in the field of leadership has been called authentic leadership development. As discussed in a special issue [edited by Avolio & Gardner (2005)] of the *Leadership Quarterly* on this topic and in an earlier theoretical piece by Luthans & Avolio

(2003), the advent of work on authentic leadership development came as a result of writings on transformational leadership, in which authors such as Bass & Steidlmeier (1999) suggest that there are pseudo versus authentic transformational leaders.

Luthans & Avolio (2003) also introduced the concept of authentic leadership development into the literature with the goal of integrating work on (Luthans 2002) positive organizational behavior with the life-span leadership development work of Avolio (1999). Their main purpose was to examine what constituted genuine leadership development including what worked and didn't work to develop leaders and leadership, as well as to bring to the foreground some of the recent work in positive psychology as a foundation for examining how one might accelerate the development. Luthans and Avolio reasoned that using some of the theoretical work in positive psychology such as Fredrickson's (2001) broaden-and-build theory, they could offer a more positive way for conceptualizing leadership development. According to Fredrickson, those individuals who have more positive psychological resources are expected to grow more effectively or to broaden themselves and build out additional personal resources to perform. Luthans and Avolio report that to a large extent, the prior leadership development work was based on a deficit-reduction model strategy, where one discovered what was wrong with a leader and then worked to correct deficits in terms of focusing on the leader's development (also see Avolio & Luthans 2006).

Authentic Leadership Defined

First and foremost, the concept of authenticity has been around for a long time, as reflected in many philosophical discussions of what constitutes authenticity (Harter et al. 2002). George (2003) popularized authentic leadership in the general practice community when he published his book on the topic, as did Luthans & Avolio (2003) for the academic community. Luthans & Avolio (2003, p. 243) defined authentic

Authentic leadership: a pattern of transparent and ethical leader behavior that encourages openness in sharing information needed to make decisions while accepting followers' inputs

Transformational leadership: leader behaviors that transform and inspire followers to perform beyond expectations while transcending self-interest for the good of the organization

Positive organizational behavior: literature that is focusing on positive constructs such as hope, resiliency, efficacy, optimism, happiness, and well-being as they apply to organizations

Broaden-and-build theory: suggests positive emotions expand cognition and behavioral tendencies, and encourage novel, varied, and exploratory thoughts and actions

leadership as "a process that draws from both positive psychological capacities and a highly developed organizational context, which results in both greater self-awareness and self-regulated positive behaviors on the part of leaders and associates, fostering positive self-development." This definition and subsequent work on authentic leadership was defined at the outset as multilevel in that it included the leader, follower, and context very specifically in the way it was conceptualized and measured. This addressed a typical criticism in the leadership literature summarized by Yammarino et al. (2005, p. 10) who concluded, "relatively few studies in any of the areas of leadership research have addressed levels-of-analysis issues appropriately in theory, measurement, data analysis, and inference drawing."

At the same time, several scholars (e.g., Cooper et al. 2005, Sparrowe 2005) expressed concerns with Luthans & Avolio's initial definition of authentic leadership. The initial conceptual differences notwithstanding, there appears to be general agreement in the literature on four factors that cover the components of authentic leadership: balanced processing, internalized moral perspective, relational transparency, and self-awareness. Balanced processing refers to objectively analyzing relevant data before making a decision. Internalized moral perspective refers to being guided by internal moral standards, which are used to self-regulate one's behavior. Relational transparency refers to presenting one's authentic self through openly sharing information and feelings as appropriate for situations (i.e., avoiding inappropriate displays of emotions). Self-awareness refers to the demonstrated understanding of one's strengths, weaknesses, and the way one makes sense of the world. These four constructs were further operationally defined by Walumbwa and colleagues (2008). Walumbwa et al. (2008) provided initial evidence using a multisample strategy involving U.S. and non-U.S. participants to determine the construct validity of a new set of authentic leadership scales. Specifically, they showed the four components described above represented unique scales that were reliable.

These four scales loaded on a higher-order factor labeled authentic leadership that was discriminantly valid from measures of transformational leadership (e.g., Avolio 1999) and ethical leadership (e.g., Brown et al. 2005) and was a significant and positive predictor of organizational citizenship behavior, organizational commitment, and satisfaction with supervisor and performance.

Future Focus Required

Work on defining and measuring authentic leadership is in the very early stages of development. Future research will need to offer additional evidence for the construct validity of this measure or other measures, and it will also need to demonstrate how authentic leadership relates to other constructs within its nomological network. This would include constructs such as moral perspective, self-concept clarity, well-being, spirituality, and judgment. Moreover, there is a need to examine how authentic leadership is viewed across situations and cultures and whether it is a universally prescribed positive root construct—meaning it represents the base of good leadership regardless of form, e.g., participative, directive, or inspiring. In the next section, we turn our attention to the second major focus on authentic leadership, which incorporates the term development.

AUTHENTIC LEADERSHIP DEVELOPMENT

Up until very recently, one would be hard-pressed to find in the leadership literature a general model of leadership development (Luthans & Avolio 2003). Even more difficult to find is evidence-based leadership development. Specifically, what evidence is there to support whether leaders or leadership can be developed using one or more specific theories of leadership? This question led to a concerted effort to explore what was known about whether leaders are born or made, as well as the efficacy of leadership interventions.

Heritability and Leadership

One avenue of research that has explored whether leaders are born versus made has involved studying identical and fraternal twins. Preliminary evidence using a behavioral genetics approach has shown that approximately 30% of the variation in leadership style and emergence was accounted for by heritability; the remaining variation was attributed to differences in environmental factors such as individuals having different role models and early opportunities for leadership development (Arvey et al. 2007). Because identical twins have 100% of the same genetic makeup and fraternal twins share about 50%, this behavioral genetics research was able to control for heritability to examine how many leadership roles the twins emerged into over their respective careers. In this and subsequent research for both men and women across cultures, similar results were obtained. The authors conducting this research conclude that the "life context" one grows up in and later works in is much more important than heritability in predicting leadership emergence across one's career.

Examining Evidence for Positive Leadership Interventions

Lord & Hall (1992, p. 153) noted, "too much research in the past has attempted to probe the complex issues of leadership using simple bivariate correlations." It seems fair to say that although most models of leadership have causal predictions, a relatively small percentage of the accumulated literature has actually tested these predictions using controlled leadership interventions, especially in field research settings (Yukl 2006).

To determine whether experimental interventions actually impacted leadership development and/or performance, a qualitative and quantitative review of the leadership intervention (i.e., studies where a researcher overtly manipulated leadership to examine its impact on some specific intermediate process variables or outcomes) literature was undertaken

(see Avolio & Luthans 2006, Avolio et al. 2009, Reichard & Avolio 2005). The focus of this meta-analytic review was unique in that up to that point, more than 30 meta-analyses had been published on leadership research, none of which had focused on leadership interventions and more than one model of leadership. For each study, the leadership intervention examined was categorized into six types: training, actor/role-play, scenario/vignette, assignments, expectations, others. Reichard & Avolio (2005) reported that regardless of the theory being investigated, results showed that leadership interventions had a positive impact on work outcomes (e.g., ratings of leader performance), even when the duration of those interventions was less than one day. In terms of utility, participants in the broadly defined leadership treatment condition had on average a 66% chance of positive outcomes versus only a 34% chance of success for the comparison group.

Future Focus Required

Relatively little work has been done over the past 100 years to substantiate whether leadership can actually be developed. Indeed, based on the meta-analysis findings reviewed above, only 201 studies were identified that fit the intervention definition. Of those 201 studies, only about one third focused on developing leadership as opposed to manipulating it for impact through role plays or scripts to test a particular proposition in one of the various models.

One of the emerging areas of interest in leadership research, which we have dedicated more attention to in its own section, concerns the linkages between cognitive science and how leaders perceive, decide, behave, and take action (Lord & Brown 2004). For example, to develop leadership, it is imperative that we examine how a leader's self-concept and/or identity is formed, changed, and influences behavior (Swann et al. 2007). This raises a key question regarding what constitutes leaders' working self-concept and/or identity with respect to how they go about influencing others

(Swann et al. 2007). For example, does an authentic leader have a different working self-concept than someone who is described by followers as transformational or transactional, and how do these differences develop in the leader over time?

We know from previous literature that although a leader's working self-concept is constructed in the current moment, it is also based on more stable self-concepts and identities stored in the individual's long-term memory. Avolio & Chan (2008) indicate there are certain trigger events that activate the leader's working self-concept. These trigger events induce self-focused attention, self-assessment, and activate a leader's working self-concept. These trigger moments can occur naturally as the leader interacts with others during leadership episodes or they can be induced through formal training exercises and self-reflection (Roberts et al. 2005).

Another very promising area of research that has not received sufficient attention in the leadership literature focuses on understanding what constitutes an individual's level of developmental readiness or one's capacity or motivational orientation to develop to one's full potential. Prior authors have defined developmental readiness as being made up of components such as one's goal orientation (Dweck 1986) and motivation to develop leadership (Maurer & Lippstreu 2005). In this literature, the authors argue that leaders who are more motivated to learn at the outset and who have higher motivation to lead will more likely embrace trigger events that stimulate their thinking about their own development as an opportunity to improve their leadership effectiveness.

In sum, a great deal of energy and interest is emerging in the leadership development literature that suggests there will be a lot more activity in trying to discover what impacts genuine leadership development at multiple levels of analysis, from cognitive through to organizational climates. This literature will no doubt link to the life-span development and cognitive psychology literatures to fuel further work in this area.

COGNITIVE PSYCHOLOGY AND LEADERSHIP

The cognitive science leadership literature is an area of research and theory containing a wide range of approaches that are united by their focus on explaining the way leaders and followers think and process information. This literature includes a broad range of topics such as self-concept theory, meta-cognitions, and implicit leadership theory (e.g., Lord & Emrich 2000), which are addressed in more detail below.

One of the more recent developments in the literature has been an attempt to develop models of leadership cognition. Lord & Hall (2005) developed a model of leadership development that emphasized the leader's cognitive attributes or abilities. A second model was developed by Mumford et al. (2003) and examined the way shared thinking contributed to leader creativity. These two approaches illustrate a fundamental way in which views of leadership cognitions vary, with the former focusing on activities with the individual leader and the latter focusing on interactions that occur between individuals (Mumford et al. 2007). We examine several of the key emerging constructs within this literature, beginning with the self-concept.

Emerging Cognitive Constructs

Recent literature on what constitutes the self-concept has distinguished between the structure of the self-concept and its contents (Altrocchi 1999). The content refers to the evaluations one makes of oneself as well as self-beliefs. The structure refers to ways in which the self-concept content is organized for processing. In a study on the structure of the self-concept, Campbell et al. (2003) examined the competing arguments that one benefits from having either unity in self-concept or pluralism. Although the literature tends to treat the two as opposite ends of a continuum, their study showed they are not necessarily related to each other. This study further showed that two measures of pluralism (self-complexity and self-concept compartmentalization) were not related to each other and that multiple measures of self-concept unity, such as self-concept differentiation, self-concept clarity, and self-discrepancies, were moderately related to each other and that each had implications for leader development.

Lord & Brown (2001) presented a model examining two specific ways that leaders can influence the way followers choose to behave in terms of the motivations they use to regulate actions/behaviors. The first way relates to values (e.g., achievement) and emphasizes making specific values (or patterns of values) salient for the follower to motivate him or her to action. The second relates to the followers' self-concept, whereby the leader activates a specific identity to which followers can relate, creating a collective identity that the follower ultimately embraces as his or her own. Both values and self-concept are viewed as mediating the linkage between the leader's actions and the behavior of the follower.

Because there are a range of peripheral and core identities that could be salient to an individual at any one point in time, the question of which identities are activated at any time is relevant to research on leadership and its impact on followers. The idea of a working self-concept refers to the identity (or combination of identities) that is salient in the moment, and it consists of three types of components: self-views, current goals, and possible selves (Lord & Brown 2004). The self-view relates to the current working model or view of oneself, whereas the possible selves may represent the ideal model an individual may be striving for and something that could be leveraged by the leader to motivate and develop followers into better followers or leaders themselves. Overall, the working self-concept has the potential to provide insight into the challenging issue of how salient one's identity is and how leadership can enhance its salience, though its use within the leadership literature has been somewhat limited so far.

One of the essential building blocks in the cognitive leadership literature is the idea of a schema, which is a broad organizing framework that helps one understand and make sense of a given context or experience. One notable example of the use of schemas with respect to leadership research is the work of Wofford et al. (1998), who proposed a cognitive model to explain the way transformational and transactional leaders view work with followers. In their field study, Wofford et al. examined schematic processes (e.g., vision, follower, self) and scripts (behaviors associated with a schema), arguing that transformational and transactional leadership use different schemas to interpret events, which then results in the choice of different leadership behaviors/actions in response to those events. Support was found for transformational leader cognitions being related to the leaders' choice of acting transformationally. Mixed support was found for the relationships between transactional leader schemas and behaviors and actions chosen.

Prototypical Abstractions of Leadership

The leadership research on social identity formation has also focused heavily on what constitutes prototypicality, which has shown that followers may be more drawn to leaders who are exemplars of groups they belong to or want to join. Early research conceptualized prototypes as being relatively static and applicable in many situations. Recent work has contested that view, arguing that prototypes are dynamic and can be applied and adapted based on the existing constraints or challenges being confronted by leaders (Lord et al. 2001).

Subsequent research has also focused on the relationship between implicit leadership theories and several relevant performance outcomes (Epitropaki & Martin 2005). We note that for more than 25 years, a great deal of the work on cognitive psychology and leadership focused on how implicit theories and prototypes affected the perceptions of leaders and followers, generally examining how it disadvantaged or biased them in views of others. More recent trends in this literature coincide nicely with emphasis

Cognitive leadership: a broad range of approaches to leadership emphasizing how leaders and followers think and process information

Transactional leadership: leadership largely based on the exchange of rewards contingent on performance

now being placed on authentic leadership development. Specifically, research is now attempting to link how leaders think about events, choose to behave, and/or develop.

Future Focus Required

Cognitive approaches to investigating leadership draw heavily on several literatures described above. This broad stream of research has potential for enhancing existing theories of leadership in terms of helping to explain how leaders and followers attend to, process, and make decisions and develop. Additional work linking self-concept and meta-cognitive theories to research on leadership will no doubt contribute to our understanding of how leaders and followers actually develop. For example, if a leader has low self-concept clarity, to what extent can we expect that same leader to be self-aware? What are the implications for enhancing a leader's self-concept clarity or working self-concept about what constitutes the roles of effective leadership in developing that leader's self-awareness and performance?

NEW-GENRE LEADERSHIP

Although prior authors have focused on what constitutes charismatic, inspirational, and visionary leadership as far back as the early 1920s, much of the attention in the literature on these newer theories of leadership has come about over the past 25 years. Burns (1978) and Bass (1985) signaled the need to shift the focus of leadership research from predominantly examining transactional models that were based on how leaders and followers exchanged with each other to models that might augment transactional leadership and were labeled charismatic, inspirational, transformational, and visionary. The early work of Bass and Burns set the stage for distinguishing what Bryman (1992) referred to as more traditional theories of leadership versus what they termed new-genre leadership theories.

New-genre leadership: leadership emphasizing charismatic leader behavior, visionary, inspiring, ideological and moral values, as well as transformational leadership such as individualized attention, and intellectual stimulation

New-Genre Versus Traditional Leadership

Bryman (1992) commented, "There was considerable disillusionment with leadership theory and research in the early 1980s. Part of the disillusionment was attributed to the fact that most models of leadership and measures accounted for a relatively small percentage of variance in performance outcomes such as productivity and effectiveness. Out of this pessimism emerged a number of alternative approaches, which shared some common features..., collectively referred to as the new leadership" (Bryman 1992, p. 21). Unlike the traditional leadership models, which described leader behavior in terms of leader-follower exchange relationships, setting goals, providing direction and support, and reinforcement behaviors, or what Bass (1985) referred to as being based on "economic cost-benefit assumptions" (p. 5), the new leadership models emphasized symbolic leader behavior; visionary, inspirational messages; emotional feelings; ideological and moral values; individualized attention; and intellectual stimulation. Emerging from these early works, charismatic and transformational leadership theories have turned out to be the most frequently researched theories over the past 20 years (Avolio 2005, Lowe & Gardner 2000).

The theory of charismatic/transformational leadership suggests that such leaders raise followers' aspirations and activate their higher-order values (e.g., altruism) such that followers identify with the leader and his or her mission/vision, feel better about their work, and then work to perform beyond simple transactions and base expectations (e.g., Avolio 1999, Bass 1985, Conger & Kanungo 1998). Accumulated research (see Avolio et al. 2004a for a summary of this literature), including a series of meta-analytic studies (e.g., Judge & Piccolo 2004), has found that charismatic/transformational leadership was positively associated with leadership effectiveness and a number of important organizational outcomes across many different types of organizations, situations, levels of analyses, and cultures such as productivity and turnover.

Over the past decade, a lot of research effort has been invested in understanding the processes through which charismatic/transformational leaders positively influence followers' attitudes, behaviors, and performance. For example, a number of studies have examined different processes through which transformational leadership effects are ultimately realized in terms of performance outcomes. These processes include followers' formation of commitment; satisfaction; identification; perceived fairness (e.g., Liao & Chuang 2007, Walumbwa et al. 2008); job characteristics such as variety, identity, significance, autonomy and feedback (e.g., Piccolo & Colquitt 2006); trust in the leader (e.g., Wang et al. 2005); and how followers come to feel about themselves and their group in terms of efficacy, potency, and cohesion (e.g., Bass et al. 2003, Bono & Judge 2003, Schaubroeck et al. 2007).

Boundary Conditions for New-Genre Leadership

After establishing the positive links between transformational leadership and the intervening variables and performance outcomes, more recent research has examined the boundary conditions in which transformational leadership is more (or less) effective in predicting follower attitudes and behaviors. For example, several studies have focused on identifying and understanding contextual variables (e.g., idiocentrism) that mediate or moderate the relationship of charismatic/transformational leadership with followers' level of motivation and performance at the individual, team or group, and organizational levels (e.g., De Cremer & van Knippenberg 2004, Keller 2006, Walumbwa et al. 2007). Additional research has focused on examining the moderating effects of follower dispositions such as efficacy (Dvir & Shamir 2003, Zhu et al. 2008), physical and structural distance (e.g., Avolio et al. 2004b), perceived environmental uncertainty (e.g., Agle et al. 2006), social networks (e.g.,

Bono & Anderson 2005), technology to support group decision-making (e.g., Sosik et al. 1997), and cultural orientations such as collectivism (e.g., Walumbwa & Lawler 2003).

Future Focus Required

Although significant progress has been made in studying charismatic/transformational leadership, a number of areas still deserve further attention. First, despite the important and positive contributions made by charismatic or transformational leadership in practice, questions remain as to what determines or predicts charismatic or transformational leadership, or why some leaders engage in charismatic or transformational leadership behavior and others do not. Limited research has examined leaders' biographies or the role of followers (Howell & Shamir 2005) as predictor variables.

Second, despite significant progress in understanding how and when charismatic and transformational leadership behaviors are more effective, further research is needed that explores the process and boundary conditions for charismatic and transformational leadership with beneficial work behaviors. For example, although scholars who have investigated charismatic and transformational leadership have discussed motivational constructs as central components in their frameworks, generally speaking, few have paid any attention to the underlying psychological processes, mechanisms, and conditions through which charismatic and transformational leaders motivate followers to higher levels of motivation and performance (Kark & Van Dijk 2007).

Yukl (1999) has called for a more concerted effort to understand both the moderating and mediating mechanisms that link charismatic/transformational leadership to follower outcomes. To date, only a few preliminary studies have simultaneously examined mediated moderation or moderated mediation (e.g., De Cremer & van Knippenberg 2004, Walumbwa et al. 2008).

Third, other areas that deserve research attention include examining how to link

Mediated moderation: a moderating relationship that is mediated by another variable

Moderated mediation: a mediating relationship that is moderated by another variable

CAS: complex adaptive system

charismatic/transformational leadership to the emerging literature on emotions and leadership. Although all of these newer theories emphasize the emotional attachment of followers to the leader, there has been a dearth of conceptual and empirical research on examining the relationships between these new leadership theories and followers' affective states (Bono & Ilies 2006).

Fourth, research on charismatic and transformational leadership at the organizational or strategic level has generally lagged behind all other areas of leadership research except perhaps the focus on leadership development (Waldman & Yammarino 1999), and the results thus far have been mixed (Agle et al. 2006). For example, Waldman and colleagues (Tosi et al. 2004, Waldman et al. 2001) found that the charisma of the chief executive officer (CEO) was not related to subsequent organizational performance as measured by net profit margin and shareholder return or return on assets, respectively. On the other hand, Agle et al. (2006) and Waldman et al. (2004) reported that CEO charisma was associated with subsequent organizational performance. Clearly, more research is needed that focuses on potential mediating and moderating variables such as external stakeholders while examining the relationship between CEO charismatic or transformational leadership and firm performance.

Finally, although cross-cultural research pertaining to charismatic/transformational leadership generally supports the relationships reported for the United States and other Western cultures, it is important to note that these studies largely involve survey-based designs. We recommend that researchers incorporate a number of alternative research designs, including but not limited to experimental designs, longitudinal designs, and qualitative designs, as well as the use of multiple sources and mixed methods studies.

COMPLEXITY LEADERSHIP

Many previous models of leadership have been designed to accommodate more traditional hierarchical structures of organizations. To the degree that organizations are hierarchical, so too are leadership models (Uhl-Bien et al. 2007). Yet, there has been a growing sense of tension in the leadership literature that models of leadership that were designed for the past century may not fully capture the leadership dynamic of organizations operating in today's knowledge-driven economy (Lichtenstein et al. 2007). Applying the concepts of complexity theory to the study of leadership has resulted in what has been referred to as complexity leadership (Uhl-Bien & Marion 2008). Based on this framework, leadership is viewed as an interactive system of dynamic, unpredictable agents that interact with each other in complex feedback networks, which can then produce adaptive outcomes such as knowledge dissemination, learning, innovation, and further adaptation to change (Uhl-Bien et al. 2007). According to complex systems leadership theory, "leadership can be enacted through *any interaction* in an organization... leadership is an *emergent* phenomenon within complex systems" (Hazy et al. 2007, p. 2).

In line with leadership fitting the needs of the situation or challenges in which it operates, complexity leadership posits that to achieve optimal performance, organizations cannot be designed with simple, rationalized structures that underestimate the complexity of the context in which the organization must function and adapt (Uhl-Bien et al. 2007). Simply viewing the leader and follower in a simple exchange process won't fly in terms of explaining the full dynamics of leadership.

Complexity and Traditional Leadership Theory

In traditional leadership theory, the unit of analysis is oftentimes the leader, the leader and follower, the leader and group, and so forth. The fundamental unit of analysis in complexity leadership is referred to as a complex adaptive system, or CAS (Uhl-Bien et al. 2007). The CAS has its roots in the physical sciences and is composed of interdependent agents that can operate simultaneously on the basis of certain rules and localized knowledge that governs the CAS, while also being able to adapt and emerge based on feedback from the system (Plowman & Duchon 2008). Complexity leadership theory (CLT; Uhl-Bien et al. 2007) has been developed as an overarching explanation of how CAS operates within a bureaucratic organization, and it identifies three leadership roles to explore: adaptive (e.g., engaging others in brainstorming to overcome a challenge), administrative (e.g., formal planning according to doctrine), and enabling (e.g., minimizing the constraints of an organizational bureaucracy to enhance follower potential).

Future Focus Required

One of the core propositions of complexity leadership theory is that "much of leadership thinking has failed to recognize that leadership is not merely the influential act of an individual or individuals but rather is embedded in a complex interplay of numerous interacting forces" (Uhl-Bien et al. 2007, p. 302). How should one then study this form of leadership? Dooley & Lichtenstein (2008) describe several methods for studying complex leadership interactions, including by focusing on (*a*) micro, daily interactions using real-time observation, (*b*) meso interactions (days and weeks) using social network analysis, where one examines a set of agents and how they are linked over time, and (*c*) macro interactions (weeks, months, and longer) through event history analysis. Finally, agent-based modeling simulations (i.e., computer simulations based on a set of explicit assumptions about how agents are supposed to operate) are also being used as a means to study complexity leadership.

In sum, the complexity leadership field clearly lacks substantive research. We suspect this is a result of the difficulties in assessing this type of emergent construct within a dynamically changing context. However, substantive research is needed if this area of leadership research is to advance beyond conceptual discussions.

SHARED, COLLECTIVE, OR DISTRIBUTED LEADERSHIP

Similar to our discussion above about complexity leadership, we see more evidence for shared or collective leadership in organizations as hierarchical levels are deleted and team-based structures are inserted. In describing shared and team leadership, it is important to point out that these forms of leadership are typically viewed as different streams of research. For example, team leadership research has typically focused on the role of an individual leading the team. In contrast, those authors examining shared leadership generally view it as a process versus a person engaging multiple members of the team. In this section, we refer to the terms "shared leadership," "distributed leadership," and "collective leadership" interchangeably, paralleling their usage in the leadership literature.

Shared Leadership Defined

According to Day et al. (2004), team and shared leadership capacity is an emergent state—something dynamic that develops throughout a team's lifespan and that varies based on the inputs, processes, and outcomes of the team. It produces patterns of reciprocal influence, which reinforce and develop further relationships between team members (Carson et al. 2007). The most widely cited definition of shared leadership is that of Pearce & Conger (2003): "a dynamic, interactive influence process among individuals in groups for which the objective is to lead one another to the achievement of group or organizational goals or both. This influence process often involves peer, or lateral, influence and at other times involves upward or downward hierarchical influence" (p. 1). The term shared leadership overlaps with relational and complexity leadership, and differs from more traditional, hierarchical, or vertical models of leadership (Pearce & Sims 2002).

Highly shared leadership is broadly distributed within a group or a team of individuals rather than localized in any one individual who serves in the role of supervisor (Pearce

CLT: complexity leadership theory

Shared leadership: an emergent state where team members collectively lead each other

& Conger 2003). More specifically, shared leadership is defined as a team-level outcome (Day et al. 2004) or as a "simultaneous, ongoing, mutual influence process within a team that is characterized by 'serial emergence' of official as well as unofficial leaders" (Pearce 2004, p. 48). Similar to what we've described with respect to complexity leadership, when shared leadership can be "viewed as a property of the whole system, as opposed to solely the property of individuals, effectiveness in leadership becomes more a product of those connections or relationships among the parts than the result of any one part of that system (such as the leader)" (O'Connor & Quinn 2004, p. 423).

Research Evidence

Although a number of authors [beginning with Mary Parker Follett (1924)] have discussed the idea of shared leadership, it has only gained attention in the academic leadership literature recently, and relatively few studies have tried to measure shared leadership. One exception is the work by Avolio & Bass (1995). In their study, instead of raters evaluating the individual leader, the target of ratings was the team itself. Avolio & Bass (1995) report that the team-level measures of transformational and transactional leadership positively predicted performance similar to the individual-level measures in previous research.

Future Focus Required

One of the criticisms of research on shared leadership involves the lack of agreement on its definition (Carson et al. 2007). For example, should there be a generic definition of shared leadership that is qualified by such terms as transactional or transformational shared leadership?

Other potential areas that have yet to be explored involve certain boundary conditions, mediators, and moderators that have been recommended as a focus for future research. For example, Pearce & Conger (2003) noted that future research was needed to examine potential moderators such as the distribution of cul-

tural values, task interdependence, task competence, task complexity, and the team life cycle. Carson et al. (2007) proposed that greater attention be paid to levels of task competence in the team, complexity of tasks, and task interdependence in terms of examining how teams function when using shared leadership. These authors have also recommended that future research focus on the team's life cycle.

Another area that has not received much research attention involves the environment in which teams function. For example, Carson et al. (2007) proposed that future research examine the type of team environment that enables shared leadership, suggesting that the environment consists of three "highly interrelated and mutually reinforcing" dimensions: shared purpose, social support, and voice. These authors described several organizational climate factors that could potentially support more shared leadership in teams, including (a) shared purpose, which "exists when team members have similar understandings of their team's primary objectives and take steps to ensure a focus on collective goals"; (b) social support, described as "team members' efforts to provide emotional and psychological strength to one another. This helps to create an environment where team members feel their input is valued and appreciated"; and (c) voice, which is "the degree to which a team's members have input into how the team carries out its purpose" (p. 1222).

Future research also needs to examine how external team leaders affect the team's ability and motivation to be self-directed and share in leadership (Carson et al. 2007). Hackman & Wageman (2005) suggest that an external leader to the team can "help team members make coordinated and task-appropriate use of their collective resources in accomplishing the team's task" (p. 269).

In a nutshell, the time for examining shared leadership may be upon us to the extent that organizations are moving into a knowledge driven era where firms are distributed across cultures. This suggests that individual-based "heroic" models of leadership may not be sustainable in and of themselves (Pearce 2004).

LEADER-MEMBER EXCHANGE

Unlike shared leadership, which has focused on groups, leader-member exchange (LMX) theory has focused on the relationship between the leader and follower (Cogliser & Schriesheim 2000). The central principle in LMX theory is that leaders develop different exchange relationships with their followers, whereby the quality of the relationship alters the impact on important leader and member outcomes (Gerstner & Day 1997). Thus, leadership occurs when leaders and followers are able to develop effective relationships that result in mutual and incremental influence (Uhl-Bien 2006).

This literature has evolved from focusing exclusively on the consequences of the LMX relationship to focusing on both antecedents and consequences. For example, Tekleab & Taylor (2003) assessed leader and follower levels of agreement on their mutual obligations and their psychological contract with each other. In a recent meta-analysis reported by Ilies et al. (2007), the authors reported that a higher-quality LMX relationship not only predicted higher levels of performance, but also organizational citizenship behaviors. Some additional areas of focus in terms of high- versus low-quality LMX relationships have been the context in which those relationships have developed. Kacmar et al. (2007) examined the conditions under which leaders and followers in low-quality exchanges exerted more effort in examining how the situation interacted with the impact of supervisors. Using control theory, the authors tried to explain how perceptions of supervisor competence, centralization, and organizational politics influenced their willingness to exert effort on the job beyond what would be typically expected in a less-than-effective exchange relationship.

Additional research on the nature of the relationship and how it is formed has focused on the use of impression management tactics and its impact on the quality of the LMX relationship. Colella & Varma (2001) investigated how a follower's perceived disability and use of in-gratiation related to LMX quality. By using ingratiation tactics, the individuals with disabilities were able to increase the quality of the relationship between the leader and follower. Similar results were reported by Sparrowe et al. (2006), who showed that downward-influence tactics used by the leader affected the quality of the LMX relationship.

LMX: leader member exchange

Extensions to LMX

The original work produced by Graen & Uhl-Bien (1995) on the role-making and role-taking processes has been extended by Uhl-Bien and colleagues (2000) to examine how leader-follower dyads transform from individual interest to shared interest based on the development of trust, respect, and obligations to each other. Similar work along these lines has examined the effects of goal congruence on the quality of the LMX relationship. This work suggests that to the extent that goals are similar or mutually reinforcing, one would expect to produce a higher-quality LMX relationship.

Additional LMX research on individual differences has examined the impact of gender on the quality of the LMX relationship, although these findings have been mixed. For instance, Adebayo & Udegbe (2004) reported that followers in opposite-sex dyads perceived a better LMX quality in comparison with those from same-sex dyads.

Recent research has moved beyond examining LMX in terms of antecedents and consequences and has examined the quality of the leader and follower relationship as a moderator and/or mediator of performance. For example, Sparrowe et al. (2006) reported that the quality of the relationship moderated the relationship between downward-influence tactics and helping behaviors. Martin et al. (2005) reported that LMX either fully or partially mediated the relationship between locus of control and several work-related outcomes such as job satisfaction, work-related well-being, and organizational commitment.

In an extension of the linkages between social network theory and LMX, Graen (2006) put forth a recent transformation of LMX theory that he refers to as the new LMX–MMX theory of sharing network leadership. Accordingly, both Uhl-Bien (2006) and Graen (2006), building on earlier LMX research, now view organizations as systems of interdependent dyadic relationships, or dyadic subassemblies, and advocate the importance of both formal and informal influences on individual, team, and network flows of behavior.

Future Focus Required

Over the years, LMX theory and research have been targets of criticism. One pervasive criticism of this literature revolves around measurement. For example, many different measures of LMX have been developed and used since the theory was first proposed (Yukl 2006). Schriesheim et al. (1999, p. 100) argued, "LMX scales seem to have been developed on ad hoc, evolutionary basis, without the presentation of any clear logic or theory justifying the changes which were made." LMX research has also been criticized for failing to conceptualize the social context in which leaders and followers are embedded. With a few exceptions, "the majority of research is, quite explicitly, located at the dyadic level, with very little theorizing or empirical work examining LMX work at the group level" (Hogg et al. 2004, p. 22). In other words, theory and research on LMX have focused on the leader-follower relationship without acknowledging that each dyadic relationship occurs within a system of other relationships (Cogliser & Schriesheim 2000, Yukl 2006). LMX theory and research also tend to assume that people simply evaluate their own LMX relationship in an absolute sense. According to Hogg et al. (2004), this is an oversimplification of how people judge relationships. The authors argue that it is much more likely that followers evaluate the quality of their LMX relationship not only in the absolute sense (i.e., low versus high), but also with reference to their perception of others' LMX relationships. Another criticism of the LMX literature is that most of it is based on correlation designs. This was a central crit-

icism made by Cogliser & Schriesheim (2000) regarding the lack of causal results reported in the extensive stream of research associated with LMX research.

LMX research has also been criticized for not including more objective measures of performance (Erdogan & Liden 2002). Frequently, research in this area has collected performance outcomes that were generated by the leader or supervisor. It is now time to extend this research by collecting independent outcome measures that logically would be influenced by the quality of LMX relationship.

Another promising area for future research is to extend work on LMX theory across cultures. Specifically, what are the implications of national culture for the formation and development of an LMX quality relationship, and in turn how would that link to key organizational outcomes? Preliminary research addressing this question across cultures has produced some interesting results. For example, Chen et al. (2006) reported that regardless of whether the manager was American or Chinese, the quality of the LMX relationship was related to cooperative goal setting or interdependence.

FOLLOWERSHIP AND LEADERSHIP

Perhaps one of the most interesting omissions in theory and research on leadership is the absence of discussions of followership and its impact on leadership. Leadership researchers treat follower attributes as outcomes of the leadership process as opposed to inputs, even though there have been a number of calls over the years to examine the role that followers play in the leadership process (e.g., Shamir 2007).

Romance of Leadership

Our examination of follower-centric views begins with a focus on what the leadership literature describes as the romance of leadership. Meindl et al. (1985) proposed a social constructionist theory to describe the relationship between leadership and followership. They argued that leadership is significantly affected by the way followers construct their understanding of the leader in terms of their interpretation of his or her personality, behaviors, and effectiveness.

Accumulated research on the romance of leadership has produced mixed findings. Schyns et al. (2007) conducted a meta-analysis to determine whether they could tease out the effects controlling for such things as measurement error and sampling bias while focusing on whether followers had a tendency to romanticize their perceptions of transformational/charismatic leadership. Their results revealed a modest relationship between the romance of leadership and perceptions of transformational/charismatic leadership, accounting for approximately 5% of the variance in leadership ratings. In another study, Kulich et al. (2007) examined the relevance of the romance of leadership theory through an experiment that compared how the performance of a male and a female leader was viewed by allowing participants to choose how much of a bonus to allocate to the leader. Their results showed that the male CEO's bonus differed substantially depending on the company's performance, whereas no differences were reported for the female CEO.

Bligh et al. (2007) found that followers' negative views of their work environment were overly attributed to their leaders' in that they viewed the leader as more responsible for these negative outcomes and situations than was warranted. Along the same lines, Weber et al. (2001) reported that group success and failure were overly attributed to the leader. However, these authors also reported that attributions of failure to the leader may have had more significant negative repercussions, with the failing team consistently voting to replace their leaders when the situation was more of the cause for the team's failure.

Updates on Follower-Centric Views

Howell & Shamir (2005) put forth some important theoretical propositions regarding how follower traits and characteristics might influence leader and follower relationships (also see Dvir & Shamir 2003). Specifically, they identified followers' self-concept clarity and collective identity as important factors in determining how followers form charismatic relationships with their leader. Howell & Shamir (2005) then suggested that followers, who have a personalized relationship with a charismatic leader, may be more likely to show blind loyalty, obedience, and deference.

Carsten et al. (2007) examined how individuals hold divergent social constructions of followership that seem to coalesce around levels of passivity or proactivity, which followers believe could lead to effectiveness in their role. Thus, like leaders, not all followers are created equal in the minds of followers. This pattern was reflected in the work of Kelley (1992), who conceptualized followers as falling into quadrants, based on their being active or passive followers as well as whether they were critical or noncritical thinkers.

Future Focus Required

Shamir (2007) suggested that leadership effectiveness is just as much a product of good followers as it is of good leaders. Shamir (2007) made some specific recommendations for future work on follower-centered research, including examining how followers' needs, identities, and implicit theories affect leader selection and emergence as well as leader endorsement and acceptance; how follower interactions/social networks influence the emergence of leadership and effectiveness; how followers' expectations, values, and attitudes determine leader behavior; how followers' expectations affect the leader's motivation and performance; how followers' acceptance of the leader and their support for the leader affect the leader's self-confidence, self-efficacy, and behavior; how followers' characteristics (e.g., self-concept clarity) determine the nature of the leadership relationship formed with the leader; and how followers' attitudes and characteristics (e.g., level of development) affect leader behavior.

In addition, more work needs to be done examining how followership is construed across different industries and cultures. It is possible that in more advanced and newly forming industries, the concept of followership may be construed and enacted differently than what we might find in more established industries with long histories of treating leaders and followers in a particular way (Schyns et al. 2007).

SUBSTITUTES FOR LEADERSHIP

The substitutes-for-leadership theory focuses on situational factors that enhance, neutralize, and/or totally substitute for leadership. For example, a group of people engaged in electronic brainstorming using technology, such as a group decision support system, may operate as though there was a participative leader who was leading the group, but in fact, leadership comes from the operating rules for using the system to engage. Kerr & Jermier (1978) proposed the substitutes-for-leadership theory to address some of the romance effects described above. This research stream focuses on a range of situational/organizational and follower characteristics that might influence the leadership dynamic (Howell et al. 2007).

Since this theory was originally proposed, a considerable amount of research has been completed to determine whether there are substitutes for leadership with respect to impacts on performance. A number of authors have concluded that evidence is not sufficient to support the main propositions in the theory (Dionne et al. 2002, Keller 2006). For example, Dionne et al. (2002) tested the moderating effects of task variability, organization formulation, organization inflexibility, and lack of control on the relationship between leadership behavior and group effectiveness. However, the authors found little support for the moderating effects proposed by the substitutes-for-leadership theory. This lack of support may be attributable to problems in measuring these substitutes for leadership. Yet, revisions to the scale and its use in subsequent research have not provided any further support for this theory.

Future Focus Required

Villa et al. (2003) recommended that future research consider including multiple moderators that may interact with each other to impact performance that might be erroneously attributed to the leader. Dionne et al. (2005) suggested that future research consider testing the five possible conditions linking leader behavior, leadership effectiveness, and other situational variables (e.g., substitutes), which include (*a*) a leadership main effects model, (*b*) a substitutes main effect model, (*c*) an interactive or joint effects model, (*d*) a mediation model, wherein the substitutes mediate leadership impact versus moderate, and (*e*) the originally proposed moderated model. Future research should also focus more on the nature of the samples to be included in tests of substitutes for leadership. For example, one might focus on the cultural background as well as quality of one's followers by sampling professional workers who function in highly independent roles, as a possible sample for studying the boundary conditions for the effects of substitutes for leadership (Howell et al. 2007).

Finally, to evaluate fairly the substitutes for theory propositions will require more longitudinal research designs. For example, leaders who are more transformational will develop followers over time to take on more leadership roles and responsibilities. The way such leaders structure the context to develop followership and the followership itself may ultimately substitute for the leader's influence (Keller 2006).

SERVANT LEADERSHIP

Building on the work of Greenleaf (1991), Spears (2004) listed ten characteristics representing a servant leader: (*a*) listening, (*b*) empathy, (*c*) healing, (*d*) awareness, (*e*) persuasion, (*f*) conceptualization, (*g*) foresight, (*h*) stewardship, (*i*) commitment, and (*j*) building community. Russell & Stone (2002) reviewed the literature on servant leadership, distinguishing such leadership into two broad categories: functional and accompany attributes. Functional attributes include having vision, being honest, trustworthy, service oriented, a role model, demonstrating appreciation of others' service, and empowerment. In terms of accompany attributes, servant leaders are described as good communicators and listeners, credible, competent, encouraging of others, teachers, and delegators. In general, the limited empirical research on servant leadership has shown that it is positively related to follower satisfaction, their job satisfaction, intrinsic work satisfaction, caring for the safety of others, and organizational commitment. Joseph & Winston (2005) examined the relationship between employee perceptions of servant leadership and organizational trust, and reported a positive relationship with both trust in the leader as well as trust in one's organization. Washington et al. (2006) examined the relationship between servant leadership and the leader's values of empathy, integrity, competence, and agreeableness, and reported that "followers' ratings of leaders' servant leadership were positively related to followers' ratings of leaders' values of empathy, integrity, and competence" (p. 700).

Future Focus Required

One major tenet of servant leadership proposed by Greenleaf (1991) was that followers of servant leaders would be expected to become "healthier, wiser, freer, more autonomous and more likely to become servants themselves" (Barbuto & Wheeler 2006, p. 321). This suggests that future research could take a more follower-centric approach in looking at the well-being of followers of servant leaders and the ways in which their well-being affects the ability of the leader and followers to perform. As with LMX, the measurement of servant leadership is problematic. Already many different measures of servant leadership have been proposed with scales and items varying based on problems with its definition. Future research needs to examine how the personal values of servant leaders differ from those of other leadership styles, such as transformational (Russell & Stone 2002).

SPIRITUALITY AND LEADERSHIP

One might ask leaders the question, Do you feel there is something missing in the work that you do and the way you lead others? Many authors have referred to that void and have attempted to examine how a greater sense of spirituality in the workplace may be fostered. The research on workplace spirituality also now includes a focus on spiritual leadership—defined as "comprising the values, attitudes, and behaviors that are necessary to intrinsically motivate one's self and others so that they have a sense of spiritual survival through calling and membership" (Fry 2003, p. 711).

Dent et al. (2005) examined how spirituality and leadership was defined in the literature and concluded, "The field of study is marked by all of the typical characteristics of paradigm development including a lack of consensus about a definition of workplace spirituality" (p. 626). Fry (2003) contends that spiritual leadership adds to the existing leadership literature components that have been explicitly missing, such as a sense of calling on the part of leaders and followers as well as the creation of organizational cultures characterized by altruistic love whereby leaders and followers express genuine care, concern, and appreciation for both self and others. Fry (2003) states, "The ultimate effect of spiritual leadership is to bring together or create a sense of fusion among the four fundamental forces of human existence (body, mind, heart, and spirit) so that people are motivated for high performance, have increased organizational commitment, and personally experience joy, peace, and serenity" (p. 727).

Future Focus Required

Part of the challenge in this area of leadership research is simply defining what spirituality means without necessarily tying it to one particular religion or philosophical base. Dent et al. (2005) summarized a number of definitions of spirituality that highlight some of the challenges in building theory and research in this area. The authors concluded that a wide array of concepts/constructs is included in the definition of spirituality, but some of the common elements are a search for meaning, reflection, an inner connection, creativity, transformation, sacredness, and energy.

Fry (2005) defines spiritual leadership as comprising the values, attitudes, and behaviors that are necessary to intrinsically motivate self and others to enhance a sense of spiritual survival through calling and membership. Yet, some authors criticize Fry's model as well as other models of spirituality and leadership for not providing a sufficient understanding of what constitutes spirituality and the ways in which it ties to leadership. For example, Benefiel (2005) criticized the work on spirituality and leadership, stating that it "inadvertently draws upon outdated, discredited, or shallow approaches to spirituality; they reinvent the wheel; they dip into credible theories of spirituality but then don't fully develop them or resolve the conflicts among them. While these theories are comprehensive and creative in the context of leadership studies, a more robust, up-to-date, and sophisticated understanding of spirituality is needed if theories of spiritual leadership are to stand up under scrutiny and be taken seriously in the wider academy" (p. 727). Finally, there still seem to be two schools of thought in this area of leadership research: In one school, a set of scholars discuss spirituality in the theological sense (Whittington et al. 2005), whereas in the other school, the focus is more on understanding the inner motivation and drive a leader creates in followers to enhance workplace spirituality (Fry 2005). Until a definition of what constitutes spirituality and leadership is agreed upon, it will be difficult to conceptualize and measure these constructs.

CROSS-CULTURAL LEADERSHIP

Although most leadership research and theory has been developed and tested within a Western context, a growing interest in research and theory focuses on the role of leadership across cultural contexts. This interest is driven in part by the globalization of organizations that encourage and, at times, require leaders to work from and across an increasingly diverse set of locations. The result is an increased focus on cross-cultural leadership research (Gelfand et al. 2007, House et al. 2004). Extensive reviews also exist for cross-cultural research that is more tangentially linked to leadership (Hofstede 2001, Kirkman et al. 2006, Leung et al. 2005).

Project GLOBE

Although there have been numerous critiques and discussions of work in this area (see *Journal of International Business Studies*, Vol. 37, No. 6), the work of Project GLOBE (global leadership and organizational behavioral effectiveness) constitutes one of the more ambitious and influential cross-cultural leadership studies. The study, as detailed in an edited book (House et al. 2004), involved a group of more than 160 researchers working in 62 societies. Research included a mix of quantitative and qualitative investigations. The study was designed to address a number of goals, the first of which was to develop cultural dimensions at both the organizational and societal level of analysis, building upon the work of Hofstede (2001). A second major goal of the project was to examine the beliefs that different cultures had about effective leaders. Although many of the leadership attributes and behaviors examined varied by culture, the research did determine that certain implicit leadership theories (e.g., charisma/transformational, team-oriented) had universal endorsement. A third phase of the research involved ethnographies of individual countries based largely on qualitative data.

Global Leadership

The goal of identifying leaders who are able to effectively lead across a variety of cultures has great appeal and has been the focus of numerous articles in both the academic (Mobley et al. 1999) and popular press (Goldsmith 2003, Green et al. 2003, Lane

2004). However, substantial differences and approaches remain in how global leadership is conceptualized and defined. One approach primarily focuses on international experience, implying that leaders must spend time living in different cultures in order to be prepared to lead (Van Dyne & Ang 2006). A second approach emphasizes the competencies a leader needs to have in order to lead effectively and successfully across cultures (Mendenhall 2001). This approach emphasizes having a broad set of experiences and competencies that allow leaders to manage across cultures rather than focusing on a deep knowledge of one or two specific cultures. This approach is reflected in the related work on global mindset (Boyacigiller et al. 2004, Clapp-Smith et al. 2007) and cultural intelligence (Earley et al. 2007, Thomas 2006).

Comparative Leadership

Comparative research on the effectiveness of leadership in different cultures was the basis of early work in this field and continues to be a major area of research (Dickson et al. 2003, Dorfman 2004, Gelfand et al. 2007, Kirkman et al. 2006). Such research compares leadership in two or more cultures, examining the degree to which a practice that was developed in one culture applies to others. A common approach examines the direct impact a cultural dimension has on leadership. For example, one major cross-cultural study examined the impact of cultural values on the selection of sources of guidance for dealing with work events that managers are likely to face in 47 countries (Smith et al. 2002). This study identified which sources of guidance were correlated with specific cultural dimensions using several major cultural value dimension frameworks.

Another common strategy examines the indirect influence of culture as it moderates the relationship between leadership practice and relevant performance outcomes. Walumbwa et al. (2007) examined the effect of allocentrism (collective orientation) and idiocentrism (individual orientation) on the relationships among leadership (transformational and transactional) and both organizational commitment and satisfaction with supervisor. Allocentrics were found to react more positively to transformational leaders, whereas idiocentrics had a more positive reaction to transactional leaders.

Future Focus Required

Although significant progress has been made in the cross-cultural leadership literature, several important issues need to be addressed. For example, the term "culture" itself refers to a complex set of constructs around which there is ongoing debate. Not surprisingly, the attempt to examine the effect that culture has on leadership brings with it the associated conceptual and methodological challenges that are already associated with cross-cultural research (Van de Vijver & Leung 2000). Despite improvements made over the years, a need remains for future research to focus on levels of analysis when conducting cross-cultural leadership research. This applies to the development of explicitly cross-level theoretical models as well as the use of appropriate statistical techniques. Although the relevance of levels is widely recognized, the implications of cross-level analysis are often not reflected in the research design in this literature, particularly when it comes to insuring a sufficient number of cultures are included to conduct the analysis. Many researchers assume they can use the country as a convenient substitute for measuring culture, which may be an erroneous level of analysis given the diversity of cultures represented in most countries. Large-scale collaborations such as the GLOBE (House et al. 2004) study and the 47-nation study of Smith et al. (2002) are likely to be required to develop the types of samples needed for such analytical approaches.

E-LEADERSHIP

Leading virtually involves leading people from different departments, organizations, countries, and sometimes even competitor companies (Avolio et al. 2001). In virtual teams, "challenges are more likely to occur when distributed work occurs in different time zones, when local communication and human infrastructures fail, when team members' hardware and software platforms are different, or when local work demands require the immediate attention of collocated managers and workers, thereby creating pressure to pursue local priorities over the objectives of distant collaborators" (A. Weisband 2008b, p. 6).

Zigurs (2003) suggested that traditional leadership models built on a foundation of face-to-face interactions may not fully explain how virtual leadership and teams work. Specifically, how one provides feedback, encouragement, rewards, and motivation needs to be re-examined where leadership is mediated through technology. Zigurs (2003) suggests that the continuing development in technology such as increased bandwidth, wireless networks, integrated handheld devices, voice input, built-in video, video walls, and automatic translation will no doubt have a significant impact on how virtual teams communicate and how leadership is manifested in such teams. To date, a great deal of the work on e-leadership focuses on either leadership in virtual work teams or groups interacting in what are called "group decision support systems." For example, Zaccaro & Bader (2003) provided an overview of the similarities and differences between face-to-face teams and e-teams. They specifically focused on the impact of leadership functions such as communication building, role clarification, team development, and effective task execution and how they differed when mediated through technology. Other authors have focused on the effects of structural factors such as distance and multiple locations on e-leadership and virtual team effectiveness (e.g., Cascio & Shurygailo 2003).

Common Questions with E-Leadership

Some of the common questions or hypotheses suggested to guide research on e-leadership and virtual teams have been summarized by Avolio et al. (2001), Barelka (2007), as well as Ahuja & Galvin (2003) and include the following: How does the nature and structure of technology impact how leadership style influences follower motivation and performance? What effect will leadership mediated through technology have on trust formation? Will the nature of the technology such as its richness or transparency be a factor in building trust in virtual teams? How will the leadership and location of teams and technology connecting members affect the quality and quantity of their communication? How will the nature of the task and its complexity influence how leadership affects virtual team performance?

Group and Virtual Teams Research

A number of studies have examined e-leadership and virtual teams. For example, Kahai & Avolio (2008) investigated the effects of leadership style and anonymity on the discussion of an ethical issue in an electronic system context. Kahai & Avolio examined how groups discussed an ethical issue by manipulating the leadership style of the target e-leader and whether the group members were anonymous or identified. They reported that frequency of group member participation in discussing how to address the ethical issue was greater when leadership style was transactional versus transformational.

Xiao et al. (2008) conducted a field experiment focusing on surgical teams operating in a real-life trauma center. In their study, the team leader either was placed in the room with the surgical team or interacted with them virtually. The authors reported that when the team leader was in the next room, the leader had greater influence on communications between the senior member in the room and other team members. However, when the senior leader was collocated, the amount of communication between the team leader, the senior member, and junior members was more balanced. With high task urgency, the team leader was more involved with the senior team member in terms of communication regardless of location, whereas the communication between the team leader and junior members was reduced.

Balthazard et al. (2008) examined the mediational role of leadership and group member interaction styles in comparing virtual and face-to-face teams. They reported that group members in face-to-face teams were generally more cohesive, were more accepting of a group's decisions, and exhibited a greater amount of synergy than did virtual teams. Face-to-face teams exhibited a greater amount of constructive interaction in comparison with virtual teams, which scored significantly higher on defensive interaction styles.

Malhotra et al. (2007) collected survey, interview, and observational data on virtual teams to identify the leadership practices of effective leaders of virtual teams. These leadership practices included the ability to (a) establish and maintain trust through the use of communication technology, (b) ensure that distributed diversity is understood and appreciated, (c) manage effectively virtual work-life cycles, (d) monitor team progress using technology, (e) enhance visibility of virtual members within the team and outside the organization, and (f) let individual team members benefit from the team.

Future Focus Required

Hambley et al. (2006) advocate that future research on e-leadership be conducted in field settings. They recommend that virtual teams working on actual problem-solving tasks and projects be examined to help capture the motivational element that may not exist with ad hoc groups working in the lab. A. Weisband (2008a) argued, "Future research may want to consider how we lead in environments that lack any central coordination mechanism, or how multiple leaders work together to innovate, create, and help others" (p. 255).

E-leadership areas recommended for future research by authors of papers on the virtual team topic include task ownership, cohesion, media richness (i.e., technology's capacity for providing immediate feedback, the number of cues and channels utilized, personalization of messages, and language variety), communica-tion quality, asynchronous and synchronous communication, task complexity, and working on multiple virtual teams simultaneously (Kozlowski & Bell 2003, Zaccaro & Bader 2003). For example, Watson et al. (1993) studied culturally diverse and homogenous virtual groups and compared their interactions over a 17-week period. They found that culturally diverse groups initially suffered in their performance but over time surpassed homogenous groups, especially in terms of the number of alternative ideas generated.

In summary, we expect that the work on virtual leadership and team interactions will continue to be a growth area for leadership research. The fundamental issue for leadership scholars and practitioners to address is how technology is transforming the traditional roles of leadership at both individual and collective levels by examining "how existing leadership styles and cultures embedded in a group and/or organization affect the appropriation of advanced information technology systems" (Avolio et al. 2001, p. 658).

CLOSING COMMENTS AND INTEGRATION

The evolution of this literature points to several important trends. The first trend involves the field of leadership taking a more holistic view of leadership. Specifically, researchers are now examining all angles of leadership and including in their models and studies the leader, the follower, the context, the levels, and their dynamic interaction. The second trend involves examining how the process of leadership actually takes place by, for example, integrating the work of cognitive psychology with strategic leadership. In this regard, we are witnessing greater interest in how the leader processes information as well as how the follower does so, and how each affects the other, the group, and organization. More work is expected on examining the various mediators and moderators that help to explain how leadership influences intended outcomes. A third trend involves deriving alternative ways to examine leadership. We expect to see a greater use of mixed-methods designs in future research. The quantitative strategies for studying leadership have dominated the literature over the past 100 years, but increasing attention is being paid to cases and qualitative research that should now be integrated with quantitative approaches.

Part of the evolution of leadership theory and research will continue to involve further defining what actually constitutes leadership from a content perspective, e.g., authentic, transformational, or visionary, and a process perspective, e.g., shared, complex, or strategic. We also expect much more attention to be paid to the area of strategic leadership, which we did not have space here to cover, and applying what we have learned about content and process to this level of analysis. Finally, we go back to the point where we started in suggesting that the time has never been better to examine the genuine development of leadership. The field of leadership has done surprisingly little to focus its energies on what contributes to or detracts from genuine leadership development. Given the forces in the global market, we expect that over the next 10 years, research and theory in this area will explode as organizations increasingly ask for ways to accelerate positive leadership development as they enter the front lines of the war for leadership talent.

In summary, the leadership field over the past decade has made tremendous progress in uncovering some of the enduring mysteries associated with leadership. These include whether leaders are born or made, how followers affect how successful leaders can be, how some charismatic leaders build up societies and others destroy them, as well as what impact leading through technology has on individual and collective performance. The period that leadership theory and research will enter over the next decade is indeed one of the most exciting in the history of this planet.

SUMMARY POINTS

1. The field of leadership is evolving to a more holistic view of leadership.

2. More positive forms of leadership are being integrated into literature.

3. Increasing attention is being given to examining how leadership causally impacts interim and ultimate outcomes.

4. The follower is becoming an integral part of the leadership dynamic system.

5. There is growing interest in what genuinely develops leadership.

6. E-leadership is becoming a commonplace dynamic in work organizations.

7. More and more leadership is being distributed and shared in organizations.

8. Leadership is being viewed as a complex and emergent dynamic in organizations.

FUTURE ISSUES

1. More future research in leadership will be mixed methods.

2. Determining the causal mechanisms that link leadership to outcomes will be a priority.

3. Assessing and developing leadership using evidence-based strategies will be a target focus.

4. Examining strategic leadership as a process and person will be an evolving area of theory and research.

5. More theoretical work and research will focus on the follower as a prime element in the leadership dynamic.

6. How to develop global mindsets among leaders will be an area of interest.

7. A top priority area will be leadership in cultures that are underrepresented in the literature, such as Muslim cultures.

8. How shared leadership evolves and develops will be a focus in face-to-face and virtual environments.

DISCLOSURE STATEMENT

The authors are not aware of any biases that might be perceived as affecting the objectivity of this review.

ACKNOWLEDGMENTS

We greatly appreciate the contributions made to this paper by Melissa Carsten, Rachel Clapp-Smith, Jakari Griffith, Yongwoon Kim, Ketan Mhatre, David Sweetman, Mary Uhl-Bien, and Kay-Ann Willis.

LITERATURE CITED

Adebayo DO, Udegbe IB. 2004. Gender in the boss-subordinate relationship: a Nigerian study. *J. Organ. Behav.* 25:515–25

Agle BR, Nagarajan NJ, Sonnenfeld JA, Srinivasan D. 2006. Does CEO charisma matter? An empirical analysis of the relationships among organizational performance, environmental uncertainty, and top management team perceptions of CEO charisma. *Acad. Manage. J.* 49:161–74

Ahuja MK, Galvin JE. 2003. Socialization in virtual groups. *J. Manage.* 29:161–85

Altrocchi J. 1999. Individual differences in pluralism in self-structure. In *The Plural Self: Multiplicity in Everyday Life*, ed. J Rowan, M Cooper, pp. 168–82. London: Sage

Arvey RD, Zhang Z, Avolio BJ, Krueger RF. 2007. Developmental and genetic determinants of leadership role occupancy among women. *J. Appl. Psychol.* 92:693–706

Avolio BJ. 1999. *Full Leadership Development: Building the Vital Forces in Organizations*. Thousand Oaks, CA: Sage. 234 pp.

Avolio BJ. 2005. *Leadership Development in Balance: Made/Born*. Hillsdale, NJ: Erlbaum

Avolio BJ. 2007. Promoting more integrative strategies for leadership theory-building. *Am. Psychol.* 62:25–33

Avolio BJ, Bass BM. 1995. Individual consideration viewed at multiple levels of analysis—a multilevel framework for examining the diffusion of transformational leadership. *Leadersh. Q.* 6:199–218

Avolio BJ, Bass BM, Walumbwa FO, Zhu W. 2004a. *Multifactor Leadership Questionnaire: Manual and Sampler Test*. Redwood City, CA: Mind Garden

Avolio BJ, Chan A. 2008. The dawning of a new era for genuine leadership development. In *International Review of Industrial and Organizational Psychology*, ed. G Hodgkinson, K Ford, pp. 197–238. New York: Wiley

Avolio BJ, Gardner WL. 2005. Authentic leadership development: getting to the root of positive forms of leadership. *Leadersh. Q.* 16:315–38

Avolio BJ, Hannah S, Reichard R, Chan A, Walumbwa F. 2009. 100 years of leadership intervention research. *Leadersh. Q.* In press

Avolio BJ, Kahai SS, Dodge GE. 2001. E-leadership: implications for theory, research, and practice. *Leadersh. Q.* 11:615–68

Avolio BJ, Luthans F. 2006. *The High Impact Leader: Moments Matter in Accelerating Authentic Leadership*. New York: McGraw-Hill. 273 pp.

Avolio BJ, Zhu WC, Koh W, Bhatia P. 2004b. Transformational leadership and organizational commitment: mediating role of psychological empowerment and moderating role of structural distance. *J. Organ. Behav.* 25:951–68

Balthazard PA, Waldman DA, Atwater LE. 2008. The mediating effects of leadership and interaction style in face-to-face and virtual teams. See S Weisband 2008, pp. 127–50

Barbuto JE, Wheeler DW. 2006. Scale development and construct clarification of servant leadership. *Group Organ. Manage.* 31:300–26

Barelka AJ. 2007. *New findings in virtual team leadership*. Unpubl. PhD thesis. Mich. State Univ.

Bass BM. 1985. *Leadership and Performance Beyond Expectations*. New York: Free Press. 256 pp.

Bass BM, Avolio BJ, Jung DI, Berson Y. 2003. Predicting unit performance by assessing transformational and transactional leadership. *J. Appl. Psychol.* 88:207–18

Bass BM, Bass R. 2008. *Handbook of Leadership: Theory, Research, and Application*. New York: Free Press. 1296 pp.

Bass BM, Steidlmeier P. 1999. Ethics, character, and authentic transformational leadership behavior. *Leadersh. Q.* 10:181–217

Benefiel M. 2005. The second half of the journey: spiritual leadership for organizational transformation. *Leadersh. Q.* 16:723–47

Bligh MC, Kohles JC, Pearce CL, Justin JEG, Stovall JF. 2007. When the romance is over: follower perspectives of aversive leadership. *Appl. Psychol.: Int. Rev. Psychol. Appl. Rev. Int.* 56:528–57

Bono JE, Anderson MH. 2005. The advice and influence networks of transformational leaders. *J. Appl. Psychol.* 90:1306–14

Bono JE, Ilies R. 2006. Charisma, positive emotions and mood contagion. *Leadersh. Q.* 17:317–34

Bono JE, Judge TA. 2003. Self-concordance at work: toward understanding the motivational effects of transformational leaders. *Acad. Manage. J.* 46:554–71

Boyacigiller NA, Beechler S, Taylor S, Levy O. 2004. The crucial yet elusive global mindset. In *Handbook of Global Management: A Guide to Managing Complexity*, ed. J McNett, pp. 81–93. Malden, MA: Blackwell Sci.

Brown ME, Trevino LK, Harrison DA. 2005. Ethical leadership: a social learning perspective for construct development and testing. *Organ. Behav. Hum. Decis. Process.* 97:117–34

Bryman A. 1992. *Charisma and Leadership in Organizations*. London/Newbury Park, CA: Sage. 198 pp.

Burns JM. 1978. *Leadership*. New York: Harper & Row. 530 pp.

Campbell JD, Assanand S, Di Paula A. 2003. The structure of the self-concept and its relation to psychological adjustment. *J. Personal.* 71:115–40

Carson JB, Tesluk PE, Marrone JA. 2007. Shared leadership in teams: an investigation of antecedent conditions and performance. *Acad. Manage. J.* 50:1217–34

Carsten M, Uhl-Bien M, Patera J, West B, McGregor R. 2007. *Social Constructions of Followership*. Presented at Acad. Manag. Conf., Philadelphia, PA

Cascio WF, Shurygailo S. 2003. E-leadership and virtual teams. *Organ. Dyn.* 31:362–76

Chen GQ, Tjosvold D, Liu CH. 2006. Cooperative goals, leader people and productivity values: their contribution to top management teams in China. *J. Manage. Stud.* 43:1177–200

Clapp-Smith R, Luthans F, Avolio BJ. 2007. The role of psychological capital in global mindset development. In *The Global Mindset: Advances in International Management*, ed. MA Hitt, R Steers, M Javidan, pp. 105–30. Greenwich, CT: JAI

Cogliser CC, Schriesheim CA. 2000. Exploring work unit context and leader-member exchange: a multi-level perspective. *J. Organ. Behav.* 21:487–511

Colella A, Varma A. 2001. The impact of subordinate disability on leader-member exchange relationships. *Acad. Manage. J.* 44:304–15

Conger JA, Kanungo RN. 1998. *Charismatic Leadership in Organizations*. Thousand Oaks, CA: Sage. 288 pp.

Cooper CD, Scandura TA, Schriesheim CA. 2005. Looking forward but learning from our past: potential challenges to developing authentic leadership theory and authentic leaders. *Leadersh. Q.* 16:475–93

Day DV, Gronn P, Salas E. 2004. Leadership capacity in teams. *Leadersh. Q.* 15:857–80

De Cremer D, van Knippenberg D. 2004. Leader self-sacrifice and leadership effectiveness: the moderating role of leader self-confidence. *Organ. Behav. Hum. Decis. Process.* 95:140–55

Dent EB, Higgins AE, Wharff DM. 2005. Spirituality and leadership: an empirical review of definitions, distinctions, and embedded assumptions. *Leadersh. Q.* 16:625–53

Dickson MW, Den Hartog DN, Mitchelson JK. 2003. Research on leadership in a cross-cultural context: making progress, and raising new questions. *Leadersh. Q.* 14:729–68

Dionne SD, Yammarino FJ, Atwater LE, James LR. 2002. Neutralizing substitutes for leadership theory: leadership effects and common-source bias. *J. Appl. Psychol.* 87:454–64

Dionne SD, Yammarino FJ, Howell JP, Villa J. 2005. Substitutes for leadership, or not. *Leadersh. Q.* 16:169–93

Dooley KJ, Lichtenstein B. 2008. Research methods for studying the dynamics of leadership. In *Complexity Leadership, Part I: Conceptual Foundations*, ed. M Uhl-Bien, R Marion, pp. 269–90. Charlotte, NC: Inform. Age

Dorfman P. 2004. International and cross-cultural leadership research. In *Handbook for International Management Research*, ed. BJ Punnett, O Shenkar, pp. 265–355. Ann Arbor, MI: Univ. Mich. Press

Dvir T, Shamir B. 2003. Follower developmental characteristics as predicting transformational leadership: a longitudinal field study. *Leadersh. Q.* 14:327–44

Dweck CS. 1986. Motivational processes affecting learning. *Am. Psychol.* 41:1040–48

Earley CP, Murnieks C, Mosakowski E. 2007. Cultural intelligence and the global mindset. In *The Global Mindset*, ed. M Javidan, RM Steers, MA Hitt, pp. 75–103. New York: Elsevier

Epitropaki O, Martin R. 2005. From ideal to real: a longitudinal study of the role of implicit leadership theories on leader-member exchanges and employee outcomes. *J. Appl. Psychol.* 90:659–76

Erdogan B, Liden R. 2002. Social exchanges in the workplace: a review of recent developments and future research directions in leader-member exchange theory. In *Leadership*, ed. IL Neider, CA Schriesheim, pp. 65–114. Greenwich, CT: Information Age

Follett MP. 1924. *Creative Experience*. New York: Logmans Green

Fredrickson BL. 2001. The role of positive emotions in positive psychology—the broaden-and-build theory of positive emotions. *Am. Psychol.* 56:218–26

Fry LW. 2003. Toward a theory of spiritual leadership. *Leadersh. Q.* 14:693–727

Fry LW. 2005. Introduction to *The Leadership Quarterly* special issue: toward a paradigm of spiritual leadership. *Leadersh. Q.* 16:619–22

Gelfand MJ, Erez M, Aycan Z. 2007. Cross-cultural organizational behavior. *Annu. Rev. Psychol.* 58:479–514

George B. 2003. *Authentic Leadership: Rediscovering the Secrets to Creating Lasting Value*. San Francisco, CA: Jossey-Bass. 217 pp.

Gerstner CR, Day DV. 1997. Meta-analytic review of leader-member exchange theory: correlates and construct issues. *J. Appl. Psychol.* 82:827–44

Goethals GR. 2005. Presidential leadership. *Annu. Rev. Psychol.* 56:545–70

Goldsmith M. 2003. *Global Leadership: The Next Generation*. Upper Saddle River, NJ: Financial Times Prentice Hall. 350 pp.

Graen GB. 2006. In the eye of the beholder: cross-cultural lesson in leadership from project GLOBE: a response viewed from the third culture bonding (TCB) model of cross-cultural leadership. *Acad. Manage. Perspect.* 20:95–101

Graen GB, Uhl-Bien M. 1995. Relationship-based approach to leadership—development of leader-member exchange (LMX) theory of leadership over 25 years—applying a multilevel multidomain perspective. *Leadersh. Q.* 6:219–47

Green S, Hassan F, Immelt J, Marks M, Meiland D. 2003. In search of global leaders. *Harvard Bus. Rev.* 81:38–45

Greenleaf RK. 1991. *The Servant as Leader*. Indianapolis, IN: Robert Greenleaf Center

Hackman JR, Wageman R. 2005. A theory of team coaching. *Acad. Manage. Rev.* 30:269–87

Hambley LA, O'Neil TA, Kline TJB. 2006. Virtual team leadership: the effects of leadership style and communication medium on team interaction styles and outcomes. *Organ. Behav. Hum. Decis. Process.* 103:1–20

Harter JK, Schmidt FL, Hayes TL. 2002. Business-unit-level relationship between employee satisfaction, employee engagement, and business outcomes: a meta-analysis. *J. Appl. Psychol.* 87:268–79

Hazy JK, Goldstein JA, Lichtenstein BB. 2007. Complex systems leadership theory: an introduction. In *Complex Systems Leadership Theory: New Perspectives from Complexity Science on Social and Organizational Effectiveness*, ed. JK Hazy, JA Goldstein, BB Lichtenstein, pp. 1–13. Mansfield, MA: ISCE Publ.

Hofstede GH. 2001. *Culture's Consequences: Comparing Values, Behaviors, Institutions, and Organizations Across Nations*. Thousand Oaks, CA: Sage. 596 pp.

Hogg MA, Martin R, Weeden K. 2004. Leader-member relations and social identity. In *Leadership and Power: Identity Processes in Groups and Organizations*, ed. D van Knippenberg, MA Hogg, pp. 18–33. London: Sage

House RJ, Hanges PJ, Javidan M, Dorfman PW, Gupta V. 2004. *Culture, Leadership, and Organizations: The GLOBE Study of 62 Societies*. Thousand Oaks, CA: Sage. 818 pp.

Howell JM, Shamir B. 2005. The role of followers in the charismatic leadership process: relationships and their consequences. *Acad. Manage. Rev.* 30:96–112

Howell JP, Bowen DE, Dorfman PW, Kerr S, Podsakoff PM. 2007. Substitutes for leadership: effective alternatives to ineffective leadership. In *Leadership: Understanding the Dynamics of Power and Influence in Organizations*, ed. RP Vecchio, pp. 363–76. Notre Dame, IN: Univ. Notre Dame Press

Ilies R, Nahrgang JD, Morgeson FP. 2007. Leader-member exchange and citizenship behaviors: a meta-analysis. *J. Appl. Psychol.* 92:269–77

Joseph EE, Winston BE. 2005. A correlation of servant leadership, leader trust, and organizational trust. *Leadersh. Organ. Dev. J.* 26:6–22

Judge TA, Piccolo RF. 2004. Transformational and transactional leadership: a meta-analytic test of their relative validity. *J. Appl. Psychol.* 89:755–68

Kacmar KM, Zivnuska S, White CD. 2007. Control and exchange: the impact of work environment on the work effort of low relationship quality employees. *Leadersh. Q.* 18:69–84

Kahai SS, Avolio BJ. 2008. Effects of leadership style and anonymity on the discussion of an ethical issue in an electronic meeting system context. See S Weisband 2008, pp. 97–126

Kark R, Van Dijk D. 2007. Motivation to lead, motivation to follow: the role of the self-regulatory focus in leadership processes. *Acad. Manage. Rev.* 32:500–28

Keller RT. 2006. Transformational leadership, initiating structure, and substitutes for leadership: a longitudinal study of research and development project team performance. *J. Appl. Psychol.* 91:202–10

Kelley RE. 1992. *The Power of Followership: How to Create Leaders People Want to Follow, and Followers Who Lead Themselves*. New York: Doubleday/Currency. 260 pp.

Kerr S, Jermier JM. 1978. Substitutes for leadership: their meaning and measurement. *Organ. Behav. Hum. Perform.* 22:376–403

Kirkman BL, Lowe KB, Gibson CB. 2006. A quarter century of Culture's Consequences: a review of empirical research incorporating Hofstede's cultural values framework. *J. Int. Bus. Stud.* 37:285–320

Kozlowski SWJ, Bell BS. 2003. Work groups and teams in organizations. In *Handbook of Psychology: Industrial and Organizational Psychology*, ed. WC Borman, DR Ilgen, RJ Klimoski, pp. 333–75. London: Wiley

Kulich C, Ryan MK, Haslam SA. 2007. Where is the romance for women leaders? The effects of gender on leadership attributions and performance-based pay. *Appl. Psychol. Int. Rev. Psychol. Appl. Rev. Int.* 56:582–601

Lane HW. 2004. *The Blackwell Handbook of Global Management: A Guide to Managing Complexity*. New York: Wiley-Blackwell. 476 pp.

Leung K, Bhagat RS, Buchan NR, Erez M, Gibson CB. 2005. Culture and international business: recent advances and their implications for future research. *J. Int. Bus. Stud.* 36:357–78

Liao H, Chuang AC. 2007. Transforming service employees and climate: a multilevel, multisource examination of transformational leadership in building long-term service relationships. *J. Appl. Psychol.* 92:1006–19

Lichtenstein BB, Uhl-Bien M, Marion R, Seers A, Orton JD, Schreiber C. 2007. Complexity leadership theory: an interactive perspective on leading in complex adaptive systems. In *Complex Systems Leadership Theory: New Perspectives from Complexity Science on Social and Organizational Effectiveness*, ed. JK Hazy, JA Goldstein, BB Lichtenstein, pp. 129–41. Mansfield, MA: ISCE Publ.

Lord RG, Brown BR. 2004. *Leadership Processes and Follower Self-Identity*. Hillsdale, NJ: Erlbaum

Lord RG, Brown DJ. 2001. Leadership, values, and subordinate self-concepts. *Leadersh. Q.* 12:133–52

Lord RG, Brown DJ, Harvey JL, Hall RJ. 2001. Contextual constraints on prototype generation and their multilevel consequences for leadership perceptions. *Leadersh. Q.* 12:311–38

Lord RG, Emrich CG. 2000. Thinking outside the box by looking inside the box: extending the cognitive revolution in leadership research. *Leadersh. Q.* 11:551–79

Lord RG, Hall RJ. 1992. Contemporary views of leadership and individual differences. *Leadersh. Q.* 3:137–57

Lord RG, Hall RJ. 2005. Identity, deep structure and the development of leadership skill. *Leadersh. Q.* 16:591–615

Lowe KB, Gardner WL. 2000. Ten years of the *Leadership Quarterly*: contributions and challenges for the future. *Leadersh. Q.* 11:459–514

Luthans F. 2002. Positive organizational behavior: developing and managing psychological strengths. *Acad. Manage. Exec.* 16:57–72

Luthans F, Avolio BJ. 2003. Authentic leadership: a positive developmental approach. In *Positive Organizational Scholarship: Foundations of a New Discipline*, ed. KS Cameron, JE Dutton, RE Quinn, pp. 241–58. San Francisco, CA: Berrett-Koehler

Malhotra A, Majchrzak A, Rosen B. 2007. Leading virtual teams. *Acad. Manage. Perspect.* 21:60–70

Martin R, Thomas G, Charles K, Epitropaki O, McNamara R. 2005. The role of leader-member exchanges in mediating the relationship between locus of control and work reactions. *J. Occup. Organ. Psychol.* 78:141–47

Maurer TJ, Lippstreu M. 2005. *Differentiating Motivation to Lead from Motivation to Develop Leadership Capability: Relevance of "Born vs Made" Beliefs.* Presented at meet. Acad. Manage., Honolulu, HI

Meindl JR, Ehrlich SB, Dukerich JM. 1985. The romance of leadership. *Adm. Sci. Q.* 30:78–102

Mendenhall ME. 2001. Introduction: new perspectives on expatriate adjustment and its relationship to global leadership development. In *Developing Global Business Leaders: Policies, Processes, and Innovations*, ed. GK Stahl, pp. 1–16. Westport, CT: Quorum

Mobley WH, Gessner MJ, Arnold V. 1999. *Advances in Global Leadership.* Stamford, CT: JAI

Mumford MD, Connelly S, Gaddis B. 2003. How creative leaders think: experimental findings and cases. *Leadersh. Q.* 14:411–32

Mumford MD, Friedrich TL, Caughron JJ, Byrne CL. 2007. Leader cognition in real-world settings: How do leaders think about crises? *Leadersh. Q.* 18:515–43

O'Connor PMG, Quinn L. 2004. Organizational capacity for leadership. In *The Center for Creative Leadership Handbook of Leadership Development*, ed. CD McCauley, E Van Velsor, pp. 417–37. San Francisco, CA: Jossey-Bass

Pearce CL. 2004. The future of leadership: combining vertical and shared leadership to transform knowledge work. *Acad. Manage. Exec.* 18:47–57

Pearce CL, Conger JA. 2003. *Shared Leadership: Reframing the Hows and Whys of Leadership.* Thousand Oaks, CA: Sage

Pearce CL, Sims HP. 2002. The relative influence of vertical vs. shared leadership on the longitudinal effectiveness of change management teams. *Group Dynamics Theory Res. Pract.* 6:172–97

Piccolo RF, Colquitt JA. 2006. Transformational leadership and job behaviors: the mediating role of core job characteristics. *Acad. Manage. J.* 49:327–40

Plowman DA, Duchon D. 2008. Dispelling the myths about leadership: from cybernetics to emergence. In *Complexity Leadership Part I: Conceptual Foundations*, ed. M Uhl-Bien, R Marion, pp. 129–53. Charlotte, NC: Inform. Age

Reichard RJ, Avolio BJ. 2005. Where are we? The status of leadership intervention research: a meta-analytic summary. In *Authentic Leadership and Practice: Origins, Effects, and Development*, ed. WL Gardner, BJ Avolio, FO Walumbwa, pp. 203–26. Oxford, UK: Elsevier Sci.

Roberts LM, Dutton JE, Spreitzer CM, Heaphy ED, Quinn RE. 2005. Composing the reflected best-self portrait: building pathways for becoming extraordinary in work organizations. *Acad. Manage. Rev.* 30:712–36

Russell RF, Stone AG. 2002. A review of servant leadership attributes: developing a practical model. *Leadersh. Organ. Dev. J.* 23:145–57

Schaubroeck J, Lam SSK, Cha SE. 2007. Embracing transformational leadership: team values and the impact of leader behavior on team performance. *J. Appl. Psychol.* 92:1020–30

Schriesheim CA, Castro SL, Cogliser CC. 1999. Leader-member exchange (LMX) research: a comprehensive review of theory, measurement, and data-analytic practices. *Leadersh. Q.* 10:63–113

Schyns B, Felfe J, Blank H. 2007. Is charisma hyper-romanticism? Empirical evidence from new data and a meta-analysis. *Appl. Psychol. Int. Rev. Psychol. Appl. Rev. Int.* 56:505–27

Shamir B. 2007. From passive recipients to active coproducers: followers' roles in the leadership process. In *Follower-Centered Perspectives on Leadership: A Tribute to the Memory of James R. Meindl*, ed. B Shamir, R Pillai, MC Bligh, M Uhl-Bien, pp. ix–xxxix. Greenwich, CT: Inform. Age

Smith PB, Peterson MF, Schwartz SH, Ahmad AH, Akande D, et al. 2002. Cultural values, sources of guidance, and their relevance to managerial behavior—a 47-nation study. *J. Cross Cult. Psychol.* 33:188–208

Sosik JJ, Avolio BJ, Kahai SS. 1997. Effects of leadership style and anonymity on group potency and effectiveness in a group decision support system environment. *J. Appl. Psychol.* 82:89–103

Sparrowe RT. 2005. Authentic leadership and the narrative self. *Leadersh. Q.* 16:419–39

Sparrowe RT, Soetjipto BW, Kraimer ML. 2006. Do leaders' influence tactics relate to members' helping behavior? It depends on the quality of the relationship. *Acad. Manage. J.* 49:1194–208

Spears LC. 2004. The understanding and practice of servant leadership. In *Practicing Servant-Leadership: Succeeding Through Trust, Bravery, and Forgiveness*, ed. LC Spears, M Lawrence, pp. 167–200. San Francisco, CA: Jossey-Bass

Swann WB, Chang-Schneider C, McClarty KL. 2007. Do people's self-views matter? Self-concept and self-esteem in everyday life. *Am. Psychol.* 62:84–94

Tekleab AG, Taylor MS. 2003. Aren't there two parties in an employment relationship? Antecedents and consequences of organization-employee agreement on contract obligations and violations. *J. Organ. Behav.* 24:585–608

Thomas DC. 2006. Domain and development of cultural intelligence—the importance of mindfulness. *Group Organ. Manage.* 31:78–99

Tosi HL, Misangyi VF, Fanelli A, Waldman DA, Yammarino FJ. 2004. CEO charisma, compensation, and firm performance. *Leadersh. Q.* 15:405–20

Uhl-Bien M. 2006. Relational leadership theory: exploring the social processes of leadership and organizing. *Leadersh. Q.* 17:654–76

Uhl-Bien M, Graen GB, Scandura TA. 2000. Implications of leader-member exchange (LMX) for strategic human resource management systems: relationships as social capital for competitive advantage. *Res. Pers. Hum. Resour. Manage.* 18:137–85

Uhl-Bien M, Marion R. 2008. *Complexity Leadership*. Charlotte, NC: Information Age

Uhl-Bien M, Marion R, McKelvey B. 2007. Complexity leadership theory: shifting leadership from the Industrial Age to the Knowledge Era. *Leadersh. Q.* 18:298–318

Van de Vijver FJR, Leung K. 2000. Methodological issues in psychological research on culture. *J. Cross-Cultural Psychol.* 31:33–51

Van Dyne L, Ang S. 2006. Getting more than you expect: global leader initiative to span structural holes and reputational effectiveness. In *Advances in Global Leadership*, ed. WH Mobley, E Weldon, pp. 101–22. New York: Elsevier

Villa JR, Howell JP, Dorfman PW, Daniel DL. 2003. Problems with detecting moderators in leadership research using moderated multiple regression. *Leadersh. Q.* 14:3–23

Waldman DA, Javidan M, Varella P. 2004. Charismatic leadership at the strategic level: a new application of upper echelons theory. *Leadersh. Q.* 15:355–80

Waldman DA, Ramirez GG, House RJ, Puranam P. 2001. Does leadership matter? CEO leadership attributes and profitability under conditions of perceived environmental uncertainty. *Acad. Manage. J.* 44:134–43

Waldman DA, Yammarino FJ. 1999. CEO charismatic leadership: levels-of-management and levels-of-analysis effects. *Acad. Manage. Rev.* 24:266–85

Walumbwa FO, Avolio BJ, Gardner WL, Wernsing TS, Peterson SJ. 2008. Authentic leadership: development and validation of a theory-based measure. *J. Manage.* 34:89–126

Walumbwa FO, Avolio BJ, Zhu W. 2008. How transformational leadership weaves its influence on individual job performance: the role of identification and efficacy beliefs. *Pers. Psychol.* In press

Walumbwa FO, Lawler JJ. 2003. Building effective organizations: transformational leadership, collectivist orientation, work-related attitudes and withdrawal behaviours in three emerging economies. *Int. J. Hum. Resour. Manage.* 14:1083–101

Walumbwa FO, Lawler JJ, Avolio BJ. 2007. Leadership, individual differences, and work-related attitudes: a cross-culture investigation. *Appl. Psychol. Int. Rev. Psychol. Appl. Rev. Int.* 56:212–30

Wang H, Law KS, Hackett RD, Wang DX, Chen ZX. 2005. Leader-member exchange as a mediator of the relationship between transformational leadership and followers' performance and organizational citizenship behavior. *Acad. Manage. J.* 48:420–32

Washington RR, Sutton CD, Field HS. 2006. Individual differences in servant leadership: the roles of values and personality. *Leadersh. Organ. Dev. J.* 27:700–16

Watson WE, Kumar K, Michaelsen LK. 1993. Cultural diversity's impact on interaction process and performance—comparing homogeneous and diverse task groups. *Acad. Manage. J.* 36:590–602

Weber R, Camerer C, Rottenstreich Y, Knez M. 2001. The illusion of leadership: misattribution of cause in coordination games. *Organ. Sci.* 12:582–98

Weisband A. 2008a. Lessons about leadership at a distance and future research directions. See S Weisband 2008, pp. 149–256

Weisband A. 2008b. Research challenges for studying leadership at a distance. See S Weisband 2008, pp. 3–12

Weisband S, ed. 2008. *Leadership at a Distance: Research in Technologically-Supported Work.* New York: Erlbaum

Whittington JL, Pitts TM, Kageler WV, Goodwin VL. 2005. Legacy leadership: the leadership wisdom of the Apostle Paul. *Leadersh. Q.* 16:749–70

Wofford JC, Goodwin VL, Whittington JL. 1998. A field study of a cognitive approach to understanding transformational and transactional leadership. *Leadersh. Q.* 9:55–84

Xiao Y, Seagull FJ, Mackenzie CF, Klein KJ, Ziegert J. 2008. Adaptation of team communication patterns. Exploring the effects of leadership at a distance: task urgency, and shared team experience. See S Weisband 2008, pp. 71–96

Yammarino FJ, Dionne SD, Chun JU, Dansereau F. 2005. Leadership and levels of analysis: a state-of-the-science review. *Leadersh. Q.* 16:879–919

Yukl G. 1999. An evaluation of conceptual weaknesses in transformational and charismatic leadership theories. *Leadersh. Q.* 10:285–305

Yukl GA. 2006. *Leadership in Organizations.* Upper Saddle River, NJ: Pearson/Prentice Hall. 542 pp.

Yukl GA, Van Fleet DD. 1992. Theory and research on leadership in organizations. In *Handbook of Industrial and Organizational Psychology*, ed. MD Dunnette, LM. Hough, pp. 147–98. Palo Alto, CA: Consulting Psychol. Press

Zaccaro SJ, Bader P. 2003. E-leadership and the challenges of leading E-teams: minimizing the bad and maximizing the good. *Organ. Dyn.* 31:377–87

Zhu W, Avolio BJ, Walumbwa FO. 2008. Moderating role of follower characteristics with transformational leadership and follower work engagement. *Group Organ. Manage.* In press

Zigurs I. 2003. Leadership in virtual teams: oxymoron or opportunity? *Organ. Dyn.* 31:339–51

Benefits of Training and Development for Individuals and Teams, Organizations, and Society

Herman Aguinis[1] and Kurt Kraiger[2]

[1]The Business School, University of Colorado Denver, Denver, Colorado 80217-3364; email: Herman.Aguinis@ucdenver.edu

[2]Department of Psychology, Colorado State University, Fort Collins, Colorado 80523-1876; email: Kurt.Kraiger@colostate.edu

Annu. Rev. Psychol. 2009. 60:451–74

First published online as a Review in Advance on October 31, 2008

The *Annual Review of Psychology* is online at psych.annualreviews.org

This article's doi: 10.1146/annurev.psych.60.110707.163505

Key Words

training benefits, training design, training delivery, training evaluation

Abstract

This article provides a review of the training and development literature since the year 2000. We review the literature focusing on the benefits of training and development for individuals and teams, organizations, and society. We adopt a multidisciplinary, multilevel, and global perspective to demonstrate that training and development activities in work organizations can produce important benefits for each of these stakeholders. We also review the literature on needs assessment and pretraining states, training design and delivery, training evaluation, and transfer of training to identify the conditions under which the benefits of training and development are maximized. Finally, we identify research gaps and offer directions for future research.

Contents

INTRODUCTION

As organizations strive to compete in the global economy, differentiation on the basis of the skills, knowledge, and motivation of their workforce takes on increasing importance. According to a recent industry report by the American Society for Training and Development (ASTD), U.S. organizations alone spend more than $126 billion annually on employee training and development (Paradise 2007). "Training" refers to a systematic approach to learning and development to improve individual, team, and organizational effectiveness (Goldstein & Ford 2002). Alternatively, development refers to activities leading to the acquisition of new knowledge or skills for pur-

poses of personal growth. However, it is often difficult to ascertain whether a specific research study addresses training, development, or both. In the remainder of this review, we use the term "training" to refer to both training and development efforts.

The importance of and scholarly interest in training in work organizations is reflected by the regular publication of training reviews in the *Annual Review of Psychology* since 1971 (Campbell 1971, Goldstein 1980, Wexley 1984, Latham 1988, Tannenbaum & Yukl 1992, Salas & Cannon-Bowers 2001). The present review covers the training literature since January 2000. We provide a review that is comprehensive though not exhaustive. Also, in contrast to previously published *Annual Review of Psychology* articles, we readily acknowledge at the outset that we take a point of view that training in work organizations produces clear benefits for individuals and teams, organizations, and society. We believe that training in work organizations is an area of applied psychological research that is particularly well suited for making a clear contribution to the enhancement of human well-being and performance in organizational and work settings as well as in society in general. Thus, in this review we first describe the benefits of training for various stakeholders and then discuss how training can be designed, delivered, and evaluated so that these benefits are maximized.

We acknowledge three unique characteristics of the present review that also differentiate it from previous *Annual Review of Psychology* articles on the same topic. First, because the training field has grown exponentially in the past decade, we cannot rely on the psychological literature to be the only or even main source of knowledge that has been generated. In preparing to write this article, we reviewed about 600 articles, books, and chapters published in psychology as well as in related fields including human resource management, instructional design, human resource development, human factors, and knowledge management. We believe this multidisciplinary approach is needed given the increasing fragmentation of

Training: the systematic approach to affecting individuals' knowledge, skills, and attitudes in order to improve individual, team, and organizational effectiveness

Development: systematic efforts affecting individuals' knowledge or skills for purposes of personal growth or future jobs and/or roles

knowledge generated by researchers in various training subfields. Second, although psychology research on training has been a topic traditionally studied at the individual level of analysis and more recently at the team level of analysis, this review also includes organization and society levels of analysis. The present article goes beyond the traditional levels of analysis because, as noted by Kaufman & Guerra (2001), "we have entered a new era in which both achieving useful results and proving that they add value to the organization and our shared society are required" (p. 319). Third, thanks in part to the availability of cheaper and faster ways to send and receive information using the Internet, human resource management interventions and training efforts in particular are taking place at a global level (Cascio & Aguinis 2008). Thus, a review of the training literature cannot limit itself to research conducted only in the United States. Accordingly, this review includes numerous studies conducted outside of North America. In short, we approached our literature review from a fundamentally necessary multidisciplinary, multilevel, and global perspective.

Organization and Overview

The present review is organized as follows. In the first section, we describe benefits of training activities. First, we focus on benefits for individuals and teams, separating these benefits into job performance and factors related to job performance (e.g., tacit skills, innovation, communication), and other benefits (e.g., empowerment, self-efficacy). Second, we describe benefits for organizations. We also separate these benefits into organizational performance, factors related to organizational performance (e.g., effectiveness, profitability, sales), and other benefits (e.g., employee and customer satisfaction, improved organizational reputation). Third, we describe benefits for society. Overall, a review of this body of literature leads to the conclusion that training activities provide benefits for individuals, teams, and organizations that improve a nation's human capital, which in turn contributes to a nation's economic growth.

The second section reviews research addressing how to maximize the benefits of training activities at the individual and team, organizational, and societal levels. First, we focus on the activities that take place before training is implemented—needs assessment and pretraining states. Then, we focus on training design and delivery, followed by a discussion of training evaluation. We review research regarding transfer of skills and knowledge acquired in training to work settings. In the third and final section, we address conclusions, including implications for practice, and suggestions for future research.

BENEFITS OF TRAINING FOR INDIVIDUALS AND TEAMS

There is documented evidence that training activities have a positive impact on the performance of individuals and teams. Training activities can also be beneficial regarding other outcomes at both the individual and team level (e.g., attitudes, motivation, and empowerment). We first review performance-related benefits.

Benefits Related to Job Performance

Training-related changes should result in improved job performance and other positive changes (e.g., acquisition of new skills; Hill & Lent 2006, Satterfield & Hughes 2007) that serve as antecedents of job performance (Kraiger 2002). Reassuringly, Arthur et al. (2003) conducted a meta-analysis of 1152 effect sizes from 165 sources and ascertained that in comparison with no-training or pretraining states, training had an overall positive effect on job-related behaviors or performance (mean effect size or $d = 0.62$). However, although differences in terms of effect sizes were not large, the effectiveness of training varied depending on the training delivery method and the skill or task being trained. For example, the most effective training programs were those including both cognitive and interpersonal skills, followed by those including psychomotor skills or tasks. Next, we describe studies to exemplify,

Human capital: the collective set of performance-relevant knowledge, skills, and attitudes within a workforce (at an organizational or societal level)

Training evaluation: the systematic investigation of whether a training program resulted in knowledge, skills, or affective changes in learners as well as go beyond, the general findings reported by Arthur et al. (2003). We emphasize that results from meta-analytic reviews should generally be given more weight than individual (i.e., primary-level) studies because they are more reliable (Aguinis et al. 2008).

Training effects on performance may be subtle (though measurable). In a qualitative study involving mechanics in Northern India, Barber (2004) found that on-the-job training led to greater innovation and tacit skills. Tacit skills are behaviors acquired through informal learning that are useful for effective performance. Regarding innovation, trained mechanics learned to build two Jeep bodies using only a homemade hammer, chisel, and oxyacetylene welder. Regarding tacit skills, Barber noted that the job of a mechanic requires "feel" to be successful. Specifically, trained mechanics developed an intuitive feel when removing dents—a complex process particularly when the fender is badly crumpled. As a result of informal training, one of the mechanics had a "good feeling of how to hit the metal at the exact spot so the work progresses in a systematic fashion" (Barber 2004, p. 134). This type of tacit skill was particularly useful in the Indian context because, although most shops in developed nations would not even attempt to repair a fender that was damaged so badly, this type of repair is common practice in the developing world (Barber 2004).

Benefits of training are also documented for technical skills. For example, Davis & Yi (2004) conducted two experiments with nearly 300 participants using behavior-modeling training and were able to improve computer skills substantially. Although behavior-modeling training has a rich history of success (e.g., Decker & Nathan 1985, Robertson 1990), a unique aspect of this research was that training was found to affect changes in worker skills through a change in trainees' knowledge structures or mental models (see also Marks et al. 2002 for an examination of mental models at the team level). Specifically, mentally rehearsing tasks allowed trainees to increase declarative knowledge and task performance, each measured 10 days after the training was completed. More recently,

Taylor et al. (2005) conducted a meta-analysis including 117 behavior-modeling training studies. They ascertained that the largest effects were for declarative and procedural knowledge (*d*s around 1.0 resulting from comparing training versus a no-training or pretest condition). Declarative knowledge is knowledge about "what" (e.g., facts, meaning of terms), whereas procedural knowledge is knowledge about "how" (i.e., how to perform skilled behavior) (see Aguinis 2009, Kraiger et al. 1993). The overall mean effect on changes in job behavior was $d = 0.27$. However, Taylor et al. (2005) reported substantial variance in the distribution of effect sizes, indicating the need to investigate moderators of the relationship between behavior-modeling training and outcomes. We address the issue of moderators below in the Suggestions for Future Research section.

Training not only may affect declarative knowledge or procedural knowledge, but also may enhance strategic knowledge, defined as knowing when to apply a specific knowledge or skill (Kozlowski et al. 2001, Kraiger et al. 1993). Smith et al. (1997) refer to this as training for adaptive expertise (see also Ford & Schmidt 2000). In addition, training may enable consistency in performance across conditions. For example, Driskell et al. (2001) conducted a study including 79 U.S. Navy technical school trainees who performed a computer-based task. Trainees participated in a stress-exposure training session. This training exposes trainees to information regarding stressors (e.g., noise, time urgency), to the stressors, and how these stressors are likely to affect performance. Results showed that training was beneficial in that trainees performed well under a novel stressor and when performing a novel task. Thus, stress training helps maintain performance consistency.

Performance consistency may also result from enhancing trainees' self-efficacy or self-management skills. Frayne & Geringer (2000) conducted a field experiment in which they administered self-management training (lectures, group discussions, and case studies) to 30 salespeople in the life insurance industry.

Results showed that salespeople who participated in the training program demonstrated higher self-efficacy, outcome expectancy (e.g., "I will increase my sense of accomplishment"), and objective outcomes (e.g., number of new policies sold) as well as subjective job performance (i.e., sales managers' ratings of each salesperson's performance). Training-related performance improvement was sustained over a 12-month period after training ended.

There are also documented benefits of training for managers and leaders. Collins & Holton (2004) conducted a meta-analysis of the benefits of managerial leadership development programs including 83 studies published between 1982 and 2001 (see also Cullen & Turnbull 2005). They found that mean ds (comparing training with no training) ranged from 0.96 to 1.37 for knowledge outcomes and from 0.35 to 1.01 for expertise/behavioral outcomes. Knowledge was defined as principles, facts, attitudes, and skills measured using both subjective (e.g., self-reports) and objective (e.g., standardized tests) measures. Expertise/behavioral outcomes were defined as changes in on-the-job behavior and were also assessed using both subjective (e.g., peer ratings) and objective (e.g., behavioral) measures.

A final illustration of training benefits related to performance is cross-cultural training, in which employees are trained to perform their jobs in a different culture and/or adjust psychologically to living in that culture (Bhawuk & Brislin 2000, Lievens et al. 2003). Morris & Robie (2001) conducted a meta-analysis of the effects of cross-cultural training on expatriate performance and adjustment. Their meta-analysis included 16 studies that investigated adjustment and 25 studies that investigated job performance as the focal dependent variable. The mean correlation for the relationship between training and adjustment was 0.12 ($p <$ 0.05), and the correlation for the relationship between training and performance was 0.23 ($p < 0.05$). However, there was substantial variability in the distribution of effect sizes, suggesting that potential moderators existed (again, we discuss the issue of moderators in

the Suggestions for Future Research section). More recently, Littrell et al. (2006) conducted a qualitative review of 25 years (1980–2005) of research addressing the effectiveness of cross-cultural training in preparing managers for an international assignment. Littrell et al. (2006) examined 29 prior conceptual reviews and 16 empirical studies. Overall, they concluded that cross-cultural training is effective at enhancing the expatriate's success on overseas assignments. They also identified many variables that moderate the effects of training on expatriate performance, including the timing of the training (e.g., predeparture, while on assignment, and postassignment), family issues (e.g., spouse's adjustment), attributes of the job (e.g., job discretion), and cultural differences between the home country and the assignment country.

Other Benefits

Other research demonstrates the impact of training on outcomes other than job performance or on variables that serve as antecedents to job performance. However, we emphasize that these additional benefits of training are not necessarily unrelated to job performance. In fact, in many cases they are indirectly related to performance and, in others, they may be related to individual and team well-being, variables arguably also indirectly related to job performance. For example, there is a renewed interest in leadership training (Collins & Holton 2004, Day 2000). Dvir et al. (2002) implemented a longitudinal randomized field experiment, using cadets in the Israel Defense Forces, in which experimental group leaders received transformational leadership training. Transformational leaders exhibit charismatic behaviors, are able to motivate and provide intellectual stimulation among followers, and treat followers with individual consideration. Results showed that transformational leadership training enhanced followers' motivation (i.e., self-actualization needs and willingness to exert extra effort), morality (i.e., internationalization of their organization's moral values), and

Cross-cultural training: training conducted for improving individual effectiveness and/or adjustment while on assignment in a new culture

empowerment (i.e., critical-independent approach, active engagement in the task, and specific self-efficacy). Towler (2003) provided 41 business students with (a) no training, (b) presentation skills training, or (c) charismatic influence training. Charismatic influence training included articulating a vision, appealing to followers' values, and using autobiography, metaphors, analogies, stories, and self-efficacy language. A sample of 102 undergraduates from a different university watched videotaped presentations by the 41 business students. Similar to results of Dvir et al. (2002), Towler (2003) found some evidence in support of the effectiveness of charismatic influence training on the performance and attitudes of the participants who watched the videotapes.

Another area that has received consistent attention is aviation human factors training. This is an important area of research because human error has been consistently identified as one of the main causes of air crashes since the late 1970s (Edkins 2002). Edkins (2002) conducted a qualitative review of the aviation human factor training literature and concluded that outcomes of safety and team-based training programs include (a) safety-related benefits, including a reduction in lost time related to injuries, and (b) teamwork-related benefits including improved team performance. Because safety-related errors in fields such as aviation and medical care are often the result of team coordination issues (e.g., Morey et al. 2002, Salas et al. 2001), team training emerges as an important intervention. Ellis et al. (2005) conducted an experiment including 65 four-person teams. Individuals participated in a dynamic command and control simulation in which participants monitor activity in a specific geographic region and defend it against invasion by ground or air. Training improved declarative knowledge within the team and, in comparison with untrained teams, trained teams demonstrated better planning and task coordination, collaborative problem solving, and communication in novel team and task environments.

The most common training intervention for improving team communication and team effectiveness is crew resource management (CRM) training. The overall goal of CRM training is to shape cockpit crew attitudes and behavior to enhance aviation safety. This type of training is usually conducted using sophisticated flight simulators, and it addresses communication, teamwork, decision-making, and awareness with respect to accidents and incidents and the role played by human error. Goeters (2002) delivered CRM training to aircrews from an eastern European airline. After participating in training, aircrews substantially improved nontechnical skills (e.g., team building) as well as situation awareness and decision-making, each of which contribute to air safety. There are two qualitative literature reviews of studies addressing CRM training: O'Connor et al. (2002) reviewed 48 studies, and Salas et al. (2001) reviewed 58 studies. Given that they included overlapping sets of primary studies, it is not surprising that the conclusions of these literature reviews converged and determined that most studies focused on the benefits regarding attitudes and knowledge at the individual and team levels of analysis. Documented benefits include positive reactions to training, knowledge of teamwork principles, and aircrew communication and performance. A more recent qualitative review by Salas et al. (2006) examined 28 studies published since the Salas et al. (2001) review and included CRM studies not only in cockpits but also in other contexts such as aircraft maintenance and health care. Salas et al. (2006) reported positive effects of CRM training on trainee reactions, but results were mixed in terms of trainee learning and on-the-job behaviors. For example, Jacobsen et al. (2001) found that trainees had high situational awareness and communicated frequently; however, trainees had difficulties diagnosing medical problems, and no team member assumed the lead or delegated tasks. In general, CRM training was more effective in aviation settings than in health care settings, where its application is more recent.

In summary, a considerable number of individual studies and meta-analytic reviews provide support for the many benefits of training for individuals and teams. These benefits include performance as well as variables that relate to performance directly (e.g., innovation and tacit skills, adaptive expertise, technical skills, self-management skills, cross-cultural adjustment) or indirectly (e.g., empowerment; communication, planning, and task coordination in teams). In the following section, we review evidence regarding benefits produced by training activities at the organizational level.

BENEFITS OF TRAINING FOR ORGANIZATIONS

Fewer than 5% of all training programs are assessed in terms of their financial benefits to the organization (Swanson 2001). The picture changes among companies recognized for their commitment to training. Specifically, the majority of organizations recognized by ASTD for innovative training programs measure training impact at some level of organizational effectiveness (Paradise 2007, Rivera & Paradise 2006). Typical organizational performance measures in this latter sample include productivity improvement, sales or revenue, and overall profitability. Overall, research regarding organizational-level benefits is not nearly as abundant as the literature on individual- and team-level benefits. Not only have there been relatively few empirical studies showing organizational-level impact, but those studies that have been done typically use self-report data and unclear causal link back to training activities (Tharenou et al. 2007). Nevertheless, we review this literature organized into two areas: benefits related to organizational performance and other benefits.

Benefits Related to Organizational Performance

Several studies conducted in European countries have documented the impact of training on organizational performance. Aragón-Sánchez et al. (2003) investigated the relationship between training and organizational performance by distributing a survey to 457 small and medium-size businesses in the United Kingdom, the Netherlands, Portugal, Finland, and Spain. Organizational performance was operationalized as (a) effectiveness (i.e., employee involvement, human resource indicators, and quality), and (b) profitability (i.e., sales volume, benefits before interest and taxes, and a ratio of benefit before taxes/sales). Results indicated that some types of training activities, including on-the-job training and training inside the organization using in-house trainers, were positively related to most dimensions of effectiveness and profitability. Ubeda García (2005) conducted a study including 78 Spanish firms with more than 100 employees. This study related organizations' training policies (e.g., functions assumed by the training unit, goals of the training unit, nature of training, and how training is evaluated) with four types of organizational-level benefits: employee satisfaction, customer satisfaction, owner/shareholder satisfaction, and workforce productivity (i.e., sales per employee). Results suggested that training programs oriented toward human capital development were directly related to employee, customer, and owner/shareholder satisfaction as well as an objective measure of business performance (i.e., sales per employee). Guerrero & Barraud-Didier (2004) administered a questionnaire to 1530 human resource directors working in large companies in France and collected financial information from the companies' financial directors or through databases approximately one year later. Five questions in the survey addressed the extent to which the company implemented training practices. The survey also included questions about social and organizational performance including work climate, employee attendance, quality of products and services, and employee productivity. Results showed that 4.6% of the variance in financial performance was explained by training (via the mediating role of social and organizational performance). Finally, Mabey & Ramirez (2005) conducted a study including 179 firms in the United Kingdom, Denmark, France, Germany, Norway, and Spain. Human resource managers or equivalent and line managers completed a survey on training practices. Financial data were gathered from the Amadeus database; a two-factor measure of financial performance was computed based on (a) operating revenue per employee and (b) cost of employees as a percentage of operating revenues. Results indicated that the manner in which management development was implemented accounted for substantive variance in the financial performance measure. Specifically, firms with line managers reporting that management development programs are valued were more likely to have a positive relationship between management development and financial performance.

Because of the paucity of primary-level studies examining the benefits of training at the organizational level, the meta-analytic reviews published to date include only a small number of studies. In the meta-analysis by Arthur et al. (2003), the researchers also examined the impact of training on organizational-level results. Only 26 studies ($N = 1748$) examined the benefits of training at the organizational level. Results showed that the benefits of training vary depending on the type of training delivery method, the skill or task being trained, and the measure used to assess effectiveness. However, the mean d for organizational results was 0.62, precisely the same effect size found for the impact of training on job-related behaviors and performance at the individual level of analysis. Similarly, the Collins & Holton (2004) meta-analysis of managerial leadership development programs included only seven studies (of 83) that included information regarding the relationship between training and tangible organizational-level benefits (e.g., reduced costs, improved quality and quantity). The total sample size in these seven studies was 418 and the overall mean d was 0.39, favoring training compared to control groups.

Other Benefits

Benefits of training have been documented for variables other than organizational performance. Again, many of these additional outcomes are related to performance indirectly.

For example, Sirianni & Frey (2001) evaluated the effectiveness of a nine-month leadership development program at a financial services company with presence in Canada, Europe, Latin America, and Asia. Participants included 29 service and operations market managers, district managers, and a regional president. The 13 training modules (e.g., managing conflict, motivating others, priority setting) were delivered in three-hour sessions every two weeks. Measures of program effectiveness included ratings offered by participants as well as other objective measures including regional scorecard results, which were collected on a monthly basis and used to determine service quality. Data collected approximately at the beginning and end of the training program suggested that, at a regional level, there were improvements on six of the seven scorecard components: overall teller errors, teller out of balance, number of deposit slips left in envelopes, business retention, teller secret shopper ratings, and new account secret shopper surveys.

Benson et al. (2004) collected data from each of the 9439 permanent, salaried employees of a large high-technology manufacturing firm to assess the effects on employee turnover of the organization's investment in employee development via a tuition reimbursement program. Investment in training via tuition reimbursement decreased turnover while employees were still taking classes. However, turnover increased once employees obtained their degrees if they were not promoted. This study points to the need to offer development opportunities on an ongoing basis and to align training efforts within an organization's performance management system (Aguinis 2009).

The nature of an organization's reputation influences how customers (and potential customers), competitors, and even employees interact with the organization. Thus, an organization's reputation can have important financial consequences. Clardy (2005) noted that an organization's reputation can be affected by its training practices. Organizations such as the SEALs (special operations force of the U.S. Navy) are legendary for their rigorous and extensive training programs. One of the goals of the SEAL training, as frequently shown on television and other media, is to "construct a reputation of SEALs as totally dedicated, ruthless, and lethally skilled operators who would be a totally invincible foe" (Clardy 2005, p. 291). Similarly, although not empirically documented yet, another possible benefit of training could be *social capital*, via relationship building, norm development, and institutional trust (Brown & Van Buren 2007). In other words, training has the potential to affect important social processes that in turn are likely to affect organizational-level outcomes.

Darch & Lucas (2002) conducted interviews with 20 small and medium-size business owners in the food industry in Queensland (Australia). These companies dealt with products such as meat, fruit, vegetables, seafood, and grains. The main goals of this study were to understand business owners' barriers to their uptake of e-commerce and to identify strategies enabling them to engage in e-commerce initiatives. Results showed that of several barriers to e-commerce, an important one was the lack of training. Study participants noted that training would be a key strategy by which they could address their need to acquire the necessary knowledge and technological skills. In short, training was seen as an important enabler for e-commerce, a key strategic direction for the success of many of these small and medium-size businesses.

In summary, many studies have gathered support for the benefits of training for organizations as a whole. These benefits include improved organizational performance (e.g., profitability, effectiveness, productivity, operating revenue per employee) as well as other outcomes that relate directly (e.g., reduced costs, improved quality and quantity) or indirectly (e.g., employee turnover, organization's reputation, social capital) to performance. In the next section, we review evidence regarding benefits produced by training activities at the societal level.

BENEFITS OF TRAINING FOR SOCIETY

Most of the research on the relationship between training activities and their benefits for society has been conducted by economists; the focal dependent variable is national economic performance. Overall, this body of literature leads to the conclusion that training efforts produce improvements in the quality of the labor force, which in turn is one of the most important contributors to national economic growth (e.g., Becker 1962, 1964). Economists coined the terms "human capital" and "capital formation in people" in referring mainly to schooling and on-the-job training (Wang et al. 2002).

An illustration of this type of analysis is a study by van Leeuwen & van Praag (2002), who calculated the costs associated with on-the-job training and the impact of such training on country-level macroeconomic variables. These researchers concluded that if employers receive a tax credit of €115 per employee trained, the total expense for the country would be €11 million, but €114 million would be generated in increased revenue resulting from the new skills acquired.

In addition to economic growth and other related financial outcomes, training activities have the potential to produce benefits such as the inclusion of the country in powerful economic blocks (e.g., European Union). This is because some of the requirements imposed on countries to be part of these blocks include human capital development. Accordingly, in recognition of the benefits of training at the societal level, many countries encourage national-scale training and development projects as a matter of national policy (Cho & McLean 2004). Consider the following selective evidence.

In the Pacific Islands, a region of Oceania with more than 10,000 islands in the South Pacific Ocean, the population is dispersed over large distances and is vulnerable to numerous environmental threats and natural disasters (Bartlett & Rodgers 2004). These islands constitute 22 different political entities, most of the economies are small, education is generally good at the elementary level but not the secondary level, and in-company training is limited. The area is very diverse economically, socially, and culturally. However, the Pacific Islands, led by the regional intergovernmental Secretariat of the Pacific Community and the Pacific Islands Forum Secretariat, have developed a common and unique vision of people as "the most important building block for economic, social, and cultural development" (Bartlett & Rodgers 2004, p. 311). This people-centered approach assumes that investment in human capital is fundamental for achieving societal prosperity.

In the United Kingdom, the government wishes to improve the skills of the workforce and encourages the development of lifelong learning practices through a variety of organizations and initiatives (Lee 2004). Although the government leads these initiatives, they give a strong voice to employers, trade unions, professional bodies, and other stakeholders in the business sector. For example, the organization Investors in People gives awards to organizations that implement excellent practices in the training of individuals to achieve business goals. Different organizations can use different means to achieve success through their people, so Investors in People does not prescribe any one method but instead provides a framework to help organizations find the most suitable means for achieving success through people (Investors in People Standard 2006).

The recognition of the importance of training activities led India in 1985 to become the first nation in the Asia-Pacific region to create a Ministry of Human Resource Development (Rao 2004). This ministry was created by then Prime Minister Rajiv Ghandi, who had a vision that investment in human capital would be an essential tool for the country's development. Accordingly, the public sector, which had traditionally been the largest employer in India, assisted in the creation of corporate training departments. Examples of organizations with such departments include Hindustan Machine Tools, Bharat Heavy Electricals, Hindustan Aeronautics, State Bank of India, Steel Authority of India, and Coal India.

Poland is an additional interesting illustration given its transition from a centralized economy under Soviet control to a member of the European Union in May 2004. Under Soviet control with a command economy, and virtually full state ownership in all sectors, a typical Polish employee was "chronically suspicious, full of sour demand, unable to take responsibility or to commit himself, ever ready to wallow in his own misery and misfortune" (Tischner 1992 as cited in Szalkowski & Jankowicz 2004, p. 347). To say the least, the majority of employees did not possess the attitudes and skills needed to meet the demands of a market economy. In addition, that thousands of employees were on the country's payroll without making value-added contributions became obvious as several industries shrunk their workforces. For example, the coal mining industry went from about 500,000 employees in the mid-1990s to about 100,000 employees a decade later (Szalkowski & Jankowicz 2004). Thus, in Poland now there is a general feeling that "further progress in the commercial sphere can only come through engagement in the process of globalization and through the development of national human resources via training, education, and research" (Szalkowski & Jankowicz 2004, p. 350).

In summary, the recognition of the benefits of training activities for society has led many countries around the world to adopt national policies to encourage the design and delivery of training programs at the national level. These policies have the goal to improve a nation's human capital, which in turn is related to greater economic prosperity.

HOW TO MAXIMIZE THE BENEFITS OF TRAINING

In the next section, we summarize recent theory and research oriented toward improving the effectiveness and impact of training. Roughly following the instructional design model (Goldstein & Ford 2002), we organize this review around stages of needs assessment and pretraining states, training design and delivery, training evaluation, and transfer of training.

Needs Assessment and Pretraining States

Conducting a thorough needs assessment before training is designed and delivered helps set appropriate goals for training and ensure that trainees are ready to participate (Blanchard & Thacker 2007). However, there continues to be little theoretical or empirical work on needs assessment (Kraiger 2003). One exception is a study by Baranzini et al. (2001), who developed and validated a needs assessment tool for the aviation maintenance industry. A second example of a theory-based approach to conducting a needs assessment is a study by Fowlkes et al. (2000), who evaluated an event-based knowledge-elicitation technique in which subject matter experts (SMEs) are asked about team situational awareness factors in response to a military helicopter operation. Results showed that more experienced experts identified a richer database of cues and were more likely to identify response strategies, supporting the conclusion that using SMEs during a needs assessment maximizes the benefits of training. The finding that expertise affects the quality of needs assessment data is consistent with the conclusions of Morgeson & Campion (1997), who reported that the accuracy of job analysis data may be compromised by up to 16 different systematic sources of error. These include social influence and self-presentation influences and limitations in information processing (cf. Ford & Kraiger 1995). More empirical research is necessary to understand how the quality of training design and delivery is affected by systematic and random influences on the quality of needs assessment data.

Consideration of the pretraining states or individual characteristics of trainees also enhances the benefits of training. Tracey et al. (2001) collected data from 420 hotel managers who attended a two-and-a-half-day managerial knowledge and skills training program. Results showed that managers' job involvement, organizational commitment, and perceptions of the work environment (i.e., perceived support and recognition) were predictive of pretraining self-efficacy, which in turn was related to pretraining motivation. Pretraining motivation was related to posttraining measures of utility reactions, affective reactions, declarative knowledge scores, and procedural knowledge scores. Pretraining motivation has also been shown to be related to trainee personality (Rowold 2007), trainee self-efficacy and training reputation (Switzer et al. 2005), as well as reactions to prior training courses (Sitzmann et al. 2007). In a field study of learners in a traditional classroom or blended learning course, Klein et al. (2006) found that learners had a higher motivation to learn when they had a high learning goal orientation (rather than a lower learning goal orientation) and when they perceived environmental conditions (e.g., time, Internet access) as learning enablers (rather than as barriers). Motivation to learn, in turn, was related to learner satisfaction, metacognition, and course grade. Kozlowski et al. (2001) showed that trait and manipulated learning orientation had independent effects on participants' self-efficacy and structural knowledge.

More generally, Colquitt et al. (2000) summarized 20 years of research on factors affecting trainee motivation. Their meta-analysis showed that training motivation was significantly predicted by individual characteristics (e.g., locus of control, conscientiousness, anxiety, age, cognitive ability, self-efficacy, valence of training, and job involvement) as well as by situational characteristics (e.g., organizational climate).

In summary, two ways to maximize the benefits of training is to conduct a needs assessment using experienced SMEs and to make sure trainees are ready and motivated for training. For example, training readiness can be enhanced by lowering trainees' anxiety about training, demonstrating the value of training before training begins, and making sure employees are highly involved and engaged with their jobs.

Transfer of training: the extent to which new knowledge and skills learned during training are applied on the job

Pretraining motivation: individual attitudes, expectancies, and self-beliefs likely to influence willingness to attend training and learning during training

Training Design and Training Delivery

Research on training design and delivery can be categorized into two general themes: research on new approaches to engage learners in meaningful learning processes and research on specific training methods. Several studies in each of these two domains provide information on how to maximize the benefits of training.

Linou & Kontogiannis (2004) compared immediate recall and follow-up retention levels (after six weeks) in four groups. Trainees were production engineering undergraduates. The primary objective of training was to help participants develop diagnostic strategies to identify symptoms and problems given a set of fault scenarios. One group received systemic training (focusing on structural, functional, and physical relationships among subsystems), two groups received either low-level or high-level diagnostic information, and one group received general training on theories related to manufacturing plants. The theory group and both diagnostic groups performed better on the immediate recall measures, whereas the systemic group performed better on the retention measure, presumably because group members built a more stable organization (mental model) of the training content. Similarly, Holladay & Quiñones (2003) showed that adding variability to practice trials resulted in better long-term retention, presumably because trainees had to exert greater effort during skill acquisition.

Researchers continued to explore error training as a strategy for increasing performance and maintaining performance under changing environmental demands. In contrast to traditional training design approaches that focus on teaching correct methods (and avoiding errors), error management training encourages trainees to make errors and engage in reflection to understand the causes of errors and strategies to avoid making them in the future. Heimbeck et al. (2003) implemented error training using a sample of undergraduate students. The task consisted of learning how to use spreadsheet software (i.e., Excel). Performance was assessed by raters who reviewed videotaped sessions and rated whether discrete tasks such as entering data correctly or formatting a table were performed correctly. Trainees who were provided the opportunity to make errors (together with explicit instructions encouraging them to learn from these errors) performed significantly higher than those in error-avoidant conditions. In a follow-up experiment, participants learning how to use presentations software (i.e., PowerPoint) performed better in the error training with metacognition prompting (i.e., instructions encouraging trainees to think explicitly about what the problem is, what they are trying to achieve, and so forth) compared to the error-avoidant condition (Keith & Frese 2005). A recent meta-analysis by Keith & Frese (2008) reported that overall, error management training was superior to either proceduralized error-avoidant training or exploratory training without error encouragement ($d = 0.44$). Effect sizes were moderated by two important factors: Effect sizes were greater for posttransfer measures compared to within-training performance, and for adaptive transfer tasks (as opposed to tasks structurally similar to training). Thus, error training may be appropriate for developing a deeper task understanding that facilitates transfer to novel tasks.

Research on error training highlights the importance of understanding and affecting learner states and answers long-standing calls to engage in research on how individuals learn, not in just the latest training fads (e.g., Campbell 1971, Kraiger et al. 1993). For example, Schmidt & Ford (2003) reported that levels of meta-cognitive activity mediated the effects of a computer-based training program on declarative knowledge, task performance, and participants' self-efficacy. An increasing amount of evidence suggests that trainees' self-regulatory processes mediate the training–learning relationship. Self-regulation refers to the extent to which executive-level cognitive systems in the learner monitor and exert control on the learner's attention and active engagement of training content (Vancouver & Day 2005). Chen et al. (2005) trained 156 individuals in 78 teams on a flight simulator task and examined adaptive performance on subsequent performance trials. Training participants' self-regulation processes mediated the effects of training on task self-efficacy and their adaptive performance across trials. Two studies reported by Sitzmann et al. (2008) used repeated trials to demonstrate that while engaging in self-regulatory processes facilitates learning, the effects improve over time.

Technology-delivered instruction (TDI) continues to become increasingly popular in industry (Paradise 2007), although researchers have been slow to study factors that facilitate or limit its effectiveness (Brown 2001, Welsh et al. 2003). TDI includes Web-based training and instruction on single workstations, PDAs and MP3 players, as well as embedded just-in-training in work-related software (Aguinis et al. 2009). One potential drawback of TDI is that it transfers more control to learners to make decisions about what and how to learn (Noe 2008). A recent meta-analysis by Kraiger & Jerden (2007) indicated that high learner control has only marginally beneficial effects on learning, and in many studies, high control has a negative effect. Low-ability or inexperienced learners under high learner-control conditions may make poor decisions about what and how to learn (DeRouin et al. 2004). One promising technique for coupling learner-driven instruction with technology is to supplement learner control with adaptive guidance. Specifically, Bell & Kozlowski (2002) concluded that providing adaptive guidance in a computer-based training environment substantively improved trainees' study and practice effort, knowledge acquired, and performance.

Better hardware and software capabilities have allowed for improvements in the delivery of various forms of remote training. Zhao et al. (2005) conducted a meta-analysis comparing face-to-face and distance education courses and found no significant differences between formats. A meta-analysis by Sitzmann et al. (2006) examined the relative effectiveness of Web-based instruction over classroom instruction. In an analysis of 96 published and unpublished studies involving 19,331 trainees, the researchers found that Web-based instruction was 6% more effective than classroom instruction for teaching declarative knowledge but was equally effective for teaching procedural knowledge. However, when the same instructional methods were used in both forms of instruction, there were no differences in the relative effectiveness of either media. Thus, the small advantage of Web-based instruction over classroom training may be due more to the use of novel (and effective) training strategies than to the medium per se.

Researchers are also exploring the impact of novel training technologies on outcomes other than learning. For example, Wesson & Gogus (2005) compared two different methods for delivering socialization training to new employees: a group social-based program and an individual computer-based program. This quasi-experiment included 261 new employees from a large technology-based consulting firm. The social-based program was substantially more successful in socializing new employees regarding people, politics, and organizational goals and values.

In summary, the application of appropriate training design and delivery methods can help maximize the benefits of training. In terms of design, recent research suggests that the benefits of training are enhanced by applying theory-based learning principles such as encouraging trainees to organize the training content, making sure trainees expend effort in the acquisition of new skills, and providing trainees with an opportunity to make errors together with explicit instructions to encourage them to learn from these errors. In terms of training delivery, recent research indicates that the benefits of using technology can be enhanced by providing trainees with adaptive guidance.

Training Evaluation

The Kirkpatrick four-levels approach to training evaluation continues to be the most widely used training evaluation model among practitioners (e.g., Sugrue & Rivera 2005, Twitchell

Adaptive guidance: providing trainees with diagnostic, future-oriented information to aid decisions about what and how much to study and practice in training

et al. 2000), although the approach continues to be criticized by researchers (e.g., Holton 2005, Kraiger 2002, Spitzer 2005). There has been little empirical work in the twenty-first century on designing and validating new evaluation measures, although there have been several conceptual contributions to frameworks guiding evaluation decisions (Holton 2005, Kraiger 2002, Spitzer 2005, Wang & Wilcox 2006).

Kraiger (2002) proposed a decision-based evaluation model. The model frames decisions about how to measure training impact around the intended purpose for evaluation—purposes of decision making, marketing, and providing feedback to participants, instructors, or instructional designers. The model also emphasizes tailoring evaluation measures to the needs and sophistication of the intended audience(s). It proposes a comprehensive taxonomy for evaluation, including assessing the training program, changes in the learner, and changes in the organization. Notably, a number of authors have criticized the lack of rigor in training evaluation designs (e.g., Edkins 2002, Littrell et al. 2006, O'Connor et al. 2002, Wang 2002). Although Kraiger's model emphasizes the importance of solid designs (as compared to more or better measures), he argued that meaningful evaluation can be done with incomplete research designs, a point raised earlier by Sackett & Mullen (1993) and Tannenbaum & Woods (1992), and later echoed by Kraiger et al. (2004). The internal referencing strategy, in which effect sizes for trained behavior (or knowledge) are compared to effect sizes for nontrained behaviors (or knowledge), was used in several studies as an alternative to more rigorous designs with a control group (Aguinis & Branstetter 2007, Frese et al. 2003).

How people react to training has continued to receive attention in the literature, particularly around the question of how best to use reactions for improving training design and delivery. Morgan & Casper (2000) factor analyzed a set of training reaction items from 9128 government employees and found evidence of two underlying factors: overall affect toward training and perceived utility of the training.

Aguinis & Branstetter (2007) also discussed the need to discriminate between affective and utility reactions because utility reactions are more strongly related to learning than are affective reactions. K.G. Brown (2005) proposed a theoretical structure with distinct factors (enjoyment, relevance, and technology satisfaction) as well as a second-order factor of overall satisfaction, related in part to trainee affect. Data from two studies reported by K.G. Brown (2005) supported this model. In a study of 181 Korean workers, Lim & Morris (2006) showed that the relationship between perceived applicability (training utility) and perceived application (transfer) decreased as the time between training and measurement increased.

There continues to be calls for establishing the return on investment for training, particularly as training continues to be outsourced and new forms of TDI are marketed as cost effective. Although the tools and strategies for showing return on investment are well known (e.g., Kraiger 2002, Phillips & Phillips 2007, Spitzer 2005), as the above review of organizational-level outcomes indicated, there remain few published studies of return on investment.

In summary, it is important not only that the benefits of training be maximized, but also that these benefits are documented. Recently proposed conceptualizations and measures of training effectiveness can enhance the perceived benefits of training from the perspective of the various stakeholders in the process, including those who participate in training, those who deliver it, and those who fund it (e.g., organizations). It is important that training evaluation include a consideration of the intended purpose of the evaluation, the needs and sophistication of the intended audience, and the variables related to various types of utility reactions (i.e., affective versus utility).

Transfer of Training

Evidence described in the previous sections forcefully makes the point that training works, in the sense that it has an impact on individuals and teams and on the organizations and the societies in which they function. However, training efforts will not yield the anticipated effects if knowledge, attitudes, and skills acquired in training are not fully and appropriately transferred to job-related activities. Thus, the study of transfer of training focuses on variables that affect the impact of training on transfer of training as well as on interventions intended to enhance transfer.

Research on moderators of the training-transfer relationship has focused primarily on workgroup factors—supervisory and peer support—as well as on organizational-level factors. Holton et al. (2003) used the Learning Transfer System Inventory (Holton et al. 2001) to examine differences in transfer characteristics across eight different organizations, three organization types, and three training types. The Learning Transfer System Inventory includes 68 items encompassing 16 conceptual constructs that in turn are organized in to four major groups: trainee characteristics (learner readiness and self-efficacy), trainee motivation (motivation to transfer, transfer effort to performance expectations, and performance to outcome expectations), work environment (performance coaching, supervisor support, supervisor sanctions, peer support, resistance-openness to change, positive personal outcomes, and negative personal outcomes), and ability (perceived content validity, personal capacity for transfer, transfer design, and opportunity to use). Analyses showed that scale scores differed across individual organizations, organization types, and training types, indicating that transfer environments are probably unique to each training application.

Regarding organizational-level factors, Kontoghiorghes (2004) emphasized the importance of both transfer climate and the work environment in facilitating transfer. Transfer climate includes a number of factors including supervisory and peer support, but also task cues, training accountability, opportunities to practice, opportunities to use new knowledge and skills, and intrinsic and extrinsic rewards for using new knowledge. Work environment factors include sociotechnical system design

variables (e.g., fostering job involvement, employee involvement, information sharing), job design variables (e.g., fostering task autonomy, job match), quality management variables (e.g., employee commitment to quality work, customer focus), and continuous learning variables (e.g., continuous learning as a priority, rewards for learning). With a sample of 300 employees in the information technology division of a large U.S. automaker, Kontoghiorghes (2004) found support for both climate and work environment factors as predictors of transfer motivation and performance.

Although there continue to be claims that the transfer climate is critical to transfer of training, empirical studies of transfer climate have yielded mixed results. Richman-Hirsch (2001) found that posttraining transfer enhancement interventions were more successful in supportive work environments. Chiaburu & Marinova (2005) found no effects for supervisory support but positive results for peer support in a study of 186 trained employees. van der Klink et al. (2001) also found no effect for supervisory support on two studies involving bank tellers. An important study for understanding these mixed results may be that of Pidd (2004), which examined the role of peer and supervisory support for transfer of training on workplace drug and alcohol awareness. Pidd reported that the influence of workplace support on transfer was moderated by the extent to which trainees identified with the groups that provided support.

A number of studies have investigated in-training strategies for improving transfer, with little or mixed success. T.C. Brown (2005) examined goal setting at the end of training by comparing three conditions: setting distal goals, setting proximal plus distal goals, and telling participants to do their best. Contrary to expectations, participants instructed to do their best out-performed trainees told to set distal goals, and did as well as participants told to set proximal plus distal goals. In contrast, Richman-Hirsch (2001) reported positive effects for a posttraining goal-setting intervention, particularly in supportive work environments.

Gaudine & Saks (2004) found no differences between a relapse prevention and transfer enhancement intervention for nurses attending a two-day training program. The researchers suggested that transfer climate and support were likely more potent determinants of transfer than were posttraining interventions. Huint & Saks (2003) examined managers' reactions to either a relapse prevention intervention or one emphasizing supervisor support. For a sample of 174 managers and students, there was no significant difference in preferences for either intervention, although there was a slight tendency to prefer the supervisor support intervention.

In summary, recent research has reported on how to ensure that the changes that take place during training are transferred back to the job environment. Taken together, this body of research points to the importance of considering interpersonal factors such as supervisory and peer support as moderators of the training-transfer of training relationship. More distal organizational-level factors such as transfer climate have not received consistent support as important moderators.

CONCLUSIONS AND SUGGESTIONS FOR FUTURE RESEARCH

We take the point of view that training leads to important benefits for individuals and teams, organizations, and society. The present review suggests that these benefits range from individual and team performance to the economic prosperity of a nation. To understand these benefits of training, we adopted a multilevel, multidisciplinary, and global perspective. We also included a discussion of how to maximize the benefits of training. These factors include paying attention to needs assessment and pretraining states of trainees (e.g., trainee motivation), training design and delivery (e.g., advantages of using error training), training evaluation (e.g., documenting training success differently depending on the stakeholder in question), and transfer of training (i.e., the importance of interpersonal factors).

Implications for Practice

The organizations that are able to realize the benefits of training that are documented in this review are able to move away from viewing the training function as an operational function or cost center to one that is value driven (Fox 2003). For example, the consulting company PricewaterhouseCoopers has cut costs in many areas but increased its investment in employee training to about $120 million per year. Another leading consulting firm, Booz Allen Hamilton, believes in developing workers as a long-term competitive advantage and manages its learning functions as revenue centers (Fox 2003). Managers and other decision makers in these organizations prefer information and data on business-related results to make decisions about how to allocate resources, including resources for training activities (Mattson 2005). Training for the sake of training, an approach that focuses on developmental ideals and supportive organizational environments, is not aligned with today's business realities, including compressed career progression pathways, budgetary cuts and constraints, highly competitive environments, and market-driven economic philosophies (McGuire et al. 2005). Designing, delivering, evaluating, and clearly documenting the benefits of training using the information included in this review will allow the human resource management function to be a strategic organizational player and to move away from the negative connotations (e.g., "welfare secretaries") associated with this function in the twentieth century (Hammonds 2005, Jacoby 2004, Kraiger et al. 2004).

Suggestions for Future Research

We also identify future directions for research. First, we suggest that the benefits of training may have a cascading effect such that individual-level benefits (e.g., individual performance) affect team-level benefits (i.e., team performance), which in turn affect organizational (i.e., profitability) and societal (i.e., human capital) outcomes. However, research is needed to understand the factors that facilitate a smooth cross-level transfer of benefits. Of special interest is the question of vertical transfer: how effects of training on individuals (increased knowledge and skills) translate directly into better functioning at the team and organizational level. Although good conceptual models of this process exist (e.g., Kozlowski & Salas 1997, Kozlowski et al. 2000), there has been little empirical research. Conceptual work on such cross-level transfers in other areas of applied psychology may prove useful in this regard (e.g., Fiol et al. 2001).

Second, a gap exists between the applied and scholarly literatures regarding the use of cycle time as a variable to assess training effectiveness (Holton 2003). Effect sizes for the quality of performance may not be the same as those for the speed at which individuals, teams, and organizations identify and implement solutions to new problems. Given competition and market-related pressures, organizations need to realize the benefits of training faster and faster. Research on this issue is lacking in the scholarly literature; work is needed regarding the factors that can accelerate the realization of the benefits of training at various levels of analysis. This research may profit from initial studies on the effects of training on innovation and performance adaptability.

Third, although the role of affect has been acknowledged in the measurement of reactions to training, affect could play a more central role in the training process in general. Prior research has focused on the relationship between liking a training program (positive reactions) and employee learning or subsequent performance (Alliger et al. 1997), but has paid less attention to relationships between affective states during training and learning. Offering employees training opportunities can be seen as a message that the organization cares for its employees (Aguinis 2009). This perception may in turn produce benefits even though training design and delivery may not be optimal. In short, future research could investigate the extent to which training opportunities are seen as a message that the organization cares, which could

be a powerful and important message in today's corporate world plagued by downsizing and employee layoffs.

Fourth, we identified the need to study moderators in several areas. Moderators explain the conditions under which an effect or relationship is likely to be present and likely to be stronger (Aguinis 2004, Aguinis et al. 2005). Training research has consistently found support for both individual and situational moderators on relationships among training interventions, trainee learning, and workplace performance (Kraiger & Aguinis 2001). For example, in this review we highlighted the importance of moderators in the study of the relationship between behavior modeling and training outcomes, the relationship between cross-cultural training and expatriate adjustment, the relationship between training and transfer. However, additional research is needed to understand fully the range and impact of these moderators. Ideally, this research would be driven by better theory on how proposed situational and individual moderators operate to effect learning and transfer. For example, how do organizational systems for accountability influence trainee motivation or cognitive effort during training? How does cognitive ability influence both the rate and depth of learning during training?

We close by emphasizing the overwhelming evidence in favor of the benefits that training produces for individuals and teams, organizations, and society. An important challenge for the practice of training is to integrate the training function with employee selection, performance management, rewards, and other human resource management practices (Aguinis 2009, Aguinis & Pierce 2008, Cascio & Aguinis 2005). Training alone may not be able to realize its benefits if it is disconnected from other human resource management functions or the organization is dysfunctional in other areas (e.g., interpersonal relationships). Training will have the greatest impact when it is bundled together with other human resource management practices and these practices are also implemented following sound principles and empirical research.

SUMMARY POINTS

1. The current review differs from previous *Annual Review of Psychology* articles on the topic of training and development because its approach is fundamentally multidisciplinary, multilevel, and global.

2. There is considerable support for the many benefits of training for individuals and teams. These benefits include performance as well as variables that relate directly (e.g., innovation and tacit skills, adaptive expertise, technical skills, self-management skills, cross-cultural adjustment) or indirectly (e.g., empowerment; communication, planning, and task coordination in teams) to performance.

3. Many studies have gathered support for the benefits of training for organizations as a whole. These benefits include improved organizational performance (e.g., profitability, effectiveness, productivity, operating revenue per employee) as well as other outcomes that relate directly (e.g., reduced costs, improved quality and quantity) or indirectly (e.g., employee turnover, organization's reputation, social capital) to performance.

4. The recognition of the benefits of training activities for society has led many countries around the world to adopt national policies to encourage the design and delivery of training programs at the national level. The goal of these policies is to improve a nation's human capital, which in turn is related to greater economic prosperity.

5. Several interventions are effective at enhancing the benefits of training. First, organizations should conduct a needs assessment using experienced subject matter experts to make sure trainees are ready and motivated for training. Second, in terms of design, organizations should apply theory-based learning principles such as encouraging trainees to organize the training content, making sure trainees expend effort in the acquisition of new skills, and providing trainees with an opportunity to make errors together with explicit instructions to encourage them to learn from these errors enhances the benefits of training. Third, in terms of training delivery, the benefits of using technology for training delivery can be enhanced by providing trainees with adaptive guidance. Fourth, it is important not only that the benefits of training be maximized, but also that these benefits are documented. Recently proposed conceptualizations and measures of training effectiveness can enhance the perceived benefits of training from the perspective of the various stakeholders in the process, including those who participate in training, those who deliver it, and those who fund it (e.g., organizations). Finally, recent research points to the importance of considering interpersonal factors such as supervisory and peer support as moderators of the relationship between training and transfer of training back to the work environment.

6. Designing, delivering, evaluating, and clearly documenting the benefits of training using the information included in this review will allow the human resource management function to be a strategic organizational player and to move away from the negative connotations (e.g., "welfare secretaries") associated with this function in the twentieth century.

7. Future research is needed in several areas. For example, the benefits of training may have a cascading effect such that individual-level benefits (e.g., individual performance) affect team-level benefits (i.e., team performance), which in turn affect organizational (i.e., profitability) and societal (i.e., human capital) outcomes. However, future research is needed

to understand the factors that facilitate a smooth cross-level transfer of benefits. Second, a gap exists between the applied and scholarly literatures regarding the use of cycle time as a variable to assess training effectiveness. Third, although the role of affect has been acknowledged in the measurement of reactions to training, affect has the potential to play a more central role in the training process in general. Finally, this review identifies the need to study moderators, including moderators of the relationship between behavior modeling and training outcomes, the relationship between cross-cultural training and expatriate adjustment, and the relationship between training and transfer.

8. Training alone may not be able to realize its benefits if it is disconnected from other human resource management functions or if the organization is dysfunctional in other areas (e.g., interpersonal relationships). Training will have the greatest impact when it is bundled together with other human resource management practices and these practices are also implemented following sound principles and practices based on empirical research.

DISCLOSURE STATEMENT

The authors are not aware of any biases that might be perceived as affecting the objectivity of this review.

ACKNOWLEDGMENTS

We thank Ken Brown, Steve Kozlowski, Chuck Pierce, and Sabine Sonnentag for constructive comments on earlier drafts. This research was conducted in part while Herman Aguinis was on sabbatical from the University of Colorado Denver and holding visiting appointments at the University of Salamanca (Spain) and the University of Puerto Rico.

LITERATURE CITED

Aguinis H. 2009. *Performance Management*. Upper Saddle River, NJ: Pearson Prentice Hall. 2nd ed.

Aguinis H. 2004. *Regression Analysis for Categorical Moderators*. New York: Guilford

Aguinis H, Beaty JC, Boik RJ, Pierce CA. 2005. Effect size and power in assessing moderating effects of categorical variables using multiple regression: a 30-year review. *J. Appl. Psychol.* 90:94–107

Aguinis H, Branstetter SA. 2007. Teaching the concept of the sampling distribution of the mean. *J. Manag. Educ.* 31:467–83

Aguinis H, Mazurkiewicz MD, Heggestad, ED. 2009. Using Web-based frame-of-reference training to decrease biases in personality-based job analysis: an experimental field study. *Pers. Psychol.* In press

Aguinis H, Pierce CA. 2008. Enhancing the relevance of organizational behavior by embracing performance management research. *J. Organ. Behav.* 29:139–45

Aguinis H, Sturman MC, Pierce CA. 2008. Comparison of three meta-analytic procedures for estimating moderating effects of categorical variables. *Organ. Res. Methods* 11:9–34

Alliger GM, Tannenbaum SI, Bennett W Jr, Traver H, Shotland A. 1997. A meta-analysis of the relations among training criteria. *Pers. Psychol.* 50:341–58

Aragón-Sánchez A, Barba-Aragón I, Sanz-Valle R. 2003. Effects of training on business results. *Int. J. Hum. Resour. Manag.* 14:956–80

Arthur WJ, Bennett WJ, Edens P, Bell ST. 2003. Effectiveness of training in organizations: a meta-analysis of design and evaluation features. *J. Appl. Psychol.* 88:234–45

Baranzini D, Bacchi M, Cacciabue PC. 2001. A tool for evaluation and identification of training needs in aircraft. *Hum. Factors Aerosp. Saf.* 1:167–93

A broad meta-analysis showing linkages between training design and evaluation features and training success at individual and organizational levels.

Barber J. 2004. Skill upgrading within informal training: lessons from the Indian auto mechanic. *Int. J. Train. Dev.* 8:128–39

Bartlett KR, Rodgers J. 2004. HRD as national policy in the Pacific Islands. *Adv. Dev. Hum. Resour.* 6:307–14

Becker G. 1962. Investment in human capital: a theoretical analysis. *J. Pol. Econ.* 70(Suppl. 5, Pt. 2):S9–49

Becker G. 1964. *Human Capital: A Theoretical and Empirical Analysis, With Special Reference to Education.* New York: Columbia Univ. Press

Bell BS, Kozlowski SWJ. 2002. **Adaptive guidance: enhancing self-regulation, knowledge and performance in technology-based training.** *Pers. Psychol.* **55:267–306**

Benson G, Finegold D, Mohrman SA. 2004. You paid for the skills, now keep them: tuition reimbursement and voluntary turnover. *Acad. Manag. J.* 47:315–31

Bhawuk DPS, Brislin RW. 2000. Cross-cultural training: a review. *Appl. Psychol.: An Int. Rev.* 49:162–91

Blanchard PN, Thacker JW. 2007. *Effective Training: Systems, Strategies, and Practices.* Upper Saddle River, NJ: Pearson Prentice Hall. 3rd ed.

Brown KG. 2001. Using computers to deliver training: Which employees learn and why? *Pers. Psychol.* 54:271–96

Brown KG. 2005. **Examining the structure and nomological network of trainee reactions: a closer look at "smile sheets."** *J. Appl. Psychol.* **90:991–1001**

Brown KG, Van Buren ME. 2007. Applying a social capital perspective to the evaluation of distance training. In *Where is the Learning in Distance Learning? Towards a Science of Distributed Learning and Training*, ed. SM Fiore, E Salas, pp. 41–63. Washington, DC: Am. Psychol. Assoc.

Brown TC. 2005. Effectiveness of distal and proximal goals as transfer-of-training interventions: a field experiment. *Hum. Resour. Dev. Q.* 16:369–87

Cascio WF, Aguinis H. 2005. *Applied Psychology in Human Resource Management.* Upper Saddle River, NJ: Pearson Prentice Hall. 6th ed.

Cascio WF, Aguinis H. 2008. Staffing twenty-first-century organizations. In *Academy of Management Annals*, ed. JP Walsh, AP Brief, 2:133–65. Mahwah, NJ: Erlbaum

Campbell JP. 1971. Personnel training and development. *Annu. Rev. Psychol.* 22:565–602

Chiaburu DS, Marinova SV. 2005. What predicts skill transfer? An exploratory study of goal orientation, training self-efficacy and organizational supports. *Int. J. Train. Dev.* 9:110–23

Chen G, Thomas B, Wallace JC. 2005. **A multilevel examination of the relationships among training outcomes, mediating regulatory processes, and adaptive performance.** *J. Appl. Psychol.* **90:827–41**

Cho E, McLean GN. 2004. What we discovered about NHRD and what it means for HRD. *Adv. Dev. Hum. Resour.* 6:382–93

Clardy A. 2005. Reputation, goodwill, and loss: entering the employee training audit equation. *Hum. Resour. Dev. Rev.* 4:279–304

Collins DB, Holton EF III. 2004. The effectiveness of managerial leadership development programs: a meta-analysis of studies from 1982 to 2001. *Hum. Resour. Dev. Q.* 15:217–48

Colquitt JA, LePine JA, Noe RA. 2000. Toward an integrative theory of training motivation: a meta-analytic path analysis of 20 years of research. *J. Appl. Psychol.* 85:678–707

Cullen J, Turnbull S. 2005. A meta-review of the management development literature. *Hum. Resour. Dev. Rev.* 4:335–55

Darch H, Lucas T. 2002. Training as an e-commerce enabler. *J. Workplace Learn.* 14:148–55

Davis FD, Yi MY. 2004. Improving computer skill training: behavior modeling, symbolic mental rehearsal, and the role of knowledge structures. *J. Appl. Psychol.* 89:509–23

Day DV. 2000. Leadership development: a review in context. *Leadersh. Q.* 11:581–614

Decker PJ, Nathan BR. 1985. *Behavior Modeling Training: Principles and Applications.* New York: Praeger

DeRouin RE, Fritzsche BA, Salas E. 2004. Optimizing e-learning: research-based guidelines for learner-controlled training. *Hum. Resour. Manag. Rev.* 43:147–62

Driskell, Hall Johnston J, Salas E. 2001. Does stress training generalize to novel settings? *Hum. Factors* 42:99–110

Dvir T, Eden D, Avolio BJ, Shamir B. 2002. Impact of transformational leadership on follower development and performance: a field experiment. *Acad. Manag. J.* 45:735–44

Blends theory and application to advance a workable compromise between advocates of highly structured and purely exploratory computer-based learning environments.

Presents both a hierarchical analysis of training reactions and a case for their value in decision making related to training.

Demonstrates the importance of trainee self-regulation during training, particularly on subsequent adaptive performance.

Edkins GD. 2002. A review of the benefits of aviation human factors training. *Hum. Factors Aerosp. Saf.* 2:201–16

Ellis APJ, Bell BS, Ployhart RE, Hollenbeck JR, Ilgen DR. 2005. An evaluation of generic teamwork skills training with action teams: effects on cognitive and skill-based outcomes. *Pers. Psychol.* 58:641–72

Fiol CM, O'Connor EJ, Aguinis H. 2001. All for one and one for all? The development and transfer of power across organizational levels. *Acad. Manag. Rev.* 26:224–42

Ford JK, Kraiger K. 1995. The application of cognitive constructs and principles to the instructional systems model of training. Implications for needs assessment, design, and transfer. In *International Review of Industrial and Organizational Psychology*, ed. CL Cooper, IT Robertson, 10:1–48. Chichester, UK: Wiley

Ford JK, Schmidt AM. 2000. Emergency response training: strategies for enhancing real-world performance. *J. Hazard. Mater.* 75:195–215

Fowlkes JE, Salas E, Baker DP, Cannon-Bowers JA, Stout RJ. 2000. The utility of event-based knowledge elicitation. *Hum. Factors* 42:24–35

Fox A. 2003. Training budgets said to be withstanding companies' economic troubles. *HR Mag.* 48(7):32, 38

Frayne CA, Geringer JM. 2000. Self-management training for improving job performance: a field experiment involving salespeople. *J. Appl. Psychol.* 85:361–72

Frese M, Beimel S, Schoenborn S. 2003. Action training for charismatic leadership: two evaluations of studies of a commercial training module on inspirational communication of a vision. *Pers. Psychol.* 56:671–97

Gaudine AP, Saks AM. 2004. A longitudinal quasi-experiment on the effects of posttraining transfer interventions. *Hum. Resour. Dev. Q.* 15:57–76

Goeters KM. 2002. Evaluation of the effects of CRM training by the assessment of nontechnical skills under LOFT. *Hum. Factors Aerosp. Saf.* 2:71–86

Goldstein IL. 1980. Training in work organizations. *Annu. Rev. Psychol.* 31:229–72

Goldstein IL, Ford JK. 2002. *Training in Organizations*. Belmont, CA: Wadsworth. 4th ed.

Guerrero S, Barraud-Didier V. 2004. High-involvement practices and performance of French firms. *Int. J. Hum. Resour. Manag.* 15:1408–23

Hammonds KH. 2005. Why we hate HR. *Fast Co.* 97:40

Heimbeck D, Frese M, Sonnentag S, Keith N. 2003. Integrating errors into the training process: the function of error management instructions and the role of goal orientation. *Pers. Psychol.* 56:333–61

Hill CE, Lent RW. 2006. A narrative and meta-analytic review of helping skills training: time to revive a dormant area of inquiry. *Psychother. Theory Res. Pract.* 43:154–72

Holladay CL, Quiñones MA. 2003. Practice variability and transfer of training: the role of self-efficacy generality. *J. Appl. Psychol.* 88:1094–103

Holton EF III. 2003. Cycle time: a missing dimension in HRD research and theory. *Hum. Resour. Dev. Rev.* 2:335–36

Holton EF III. 2005. Holton's evaluation model: new evidence and construct elaborations. *Adv. Dev. Hum. Resour.* 7:37–54

Holton EF III, Bates RA, Ruona WEA. 2001. Development of a generalized learning transfer system inventory. *Hum. Resour. Dev. Q.* 11:333–60

Holton EF III, Chen H-C, Naquin SS. 2003. An examination of learning transfer system characteristics across organizational settings. *Hum. Resour. Dev. Q.* 14:459–82

Huint H, Saks AM. 2003. Translating training science into practice: a study of managers' reactions to post-training transfer interventions. *Hum. Resour. Dev. Q.* 14:181–98

Investors in People Standard. 2006. **http://www.investorsinpeople.co.uk/**

Jacobsen J, Lindekaer AL, Ostergaard HT, Nielsen K, Ostergaard D, Laub M, et al. 2001. Management of anaphylactic shock evaluated using a full-scale anaesthesia simulator. *Acta Anaesthesiol. Scand.* 45:315–19

Jacoby SM. 2004. *Employing Bureaucracy*. Mahwah, NJ: Erlbaum. 2nd ed.

Kaufman R, Guerra I. 2001. A perspective adjustment to add value to external clients (including society). *Hum. Resour. Dev. Q.* 12:319–24

Keith N, Frese M. 2005. Self-regulation in error management training: emotion control and metacognition as mediators of performance effects. *J. Appl. Psychol.* 90:677–91

Keith N, Frese M. 2008. Effectiveness of error management training: a meta-analysis. *J. Appl. Psychol.* 93:59–69

Empirical study that highlights two trainee states that likely mediate the effectiveness of increasingly popular error management training.

Klein HJ, Noe RA, Wang C. 2006. Motivation to learn and course outcomes: the impact of delivery mode, learning goal orientation, and perceived barriers and enablers. *Pers. Psychol.* 59:665–702

Kontoghiorghes C. 2004. Reconceptualizing the learning transfer conceptual framework: empirical validation of a new systemic model. *Int. J. Train. Dev.* 8:210–21

Kozlowski SWJ, Brown KG, Weissbein DA, Cannon-Bowers JA, Salas E. 2000. A multi-level perspective on training effectiveness: enhancing horizontal and vertical transfer. In *Multilevel Theory, Research, and Methods in Organizations*, ed. KJ Klein, SWJ Kozlowski, pp. 157–210. San Francisco, CA: Jossey-Bass

Kozlowski SWJ, Gully SM, Brown KG, Salas E, Smith EM, Nason ER. 2001. Effects of training goals and goal orientation traits on multidimensional training outcomes and performance adaptability. *Organ. Behav. Hum. Decis. Process.* 85:1–31

Kozlowski SWJ, Salas E. 1997. An organizational systems approach for the implementation and transfer of training. In *Improving Training Effectiveness in Work Organizations*, ed. K Ford, SW Kozlowski, K Kraiger, E Salas, M Teachout, pp. 247–87. Mahwah, NJ: Erlbaum

Kraiger K. 2002. Decision-based evaluation. In *Creating, Implementing, and Maintaining Effective Training and Development: State-of-the-Art Lessons for Practice*, ed. K Kraiger, pp. 331–75. San Francisco, CA: Jossey-Bass

Kraiger K. 2003. Perspectives on training and development. In *Handbook of Psychology: Volume 12, Industrial and Organizational Psychology*, ed. WC Borman, DR Ilgen, RJ Klimoski, pp. 171–92. Hoboken, NJ: Wiley

Kraiger K, Aguinis H. 2001. Training effectiveness: assessing training needs, motivation, and accomplishments. In *How People Evaluate Others in Organizations: Person Perception and Interpersonal Judgment in I/O Psychology*, ed. M London, pp. 203–19. Mahwah, NJ: Erlbaum

Kraiger K, Ford JK, Salas E. 1993. Application of cognitive, skill-based, and affective theories of learning outcomes to new methods of training evaluation. *J. Appl. Psychol.* 78:311–28

Kraiger K, Jerden E. 2007. A new look at learner control: meta-analytic results and directions for future research. In *Where is the Learning in Distance Learning? Towards a Science of Distributed Learning and Training*, ed. SM Fiore, E Salas, pp. 65–90. Washington, DC: APA Books

Kraiger K, McLinden D, Casper WJ. 2004. Collaborative planning for training impact. *Hum. Resour. Manag. Rev.* 43:337–51

Latham GP. 1988. Human resource training and development. *Annu. Rev. Psychol.* 39:545–82

Lee M. 2004. National human resource development in the United Kingdom. *Adv. Dev. Hum. Resour.* 6:334–45

Lievens F, Harris MM, Van Keer E, Bisqueret C. 2003. Predicting cross-cultural training performance: the validity of personality, cognitive ability, and dimensions measured by an assessment center and a behavior description interview. *J. Appl. Psychol.* 88:476–89

Lim DH, Morris ML. 2006. Influence of trainee characteristics, instructional satisfaction, and organizational climate on perceived learning and transfer training. *Hum. Resour. Dev. Q.* 17:85–115

Linou N, Kontogiannis T. 2004. The effect of training systemic information on the retention of fault-finding skills in manufacturing industries. *Hum. Factors Ergon. Manufacturing* 14:197–217

Littrell LN, Salas E, Hess KP, Paley M, Riedel S. 2006. Expatriate preparation: a critical analysis of 25 years of cross-cultural training research. *Hum. Resour. Dev. Rev.* 5:355–88

Mabey C, Ramirez M. 2005. Does management development improve organizational productivity? A six-country analysis of European firms. *Int. J. Hum. Resour. Manag.* 16:1067–82

Marks MA, Sabella MJ, Burke CS, Zaccaro SJ. 2002. The impact of cross-training on team effectiveness. *J. Appl. Psychol.* 87:3–13

Mattson B. 2005. Using the critical outcome technique to demonstrate financial and organizational performance results. *Adv. Dev. Hum. Resour.* 7:102–20

McGuire D, Cross C, O'Donnell D. 2005. Why humanistic approaches in HRD won't work. *Hum. Resour. Dev. Q.* 16:131–37

Morey JC, Simon R, Jay GD, Wears RL, Salisbury M, et al. 2002. Error reduction and performance improvement in the emergency department through formal teamwork training: evaluation results of the MedTeams Project. *Health Serv. Res.* 37:1553–81

Morgan RB, Casper WJ. 2000. Examining the factor structure of participant reactions to training: a multidimensional approach. *Hum. Resour. Dev. Q.* 11:301–17

Introduces perceived barriers and enablers as factors in choosing and benefiting from traditional and blended learning environments.

Critiques past approaches to training evaluation models and presents a theory- and practice-based new evaluation model for practitioners and researchers.

Morgeson FP, Campion MA. 1997. Social and cognitive sources of potential inaccuracy in job analysis. *J. Appl. Psychol.* 82:627–55

Morris MA, Robie C. 2001. A meta-analysis of the effects of cross-cultural training on expatriate performance and adjustment. *Int. J. Train. Dev.* 5:112–25

Noe RA. 2008. *Employee Training and Development.* Boston, MA: Irwin-McGraw. 4th ed.

O'Connor P, Flin R, Fletcher G. 2002. Techniques used to evaluate crew resource management training: a literature review. *Hum. Factors Aerosp. Saf.* 2:217–33

Paradise A. 2007. State of the Industry: ASTD's Annual Review of Trends in Workplace Learning and Performance. Alexandria, VA: ASTD

Phillips JJ, Phillips P. 2007. Measuring return on investment in leadership development. In *The Handbook of Leadership Development Evaluation*, ed. KM Hannum, JW Martineau, C Reinelt, pp. 137–66. Hoboken, NJ: Wiley

Pidd K. 2004. The impact of workplace support and identity on training transfer: a case study of drug and alcohol safety training in Australia. *Int. J. Train. Dev.* 8:274–88

Rao TV. 2004. Human resource development as national policy in India. *Adv. Dev. Hum. Resour.* 6:288–96

Richman-Hirsch WL. 2001. Posttraining interventions to enhance transfer: the moderating effects of work environments. *Hum. Resour. Dev. Q.* 12:105–19

Rivera RJ, Paradise A. 2006. *State of the Industry: ASTD's Annual Review of Trends in Workplace Learning and Performance.* Alexandria, VA: ASTD

Robertson IT. 1990. Behaviour modelling: its record and potential in training and development. *Br. J. Manag.* 1:117–25

Rowold J. 2007. The impact of personality on training-related aspects of motivation: test of a longitudinal model. *Hum. Resour. Dev. Q.* 18:9–31

Sackett PR, Mullen EJ. 1993. Beyond formal experimental design: towards an expanded view of the training evaluation process. *Pers. Psychol.* 46:613–27

Salas E, Burke CS, Bowers CA, Wilson KA. 2001. Team training in the skies: Does crew resource management (CRM) training work? *Hum. Factors* 42:641–74

Salas E, Cannon-Bowers JA. 2001. The science of training: a decade of progress. *Annu. Rev. Psychol.* 52:471–99

Salas E, Wilson KA, Burke CS. 2006. Does crew resource management training work? An update, an extension, and some critical needs. *Hum. Factors* 48:392–412

Satterfield JM, Hughes E. 2007. Emotion skills training for medical students: a systematic review. *Med. Educ.* 41:935–41

Schmidt A, Ford JK. 2003. Learning within a learner control training environment: the interactive effects of goal orientation and metacognitive instruction on learning outcomes. *Pers. Psychol.* 56:405–30

Sirianni PM, Frey BA. 2001. Changing a culture: evaluation of a leadership development program at Mellon Financial Services. *Int. J. Train. Dev.* 5:290–301

Sitzmann T, Bell B, Kraiger K. 2008. A multi-level analysis of the effect of prompting self-regulation in technology-delivered instruction. *Pers. Psychol.* Manuscr. under review

Sitzmann T, Brown KG, Ely K, Kraiger K. 2008. Motivation to learn in a military training curriculum: a longitudinal investigation. *Mil. Psychol.* Manuscr. under review

Sitzmann T, Kraiger K, Stewart D, Wisher R. 2006. The comparative effectiveness of Web-based and classroom instruction: a meta-analysis. *Pers. Psychol.* 59:623–64

Smith EM, Ford JK, Kozlowski SWJ. 1997. Building adaptive expertise: implications for training design. In *Training for a Rapidly Changing Workplace: Applications of Psychological Research*, ed. MA Quiñones, A Ehrenstein, pp. 89–118. Washington, DC: APA Books

Spitzer DR. 2005. Learning effectiveness measurement: a new approach for measuring and managing learning to achieve business results. *Adv. Dev. Hum. Resour.* 7:55–70

Sugrue B, Rivera RJ. 2005. *State of the Industry: ASTD's Annual Review of Trends in Workplace Learning and Performance.* Alexandria, VA: ASTD

Swanson RA. 2001. *Assessing the Financial Benefits of Human Resource Development.* Cambridge, MA: Perseus

Switzer KC, Nagy MS, Mullins ME. 2005. The influence of training reputation, managerial support, and self-efficacy on pretraining motivation and perceived training transfer. *Appl. HRM Res.* 10:21–34

Latest in an annual series that documents training practices in a large sample of U.S. corporations.

Large-scale meta-analysis that evaluates the effectiveness of Web-based instruction and suggests design factors for optimizing effectiveness.

Szalkowski A, Jankowicz D. 2004. The development of human resources during the process of economic and structural transformation in Poland. *Adv. Dev. Hum. Resour.* 6:346–54

Tannenbaum SI, Woods SB. 1992. Determining a strategy for evaluating training: operating within organizational constraints. *Hum. Resour. Plann.* 15(2):63–81

Tannenbaum SI, Yukl G. 1992. Training and development in work organizations. *Annu. Rev. Psychol.* 43:399–441

Taylor PJ, Russ-Eft DF, Chan DWL. 2005. A meta-analytic review of behavior modeling training. *J. Appl. Psychol.* 90:692–709

Tharenou P, Saks AM, Moore C. 2007. A review and critique of research on training and organizational-level outcomes. *Hum. Resour. Manag. Rev.* 17:251–73

Towler AJ. 2003. Effects of charismatic influence training on attitudes, behavior, and performance. *Pers. Psychol.* 56:363–81

Tracey JB, Hinkin TR, Tannenbaum S, Mathieu JE. 2001. The influence of individual characteristics and the work environment on varying levels of training outcomes. *Hum. Resour. Dev. Q.* 12:5–23

Twitchell K, Holton E III, Trott JW Jr. 2000. Technical training evaluation practices in the United States. *Perform. Improv. Q.* 13(1):84–109

Ubeda García M. 2005. Training and business performance: the Spanish case. *Int. J. Hum. Resour. Manag.* 16:1691–710

Van Der Klink M, Gielen E, Nauta C. 2001. Supervisory support as a major condition to enhance transfer. *Int. J. Train. Dev.* 5:52–63

van Leeuwen MJ, van Praag BM. 2002. The costs and benefits of lifelong learning: the case of the Netherlands. *Hum. Resour. Dev. Q.* 13:151–68

Vancouver JB, Day DV. 2005. Industrial and organisation research on self-regulation: from constructs to applications. *Appl. Psychol.* 54:155–85

Wang G. 2002. Control groups for human performance technology (HPT) evaluation and measurement. *Perform. Improv. Q.* 15(2):34–48

Wang GG, Dou Z, Li N. 2002. A systems approach to measuring return on investment for HRD interventions. *Hum. Resour. Dev. Q.* 13:203–24

Wang GG, Wilcox. 2006. Training evaluation: knowing more than is practiced. *Adv. Dev. Hum. Resour.* 8:528–39

Welsh ET, Wanberg CR, Brown KG, Simmering MJ. 2003. E-learning: emerging uses, empirical results and future directions. *Int. J. Train. Dev.* 7:245–58

Wesson MJ, Gogus CI. 2005. Shaking hands with a computer: an examination of two methods of organizational newcomer orientation. *J. Appl. Psychol.* 90:1018–26

Wexley KN. 1984. Personnel training. *Annu. Rev. Psychol.* 35:519–51

Zhao Y, Lei J, Lai BYC, Tan HS. 2005. What makes the difference? A practical analysis of research on the effectiveness of distance education. *Teach. Coll. Rec.* 107:1836–84

Conceptual Consumption

Dan Ariely[1] and Michael I. Norton[2]

[1]Duke University, Durham, North Carolina 27708; email: dandan@duke.edu

[2]Harvard Business School, Boston, Massachusetts 02163; email: mnorton@hbs.edu

Annu. Rev. Psychol. 2009. 60:475–99

First published online as a Review in Advance on September 2, 2008

The *Annual Review of Psychology* is online at psych.annualreviews.org

This article's doi:
10.1146/annurev.psych.60.110707.163536

0066-4308/09/0110-0475$20.00

Key Words

consumer behavior, expectancies, goals, fluency, regulatory fit

Abstract

As technology has simplified meeting basic needs, humans have cultivated increasingly psychological avenues for occupying their consumption energies, moving from consuming food to consuming concepts; we propose that consideration of such "conceptual consumption" is essential for understanding human consumption. We first review how four classes of conceptual consumption—consuming expectancies, goals, fluency, and regulatory fit—impact physical consumption. Next, we benchmark the power of conceptual consumption against physical consumption, reviewing research in which people forgo positive physical consumption—and even choose negative physical consumption–in order to engage in conceptual consumption. Finally, we outline how conceptual consumption informs research examining both preference formation and virtual consumption, and how it may be used to augment efforts to enhance consumer welfare.

Contents

INTRODUCTION

Although consumption is fundamental to all forms of life, human consumption is extraordinary in its variety and sheer inventiveness. Some physical consumption, such as food and water, is essential for basic survival and thus shared with other organisms, but humans are remarkable in the scale of consumption over and above meeting basic needs, and indeed in the way that even "basic" consumption is embellished and elaborated—consider, for example, the sheer number of brands of bottled water. The centrality of consumption is not unique to the modern age, of course, nor is it unique to humans. Animals spend much of their time searching for food and consuming it; similarly, our ancestors spent much of their time foraging for, preparing, and consuming food (Kaplan 2000, Sahlins 1972). With modern technology, however, the nature of consumption has changed: Whereas our ancestors needed a minimum of some 15–20 hours per week to gather and prepare food,

the current U.S. consumer can accomplish the same tasks with one 30-minute trip to a supermarket per week and 30 minutes per day preparing meals, thanks to innovations such as microwave ovens and instant meals.

But how do humans use this additional time? One avenue that humans clearly pursue is overconsumption of food; having evolved in an environment where food was both scarce and unpredictable such that eating to our physical limit when food was available was a dominant strategy, continuing to apply this rule mindlessly when food is abundant underlies modern obesity epidemics (Pinel et al. 2000, Wansink 2006). In addition to hunger for food and thirst for water shared with other animals, however, humans use this additional time to address their unique—and seemingly—insatiable appetite for consumption of information, so much so that Schelling (1984) famously called the mind a "consuming organ," and Borgmann (2000) wrote that "to live is to consume." The staggering amount of time people spend reading blogs about celebrities attests to this appetite; more broadly, evidence can be found in human desires for stories (originally through oral storytelling, and increasingly through books and movies), for rumors and gossip, for news, for cultural memes, and so on (see Allport & Postman 1947, Dawkins 1976, Heath et al. 2001, Sinaceur & Heath 2005). Thus, in some sense people have switched from consuming food (foraging for nuts) to consuming ideas (foraging for information in blogs). Although not a literal one-to-one exchange of consumption of food for consumption of ideas, we suggest a basic property of human consumption: As basic needs are met with greater ease and celerity, humans find a wide variety of increasingly psychological avenues for quenching their consumption thirst. Even the labor with which humans have replaced hunting and foraging is telling, as countries transition from manufacturing to knowledge economies (Drucker 1959), where both the production and consumption of ideas are paramount. Shirky (2008), for example, has noted that whereas Americans spend some 200 billion hours per year watching television, Wikipedia—the online dictionary whose intellectual content is generated entirely by unpaid contributors—now represents roughly 100 million hours of human thought, a novel and promising use of excess consumption energy.

In fact, we suggest that the desire for consuming information in these forms (stories, blogs, and so on) merely scratches the surface of the fundamental role that ideas and concepts play in the consumption experience, and that a large portion of human consumption can be better understood by considering "conceptual consumption," psychological consumption that can occur independent of, and in some cases can even trump, physical consumption. As sociologists and anthropologists in the field of consumer behavior have pointed out for many years, physical consumption (of consumer products, of brands) is used not just to satisfy basic needs but also to signal to ourselves and others our beliefs, attitudes, and social identities (e.g., Belk 1988, Fournier 1998, Hirschman & Holbrook 1982, Holbrook & Hirschman 1982, Holt 1995, Mick 1986). Thus, although one view of consumption divides consumption into consuming the physical (food, water) compared with consuming the psychological (ideas, information), the sociological/anthropological view suggests that this division may be artificial: Conceptual consumption is implicated in even the most basic consumption acts, such as eating or drinking, and is therefore paramount.

Take the deceptively simple case of the decision to eat a chocolate chip cookie. Certainly, because the cookie counts as food, we could analyze the decision from a physical consumption standpoint, measuring the cookie's fat content and nutritional value (Berthoud & Morrison 2008). We could also analyze the decision from a marketer's perspective, by examining how willingness to pay varied as a function of the number of chocolate chips in the cookie, or its size, or its placement on a shelf. Both of these approaches, of course, are fruitful in understanding the consumption act. Our concern, however, is with the psychology behind the consumption act, the surprisingly complicated nature of the conceptual consumption underlying even such seemingly simple physical consumption decisions.

Compare and contrast the decision to consume a cookie from the perspective of a dog or a human. From our experience with canines, the dog's psychology with regard to the cookie goes something like, "Yes," followed one second later by immediate consumption of the cookie. Contrast this to the human psychology of eating the cookie. Faced with a cookie on a plate, humans might think, "How many cookies have I had today?" "How does eating this cookie jibe with my weekly goal to lose two pounds?" "What will my coworkers think if I take the last cookie?" "I wonder if this cookie is organic?" "And if it is organic, is it even worth eating?" "Are any of the ingredients in this cookie produced by exploited third-world workers?" and so on. Indeed, the extraordinary human capacity for mental simulation of both past and future events (Gilbert & Wilson 2007, Kahneman & Miller 1986, et al. 2008, Roese 1997, Taylor et al. 1998, Tulving 2002) and general proclivity for mind-wandering (Mason et al. 2007, Smallwood & Schooler 2006) suggests that the potential list of questions may well be endless.

In this example, notice that regardless of the questions the consumer asks—the concepts brought to mind—the physical consumption object (the cookie) remains exactly the same; conceptual consumption, on the other hand, will be markedly different depending on whether consumers are thinking about a goal to lose weight compared with a desire to promote fair labor practices. In the current review, we explore the interactions between physical and conceptual consumption, outlining and providing representative research examples of what experimentalists in consumer behavior have learned about the psychological aspects of consumption. In doing so, we also attempt to provide a framework for thinking about what the study of consumer behavior is and is not to a field that continually seeks to differentiate itself from related disciplines such as psychology and economics, and even to differentiate how research in consumer behavior differs from marketing research (Deighton 2007, Loken 2006, Mick 2003, Simonson et al. 2001). We suggest that consumer behavior is fundamentally and increasingly the study of conceptual consumption, broadly defined across many domains of consumption.

OVERVIEW

The bulk of this review is divided into two parts. In Part I, we consider several streams of literature that have received attention from consumer behavior researchers that we feel best demonstrate people's desire to consume concepts: the impact of expectancies, goals, fluency, and regulatory fit on physical consumption. In Part II, we then explore the relative strength of conceptual consumption compared with physical consumption, finding cases in which the desire to consume concepts trumps the desire to engage in physical consumption even when that physical consumption offers utility, exploring cases in which people forgo positive physical consumption to consume a concept, and even more puzzling, cases in which they choose negative physical consumption. Finally, we end by outlining the potential for a better understanding of conceptual consumption to contribute to three areas of research: preference formation and perpetuation, virtual and online consumption, and research focused on increasing consumer welfare by improving people's consumption decisions.

PART I: CONSUMING CONCEPTS

In this first section, our goal is to outline several different classes of conceptual consumption. Our goal is not to be exhaustive—there are many more concepts that people consume than those we review below—but we have selected four that have received attention recently in consumer behavior as a jumping off point: expectancies, goals, fluency, and regulatory fit. For each concept, we provide a brief review of the existing research—we encourage readers to look elsewhere for more comprehensive reviews of these topics—and then describe in

greater detail specific investigations that we feel highlight a unique aspect of conceptual consumption. In particular, we focus on research that holds physical consumption constant, and varies only the concepts available for consumption, to demonstrate an independent role for consuming concepts in determining the utility of an experience over and above utility from physical consumption.

Consuming Expectancies

One of the concepts that has received the most attention in consumer behavior for its impact on consumption is how people's expectations influence and alter their consumption, even holding the physical consumption object constant. Indeed, one of the classic studies in consumer behavior (Allison & Uhl 1964) is at heart a study about expectancies: Consumers who drank beer with visible brands saw those beers as highly variable in their taste and preferred beers with their favorite brand label, whereas consumers who drank unbranded beers tended to rate them all as tasting similar to each other. Thus, expectations set by associations with advertising and branding can influence and sometimes supersede physical consumption of both products and services (Boulding et al. 1993, 1999; Braun 1999; Kopalle & Lehmann 2001, 2006; Nevid 1981; Wansink & Chandon 2006). Because people tend to seek confirmation for their beliefs (Lord et al. 1979, Snyder & Swann 1978), expectations can guide perception and shape behavior; the impact of expectancies on perception has been documented in many domains (for a review, see Fiske & Taylor 2008), including demonstrations of stereotypes influencing perceptions of individuals (Darley & Gross 1983, Klein & Snyder 2003, Norton et al. 2004), of expectancies of humor influencing people's enjoyment of cartoons (Wilson et al. 1989), of the spin doctoring of political consultants influencing perceptions of politicians' performances in televised debates (Norton & Goethals 2004), and of the influence of health information on the enjoyment of food (Levin & Gaeth 1988, Wansink et al.

2000). In addition, expectancies seem to have a life of their own; merely stating that one expects to engage in some behavior can increase the likelihood of performing it (Fitzsimons & Morwitz 1996, Greenwald et al. 1987, Morwitz et al. 1993).

In one recent investigation, Lee et al. (2006) asked patrons of a pub to drink a small glass of a commercially available beer and a small glass of their own "MIT brew," which consisted of the same beer with the addition of one ingredient—balsamic vinegar. They asked people to sample the two beers and to choose which they wanted a full glass of, but they varied when they told participants about the secret ingredient. One-third of the participants were never told about the balsamic vinegar, another third were told up front about the balsamic vinegar, and the final third first tested the two beers without knowing anything about the vinegar (as in the first condition) but then were told about the vinegar prior to making their choice. Thus, the final group knew about the balsamic vinegar but learned about it only after the tasting experience itself ended. The results showed that the timing of disclosure of the secret ingredient significantly affected people's preference for the MIT brew compared to a regular beer. The beer with balsamic vinegar was perceived to be repulsive only when that disclosure preceded drinking the beer. This difference suggests that concepts are not just an additional input for decisions, but that conceptual consumption can actually change the physical consumption experience itself: When people learned that the MIT brew had vinegar after drinking it, they liked the beer just fine, but when they expected the MIT brew to be bad (when they knew about the vinegar up front), they thought the beer was bad.

Indeed, the impact of expectancies on consumption is powerful enough that changing conceptual consumption can affect physical consumption at a level that can be observed in brain imaging studies, evidence that expectancies offer utility independent of physical consumption. McClure et al. (2004), for example, asked participants who preferred Coke to Pepsi to drink Coke and Pepsi when they knew what drink they were about to consume and when they did not; participants preferred Coke, but only when they knew it was Coke. This finding suggests that controlling for physical consumption, the conceptual consumption made possible by brand associations had an impact over and above the utility of Coke itself. Most interestingly, McClure et al. (2004) conducted this study while participants were scanned using functional magnetic resonance imaging, and analyses revealed that these preferences were reflected by recruitment of brain regions associated with the processing of reward, offering evidence for the deep impact of concepts on physical consumption. In a similar investigation that utilized the well-documented consumer inference that price serves as a signal of product quality (Rao & Monroe 1989; though see Gerstner 1985), Plassmann et al. (2008) asked participants to taste one wine several times but told them that they were actually sampling different wines; across trials, they told participants that the wine they were about to taste was cheap or expensive. Offering converging evidence with McClure et al. (2004), Plassmann et al. (2008) found that consumption of "higher-priced" wines was related to greater recruitment of reward circuitry; once again, controlling for physical consumption, conceptual consumption affected experienced utility.

Expectancies can be so powerful that they can influence not just perception and internal experiences but also external events through what Merton (1948) termed "self-fulfilling prophecies," and these prophecies can occur without conscious awareness (Chen & Bargh 1997). Males who believe that a woman with whom they are interacting is attractive elicit greater sociability from her (Snyder et al. 1977), students perform better if their teachers are led to believe that they are late bloomers (Jussim & Harber 2005, Rosenthal & Jacobson 1968), and parents' erroneous beliefs about their children's drinking habits come to shape how much their children drink (Madon et al. 2003).

One of the most compelling demonstrations of the impact of self-fulfilling prophecies in the domain of consumer behavior is in the domain of placebo effects, an area of research that has received increasing attention in the medical literature (Price et al. 2008). Shiv et al. (2005) asked students to engage in mental tasks such as solving puzzles, but allowed participants to purchase energy drinks before the task began. Some participants purchased the drink at full price, while others were given the opportunity to buy the drink at a discount. Participants who bought the drink at a discount subsequently performed worse on the task. These results extended beyond the laboratory as well: In a field study, Shiv et al. (2005) showed that people who had caught colds rated their cold remedies as more effective if they had paid full price for them. Another investigation demonstrated similar placebo effects for a pill purported to relieve pain: Participants who were told the pill had been discounted were unable to tolerate as much physical pain as those who were told the pill was not discounted (Waber et al. 2008). In a related investigation, Irmak et al. (2005) showed that people's desire for treatments to work influences the effectiveness of placebos.

Taken together, these studies on expectancies suggest that preconceptions and ideas about consumption can act to modify the physical consumption experience itself. As the MIT Brew, Coke, and placebo examples illustrate, higher-order mental processes are deeply implicated in even the simplest of experiences (tasting beer, drinking Coke, and taking cold medication), making conceptual consumption an integral part of any physical consumption.

Consuming goals. Recent years have seen a large increase in research exploring the nature and function of goals in psychology and consumer behavior (Bagozzi & Dholakia 1999, Baumgartner & Pieters 2008), with investigations of factors that influence goal completion—such as setting deadlines (Ariely & Wertenbroch 2002) or coping with distractions (Fishbach et al. 2003)—as well as research exploring how people manage conflicting goals (Fishbach & Dhar 2005). There is little doubt that goal setting serves as a strong motivator

for humans; researchers have demonstrated the power of goals in shaping behavior in countless domains, from relationships with others (Chartrand et al. 2007, Fitzsimons & Bargh 2003) to prosocial behavior (Nelson & Norton 2005, Trötschel & Gollwitzer 2007) to weight loss (Bagozzi & Edwards 1998). Indeed, people are willing to overcome obstacles to meet goals, returning to tasks relevant to a desired goal when such goal-directed behavior is interrupted (Bargh et al. 2001), and goals are even contagious, spreading from one person to another with relative ease (Aarts et al. 2004).

Gollwitzer (1990, 1999) introduced the concept of implementation intentions, or how goals lead people to behave in ways consistent with those goals. When an individual decides on 40 push-ups as part of a new exercise regimen, they then treat that number as a reference point, leading to increased effort as they approach that number (in line with having implementation intentions to reach that goal) but a rapid drop-off after that point (Heath et al. 1999). In this case, of course, the individual has set this goal herself, and 40 push-ups may have some real meaning in that it is an appropriate level for which to aim. But what about cases in which researchers set goals? The research reviewed above suggests that experimentally induced goals have a powerful impact on human behavior; in one recent investigation, people's choices for tasks were dramatically impacted by the number of "points" those tasks offered—even when the points in fact had no value (Hsee et al. 2003).

We are particularly interested in how a goal can come to serve not as a motivator to engage in some desired behavior, but, ironically, as a goal in and of itself. In other words, we explore cases in which goals serve as concepts that humans wish to consume, leading goals to supersede physical consumption. Below, we describe three investigations that demonstrate goal consumption, two in which the desire to consume a goal leads to increased physical consumption, and one in which goal consumption leads to decreased physical consumption.

In a field study, Nunes & Dreze (2006) demonstrated how making salient a goal to complete a task can increase consumption of a good. They gave 300 loyalty cards to customers of a car wash. For half of the customers, the cards required ten additional purchases in order to receive a free car wash, but the researchers kindly affixed two stickers as a head start; for the other customers, the cards required eight purchases to obtain the free car wash, but no stickers were already attached. Thus, in both conditions, customers needed to pay for eight additional car washes to receive a free wash, but in the first condition, they were endowed with the illusion of progress toward that goal. When the researchers counted how many cards were redeemed, they found that nearly twice as many customers paid for the additional eight washes and redeemed their card when they had been given two stickers. Given that the price of eight car washes is the same for customers in each condition, those customers endowed with progress toward a goal therefore spent much more money at the car wash than those for whom this goal was not made salient. Because the car washes were all of similar quality, this suggests that consuming the goal offered these participants additional utility over and above consuming the physical product. Kivetz et al. (2006) demonstrated similar results for consumers completing loyalty cards at coffee shops. Indeed, by this reckoning, one reason that sunk costs are so difficult to let "sink" (Arkes & Blumer 1985, Staw 1981) may be that initial investment sets in motion a goal to complete the underlying task, and giving up the opportunity to consume that goal at the task's completion creates too much disutility.

But are such desires to complete tasks specifically related to consuming a goal? A related study suggests this may be the case, providing direct evidence of increased physical consumption driven by the desire to complete a relevant goal. Dhar et al. (2007) gave participants in one study the opportunity to buy a 7-rupee keychain; before considering that purchase, however, some participants were given the opportunity to buy a desirable CD while others were given the opportunity to buy a somewhat less exciting light bulb. Because more

participants bought the CD than the light bulb, more of the individuals who had the opportunity to buy the CD subsequently bought the keychain, demonstrating "shopping momentum." Indeed, regardless of whether the first purchase was of a light bulb or a CD, participants were more likely to buy the keychain as long as they had simply purchased something before receiving the 7-rupee-keychain offer. Most important for our account, these purchases were driven by goal-related cognitions; initial purchases caused participants to shift to an implemental mindset (Gollwitzer 1990), which spurred subsequent purchases. Note that in all cases, participants were faced with the same physical consumption decision: a 7-rupee keychain. When purchasing goals were active, however, participants acted as though that keychain was more valuable, suggesting—in line with our account—that completing the goal, and thus consuming that concept, was the driver of their behavior. Indeed, other research demonstrates that merely considering whether or not to buy an item promotes a purchasing mindset that induces subsequent purchasing (Xu & Wyer 2007), suggesting the ease with which the desire to consume goals may be instantiated.

The above examples, however, all suggest that the desire to consume goals also leads to increased physical consumption. Our account suggests that the desire to consume concepts is separable from the desire to consume things and that it can therefore decrease physical consumption as well. Evidence for such a claim would come from data showing that the desire to consume a completed goal can reduce people's typical physical consumption behavior. Lee & Ariely (2006), in an investigation of consumer responses to promotional coupons, demonstrate just this. In a series of field studies at a convenience store where the average total purchase was $4, they gave customers conditional coupons of the form: "spend $X or more and get $Y off." Some customers received a coupon that offered $1 off any purchase of $6 and above, while others received a coupon that offered $1 off of any purchase of $2 and above.

Consumers who received the coupon that required a $6 purchase increased their average spending above their usual $4 in an effort to receive their dollar off (see also Milkman et al. 2008). Most importantly for our account, those customers who received the coupon that required only a $2 purchase to receive $1 actually decreased their spending from their typical $4—even though they would have received their dollar off had they spent $4. These results suggest that goals can be separate from economic incentives involved in decisions about purchasing; the fact that customers left the store with fewer items than they had intended to buy after receiving the conditional $2 coupon demonstrates that consuming the goal implied by the coupon did in fact trump physical consumption.

Consuming fluency. Another area that has received increased attention in recent years is the impact of fluency—broadly defined, the ease with which stimuli are processed and experienced—on consumer behavior. The classic studies in this domain are Zajonc and colleagues' investigations of mere exposure, where simply being exposed to a stimulus—whether above or below consciousness—leads to more positive affective reactions (Kunst-Wilson & Zajonc 1980, Zajonc 1968) due to the perceptual fluency that results from familiarity (Whittlesea 1993). Indeed, so strong is the link between familiarity and liking that people make two related mistakes: the reverse inference that things they like must be familiar (Monin 2003) and that increased exposure invariably leads to liking even in cases when it does not (Norton et al. 2007). Building off the core concept in Tversky & Kahneman's (1973) availability heuristic—that instances that spring to mind more readily exert greater influence in judgment—Schwarz and his colleagues have explored the more general impact of ease of retrieval (Schwarz 2004, Schwarz & Clore 1996). Such feelings of fluency—of things "feeling right"—have been shown to impact judgments and behavior ranging from brand and product evaluations (Ferraro et al. 2008, Janiszewski 1993, Labroo et al. 2008, Lee & Labroo 2004, Menon & Raghubir 2003), to responses to advertising (Fang et al. 2007, Petrova & Cialdini 2005), to creativity (Csikszenthmihalyi 1990), to gambling behavior (Simmons & Nelson 2006), to performance in school (Nelson & Simmons 2007).

Our interest is in how fluency might affect behavior over and above physical consumption. In one particularly striking example using real data from the New York Stock exchange, Alter & Oppenheimer (2006) showed that stocks with fluent stock ticker codes (those whose abbreviations were pronounceable) outperformed stocks with more disfluent names: Given a $1000 investment, the ten most fluently named shares would have yielded a profit of more than $100 in the first day of trading and more than $300 after one year compared with the ten most disfluently named shares. This study offers particularly compelling evidence for the impact of conceptual consumption: Since stock prices are meant to be driven by market factors reflecting the true value of corporations (though see Shleifer & Summers 1990), and stock ticker codes are unrelated to the actual profitability of the companies they represent, these data suggest that fluency alone leads people to value the consumption of stocks with fluent names.

If the desire to consume fluency leads to greater consumption, can disfluency also reduce physical consumption? Novemsky et al. (2007) asked participants to choose between two similar cell phones, while also giving them the option to defer choice. Previous research has demonstrated that as the difficulty of choice increases, people are more likely to defer such choices, avoiding decisional conflict and regret (Anderson 2003, Dhar 1997, Dhar & Simonson 2003, Tversky & Shafir 1992). Whereas these earlier investigations have generally manipulated features of the choice set to induce deferral, Novemsky et al. (2007) subtly manipulated the fluency of the decision by simply making the font in which the product descriptions appeared easier (fluent) or harder (disfluent) to read. Thus, this study explores the impact of fluency on choice, controlling for the actual physical consumption experience (the cell phones were identical in both conditions). Participants were significantly more likely to defer choice in the disfluent condition, suggesting that their negative consumption of fluency affected their physical consumption (see also Alter et al. 2007).

Consuming "fit." Consumption of fluency—the feeling of ease that accompanies stimuli that are easy to process—shares characteristics with another area of research that continues to grow in scope and scale: Regulatory "fit," when people "feel right" when engaged in a task in which their motivations align with their behavior (Higgins 2000, 2005). Regulatory fit has been shown to impact phenomena ranging from the amount of effort people devote to tasks (Vaughn et al. 2006), to their susceptibility to persuasive appeals (Cesario et al. 2004), to their ability to engage in effective self-control (Hong & Lee 2008). Although fluency and fit are conceptually and likely experientially distinct, we suggest that both offer opportunities for conceptual consumption: People can receive value from fit such that the desire to conceptually consume regulatory fit alters physical consumption.

Regulatory fit has been of particular interest in recent years to researchers in consumer behavior (see Aaker & Lee 2006, Avnet & Higgins 2006), with studies exploring the impact of regulatory focus on information processing in consumer choice (Wang & Lee 2006) and on product decisions made in the moment or for the future (Mogilner et al. 2008). Most importantly for our account, research in consumer behavior has demonstrated that fit qualifies as another class of conceptual consumption. In one investigation, Higgins et al. (2003) first assessed participants' chronic regulatory orientations, sorting them into promotion-focused or prevention-focused individuals. They then offered participants the chance to buy a mug or a pen, but manipulated whether participants considered how much they would gain from choosing one (matching a promotion focus) or how much they would lose from choosing one (matching a prevention focus). Participants whose chronic orientation matched the mode with which they were asked to make their bids for the item (i.e., who were experiencing fit) offered a 50% price premium over those who were experiencing a mismatch between chronic orientations and task instructions. In a related investigation, Avnet & Higgins (2003) induced participants to adopt either a locomotion or assessment orientation, then asked them to choose book lights either by an elimination strategy (matching the locomotion orientation) or a full-evaluation strategy (matching the assessment orientation). Again, participants' valuation of the book light was higher when they were experiencing fit than when they were not. Finally, Levav et al. (2008) demonstrated that when multiple products offer an opportunity to consume fit, the conflict between consuming these concepts leads to choice deferral in the same way that conflict between consuming similar physical products does (see Chernev 2004), further evidence of the impact of concepts on consumption. In sum, holding physical consumption constant (the mugs, pens, and book lights in the above experiments were the same in all conditions), the experience of consuming fit appears to offer utility—and the lack of fit or conflicting fit, disutility—suggesting that, like fluency, regulatory fit is conceptually consumed.

PART II: SACRIFICING PHYSICAL CONSUMPTION FOR CONCEPTUAL CONSUMPTION

As we mentioned above, we are far from the first to identify how the desire to consume concepts can influence physical consumption. Indeed, conspicuous consumption offers just such an example, in which people purchase high-priced consumer goods not merely to enjoy the utility of the quality product but also to display their wealth to others, consuming the social status that results (Veblen 1899; see also Amaldoss & Jain 2005, Corneo & Jeanne 1997). With conspicuous consumption, however, physical and conceptual consumption go hand in hand, as people get both consumption utility and social utility from spending more money. A strong test of the importance of conceptual consumption would be to pit conceptual versus physical consumption and find cases where people are willing to sacrifice utility from physical consumption for the sake of conceptual consumption. Just as Foa (1971) demonstrated that humans trade one form of consumption for another between individuals (e.g., money for goods or love for status), we suggest they may also trade off different kinds of consumption within themselves.

Indeed, we suggest that one of the uses of the construct of conceptual consumption is that it helps to explain—or at minimum bring together under one umbrella—several seemingly paradoxical or self-abnegating behaviors that consumer researchers have identified. When people make choices that are seemingly suboptimal from a utility maximization perspective—forgoing positive experiences, and even more oddly, choosing negative experiences—we suggest that they are very likely to be engaging in some form of conceptual consumption, the utility from which outweighs the loss of utility from forgoing positive or choosing negative experiences. The task for consumer behavior researchers is therefore to identity what class of conceptual consumption is at play and to measure the impact of that concept. Below, we review five domains in which people forgo positive experiences—variety seeking, feature fatigue, strategic memory protection, contamination, and charitable giving—and two in which they not only forgo the positive but seek the negative—via consumption of negative emotions and negative experiences—in order to engage in conceptual consumption.

Forgoing Positive Consumption

Variety seeking. A great deal of attention in the literature has been paid to the notion that people seek variety, or, more accurately, that they seek too much variety—more variety than will make them happy. This tendency to over-

invest in variety is the result of individuals' tendency to spread their consumption evenly across available sets of options (Fox et al. 2005, Read & Loewenstein 1995, Simonson 1990) and even to vary their decision rules from choice to choice (Drolet 2002). For instance, in an experiment in which participants chose between five investment funds, participants presented with four equity funds and one fixed-income fund allocated 68% to equities, whereas those presented with just one equity fund and four fixed-income funds allocated just 43% to equities (Benartzi & Thaler 2001). In another well-known example, when people choose yogurts for each of the days in the coming week at the same time, they tend to choose more variety (selecting some of each flavor), but when they choose a yogurt on each individual day, they tend to diversify much less, picking their favorite (say, blueberry) much more frequently (see Kahneman & Snell 1992). In short, the tendency to seek variety can lead people to end up with suboptimal physical consumption (Ratner et al. 1999).

This tendency is particularly highlighted in social situations, and researchers have focused a great deal of attention on the social aspects of variety seeking. Ariely & Levav (2000), for example, examined the variety-seeking behavior of groups of patrons at a microbrewery as a function of the method of ordering beer. They contrasted the regular method for ordering, in which people stated their order aloud in sequence (such that they could be influenced by one another), with a condition in which individuals marked their orders privately on their menu; patrons who ordered aloud opted for more variety, suggesting that social pressures increased variety seeking. In addition, this variety seeking had consequences: Patrons announcing their orders publicly were less satisfied with the beer they consumed and reported feeling more regret than those who selected their beer privately (and who therefore were immune from variety-seeking norms), offering direct evidence that they sacrificed physical consumption utility as a result of social pressures.

Why would people seek more variety in social settings if it makes them unhappy? We suggest that they were trading off physical consumption for conceptual consumption, in this case, wanting others to see them—and wanting to see themselves—as interesting and unique (Tian et al. 2001). Evidence suggests that variety-seeking is likely effective at accomplishing both goals: Ratner & Kahn (2002) demonstrated that individuals who seek variety are accorded more social status than those who do not, and Sande et al. (1988) offer evidence that in many cases, people wish to see themselves as more multifaceted and unpredictable than others even removed from social settings. Of course, it is not necessarily the case that variety seeking per se is the key to seeing oneself in a positive light and gaining approval from others. For example, individuals in more collectivistic cultures seem to prefer consensus to unique options (Kim & Drolet 2003). We might expect individuals in such cultures to make the opposite tradeoffs in their variety-seeking behavior, choosing less-preferred options to fit in rather than to stand out, in an effort to see themselves as embedded in the social fabric and receive social approval for following cultural norms. In sum, people's variety-seeking behavior may be better understood by taking into account the benefits of physical consumption weighed against the conceptual consumption of social utility made available by such behavior.

Feature fatigue. Similar to research on variety seeking—that when making decisions for future consumption, people choose too much variety that they come to regret—recent work exploring "feature fatigue" demonstrates that people prefer products with more features at the moment of purchase but that feature-rich products subsequently can be difficult if not impossible to use, leaving them dissatisfied with their purchase (Thompson et al. 2005). Why would people make this seeming mistake, choosing products that they can barely use, rather than sticking with simpler products? As with variety seeking, research suggests that one explanation for this behavior is that people may be

trading off satisfaction with their choices for social status. Thompson & Norton (2008) found that making social concerns salient, for example, by informing participants that their choices would be made public to other participants, increased the choice share of feature-rich products; most importantly, observers did accord those who chose feature-rich options higher social status, seeing them as smarter, more interesting, and more cutting-edge. Thus, as with variety-seeking behavior, people seem willing to sacrifice physical consumption (struggling with difficult-to-use cameras) in order to engage in conceptual consumption, the social utility gained from displaying such products to others (see also Berger & Heath 2007).

Strategic memory protection. An even more nuanced behavior involving the sacrifice of physical consumption is evident in a recent investigation by Zauberman et al. (2008). Zauberman and colleagues investigate the odd cases where, when people truly enjoy an experience—deriving utility and satisfaction from it—they forgo ever repeating it. Zauberman et al. (2008) suggest that this behavior is driven by the desire to protect the memory of the past experience from possible contamination by future experiences that might not be as pleasurable. In one study, participants in one condition were asked to recall a special evening out; in the other, they were asked to recall a typical evening out. Not surprisingly, special evenings were rated more highly than typical ones. But when the researchers then asked participants which experience they would want to repeat—with just one change, that they would have to repeat it with a different person or people—participants were more likely to want to repeat the typical evening than the special evening, even though they had just rated this experience as providing less utility.

Why would people engage in this type of behavior, forgoing a repeat of a superior experience to an inferior one? One explanation of this result is that special evenings occur with one's favorite people (e.g., one's partner), and therefore the second evening with a less significant person is by definition less special. Even given this loss of utility from the company one keeps, however, one would predict from a strict physical consumption standpoint that the special evening (say, dinner at a fancy restaurant) would still be more positive than a typical one (dinner at McDonald's). From a conceptual consumption standpoint, however, this behavior makes perfect sense. Zauberman et al. argue that people are preserving their ability to consume the memory of that event (the concept of that evening) indefinitely, gaining utility from each memory; although repeating the special evening with someone else might be pleasant, depriving oneself of the ability to consume the memory of that one perfect evening is too high a tradeoff. Indeed, previous work has explored how memory serves just this function, of placing people in time and space and giving them a sense of meaning (Cowley 2007, Elster & Loewenstein 1992, Holbrook 1993, Wildschut et al. 2006).

Contamination. Strategic memory protection involves a symbolic desire to prevent future experiences from contaminating memories for special experiences in the past, but fear of contamination is more broadly manifested in physical consumption as well (Rozin & Fallon 1987). For instance, drinks that are in contact even briefly with a sterilized cockroach are seen as contaminated, as are sweaters worn by disliked individuals such as Adolf Hitler (Rozin et al. 1986, 1989). These results suggest that the consumption of disgust—independent of the stimulus to be consumed and independent of any actual harmful contamination—can affect physical consumption. Argo et al. (2006), for example, asked participants to try on T-shirts and rate them but varied whether participants thought that the T-shirt had not been worn or had recently been worn (leading participants to a T-shirt hanging in a dressing room that a confederate had just exited). They found that, despite the fact that participants never witnessed any physical contact with the shirt, the specter of the shirt having been worn raised sufficient disgust to decrease their liking for the shirt. Morales & Fitzsimons (2007) explored disgust in a nonsocial context, varying whether one product (a box of cookies) either was or was not touching a product that elicited disgust (a box of feminine napkins). Similar to the findings of Argo et al. (2006), even though no actual contamination had been witnessed, the cookies were liked less when their box had been touching the box of feminine items. In sum, people reduced physical consumption of desirable products—T-shirts and cookies—because their conceptual consumption of disgust affected their perceived utility of those products, even though the products remained the same.

So powerful are the effects of consumption of disgust on physical consumption that the mere association of contamination with a food can be enough to reduce physical consumption of that food. In general, such taste aversion learning—in which becoming ill after eating a food creates an aversion to that food— is adaptive in that it can protect humans from ingestion of lethal toxins (Revusky & Bedarf 1967, Rozin & Kalat 1971). Bernstein et al. (2005), however, showed that merely implanting a false memory of experiencing disgust after eating a food was sufficient to lead to avoidance of that food. In one experiment, some 20% of adult participants came to believe that they had become ill after eating strawberry ice cream as a child when the researchers suggested that this experience had actually occurred, and these false beliefs then led them to profess an intention to avoid strawberry ice cream in the future. Thus, the impact of consuming disgust on physical consumption can extend not only forward in time—as demonstrated by Argo et al. (2006) and Morales & Fitzsimons (2007)—but also backward in time, further evidence for the impact of conceptual consumption, in this case the mere memory of contamination, on physical consumption.

Charitable giving. Driven in part by natural disasters that required and elicited enormous amounts of charitable giving (e.g., 9/11, the 2004 tsunami, and Hurricane Katrina), consumer behavior researchers have devoted increasing attention to the study of charitable donations. From our perspective, charitable donations offer an interesting case of forgoing positive physical consumption, since any donation to another person necessarily precludes givers from using that money to pursue their own happiness. Some cases of such donations may be self-interested, of course. For instance, there are sound evolutionary reasons to behave more altruistically toward genetically related kin (Burnstein et al. 1994, Hamilton 1964; for a recent review, see de Waal 2008), and donating more to charities that seek a cure for an illness that afflicts a loved one might improve that person's chance of survival (Small & Simonsohn 2008).

But what about giving to complete strangers, where there is no chance of any physical benefit coming back (Trivers 1971), as with those whites who donated money to the predominantly minority victims of Hurricane Katrina (Cuddy et al. 2007, Fong & Luttmer 2008)? Researchers have identified a number of factors that influence such donations. People are more generous toward individualized victims than they are toward statistical/aggregated victims (Small & Loewenstein 2003). For example, using personalizing information to single out an individual child with cancer—rather than referring to a group of children with cancer—increases donations to cancer funds (Kogut & Ritov 2005a,b). Although the investigations cited above are important for increasing the frequency and amount of charitable giving, they do not offer an understanding of why people choose to sacrifice their own physical consumption for the physical consumption of strangers. We suggest that they do so to engage in conceptual consumption, to consume a view of themselves as altruistic individuals, leading to the benefit of increased well-being.

The debate between whether helping others is altruistic or self-motivated (making oneself feel better about the another's pain as opposed to helping them unselfishly) has long raged in social science, with psychologists often focusing on why people don't help enough and economists on why they help at all (Andreoni 1990, Batson et al. 1997, Cialdini et al. 1997, Fehr & Schmidt 1999, Loewenstein et al. 1989; also see Ariely & Norton 2007). In this vein, several recent investigations have explored whether giving is actually a function of social goals, such as signaling one's morality (Ariely et al. 2008) or financial success (Griskevicius et al. 2007).

Recent research suggests that whatever the initial motivation for the behavior, giving to others does confer benefits on the giver in both the short and long term. Dunn et al. (2008) specifically explored the tradeoff between spending a given amount of money on oneself (engaging in physical consumption) and enabling another to engage in physical consumption by giving that money to someone else (thus offering the giver the opportunity to engage in conceptual consumption). A field study showed that employees who spent more of a bonus on others than on themselves reported being happier as a result; indeed, the manner in which they spent that bonus was a more important predictor of their happiness than the size of the bonus itself. In addition, when people were given money one morning and randomly assigned either to spend the money on themselves or on someone else over the course of the day, those who spent it on others were significantly happier that night. These results suggest that when individuals sacrifice their own physical consumption for the physical consumption of others, they successfully trade off positive physical consumption for positive conceptual consumption, as reflected in their greater happiness. Unfortunately, because the mere thought of money can inhibit people from giving to others (Vohs et al. 2006), people may underutilize this path to happiness. We discuss the issue of how to encourage optimal consumer behavior in the Conclusions section.

Choosing Negative Consumption

The odd nature of forgoing positive experiences for the sake of conceptual consumption pales in comparison to research exploring the strange cases in which people actually choose the negative over the positive. For instance, skydiving is clearly a terrifying experience—even offering a chance, albeit small, of death—yet people pay money for and clearly derive utility from this activity (Celsi et al. 1993). Mountaineering, which offers an even higher chance of death, seems to be similarly and puzzlingly attractive (Loewenstein 1999). We suggest, and some recent research shows, that people may choose negative physical consumption experiences precisely because such experiences offer positive conceptual consumption.

Negative emotions. Research on the consumption of negative emotions has its antecedents in work exploring cases in which people experience mixed emotional and cognitive reactions. In contrast to earlier psychological models that stressed the strong human desire for cognitive consistency, such as Heider's (1958) balance theory and Festinger's (1957) theory of cognitive dissonance, more recent research has focused on how people are not just capable of experiencing mixed emotions (Lau-Gesk 2005, Williams & Aaker 2002) and attitudinal ambivalence (Newby-Clark et al. 2002, Priester & Petty 1996, Priester et al. 2007), but also on how such experiences are quite common. Choosing to engage in experiences that offer mixed emotions, however, means that such experiences by their nature contain at least some positive elements. Larsen et al. (2001) offer the example of viewers seeing the movie *Life is Beautiful*: Viewers are likely to cry during the movie, but writer/director Benigni inserts comedic moments to break the drama.

What can explain consumption of purely negative emotions and experiences? *Life is Beautiful* contains at least some light moments, but what about watching a horror movie where one experiences unabated fear for the duration of the experience? Any model of utility maximization has at its heart the notion that people seek to maximize their hedonic utility, which hardly seems to map onto watching *The Exorcist*. Andrade & Cohen (2007) investigated just these situations—watching horror

movies—to understand how people might benefit from these experiences. They found that, at least for people predisposed to horror movies, the negative emotions elicited by such movies are coactivated with positive emotions. Engaging in negative physical consumption thus ironically provides an opportunity to engage in positive conceptual consumption, perhaps providing a source of utility in addition to that which comes from consuming purely positive experiences.

Negative experiences. Although Andrade & Cohen (2007) focus specifically on negative emotions elicited by movies, Keinan & Kivetz (2008) examine a wider range of seemingly suboptimal behavior, from sleeping in ice houses to eating bacon ice cream. In one study, Keinan & Kivetz (2008) asked participants to make a choice between staying at a Marriott in Florida or an ice hotel in Quebec; despite the fact that participants thought the Marriott would be more pleasurable, they preferred the ice hotel. As with the variety-seeking research reviewed above, one view of choosing bacon ice cream is that people are simply behaving suboptimally by engaging in negative physical consumption; our view is that they are trading off the negative physical consumption for positive conceptual consumption.

Indeed, Keinan & Kivetz (2008) share our view that this seemingly baffling behavior may be more rational than it appears, writing about how people use such experiences to check off boxes on their "experiential CVs." Other researchers have explored how collecting can provide people with a sense of purpose (Belk 1995); in fact, individuals can become so preoccupied with completing collections that collecting can develop into pathological hoarding (Tolin et al. 2007). In one study, Keinan & Kivetz (2008) checked participants' watches to see if they were set ahead as an index of how concerned people were with using their time productively, and found that people who set their watches ahead—individuals most concerned about using their time to complete tasks (such as collecting experiences)—were precisely those individuals likely to choose exotic options. Thus, people appear to engage in negative consumption—sleeping on ice instead of pillows—because such negative physical consumption allows them to experience positive conceptual consumption, allowing them to enjoy a view of themselves as productive people who are adding to their collections of experiences.

CONCLUSIONS AND FUTURE DIRECTIONS

In this review, we have tried to provide a framework for categorizing and linking a variety of phenomena that have been studied in isolation. In particular, our goal was to suggest that these seemingly unrelated phenomena—for instance, the impact of fluency on consumer behavior and the odd cases when people choose to consume negative experiences—can be understood by considering the extent to which they implicate conceptual consumption. Our goal was not to cover every topic in consumer behavior, nor even to be comprehensive on each topic that we chose to include—the literature on goals alone likely would fill an Annual Review chapter—but rather to describe those investigations that best demonstrate the nature and impact of conceptual consumption. We again stress that we are far from the first researchers to note the role of psychological factors in influencing consumption, but we hope that by highlighting the connections between consumer behavior researchers who take a sociological or anthropological approach to those who take an experimental approach, conceptual consumption might serve as a link between these different orientations.

In the remainder of this review, we discuss potential contributions for conceptual consumption in three different areas of research. We first focus on the impact of conceptual consumption on the formation and perpetuation of preferences. We next focus on how a deeper consideration of conceptual consumption might be used to inform scholarship in two areas with implications for public policy:

research investigating people's willingness to enact virtual social lives—and spend money constructing those lives—on the Internet, and research devoted to helping consumers make better consumption decisions in both the short and long term.

Conceptual Consumption Over Time: Inferring Preferences from Actions

In this review, we particularly focus on research demonstrating the impact of conceptual consumption on physical consumption in the short term, such as how consuming goals changes purchasing behavior on one shopping trip. Elsewhere, we have described a two-stage model outlining how, in contrast to the economic model that actions reflect underlying preferences, actions can in fact create preferences (Ariely & Norton 2008). As an example, imagine a woman who moves to a new city and is hungry on her first evening in her new building. It just so happens that a pizza vendor a few blocks away placed flyers in that building earlier that day; our new tenant sees the flyer, calls that restaurant (not knowing any others), and has what is likely at least a decent pizza. What happens the next time she wants pizza? She recalls the pizza she had before and does not infer that her "preference" was caused by the fact that this pizza shop happened to inundate the building with flyers that day (whereas had she moved in one day earlier or later, a different vendor may have placed flyers, leading her to develop a "preference" for that shop instead). Rather, she recalls that this store actually offers better pizza than other stores. In this way, people can develop preferences for "their" pizza shop that are caused by their actions, rather than act in ways that reveal their preferences (see also Bem 1972). Indeed, people may even incorporate this preference into their self-concepts, deriving utility from seeing themselves as the kind of person who frequents such "quality" establishments.

Certainly, the first stage of this model is not controversial. Abundant evidence demonstrates that people's preferences are frequently constructed in the moment and are susceptible to fleeting situational factors (Bettman et al. 1998, Payne et al. 1993, Shafir et al. 1993, Slovic 1995), such as subtle primes (Bargh & Chartrand 1999, Fitzsimons et al. 2002), incidental emotions (Cryder et al. 2008, Lerner et al. 2004), or even the weather (Simonsohn 2007). Indeed, much of the bulk of this review is a catalogue of the way that different concepts— from fluency to fit to contamination—serve to shape people's preferences without their awareness. To take just one example, participants' choice of cell phones as described in Novemsky et al. (2007) was driven by the fluency of the advertisements for those phones; we suggest that they would be very unlikely to attribute their behavior to those fonts, instead believing that they valued the phone at the price they paid.

This second stage, where we propose that individuals are insensitive to the impact of situational factors on their behavior, misattributing utility caused by irrelevant factors to stable underlying preferences that then guide subsequent behavior in the longer term, requires future research. Ariely et al. (2003) showed that when participants were asked to indicate whether they would pay a given price— arbitrarily set by the last two digits of their social security number—for a bottle of wine, those with higher social security numbers bid more. In addition, bids for subsequent bottles of wine followed in a coherent manner, such that better bottles of wine fetched higher prices, even though the initial price had been arbitrarily induced. These results offer some evidence that people do observe their past behavior and see it as reflective of preferences even when these preferences were actually determined by situational factors.

We believe that studies that explore conceptual and physical consumption in tandem offer an excellent opportunity to better understand the psychology of actions leading to preferences and thus advance the field's knowledge of this key debate between psychology and economics. By measuring conceptual consumption as an important input into total utility, researchers not only can better understand seeming violations of utility maximization (such as sleeping in ice hotels), but also can be better able to predict the circumstances under which people might both choose these seemingly suboptimal outcomes and turn them into longer-lasting patterns of behavior.

Virtual Consumption as Conceptual Consumption

As consumers increasingly move their physical consumption online, buying their books, music, clothes, and computers sight unseen, researchers in consumer behavior have begun to investigate the impact of this new channel on both consumer decision-making and subsequent satisfaction (Alba et al. 1997, Bellman et al. 2006, Deighton & Kornfeld 2007, Hamilton & Thompson 2007). Perhaps one of the most fascinating changes to consumption as a result of online consumer behavior is the seemingly unstoppable popularity of social networking sites and virtual worlds such as Myspace and Second Life: Some 55% of Americans aged 12–17 have created online profiles, and 16 million Americans have used an online dating Web site (Amichai-Hamburger & Furnham 2007, Castronova 2005, Frost et al. 2008, Lenhart & Madden 2007, Madden & Lenhart 2006). Even more interestingly, people engage in virtual commerce on such sites, converting real money into virtual currency, then using that currency to decorate their virtual apartments and dress their avatars, buying virtual consumer goods from the many companies, such as Nike and American Apparel, that have opened virtual stores in Second Life.

Why are people happy to conduct their social lives online and "waste" their real money on buying imaginary products? Examined from the viewpoint of conceptual consumption, both behaviors are less inexplicable. Face-to-face interaction offers some utility that virtual interaction cannot (physical contact, for example), whereas social utility is conceptual, available for consumption in person or at a remove. As a result, virtual interaction at such sites may in fact meet people's consumption needs. Similarly, although buying virtual Nikes for one's avatar removes some physical utility derived from using the shoes (though Nike cleverly designed shoes that allow avatars to run faster), the conceptual consumption engendered by identifying with and displaying brands (Aaker 1997, Belk 1988) means that forgoing the physical product may detract very little from the enjoyable conceptual consumption that owning a Nike product allows. Although the enduring popularity of any specific social networking site or virtual world is difficult to predict—witness the rapid rise and fall of Friendster—we suggest that sites that offer more opportunities for conceptual consumption are likely to gain more traction.

Conceptual Consumption and "Improved" Consumer Behavior

We conclude by discussing how consideration of the importance of conceptual consumption can be used to inform efforts to help consumers better manage their consumption in both the short and long term. There has been an increase in recent years in calls for consumer behavior researchers to engage in research designed to benefit consumers (Bazerman 2001), using the knowledge acquired from previous research to improve public policy (Mick 2007, Ratner et al. 2008, Thaler & Sunstein 2008). Indeed, our review of the literature on charitable giving above offers one domain in which such work is already under way. Much of the focus on changing people's behavior for the better has been on exploring ways to move them from engaging in "want" behaviors and indulging their sometimes shortsighted passions to "should" behaviors such as planning for the future (Bazerman et al. 1998, Loewenstein 1996, Schelling 1984; for a recent review, see Milkman et al. 2008). We suggest that offering people a chance to engage in conceptual consumption when they are required to trade off physical consumption may be an effective means of reaching this goal. Given that people will not be able to eat all the ice cream they want, researchers can explore ways in which consuming some concept might

substitute—at least in part—for that foregone physical consumption.

We close with an illustrative example of a successful intervention from political science that is close in spirit to our proposition, one that utilizes people's desire to consume social utility as a trigger for overcoming people's resistance to civic engagement. Of course, countless studies in social psychology have demonstrated the impact of social norms on behavior, from Asch's (1951) famous conformity studies to Goldstein et al.'s (2008) demonstration of the impact of social norms on towel reuse in hotels (see Cialdini & Goldstein 2004). These studies, however, often have the flavor of twisting people's arms to comply with some norm; from our standpoint, such appeals may be effective because they give individuals the opportunity to consume social utility. In a field study designed to increase voting, Gerber et al. (2008) mailed flyers to prospective voters: In one condition, the flyer merely reminded people that voting was their civic duty, while in another, the flyer revealed both the household's voter turnout and their neighbors' turnout and suggested that a follow-up mailing after the election would report whether or not the recipient voted. In contrast to the first condition, then, the latter condition forces people who fail to vote to sacrifice social utility, whereas voting offers them a chance to display their good behavior to their neighbors and to consume social utility. This social utility condition increased turnout by more than 8% compared to a control condition, whereas the civic duty reminder increased voting by less than 2%.

In addition, in line with Ariely & Norton's (2008) contention that preferences caused by situational factors can lead people to infer underlying preferences, research suggests that voting is habit forming, in that if people vote just once they are much more likely to become voters (Gerber et al. 2003), suggesting a possible longer-term impact of conceptual consumption on behavior. Assuming that higher voter turnout is desirable in a democratic society, these studies serve as promising evidence that increasing opportunities for conceptual consumption when asking consumers to alter physical consumption can increase social welfare. We hope that consumer behavior researchers will continue the trend of engaging in research designed to help consumers make wiser decisions.

DISCLOSURE STATEMENT

The authors are not aware of any biases that might be perceived as affecting the objectivity of this review.

ACKNOWLEDGMENTS

We thank Jim Bettman, John Deighton, Anat Keinan, and Kathleen Vohs for their helpful suggestions, and Megan Hogerty for her assistance.

LITERATURE CITED

Aaker JL. 1997. Dimensions of brand personality. *J. Mark. Res.* 34:347–56

Aaker JL, Lee AY. 2006. Understanding regulatory fit. *J. Mark. Res.* 43:15–19

Aarts H, Gollwitzer PM, Hassin R. 2004. Goal contagion: Perceiving is for pursuing. *J. Personal. Soc. Psychol.* 87:23–37

Alba J, Lynch J, Weitz B, Janiszewski C, Lutz R, et al. 1997. Interactive home shopping: consumer, retailer, and manufacturer incentives to participate in electronic marketplaces. *J. Mark.* 61:38–53

Allison RI, Uhl KP. 1964. Influence of beer brand identification on taste perception. *J. Mark. Res.* 1:36–39

Allport GW, Postman L. 1947. *The Psychology of Rumor*. New York: Holt

Alter AL, Oppenheimer DM. 2006. Predicting short-term stock fluctuations by using processing fluency. *Proc. Natl. Acad. Sci. USA* 103:9369–72

Alter AL, Oppenheimer DM, Epley N, Eyre RN. 2007. Overcoming intuition: metacognitive difficulty activates analytic reasoning. *J. Exp. Psychol.: Gen.* 136:569–76

Amaldoss W, Jain S. 2005. Conspicuous consumption and sophisticated thinking. *Manage. Sci.* 51(10):1449–66

Amichai-Hamburger Y, Furnham A. 2007. The positive net. *Comput. Hum. Behav.* 23:1033–45

Anderson CJ. 2003. The psychology of doing nothing: Forms of decision avoidance result from reason and emotion. *Psychol. Bull.* 129:139–67

Andrade EB, Cohen JB. 2007. On the consumption of negative feelings. *J. Consum. Res.* 34:283–300

Andreoni J. 1990. Impure altruism and donations to public goods: a theory of warm-glow giving. *Econ. J.* 100:464–77

Argo JJ, Dahl DW, Morales AC. 2006. Consumer contamination: how consumers react to products touched by others. *J. Mark.* 70:81–94

Ariely D, Bracha A, Meier S. 2008. Doing good or doing well? Image motivation and monetary incentives in behaving prosocially. *Am. Econ. Rev.* In press

Ariely D, Levav J. 2000. Sequential choice in group settings: taking the road less traveled and less enjoyed. *J. Consum. Res.* 27:279–90

Ariely D, Loewenstein G, Prelec D. 2003. Coherent arbitrariness: stable demand curves without stable preferences. *Q. J. Econ.* 118:73–105

Ariely D, Norton MI. 2007. Psychology and experimental economics: a gap in abstraction. *Curr. Dir. Psychol. Sci.* 16:336–39

Ariely D, Norton MI. 2008. How actions create—not just reveal—preferences. *Trends Cogn. Sci.* 12:13–16

Ariely D, Wertenbroch K. 2002. Procrastination, deadlines, and performance: self-control by precommitment. *Psychol. Sci.* 13:219–24

Arkes HR, Blumer C. 1985. The psychology of sunk cost. *Organ. Behav. Hum. Dec.* 35:124–40

Asch SE. 1951. Effects of group pressure upon the modification and distortion of judgment. In *Groups, Leadership and Men*, ed. H Guetzkow, pp. 177–90. Pittsburgh, PA: Carnegie Press

Avnet T, Higgins ET. 2003. Locomotion, assessment, and regulatory fit: value transfer from "how" to "what." *J. Exp. Soc. Psychol.* 39:525–30

Avnet T, Higgins ET. 2006. How regulatory fit affects value in consumer choices and opinions. *J. Mark. Res.* 43:1–10

Bagozzi RP, Dholakia UM. 1999. Goal setting and goal striving in consumer behavior. *J. Mark.* 63:19–32

Bagozzi RP, Edwards EA. 1998. Goal setting and goal pursuit in the regulation of body weight. *Psychol. Health* 13:593–621

Bargh JA, Chartrand TL. 1999. The unbearable automaticity of being. *Am. Psychol.* 54:462–79

Bargh JA, Gollwitzer PM, Chai AL, Barndollar K, Trötschel R. 2001. Automated will: nonconscious activation and pursuit of behavioral goals. *J. Personal. Soc. Psychol.* 81:1014–27

Batson CD, Sager K, Garst E, Kang M, Rubchinsky K, Dawson K. 1997. Is empathy-induced helping due to self-other merging? *J. Personal. Soc. Psychol.* 73:495–509

Baumgartner H, Pieters FGM. 2008. Goal-directed consumer behavior. In *Handbook of Consumer Psychology*, ed. C Haugtvedt, P Herr, F Kardes, pp. 367–92. Mahwah, NJ: Psychol. Press

Bazerman MH. 2001. Consumer research for consumers. *J. Consum. Res.* 27:499–504

Bazerman MH, Tenbrunsel AE, Wade-Benzoni KA. 1998. Negotiating with yourself and losing: making decisions with competing internal preferences. *Acad. Manage. Rev.* 23:225–41

Belk RW. 1988. Possessions and the extended self. *J. Consum. Res.* 15:139–67

Belk RW. 1995. *Collecting in a Consumer Society*. London: Routledge

Bellman S, Johnson EJ, Lohse GL, Mandel N. 2006. Designing marketplaces of the artificial with consumers in mind: four approaches to understanding consumer behavior in electronic environments. *J. Interact. Mark.* 20:21–33

Bem DJ. 1972. Self-perception theory. *Adv. Exp. Soc. Psychol.* 6:1–62

Benartzi S, Thaler RH. 2001. Naive diversification strategies in retirement saving plans. *Am. Econ. Rev.* 91(1):79–98

Berger J, Heath C. 2007. Where consumers diverge from others: identity-signaling and product domains. *J. Consum. Res.* 34:121–34

Bernstein DM, Laney C, Morris EK, Loftus EF. 2005. False beliefs about fattening foods can have healthy consequences. *Proc. Natl. Acad. Sci. USA* 102:13724–31

Berthoud H, Morrison C. 2008. The brain, appetite, and obesity. *Annu. Rev. Psychol.* 59:55–92

Bettman JR, Luce MF, Payne JW. 1998. Constructive consumer choice processes. *J. Consum. Res.* 25:187–217

Borgmann A. 2000. The moral complexion of consumption. *J. Consum. Res.* 26:418–22

Boulding W, Kalra A, Staelin R. 1999. The quality double whammy. *Mark. Sci.* 18:463–84

Boulding W, Kalra A, Staelin R, Zeithaml VA. 1993. A dynamic process model of service quality: from expectations to behavioral intentions. *J. Mark. Res.* 30:7–27

Braun KA. 1999. Postexperience advertising effects on consumer memory. *J. Consum. Res.* 25:319–34

Burnstein E, Crandall C, Kitayama S. 1994. Some neo-Darwinian decision rules for altruism: weighing cues for inclusive fitness as a function of the biological importance of the decision. *J. Personal. Soc. Psychol.* 67:773–89

Castronova E. 2005. *Synthetic Worlds: The Business and Culture of Online Games*. Chicago: Univ. Chicago Press

Celsi RL, Rose RL, Leigh TW. 1993. An exploration of high-risk leisure consumption through skydiving. *J. Consum. Res.* 20:1–20

Cesario J, Grant H, Higgins ET. 2004. Regulatory fit and persuasion: transfer from "feeling right." *J. Personal. Soc. Psychol.* 86:388–404

Chartrand TL, Dalton AN, Fitzsimons GJ. 2007. Nonconscious relationship reactance: when significant others prime opposing goals. *J. Exp. Soc. Psychol.* 43:719–26

Chen M, Bargh JA. 1997. Nonconscious behavioral confirmation processes: the self-fulfilling consequences of automatic stereotype activation. *J. Exp. Soc. Psychol.* 33:541–60

Chernev A. 2004. Goal-attribute compatibility in consumer choice. *J. Consum. Psychol.* 14:141–50

Cialdini RB, Brown SL, Lewis BP, Luce C, Neuberg SL. 1997. Reinterpreting the empathy-altruism relationship: When one into one equals oneness. *J. Personal. Soc. Psychol.* 73:481–94

Cialdini RB, Goldstein NJ. 2004. Social influence: compliance and conformity. *Annu. Rev. Psychol.* 55:591–621

Corneo G, Jeanne O. 1997. Conspicuous consumption, snobbism and conformism. *J. Public Econ.* 66:55–71

Cowley E. 2007. How enjoyable was it? Remembering an affective reaction to a previous consumption experience. *J. Consum. Res.* 34:494–505

Cryder CE, Lerner JS, Gross JJ, Dahl RE. 2008. Misery is not miserly: sad and self-focused individuals spend more. *Psychol. Sci.* 19:525–30

Cuddy AJC, Rock MS, Norton MI. 2007. Aid in the aftermath of Hurricane Katrina: inferences of secondary emotions and intergroup helping. *Group. Process. Intergroup Relat.* 10:107–18

Csikszenthmihalyi M. 1990. *Flow: The Psychology of Optimal Experience.* New York: Harper Perennial

Darley JM, Gross PH. 1983. A hypothesis-confirming bias in labeling effects. *J. Personal. Soc. Psychol.* 44:20–33

Dawkins RM. 1976. *The Selfish Gene.* London: Oxford Univ. Press

Deighton J. 2007. The territory of consumer research: walking the fences. *J. Consum. Res.* 34:279–82

Deighton J, Kornfeld L. 2007. *Digital interactivity: unanticipated consequences for markets, marketing, and consumers.* Work. pap., Harvard Business School, Boston, MA

De Waal FBM. 2008. Putting the altruism back into altruism: the evolution of empathy. *Annu. Rev. Psychol.* 59:279–300

Dhar R. 1997. Consumer preference for a no-choice option. *J. Consum. Res.* 24:215–31

Dhar R, Huber J, Khan U. 2007. The shopping momentum effect. *J. Mark. Res.* 64:370–78

Dhar R, Simonson I. 2003. The effect of forced choice on choice. *J. Mark. Res.* 40:146–60

Drolet A. 2002. Inherent rule variability in consumer choice: changing rules for change's sake. *J. Consum. Res.* 29:293–305

Drucker PF. 1959. *Landmarks of Tomorrow: A Report On the New "Post-Modern" World.* New York: Harper & Row

Dunn EW, Aknin LB, Norton MI. 2008. Spending money on others promotes happiness. *Science* 319:1687–88

Elster J, Loewenstein G. 1992. Utility from memory and anticipation. In *Choice Over Time*, ed. G Loewenstein, J Elster, pp. 213–34. New York: Sage Found.

Fang X, Singh S, Ahluwalia R. 2007. An examination of different explanations for the mere exposure effect. *J. Consum. Res.* 34:97–103

Fehr E, Schmidt KM. 1999. A theory of fairness, competition and co-operation. *Q. J. Econ.* 114:817–68

Ferraro R, Bettman JR, Chartrand TL. 2008. The power of strangers: the effect of incidental consumer-brand encounters on brand choice. *J. Consum. Res.* In press

Festinger L. 1957. *A Theory of Cognitive Dissonance.* Evanston, IL: Row, Peterson

Fishbach A, Dhar R. 2005. Goals as excuses or guides: the liberating effect of perceived goal progress on choice. *J. Consum. Res.* 32:370–77

Fishbach A, Friedman RS, Kruglanski AW. 2003. Leading us not unto temptation: momentary allurements elicit overriding goal activation. *J. Personal. Soc. Psychol.* 84:296–309

Fiske ST, Taylor SE. 2008. *Social Cognition: From Brains to Culture.* New York: McGraw-Hill

Fitzsimons GJ, Hutchinson JW, Alba JW, Chartrand TL, Huber J, et al. 2002. Non-conscious influences on consumer choice. *Mark. Lett.* 13:267–77

Fitzsimons GJ, Morwitz VG. 1996. The effect of measuring intent on brand-level purchase behavior. *J. Consum. Res.* 23:1–11

Fitzsimons GM, Bargh JA. 2003. Thinking of you: nonconscious pursuit of interpersonal goals associated with relationship partners. *J. Personal. Soc. Psychol.* 84:148–64

Foa UG. 1971. Interpersonal and economic resources. *Science* 171:345–51

Fong CM, Luttmer EFP. 2008. *What determines giving to Hurricane Katrina victims? Experimental evidence on racial group loyalty.* Work. pap., NBER, Harvard Univ., Cambridge, MA

Fournier S. 1998. Consumers and their brands: developing relationship theory in consumer research. *J. Consum. Res.* 24:343–73

Fox CR, Ratner RK, Lieb DS. 2005. How subjective grouping of options influences choice and allocation: diversification bias and the phenomenon of partition dependence. *J. Exp. Psychol.: Gen.* 134(4):538–51

Frost JH, Chance Z, Norton MI, Ariely D. 2008. People are experience goods: improving online dating with Virtual Dates. *J. Interact. Mark.* 22:51–61

Gerber AS, Green DP, Larimer CW. 2008. Social pressure and voter turnout: evidence from a large-scale field experiment. *Am. Polit. Sci. Rev.* 102:33–48

Gerber AS, Green DP, Shachar R. 2003. Voting may be habit-forming: evidence from a randomized field experiment. *Am. J. Polit. Sci.* 47:540–50

Gerstner E. 1985. Do higher prices signal higher quality? *J. Mark. Res.* 22:209–15

Gilbert DT, Wilson TD. 2007. Prospection: experiencing the future. *Science* 317:1351–54

Goldstein NJ, Cialdini RB, Griskevicius V. 2008. A room with a viewpoint: using social norms to motivate environmental conservation in hotels. *J. Consum. Res.* In press

Gollwitzer PM. 1990. Action phases and mind-sets. In *The Handbook of Motivation and Cognition: Foundations of Social Behavior*, ed. ET Higgins, RM Sorrentino, 2:53–92. New York: Guilford

Gollwitzer PM. 1999. Implementation intentions: strong effects of simple plans. *Am. Psychol.* 54:493–503

Greenwald AF, Carnot CG, Beach R, Young B. 1987. Increasing voting behavior by asking people if they expect to vote. *J. Appl. Psychol.* 72:315–18

Griskevicius V, Tybur JM, Sundie JM, Cialdini RB, Miller GF, Kenrick DT. 2007. Blatant benevolence and conspicuous consumption: when romantic motives elicit strategic costly signals. *J. Personal. Soc. Psychol.* 93:85–102

Hamilton RW, Thompson DV. 2007. Is there a substitute for direct experience? Comparing consumers' preferences after direct and indirect product experiences. *J. Consum. Res.* 34:546–55

Hamilton WD. 1964. The genetical evolution of social behaviour I and II. *J. Theor. Biol.* 7:1–16

Heath C, Bell C, Sternberg E. 2001. Emotional selection in memes: the case of urban legends. *J. Personal. Soc. Psychol.* 81:1028–41

Heath C, Larrick RP, Wu G. 1999. Goals as reference points. *Cogn. Psychol.* 38:79–109

Heider F. 1958. *The Psychology of Interpersonal Relations*. New York: Wiley

Higgins ET. 2000. Making a good decision: value from fit. *Am. Psychol.* 55:1217–30

Higgins ET. 2005. Value from regulatory fit. *Curr. Dir. Psychol. Sci.* 14:209–13

Higgins ET, Idson LC, Freitas AL, Spiegel S, Molden DC. 2003. Transfer of value from fit. *J. Personal. Soc. Psychol.* 84:1140–53

Hirschman EC, Holbrook MB. 1982. Hedonic consumption: emerging concepts, methods and propositions. *J. Mark.* 46:92–101

Holbrook MB. 1993. Nostalgia and consumption preferences. *J. Consum. Res.* 20:245–56

Holbrook MB, Hirschman EC. 1982. The experiential aspects of consumption—consumer fantasies, feelings, and fun. *J. Consum. Res.* 9:132–40

Holt DB. 1995. How consumers consume: a typology of consumption practices. *J. Consum. Res.* 22:1–16

Hong JW, Lee AY. 2008. Be fit and be strong: mastering self-regulation through regulatory fit. *J. Consum. Res.* 34:682–95

Hsee CK, Yu F, Zhang J, Zhang Y. 2003. Medium maximization. *J. Consum. Res.* 30:1–14

Irmak C, Block LG, Fitzsimons GJ. 2005. The placebo effect in marketing: Sometimes you just have to want it to work. *J. Mark. Res.* 42:406–9

Janiszewski C. 1993. Preattentive mere exposure effects. *J. Consum. Res.* 20:376–92

Jussim L, Harber KD. 2005. Teacher expectations and self-fulfilling prophecies: knowns and unknowns, resolved and unresolved controversies. *Personal. Soc. Psychol. Rev.* 9:131–55

Kahneman D, Miller DT. 1986. Norm theory: comparing reality to its alternatives. *Psychol. Rev.* 93:126–53

Kahneman D, Snell J. 1992. Predicting a changing taste: Do people know what they will like? *J. Behav. Decis. Making* 5:187–200

Kaplan P. 2000. The darker side of the original affluent society. *J. Anthropol. Res.* 56:301–24

Keinan A, Kivetz R. 2008. *Productivity mindset and the consumption of collectible experiences*. Work. pap., Harvard Business School, Boston, MA

Kim HS, Drolet A. 2003. Choice and self-expression: a cultural analysis of variety-seeking. *J. Personal. Soc. Psychol.* 85:373–82

Kivetz R, Urminsky O, Zheng Y. 2006. The goal-gradient hypothesis resurrected: purchase acceleration, illusionary goal progress, and customer retention. *J. Mark. Res.* 43:39–58

Klein O, Snyder M. 2003. Stereotypes and behavioral confirmation: from interpersonal to intergroup perspectives. *Adv. Exp. Soc. Psychol.* 35:153–234

Kogut T, Ritov I. 2005a. The singularity effect of identified victims in separate and joint evaluations. *Organ. Behav. Hum. Dec.* 97:106–16

Kogut T, Ritov I. 2005b. The "identified victim" effect: an identified group, or just single individual? *J. Behav. Decis. Making* 18:157–67

Kopalle PK, Lehmann DR. 2001. Strategic management of expectations: the role of disconfirmation sensitivity and perfectionism. *J. Mark. Res.* 38:386–94

Kopalle PK, Lehmann DR. 2006. Setting quality expectations when entering a market: What should the promise be? *Mark. Sci.* 25:8–24

Kunst-Wilson WR, Zajonc RB. 1980. Affective discrimination of stimuli that cannot be recognized. *Science* 207:557–58

Labroo A, Dhar R, Schwarz N. 2008. Of frowning watches and frog wines: semantic priming and visual fluency. *J. Consum. Res.* 34:819–31

Larsen JT, McGraw AP, Cacioppo JT. 2001. Can people feel happy and sad at the same time? *J. Personal. Soc. Psychol.* 81:684–96

Lau-Gesk L. 2005. Understanding consumer evaluations of mixed affective experiences. *J. Consum. Res.* 32:23–28

Lee AY, Labroo A. 2004. The effect of conceptual and perceptual fluency on brand evaluation. *J. Mark. Res.* 41:151–65

Lee L, Ariely D. 2006. Shopping goals, goal concreteness, and conditional promotions. *J. Consum. Res.* 33:60–70

Lee L, Frederick S, Ariely D. 2006. Try it, you'll like it: the influence of expectation, consumption, and revelation on preferences for beer. *Psychol. Sci.* 17:1054–58

Lenhart A, Madden M. 2007. *Social Networking Websites and Teens: An Overview*. Washington, DC: Pew Internet Am. Life Proj.

Lerner JS, Small DA, Loewenstein G. 2004. Heart strings and purse strings: carryover effects of emotions on economic decisions. *Psychol. Sci.* 15:337–40

Levav J, Kivetz R, Cho CK. 2008. *Too much fit? How regulatory fit can turn us into Buridan's asses*. Work. pap., Columbia Univ., New York, NY

Levin IP, Gaeth GJ. 1988. How consumers are affected by the framing of attribute information before and after consuming the product. *J. Consum. Res.* 15:374–78

Loewenstein G. 1996. Out of control: visceral influences on behavior. *Organ. Behav. Hum. Dec.* 65:272–92

Loewenstein G. 1999. Because it is there: the challenge of mountaineering . . . for utility theory. *Kyklos* 52:315–44

Loewenstein G, Thompson L, Bazerman M. 1989. Social utility and decision making in interpersonal contexts. *J. Personal. Soc. Psychol.* 57:426–41

Loken B. 2006. Consumer psychology: categorization, inferences, affect, and persuasion. *Annu. Rev. Psychol.* 57:453–85

Lord CG, Ross L, Lepper MR. 1979. Biased assimilation and attitude polarization: the effects of prior theories on subsequently considered evidence. *J. Personal. Soc. Psychol.* 37:2098–109

Madden M, Lenhart A. 2006. *Online Dating*. Washington, DC: Pew Internet Am. Life Proj.

Madon S, Guyll M, Spoth RL, Cross SE, Hilbert SJ. 2003. The self-fulfilling influence of mother expectations on children's underage drinking. *J. Personal. Soc. Psychol.* 84:1188–205

Mason MF, Bar M, Macrae CN. 2008. Exploring the past and impending future in the here and now: mind-wandering in the default state. *Cognitive Sci.* In press

Mason MF, Norton MI, Van Horn JD, Wegner DM, Grafton ST, Macrae CN. 2007. Wandering minds: the default network and stimulus-independent thought. *Science* 315:393–95

McClure SM, Li J, Tomlin D, Cypert KS, Montague LM, Montague PR. 2004. Neural correlates of behavioral preference for culturally familiar drinks. *Neuron* 44:379–87

Menon G, Raghubir P. 2003. Ease-of-retrieval as an automatic input in judgments: a mere-accessibility framework? *J. Consum. Res.* 30:230–43

Merton RK. 1948. The self-fulfilling prophecy. *Antioch Rev.* 8:193–210

Mick DG. 1986. Consumer research and semiotics—exploring the morphology of signs, symbols, and significance. *J. Consum. Res.* 13:196–213

Mick DG. 2003. From the editor: appreciation, advice, and some aspirations for consumer research. *J. Consum. Res.* 29:i–viii

Mick DG. 2007. The end(s) of marketing and the neglect of moral responsibility by the American Marketing Association. *J. Public Policy Mark.* 26:289–92

Milkman KL, Beshears J, Rogers T, Bazerman M. 2008. *Mental accounting and small windfalls: evidence from an online grocer.* Work. pap., Harvard Business School, Boston, MA

Milkman KL, Rogers T, Bazerman MH. 2008. Harnessing our inner angels and demons: what we have learned about want/should conflicts and how that knowledge can help us reduce short-sighted decision making. *Perspect. Psychol. Sci.* 3:324–38

Mogilner C, Aaker J, Pennington G. 2008. Time will tell: the distant appeal of promotion and imminent appeal of prevention. *J. Consum. Res.* 34:670–81

Monin B. 2003. The warm glow heuristic: when liking leads to familiarity. *J. Personal. Soc. Psychol.* 85:1035–48

Morales AC, Fitzsimons GJ. 2007. Product contagion: changing consumer evaluations through physical contact with "disgusting" products. *J. Mark. Res.* 44:272–83

Morwitz VG, Johnson E, Schmittlein D. 1993. Does measuring intent change behavior? *J. Consum. Res.* 20:46–61

Nelson LD, Norton MI. 2005. From student to superhero: situational primes shape future helping. *J. Exp. Soc. Psychol.* 41:423–30

Nelson LD, Simmons JP. 2007. Moniker maladies: when names sabotage success. *Psychol. Sci.* 18:1106–1112

Nevid JS. 1981. Effects of brand labeling on ratings of product quality. *Percept. Mot. Skills* 53:407–10

Newby-Clark IR, McGregor I, Zanna MP. 2002. Thinking and caring about cognitive inconsistency: When and for whom does attitudinal ambivalence feel uncomfortable? *J. Personal. Soc. Psychol.* 82:157–66

Norton MI, Frost JH, Ariely D. 2007. Less is more: the lure of ambiguity, or why familiarity breeds contempt. *J. Personal. Soc. Psychol.* 92:97–105

Norton MI, Goethals GR. 2004. Spin (and pitch) doctors: campaign strategies in televised political debates. *Polit. Behav.* 26:227–48

Norton MI, Vandello JA, Darley JM. 2004. Casuistry and social category bias. *J. Personal. Soc. Psychol.* 87:817–31

Novemsky N, Dhar R, Schwarz N, Simonson I. 2007. Preference fluency in choice. *J. Mark. Res.* 44:347–56

Nunes JC, Dreze X. 2006. The endowed progress effect: how artificial advancement increases effort. *J. Consum. Res.* 32:504–12

Payne JW, Bettman JR, Johnson EJ. 1993. *The Adaptive Decision Maker.* New York: Cambridge Univ. Press

Petrova PK, Cialdini RB. 2005. Fluency of consumption imagery and the backfire effects of imagery appeals. *J. Consum. Res.* 32:442–52

Pinel JPJ, Assanand S, Lehman DR. 2000. Hunger, eating, and ill health. *Am. Psychol.* 55:1105–16

Plassmann H, O'Doherty J, Shiv B, Rangel A. 2008. Marketing actions can modulate neural representations of experienced pleasantness. *Proc. Natl. Acad. Sci. USA* 105:1050–54

Price DD, Finniss DG, Benedetti F. 2008. A comprehensive review of the placebo effect: recent advances and current thought. *Annu. Rev. Psychol.* 59:565–90

Priester JR, Petty RE. 1996. The gradual threshold model of ambivalence: relating the positive and negative bases of attitudes to subjective ambivalence. *J. Personal. Soc. Psychol.* 71:431–49

Priester JR, Petty RE, Park K. 2007. Whence univalent ambivalence? From the anticipation of conflicting reactions. *J. Consum. Res.* 34:11–21

Rao A, Monroe KB. 1989. The effect of price, brand name, and store name on buyers' perceptions of product quality: an integrative review. *J. Mark. Res.* 26:351–57

Ratner RK, Kahn BK. 2002. The impact of private versus public consumption on variety-seeking behavior. *J. Consum. Res.* 29:246–57

Ratner RK, Kahn BE, Kahneman D. 1999. Choosing less-preferred experiences for the sake of variety. *J. Consum. Res.* 26:1–15

Ratner RK, Soman D, Zauberman G, Ariely D, Carmon Z, et al. 2008. How behavioral decision research can enhance consumer welfare: from freedom of choice to paternalistic intervention. *Mark. Lett.* In press

Read D, Loewenstein G. 1995. Diversification bias: explaining the discrepancy in variety seeking between combined and separated choices. *J. Exp. Psychol.: Appl.* 1:34–49

Revusky SH, Bedarf EW. 1967. Association of illness with prior ingestion of novel foods. *Science* 155:219–20

Roese NJ. 1997. Counterfactual thinking. *Psychol. Bull.* 121:133–48

Rosenthal R, Jacobson L. 1968. *Pygmalion in the Classroom: Teacher Expectation and Pupils' Intellectual Development*. New York: Rinehart & Winston

Rozin P, Fallon AE. 1987. A perspective on disgust. *Psychol. Rev.* 94:23–41

Rozin P, Kalat JW. 1971. Specific hungers and poison avoidance as adaptive specializations of learning. *Psychol. Rev.* 78:459–86

Rozin P, Millman L, Nemeroff C. 1986. Operation of the laws of sympathetic magic in disgust and other domains. *J. Personal. Soc. Psychol.* 40:703–12

Rozin P, Nemeroff C, Wane M, Sherrod A. 1989. Operation of the sympathetic magical law of contagion in interpersonal attitudes among Americans. *Bull. Psychon. Soc.* 27:367–70

Sahlins M. 1972. *Stone Age Economics*. Chicago, IL: Aldine

Sande GN, Goethals GR, Radloff CE. 1988. Perceiving one's own traits and others': the multifaceted self. *J. Personal. Soc. Psychol.* 54:13–20

Schelling TC. 1984. The mind as a consuming organ. In *Choice and Consequence: Perspectives of an Errant Economist*, pp. 328–46. Cambridge, MA: Harvard Univ. Press

Schwarz N. 2004. Metacognitive experiences in consumer judgment and decision making. *J. Consum. Psychol.* 14:332–48

Schwarz N, Clore GL. 1996. Feelings and phenomenal experiences. In *Social Psychology: Handbook of Basic Principles*, ed. ET Higgins, A Kruglanski, pp. 433–65. New York: Guilford

Shafir E, Simonson I, Tversky A. 1993. Reason-based choice. *Cognition* 49:11–36

Shirky C. 2008. *Gin, television, and social surplus*. **http://www.herecomeseverybody.org/2008/04/looking-for-the-mouse.html**

Shiv B, Carmon Z, Ariely D. 2005. Placebo effects of marketing actions: Consumers may get what they pay for. *J. Mark. Res.* 42:383–93

Shleifer A, Summers L. 1990. The noise trader approach to finance. *J. Econ. Perspect.* 4:19–33

Simmons J, Nelson LD. 2006. Intuitive confidence: choosing between intuitive and nonintuitive alternatives. *J. Exp. Psychol.: Gen.* 135:409–28

Simonsohn U. 2007. *Weather to go to college*. Work. pap., Univ. Calif., San Diego

Simonson I. 1990. The effect of purchase quantity and timing on variety-seeking behavior. *J. Mark. Res.* 27:150–62

Simonson I, Carmon Z, Dhar R, Drolet A, Nowlis S. 2001. Consumer research: in search of identity. *Annu. Rev. Psychol.* 52:249–75

Sinaceur M, Heath C. 2005. Emotional and deliberative reactions to a public crisis: mad cow disease in France. *Psychol. Sci.* 16:247–54

Slovic P. 1995. The construction of preference. *Am. Psychol.* 50:364–71

Small DA, Loewenstein G. 2003. Helping "A" victim or helping "THE" victim: altruism and identifiability. *J. Risk Uncertainty* 26:5–16

Small DA, Simonsohn U. 2008. Friends of victims: personal experience and prosocial behavior. *J. Consum. Res.* In press

Smallwood J, Schooler JW. 2006. The restless mind. *Psychol. Bull.* 132:946–58

Snyder M, Swann WB. 1978. Hypothesis-testing processes in social interaction. *J. Personal. Soc. Psychol.* 36:1202–12

Snyder M, Tanke ED, Berscheid E. 1977. Social perception and interpersonal behavior: on the self-fulfilling nature of social stereotypes. *J. Personal. Soc. Psychol.* 35:656–66

Staw BM. 1981. The escalation of commitment to a course of action. *Acad. Manage. Rev.* 6:577–87

Taylor SE, Pham LB, Rivkin ID, Armor DA. 1998. Harnessing the imagination: mental simulation, self-regulation, and coping. *Am. Psychol.* 53:429–39

Thaler RH, Sunstein CR. 2008. *Nudge: Improving Decisions About Health, Wealth, and Happiness*. New Haven, CT: Yale Univ. Press

Thompson DV, Hamilton RW, Rust R. 2005. Feature fatigue: when product capabilities become too much of a good thing. *J. Mark. Res.* 42:431–42

Thompson DV, Norton MI. 2008. *The social utility of feature creep*. Work. pap., Georgetown Univ., Washington, DC

Tian KT, Bearden WO, Hunter GL. 2001. Consumers' need for uniqueness: scale development and validation. *J. Consum. Res.* 28:50–66

Tolin DF, Frost RO, Steketee G. 2007. *Buried in Treasures: Help for Compulsive Acquiring, Saving, and Hoarding.* New York: Oxford Univ. Press

Trivers RL. 1971. The evolution of reciprocal altruism. *Q. Rev. Biol.* 46:35–57

Trötschel R, Gollwitzer PM. 2007. Implementation intentions and the willful pursuit of prosocial goals in negotiations. *J. Exp. Soc. Psychol.* 43:579–98

Tulving E. 2002. Episodic memory: from mind to brain. *Annu. Rev. Psychol.* 53:1–25

Tversky A, Kahneman D. 1973. Availability: a heuristic for judging frequency and probability. *Cogn. Psychol.* 5:207–32

Tversky A, Shafir E. 1992. Choice under conflict: the dynamics of deferred decision. *Psychol. Sci.* 3:358–61

Vaughn LA, Malik J, Schwartz S, Petkova Z, Trudeau L. 2006. Regulatory fit as input for stop rules. *J. Personal. Soc. Psychol.* 91:601–11

Veblen T. 1975 (1899). *The Theory of the Leisure Class.* New York: A.M. Kelley

Vohs KD, Mead NL, Goode MR. 2006. The psychological consequences of money. *Science* 314:1154–56

Waber RL, Shiv B, Carmon Z, Ariely D. 2008. Commercial features of placebo and therapeutic efficacy. *J. Am. Med. Assoc.* 299:1016–17

Wang J, Lee AY. 2006. The role of regulatory focus in preference construction. *J. Mark. Res.* 43:28–38

Wansink B. 2006. *Mindless Eating: Why We Eat More Than We Think.* New York: Bantam-Dell

Wansink B, Chandon P. 2006. Can "low-fat" nutrition labels lead to obesity? *J. Mark. Res.* 43:605–17

Wansink B, Park SB, Sonka S, Morganosky M. 2000. How soy labeling influences preference and taste. *Int. Food Agribusiness Manag. Rev.* 3:85–94

Whittlesea BWA. 1993. Illusions of familiarity. *J. Exp. Psychol.: Learn.* 19:1235–53

Wildschut T, Sedikides C, Arndt J, Routledge C. 2006. Nostalgia: content, triggers, functions. *J. Personal. Soc. Psychol.* 91:975–93

Williams P, Aaker J. 2002. Can mixed emotions peacefully coexist? *J. Consum. Res.* 28:636–49

Wilson TD, Lisle DJ, Kraft D, Wetzel CG. 1989. Preferences as expectation-driven inferences: effects of affective expectations on affective experience. *J. Personal. Soc. Psychol.* 56:519–30

Xu AJ, Wyer RS. 2007. The effect of mind-sets on consumer decision strategies. *J. Consum. Res.* 34:556–66

Zajonc RB. 1968. Attitudinal effects of mere exposure. *J. Personal. Soc. Psychol.* 9:1–27

Zauberman G, Ratner RK, Kim BK. 2008. Memories as assets: strategic memory protection in choice over time. *J. Consum. Res.* In press

Health Psychology: Developing Biologically Plausible Models Linking the Social World and Physical Health

Gregory Miller,[1] Edith Chen,[1] and Steve W. Cole[2]

[1]Department of Psychology, University of British Columbia, Vancouver, V6T 1Z4, British Columbia; email: gemiller@psych.ubc.ca

[2]Department of Medicine, Division of Hematology-Oncology, UCLA School of Medicine, UCLA AIDS Institute, UCLA Molecular Biology Institute, Jonsson Comprehensive Cancer Center and the Norman Cousins Center at UCLA, University of California, Los Angeles, California 90095

Annu. Rev. Psychol. 2009. 60:501–24

The *Annual Review of Psychology* is online at psych.annualreviews.org

This article's doi: 10.1146/annurev.psych.60.110707.163551

Key Words

stress, social relationships, socioeconomic status, coronary heart disease, HIV/AIDS, inflammation, psychoneuroimmunology

Abstract

Research over the past several decades has documented psychosocial influences on the development and progression of several major medical illnesses. The field is now increasingly focused on identifying the biological and behavioral mechanisms underlying these effects. This review takes stock of the knowledge accumulated in the biological arena to date and highlights conceptual and methodological approaches that have proven especially productive. It emphasizes the value of a disease-centered approach that "reverse engineers" adverse health outcomes into their specific biological determinants and then identifies psychologically modulated neuroendocrine and immunologic dynamics that modulate those pathological processes at the cellular and molecular levels.

Contents

INTRODUCTION

Over the past several decades, there has been an explosion of interest in the area of health psychology, fueled by mounting evidence that psychological factors have important implications for health. The data from this line of work have been sufficiently compelling that a sizeable number of our biomedical colleagues—who were initially and rightfully skeptical of the idea—now believe that factors such as chronic stress, depression, hostility, and social isolation influence vulnerability to certain diseases (Cohen et al. 2007, Glaser et al. 1999, Kiecolt-Glaser et al. 2002). As consensus opinion has come to support a role of psychosocial factors in influencing physical health, research has increasingly focused on identifying the biological and behavioral mechanisms underlying these effects.

The objectives of this review are to take stock of the knowledge accumulated in the biological arena to date and to highlight conceptual and methodological approaches that have proven especially productive. We organize the review around four lines of work that are critical for identifying psychobiological mechanisms: (*a*) research linking psychosocial factors to disease outcomes, (*b*) research linking psychosocial factors to biological intermediaries, (*c*) research identifying biological chains of causality, and (*d*) research connecting discoveries across these three domains. We take a disease-centered approach that "reverse engineers" adverse health outcomes into their specific biological determinants and then identifies psychologically modulated neuroendocrine and immunologic dynamics that modulate those pathological processes at the cellular and molecular levels. Much of our mediational discussion focuses on the sympathetic nervous system (SNS), the hypothalamic pituitary adrenocortical (HPA) axis, and the immune system. These are certainly not the only potential mediators linking mind and body, but they are the most extensively studied intermediates and influence each of the diseases we consider.

PSYCHOSOCIAL FACTORS AND DISEASE OUTCOMES

The starting point for mechanistic health psychology research should be a robust clinical phenomenon. By this, we mean a well-established association between a psychosocial characteristic and the incidence or progression of a serious medical illness (i.e., changes in experienced symptoms or biological processes that drive disease progression). We say this because research that simply documents linkages between psychosocial factors and biological parameters that do not have clear implications for health or disease will have limited theoretical utility. For example, many studies have documented relationships between acute stress and transient alterations in the distribution of certain leukocyte subtypes in circulating blood (particularly natural killer cells). However, no evidence indicates that these small variations in leukocyte trafficking have any material health impact. A surer approach for identifying health-relevant psychobiologic interactions is to begin with a particular disease of interest, ask first which biological processes are involved in the development and progression of that disease, and then empirically analyze those processes to determine which are subject to regulation by the social world and the behavioral and biological processes it modulates. For example, dozens of studies now link depressive symptoms with morbidity and mortality from heart disease (see reviews by Rugulies 2002, van Melle et al. 2004, Wulsin & Singal 2003). These data provide a strong rationale for moving forward with studies of depression's association with coagulation, inflammation, and other processes that drive atherosclerosis. Likewise, multiple studies link psychosocial risk factors to HIV-1 disease progression (Cole 2006, Cole et al. 1997, Sloan et al. 2007c). This link provided researchers with a rationale for subsequent analyses of the upstream biological processes that drive clinical disease progression (e.g., viral replication, innate immune responses; Cole et al. 2001, 2003), which ultimately led to the identification of specific molecular mechanisms mediating the effects of stress-induced neuroendocrine dynamics on HIV-1 pathogenesis (Cole et al. 1998, 1999, 2001; Collado-Hidalgo et al. 2006; Sloan et al. 2006, 2007a,b, 2008). Thus, successful discovery of pathways mediating biobehavioral influences on disease depends critically on the availability of a good basic understanding of disease pathogenesis (to guide the bottom-up selection of specific pathophysiologic targets) and the identification of a robust clinical phenomenon (to guide the top-down targeting of specific psychobiologic pathways).

What, then, constitutes a robust clinical phenomenon? Ideally, a relationship between psychosocial risk factors and clinical disease outcomes would be documented in a series of independent prospective epidemiologic studies that are well powered, carefully evaluate potential sources of confounding, and utilize meaningful clinical outcomes such as morbidity and mortality as endpoints. For example, several studies have shown that high levels of chronic stress are associated with subsequent increases in morbidity and mortality from a variety of diseases, including respiratory infection, cardiovascular disease, and HIV/AIDS (see reviews by Cohen et al. 2007, Krantz & McCeney 2002), as well as adverse clinical outcomes such as impaired wound healing (Kiecolt-Glaser et al. 1995, 2005). A number of individual psychological characteristics have also emerged as robust risk factors for some diseases. For example, both hostility and depression have been linked repeatedly with the incidence and progression of cardiovascular disease (see reviews by Miller et al. 1996, Rugulies 2002, Smith 1992, van Melle et al. 2004, Wulsin & Singal 2003). At the broader level of analysis, features of the larger social environment such as low socioeconomic status (SES; see reviews by Adler et al. 1993, Chen et al. 2002, Marmot & Wilkinson 2000) and social isolation (see reviews by Berkman et al. 1979, Berkman & Kawachi 2000, House et al. 1988) have proven to be robust predictors of adverse outcomes in the context of cardiovascular, respiratory, and infectious diseases, as well as certain cancers.

Although these results linking psychosocial factors with medical outcomes are provocative, it is important to remember that they come from observational studies that cannot clearly determine the direction of causality among the variables analyzed. Thus, when embarking on a mechanistic program of research in health psychology, it is often useful to consider whether the linkage of interest might be causally substantiated with other methodologies. For ethical reasons, human subjects cannot be randomly assigned to most of the psychosocial circumstances of interest in health psychology. However, they can be randomly assigned to interventions that alter the psychosocial or biomedical consequences of those circumstances. To the extent that such interventions are successful at influencing biomedical endpoints, they provide convincing evidence that a psychosocial characteristic is acting on disease in a causal fashion. For example, in a classic intervention trial, coronary heart disease (CHD) patients were randomized to rehabilitation programs with or without counseling for the behavior pattern known as Type A. Patients who received the counseling not only showed declines in Type A behaviors, but were significantly less likely to have a recurrent myocardial infarction over follow-up (Friedman et al. 1986). In a more recent trial of patients with ischemic heart disease, routine medical care was delivered with or without stress management. Afterward, patients who received stress management showed better endothelial function and fewer wall motion abnormalities than the patients who did not receive stress management (Blumenthal et al. 2005).

Unfortunately, only a handful of trials targeting psychosocial parameters have reported positive clinical outcomes. Notably, a recent large multisite trial aimed at alleviating low social support and depression in cardiac patients found no effects of intervention on mortality across the whole sample (Berkman et al. 2003). A critical review of the literature on psychosocial interventions for cancer patients also found little evidence that such treatments reduce morbidity or mortality (Coyne et al. 2007). Null findings such as these do not exclude the possibility of a causal influence for psychosocial circumstances, as there may be many other reasons why a psychosocial intervention would fail to influence morbidity or mortality (e.g., poor measurement, insufficient statistical power, weak adherence to the intervention, or weakness in the intervention's ability to significantly impact the behavioral risk factor or the key pathophysiologic process in

the disease; Carney et al. 1999, Coyne et al. 2007, Miller & Cohen 2001). However, when negative findings emerge from intervention trials, it implies that the mechanistic researcher needs to look to other approaches to substantiate the epidemiologic phenomenon s/he is trying to unpack.

Animal models can often provide good mechanistic evidence relating psychosocial risk factors to physical health. Unlike humans, animals can be randomly assigned to psychologically difficult circumstances and monitored over time to determine whether these experiences influence disease outcomes. Many studies of this nature have been performed and, encouragingly, their findings often converge with correlational evidence from human epidemiologic research. Some notable examples include the results linking long-term stress with vulnerability to respiratory infection, CHD, and accelerated progression of HIV/AIDS, as well as data linking subordinate social status to greater morbidity and mortality (see reviews by Bailey et al. 2007, Manuck et al. 1995, Sloan et al. 2007c, Verrier & Lown 1984). Not all psychosocial circumstances can be accurately modeled in animals, but mechanistic research can operate on firmer ground when animal models are available to establish causal relationships and access biological tissues for mechanistic analyses.

PSYCHOSOCIAL FACTORS AND BIOLOGICAL INTERMEDIARIES

Once a robust linkage between a psychosocial factor and a clinical health outcome has been identified, the next step is to determine what biological processes convey those effects into the physical environment of disease pathogenesis (i.e., what biological mediators carry psychosocial influences "under the skin"). Significant progress has been made in understanding the biological correlates of stress, depression, social support, and SES. These data provide new substantive insights and establish a conceptual approach for future studies mapping relationships between extraindividual social risk factors and their intraindividual impact on physiology and disease.

Psychological Stress

Decades of research have catalogued the endocrine and immune changes that result from stressful experience. Early studies identified general relationships between differing psychological states (e.g., relaxed vegetative states versus acute stress–active coping responses versus more severe overwhelming threat) and distinct patterns of neuroendocrine response (e.g., parasympathetic nervous system activity, SNS activity, and HPA activation, respectively; reviewed in Weiner 1992). Recent studies have clarified the psychological antecedents that drive human neuroendocrine responses. An influential meta-analysis by Dickerson & Kemeny (2004) indicates that human cortisol responses to acute laboratory stressors are most pronounced in situations that pose a social threat to the individual. Increased secretion of cortisol is also seen in persons facing real-life stressors that are more chronic in nature. However, meta-analysis also shows that these dynamics shift as time passes (Miller et al. 2007). Early in the course of a chronic stressor, there is robust activation of the HPA axis, which results in elevated concentrations of adrenocorticotrophic hormone and cortisol. As time passes, HPA axis activity diminishes, and cortisol secretion rebounds to normal and later to below normal. Recent theoretical analyses have also linked differential profiles of autonomic nervous system response to distinct psychological appraisals of a stressful situation (e.g., threat versus challenge; Tomaka et al. 1997). As with the HPA axis, data increasingly suggest that social threat or uncertainty may be a particularly powerful determinant of SNS activity (Cole et al. 2003, Kagan 1994). Thus, many of the physiologic and health dynamics that were once construed as driven by stress are increasingly being analyzed in terms of the social etiology of individual neuroendocrine activity. This provides a conceptual bridge between epidemiologic data that emphasize socioenvironmental risk factors in health at the population level and traditional intraindividual analyses of stress effects on physiology.

Three decades of research in psychoneuroimmunology (PNI) have also identified distinct immunobiological correlates of differing psychological states. A meta-analysis of human PNI studies found that the chronicity and severity of stressors played a key role in moderating the nature and intensity of associated alterations in immunologic parameters (Segerstrom & Miller 2004). Acute stresses such as public speaking amplify several features of the innate immune response (e.g., natural killer cell trafficking and cytotoxicity). These effects are transient and may represent an immunologic component of the broader fight-or-flight response to threat. Stressors that persist for longer durations, such as school exams, are associated with alterations in adaptive immune responses (e.g., humoral immune responses mediated by B-lymphocytes versus cellular immune responses mediated by cytotoxic T-lymphocytes). Several studies suggest that antibody-mediated humoral immune responses can be enhanced by chronic stress, whereas some aspects of cell-mediated response are suppressed. Stressors that are both severe and stable, such as serving as a caregiver for a demented relative, often impair multiple aspects of the immune response. For example, relative to age-matched controls, caregivers produce fewer virus-specific antibodies following influenza vaccination, show delayed healing of experimentally administered wounds, and show down-regulation of several immunobiological processes in ex vivo assays of leukocyte function (e.g., Kiecolt-Glaser et al. 1991, 1995, 1996; Vedhara et al. 1999). However, research increasingly shows that stress is not globally immunosuppressive. Whereas chronic stress can suppress several aspects of adaptive immune function, it also appears to induce a chronic and systemic state of mild inflammation (Kiecolt-Glaser et al. 2003, Miller et al. 2008, Ranjit et al. 2007a). This is manifest by increased circulating concentrations of the inflammatory biomarkers C-reactive protein (CRP) and interleukin-6 (IL-6). Because inflammation is a key pathogenic mechanism in many infectious, cardiovascular, and neoplastic diseases (Coussens & Werb 2002, Eccles 2005, Libby & Theroux 2005, Perkins 2007), stress enhancement of inflammatory signaling has provided a new set of mechanistic hypotheses for understanding the pathways that link psychosocial characteristics with morbidity and mortality (also see Kiecolt-Glaser et al. 2002).

Depression

Severe depression is often associated with increased circulating levels of HPA and SNS neuroendocrine mediators (see reviews by Musselman et al. 1998, Plotsky et al. 1995). About half of patients with severe forms of depression also show dysregulation of the negative-feedback circuit that regulates HPA output (Haskett 1993). However, these patterns of excess HPA and SNS activity are seldom found in patients with milder versions of depression (Anisman et al. 1999, Miller et al. 1999, Ravindran et al. 1995, Stetler et al. 2004, Strickland et al. 2002).

Depressed individuals also show patterns of immune alteration similar to those observed in chronic stress; e.g., impairments in some cellular immune parameters, delayed healing of experimentally administered wounds, and blunted antibody responses to vaccination, accompanied by increased systemic inflammatory activity (e.g., Bosch et al. 2007; Glaser et al. 2003; Irwin et al. 1998; Kop et al. 2002; Lesperance et al. 2004; Miller et al. 2002b, 2005; see reviews by Irwin 2001, 2002; Raison et al. 2006). Similar patterns are seen in both clinically depressed patients and those with high levels of dysphoric affect. The linkage between depressive symptoms and systemic inflammation has been of special interest to researchers lately because it may help to explain the excess cardiovascular morbidity and mortality associated with depression. Inflammation is a key pathologic mechanism underlying heart disease, and elevated levels of biomarkers such as CRP and IL-6 forecast clinical events such as myocardial infarction and coronary death (see review by Libby & Theroux 2005).

Social Support

Some data suggest that people who are socially isolated show higher circulating levels of cortisol, epinephrine, and norepinephrine (see reviews by Seeman & McEwen 1996, Uchino et al. 1996), although other studies find no substantial differences (e.g., Cole 2008, Cole et al. 2007). However, recent data suggest that alterations in glucocorticoid receptor (GR) signaling associated with subjective social isolation may result in impaired physiologic control of inflammation by the HPA axis, despite normal circulating cortisol levels (e.g., Cole 2008, Cole et al. 2007). These alterations in hormonal receptor sensitivity result in altered gene expression profiles in immune cells (Cole et al. 2007), which could potentially explain why socially isolated people also show weaker antibody responses, and greater vulnerability to respiratory infection following exposure to a virus (e.g., Cohen et al. 1997, Pressman et al. 2005; see review by Cohen 2004). Data from experimental primate models also show that stressful social relationships can exacerbate viral infections by altering SNS neural regulation of the lymphoid organs in which leukocytes generate antiviral responses, resulting in suboptimal gene expression responses to infection (Sloan et al. 2007b). Consistent with these alterations in immune cell sensitivity to regulation by the HPA axis and SNS, people with low social support also show elevated circulating levels of C-reactive protein and interleukin-6 (Loucks et al. 2006a,b). Most of these physiological correlates of the social world are evident in persons who report feeling lonely on a chronic basis, irrespective of their objective social conditions (e.g., Adam et al. 2006, Cole et al. 2007, Pressman et al. 2005; see reviews by Hawkley & Cacioppo 2007, Kiecolt-Glaser 1999).

Socioeconomic Status

Several studies have also linked low socioeconomic status to higher levels of cortisol and epinephrine during daily life (Cohen et al. 2006a,b; Evans & English 2002; Janicki-Deverts et al. 2007; Lupien et al. 2000, 2001) as well as to increased circulating concentrations of inflammatory biomarkers for CHD such as CRP and IL-6 (Hemingway et al. 2003, Panagiotakos et al. 2005; see review by Chen & Miller 2007a).

CONCEPTUALIZING LINKS BETWEEN THE SOCIAL WORLD AND BIOLOGY

In many cases, the starting point phenomenon for the above studies is a link between an individual-level psychosocial characteristic (e.g., chronic stress) and a specific clinical outcome (e.g., respiratory infection). As researchers develop more complete psychobiological theories of disease, it is important to create rich and comprehensive models of the social context of disease by considering factors at multiple social levels (e.g., individual, peer, community, culture). For researchers starting with distal social environment factors such as SES, the challenge is to uncover the more proximal psychosocial mechanisms that bring the larger social environment down to the level of the individual. For researchers starting with individual psychological characteristics such as stress, the challenge is to gain a richer understanding of the broader social forces that contribute to stress by studying factors beyond the individual level. These more integrative approaches provide a broader understanding of the social context of disease as well as novel insights into developmental structure and even potential interventions targeting specific psychosocial risk factors.

Early-Life Environments and Health

Findings from a number of studies suggest that early-life social environments can have long-lasting impacts on health that persist well into adulthood (see reviews by Barker 1997, Hertzman 1999, Repetti et al. 2002). These findings have been substantiated in experimental research in animal models (see Coe & Lubach 2005, Hodgson & Coe 2005, Meaney & Szyf 2005). One psychosocial model explaining

this phenomenon implicates exposure to risky family environments early in life (Repetti et al. 2002). Risky families are cold, have high levels of conflict and aggression, and rarely undertake nurturing behaviors. The model states that these types of families engage in more harsh, inconsistent parenting, which in turn leads children to have greater difficulty regulating their emotions. As a result, biological stress response systems become dysregulated, leading to risk for a variety of health problems over time (Repetti et al. 2002). Recently, empirical evidence has begun to emerge for a psychosocial model linking early-life environments to adult biological profiles. For example, young adults who reported more difficult family environments in childhood had higher levels of current negative emotions such as depression and anxiety, which in turn were associated with higher basal levels of cortisol (Taylor et al. 2004). Similarly, adults who reported difficult early-life family environments had higher current levels of depression and less mastery, which in turn were associated with greater elevations in the inflammatory marker CRP (Taylor et al. 2006). These findings suggest pathways by which the broader social context (early family environment) may shape the development of individual characteristics (negative emotions), which in turn have implications for individual hormonal and immune profiles.

Socioeconomic Status and Health

Psychosocial factors are also thought to play an important role in the relationship between SES and health (Marmot & Wilkinson 2000), with stress being one commonly implicated pathway. Low-SES individuals experience greater numbers of stressful life events (Brady & Matthews 2002), and greater stress has been found to partially explain relationships between low SES and poor self-reported health (Cohen et al. 1999). However, in seeking to understand how larger social forces such as SES and external stimuli such as negative life events might have biological effects, a theory is needed to explain how these factors operate at the individual level.

Our research group has proposed that external social environments have to be perceived by the individual in negative ways in order to have detrimental biological effects (Chen & Miller 2007b). In particular, we postulate that children who grow up in low-SES neighborhoods are more likely to experience negative life events, especially ones that are unpredictable. As a result, low-SES children will be more likely to develop a sense of vigilance and a lowered threshold for perceiving threat in new situations. In life situations that are ambiguous (where the outcome and intention of another person are unclear), we argue that differences between low- and high-SES children will be most pronounced, and that low-SES children will interpret these situations in a much more threatening manner than high-SES children. In turn, these types of threat interpretations are hypothesized to affect biological responses.

Empirically, we tested this theory by devising a set of videos depicting different types of life situations. Children and adolescents watched these videos and were interviewed about their interpretations. Through this approach, we were able to hold the exposure (the situation) constant and assess variability in interpretations. We found that low SES was associated with greater interpretations of threat during ambiguous, but not negative, social situations (Chen & Matthews 2003). We further documented that threat interpretations during ambiguous social situations statistically mediated the relationship between low SES and heightened cardiovascular reactivity in healthy adolescents, and heightened inflammatory profiles in children with asthma (Chen et al. 2004, 2006). These findings suggest that the larger social environment is able to affect biological responses in an individual via the ways they perceive their social environment.

Social Context of Emotions

The above studies provide examples of how to connect larger social factors such as SES to individual processes. However, many researchers interested in mechanisms have an individual psychosocial characteristic such as stress or depression as their starting point. In these cases, a more comprehensive model would also seek to understand the broader context that underlies the development of these individual characteristics. One example of this approach is the proposal by Dickerson & Kemeny (2004) that the social evaluative nature of a threat—the extent to which a person could potentially be judged negatively by others—plays a significant role in determining the intensity of cortisol response to a fixed challenge (the Trier Social Stress Test). In their theory, the subjective experience of shame represents a key psychological driver of the stress response and thereby serves as a portal between external conditions and the biology of the body. Extending this approach to an evolutionary context, Dickerson and Kemeny theorized that just as humans have evolved a physical response system designed to protect the self from harm, by eliciting emotions (e.g., fear) and biological responses (e.g., fight-or-flight response) in the face of danger, they have also evolved a parallel social self-preservation system that mobilizes emotions (e.g., shame) and biological responses (cortisol secretion and systemic inflammation) in the face of threats to one's social standing within a group (Dickerson et al. 2004).

Empirical evidence is beginning to emerge in support of this theory. When participants were asked to undergo an acute laboratory stressor either in the presence of an audience (social evaluation) or alone (no social evaluation), the audience condition elicited more shame and greater cortisol responses compared to doing the same task alone (Gruenewald et al. 2004). In a study of competitive ballroom dancers, cortisol levels increased on competition days but not on training days in which identical routines were performed (but without evaluation by judges). Furthermore, cortisol increases were greater during competition for couples dancers (where each individual had a greater focus of evaluation from judges and audience members) compared to group dancers (Rohleder et al. 2007). Collectively, this line of work provides an intriguing example of building a broader theoretical model around empirical evidence tying a context (social evaluation by others) to a specific individually experienced emotion (shame) and in turn to specific biological responses (cortisol output).

DEVELOPING A CAUSAL BIOLOGICAL CHAIN FOR PSYCHOSOCIAL FACTORS

Much of the existing mechanistic research in health psychology relates a single psychosocial characteristic (e.g., depression) to a single presumptive biological mediator (e.g., cortisol) or to a small group of conceptually related mediators (e.g., IL1-β and IL-6). Although this approach has proven useful, we argue that the field now must move beyond assessments of solitary biomarkers toward more sophisticated causal models of how psychosocial factors come to influence the course of disease.

In order to proceed on a theoretically informed search for mechanisms, one must understand the biological processes that drive initiation and progression of a specific disease. Hence, one approach to developing comprehensive biological models is to map out the pathophysiology of the disease and then identify specific elements of that system that might be regulated by proposed biobehavioral mediators (e.g., the HPA axis or SNS). Research utilizing this approach could then proceed in a systematic explanatory progression, whereby one would (*a*) identify the most proximal biological pathways linked to clinical disease outcomes (i.e., mechanism of pathogenesis), (*b*) test whether the psychosocial factor of interest is associated with these proximal biological mechanisms, and then (*c*) identify the biobehavioral mediators that regulate these proximal biological mechanisms. One could then test whether the psychosocial factor of interest is associated with these regulatory mechanisms in standard correlational mediation analyses or, ideally, manipulate putative mediators and observe alterations in the basic relationship between psychosocial factors and disease-proximal biology. In this way, researchers can begin to build a

systematic and convincing argument about the causal chain of biological relationships that underlie the link between a social factor and a clinical health outcome.

Stress and Asthma

We provide one example of this type of approach based on our work in childhood asthma. Psychological stress has been linked to poorer clinical asthma outcomes, such as an increased risk of asthma exacerbations (Sandberg et al. 2000, 2004). Asthma is an inflammatory disease, wherein activation of eosinophils, production of immunoglobulin E, and degranulation of mast cells form key events leading to the release of allergic mediators such as histamines and leukotrienes. These molecules bring about edema, smooth muscle constriction, and mucus production in the airways, resulting in clinical symptoms such as wheezing, chest tightness, and shortness of breath. Based on these working biological models, we tested whether psychological stress would be associated with the above types of inflammatory markers in children who had been physician-diagnosed with asthma. Children were interviewed about life stress, and peripheral blood samples were collected to measure eosinophils. We documented that children with asthma who experienced higher levels of chronic home-life stress had greater eosinophil counts, even after controlling for a variety of medical and demographic characteristics (Chen et al. 2006). This study provided a biological starting point (increased eosinophil counts) for understanding why psychological stress would be linked to clinical outcomes such as increased asthma exacerbations.

We then asked what immune processes might foster the production and activation of eosinophils. It turns out that certain cytokines—primarily IL-5—are responsible for activating eosinophils and recruiting them to the airways. Because cytokines are only released when immune cells are activated, we set up a laboratory model for activating immune cells in vitro, and we tested whether stress would be associated with the production of IL-5 after participants' mononuclear cells were stimulated with a mitogen. We found that higher levels of chronic home stress were also associated with greater stimulated production of IL-5 (Chen et al. 2006). This finding suggests that given an equivalent exposure to asthma-inducing allergens, children with asthma who are experiencing stress will exhibit heightened inflammatory responses compared to children with asthma who are under low stress. This now provided us with a second piece of evidence of a social factor (stress) linked with biological processes (increase in both stimulated cytokine production and eosinophil counts), and in a direction that is consistent with the clinical evidence of greater risk for asthma morbidity.

From there, we went one step deeper and asked what cellular processes might regulate inflammatory responses such as cytokine production. Immune cells are equipped with mechanisms to both activate and terminate inflammatory responses. Hormones such as cortisol are known to provide anti-inflammatory signals to immune cells. Because stress is known to activate the HPA as well as the SNS, we hypothesized that under conditions of chronic stress, persistent elevations in the hormonal products of these axes (cortisol, epinephrine, and norepinephrine) would result in a compensatory down-regulation of the receptors for these hormones—for example, the GR as well as the β2 adrenergic receptor (β2AR). As a result, the immune system's ability to respond to anti-inflammatory signals from these hormones would be reduced, and inflammatory processes would flourish (Miller et al. 2002a). In a sample of children with asthma, we tested whether life stress was associated with the expression of messenger RNA (mRNA) for the GR and β2AR. We found that children with asthma who simultaneously experienced high levels of both acute and chronic stress exhibited a 5.5-fold reduction in GR mRNA and a 9.5-fold reduction in β2AR mRNA relative to children with asthma without comparable stressor exposure (Miller & Chen 2006). This diminished expression of the GR and β2AR genes suggests that children with asthma who are experiencing acute and chronic stress may be both more vulnerable to inflammation and less responsive to asthma medications (such as inhaled corticosteroids and beta-agonists, which act through these receptors). Overall, these patterns suggest that even molecular pathways involved in the regulation of inflammation are patterned by psychological stress in children with asthma and hence may help explain biologically why children under stress would experience poorer asthma outcomes.

Stress and Cortisol

Another approach to developing comprehensive biological models is to start with a well-defined psychobiological effect and then systematically explore its implications at the level of tissues and organs. For example, there are well-documented relationships between a variety of psychosocial characteristics we discuss and the output of cortisol (see reviews by Dickerson & Kemeny 2004, Haskett 1993, Miller et al. 2007). However, circulating cortisol is only the starting point for a complex and tightly regulated chain of events and by itself does not explain the differential disease risk attributed to these characteristics. Instead, the consequences of cortisol's action on the behavior of disease-related cells constitute a mechanism of disease. A long chain of events is required to translate alterations in circulating cortisol levels into differential disease risk. Once it is released, cortisol must bind to GRs or mineralocorticoid receptors (MRs) located in the cytosol of a cell. The newly formed receptor-hormone complex must then translocate to the nucleus, where it can modify the gene expression routines that govern cellular behavior.

Most tissues are equipped with a host of counterregulatory mechanisms that can potentially intervene in this process to insure that acute changes in cortisol do not drastically disrupt homeostasis. This means that even if cortisol levels are increased markedly by a psychosocial circumstance, the bodily tissues this hormone regulates may not be affected commensurately because counterregulatory mechanisms may alter how loudly cortisol's signals are heard. One way in which tissues undertake counterregulatory actions is by altering characteristics of the receptors to which cortisol binds. To counterbalance the fact that cortisol levels have increased, cells can reduce the density or activity of their GRs and MRs. Receptors that are downregulated or desensitized will pass on fewer of cortisol's signals to the nucleus of the cell, where the gene expression routines that govern cellular behavior are carried out (Cole et al. 2007).

To evaluate how these dynamics play out with regard to psychosocial characteristics, some researchers have begun studying how bodily tissues respond to bursts of cortisol (see Ebrecht et al. 2000, Rohleder et al. 2001). For research focused on the immune system, this can be done by collecting white blood cells, stimulating them with bacterial products, and then adding a dose of cortisol to the culture. Because cortisol has powerful anti-inflammatory properties, its presence should dampen the cellular response to bacterial stimulation. If it does not, one can infer that the system has lost an important regulatory constraint. Some research suggests that this may occur with stress. For example, one study found that among people facing a severe chronic stressor—being the parent of a child with cancer—white blood cells' sensitivity to inhibition by dexamethasone was reduced (Miller et al. 2002a). This was manifest by a reduction in the ability of dexamethasone to suppress bacterially stimulated production of IL-6, a molecule that plays a key role in organizing inflammatory responses. Together, these findings suggest that psychological circumstances not only modify hormonal outputs, such as cortisol levels, but also modify the way the immune system responds to signals from cortisol. In turn, these responses to cortisol will influence the ability of certain genes to get activated and engage in protein synthesis.

The cortisol challenge paradigms outlined above measure the capacity of an immune cell to respond to a hormonal stimulus in vitro, but they do not tell us how such dynamics are actually playing out under physiologic conditions.

The latter has been a challenging question to answer, but recent developments in functional genomics and bioinformatics have provided new methodologies for gauging the steady-state regulatory actions of hormones such as cortisol. One approach uses microarray technology to monitor the activity of all ~22,000 human genes in a tissue of interest (e.g., immune cells collected from peripheral blood). This analysis reveals a subset of genes that are differentially expressed by two groups of patients, e.g., those who have and have not been exposed to some psychosocial circumstance of interest. Bioinformatics technology is then used to discern what these genes have in common. This can be done by scanning the upstream regulatory DNA sequences (promoter regions) of differentially expressed genes to determine the prevalence of DNA motifs that serve as targets for hormone- and cytokine-activated transcription factors (Cole et al. 2005). With these data in hand, one can make reverse-inferences about how active certain signaling pathways have been in vivo. For example, if the genes that tend to be overexpressed in one set of patients show a disproportionate prevalence of transcription factor-binding motifs for the GR, one can infer that their tissue has been exposed to greater cortisol-mediated signaling. These methods enable researchers to quantify how loudly cortisol signals are being heard by the genome and what effect this is having on the ability of genes to get switched on to initiate protein synthesis. Because this approach measures postreceptor gene transcription, it integrates the effect of differential HPA axis output (e.g., bioavailable cortisol) and differential GR-mediated signal transduction.

Our team recently used this strategy to evaluate how a severe chronic stressor—caring for a family member with brain cancer—influenced cortisol-mediated signaling in the white blood cells that drive inflammation (monocytes). This analysis revealed that stressed patients had diminished expression of genes bearing response elements for GR and at the same time heightened expression of transcripts with response elements for proinflammatory transcription factors such as nuclear factor κ-B (Miller et al. 2008). In other words, these data showed that caregivers' monocytes were registering fewer cortisol signals than were monocytes of controls. As a result, genes that cortisol usually switches on were not being expressed as strongly in monocytes from caregivers as those from controls, and genes that cortisol usually silences were more active in caregivers than in controls. This in vivo readout suggests an intriguing scenario for how chronic stressors influence disease: By interfering with the ability of cortisol to deliver signals to white blood cells, stressors may facilitate the kinds of proinflammatory gene expression cascades that contribute to coronary disease, autoimmune disorders, and infectious diseases (also see Miller et al. 2002a, Raison & Miller 2003).

By targeting multiple levels of analysis in the biological domain, researchers also gain an important advantage of being able to uncover patterns that may have been missed by focusing on only one level of biological mechanisms. For example, in the above study, we collected daily saliva samples from participants, but chronic stress was not associated with differential cortisol levels. Similarly, we measured the expression of GR in white blood cells, but this too was unrelated to chronic stress. If we had constrained our analysis to include only hormonal outputs or receptor expression, we would have mistakenly concluded that cortisol, and the tissues it regulates, are unaffected by caregiving. But as the gene expression profile revealed, this was not the case. Instead, we were able to discover that the monocytes of chronically stressed individuals are not hearing cortisol signals from the body as loudly as they should, even though this hormone is being secreted in sufficient quantities and sufficient numbers of receptors are available to bind it. As a consequence of that alteration, proinflammatory genes were overexpressed, leading to a change in circulating indicators of inflammation (e.g., CRP).

One criticism sometimes leveled at microarrays is based on the assumption that they inherently involve nonhypothesis-driven exploratory analyses. However, the application we describe above shows how microarrays can be used to test a priori mechanistic hypotheses (i.e., that stress-induced alterations in inflammation are mediated by desensitization of the GR-mediated gene transcription control pathway). Of course, microarray technology can also be used for "unbiased discovery" studies to reveal patterns in the data that an investigator may have otherwise overlooked. We believe that hypothesis-free discovery-based approaches can be quite useful, especially in areas where there is little pre-existing biological theory to guide research, and only a fraction of the potential mechanisms have been seriously explored. Theory-driven research is of course preferable in cases where strong theories exist. In that sense, microarrays as a technology are much like any other tool (e.g., an inferential statistical test or a CRP assay)—their epistemological strength derives from the research context in which they are used (e.g., in experimental studies or hypothesis-driven observational analyses) and is not a property of the methodology per se.

PUTTING IT ALL TOGETHER

Ultimately, the most convincing mechanistic programs of research methodically piece together both the psychosocial and biological sides in a way that paints a detailed picture of the linear progression from social environment to disease outcome. As research moves deeper into the pathophysiology of a disease, it should continue to test whether the target psychosocial factor remains associated with each step in the disease process, in order to identify the biological pathways that are the most plausibly influenced by the social world. In addition, as the work moves across different levels on the psychosocial end, it should continue to test whether each level (e.g., cultural influences, community influences, family factors, and individual characteristics) remains associated with biological processes that contribute to disease outcomes. In this way, research can start broadly on the social end (e.g., with a construct such as SES) and broadly on the clinical end (e.g., with an outcome like mortality), and systematically establish the links in between that bring the social world and the clinical endpoints closer together. The ultimate goal is to lay out a step-by-step mechanistic model of how the larger social environment gets embedded within an individual and comes to alter biological processes that influence the course of disease. **Figure 1** (see color insert) provides examples of how such models might look, both generally and in the context of specific conditions such as heart disease, asthma, and HIV/AIDS.

We now provide two examples of research that have sought to connect mechanisms at multiple levels along a model of psychological factors to biological processes to disease outcomes. Both investigate the immunologic basis for the link between stress and viral infection—perhaps the best established of all psychoneuroimmunologic phenomena. The first example involves the role of stress in increasing vulnerability to the common cold. High levels of stress have been found to predict increased risk of developing respiratory infections following exposure to various viruses (Cohen et al. 1991, 1998). Production of the proinflammatory cytokine IL-6 is thought to be a key contributor to this process because increases in the concentration of this cytokine precede the development of and correlate strongly with clinical respiratory symptoms. Hence, researchers tested whether psychological stress might activate the production of IL-6, in turn leading to illness symptoms (Cohen et al. 1999). Healthy participants were quarantined, exposed to a respiratory virus, and symptoms and mucus production were monitored over the following week. Higher levels of perceived stress were associated with higher levels of IL-6 during the week following viral exposure. In turn, higher levels of IL-6 were associated with greater symptoms and mucus production. Finally, when the effects of IL-6 were partialled out statistically, the relationship between stress and clinical symptoms/mucus weight dropped by 58% to 67%, suggesting that one biological effect of stress is to heighten inflammatory responses to viral exposure, which

in turn increase respiratory infection symptoms (Cohen et al. 1999).

A second example involves the relationship between stress and accelerated progression of HIV-1 infection. This line of research emerged from early epidemiologic observations showing that gay men who concealed their homosexual identity from others showed more rapid progression of HIV-1 infection, including accelerated declines in CD4+ T lymphocyte levels, shorter times to onset of AIDS-defining clinical conditions, and shorter times to death (Cole et al. 1996). Subsequent analyses unpacked the risk factor of "closeting" into its internal psychological motivation—individual differences in sensitivity to social threat (Cole 2006, Cole et al. 1997). That specific intrapsychic translation allowed the generation of hypotheses regarding the biobehavioral mediators involved through analogy to previous research linking social threat sensitivity to individual differences in SNS activity (Kagan 1994). Based on those hypotheses, laboratory studies probed the relationships between closeted social behavior, psychological sensitivity to social threat, increased SNS activity, and the biological process that fundamentally drives HIV-1 disease progression—the rate of viral replication. Findings showed that as much as 90% of the total association between social threat sensitivity and HIV-1 replication could potentially be explained by intervening differences in SNS activity (Cole et al. 2003). To evaluate the plausibility of this relationship from a molecular virologic standpoint, subsequent laboratory studies explored the capacity of the SNS neurotransmitter norepinephrine to enhance HIV-1 replication in cellular model systems (Cole et al. 1998). Those studies identified several molecular mechanisms by which norepinephrine could accelerate viral replication, including increased T cell vulnerability to infection (Cole et al. 1999), increased transcription of the HIV-1 genome (Cole et al. 2001), and decreased antiviral response by host cell cytokines (Cole et al. 1998, Collado-Hidalgo et al. 2006).

Together, those observations utilized an array of different analytic systems to document a chain of binary mechanistic relationships from an observable behavioral risk factor (closeting) to a measurable intrapsychic response (perceived social threat) that activated a known biobehavioral signaling pathway (the SNS/ norepinephrine system), which was shown to enhance activity of the key pathogenetic processes known to drive differential risk of disease (HIV-1 replication, antiviral response). Initiating this chain was a cultural context in which homosexual social identity constituted a potential basis for social rejection and consequent subjective threat (Cole 2006). In its system of individual binary relationships, this mechanistic hypothesis was plausible and not particularly complicated. Nevertheless, it still involved more levels of analysis than could be studied tractably in a human research setting (cultural attitudes, individual psychological responses, neural signaling pathways, and the molecular biology of viral replication). To assess the simultaneous plausibility of the system as a whole, the researchers turned to a socially manipulable and tissue-accessible experimental animal model of social threat effects on replication of the Simian immunodeficiency virus (SIV; a close analogue of HIV-1 that infects rhesus macaques). Analyses of animals experimentally infected with SIV and randomly assigned to chronically threatening social conditions versus less stressful stable social conditions showed that social stress did indeed simultaneously increase SNS regulation of immune cells, undermine expression of antiviral cytokines, and accelerate replication of SIV (Sloan et al. 2006, 2007b, 2008). Additional analyses showed that constitutional individual differences in sensitivity to social threat were also associated with increased SNS regulation of the lymph node tissues in which immune responses are initiated (Sloan et al. 2007a). Thus, experimental model systems and naturally occurring analogues of the original socioepidemiologic relationship both support the overarching hypothesis that relationships between social behavior and

HIV-1 disease progression are mediated by psychological threat responses that increase SNS signaling to the immune system and thereby alter leukocyte gene expression in ways that facilitate viral replication and accelerate the progression of clinical disease. In this case, refinement of the sociobehavioral risk factor into a psychological process with identifiable neurobiological correlates played a crucial role in developing a plausible mechanistic theory, and its subsequent validation required convergent testing through a variety of methodological approaches (social epidemiology, observational human clinical studies, experimental animal models, and cellular model systems) and across diverse levels of analysis (social, personal, neuroendocrine, cellular, and molecular). This is one of the most ambitious PNI analyses to date, and its empirical success underscores our confidence that complex health psychology phenomena can be successfully analyzed using the simultaneous top-down and bottom-up strategic approach outlined above.

DEALING WITH TEMPORAL DYNAMICS

Analytic models in health psychology often (and usually implicitly) assume that psychosocial characteristics are static and therefore can be measured at any time, and as well, that disease-relevant biological processes will be evident at any point that they are measured. Although this is a reasonable starting point for researchers seeking to clarify the relevant psychosocial and biological processes to include in a model, a full account of health psychology dynamics requires insight into how these relationships originally emerged and how they evolve and change over time.

Connecting the Time Frame of Psychological Constructs to Disease Processes

Psychosocial factors can range in time from those that are briefly experienced to those that

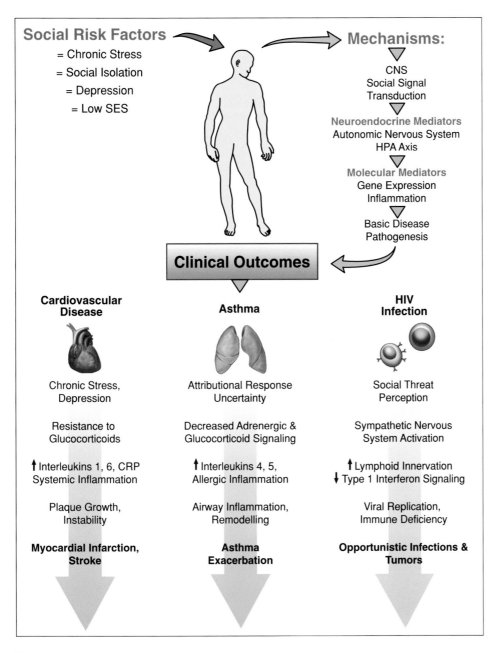

Figure 1

(*Top*) The mechanistic chain of events through which the social world "gets inside the body" to influence disease pathogenesis. (*Bottom*) More-specific mechanistic pathways are hypothesized in the context of heart disease, asthma, and HIV/AIDS.

persist for years. Short-lived psychosocial factors typically have a clear onset and offset, and might last anywhere from seconds to several days (e.g., a near-miss traffic accident; failing an exam). Longer-lasting psychosocial factors might persist for months to years, with no clear end. This could include exposures to chronic stress (repeated conflict in the family) or stable characteristics of an individual, such as personality. Similarly, biological mechanisms also may be short acting or long acting. As with psychosocial factors, short-acting biological mechanisms typically have a clear onset and offset and last from seconds to hours (e.g., sympathetic nervous system activation). In contrast, long-lasting biological mechanisms might develop and persist over the course of years (e.g., blood pressure levels). Diseases also often have both acute and chronic manifestations. For example, in asthma patients, exposure to allergic triggers often elicits a short-lived early-phase response that causes bronchial chest tightening and a more chronic late-phase response that leads to persistent airway inflammation. Similarly, heart disease results from atherosclerotic plaques that grow over a period of decades, whereas heart attacks occur when these plaques abruptly burst, causing the formation of thrombi that occlude the heart's blood supply.

Because of these temporal dynamics, mechanistic research programs are most likely to be most successful when their predictors, mediators, and outcomes operate along similar timelines. This perspective is evident, for example, in Kop's model of psychosocial contributions to CHD (Kop & Cohen 2001, 2007). This model classifies the major psychosocial risk factors for CHD according to their duration of exposure (acute versus episodic versus chronic) and temporal proximity to clinical outcomes (hours versus years versus decades). It goes on to propose that each kind of psychosocial circumstance operates through a different underlying biological mechanism to accentuate vulnerability to a different pathological component of CHD. For example, chronic psychosocial factors such as hostility are thought to foster hypertension, sympathetic activation, and lipid abnormalities,

which in turn accelerate the earlier and middle stages of the atherosclerosis. Episodic factors such as depression are thought to increase coagulation and inflammation, and by doing so destabilize plaque in patients in the later phases of disease. Finally, acute risks like outbursts of anger are thought to precipitate the transition from asymptomatic atherosclerosis to clinically manifest CHD. By increasing activity of the autonomic nervous system and compromising myocardial oxygen supply, these brief events foster plaque rupture, ventricular arrhythmia, and other clinical phenomena. Although decisive empirical evidence for these distinctions is still required, this model provides a promising integrative approach because it focuses attention on the natural history of the disease, suggests places where psychosocial circumstances are likely to intersect with it, and proposes mediators that are biologically and temporally plausible.

Understanding the Temporal Dynamics of Psychobiological Effects

Some have argued that psychosocial factors may not always have immediate, observable effects on biology and health, but rather that there may be critical time periods in life when the biological effects of a psychosocial factor are most likely to occur (e.g., Coe & Lubach 2003). For example, there is mounting evidence that unfavorable socioeconomic circumstances in the early years of life are associated with increased vulnerability to various diseases in adulthood (Cohen et al. 2004, Kittleson et al. 2006, Lawlor et al. 2006; see review by Galobardes et al. 2004). However, it is challenging to develop biological models that can account for the 40- to 50-year "incubation period" between childhood exposure and adulthood disease. To get traction on this problem, a research program needs not only to specify how early-life events get under the skin, but also how they stay there over multiple decades to promote disease later in life.

The biological programming hypotheses advanced by Barker (1997), Hertzman (1999), and others suggest that during critical periods of development, unfavorable environmental circumstances can program biological systems in ways that persist across the lifespan. These models provide a useful heuristic for thinking about early-life influences, but they did not specify the mechanism by which this occurs. However, recent developments in the biology of epigenetics, transcriptional control circuits, and tissue remodeling have begun to suggest possible biological mechanisms for such developmental influences.

Epigenetics describes stable changes in the activity of a gene that arise without alterations to its DNA sequence (see review by Jirtle & Skinner 2007). Epigenetic alterations allow organisms to establish and maintain different gene expression programs in different cells (which enables cells with the same genetic information to be phenotypically different). Epigenetic control of gene expression occurs in two main ways: either the DNA itself is chemically altered (DNA methylation) or the histone proteins that package DNA into chromosomes are modified. Epigenetic modifications can be mitotically and meiotically heritable, meaning they can be passed across generations of both somatic and germline cells. This allows them to have long-term (and potentially cross-generational) influences (Richards 2006).

Recent evidence suggests that epigenetic modifications constitute one potential pathway through which the early-life environment, both physical and social, influences patterns of genomic activity. For example, studies in animals indicate that some in utero or early-life exposures, such as exposure to cigarette smoking, vitamin B12, and folic acid, can induce epigenetic alterations that persist through the organism's lifetime (Jirtle & Skinner 2007). Moreover, animal models suggest that these alterations may contribute to phenotypic differences and vulnerability to some diseases (see overview by Jirtle & Skinner 2007). Although they can be much more stable over time than are levels of hormone activity or transcription factor activity, epigenetic effects are subject to environmental modification and are therefore less stable than DNA sequence characteristics. A recent study found that human monozygotic twin pairs were epigenetically similar during early life, but showed markedly diverging patterns of DNA methylation and histone acetylation as they aged (Fraga et al. 2005). These disparities were most pronounced in twin pairs who had been separated early in life, suggesting that environmental influences play a major role in driving divergence. Such findings underscore the semiplastic nature of epigenetic modifications.

A provocative research program in animals (Meaney & Szyf 2005) indicates that social exposures in early life can have long-lasting epigenetic and phenotypic influences. This work shows that neonatal rodents who receive high levels of nurturing from their mothers in the first week of life exhibit diminished cortisol responses to stressful experience when they reach adulthood (e.g., Liu et al. 1997). This hormonal resilience to stressors arises from nurturing-induced epigenetic modifications, such as demethylation of DNA and acetylation of histone proteins, that facilitate expression of the GR in hippocampal tissue (Weaver et al. 2004). (Greater expression of GR enables tighter regulation of the hormonal system that controls the release of cortisol.)

Stress-induced epigenetic dynamics provide one mechanistic solution to the incubation problem outlined above. To the extent that future research in humans is able to substantiate Meaney & Syzf's (2005) findings in rodents, epigenetic processes may serve as a mechanistic and conceptual bridge linking temporally distant phenomena. Some preliminary work of this nature has begun to appear. For example, in a cohort of healthy teenagers, we tested associations of SES at different periods of life with current expression of genes that code for GR and other molecules that regulate inflammation (Miller & Chen 2007). Interestingly, the current SES of these subjects did not predict gene expression patterns, but their family's social standing when they were 2–3 years of age did predict patterns. Subjects who spent their early years in a lower-SES setting had lesser quantities of GR mRNA and more mRNA for proinflammatory genes than did those who spent their early years in a higher-SES setting. This pattern was evident regardless of the subject's current family SES. Though the mechanisms underlying these findings remain unclear, they suggest that low early-life SES may alter the epigenome of immune cells in ways that foster the emergence a proinflammatory phenotype. If corroborated, patterns of this nature could begin to explain early-life influences on diseases of adulthood as well as other temporally distant phenomenon, such as the links between traumatic experiences and health problems that emerge decades later (Dong et al. 2004; Li et al. 2002a,b).

Transcriptional control circuits and posttranslational modification of proteins provide additional molecular mechanisms by which environmental factors can induce persistent alterations in physiologic function. Transcription control circuits involve sequential gene expression relationships that induce positive (or negative) feedback cycles. For example, pathogen-induced inflammatory signaling can activate the proinflammatory cytokine gene *IL1B* (encoding interleukin 1β), which, when it subsequently signals through the IL-1 receptor, can activate the MAP kinase pathway and thereby phosphorylate the GR (Pace et al. 2007). MAP kinase phosphorylation is a posttranslational modification of the GR protein that desensitizes it to the effects of cortisol, resulting in decreased anti-inflammatory signaling from the HPA axis and complementary increases in inflammatory gene transcription by nuclear factor-κB. Continuing inflammatory signaling, in turn, drives increased *IL1B* gene expression, providing a positive feedback cycle that locks out anti-inflammatory signaling and perpetuates inflammation. Many physiologic systems involve such feedback loops and thus provide opportunities for significant environmental influences at one point to shape subsequent physiologic responses to environmental stimuli.

Another biological mechanism that can perpetuate the physiologic effect of transient environmental influences is tissue remodeling. By altering patterns of gene expression in cells,

receptor-mediated signaling pathways essentially change the nature of the tissues composed of those cells. This can endow the remodeled tissue with altered sensitivity to subsequent environmental stimuli that persists for the life of a cell or for a generation of its protein structure (e.g., months to years). One example of this comes from the studies of social stress effects on the replication of SIV in rhesus macaques (Sloan et al. 2007b). One consequence of unstable social conditions involves increasing density of SNS neural fibers within the lymph node environment that structures the initiation of immune responses (and serves as a site for viral replication). Stress-induced increase in SNS innervation provides a neurobiological structure that can deliver more norepinephrine into the immunobiological environment of the lymph node in response to a subsequent stressful experience. This dynamic shows similar positive feedback properties to the glucocorticoid resistance dynamic outlined above and can have a substantial impact on immune response to pathogens (Sloan et al. 2007b, 2008). Another instance of tissue remodeling occurs in asthma, when transient inflammatory reactions induce long-term remodeling of airway tissues in ways that render the lungs hypersensitive to subsequent challenges. Thus, the physiologic composition of our current bodies is shaped to some extent by our historical interactions with previous environments. These dynamics provide a concrete molecular manifestation of Barker's (1997) and Hertzman's (1999) notion of biological programming, as well as longitudinal conceptions of allostatic load (McEwen 1998).

The preceding examples describe mechanisms by which relatively transient psychosocial conditions can bring about long-term (even permanent) changes in the ways that cells and tissues behave. However, recent evidence suggests that psychobiologic influences can play out in more temporally dynamic ways as well, where the biology itself becomes a moving target. The most concrete example of this comes from work on chronic stress and cortisol output (see Miller et al. 2007 for a review). It shows that when chronic stress first begins, there is an initial activation of the HPA axis, which leads to an increased output of cortisol. But as time passes, this activity subsides and cortisol secretion rebounds to normal, and if the stressor persists, to below normal. These findings show that the impact of chronic stress on HPA activity does not unfold in the static and linear fashion that most models in health psychology presume. Instead, the body seems to make use of counterregulatory mechanisms to adapt to the demands imposed by the stressor, just as it does when faced with physical stimuli such as changes in oxygen supply, nutrient availability, or temperature. Characterizing these adaptations and refining models of stress and disease accordingly poses an important challenge for health psychology in the coming decade (for examples of this kind of thinking, see Mohr & Pelletier 2006).

CONCLUSIONS

The health psychology literature has shown substantial growth in phenomenological documentations relating psychosocial factors to disease outcomes (Cohen et al. 2007, Rozanski et al. 1999). The most significant challenge now involves identifying the biological processes mediating those relationships. Success in this arena will strengthen the empirical corpus of health psychology by providing epistemologically satisfying causal explanations for the observed phenomenon and suggesting therapeutic strategies for protecting individuals against the adverse health effects of known risk factors such as low SES, social isolation, stress, and depression. A host of new methodological strategies and conceptual frameworks has emerged to support these endeavors. Some particularly promising technical opportunities involve (*a*) the use of massively parallel molecular assay systems to capture genome-wide patterns of gene transcription, epigenetic dynamics, protein distributions, and posttranslational modifications; (*b*) the advent of sophisticated statistical methods for testing mediational hypotheses in correlational analyses and experimental manipulations of putative mediators; (*c*) the increasing availability of noninvasive imaging systems and validated biomarkers such as CRP that can provide penetrating insights into disease pathophysiology in human populations; and (*d*) meta-analytic statistical strategies that can abstract general theoretical principles from a diverse array of primary literature. Leveraging these methodological advances are new conceptual frameworks for understanding interactions between environmental conditions and health-related physiology, including (*a*) a growing appreciation of inflammation's common contribution to a wide variety of prevalent chronic diseases and its sensitivity to biobehavioral regulation; (*b*) deepening biobehavioral theories that map distinct psychological states and processes onto distinct neuroendocrine and immunologic signatures; and (*c*) new insights into the regulatory plasticity of neuroimmune interactions, including persistent alterations in neurobiological signaling regimes that stem from transient environmental influences (e.g., epigenetic alterations, glucocorticoid resistance, stress-induced innervation dynamics, transcriptional feedback circuits, and tissue remodeling).

Ironically, as the novelty of PNI has waned during the past decade, the field has also begun to yield its first comprehensive mechanistic explanations for biobehavioral relationships in health. That yield emerged first in the context of viral infections, as well-crystallized theories of disease pathogenesis interacted with developing PNI principles to clarify the key role of environmentally sensitive host factors in shaping the biology of viral infections (Glaser et al. 1999, Glaser & Kiecolt-Glaser 2005, Miller & Cohen 2005, Sloan et al. 2007c). As the role of inflammation in atherosclerosis has become more fully appreciated, a rich literature on psychosocial risk factors for CHD has incorporated new pathophysiologic concepts that now promise to define more clearly the specific biological mechanisms involved (Krantz & McCeney 2002, Rozanski et al. 1999). Relationships between stress and the biology of inflammation and tissue regeneration have also begun to accelerate mechanistic analyses of biobehavioral relationships in cancer (Antoni et al. 2006, Thaker et al. 2006). Progress in all of these areas has been accelerated by the confluence of new perspectives on basic disease pathophysiology and new conceptions of biobehavioral regulation in the common language of molecular biology. In this review, we hope to advance some overarching conceptual approaches that will spur health psychologists to capitalize on these emerging opportunities to the fullest extent possible.

DISCLOSURE STATEMENT

The authors are not aware of any biases that might be perceived as affecting the objectivity of this review.

LITERATURE CITED

Adam EK, Hawkley LC, Kudielka BM, Cacioppo JT. 2006. Day-to-day dynamics of experience—cortisol associations in a population-based sample of older adults. *Proc. Natl. Acad. Sci. USA* 103:17058–63

Ader R, ed. 2007. *Psychoneuroimmunology*. Boston, MA: Elsevier. 4th ed.

Ader R, Felten D, Cohen N, eds. 2001. *Psychoneuroimmunology*. New York: Academic. 3rd ed.

Adler NE, Boyce WT, Chesney MA, Folkman S, Syme SL. 1993. Socioeconomic inequalities in health: no easy solution. *J. Am. Med. Assoc.* 269:3140–45

Anisman H, Ravindran AV, Griffiths J, Merali Z. 1999. Endocrine and cytokine correlates of major depression and dysthymia with typical or atypical features. *Mol. Psychiatry* 4:182–88

Antoni MH, Lutgendorf SK, Cole SW, Dhabhar FS, Sephton SE, et al. 2006. The influence of bio-behavioural factors on tumour biology: pathways and mechanisms. *Nat. Rev. Cancer* 6:240–48

Bailey MT, Padgett DA, Sheridan JF. 2007. Stress-induced modulation of innate resistance and adaptive immunity to influenza viral infection. See Ader 2007, pp. 1097–106

Barker DJ. 1997. The fetal origins of coronary heart disease. *Acta Paediatr. Suppl.* 422:78–82

Berkman LF, Blumenthal J, Burg M, Carney RM, Catellier D, Cowan MJ. 2003. Writing Committee for the ENRICHD Investigators. Effects of treating depression and low-perceived social support on clinical events after myocardial infarction: the Enhancing Recovery in Coronary Heart Disease Patients (ENRICHD) Randomized Trial. *J. Am. Med. Assoc.* 289:3106–16

Berkman LF, Kawachi I. 2000. *Social Epidemiology*. New York: Oxford Univ. Press

Berkman LF, Syme SL. 1979. Social networks, host resistance, and mortality: a nine-year follow-up study of Alameda County residents. *Am. J. Epidemiol.* 109:186–204

Blumenthal JA, Sherwood A, Babyak MA, Watkins LL, Waugh R, et al. 2005. Effects of exercise and stress management training on markers of cardiovascular risk in patients with ischemic heart disease: a randomized controlled trial. *J. Am. Med. Assoc.* 293:1626–34

Bosch JA, Engeland CG, Cacioppo JT, Marucha PT. 2007. Depressive symptoms predict mucosal wound healing. *Psychosom. Med.* 69:597–605

Brady SS, Matthews KA. 2002. The effect of socioeconomic status and ethnicity on adolescents' exposure to stressful life events. *J. Pediatr. Psychol.* 27:575–83

Carney RM, Freedland KE, Veith RC, Jaffe AS. 1999. Can treating depression reduce mortality after an acute myocardial infarction? *Psychosom. Med.* 61:666–75

Chen E, Hanson MD, Paterson LQ, Griffin MJ, Walker HA, Miller GE. 2006. Socioeconomic status and inflammatory processes in childhood asthma: the role of psychological stress. *J. Allergy Clin. Immunol.* 117:1014–20

Chen E, Langer DA, Raphaelson YE, Matthews KA. 2004. Socioeconomic status and health in adolescents: the role of stress interpretations. *Child Dev.* 75:1039–52

Chen E, Matthews KA. 2003. Development of the Cognitive Appraisal and Understanding of Social Events (CAUSE) Videos. *Health Psychol.* 22:106–10

Chen E, Matthews KA, Boyce WT. 2002. Socioeconomic differences in children's health: How and why do these relationships change with age? *Psychol. Bull.* 128:295–329

Chen E, Miller GE. 2007a. Social context as an individual difference in psychoneuroimmunology. See Ader 2007, pp. 497–508

Chen E, Miller GE. 2007b. Stress and inflammation in exacerbations of asthma. *Brain Behav. Immun.* 21:993–99

Coe CL, Lubach GR. 2003. Critical periods of special health relevance for psychoneuroimmunology. *Brain Behav. Immun.* 17:3–12

Coe CL, Lubach GR. 2005. Prenatal origins of individual variation in behavior and immunity. *Neurosci. Biobehav. Rev.* 29:39–49

Cohen S. 2004. Social relationships and health. *Am. Psychol.* 59:676–84

Cohen S, Doyle WJ, Baum A. 2006a. Socioeconomic status is associated with stress hormones. *Psychosom. Med.* 68:414–20

Cohen S, Doyle WJ, Skoner DP. 1999. Psychological stress cytokine production and severity of upper respiratory illness. *Psychosom. Med.* 61:175–80

Cohen S, Doyle WJ, Skoner DP, Rabin BS, Gwaltney JM Jr. 1997. Social ties and susceptibility to the common cold. *J. Am. Med. Assoc.* 277:1940–44

Cohen S, Doyle WJ, Turner RB, Alper CM, Skoner DP. 2004. Childhood socioeconomic status and host resistance to infectious illness in adulthood. *Psychosom. Med.* 66:553–58

Cohen S, Frank E, Doyle WJ, Skoner DP, Rabin BS, Gwaltney JM Jr. 1998. Types of stressors that increase susceptibility to the common cold in healthy adults. *Health Psychol.* 17:214–23

Cohen S, Janicki-Deverts D, Miller GE. 2007. Psychological stress and disease. *J. Am. Med. Assoc.* 298:1685–87

Cohen S, Kaplan GA, Salonen JT. 1999. The role of psychological characteristics in the relation between socioeconomic status and perceived health. *J. Appl. Soc. Psychol.* 29:445–68

Cohen S, Schwartz JE, Epel E, Kirschbaum C, Sidney S, Seeman T. 2006b. Socioeconomic status, race, and diurnal cortisol decline in the Coronary Artery Risk Development in Young Adults (CARDIA) Study. *Psychosom. Med.* 68:41–50

Cohen S, Tyrrell DA, Smith AP. 1991. Psychological stress and susceptibility to the common cold. *N. Engl. J. Med.* 325:606–12

Cole SW. 2006. Social threat, personal identity, and physical health in closeted gay men. In *Sexual Orientation and Mental Health*, ed. AM Omoto, HS Kurtzman, pp. 245–68. Washington, DC: Am. Psychol. Assoc.

Cole SW. 2008. Social regulation of leukocyte homeostasis: the role of glucocorticoid sensitivity. *Brain Behav. Immun.* In press

Cole SW, Hawkley LC, Arevalo JM, Sung CS, Rose RM, Cacioppo JT. 2007. Social regulation of gene expression: inflammation and the human transcriptional response to loneliness. *Genome Biol.* 8:R189

Cole SW, Jamieson BD, Zack JA. 1999. cAMP externalizes lymphocyte CXCR4: implications for chemotaxis and HIV infection. *J. Immunol.* 162:1392–400

Cole SW, Kemeny ME, Fahey JL, Zack JA, Naliboff BD. 2003. Psychological risk factors for HIV pathogenesis: mediation by the autonomic nervous system. *Biol. Psychiatry* 54:1444–56

Cole SW, Kemeny ME, Taylor SE. 1997. Social identity and physical health: accelerated HIV progression in rejection-sensitive gay men. *J. Personal. Soc. Psychol.* 72:320–36

Cole SW, Kemeny ME, Taylor SE, Visscher BR, Fahey JL. 1996. Accelerated course of human immunodeficiency virus infection in gay men who conceal their homosexual identity. *Psychosom. Med.* 58:219–31

Cole SW, Korin YD, Fahey JL, Zack JA. 1998. Norepinephrine accelerates HIV replication via protein kinase A-dependent effects on cytokine production. *J. Immunol.* 161:610–16

Cole SW, Naliboff BD, Kemeny ME, Griswold MP, Fahey JL, Zack JA. 2001. Impaired response to HAART in HIV-infected individuals with high autonomic nervous system activity. *Proc. Natl. Acad. Sci. USA* 98:12695–700

Cole SW, Yan W, Galic Z, Arevalo J, Zack JA. 2005. Expression-based monitoring of transcription factor activity: the TELiS database. *Bioinformatics* 21:803–10

Collado-Hidalgo A, Sung C, Cole S. 2006. Adrenergic inhibition of innate antiviral response: PKA blockade of Type I interferon gene transcription mediates catecholamine support for HIV-1 replication. *Brain Behav. Immun.* 20:552–63

Coussens LM, Werb Z. 2002. Inflammation and cancer. *Nature* 420:860–67

Coyne JC, Stefanek M, Palmer SC. 2007. Psychotherapy and survival in cancer: the conflict between hope and evidence. *Psychol. Bull.* 133:367–94

Dickerson SS, Gruenewald TL, Kemeny ME. 2004. When the social self is threatened: shame physiology and health. *J. Personal.* 72:1191–216

Dickerson SS, Kemeny ME. 2004. Acute stressors and cortisol responses: a theoretical integration and synthesis of laboratory research. *Psychol. Bull.* 130:355–91

Dong M, Giles WH, Felitti VJ, Dube SR, Williams JE, et al. 2004. Insights into causal pathways for ischemic heart disease: adverse childhood experiences study. *Circulation* 110:1761–66

Ebrecht M, Buske-Kirschbaum A, Hellhammer D, Kern S, Rohleder N, et al. 2000. Tissue specificity of glucocorticoid sensitivity in healthy adults. *J. Clin. Endocrinol. Metab.* 85:3733–39

Eccles R. 2005. Understanding the symptoms of the common cold and influenza. *Lancet Infect. Dis.* 5:718–25

Evans GW, English K. 2002. The environment of poverty: multiple stressor exposure, psychophysiological stress, and socioemotional adjustment. *Child Dev.* 73:1238–48

Fraga MF, Ballestar E, Paz MF, Ropero S, Setien F, et al. 2005. Epigenetic differences arise during the lifetime of monozygotic twins. *Proc. Natl. Acad. Sci. USA* 102:10604–9

Friedman M, Thoresen CE, Gill JJ, Ulmer D, Powell LH, et al. 1986. Alteration of Type A behavior and its effect on cardiac recurrences in post-myocardial infarction patients: summary results of the recurrent coronary prevention project. *Am. Heart J.* 112:653–65

Galobardes B, Lynch JW, Davey Smith G. 2004. Childhood socioeconomic circumstances and cause-specific mortality in adulthood: systematic review and interpretation. *Epidemiol. Rev.* 26:7–21

Glaser R, Kiecolt-Glaser JK. 2005. Stress-induced immune dysfunction: implications for health. *Nat. Rev. Immunol.* 5:243–51

Glaser R, Rabin B, Chesney M, Cohen S, Natelson B. 1999. Stress-induced immunomodulation: implications for infectious diseases. *J. Am. Med. Assoc.* 281:2268–70

Glaser R, Robles TF, Sheridan J, Malarkey WB, Kiecolt-Glaser JK. 2003. Mild depressive symptoms are associated with amplified and prolonged inflammatory responses after influenza virus vaccination in older adults. *Arch. Gen. Psychiatry* 60:1009–14

Gruenewald TL, Kemeny ME, Aziz N, Fahey JL. 2004. Acute threat to the social self: shame, social self-esteem, and cortisol activity. *Psychosom. Med.* 66:915–24

Haskett RF. 1993. The HPA axis and depressive disorders. In *Biology of Depressive Disorders*, ed. JJ Mann, DJ Kupfer, pp. 171–88. New York: Plenum

Hawkley LC, Cacioppo JT. 2007. Aging and loneliness: downhill quickly? *Curr. Dir. Psychol. Sci.* 16:187–91

Hemingway H, Shipley M, Mullen MJ, Kumari M, Brunner E, et al. 2003. Social and psychosocial influences on inflammatory markers and vascular function in civil servants (The Whitehall II Study). *Am. J. Cardiol.* 92:984–87

Hertzman C. 1999. The biological embedding of early experience and its effects on health in adulthood. *Ann. N. Y. Acad. Sci.* 896:85–95

Hodgson D, Coe CL. 2005. *Perinatal Programming. Early-Life Determinants of Adult Health and Disease.* Boston, MA: Informa Healthcare

House JS, Landis KR, Umberson D. 1988. Social relationships and health. *Science* 241:540–45

Irwin MR. 2001. Depression and immunity. See Ader et al. 2001, pp. 383–98

Irwin MR. 2002. Psychoneuroimmunology of depression: clinical implications. *Brain Behav. Immun.* 16:1–16

Irwin MR, Costlow C, Williams H, Artin KH, Chan CY, et al. 1998. Cellular immunity to varicella-zoster virus in patients with major depression. *J. Infect. Dis.* 178:S104–8

Janicki-Deverts D, Cohen S, Adler NE, Schwartz JE, Matthews KA, Seeman TE. 2007. Socioeconomic status is related to urinary catecholamines in the Coronary Artery Risk Development in Young Adults (CARDIA) study. *Psychosom. Med.* 69:514–20

Jirtle RL, Skinner MK. 2007. Environmental epigenomics and disease susceptibility. *Nat. Rev. Genet.* 8:253–62

Kagan J. 1994. *Galen's Prophecy: Temperament in Human Nature.* New York: Basic Books

Kiecolt-Glaser JK. 1999. Stress personal relationships and immune function: health implications. *Brain Behav. Immun.* 13:61–72

Kiecolt-Glaser JK, Dura JR, Speicher CE, Trask OJ, Glaser R. 1991. Spousal caregivers of dementia victims: longitudinal changes in immunity and health. *Psychosom. Med.* 53:345–62

Kiecolt-Glaser JK, Glaser R, Gravenstein S, Malarkey WB, Sheridan JF. 1996. Chronic stress alters the immune response to influenza virus vaccine in older adults. *Proc. Natl. Acad. Sci. USA* 93:3043–47

Kiecolt-Glaser JK, Loving TJ, Stowell JR, Malarkey WB, Lemeshow S, et al. 2005. Hostile marital interactions, proinflammatory cytokine production, and wound healing. *Arch. Gen. Psychiatry* 62:1377–84

Kiecolt-Glaser JK, Marucha PT, Malarkey WB, Mercado AM, Glaser R. 1995. Slowing of wound healing by psychological stress. *Lancet* 346:1194–96

Kiecolt-Glaser JK, McGuire L, Robles T, Glaser R. 2002. Emotions morbidity and mortality: new perspectives from psychoneuroimmunology. *Annu. Rev. Psychol.* 53:83–107

Kiecolt-Glaser JK, Preacher KJ, MacCallum RC, Atkinson C, Malarkey WB, Glaser R. 2003. Chronic stress and age-related increases in the proinflammatory cytokine IL-6. *Proc. Natl. Acad. Sci. USA* 100:9090–95

Kittleson MM, Meoni LA, Wang NY, Chu AY, Ford DE, Klag MJ. 2006. Association of childhood socioeconomic status with subsequent coronary heart disease in physicians. *Arch. Intern. Med.* 166:2356–61

Kop WJ, Cohen N. 2001. Psychological risk factors and immune system involvement in cardiovascular disease. See Ader et al. 2001, pp. 525–44

Kop WJ, Cohen N. 2007. Psychoneuroimmunological pathways involved in acute coronary syndromes. See Ader 2007, pp. 921–44

Kop WJ, Gottdiener JS, Tangen CM, Fried LP, McBurnie MA, et al. 2002. Inflammatory and coagulation factors in persons >65 years of age with symptoms of depression but without evidence of myocardial ischemia. *Am. J. Cardiol.* 89:419–24

Krantz DS, McCeney MK. 2002. Effects of psychological and social factors on organic disease: a critical assessment of research on coronary heart disease. *Annu. Rev. Psychol.* 53:341–69

Lawlor DA, Sterne JA, Tynelius P, Davey Smith G, Rasmussen F. 2006. Association of childhood socioeconomic position with cause-specific mortality in a prospective record linkage study of 1,839,384 individuals. *Am. J. Epidemiol.* 164:907–15

Lesperance F, Frasure-Smith N, Theroux P, Irwin M. 2004. The association between major depression and levels of soluble intercellular adhesion molecule 1 interleukin-6 and C-reactive protein in patients with recent acute coronary syndromes. *Am. J. Psychiatry* 161:271–77

Li J, Hansen D, Mortensen PB, Olsen J. 2002a. Myocardial infarction in parents who lost a child: a nationwide prospective cohort study in Denmark. *Circulation* 106:1634–39

Li J, Johansen C, Hansen D, Olsen J. 2002b. Cancer incidence in parents who lost a child. *Cancer* 95(10):2237–42

Libby P, Theroux P. 2005. Pathophysiology of coronary artery disease. *Circulation* 111:3481–88

Liu D, Diorio J, Tannenbaum B, Caldji C, Francis D, et al. 1997. Maternal care hippocampal glucocorticoid receptors and hypothalamic-pituitary-adrenal responses to stress. *Science* 277:1659–62

Loucks EB, Berkman LF, Gruenewald TL, Seeman TE. 2006a. Relation of social integration to inflammatory marker concentrations in men and women 70 to 79 years. *Am. J. Cardiol.* 977:1010–16

Loucks EB, Sullivan LM, D'Agostino RBS, Larson MG, Berkman LF, Benjamin EJ. 2006b. Social networks and inflammatory markers in the Framingham Heart Study. *J. Biosoc. Sci.* 386:835–42

Lupien SJ, King S, Meaney MJ, McEwen BS. 2000. Child's stress hormone levels correlate with mother's socioeconomic status and depressive state. *Biol. Psychiatry* 48:976–80

Lupien SJ, King S, Meaney MJ, McEwen BS. 2001. Can poverty get under your skin? Basal cortisol levels and cognitive function in children from low and high socioeconomic status. *Dev. Psychopathol.* 13:653–76

Manuck SB, Marsland AL, Kaplan JR, Williams JK. 1995. The pathogenicity of behavior and its neuroendocrine mediation: an example from coronary artery disease. *Psychosom. Med.* 57:275–83

Marmot M, Wilkinson RG. 2000. *Social Determinants of Health*. New York: Oxford Univ. Press

McEwen BS. 1998. Protective and damaging effects of stress mediators. *N. Engl. J. Med.* 338:171–79

Meaney MJ, Szyf M. 2005. Environmental programming of stress responses through DNA methylation: life at the interface between a dynamic environment and a fixed genome. *Dialogues Clin. Neurosci.* 7:103–23

Miller GE, Chen E. 2006. Stressful experience and diminished expression of genes encoding the glucocorticoid receptor and b2-adrenergic receptor in children with asthma. *Proc. Natl. Acad. Sci. USA* 103:5496–501

Miller GE, Chen E. 2007. Unfavorable socioeconomic conditions in early life presage expression of proinflammatory phenotype in adolescence. *Psychosom. Med.* 69:402–9

Miller GE, Chen E, Sze J, Marin TJ, Doll RM, et al. 2008. A functional genomic fingerprint of chronic stress in humans: decreased glucocorticoid and increased NF-κB signaling. *Biol. Psychiatry.* In press

Miller GE, Chen E, Zhou E. 2007. If it goes up must it come down? Chronic stress and the hypothalamic-pituitary-adrenocortical axis in humans. *Psychol. Bull.* 133:25–45

Miller GE, Cohen S. 2001. Psychological interventions and the immune system: a meta-analytic review and critique. *Health Psychol.* 20:47–63

Miller GE, Cohen S. 2005. Infectious disease and psychoneuroimmunology. In *Human Psychoneuroimmunology*, ed. K Vedhara, MR Irwin, pp. 219–42. New York: Oxford Univ. Press

Miller GE, Cohen S, Herbert TB. 1999. Pathways linking major depression and immunity in ambulatory female patients. *Psychosom. Med.* 61:850–60

Miller GE, Cohen S, Ritchey AK. 2002a. Chronic psychological stress and the regulation of proinflammatory cytokines: a glucocorticoid resistance model. *Health Psychol.* 21:531–41

Miller GE, Freedland KE, Duntley S, Carney RM. 2005. Relation of depressive symptoms to C-reactive protein and pathogen burden (cytomegalovirus, herpes simplex virus, Epstein-Barr virus) in patients with earlier acute coronary syndromes. *Am. J. Cardiol.* 95:317–21

Miller GE, Stetler CA, Carney RM, Freedland KE, Banks WA. 2002b. Clinical depression and inflammatory risk markers for coronary heart disease. *Am. J. Cardiol.* 90:1279–83

Miller TQ, Smith TW, Turner CW, Guijarro ML, Hallet AL. 1996. A meta-analytic review of research on hostility and physical health. *Psychol. Bull.* 119(2):322–48

Mohr DC, Pelletier D. 2006. A temporal framework for understanding the effects of stressful life events on inflammation in patients with multiple sclerosis. *Brain Behav. Immun.* 201:27–36

Musselman DL, DeBattista C, Nathan KI, Kilts CD, Schatzberg AF, Nemeroff CB. 1998. Biology of depression. *Textbook of Psychopharmacology*, ed. AF Schatzberg, CB Nemeroff, pp. 549–88. Washington, DC: Am. Psychiatr. Press

Pace TW, Hu F, Miller AH. 2007. Cytokine-effects on glucocorticoid receptor function: relevance to glucocorticoid resistance and the pathophysiology and treatment of major depression. *Brain Behav. Immun.* 21:9–19

Panagiotakos DB, Pitsavos C, Manios Y, Polychronopoulos E, Chrysohoou CA, Stefanadis C. 2005. Socioeconomic status in relation to risk factors associated with cardiovascular disease in healthy individuals from the ATTICA study. *Eur. J. Cardiovasc. Prev. Rehabil.* 12:68–74

Perkins ND. 2007. Integrating cell-signalling pathways with NF-κB and IKK function. *Nat. Rev. Mol. Cell Biol.* 8:49–62

Plotsky PM, Owens MJ, Nemeroff CB. 1995. Neuropeptide alterations in mood disorders. In *Psychopharmacology: The Fourth Generation of Progress*, ed. F Bloom, DJ Kupfer, pp. 971–81, New York: Raven

Pressman SD, Cohen S, Miller GE, Barkin A, Rabin BS. 2005. Loneliness, social network size, and immune response to influenza vaccination in college freshmen. *Health Psychol.* 24:297–306

Raison CL, Capuron L, Miller AH. 2006. Cytokines sing the blues: inflammation and the pathogenesis of depression. *Trends Immunol.* 27:24–31

Raison CL, Miller AH. 2003. When not enough is too much: the role of insufficient glucocorticoid signaling in the pathophysiology of stress-related disorders. *Am. J. Psychiatry* 160:1554–65

Ranjit N, Diez-Roux AV, Shea S, Cushman M, Ni H, Seeman T. 2007a. Socioeconomic position race/ethnicity and inflammation in the multi-ethnic study of atherosclerosis. *Circulation* 116:2383–90

Ravindran AV, Griffiths J, Merali Z, Anisman H. 1995. Lymphocyte subsets associated with major depression and dysthymia: modification by antidepressant treatment. *Psychosom. Med.* 57:555–63

Repetti RL, Taylor SE, Seeman T. 2002. Risky families: family social environments and the mental and physical health of offspring. *Psychol. Bull.* 128:330–66

Richards EJ. 2006. Inherited epigenetic variation—revisiting soft inheritance. *Nat. Rev. Genet.* 8:395–401

Rohleder N, Beulen SE, Chen E, Wolf JM, Kirschbaum C. 2007. Stress on the dance floor: the cortisol stress response to social-evaluative threat in competitive ballroom dancers. *Personal. Soc. Psychol.* 33:69–84

Rohleder N, Schommer NC, Hellhammer DH, Engel R, Kirschbaum C. 2001. Sex differences in the glucocorticoid sensitivity of proinflammatory cytokine production after psychosocial stress. *Psychosom. Med.* 63:966–72

Rozanski A, Blumenthal JA, Kaplan JR. 1999. Impact of psychological factors on the pathogenesis of cardiovascular disease and implications for therapy. *Circulation* 99:2192–217

Rugulies R. 2002. Depression as a predictor for coronary heart disease. A review and meta-analysis. *Am. J. Prev. Med.* 23:51–61

Sandberg S, Jarvenpaa S, Penttinen A, Paton JY, McCann DC. 2004. Asthma exacerbations in children immediately following stressful life events: a Cox's hierarchical regression. *Thorax* 59:1046–51

Sandberg S, Paton JY, Ahola S, McCann DC, McGuinness D, Hillary CR. 2000. The role of acute and chronic stress in asthma attacks in children. *Lancet* 356:982–87

Seeman TE, McEwen BS. 1996. Impact of social environment characteristics on neuroendocrine regulation. *Psychosom. Med.* 58:459–71

Segerstrom SC, Miller GE. 2004. Psychological stress and the human immune system: a meta-analytic study of 30 years of inquiry. *Psychol. Bull.* 130:601–30

Sloan EK, Capitanio JP, Cole SW. 2008. Stress-induced remodeling of lymphoid innervation. *Brain Behav. Immun.* In press

Sloan EK, Capitanio JP, Tarara RP, Cole SW. 2007a. Social temperament and lymph node innervation. *Brain Behav. Immun.* E-pub ahead of print

Sloan EK, Capitanio JP, Tarara RP, Mendoza SP, Mason WA, Cole SW. 2007b. Social stress enhances sympathetic innervation of primate lymph nodes: mechanisms and implications for viral pathogenesis. *J. Neurosci.* 27(33):8857–65

Sloan EK, Collado-Hidalgo A, Cole SW. 2007c. Psychobiology of HIV infection. See Ader 2007, pp. 1053–76

Sloan EK, Tarara RP, Capitanio JP, Cole SW. 2006. Enhanced replication of simian immunodeficiency virus adjacent to catecholaminergic varicosities in primate lymph nodes. *J. Virol.* 80(9):4326–35

Smith TW. 1992. Hostility and health: current status of a psychosomatic hypothesis. *Health Psychol.* 11:139–50

Stetler C, Dickerson SS, Miller GE. 2004. Uncoupling of social zeitgebers and diurnal cortisol secretion in clinical depression. *Psychoneuroendocrinology* 29:1250–59

Strickland PL, Deakin JF, Percival C, Dixon J, Gater RA, Goldberg DP. 2002. Bio-social origins of depression in the community. Interactions between social adversity cortisol and serotonin neurotransmission. *Br. J. Psychiatry* 180:168–73

Taylor SE, Lehman BJ, Kiefe CI, Seeman TE. 2006. Relationship of early life stress and psychological functioning to adult C-reactive protein in the Coronary Artery Risk Development in Young Adults Study. *Biol. Psychiatry* 60:819–24

Taylor SE, Lerner JS, Sage RM, Lehman BJ, Seeman TE. 2004. Early environment, emotions, responses to stress, and health. *J. Personal.* 72:1365–93

Thaker PH, Han LY, Kamat AA, Arevalo JM, Takahashi R, et al. 2006. Chronic stress promotes tumor growth and angiogenesis in a mouse model of ovarian carcinoma. *Nat. Med.* 12:939–44

Tomaka J, Blascovich J, Kibler J, Ernst JM. 1997. Cognitive and physiological antecedents of threat and challenge appraisal. *J. Personal. Soc. Psychol.* 731:63–72

Uchino BN, Cacioppo JT, Kiecolt-Glaser JK. 1996. The relationship between social support and physiological processes: a review with emphasis on underlying mechanisms and implications for health. *Psychol. Bull.* 119:488–531

van Melle JP, de Jonge P, Spijkerman TA, Tijssen JG, Ormel J, et al. 2004. Prognostic association of depression following myocardial infarction with mortality and cardiovascular events: a meta-analysis. *Psychosom. Med.* 66:814–22

Vedhara K, Cox NK, Wilcock GK, Perks P, Hunt M, et al. 1999. Chronic stress in elderly caregivers of dementia patients and antibody response to influenza vaccination. *Lancet* 353:627–31

Verrier RL, Lown B. 1984. Behavioral stress and cardiac arrhythmias. *Annu. Rev. Physiol.* 46:155–76

Weaver ICG, Cervoni N, Champagne FA, D'Alessio AC, Sharma S, et al. 2004. Epigenetic programming by maternal behavior. *Nat. Neurosci.* 7:847–54

Weiner H. 1992. *Perturbing the Organism: The Biology of Stressful Experience.* Chicago: Univ. Chicago Press

Wulsin LR, Singal BM. 2003. Do depressive symptoms increase the risk for the onset of coronary disease? A systematic quantitative review. *Psychosom. Med.* 65:201–10

The Case for Cultural Competency in Psychotherapeutic Interventions

Stanley Sue,[1] Nolan Zane,[1]
Gordon C. Nagayama Hall,[2] and Lauren K. Berger[1]

[1]Department of Psychology, University of California, Davis, California 95616;
[2]Department of Psychology, University of Oregon, Eugene, Oregon 97403;
email: ssue@ucdavis.edu, nwzane@ucdavis.edu, gnhall@uoregon.edu, lkberger@ucdavis.edu

Annu. Rev. Psychol. 2009. 60:525–48

First published online as a Review in Advance on August 25, 2008

The *Annual Review of Psychology* is online at psych.annualreviews.org

This article's doi:
10.1146/annurev.psych.60.110707.163651

0066-4308/09/0110-0525$20.00

Key Words

cultural adaptation, ethnic minority, evidence-based practice, treatment outcomes, mental health

Abstract

Cultural competency practices have been widely adopted in the mental health field because of the disparities in the quality of services delivered to ethnic minority groups. In this review, we examine the meaning of cultural competency, positions that have been taken in favor of and against it, and the guidelines for its practice in the mental health field. Empirical research that tests the benefits of cultural competency is discussed.

Contents

INTRODUCTION

The notion that culturally competent services should be available to members of ethnic minority groups has been articulated for at least four decades. Multiculturalism, diversity, and cultural competency are currently hot and important topics for mental health professionals (Pistole 2004, Whaley & Davis 2007). Originally conceptualized as cultural responsiveness or sensitivity, cultural competency is now advocated and, at times, mandated by professional organizations; local, state, and federal agencies; and various professions. Yet, the concept has also been a source of controversy concerning its necessity, empirical research base, and political implications. This review examines many of the key issues surrounding cultural competency—namely, its definition, rationale, empirical support, and effects. We have not attempted to be exhaustive in our review of the relevant research; instead, we have examined the major issues and trends in cultural competency.

Many prominent health care organizations are now calling for culturally competent health care and culturally competent professionals (Herman et al. 2004). Appeals for cultural competency grew out of concerns for the status of ethnic minority group populations (i.e., African Americans, American Indians and Alaska Natives, Asian Americans, and Hispanics). These concerns were prompted by the growing diversity of the U.S. population, which necessitated changes in the mental health system to meet the different needs of multicultural populations. Further troubling were the well-documented health status disparities between different ethnic and racial groups, as well as the nationally publicized studies regarding cultural bias in health care decision making and recommendations (Schulman et al. 1999). The evidence revealed that mental health services were not accessible, available, or effectively delivered to these populations. Compared to white Americans, ethnic minority groups were found to underutilize services or prematurely terminate treatment (Pole et al. 2008, Sue 1998). Racial and ethnic minorities receive a lower quality of health care than do nonminorities, have less access to care, and are not as likely to be given effective, state-of-the-art treatments (U.S. Surgeon General 2001). The disparities exist because of service inadequacies rather than any possible differences in need for services or access-related factors, such as insurance status (Smedley et al. 2003).

Justice or ethical grounds have also propelled cultural competency (Whaley & Davis 2007). The goals of many professional organizations include equity and fairness in the delivery of services. For example, one of the guiding principles of the American Psychological Association (2002, pp. 1062–1063) is that:

> Psychologists recognize that fairness and justice entitle all persons to access to and benefit from the contributions of psychology and to equal quality in the processes, procedures, and services being conducted by psychologists. Psychologists exercise reasonable judgment and take precautions to ensure that their potential biases, the boundaries of their competence, and the limitations of their expertise do not lead to or condone unjust practices.

Ridley (1985) has argued that cultural competence is an ethical obligation and that cross-cultural skills should be placed on a level of parity with other specialized therapeutic skills. As an alternative to the passive "do no harm" approach in ethical standards in many helping professions, Hall et al. (2003) advocated that ethical standards mandate cultural competence via collaboration with, and sometimes deference to, ethnic minority communities and experts.

The delivery of quality services is especially difficult because of cultural and institutional influences that determine the nature of services. For example, Bernal & Scharrón-Del-Río (2001) maintain that ethnic and cultural factors should be considered in psychosocial treatments for many reasons. They propose that psychotherapy itself is a cultural phenomenon that plays a key role in the treatment process. In addition, ethnic and cultural concepts may clash with mainstream values inherent to traditional psychotherapies. The sources of treatment disparities are complex, are based on historic and contemporary inequities, and involve many players at several different levels, including health systems, their administrative and bureaucratic processes, utilization managers, health care professionals, and patients (Smedley et al. 2003).

Although the problems giving rise to the cultural competency movement are multifaceted, our focus in this review is to analyze therapist and treatment tactics that are considered culturally competent. In the focus on cultural competency, we acknowledge the social and psychological diversity that exists among members of any ethnic minority group and the tendency to generalize information across distinct ethnic groups. The discussion of cultural competence issues for a particular ethnic minority group becomes even more challenging in view of the limited amount of empirically based information available on cultural influences in mental health treatment. Considering these limitations, we proceed as judiciously as we can, examining key cultural tendencies and issues likely to be encountered in psychotherapy and counseling, drawing out some implications from the extant research, and offering some suggestions for research that may produce more culturally informed mental health practices. We also recognize that culture is only one relevant factor in providing effective mental health treatment and that depending on the circumstances, other aspects of clients may be more influential. The literature reviewed represents trends that have been observed and should be considered as guidelines or working hypotheses often linked with culturally competent mental health care for ethnic minority clientele.

WHAT IS CULTURAL COMPETENCY?

From the outset, we want to indicate that our coverage is limited. In cultural competence, it is important to distinguish between three levels of analysis: provider and treatment level, agency or institutional level (e.g., the operations of a mental health agency), and systems level (e.g., systems of care in a community). Our focus is on the first level—that of the provider, therapist, or counselor and that of the specific treatment used.

To evaluate the validity, utility, and empirical basis of cultural competency, one must first be able to define the construct. Competence is usually defined as an ability to perform a task or the quality of being adequately prepared or qualified. If therapists or counselors are generally competent to conduct psychotherapy, they should be able to demonstrate their skills with a range of culturally diverse clients. Proponents of cultural competency, however, believe that competency is largely a relative skill or quality, depending on one's cultural expertise or orientation. Their definitions of cultural competency assume that expertise or effectiveness in treatment can differ according to the client's ethnic or racial group. As Hall (2001) noted, advocates of cultural competency or sensitivity appreciate the importance of cultural mechanisms and argue that simply exporting a method from one cultural group to another is inadequate.

Can Cultural Competency be Distinguished from Competency in General?

Is there evidence that cultural competency can be distinguished from competency in general? The two may overlap but also have some distinct effects. Fuertes and colleagues (2006) found that ethnic minority clients rated their therapists as being higher in multicultural competency if the therapists were rated high on therapeutic alliance and empathy. These two characteristics are considered good ingredients in all treatments. Fuertes et al. (2006) recommend that therapists receive training in traditional areas such as relationship building and in communicating empathy. At the same time, they believe it is important that therapists be trained to competently handle the culture-based concerns that their clients bring to therapy. Another study suggests that the two are somewhat distinct. Constantine (2002) correlated African American, American Indian, Asian American, and Hispanic clients' treatment satisfaction with two measures of competency: one that assessed counselors' competency in general (i.e., the Counselor Rating Form–Short) and the other that measured cross-cultural competence in particular (Cross-Cultural Counseling Inventory–Revised). Although the two well-established competency measures were somewhat related, the cross-cultural competency measure contributed significantly to client

satisfaction beyond general competency. There was also evidence that ethnic minority clients' perceptions of their counselors' multicultural counseling competence partially mediated the relationship between general counseling competence ratings and satisfaction with counseling. Thus, cultural competency may be meaningfully distinguished from competency in general.

Differing Definitions

But how does one define the concept? In the past, terms such as "cultural sensitivity," "cultural responsiveness," and "multicultural competence" were used to convey the significance of attending to cultural issues in therapy and counseling. Despite consensus over the importance and significance of cultural values and behaviors in treatment, investigators have actually varied in their specific assumptions or focus for cultural competency. Many models of culturally sensitive therapy have been developed (Hall et al. 2003). Some describe characteristics of cultural competency. For example, ingredients viewed by some as essential for cultural competence include having an understanding, appreciation, and respect for cultural differences and similarities within, among, and between culturally diverse patient groups (U.S. Dept. Health Human Serv. 2002). Culturally competent care has been defined as a system that acknowledges the importance and incorporation of culture, assessment of cross-cultural relations, vigilance toward the dynamics that result from cultural differences, expansion of cultural knowledge, and adaptation of interventions to meet culturally unique needs (Whaley & Davis 2007).

Others emphasize the outcome of cultural expertise. Thus, having cultural knowledge or skills is important to the extent that positive outcomes are achieved, such as:

- The capacity to perform and obtain positive clinical outcomes in cross-cultural encounters (Lo & Fung 2003).
- The acquisition of awareness, knowledge, and skills needed to function effectively in

a pluralistic democratic society (i.e., the ability to communicate, interact, negotiate, and intervene on behalf of clients from diverse backgrounds) (Alvarez & Chen 2008, D.W. Sue & Torino 2005).

- The possession of cultural knowledge and skills of a particular culture to deliver effective interventions to members of that culture (S. Sue 1998).
- The ability to work effectively in cross-cultural situations using a set of congruent behaviors, attitudes, and policies that come together in a system, agency, or among professionals (Agency for Healthcare Research and Quality 2004).

Although the varying definitions overlap to some degree, one meaningful way of conceptualizing the definitions of competency is to note that some emphasize the (*a*) kind of person one is, (*b*) skills or intervention tactics that one uses, or (*c*) processes involved. In terms of the kind of person one is, D.W. Sue and colleagues (Sue et al. 1982, 1992) argue that the culturally competent counselor has:

- Cultural awareness and beliefs: The provider is sensitive to her or his personal values and biases and how these may influence perceptions of the client, the client's problem, and the counseling relationship.
- Cultural knowledge: The counselor has knowledge of the client's culture, worldview, and expectations for the counseling relationship.
- Cultural skills: The counselor has the ability to intervene in a manner that is culturally sensitive and relevant.

In this view, cultural competency involves a constellation of the right personal characteristics (awareness, knowledge, and skills) that a counselor or therapist should have. Every counselor should possess these characteristics. This model for cultural competency is the most widely recognized framework, and it formed the basis for much of the multicultural guidelines adopted by the American Psychological Association (Am. Psychol. Assoc. 2003) as well as the

multicultural counseling competencies adopted by the organization's Division 17.

The skills or tactics model views cultural competency as a skill to be learned or a strategy to use in working with culturally diverse clients. One chooses to exercise the skill or to use a cultural adaptation under the appropriate circumstances. Cultural competency is essentially similar to other specialized therapeutic skills such as expertise in sexual dysfunctions and depressive disorders (Ridley 1985). In this view, acquisition of multicultural competence would involve in-depth training and supervised experience as found in the development of other psychotherapeutic competencies (Whaley & Davis 2007).

Finally, process-oriented models focus on the complex client-therapist-treatment interactions and processes involved. For example, López (1997) considers the essence of cultural competence to be "the ability of the therapist to move between two cultural perspectives in understanding the culturally based meaning of clients from diverse cultural backgrounds" (p. 573). S. Sue (1998) views cultural competence as a multidimensional process. He proposes that three important characteristics underlie cultural competency among providers: scientific mindedness (i.e., forming and testing hypotheses), dynamic sizing (i.e., flexibility in generalizing and individualizing), and culture-specific resources (i.e., having knowledge and skills to work with other cultures) in response to different kinds of clients.

The definitions of cultural competence have points of convergence and divergence (Whaley & Davis 2007). They all agree that knowledge, skills, and problem solving germane to the cultural background of the help seeker are fundamental. Nevertheless, the different definitions vary with respect to their emphasis on global characteristics, knowledge, skills, awareness, problem-solving abilities, aspirations, processes, etc. The definitions also vary as to how amenable they are to research testing. The kind-of-person model and the process model pose problems in terms of empirical testing. In both models, characteristics of culturally competent therapists or interacting processes are difficult to specify and operationalize for research. On the other hand, the skills or cultural adaptation model can be more readily tested. In this model, researchers introduce the skill or cultural adaptation of treatment and compare the effects with other treatment or no-treatment control groups.

In general, it has been difficult to develop research strategies, isolate components, devise theories of cultural competency, and implement training strategies. Some limitations in cultural sensitivity or competency are that it (a) has various meanings, (b) includes inadequate descriptors, (c) is not theoretically grounded, and (d) is restricted by a lack of measurements and research designs for evaluating its impact in treatment.

RESISTANCE TO CULTURAL COMPETENCY

It is not surprising that cultural competency or multiculturalism has come under attack. Because of the lack of research on cultural competency, some have challenged it as being motivated by "political correctness" (Satel & Forster 1999) and untested in clinical trials (Satel 2000).

One of the important debates in the literature concerning cultural competency can be found in the attempt to establish multicultural counseling competencies or multicultural guidelines for the American Mental Health Counseling Association. The guidelines, many of which are highly similar to the ones adopted by the American Psychological Association (2003), stimulated civil but contentious exchanges. The debated issues revolved around several key questions, articulated largely by Thomas & Weinrach (2004), Weinrach & Thomas (2002, 2004), Vontress & Jackson (2004), and Patterson (2004):

1. Are cultural competency proponents stereotyping ethnic minority clients?

    Because cultural competency advocates emphasize the need to understand the cultural values and worldviews of

members of different cultural groups, Weinrach & Thomas (2002, 2004) have suggested that the position that members of these groups behave similarly is inadvertently racist, stereotypic, and prejudicial. Herman et al. (2007) and Hwang (2006) made similar points more recently. They ask whether it is possible to conduct culturally competent counseling given the risks associated with implementing counseling in a manner that fails to attend to a client's individual differences and inadvertently promotes culture-related stereotypes of clients. For example, important individual differences among American Indian clients include ethnic identity, acculturation, residential situation, and tribal background (Trimble 2003, 2008). By addressing presumed cultural orientations of, say, American Indians, therapists may fail to consider acculturated American Indian clients who do not hold traditional Native American perspectives.

2. By advocating for multicultural competencies for ethnic minority groups, are we discriminating against or ignoring other diversity characteristics such as gender, sexual orientation, and social class?

    The cultural competency movement, for the most part, has been addressed to the needs of African Americans, American Indians and Native Alaskans, Asian Americans, and Hispanics. Weinrach & Thomas (2002) believe that the designation of only a few minority groups as worthy of the profession's attention is profoundly demeaning to those minorities not included and that the concerns of other diverse populations, such as women and persons with disabilities, are ignored.

3. Is the role of culture and minority group status in mental health overemphasized in multiculturalism?

    Weinrach & Thomas (2002, 2004) have also raised the issue that multicultural proponents have emphasized that external or environmental forces, such as racism and oppression, largely cause clients' emotional disturbance. Intrapsychic causes are minimized. Weinrach & Thomas argue that a focus on race is an outmoded notion. Race does not provide an adequate explanation of the human condition. Attempts to invoke race as such have been appropriately labeled as racist and inadvertently contribute to America's preoccupation with the pigmentation of a person's skin. Vontress & Jackson (2004) maintain that mental health counselors should look at all factors that affect a client's situation. Race may or may not be one of them. They believe that in general, race is not the real problem in the United States today. The significance that clients attach to it is the most important consideration. However, Vontress & Jackson (2004) believe that in this country, the attention given to discussing cultural differences and similarities is good for society and for our profession.

Finally, Patterson (2004) is concerned over the emphasis on cultural differences. He notes that it has not been fruitful to assume that simply having knowledge of the culture of the client will lead to more appropriate and effective therapy. The first faulty assumption is that counseling or psychotherapy is a matter of information, knowledge, practices, skills, or techniques. Rather, the competent mental health counselor is one who provides an effective therapeutic relationship. The second faulty assumption is that client differences are more important than client similarities. He argues that a treatment such as client-centered therapy is a universal system that cuts across cultures. However, methods that are considered universal usually are Western methods that are assumed to apply to other groups. Most Western therapeutic methods rely heavily on verbal and emotional expression. Yet, among persons of East Asian ancestry, talking has been found to interfere with thinking (Kim 2002), and emo-

tional expression may be dependent on cultural norms (Chentsova-Dutton et al. 2007). In fact, recent research indicates that the psychological consequences of emotional suppression and control can differ depending on the cultural context (Butler et al. 2007).

4. Is the emotional and political context of the debate creating incivility?

Weinrach & Thomas (2004) have indicated that support for cultural competency, created as a logical consequence of the 1960s civil rights movement, is often used as a litmus test of one's commitment to a nonracist society. Weinrach & Thomas (2004, pp. 90–91) state:

Among other goals, they were intended to sensitize White mental health professionals to the unique cultural distinctiveness of male clients on the basis of membership in four visible minority groups. At the symbolic level, they have successfully brought to professional counselors' awareness the importance of attending to the diverse counseling needs of visible minorities. On the applied level, they have been a failure, as we see it. We would prefer to see their demise in order to foster the recognition that client needs should not be assumed to be based upon group membership alone, but rather on the unique constellation of individual client characteristics, including but not limited to cultural distinctiveness.

They lament the fact that persons who refuse to adopt the competencies may be accused of displaying "unintentional racism" or the results of "the insidious ethnocentric aspect of our cultural conditioning" (see Ivey & Ivey 1997, D.W. Sue 1996).

Although heated at times, the debates in the literature have been instructive. First, they help to clarify positions and misunderstandings. For example, most advocates of cultural competency do not see external factors (e.g., racism) as the sole or primary cause of mental disorders or that attention to ethnicity and race lessens concern over other diversity or individual differences (e.g., gender, sexual orientation, social class, etc.) factors (Arredondo & Toporek 2004, Coleman 2004). They recognize individual differences within various ethnic groups, such as the multitude of groups considered Hispanic (e.g., Mexican, Puerto Rican, and Cuban American). Even within a particular group, such as Mexican Americans, there may be considerable variations in level of acculturation that affect the outcomes of cultural competency interventions, as we note below. The emphasis on ethnicity and race is a reaction to centuries of ethnocentric bias against, and inattention to, the importance of culture and minority group status. If, as Bernal & Scharrón-Del-Río (2001) have argued, psychotherapy itself is a cultural phenomenon, ethnic minority concepts may conflict with mainstream values inherent to traditional psychotherapies. Cultural values of interdependence and spirituality, and discrimination in the psychotherapy of ethnic minorities, are often ignored in treatment approaches to ethnic minority clients (Hall 2001). In order to achieve the ecological validity of interventions, these cultural values must be considered in all treatments (Bernal 2006). Given the growing ethnic minority populations and the existing disparities in health and treatment, special attention to race and ethnicity is needed.

Second, there is no single multicultural orientation or cultural competency viewpoint, as noted in our discussion of the definitions of cultural competency. Yet, critics often attack cultural competency by characterizing it with extreme positions (a straw man approach). Satel & Forster (1999) have asserted that the most radical vision of cultural competence claims that membership in an oppressed group is a client's most clinically important attribute. This assertion is misleading because few, if any, would advocate such a view. In addition, cultural competency tactics appear to vary according to the kind of client and the kind of disorders experienced by the client (discussed below).

Third, discussions of culture, ethnicity and race, and multiculturalism are frequently heated and emotional. Emotional reactions to the issues are not unexpected. Race and ethnicity have been highly controversial throughout the history of the United States. As noted by Pope-Davis et al. (2001, pp. 128–129):

> It is our contention that multiculturalism is infused with political meaning. The word itself is a symbol—a trigger—of change that often elicits a range of emotional responses.... We believe that it is also important to acknowledge that, given the history of psychology's inadequacies with diverse populations, multiculturalism is not an apoliticized theory. Much of the research done in the multicultural arena attempts to shift current thinking and institutional practices toward greater equality and recognition of diverse needs and perspectives. This agenda ... implicates the subjective motivation of the researchers in the product.

Finally, much consensus exists over the necessity for more research and over the multitude of unanswered questions and issues. Ridley et al. (1994) indicate that cultural competency lacks theoretical grounding and adequate measures of the construct. Moreover, little research examines ethnic variations in response to treatment (Mak et al. 2007). Despite the questions raised over cultural competency adaptations, the magnitude of mental health disparities in access to and quality of services for ethnic minority populations has spurred actions to address the problems.

WHAT HAS BEEN ACCOMPLISHED SO FAR?

Awareness of treatment disparities and the effects on mental health have stimulated the establishment of local, state, and federal guidelines for the delivery of culturally competent services. For example, the following federal agencies are among the many that have Websites that explain their cultural competency recommendations and guidelines:

- Administration on Aging, U.S. Department of Health & Human Services (HHS) (**http://www.aoa.dhhs.gov/prof/adddiv/cultural/addiv_cult.asp**)

- Office of Minority Health, HHS (**http://www.omhrc.gov/templates/browse.aspx?lvl=1&lvlID=3**)
- Health Resources and Services Administration (**http://www.hrsa.gov/culturalcompetence/**)
- Substance Abuse and Mental Health Services Administration (**http://mentalhealth.samhsa.gov/dtac/CulturalCompetency.asp**)

In terms of psychology organizations, counseling psychologists were among the first to extensively discuss and debate cultural competency issues through organizations such as the Association for Non-White Concerns in Personnel and Guidance in the 1970s and the Association for Multicultural Counseling and Development in the 1980s. Subsequently, many counseling psychologists through APA Division 17 (Counseling Psychology) and the National Institute for Multicultural Competence advocated for multicultural guidelines. Among clinical psychologists, APA Division 12 (Society of Clinical Psychology) established the section on the Clinical Psychology of Ethnic Minorities.

The APA has also had a history of involvement in ethnic, culture, and professional practice. The adoption of the *Guidelines on Multicultural Education, Training, Research, Practice, and Organizational Change for Psychologists* had implications not only for mental health services but also for education, training, and research (Am. Psychol. Assoc. 2003). These guidelines provided a context for service delivery: "Psychologists are encouraged to apply culturally appropriate skills in clinical and other applied psychological practices..." (p. 390). Cross-culturally sensitive practitioners are encouraged to develop skills and practices that are attuned to the unique worldviews and cultural backgrounds of clients by striving to incorporate understanding of a client's ethnic, linguistic, racial, and cultural background into therapy" (p. 391).

Other professional organizations have issued statements, guidelines, or policies regarding cultural competency. For example, the American Psychiatric Association's Steering Committee to Reduce Disparities in Access to Psychiatric Care (2004) developed an action plan to reduce disparities and to increase cultural awareness. Similarly, the National Association of Social Workers defined cultural competency as a set of congruent behaviors, attitudes, and policies that come together in a system or agency or among professionals and enable the system, agency, or professionals to work effectively in multicultural situations. It then developed standards for cultural competence in social work practice (Natl. Assoc. Social Workers 2007).

In the past two decades, cultural competency has been mandated to reduce mental health disparities; at the very least, cultural competency is recommended by various institutions, governmental bodies, and professional organizations. However, the mandates are rather hortatory or aspirational in nature because precise tactics and implementation strategies are unclear. Research is needed to gain knowledge about what works in cultural competency and how it works. It should be noted that most definitions of cultural competency do not include treatment outcomes as the major criteria for competence. This is surprising since it seems reasonable that if certain therapist skills or orientations are more culturally competent, these should be related to better treatment outcomes for ethnic minority clients (or at the minimum, equitable outcomes relative to those of mainstream clients). The proliferation of operational definitions of cultural competence may stem from the fact that these notions of competence have not been held empirically accountable to treatment outcomes—the gold standard (U.S. Surgeon General 2001).

We indicate below the kinds of interventions that characterize cultural competency. We examine the research studies that have tested the effects of culturally competent interventions and discuss outcomes of these studies in the final section.

WHAT KINDS OF CULTURAL COMPETENCY INTERVENTIONS HAVE BEEN ATTEMPTED?

Considerable variation exists in the studies of culturally competent interventions. The interventions have ranged in terms of:

- Intervention approach. A narrow intervention is changing a specific feature of standard treatment practice such as conducting treatment in the ethnic language of the client. Broader interventions are those in which the general treatment approach is determined by the client's ethnicity or in which many different features are based on cultural considerations (e.g., not only having a language match between client and therapist but also an ethnic and cultural match).
- Client problems and issues (e.g., rape prevention, treatment of schizophrenia, prevention of drug abuse, depression, and self-esteem).
- Ethnic/racial groups (African American, American Indian and Alaskan Natives, Asian Americans, and Hispanics). Most studies have been conducted on African Americans and Hispanics. Very few have included American Indians and Alaskan Natives. Some investigations involve more than one ethnic/racial group.
- Intervention type. Studies vary according to individual versus group interventions, treatment versus prevention, and use of standard treatments (e.g., cognitive behavioral treatment) versus specially developed interventions (e.g., *cuento* therapy for Puerto Ricans).

The studies also vary considerably on the type of research design (experimental, correlational, and archival), outcome measures used, the inclusion of control or alternative intervention groups, rigor in design, follow-up assessment, and sample size. In any event, we have classified the studies into certain categories for heuristic purposes only. We discuss culture competency in terms of method of delivery, content, and specialized interventions, which have been programmatically examined, such as cognitive behavioral treatments, storytelling interventions, and family therapies.

Method of Delivery

Method of delivery is intended to make the intervention more culturally consistent, increase credibility of the treatment or provider, or make the treatment understandable to ethnic minority clients. Delivery methods include intervention tactics that respond to the ethnic language of clients (e.g., translating materials or having bilingual therapists), varying the interpersonal style of the intervention (e.g., showing *respeto* or culturally appropriate respect with Hispanics), or providing a cultural context for interventions (Andrés-Hyman et al. 2006). These changes share a common feature in that they involve generic applications; they can be implemented across most types of treatment (e.g., psychodynamic, behavioral, and cognitive-behavioral).

A minimum requirement of the intervention is that therapists must be able to communicate with clients in a manner that is culturally acceptable and appropriate. Clients who have limited English proficiency have difficulties entering, continuing, and benefiting from treatment (Snowden et al. 2007) and appear to need culturally adapted interventions more than do clients who are acculturated and have greater English proficiency (Sue et al. 1991). A number of investigations used therapists who speak the ethnic language of clients who have limited English proficiency. These studies explicitly report that treatment was conducted by therapists who were bilingual or who spoke the language of their clients. The languages have included Spanish (e.g., Armengol 1999, Gallagher-Thompson et al. 2001, Guinn & Vincent 2002, Kopelowicz et al. 2003, Martinez & Eddy 2005), Korean (Shin 2004, Shin & Lukens 2002), and Chinese (Dai et al. 1999). Some studies attempted to see if ethnic match or a related form of match (e.g., cognitive match) between provider and client affected intervention outcomes or processes (Campbell & Alexander 2002, Flaskerud 1986, Flaskerud

& Hu 1994, Mathews et al. 2002, Sue et al. 1991, Takeuchi et al. 1995, Zane et al. 2005). Rather than examining specific therapist-client matches in language or other aspects, some studies have simply examined institutional resources (e.g., the extent to which agencies had therapists who could conduct treatment in the ethnic language of clients) and then correlated treatment outcomes for ethnic clients (Campbell & Alexander 2002, Flaskerud 1986, Flaskerud & Hu 1994, Gamst et al. 2003, Lau & Zane 2000, S. Sue et al. 1991, Yeh et al. 1994). In all of the studies, it is difficult to ascertain the precise factors that account for client outcomes. As mentioned above, most investigations have included many different features of cultural competency, and language was only one of them. For example, having bilingual staff may provide not only language match but also cultural or ethnic match.

Besides language, other cultural competency adaptations were reflected in communication patterns. For instance, patterns of interactions common among less-acculturated Hispanic/Latinos were followed in Armengol's (1999) study involving support group therapy. A formal mode of address was used if that was the stated preference of participants. Even when first names were preferred, the more formal personal pronoun form of "you" (i.e., "*usted*") was employed. Participants also addressed the group facilitator by her professional title (*Doctora*), even when using her first name. The use of such practices is consistent with cultural values involving *respeto* and deference toward authority figures. These communication patterns have also been employed in other intervention strategies such as cognitive behavioral treatment and interpersonal psychotherapy (Miranda et al. 2003a, Rossello et al. 2008). Although showing respect is desirable regardless of the client's culture, knowledge of the culture determines how effectively that respect is shown and delivered.

In some intervention approaches, culturally consistent adaptations have involved the initiation of ceremonies that reflect cultural rituals such as a unity circle, a drum call, the pouring of libation to the ancestors, and a blessing for the day, which are African-based rituals (Harvey & Hill 2004), and use of ethnic foods during intervention (Longshore & Grills 2000).

Content

Content refers to the discussion of, or dealing with, cultural patterns, immigration, minority status, racism, and cultural background experiences in the intervention. The introduction of content may serve to increase understandability and credibility of the intervention and to demonstrate the pertinence of the intervention to the real-life problems experienced by clients (Ponterotto et al. 2006). Most interventions have both delivery and content elements. For example, in a culturally adapted management training intervention for Latino parents, Martinez & Eddy (2005) not only conducted training sessions in Spanish but also addressed culturally relevant immigration and acculturation issues. Similarly, relevant cultural content was included in a support group intervention for Hispanic traumatic brain injury survivors (Armengol 1999) and in an educational intervention program for low-acculturated Latinas (Guinn & Vincent 2002). The interventions included discussions of language, acculturation, spirituality, stressors inherent in the migratory experience, attitudes and beliefs about disability and health care, and support networks.

Interventions involving African American girls (Belgrave 2002, Belgrave et al. 2000), youths (Cherry et al. 1998, Harvey & Hill 2004, Jackson-Gilfort et al. 2001), and adults (Longshore & Grills 2000) have incorporated principles of spirituality, harmony, collective responsibility, oral tradition, holistic approach, experiences with prejudice and discrimination, racial socialization, and interpersonal/communal orientation that are often found in African American worldviews. In a rape prevention program that included many African Americans, Heppner et al. (1999) introduced culturally relevant content (e.g., including specific information about race-related rape myths and statistics on prevalence rates for both blacks and whites and having black and white guest speakers discuss their sexual violence experiences in a cultural context to increase the personal relevancy of the message). Robinson et al. (2003) studied the effects of school-based health center programs for African American students. All of the programs were intended to promote an African American atmosphere and theme. Features ranged from having school decorations and posters (representing Afrocentric perspectives and positive African American role models) to employing African American staff and tailoring services to be delivered in a culturally sensitive manner.

Culturally adapted content has also been used with other ethnic minority groups such as American Indians and Alaska Natives (De Coteau et al. 2006). Fisher et al. (1996) used spiritual groups and cultural awareness training in a residential treatment program in Alaska. Schinke et al. (1988) provided biculturally relevant examples of verbal and nonverbal means of refusing substance use. For instance, leaders modeled how subjects could turn down offers of tobacco, alcohol, and drugs from peers without offending their American Indian and non-American Indian friends. While subjects practiced their communication skills, leaders offered coaching, feedback, and praise. Zane and colleagues (1998) report an example of a preventive intervention program for Asian Americans. The program was intended to prevent substance use and to increase the resiliency of high-risk Asian youths and their families. Group discussions and skill-building exercises for youths focused on Asian familial values, acculturation issues, and intergenerational communication. Parents participated in small-group workshops that also included topics involving cultural values, intergenerational communication, and family.

The studies indicate that cultural competency adaptations can range from simply providing ethnic language provisions to introducing multifaceted changes in intervention philosophy, delivery, and format. Some studies compared cultural adaptations to no-intervention or no-adaptation control groups.

Furthermore, components of cultural competency were not subjected to testing, so it is not possible to attribute possible positive effects of intervention to any particular component (e.g., determining whether treatment outcomes were caused by ethnic language translations or introduction of particular ethnic contents). Before we examine the outcome of cultural competency interventions, we discuss specific kinds of interventions, developed through more programmatic research, that have used cultural adaptations: storytelling, family interventions, and cognitive behavioral therapy.

Storytelling

Many Latinos answer questions by telling a story, thereby allowing the answer to emerge out of their narrative (Comas-Díaz 2006). In order to improve the self-concept, emotional well-being, and adaptive behaviors of Puerto Rican children, researchers (Costantino et al. 1986; Malgady et al. 1990a,b) used *cuentos* (Puerto Rican folktales) or biographies of heroic persons. Folktales often convey a message or a moral to be emulated by others. The investigators incorporated themes such as social judgment, control of aggression, and delay of gratification within Puerto Rican American culture and experiences. By presenting culturally familiar characters of the same ethnicity as the children, they felt that the folktales would serve to motivate attentional processes; make it easier to identify with the beliefs, values, and behaviors portrayed in the adapted *cuentos*; and model functional relationships with parental figures. Therapists, mothers, or group leaders read the *cuentos* bilingually, typically to children at risk for emotional or behavioral problems.

The research designs of the studies often compared adapted *cuento* intervention with original folktales (not adapted to U.S. experiences) to other forms of intervention (e.g., art/play therapy) or to a no-intervention control group. Children were randomly assigned to groups. Results across the various studies yielded favorable emotional and behavioral outcomes for the adapted *cuento* intervention compared with the other groups.

Family

Szapocznik, Santisteban, and their colleagues (Santisteban et al. 1997, 2003, 2006; Szapocznik et al. 1984, 1986, 1989, 1990, 2003) have systematically investigated the effects of specially designed, culturally adapted treatment interventions in families. Brief structural family therapy (BSFT) is an integration of structural and strategic theory and principles. BSFT was created because it was found to be adaptable and acceptable for work with Hispanic families. The investigators believe that the modality is especially suited to the needs of the targeted populations because it emerged out of experience in working with urban minority group families (particularly African American and Puerto Rican) that were disadvantaged in terms of social, cultural, educational, and political position in American society. Some components of the model are used with all families, and others are family specific and may be unique to certain cultural groups (i.e., immigration issues, racial prejudice issues). In BSFT, therapists take an active, directive, present-oriented leadership role that matches the expectations of the population.

Moreover, a structural family approach is consistent with Hispanics' preference for clearly delineated hierarchies within the family. BSFT was able to directly address common acculturation-related stressors, such as acculturation differences and intergenerational conflicts between children and their parents. Research designs for the studies of BSFT often included randomized control trials. In general, BSFT was found to be as good as or (typically) superior to control conditions in reducing parent and youth reports of problems associated with conduct, family functioning, and treatment engagement.

Cognitive Behavioral Therapy

A number of studies have examined whether culturally adapted forms of cognitive behavioral therapy (CBT) are more effective than are nonadapted forms of CBT, whether culturally adapted treatment demonstrates positive outcomes, or whether certain components of CBT are more helpful than others (Jackson et al. 2006, Shen et al. 2006). These studies are important because CBT is effective for many different problems (e.g., anxiety and depression) and for different ethnic populations. Furthermore, because CBT is often delivered with a fixed format or manualized script, it can readily incorporate cultural adaptations and be tested. For example, Kohn and colleagues (2002) examined the degree to which a manualized CBT intervention could be adapted in a culturally sensitive manner in treating depressed low-income African American women experiencing multiple stressors. The adaptations included changes in the language used to describe cognitive-behavioral techniques and inclusion of culturally specific content (e.g., African American family issues) in order to better situate the intervention in an African American context. Compared with a nonadapted CBT intervention group, women in the adapted CBT group exhibited a larger drop in depression. De Coteau et al. (2006) have offered general guidelines for modifying manualized treatments that are particularly applicable to Native Americans living on reservations or in rural tribal communities.

Miranda and her colleagues (2003a) have studied whether cultural adaptations to CBT improve the outcomes of treatment for Hispanics. In randomized trials, the adapted form of CBT consisted of having bilingual and bicultural providers, translating all materials into Spanish, training staff to show *respeto* and *simpatia* to patients, and allowing for somewhat warmer, more personalized interactions than are typical for English-speaking patients. These adaptations were considered to be culturally responsive. The patients who received the adapted CBT had lower dropout rates than those who received CBT alone. There was indication that the effects of adapted CBT were stronger among those whose first language was Spanish rather than English in terms of greater improvement in symptoms and functioning.

Miranda et al. (2003b) have also shown that quality improvement interventions for depressed primary care patients can improve

BSFT: brief structural family therapy

IPT: interpersonal psychotherapy

treatment outcomes for ethnic minority groups. Because ethnic minority clients often receive poorer quality of services than do white clients (U.S. Surgeon General 2001), the investigators wanted to study the effects of quality improvements to care. The culturally adapted improvements included the availability of materials in English and Spanish. Hispanic and African American providers were included in videotaped materials for patients. In addition, providers were given training materials that dealt with cultural beliefs and ways of overcoming barriers to care for Latino and African American patients. The quality improvement interventions resulted in beneficial outcomes. However, because the study included general improvements as well as culturally relevant interventions, it was not possible to determine what factors in the interventions caused the favorable outcomes.

Rossello & Bernal (1999) found that cultural adaptations to CBT and interpersonal psychotherapy (IPT) were more effective than a wait-list control group in reducing depression among Puerto Rican youths. Rossello et al. (2008) maintain that certain treatment approaches, such as CBT and IPT, may intrinsically appeal to the cultural orientation of Latinos. CBT has (*a*) a didactic orientation that provides structure to treatment and education about the therapeutic process; (*b*) a classroom format that reduces the stigma of psychotherapy; (*c*) a match with client expectations of receiving a directive and active intervention from the provider; (*d*) an orientation focused on the present and on problem solving; and (*e*) concrete solutions and techniques to be used when facing problems. On the other hand, IPT focuses largely on the present interpersonal conflicts that are pertinent to Latino values of *familismo* (family) and *personalismo* (personal considerations). The congruence of CBT and IPT with Latino values made it easier for the investigators to adapt them for use with Puerto Rican adolescents. The adolescents were randomly assigned to CBT (individual or group treatment) or IPT (individual or group treatment). Results revealed that all groups demon-

strated decreases in depressive symptoms with CBT that were superior to IPT.

Other studies have introduced cultural adaptations in cognitive behavioral training. Gallagher-Thompson et al. (2001) designed a culturally sensitive eight-week class that taught specific cognitive and behavioral skills for coping with the frustrations associated with caregiving. Hispanic caregivers of dementia victims were assigned to the training class or to a wait-list control group. At the end of the intervention, trained caregivers reported significantly fewer depressive symptoms than did those in the control group. Hinton et al. (2005) has also used CBT to treat Cambodian refugees by using culturally appropriate visualization tasks.

Findings from the CBT studies provide consistent indication that cultural competency interventions are effective, and two of the studies (Kohn et al. 2002, Miranda et al. 2003a) found that cultural competency adaptations to CBT were superior to nonadapted CBT.

IS TREATMENT GENERALLY EFFECTIVE WITH ETHNIC MINORITY POPULATIONS?

As mentioned above, ethnic and racial disparities exist in treatment access and quality. Does this mean that treatment is not effective with ethnic minority populations or that ethnic clients should not seek treatment for mental health problems? Despite the disparities, treatment is needed and can be helpful for all populations (President's New Freedom Commission 2003, U.S. Surgeon General 2001). Ethnic minority populations need access to the best forms of treatment. The questions to be answered include what are the best forms of treatment for ethnic minority populations and whether cultural competency interventions add to positive treatment outcomes.

In the mental health field, widespread attempts have been made to define the best forms of treatment. Outcomes of mental health care are evaluated through two types of research, efficacy and effectiveness studies (Miranda et al. 2005). Efficacy studies, or randomized, controlled trials, are valuable in determining the treatment factors that determine outcomes. They are designed to maximize internal validity and are rigorously conducted, often in strictly controlled settings. Effectiveness research is typically conducted in more real-life situations and may not achieve the rigor and controls found in efficacy studies. It often provides greater external validity than internal validity compared to efficacy studies. Efficacy and effectiveness research is used to guide treatment recommendations. The use of research to establish best practices has resulted in the designation of evidence-based practices (EBPs) and empirically supported treatments (ESTs). EBPs are those psychotherapeutic practices that have demonstrated value through either effectiveness or efficacy research. ESTs are certain types of EBPs that have been shown through rigorous efficacy research to result in positive outcomes. However, little research has been conducted on the value of EBPs and ESTs for ethnic minority populations (Constantine et al. 2008). As late as 1996, Chambless and colleagues (1996) could not find even one EST study that analyzed ethnicity as a variable. More recently, Mak et al. (2007) conducted a review of clinical trial studies. They found that most of the studies reported gender information, and gender representation was balanced across studies. However, less than half of the studies provided complete racial/ethnic information with respect to their samples. Except for whites and African Americans, all racial/ethnic groups were underrepresented, and less than half of the studies had potential for subgroup analyses by gender and race/ethnicity (Mak et al. 2007). Given the paucity of research, the external validity of EBPs has not been clearly established (Whaley & Davis 2007). The lack of research has led many to conclude that the answers are still unclear as to whether EBPs and ESTs are effective with these populations and the conditions under which such treatments are beneficial (Castro et al. 2004, Sue & Zane 2006).

Studies of treatment and preventive intervention effects for ethnic minorities were reviewed by Miranda et al. (2005). In general,

their review concluded that EBPs were effective with different ethnic minority groups and ethnic minority children and adults for a wide range of mental disorders and problem behaviors (e.g., depression, anxiety, and family problems). A meta-analysis of evidence-based treatments for ethnic minority youths was conducted by Huey & Polo (2008). They found that these interventions produced positive overall treatment effects of medium magnitude. However, the investigators raised the possibility that the EBPs and ESTs may sometimes have included cultural adaptations such as performing the interventions in the cultural context of the client, using the client's ethnic language, or integrating cultural elements. We do not know the extent to which research studies use culturally adapted elements but fail to report them. Given the preponderance of evidence that EBPs and ESTs are often effective, are culturally competent adaptations needed?

EBPs: evidence-based practices

ESTs: empirically supported treatments

DO CULTURAL COMPETENCY ADAPTATIONS DEMONSTRATE POSITIVE AND INCREMENTAL EFFECTS ON TREATMENT?

What does research reveal about the effects of cultural competency interventions? Two meta-analyses are pertinent to this question. Griner & Smith (2006) directly examined the effects of cultural competency interventions. Huey & Polo (2008) confined their meta-analysis to ethnic minority youths and indirectly addressed the question after examining the outcomes of evidence-based treatments (and not necessarily cultural-competency studies) for ethnic minority youths.

Because Griner & Smith (2006) is the only meta-analysis to date that has examined the effects of culturally competent interventions, we want to elaborate on its findings. Their meta-analysis revealed that there are controlled, experimental studies of cultural competency. For more than two decades, such studies have appeared, albeit few in number and varying in methodological soundness. Studies included in their meta-analysis largely involved the comparison of culturally adapted mental health interventions to traditional mental health interventions. Griner & Smith (2006) identified 76 studies. Their analysis revealed a moderate effect size for culturally competent interventions [the random effects weighted average effect size was d = 0.45 (SE = 0.04, p < 0.0001), with a 95% confidence interval of d = 0.36 to d = 0.53. The data consisted of 72 nonzero effect sizes, of which 68 (94%) were positive and 4 (6%) were negative. Effect sizes ranged from d = −0.48 to d = 2.7].

Importantly, Griner & Smith (2006) attempted to control for or clarify the effects of other possible confounding variables.

   (a) Publication bias (e.g., studies with statistically significant results are more likely to be published than are studies with statistically nonsignificant results). Their analysis indicated that publication bias does not appear to be a substantial threat to the results obtained in the meta-analysis.
   (b) Participant characteristics (i.e., participant age, clinical status, gender, ethnicity, and level of acculturation). Older individuals had higher effect sizes than younger persons. In general, ethnicity of the client did not moderate the results obtained. In addition, for Hispanic clients, ethnicity tended to interact with acculturation in that low levels of acculturation appeared to profit greatly from culturally competent interventions.
   (c) Research procedures (e.g., experimental versus single-group designs). Overall results were not altered by studies that varied as to the research design, inclusion of control groups, or nature of the control group.
   (d) Type of cultural adaptations. Some studies involved individual therapy whereas many others involved group interventions or a combination of the two. The format of the intervention did not moderate the overall results, nor did the duration of interventions. However, studies that were focused on one ethnic/racial population yielded higher effect sizes

than those in which mixed racial populations were included. Studies in which there were no reports of attempting to match clients and therapists based on ethnicity had average effect sizes that were higher than those of studies in which ethnic matching was generally attempted (but not consistently conducted). Studies in which the client was matched with a therapist based on language (if other than English) had outcomes that were twice as effective as were studies that did not match language.

The contribution of Griner & Smith (2006) is highly significant. Not only do they provide evidence for the value of cultural competency, but they also examine possible confounding effects associated with cultural competency. As recognized by the investigators, their meta-analysis was the first one to be applied to cultural competency studies. Therefore, it included all research reports available, regardless of quality and rigor. Indeed, the reports varied considerably in terms of population studied (problems/disorders, age groups, ethnicity, etc.), methodology (random versus nonrandom assignment to treatment/control conditions, follow-up design, measures used, etc.), and type of treatment (e.g., from English translations of materials to contextual changes in the setting of treatment). Given the diversity of the studies, cultural competency has positive effects on treatment outcomes even though the precise factors that account for the effects cannot be easily specified at this time.

Three positions, ranging in favorability to cultural competency adaptations, have been articulated from reviews. First, Griner & Smith (2006) conclude in their meta-analysis that cultural competency interventions have a moderate positive effect. Second, Miranda et al. (2005) take a more cautious position because of the lack of adequate tests for cultural competency effects. Nevertheless, they state, "In the absence of efficacy studies, the combined used of protocols or guidelines that consider culture and context with evidence-based care is likely to facilitate engagement in treatment and probably to enhance outcomes." Third, in contrast to the conclusions of Smith & Griner (2006), Huey & Polo (2008) state in their meta-analysis:

> ...there is no compelling evidence as yet that these adaptations actually promote better clinical outcomes for ethnic minority youth. Overemphasizing the use of conceptually appealing but untested cultural modifications could inadvertently lead to inefficiencies in the conduct of treatment with ethnic minorities.

Thus, the most discrepant conclusions are derived from the two meta-analyses. The differing conclusions may simply be the result of the nature of the studies. Griner & Smith (2006) included interventions with adults and children, whereas Huey & Polo (2008) focused on children and youths. Interestingly, little overlap exists in the cultural competency adaptation studies that were included in their respective meta-analyses, even when one takes into account the dissimilar time periods for the reviews. This may reflect different inclusion/exclusion criteria used in the two meta-analyses. In addition, differences may exist in how the studies are interpreted. The relatively few rigorous studies that directly compare culturally adapted interventions with nonculturally adapted interventions also add to the problems in trying to draw conclusions. Two studies (Kohn et al. 2002, Miranda et al. 2003a) comparing culturally adapted CBT with nonculturally adapted CBT demonstrated the superiority of the cultural interventions. Finally, it is possible that interventions not considered culturally adapted may contain cultural features. As mentioned above, treatments may include discussions of cultural content even though they are not intended to be culturally adapted interventions. Or the treatments (e.g., CBT) may be inherently consistent with one's cultural orientation, as argued by Rossello et al. (2008). In either case, the manipulation of "not adapted" may be contaminated.

FINAL THOUGHTS

1. The preponderance of evidence shows that culturally adapted interventions provide benefit to intervention outcomes. This added value is more apparent in the research on adults than on children or youths. The additive effect of culturally adapted interventions is consistent with research examining the extent to which an intervention is implemented according to its original design, namely, its fidelity or is adapted. Blakely et al. (1987) found that adaptations involving adding certain features to an intervention were more effective than were adaptations involving replacing a component of the intervention.

2. Culturally competent interventions cover a whole range of activities (e.g., language match, discussions of cultural issues, and delivery of treatment in a culturally consistent manner).

3. Given the relatively few empirical studies of cultural competency, more research is needed, especially randomized clinical trials and "unpackaging" research that examines which cultural adaptations are effective.

4. Therapist, client, and intervention factors probably influence who is most likely to benefit from specific culturally adapted interventions. For example, cultural competency methods are probably more important with unacculturated than with acculturated ethnic minority clients. Individual differences as well as ethnic and cultural differences should be considered in the nature of the intervention delivery styles and content.

5. Little consensus currently exists as to when to use cultural interventions. Some believe that all interventions should be culturally competent in that therapists need to have appropriate cultural awareness, knowledge, and skills to work with clients. The kind-of-person model for

cultural competency argues for cultural competency as an integral part of any treatment. For other multiculturalists, cultural interventions should be introduced under certain conditions. Leong & Lee (2006) have developed a model intended to identify cultural gaps in particular treatments and then to adopt adaptations that address the gaps. Lau (2006) maintains that culturally adapted treatments should be judiciously applied and are warranted (*a*) if evidence exists that a particular clinical problem encountered by a client emerges within a distinct set of risk and resilience factors in a given ethnic community or (*b*) if clients from a given ethnic community respond poorly to certain EBT approaches. In other words, cultural adaptations to EBT should be used if the problems encountered by individuals are influenced by membership in a particular (e.g., ethnic minority) community or if members of that community respond poorly to a standard EBT treatment. Similarly, Zavfert (2008) proposes that an ideographic approach should be taken that would rely on assessment of key cultural factors that are empirically determined to be most relevant to development and maintenance of a particular problem. When specifying culturally competent adaptations, the particular cultural factors affecting the client are considered as well as individual differences in acculturation, experiential background, type of disorder, etc.

6. A major disconnect appears to exist between cultural competency guidelines or recommendations and psychotherapy research examining cultural issues in treatment. The former has tended to focus on characteristics, values, attitudes, and skills on the part of the therapist that can minimize the social and cultural distance between care provider and client, whereas the latter has tended to examine changes in treatment procedures and content that more adequately ad-

dress the cultural experiences of ethnic minority clients. This difference in emphasis on therapist adaptation as opposed to treatment adaptation may partially account for the slow progress made in developing culturally competent mental health care. Norcross & Goldfried (1992) found that therapist and relationship factors accounted for 30% of the improvement in psychotherapy patients, whereas client, family, and other environmental factors accounted for 40%. Specific treatment techniques when combined with the expectancy factors commonly associated with placebo effects accounted for the other 30% of improvement. This research strongly suggests that both therapist and treatment adaptations warrant attention in cultural competency studies. Clearly, research is needed that investigates how these two types of adaptations interact and the separate and combined effects they have on treatment outcomes. For example, in most treatment adaptation studies, the level of therapist skill related to cultural competency is unknown or not assessed. On the other hand, when therapist cultural competency skills are examined, it is unclear if therapists who are deemed culturally competent also may be using certain cultural adaptations in their treatment practices. At the very least, these types of adaptations must be examined or controlled for if research on cultural competence is to proceed in a more informed manner.

7. Finally, the evaluation of the extent to which therapists and interventions effectively address cultural issues is situated in the complex interplay of processes that account for behavior and attitudinal change in psychotherapy. We have noted that theoretical and methodological inadequacies in psychotherapy research have combined to perpetuate imprecise models of change. When it is unclear how people change in psychotherapy and what they have learned in this process, the task

of identifying those aspects of treatment that would make it culturally responsive or competent becomes even more difficult (Zane & Sue 1991).

SUMMARY POINTS

1. There is a growing movement to make services more culturally competent.

2. Cultural competency has been defined in many different ways, and it has provoked considerable controversy over its assumptions, effects, and necessity.

3. Cultural competency interventions have varied considerably, ranging from encompassing an entire treatment program to selected adaptations to existing treatment procedures.

4. Research on cultural competency has increased over time, although research designs have differed in the degree of rigor.

5. The available evidence indicates that cultural competency in psychological interventions and treatments is valuable and needed.

FUTURE ISSUES

Further research is needed to answer the following questions.

1. Is cultural competency better conceptualized as a concrete skill that can be learned by anyone or as a complex process that depends on social interactions?

2. Can a theoretical model be devised that explains cultural competency and why it works?

3. Why do research findings on the effects of culturally competent interventions show so much variability?

4. How can the multicultural guidelines adopted by the American Psychological Association be implemented in research, practice, and training?

5. Can universally beneficial treatment strategies (that apply to everyone) versus beneficial culture-specific interventions (that apply to specific populations) be identified?

DISCLOSURE STATEMENT

The authors are not aware of any biases that might be perceived as affecting the objectivity of this review.

ACKNOWLEDGMENT

This study was supported in part by the Asian American Center on Disparities Research (National Institute of Mental Health grant 1P50MH073511-01A2).

LITERATURE CITED

Agency Healthcare Res. Qual. 2004. *Setting the Agenda on Cultural Competence in Health Care*. Rockville, MD: U.S. Dept. Health Human Serv.

Alvarez AN, Chen GA. 2008. Ruth as an Asian American: a multicultural, integrative perspective. In *Case Approach to Counseling and Psychotherapy*, ed. G Corey. Belmont, CA: Wadsworth

Am. Psychol. Assoc. 2002. Ethical principles of psychologists and code of conduct. *Am. Psychol.* 57(12):1060–73

Am. Psychiatr. Assoc. Steering Comm. to Reduce Disparities in Access to Psychiatr. Care. 2004. *Reducing Mental Health Disparities for Racial and Ethnic Minorities: A Plan of Action.* Washington, DC: Am. Psychiatr. Publ.

Am. Psychol. Assoc. 2003. **Guidelines on multicultural education, training, research, practice, and organizational change for psychologists.** *Am. Psychol.* 58(5):377–402

Andrés-Hyman RC, Ortiz J, Anez LM, Paris M, Davidson L. 2006. Culture and clinical practice: recommendations for working with Puerto Ricans and other Latinas (os) in the United States. *Prof. Psychol. Res. Prac.* 37(6):694–701

Armengol C. 1999. A multimodel support group with Hispanic traumatic brain injury survivors. *J. Head Trauma Rehab.* 14(3):233–46

Arredondo P, Toporek R. 2004. Multicultural counseling competencies=ethical practice. *J. Ment. Health Couns.* 26(1):44–55

Belgrave FZ. 2002. Relational theory and cultural enhancement interventions for African American adolescent girls. *Public Health Rep.* 117(1):76–81

Belgrave FZ, Chase-Vaughn G, Gray F, Addison JD, Cherry VR. 2000. The effectiveness of a culture- and gender-specific intervention for increasing resiliency among African American preadolescent females. *J. Black Psychol.* 26(2):133–47

Bernal G. 2006. Intervention development and cultural adaptation research with diverse families. *Fam. Process.* 45(2):143–51

Bernal G, Scharrón-Del-Río MR. 2001. Are empirically supported treatments valid for ethnic minorities? Toward an alternative approach for treatment research. *Cultur. Divers. Ethnic Minor. Psychol.* 7(4):328–42

Blakely C, Mayer J, Gottschalk R, Schmitt N, Davidson W, et al. 1987. The fidelity-adaptation debate: implications for the implementation of public sector social programs. *Am. J. Commun. Psychol.* 15(3):253–68

Butler EA, Lee TL, Gross JJ. 2007. Emotion regulation and culture: Are the social consequences of emotion suppression culture-specific? *Emotion* 7(1):30–48

Campbell CI, Alexander JA. 2002. Culturally competent treatment practices and ancillary service use in outpatient substance abuse treatment. *J. Subst. Abuse Treat.* 22(3):109–19

Castro FG, Barrera M, Martinez CR. 2004. The cultural adaptation of prevention interventions: resolving tensions between fidelity and fit. *Prevent. Sci.* 5(1):41–45

Chambless DL, Sanderson WC, Shoham V, Bennett-Johnson S, Pope KS, et al. 1996. An update on empirically validated therapies. *Clin. Psychol.* 49(3):5–18

Chentsova-Dutton YE, Chu JP, Tsai JL, Rottenberg J, Gross JJ, Gotlib IH. 2007. Depression and emotional reactivity: variation among Asian Americans of East Asian descent and European Americans. *J. Abnorm. Psychol.* 116(4):776–85

Cherry VR, Belgrave FZ, Jones W, Kennon DK, Gray FS, Phillips S. 1998. NTU: an Africentric approach to substance abuse prevention among African American youth. *J. Primary Prev.* 18(3):319–39

Coleman HLK. 2004. Multicultural counseling competencies in a pluralistic society. *J. Mental Health Couns.* 26(1):56–66

Comas-Díaz L. 2006. Latino healing: the integration of ethnic psychology into psychotherapy. *Psychother. Theory Res. Pract. Train.* 43(4):453–63

Constantine MG. 2002. Predictors of satisfaction with counseling: racial and ethnic minority clients' attitudes toward counseling and ratings of their counselors' general and multicultural counseling competence. *J. Couns. Psychol.* 49(2):255–63

Constantine MG, Miville ML, Kindaichi MM. 2008. Multicultural competence in counseling psychology practice and training. In *Handbook of Counseling Psychology,* ed. SD Brown, RW Lent, pp. 141–58. New York: Wiley

Costantino G, Magady RG, Rogler LH. 1986. Cuento therapy: a culturally sensitive modality for Puerto Rican children. *J. Consult. Clin. Psychol.* 54(5):639–45

Dai Y, Zhang S, Yamamoto J, Ao M, Belin TR, et al. 1999. Cognitive behavioral therapy of minor depressive symptoms in elderly Chinese Americans: a pilot study. *Community Ment. Health J.* 35(6):537–42

De Coteau T, Anderson J, Hope D. 2006. Adapting manualized treatments: treating anxiety disorders among Native Americans. *Cogn. Behav. Pract.* 13(4):304–9

Lists guidelines adopted by the American Psychological Association for multicultural research, practice, and training.

Fisher DG, Lankford BA, Galea RP. 1996. Therapeutic community retention among Alaska Natives: Akeela House. *J. Subst. Abuse Treat.* 13(3):265–71

Flaskerud JH. 1986. The effects of culture-compatible intervention on the utilization of mental health services by minority clients. *Community Ment. Health J.* 22(2):127–41

Flaskerud JH, Hu L. 1994. Participation in and outcome of treatment for major depression among low income Asian-Americans. *Psychiatr. Res.* 53(3):289–300

Fuertes JN, Stracuzzi TI, Bennett J, Scheinholtz J, Mislowack A, et al. 2006. Therapist multicultural competency: a study of therapy dyads. *Psychother. Theory Res. Pract. Train.* 43(4):480–90

Gallagher-Thompson D, Arean P, Rivera P, Thompson LW. 2001. A psychoeducational intervention to reduce distress in Hispanic family caregivers: results of a pilot study. *Clin. Gerontol.* 23(1–2):17–32

Gamst G, Aguilar-Kitibutr A, Herdina A, Hibbs S, Krishtal E, et al. 2003. Effects of racial match on Asian American mental health consumer satisfaction. *Ment. Health Serv. Res.* 5(4):197–208

Griner D, Smith TB. 2006. Culturally adapted mental health intervention: a meta-analytic review. *Psychother. Theory Res. Pract. Train.* 43(4):531–48

Guinn B, Vincent V. 2002. A health intervention on Latina spiritual well-being constructs: an evaluation. *Hispanic J. Behav. Sci.* 24(3):379–91

Hall GCN. 2001. Psychotherapy research with ethnic minorities: empirical, ethical, and conceptual issues. *J. Consult. Clin. Psychol.* 69(3):502–10

Hall GCN, Iwamasa GY, Smith JN. 2003. Ethical principles of the psychology profession and ethnic minority issues. In *Handbook of Professional Ethics for Psychologists: Issues, Questions, and Controversies*, ed. W O'Donohue, KE Ferguson, pp. 301–18. Thousand Oaks, CA: Sage

Harvey AR, Hill RB. 2004. Africentric youth and family rites of passage program: promoting resilience among at-risk African American youths. *Soc. Work* 49(1):65–71

Heppner MJ, Neville HA, Smith K, Kivlighan DM Jr, Gershuny BS. 1999. Examining immediate and long-term efficacy of rape prevention programming with racially diverse college men. *J. Couns. Psychol.* 46(1):16–26

Herman KC, Merrell KW, Reinke WM, Tucker CM. 2004. The role of school psychology in preventing depression. *Psychol. Schools* 41(7):763–75

Herman KC, Tucker CM, Ferdinand LA, Mirsu-Paun A, Hasan NT, Beato C. 2007. Culturally sensitive health care and counseling psychology: an overview. *Couns. Psychol.* 35(5):633–49

Hinton DE, Chhean D, Pich V, Safren SA, Hofmann SG, Pollack MH. 2005. A randomized controlled trial of cognitive-behavior therapy for Cambodian refugees with treatment-resistant PTSD and panic attacks: a cross-over design. *J. Trauma Stress* 18(6):617–29

Huey SJ Jr, Polo AJ. 2008. Evidence-based psychosocial treatments for ethnic minority youth: a review and meta-analysis. *J. Clin. Child Adolesc. Psychol.* 37(1):262–301

Hwang W. 2006. The psychotherapy adaptation and modification framework: application to Asian Americans. *Am. Psychol.* 61(7):702–15

Ivey MB, Ivey AE. 1997. And now we begin. *Couns. Today* 40:42

Jackson LC, Schmutzer PA, Wenzel A, Tyler JD. 2006. Applicability of cognitive-behavior therapy with American Indian individuals. *Psychother. Theory Res. Pract. Train.* 43(4):505–17

Jackson-Gilfort A, Liddle HA, Tejeda MJ, Dakof GA. 2001. Facilitating engagement of African American male adolescents in family therapy: a cultural theme process study. *J. Black Psychol.* 27(3):321–40

Kim HS. 2002. We talk, therefore we think? A cultural analysis of the effect of talking on thinking. *J. Personal. Soc. Psychol.* 83(4):828–42

Kohn LP, Oden T, Munoz RF, Robinson A, Leavitt D. 2002. Adapted cognitive behavioral group therapy for depressed low-income African American women. *Community Ment. Health J.* 38(6):497–504

Kopelowicz A, Zarate R, Smith VG, Mintz J, Liberman RP. 2003. Disease management in Latinos with schizophrenia: a family-assisted, skills training approach. *Schizophrenia Bull.* 29(2):211–28

Lau AS. 2006. Making the case for selective and directed cultural adaptations of evidence-based treatments: examples from parent training. *Clin. Psychol. Sci. Pract.* 13(4):295–310

Lau AS, Zane N. 2000. Examining the effects of ethnic-specific services: an analysis of cost-utilization and treatment outcome for Asian American clients. *J. Community Psychol.* 28(1):63–77

Provides a meta-analysis of research pertaining to evidence-based treatments for ethnic minority youths.

Discusses the conditions under which cultural adaptations should be utilized.

Leong FTL, Lee S. 2006. A cultural accommodation model for cross-cultural psychotherapy: illustrated with the case of Asian Americans. *Psychother. Theory Res. Pract. Train.* 43(4):410–23

Lo HT, Fung KP. 2003. Culturally competent psychotherapy. *Can. J. Psychiatry* 48(3):161–70

Longshore D, Grills C. 2000. Motivating illegal drug use recovery: evidence for a culturally congruent intervention. *J. Black Psychol.* 26(3):288–301

López SR. 1997. Cultural competence in psychotherapy: a guide for clinicians and their supervisors. In *Handbook for Psychotherapy Supervision*, ed. CE Watkins Jr, pp. 570–88. Hoboken, NJ: Wiley

Mak WWS, Law RW, Alvidrez J, Perez-Stable EJ. 2007. Gender and ethnic diversity in NIMH-funded clinical trials: review of a decade of published research. *Adm. Policy Ment. Health* 34(6):497–503

Malgady R, Rogler LH, Costantino G. 1990a. Culturally sensitive psychotherapy for Puerto Rican children and adolescents: a program of treatment outcome research. *J. Consult. Clin. Psychol.* 58:704–12

Malgady R, Rogler LH, Costantino G. 1990b. Hero/heroine modeling for Puerto Rican adolescents: a preventive mental health intervention. *J. Consult. Clin. Psychol.* 58:469–74

Martinez CR, Eddy JM. 2005. Effects of culturally adapted parent management training on Latino youth behavioral health outcomes. *J. Consult. Clin. Psychol.* 73(5):841–51

Mathews CA, Glidden D, Murray S, Forster P, Hargreaves WA. 2002. The effect of treatment outcomes of assigning patients to ethnically focused inpatient psychiatric units. *Psychiatr. Serv.* 53:830–35

Miranda J, Azocar F, Organista K, Dwyer E, Areane P. 2003a. Treatment of depression among impoverished primary care patients from ethnic minority groups. *Psychiatr. Serv.* 54:219–25

Miranda J, Bernal G, Lau A, Kohn L, Hwang W, La Fromboise T. 2005. State of the science on psychosocial interventions for ethnic minorities. *Annu. Rev. Clin. Psychol.* 1:113–42

Miranda J, Duan N, Sherbourne C, Schoenbaum M, Lagomasino I, et al. 2003b. Improving care for minorities: Can quality improvement interventions improve care and outcomes for depressed minorities? Results of a randomized, controlled trial. *Health Serv. Res.* 38(2):613–30

Natl. Assoc. Social Workers. 2007. Indicators for the achievement of the NASW standards for cultural competence in social work practice. Washington, DC: Natl. Assoc. Social Workers

Norcross JC, Goldfried MR. 1992. *Handbook of Psychotherapy Integration*. New York: Basic Books

Patterson CH. 2004. Do we need multicultural counseling competencies? *J. Ment. Health Couns.* 26(1):67–73

Pistole MC. 2004. Editor's note of multicultural competencies. *J. Ment. Health Couns.* 26(1):39–40

Pole N, Gone JP, Kulkarni M. 2008. Posttraumatic stress disorder among ethnoracial minorities in the United States. *Clin. Psychol. Sci. Pract.* 15(1):35–61

Ponterotto JG, Utsey SO, Pedersen PB. 2006. *Preventing Prejudice: A Guide for Counselors, Educators, and Parents*. Los Angeles, CA: Sage

Pope-Davis DB, Liu WM, Toporek RL, Brittan-Powell CS. 2001. What's missing from multicultural competency research: review, introspection, and recommendations. *Cult. Divers. Ethnic Minority Psychol.* 7(2):121–38

President's New Freedom Commission on Mental Health. 2003. Achieving the Promise: Transforming Mental Health care in America. *Report of the President's New Freedom Commission on Mental Health.* Rockville, MD

Ridley CR. 1985. Imperatives for ethnic and cultural relevance in psychology training programs. *Prof. Psychol. Res. Pract.* 16(5):611–22

Ridley C, Mendoza D, Kanitz B. 1994. Multicultural training: reexamination, operationalization, and integration. *Couns. Psychol.* 22:227–89

Robinson W, Harper G, Schoeny M. 2003. Reducing substance use among African American adolescents: effectiveness of school-based health centers. *Clin. Psychol. Sci. Pract.* 10(4):491–504

Rossello J, Bernal G. 1999. The efficacy of cognitive-behavioral and interpersonal treatments for depression in Puerto Rican adolescents. *J. Consult. Clin. Psych.* 67:734–45

Rossello J, Bernal G, Rivera-Medina C. 2008. Individual and group CBT and IPT for Puerto Rican adolescents with depressive symptoms. *Cult. Divers. Ethnic Minority Psychol.* 14(3):234–45

Santisteban DA, Coatsworth JD, Perez-Vidal A, Mitrani V, Jean-Gilles M, Szapocznik J. 1997. Brief structural strategic family therapy with African American and Hispanic high-risk youth: a report of outcome. *J. Community Psychol.* 25:453–71

Serves as a model for devising and testing cultural interventions with ethnic minority groups.

Santisteban DA, Coatsworth JD, Perez-Vidal A, Kurtines WM, Schwartz SJ, et al. 2003. Efficacy of brief strategic family therapy in modifying Hispanic adolescent behavior problems and substance use. *J. Fam. Psychol.* 17(1):121–33

Santisteban DA, Suarez-Morales L, Robbins MS, Szapocznik J. 2006. Brief strategic family therapy: lessons learned in efficacy research and challenges to blending research and practice. *Fam. Process.* 45(2):259–71

Satel S. 2000. *PC, M.D.: How Political Correctness is Corrupting Medicine.* New York: Basic Books

Satel S, Forster G. 1999. *Multicultural Mental Health: Does Your Skin Color Matter More Than Your Mind?* Washington, DC: Center for Equal Opportunity

Schinke S, Orlandi M, Botvin G, Gilchrist L, Trimble J, Locklear V. 1988. Preventing substance abuse among American-Indian adolescents: a bicultural competence skills approach. *J. Couns. Psychol.* 35:87–90

Schulman KA, Berlin JA, Harless W, Kerner JF, Sistrunk S, et al. 1999. The effect of race and sex on physicians' recommendations for cardiac catheterization. *New Engl. J. Med.* 340(8):618–26

Shen EK, Alden LE, Sochting I, Tsang P. 2006. Clinical observations of a Cantonese cognitive-behavioral treatment program for Chinese immigrants. *Psychother. Theory Res. Pract. Train.* 43(4):518–30

Shin S. 2004. Effects of culturally relevant psychoeducation for Korean American families of persons with chronic mental illness. *Res. Social Work Pract.* 14:231–39

Shin S, Lukens E. 2002. Effects of psychoeducation for Korean Americans with chronic mental illness. *Psychiatr. Serv.* 53:1125–31

Smedley BD, Smith AY, Nelson AR, eds. 2003. *Unequal Treatment: Confronting Racial and Ethnic Disparities in Health Care.* Washington, DC: Natl. Acad. Press. 764 pp.

Snowden L, Masland M, Guerrero R. 2007. Federal civil rights policy and mental health treatment access for persons with limited English proficiency. *Am. Psychol.* 62(2):109–17

Sue DW. 1996. ACES endorsement of the multicultural counseling competencies: Do we have the courage? *ACES Spectrum* 57(1):9–10

Sue DW, Arredondo P, McDavis R. 1992. Multicultural counseling competencies and standards: a call to the profession. *J. Couns. Dev.* 70:477–86

Sue DW, Bernier JB, Duran M, Feinberg L, Pedersen P, et al. 1982. Position paper: cross-cultural counseling competencies. *Couns. Psychol.* 10(2):45–52

Sue DW, Torino GC. 2005. Racial-cultural competence: awareness, knowledge, and skills. In *Handbook of Racial-Cultural Psychology and Counseling: Training and Practice. Vol. 2*, ed. RT Carter, pp. 3–18. Hoboken, NJ: Wiley

Sue S. 1998. In search of cultural competence in psychotherapy and counseling. *Am. Psychol.* 53:440–48

Sue S, Fujino D, Hu L, Takeuchi D, Zane N. 1991. Community mental health services for ethnic minority groups: a test of the cultural responsiveness hypothesis. *J. Clin. Consult. Psychol.* 59:533–40

Sue S, Zane N. 2006. Ethnic minority populations have been neglected by evidence-based practices. In *Evidence-Based Practices in Mental Health: Debate and Dialogue on the Fundamental Questions*, ed. JC Norcross, LE Beutler, RF Levant, pp. 338–45, 359–61. Washington, DC: Am. Psychol. Assoc.

Szapocznik J, Amaro H, Gonzalez G, Schwartz SJ, Castro FG, et al. 2003. Drug abuse treatment for Hispanics. In *National Strategic Plan on Hispanic Drug Abuse Research: From the Molecule to the Community*, ed. H Amaro, DE Cortés, pp. 91–117. Boston: Northeastern Univ. Inst. Urban Health Res.

Szapocznik J, Kurtines W, Santisteban DA, Rio AT. 1990. Interplay of advances between theory, research, and application in treatment interventions aimed at behavior problem children and adolescents. *J. Consult. Clin. Psychol.* 58(6):696–703

Szapocznik J, Rio A, Perez-Vidal A, Kurtines W, Hervis O, Santisteban D. 1986. Bicultural effectiveness training (BET): an experimental test of an intervention modality for families experiencing intergenerational/intercultural conflict. *Hispanic J. Behav. Sci.* 8:303–30

Szapocznik J, Santisteban D, Kurtines W, Perez-Vidal A, Hervis O. 1984. Bicultural effectiveness training (BET): a treatment intervention for enhancing intercultural adjustment. *Hispanic J. Behav. Sci.* 6:317–44

Szapocznik J, Santisteban D, Rio A, Perez-Vidal A, Kurtines W. 1989. Family effectiveness training: an intervention to prevent drug abuse and problem behaviors in Hispanic adolescents. *Hispanic J. Behav. Sci.* 11:4–27

Evaluates the programmatic research using brief strategic family therapy primarily with Hispanic families.

Presents issues that later deeply influenced the multicultural guidelines adopted by the American Psychological Association.

Notes the complexities and complications in using evidence-based practices with ethnic minority populations.

Takeuchi D, Sue S, Yeh M. 1995. Return rates and outcomes from ethnicity-specific mental health programs in Los Angeles. *Am. J. Public Health* 85:638–43

Thomas K, Weinrach S. 2004. Mental health counseling and the AMCD multicultural counseling competencies: a civil debate. *J. Ment. Health Couns.* 26:41–43

Trimble JE. 2003. Cultural sensitivity and cultural competence. In *The Portable Mentor: Expert Guide to a Successful Career in Psychology*, ed. M Prinstein, M Patterson, pp. 13–32. New York: Kluwer Acad./Plenum

Trimble JE. 2008. Cultural considerations and perspectives for providing psychological counseling for Native American Indians. In *Counseling Across Cultures*, ed. PB Pedersen, JG Draguns, WJ Lonner, JE Trimble, pp. 93–111. Los Angeles, CA: Sage

U.S. Dep. Health Human Serv. 2002. Health Resources and Services Administration. *Definitions of cultural competence.* **http://bhpr.hrsa.gov/diversity/cultcomp.htm**

U.S. Surgeon General. 2001. *Mental health: culture, race, and ethnicity. A supplement to mental health: a report of the Surgeon General*. Rockville, MD: U.S. Dep. Health Human Serv.

Vontress C, Jackson M. 2004. Reactions to the multicultural counseling competencies debate. *J. Ment. Health Couns.* 26:74–80

Weinrach SG, Thomas KR. 2002. A critical analysis of the multicultural counseling competencies: implications for the practice of mental health counseling. *J. Ment. Health Couns.* 24(1):20–35

Weinrach SG, Thomas KR. 2004. The AMCD multicultural counseling competencies: a critically flawed initiative. *J. Ment. Health Couns.* 26:81–93

Whaley A, Davis K. 2007. Cultural competence and evidence-based practice in mental health services: a complementary perspective. *Am. Psychol.* 62:563–74

Yeh M, Takeuchi DT, Sue S. 1994. Asian American children in the mental health system: a comparison of parallel and mainstream outpatient service centers. *J. Clin. Child Psychol.* 23(1):5–12

Zane N, Aoki B, Ho T, Huang L, Jang M. 1998. Dosage-related changes in a culturally-responsive prevention program for Asian American youth. *Drugs Soc.* 12:105–25

Zane N, Sue S. 1991. Culturally-responsive mental health services for Asian Americans: treatment and training issues. In *Ethnic Minority Perspectives on Clinical Training and Services in Psychology*, ed. H Myers, P Wohlford, P Guzman, R Echemendia, pp. 48–59. Washington, DC: Am. Psychol. Assoc.

Zane N, Sue S, Chang J, Huang L, Huang J, et al. 2005. Beyond ethnic match: effects of client-therapist cognitive match in problem perception, coping orientation, and treatment goals on treatment outcomes. *J. Community Psychol.* 33(5):569–85

Zavfert C. 2008. Culturally competent treatment of posttraumatic stress disorder in clinical practice: an ideographic, transcultural approach. *Clin. Psychol. Sci. Pract.* 15(1):68–73

The best single source on mental health issues faced by ethnic minority populations in the United States.

Missing Data Analysis:
Making It Work
in the Real World

John W. Graham

Department of Biobehavioral Health and the Prevention Research Center, The Pennsylvania State University, University Park, Pennsylvania 16802; email: jgraham@psu.edu

Annu. Rev. Psychol. 2009. 60:549–576

First published online as a Review in Advance on July 24, 2008

The *Annual Review of Psychology* is online at psych.annualreviews.org

This article's doi:
10.1146/annurev.psych.58.110405.085530

Key Words

multiple imputation, maximum likelihood, attrition, nonignorable missingness, planned missingness

Abstract

This review presents a practical summary of the missing data literature, including a sketch of missing data theory and descriptions of normal-model multiple imputation (MI) and maximum likelihood methods. Practical missing data analysis issues are discussed, most notably the inclusion of auxiliary variables for improving power and reducing bias. Solutions are given for missing data challenges such as handling longitudinal, categorical, and clustered data with normal-model MI; including interactions in the missing data model; and handling large numbers of variables. The discussion of attrition and nonignorable missingness emphasizes the need for longitudinal diagnostics and for reducing the uncertainty about the missing data mechanism under attrition. Strategies suggested for reducing attrition bias include using auxiliary variables, collecting follow-up data on a sample of those initially missing, and collecting data on intent to drop out. Suggestions are given for moving forward with research on missing data and attrition.

Contents

INTRODUCTION AND OVERVIEW

Missing data have challenged researchers since the beginnings of field research. The challenge has been particularly acute for longitudinal research, that is, research involving multiple waves of measurement on the same individuals. The main issue is that the analytic procedures researchers use, many of which were developed early in the twentieth century, were designed to have complete data. Until relatively recently, there was simply no mechanism for handling the responses that were sometimes missing within a particular survey, or whole surveys that were missing for some waves of a multiwave measurement project.

Problems brought about by missing data began to be addressed in an important way starting in 1987, although a few highly influential articles did appear before then (e.g., Dempster et al. 1977, Heckman 1979, Rubin 1976). What happened in 1987 was nothing short of a revolution in thinking about analysis of missing data. The revolution began with two major books that were published that year. Little & Rubin (1987) published their classic book, *Statistical Analysis with Missing Data* (the second edition was published in 2002). Also, Rubin

(1987) published his book, *Multiple Imputation for Nonresponse in Surveys*. These two books, coupled with the advent of powerful personal computing, would lay the groundwork for missing data software to be developed over the next 20 years and beyond. Also published in 1987 were two articles describing the first truly accessible method for dealing with missing data using existing structural equation modeling (SEM) software (Allison 1987, Muthén et al. 1987). Finally, Tanner & Wong (1987) published their article on data augmentation, which would become a cornerstone of the multiple imputation (MI) software that would be developed a decade later.

Goals of This Review

A major goal of this review is to present ideas and strategies that will make missing data analyses useful to researchers. My aim here is to encourage researchers to use the missing data procedures that are already known to be good ones. Efforts toward this goal involve summarizing the major research in missing data analysis over the past several years. However, much of the reluctance to adopt these procedures is related to the myths and misconceptions that continue to abound about the impact of missing data with and without using these procedures. Thus, a goal of this review is to clear up many of the myths and misconceptions surrounding missing data and analysis with missing data.

Work is required to become a practiced user of the acceptable (i.e., MI and maximum-likelihood, or ML) procedures. But that work would be a lot less onerous if one had confidence that learning these procedures would truly make one's work better and that criticisms surrounding missing data would be materially reduced.

Researchers should use MI and ML procedures (see Schafer & Graham 2002). They are good procedures that are based on strong statistical traditions. They can certainly be improved on, but by how much? I would argue that using MI and ML procedures gets us at least 90% of the way to the hypothetical ideal from where

we were 25 years ago. Newer procedures will continually fine-tune the existing MI and ML procedures, but the main missing data solutions are already available and should be used now.

Above all, my goal is that this review will be of practical value. I hope that my words will facilitate the use of MI and ML missing data methods. This is not intended to be a thorough review of all work and methods relating to missing data. I have focused on what I believe to be most useful.

What's to Come

In the following sections, I discuss three major missing data topics: missing data theory, analysis in practice, and attrition and missingness that is not missing at random. In the first major section, I lay out the main tenets of what I refer to as "missing data theory." One central focus in this section is the causes or mechanisms of missingness. In this section, I discuss what I refer to as the "old" methods for dealing with missing data, but as much as possible, my discussion is limited to methods that remain useful at least in some circumstances. This section briefly presents the methods I fully endorse: MI and ML.

In the second major section, I focus on the practical side of performing missing data analyses. Over the years, I have faced all of these problems as a data analyst; these are real solutions. Sometimes the solutions are a bit ad hoc. Better solutions may become available in the future, but the solutions I present are known to have minimal harmful impact on statistical inference, and they will keep you doing analysis, which is the most important thing. In this section, I also touch on the developing area of planned missingness designs, an area that opens up new design possibilities for researchers who are already making use of the recommended MI and ML missing data procedures. Contrary to the old adage that the best solution to missing data is not to have them, there are times when building missing data into the overall measurement design is the best use of limited resources.

In the final major section, I describe the area of attrition and missingness that is not missing at random. This kind of missingness has proven to be a major obstacle, especially in longitudinal and intervention research. A good bit of the problem in this area stems from the fact that the framework for thinking about these issues was developed and solidified well before the missing data revolution. In this section, I propose a different framework for thinking about attrition and make several suggestions (pleas?) as to how researchers might proceed in this area.

MISSING DATA THEORY

Causes or Mechanisms of Missingness

Statisticians talk about missingness mechanisms. But what they mean by that term differs from what social and behavioral scientists think of as mechanisms. When I (trained as an experimental social psychologist) use that word, I think of causal mechanisms. What is the reason the data are missing? Statisticians, on the other hand, often are thinking more along the lines of a description of the missingness. For example, it is not uncommon to talk about a vector R for each variable, which takes on the value "1" if the variable has data for that case, and "0" if the value is missing for that case. This leads naturally to descriptions of the missing data, that is, patterns of missingness. For example, suppose that one has three variables (X, Y_1, and Y_2), and suppose that X is never missing but Y_1 is missing for some individuals, and Y_2 is missing for a few more. Or, thinking about it the other way, suppose one has data for all three variables for some number of cases, but partial data (X and Y_1) for some number of cases and partial data (X only) for some other number of cases. The patterns of missingness for a hypothetical $N = 100$ cases might look like those shown in **Table 1**. Also, as shown in **Table 1**, it not uncommon for a small number of cases to be present at one wave, missing at a later wave, and then give data at a still later wave.

When people talk about the mechanisms of missingness, three terms come up: miss-

Table 1 Hypothetical patterns of missingness

Variable			
X	Y_1	Y_2	N
1	1	1	65
1	1	0	20
1	0	0	10
1	0	1	5

1 = value present; 0 = value missing.

ing completely at random (MCAR), missing at random (MAR), and missing not at random (MNAR). Although statisticians prefer not to use the word "cause," they do often use the words "due to" or "depends on" in this context.

With MAR, the missingness (i.e., whether the data are missing or not) may depend on observed data, but not on unobserved data (Schafer & Graham 202).

MCAR is a special case of MAR in which missingness does not depend on the observed data either (Schafer & Graham 2002).

With MNAR, missingness does depend on unobserved data.

More about MAR, MCAR, and MNAR. Although these three important terms do have specific statistical definitions, their practical meaning is often elusive. MCAR is perhaps the easiest to understand. If the cases for which the data are missing can be thought of as a random sample of all the cases, then the missingness is MCAR. This means that everything one might want to know about the data set as a whole can be estimated from any of the missing data patterns, including the pattern in which data exist for all variables, that is, for complete cases (e.g., see the top row in **Table 1**).

Another aspect of MCAR that is particularly easy to understand for psychologists is that the word "random" in MCAR means what psychologists generally think of when they use the term. The word "random" in MAR, however, means something rather different from what psychologists typically think of as random. In fact, the randomness in MAR missingness means that once one has conditioned on (e.g., controlled for) all the data one has, any remaining missingness is completely random (i.e., it does not depend on some unobserved variable). Because of this, I often say that a more precise term for missing at random would be conditionally missing at random. However, if such a term were in common use, its acronym (CMAR) would often be confused with MCAR. Thus, my feeling about this is that psychologists should continue to refer to MCAR and MAR but simply understand that the latter term refers to conditionally missing at random.

Another distinction that is often used with missingness is the distinction between ignorable and nonignorable missingness. Without going into detail here, suffice it to say that ignorable missingness applies to MCAR and MAR, whereas nonignorable missingness is often used synonymously with MNAR.

An important wrinkle with these terms, especially MAR and MNAR (or ignorable and nonignorable), is that they do not apply just to the data. Rather they apply jointly to the data and to the analysis that is being used. For example, suppose one develops a smoking prevention intervention and has a treatment group and a control group (represented by a dummy variable called Program). Suppose that one measures smoking status at time 2, one year after implementation of the prevention intervention (Smoking$_2$). Finally, suppose that some people have missing data for Smoking$_2$, and that missingness on Smoking$_2$ depends on smoking status measured at time 1, just before the program implementation (Smoking$_1$). If one includes Smoking$_1$ in one of the acceptable missing data procedures (MI or ML), then the missingness on Smoking$_2$ is conditioned on Smoking$_1$ and is thus MAR (note that even with complete case analysis, the regression analysis of Program predicting Smoking$_2$ is MAR as long as Smoking$_1$ is also included in the model; e.g., see Graham & Donaldson 1993). However, if the researcher tested a model in which the Program alone predicted Smoking$_2$, then the missingness would become MNAR because the researcher failed to condition on Smoking$_1$, the cause of missingness.

Many researchers have suggested modifying the names of the missing data mechanisms in order to have labels that are a bit closer to regular language usage. However, missing data theorists believe that these mechanism names should remain as is. I agree. I now believe we would be doing psychologists a disservice if we encouraged them to abandon these terms, which are so well entrenched in the statistics literature. Rather, we should continue to use these terms (MCAR, MAR, and MNAR), but always define them very carefully using regular language.

Consequences of MCAR, MAR, and MNAR. The main consequence of MCAR missingness is loss of statistical power. The good thing about MCAR is that analyses yield unbiased parameter estimates (i.e., estimates that are close to population values). MAR missingness (i.e., when the cause of missingness is taken into account) also yields unbiased parameter estimates. The reason MNAR missingness is considered a problem is that it yields biased parameter estimates (discussed at length below).

Old Analyses: A Brief Summary

This summary is not intended to be a thorough examination of the "old" approaches for dealing with missing data. Rather, in order to be of most practical value, the discussion below focuses on the old approaches that can still be useful, at least under some circumstances.

Yardsticks for evaluating methods. I have judged the various methods (old and new) by three means. First, the method should yield unbiased parameter estimates over a wide range of parameters. That is, the parameter estimate should be close to the population value for that parameter. Some of the methods I would judge to be unacceptable (e.g., mean substitution) may yield a mean for a particular variable that is close to the true parameter value (e.g., under MCAR), but other parameters using this method can be seriously biased. Second, there should be a method for assessing the degree of uncertainty about parameter estimates. That is, one should be able to obtain reasonable estimates of the standard error or confidence intervals. Third, once bias and standard errors have been dealt with, the method should have good statistical power.

Complete cases analysis (AKA, listwise deletion). This approach can be very useful even today. One concern about listwise deletion is that it may yield biased parameter estimates (e.g., see Wothke 2000). For example, groups with complete data, especially in a longitudinal study, often are quite different from those that have missing data. Nevertheless, the difference in those two groups often is embodied completely in the pretest variables (for which everyone has data). Thus, as long as those variables can reasonably be included in the model as covariates, the bias is often minimal, even with listwise deletion, especially for multiple regression models (e.g., see Graham & Donaldson 1993).

However, there will always be some loss of power with listwise deletion because of the unused partial data. And in some instances, this loss of power can be huge, making this method an undesirable option. Still, if the loss of cases due to missing data is small (e.g., less than about 5%), biases and loss of power are both likely to be inconsequential. I, personally, would still use one of the missing data approaches even with just 5% missing cases, and I encourage you

to get used to doing the same. However, if a researcher chose to stay with listwise deletion under these special circumstances, I believe it would be unreasonable for a critic to argue that it was a bad idea to do so. It is also important that standard errors based on listwise deletion are meaningful.

Pairwise deletion. Pairwise deletion is usually used in conjunction with a correlation matrix. Each correlation is estimated based on the cases having data for both variables. The issue with pairwise deletion is that different correlations (and variance estimates) are based on different subsets of cases. Because of this, it is possible that parameter estimates based on pairwise deletion will be biased. However, in my experience, these biases tend to be small in empirical data. On the other hand, because different correlations are based on different subsets of cases, there is no guarantee that the matrix will be positive definite (see sidebar Positive Definite). Nonpositive definite matrices cannot be used for most multivariate statistical analyses. A bigger concern with pairwise deletion is that there is no basis for estimating standard errors.

Because of all these problems, I cannot recommend pairwise deletion as a general solution. However, I do still use pairwise deletion in one specific instance. When I am conducting preliminary exploratory factor analysis with a large number of variables, and publication of the factor analysis results, per se, is not my goal, I sometimes find it useful to conduct this analysis with pairwise deletion. As a preliminary analysis for conducting missing data analysis, I sometimes examine the preliminary eigenvalues from principal components analysis (see sidebar Eigenvalue). If the last eigenvalue is positive, then the matrix is positive definite. Many failures of the expectation-maximization (better known as EM) algorithm (and MI) are due to the correlation matrix not being positive definite.

Other "old" methods. Other old methods include mean substitution, which I do not recommend. In the "Modern" Missing Data Analysis

---

POSITIVE DEFINITE

One good way to think of a matrix that is not positive definite is that the matrix contains less information than implied by the number of variables in the matrix. For example, if a matrix contained the correlations of three variables (A, B, and C) and their sum, then there would be just three variables worth of information, even though it contained four variables. Because the sum is perfectly predicted by the three variables, it adds no new information, and the matrix would not be positive definite.

Methods section, I describe a method based on the EM algorithm that is much preferred over mean substitution (see the sections on Good Uses of the EM Algorithm and Imputing a Single Data Set from EM Parameters). A second method that has been described in the literature involves using a missingness dummy variable in addition to the specially coded missing value. This approach has been discredited and should not be used (e.g., see Allison 2002). Finally, regression-based single imputation has been employed in the past. Although the concept is a sound one and is the basis for many of the modern procedures, this method is not recommended in general.

"Modern" Missing Data Analysis Methods

The "modern" missing data procedures I consider here are (a) the EM algorithm, (b) multiple imputation under the normal model, and (c) ML methods, often referred to as full-information maximum likelihood (FIML) methods.

EM algorithm. It is actually a misnomer to refer to this as "the" EM algorithm because there are different EM algorithms for different applications. Each version of the EM algorithm reads in the raw data and reads out a different product, depending on the application. I describe here the EM algorithm that reads in the raw data, with missing values, and reads out an ML variance-covariance matrix and vector of means. Definitive technical treatments of various EM algorithms are given in Little & Rubin (1987, 2002) and Schafer (1997). Graham and colleagues provide less-technical descriptions of the workings of the EM algorithm for covariance matrices (Graham & Donaldson 1993; Graham et al. 1994, 1996, 1997, 2003).

In brief, the EM algorithm is an iterative procedure that produces maximum likelihood estimates. For the E-step at one iteration, cases are read in, one by one. If a value is present, the sums, sums of squares, and sums of cross-products are incremented. If the value is missing, the current best guess for that value is used instead. The best guess is based on regression-

> ## EIGENVALUE
>
> Eigenvalues are part of the decomposition of a correlation matrix during factor analysis or principal components analysis. Each eigenvalue represents the variance of the linear combination of items making up that factor. In principal components, the total variance for the correlation matrix is the number of items in the matrix. If the matrix is positive definite, the last eigenvalue will be positive, that is, it will have variance. However, if the matrix is not positive definite, one or more of the eigenvalues will be 0, implying that those factors have no variance, or that they add no new information over and above the other factors.

based single imputation with all other variables in the model used as predictors. For the sums, the best guess value is used as is. For sums of squares and sums of cross-products, if just one value is missing, then the quantity is incremented directly. However, if both values are missing, then the quantity is incremented, and a correction factor is added. This correction is conceptually equivalent to adding a random residual error term in MI (described below).

In the M-step of the same iteration, the parameters (variances, covariances, and means) are estimated (calculated) based on the current values of the sums, sums of squares, and sums of cross-products. Based on the covariance matrix at this iteration, new regression equations are calculated for each variable predicted by all others. These regression equations are then used to update the best guess for missing values during the E-step of the next iteration. This two-step process continues until the elements of the covariance matrix stop changing. When the changes from iteration to iteration are so small that they are judged to be trivial, EM is said to have converged.

Being ML, the parameter estimates (means, variances, and covariances) from the EM algorithm are excellent. However, the EM algorithm does not provide standard errors as an automatic part of the process. One could obtain an estimate of these standard errors using bootstrap procedures (e.g., see Graham et al. 1997). Although bootstrap procedures (Efron

1982) are often criticized, they can be quite useful in this context as a means of dealing with nonnormal data distributions.

Good uses of the EM algorithm. Although the EM algorithm provides excellent parameter estimates, the lack of convenient standard errors means that EM is not particularly good for hypothesis testing. On the other hand, several important analyses, often preliminary analyses, don't use standard errors anyway, so the EM estimates are very useful. First, it is often desirable to report means, standard deviations, and sometimes a correlation matrix in one's paper. I would argue that the best estimates for these quantities are the ML estimates provided by EM. Second, data quality analyses, for example, coefficient alpha analyses, because they typically do not involve standard errors, can easily be based on the EM covariance matrix (e.g., see Enders 2003; Graham et al. 2002, 2003). The EM covariance matrix is also an excellent basis for exploratory factor analysis with missing data. This is especially easy with the SAS/STAT® software program (SAS Institute); one simply includes the relevant variables in Proc MI, asking for the EM matrix to be output. That matrix may then be used as input for Proc Factor using the "type = cov" option.

Although direct analysis of the EM covariance matrix can be useful, a more widely useful EM tool is to impute a single data set from EM parameters (with random error). This procedure has been described in detail in Graham et al. (2003). This single imputed data set is known to yield good parameter estimates, close to the population average. But more importantly, because it is a complete data set, it may be read in using virtually any software, including SPSS. Once read into the software, coefficient alpha and exploratory factor analyses may be carried out in the usual way. One caution is that this data set should not be used for hypothesis testing. Standard errors based on this data set, say from a multiple regression analysis, will be too small, sometimes to a substantial extent. Hypothesis testing should be carried out with MI or one of the FIML procedures. Note that

the procedure in SPSS for writing out a single imputed data set based on the EM algorithm is not recommended unless random error residuals are added after the fact to each imputed value; the current implementation of SPSS, up to version 16 at least, writes data out without adding error (e.g., see von Hippel 2004). This is known to produce important biases in the data set (Graham et al. 1996).

Implementations of the EM algorithm. Good implementations of the EM algorithm for covariance matrices are widely available. SAS Proc MI estimates the EM covariance matrix as a by-product of its MI analysis (SAS Institute). Schafer's (1997) NORM program, a stand-alone Microsoft Windows program, also estimates the EM covariance matrix as a step in the MI process. Graham et al. (2003) have described utilities for making use of that covariance matrix. Graham & Hofer (1992) have created a stand-alone DOS-based EM algorithm, EMCOV, which can be useful in simulations.

Multiple imputation under the normal model. I describe in this section MI under the normal model as it is implemented in Schafer's (1997) NORM program. MI as implemented in SAS Proc MI is also based on Schafer's (1997) algorithms, and thus is the same kind of program as NORM. Detailed, step-by-step instructions for running NORM are available in Graham et al. (2003; also see Graham & Hofer 2000, Schafer 1999, Schafer & Olsen 1998). Note that Schafer's NORM program is also available as part of the Splus missing data library (**http://www.insightful.com/**).

The key to any MI program is to restore the error variance lost from regression-based single imputation. Imputed values from single imputation always lie right on the regression line. But real data always deviate from the regression line by some amount. In order to restore this lost variance, the first part of imputation is to add random error variance (random normal error in this case). The second part of restoring lost variance relates to the fact that each imputed value is based on a single regression equation, because the regression equation, and the underlying covariance matrix, is based on a single draw from the population of interest.

In order to adjust the lost error completely, one should obtain multiple random draws from the population and impute multiple times, each with a different random draw from the population. Of course, this is almost never possible; researchers have just a single sample. One option might be to simulate random draws from the population by using bootstrap procedures (Efron 1982). Another approach is to simulate random draws from the population using data augmentation (DA; Tanner & Wong 1987).

The key to Schafer's NORM program is DA. NORM first runs EM to obtain starting values for DA. DA can be thought of as a kind of stochastic (probabilistic) version of EM. It, too, is an iterative, two-step process. There is an imputation step during which DA simulates the missing data based on the current parameter estimates, and a posterior step during which DA simulates the parameters given the current (imputed) data. DA is a member of the Markov-Chain Monte Carlo family of algorithms. It is Markov-like in the sense that all of the information from one step of DA is contained in the previous step. Because of this, the parameter estimates and imputed values from two adjacent steps of DA are more similar than one would expect from two random draws from the population. However, after, say, 50 steps of DA, the parameter estimates and imputed values from the initial step and those 50 steps removed are much more like two random draws from the population. The trick is to determine how many steps are required before the two imputed data sets are sufficiently similar to two random draws from the population. Detailed guidance for this process is given in Graham et al. (2003). In general, the number of iterations it takes EM to converge is an excellent estimate of the number of steps there should be between imputed data sets from DA (this rule applies best to the NORM program; different MI programs have different convergence criteria, and this rule may be slightly different with those MI programs). In addition, diagnostics are available in NORM

and Proc MI to verify that the number of DA steps selected was good enough.

Implementations of MI under the normal model. Implementations of MI under the normal model are also widely available. Schafer's (1997) NORM software is a free program (see **http://methodology.psu.edu/** for the free download). SAS Proc MI (especially version 9, but to a large extent version 8.2; SAS Institute) provides essentially the same features as NORM. For analyses conducted in SAS, Proc MI is best. Other implementations of MI are not guaranteed to be as robust as are those based on DA or other Markov-Chain Monte Carlo routines, although such programs may be useful under specific circumstances. For example, Amelia II (see Honaker et al. 2007, King et al. 2001) and IVEware (Raghunathan 2004) are two MI programs that merit a look. See Horton & Kleinman (2007) for a recent review of MI software.

Special MI software for categorical, longitudinal/cluster, and semi-continuous data. In this category are Schafer's (1997) CAT program (for categorical data) and MIX program (for mixed continuous and categorical problems). Both of these are available (along with NORM) as special commands in the latest version of Splus. Although CAT can certainly be used to handle imputation with categorical data, it presents the user with some limitations. Most importantly, the default in CAT involves what amounts to the main effects and all possible interactions. Thus, even with a few variables, the default model can involve a huge number of parameters. For example, with just five input variables, CAT estimates parameters for 31 variables (five main effects, ten 2-way interactions, ten 3-way interactions, five 4-way interactions, and one 5-way interaction).

Also included in this category is the PAN program (for special panel and cluster-data designs, see Schafer 2001, Schafer & Yucel 2002). PAN was created for the situation in which a variable, Posatt (beliefs about the positive social consequences of alcohol use), was measured in grades 5, 6, 7, 9, and 10 of a longitudinal study, but was omitted for all subjects in grade 8. Other variables (e.g., alcohol use), however, were measured in all six grades. Because no subject had data for Posatt measured in eighth grade, MI under the normal model could not be used to impute that variable. However, because PAN also takes into account growth (change) over time, Posatt 8 can be imputed with PAN. PAN is also very good for imputing clustered data (e.g., students within schools) where the number of clusters is large. Although the potential for the PAN program is huge, its availability remains limited.

Olsen & Schafer (2001) have described multiple imputation for semi-continuous data, especially in the growth modeling context. Semi-continuous data come from variables that have many responses at one value (e.g., 0) and are more or less normally distributed for values greater than 0.

Imputing a single data set from EM parameters. An often useful alternative to analyzing the EM covariance matrix directly is to impute a single data set based on EM parameters (+random error, an option available in Schafer's NORM program; see Graham et al. 2003 for details). With data sets imputed using data augmentation, parameter estimates can be anywhere in legitimate parameter space. However, when the single imputation (+error) is based on the EM covariance matrix, all parameter estimates are near the center of the parameter space. For this reason, if one analyzes just one imputed data set, it should be this one. This data set is very useful for analyses that do not require hypothesis testing, such as coefficient alpha analysis and exploratory factor analysis (see Graham et al. 2003 for additional details).

FIML methods. FIML methods deal with the missing data, do parameter estimation, and estimate standard errors all in a single step. This means that the regular, complete-cases algorithms must be completely rewritten to handle missing data. Because this task is somewhat daunting, software written with the FIML missing data feature is limited. At present, the feature is most common in SEM software (in alphabetical order, Amos: Arbuckle & Wothke 1999; LISREL: Jöreskog & Sörbom 1996, also see du Toit & du Toit 2001; Mplus: Muthén, & Muthén 2007; and Mx: Neale et al. 1999). Although each of these programs was written specifically for SEM applications, they can be used for virtually any analysis that falls within the general linear model, most notably multiple regression. For a review of FIML SEM methods, see Enders (2001a).

Other FIML (or largely FIML) software for latent class analysis includes Proc LTA (e.g., Lanza et al. 2005; also see **http://methodology. psu.edu**) and Mplus (Muthén & Muthén 2007).

Other "older" methods. One other method deserves special mention in this context. Although SEM analysis with missing data is currently handled almost exclusively by SEM/FIML methods (see previous section), an older method involving the multiple group capabilities of SEM programs is very useful for some applications. This approach was described initially by Allison (1987) and Muthén et al. (1987). Among other things, this method has proven to be extremely useful with simulations involving missing data (e.g., see Graham et al. 2001, 2006).

This method also continues to be useful for measurement designs described as "accelerated longitudinal" or "cohort sequential" (see Duncan & Duncan 1994; Duncan et al. 1994, 1996; McArdle 1994; McArdle & Hamagami 1991, 1992). With these designs, one collects data for two or more sets of participants of different ages over, say, three consecutive years. For example, one group is 10, 11, and 12 years old over the three years of a study, and another group is 11, 12, and 13 years old over the same three study years. Because no participants have data for both ages 10 and 13, regular FIML-based SEM software and normal-model MI cannot be used in this context. However, the multiple-group SEM approach may be used to test a growth model covering growth over all four ages.

Dispelling Myths About MAR Missing Data Methods

Myths abound regarding missing data and analysis with missing data. Many of these myths originated with thinking that was developed well before the missing data revolution. Parts of that earlier thinking, of course, remain an important element of modern psychological science. But the parts relating to missing data need to be revised. I address three of the most common myths in this section. Other myths are dealt with in the sections that follow.

Imputation is making up the data. It is true that imputation is the process of plugging in plausible values where none exist. But the point of this process is not to obtain the individual values themselves. Rather, the point is to plug in these values (multiple times) in order to preserve important characteristics of the data set as a whole. By "preserve," I mean that parameter estimates should be unbiased. That is, the estimated mean, for example, should be close to the true population value for the mean; the estimated variance should be close to the true population value for the variance. In this review, I talk mainly about multiple imputation under the normal model. Normal-model MI "preserves" means, variances, covariances, correlations, and linear regression coefficients.

You are unfairly helping yourself by imputing (AKA, it is okay to impute the independent variable, but not the dependent variable). There are several versions of this myth. In the past, some researchers were convinced that imputation procedures such as normal-model MI were fine for imputing missing data that might occur within the set of independent variables (IVs) (and covariates) of a study. However, these researchers were very reluctant to include the dependent variable (DV) in the MI model when it, too, included missing values. They felt that it was somehow unfair to impute the DV.

The truth is that all variables in the analysis model must be included in the imputation model. The fear is that including the DV in the imputation model might lead to bias in estimating the important relationships (e.g., the regression coefficient of a program variable predicting the DV). However, the opposite actually happens. When the DV is included in the model, all relevant parameter estimates are unbiased, but excluding the DV from the imputation model for the IVs and covariates can be shown to produce biased estimates. The problem with leaving the DV out of the imputation model is this: When any variable is omitted from the model, imputation is carried out under the assumption that the correlation is $r = 0$ between the omitted variable and variables included in the imputation model. Thus, when the DV is omitted, the correlations between it and the IVs (and covariates) included in the model are all suppressed (i.e., biased) toward 0.

MAR methods don't work if the MAR assumption does not hold (AKA, complete cases are preferred if MAR does not hold). With some procedures, such as multiple linear regression, it is assumed that the data are multivariate normal. Violation of this assumption is known to affect the results (most notably the standard errors of the regression coefficients). So with multiple regression, if the normality assumption has been violated, one should use a different procedure. This logic makes good sense with multiple regression analysis, but it does not apply to analysis with missing data because with multiple regression, when the normality assumption is violated, other common procedures work better. But with missing data, when the MAR assumption has been violated, the violation affects the old procedures (e.g., listwise deletion) as well, and typically this violation has greater effect on the old procedures. In short, MI and ML methods are always at least as good as the old procedures (e.g., listwise deletion, except in artificial, unrealistic circumstances), and MI/ML methods are typically better than old methods, and often very much better.

An important difference between MI/ML methods and complete cases analysis is that auxiliary variables (see next section) may be used with MI/ML in order to reduce the impact of MNAR missingness. However, there is no good way of incorporating auxiliary variables into a complete cases model unless they can reasonably be incorporated (e.g., as covariates) into the model of substantive interest.

PRACTICAL ISSUES: MAKING MISSING DATA ANALYSIS WORK IN THE REAL WORLD

The suggestions given here are designed to make missing data analyses useful in real-world data situations. Some of the suggestions given here are necessarily brief. Many other practical suggestions are given in Graham et al. (2003) and elsewhere.

Inclusive versus Restrictive Variable Inclusion Strategies (MI versus FIML)

In some ways, this is the most important lesson that can be learned when doing missing data analysis in the real world. Collins et al. (2001) discussed the differences between "inclusive" and "restrictive" variable inclusion strategies in missing data analysis. An inclusive strategy is one in which auxiliary variables are included in the model. An auxiliary variable is a variable that is not part of the model of substantive interest, but is highly correlated with the variables in the substantive model. Collins et al. (2001) showed that including auxiliary variables in the missing data model can be very helpful in two important ways. It can reduce estimation bias due to MNAR missingness, and it can partially restore lost power due to missingness.

Collins et al. (2001) note that the potential auxiliary variable benefit is the same for MI and FIML analyses but that the typical use of MI is different from typical use of FIML. For MI analyses, including auxiliary variables in the imputation model has long been practiced and is very easy to accomplish: Simply add the variables to the imputation model. Furthermore, once the auxiliary variables have been included in the imputation model, subsequent analyses

involving the imputed data benefit from the auxiliary variables, whether or not those variables appear in the analysis of substantive interest (this latter benefit also applies to analysis of the EM covariance matrix). On the other hand, FIML analyses have typically included only the variables that are part of the model of substantive interest. Thus, researchers who use FIML models have found it difficult to incorporate auxiliary variables in a reasonable way. Fortunately, reasonable approaches for including auxiliary variables into SEM/FIML models now exist (e.g., see Graham 2003; also see the recently introduced feature in Mplus for easing the process of including auxiliary variables). Note that although these methods work well for SEM/FIML models, no corresponding strategies are available at present for incorporating auxiliary variables into latent class FIML models.

Small Sample Sizes

Graham & Schafer (1999) showed that MI performs very well in small samples (as low as N = 50), even with very large multiple regression models (as large as 18 predictors) and even with as much as 50% missing data in the DV. The biggest issue with such small samples is not the missingness, per se, but rather that one simply does not have much data to begin with and missingness depletes one's data even further. MI was shown to perform very well under these circumstances; the analyses based on MI data were as good as the same analyses performed on complete data.

The simulations performed by Graham & Schafer (1999) also showed that normal-model MI with nonnormal data works well, as well as analysis with the same data with no missing values. Although analysis of imputed data works as well as analysis with complete datasets, nothing in the imputation process, per se, fixes the nonnormal data. Thus, in order to correct the problems with standard errors often found with nonnormal data, analysis procedures must be used that give correct standard errors (e.g., the correction given for SEM by Satorra & Bentler

1994). Enders (2001b) has drawn similar conclusions regarding the use of the FIML missing data feature for SEM programs.

Rounding

Rounding should be kept to a minimum. MI was designed to restore the lost variability found in single imputation, and the MI strategy was designed to yield the correct variability. Rounding is tantamount to adding more variability to the imputed values. The added variability is random, to be sure, but there is definitely more of it with rounding than without. This additional variance is evident in coefficient alpha analyses with rounded and unrounded imputed values in a single data set imputed from EM parameters. Coefficient alpha is always a point or two lower (showing more random error variance) with rounding than without (also, see the Categorical Missing Data and Normal-Model MI section below for a discussion regarding rounding for categorical variables).

Number of Imputations in MI

Missing data theorists have often claimed that good inferences can be made with the number of imputed data sets (m) as few as $m = 3$ to 5. They have argued that the relative efficiency of estimation is very high under these circumstances, compared to an infinite number of imputations. However, Graham et al. (2007) have recently shown that the effects of m on statistical power for detecting a small effect size ($\rho = 0.10$) can be strikingly different from what is observed for relative efficiency. They showed that if statistical power is the main consideration, the number of imputations typically must be much higher than previously thought. For example, with 50% missing information, Graham et al. (2007) showed that MI with $m = 5$ has a 13% power falloff compared to the equivalent FIML analysis; with 30% missing information and $m = 5$, there was a 7% power falloff compared to FIML. Graham et al. (2007) recommend that at least $m = 40$ imputations are needed with 50% missing informa-tion to guarantee less than a 1% power falloff compared to the comparable FIML analysis.

Making EM (and MI) Perform Better (i.e., Faster)

Factors that affect the speed of MI are the same as those that affect the speed of EM, so I focus here on the latter. EM involves matrix manipulations to a large extent, so sample size has relatively little effect. However, the number of variables (k) affects EM tremendously. Consider that EM estimates $[k(k+1)/2 + k]$ parameters [k variances, $(k(k-1)/2)$ covariances, and k means]. That means that with 25, 50, 100, 150, and 200 variables, EM must estimate 350, 1325, 5150, 11,475, and 20,300 parameters, respectively. Note that as the number of variables gets large, the number of estimated parameters in EM gets huge. Although there is leeway here, I generally try to keep the total number of variables under 100 even with large sample sizes of N = 1000 or more. With smaller sample sizes, a smaller number of variables should be used.

Also affecting the speed of EM and MI is the amount of missing information (similar to, but not the same as, the amount of missing data). More missing information means EM converges more slowly. Finally, the distributions of the variables can affect speed of convergence. With highly skewed data, EM generally converges much more slowly. For this reason, it is often a good idea to transform the data (e.g., with a log transformation) prior to imputation. The imputed values can be back-transformed (e.g., using the antilog) after imputation, if necessary.

If EM is very slow to converge, for example, if it takes more than about 200 iterations, the speed of convergence can generally be improved. If EM converges in 200 iterations, then one should ask for 200 steps of data augmentation between each imputed data set. With $m = 40$ imputed data sets, one would need to run $40 \times 200 = 8000$ steps of DA. If EM converged in 1000 iterations, one would need to run $40 \times 1000 = 40,000$ steps of DA. The additional time can be substantial, especially if the time between iterations is large.

Including Interactions in the Missing Data Model

An issue that comes up frequently in missing data analysis has to do with omitting certain variables from the missing data model. This issue is sometimes referred to as being sure that the imputation model is at least as general as the analysis model. A clear example is a test of the effect of an interaction (e.g., the product) of two variables on some third variable. Because the product is a nonlinear combination of the two variables, it is not part of the regular linear imputation model. The problem with excluding such variables from the imputation model is that all imputation is done under the assumption that the correlation is r = 0 between the omitted variable and all other variables in the imputation model. In this case, the correlation between the interaction term and the DVs of interest will be suppressed toward 0. The solution is to anticipate any interaction terms and include the relevant product terms in the imputation model.

Another way to conceive of an interaction is to think of one of the variables as a grouping variable (e.g., gender). The interaction in this case means that the correlation between two variables is different for males and females. In the typical imputation model, one imputes under the model that all correlations are the same for females and males. A good way to impute under a model that allows these correlations to be different is to impute separately for males and females. The advantage of this approach is that all interactions involving gender can be tested during analysis even if a specific interaction was not anticipated beforehand. This approach works very well in program effects analyses. If the program and control groups are imputed separately, then it is possible to test any interaction involving the program dummy variable after the fact. One drawback to imputing separately within groups is that it cuts the sample size at least in half. This may be accept-

able with a large sample. But if the sample is too small for this strategy, then including a few carefully selected product terms may be the best option.

Longitudinal Data and Special Longitudinal Missing Data Models

Missing data models have been created for handling special longitudinal data sets (e.g., the PAN program; Schafer 2001). Some people believe that programs such as PAN must be used to impute longitudinal data, for example, in connection with growth curve modeling (see "Modern" Missing Data Analysis Methods section above). However, this is not the case. It is easiest to see this by examining the various ways in which growth curve analyses can be performed. Special hierarchical linear modeling programs (e.g., HLM; Raudenbush & Bryk 2002) can be used for this purpose. However, standard SEM programs can also be used (e.g., see Willett & Sayer 1994). When analyses are conducted with these models under identical conditions (e.g., assuming homogeneity of error variances over time), the results of these two procedures are identical.

The key for the present review is that a variance-covariance matrix and vector of means provide all that is needed for performing growth modeling in SEM. Thus, any missing data procedure that preserves (i.e., estimates without bias) variances, covariances, and means is acceptable. This is exactly what results from the EM algorithm, and, asymptotically, with normal-model MI. In summary, MI under the normal model, or essentially equivalent SEM models with a FIML missing data feature, may safely be used in conjunction with longitudinal data.

Categorical Missing Data and Normal-Model MI

Although some researchers believe that missing categorical data requires special missing data procedures for categorical data, this is not true in general. The proportion of people giving the

"1" response for a two-level categorical variable coded "1" and "0" is the same as the mean for that variable. Thus, the important characteristics of this variable are preserved, even using normal-model MI. If the binary variable (e.g., gender) is to be used as a covariate in a regression analysis, then the imputed values should be used, as is, without rounding (see Rounding section above). If the binary variable must be used in analysis as a binary variable, then each imputed value should be rounded to the nearest observed value (0 or 1). There are variations on this rounding procedure (e.g., see Bernaards et al. 2007), but the simple rounding is known to perform very well in empirical data.

With normal-model MI (this also applies to SEM analysis with FIML), categorical variables with two levels may be used directly. However, categorical variables with more than two levels must first be dummy coded. If there are p levels in the categorical variable, then $p - 1$ dummy variables must be created to represent the categorical variable. For example, with a categorical variable with four levels, this dummy coding is completed as shown in **Table 2**.

If the original categorical variable has no missing data, then creating these dummy variables and using them in the missing data analysis is all that must be done. However, if the original categorical variable does have missing data, then imputation under the normal model may not work perfectly, and an ad hoc fix must be used. The problem is that dummy coding has precise meaning when all dummy-code values for a particular person are 0 or if there is exactly one 1 for the person. If there is a missing value for the original categorical variable, then all of the dummy variables will also be missing and it

is possible that a missing value for two (or more) of the dummy variables could be imputed as a 1 after rounding. If any people have 1 values for more than one of these dummy variables, then the meaning of the dummy variables is changed.

If the number of "illegal" imputed values in this situation is small compared with the overall sample size, then one could simply leave them. However, a clever, ad hoc fix for the problem has been suggested by Paul Allison (2002). To employ Allison's fix, it is important to impute without rounding. Whenever there is an illegal pattern of imputed values (more than a single 1 for the dummy variables), the value 1 is assigned to the dummy variable with the highest imputed value, and 0 is assigned to all others in the dummy variable set. The results of this fix will be excellent under most circumstances.

Estimating proportions and frequencies with normal-model MI. Although normal-model MI does a good job of preserving many important characteristics of the data set as a whole, it is important to note that it does not preserve proportions and frequencies, except in the special case of a variable with just two levels (e.g., yes and no coded as 1 and 0), in which case the proportion of people giving the 1 response is the same as the mean and is thus preserved. However, consider the question, "How many cigarettes did you smoke yesterday?" (0 = none, 1 = 1–5, 2 = 6 or more). Researchers may be interested in knowing the proportion of people who have smoked cigarettes. This is the same as the proportion of people who did not respond 0, or one minus the proportion who gave the 0 response. Although the mean of this three-level smoking variable will be correct with normal-model MI, the proportion of people with the 0 response is not guaranteed to be correct unless the three-level smoking variable happens to be normally distributed (which is unlikely in most populations). This problem can be corrected simply by performing a separate EM analysis with the two-level version of this smoking variable (e.g., 0 versus other). The EM mean provides the correct proportion. Correct frequencies for all

Table 2 Example of dummy coding with four-level categorical variable

Original category	Dummy variable		
	D1	D2	D3
1	1	0	0
2	0	1	0
3	0	0	1
4	0	0	0

response categories, if needed, may be obtained in this case by recasting the three-level categorical variable as two dummy variables.

Normal-Model MI with Clustered Data

The term "clustered data" refers to the situation in which cases are clustered in naturally occurring groups, for example, students within schools. In this situation, the members of each cluster are often more similar to one another in some important ways than they are to members of other clusters. This type of multilevel structure requires special methods of analysis (e.g., Raudenbush & Bryk 2002; also see Murray 1998). These multilevel analysis models allow variable means to be different across the different clusters (random intercepts model), and sometimes they allow the covariances to be different in the different clusters (random slopes and intercepts model). If the analysis of choice is a random slopes and intercepts model, then, just as described above, the imputation model should involve imputing separately within each cluster. However, if the analysis of choice involves only random intercepts, then a somewhat easier option is available. In this situation, the cluster membership variable can be dummy coded. That is, for p clusters, $p - 1$ dummy variables would be specified (see **Table 2** for a simple dummy variable example).

With the dummy coding strategy, the $p - 1$ dummy variables are included in the imputation model. As long as the number of clusters is relatively small compared with the sample size, this dummy coding strategy works well. I have seen this strategy work well with as many as 35 dummy variables, although a smaller number is desirable. Remember that the number of dummy variables takes away from the number of substantive variables that reasonably can be used in the imputation model.

When the number of clusters is too high to work with normal-model MI, several options are available. A specialty MI model (such as PAN; Schafer 2001) can be employed, but that strategy can sometimes be costly in terms of learning new procedures. In addition, the performance of PAN has not been adequately evaluated at this time. Alternatively, the number of clusters can be reduced in a reasonable way. For example, if it is known that certain clusters have similar means, then these clusters could be combined (i.e., they would have the same dummy variable) prior to imputation (note that this kind of combining of clusters must be done within experimental groups). For every combination of this sort that can be reasonably formed, the number of dummy variables is reduced by one. I have even seen the strategy of performing a k-means cluster analysis on the key study variables using school averages as input. This type of analysis would help identify the clusters of clusters for which means on key variables are similar.

One factor to take into consideration when employing the dummy variable approach to handling cluster data is that sometimes variables, especially binary variables, that have very low counts (e.g., marijuana use among fifth graders) will be constants within one or more of the clusters. The data should be examined for this kind of problem prior to attempting the dummy variable approach. A good way to start is to perform a principal components analysis on the variables to be included in the imputation model, along with the dummy variables. If the last eigenvalue from this analysis is positive, the dummy coding strategy will most likely work.

Large Numbers of Variables

This problem represents perhaps the biggest challenge for missing data analyses in large field studies, especially longitudinal field studies. Consider that most constructs are measured with multiple items. Five constructs with four items per construct translates into 20 individual variables. Five waves of measurement produce 100 variables. If more constructs are included in the analysis, it is difficult to keep the total down to the $k = 100$ that I have recommended. It is even more difficult to keep the variables in the imputation model to a reasonable number if one has cluster data and is employing the dummy variable strategy (see previous section). Below, I describe briefly two strategies that have worked well in practice.

Imputing whole scales. If the analysis involves latent variable analysis (e.g., SEM) such that the individual variables must be part of the analysis, then imputing whole scales is not possible. However, analyses often involve the whole scales anyway, so imputing at that level is an excellent compromise. As long as study participants have data either for all or for none of the scale items, then this strategy is easy. The problem with using this strategy is how to deal with the partial data on the scale. Schafer & Graham (2002) suggested that forming a scale score based on partial data can cause problems in some situations, but may be fine in others. In my experience, forming a scale score based on partial data will be acceptable (*a*) if a relatively high proportion of variables are used to form the scale score (and never fewer than half of the variables), and (*b*) when the variables are consistent with the domain sampling model (Nunnally 1967), and (*c*) when the variables have relatively high coefficient alpha. Variables can be considered consistent with the domain sampling model when the item-total correlations (or factor loadings) for the variables within the scale are all similar. Conceptually, it must be reasonable that dropping one variable from the scale has essentially the same meaning as dropping any other variables from the scale. Otherwise, one must either discard any partial data or impute at the individual item level for that scale. Imputing at the scale level for even some of the study scales will often help with the problem of having too many variables.

Think FIML. Another strategy that works well in practice is to start with the variables that would be included in the analysis model of substantive interest. If the FIML approaches are used, then these are the only variables that would be included using the typical practice. In addition, one should carefully select the few auxiliary variables that will have the most beneficial impact on the model. Adding auxiliary variables that are correlated r = 0.50 or better with the variables of interest will generally help the analysis to have less bias and more power. However, adding auxiliary variables with lower correlations will typically have little incremental benefit, especially when these additional variables are correlated with the auxiliary variables already being used.

Good candidates for auxiliary variables are the same variables used in the analytic model, but measured at different waves. For example, in a test of a program's effect on smoking at wave 4, with smoking at wave 1 as a covariate, smoking at waves 2 and 3 is not being used in the analysis model but should be rather highly correlated with smoking at wave 4. These two variables would make excellent auxiliary variables.

A related strategy is to impute variables that are relatively highly correlated with one another. Suppose, for example, that one would like to conduct program effect analyses on a large number of DVs, say 30. But including 30 DVs, 30 wave-1 covariates, and the corresponding 60 variables from waves 2 and 3 (as auxiliary variables) would be too many, especially considering that there are perhaps 10 background variables as covariates and perhaps 20 dummy variables representing cluster membership. All these hypothetical variables total 150 variables in the imputation model.

In this instance, a principal components analysis on the 30 DVs could identify three or four sets of items that are relatively highly correlated. This approach does not need to be precise; it is simply used as a device for identifying variables that are more correlated. These groupings of variables would then be imputed together. By conducting imputation analyses and analyses in these groupings, nearly all of the benefits of the auxiliary variables would be gained at a minimum cost of time for imputation and analysis.

Practicalities of Measurement: Planned Missing Data Designs

In this section, I outline the developing area of planned missingness designs. If you are following my advice, you are already (or soon will be) using the recommended MI and ML missing data procedures. Thus, it is time to explore new possibilities with respect to data collection.

3-Form design. Measurement is the cornerstone of science. Without measurement, there is no science. When researchers design the measurement component of their study, they are universally faced with the dilemma of wanting to ask more questions than their study participants are willing to answer, given what they are being paid. Invariably, researchers are faced with the choice of asking fewer questions or paying their participants more. The 3-form design (Graham et al. 2006), which has been in use since the early 1980s (e.g., see Graham et al. 1984), gives researchers a third choice. In its generic form, the 3-form design allows researchers to increase by 33% the number of questions for which data are collected without changing the number of questions asked of each respondent. The trick is to divide all questions asked into four items sets. The X set, which contains questions most central to the study outcomes, is asked of everyone. But the A, B, and C sets of items are rotated, such that one set is omitted from each of the three forms. **Table 3** describes the basic idea of the design (Raghunathan & Grizzle 1995 suggested a similar design involving all possible two-set combinations of five items sets).

The benefit of the 3-form design is that one gathers data for 33% more questions than can be asked of any one participant. Also, importantly, at least one-third of the participants provide data for every pair of questions. That is, all correlations are estimable. This feature is not shared by most other measurement designs of this general sort (generically described as matrix sampling). The drawback to the 3-form design is that some correlations, because they are based on only one-third of the sample, are tested with lower power. However, as Graham et al. (2006) show, virtually all of the possible drawbacks are under the researcher's control and can generally be avoided.

Two-method measurement. Graham et al. (2006) also described a planned missingness design called two-method measurement (also see Allison & Hauser 1991, who describe a related design). The two-method measurement design stems from the need to obtain good, valid measures of the main DV. Researchers in many domains face a dilemma: (*a*) collect data from everyone with a relatively inexpensive, but questionably valid measure (e.g., a self-administered, self-report measure of recent physical activity), or (*b*) collect data from a small proportion of study participants using a more valid, but much more expensive, measure (e.g., using an expensive accelerometer). The two-method measurement design allows the collection of both kinds of data: complete data for the less expensive measure, and partial data (on a random sample of participants) for the expensive measure. SEM models are then tested in which the two kinds of data are both used as indicators of a latent variable of the construct of interest (e.g., recent physical activity). If certain assumptions are met (and they are commonly met), then this SEM approach allows for the test of the main study hypotheses with more statistical power than is possible with the expensive measure alone and with more construct validity than is possible with the inexpensive measure alone. For details on this design, see Graham et al. (2006).

ATTRITION AND MNAR MISSINGNESS

The methods described up to this point are clear. I believe that the directions we have

Table 3   3-form design

Form	Respondent received item set?			
	X	**A**	**B**	**C**
1	Yes	Yes	Yes	No
2	Yes	Yes	No	Yes
3	Yes	No	Yes	Yes

headed, and the MI and ML methods that have been developed, are the right way to go. My advice continues to be to learn and use these methods. I am certain that the major software writers will continue to help in this regard, and in a very few years, the software solutions will be abundant (e.g., see these recent missing data developments: the feature in Mplus for easing the process of including auxiliary variables; the association between SPSS and Amos software; and the inclusion of MI into SAS/STAT® software). But as we move forward into the arena of attrition and MNAR missingness, the waters get a bit murky. The following section describes more of a work in progress. Nevertheless, I believe that we are making strides, and the way to move forward is becoming clearer.

It has been said that attrition in longitudinal studies is virtually ubiquitous. Although that may be true in large part, also ubiquitous is the fear researchers and critics express that attrition is a threat to the internal validity of the study and the readiness with which researchers are willing to discount study results when more than a few percent of the participants have dropped out along the way. To make matters worse, even the missing data experts often make statements that, if taken out of context, seem to verify that the fears about attrition were well founded. To be fair, the concerns about attrition began well before the missing data revolution, and in the absence of the current knowledge base about missing data, perhaps taking the conservative approach was the right thing to do.

But now we have this knowledge base, and it is time to take another, careful look at attrition. It is important to acknowledge that the conclusions in some studies will be adversely affected by attrition and MNAR missingness, and I am not suggesting that we pretend that isn't the case. But I do believe that the effects of attrition on study conclusions in a general sense are not nearly as severe as commonly feared. In this section, I describe the beginnings of a framework for measuring the extent to which attrition has biasing effects, and I present evidence that the biasing effects of attrition can be tolerably low, even with what is normally considered substantial attrition. Furthermore, I cite research showing that if the recommended safeguards are put in place, the effects of attrition can be further diminished.

With MAR missingness, missing scores at one wave can be predicted from the scores at previous waves. This is true even though the previous scores might be markedly different for stayers and leavers. With MNAR missingness, the missing scores cannot be predicted based on the previous scores; the model that applies to complete cases for describing how scores change over time does not apply to those who have missing data. The practical problem with MNAR missingness is that the missing scores could be anywhere (high or low). And because of this uncertainty, it is possible that clear judgments cannot be made about the study conclusions. The strategies I present in this section serve to reduce that uncertainty. Some of these strategies can be employed after the fact (especially for longitudinal studies), but many of the strategies must be planned in advance for maximum effectiveness.

Some Clarifications About Missing Data Mechanisms

The major three missingness mechanisms are MCAR, MAR, and MNAR. These three kinds of missingness should not be thought of as mutually exclusive categories of missingness, despite the fact that they are often misperceived as such. In particular, MCAR, pure MAR, and pure MNAR really never exist because the pure form of any of these requires almost universally untenable assumptions. The best way to think of all missing data is as a continuum between MAR and MNAR. Because all missingness is MNAR (i.e., not purely MAR), then whether it is MNAR or not should never be the issue. Rather than focusing on whether the MI/ML assumptions are violated, we should answer the question of whether the violation is big enough to matter to any practical extent.

Measuring the Biasing Effects of Attrition

In order for researchers to move toward a missing data approach that focuses on the likely impact of MNAR missingness, they need tools for measuring the effects of missingness (attrition) on estimation bias. Collins et al. (2001) made effective use of the standardized bias (presented as a percent of the standard error) for this purpose: Standardized Bias = $100 \times$ (average parameter estimate − population value)/SE, where SE = the standard error of the estimate, or the standard deviation of the sampling distribution for the parameter estimate in question. Collins et al. (2001) argued that standardized bias greater than 40% (i.e., more than 40% of a standard error) represented estimation bias that was of practical significance. Armed with this tool for judging whether MNAR bias was of practical significance, Collins et al. (2001) showed that the regression coefficient (X predicting Y), where the cause of missingness was Z, was biased to a practical degree only when there was 50% missing on Y and $r_{ZY} = 0.90$. With 50% missing on Y and $r_{ZY} = 0.40$, 25% missing on Y and $r_{ZY} = 0.90$, and 25% missing on Y and $r_{ZY} = 0.40$, the bias was judged not to be of practical significance when the cause of missingness was omitted from the model (i.e., for MNAR missingness). (Note that although Collins et al. 2001 found that the regression coefficient was largely unbiased, the mean of Y did show a practical level of bias in all four of their missingness and r_{ZY} scenarios described above. This may be an issue in some studies.)

The findings of the Collins et al. (2001) study are important for a variety of reasons: (a) they demonstrated the usefulness of standardized bias as a way of measuring the practical effects of bias due to attrition, and (b) they showed that MNAR missingness alone is often not sufficient to affect the internal validity of an experimental study to any practical extent.

Suppression and inflation bias. Two kinds of attrition bias are inflation and suppression bias. Inflation bias makes a truly ineffective program, or experimental manipulation, appear to be effective. Suppression bias, on the other hand, makes a truly effective program look less effective or an ineffective program look as if it had a harmful effect. When evaluation researchers write about attrition bias, they usually are talking about inflation bias, which is a major concern because it calls into question the internal validity of a study. Suppression bias is much less important if it occurs along with a significant program effect in the desired direction and thus does not undermine the internal validity of the study. On the other hand, suppression bias can be a significant factor if it keeps the truly effective nature of a program from being observed. The possibility of suppression bias is an especially important factor during the planning (and proposal) stages of a project. The chances are reduced that a project will be funded if the power to detect true effects is likely to be diminished unduly because of suppression bias.

Important quantities in describing missingness. In any discussion of missing data and attrition, three quantities are prominently featured: (a) the amount of missingness (i.e., percent missing or percent attrition), (b) r_{ZY}, the correlation between the cause of missingness, Z, and the model variable containing missingness, Y, and (c) r_{ZR}, the correlation between the cause of missingness, Z, and missingness itself, R. This last quantity, r_{ZR}, is often manipulated as MAR linear by allowing the probability of a missing Y to be dependent on the quartiles of Z. In Collins et al. (2001), for example, the probabilities of missing on Y were 0.20, 0.40, 0.60, and 0.80 for the first, second, third, and fourth quartiles of Z, respectively. The magnitude of this correlation, r_{ZR}, which depends on the range of these probabilities, can be thought of as the strength of the lever for missingness. That is, a wide range means greater impact on missingness (higher r_{ZR}), and a narrow range means less impact (lower r_{ZR}). Collins et al.

(2001) used a rather strong lever for missingness in their simulations. Their lever for 50% missingness produces $r_{ZR} = 0.447$. A weaker lever for missingness would involve setting the four probabilities for Y missing to different values, for example, 0.35, 0.45, 0.55, and 0.65 for the four quartiles of Z. This lever also produces 50% missingness on Y, but corresponds to $r_{ZR} = 0.224$.

Missing Data Diagnostics

Researchers often want to examine the difference between stayers and leavers on the pretest variables of a longitudinal study. Knowledge will be gained from this practice, but not as much as researchers might think. Because the missingness is not MCAR, any differences observed on pretest variables should not be unexpected. And the information gained cannot indicate the degree to which the missingness is MNAR. Perhaps the best value of this kind of analysis is to identify the pretest variables that most strongly predict missingness later in the study; these variables can be included in the missing data model (e.g., see Heckman 1979, Leigh et al. 1993).

The diagnostics of Hedeker & Gibbons. However, making use of longitudinal data and examining the missingness and the patterns of change over time on the main DV can be very enlightening. Hedeker & Gibbons (1997) provided an excellent example of this kind of diagnostic. In the empirical study they used to illustrate their analytic technique (a pattern mixture model), they plotted the main DV over the four main measurement points in four groups: (*a*) drug group, data for week 6; (*b*) placebo group, data for week 6; (*c*) drug group, data missing for week 6; (*d*) placebo group, data missing for week 6 (where week 6 was the final measure in the study).

These plots (Hedeker & Gibbons 1997, p. 72) show clearly that the changes over time in all four groups were nearly linear. Among those with data for the last time point, the participants in the drug group were clearly doing better than those in the placebo group. Among those who

did not have data for the last measure (week 6), the people in the drug condition appeared to be doing even better, and those in the placebo condition appeared to be doing even worse.

Although it is highly speculative to extrapolate from a single pretest to the last posttest, extrapolation to the last posttest makes much more sense when one is working from a clearly established longitudinal trend. That is, there is much less uncertainty about what the missing scores might be on the final measure. In the Hedeker & Gibbons (1997) study, for example, it can be safely assumed that those without data for the final wave continued along the same (or similar) trajectory that could be observed through three of the four time points.

Figure 1 displays the same kind of data from the Adolescent Alcohol Prevention Trial (AAPT; Hansen & Graham 1991). The figure illustrates the same four plots, this time for the program group (Norm) and comparison group (No Norm) for those who did have data for the final follow-up measure at eleventh grade and for those who did not. It is evident that just as in the study described by Hedeker & Gibbons (1997), the plots look reasonably smooth, and it would be a reasonable to assume

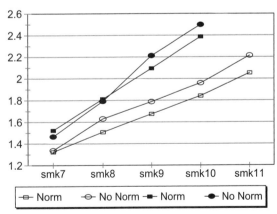

Figure 1

Smoking levels over time for those with and without data for the last wave of measurement. Students in the Norm program group (*square markers*) reported lower levels of cigarette smoking than did students in the Comparison group (*circle markers*) for those who had data for the last wave of measurement (eleventh grade; *white markers*) as well as for those who had missing data for the last wave of measurement (*black markers*).

that the missing smoking scores for eleventh grade followed this same or a similar trajectory.

All of these plotted points make it more difficult to imagine that the missing points are hugely different from where one would guess they would be based on the observed trajectories. On the other hand, it would make little sense to try to predict the missing eleventh-grade data based on the seventh-grade pretest data alone. Based only on those pretest scores, the missing eleventh-grade scores could indeed be anywhere.

The data described by Hedeker & Gibbons (1997) and the data presented here are very well behaved. However, not all plots of the main DV over time will be this smooth. In a longitudinal study, for example, the changes in the DV over time may not conform to a simple, well-defined curve (linear or curvilinear). Under those conditions, predicting the missing final data point would be much more difficult.

Nonignorable (MNAR) Methods

Nonignorable methods (e.g., see Demirtas 2005; Demirtas & Schafer 2003; Hedeker & Gibbons 1997; Little 1993, 1994, 1995) may be very useful. However, it is not necessarily true that any particular method will be better than MAR methods (e.g., normal-model MI or ML) for any particular empirical study. It is well known that methods for handling nonignorable data require the analyst to make assumptions about the model of missingness. If this model is incorrect, the MNAR model may perform even less well than standard MAR methods (e.g., see Demirtas & Schafer 2003).

On the other hand, MNAR methods such as pattern mixture models may, as argued above, be excellent tools for describing the missingness in longitudinal fashion, thereby increasing one's confidence in many instances about the true nature of the missingness. As suggested by Little (1993, 1994, 1995), this type of model can be a good way to perform sensitivity analyses about the model structure. If the same general study conclusions are made over a wide variety of possible missing data models, then one has greater

confidence in those study conclusions. In addition, the models suggested by Hedeker & Gibbons (1997) may prove to be especially useful when the longitudinal patterns of the main DV are as smooth as they described.

Strategies for Reducing the Biasing Effects of Attrition

Use auxiliary variables. Probably the single best strategy for reducing bias (and increasing statistical power lost owing to missing data) is to include good auxiliary variables in the missing data model (see Collins et al. 2001). As Little (1995) put it, "one should collect covariates that are useful for predicting missing values." It is important that these variables need only be good for predicting the missing values; they need not be related to missingness, per se. Good candidate variables for auxiliary variables are measures of the main DV that happen not to be in the analysis model. However, if the analysis already involves all measures of the DV (e.g., with latent growth modeling analyses), then the incremental benefit of other potential auxiliary variables is likely to be small.

Collins et al. (2001) showed that including an auxiliary variable with $r_{ZY} = 0.40$ reduced relatively little bias in any of the parameters examined. However, including an auxiliary variable with $r_{ZY} = 0.90$ had a major impact on bias. Later simulations have suggested that the benefit from auxiliary variables begins to be noticeable at about $r_{ZY} = 0.50$ or 0.60. Furthermore, it appears that one or two auxiliary variables with $r_{ZY} = 0.60$ are better than 20 auxiliary variables whose correlations with Y are all less than $r_{ZY} = 0.40$. This is true because such variables are often intercorrelated, and the incremental benefit of adding them to the model is very small.

Longitudinal missing data diagnostics. The excellent strategy described by Hedeker & Gibbons (1997) is discussed above. If longitudinal data are available, this strategy is a good way to describe the missingness patterns. Not all patterns will be good. The best longitudinal patterns are those that reduce the uncertainty about what the missing scores might be at the last waves of measurement.

Measuring intent to drop out. Schafer & Graham (2002) suggested that a potentially good way of reducing attrition bias is to measure participants' intent to drop out of the study. Some people say they will drop out and do drop out, whereas others say they will drop out and do not. Those who do not drop out provide a good basis for imputing the scores of those who do. Demirtas & Schafer (2003) suggested that this approach might be one good way of dealing with MNAR missingness. Leon et al. (2007) performed a simulation that suggested that this approach can be useful.

Collecting follow-up data from those initially missing. Perhaps the best way of dealing with MNAR missingness is to follow up and measure a random sample of those initially missing from the measurement session (e.g., see Glynn et al. 1993, Graham & Donaldson 1993). This strategy is not easy, and it is impossible in some research settings (e.g., where study participants have died). However, even if some studies are conducted that include these follow-up measures from a random sample of those initially missing, it could shed enormous light on the issues surrounding MNAR missingness. With a few well-placed studies of this sort, we would be an excellent position to establish the true bias from using MAR methods and a variety of MNAR methods.

One wrinkle with this approach is that although collecting data from a random sample of those initially missing can be very difficult, collecting data from a nonrandom sample of those initially missing is much easier. Although inferences from this nonrandom sample are generally weaker than inferences possible from a random sample, data such as these may be of much value (e.g., see Glynn et al. 1993).

Suggestions for Reporting About Attrition in an Empirical Study

1. Avoid generic, possibly misleading, statements about the degree to which attrition plagues longitudinal research.
2. Be precise about the amount of attrition; avoid vague terms that connote a missing data problem. Use precise percentage of dropout from treatment and control groups if that is relevant.
3. Missingness on the main DV can be caused by (*a*) the program itself, (*b*) the DV itself, (*c*) the program × DV interaction, or (*d*) any combination of these factors. Perform analyses that lay out as clearly as possible which version of attrition is most likely in the particular study (e.g., see Hedeker & Gibbons 1997).
4. Based on longitudinal diagnostics, assess the degree of estimation bias, for example, using standardized bias (e.g., see Collins et al. 2001) for this configuration and percent of attrition, and determine the kind of bias (suppression or inflation).
5. Draw study conclusions in light of these facts.

Suggestions for Conduct and Reporting of Simulation Studies on Attrition

1. Avoid generic, possibly misleading, statements about the degree to which attrition plagues longitudinal research. Limit the number of assertions about the possible problems associated with attrition. Those of us who do this kind of simulation study must shoulder the responsibility of being precise in how we talk about these topics—what we say can be very influential. Be careful to give proper citations for any statement about the degree to which attrition is known to be a problem or not. Try to focus on the constructiveness of taking proper steps to minimize any biasing effects of attrition.
2. Be precise about the amount of attrition in the simulation study. Provide a

sufficient number of citations to demonstrate that this amount of attrition is of plausible relevance in the substantive area to which the simulation study applies.

3. Be precise about the configuration of attrition simulated in the study. If the configuration of attrition is simulated in a manner different from that used in other simulation studies, then provide a description of the procedure in plain terms and in comparison with the approaches of other simulation researchers (e.g., see the difference in style between Collins et al. 2001 and Leon et al. 2007). Different approaches are all valuable; readers with varying degrees of technical skill just need to know how they relate to one another.

Be precise about the strength of attrition used in the simulation. For example, Collins et al. (2001) specified increasing missingness probabilities for the four quartiles of the variable Z (0.20 for Q1, 0.40 for Q2, 0.60 for Q3, and 0.80 for Q4). As it turns out, this was very strong attrition compared to what it could have been (e.g., 0.35 for Q1, 0.45 for Q2, 0.55 for Q3, and 0.65 for Q4). This is important because the strength used produced bias in the Collins et al. (2001) study that would present practical problems, whereas the latter strength would produce a level of bias that Collins and coworkers would have judged to be acceptably low, even with 50% missingness on Y, and $r_{ZY} = 0.90$ in both cases. Also, present a sufficient number of citations from the empirical literature to demonstrate that the strength of effect used in the simulation actually occurs in empirical research to an extent that makes the study useful. As noted above, the strength of attrition used in the Collins et al. (2001) study was greater than is typically seen in empirical research.

More Research is Needed

Collins et al. (2001) did a nice job of describing the standardized bias concept, which they used as one of the primary yardsticks of practical importance of missing data bias. In their study, they used 40% bias (parameter estimate is four-tenths of a standard error different from the population value) as the cutoff for MNAR bias that would be of practical concern. Anything greater than 40% would be considered to be of practical concern. This implies that anything 40% or less would be considered to be of no practical concern.

Collins et al. (2001) went out on a limb with an estimate of a cutoff for practical effect of MNAR bias, and this study is an excellent starting place for this kind of research. I am reminded of the early days of SEM research, when researchers were struggling to find indices of practical model fit and to find cutoffs for such indices above which a model's fit might be judged as "good." Bentler & Bonett (1980) were the first to provide any kind of cutoff (0.90 for their nonnormed fit index). SEM researchers were eager to employ this 0.90 cutoff, but with considerable experience with this fit index, eventually began to realize that perhaps 0.95 was a better cutoff.

I suggest that researchers involved with work where attrition is a factor (both empirical and simulation studies) begin to develop experience with the standardized bias concept used by Collins et al. (2001). But after years of experience, will we still believe that 40% bias is the best cutoff? It is easy to show that a standardized bias of 40% corresponds to a change in the t-value of 0.4. Can we tolerate such a change? Other issues surround the use of standardized bias. For example, larger sample sizes produce more standardized bias. Future research should address the possibility that different cut points are needed for different sample sizes.

Other indices of the practical impact of attrition bias. In the SEM literature, researchers now enjoy a plethora of indices of practical fit. There are even three or four fundamentally different approaches to these indices of practical fit. We need more such approaches to the practical effects of attrition. I encourage the development of such indices.

Collecting data on a random sample of those initially missing. Many authors have recommended collecting data on a random sample of those initially missing. However, most of this has involved simulation work and not actual data collection. Carefully conducted empirical studies along the lines suggested by Glynn et al. (1993) and Graham & Donaldson (1993) to determine the actual extent of MNAR biases would be valuable, not just to the individual empirical study, but also to the study of attrition in general. If this type of study is conducted properly, it will give us much-needed information about the effect of MNAR processes on estimation bias. It is possible that the kinds of studies for which MNAR biases are greatest are precisely the studies for which collection of additional data on the initial dropouts is most difficult. Nevertheless, even a few such studies will be a great benefit.

Empirical studies testing benefit of intent to drop out questions. The simulation study conducted by Leon et al. (2007) suggests that this strategy is promising. However, empirical studies are needed that make use of these kinds of procedures. Best, perhaps, would be a few carefully conducted studies that examined the combination of this approach with the approach of collecting data on a random sample of those initially missing.

SUMMARY AND CONCLUSIONS

1. Several excellent, useful, and accessible programs exist for performing analysis with missing data with multiple imputation under the normal model and maximum-likelihood (or FIML) methods. Use them! My wish is that 10 years from now, everyone will be making use of these procedures as a matter of course. Having these methods serve as our basic platform will raise the quality of everyone's research.

2. Gain experience with MNAR missing data (e.g., from attrition), especially with the measures of the practical effect of MNAR data. Use the indices that exist, and evaluate them. Come up with your own levels of what constitutes acceptable levels of estimation bias. Where possible, publish articles describing a new approach to evaluating the practical impact of MNAR missingness on study conclusions.

3. Try to move away from the fear of missing data and attrition. Situations will occur in which missing data and attrition will affect your research conclusions in an undesirable way. But don't fear that eventuality. Embrace the knowledge that you will be more confident in your research conclusions, either way. Don't see this possible situation as a reason not to understand missing data issues. Focus instead on the idea that your new knowledge means that when your research conclusions are desirable, you needn't have the fear that you got away with something. Rather, you can go ahead with the cautious optimism that your study really did work.

DISCLOSURE STATEMENT

The author is not aware of any biases that might be perceived as affecting the objectivity of this review.

LITERATURE CITED

Allison PD. 1987. Estimation of linear models with incomplete data. In *Sociological Methodology 1987*, ed. C Clogg, pp. 71–103. San Francisco, CA: Jossey-Bass
Allison PD. 2002. *Missing Data*. Thousand Oaks, CA: Sage

Allison PD, Hauser RM. 1991. Reducing bias in estimates of linear models by remeasurement of a random subsample. *Soc. Method Res.* 19:466–92

Arbuckle JL, Wothke W. 1999. *Amos 4.0 User's Guide.* Chicago: Smallwaters

Bentler PM, Bonett DG. 1980. Significance tests and goodness of fit in the analysis of covariance structures. *Psychol. Bull.* 88:588–606

Bernaards CA, Belin TR, Schafer JL. 2007. Robustness of a multivariate normal approximation for imputation of incomplete binary data. *Stat. Med.* 26:1368–82

Collins LM, Schafer JL, Kam CM. 2001. A comparison of inclusive and restrictive strategies in modern missing data procedures. *Psychol. Methods* 6:330–51

Demirtas H. 2005. Multiple imputation under Bayesianly smoothed pattern-mixture models for nonignorable drop-out. *Stat. Med.* 24:2345–63

Demirtas H, Schafer JL. 2003. On the performance of random-coefficient pattern-mixture models for non-ignorable dropout. *Stat. Med.* 21:1–23

Dempster AP, Laird NM, Rubin DB. 1977. Maximum likelihood from incomplete data via the EM algorithm (with discussion). *J. R. Stat. Soc.* B39:1–38

Duncan SC, Duncan TE. 1994. Modeling incomplete longitudinal substance use data using latent variable growth curve methodology. *Multivar. Behav. Res.* 29:313–38

Duncan SC, Duncan TE, Hops H. 1996. Analysis of longitudinal data within accelerated longitudinal designs. *Psychol. Methods* 1:236–48

Duncan TE, Duncan SC, Hops H. 1994. The effect of family cohesiveness and peer encouragement on the development of adolescent alcohol use: a cohort-sequential approach to the analysis of longitudinal data. *J. Stud. Alcohol* 55:588–99

du Toit M, du Toit S. 2001. *Interactive LISREL: User's Guide.* Lincolnwood, IL: Sci. Software Intl.

Efron B. 1982. *The Jackknife, the Bootstrap, and Other Resampling Plans.* Philadelphia, PA: Soc. Industrial Appl. Math.

Enders CK. 2001a. A primer on maximum likelihood algorithms available for use with missing data. *Struct. Equ. Model.* 8:128–41

Enders CK. 2001b. The impact of nonnormality on full information maximum-likelihood estimation for structural equation models with missing data. *Psychol. Methods* 6:352–70

Enders CK. 2003. Using the expectation maximization algorithm to estimate coefficient alpha for scales with item-level missing data. *Psychol. Methods* 8:322–37

Glynn RJ, Laird NM, Rubin DB. 1993. Multiple imputation in mixture models for nonignorable nonresponse with followups. *J. Am. Stat. Assoc.* 88:984–93

Graham JW. 2003. Adding missing-data relevant variables to FIML-based structural equation models. *Struct. Equ. Model.* 10:80–100

Graham JW, Cumsille PE, Elek-Fisk E. 2003. Methods for handling missing data. In *Research Methods in Psychology,* ed. JA Schinka, WF Velicer, pp. 87–114. Volume 2 of *Handbook of Psychology,* ed. IB Weiner. New York: Wiley

Graham JW, Donaldson SI. 1993. Evaluating interventions with differential attrition: the importance of nonresponse mechanisms and use of followup data. *J. Appl. Psychol.* 78:119–28

Graham JW, Flay BR, Johnson CA, Hansen WB, Grossman LM, Sobel JL. 1984. Reliability of self-report measures of drug use in prevention research: evaluation of the Project SMART questionnaire via the test-retest reliability matrix. *J. Drug Educ.* 14:175–93

Graham JW, Hofer SM. 1992. *EMCOV Users Guide.* Univ. S. Calif. Unpubl. documentation

Graham JW, Hofer SM. 2000. Multiple imputation in multivariate research. In *Modeling Longitudinal and Multiple-Group Data: Practical Issues, Applied Approaches, and Specific Examples,* ed. TD Little, KU Schnabel, J Baumert, 1:201–18. Hillsdale, NJ: Erlbaum

Graham JW, Hofer SM, Donaldson SI, MacKinnon DP, Schafer JL. 1997. Analysis with missing data in prevention research. In *The Science of Prevention: Methodological Advances from Alcohol and Substance Abuse Research,* ed. K Bryant, M Windle, S West, 1:325–66. Washington, DC: Am. Psychol. Assoc.

Graham JW, Hofer SM, MacKinnon DP. 1996. Maximizing the usefulness of data obtained with planned missing value patterns: an application of maximum likelihood procedures. *Multivar. Behav. Res.* 31:197–218

Graham JW, Hofer SM, Piccinin AM. 1994. Analysis with missing data in drug prevention research. In *Advances in Data Analysis for Prevention Intervention Research, National Institute on Drug Abuse Research Monograph*, ed. LM Collins, L Seitz, 142:13–63. Washington, DC: Natl. Inst. Drug Abuse

Graham JW, Olchowski AE, Gilreath TD. 2007. How many imputations are really needed? Some practical clarifications of multiple imputation theory. *Prev. Sci.* 8:206–13

Graham JW, Roberts MM, Tatterson JW, Johnston SE. 2002. Data quality in evaluation of an alcohol-related harm prevention program. *Evaluation Rev.* 26:147–89

Graham JW, Schafer JL. 1999. On the performance of multiple imputation for multivariate data with small sample size. In *Statistical Strategies for Small Sample Research*, ed. R Hoyle, 1:1–29. Thousand Oaks, CA: Sage

Graham JW, Taylor BJ, Cumsille PE. 2001. Planned missing data designs in analysis of change. In *New Methods for the Analysis of Change*, ed. LM Collins, A Sayer, 1:335–53. Washington, DC: Am. Psychol. Assoc.

Graham JW, Taylor BJ, Olchowski AE, Cumsille PE. 2006. Planned missing data designs in psychological research. *Psychol. Methods* 11:323–43

Hansen WB, Graham JW. 1991. Preventing alcohol, marijuana, and cigarette use among adolescents: peer pressure resistance training versus establishing conservative norms. *Prev. Med.* 20:414–30

Heckman JJ. 1979. Sample selection bias as a specification error. *Econometrica* 47:153–61

Hedeker D, Gibbons RD. 1997. Application of random-effects pattern-mixture models for missing data in longitudinal studies. *Psychol. Methods* 2:64–78

Honaker J, King G, Blackwell M. 2007. *Amelia II: A Program for Missing Data*. Unpubl. users guide. Cambridge, MA: Harvard Univ. **http://gking.harvard.edu/amelia/**

Horton NJ, Kleinman KP. 2007. Much ado about nothing: a comparison of missing data methods and software to fit incomplete data regression models. *Am. Stat.* 61:79–90

Jöreskog KG, Sörbom D. 1996. *LISREL 8 User's Reference Guide*. Chicago: Sci. Software

King G, Honaker J, Joseph A, Scheve K. 2001. Analyzing incomplete political science data: an alternative algorithm for multiple imputation. *Am. Polit. Sci. Rev.* 95:49–69

Lanza ST, Collins LM, Schafer JL, Flaherty BP. 2005. Using data augmentation to obtain standard errors and conduct hypothesis tests in latent class and latent transition analysis. *Psychol. Methods* 10:84–100

Leigh JP, Ward MM, Fries JF. 1993. Reducing attrition bias with an instrumental variable in a regression model: results from a panel of rheumatoid arthritis patients. *Stat. Med.* 12:1005–18

Leon AC, Demirtas H, Hedeker D. 2007. Bias reduction with an adjustment for participants' intent to drop out of a randomized controlled clinical trial. *Clin. Trials* 4:540–47

Little RJA. 1993. Pattern-mixture models for multivariate incomplete data. *J. Am. Stat. Assoc.* 88:125–34

Little RJA. 1994. A class of pattern-mixture models for normal incomplete data. *Biometrika* 81:471–83

Little RJA. 1995. Modeling the drop-out mechanism in repeated-measures studies. *J. Am. Stat. Assoc.* 90:1112–21

Little RJA, Rubin DB. 1987. *Statistical Analysis with Missing Data*. New York: Wiley

Little RJA, Rubin DB. 2002. *Statistical Analysis with Missing Data*. New York: Wiley. 2nd ed.

McArdle JJ. 1994. Structural factor analysis experiments with incomplete data. *Multivar. Behav. Res.* 29(4):409–54

McArdle JJ, Hamagami F. 1991. Modeling incomplete longitudinal and cross-sectional data using latent growth structural models. *Exp. Aging Res.* 18:145–66

McArdle JJ, Hamagami F. 1992. Modeling incomplete longitudinal data using latent growth structural equation models. In *Best Methods for the Analysis of Change*, ed. L Collins, JL Horn, 1:276–304. Washington, DC: Am. Psychol. Assoc.

Murray DM. 1998. *Design and Analysis of Group-Randomized Trials*. New York: Oxford Univ. Press

Muthén B, Kaplan D, Hollis M. 1987. On structural equation modeling with data that are not missing completely at random. *Psychometrika* 52:431–62

Muthén LK, Muthén BO. 2007. *Mplus User's Guide*. Los Angeles, CA: Muthén & Muthén. 4th ed.

Neale MC, Boker SM, Xie G, Maes HH. 1999. *Mx: Statistical Modeling*. Richmond: Virginia Commonwealth Univ. Dept. Psychiatry. 5th ed.

Nunnally JC. 1967. *Psychometric Theory*. New York: McGraw-Hill

Olsen MK, Schafer JL. 2001. A two-part random-effects model for semicontinuous longitudinal data. *J. Am. Stat. Assoc.* 96:730–45

Raghunathan TE. 2004. What do we do with missing data? Some options for analysis of incomplete data. *Annu. Rev. Public Health* 25:99–117

Raghunathan TE, Grizzle J. 1995. A split questionnaire survey design. *J. Am. Stat. Assoc.* 90:54–63

Raudenbush SW, Bryk AS. 2002. *Hierarchical Linear Models.* Thousand Oaks, CA: Sage. 2nd ed.

Rubin DB. 1976. Inference and missing data. *Biometrika* 63:581–92

Rubin DB. 1987. *Multiple Imputation for Nonresponse in Surveys.* New York: Wiley

SAS Institute. 2000–2004. *SAS 9.1.3 Help and Documentation.* Cary, NC: SAS Inst.

Satorra A, Bentler PM. 1994. Corrections to test statistics and standard errors in covariance structure analysis. In *Latent Variables Analysis: Applications for Developmental Research*, ed. A von Eye, CC Clogg, 1:399–419. Thousand Oaks, CA: Sage

Schafer JL. 1997. *Analysis of Incomplete Multivariate Data.* New York: Chapman & Hall

Schafer JL. 1999. Multiple imputation: a primer. *Stat. Methods Med. Res.* 8:3–15

Schafer JL. 2001. Multiple imputation with PAN. In *New Methods for the Analysis of Change*, ed. LM Collins, AG Sayer, 1:357–77. Washington, DC: Am. Psychol. Assoc.

Schafer JL, Graham JW. 2002. Missing data: our view of the state of the art. *Psychol. Methods* 7:147–77

Schafer JL, Olsen MK. 1998. Multiple imputation for multivariate missing data problems: a data analyst's perspective. *Multivar. Behav. Res.* 33:545–71

Schafer JL, Yucel RM. 2002. Computational strategies for multivariate linear mixed-effects models with missing values. *J. Comput. Graph. Stat.* 11:437–57

Tanner MA, Wong WH. 1987. The calculation of posterior distributions by data augmentation (with discussion). *J. Am. Stat. Assoc.* 82:528–50

von Hippel PT. 2004. Biases in SPSS 12.0 Missing Value Analysis. *Am. Stat.* 58:160–64

Willett JB, Sayer AG. 1994. Using covariance structure analysis to detect correlates and predictors of individual change over time. *Psychol. Bull.* 116(2):363–81

Wothke W. 2000. Longitudinal and multigroup modeling with missing data. In *Modeling Longitudinal and Multiple-Group Data: Practical Issues, Applied Approaches, and Specific Examples*, ed. TD Little, KU Schnabel, J Baumert, 1:219–40. Hillsdale, NJ: Erlbaum

Latent Variable Modeling of Differences and Changes with Longitudinal Data

John J. McArdle

Department of Psychology, University of Southern California, Los Angeles, California 90089-1061; email: jmcardle@usc.edu

Annu. Rev. Psychol. 2009. 60:577–605

First published online as a Review in Advance on September 25, 2008

The *Annual Review of Psychology* is online at psych.annualreviews.org

This article's doi: 10.1146/annurev.psych.60.110707.163612

0066-4308/09/0110-0577$20.00

Key Words

linear structural equations, repeated measures

Abstract

This review considers a common question in data analysis: What is the most useful way to analyze longitudinal repeated measures data? We discuss some contemporary forms of structural equation models (SEMs) based on the inclusion of latent variables. The specific goals of this review are to clarify basic SEM definitions, consider relations to classical models, focus on testable features of the new models, and provide recent references to more complete presentations. A broader goal is to illustrate why so many researchers are enthusiastic about the SEM approach to data analysis. We first outline some classic problems in longitudinal data analysis, consider definitions of differences and changes, and raise issues about measurement errors. We then present several classic SEMs based on the inclusion of invariant common factors and explain why these are so important. This leads to newer SEMs based on latent change scores, and we explain why these are useful.

Contents

INTRODUCTION: LONGITUDINAL DATA AND THE STRUCTURAL EQUATION MODELING APPROACH

This review describes contemporary methods for longitudinal data analysis. So let us start by considering situations in which individuals (N) from different groups (G) have been measured over several discrete periods of time ($T < N$) on a repeated set of measurements (Y_m). In an experimental design, this could represent a classical layout wherein we randomize individuals to different conditions and measure everyone at multiple time points on multiple variables (Bock 1975). In an observational study, or longitudinal panel design, we could measure different demographic groups on multiple occasions over many years (Hsiao 2003). Of course, a variety of classical techniques are used for analyzing such data, including repeated measures analysis of variance, time series analysis, and growth curve analysis (Nesselroade & Baltes 1979). There are also many newer techniques that serve similar purposes (Hedecker & Gibbons 2006, Muller & Stewart 2006, Singer & Willett 2003, Verbeke & Molenberghs 2000, Walls & Schafer 2006).

A brief glance of the past few decades of Annual Review volumes shows the importance placed on statistical models for data analyses, and a few previous reviews have already focused on SEM principles and techniques (Bentler 1980, Bentler & Dudgeon 1996, Bollen 2002, MacCallum & Austin 2000, Tomarken & Waller 2005). These reviews discuss technical aspects of SEM, the nature of latent variables, SEM hypothesis formation and statistical testing, and even the misuse of SEM. Other Annual Review articles provide informative discussions about the key issues in repeated measures analysis (e.g., Collins 2006, Cudeck & Harring 2007, MacKinnon et al. 2007, Maxwell et al. 2008, Raudenbush 2001). The many good general references to SEM (e.g., Kline 2005, McDonald 1985) include several new books specifically about SEM for repeated measures (e.g., Bollen & Curran 2006, Duncan et al. 2006). In contemporary work, it has become popular to focus on the trajectory over time as the key feature of a repeated measures analysis (e.g., MacCallum et al. 1997; McArdle 1986, 1989; Raudenbush 2001). The trajectory approach has gained popularity, and for the most part, it nicely matches the scientific goals of longitudinal research (Nesselroade & Baltes 1979). Adding something new and useful to this impressive collection is not so easy.

In this review, we survey a variety of different ideas about data analysis, but we try to bring these together by our explicit focus on what we term the "latent change score" model. It is expected that readers well versed in the techniques of regression analysis and factor analysis will find this review to be elementary reading

and probably to be missing many technical details. But this is intentional. To reach a wider audience, we do not present the typical algebraic expressions or computer program SEM scripts, and all the new models are explained using simple plots or path diagrams. Because we survey models from a wide variety of scientific disciplines, where alternative terms are often used for the same mathematical and statistical concepts, we do not include all aspects of these models. Our hope is that our extensive use of path diagrams will help the reader see the common features of these theoretically appealing and practically useful ideas. And we hope this approach will clarify our main recommendation: When thinking about any repeated measures analysis it is best to ask first, what is your model for change?

Separating Differences from Changes

The many semantic conventions and colloquialisms used by psychological researchers do not always precisely match their formal definitions. A first issue here is the distinction between inferences about (*a*) differences between people and (*b*) changes within people. We use the plots of fictional scores over time in **Figure 1** to clarify this key distinction.

In **Figure 1a**, we have plotted six pairs of *X-Y* data points to show hypothetical data obtained from six different individuals. To provide a substantive context, we label the *Y*-axis "Alert" and we label the *X*-axis "Time of Day." We add a regression line where $X \rightarrow Y$ (with intercept β_0 and slope β_1). Because this regression line has a negative slope, our substantive interpretation might be that alertness decreases as the day goes on. In more technical terms, the difference between people on predictor X leads to an expected difference in outcome Y. To avoid causal language, we can express the slope (β_1) as the expected change in Y for a one-unit change in X. Notice we use the word "change" to describe the "difference" between persons.

Next consider the different data layout of **Figure 1b**. Here we view the same six pieces

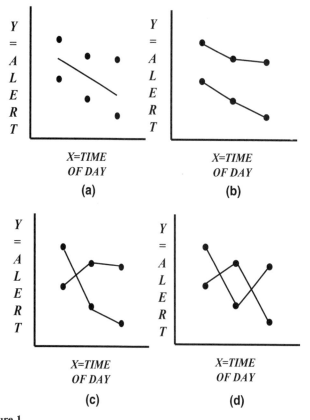

Y = A L E R T

X=TIME OF DAY

(a)

Y = A L E R T

X=TIME OF DAY

(b)

Y = A L E R T

X=TIME OF DAY

(c)

Y = A L E R T

X=TIME OF DAY

(d)

Figure 1

Alternative plots of cross-sectional and longitudinal data. (*a*) Cross-sectional measurements, (*b*) longitudinal measurements, (*c*) one longitudinal alternative, and (*d*) another longitudinal alternative.

of information as coming from just two people measured at three time points on the same measure (i.e., $Y[1]$, $Y[2]$, and $Y[3]$). To indicate the same person over time, we can connect the dots with lines, and now see both lines go down as the time-of-day increases. A simple subtraction of any two scores for any person is termed a "difference score" (e.g., $D = Y[2]-Y[1]$), and these are changes within a person over occasions. Now we use the word "difference" to define a "change."

The six data points in **Figures 1***a* and **1***b* are in exactly the same positions, and there is no alteration of the inference about X producing Y. Of course, in **Figure 1***b* we measure fewer people. To anticipate a reasonable statistical question, we can state (without proof) that, given the same number of data points, there is typically a

gain in statistical precision by adding more occasions of measurement with the same people—i.e., repeated measures lead to increased power (Bock 1975, Hertzog et al. 2006, Muthén & Curran 1997).

In **Figure 1***c* and **1***d*, the same six data points are plotted, but we connect these data across two people in a different way. In **Figure 1***c*, it appears as if the two people shift in their position from Time 1 to Time 2—one line goes down while the other line goes up. In **Figure 1***d*, we connect other points, and now both lines appear to be fluctuating between ups and downs. By using the same data points, we can see that many different longitudinal patterns are possible underneath any set of cross-sectional scores. This highlights the key purpose of most longitudinal repeated measures data—to detect differences in the patterns of individual changes.

In theory, we can calculate the change scores and write another regression equation in which change is the dependent variable predicted by some difference between the people. This is an elementary description of the well-known mixed model, which attempts to identify the "between-person differences in within-person changes" (Nesselroade & Baltes 1979). It is worth noting that seminal statements made by some of the most important leaders of our field strongly advocated the need to avoid change scores (e.g., Cronbach & Furby 1970, Lord 1958). These statements focused primarily on the very real problems of measurement error in the change scores. In contrast, other researchers who investigated these statistical issues emphasized the benefits of using change scores (i.e., Allison 1990, Nesselroade & Cable 1974, Rogosa 1979, Rogosa & Willett 1983). It is not surprising that the appropriate use of change scores remains a conundrum for many researchers.

The Structural Equation Modeling Approach

It is well known that SEMs are used to express a theoretical model in terms of linear and nonlinear expressions with observed and unobserved variables (Goldberger & Duncan 1973). SEM expressions lead to predictions or expectations for the means, standard deviations, and correlations, and these can then be compared to observed statistics. A series of alternative models, often based on radically different ideas, can be organized in this way and then compared with one another using a variety of goodness-of-fit tests. In the early years of SEM, only a few reliable computer programs were able to carry out these calculations (e.g., ACOVSM, Jöreskog et al., 1971; LISREL, Jöreskog & Sörbom 1979; COSAN; McDonald 1985). Today, many SEM programs exist, ranging from the most flexible (Mplus; Muthén & Muthén 2002), to the most graphic (AMOS; Arbuckle & Wotke 2004), to the least expensive (Mx; Neale et al. 1999). SEM programs are often hard to choose among, and alternative computer scripts can be very helpful (e.g., Ferrer et al. 2004). All SEM programs can carry out the calculations for the models described here, so computer program differences are not highlighted.

Important lessons have been learned from statistical research on the classical tests of mean differences using repeated measures analysis of variance (ANOVA). Research in the early 1970s showed that the most popular ANOVA tests were based on an assumption of an equal variance and an equal correlation over time, a pattern termed "compound symmetry" (e.g., McCall & Applebaum 1973). Unfortunately, these assumptions seemed highly improbable with real longitudinal data. As it turned out, features of the tests of the mean differences over time were influenced by the adequacy of the covariance structure assumptions. In standard testing of the mean differences, (*a*) the Type I error rate (e.g., $\alpha = 0.05$) is inflated if the simple covariance assumptions are not met, but (*b*) the Type II error (e.g., 1-*power*) is inflated if no structure is placed on the covariances. The suggested correction at the time was to alter the degrees-of-freedom by a coefficient (termed ε) computed from the covariance matrix or to use the unstructured but less-powerful multivariate approach (MANOVA; McCall &

Applebaum 1973, O'Brien & Kaiser 1985). At the same time, other researchers were promoting a different kind of data analysis approach, eventually termed SEM (e.g., Jöreskog et al. 1971), wherein the mean and the covariance hypotheses could be considered jointly by what are now termed "shared parameters" (McArdle et al. 2005).

The approach presented here emphasizes the need for explicit structural hypotheses about means and covariances and for the direct inclusion of latent change scores to express specific developmental hypotheses about individuals and groups (e.g., McArdle & Nesselroade 1994, Nesselroade & Baltes 1979). SEM techniques are used to translate these specific hypotheses into structural expectations for the means and covariances over time so these expectations can be compared with a real set of longitudinal data. SEM path diagrams are used as a shorthand to convey aspects of the required matrix algebra. These diagrams highlight the key parameters we can test as well as the assumptions we cannot test. The path diagrams used here are intentionally more elaborate than are other SEM representations because these diagrams express every algebraic relationship among the scores.

STRUCTURAL EQUATION MODELS FOR REPRESENTING CHANGES

We first consider some of the key longitudinal questions about change using popular models for two occasions of data. The basic techniques described here are used in most of the other SEM examples to follow.

Auto-Regression Models

The first kind of model to be considered here is the familiar auto-regression model, drawn in **Figure 2a**. We label the two repeated scores as $Y[1]$ and $Y[2]$, and we presume $Y[1]$ "precedes" $Y[2]$ in time. This order of events suggests we add a regression (β) where $Y[1]$ is used to "predict" $Y[2]$ at the later time (i.e., $Y[2]$ is

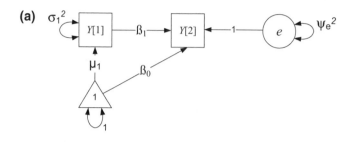

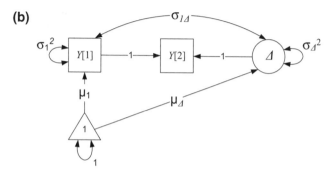

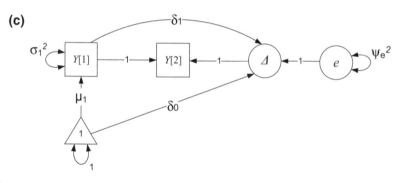

Figure 2

Alternative structural equation models for two-occasion data. (*a*) Traditional regression, (*b*) latent change score, and (*c*) change regression.

regressed on $Y[1]$). As in any regression calculation, we further assume that the unobserved residual term e is uncorrelated with the initial score $Y[1]$. In the traditional path diagram, there are no intercepts, and variables are often assumed to be standardized. But in this diagram, we explicitly draw all model parameters: (*a*) observed variables $Y[1]$ and $Y[2]$ as squares, (*b*) the unobserved variable e as a circle, (*c*) the implied constant of *1* as a triangle, (*d*) one-headed arrows to represent "fixed" or group effects (μ_1, β_0, β_1), and (*e*) two-headed arrows to represent "random" or individual effects (σ_1^2, ψ_e^2, 1). Al-

though these parameters complicate this simple figure, they prove very useful in subsequent model comparisons.

We can now use any SEM program to estimate values for this model. We start by calculating the means and covariances (or average cross-products) formed from observed raw scores. Numerical estimates for all unknown parameters (i.e., Greek letters) are obtained as well as a single index of goodness-of-fit of the model to the data (i.e., the likelihood L). To create a formal test of this model, we need to compare it to an alternative model, usually with different parameters. The SEM approach proves remarkably flexible here because parameters can be (*a*) free to vary, (*b*) fixed at any known value, or (*c*) set equal to any other parameter. For example, one typical alternative to model 2a is another in which there is "no stability" over time, and this can be formed by restricting the regression slope to be fixed at zero ($\beta_1 = 0$). Under standard regularity conditions (e.g., normality of the residuals), the difference in fit between the two models ($L_d = L_a - L_b$) is distributed as a chi-square (χ^2) variate with one degree-of-freedom ($df_d = df_a - df_b$). This SEM approach is not novel and it yields the same results we could obtain using any standard linear regression program.

Change Score Models

It is simple to subtract the two scores for each person using the observed data ($D = Y[2] - Y[1]$), with the results known as "gain scores" or "difference scores." But, as basic as this seems, calculating differences from raw data is not the most promising route to take here. Instead, the model of **Figure 2b** is a change score model for the same initial observations. We start with the same data ($Y[1]$ and $Y[2]$), but we add an unobserved variable labeled Δ. To this we add a set of fixed values ($=1$) on the specific arrows so we can mimic the result of a subtraction ($Y[2] = 1^*Y[1] + 1^*\Delta$). This change score ($\Delta$) is now explicitly defined as "the part of the score of $Y[2]$ that is not identical to $Y[1]$." This change score is not directly measured, so it can be considered as our first latent change score (McArdle & Nesselroade 1994; cf., Bollen 2002).

We can now use SEM software to estimate and test questions about changes directly from the original two-occasion data. The traditional statistical features of the change score are all included as model parameters—the mean of the changes (μ_Δ), the variance of the changes (σ_Δ^2), and the covariance of the initial scores with the changes ($\sigma_{1\Delta}$). For example, we can now test the hypothesis of "no mean differences over time"

by forcing the mean of the difference to be zero ($\mu_\Delta = 0$). This model leads to expectations of equal means over time, and the difference in fit is indexed by a chi-square test (χ^2). We can use the same model to test hypotheses about individual differences in change ($\sigma_\Delta^2 = 0$, $\sigma_{1\Delta} = 0$).

We do not need to calculate the change scores directly to examine their statistical properties when we use the model of **Figure 2b**. Instead, we define a latent change score by using fixed unit values; this simple SEM technique also proves valuable in the more-complex models presented below. The auto-regression model of **Figure 2b** is fit to observed data that are identical to those of the change score model of **Figure 2b**, and both models have the same number of parameters and achieve the same fit—i.e., these models are not testable alternatives of one another. Instead, the fundamental difference between auto-regression and change score models is in the way we represent and test hypotheses about the within-person changes. The change statistics are nearly impossible to describe in **Figure 2a**, but these are explicit parameters of **Figure 2b**.

Change-Regression Models

Further consideration about the two models discussed above leads to another question in change research: Should we remove the part of the individual change that is related to the initial level? In **Figure 2c**, we draw a slightly revised version of **Figure 2b**, in which we transform the covariance ($\sigma_{1\Delta}$) into a regression coefficient (δ_1) to estimate a model with a base-free measure of change. This is also a transformation of parameters in **Figure 2a** (i.e., with $\delta_0 = \beta_0$, $\delta_1 = \beta_1 - 1$) and is useful to formalize this simple interpretation. In addition, the transformation provides one way to deal with the classic problem known as Lord's Paradox (Lord 1967)— the difference in results obtained from the regression in **Figure 2a** and the change model in **Figure 2b** are avoided if we use the change-regression model in **Figure 2c** (with group information).

Estimating this change score regression (δ_1) is mainly useful when the changes have not taken place by the time of the initial occasion. This is assured, for example, in an experiment wherein a manipulation occurs between Time 1 and Time 2. In contrast, in observational research, the two occasions may be arbitrary selections from an ongoing process unfolding over time, possibly in different ways for different persons. In this case, the changes may already be apparent at the time of the initial data collection, so this change regression is only an arbitrary transformation. This is a case where SEMs regressions yield parameter estimates that may be very difficult to interpret.

STRUCTURAL EQUATION MODELS FOR ADDING GROUP DIFFERENCES

Group differences are important aspects of both experimental and observational longitudinal studies. As is well known, the use of random assignment to groups provides a direct basis for causal inference. In observational studies, a frequent goal is to separate groups that are not following the same process (i.e., heterogeneity). Group information may be considered in many ways, and the techniques described in this section are relevant to all SEMs in the discussion that follows.

Group Information as Contrast Codes

Let us assume that an important difference exists between groups of people (e.g., due to a manipulation, based on gender, linked to high test scores), and we want to examine how these differences impact some outcome. One popular model for this purpose is drawn as **Figure 3a**. This is a change score path model that also includes the group information as a measured variable (G) using dummy codes ($G = 0$ or 1) or effect code ($G = -1/2$ or $+1/2$). This typical use of group differences as a coded variable allows standard regression parameters to estimate mean differences between groups. With dummy codes, these path coefficients represent

a 2-by-2 ANOVA with four parameters: (*a*) an initial mean ($\beta_0 = 1 \to Y[1]$), (*b*) a between-group effect ($\beta_1 = G \to Y[1]$), (*c*) a within-group effect ($\alpha_0 = 1 \to \Delta$), and (*d*) a within-by-between effect ($\alpha_1 = G \to \Delta$). Other aspects of the ANOVA include the variances and covariance of the residuals of the level and change score (ψ_e^2, ψ_z^2, ψ_{ez}).

As in any regression formulation of ANOVA among K independent groups, we need K-1 contrasts to fully represent the mean differences. A common variation of this model is the use of "adjusted" change parameters in the analysis of covariance (ANCOVA). This is drawn in the same way as **Figure 3a**, but with the addition of a continuous variable X as an observed predictor of both the initial level and changes. In ANCOVA, the model parameters are conditional on the expected values of the measured X variable. Many researchers use the term "controlled" for this form of statistical adjustment, and this is reasonable in some cases. We must recognize that the statistics are under our control but the individuals are not. The ANCOVA interaction term, representing potential differences in the slopes of the covariate between groups, can be introduced in path models using product terms as measured variables ($P = G^*X$). In this way, any ANCOVA can be carried out as an SEM.

Multiple-Group Latent-Difference Models

This previous use of group coding is limiting in a number of ways. The focus of this kind of analysis is on differences in the mean changes over groups, and other forms of group differences in change processes are not typically considered. Different groups of people may have different means, but they may also have different amounts of variability in their changes (σ_Δ^2). The SEM approach expands our options for considering aspects of group differences.

Figure 3b represents a latent change score model in which we have assumed there are two independent groups of individuals, perhaps differentiated by an experimental

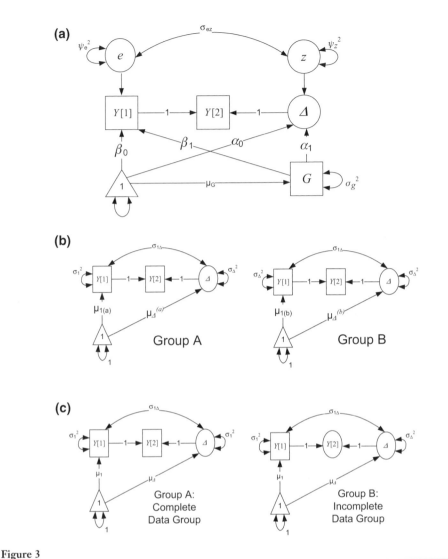

(a)

(b)

Group A

Group B

(c)

Group A:
Complete
Data Group

Group B:
Incomplete
Data Group

Figure 3

Alternative two-occasion structural equation models with group differences. (*a*) Adding group codes,
(*b*) multiple group model, and (*c*) incomplete data groups.

treatment (e.g., treatment versus controls), a demographic difference (e.g., males versus females), or an observational difference (e.g., high versus low math scores). This organization of the data into groups allows for tests of group differences by using a multiple-group SEM. In this example, the group means are represented as regressions from the constant within each group $(1 \rightarrow Y[1] = \mu_1^{(a)}, \mu_1^{(b)})$. A test of the equality of these coefficients is termed "invariance over groups" $(\mu_1^{(a)} = \mu_1^{(b)})$, and this can be carried

out using the SEM programs. These invariance constraints will result in a misfit (χ^2) of the same magnitude as tests of no mean differences between coded groups $(\beta_1 = 0$ in **Figure 3a**). Next, the mean of the changes $(\mu_\Delta^{(a)}, \mu_\Delta^{(b)})$ can be tested for invariance over groups $(\mu_\Delta^{(a)} = \mu_\Delta^{(b)})$ as a test of group-by-time interaction.

This multiple-group SEM allows testing the invariance of any model parameter. In this case, we might want to add a test of the equality-of-change variation over groups $(\sigma_\Delta^{2(a)} = \sigma_\Delta^{2(b)})$

to see if there are group differences in the amount of changes (using the χ^2). A more complex expression can be formed to test the equality of the "coefficient of variation" or effect sizes ($\mu_\Delta^{(a)}/\sigma_\Delta^{(a)} = \mu_\Delta^{(b)}/\sigma_\Delta^{(b)}$). Following a similar logic, we can easily represent and test interactions, even interactions including latent variables, without creating product variables. In the typical MANOVA analyses, we require complete homogeneity of covariance over groups (e.g., Bock 1975, O'Brien & Kaiser 1985), but some SEM alternatives, with less-extreme forms of invariance, may be more realistic and useful.

Multiple Group Structural Equation Model Estimation with Incomplete Data

In practical situations, we often have repeated measures data wherein some individuals are not measured at all occasions. In some designed experiments, we may plan not to measure some of the subjects to estimate the impact of measurement (e.g., incomplete blocks design, Solomon 4-group design). But in most observational studies, some participants drop out after the first occasion, usually for a variety of different reasons. As pointed out above, it is difficult to estimate changes when only one measurement occasion is available. So unless there is a compelling reason to do otherwise, persons who drop out of the study are typically dropped from all subsequent data analysis. This use of complete cases often seems to be the only possible analysis, and we generally view this as a conservative approach that avoids overstating our results.

Recent statistical research has focused on this incomplete data problem and has demonstrated how the previous statements about complete-case analysis are not typically true (Enders 2001, Little & Rubin 2002). In fact, well-intentioned complete-case analyses are likely to yield unintentionally biased results. A typical indicator of attrition bias due to dropouts is expressed as the mean differences at Time 1 between groups that (*a*) participate at

both occasions and (*b*) those that are not available at the second occasion. When we find mean differences between these groups we have selection bias, and the question becomes, what inferences are now possible?

One of the more popular features of SEM is the ability to deal directly with common problems of incomplete data. Following the well-developed lead of many statisticians (Hsiao 2003, Jöreskog & Sörbom 1979, Little & Rubin 2002), any change model can be written in terms of a sum of misfits (L_g) for multiple groups, where groups are defined as persons with the identical pattern of complete data. In **Figure 3c**, we present a change-score model for two occasions for one group with complete data ($Y[1]$ and $Y[2]$) and a second change-score model for the group of individuals who are missing data at Time 2. The difference between the groups is only that $Y[2]$ is observed in group A (drawn as a square) but is unobserved in group B (drawn as a circle; Horn & McArdle 1980, McArdle & Bell 2000).

Many alternative estimation techniques are available to deal with these problems (e.g., multiple imputation; Little & Rubin 2002), but the SEM approach is relatively easy to understand (McArdle & Bell 2000, Enders 2001). If we want to make an inference about all people as if they were from the same population of interest, we must assume invariance of all parameters over all groups (e.g., $\mu_1^{(a)} = \mu_1^{(b)}$, $\mu_\Delta^{(a)} = \mu_\Delta^{(b)}$, $\sigma_\Delta^{2(a)} = \sigma_\Delta^{2(b)}$). If these invariance assumptions yield a reasonable fit, we may conclude the incomplete data are missing completely at random (MCAR). However, if the multiple-group invariance constraints do not fit well (i.e., a significant χ^2), we may conclude that they are missing at random (MAR). In either event, requiring invariance of all parameters provides the best estimate of the population parameters of the latent differences as if everyone had continued to participate. Thus, we accept any loss of fit associated with this form of invariance, and we compare alternative models with this misfit as our new baseline.

In general, this multiple-group SEM approach uses all available data on any measured variable, so it is a reasonable starting point for all further change analysis. The inclusion of all the cases, both complete and incomplete, allows us to examine the impact of attrition and possibly to correct for these biases. MAR results represent a convenient starting point, but many more techniques are available for dealing with incomplete data. We should try to measure the reasons why people do not participate, because nonrandom selection can create additional biases (e.g., McArdle et al. 2005, McArdle & Bell 2000, Raudenbush 2001). We are able to analyze all the data collected using these and other incomplete-data techniques.

STRUCTURAL EQUATION MODELS FOR INCLUDING LATENT COMMON FACTORS

The SEMs described above do not attempt to solve the potential problems of compounding measurement error in using change scores. To deal with these problems, we rely on multiple measurements of the same construct within each occasion. With multiple measures, we first examine the hypotheses about common factors (McArdle 2007b, McDonald 1985, Meredith & Horn 2001), and we then expand these common factors into more complete mean and covariance structures.

Regression with Common Factors

The path diagram in **Figure 4a** represents a structural hypothesis for multivariate observations (squares $X[t]$, $Y[t]$, $Z[t]$) repeated over two occasions of measurement. Within each occasion, we include a latent variable at each occasion (circles $f[1]$ and $f[2]$) with factor loadings (one-headed arrows labeled λ_m). The unique variation for each variable is also included (ψ_m^2 as double-headed arrows). Following classical factor-analysis theory, unique factor scores are thought to be decomposable into two parts— one part that is specific to the test and represents valid measurement, and a second part that is random error. We assume each unique factor contributes variation at a given time but

is independent of other scores within and across occasions (Meredith & Horn 2001).

Common factors are used to represent the testable hypothesis that a single unobserved variable can account for the covariation among the observed scores within each occasion. We next require the factor loading for each to be the same value at all time points—factor loading invariance ($\lambda_m[1] = \lambda_m[2]$). This is a formal way to assert that this factor score has the same substantive meaning at each time of measurement. It is typical in SEM to introduce a regression in which common factors at later times are regressed on common factors at earlier times (β_f). In theory, these factor scores reflect only the common variance, and they do not contain measurement error. Thus, to the degree the invariant common-factor model is correct, this factor score regression represents the stability of only the reliable components of our measures.

Latent Changes in Common-Factor Scores

In cases in which the factor loading invariance restrictions are reasonable, we can write an alternative form of the model. In **Figure 4b**, we introduce a third latent score (Δf) that represents the latent change between the two common-factor scores. In SEM, we typically do not estimate the factor scores, so we cannot calculate this true change score directly. Instead, we follow the logic of the SEM in **Figure 2b** and include a set of fixed unit-valued coefficients ($= 1$), so the second latent factor ($f[2]$) is defined as a simple sum of the other two ($f[1] + \Delta f$). Because the latent change score (Δf) now is part of the model, the model parameters include the variation in latent changes across individuals (ϕ_Δ^2) as well as covariation of change with the initial common factor ($\phi_{1\Delta}$). As in the factor-regression model of **Figure 5a**, these common factors do not include errors of measurement, and this variance in latent change score is not confounded by errors of measurement. When used in this way, this multivariate SEM avoids the classical problems of using

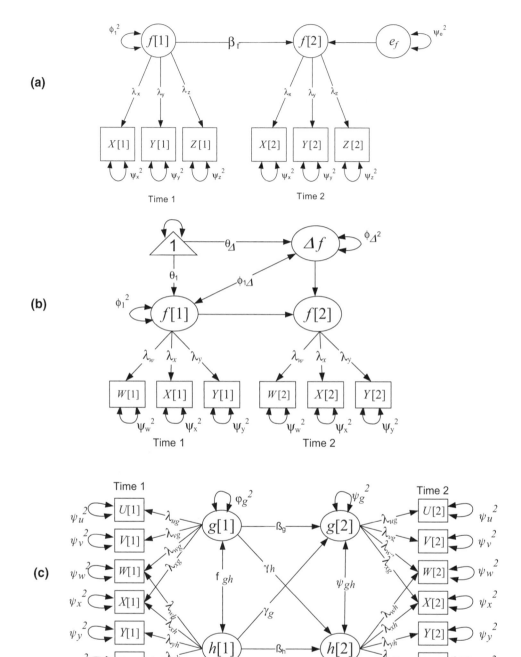

Figure 4

Alternative two-occasion structural equation models for multivariate data. (*a*) Common-factor regression, (*b*) common-factor latent change score, and (*c*) multiple-common-factors crossed-lagged regression.

inherently unreliable difference scores and the random errors cannot create regression to the mean (McArdle & Nesselroade 1994, Nesselroade et al. 1980).

This SEM also allows us to test hypotheses about mean changes over time in the reliable common-factor scores. By including observed variable means, we can additionally estimate a latent level mean (θ_1) and a latent change score mean (θ_Δ). From this multivariate SEM, we can calculate a nonstandard repeated-measure t-test among the common-factor scores and examine whether the mean of the latent change factor is zero ($\theta_\Delta = \theta_2 - \theta_1 = 0$?). A more complete description of these tests would include intercepts for each variable (ν_m), but these are not drawn here.

This new SEM offers a powerful way to answer questions typically asked by both the classical ANOVA and factor analysis techniques. In MANOVA, we estimate the linear combination weights that maximize the mean differences over time using canonical variates, which do not attempt to account for the correlations within time or across residuals. In contrast, the SEM in **Figure 4b** provides a highly structured approach for the repeated-measures ANOVA question. We are asking whether all the mean changes over time in this set of variables ($W[t]$, $X[t]$, $Y[t]$) are accounted for by mean changes in the common factors ($f[t]$). This is often exactly the question we want to answer.

Questions of Factorial Invariance Over Time

The search for factorial invariance over time is viewed by many as an empirical issue (Meredith & Horn 2001). As a first question, we typically ask whether the number of factors is equal over time. Assuming no substantial misfit, we can then ask questions about the invariance of all factor loadings over time: Does $\Lambda[1] = \Lambda[2]$? Other questions of factor equivalence over time can be asked, such as whether the person's unobserved factor scores are equal over time ($f[1]_n = f[2]_n$). This is a more difficult question that is examined indirectly by asking if the

factor means equal ($\theta[1] = \theta[2]$), if the factor variances equal ($\phi[1]^2 = \phi[2]^2$), and if the factors perfectly correlated ($\rho[1,2] = 1$). In repeated measures data, it is also reasonable to add specific covariances for each measurement over time (ψ_{mm}; not drawn) to remove additional confounds.

Further relaxations of the factor invariance model (**Figure 4a**) can be tested and may fit the data better, but the results may not be easy to interpret. In the absence of the same number of factors, we would need to interpret each factor separately. In the absence of factor loading invariance, we cannot assert the same common factors are measured at each measurement occasion. Although we might be interested in this kind of evidence for qualitative change, it is difficult to go much further in SEM because we do not have analytic tools to compare apples and oranges. Using repeated measures with the same number of factors and invariant-factor loadings allows us to say we have repeated constructs.

Because factor invariance is both practical and desirable, it seems appropriate to search for a metric invariant model of measurement until such a solution is found. In **Figure 4c**, we assume six variables are measured at each of two occasions and are indicators of two factors ($g[t]$ and $h[t]$). Each pair of factor scores are assumed to be correlated with each other and with the Time 1 factor scores (as drawn here). Here the factor loadings are invariant over time, but the factor pattern within each time is complex. The pattern is simple for the first two variables ($U[t]$ and $V[t]$ load on $g[t]$) as well as for the last two ($Y[t]$ and $Z[t]$ load on $h[t]$). But the invariant pattern is more complicated for the middle two variables, which have two loadings each ($W[t]$ and $X[t]$ load on both $g[t]$ and $h[t]$). Typically, a variable with multiple loadings does not contribute to the factorial description, but this is helpful because these multiple loadings are the same over time. So, although all variables do not exhibit a simple structure, a complex but invariant factor pattern may end up being more practically useful because it establishes the identity of factors across occasions.

STRUCTURAL EQUATION MODELS USING TIME-SERIES CONCEPTS

Many SEMs for repeated measures data come from the time-series literature (e.g., Browne & Nesselroade 2005, Nesselroade et al. 2001). These models typically do not deal with group averages, or even invariant common factors, but are based solely on time-to-time dependencies indicated by the covariance structures. Here we discuss several popular variations based on time-series regressions among invariant common factors over time.

Crossed-Lagged Regression of Factors

The introduction of multiple constructs within each longitudinal occasion of measurement leads naturally to questions about time-dependent relationships among changes in these factors. A classical SEM for multiple factors over time is based on a latent variable cross-lagged regression model (Gollob & Reichardt 1987, Rogosa 1979, Shadish et al. 2002). In **Figure 4c**, we assumed that each common factor influences itself over time with lagged autoregressions (β_g and β_b) and that each factor crosses over to influence the other factor at subsequent times (γ_g and γ_b).

This basic two-occasion two-factor model is used in an attempt to isolate the pattern of influences across the constructs over time. Indeed, this cross-lagged setup inspired the optimistic label of "causal modeling" for all SEMs (Bentler 1980; cf. McDonald 1985). However, for proper time-series causal inference, the variances and covariances of the factors (ϕ_g^2, ϕ_b^2, ϕ_{gb}) are required to be equal over time—these restrictions imply the common factors have reached a stationary state or a point of equilibrium. As with most other invariance hypotheses, these tests are fitted to raw score covariances and not merely to correlations (Meredith & Horn 2001). These important tests require a complex set of model constraints, so they are often simply ignored (Browne & Nesselroade 2005).

The lagged coefficients (β_g and β_b) provide information about the general stability within each variable, and the crossed coefficients (γ_g and γ_b) give information about the impact of one factor upon the other. If we can force one of these crossed coefficients to zero without a large misfit ($\gamma_g = 0$), then we can say that this factor ($g[t]$) is not a leading indicator over time of the other factor ($b[t+1]$). It is also possible to fit a model in which both influences are zero ($\gamma_g = \gamma_b = 0$), and if this fits well, then we can assert that the common factors do not influence one another. Except in rare cases (e.g., dyads), it is not reasonable to examine the exact equality of the processes ($\gamma_g = \gamma_b$) because different common factors are not in the same scale of measurement. A simpler alternative that also needs to be rejected is that only one common factor is needed over all times so there are no crossed effects at all (e.g., **Figure 4a**).

Under this set of assumptions, any significant cross-regression indicates a prediction over time independent of the outcome variable's own history, and this is a classic definition of a causal influence in observational data (e.g., Hsiao 2003). It has recently been pointed out that the longitudinal cross-lagged coefficient provides a reasonable test of a mediation hypothesis, and longitudinal data may be necessary for mediation theory (Cole & Maxwell 2003, MacKinnon et al. 2007). Nevertheless, the main problem with making any such causal assertions from longitudinal data is that they may be wrong, and we might not know it from our model fitting (Shadish et al. 2002). These inferences may be wrong because the variables have not reached equilibrium, or other variables are missing from the model that alter the influences, or these common factors are not invariant, and so on. These are not easy problems to overcome in longitudinal observational data.

It may be useful to point out that the latent change score model (**Figure 4b**) can be extended for use with multiple constructs with sets of latent changes (Δg and Δb). These change equations can directly represent the parameters of most interest, but they have the misfortune of appearing far more complicated than the cross-lagged model so they are not drawn here. Still, these SEMs can directly represent common questions, such as whether a change in X produces a change in Y, by turning a passive factor covariance (i.e., $\Delta g \rightarrow \Delta h$) into an active regression of factor changes (i.e., $\Delta g \rightarrow \Delta h$). We must consider if this question might be best represented using a model with regressions of changes on levels (as in **Figure 2c**), and we return to this issue below. In either case, it is certainly possible to specify some additional change questions as formal hypotheses.

The overall benefit of any crossed-lagged SEM comes when the model alternatives are clear and testable or when they can suggest a need for the collection of additional data. Patterns of causal influences are more complex and are not so easy to test, especially shorter-term feedback loops, different patterns of causal influence at different times, or different influences for subgroups of persons. In many cases, we can use SEM to ensure that these tests are meaningful statements of the hypotheses, but these models certainly cannot deal with all threats to the validity of all time-based causal assertions (see Shadish et al. 2002).

Extending Time-Series Factor Models to Multiple Occasions

We next consider more than two occasions of repeated measures data. Let's assume the common-factor scores at a current time ($f[t]$) are fully predicted by scores on the same factor at an earlier time ($f[t-1]$) with the classical inclusion of a disturbance term ($z[t]$). This type of model is presented in **Figure 5a** for four time points with invariant factor loadings (Λ) for the observed variables ($Y[t]$). As in most time-series models, the means are not usually restricted, so neither intercepts nor changes in the means are considered here.

In classical time-series analysis, the specific time of observation does not matter, but we do focus on the interval of time (Δt) between observations. For this reason, we only draw one regression weight (β) for a specific unit of time, and one disturbance variance (ω^2), and we as-

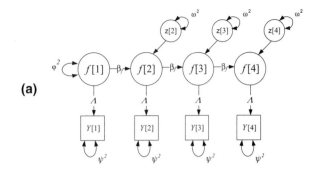

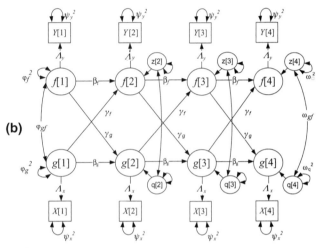

Figure 5

Alternative multiple-occasion structural equation models based on time-series concepts. (*a*) Quasi-Markov simplex with one common factor and (*b*) cross-lagged regression over many occasions.

sume this is invariant (stationary) over time. This is a highly restricted structure over time—a Markov simplex—wherein each covariance is a function of these parameters and the time interval (for occasions j and k, $\sigma_{jk} = \phi_1^2\, \beta^{k-j}$). As a start, we assume that the current scores are based only on immediately past behaviors, and this is a testable hypothesis. In early work on this topic, it was shown how all the errors of measurement could be separately estimated from observed variables with only a few occasions of measurement (i.e., $T = 4$). In later research, models with more-complete common factors were included ($f[t]$ in a quasi-Markov simplex; Jöreskog & Sörbom 1979). Assuming the common-factor loadings are invariant over time, we can test a broad hypothesis of equilibrium by asking if there is equality (i.e., stationarity) of the common-factor covariances within each time.

This time-series framework leads to a highly restricted covariance structure, so the simple auto-regressive factor model of **Figure 5a** does not always provide a good fit to the data, and more complexity may be needed (Nesselroade et al. 2001). Many alternatives can be considered at this point, including the introduction of more predictors from earlier times (i.e., using multiple back-shifts or lags $f\,[t-2], f\,[t-3]$, etc.), and other concepts about correlations of nearest points (i.e., latent moving average terms; Browne & Nesselroade 2005). However, it is clear that most SEM researchers avoid these issues and simply allow some or all of these parameters to vary, especially the auto-regressions (i.e., $\beta[1]$, $\beta[2]$, etc.) and disturbances (i.e., $\omega[1]^2$, $\omega[2]^2$, etc.). In real longitudinal data collections, the time period sampled may span different causal systems, and the crossed-lagged coefficients across time may need to vary, but this may lead to a more complex causal interpretation (Gollob & Reichardt 1987). This is another case in which standard SEM programs can be used to estimate parameters outside the bounds of the usual time-series interpretation.

Extending Cross-Lagged Factor Regression to Multiple Occasions

In **Figure 5b**, we presume each common factor is predicted by itself with lagged regressions (β) and by the other common factor with crossed regressions (γ). This simplified model extends the formal basis of cross-lagged common factors (**Figure 4c**) to many more occasions ($T > 2$). As a starting point, the effects over time are only included for factor scores at the immediately preceding time point. This framework allows us to evaluate whether any variable ($g[t]$) is an outcome of both itself at an earlier time ($g[t-1]$) and also an outcome of a different variable ($f\,[t-1]$) at an earlier time. As stated above, we may need to consider more complex models

that include effects from other time lags (e.g., $t-2$, $t-3$). In multivariate time-series analysis, we assume all common factors have reached a state of equilibrium, and we assume the pattern of causal influences is identical over equal distances in time. The invariance constraints of the factor loadings and the cross-lagged coefficients lead to a simplicity that requires empirical evaluation, but these simplifications can be effective when dealing with a lot of data.

This multi-occasion cross-lagged factors model provides a rigorous way to evaluate whether the phenomena under study are linked in a stationary (i.e., nonevolving) process. In practice, this model is often applied in observational panel studies without a time-series foundation, and a multitude of additional coefficients are needed for each occasion (e.g., Cillessen & Mayeux 2004). These kinds of longitudinal analyses might isolate causal/control features among the factors, but the resulting effects must be further studied in more rigorously controlled experiments before we could be certain about the true causal influences (Shadish et al. 2002). Of course, this is not to imply that randomization solves all problems—a randomized treatment may affect any model parameter, so group differences in the cross-lagged coefficients may be key (McArdle 2007a).

STRUCTURAL EQUATION MODELS USING LATENT-CURVE CONCEPTS

The popular time-series models do not deal with the group averages over time, but previous SEM research has considered many models that include both means and covariances (Harris 1963, Horn 1972, Horn & McArdle 1980, Jöreskog 1973, Jöreskog & Sörbom 1979). In a novel and comprehensive approach to this problem, Meredith & Tisak (1990) demonstrated how classical growth-curve models could be represented and fitted using a standard SEM based on restricted common factors for means and covariances. These representations of latent-curve SEMs were critical because they offered a wide range of alternatives to stationarity and equal-interval assumptions. This new SEM approach quickly spawned methodological and substantive applications (e.g., Bollen & Curran 2006; Duncan et al. 2006; McArdle 1986, 2001).

Latent Growth-Curve Models

One form of the latent-curve model is depicted in **Figure 6a**. In this model, we assume that each set of observed variables ($Y[t]$) reflects a set of invariant common factors ($f[t]$) separated from unique factors. Here, the common factors are organized to have three unobserved or latent scores: (*a*) a latent intercept or initial level (f_i), (*b*) a latent slope (f_s) representing the change over time, and (*c*) a time-specific independent state ($z[t]$). To indicate the average changes over time, we define a set of group coefficients or basis weights (e.g., slope loadings $\alpha[t]$) based on time since some event (e.g., time since surgery, time since birth). These model parameters are used to form the shape of the trajectory over occasions.

In path diagrams such as **Figure 6a**, the level and slope are often assumed to be random variables with fixed means (θ_i, θ_s) with random variances (ϕ_i^2, ϕ_s^2) and covariance (ϕ_{is}). We assume there is a within-time-state variance (ω^2) common to all observed measures (Horn 1972, McArdle & Woodcock 1997) and one unique variance (ψ_m^2) specific to each measure. For simplicity, these variance terms are assumed to be invariant over time and uncorrelated with all other components, but we recognize these restrictions may not be appropriate for real data.

This type of path diagram is a direct translation of the average cross-products matrix algebra used to estimate these models (Grimm & McArdle 2005). This inclusion of the basis coefficients ($\alpha[t]$) in this way means these parameters are shared in all model restrictions. Specifically, this includes a proportional relationship over time for the means (i.e., $\mu[t] = \theta_i + \theta_s \alpha[t]$) and the standard deviations ($\sigma[t]$, including $\alpha[t]$), and a more complex relationship with the over-time correlations ($\rho[t,t+1]$, including $\alpha[t]$ and $\alpha[t+1]$). Notice that the mean structure is formed as in an ANOVA, but the covariance structure lies in between the restrictions of ANOVA and the unrestricted MANOVA. This is important because the inclusion of appropriate restrictions on the covariance structure from the latent-curve model increases the statistical power of tests of mean differences (Muller & Stewart 2006, Muthén & Curran 1997).

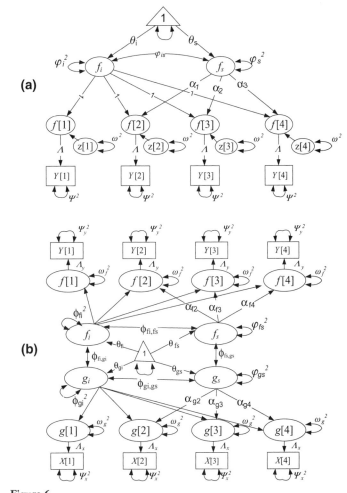

Figure 6

Alternative multiple-occasion structural equation models based on latent-growth concepts. (*a*) Latent-curve model for one common factor and (*b*) bivariate latent-curve model for two common factors.

Fitting Latent-Curve Hypotheses

Different organizations of the basis parameters represent specific hypothesis to be tested.

For example, if the basis is set to zero ($\alpha[t] = 0$), this eliminates the slope impacts and produces a level-only model with equal means and a compound symmetry structure. If we fix the basis to be the specific time of measurement ($\alpha[t] = t-1$), we can represent a straight-line or linear growth curve with a more complex shared parameter structure. Other popular nonlinear models include polynomial models (quadratic, cubic) and exponential forms (e.g., Ghisletta & McArdle 2001, Grimm et al. 2007). Although not as popular, we can also estimate latent-basis coefficients as we do any other set of factor loading where, because these are essentially factors of time, this leads to an estimate of an optimal shape for the group curve and individual differences (i.e., McArdle 1986, 1989; McArdle & Bell 2000; Meredith & Tisak 1990).

This latent-curve model is often expanded into what is popularly known as a multilevel, hierarchical, or random coefficient form. From an SEM perspective, we simply add a group-regression model that follows our use of group coding described above (**Figure 3a**). Here the predictors are group codes (G) or covariates (X) and the outcomes are the latent levels (f_i) and latent slopes (f_s). Because these outcomes are latent levels and latent slopes, this is termed a "second-level equation." There are some minor points of disagreement about exactly which random-coefficients models can and cannot be fit using standard SEM software (Cudeck & Harring 2007), but newer SEM software offers an effective way to deal with most practical problems (e.g., Ferrer et al. 2004).

We can compare the latent-curve model to standard ANOVA approaches. MANOVA makes no explicit provision for the structure of the covariances or even for uncorrelated residuals, so the otherwise comparable MANOVA tests (of linearity, etc.) require far more parameters and can be expected to yield far less power. This is not to suggest that SEM is best used with very small samples, but it does suggest that estimating a minimal number of parameters is a powerful idea. It is also well known that the standard MANOVA equations can be dif-

ficult to use with incomplete data (Bock 1975, Hedecker & Gibbons 2006). The additional requirement of homogeneity of the covariances over groups, a test often ignored in practice, may be more realistic if this test is formed as an SEM with latent-curve invariance over groups.

Considering Multiple Latent Curves

Assuming we have two common factors measured at multiple times, we can fit what appears to be an entirely different model—a model based on multiple latent curves (McArdle 1989). One popular version of this model is displayed in **Figure 6b**. In this model, we assume that each series is based on its own latent curve, with unlabelled arrows but different shapes ($\alpha_f[t]$, $\alpha_g[t]$) and with different parameters for the respective levels and slopes. However, the new information in this bivariate model comes from the cross-covariances of the levels and slopes. This model has recently become a popular way to represent a parallel-growth process (Bollen & Curran 2006, Duncan et al. 2006, Singer & Willett 2003). Of interest here is the correlation of the two latent slopes ($\phi_{fs,gs}$), this is an error-free index of simultaneous changes across different variables (f_s and g_s). Given other restrictions ($\phi_{fi,fs} = 0$, $\phi_{gi,gs} = 0$), we can test the hypothesis of "no connection in changes" among the factor scores ($\phi_{fs,gs} = 0$; Hertzog et al. 2006).

A problem of inference emerges when the direct test of correlated slopes is interpreted as the test of a dynamic impact (e.g., as in McArdle 1989; cf., MacCallum et al. 1997). The correlation of latent changes across different variables does not change over time and it does not represent a directional dynamic hypothesis. In the hope of obtaining time-dependent dynamic information, some researchers have tried to substitute a cross-lagged regression of the latent slopes on the latent levels (e.g., Bollen & Curran 2006, Singer & Willett 2003, Snyder et al. 2003). Although this model offers new latent-variable parameters, the only reasonable situation for this change regression comes when the latent levels are known to precede the latent slopes. That is, this levels → slopes model may be useful in experimental situations when there is a similar starting point for all subjects, but these same model parameters may be quite arbitrary with most observational data.

A related form of the latent-curve model with widespread usage in epidemiology and biostatistics is the time-varying covariate model adapted from work on survival analysis regression (Cox 1972). When applied in SEM (e.g., Bollen & Curran 2006), one of the variables ($X[t]$) is thought to be responsible for some part of the curvature of the other ($Y[t]$), so its influence is removed from the outcome scores within each time (or at lagged times). These time-varying covariate models are relatively easy to implement using existing computer software (e.g., Mplus, MIXED), so they are rapidly growing in popularity. Although covariate adjustment may be needed, this time-varying covariate approach is designed to remove all impacts, and this approach may not tell us much about the dynamic interplay among variables.

STRUCTURAL EQUATION MODELS USING LATENT-CHANGE CONCEPTS

In any data analysis problem where multiple constructs have been measured at multiple occasions, we need to consider the importance of causal sequences and determinants of changes (Nesselroade & Baltes 1979). The goal of evaluating time-based sequences, especially when things are changing, is one of the main reasons for collecting longitudinal repeated-measure data in the first place. We have pointed out above the useful benefits of the classical models, but we have also seen that each is limited to specific forms of dynamic inference. Of course, the statistical evaluation of dynamic sequences is not an easy problem, and these problems have puzzled researchers for decades. We describe below how the prior SEMs lead directly to new SEMs that can provide a more flexible framework for causal-dynamic questions.

Mixing Models for Means and Covariances

The time-series and latent-curve models discussed in the previous two sections are not identical, but they can be fit to the same repeated measures data. The distinguishing feature of time-series factor models (**Figure 5a**) is the use of time of measurement as a guide to organize the predictive regressions—i.e., moving forward in time. In contrast, in the latent-curve model (**Figure 6a**), we use the data at any time to define group curves and individual differences around a trajectory, so time-to-time predictions are not essential. Typically, these models do not use the same parameters, so they cannot be directly compared using standard goodness-of-fit tests. This has led some researchers to use both types of models with the same data, and the use of a multiple-model strategy often seems sensible in practice (e.g., Cillessen & Mayeux 2004).

Other researchers have tried to combine aspects of these models. In recent statistical work, ANOVA researchers have recognized that when the standard models do not fit well enough, a variety of built-in covariance assumptions can be added that are not strictly connected to the hypotheses about the means (e.g., AR[t]; for details, see Muller & Stewart 2006). A similar strategy was initially suggested for SEM (Jöreskog 1973), and it became easy to follow this lead and simply paste the two diagrams (in **Figure 5a** and **Figure 6b**) together as a composite model in the hopes achieving better fit (e.g., Curran & Bollen 2001, Horn & McArdle 1980). This composite strategy should end up with a better-fitting model, but the estimated parameters may still only be interpreted as separate parts.

A different way to approach this problem is to examine the specific theory generating the expectations. One common feature of contemporary repeated measures SEMs is that we are defining a trajectory over time (or an integral) in the scores, and the changes are implied using some difference (or differential) operator. However, if we look back to the classic literature on growth-curve analysis, the derivative (difference) was typically defined at the start, and this model of change then led to the expected integral (or trajectory) for the outcome of interest (Boker 2001, McArdle & Nesselroade 2003). Repeated measures SEMs can now be considered in this same way.

Latent Change Score Models

Figure 7a is a path diagram based on this concept of multiple latent change scores over time. Once again, we start with the separation of com-

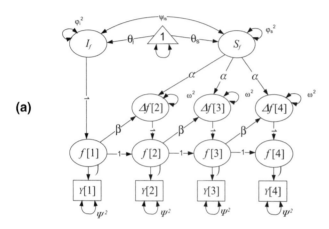

(a)

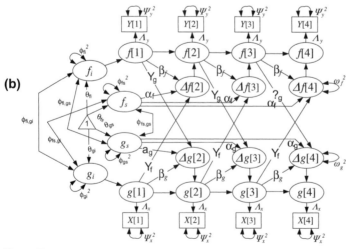

(b)

Figure 7

Alternative multiple-occasion structural equation models based on latent change concepts. (*a*) Latent change score model for one common factor and (*b*) bivariate latent change score model for two common factors.

mon from unique factors using invariant factor loadings (Λ). For single variables, this definition is similar to separating the latent or true score from the random error of measurement. We next follow the latent change score concept and consider each common-factor score (f [t]) to be the sum of the immediately previous factor score (f [t−1]) and some unobserved or latent change score (Δf [t]). If we then repeat this process for each time point, we add a layer of (t−1) new latent change scores to the model.

This approach is a natural generalization of the previous models in which difference scores are included as unobserved variables (**Figures 2b, 4b, 5b**). **Figure 7a** includes latent change scores (Δf [t]) at each occasion (after Time 1), and we assume these latent variables are equidistant in time ($\Delta t = 1$) even if the observed scores are not. That is, the observed data may be unbalanced (Hamagami & McArdle 2000, 2007). This definition of an equal-interval latent time scale is nontrivial because it allows us to eliminate the time lag (Δt) from all equations. The use of many fixed unit coefficients, a deceptively simple algebraic device, allows us to start with a change equation and then define any trajectory equation. That is, we do not directly define auto-regressions (β [t]) or slope coefficients (α [t]). Instead, we directly define the model of change and indirectly create overtime expectations from the accumulation of latent changes among latent variables.

This latent change equation produces many unusual-looking path diagrams (**Figure 7a**; see Collins & Sayer 2001), but because we have included all model parameters, the standard path-tracing rules of expectations remain intact. In these tracings, any change that occurs earlier accumulates and is expressed in the later occasions. The first term in the accumulation process may be traced in the diagram by starting at the first change score (Δf [2]). This change does not affect the prior score (f [1]), but it does influence the second time directly (by the fixed 1), and it is an indirect part of all the other latent common factors through the sequence of fixed-unit values (from f [t] to f [t+1]). Similarly, the next change score (Δf [3]) does not affect prior times, but it is a part of all future times. This sequence is used to form a set of expectations for the means, variances, and covariances over time, but potentially complex expectations are automatically generated using any standard SEM software (Grimm & McArdle 2005; Hamagami & McArdle 2000, 2007; McArdle 2001).

This approach to latent change scores can represent all difference and change concepts from the models discussed above. For example, the latent intercept term (f_i) has effects along the one-headed arrows (from f [t] to f [t+1]), so the intercept mean (θ_i) and variance (ϕ_i^2) are part of the expected value of every time point. Next we add a latent slope score (f_s) with loadings (α[t]) and with a mean (θ_s). The latent slope is not connected to the first factor score (f [1]), but it affects the changes (Δf [t]), and this influence is accumulated over subsequent time points. We can also include a prediction of the latent change score (Δf [t]) as a linear function (β) of the factor score at the previous time (f [t−1]), plus a state residual (z[t]), and these effects are multiplied over time. Because of the common-factor model separation, the error variances (ψ_m^2) are assumed to be constant over time and are not part of this accumulation.

The resulting model in **Figure 7a** is termed a dual-change score model. In this expression of change, we permit both a systematic constant change (α) from the linear slope and a systematic proportional change (β) over time. As a simple start, these change coefficients (α, β) can be considered invariant over time (e.g., ergodic). The invariance of dynamic parameters does not mean the expectations are constant—the latent scores can grow and change—but it does mean that the expectations accumulate in a systematic fashion. This simple linear-difference model with multiple control parameters leads to a nonlinear growth trajectory from the accumulation of latent changes and comes from a family of curves based on linear and exponential trajectories (Ghisletta & McArdle 2001, Grimm et al. 2007, Hamagami & McArdle 2007).

Multiple Latent Change Score Models

Figure 7b is a latent change score model for two common factors. Here we draw the dual-change model for each set of observed variables (Y[t] and X[t]) in terms of their common factors (f [t] and g[t]). We assume the sets of observed scores are measured over a defined interval of time and the latent variables are defined over an equal interval of time ($\Delta t = 1$), and we add layers of latent difference scores (Δf [t] and Δg[t]). This model includes the use of fixed-unit values (unlabeled arrows) to define pairs of latent changes (Δf [t] and Δg[t]), and equality (invariance) constraints over time within a factor (for the α, β, and γ parameters) to simplify estimation and identification. Most critically, in this model a coupling parameter (γ_f) represents the time-dependent effect of one construct (g[t−1]) on the subsequent change in the other (Δf [t]). We can include both directions (γ_f and γ_g) and consider many different SEMs for multiple latent changes.

This new change model subsumes all aspects of the previous models as special cases to be tested. We can fit the standard cross-lagged factor model (**Figure 5b**) by eliminating the latent intercepts and the latent slopes. The standard cross-lagged models do not allow for systematic growth components, but this is now a testable feature of this change model. To obtain a bivariate latent curve (**Figure 6b**), we eliminate both the autoregressive ($\beta_f = \beta_g = 0$) and coupling parameters ($\gamma_f = \gamma_g = 0$). The bivariate latent growth models may represent parallel latent processes, even including regressions of slopes on levels, but they do not allow for cross-lagged dynamic coupling of the key factors over time, so such a simple model may not capture the systematic changes or fit the data.

The inclusion of latent changes in a bivariate model allows a variety of dynamic models to be tested using the standard SEM statistical approach. These bivariate trajectories can be complex, but they are automatically created as a linear accumulation of first differences for each variable by standard SEM programs. These bivariate latent change score models can be expanded in many other ways lead to more-complex nonlinear-trajectory equations (e.g., nonhomogeneous equations; Hamagami & McArdle 2000, 2007). These dynamic models can easily be extended to multivariate form to estimate the time-dependent interplay among multiple factors (Ghisletta & Lindenberger 2005, McArdle et al. 2001). Additional dynamic features will be possible to estimate with more common factors and more occasions of measurement.

ADDITIONAL RELEVANT RESEARCH ISSUES

We have discussed a variety of new options for repeated measures data analysis from an SEM perspective. We have tried to show how SEMs permit researchers to make very specific hypotheses about longitudinal data and then to use traditional multivariate statistical tests about mean and covariance structures to form test statistics. In areas where the a priori hypotheses are straightforward, using SEM is relatively easy. But when the hypotheses are more complex and flexibility is needed, SEM may prove even more useful. In this final section, we discuss some new applications, some additional but overlooked topics, and offer some concluding thoughts.

New Dynamic Structural Equation Model Applications

This review does not emphasize substantive applications, but each model discussed here has been used to analyze real data. Latent cross-lagged models were widely used in the 1970s and 1980s, and latent-curve applications increased rapidly during the 1990s and 2000s. The bivariate dual-change model has only been available a short time (post 2000), but many researchers have already applied this dynamic SEM to their substantive problems. In our own recent applications, we have used dynamic SEM to investigate the lead-lag relationships in (a) Wechsler Intelligence Scale for Children (McArdle 2001), (b) Wechsler Adult

Intelligence Scale factors changing over adulthood (McArdle et al. 2001), (c) anti-social behaviors and reading achievement in the National Longitudinal Study of Youth cohort (McArdle & Hamagami 2001), (d) cognitive dynamics in longitudinal twin data (McArdle & Hamagami 2003), (e) Experimental impacts of cognitive training (McArdle 2007a), and (f) brain changes in lateral ventricle size (LVS) and the Wechsler Memory Scale (WMS) (McArdle et al. 2004).

Some aspects of our final study illustrate the substantive utility of dynamic modeling. These brain-behavior data were collected at two occasions over a seven-year longitudinal period for people of a wide range of ages (30–90). As shown in **Figure 8a**, we organized and plotted the raw data over age-at-testing. The two plots on the left-hand side show that the two-point raw data connected by small lines (over seven years) and the age coverage per person is sparse at best. To minimize selection biases, we also included persons who only participated once (shown as circles). We initially fit models to each variable separately using a latent change score model (**Figure 7a**) over age, and the results are given in the two plots on the right-hand side. From these analyses, we found that the brain changes (ΔLVS[t]) were linearly increasing, so the trajectories were increasing exponentially over age, probably reflecting shrinkage of related neural structures. At the same time, we found that the memory changes (ΔWMS[t]) had both constant and proportional changes and the trajectories were decreasing over age, indicating rapid losses of memory in the oldest ages. Although it seems reasonable to make statements about the likely causes and effects at this point, this raises the classic problem of the ecological fallacy—from the prior trajectories, we do not know if the persons who are increasing the most in lateral ventricle size are also the same persons who are subsequently losing their memory abilities. However, we joined the two series, and from the bivariate change model (**Figure 7b**) analysis, we estimated a coupling coefficient from LVS$\rightarrow \Delta$WMS ($\gamma_{WMS} = -0.2$) that dominated the coupling of WMS$\rightarrow \Delta$LVS

(a)

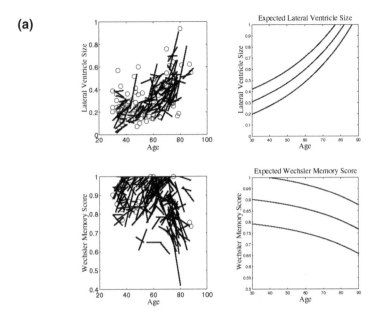

(b)

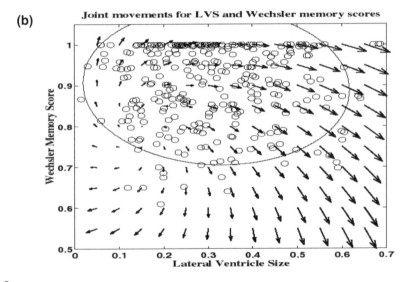

Figure 8

Results from bivariate latent change score analysis (from McArdle et al. 2004). (*a*) Aging data and latent-curve score expectations for lateral ventricle size (LVS) and Wechsler Memory Scores (WMS) and (*b*) statistical vector field result of expected changes in LVS and WMS over time.

($\gamma_{LVS} = 0$). This new dynamic SEM evidence suggested the brain changes were a leading indicator in time of the memory changes and not the other way around.

To summarize the bivariate dynamic results, we also expressed the final model coefficients using a statistical vector field, shown in **Figure 8*b***. Each arrow in this figure starts at a pair of scores, representing the bivariate starting point, and the direction of the arrow illustrates the changes expected over the next time point in the set of scores. This figure illustrates one of the major outcomes of a true score dynamic model—the "pulling" of memory changes downward by increasing size of the lateral ventricles. For many knowledgeable scientists, this illustrates an obvious dynamic relationship (i.e., brain → Δbehavior), but ours is an empirical observation. This pictorial description sets the stage for further work in simplifying the dynamic concepts and the corresponding multivariate results.

Research led by others has used similar bivariate latent change score models to examine different lead-lag relationships, including (a) personality disorders and changes (Hamagami et al. 2000), (b) perceptual speed and knowledge changes in older ages (Ghisletta & Lindenberger 2003, 2005), (c) specific cognitive abilities and achievement using the Woodcock-Johnson scales (Ferrer & McArdle 2004), (d) social participation and perceptual speed in aging (Lövdén et al. 2005), (e) physical activity and cognitive declines (Ghisletta et al. 2006), (f) reading and cognition over all ages (Ferrer et al. 2007), and (g) forgiveness and psychological adjustment (Orth et al. 2008).

Other Promising Directions

Many topics that are relevant to longitudinal SEM and multivariate data analysis have not been considered here. In practice, we need to know how to best select measures, score or scale the measures, deal with different (unbalanced) intervals of time, design how many occasions and participants are needed, deal with outliers, choose appropriate estimation techniques, and select indices of goodness-of-fit. All of these problems have new and elegant statistical solutions and are worthy of more detailed discussions.

New forms of multiple group and incomplete data approaches can be used with the dynamic models described here. By using a multilevel approach, we can also effectively analyze cases in which each person has different amounts of longitudinal data (i.e., unbalanced data or incomplete data), and some of the new SEM programs make this an easy

task. These possibilities lead directly to the revival of practical experimental options based on incomplete data (e.g., McArdle & Woodcock 1997). Incomplete data models have also been used to describe the potential benefits of a mixture of age-based and time-based models using only two time points of data collection—an accelerated longitudinal design (Duncan et al. 2006, McArdle & Bell 2000, Raudenbush 2001).

Factorial invariance, especially factor-loading invariance, was considered as a major requirement for any longitudinal analysis. As presented here, the goal of measurement invariance needs to be achieved before we can consider any SEMs of latent changes. Although only scale-level data are considered here, practical problems with measurement invariance at the scale level may indicate more basic measurement problems at the item level (McDonald 1985). Using incomplete data principles, item invariance is possible even if the items are originally used in the context of different scales (Grimm et al. 2007, McArdle & Nesselroade 2003). There are many techniques for linkage across measurement scales with sparse longitudinal data, and invariant item-response models may be very useful for these purposes (McArdle et al. 2002, McArdle & Nesselroade 2003).

A great deal of interest has focused on another fundamental repeated measures problem—the separation of latent groupings of people with different patterns of changes. Recent theoretical work on latent mixture models has been carefully developed (McLachlan & Peel 2000) and can be used for this purpose. In these analyses, the distribution of the latent parameters is assumed to come from a mixture of two or more overlapping distributions or latent classes. Mixture modeling of this variety is a recent addition to some SEM programs (e.g., Mplus; see Grimm et al. 2007). This interesting concept of a latent grouping seems very reasonable from a substantive point of view, but critics of these techniques point out the possibility of finding multiple latent classes when only one actually exists (e.g., Bauer & Curran 2003). Still, as with any multivariate cluster analysis result, our hope is that latent mixtures of group changes will be treated as an exploratory result that can be useful in guiding subsequent research.

Finally, there are many other elegant statistical models for longitudinal data. There have been several important breakthroughs in work on dynamic modeling of continuous time data using SEM software (e.g., Boker 2001, Chow et al. 2007, Montfort et al. 2007, Oud & Jansen 2000). These differential models offer many more dynamic possibilities, and this is increasingly important when large amounts of time points of data are collected ($T > N$). Other repeated-measures SEMs are based on the logic of partitioning variance components across multiple modalities (Kenny & Zautra 2001, Kroonenberg & Oort 2003, Steyer et al. 2001). These models decompose factorial influences into orthogonal common and specific components, with an emphasis on separating trait factors from state factors. These models have interesting interpretations, and they may be useful when combined with other SEMs described here.

Final Comments

The statistical training for most psychologists is still based on classical logic of ANOVA, multiple regression, and factor analysis techniques. A common theme of all this training is that statistical techniques are calculations based on specific assumptions, and the scientific inferences are limited by the accuracy of our statistical assumptions. This way of thinking about data analysis allows us to face new problems and is essential as the problems become more complex.

This review has attempted to highlight what has been learned from applying newer forms of SEM thinking to repeated-measures data designs. In some cases, advances are obvious, and in other cases, cautions have been suggested. From a broad perspective, a central conclusion of this review is that any repeated measures analysis should not start by asking, "What is your data collection design?" or "What computer program can you use?" The corollary conclusion is that all repeated measures analyses should start with the question, "What is your model for change?"

DISCLOSURE STATEMENT

The author is not aware of any biases that might be perceived as affecting the objectivity of this review, and he has no financial interest in any specific SEM computer program.

ACKNOWLEDGMENTS

The work described here has been supported since 1980 by the National Institute on Aging (grant #AG-07137). I am especially grateful to the collaboration of my close friend and colleague, John R. Nesselroade. This research was also helped by the support of many others, including the editors, and Steven Boker, Emilio Ferrer, Paolo Ghisletta, Kevin Grimm, Kelly Kadlec, Carol Prescott, John Prindle, Dick Woodcock, and Yan Zhou.

LITERATURE CITED

Allison PD. 1990. Change scores as dependent variables in regression analysis. In *Sociological Methodology 1990*, ed. CC Clogg, pp. 93–114. San Francisco, CA: Jossey-Bass

Arbuckle JL, Wotke W. 2004. *AMOS 5.0 User's Guide*. Chicago: Smallwaters

Bauer DJ, Curran PJ. 2003. Distributional assumptions of growth mixture models: implications for overextraction of latent trajectory classes. *Psychol. Methods* 8(3):338–63

Bentler PM. 1980. Multivariate analysis with latent variables: causal modeling. *Annu. Rev. Psychol.* 31:419–56

Bentler PM, Dudgeon P. 1996. Covariance structure analysis: statistical practice, theory, and directions. *Annu. Rev. Psychol.* 47:563–92

Bock RD. 1975. *Multivariate Statistical Methods in Behavioral Research*. New York: McGraw-Hill

Boker SM. 2001. Differential structural equation modeling of intraindividual variability. See Collins & Sayer 2001, pp. 3–28

Bollen KA. 2002. Latent variables in psychology and the social sciences. *Annu. Rev. Psychol.* 53:605–34

Bollen K, Curran PJ. 2006. *Latent Curve Models: A Structural Equation Perspective*. New York: Wiley

Browne M, Nesselroade JR. 2005. Representing psychological processes with dynamic factor models: some promising uses and extensions of autoregressive moving average time series models. In *Contemporary Advances in Psychometrics*, ed. A Madeau, JJ McArdle, pp. 415–52. Mahwah, NJ: Erlbaum

Chow S-M, Ferrer E, Nesselroade JR. 2007. An unscented Kalman filter approach for the estimation of nonlinear dynamic systems models. *Multivariate Behav. Res.* 42(2):283–321

Cillessen A, Mayeux L. 2004. From censure to reinforcement: developmental changes in the association between aggression and social status. *Child Dev.* 75:147–63

Cole DA, Maxwell SE. 2003. Testing mediational models with longitudinal data: questions and tips in using structural equation models. *J. Abnorm. Psychol.* 112:558–77

Collins LM. 2006. Analysis of longitudinal data: the integration of theoretical model, temporal design, and statistical model. *Annu. Rev. Psychol.* 57:505–28

Collins LM, Sayer A. 2001. *New Methods for the Analysis of Change*. Washington, DC: Am. Psychol. Assoc. Press

Cox DR. 1972. Regression models and life-tables. *J. R. Stat. Soc. B* 34:187–220

Cronbach LJ, Furby L. 1970. How we should measure change—or should we? *Psychol. Bull.* 74:68–80

Cudeck R, Harring JR. 2007. Analysis of nonlinear patterns of change with random coefficient models. *Annu. Rev. Psychol.* 58:615–37

Curran PJ, Bollen K. 2001. The best of both worlds: combining autoregressive and latent curve models. See Collins & Sayer 2001, pp. 105–36

Duncan TE, Duncan SC, Strycker LA, Li F. 2006. *An Introduction to Latent Variable Growth Curve modeling: Concepts, Issues, and Applications*. Mahwah, NJ: Erlbaum. 2nd ed.

Enders CK. 2001. A primer on maximum likelihood algorithms for use with missing data. *Struct. Equation Model.* 8:128–41

Ferrer E, Hamagami F, McArdle JJ. 2004. Modeling latent growth curves with incomplete data using different types of structural equation modeling and multilevel software. *Struct. Equation Model.* 11(3):452–83

Ferrer E, McArdle JJ. 2004. An experimental analysis of dynamic hypotheses about cognitive abilities and achievement from childhood to early adulthood. *Dev. Psychol.* 40:935–52

Ferrer E, McArdle JJ, Shaywitz BA, Holahan JM, Marchione K, Shaywitz SE. 2007. Longitudinal models of developmental dynamics between reading and cognition from childhood to adolescence. *Dev. Psychol.* 43:1460–73

Ghisletta P, Bickel J-F, Lövdén M. 2006. Does activity engagement protect against cognitive decline in old age? Methodological and analytical considerations. *J. Gerontol. B Psychol. Sci.* 61:253–61

Ghisletta P, Lindenberger U. 2003. Age-based structural dynamics between perceptual speed and knowledge in the Berlin Aging Study: direct evidence for ability dedifferentiation in old age. *Psychol. Aging* 18(4):696–713

Ghisletta P, Lindenberger U. 2005. Exploring the structural dynamics of the link between sensory and cognitive functioning in old age: longitudinal evidence from the Berlin Aging Study. *Intelligence* 33:555–87

Ghisletta P, McArdle JJ. 2001. Latent growth curve analyses of the development of height. *Struct. Equation Model.* 8(4):531–55

Goldberger AS, Duncan OD. 1973. *Structural Equation Models in the Social Sciences*. New York: Seminar Press

Gollob HF, Reichardt CS. 1987. Taking account of time lags in causal models. *Child Dev.* 58:80–92

Grimm KJ, Hamagami F, McArdle JJ. 2007. Nonlinear growth models in research on cognitive aging. See Montfort et al. 2007, pp. 267–94

Grimm KJ, McArdle JJ. 2005. A note on the computer generation of mean and covariance expectations in latent growth curve analysis. In *Multi-Level Issues in Strategy and Methods*, ed. F Danserau, FJ Yammarino, pp. 335–64. New York: Elsevier

Hamagami F, McArdle JJ. 2000. Advanced studies of individual differences linear dynamic models for longitudinal data analysis. In *New Developments and Techniques in Structural Equations Modeling*, ed. G Marcoulides, R Schumacker, pp. 203–46. Mahwah, NJ: Erlbaum

Hamagami F, McArdle JJ. 2007. Dynamic extensions of latent difference score models. In *Quantitative Methods in Contemporary Psychology*, ed. SM Boker, ML Wegner, pp. 47–85. Mahwah, NJ: Erlbaum

Hamagami F, McArdle JJ, Cohen P. 2000. Bivariate dynamic systems analyses based on a latent difference score approach for personality disorder ratings. In *Temperament and Personality Development Across the Life Span*, ed. VJ Molfese, DL Molfese, pp. 253–80. Mahwah, NJ: Erlbaum

Harris CW, ed. 1963. *Problems in Measuring Change*. Madison: Univ. Wisc. Press

Hedecker D, Gibbons R. 2006. *Longitudinal Data Analysis*. New York: Wiley

Hertzog C, Lindenberger U, Ghisletta P, Oertzen TV. 2006. On the power of multivariate latent growth curve models to detect correlated change. *Psychol. Methods* 11(3):244–52

Horn JL. 1972. State, trait, and change dimensions of intelligence. *Br. J. Math. Stat. Psychol.* 42(2):159–85

Horn JL, McArdle JJ. 1980. Perspectives on Mathematical and Statistical Model Building (MASMOB) in research on aging. In *Aging in the 1980's: Psychological Issues*, ed. L Poon, pp. 503–41. Washington, DC: Am. Psychol. Assoc.

Hsiao C. 2003. *Analysis of Panel Data*. London: Cambridge Univ. Press. 2nd ed.

Jöreskog KG, Sörbom D. 1979. *Advances in Factor Analysis and Structural Equation Models*. Cambridge, MA: Abt Books

Jöreskog KG, van Thillo M, Gruvaeus GT. 1971. *ACOVSM: a general computer program for analysis of covariance structures including generalized MANOVA*. Res. bull., Educ. Test. Serv., Princeton, NJ

Kenny DA, Zautra A. 2001. The trait-state model for longitudinal data. See Collins & Sayer 2001, pp. 241–64

Kline R. 2005. *Principles and Practices in Structural Equation Modeling*. New York: Guilford

Kroonenberg PM, Oort FJ. 2003. Three-mode analysis of multimode covariance matrices. *Br. J. Math. Stat. Psychol.* 56(2):305–35

Little RJA, Rubin DJ. 2002. *Statistical Analysis with Missing Data*. New York: Wiley. 2nd ed.

Lord F. 1958. Further problems in the measurement of growth. *Educ. Psychol. Meas.* 18:437–54

Lord F. 1967. A paradox in the interpretation of group comparisons. *Psychol. Bull.* 68(5):304–5

Lövdén M, Ghisletta P, Lindenberger U. 2005. Social participation attenuates decline in perceptual speed in old and very old age. *Psychol. Aging* 20:423–34

MacCallum RC, Austin JT. 2000. Applications of structural equation modeling in psychological research. *Annu. Rev. Psychol.* 51:201–26

McCallum RC, Kim C, Malarkey WB, Kiecolt-Glaser JK. 1997. Studying multivariate change using multilevel models and latent curve models. *Multivariate Behav. Res.* 32:215–53

MacKinnon DP, Fairchild AJ, Fritz MS. 2007. Mediation analysis. *Annu. Rev. Psychol.* 58:593–614

Maxwell SE, Kelley K, Rausch JR. 2008. Sample size planning for statistical power and accuracy in parameter estimation. *Annu. Rev. Psychol.* 59:537–63

McArdle JJ. 1986. Latent variable growth within behavior genetic models. *Behav. Genet.* 16(1):163–200

McArdle JJ. 1989. Structural modeling experiments using multiple growth functions. In *Learning and Individual Differences: Abilities, Motivation, and Methodology*, ed. P Ackerman, R Kanfer, R Cudeck, pp. 71–117. Hillsdale, NJ: Erlbaum

McArdle JJ. 2001. A latent difference score approach to longitudinal dynamic structural analyses. In *Structural Equation Modeling: Present and Future*, ed. R Cudeck, S du Toit, D Sorbom, pp. 342–80. Lincolnwood, IL: Sci. Softw. Int.

McArdle JJ. 2007a. Dynamic structural equation modeling in longitudinal experimental studies. See Montfort et al. 2007, pp. 159–88

McArdle JJ. 2007b. Five steps in the structural factor analysis of longitudinal data. In *Factor Analysis at 100 Years*, ed. R Cudeck, R MacCallum, pp. 99–130. Mahwah, NJ: Erlbaum

McArdle JJ, Bell RQ. 2000. An introduction to latent growth curve models for developmental data analysis. In *Modeling Longitudinal and Multiple-Group Data: Practical Issues, Applied Approaches, and Scientific Examples*, ed. TD Little, KU Schnabel, J Baumert, pp. 69–107. Mahwah, NJ: Erlbaum

McArdle JJ, Grimm K, Hamagami F, Bowles R, Meredith W. 2002. A dynamic structural equation analysis of vocabulary abilities over the life-span. Presented at annu. meet. *Soc. Multivariate Exp. Psychol.*, Charlottesville, VA

McArdle JJ, Hamagami F. 2001. Linear dynamic analyses of incomplete longitudinal data. See Collins & Sayer 2001, pp. 137–76

McArdle JJ, Hamagami F. 2003. Structural equation models for evaluating dynamic concepts within longitudinal twin analyses. *Behav. Genet.* 33(2):137–59

McArdle JJ, Hamagami F, Jones K, Jolesz F, Kikinis R, et al. 2004. Structural modeling of dynamic changes in memory and brain structure using longitudinal data from the normative aging study. *J. Gerontol. Psychol. Sci.* 59B(6):P294–304

McArdle JJ, Hamagami F, Meredith W, Bradway KP. 2001. Modeling the dynamic hypotheses of Gf-Gc theory using longitudinal life-span data. *Learn. Individ. Differences* 12:53–79

McArdle JJ, Nesselroade JR. 1994. Structuring data to study development and change. In *Life-Span Developmental Psychology: Methodological Innovations*, ed. SH Cohen, HW Reese, pp. 223–67. Hillsdale, NJ: Erlbaum

McArdle JJ, Nesselroade JR. 2003. Growth curve analyses in contemporary psychological research. In *Comprehensive Handbook of Psychology, Volume Two: Research Methods in Psychology*, ed. J Schinka, W Velicer, pp. 447–80. New York: Pergamon

McArdle JJ, Small BJ, Backman L, Fratiglioni L. 2005. Longitudinal models of growth and survival applied to the early detection of Alzheimer's disease. *J. Geriatr. Psychiatry Neurol.* 18(4):234–41

McArdle JJ, Woodcock JR. 1997. Expanding test-rest designs to include developmental time-lag components. *Psychol. Methods* 2(4):403–35

McCall RB, Applebaum MI. 1973. Bias in the analysis of repeated measures designs: some alternative approaches. *Child Dev.* 44:401–15

McDonald RP. 1985. *Factor Analysis and Related Methods*. Hillsdale, NJ: Erlbaum

McLachlan G, Peel D. 2000. *Finite Mixture Models*. New York: Wiley

Meredith W, Horn JL. 2001. The role of factorial invariance in measuring growth and change. See Collins & Sayer 2001, pp. 201–40

Meredith W, Tisak J. 1990. Latent curve analysis. *Psychometrika* 55:107–22

Montfort K, Oud H, Satorra A. 2007. *Longitudinal Models in the Behavioural and Related Sciences*. Mahwah, NJ: Erlbaum

Muller KE, Stewart PW. 2006. *Linear Model Theory*. New York: Wiley

Muthén BO, Curran P. 1997. General longitudinal modeling of individual differences in experimental designs: a latent variable framework for analysis and power estimation. *Psychol. Methods* 2:371–402

Muthén LK, Muthén BO. 2002. *Mplus, the Comprehensive Modeling Program for Applied Researchers User's Guide*. Los Angeles, CA: Muthen & Muthen

Neale MC, Boker SM, Xie G, Maes HH. 1999. *Mx Statistical Modeling*. Unpubl. program manual, VA Inst. Psychiatr. Behav. Genet., Med. Coll. VA, VA Commonwealth Univ., Richmond, VA. 5th ed.

Nesselroade JR, Baltes PB. 1979. *Longitudinal Research in the Study of Behavior and Development*. New York: Academic

Nesselroade JR, Cable DG. 1974. Sometimes it's okay to factor difference scores—the separation of state and trait anxiety. *Multivariate Behav. Res.* 9:273–82

Nesselroade JJ, McArdle JJ, Aggen SH, Meyers J. 2001. Dynamic factor analysis models for multivariate time series analysis. In *Modeling Individual Variability with Repeated Measures Data: Advances and Techniques*, ed. DM Moskowitz, SL Hershberger, pp. 233–66. Mahwah, NJ: Erlbaum

Nesselroade JR, Stigler SM, Baltes PB. 1980. Regression toward the mean and the study of change. *Psychol. Bull.* 88(3):622–37

O'Brien RG, Kaiser MK. 1985. MANOVA method for analyzing repeated measures designs: an extensive primer. *Psychol. Bull.* 97(2):316–33

Orth U, Berking M, Walker N, Meier LL, Znoj H. 2008. Forgiveness and psychological adjustment following interpersonal transgressions: a longitudinal analysis. *J. Res. Personal.* 42:365–85

Oud JHL, Jansen RARG. 2000. Continuous time state space modeling of panel data by means of SEM. *Psychometrika* 65:199–215

Raudenbush SW. 2001. Comparing personal trajectories and drawing causal inferences from longitudinal data. *Annu. Rev. Psychol.* 52:501–25

Rogosa D. 1979. Causal models in longitudinal research: rationale, formulation, and interpretation. In *Longitudinal Research in the Study of Behavior and Development*, ed. JR Nesselroade, PB Baltes, pp. 263–302. New York: Academic

Rogosa D, Willett J. 1983. Demonstrating the reliability of the difference score in the measurement of change. *J. Educ. Meas.* 20(4):335–43

Singer JD, Willett J. 2003. *Applied Longitudinal Data Analysis*. New York: Oxford Univ. Press

Shadish W, Cook TD, Campbell DT. 2002. *Experimental and Quasi-Experimental Design for Generalized Causal Inference*. Boston, MA: Houghton-Mifflin

Snyder J, Brooker M, Patrick MR, Snyder A, Schrepferman L, Stoolmiller M. 2003. Observed peer victimization during early elementary school: continuity, growth, and relation to risk for child antisocial and depressive behavior. *Child Dev.* 74(6):1881–98

Steyer R, Partchev I, Shanahan MJ. 2001. Modeling true intraindividual change in structural equation models: the case of poverty and children's psychological adjustment. In *Modeling Longitudinal and Multiple-Group Data: Practical Issues, Applied Approaches, and Scientific Examples*, ed. TD Little, KU Schnabel, J Baumert, pp. 109–27. Mahwah, NJ: Erlbaum

Tomarken AJ, Waller NJ. 2005. Structural equation modeling: strengths, limitations, and misconceptions. *Annu. Rev. Clin. Psychol.* 1:31–65

Verbeke G, Molenberghs G. 2000. *Linear Mixed Models for Longitudinal Data*. New York: Springer

Walls TA, Schafer JL. 2006. *Models of Intensive Longitudinal Data*. New York: Oxford Univ. Press

The Renaissance of Field Experimentation in Evaluating Interventions

William R. Shadish[1] and Thomas D. Cook[2]

[1] University of California, Merced, California 95344; email: wshadish@ucmerced.edu

[2] Institute for Policy Research, Northwestern University, Evanston, Illinois 60208-4100; email: t-cook@northwestern.edu

Annu. Rev. Psychol. 2009. 60:607–29

First published online as a Review in Advance on July 9, 2008

The *Annual Review of Psychology* is online at psych.annualreviews.org

This article's doi: 10.1146/annurev.psych.60.110707.163544

Key Words

experiment, quasi-experiment, regression discontinuity, propensity scores, matching, time series

Abstract

Most experiments are done in laboratories. However, there is also a theory and practice of field experimentation. It has had its successes and failures over the past four decades but is now increasingly used for answering causal questions. This is true for both randomized and—perhaps more surprisingly—nonrandomized experiments. In this article, we review the history of the use of field experiments, discuss some of the reasons for their current renaissance, and focus the bulk of the article on the particular technical developments that have made this renaissance possible across four kinds of widely used experimental and quasi-experimental designs—randomized experiments, regression discontinuity designs in which those units above a cutoff get one treatment and those below get another, short interrupted time series, and nonrandomized experiments using a nonequivalent comparison group. We focus this review on some of the key technical developments addressing problems that previously stymied accurate effect estimation, the solution of which opens the way for accurate estimation of effects under the often difficult conditions of field implementation—the estimation of treatment effects under partial treatment implementation, the prevention and analysis of attrition, analysis of nested designs, new analytic developments for both regression discontinuity designs and short interrupted time series, and propensity score analysis. We also cover the key empirical evidence showing the conditions under which some nonrandomized experiments may be able to approximate results from randomized experiments.

Contents

HISTORY IN BRIEF

The modern use of field experiments in the social sciences first became widespread in the 1960s (Cook & Shadish 1994, Riecken et al. 1974, Shadish et al. 1991). An exemplar is the New Jersey Negative Income Tax Experiment (Nathan 1989, Rossi & Lyall 1978), which was designed in the late 1960s to test whether guaranteeing working poor families an income they could spend at their own discretion might serve as an alternative to the welfare system of the day that was heavy with professional services. The fear was widespread that providing cash instead of services would undermine the work motivation of individuals and would lead to welfare as a lifestyle. Hence, the major purpose of

Randomized experiment: a design that assigns units to conditions based on some chance process such as the toss of a coin

the demonstration was to estimate how different income guarantees, combined with different marginal tax policies, affected labor force participation. This was tested in a large randomized experiment that took many years and many millions of dollars to complete.

However, all did not go smoothly. The basic idea was very controversial. Some commentators believed that it promoted the wrong values, while many bureaucratic and professional groups felt that their own welfare would be compromised if cash were substituted for services. The length of the experiment meant that by the time the results were available, the policymakers who were originally interested in the idea—the Nixon administration in this case—were no longer in office, and a new set of policy questions were at the fore. Questions also arose about how to analyze the data, given that the participants did not always accept the conditions to which they were assigned, and others dropped out before completing the study. For all these reasons, many observers wondered whether the time and effort invested in this experiment were worthwhile.

This study is just one example of the large-scale field experiments conducted beginning in the 1960s and 1970s. Others include the National Institute of Mental Health Collaborative Depression Project (Elkin et al. 1985, 1989), the Head Start and Follow Through evaluations (Wholey et al. 1970), and the Manhattan Bail Bond Experiment (Botein 1965). These experiments were partly fueled by demand for data about the implementation and effects of the many social programs introduced under President Lyndon Johnson's Great Society initiatives. Such experiments were time consuming and expensive, and hopes were high that their results would be definitive and useful for policy.

However, these pioneering experiments seemed neither as definitive nor as useful as had first been hoped. Some problems were logistical. For example, some experiments were unable to recruit enough participants, and various participants were unwilling to accept random assignment. Other problems reflected an unexpectedly diverse set of social reactions to the design of the experiment. For instance, some groups with a stake in the intervention or its outcomes began to challenge whether the treatment really reflected what participants needed and whether the outcomes measured were what the treatment was designed to accomplish. Still other problems were technical. In randomized experiments, poorly implemented random assignment procedures and differential attrition from conditions compromised the group equivalence that randomization aimed to achieve, and it was unclear what analyses might compensate. In nonrandomized experiments, selection biases at the start of the study led to similar compromises, exacerbated because no statistical method for adjusting those biases had either a clear theoretical or an empirical warrant. In all experiments, both partial treatment implementation and participant crossover from one condition to another led to confusion about what inferences about treatment effects were justified. Similarly, both randomized and nonrandomized experiments encountered problems of units nested within conditions (e.g., students nested within classrooms) that violated independence assumptions of ordinary least squares statistics in a manner that led to increased Type I errors—concluding that an intervention worked when a proper analysis might not support that conclusion.

When social experiments were finally completed and reported, years had usually passed since raising the question the experiment addressed. Often the stakeholders who first asked the question were no longer players in the policy-shaping community, having left political office, been removed or resigned from appointed positions, or moved on to other social issues. Even when the policy-shaping community retained interest in the original question, the experimental results proved less than definitive. This was because of not only the implementation and technical problems described above, but also because different stakeholders could legitimately debate the meaning and value of the observed outcomes and because decisions about adopting an intervention turned out to be far less driven by whether an inter-

vention works than by other social, economic, and political factors.

These problems caused many scholars and practitioners to raise serious and sustained questions about whether field experiments were a viable or valuable contribution to either science or policy (e.g., Cronbach 1982, Cronbach et al. 1980). Critics questioned whether causal questions were worth asking, whether field experiments were capable of answering any questions that might be worth asking, and whether the disputed answers that experiments provided would be useful in the cases in which they were possible. Consequently, the 1970s and 1980s saw a proliferation of alternative methods for studying social interventions, ranging from nonexperimental econometric methods to qualitative and anthropological case studies, as well as a demotion of causal questions in the understanding of which questions were worth asking. Entire fields, particularly education but also some parts of economics and sociology, largely rejected experimentation in favor of these and other alternatives.

Yet interest in field experimentation remained strong in some areas, especially in medicine, public health, and a few subdisciplines. Examples include parts of labor economics where funding for large-scale experiments continued, and parts of clinical psychology where the implementation and technical problems of experimentation were never as great because researchers had high levels of control over the intervention and its setting. Slowly over four decades, the sustained attention in these areas to solving the early problems of field experimentation laid the foundations for today's renaissance.

After reviewing the reasons why field experimentation has staged such a dramatic comeback, this article then examines the key issues on which progress has been made. We organize the review around the major kinds of experiments in order of their strength for causal inference, from the strongest randomized designs through the presumed weakest designs with nonrandomized controls. In each of these designs, we show how progress had been made in addressing all of the key problems that emerged with the design in the early years for field experimentation, and we discuss the empirical evidence suggesting the conditions under which each of the nonrandomized designs might provide effect estimates comparable to randomized designs. We conclude with a discussion of some of the issues that remain to be addressed, some technical issues, but mostly social and political issues concerning the use of results in practice and policy.

MODERN RENAISSANCE OF FIELD EXPERIMENTATION

A number of developments in the past two decades created the technical and social conditions under which field experimentation could again flourish on a wide scale.

Evidence-Based Practice

We do not know who first used the term evidence-based practice, but the term or its cognates—and more importantly the policy of using fiscal and organizational incentives to encourage practitioners and administrators to develop and adopt interventions with demonstrated empirical effectiveness—are now widespread in nearly all fields where practitioners intervene with people. Medicine and public health pioneered in developing the ideology and social infrastructure to support evidence-based practice, as best seen in the Cochrane Collaboration, an organization in the United Kingdom begun in 1993 and dedicated to improving health care globally through systematic reviews of the effectiveness of health care interventions (**www.cochrane.org**). In that regard, a nod must also go to the development of meta-analysis (Glass 1976), the methodology for creating quantitative syntheses of evidence often applied to studies about the effects of treatments. A host of scholarly and governmental organizations both adopted the ideology and contributed to the methodology in areas such as prevention research, clinical psychology, and public health. Interest in evidence-based prac-

tice was partly ideological but also economic. In clinical psychology, for example, insurance companies stressed the role that demonstrated efficacy would play in reimbursing psychotherapists.

In fields where ideology and recent practice had rejected experimentation, most notably education, the turn of the twenty-first century saw federal mandates for the use both of experiments and of interventions with experimental support, and funding priorities underwent a large shift to back this mandate. An example is the creation of the Institute of Education Sciences within the U.S. Department of Education under the leadership of R. Grover Whitehurst. Among other things, the Institute of Education Sciences gave preferential funding to randomized experiments (and sometimes high-quality nonrandomized experiments such as the regression discontinuity design), created the What Works Clearinghouse to synthesize research about effective educational interventions, and initiated a new professional association (the Society for Research on Educational Effectiveness) to counter resistance in the traditional educational establishment to experimentation. The result was a detectable increase in the use of experimental methods in education (Constas 2007).

Renewed Interest from Economists and Statisticians

Simultaneous developments in economics and statistics also played a major role in the renaissance. The majority of economists interested in causal inference had long subordinated experimental design to statistical analyses that adjust nonexperimental data for selection bias, most notably using selection bias models like those developed by Heckman (e.g., Heckman 1979, 1992). Yet a subset of economists retained an interest in experiments, fueled in part by demonstrations that selection bias models could not reproduce gold standard experimental results (Glazerman et al. 2003, LaLonde & Maynard 1987). At the same time, a few private sector research corporations staffed mostly by economists were solving some of the practical and technical problems in early economic experiments, most notably the Manpower Development Research Corporation (now simply MDRC) headed by economist Judith Gueron (Gueron 1985). Consequent to such developments, by the twenty-first century, many economists—especially young labor economists at the best universities—renewed their interests in strong experimental design. This included both randomized experiments and the regression discontinuity design that was revived from obscurity almost single-handedly by its widespread adoption in economics (Cook 2007).

Similarly, although statisticians had always expressed a preference for randomized experiments, they rarely contributed to the solution of practical problems with them and even more rarely addressed the problems of nonrandomized experiments. That changed with widespread interest in work by statistician Donald Rubin (e.g., Rosenbaum & Rubin 1983, Rubin 1974), himself a student of one of the few statisticians with sustained interest in nonrandomized experiments, William G. Cochran. A good summary of what is often referred to as Rubin's Causal Model, or more precisely the potential outcomes model, is found in Rubin (2004). The three key elements of Rubin's Causal Model are units, treatments, and potential outcomes. If Y is the outcome measure, define $Y(1)$ as the potential outcome that would be observed if the unit is exposed to a treatment ($W = 1$), and define $Y(0)$ as the potential outcome that would be observed if that same unit is not exposed to the treatment ($W = 0$). If so, then the (potential) effect is the difference between these two potential outcomes, $Y(1)$–$Y(0)$. This effect is defined on each unit, and the average of individual causal effects is the average causal effect. However, these are potential outcomes only until treatment begins. After treatment begins, only $Y(1)$ or $Y(0)$ can be observed, with the other being missing, so that the fundamental problem of causal inference in Rubin's Causal Model is how to estimate the missing outcome. These missing outcomes are sometimes called counterfactuals because they are not, in fact, what happened. Furthermore, after treatment begins, individual causal effects cannot actually be observed as defined [$Y(1)$–$Y(0)$], although the average causal effect over all units can be observed under conditions such as random assignment. When presented in detail (Rubin 2004; W.R. Shadish, manuscript submitted), this model provides a statistical definition of an effect, a set of assumptions that allowed the effect to be calculated, and most importantly, statistical tools for approaching the estimation of effects in nonrandomized experiments that heretofore had resisted such solution (Morgan & Winship 2007; Rubin 2004; W.R. Shadish, manuscript submitted). The model and its attendant developments gave new credibility to causal estimates from nonrandomized experiments, though the limits of this claim are still being contested today.

The Empirical Program of Experimentation

A crucial development was the increased attention to developing empirical evidence about which methodologies and statistical analyses live up to their promise to provide accurate answers to causal questions (Shadish 2000). Early examples were by economists who compared results from randomized and adjusted nonrandomized experiments (Fraker & Maynard 1987, LaLonde & Maynard 1987), but examples today are so widespread that they themselves are the subject of quantitative and narrative reviews (Cook et al. 2008, Glazerman et al. 2003, Heinsman & Shadish 1996, Shadish & Ragsdale 1996). Though consensus has yet to emerge on the results of such inquiries, the methods for doing such empirical work are improving (Shadish et al. 2008), the standards for interpreting such work are becoming more clear (Cook et al. 2008), and there is reason to believe that better understanding is emerging of some of the conditions under which both randomized and nonrandomized experiments can live up to their promise of providing good answers to causal questions. We discuss such matters below.

RANDOMIZED EXPERIMENTS

Key to the ability to meet the demand for randomized experiments is the creation of an infrastructure to support the effort. Areas such as medicine and public health developed the infrastructure earliest, building a preference for experiments into grant funding, journal publication, and graduate education whenever causal issues were at stake. The wide availability of health-related funding provided the experiential learning necessary to identify and solve practical problems with large-scale experiments. The funding also permitted hiring biostatisticians who developed and applied statistical solutions. Some parts of psychology did likewise, so that a strong tradition of randomized field experiments developed in the evaluation of the effects of psychotherapy, of large-scale behavioral medicine interventions, and of some interventions in school settings to manage classroom behavior and achievement. To a lesser extent, this is also true of labor economics as it persisted in the task of identifying effective interventions after some early problems with experiments (Gueron 1985). In education, which provides a primary outlet for applying psychological ideas, developing an infrastructure similar to that in health or clinical psychology has only recently begun, and without that infrastructure, it will be impossible to counter claims that experiments cannot be conducted in education. A successful tradition of experimentation requires the kind of persistence that many health researchers, many psychologists, and labor economists displayed but that has been lacking in educational research heretofore. Several key methodological developments that improved the yield from experimental work have made the institutionalization task easier.

Implementing Successful Experiments

Some of the early experimental disappointments led to developing methods for dealing with the human, organizational, and political factors required to implement a randomized experiment successfully (Boruch 1997, Gueron 1985, Shadish et al. 2002). These matters, such as ways to discuss random assignment with stakeholders hostile to the idea, seem mundane but are nonetheless crucial to successful experimentation to ensure that enough qualified participants can be recruited to the study, to maximize the chances that random assignment occurs properly, to coordinate large multisite trials, to monitor the implementation of treatment and outcome protocols to ensure fidelity, to review early results for possible adverse outcomes, and to ensure the collected data are digitized rapidly and accurately for later analysis. Workers in some professions, such as labor economics or public health in school settings, stuck with the task of solving these early problems and are now lending their expertise to those in fields that gave up early, such as education, thus cutting short the time it will take the latter to develop solutions. However, professionals in education subfields will inevitably present their own contextual problems that will require at least partially novel solutions.

Partial Treatment Implementation

A key problem in randomized experiments was how to estimate effects when treatments are only partially implemented or when participants cross over from one condition to another in an uncontrolled way. The classic solution is an intent-to-treat (ITT) analysis in which the researcher measures outcomes on all participants no matter what their treatment status, and then analyzes their outcomes in the condition to which they were originally assigned. This analysis preserves the integrity of the initial random assignment and provides an unbiased estimate of the intent to treat that is often of special policy interest. After all, policymakers can rarely make policies that force citizens to accept a treatment; they are still interested in estimating causal effects if only a fraction of those assigned actually receive their assigned treatment.

Other stakeholders are interested in a different causal question: What is the effect of the treatment on the treated (TOT)? This previously was estimated (suboptimally) by comparing those who self-selected treatment with those who self-selected the control (or other treatment comparison) condition, conditioning on whatever covariates are available. This estimate is suboptimal because of error in the covariates and the need for covariates that completely account for the selection process or the outcome. However, some economists and statisticians have outlined a practical solution to this dilemma by combining an instrumental variables tradition in economics with the potential outcomes tradition in statistics (Angrist et al. 1996). An instrumental variable is related to the treatment but not to the outcome except through its relationship on the treatment. With such an instrument, one can obtain an unbiased effect of a treatment despite selection bias. Therefore, instrumental variables have been a mainstay of econometric causal inference for decades even though establishing that one has actually chosen an instrument that meets all the analytic assumptions may be as much a matter of rhetoric as it is a matter of producing evidence. Yet one instrument is undoubtedly bias-free: random assignment to conditions, which by definition can only be related to outcome through its effects on the receipt of treatment. Capitalizing on this, Angrist et al. (1996) made random assignment an instrument for receipt of treatment, thereby providing an unbiased estimate of the effects of treatment on the treated. They also outlined the assumptions needed, which are more stringent than for an ITT analysis but nonetheless often plausible.

Angrist et al. (1996) illustrated the method and its assumptions with the example of the Vietnam draft lottery. Birth dates were assigned random numbers from 1 to 365, and those below a certain number were then subject to the draft (in effect, being randomly assigned to draft eligibility). However, not all those subject to the draft actually served in the military. Suppose the question of interest is whether actually serving in the military increases mortality, the TOT estimator, rather than draft eligibility, the ITT estimator. The standard ITT analysis uses randomization to examine whether draft eligibility increases mortality. Although this yields an unbiased estimate of effects, it will not be the question of greatest interest for all stakeholders. But to compare the mortality of those who did or did not serve in the military is biased by the many unknown factors, in addition to the draft, that caused people to serve (e.g., volunteering because of a family tradition or being cajoled by peers who have enlisted). The Angrist et al. (1996) method provides an unbiased instrumental variable estimate of the TOT question when its assumptions are met.

When both treatment implementation and outcome are dichotomous, the computations require only a hand calculator. The following computations are for the draft example. Because 35.3% of those who were draft eligible actually served in the military, and 19.4% of those who were not eligible also served in the military, we can say that the lottery (random assignment) caused 15.9% to serve in the military. This is the usual ITT analysis of a randomized experiment with military service as the outcome. In addition, 2.04% of the draft eligible died, as did 1.95% of those not eligible. So being draft eligible caused 0.09% to die. This is an ITT analysis with death as the outcome. The unbiased TOT estimate of actually serving in the military on death is simple to calculate, being 0.0009/.159 = 0.0058 = 0.56%. So serving in the military caused the death of about one-half of 1% of those soldiers.

Variations on this method rapidly appeared for use in studies with nondichotomous measures of treatment intensity, such as the extent of drug dosage or hours of exam preparation. These variations used multivalued instrumental variables, providing bounds on estimates rather than point estimates (Angrist & Imbens 1995; Balke & Pearl 1997; Barnard et al. 1998; Efron & Feldman 1991; Fischer-Lapp & Goetghebeur 1999; Goetghebeur & Molenberghs 1996; Imbens & Rubin 1997a,b; Little & Yau 1996; Oakes et al. 1993; Robins 1998). The plausibility of assumptions decreases in some of these applications, and new developments are so rapid that readers are advised to search the most recent literature before relying solely on the references above.

When faced with partial treatment implementation, an ITT analysis remains the method of choice because of its fewer and more transparent assumptions and its frequent policy interest. Nonetheless, the instrumental variables analysis now allows researchers to estimate and report TOT effects that are unbiased in theory and will likely be so in much research practice. Both estimates are usually worth computing.

Attrition

Large amounts of attrition from randomized experiments, that is, loss of participants to outcome measurement, can decrease power and damage the credibility of a randomized experiment. Much worse is differential attrition—when dropouts in one condition differ from dropouts in another in ways related to the outcome. Such attrition is selection bias that occurs after random assignment, and it calls into question whether the resulting effect estimate is unbiased. The problem of attrition is by no means solved, but it has been constructively addressed in two ways. First, we know more about how to prevent attrition from occurring in the first place. This knowledge was developed, by necessity, among researchers working with populations that are hard to find or do not wish to be found, such as abused women, illegal drug users, or homeless persons with severe and persistent mental problems (e.g., Ribisl et al. 1996). Successful strategies are expensive, require staff dedicated solely to the task, and of greatest significance, require researchers to leave the office, but they can also result in retention rates as high as 98% over two years with difficult-to-track populations.

Second, since some loss to outcome measurement will typically occur even with the best preventive efforts, researchers have developed sensitivity analyses about the potential effects of attrition on effect estimates (Shadish et al. 1998, Shih & Quan 1997). Results are encouraging, especially when effect sizes are not too small. Shadish et al. (1998) developed a method and computer program for examining the potential effects of attrition on effect estimates with dichotomous outcomes, varying assumptions about whether dropouts succeeded or failed for each condition. They applied the method to a set of randomized experiments on the effects of family therapy on substance abusers, a population that has high attrition from treatment. Results suggested the therapy would be successful under any plausible assumption about what happens to dropouts. Shih & Quan (1997) do similar kinds of analysis for continuous outcomes.

Because of all these developments, today we can field randomized experiments with much greater confidence that the results will be accurate despite problems that four decades ago would have spelled trouble. As a result of the policy emphasis on evidence-based practice, confidence is also higher that results will be useful in practice both conceptually and instrumentally.

Nested Designs

It is common in field experimentation for units to be nested within aggregated groups that are themselves nested within conditions. Examples include students nested within classrooms, clients nested within psychotherapy groups or psychotherapists, patients nested within physician practices, or workers nested within worksites. When aggregates (e.g., classrooms) rather than individuals (e.g., students) are assigned to conditions, the designs are often called group-randomized or cluster-randomized (Murray 1998). Regardless of whether aggregates or individuals are assigned to conditions, however, such nesting must be presumed to induce a dependency among nested units, which leads to violations of the independence assumptions of most ordinary statistics such as t-tests, analysis of variance, correlation, and regression. Such violations dramatically affect the Type I error rates (usually $\alpha = 0.05$), so that even the most modest dependencies could change α from 0.05

to as much as 0.20 to 0.50. Until the 1980s, no strong solution to this problem existed, so researchers tended to ignore it.

Progress has occurred in two areas. First is the invention and wide dissemination of statistical models and associated computer programs that appropriately analyze such data (Donner & Klar 1996, Goldstein 1986, Murray 1998, Raudenbush & Bryk 2002). The statistical models are variously called hierarchical linear models, multilevel models, or random coefficients models, and they are implemented in free-standing computer programs such as HLM (Raudenbush et al. 2004) and MLwiN (Rasbash et al. 2005) as well as popular computer packages such as SAS Proc Mixed (Littell 2006). Though these models have not been as widely adopted as they should have been, given the prevalence of nested data in field experimentation (e.g., Baldwin et al. 2005), they do solve the basic underlying statistical problem, yielding appropriate Type I error rates.

The second area of progress has been improving power in nested designs. The underlying problem here is that a proper analysis with a multilevel model often requires a large number of aggregate units (e.g., classrooms) to achieve the desired statistical power of 0.80. Because gathering data on, say, 50 classrooms per condition may be prohibitive for all but the best-funded research, investigators are faced with the choice between a properly analyzed study with too few aggregate units resulting in low power or a study improperly examined by an analysis that ignores nesting but that results in statistical significant results, albeit artifactually. This tradeoff encouraged many researchers simply to ignore the proper analysis. Yet it turns out that power can be improved, often dramatically, by using some simple design features such as matching or stratification, repeated measures, or most effectively, covarying a pretest measure that is highly correlated with the outcome measure. Exact results vary somewhat depending on the assumptions one makes about the intraclass correlation (the measure of how dependent units within aggregates really are) and the pretest-outcome correlation, but they suggest

that as few as 10–12 classrooms per condition might yield desired power levels. The latter is logistically feasible for many more researchers.

Initially, all these developments in the analysis of nested models, partial treatment implementation, and attrition occurred independently. Today, models are being developed that incorporate more than one analysis. An example is Jo et al. (2008), who show how to combine proper nested design analysis with the Angrist et al. (1996) partial-treatment implementation analysis discussed above. Similar progress is occurring that combines these analyses with modern missing data analysis methods. Software for the latter may not yet be quite as widely available and transparent as that for the basic developments themselves, but rapid computerization seems likely.

REGRESSION DISCONTINUITY DESIGNS

Regression discontinuity designs (RDDs) are sometimes also called cutoff-based designs. They assign units to conditions based on a cutoff score on an ordered assignment variable, with units that fall on one side of the cutoff receiving treatment and those on the other side receiving the comparison condition. A regression is then fit to predict outcome from the assignment variable (minus the cutoff) and a treatment dummy variable. An effect is inferred if the regression line displays a discontinuity—a change in slope or intercept—at the cutoff between treatment and control. For example, the State of California passed legislation giving unemployment compensation to newly released prisoners, but only if they had worked more than 652 hours over the previous 12 months while in prison. Those who worked fewer hours than the cutoff value of 652 were ineligible. Berk & Rauma (1983) found that those receiving unemployment compensation had a recidivism rate 13% lower than controls.

First Goldberger (1972) and then Rubin (1977) showed that the regression discontinuity at the cutoff is an unbiased effect estimate under a proper analysis. Yet the design

Matching: equating two nonequivalent groups by selecting pairs of units with similar values on a variable correlated with outcome was rarely used for 30 years after Thistlewaite & Campbell (1960) invented it. In the 1990s, however, economists and a few others began to use the design more often, taking advantage of many naturally occurring cases of assignment to treatment using a cutoff—for example, students to remedial writing training if they scored lower than a cutoff on a measure of writing skills (Aiken et al. 1998), or villages to receipt of social welfare assistance if they scored lower than a cutoff on a measure of village development (Buddelmeyer & Skoufias 2003). Combining the statistical developments from Rubin's potential outcomes model with standard econometric regression methods, they simultaneously made progress toward solving two problems with the RDD—modeling nonlinearities in the relationship between the assignment and outcome variables, and dealing with failures to assign to treatment by the cutoff score and nothing else. Once the design came back into vogue with these developments, researchers began to see opportunities to use it in many other naturally occurring situations where assignment is by cutoff (Cook 2007).

Modeling Nonlinearities

In RDD, the size of the effect is measured by the size of the discontinuity between treatment and control group regression lines at the cutoff. This estimate is unbiased only if the form of the relationship between the assignment and outcome variables is correctly modeled. The standard RDD analysis uses ordinary linear regression and so usually assumes a linear relationship. If the true relationship is nonlinear, though, a reliable discontinuity may be discovered that is an artifact of the wrong model rather than a true effect. This would happen, for example, if the true relationship is quadratic because those with higher assignment variable scores benefit more from treatment than those with lower scores—as when economically advantaged children learn more from Sesame Street than disadvantaged ones. Often there is no independent way to know the form of the true relationship. Standard advice to reduce the prob-

lem (e.g., Shadish et al. 2002, Trochim 1984) is (*a*) to examine the plot visually to try to identify nonlinearities; (*b*) to overfit the linear model by adding nonlinear functions of the assignment variable and interaction terms between assignment and outcome until all these terms are nonsignificant; (*c*) to compare the RDD data to preintervention data using the same variables, thus treating the preintervention regression as a control against which underlying nonlinearities can be distinguished from a treatment effect; and (*d*) to use nonparametric regression techniques that do not assume linearity. Economists particularly like the last solution (as well as the third one), which uses kernel density functions, lowess smoothers, and local linear regression techniques. These techniques are sensitive to exploring and modeling nonlinearities and allow estimating the causal impact locally at the cutoff point where an RDD estimate is most valid anyway. After all, this is where the treatment and comparison groups are most similar, sometimes differing only by measurement error in the assessment of the assignment variable. But nonparametric methods do entail additional assumptions of their own. Modern practice in the analysis of RDD emphasizes using all or most of the approaches listed above. It has become normal to present multiple estimates of the causal effect to test the sensitivity of results to the assumptions made about functional form. Robust results imply great confidence; more variable ones, less confidence. A good example of such recent practice can be found in Wong et al. (2008).

Fuzzy Regression Discontinuity

Effect estimates from RDDs are only unbiased if assignment is strictly by cutoff. This is similar to the assumption in randomized experiments that assignment adheres strictly to a chance process like the flip of a coin. The term "fuzzy regression discontinuity" refers to the case where some participants are assigned to conditions in violation of the cutoff, or where they cross over from their assigned condition to another condition. Biased estimates can then result. Just as in a randomized experiment, the importance of such misassignment depends on its magnitude. Traditionally, the claim is that 5% fuzziness is unlikely to be much of a problem; but this is itself a fuzzy criterion, particularly when an effect is quite small. The likely severity of the problem can be diagnosed with an assessment of the amount of crossover, especially graphically around the cutoff. A precondition for diagnosis of severity is measurement of both the treatment intended for each unit and the treatment each unit actually received.

An ITT analysis should be done to assess the effects of the intended intervention irrespective of the received intervention. This unbiased ITT analysis is analogous to standard practice in a randomized experiment. However, when effects of TOT are of interest, a second unbiased analysis is possible with an RDD that takes advantage of the same instrumental variable analysis described previously for the randomized experiment (Angrist et al. 1996). As with the randomized experiment, the treatment dummy variable serves as the instrument for examining the effects of the treatment actually implemented. Examples of the analysis are in Angrist & Lavy (1999) and Wong et al. (2008), and the proof is in Hahn et al. (2001).

However, RDD must always be prospective in the sense that a cutoff is set and assignment made before the intervention is administered according to the side of the cutoff on which a unit falls. This also applies to experiments where random assignment must always precede treatment delivery. Otherwise, in both RDD and the experiment, one only has the kind of retrospective observational survey in which uncontrolled selection into conditions is the source of selection bias that is routinely much more problematic than when the assignment process is known.

Several studies have deliberately compared the causal results from randomized experiments to those from similar regression discontinuity designs (Aiken et al. 1998; D. Black, J. Galdo, & J.C. Smith, unpublished manuscript; Buddelmeyer & Skoufias 2003). The results are summarized by Cook and colleagues (Cook et al. 2008), illustrating reasonably close agreement in their estimates of the size and direction of effects. This agreement is not surprising theoretically, given the known conditions under which RDDs yield unbiased estimates. It is, however, gratifying given that RDDs, like any other design, are rarely implemented in perfect accord with the ideal and then are validated against randomized experiments that are also often not implemented as one might wish.

Still, both the analytic advances and the increased use of RDD in recent years suggest that, after a long hibernation, RDD has finally emerged as both a desirable and a feasible method for estimating causal effects (Cook 2007). It is especially useful, and now more widely used, when assignment is made on the basis of need or merit, and the latter can be measured for use as an assignment variable.

INTERRUPTED TIME SERIES

A traditional interrupted time series (ITS) design has about 100 observations on one unit, during which a treatment is introduced at some known time. This large number of observations is needed in order to accurately identify the statistical model including cycles, autocorrelations, and trends. Similar to RDD, an effect is measured as a change in the slope or intercept of the time series at the point of treatment introduction. Also similar to RDD, correct identification of the functional form of the relationship between time and outcome is crucial. Analytic methods for analyzing such designs are well developed, but it is rare for researchers to have the opportunity to gather so many data points over time, although some daily diary methods do permit this. Thus, recent years have seen more interest and progress in the design and analysis of short interrupted time series, having say, 10–50 time points but all the other characteristics of traditional ITS.

A major realization has been the limited set of circumstances permitting interpretable simple ITS without a control series. Such simple designs are most interpretable when a series of

Time series: a quasi-experimental design that measures a single unit many consecutive times on the same outcome measure

circumstances are on hand that rarely co-occur. These are basically an abrupt intervention at a known point in time, the immediate or very rapid onset of a response, and either a large effect or a pretest time series with very little random variation around a clear trend line. Reality teaches us that many interventions seep into units gradually rather than enter all of them at the same time and with high intensity, regardless of what the dissemination plan specified, and that responses can be delayed. This delay makes plausible some alternative explanations for the effect, such as other events that also occurred in the period after treatment was implemented. As a result, practice has moved toward ITS designs with a control series, whether created from nonintervention units or from nonequivalent dependent variables—those that the intervention should not affect but that other alternative causes should affect.

In some ways, the most well developed part of the short-term ITS literature concerns single case designs. These are particularly prevalent in some parts of clinical psychology (Marascuilo & Busk 1988, Morgan & Morgan 2001, Wampold & Worsham 1986), education (Phye et al. 2005), and medicine (McLeod et al. 1986, Weiss et al. 1980). They are sometimes called ABAB designs to indicate measurement of outcome over repeated alternations of baseline (A), treatment (B), withdrawal of treatment but continued assessment of the outcome (A), and reintroduction of treatment (B). The causal prediction is that two spikes occur in the response function soon after each occurrence of B is put into place.

Such designs have been well developed since the 1950s. What is new today is analytic models, especially the use of pooled time series (Hoeppner et al. 2008) and multilevel models that can often estimate treatment effects when many independent short-time series assessing the same intervention on the same outcome are available (Van den Noortgate & Onghena 2003). Such designs are more widely feasible when the research can recruit, for example, 20–40 schools that are each measured 4–8 times or 20 or 40 students each measured the same number of times. The multilevel analyses treat observations within units in the Level 1 model (e.g., within schools in one case or within persons in another), whereas unit variables (e.g., person or school characteristics) are treated at Level 2. The treatment indicator is a time-varying covariate at Level 1 because different cases can introduce and remove treatment at different times and can even have different numbers of total observations and missing data patterns. The resulting effect estimate is not known to be statistically unbiased. Instead, it relies on demonstrating that the effect is present when the treatment is present and is absent or at least reduced when the treatment is absent. To the extent that the intervention and its removal are applied at different times with different units, the possibility of a cyclical maturation pattern mimicking the theoretically expected pattern of results can be ruled out. The practical difficulty is failing to detect true causal relationships because of measurement artifacts and temporal persistence patterns. If the first B leads to a spike whose effect persists over time, it will then be difficult to detect a second spike; if removing the first intervention engenders special individual or social processes associated with its removal, then these too can affect data in the subsequent AB sequence and obscure obtaining data that correspond to the theoretically expected pattern.

Several analytic problems continue to be examined in the literature on single case studies and their aggregation. Of particular interest is how many independent series, and how many time points within those series, are needed to obtain powerful and accurate causal estimates. Some evidence suggests the analysis may be feasible with as few as 10 times series with 10–15 time points each when all trends are linear, though clearly more of both is better. Conversely, for the most complex analyses involving latent variables, hundreds of cases may be needed, though the number of time points can still be relatively small (duToit & Browne 2008). For example, the latter authors used 455 schoolchildren measured at only five points in time. The main challenge is with correct modeling of the form of trends over time, and control time series clearly help with this in all contexts, including ABAB. A second challenge is modeling the error structure of the residuals, given that the assumption of independent errors is often violated in time series work. Most software for hierarchical linear modeling builds in some form of correction for nonindependent error, and economists frequently use a series of techniques, all predicated on a variety of assumptions. Though closure on functional forms and nonindependent errors is not yet upon us, the promise is sufficient that we expect more widespread use of short-term ITS for examining the effects of social interventions across, for example, schools over time or individuals over time What is clear, though, is that in most circumstances beyond the tightly controlled ABAB design, control ITS will be needed as well as intervention ITS. Most social interventions do not have an abrupt onset, the responses to them are not immediate, the expected effects are not large, and the preintervention slopes are too short and varied for the accurate assessment of functional form that provides the counterfactual.

NONEQUIVALENT COMPARISON GROUP EXPERIMENTS

The nonequivalent comparison group experiment design, which is characterized by both a pretest and a nonequivalent comparison group, is probably the workhorse design for causal inference in many substantive areas including education. Its low repute is due to its vulnerability to selection bias—treatment effects that are confounded with characteristics of units correlated with outcome. The advances in addressing this vulnerability have been significant in the past few decades, first in design and then in analysis.

The Importance of Good Design

Focal local controls. Decades of methodological advice stress the importance of control groups that are as similar as possible to the treatment group. Indeed, that is a key purpose of random assignment. Yet many observational studies, particularly in education and economics, fail to obtain similar control groups, for example, when a locally implemented treatment is compared with a patently nonlocal control group drawn from a national random sample (Hill et al. 2004). Borrowing a turn of phrase that Campbell (1976) once used in regard to a related issue in time series designs, the desirable control in a nonequivalent comparison group experiment is a focal local control group: in the same locale as the treatment group and focused on persons with the same kinds of characteristics as those in the treatment group, most particularly the characteristics that are most highly correlated with selection into conditions and with the outcome under investigation. Often control groups are one or the other, but not both. For instance, national random samples cannot be local for a locally conducted experiment, even if they approximate some of the desired focal characteristics. Conversely, local controls are not always focal when the units have characteristics demonstrably different from those in the treatment group, as when the quasi-experiment used by Cicirelli et al. (1969) compared local Head Start children who were disadvantaged enough to meet the eligibility criteria for Head Start with other local children who were not enrolled in Head Start because they were not as disadvantaged. A fundamental element of good quasi-experimental design is that a focal local control makes the job of estimating causal effects much easier from the start.

For example, Aiken et al. (1998) used both a randomized and a quasi-experiment to test the effects of a remedial writing program for new students registering at a university. Their control group was students who were also eligible for the program but who registered for classes too late to be in the randomized experiment. The control group's focal characteristics were plausibly similar to those eligible students who registered on time. Aiken and coworkers indeed showed that this control group did not differ significantly or substantially from the treatment group on a host of pretest measurements that

Nonequivalent comparison group experiment design: a quasi-experimental design with more than one condition and a posttest

Quasi-experiment: a design that manipulates the presumed cause and measures the presumed outcome but does not randomly assign participants to conditions

were correlated with posttest. Of course, one can never be certain that the two groups are similar on all unobserved variables, but the claim here is that fewer selection biases are likely to be present than if the control were not locally or focally similar, such as students from another university or whose ACT scores made them ineligible for the program. In their study, Aiken et al. (1998) found that program effects from the randomized experiment were virtually identical to effects when the nonrandomized focal local control was substituted for the randomized control.

Matching on stable covariates. The quality of a nonequivalent control also can be improved by selecting one that is well matched to the treatment group on stable covariates, especially pretest measures of the outcome variable. Many of the early problems with matching in nonrandomized experiments were due to poor matching practices. In an early evaluation of Head Start by Cicirelli et al. (1969), groups were matched on unreliable measures of individual child achievement. High-achieving students in the Head Start group were matched with lower-achieving control group students, which was necessary because the control population was higher achieving in general. Systematically higher levels of positive measurement error in the treatment group scores and of negative measurement error in the control group scores at pretest were less positive or negative by chance at posttest, causing the two group scores to regress to different means that made it appear that Head Start hurt children. However, reanalysis correcting for unreliability in the matching variables showed that this finding was not correct (Magidson 1977).

The lesson is that it it important to match on variables that are less likely to contain much measurement error. One way to do so is to match on composite variables because adding equivalent items to a measure will increase its reliability. An example of this kind of matching is an evaluation of the Comer whole-school reform program in Detroit public schools by Millsap et al. (2000), who wanted to create controls matched on pretest student achievement levels. To increase the reliability of this matching variable, the investigators matched on achievement test scores that were aggregated across individual students to the school level and also aggregated over several years of pretest data. Such multiyear average school-level scores tend to be extremely reliable. In this study, the control schools were also focal local controls in the sense discussed above. They were from similar parts of Detroit, with similar school-level and individual student characteristics.

We stress two characteristics that are needed for stable matching. One is the reduction of measurement error described above, but the other is matching on a variable that either is a pretest measure of the outcome or is another variable that is as highly correlated as possible with that outcome. Measurement error is not the only cause of regression to the mean (Campbell & Kenny 1999). Such regression will occur any time two variables are imperfectly correlated—the person who is the tallest will not necessarily be the heaviest even though both variables are measured with extremely high reliability. In the absence of a treatment effect, school-level pretest achievement scores are likely to be very highly correlated with school-level posttest achievement scores, further reducing any potential impact of regression artifacts. Combining matching on stable covariates from a pool of focal local controls can greatly improve the chances of correctly estimating effects.

Propensity Score and Other Analyses

The previous two sections emphasize the importance of good design in nonrandomized studies. Another tradition emphasizes statistical adjustments to nonrandomized results so the resulting effects might better approximate those from randomized experiments. Such adjustments almost certainly work best when used with studies that are well designed at the start, especially using the design features described above. Currently, the most popular adjustment is propensity score analysis.

Propensity score analysis is another development from Rubin's potential outcomes model. Propensity scores are the predicted probabilities of being in treatment or control given the available covariates. They are usually constructed using logistic regression, but a host of other methods can be used. Groups that are balanced on the true propensity scores are also balanced on all the covariates used to create those propensity scores, where balance is assessed using methods described in Rubin (2001). However, because the true propensity scores are unknown and must be estimated, assessing balance on the propensity scores must be supplemented with assessing balance on the individual covariates as well. The idea is to mimic the balance achieved by random assignment between groups, where groups are equivalent on all measured and unmeasured covariates. The difference is that propensity score matching only succeeds in matching on the measured covariates, making balance a necessary but not sufficient condition for unbiased effects. Hence the use of propensity scores also requires the assumption of strong ignorability, that potential outcomes are orthogonal to treatment assignment conditional on the observed variables, or in other words, that there are no unmeasured variables that cause a hidden bias. If the strong ignorability assumption is not met, propensity score matching should not produce the same results as a randomized experiment; conversely, if the strong ignorability assumption is met, it should produce the same results. Strong ignorability requires measurement of all covariates related to both treatment and outcome. A key need is to develop measures indicating how well this assumption is met. In the meantime, when data are clearly imbalanced at the start, assessing how well available covariates predict both assignment and outcome is a weak but necessary fallback. It is weak because standards for how much prediction is enough are lacking; it is necessary because demonstrably poor prediction is a cause for concern—in such cases, propensity score adjustments can increase rather than decrease bias.

To illustrate, Shadish et al. (2008) randomly assigned participants to be in a randomized or nonrandomized experiment. Those in the randomized experiment were randomly assigned to mathematics or vocabulary training, while the remaining students got to choose their training. Participants were otherwise treated identically and simultaneously and were not aware of the manipulation of assignment method. Shadish et al. (2008) created propensity scores from a very extensive set of pretest covariates that might predict treatment choice (e.g., math anxiety and preference) and outcome (e.g., math and vocabulary skills at pretest). They were then able to reproduce closely the results from the randomized experiment using several different kinds of propensity score analyses, and even using simple linear regression of the original covariates without propensity scores. However, they also showed that propensity scores based on a weak set of predictors (i.e., gender, age, ethnicity, and marital status) failed to reduce bias much, or sometimes increased it. Subsequent reanalyses of the data using an indirect test of strong ignorability—one that was possible only because the yoked randomized experiment was present—suggested convincingly that balance was not sufficient for bias reduction but that balance plus strong ignorability was sufficient (Steiner et al. 2008).

Summaries of Empirical Evidence

A considerable amount of empirical literature compares results from nonrandomized to randomized experiments. Some reviews of that literature have questioned whether statistical adjustments can reproduce results from randomized experiments (Glazerman et al. 2003). Those results are questionable because the comparisons were commonly quite poor in many ways. Cook and colleagues (Cook et al. 2008) suggested that good comparisons of experimental and quasi-experimental estimators must meet seven criteria:

1. The studies must compare one randomly formed control group and one

nonrandomly formed control group. Without this, no comparison can be made.

2. The randomized and nonrandomized experiment should both estimate the same estimator, be it treatment on treated or intent to treat, because otherwise agreement in results would not be expected.

3. The randomized and nonrandomized groups should differ from each other only in assignment method, for otherwise any differences in estimators might be due to confounds rather than assignment method.

4. The person producing the nonrandomized estimate of effect should not know the results from the randomized experiment or else they may keep searching for a nonrandomized estimator until they find one that matches the randomized one.

5. The randomized experiment should be an exemplar of its kind, not subject to large attrition or partial treatment implementation problems that statistical adjustments such as propensity scores are not designed to fix.

6. The nonrandomized design should similarly be an exemplar of its kind, similarly without attrition or partial treatment implementation problems, with focal local controls and good pretest measurement of variables related to treatment and outcome. Otherwise, we would not expect it to match a randomized result.

7. A defensible standard for what counts as a match in randomized and nonrandomized results is used. This is difficult both because reasonable people might disagree on substantive criteria that would make a difference to policy decisions and because statistical criteria will inevitably be subject to power problems.

This is a stringent set of criteria, only fully met in one comparison of random and nonrandom assignment, but met substantially by several more experiments. Cook and colleagues (Cook et al. 2008) showed that when most or all of these seven criteria were met, results from various different kinds of nonrandomized experiments yielded a reasonable match to results from randomized experiments. This was true for regression discontinuity designs, well-designed nonrandomized experiments with focal local controls and stable matching, and statistical analyses such as propensity scores. A key conclusion is, of course, that it is essential to use good design on the front end, on the presumption that good design limits the amount of bias needing to be reduced by any such adjustment.

PATTERN MATCHING DESIGNS

Sometimes none of the preceding options is feasible, and even when the options are feasible, the researcher may wish to improve causal inference by supplementing the study design. Several design strategies have proven useful in producing plausible causal inferences. The set of those strategies is termed "pattern matching designs" to emphasize that they combine various design features so as to produce multiple probes of a causal hypothesis that inform different threats to internal validity without all sharing the same threat. When such probes all converge on the same effect, the plausibility of a causal inference is increased due to the more numerous alternative interpretations informed and the absence of shared bias.

A good example of a pattern matching design is the Reynolds & West (1987) study of the effects of Arizona's "Ask for the Sale" campaign to sell lottery tickets. Participating stores selling lottery tickets agreed to post a sign reading, "Did we ask you if you want a lottery ticket? If not, you get one free"; they also agreed to give a free ticket to those customers whom they neglected to ask the question but who then requested one. Because participation was voluntary, the resulting nonequivalent control group design was supplemented in four ways. First, the authors matched treatment to control stores from the same chain (and where possible, the same zip code) as well as on the pretest market share of ticket sales. Second, they added multiple pretest and posttest assessments by examining mean weekly ticket sales for four weeks before and four weeks after the treatment started. They then observed that pretest sales trends were decreasing nearly identically in both the treatment and control groups, and so maturation differences could not explain increasing ticket sales. Similarly, regression to the mean was unlikely because the treatment group sales were continuously decreasing over four consecutive pretests, and because control group ticket sales continued to decrease after treatment began. Third, Reynolds & West (1987) studied treatment effects on three nonequivalent dependent variables in the treatment group, discovering that the intervention increased ticket sales but not sales of gas, cigarettes, or grocery items. Fourth, they located some stores in which the treatment was removed and then repeated, or was initiated later than in other stores, and found that the outcome tracked the introduction, removal, and reinstatement of treatment over time while sales in the matched controls remained unchanged. Nearly all of these analyses suggested that the "Ask for the Sale" intervention increased ticket sales after the program began, making it difficult to think of an alternative explanation for the effect.

Pattern matching designs counter the unfortunate notion that researchers should choose from a small and fixed set of designs. Campbell & Stanley (1963) inadvertently encouraged such oversimplifications with their table of simple designs and associated plus and minus signs indicating which validity threats are controlled—which they themselves acknowledged at the end of their text might be so simple that they mislead. Instead, pattern matching designs attend to a less often noticed piece of advice, to predict a diverse pattern of results whose strong testing might require multiple nonrandomized designs each with different presumed biases, "the more numerous and independent the ways in which the experimental effect is demonstrated, the less numerous and less plausible any singular rival invalidating hypothesis becomes" (Campbell & Stanley 1963, p. 206). The spirit of this recommendation is the same

as that of R.A. Fisher, who advised to "make your theories elaborate" (cited in Rosenbaum 1984, p. 41) in order to improve causal inference from nonrandomized experiments.

Given such a pattern matching logic, statistical analyses are required that test the overall fit of all the hypothesis tests, not just the difference between adjacent means as in the simple designs. But such tests are not as well developed as those for testing the difference among a small number of means. It may be that testing effects in pattern matching designs requires an approach more resembling meta-analysis, such as combined probability tests. This is a topic needing considerable attention.

CONCLUSION

Great progress has been made in the past four decades about how to solve the implementation and technical problems associated with experiments. In this sense, it is today possible to entertain a vision in which we understand the conditions under which many different kinds of experimental methods, both randomized and nonrandomized, are known to yield accurate effect estimates. Such a vision was hard to conceive four decades ago, but its very possibility points to the extent of the advances that have been made. Scientific progress of this potential magnitude takes decades of effort, persistent research attention, and perhaps a partly fortuitous combination of technical developments.

That being said, we do not claim that the vision has been achieved in practice, on several counts. Randomized experiments remain the method of choice, all things being equal and when they are feasible and ethical, for their strong statistical warrant has no peer among the nonrandomized alternatives. The conditions under which those nonrandomized alternatives seem to produce accurate results are only tentatively understood and place demands on the researcher for good measurement and careful attention to design that cannot be routinely assumed to occur in practice. Many researchers will not know how to implement the best approaches to analysis of nonrandomized experiments or will implement them under conditions of poor pretest measurement that probably yield poor results. And a great deal more empirical research is needed to tease out the nuances of good quasi-experimental design and analysis in a manner that further clarifies the conditions under which they work better or worse. It may take another several decades of that kind of work before we can know how much confidence we should place in nonexperimental estimators.

Also, this review primarily addresses progress in the technical aspects of experimentation. These are crucial developments in many ways. Yet we must remember that field experimentation exists in a policy context. As we said at the start of this review, one of the factors contributing to the renaissance of field experimentation is the evidence-based practice movement. The presumption is that the policy environment today is more open to influence based on information about what works. Yet this presumption badly needs empirical examination. A key lesson of the early rounds of experiments in the 1970s was indeed that policy responds surprisingly little to information about what works (Shadish et al. 1991). The current environment does indeed seem to produce information about what works, information that is of much higher quality than was the case in the 1970s. Much of that information is produced in response to mandates, however, leaving open the possibility that the information will again have little impact on practice and policy. We know of few researchers seriously investigating this possibility.

Fortunately, researchers interested in studying the use of experimental results do not have to start from scratch either conceptually or empirically. Program evaluators have studied the use of evaluation results extensively, developed conceptual systems to help us understand the kinds of uses that can occur and the conditions that facilitate each of these uses. The literature is more extensive than we can summarize here, but good starting points for those interested in such research are in Shadish et al. (1991), Shulha & Cousins (1997), Weiss (1998), and Weiss et al. (2008). The most likely findings will be that short-term instrumental use of experimental evidence to change policy are rare but do occur, especially in cases where the intervention is of interest to the practitioner and has a naturally high turnover rate so that substitution occurs easily. Nevertheless, these results will have significant impact both on how policymakers and practitioners think and on the education received by their replacements that are still in training. In the end, though, significant empirical investigation of such uses is the only way to know for sure if current investments in experimental work really do lead to evidence-based practice.

We have been involved in reviewing the state of social experimentation for more than 20 years (e.g., Cook & Shadish 1986, 1994; W.R. Shadish, manuscript submitted; Shadish et al. 1991). It is fair to say that the present review leaves us more optimistic about the state of experimentation, both technically and socially, than at any time before. We hope—indeed, anticipate—that a review that is written 10 to 20 years from now will yield even more encouraging conclusions.

SUMMARY POINTS

1. A round of early social experiments in the 1960s and 1970s led to disappointing results given technical problems and a perceived failure to use the results. Some fields stopped using experiments as a result.

2. Experimentation is experiencing a renaissance today due to the emphasis on evidence-based practice, the increased involvement of economists and statisticians, and the growing empirical literature that clarifies the effects of certain design and analytic practices.

3. Progress in randomized experiments has involved increased understanding of how to implement them well, better analytic methods for coping with partial treatment implementation, and more knowledge of how to prevent attrition and bracket its possible effects.

4. Progress in regression discontinuity designs has come from vastly increased usage of the design in the past decade by economists who have provided new analytic methods for how to model nonlinearities and how to cope with violations of assignment by cutoff score.

5. Evidence suggests that nonequivalent comparison group designs can approximate answers from randomized designs when they use focal local controls, careful matching on stable covariates, and measure a rich set of pretest predictors of treatment and outcome that can be used in statistical adjustments such as propensity score analysis.

6. When none of the other designs is feasible, researchers should assemble more than one design that predicts a pattern of causal results, for if the results match the predicted pattern, there are fewer plausible alternative explanations.

7. We have made great progress toward understanding the conditions under which a wide variety of kinds of randomized and nonrandomized designs are known to yield accurate effect estimates.

FUTURE ISSUES

1. We need much more knowledge of the conditions under which propensity score analysis can be useful. What sample sizes are needed? How can we best measure the strong ignorability assumption? What approach to missing data in the pretest covariates is best?

2. Methods for the analysis of short interrupted time series need continued development. Especially needed is work on producing estimates of effects that are in the same metric as estimates from between-group designs so that we can know how well the former approximate the latter.

3. The concept of a focal local control needs clarification so that researchers can better know when such a control is present and likely to be comparable to a nonrandomized treatment group.

4. Methods for the analysis of pattern-matching designs have received virtually no attention and are badly needed.

5. Propensity score analysis would benefit from ways to test the strong ignorability assumption.

6. The quality of studies comparing results from randomized and nonrandomized experiments needs improvement in general, and much more of this kind of research needs to be done.

DISCLOSURE STATEMENT

The authors are not aware of any biases that might be perceived as affecting the objectivity of this review.

ACKNOWLEDGMENTS

This work was supported in part by grants H324U050001-06 and R305U07003/01 from the U.S. Department of Education, Institute of Education Sciences.

LITERATURE CITED

Aiken LS, West SG, Schwalm DE, Carroll JL, Hsiung S. 1998. Comparison of a randomized and two quasi-experimental designs in a single outcome evaluation: efficacy of a university-level remedial writing program. *Eval. Rev.* 22:207–44

Angrist JD, Imbens GW. 1995. Two-stage least squares estimation of average causal effects in models with variable treatment intensity. *J. Am. Stat. Assoc.* 90:431–42

Angrist JD, Imbens GW, Rubin DB. 1996. Identification of causal effects using instrumental variables. *J. Am. Stat. Assoc.* 91:444–55

> Shows how to obtain an unbiased estimate of treatment on the treated in the presence of partial treatment implementation.

Angrist JD, Lavy V. 1999. Using Maimonides' rule to identify the effects of class size on scholastic achievement. *Q. J. Econ.* 114:533–75

Baldwin SA, Murray DM, Shadish WR. 2005. Empirically supported treatments or Type I errors? Problems with the analysis of data from group-administered treatments. *J. Consult. Clin. Psychol.* 73:924–35

Balke A, Pearl J. 1997. Bounds on treatment effects from studies with imperfect compliance. *J. Am. Stat. Assoc.* 92:1171–76

Barnard J, Du J, Hill JL, Rubin DR. 1998. A broader template for analyzing broken randomized experiments. *Sociol. Methods Res.* 27:285–317

Berk RA, Rauma D. 1983. Capitalizing on nonrandom assignment to treatment: a regression discontinuity evaluation of a crime control program. *J. Am. Stat. Assoc.* 78:21–27

Boruch RF. 1997. *Randomized Field Experiments for Planning and Evaluation: A Practical Guide.* Thousand Oaks, CA: Sage

Botein B. 1965. The Manhattan Bail Project: its impact on criminology and the criminal law process. *Texas Law Rev.* 43:319–31

Buddelmeyer H, Skoufias E. 2003. *An Evaluation of the Performance of Regression Discontinuity Design on PROGRESA.* Bonn, Germany: IZA

Campbell DT. 1976. Focal local indicators for social program evaluation. *Soc. Indicators Res.* 3:237–56

Campbell DT, Kenny DA. 1999. *A Primer on Regression Artifacts.* New York: Guilford

Campbell DT, Stanley JC. 1963. *Experimental and Quasi-Experimental Designs for Research.* Chicago: Rand-McNally

> Summarizes the history, repeated reinvention, and current revival of the regression discontinuity design.

Cicirelli VG. 1969. *The Impact of Head Start: An Evaluation of the Effects of Head Start on Children's Cognitive and Affective Development. Vol. 1 & 2. A Report to the Office of Economic Opportunity.* Athens: Ohio Univ. Westinghouse Learning Corp.

Constas MA. 2007. Reshaping the methodological identity of education research: early signs of the impact of Federal policy. *Eval. Rev.* 31:391–400

Cook TD. 2007. "Waiting for life to arrive": a history of the regression-discontinuity design in psychology statistics and economics. *J. Econometrics* 142:636–54

Cook TD, Shadish WR. 1986. Program evaluation: the worldly science. *Annu. Rev. Psychol.* 37:193–232

Cook TD, Shadish WR. 1994. Social experiments: some developments over the past 15 years. *Annu. Rev. Psychol.* 45:545–80

> Summarizes evidence that well-done nonrandomized experiments can approximate results from randomized experiments.

Cook TD, Shadish WR, Wong VC. 2008. Three conditions under which experiments and observational studies often produce comparable causal estimates: new findings from within-study comparisons. J. Policy Anal. Manag. In press

Cronbach LJ. 1982. *Designing Evaluations of Educational and Social Programs*. San Francisco, CA: Jossey-Bass

Cronbach LJ, Ambron SR, Dornbusch SM, Hess RD, Hornik RC, et al. 1980. *Toward Reform of Program Evaluation*. San Francisco, CA: Jossey-Bass

Donner A, Klar N. 1996. Statistical considerations in the design and analysis of community intervention trials. *J. Clin. Epidemiol.* 49:435–39

duToit SHC, Browne MW. 2008. Structural equation modeling of multivariate time series. *Multivariate Behav. Res.* 42:67–101

Efron B, Feldman D. 1991. Compliance as an explanatory variable in clinical trials. *J. Am. Stat. Assoc.* 86:9–26

Elkin I, Parloff MB, Hadley SW, Autry JH. 1985. NIMH Treatment of Depression Collaborative Research Program: background and research plan. *Arch. Gen. Psychiatry* 42:305–16

Elkin I, Shea T, Watkins JT, Imber SD, Sotsky SM, et al. 1989. National Institute of Mental Health Treatment of Depression Collaborative Research Program: general effectiveness of treatments. *Arch. Gen. Psychiatry* 46:971–82

Fischer-Lapp K, Goetghebeur E. 1999. Practical properties of some structural mean analyses of the effect of compliance in randomized trials. *Control. Clin. Trials* 20:531–46

Fraker T, Maynard R. 1987. Evaluating comparison group designs with employment-related programs. *J. Hum. Resour.* 22:194–227

Glass GV. 1976. Primary, secondary and meta-analysis. *Educ. Res.* 5:3–8

Glazerman S, Levy DM, Myers D. 2003. Nonexperimental versus experimental estimates of earnings impacts. *Ann. Am. Acad. Pol. Soc. Sci.* 589:63–93

Goetghebeur E, Molenberghs G. 1996. Causal inference in a placebo-controlled clinical trial with binary outcome and ordered compliance. *J. Am. Stat. Assoc.* 91:928–34

Goldberger AS. 1972. *Selection bias in evaluating treatment effects: some formal illustrations*. Discuss. pap. #123, Inst. Res. Poverty, Univ. Wisc., Madison

Goldstein H. 1986. Multilevel mixed linear model analysis using generalized least squares. *Biometrika* 73:43–56

Gueron JM. 1985. The demonstration of state work/welfare initiatives. In *Randomization and Field Experimentation*, ed. RF Boruch, W Wothke, pp. 5–13. San Francisco, CA: Jossey-Bass

Hahn J, Todd P, Van Der Klaauw W. 2001. Identification and estimation of treatment effects with a regression-discontinuity design. *Econometrica* 69:201–9

Heckman JJ. 1979. Sample selection bias as a specification error. *Econometrica* 47:153–61

Heckman JJ. 1992. Randomization and social policy evaluation. In *Evaluating Welfare and Training Programs*, ed. CF Manski, I Garfinkel, pp. 201–30. Cambridge, MA: Harvard Univ. Press

Heinsman DT, Shadish WR. 1996. Assignment methods in experimentation: When do nonrandomized experiments approximate the answers from randomized experiments? *Psychol. Methods* 1:154–69

Hill JL, Reiter JP, Zanutto EL. 2004. A comparison of experimental and observational data analyses. In *Applied Bayesian Modeling and Causal Inference from Incomplete Data Perspectives*, ed. A Gelman, X-L Meng, pp. 51–60. New York: Wiley

Hoeppner BB, Goodwin MS, Velicer WF, Heltshe J. 2008. An example of pooled time series analysis: cardiovascular reactivity to stressors in children with autism. *Multivariate Behav. Res.* 42:707–27

Imbens GW, Rubin DB. 1997a. Bayesian inference for causal effects in randomized experiments with noncompliance. *Ann. Stat.* 25:305–27

Imbens GW, Rubin DB. 1997b. Estimating outcome distributions for compliers in instrumental variables models. *Rev. Econ. Stud.* 64:555–74

Jo B, Asparouhov T, Muthén BO, Ialongo NS, Brown CH. 2008. Cluster randomized trials with treatment noncompliance. *Psychol. Methods* 13:1–18

LaLonde R, Maynard R. 1987. How precise are evaluations of employment and training experiments: evidence from a field experiment. *Eval. Rev.* 11:428–51

Littell RC. 2006. *SAS for Mixed Models*. Cary, NC: SAS Publ.

Little RJ, Yau L. 1996. Intent-to-treat analysis for longitudinal studies with dropouts. *Biometrics* 52:1324–33

Magidson J. 1977. Toward a causal model approach for adjusting for preexisting differences in the nonequivalent control group situation. *Eval. Q.* 1:399–420

Marascuilo LA, Busk PL. 1988. Combining statistics for multiple-baseline AB and replicated ABAB designs across subjects. *Behav. Assess.* 10:1–28

Provides methods for estimating effects in regression discontinuity designs in the face of violations of the cutoff.

McLeod RS, Taylor DW, Cohen A, Cullen JB. 1986. Single patient randomized clinical trial: its use in determining optimal treatment for patient with inflammation of a Kock continent ileostomy reservoir. *Lancet* 1(March 29):726–28

Millsap MA, Chase A, Obeidallah D, Perez-Smith AP, Brigham N, Johnston K. 2000. *Evaluation of Detroit's Comer Schools and Families Initiative: Final Report.* Cambridge, MA: Abt Assoc.

Morgan DL, Morgan RK. 2001. Single participant research design: bringing science to managed care. *Am. Psychol.* 56:119–27

Morgan SL, Winship C. 2007. *Counterfactuals and Causal Inference.* London: Cambridge Univ. Press

Murray DM. 1998. *Design and Analysis of Group-Randomized Trials.* New York: Oxford Univ. Press

Nathan RP. 1989. *Social Science in Government: Uses and Misuses.* New York: Basic Books

Oakes D, Moss AJ, Fleiss JL, Bigger JT Jr, Therneau T, et al. 1993. Use of compliance measures in an analysis of the effect of diltiazem on mortality and reinfarction after myocardial infarction. *J. Am. Stat. Assoc.* 88:44–49

Phye GD, Robinson DH, Levin J, eds. 2005. *Empirical Methods for Evaluating Educational Interventions.* New York: Academic

Rasbash J, Steele F, Browne WJ, Prosser B. 2005. *A User's Guide to MLwiN Version 2.0.* Bristol, UK: Univ. Bristol

Raudenbush SW, Bryk AS. 2002. *Hierarchical Linear Models: Applications and Data Analysis Methods.* Thousand Oaks, CA: Sage

Raudenbush SW, Bryk A, Cheong YF, Congdon R. 2004. *HLM6: Hierarchical Linear and Nonlinear Modeling.* Chicago: Sci. Software Intl.

Reynolds KD, West SG. 1987. A multiplist strategy for strengthening nonequivalent control group designs. *Eval. Rev.* 11:691–714

Ribisl KM, Walton MA, Mowbray CT, Luke DA, Davidson WS, Bootsmiller BJ. 1996. Minimizing participant attrition in panel studies through the use of effective retention and tracking strategies: review and recommendations. *Eval. Program Planning* 19:1–25

Riecken HW, Boruch RF, Campbell DT, Caplan N, Glennan TK, et al. 1974. *Social Experimentation: A Method for Planning and Evaluating Social Intervention.* New York: Academic

Robins JM. 1998. Correction for noncompliance in equivalence trials. *Stat. Med.* 17:269–302

Rosenbaum PR. 1984. From association to causation in observational studies: the role of tests of strongly ignorable treatment assumptions. *J. Am. Stat. Assoc.* 79:41–48

Rosenbaum PR, Rubin DB. 1983. The central role of the propensity score in observational studies for causal effects. *Biometrika* 70:141–55

Rossi PH, Lyall KC. 1978. An overview evaluation of the NIT experiment. In *Evaluation Studies Review Annual,* ed. TD Cook, ML DelRosario, KM Hennigan, MM Mark, WMK Trochim, 3:412–28. Newbury Park, CA: Sage

Rubin DB. 1974. Estimating causal effects of treatments in randomized and nonrandomized studies. *J. Educ. Psychol.* 66:688–701

Rubin DB. 1977. Assignment to treatment group on the basis of a covariate. *J. Educ. Stat.* 2:1–26

Rubin DB. 2001. Using propensity scores to help design observational studies: application to the tobacco litigation. *Health Serv. Outcomes Res. Methodol.* 2:169–88

Rubin DB. 2004. Teaching statistical inference for causal effects in experiments and observational studies. *J. Educ. Behav. Stat.* 29:343–67

Shadish WR. 2000. The empirical program of quasi-experimentation. In *Validity and Social Experimentation: Donald Campbell's Legacy,* ed. L Bickman, pp. 13–35. Thousand Oaks, CA: Sage

Shadish WR. 2008. *Bandwidth versus fidelity: working through commensurability of Campbell and Rubin for causal inference.* Manuscr. submitted

Shadish WR, Clark MH, Steiner PM. 2008. Can nonrandomized experiments yield accurate answers? A randomized experiment comparing random to nonrandom assignment. *J. Am. Stat. Assoc.* In press

Shadish WR, Cook TD, Campbell DT. 2002. *Experimental and Quasi-Experimental Designs for Generalized Causal Inference.* Boston, MA: Houghton-Mifflin

Shadish WR, Cook TD, Leviton LC. 1991. *Foundations of Program Evaluation: Theories of Practice.* Newbury Park, CA: Sage

Presents the best available summary of methods for preventing attrition.

Provides an exemplar of how to assess balance using propensity scores in observational studies.

Furnishes a good general introduction to Rubin's potential outcomes model.

Serves as a good general reference to many aspects of experimental and quasi-experimental design.

Shadish WR, Hu X, Glaser RR, Kownacki RJ, Wong T. 1998. A method for exploring the effects of attrition in randomized experiments with dichotomous outcomes. *Psychol. Methods* 3:3–22

Shadish WR, Ragsdale K. 1996. Random versus nonrandom assignment in psychotherapy experiments: Do you get the same answer? *J. Consult. Clin. Psychol.* 64:1290–305

Shih WJ, Quan H. 1997. Testing for treatment differences with dropouts present in clinical trials—a composite approach. *Stat. Med.* 16:1225–39

Shulha LM, Cousins JB. 1997. Evaluation use: theory, research and practice since 1986. *Am. J. Eval.* 18:195–208

Steiner PM, Cook TD, Shadish WR, Clark MH. 2008. *The Importance of Covariate Selection in Controlling for Selection Bias in Observational Studies.* Manuscr. submitted

Thistlewaite DL, Campbell DT. 1960. Regression-discontinuity analysis: an alternative to the ex post facto experiment. *J. Educ. Psychol.* 51:309–17

Trochim WMK. 1984. *Research Design for Program Evaluation: The Regression-Discontinuity Approach.* Newbury Park, CA: Sage

Van Den Noortgate W, Onghena P. 2003. Hierarchical linear models for the quantitative integration of effect sizes in single-case research. *Behav. Res. Methods Instrum. Comput.* 351:1–10

Wampold BE, Worsham NL. 1986. Randomization tests for multiple-baseline designs. *Behav. Assess.* 8:135–43

Weiss B, Williams JH, Margen S, Abrams B, Caan B, et al. 1980. Behavioral responses to artificial food colors. *Science* 207:1487–89

Weiss CH. 1998. Have we learned anything new about the use of evaluation? *Am. J. Eval.* 19:21–33

Weiss CH, Murphy-Graham E, Petrosino A, Gandhi AG. 2008. The Fairy Godmother—and her warts: making the dream of evidence-based policy come true. *Am. J. Eval.* 29:29–47

Wholey JS, Scanlon JW, Duffy HG, Fukumoto JS, Vogt LM. 1970. *Federal Evaluation Policy: Analyzing the Effects of Public Programs.* Washington, DC: Urban Inst.

Wong VC, Cook TD, Barnett WS, Jung K. 2008. An effectiveness-based evaluation of five state prekindergarten programs. *J. Policy Anal. Manag.* 27:122–54

Adolescent Romantic Relationships

W. Andrew Collins,[1] Deborah P. Welsh,[2]
and Wyndol Furman[3]

[1] Institute of Child Development, University of Minnesota, Minneapolis,
Minnesota 55455-0345; email: wcollins@umn.edu

[2] Department of Psychology, University of Tennessee, Knoxville, Tennessee 37996-0900;
email: dwelsh@utk.edu

[3] Department of Psychology, University of Denver, Denver, Colorado 80209;
email: wfurman@nova.psych.du.edu

Annu. Rev. Psychol. 2009. 60:631–52

The *Annual Review of Psychology* is online at
psych.annualreviews.org

This article's doi:
10.1146/annurev.psych.60.110707.163459

0066-4308/09/0110-0631$20.00

Key Words

adolescence, contexts, peers, development

Abstract

In this article, we review theoretical and empirical advances in research
on romantic relationships between age 10 and the early twenties. First,
we describe key themes in this area of research. Next, we briefly characterize the most influential theoretical formulations and distinctive
methodological issues. We then describe research findings regarding
pertinent social and developmental processes. We summarize the extensive findings on relationships with parents and peers as a context for
romantic relationships. Finally, we characterize the growing evidence
that adolescent romantic relationships are significant for individual adjustment and development, and we note promising directions for further
research.

Contents

Romantic relationships: mutually acknowledged ongoing voluntary interactions, commonly marked by expressions of affection and perhaps current or anticipated sexual behavior

Romantic experiences: varied behavioral, cognitive, and emotional phenomena with romantic content; may or may not include direct experiences with a romantic partner

INTRODUCTION AND OVERVIEW

Romantic relationships are a hallmark of adolescence. Only in the past decade, however, has scientific interest begun to match the hold of this topic on the popular and artistic imagination. Once regarded as trivial, transitory, or merely artifacts of social dysfunction, adolescent romantic relationships increasingly are regarded as potentially significant relational factors in individual development and well-being (Collins 2003, Furman & Collins 2008, Furman & Shaffer 2003). The intellectual forebears of this contemporary perspective come not only from the study of adolescent psychology and development (Smetana et al. 2006), but also from the remarkable expansion and refinement of scientific research on interpersonal relationships (Reis et al. 2000). The scope and vitality of current research in the area are remarkable. Several edited volumes have been published (e.g., Crouter & Booth 2006, Florsheim 2003, Furman et al. 1999); research laboratories in North America, South America, Europe, Australia, and the Middle East pursue research programs on the nature and processes of adolescent romantic relationships; and the number of journal articles and scientific program slots devoted to the topic have increased annually since 2000.

The term "romantic relationships" refers to mutually acknowledged ongoing voluntary interactions. Compared to other peer relationships, romantic ones typically have a distinctive intensity, commonly marked by expressions of affection and current or anticipated sexual behavior. This definition applies to same-gender, as well as mixed-gender, relationships. The term "romantic experiences" refers to a larger category of activities and cognitions that includes relationships and also varied behavioral, cognitive, and emotional phenomena that do not involve direct experiences with a romantic partner. This category includes fantasies and one-sided attractions ("crushes"), as well as interactions with potential romantic partners and brief nonromantic sexual encounters (e.g., "hooking up," or casual involvement in activities usually thought to take place with romantic partners, from "making out" to intercourse) (B. Brown et al. 1999, Furman & Collins 2008, Manning et al. 2006). Little research has been devoted to romantic experiences other than actual relationships.

Romantic relationships are more common during adolescence than has usually been assumed. More than half of U.S. adolescents report having had a special romantic relationship in the past 18 months (Carver et al. 2003). The proportions are even higher with more inclusive definitions of romantic relationships (e.g., dating, spending time with or going out with someone for a month or longer) (Furman & Hand 2006). Incidence varies, however, across the three commonly recognized subperiods of adolescence: early adolescence (typically ages 10–13); middle adolescence (ages 14–17); and late adolescence (18 until the early twenties) (Smetana et al. 2006). For example, 36% of 13-year-olds, 53% of 15-year-olds, and 70% of 17-year-olds report having had a "special" romantic relationship in the previous 18 months. By middle adolescence, most individuals have been involved in at least one romantic relationship (Carver et al. 2003). High school students commonly report more frequent interactions with romantic partners than with parents, siblings, or friends (Laursen & Williams 1997). The percentage of adolescents who report having a romantic relationship increases during the teenage years (Carver et al. 2003).

Research on adolescent romantic relationships has increased more in the past decade than in all of the previous century. Before 1999, the small amount of available information was largely descriptive. The primary foci were adolescents' perceptions of potential partners and the extent of dating activity; interest in the significance for individual development was limited to the association with maladaptation and negative behavior (see Collins 2003 for a historical perspective). Contemporary researchers have expanded their purview in several respects. First, greater attention has been given to the quality of these relationships and their potential implications for positive, as well as negative, developmental outcomes for adolescents. Second, research questions have been broadened to encompass the processes associated with involvement in and qualities of adolescent relationships (e.g., cognitions and perceptions, emotions, and intimacy). In both of these first two research trends, researchers also have shifted from almost exclusive reliance on questionnaires to incorporating observational methods, detailed interviews, and other methods. Third, research on romantic relationships, like research on adolescents generally, has become more inclusive. Researchers now give greater attention to cultural, racial, and socioeconomic diversity in the characteristics and significance of adolescent romantic relationships. Research on the roman-

tic experiences of nonheterosexual youths is increasing, as well.

In this review, we first briefly describe especially influential theoretical and methodological considerations in current research. We next summarize current knowledge about key features of adolescent romantic relationships: the nature, degree, and timing of involvement in romantic relationships; the nature and psychological significance of relationship quality; the contributions of the characteristics of romantic partners; salient features of the content of these relationships, such as sexual behavior and partner aggression; and the cognitive and emotional processes associated with romantic relationships. For each of these features, we consider both developmental changes and individual differences. We then address the role of relationship networks in adolescent relationships. Finally, we discuss the evidence regarding the psychological and developmental significance of participating in adolescent romantic relationships. The review concludes by identifying especially promising directions for further research.

THEORETICAL AND METHODOLOGICAL CONSIDERATIONS

Theories

The theories that commonly serve as touchstones in current research ground romantic relationships in normative social experiences of childhood and adolescence. They include biosocial perspectives, such as evolutionary theory, more specific formulations emphasizing neuroendocrine functioning, and genetics; ecological perspectives; and interpersonal formulations, such as attachment and interdependence theories.

Biosocial perspectives. Biosocial perspectives emanate largely from evolutionary psychology and research on neuroendocrine processes. A common premise is that changes in social relationships that enhance reproductive

"Hooking up": casual involvement in activities usually thought to take place with romantic partners (e.g., "making out," intercourse)

Relationship quality: degree to which partners manifest intimacy, affection, and nurturance

fitness should co-occur with attaining reproductive capability (Weisfeld 1999). This premise undergirds much of the existing research on the implications of pubertal development for the changing distribution of adolescents with adults and peers, especially other-sex peers. Research findings from studies of both human and nonhuman adolescents suggest that reproductive maturation may be inhibited by physical closeness to parents and accelerated by distance from them, which would minimize inbreeding and thereby increase reproductive fitness. Although the timing of puberty is associated with romantic and sexual behavior (e.g., Dornbusch et al. 1981, Ellis 2004), recent research findings raise expectations for more specific targeted studies of the implications of changes predicted by evolutionary theory to play a role in adolescent romantic relationships (Susman 2006).

A related line of research involves examining neurotransmitters such as oxytocin and vasopressin in relation to the behavioral features of adolescent sexuality and romantic relationships (Reis et al. 2000). Behavioral genetics has not yet been used to inform research on behaviors peculiar to early sexual activity or romantic relationships (Collins & Steinberg 2006). Evolutionary perspectives have guided a significant amount of research on adult romantic relationships (Buss 2005), but the application to adolescent romantic relationships has primarily consisted of theoretical papers (e.g., Laursen & Jensen-Campbell 1999). Thus, research activities derived from biosocial theories of adolescent romantic relationships promise potential growth but have yielded little thus far.

Ecological perspectives. Ecological perspectives emphasize the social and cultural contexts that encourage or constrain close relationships and endow them with meaning and significance. In this view, events that occur in other settings and relationships inevitably affect adolescent romantic relationships, which in turn can impinge on those settings. Among the potentially influential ecological features are histor-ical, social, economic, political, geographical, cultural, and institutional and community conditions and characteristics that shape proximal experiences (Larson & Wilson 2004). Among the most frequently studied contexts of adolescent romantic relationships are networks of families and peers, ethnic/cultural contexts, religious institutions, and the mass media (e.g., J. Brown et al. 2002, Connolly et al. 2000, Giordano et al. 2005, Rostosky et al. 2004).

Interpersonal perspectives. Interpersonal perspectives emphasize the nature and processes of changes in adolescents' social relationships and the contribution of these changes to individual development. In interdependence models, joint patterns of actions, cognitions, and emotions between two individuals are the primary locus of interpersonal influences (Hinde 1997, Kelley et al. 2002, Laursen & Bukowski 1997). During adolescence, interdependencies in family relationships continue, though often in different forms than in earlier life, and interdependencies with friends and romantic partners become more apparent (Collins 2003). Research inspired by interdependence views typically focuses on the aspects of couple interactions that may favor stability or change in romantic relationships.

A particularly influential interdependence view, attachment theory, holds that a history of sensitive, responsive interactions and strong emotional bonds with caregivers in childhood facilitates adaptation to the transitions of adolescence (Allen & Land 1999, Collins & Sroufe 1999). Mature romantic attachments, however, require the cognitive and emotional maturity to integrate attachment, caregiving, and sexual/reproductive components (Waters & Cummings 2000). Although the necessary maturity level rarely is achieved before late adolescence (Allen & Land 1999), the developmental process begins earlier with a redistribution of attachment-related functions (for example, a desire for proximity, relying on the other person for unconditional acceptance) to friends and boyfriends or girlfriends (Furman & Wehner 1997).

These theories address different levels of analysis and, thus, are complementary rather than mutually exclusive or incompatible. Despite the apparent relevance of biosocial, ecological, and interdependence formulations, however, theories in this area have not developed to the point of widespread influence over research in the area. The time is right for further theoretical development to guide future progress in the area. One fruitful direction may be more integrative theorizing. For example, developmental systems models (e.g., Magnusson & Stattin 1998), though conceptually and methodologically daunting, call attention to the contrasting and the overlapping implications of multiple perspectives for adolescent romantic relationships.

Methodological Issues

Four methodological challenges confront researchers when designing and interpreting studies of adolescents' romantic relationships: (*a*) issues of operational definition, (*b*) representativeness of samples, (*c*) the ephemeral nature and instability of adolescent relationships, and (*d*) the interdependence of dyadic data.

Operational definitions. Conceptualizations of adolescent romantic relationships have been remarkably consistent across existing studies, yet no standard operational definitions exist nor has the broader domain of romantic experiences been well specified. Researchers typically have asked participants if they have a romantic relationship (or a boyfriend or girlfriend), and the participants decide on the basis of their own definition. A brief description is sometimes provided for clarification (e.g., "when you like a guy [girl] and he [she] likes you back") (Giordano et al. 2006). Researchers often also specify a minimum duration (e.g., at least one month long) in an effort to narrow the criteria (Welsh & Dickson 2005). Differences in definition affect estimates of the frequency and duration of romantic relationships and, very likely, findings from research (Furman & Hand 2006).

Obtaining representative samples. The nature and some features of adolescent romantic relationships may vary across diverse cultural, racial, and socioeconomic contexts. Researchers seek to capture the range of this diversity in their sampling strategies, but the task is difficult. Recruiting from schools is one of the best strategies for obtaining representative samples. However, school administrators are often reluctant to endorse research focused on controversial issues such as adolescent romantic relationships. Creative ways of addressing the concerns of school administrators may be needed to obtain such samples (Welsh et al. 2005). Some researchers attempt to recruit participants from community organizations or locations (e.g., churches, shopping malls); adolescents found in particular community organizations or locations may be less likely than are those recruited from schools to represent the adolescent population. Increasingly, researchers use Internet social networking Web sites (e.g., Facebook and MySpace) to recruit research participants. This strategy potentially offers access to larger numbers of potential participants than the recruiting methods mentioned above. Recent statistics show that 87% of U.S. teens use the Internet, and the number of adolescents using the Internet to communicate continues to increase (Lenhart et al. 2005).

Regardless of how the sample is obtained, adolescents and parents who consent to participate in research on adolescent romantic relationships may differ systematically from adolescents who are unwilling to participate. For example, some researchers have found that ideologically conservative parents and adolescents are often less willing to participate in research on romantic relationships than are more liberal parents. Some researchers address this problem by using samples originally recruited for broader purposes. For example, researchers can use publicly available datasets of nationally representative samples collected to assess adolescent health broadly rather than romantic relationships specifically (e.g., Bearman et al. 1997). Two limitations are inherent in this approach. One is that researchers are restricted to the variables collected in the original study. The second is that the data likely come only from self-report questionnaires, potentially confounding the findings with common method variance. A variation on this strategy is collecting new data from participants of a previous intensive longitudinal study in which the participants are already committed to the larger developmental project (e.g., Capaldi et al. 2001, Sroufe et al. 2005). The problem associated with this approach is that the intensive data collection typical of well-conceptualized longitudinal studies often necessitates relatively small sample sizes. Thus, the goal of recruiting representative samples typically requires carefully reasoned trade-offs among the strengths and weaknesses of various strategies and detailed reporting of the decision processes associated with a particular study.

Regardless of research design, the possibility of bias from untruthful reporting always looms. It is unclear whether adolescent participants are any more or less likely than those of other ages to either exaggerate or suppress reports of dating, sexual activity, and so forth. Prudent researchers provide for other, as well as self, reports and additional checks on the reliability and validity of data.

Short duration and instability of relationships. Researchers interested in development face the particular challenge of the relatively transitory phenomena of adolescents' romantic relationships (B. Brown et al. 1999). Relationships may come and go before the researcher has had the opportunity to study them. Traditional longitudinal designs typically specify data collection at regular time intervals (often one year) rather than sampling at the time a new relationship emerges. Studies of the initiation, development, and decline of particular relationships are needed, however, to discern how each relationship contributes to choice of partners and behavior in future relationships. Some methodological techniques used to address this complex issue are daily diary studies (Bolger et al. 2003, Downey et al. 1998), regular

brief phone calls inquiring about relationship transitions, and regular intensive relationship histories (Giordano et al. 2006).

Interdependence of data. Romantic relationships are dyadic; thus, data from the two participants are not independent. The recent widespread use of multilevel modeling techniques allows romantic relationship researchers to separate the variance in outcome variables into individual and dyadic components. Such techniques also address the lack of independence in the couple members' responses. Non-independence violates the assumptions of common statistical techniques such as multiple regression by incorrectly estimating error terms (for a definitive treatment of statistical analysis of dyadic data, see Kenny et al. 2006).

ROMANTIC RELATIONSHIP PROCESSES DURING ADOLESCENCE

A fundamental challenge in research on adolescent romantic experiences is identifying the relevant dimensions of variation. Collins (2003) has delineated five features with documented relevance to the current and/or long-term significance for individual functioning and further development: romantic involvement; partner identity; relationship content; relationship quality; and cognitive and emotional processes in the relationship. Romantic involvement or activity refers to whether or not a person dates, when s/he began dating, the duration of the relationship, and the frequency and consistency of dating and relationships. Partner identity is concerned with the characteristics of the person with whom an adolescent has a romantic experience (e.g., dating). Content refers to what the members of the dyad do and do not do together. Relationship quality pertains to the relative degree of positive, supportive, beneficent experiences as compared to the negative, potentially detrimental ones. Cognitive and emotional processes include perceptions, attributions, and representations of oneself, the partner, and the relationship, as well as the emotions and moods elicited in romantic encounters and affective statements associated with involvement in and the dissolution of relationships (e.g., depressive symptoms).

Involvement in Romantic Relationships

Becoming involved in romantic relationships and the frequency of romantic experiences are embedded in the adolescent social system. Prior to adolescence, interactions typically occur with peers of the same gender; most friendship pairs are of the same gender (Kovacs et al. 1996). Affiliation with mixed-gender groups typically follows in early to middle adolescence and facilitates the progression from same-gendered friendships to dyadic romantic relationships (Connolly et al. 2004). Across the teenage years, young people spend increasing amounts of time with other gender peers and romantic partners (Laursen & Williams 1997, Richards et al. 1998). By early adulthood, time with romantic partners increases further at the expense of involvement with friends and crowds (Reis et al. 1993).

The timing of involvement is often attributed to the onset of puberty; however, researchers now have demonstrated that gonadarche (development of the gonads, with increased release of estrogen in females and testosterone in males) is distinct from changes that may be relevant to romantic interest. Adrenarche, or the increased activity of the adrenal glands just prior to puberty, appears to be more strongly predictive of sexual interest and awareness than gonadarche, which occurs later (e.g., Halpern 2003, McClintock & Herdt 1996). Moreover, researchers repeatedly have demonstrated the independent contributions of social expectations, especially age-graded behavior norms, to the initiation of dating in Western countries (e.g., Dornbusch et al. 1981). Cultural norms also affect the activities that are expected and approved within dating relationships (Feldman et al. 1999, Seiffge-Krenke 2006, Silbereisen & Schwarz 1998). For example, Asian American adolescents are less likely to have had a romantic relationship in the past 18 months than are adolescents in African American, Hispanic, Native American, and European American groups (Carver et al. 2003). Latina early-adolescent girls described being more closely supervised in contexts in which they interacted with males than African American early-adolescent girls report. Both Latina and African American early-adolescent girls kept their early boyfriends a secret from their family members, especially their mothers. They explained that they kept these relationships secret because they feared being forced to end the relationship (O'Sullivan & Meyer-Bahlburg 2003).

Less is known about the developmental course of the relationships of gay, lesbian, and bisexual adolescents. Among sexual-minority adolescents, approximately 93% of boys and 85% of girls report having had some same-sex activity (Savin-Williams & Diamond 2000). The number of romantic relationships reported by youths involved in organizations for sexual minorities is comparable to the number for heterosexual youths (Diamond & Lucas 2004). The average age of a first "serious" same-gender relationship is 18 years (Floyd & Stein 2002). Same-gender dating can be uncommon, however, in locations where fewer adolescents are openly identified as gay, lesbian, or bisexual (Diamond et al. 1999). In many instances, same-sex romantic attraction puts adolescents at risk for violence; youths who report same-sex or both-sex romantic attraction are more likely to experience extreme forms of violence than are those who report only other-sex romantic interests (Russell et al. 2001).

An important caveat is that the early romantic experiences of many youths include both same-sex and other-sex partners. The majority of sexual-minority youths report dating members of the other sex (Savin-Williams 1996). Approximately 42% of sexual-minority adolescent girls and 79% of sexual-minority adolescent boys report some sexual activity with a member of the other sex (D'Augelli 1998). Such dating can either provide a cover for a minority sexual identity or help clarify one's identity (Diamond et al. 1999). A significant

Gonadarche: increased release of estrogen in females and testosterone in males

Adrenarche: increased activity of the adrenal glands just prior to puberty

proportion of women also characterize themselves as "mostly heterosexual" (Austin et al. 2007). Same-gender attraction, sexual behavior, and identity are not perfectly correlated with one another (Diamond 2003, Savin-Williams 2006); thus, sexual identity and the gender of the person one is attracted to can be quite fluid over time, especially for women. Not surprisingly, then, estimates of the prevalence of homosexuality can range from 1% to 21% depending upon the definition. Such variability underscores the idea that no simple dichotomy exists between heterosexuality and homosexuality.

Partner Characteristics

The characteristics of romantic partners contribute to both the distinguishing features and potential developmental sequelae of an adolescent romantic relationship. Little is known, however, about adolescents' selection of partners or the extent to which partner characteristics are important to the development of each member of the adolescent couple (Furman & Simon 2008). The small amount of available information is largely descriptive. Like adults, adolescents report that their ideal partners are intelligent, interpersonally skillful, and physically appealing (Regan 2003, Roscoe et al. 1987), but the match between ideal and actual partners has not been studied (Collins 2003). For many adolescents, community and cultural norms determine the field of availability, or standards for who is acceptable as a romantic target. Whether relationships conform to a culturally or socially prescribed field of availability affects both the individual and the relationship in multiple ways (e.g., Coates 1999).

Most is known about the demographic match between the two adolescents in a couple. Among heterosexual adolescents, males tend to choose dating partners close to their own age, whereas females' dating partners are often older than they are. Dating partners are similar in race, ethnicity, and other demographic characteristics (Carver et al. 2003). Recent findings also show young adolescent partners to be sig-

nificantly alike on certain social and psychological characteristics, e.g., popularity, physical attraction, and depressive symptoms (Simon et al. 2008). This "selective partnering" is also evident in patterns of psychological and physical aggression in young at-risk couples (Capaldi & Crosby 1997).

Emotional dimensions of selective partnering generally have been neglected in research. An exception is reports of partner choice among sexual-minority adolescents. Sexual-minority males typically report that they were first sexually rather than emotionally attracted to another male, whereas sexual-minority females were evenly divided between first having had an emotional or sexual attraction to another female or a male, as was the case with their first same-gender sexual partners (Savin-Williams & Diamond 2000). The emotional and sexual attraction processes associated with the demographic correspondence between heterosexual partners is a promising future research direction.

The influence of partner characteristics has thus far been neglected in research. Girls' working models of romantic relationships are related to their partners' behavior, as well as their own (Furman & Simon 2006), but it is not clear if these relations reflect "selective partnering" or socialization in the relationship. In one of the few studies to distinguish socialization and selection effects, partners' popularity, depressive symptoms, relational aggression, and relational victimization reliably predicted changes over time in adolescents' status on these same variables, controlling for initial similarity between partners. The magnitude and direction of change varied according to adolescents' and partners' functioning prior to the relationship, even when best friend characteristics are controlled (Simon et al. 2008). Further research addressing similar questions in later, as well as early, adolescence is needed to fill this gap in the literature.

Content

Relationship content refers to partners' shared activities. Adolescents engage in distinct

---

Field of availability: range of persons acceptable as potential romantic partners; commonly determined by community and cultural norms

patterns of interaction that differ from their interactions with parents or peers. Interactions with romantic partners contain more conflict than with friends and less responsiveness than either interactions with best friends or those with mothers. Despite these interactional differences, adolescents nevertheless perceived more support from their romantic partners than from their mothers (Furman & Shomaker 2008). One explanation for these unexpected findings may come from studies showing that adolescents project their perceptions of their own behaviors onto their perceptions of their partner's behaviors (Welsh & Dickson 2005). In these studies, adolescent couples, as well as independent observers of their interactions, also tended to describe the couple relationships as egalitarian. In most of the couples, adolescents perceived themselves and their partners as equally contributing emotional resources, sharing power in interaction, and sharing decision-making responsibility. Perceived inequality in these respects has repeatedly been associated with more psychological symptoms in the members of the couple, especially females (Galliher et al. 2004). Two forms of relationship content have been the focus of considerable popular, as well as scholarly, attention: sexual behavior and aggression between partners.

Sexual behavior. Romantic relationships are the context in which the majority of adolescents' sexual behavior occurs (Manning et al. 2000). Adolescent relationships have rarely been the focus of investigations of sexual behavior, however (Bouchey & Furman 2003, Crockett et al. 2003, Florsheim 2003). Only in the past decade have researchers, under the influence of developmental theories, begun to examine the development of adolescent sexuality from a normative perspective and to investigate the contexts in which sexual behavior occurs (Diamond & Savin-Williams 2003, Florsheim 2003, Welsh et al. 2000). Such studies have shown, for example, that adolescent females perceive strong norms that sexual behavior should occur within the context of romantic relationships and not outside of it.

Themes of shame and degradation are associated with sexual activity outside of romantic relationships, although these themes are less strong for African American adolescents than for European American youths (O'Sullivan & Meyer-Bahlburg 2003). These views may explain the association between depressive symptoms and sexual behavior outside of romantic relationships in female adolescents and early adults (Grello et al. 2003, 2006).

Normative models also have stimulated research on sexual behaviors other than intercourse. These studies have revealed that "lighter" sexual behaviors such as kissing, holding hands, and hugging are positively associated with positive parent-child relationships and with romantic relationship satisfaction and commitment (Welsh et al. 2005, Williams et al. 2008). An important agenda for future research is examining the developmental significance of these more affectionate sexual behaviors in the context of adolescents' romantic relationships.

The potential significance of sexual behavior for adolescent development depends more than is commonly recognized on the moderating influences of developmental status, the nature of the relationship, and the implicit meaning of sexual activity for the adolescent. For example, engaging in genitally stimulating or "heavy" sexual behaviors in early adolescence is consistently associated with numerous problems (e.g., depression, violence, substance use, hostile family processes, poor academic participation, and poor romantic relationship quality) (Welsh et al. 2005, Williams et al. 2008). However, engaging in these behaviors, including intercourse, within the context of a romantic relationship in late adolescence has not been linked with greater incidence of problems (Grello et al. 2003, Welsh et al. 2005). The subjective meaning of sexual behaviors within romantic relationships varies in different stages of development (Welsh et al. 2000). As romantic relationships become more intimate and committed during late adolescence, sexual behaviors may represent a physical expression of the partners' intimacy and commitment, whereas sexual behavior in early adolescence is more likely to signify an effort to avoid losing the relationship (O'Sullivan & Meyer-Bahlburg 2003) or a difficulty communicating about sexual behavior (Widman et al. 2006).

Dating aggression. Aggression between romantic partners is common in both other-sex and same-sex romantic relationships in adolescence. Although estimates vary widely across sample and assessment methods, 10% to 48% of adolescents report experiencing physical aggression in their dating relationships, and one-quarter to one-half of adolescents report psychological aggression (Halpern et al. 2001, 2004; Jouriles et al. 2005). Moreover, although physical aggression was once believed to be primarily inflicted by males upon females, recent investigations reveal either no gender differences or higher prevalence rates for adolescent females as aggressors or initiators of aggression (Archer 2000; Capaldi et al. 2007; Halpern et al. 2001, 2004). The meaning and developmental implications of adolescent female dating aggression, however, likely differs from the implications of male aggression. Further research is needed to examine this particular hypothesis and to examine female dating aggression in general.

Both physical and relational aggression (attempting to cause harm by damaging one's relationships) increase from early to middle adolescence (Halpern et al. 2001, Pepler et al. 2006). Investigations have linked dating aggression in adolescent romantic relationships to parental and peer influences (Arriaga & Foshee 2004, Capaldi et al. 2001, Kinsfogel & Grych 2004). Adolescent males exposed to greater parental conflict are more likely to perceive aggression as justifiable in romantic relationships and report higher levels of verbal and physical aggression in their romantic relationships. Females' aggressive behavior in romantic relationships, on the other hand, is generally not linked with parental conflict (Kinsfogel & Grych 2004), highlighting the different trajectories associated with male and female aggression. Peers also play a formative role in the development of males' dating aggression. Males' aggression

toward their girlfriends is associated with recent hostile discussions about women with close friends (Capaldi et al. 2001). These accumulating findings have prompted researchers to shift their attention from questions of whether and how much aggression occurs in adolescent romantic relationships to examine the processes that account for differential manifestations of dating aggression and the conditions under which it is more or less likely (e.g., Buzy et al. 2004).

Relationship Quality

Relationship quality refers to the degree to which partners manifest intimacy, affection, and nurturance. Low-quality relationships are marked by irritation, antagonism, and notably high levels of conflict or controlling behavior (Galliher et al. 2004). High-quality relationships characterized by supportiveness and intimacy are associated with measures of functioning and well-being for the individuals involved; similarly, quality romantic relationships in adolescence are associated with increased likelihood of positive relationships and relationship commitment in early adulthood (Seiffge-Krenke & Lang 2002). More negative qualities likewise have been linked to varied negative outcomes (for a review, see Furman & Collins 2008). Intimacy is widely regarded as a likely component of relationship quality. However, little research has examined this construct in the context of adolescent romantic relationships.

Longitudinal findings confirm links between the quality of adolescents' relationships and the quality of family relationships from birth forward (Collins & Van Dulmen 2006, Furman & Collins 2008). Qualities of friendships in middle and late adolescence are associated with concurrent qualities of romantic relationships (Collins & Van Dulmen 2006, Furman et al. 2002). The nature and processes of these developmentally significant relations among relationships is a promising area for further study.

Up to now, research findings have revealed more about the observable characteristics of adolescents' friendships and romantic relationships than about the meaning of deeper, less-discernible qualities such as intimacy. As interest in adolescent romantic relationships increases and diversifies, attention to these subjective features likely will do so as well.

Little is known about the likelihood or the determinants of either successful or unsuccessful adolescent romantic relationships. In particular, it is unclear how serious or long lasting these relationships ideally should be. Most appear to be relatively brief, lasting between 6–12 months, but variation around this norm is considerable (Connolly & McIsaac 2008). Depending on duration and the content and quality of the relationship, adolescent romantic involvement has been found to be associated with both social competence and risk (Furman et al. 2008). A series of very short-term relationships is associated with greater depressive symptomatology (Joyner & Udry 2000) and increased rates of problem behavior in the partners (Zimmer-Gembeck et al. 2001). A particularly persistent finding is that teenage relationships that result in early marriage have generally been associated with high risk for marital dissatisfaction and divorce (Karney & Bradbury 1995). At the same time, recent findings show that adolescent relationships of moderate length (e.g., several weeks to several months) appear to be effective preparation for high-quality romantic relationships in early adulthood (Madsen & Collins 2005). Variability in the timing, duration, and quality clearly are significant determinants of the psychological and social impact of teenage relationships and thus warrant additional emphasis in the next phase of research in the area.

Cognitive and Emotional Processes

Concepts of relationships and perceptions of their social functions change with increasing age. In a longitudinal analysis of relationship narratives (Waldinger et al. 2002), the structure and complexity of narratives increased between middle adolescence and age 25, whereas narra-

tive themes were surprisingly similar across the 8- to 10-year gap between waves of the study. A desire for closeness and distance were a dominant theme in the relationships of participants at both ages. In longitudinal research, adolescents increasingly report that their first recognizable feelings of love occurred at a later age than they had reported at earlier time points. This pattern likely reflects changes in personal definitions of love, perhaps resulting from increasing cognitive and emotional maturity and wider experience in relationships (Montgomery & Sorell 1998, Shulman & Scharf 2000).

Heterosexual adolescents report that association with other-gender peers is the most common source of their positive affect (Wilson-Shockley 1985 as cited in Larson et al. 1999; Larson & Richards 1998). Moreover, having a romantic relationship and the quality of that relationship commonly are associated positively with feelings of self-worth (Connolly & Konarski 1994, Harter 1999). By late adolescence, self-perceived competence in romantic relationships emerges as a reliable component of general competence (Masten et al. 1995). At the same time, adolescents in romantic relationships report experiencing more conflict than other adolescents report (Laursen 1995), and mood swings—a stereotype of adolescent emotional life—are more extreme for those involved in romantic relationships (Larson et al. 1999, Savin-Williams 1996). In a widely cited finding, adolescents who had begun romantic relationships in the past year manifested more symptoms of depression than did adolescents not in romantic relationships (Joyner & Udry 2000). Indeed, the most common trigger of the first episode of a major depressive disorder is a romantic break-up (Monroe et al. 1999). Subsequent studies have identified important moderators of this association (e.g., Ayduk et al. 2001, Davila et al. 2004, Grello et al. 2003, Harper & Welsh 2007). For example, break-ups, rather than involvement in romantic relationships per se, may explain the frequent reports of elevated depressive symptoms.

Individual differences in cognitive and emotional processes also play a key role in romantic

Rejection sensitivity:
an individual's
tendency to anxiously
expect, perceive, and
overreact to rejection

relationships. A striking case is the phenomenon of rejection sensitivity, which refers to individuals' tendency to anxiously expect, perceive, and overreact to rejection (Downey et al. 1999). This cognitive and behavioral syndrome is hypothesized to arise from experiences of rejection in parent-child relationships and also in relations with peers and, possibly, romantic partners (Downey et al. 1999). Compared to adolescents with low scores on a standardized measure of rejection sensitivity, those with high scores characteristically expect romantic partners to reject them and, indeed, do experience disproportionately frequent rejection. Furthermore, the high-rejection-sensitive individuals report less satisfaction in their relationships and more depressive symptoms (Ayduk et al. 2001, Downey et al. 1999).

Concluding Comment

Although some adolescents at every age experience beginnings and endings of romantic relationships (Connolly & McIsaac 2008), relative contrasts can be seen in the features of relationships in early, middle, and late adolescence. Involvement in dating increases notably between the ages of 12 and 18, and ending a romantic relationship becomes less likely during the same period (Connolly & McIsaac 2008). Early and later adolescents' criteria for partner selections differ, as does the content of exchanges between partners. Perceptions of partner supportiveness, interdependence, and closeness increase with age (Laursen & Williams 1997, Zimmer-Gembeck 1999). Collins (2003) has suggested that a shift occurs between ages 15 and 17 in the features and implications of romantic relationships. This apparent mid-adolescent shift undoubtedly represents an accumulation of gradual changes that appear abrupt because most studies are cross-sectional comparisons of age groups. As evidence of age-related patterns in key aspects of romantic relationships accumulates, however, pressures are increasing for developmental accounts that explain the find-

ings. The eventual explanation almost certainly will implicate cognitive and emotional maturation, achievements regarding identity and autonomy, increasing diversification of social networks, and contextual changes associated with impending adulthood.

INTERPERSONAL CONTEXTS

Romantic relationships occur in multiple contexts, representing varied levels of analysis, and these contexts may shape and constrain the features of relationships, from the timing and forms of involvement to partner choice and permissible activities (Seiffge-Krenke 2006). Evidence of cultural and subcultural variations is cited above. This section is devoted to the most extensively studied contextual influences on adolescent romantic relationships, each partner's current and past experiences with parents and peers (Collins & Van Dulmen 2006, Connolly & McIsaac 2008).

Peer Affiliations and Friendships

The assumption that the peer social system is the staging ground for romantic relationships during adolescence pervades research on the topic. Having a large number of other-gender friends and being liked by many of one's peers in adolescence is correlated with current and future dating patterns (Connolly et al. 2000, Kuttler & LaGreca 2004). General social competence with peers is associated with romantic relationship activity in early and middle adolescence (Furman et al. 2008). Moreover, for early adolescents, having a boyfriend or girlfriend confers social status and facilitates "fitting in." For example, both Latina and female African American early adolescents described wanting to have a boyfriend in order to demonstrate their popularity among their peers. Boyfriends who were attractive, popular, somewhat older than them, or who brought them gifts were especially desired (O'Sullivan & Meyer-Bahlburg 2003).

The potential role of friendship in the development of romantic relationships is both fundamental and multifaceted. Relationships with friends function both as prototypes of interactions compatible with romantic relationships and as testing grounds for experiencing and managing emotions in the context of voluntary close relationships (Connolly et al. 2004). Friends also serve as models and sources of social support for initiating and pursuing romantic relationships and also for weathering periods of difficulty in them, thus potentially contributing to variations in the qualities of later romantic relationships (Connolly & Goldberg 1999). Cognitive representations of friendships and the perceived qualities of interactions within them are associated significantly with interactions in romantic relationships (Furman & Shomaker 2008, Furman et al. 2002). Relatively little is known about the links between sexual minorities' friendships and romantic relationships. Number of friends appears to be unrelated to romantic relationship involvement, although those who have had more romantic relationships report more worries about losing friends (Diamond & Lucas 2004).

Contrary to common stereotypes of cross-purposes between parents and peers, the peer and family domains are often similar, and family and peer influences commonly act in concert with one another with respect to romantic relationships. For example, a stable, harmonious family life reduces the risk of affiliation with deviant peers, and the two jointly reduce the risk of choosing deviant romantic partners (Donnellan et al. 2005, Zimmer-Gembeck et al. 2001). Family and peer influences also may moderate each other. Parental support is associated with a reduction in criminality for those without a romantic partner, but the support of a partner is the more important factor for those with a romantic partner (Van Dulmen et al. 2008).

Relationships with Parents

Nurturant-involved parenting in adolescence is predictive of warmth, support, and low hostility toward romantic partners in early adulthood. Moreover, the degree of flexible control,

cohesion, and respect for privacy experienced in families is related positively to intimacy in late-adolescent romantic relationships, with especially strong links emerging for women. Parent-adolescent conflict resolution is also associated with later conflict resolution with romantic partners (Conger et al. 2000, Cui & Conger 2008, Donnellan et al. 2005, Feldman et al. 1998). In contrast, unskilled parenting and aversive family communications are associated with later aggression toward romantic partners, and the degree of negative emotionality in parent-adolescent dyads is correlated with negative emotionality and poor quality interactions with romantic partners in early adulthood (Conger et al. 2000, K. Kim et al. 2001). This association appears to be mediated by negative affect and ineffective monitoring and discipline in parent-adolescent relationships (Conger et al. 2000).

Interactions with parents in earlier periods of development also have been implicated in the stability and quality of early-adult romantic relationships (Simpson et al. 2007). Parent-child relationships appear to account for more variance in romantic-relationship behavior than either sibling relationships or the models provided by parents' own marriages. Contrary to common speculation, the majority of findings from studies that include assessment of sibling relationships have revealed no significant associations with the features of interactions with romantic partners (Conger et al. 2000). Similarly, parental conflict and marital disharmony appear to affect the romantic relationships of offspring indirectly, through the deleterious effects of marital stressors on nurturant, involved parenting (Conger et al. 2000, Cui & Conger 2008). One avenue through which marital stress and parental separation affect adolescents' romantic lives is through increased risk for early romantic involvement, which in turn is associated with poor individual adjustment (Furman & Collins 2008).

Not surprisingly, the characteristics of relationships with parents and with peers become more extensively interrelated with features of

Nurturant-involved parenting: parent behavior marked by warmth, active interest in and acceptance of the adolescent, and encouragement of positive behaviors

romantic relationships during late adolescence and early adulthood (Meeus et al. 2007). Perhaps the growing importance of romantic relationships calls attention to the commonalities across types of relationships. It is equally likely, however, that the correlations among early adults' relationships reflect their common associations with parents and with peers prior to adolescence (Collins & Van Dulmen 2006, Waters & Cummings 2000). The processes that account for these developmentally significant relations among differing relationships are a promising area for further study.

SIGNIFICANCE OF ADOLESCENT ROMANTIC RELATIONSHIPS

The developmental significance of romantic relationships depends on the behavioral, cognitive, and emotional processes occurring within the relationship, on the individual characteristics of the adolescents (age, attachment styles, rejection sensitivity, self-silencing, gender), and on the contexts in which they occur (Furman & Collins 2008, Furman & Shaffer 2003). Accumulating findings document statistically reliable associations between adolescents' romantic experiences and multiple aspects of individual development: forming a personal identity, adjusting to changes in familial relationships, furthering harmonious relations with peers, succeeding (or not) in school, looking ahead to future careers, and developing sexuality (regardless of the extent of sexual activity) (Furman & Collins 2008, Furman & Shaffer 2003). The nature and quality of romantic experiences are correlated with self-esteem, self-confidence, and social competence (Pearce et al. 2002; Zimmer-Gembeck et al. 2001, 2004). Conversely, anxiety over preserving a relationship often results in self-silencing, in which individuals suppress their thoughts and opinions out of fear of losing their intimate partner and relationship. Self-silencing in turn is associated with poorer communication between partners, higher levels of depressive symptoms, and greater rejection sensitivity

(Harper et al. 2006, Harper & Welsh 2007). Poor-quality romantic relationships are further associated with alcohol and drug use, poor academic performance, externalizing and internalizing symptoms, poor emotional health, and low job competence (Zimmer-Gembeck et al. 2001, 2004).

Contrary to widespread skepticism, romantic experiences also appear to be positively related to qualities of romantic relationships in later life. Longitudinal research in Germany showed that quality of romantic relationships in middle adolescence was significantly and positively related to commitment in other relationships in early adulthood (Seiffge-Krenke & Lang 2002). Apparently, romantic relationships can be associated with healthy, normative development in some adolescents and can be symptomatic of pathology in others (Welsh et al. 2003). Better understanding is needed of the factors that differentiate adolescents whose romantic relationships are evidence of normal, developmental processes and those whose romantic relationships are symptomatic of or may cause psychological turmoil (Florsheim 2003).

These cross-sectional correlations plausibly could reflect either the effects of romantic experience on adjustment or the converse. For example, "off-time" dating or romantic experience beginning in late childhood and early adolescence is associated with subsequent misconduct and poor academic performance, which in turn are risk factors for further negative romantic relationships (Furman et al. 2008, Zimmer-Gembeck et al. 2001). Similarly, romantic involvement has repeatedly been linked to depressive symptoms, especially for adolescents engaging in casual sex or with a history of unresponsive familial relationships, and these conditions further increase the risk of negative romantic experiences (e.g., Ayduk et al. 2001, Davila et al. 2004, Grello et al. 2003, Harper & Welsh 2007). Inferences of causality aside, current findings provide an impetus for testing numerous hypotheses about the nature and extent of links between features of romantic relationships and individual functioning.

ISSUES AND FUTURE DIRECTIONS

Two recurring themes in this review are that romantic relationships during adolescence are more multifaceted than is often assumed and that their significance for development is multidimensional rather than unidimensional. It is not surprising, therefore, that researchers have had to move quickly to advance beyond the largely descriptive correlational work of the late-twentieth century to the more nuanced research designs that now typify research in the area. Contemporary research on adolescent romantic relationships potentially broadens understanding of the significance of close relationships in the development of individual well being and social competence.

Many questions remain. Research on the interpersonal processes associated with adolescent romantic relationships is still at an early stage. For example, partner characteristics play a still-unspecified role in the significance of adolescent romantic relationships. Adolescents' reports of the quality of their relationships with different partners are moderately consistent (Connolly et al. 2000), but it is unclear how much carryover occurs from one adolescent romantic relationship to the next or how much having a new partner may lead to a different experience. Among the topics that could profitably be considered are the processes associated with continuity and discontinuity of aggression across diverse relationships, including between adolescent partners (Capaldi et al. 2003). In addition, although research findings consistently document the importance of peer relationship quality to romantic relationships, relatively little is known about the similarities and differences in the characteristics of same- and cross-gender friendships and heterosexual romantic relationships (Hand & Furman 2008). Even less is known about the functional relations between friendships and romantic relationships in sexual-minority adolescents. In general, researchers must integrate behavioral and neurobiological processes into research on adolescent romantic relationships (Bartels & Zeki 2004, Diamond & Lucas 2004).

More extensive and systematic research is needed on the processes and effects of contextual influences on romantic relationships during adolescence, as well, to supplement the existing fragmentary evidence of influences from cultural and community factors. Particularly needed are cross-ethnic and cross-national comparisons regarding the incidence of such relationships, as well as their correlates and the associated processes. Such comparisons, for example, should examine the implications of timing and interpersonal networks on romantic experiences generally and romantic relationships in particular. Similarly, comparative studies of the content of adolescent romantic relationships could be suggestive of explanatory mechanisms for variations across contexts. Collaborations among international teams of researchers could provide especially rich and valuable information (Connolly & McIsaac 2008, Seiffge-Krenke 2006).

The short history of concerted research activity in this area has yielded path-breaking findings and a flexible, broadly applicable conceptual framework and expanded array of research methods and measurement protocols. In the next phase of research, those resources should be used to assemble evidence that more fully represents the range of romantic experiences common to the age period. Addressing these issues will provide us a more complete picture of romantic experiences and their significance for human development.

SUMMARY POINTS

1. Having a mutual romantic interest in or actively dating someone is common in adolescence and of longer duration than is usually assumed. Participation increases steadily throughout adolescence.

2. Since 1999, research on adolescent romantic relationships has shifted from a descriptive focus to an interest in the content and qualities of these relationships and their correlates and potential sequelae for individuals.

3. Interpersonal theories are most evident in previous research. Perspectives from biosocial and ecological theorists have played a role as well. Methodological challenges include establishing workable operational definitions, obtaining representative samples, capturing relationships that are often unstable or of short duration, and applying statistical methods appropriate for nonindependent data sources.

4. The significance to individuals of participating in a romantic relationship during adolescence appears to depend on the timing and duration of the relationship, characteristics of (the) partner(s), content of interactions between partners, quality of interactions, and cognitive and emotional processes associated with the relationship(s).

5. Between ages 15 and 17, notable changes commonly occur in whether one experiences a romantic relationship, the likely duration of the relationship, implicit criteria for selecting a partner, the content of exchanges between partners, and the degree to which of the affected individuals attend to perceptions of closeness, supportiveness, and interdependence between partners.

FUTURE ISSUES

1. Correlations between involvement in adolescent romantic relationships and adolescents' psychosocial maturation, social acceptance, and skills for engaging in relationships have been documented repeatedly, but explanations for these associations are largely speculative. The role of age-graded community and societal norms, in relation to biological maturation, are especially poorly understood. Large-sample longitudinal studies, designed to address developmental change processes, are needed.

2. Families and peers both appear to play a significant role in most if not all constituent processes of adolescent romance. However, the effects vary across features of relationships and between families and peers, depending on the features(s) of interest. Some effects are additive; and some are compensatory. Little is known about how these influences operate, separately and jointly, in romantic relationship processes.

3. Although adolescents report moderately consistent relationship quality with different partners, it is unclear how much carryover occurs from one adolescent romantic relationship to the next.

4. Little reliable evidence is available regarding common assumptions of consistency in aggression across adolescent romantic relationships and between romantic and nonromantic partners.

5. The nature and extent of similarities and differences between the romantic relationships of sexual-minority adolescents and those of heterosexual adolescents have generally been neglected, as have comparisons of cross-ethnic and cross-national samples.

DISCLOSURE STATEMENT

The authors are not aware of any biases that might be perceived as affecting the objectivity of this review.

LITERATURE CITED

Adams GR, Berzonsky M. 2003. *The Blackwell Handbook of Adolescence*. Oxford, UK: Blackwell Sci.

Allen JP, Land D. 1999. Attachment in adolescence. In *Handbook of Attachment: Theory, Research, and Clinical Applications*, ed. J Cassidy, PR Shaver, pp. 319–35. New York: Guilford

Archer J. 2000. Sex differences in aggression between heterosexual partners: a meta-analytic review. *Psychol. Bull.* 126:651–80

Arriaga XB, Foshee VA. 2004. Adolescent dating violence: Do adolescents follow in their friends' or their parents' footsteps? *J. Interpers. Violence* 19:162–84

Austin SB, Roberts AL, Corliss HL, Molnar BE. 2007. Sexual violence victimization history and sexual risk indicators in a community-based urban cohort of "mostly heterosexual" and heterosexual young women. *Am. J. Publ. Health* 98:1015–20

Ayduk O, Downey G, Kim M. 2001. Rejection sensitivity and depressive symptoms in women. *Personal. Soc. Psychol. Bull.* 27:868–77

Bartels A, Zeki S. 2004. The neural basis of romantic love. *NeuroReport* 2:12–15

Bearman PS, Jones J, Udry JR. 1997. The National Longitudinal Study of Adolescent Health: research design. Available at **http://www.cpc.unc.edu/addhlth**

Bolger N, Davis A, Raffaelli E. 2003. Diary methods: capturing life as it is lived. *Annu. Rev. Psychol.* 54:579–616

Bouchey HA, Furman W. 2003. Dating and romantic experiences in adolescence. See Adams & Berzonsky 2003, pp. 313–39

Brown BB, Feiring C, Furman W. 1999. Missing the love boat: why researchers have shied away from adolescent romance. See Furman et al. 1999, pp. 1–16

Brown J, Steele J, Walsh-Childers K. 2002. *Sexual Teens, Sexual Media: Investigating Media's Influences on Adolescent Sexuality*. Mahwah, NJ: Erlbaum

Buss D, ed. 2005. *The Handbook of Evolutionary Psychology*. Hoboken, NJ: Wiley

Buzy WM, McDonald R, Jouriles EN, Swank P, Rosenfield D, et al. 2004. Adolescent girls' alcohol use as a risk factor for relationship violence. *J. Res. Adolesc.* 14:449–70

Capaldi DM, Crosby L. 1997. Observed and reported psychological and physical aggression in young, at-risk couples. *Soc. Dev.* 6:184–206

Capaldi DM, Dishion TJ, Stoolmiller M, Yoerger K. 2001. Aggression toward female partners by at-risk young men. *Dev. Psychol.* 37:61–73

Capaldi DM, Kim HK, Short JW. 2007. Observed initiation and reciprocity of physical aggression in young, at-risk couples. *J. Fam. Violence* 22:101–11

Capaldi DM, Short J, Crosby L. 2003. Physical and psychological aggression in at-risk young couples: stability and change in young adulthood. *Merrill-Palmer Q.* 49:1–27

Carver K, Joyner K, Udry JR. 2003. National estimates of adolescent romantic relationships. In *Adolescent Romantic Relationships and Sexual Behavior: Theory, Research, and Practical Implications*, ed. P Florsheim, pp. 291–329. New York: Cambridge Univ. Press

Coates DL. 1999. The cultured and culturing aspects of romantic experience in adolescence. See Furman et al. 1999, pp. 330–63

Collins WA. 2003. More than myth: the developmental significance of romantic relationships during adolescence. *J. Res. Adolesc.* 13:1–25

Collins WA, Sroufe LA. 1999. Capacity for intimate relationships: a developmental construction. In *Contemporary Perspectives on Adolescent Romantic Relationships*, ed. W Furman, C Feiring, BB Brown, pp. 123–47. New York: Cambridge Univ. Press

Collins WA, Steinberg L. 2006. Adolescent development in interpersonal context. In *The Handbook of Child Psychology: Vol. 3. Social, Emotional and Personality Development*, ed. W Damon, R Lerner, N Eisenberg, pp. 1003–67. New York: Wiley. 6th ed.

Landmark consideration of the implications of attachment theory for developmental and individual differences in romantic as well as nonromantic adolescent relationships.

Outlines a framework for systematic research on the nature and developmental significance of adolescent romantic relationships.

Collins WA, Van Dulmen M. 2006. "The course of true love(s). . .": origins and pathways in the development of romantic relationships. In *Romance and Sex in Adolescence and Emerging Adulthood: Risks and Opportunities*, ed. A Booth, A Crouter, pp. 63–86. Mahwah, NJ: Erlbaum

Conger RD, Cui M, Bryant CM, Elder GH Jr. 2000. Competence in early adult romantic relationships: a developmental perspective on family influences. *J. Personal. Soc. Psychol.* 79:224–37

Connolly JA, Craig W, Goldberg A, Pepler D. 2004. Mixed-gender groups, dating, and romantic relationships in early adolescence. *J. Res. Adolesc.* 14:185–207

Connolly JA, Furman W, Konarski R. 2000. The role of peers in the emergence of heterosexual romantic relationships in adolescence. *Child Dev.* 71:1395–408

Connolly JA, Goldberg A. 1999. Romantic relationships in adolescence: the role of friends and peers in their emergence and development. See Furman et al. 1999, pp. 266–90

Connolly JA, Konarski R. 1994. Peer self-concept in adolescence: analysis of factor structure and of associations with peer experience. *J. Res. Adolesc.* 4:385–403

Connolly JA, McIsaac C. 2008. Adolescent romantic relationships: beginnings, endings, and psychosocial challenges. *Newsl. Int. Soc. Stud. Behav. Dev.* 32:1–5

Crockett L, Raffaelli M, Moilanen KL. 2003. Adolescent sexuality: behavior and meaning. See Adams & Berzonsky 2003, pp. 371–92

Crouter A, Booth A, eds. 2006. *Romance and Sex in Adolescence and Emerging Adulthood: Risks and Opportunities.* Mahwah, NJ: Erlbaum

Cui M, Conger RD. 2008. Parenting behavior as mediator and moderator of the association between marital problems and adolescent maladjustment. *J. Adolesc. Res.* 18:261–84

D'Augelli AR. 1998. Lesbian, gay, and bisexual youth and their families: disclosure of sexual orientation and its consequences. *Am. J. Orthopsychiatry* 68:361–71

Davila J, Steinberg S, Kachadourian L, Cobb R, Fincham F. 2004. Romantic involvement and depressive symptoms in early and late adolescence: the role of a preoccupied relational style. *Personal Relat.* 11:161–78

Diamond LM. 2003. Was it a phase? Young women's relinquishment of lesbian/bisexual identities over a 5-year period. *J. Personal. Soc. Psychol.* 84:352–64

Diamond LM, Lucas S. 2004. Sexual-minority and heterosexual youths' peer relationships: experiences, expectations, and implications for well-being. *J. Res. Adolesc.* 14:313–40

Diamond LM, Savin-Williams RC. 2003. The intimate relationships of sexual-minority youths. See Adams & Berzonsky 2003, pp. 393–12

Diamond LM, Savin-Williams RC, Dubé EM. 1999. Sex, dating, passionate friendships, and romance: intimate peer relations among lesbian, gay, and bisexual adolescents. See Furman et al. 1999, pp. 175–210

Donnellan M, Larsen-Rife D, Conger R. 2005. Personality, family history, and competence in early adult romantic relationships. *J. Personal. Soc. Psychol.* 88:562–76

Dornbusch S, Carlsmith JM, Gross R, Martin J, Jennings D, et al. 1981. Sexual development, age, and dating: a comparison of biological and social influences upon one set of behaviors. *Child Dev.* 52:179–85

Downey G, Bonica C, Rincón C. 1999. Rejection sensitivity and adolescent romantic relationships. See Furman et al. 1999, pp. 148–74

Downey G, Freitas AL, Michaelis B, Khouri H. 1998. The self-fulfilling prophecy in close relationships: rejection sensitivity and rejection by romantic partners. *J. Personal. Soc. Psychol.* 75:545–60

Ellis B. 2004. Timing of pubertal maturation in girls: an integrated life history approach. *Psychol. Bull.* 130:920–58

Feldman SS, Gowen LK, Fischer L. 1998. Family relationships and gender as predictors of romantic intimacy in young adults: a longitudinal study. *J. Res. Adolesc.* 8:263–86

Feldman SS, Turner R, Araujo K. 1999. The influence of the relationship context on normative and personal sexual timetables in youths. *J. Res. Adolesc.* 9:25–52

Florsheim P. 2003. *Adolescent Romantic Relations and Sexual Behavior: Theory, Research, and Practical Implications.* Mahwah, NJ: Erlbaum

Floyd FJ, Stein TS. 2002. Sexual orientation identity formation among gay, lesbian, and bisexual youths: multiple patterns of milestone. *J. Res. Adolesc.* 12:167–91

Supplies a rationale for differentiating among the relationships of sexual-minority youth and recognizing the similarities and differences (cf., heterosexual youth).

Extends the concept of rejection sensitivity to adolescents in romantic relationships.

Furman W, Brown BB, Feiring C, eds. 1999. *The Development of Romantic Relationships in Adolescence.* New York: Cambridge Univ. Press

Furman W, Collins WA. 2008. Adolescent romantic relationships and experiences. In *Handbook of Peer Interactions, Relationships, and Groups*, ed. KH Rubin, W Bukowski, B Laursen. New York: Guilford. In press

Furman W, Hand LS. 2006. The slippery nature of romantic relationships: issues in definition and differentiation. In *Romance and Sex in Adolescence and Emerging Adulthood: Risks and Opportunities*, ed. A Crouter, A Booth, pp. 171–78. Mahwah, NJ: Erlbaum

Furman W, Ho MH, Low SM. 2008. The rocky road of adolescent romantic experience: dating and adjustment. In *Friends, Lovers, and Groups: Key Relationships in Adolescence*, ed. RCME Engels, M Kerr, H Stattin, pp. 61–80. New York: Wiley

Furman W, Shaffer L. 2003. The role of romantic relationships in adolescent development. In *Adolescent Romantic Relations and Sexual Behavior: Theory, Research, and Practical Implications*, ed. P Florsheim, pp. 3–22. Mahwah, NJ: Erlbaum

Furman W, Shomaker L. 2008. Patterns of interaction in adolescent romantic relationships: distinct features and associations with other close relationships. *J. Adolesc.* In press

Furman W, Simon VA. 2006. Actor and partner effects of adolescents' working models and styles on interactions with romantic partners. *Child Dev.* 77:588–604

Furman W, Simon VA. 2008. Homophily and influence in adolescent romantic relationships. In *Understanding Peer Influence in Children and Adolescents*, ed. M Prinstein, KA Dodge, pp. 203–24. New York: Guilford

Furman W, Simon VA, Shaffer L, Bouchey HA. 2002. Adolescents' working models and styles for relationships with parents, friends, and romantic partners. *Child Dev.* 73:241–55

Furman W, Wehner EA. 1997. Adolescent romantic relationships: a developmental perspective. In *Romantic Relationships in Adolescence: Developmental Perspectives*, ed. S Shulman WA Collins, pp. 21–36. San Francisco, CA: Jossey-Bass

Galliher RV, Welsh DP, Rostosky SS, Kawaguchi MC. 2004. Interaction and relationship quality in late adolescent romantic couples. *J. Soc. Personal. Relat.* 21:203–16

Giordano P, Longmore MA, Manning WD. 2006. Gender and the meanings of adolescent romantic relationships: a focus on boys. *Am. Sociol. Rev.* 71:360–87

Giordano P, Manning W, Longmore M. 2005. The romantic relationships of African-American and white adolescents. *Sociol. Q.* 46:545–68

Grello CM, Welsh DP, Harper MS. 2006. No strings attached: the nature of casual sex in college students. *J. Sex Res.* 43:255–67

Grello CM, Welsh DP, Harper MS, Dickson J. 2003. Dating and sexual relationship trajectories and adolescent functioning. *Adolesc. Fam. Health* 3:103–12

Halpern CT. 2003. Biological influences on adolescent romance and sexual behavior. In *Adolescent Romantic Relations and Sexual Behavior: Theory, Research, and Practical Implications*, ed. P Florsheim, pp. 57–84. Mahwah, NJ: Erlbaum

Halpern CT, Oslak SG, Young ML, Martin SL, Kupper LL. 2001. Partner violence among adolescents in opposite-sex romantic relationships: findings from the National Longitudinal Study of Adolescent Health. *Am. J. Publ. Health* 91:1679–85

Halpern CT, Young ML, Waller MW, Martin, SL, Kupper LL. 2004. Prevalence of partner violence in same-sex romantic and sexual relationships in a national sample of adolescents. *J. Adolesc. Health* 35:124–31

Hand LS, Furman W. 2008. Rewards and costs in adolescent other-sex friendships: comparisons to same-sex friendships and romantic relationships. *Soc. Dev.* In press

Harper MS, Dickson JW, Welsh DP. 2006. Self-silencing and rejection sensitivity in adolescent romantic relationships. *J. Youth Adolesc.* 35:459–67

Harper MS, Welsh DP. 2007. Keeping quiet: self-silencing and its association with relational and individual functioning among adolescent romantic couples. *J. Soc. Personal. Relat.* 24:99–116

Harter S. 1999. *The Construction of the Self.* New York: Guilford

Hinde RA. 1997. *Relationships: A Dialectical Perspective.* Sussex, UK: Psychol. Press

Jouriles EN, McDonald R, Garrido E, Roselfield D, Brown AS. 2005. Assessing aggression in adolescent romantic relationships: Can we do it better? *Psychol. Assess.* 17:469–75

Provides an influential compendium of conceptual and empirical foundations for recent growth of research in the area.

Provides a conceptual rationale for a developmental approach to the psychological significance of romantic relationships during adolescence.

Systematically analyzes the relation of biological maturation in adolescence to romantic interests and behavior and sexual behavior.

Relates research finding of a correlation between participation in romantic relationships and depression in adolescent females.

Joyner K, Udry JR. 2000. You don't bring me anything but down: adolescent romance and depression. *J. Health Soc. Behav.* 41:369–91

Karney B, Bradbury T. 1995. The longitudinal course of marital quality and stability: a review of theory, methods, and research. *Psychol. Bull.* 118:3–34

Kelley HH, Berscheid E, Christensen A, Harvey JH, Huston TL, et al. 2002/1983. *Close Relationships.* Clinton Corners, NY: Percheron

Kenny DA, Kashy DA, Cook WL. 2006. *Dyadic Data Analysis.* New York: Guilford

Kim K, Conger RD, Lorenz FO, Elder GH Jr. 2001. Parent-adolescent reciprocity in negative affect and its relation to early adult social development. *Dev. Psychol.* 37:775–90

Kinsfogel KM, Grych JH. 2004. Interparental conflict and adolescent dating relationships: integrating cognitive, emotional, and peer influences. *J. Fam. Psychol.* 8:505–15

Kovacs DM, Parker JG, Hoffman LW. 1996. Behavioral, affective, and social correlates of involvement in cross-sex friendship in elementary school. *Child Dev.* 67:2269–86

Kuttler A, LaGreca A. 2004. Linkages among adolescent girls' romantic relationships, best friendships, and peer networks. *J. Adolesc.* 27:395–414

Larson RW, Clore GL, Wood GA. 1999. The emotions of romantic relationships: Do they wreck havoc on adolescents? See Furman et al. 1999, pp. 19–49

Larson RW, Richards M. 1998. Waiting for the weekend: Friday and Saturday night as the emotional climax of the week. In *Temporal Rhythms in Adolescence: Clocks, Calendars, and the Coordination of Daily Life*, ed. A Crouter, R Larson, pp. 37–51. San Francisco, CA: Jossey-Bass

Larson RW, Wilson S. 2004. Adolescence across place and time: globalization and the changing pathways to adulthood. In *Handbook of Adolescent Psychology*, ed. R Lerner L Steinberg, pp. 299–30. New York: Wiley. 2nd ed.

Laursen B. 1995. Conflict and social interaction in adolescent relationships. *J. Res. Adolesc.* 5:55–70

Laursen B, Bukowski WM. 1997. A developmental guide to the organization of close relationships. *Int. J. Behav. Dev.* 21:747–70

Laursen B, Jensen-Campbell LA. 1999. The nature and functions of social exchange in adolescent romantic relationships. See Furman et al. 1999, pp. 50–74

Laursen B, Williams VA. 1997. Perceptions of interdependence and closeness in family and peer relationships among adolescents with and without romantic partners. In *Romantic Relationships in Adolescence: Developmental Perspectives*, ed. S Shulman, WA Collins, pp. 3–20. San Francisco, CA: Jossey-Bass

Lenhart A, Madden M, Hitlin P. 2005. *Teens and Technology: Youth are Leading the Transition to a Fully Wired and Mobile Nation.* Washington, DC: Pew Internet Am. Life Proj.

Madsen S, Collins WA. 2005. Differential predictions of young adult romantic relationships from transitory vs. longer romantic experiences during adolescence. Presented at *Bienn. Meet. Soc. Res. Child Dev.*, Atlanta, GA

Magnusson D, Stattin H. 1998. Person-context interaction theories. In *Handbook of Child Psychology. Volume 1: Theoretical Models of Human Development*, ed. W Damon, RM Lerner, pp. 685–759. New York: Wiley

Manning WD, Giordano PC, Longmore MA. 2006. Hooking up: the relationship contexts of "nonrelationship" sex. *J. Adolesc. Res.* 21:459–83

Manning WD, Longmore MA, Giordano PC. 2000. The relationship context of contraceptive use at first intercourse. *Fam. Plann. Perspec.* 32:104–10

Masten AS, Coatsworth JD, Neemann JL, Gest SD, Tellegen A, et al. 1995. The structure and coherence of competence from childhood through adolescence. *Child Dev.* 66:1635–59

McClintock MK, Herdt G. 1996. Rethinking puberty: the development of sexual attraction. *Curr. Dir. Psychol. Sci.* 5:178–83

Meeus W, Branje S, Van Der Valk I, de Wied M. 2007. Relationships with intimate partner, best friends, and parents in adolescence and early adulthood: a study of the saliency of the intimate partnership. *Int. J. Behav. Dev.* 31:449–60

Monroe SM, Rohde P, Seeley JR, Lewinsohn PM. 1999. Life events and depression in adolescence: relationship loss as a prospective risk factor for first onset of major depressive disorder. *J. Abnorm. Psychol.* 108:606–14

Montgomery MJ, Sorell GT. 1998. Love and dating experience in early and middle adolescence: grade and gender comparisons. *J. Adolesc.* 21:677–89

O'Sullivan LF, Meyer-Bahlburg HFL. 2003. African-American and Latina inner-city girls' reports of romantic and sexual development. *J. Soc. Personal. Relat.* 20:221–38

Pearce MJ, Boergers J, Prinstein MJ. 2002. Adolescent obesity, overt and relational peer victimization, and romantic relationships. *Obesity Res.* 10:386–93

Pepler DJ, Craig WM, Connolly JA, Yuile A, McMaster L, Jiang D. 2006. A developmental perspective on bullying. *Aggressive Behav.* 32:376–84

Regan JA. 2003. Ideal partner preferences among adolescents. *Soc. Behav. Personal.* 31:13–20

Reis HT, Collins WA, Berscheid E. 2000. Relationships in human behavior and development. *Psychol. Bull.* 126:844–72

Reis HT, Lin Y, Bennett ME, Nezlek JB. 1993. Change and consistency in social participation during early adulthood. *Dev. Psychol.* 29:633–45

Richards MH, Crowe PA, Larson R, Swarr A. 1998. Developmental patterns and gender differences in the experience of peer companionship during adolescence. *Child Dev.* 69:154–63

Roscoe B, Diana MS, Brooks RH. 1987. Early, middle, and late adolescents' views on dating and factors influencing partner selection. *Adolescence* 22:59–68

Rostosky SS, Wilcox BL, Wright MLC, Randall BA. 2004. The impact of religiosity on adolescent sexual behavior: a review of the evidence. *J. Adolesc. Res.* 19:677–97

Russell ST, Franz BT, Driscoll AK. 2001. Same-sex romantic attraction and experiences of violence in adolescence. *Am. J. Publ. Health* 91:903–6

Savin-Williams RC. 1996. Dating and romantic relationships among gay, lesbian, and bisexual youths. In *The Lives of Lesbians, Gays, and Bisexuals: Children to Adults*, ed. RC Savin-Williams, KM Cohen, pp. 166–80. Fort Worth, TX: Harcourt Brace

Savin-Williams RC. 2006. Who's gay? Does it matter? *Curr. Dir. Psychol. Sci.* 15:40–44

Savin-Williams RC, Diamond LM. 2000. Sexual identity trajectories among sexual-minority youths: gender comparisons. *Arch. Sex. Behav.* 29:607–27

Seiffge-Krenke I. 2006. *Nach Pisa. Stress in der Schule und mit den Eltern. Bewältigungskompetenz deuscher Jugendlicher im internationalen Vergleich*. Göttingen: Vandenhoeck & Ruprecht

Seiffge-Krenke I, Lang J. 2002. Forming and maintaining romantic relations from early adolescence to young adulthood: evidence of a developmental sequence. Presented at Bienn. Meet. Soc. Res. Adolesc., 19th, New Orleans, LA

Shulman S, Scharf M. 2000. Adolescent romantic behaviors and perceptions: age- and gender-related differences, and links with family and peer relationships. *J. Res. Adolesc.* 10:91–118

Silbereisen RK, Schwarz B. 1998. Timing of first romantic involvement: commonalities and differences in the former Germanys. In *Adolescence, Cultures, and Conflicts: Growing up in Europe*, ed. J-E Nurmi, pp. 129–48. New York: Garland

Simon VA, Aikins JW, Prinstein MJ. 2008. Romantic partner selection and socialization during early adolescence. *Child Dev.* In press

Simpson JA, Collins WA, Tran S, Haydon KC. 2007. Attachment and the experience and expression of emotions in romantic relationships: a developmental perspective. *J. Personal. Soc. Psychol.* 72:355–67

Smetana JG, Campione-Barr N, Metzger A. 2006. Adolescent development in interpersonal contexts. *Annu. Rev. Psychol.* 57:255–84

Sroufe LA, Egeland B, Carlson EA, Collins WA. 2005. *The Development of the Person: The Minnesota Study of Risk and Adaptation from Birth to Adulthood*. New York: Guilford

Susman EJ. 2006. *Puberty revisited: models, mechanisms, and the future*. Presented at Bienn. Meet. Soc. Res. Adolesc., 21st, San Francisco, CA

Van Dulmen M, Goncy E, Haydon KC, Collins WA. 2008. Distinctiveness of adolescent and emerging adult romantic relationship features in predicting externalizing behavior problems. *J. Youth Adolesc.* 37:336–45

Waldinger RJ, Diguer L, Guastella F, Lefebvre R, Allen J, et al. 2002. The same old song? Stability and change in relationship schemas from adolescence to young adulthood. *J. Youth Adolesc.* 31:17–29

Waters E, Cummings EM. 2000. A secure base from which to explore close relationships. *Child Dev.* 71:164–72

Weisfeld G. 1999. *Evolutionary Principles of Human Adolescence*. New York: Basic Books

Welsh DP, Dickson JW. 2005. Video-recall procedures for examining observational data and subjective understanding in family psychology. *J. Fam. Psychol.* 19:62–71

Welsh DP, Grello CM, Harper MS. 2003. When love hurts: depression and adolescent romantic relationships. In *Adolescent Romantic Relations and Sexual Behavior: Theory, Research and Practical Implications*, ed. P Florsheim, pp. 185–211. Mahwah, NJ: Erlbaum

Welsh DP, Haugen PT, Widman L, Darling N, Grello CM. 2005. Kissing is good: a developmental investigation of sexuality in adolescent romantic couples. *Sexuality Res. Soc. Policy* 2:32–41

Welsh DP, Rostosky SS, Kawaguchi MC. 2000. A normative perspective of adolescent girls' developing sexuality. In *Sexuality, Society, and Feminism: Psychological Perspectives on Women*, ed. CB Travis, JS White, pp. 111–40. Washington, DC: APA

Widman L, Welsh DP, McNulty JK, Little KC. 2006. Sexual communication and contraceptive use in adolescent dating couples. *J. Adolesc. Health* 39:893–99

Williams T, Connolly J, Cribbie R. 2008. Light and heavy heterosexual activities of young Canadian adolescents: normative patterns and differential predictors. *J. Res. Adolesc.* 18:145–72

Zimmer-Gembeck MJ. 1999. Stability, change and individual differences in involvement with friends and romantic partners among adolescent females. *J. Youth Adolesc.* 28:419–38

Zimmer-Gembeck MJ, Siebenbruner J, Collins WA. 2001. Diverse aspects of dating: associations with psychosocial functioning from early to middle adolescence. *J. Adolesc.* 24:313–36

Zimmer-Gembeck MJ, Siebenbruner J, Collins WA. 2004. A prospective study of intraindividual and peer influences on adolescents' heterosexual romantic and sexual behavior. *Arch. Sex. Behav.* 33:381–94

Imitation, Empathy, and Mirror Neurons

Marco Iacoboni

Ahmanson-Lovelace Brain Mapping Center, Department of Psychiatry and Biobehavioral Sciences, Semel Institute for Neuroscience and Social Behavior, Brain Research Institute, David Geffen School of Medicine at UCLA, Los Angeles, California 90095; email: iacoboni@loni.ucla.edu

Annu. Rev. Psychol. 2009. 60:653–70

First published online as a Review in Advance on September 15, 2008

The *Annual Review of Psychology* is online at psych.annualreviews.org

This article's doi: 10.1146/annurev.psych.60.110707.163604

0066-4308/09/0110-0653$20.00

Key Words

social cognition, theory of mind, mirror neuron system, embodiment

Abstract

There is a convergence between cognitive models of imitation, constructs derived from social psychology studies on mimicry and empathy, and recent empirical findings from the neurosciences. The ideomotor framework of human actions assumes a common representational format for action and perception that facilitates imitation. Furthermore, the associative sequence learning model of imitation proposes that experience-based Hebbian learning forms links between sensory processing of the actions of others and motor plans. Social psychology studies have demonstrated that imitation and mimicry are pervasive, automatic, and facilitate empathy. Neuroscience investigations have demonstrated physiological mechanisms of mirroring at single-cell and neural-system levels that support the cognitive and social psychology constructs. Why were these neural mechanisms selected, and what is their adaptive advantage? Neural mirroring solves the "problem of other minds" (how we can access and understand the minds of others) and makes intersubjectivity possible, thus facilitating social behavior.

Contents

INTRODUCTION

Although mimicry is a pervasive phenomenon in the animal kingdom, imitation certainly achieves its highest form in humans. Past authors—for instance, de Montaigne (1575), Adam Smith (1759), Poe (1982), Nietzsche (1881), and Wittgenstein (1980)—have often associated imitation with the ability to empathize and understand other minds. The evolutionary, functional, and neural mechanisms linking imitation to empathy, however, have been unclear for many years. Recently, there has been a convergence between cognitive models of imitation, social psychology accounts of its pervasiveness and its functional links with empathy and liking, and the neuroscience discoveries of neural mechanisms of imitation and empathy. This convergence creates a solid framework in which theory and empirical data reinforce each other.

Hebbian learning: associative learning is implemented by simultaneous activation of cells that would lead to increased synaptic strength between the cells

Among cognitive models of imitation, the ideomotor model and the associative sequence learning model seem to map well onto neurophysiological mechanisms of imitation. The ideomotor model assumes a common representational format for action and perception, whereas the associative sequence learning model puts at center stage Hebbian learning as a fundamental mechanism linking sensory representations of the actions of others to motor plans. Furthermore, social psychology studies have documented the automaticity of imitation and mimicry in humans, a feature that also maps well onto some recently disclosed neurophysiological bases of imitation.

This review discusses cognitive models, social psychology constructs, and neural mechanisms of imitation under the hypothesis that these mechanisms were selected because they offer the adaptive advantage of enabling the understanding of the feelings and mental states of others, a cornerstone of social behavior.

COGNITIVE MECHANISMS OF IMITATION

The Ideomotor Framework of Imitation

Theories of action can be divided into two main frameworks. The most dominant framework may be called the sensory-motor framework of action. It assumes that actions are initiated in response to external stimuli. In this framework, perception and action have independent representational formats. Stimuli must be translated into motor responses by stimulus-response mapping mechanisms. This framework has generated a large literature and elegant experimental paradigms, as for instance the work on stimulus-response compatibility (Hommel & Prinz 1997, Proctor & Reeve 1990). Stimulus-response translational mechanisms, however, do not easily account for the similarity between the observed action and the action performed by the imitator that is required by imitation. Indeed, one of the main problems of imitation often discussed in the literature inspired by sensory-motor models is the so-called correspondence problem (Nehaniv & Dautenhahn 2002). This problem can be summarized with the question: how is the sensory input from somebody else's action transformed into a matching motor output by the imitator?

For the ideomotor framework of action, the correspondence problem of imitation is not a problem at all. Indeed, the ideomotor framework assumes a common representational format for perception and action, an assumption that makes translational processes between stimuli and responses rather unnecessary. The roots of the ideomotor framework were established by the work of Hermann Martin Lotze (Prinz 2005) and William James (1890). The starting point of actions, for Lotze and James, is not a response to a sensory stimulation, but rather the representation of the goal that the agent intends to achieve. When an intention is unchallenged by a conflicting one, it activates the representation of the intended goal and the motor plan necessary to achieve it. The coactivation of the intended goal and the motor plan required to achieve it—according to the ideomotor framework—is the result of our experience. We have learned the effects of our own actions, and we expect certain effects when we perform certain acts. This previous learning makes it possible that just thinking about the intended goal automatically activates the representation of the action necessary to obtain it. Thus, when I think about rebooting my computer, I automatically activate the representation of the finger movement necessary to press the appropriate key.

The ideomotor framework naturally accounts for imitation. According to this framework, when I see somebody else's actions and their consequences, I activate the representations of my own actions that would produce those consequences. Here, consequences are construed in a very broad sense. For instance, a simple finger lifting has multiple perceptual consequences, among them the sight of the finger lifting. Thus, simply watching somebody else lifting a finger should activate my own mo-

tor plan to lift the same finger. Brass and colleagues tested this hypothesis in elegantly simple experiments (Brass et al. 2000, 2001). Subjects were shown two movements of the index finger from the same starting position. In half of the trials the finger would move upward, and in the other half it would move downward. Subjects were instructed to respond as fast as possible using their own index finger. Within each block of trials, subjects were instructed to use always the same motor response, either an upward or a downward movement. Thus, although perceptually subjects were seeing both upward and downward movements, motorically they were only executing one of the two movements. Given that response selection was not required, the identity of the stimulus was completely irrelevant for the initiation of the motor response. Here, the sensory-motor framework would predict similar reaction times for responses that were identical to the stimulus (e.g., upward motor response for a stimulus showing an upward finger movement) and for responses that were different from the stimulus (e.g., upward motor response for a stimulus showing a downward finger movement). In contrast, the ideomotor framework would predict faster reaction times for motor responses identical to the stimulus compared to motor responses different from the stimulus. The results demonstrated a large chronometric advantage for responses identical to the stimuli, in line with the predictions of the ideomotor framework (Brass et al. 2000, 2001).

The ideomotor framework also predicts that goals have higher priority than movements in imitation. Imitation experiments in children have confirmed this prediction. In one of these experiments (Bekkering et al. 2000), children and experimenters were sitting on the opposite sides of a desk. In half of the trials the experimenter would place her or his left hand on the left side of the desk (left ipsilateral movement) or on the right side of the desk (left contralateral movement); in the remaining half of the trials the experimenter would place her or his right hand on the right side of the desk (right ipsilateral movement) or on the left side of the desk

Associative sequence learning: imitation is based on associative, Hebbian-like learning, creating "vertical links" between sensory and motor representations

(right contralateral movement). Children were instructed to "Do what I do," and in all cases, they imitated all these movements well. In a separate session, children and experimenters were again sitting on the opposite sides of the desk. Now, however, there were two big red dots, one on the left and one on the right side of the desk. Whenever the experimenter made a movement, either ipsilateral or contralateral with either the left or the right hand, the hand of the experimenter would end up covering the big red dot. Children were again instructed to "Do what I do." In this situation, children imitated well the ipsilateral movements but made frequent mistakes when trying to imitate the contralateral movements. Note that these movements had been imitated well in absence of the big red dot. The presence of the big red dot had changed the goal of the action to be imitated. Whereas in the absence of the dot, the action itself was the goal to be imitated, the presence of the dot had changed the goal of the action in covering the dot. Indeed, children made mistakes when imitating contralateral movements because they used ipsilateral movements to cover the same dot that had been covered by the experimenter. In other words, children would copy the goal but used a simpler movement to achieve this goal (Bekkering et al. 2000).

One of the main assumptions of the ideomotor framework is that action and perception share a common representational format. This assumption fits well recent neuroscience discoveries, as discussed below. Another important assumption of the ideomotor framework is that our perceptual and motor experience is very important in shaping the functional aspects of imitation. This assumption is also shared by the associative sequence learning model (Heyes 2005), as described in the next section.

Associative Sequence Learning

The associative sequence learning model of imitation proposes that imitative abilities are based on associations between the sensory and motor representation of actions. These associations would be mostly shaped by experience, although a small number of these associations may be innate. Several environmental situations may favor the establishment of these associations between sensory and motor representation of actions, for instance, visually guided actions, such as reaching and grasping, during which we can observe our own arm and hand reach and grasp for objects surrounding us. Also, mirrors and other reflecting surfaces allow the observation of one's own facial and body movement as if they were performed by somebody else. Furthermore, early in human development, adults tend to imitate the baby (Nadel 2002), thus favoring the formation of the associations between sensory and motor representations of actions.

The basic assumption of the associative sequence learning model is that imitation is not based on dedicated functional (and neural) mechanisms. General sensory and motor systems may implement imitative abilities through mechanisms that are strongly reminiscent of Hebbian learning. One of the corollaries of this assumption is that imitation should not be confined to specific lineages. Indeed, although primates clearly show varying degrees of imitative abilities, birds (Akins et al. 2002) and dolphins (Herman 2002) also seem able to imitate. Thus, imitative behavior appears to be the product of convergent evolution. If this is true, then the hypothesis that imitation is mostly shaped by experience—as assumed by the associative sequence learning model—is obviously supported.

The role of experience and the environment in shaping imitative abilities may also account for evidence that at first sight seems at odds with the basic assumptions of the associative sequence learning model. Many animals share similar basic sensory and motor functional and neural mechanisms. In principle, this should lead to similar imitative skills in many animals. Imitation abilities, however, vary substantially between species (Boysen & Himes 1999, Hurley & Chater 2005). Is this evidence a fatal blow to the main assumption of the associative sequence learning model? Probably not. Indeed, different kinds of environments may account for the differences in imitative abilities observed in different species. As discussed above, some elements that are quite specific to the human environment should favor the formation of the associations between sensory and motor representations posited by the associative sequence learning model. In keeping with these ideas, humans are by far the best imitators (Hurley & Chater 2005).

Empirical evidence in well-controlled laboratory experiments seems to support the role of experience in shaping imitation, as hypothesized by the associative sequence learning model. For instance, hand-opening and hand-closing gestures are typically facilitated by the observation of the same movement compared to the observation of a different movement. However, this facilitation can be abolished by a relatively short period of training during which subjects are instructed to open the hand while observing hand closing, and to close the hand while observing hand opening (Heyes et al. 2005).

In another experiment, the effect of training was measured on the speed of imitation induced by the observation of human motion versus robotic motion. A typical finding is that humans imitate more quickly the movements of another human compared to the movements of a robot. This effect, however, may be simply because humans tend to interact more with other humans than with robots. Indeed, subjects who were trained to execute hand movement in response to a robotic movement demonstrated no difference in speed of imitation while observing human and robotic movements (Press et al. 2007).

Although the associative sequence learning model and the ideomotor framework of imitation share the main idea that experience is extremely important for imitation, they also seem to differ on an important point. The associative sequence learning model assumes that separate sensory and motor representations are linked by experience. In contrast, the ideomotor framework assumes that sensory and motor functional mechanisms share a common represen-

tational format. In psychological terms, these differences are not negligible. The translation of these different concepts into neural activity, however, as discussed below, may not differ dramatically (Glimcher 2005). Indeed, the main assumptions of both the associative sequence learning model and the ideomotor framework of imitation fit well with recent neuroscience findings on imitation.

IMITATION AND EMPATHY IN SOCIAL BEHAVIOR

Pervasiveness and Automaticity of Human Imitation

Humans seem to have a strong tendency to align their behavior with their fellows during social interactions (Lieberman 2007). Some of these forms of imitation and mimicry are not only pervasive and automatic, but also operate on a quite complex level. Ap Dijksterius (2005)—following LeDoux's terminology on processing of fearful stimuli (LeDoux 1996)—suggests that there are two roads to human imitation. A low road leads to imitation in a direct fashion, such that the perceiver acts the gestures, postures, facial expressions, and speech perceived in other people. A high road leads to complex and rather subtle forms of imitation, as shown by a number of experiments with priming manipulations that lead to stereotype activation or trait activation.

An example of stereotype activation on motor behavior is provided by the following experiment. Participants performed a scrambled-sentence language task. Some subjects were exposed to words such as Florida, bingo, gray; that is, words typically associated with the elderly. Some other subjects were not. After the experiment, participants left the laboratory and walked back to the elevator to leave the building. An experimenter timed this walk back to the elevator. Subjects who had been primed with the elderly stereotype were reliably slower than subjects who had not been primed (Bargh et al. 1996). The primed subjects imitated—obviously in an unconscious way—the slowness of old people.

The high road to imitation is also at work in memory and general knowledge tasks. In one experiment, subjects sat in front of a desk full of objects. The stereotype of the elderly was primed again in some subjects by asking them questions on elderly people. Other subjects, in contrast, were asked questions about college students. Subsequently, subjects were transferred to another room and were asked to remember the objects that were on the desk in front of them. The subjects primed with the elderly stereotype remembered far fewer objects than did the other participants (Dijksterhuis et al. 2000).

In a series of experiments, participants were either asked to think about college professors (a group of people typically associated with intelligence) and to write down everything that came to mind about college professors, or they were asked to think about soccer hooligans (a group of people typically not associated with intelligence) and to write down everything that came to mind about soccer hooligans. In a later task involving general knowledge questions, a task that was ostensibly unrelated to the first one, the participants who were asked to think about college professors outperformed the participants who were asked to think about soccer hooligans. Indeed, the participants who were asked to think about college professors even outperformed participants who were not asked anything at all, and the participants who were asked to think about soccer hooligans were outperformed by participants who were not asked anything at all (Dijksterhuis & van Knippenberg 1998).

Many more studies support the concept that the high road to imitation is pervasive and automatic (Dijksterhuis 2005). The question is why pervasiveness and automaticity have been selected as distinctive properties of the high road to imitation. One possibility is that imitation facilitates social interactions, increases connectedness and liking, gets people closer to each other, and fosters mutual care. If this account

is correct, it should follow that good imitators should also be good at recognizing emotions in other people, which in turn may lead to greater empathy. Thus, this account would predict a correlation between the tendency to imitate others and the ability to empathize with them. This hypothesis was tested in a series of experiments (Chartrand & Bargh 1999). In the first experiment, subjects were asked to choose pictures in a set of photographs. The cover story was that the researchers needed some of these pictures for a psychological test and wanted to know from the subjects which pictures they considered more stimulating. While subjects were choosing the pictures, a confederate was sitting in the same room with the real subject. The confederate pretended to be another subject who was also choosing good stimulating pictures. During the experimental sessions, some confederates deliberately rubbed their nose while the others shook their foot. Subjects were videotaped and their motor behavior was measured. It was found that the real subjects unintentionally mimicked the motor behavior of the confederate with whom they were sharing the room. Subjects who shared the room with confederates who rubbed their nose, rubbed their nose more than did subjects who shared the room with confederates who shook their foot. Furthermore, subjects who shared the room with confederates who shook their foot, shook their foot more than did subjects who shared the room with confederates who rubbed their nose. These results are in line with the idea that imitation is automatic and provide the necessary prelude to the following experiments.

The second experiment tested the hypothesis that one of the functions of this automatic tendency to imitate is to increase liking between individuals. Participants were again asked to choose pictures, and confederates were again sitting with them, pretending to be participants of the study. In this second experiment, the cover task required participants and confederates to take turns in describing what they saw in various photos. At the end of the interaction

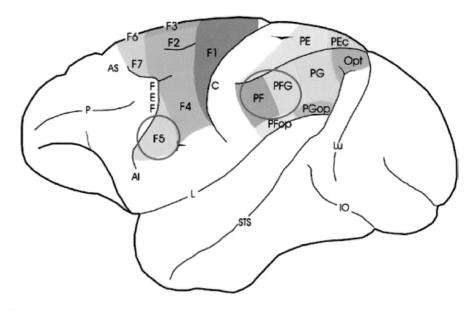

Figure 1

Schematic drawing of the lateral wall of the macaque brain. The inferior frontal (ventral premotor area F5) and inferior parietal (PF and PFG) areas circled in red contain mirror neurons. (Modified from figure 1 of Rizzolatti & Craighero 2004.)

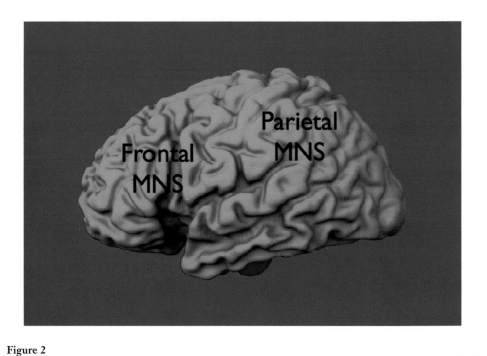

Figure 2

Lateral wall of the human brain. Human areas presumed to contain mirror neurons are in the posterior part of the inferior frontal gyrus and in the anterior part of the inferior parietal lobule.

between participants and confederates, the participants were also asked to complete a questionnaire to report how much they liked the other participant (that is, the confederate) and how smoothly they thought the interaction had gone. In this second experiment, the confederates either imitated the spontaneous postures, movements, and mannerisms of the subjects or kept a neutral posture. The participants who were mimicked by confederates during the interaction liked the confederates much more than did the participants who were not imitated. Furthermore, mimicked subjects rated the smoothness of the interaction higher than did the participants who were not imitated. This experiment demonstrated that imitation and liking tend to go together. When someone is imitating us, we tend to like him or her more.

A third experiment tested the hypothesis that the more people tend to imitate others, the more they are concerned with the feelings of other people. The setting of this third experiment was identical to the first experiment. The novel aspect of this last experiment was that the participants responded to a questionnaire that measured their empathic tendencies. The experiment found a strong correlation between the tendency to empathize and the amount of imitative behavior displayed by the participants. The more a subject imitated the confederate, the more that subject was an empathic individual (Chartrand & Bargh 1999). This result suggests that through imitation and mimicry, we are able to feel what other people feel. By being able to feel what other people feel, we are also able to respond compassionately to other people's emotional states (Eisenberg 2000, Tangney et al. 2007).

Many other empirical results are consistent with these ideas (Braten 2007, Niedenthal et al. 2005). What are the neural correlates of these complex forms of human behavior? A recent discovery in the monkey premotor cortex has sparked a whole series of new studies, in monkeys and humans, that are relevant to this question.

NEURAL MECHANISMS OF IMITATION

Neural Precursors in Nonhuman Primates

The premotor cortex of the macaque brain, a cortical region important for the planning, preparation, and selection of movements and coordinated actions, is not homogeneous (Matelli et al. 1985). It is composed of several cito-architectonic fields with different physiological properties. In the lateral wall of the macaque brain, the ventral sector of the premotor cortex is composed of two main fields, area F4 and area F5 (Matelli et al. 1985). Area F5 has physiological properties relevant to the neural control of mouth and hand movements, especially grasping (Rizzolatti et al. 1988). Within area F5, there are neurons that discharge not only when the monkey performs goal-oriented actions such as grasping an object, holding it, manipulating it, and bringing it to the mouth, but also when the monkey, completely still, simply observes somebody else performing these actions. Because of these properties, which almost suggest that the monkey is observing its own actions reflected by a mirror, these cells were called mirror neurons (di Pellegrino et al. 1992, Gallese et al. 1996).

The properties of mirror neurons call to mind the concepts of the ideomotor framework of actions, according to which perception and action share common representational formats. Indeed, mirror neurons embody the overlap between perception and action predicted by the ideomotor framework by discharging both during action execution and during action observation.

The initial hypothesis about the functional role of mirror neurons focused on action recognition. By firing during actions of the self and of other individuals, mirror neurons may provide a remarkably simple neural mechanism for recognizing the actions of others. Early observations on firing-rate changes in mirror neurons demonstrated that these cells do not fire at the sight of a pantomime (Rizzolatti et al. 1996,

Premotor cortex: anterior sector of the agranular frontal cortex containing neurons that are relevant to the planning, preparation, and selection of actions

Mirror neurons: neurons with motor properties in premotor and posterior parietal cortex that fire not only during action execution, but also while observing somebody else performing the same or a similar action

Rizzolatti & Arbib 1998). For instance, the pantomime of whole-hand grasp (when the whole hand is used to grasp a relatively large object, as an orange) does not trigger the discharge of a mirror neuron that fires during execution and observation of whole-hand grasps. This makes sense because monkeys typically do not pantomime. These early findings suggested that the properties of this neural system were remarkable but relatively simple, some sort of "monkey see, monkey do" neural mechanisms. However, many other findings contradict this view and rather suggest that mirror neurons form a sophisticated, nuanced system for shared coding of motor and perceptual aspects of actions of self and others (Rizzolatti & Craighero 2004).

For instance, although the term "mirror" implies a strong similarity between the executed and the observed actions, only one third of mirror neurons—the so-called strictly congruent mirror neurons—fire for the same executed and observed action. The remaining two-thirds of mirror neurons—the so-called broadly congruent mirror neurons—fire for executed and observed actions that are not the same but either achieve the same goal or are logically related (di Pellegrino et al. 1992, Gallese et al. 1996, Rizzolatti & Craighero 2004), thus forming some sort of sequence of acts, as for instance observed placing food on the table and executed grasping food and bringing it to the mouth.

The properties of broadly congruent mirror neurons suggest that these cells provide a flexible coding of actions of self and others. This flexibility is an important property for successful social interactions because even though imitation is a pervasive phenomenon in humans, people do not imitate each other all the time but rather often perform coordinated, cooperative, complementary actions. Broadly congruent mirror neurons seem ideal cells to support cooperative behavior among people (Newman-Norlund et al. 2007).

Following the initial observations (di Pellegrino et al. 1992, Gallese et al. 1996), a series of more recent experiments have demonstrated other complex properties of mirror neurons. For instance, we often easily recognize actions that are partially occluded. The role of mirror neurons in the recognition of hidden actions was tested by using a screen that occluded the completion of the grasping action (Umiltà et al. 2001). In two baseline conditions, the firing of the cells was measured for observation of grasping and of grasp pantomime. As expected, mirror neurons fired for grasping observation but not for observation of the pantomime. In a new experimental condition, the subject watched a graspable object placed on a desk in front of the monkey. Subsequently, a screen occluded the sight of the graspable object and a human experimenter reached with her or his hand behind the screen. The monkey was able to see the experimenter's hand moving toward the object but was not able to see the actual grasping action, which was occluded by the screen. Approximately half of the mirror neurons tested in this experiment discharged even though the grasping action was occluded. The firing rate changes of these neurons were tested also in an additional control condition. Here, at the beginning of the trial, the monkey saw that there was no graspable object on the table. As in the previous experimental conditions, a screen subsequently occluded the sight of the table and a human experimenter reached with her or his hand behind the screen. Consider that at this point, this additional control condition is visually identical to the previous experimental conditions involving the screen occluding the sight of the grasping action. The only difference here is the prior knowledge of the absence of a graspable object behind the screen. Mirror neurons tested under this experimental condition did not change their firing rate, suggesting that the unseen action behind the screen was indeed coded as a pantomime (or, better, as a nongrasping action) (Umiltà et al. 2001).

The experiment on hidden actions demonstrates another aspect of the properties of mirror neurons that suggests that these cells code actions in a fairly sophisticated way. The same visual information is coded differently, on the basis of prior knowledge about the presence or absence of a graspable object behind the screen. A subsequent experiment demonstrated that mirror neurons also code in absence of any visual input (Kohler et al. 2002). In this study, after the necessary baseline conditions were performed and mirror neurons were identified, the experimenters measured the firing-rate changes of mirror neurons to the sound of actions. The sound stimuli used in this study were associated with common actions such as tearing a piece of paper, breaking peanuts, and so on. Control sounds not associated with actions, for instance white noise, were also used (Keysers et al. 2003, Kohler et al. 2002). The single-cell recordings demonstrated that mirror neurons can also discharge to the sound of an action, even in absence of the visual input related to the action. These auditory properties of mirror neurons have two important theoretical implications. One implication is relevant to the evolution of language. Area F5 of the macaque brain (where mirror neurons were originally discovered) is the anatomical homologue of Brodmann area 44 of the human brain (Rizzolatti & Arbib 1998), a brain area with important language properties. This anatomical correspondence, together with other considerations, led to the hypothesis that mirror neurons may have facilitated the emergence of language in the human brain (Rizzolatti & Arbib 1998). However, language is not only written and read but also (and mostly) spoken and heard. Mirror neuron responses to auditory stimuli are essential evidence for the hypothesis that mirror neurons are important neural elements in language evolution. The other implication of the auditory properties of mirror neurons is that they show that mirror neurons are multimodal cells. This functional property is theoretically important because it is compatible with associative models of how mirror neurons may be formed, which is discussed in more detail below. When we break a peanut, the visual input of our fingers breaking the peanut and the auditory input of the sound of breaking the peanut almost always co-occur, especially when we are initially learning to perform the action. Associative models can easily account for multimodal responses that are produced by the co-occurrence of sensory stimuli from multiple modalities (Fanselow & Poulos 2005, Keysers & Perrett 2004, Wasserman & Miller 1997).

A recent study on mirror neuron responses to the sight of actions involving the use of tools is also consistent with the hypothesis that the properties of mirror neurons are shaped by experience. Early observations on mirror neuron responses to observed actions suggested that these cells do not fire at the sight of an action involving the use of a tool. For instance, a mirror neuron discharging during the execution and observation of precision grips (when grasping small objects with two fingers) would not fire at the sight of the experimenter using a hand tool such as a pliers to grasp the same small object (Rizzolatti & Arbib 1998). However, a recent study recording in the inferolateral aspect of area F5 has reported robust discharges in approximately 20% of recorded mirror neurons when the monkey observed the experimenters using tools (Ferrari et al. 2005). Indeed, these discharges were even more robust than the discharges of the same cells during the observation of a grasping action without the tool (Ferrari et al. 2005). Although it is not possible to demonstrate unequivocally that the mirror neuron responses to tool use actions were acquired through the daily experience of observing human experimenters using tools in the lab, this seems a likely explanation. It is unlikely that tool-use mirror neurons were already present in area F5 of the macaque brain but never recorded for more than ten years. This recently discovered functional property of mirror neurons and its likely underlying forming mechanisms is also obviously relevant to the psychological theories discussed above.

Furthermore, described above, the ideomotor framework of action puts intentions front and center. Is it possible that the discharge of mirror neurons may represent the coding of the intention associated with the performed and observed action rather than the action itself? A recent single-cell recording study has addressed this question (Fogassi et al. 2005). The depth electrode recordings first demonstrated that neurons in area PF/PFG—a cortical area located in the anterior part of the inferior parietal lobule that is anatomically connected with area F5 in the ventral premotor cortex (see **Figure 1**, see color insert) and that also contains mirror neurons—had differential discharges for the same grasping action that led to, say, eating food rather than placing the food in a container (note that the monkeys were rewarded after placing the food in the container; thus, the amount of reward was identical for both actions). Not surprisingly, grasping for eating was preferred by the majority of grasping cells in this parietal area, although approximately 25% of neurons coding differently the same grasping action on the basis of its intention preferred grasping for placing over grasping for eating (Fogassi et al. 2005).

This pattern of firing-rate changes demonstrates that these cells code the same executed grasping action rather differently, according to the intention (or the goal) associated with the grasping action. The same pattern of firing-rate changes was also observed during action observation. Here, the monkey was simply observing the human experimenter performing grasping actions. The intention of the experimenter was cued by the presence of a container. When the container was present, the experimenter grasped the food and placed it in the container. When the container was absent, the experimenter grasped the food and ate it. At the time of grasping, the cells that discharged more robustly for grasping to eat when the monkey performed the actions also discharged more robustly when the monkey simply observed the human experimenter grasping the food in order to eat it. Likewise, the cells that discharged more robustly for grasping to place when the monkey performed the actions also discharged more robustly when the monkey simply observed the human experimenter grasping the food in order to place it in the container (Fogassi et al. 2005). Thus, rather than coding the observed grasping action, these neurons seem to be coding the goal associated with the action, the intention to eat or to place.

The most dramatic demonstration of the role of goal coding in these cells has been provided by a very recent study (Umiltà et al. 2008). Here, single-cell recordings in area F5 were performed after monkeys were trained to use pliers to grasp objects. Ventral premotor neurons active during grasping actions were also active when the monkey used pliers to grasp objects. Monkeys were trained to use reverse pliers that required hand opening rather than hand closing (as in natural grasps). Remarkably, neurons that fired during hand closing in natural grasps and during use of normal pliers did fire during hand opening when the monkeys used the reverse pliers. The activity of these motor neurons is evidently centered on coding the goal of the action rather than the motor detail of hand closing or opening. Among these motor neurons, the cells with mirroring properties also demonstrated a pattern of firing-rate changes centered on goal coding, discharging when the tips of the pliers were closing on the objects to be grasped during observation of action with both normal and reverse pliers (Umiltà et al. 2008).

Mirror neurons do not mirror only grasping actions performed with the hand or with tools controlled by the hand. There is evidence of mirror neurons coding facial actions, in particular with the mouth. Both ingestive (such as biting and sucking) and communicative actions are coded by mirror neurons (Ferrari et al. 2003). This is especially important for the hypothesis that mirror neurons may facilitate our understanding of the emotions of other people, because the face is the body part that we use most often to express our own emotions.

Macaque Mirror Neurons and Imitation in Monkeys

Do monkeys imitate? This is a contentious issue, and the answer to this question is heavily dependent on the definition of imitation. Among scholars, it was widely held at the end of the nineteenth century that monkeys not only are able to imitate, but they actually do it "...at ludicrous length." (Romanes 1883). In those times, imitation was not typically associated with high forms of intelligence. This view of imitation has changed considerably in the past 30 years (Hurley & Chater 2005), calling also for a revision of previously held ideas on monkeys' ability to imitate. Indeed, such revision had at some point taken the form of a true backlash, with many scholars denying that monkeys had any imitative ability. This position raised the issue of what is the adaptive advantage of mirror neurons for monkeys and inspired new and better-controlled studies. There is now well-controlled evidence that monkeys are indeed able to imitate (Ferrari et al. 2006; Subiaul et al. 2004; Voelkl & Huber 2000, 2007), and it is likely—although there is no direct evidence yet—that this ability is supported by mirror neurons. For instance, marmosets observed a demonstrator removing the lids from a series of plastic canisters to obtain a mealworm. Subsequently, marmosets that observed a demonstrator using its hands to remove the lids used only their hands, whereas marmosets that observed a demonstrator using its mouth used their mouth to remove the lids (Voelkl & Huber 2000). In another study, marmosets observed another marmoset (the model) that was previously trained to open a box in a peculiar way. Detailed motion analyses demonstrated that the highly unusual movement pattern of the model was faithfully replicated by the observers (Voelkl & Huber 2007). A recent study has also shown that rhesus macaques display neonatal imitation abilities that are similar to the abilities displayed by human neonates (Ferrari et al. 2006).

It is evident, however, that imitative learning is not developed in monkeys as it is in humans (Hurley & Chater 2005). What then would be the main function of mirror neurons in the monkey brain? One possibility might be that mirror neurons facilitate the ability to recognize the actions of others. A recent behavioral study, however, has also revealed that monkeys are able to recognize when they are being imitated (Paukner et al. 2005). In this study, monkeys observed two experimenters, each manipulating a wooden cube with a hole in each side. Initially, the monkeys did not show any preferential looking between the two experimenters.

Subsequently, a cube was given to the monkey. When the monkey started manipulating the cube, one of the two experimenters imitated accurately the monkey's actions directed at the cube. The second experimenter, in contrast, performed different actions. At this point, the monkey preferentially looked at the experimenter imitating her own actions. This capacity, which is likely supported by mirror neurons, may have an important social function and may be one of the early functional precursors of the highly developed imitative behavior of humans.

Human Brain Mechanisms of Mirroring

The exquisite spatial and temporal resolution afforded by depth electrode recordings of single-cell activity can be obtained only with techniques of brain investigation that are quite invasive. These techniques cannot typically be used in humans. The neural properties revealed by single-unit recordings in monkeys are usually investigated in humans at the system level, with lesion studies (behavioral observations on neurological patients), brain imaging, and recently transcranial magnetic stimulation (TMS). Although the relationships between all these markers of brain activity are far from being fully defined, there is evidence that they tend to correlate relatively well. Spiking neuronal activity recorded with in-depth electrodes correlates well with the blood-oxygenation-level dependent (BOLD) signal measured by functional magnetic resonance imaging (fMRI) (Logothetis et al. 2001). In some cases, however, spiking activity and BOLD seem to dissociate (Logothetis & Wandell 2004), for instance when spiking responses show adaptation (that is, a reduced response to repeated stimuli) while BOLD does not (Goense & Logothetis 2008). Nevertheless, a recent TMS study has shown similar stimulation effects on both neural and hemodynamic signals (Allen et al. 2007), supporting the practice of inferring neural activity from signals based on hemodynamic changes, such as BOLD fMRI.

TMS: transcranial magnetic stimulation

BOLD: blood-oxygenation-level dependent

fMRI: functional magnetic resonance imaging

Indeed, this practice is widely used in systems neuroscience. For instance, single-cell recordings with depth electrodes have revealed in the dorsal premotor cortex of macaques cellular mechanisms of conditional motor learning, the fundamental ability that allows the association of motor responses to arbitrary sensory stimuli, as when we brake at a red traffic light. In humans, the dorsal premotor cortex has also been associated with conditional motor learning by brain imaging and lesion studies (Passingham 1993). Even though single-cell recordings of human dorsal premotor neurons have not been performed, the obvious assumption is that the human brain must have dorsal premotor cellular mechanisms that enable conditional motor learning and that are likely similar to—albeit probably more sophisticated than—the ones recorded in monkeys.

This very same logic applies to the investigation of mirror neurons in the human brain. Given that the information typically obtained in human studies is at system level, the term "mirror neuron system" is often used in these studies. Two positron emission tomography studies (Grafton et al. 1996, Rizzolatti et al. 1996) and a TMS study (Fadiga et al. 1995) provided early evidence compatible with the idea that the human ventral premotor and inferior frontal cortex had mirroring properties. However, these studies did not investigate the role of these human brain areas in imitation. In a later fMRI study (Iacoboni et al. 1999), subjects were required to imitate simple finger movements and to perform motor and visual control tasks. The logic of the study was as follows: The neuronal discharge measured by depth electrode recordings in macaques during action observation is approximately 50% of the discharge measured during action execution (Gallese et al. 1996). Thus, human brain areas with mirror neurons should also have an increased BOLD signal (which roughly correlates with brain activity in fMRI) during action observation that is approximately 50% of the BOLD increase measured during action execution. Furthermore, during imitation, subjects were simultaneously watch-

ing the finger movement and copying it. Thus, mirror neuron areas may have a BOLD signal increase during imitation that is approximately the sum of the BOLD signal increases observed during action observation and during action execution. The fMRI study found that two cortical areas had this predicted pattern of activity: They were located in the posterior part of the inferior frontal gyrus and in the rostral part of the posterior parietal cortex (Iacoboni et al. 1999), in anatomical locations (see **Figure 2**, see color insert) that were homologous to the anatomical locations of the macaque brain areas with mirror neurons, that is, area F5 in the ventral premotor cortex and area PF/PFG in the rostral sector of the inferior parietal lobule.

The inferior frontal area with mirroring properties overlapped with the posterior part of Broca's area, a major language area. On one hand, these findings supported the evolutionary hypothesis about the role of mirror neurons in language (Rizzolatti & Arbib 1998). On the other hand, an activation in a language area during a nonlanguage task may be induced by covert verbalization occurring during the activation tasks. It is unclear why imitation should induce more covert verbalization than motor execution, which in turn should induce more covert verbalization than action observation (the pattern predicted for a mirror neuron area and observed in the posterior part of the inferior frontal gyrus and in the rostral part of the posterior parietal cortex), and this issue cannot be conclusively resolved by fMRI, which is a technique that provides only correlational data between brain areas and human behavior. TMS, on the other hand, provides information on the causal role of the activity in a brain area and human behavior. A high-frequency repetitive TMS study indeed demonstrated later that activity in the pars opercularis, the posterior part of the inferior frontal gyrus, is essential to imitation (Heiser et al. 2003).

A series of brain-imaging studies has suggested a core cortical circuitry for imitation composed of the posterior part of the superior temporal sulcus, a higher-order visual area that responds to watching biological motion and intentional actions (Allison et al. 2000, Jellema et al. 2000, Perrett et al. 1989, Puce & Perrett 2003, Puce et al. 1998), and by the parietal and frontal mirror neuron areas. Within this cortical circuitry, the superior temporal cortex would provide a higher-order visual description of the actions of other people and would feed this information to the fronto-parietal mirror neuron areas (Iacoboni et al. 2001). The parietal mirror neuron area would code the motor aspect of the action (Iacoboni et al. 1999), whereas the frontal mirror neuron area would be more concerned with the goal of the action (Iacoboni 2005, Iacoboni et al. 2005, Iacoboni & Dapretto 2006, Koski et al. 2002).

Imitative behavior can take many forms (Hurley & Chater 2005). The core circuitry for imitation, composed of superior temporal cortex, inferior parietal lobule, and inferior frontal cortex, interacts with other neural systems to support different forms of imitative behavior. For instance, the interactions between the core circuitry for imitation and the dorsolateral prefrontal cortex seem critical during imitative learning (Buccino et al. 2004). In contrast, social mirroring and the ability to empathize with others may be supported by the interactions between the core circuitry for imitation and the limbic system (Iacoboni 2005). An fMRI study of imitation and observation of facial emotional expressions (Carr et al. 2003) tested the hypothesis that empathy is enabled by a large-scale neural network composed of the mirror neuron system, the limbic system, and the insula connecting these two neural systems. Within this network, mirror neurons would support the simulation of the facial expressions observed in other people, which in turn would trigger activity in limbic areas, thus producing in the observer the emotion that other people are feeling. This model predicts activation of mirror neuron areas, insula, and limbic areas during both observation and imitation of facial emotional expressions. Furthermore, the model predicts that the increased activity in mirror neuron ar-

eas during imitation should also spread to insula and limbic areas, if these brain centers are indeed functionally connected with mirror neuron areas. Both predictions were supported by the empirical findings (Carr et al. 2003).

In functional terms, the large-scale network composed of mirror neuron areas, insula, and the limbic system likely provides a simulation-based form of empathy (Goldman 2006, Goldman & Sripada 2005). Recent data also suggest that the activity in this network provides a biomarker of sociality and empathy. Indeed, an fMRI study of imitation and observation of facial expressions in children with autism and in typically developing children demonstrated not only a deficit in mirror neuron areas in the children with autism, but also a correlation between the severity of the disease and activity in these areas: The lower the activity in mirror neuron areas, the more severe the autism (Dapretto et al. 2006). Furthermore, a separate fMRI study on typically developing preadolescents—in which the activation task was again the observation and imitation of facial emotional expressions—has recently demonstrated that activity in mirror neuron areas was positively correlated with interpersonal competence and empathic concern (Pfeifer et al. 2008). Two additional fMRI studies on adults also support the findings obtained in children. In one study, subjects observed simple grasping actions (Kaplan & Iacoboni 2006). In the other study, subjects listened to action sounds (Gazzola et al. 2006). Both studies found a positive correlation between empathy scores and activity in premotor areas activated during action observation and while listening to action sounds, thus likely containing mirror neurons.

Neural Mirroring and Psychological Theories of Imitation

The ideomotor model of imitation and the associative sequence learning model share many concepts but diverge on a fundamental one: The former assumes overlap between perceptual and motor representations, whereas the latter assumes that sensory and motor representations are separated but functionally connected through vertical links formed by associative learning. Both models also map well onto the functional properties of mirror neurons and neural systems for mirroring. Do the neuroscience findings on mirror neurons better support the assumptions of the ideomotor model on perceptual and motor representations or those of the associative sequence learning model? It is difficult to answer this question because the levels of description of psychological theories and those of neuroscience empirical work are radically different.

The discharge of mirror neurons during action execution and action observation seems to fulfill the main assumption of the ideomotor model, a common representational format for perception and action. Preliminary results on individual neuronal activity obtained with depth electrode recordings in humans (R. Mukamel, A. Ekstrom, J. Kaplan, M. Iacoboni and I. Fried, unpublished observations) seem also to support the ideomotor model. Using a rare clinical opportunity, we recently recorded single-cell activity in epileptic patients implanted for surgical evaluation. We found human neurons with mirror properties in the frontal lobe as well as in the medial temporal cortex. Although the discharge of these cells during action execution and action observation seems to imply a common representational format for perception and action implemented at single cell level, it is also true that lesions in the frontal lobe are more often associated with motor deficits, and lesions in the medial temporal lobe are more often associated with perceptual deficits. Perception and action, which are united at the level of single cells, seem to be more easily separated at the system level. In principle, the discharge during action execution and during action observation of frontal and medial temporal neurons may represent in neural terms the "vertical links" posited by the associative sequence learning model between a sensory unit (the medial temporal neuron) and

a motor unit (the frontal neuron) that fire together as a result of associative learning.

WHY NEURAL MIRRORING AND IMITATION?

The fundamental Darwinian question is why mirror neurons were selected by evolution. What is the adaptive advantage of having these neurons? The properties of these cells seem to solve—or better, dis-solve—what is called the "problem of other minds": if one has access only to one's own mind, how can one possibly understand the minds of other people? How can one possibly share one's own mental states with others, making intersubjectivity possible?

A classical solution to the problem of other minds is the so-called argument from analogy. The argument from analogy posits that we first observe certain relations between our mental states and our bodily states and then find an analogy between our body and the body of other people. If there is an analogy between our body and the body of others, there may be also an analogy between our mental states/bodily states relations and those of other people. This way of reasoning about the mental states of other people seems too complex for something we seem to accomplish so naturally, effortlessly, and quickly. Mirror neurons, in contrast, provide a prereflective, automatic mechanism of mirroring what is going on in the brain of other people that seems more compatible with our ability to understand others effortlessly and with our tendency to imitate others automatically, as we have discussed in this review.

A further implication of the recent work on the relationships between mirror neurons, imitation, and empathy is the consideration that the evolutionary process made us wired for empathy. This is a major revision of widely held beliefs. Traditionally, our biology is considered the basis of self-serving individualism, whereas our ideas and our social codes enable us to rise above our neurobiological makeup. The research on mirror neurons, imitation, and empathy, in contrast, tells us that our ability to empathize, a building block of our sociality (Adolphs 2009) and morality (de Waal 2008, Tangney et al. 2007), has been built "bottom up" from relatively simple mechanisms of action production and perception (Iacoboni 2008).

SUMMARY POINTS

1. Imitation is pervasive and automatic in humans.

2. Psychological models of imitation that assume an overlap or strong associative links between perception and action are supported by neural mirroring.

3. The core neural circuitry of imitation is composed of a higher-order visual area (the posterior part of the superior temporal sulcus) and by the fronto-parietal mirror neuron system.

4. Empathy is implemented by a simulation of the mental states of other people.

5. A large-scale network for empathy is composed of the mirror neuron system, the insula, and the limbic system.

6. Mirror neurons were selected because they provide the adaptive advantage of intersubjectivity.

FUTURE ISSUES

1. What are the anatomical locations and physiological properties of mirror neurons in humans? Depth electrode recordings in neurological patients may be able to investigate this issue.

2. How can we more precisely map the predictions of psychological models onto empirical findings from the neurosciences?

3. What are the developmental mechanisms that shape the mirror neuron system?

4. What are the factors that influence the ability to empathize with other people?

DISCLOSURE STATEMENT

The author is not aware of any biases that might be perceived as affecting the objectivity of this review.

ACKNOWLEDGMENTS

For generous support, I thank the Brain Mapping Medical Research Organization, Brain Mapping Support Foundation, Pierson-Lovelace Foundation, The Ahmanson Foundation, William M. and Linda R. Dietel Philanthropic Fund at the Northern Piedmont Community Foundation, Tamkin Foundation, Jennifer Jones-Simon Foundation, Capital Group Companies Charitable Foundation, Robson Family, and Northstar Fund.

LITERATURE CITED

Adolphs R. 2009. The social brain: neural basis of social knowledge. *Annu. Rev. Psychol.* 60:693–716

Akins CK, Klein ED, Zentall TR. 2002. Imitative learning in Japanese quail (*Coturnix japonica*) using the bidirectional control procedure. *Anim. Learn. Behav.* 30:275–81

Allen EA, Pasley BN, Duong T, Freeman RD. 2007. Transcranial magnetic stimulation elicits coupled neural and hemodynamic consequences. *Science* 317:1918–21

Allison T, Puce A, McCarthy G. 2000. Social perception from visual cues: role of the STS region. *Trends Cogn. Sci.* 4:267–78

Bargh JA, Chen M, Burrows L. 1996. Automaticity of social behavior: direct effects of trait construct and stereotype-activation on action. *J. Personal. Soc. Psychol.* 71:230–44

Bekkering H, Wohlschläger A, Gattis M. 2000. Imitation of gestures in children is goal-directed. *Q. J. Exp. Psychol. A* 53:153–64

Boysen ST, Himes GT. 1999. Current issues and emerging theories in animal cognition. *Annu. Rev. Psychol.* 50:683–705

Brass M, Bekkering H, Prinz W. 2001. Movement observation affects movement execution in a simple response task. *Acta Psychol. (Amst.)* 106:3–22

Brass M, Bekkering H, Wohlschläger A, Prinz W. 2000. Compatibility between observed and executed finger movements: comparing symbolic, spatial, and imitative cues. *Brain Cogn.* 44:124–43

Braten E. 2007. *Advances in Consciousness Research*. Amsterdam: John Benjamins

Buccino G, Vogt S, Ritzl A, Fink GR, Zilles K, et al. 2004. Neural circuits underlying imitation learning of hand actions: an event-related fMRI study. *Neuron* 42:323–34

Carr L, Iacoboni M, Dubeau MC, Mazziotta JC, Lenzi GL. 2003. Neural mechanisms of empathy in humans: a relay from neural systems for imitation to limbic areas. *Proc. Natl. Acad. Sci. USA* 100:5497–502

Chartrand TL, Bargh JA. 1999. The chameleon effect: the perception-behavior link and social interaction. *J. Personal. Soc. Psychol.* 76:893–910

Dapretto M, Davies MS, Pfeifer JH, Scott AA, Sigman M, et al. 2006. Understanding emotions in others: mirror neuron dysfunction in children with autism spectrum disorders. *Nat. Neurosci.* 9:28–30

de Montaigne M. 1575. *Essays*. Harmondsworth, UK: Penguin

de Waal FB. 2008. Putting the altruism back into altruism: the evolution of empathy. *Annu. Rev. Psychol.* 59:279–300

di Pellegrino G, Fadiga L, Fogassi L, Gallese V, Rizzolatti G. 1992. Understanding motor events: a neurophysiological study. *Exp. Brain Res.* 91:176–80

Dijksterhuis A. 2005. Why we are social animals: the high road to imitation as social glue. See Hurley & Chater 2005, 2:207–20

Dijksterhuis A, Bargh J, Miedema J. 2000. Of men and mackerels: attention and automatic behavior. In *Subjective Experience in Social Cognition and Behavior*, ed. H Bless, JP Forgas, pp. 36–51. Philadelphia, PA: Psychol. Press

Dijksterhuis A, van Knippenberg A. 1998. The relation between perception and behavior, or how to win a game of Trivial Pursuit. *J. Personal. Soc. Psychol.* 74:865–77

Eisenberg N. 2000. Emotion, regulation, and moral development. *Annu. Rev. Psychol.* 51:665–97

Fadiga L, Fogassi L, Pavesi G, Rizzolatti G. 1995. Motor facilitation during action observation: a magnetic stimulation study. *J. Neurophysiol.* 73:2608–11

Fanselow MS, Poulos AM. 2005. The neuroscience of mammalian associative learning. *Annu. Rev. Psychol.* 56:207–34

Ferrari PF, Gallese V, Rizzolatti G, Fogassi L. 2003. Mirror neurons responding to the observation of ingestive and communicative mouth actions in the monkey ventral premotor cortex. *Eur. J. Neurosci.* 17:1703–14

Ferrari PF, Rozzi S, Fogassi L. 2005. Mirror neurons responding to observation of actions made with tools in monkey ventral premotor cortex. *J. Cogn. Neurosci.* 17:212–26

Ferrari PF, Visalberghi E, Paukner A, Fogassi L, Ruggiero A, Suomi SJ. 2006. Neonatal imitation in rhesus macaques. *PLoS Biol.* 4:e302

Fogassi L, Ferrari PF, Gesierich B, Rozzi S, Chersi F, Rizzolatti G. 2005. Parietal lobe: from action organization to intention understanding. *Science* 308:662–67

Gallese V, Fadiga L, Fogassi L, Rizzolatti G. 1996. Action recognition in the premotor cortex. *Brain* 119(Pt. 2):593–609

Gazzola V, Aziz-Zadeh L, Keysers C. 2006. Empathy and the somatotopic auditory mirror system in humans. *Curr. Biol.* 16:1824–29

fMRI study that demonstrated that the reduced activity in putative mirror neuron areas in patients with autism correlates with the severity of the disease.

First article to describe mirror neurons. Although the term "mirror neuron" had not been coined yet, the cells described in this article are mirror neurons.

Describes single-cell recordings in macaques demonstrating that the majority of mirror neurons code the intention associated with an observed action, rather than the action itself.

Describes in detail the most important basic properties of mirror neurons and proposes the distinction between strictly congruent and broadly congruent mirror neurons.

Glimcher PW. 2005. Indeterminacy in brain and behavior. *Annu. Rev. Psychol.* 56:25–56

Goense JB, Logothetis NK. 2008. Neurophysiology of the BOLD fMRI signal in awake monkeys. *Curr. Biol.* 18:631–40

Goldman AI. 2006. *Simulating Minds: The Philosophy, Psychology, and Neuroscience of Mindreading.* New York: Oxford Univ. Press

Goldman AI, Sripada CS. 2005. Simulationist models of face-based emotion recognition. *Cognition* 94:193–213

Grafton ST, Arbib MA, Fadiga L, Rizzolatti G. 1996. Localization of grasp representations in humans by positron emission tomography. 2. Observation compared with imagination. *Exp. Brain Res.* 112:103–11

Heiser M, Iacoboni M, Maeda F, Marcus J, Mazziotta JC. 2003. The essential role of Broca's area in imitation. *Eur. J. Neurosci.* 17:1123–28

Herman L. 2002. Vocal, social, and self-imitation by bottlenose dolphins. In *Imitation in Animals and Artifacts*, ed. K Dautenhahn, C Nehaniv, pp. 63–106. Cambridge, MA: MIT Press

Heyes C. 2005. Imitation by association. See Hurley & Chater 2005, 1:157–76

Heyes C, Bird G, Johnson H, Haggard P. 2005. Experience modulates automatic imitation. *Brain Res. Cogn. Brain Res.* 22:233–40

Hommel B, Prinz W. 1997. *Theoretical Issues in Stimulus-Response Compatibility.* Amsterdam: Elsevier

Hurley S, Chater N. 2005. *Perspectives on Imitation: From Neuroscience to Social Science.* Cambridge, MA: MIT Press

Iacoboni M. 2005. Neural mechanisms of imitation. *Curr. Opin. Neurobiol.* 15:632–37

Iacoboni M. 2008. *Mirroring People.* New York: Farrar, Straus & Giroux

Iacoboni M, Dapretto M. 2006. The mirror neuron system and the consequences of its dysfunction. *Nat. Rev. Neurosci.* 7:942–51

Iacoboni M, Koski LM, Brass M, Bekkering H, Woods RP, et al. 2001. Reafferent copies of imitated actions in the right superior temporal cortex. *Proc. Natl. Acad. Sci. USA* 98:13995–99

Iacoboni M, Molnar-Szakacs I, Gallese V, Buccino G, Mazziotta JC, Rizzolatti G. 2005. Grasping the intentions of others with one's own mirror neuron system. *PLoS Biol.* 3:e79

Iacoboni M, Woods RP, Brass M, Bekkering H, Mazziotta JC, Rizzolatti G. 1999. Cortical mechanisms of human imitation. *Science* 286:2526–28

James W. 1890. *Principles of Psychology.* New York: Holt

Jellema T, Baker CI, Wicker B, Perrett DI. 2000. Neural representation for the perception of the intentionality of actions. *Brain Cogn.* 44:280–302

Kaplan JT, Iacoboni M. 2006. Getting a grip on other minds: mirror neurons, intention understanding and cognitive empathy. *Soc. Neurosci.* 1:175–83

Keysers C, Kohler E, Umiltà MA, Nanetti L, Fogassi L, Gallese V. 2003. Audiovisual mirror neurons and action recognition. *Exp. Brain Res.* 153:628–36

Keysers C, Perrett DI. 2004. Demystifying social cognition: a Hebbian perspective. *Trends Cogn. Sci.* 8:501–7

Kohler E, Keysers C, Umiltà MA, Fogassi L, Gallese V, Rizzolatti G. 2002. Hearing sounds, understanding actions: action representation in mirror neurons. *Science* 297:846–48

Koski L, Wohlschläger A, Bekkering H, Woods RP, Dubeau MC, et al. 2002. Modulation of motor and premotor activity during imitation of target-directed actions. *Cereb. Cortex* 12:847–55

LeDoux JA. 1996. *The Emotional Brain.* New York: Simon & Schuster

Lieberman MD. 2007. Social cognitive neuroscience: a review of core processes. *Annu. Rev. Psychol.* 58:259–89

Logothetis NK, Pauls J, Augath M, Trinath T, Oeltermann A. 2001. Neurophysiological investigation of the basis of the fMRI signal. *Nature* 412:150–57

Logothetis NK, Wandell BA. 2004. Interpreting the BOLD signal. *Annu. Rev. Physiol.* 66:735–69

Matelli M, Luppino G, Rizzolatti G. 1985. Patterns of cytochrome oxidase activity in the frontal agranular cortex of the macaque monkey. *Behav. Brain Res.* 18:125–36

Nadel J. 2002. Imitation and imitation recognition: functional use in preverbal infants and nonverbal children with autism. In *The Imitative Mind: Development, Evolution, and Brain Bases*, ed. AN Meltzoff, W Prinz, KW Fischer, G Hatano, pp. 42–62. London: Cambridge Univ. Press

Nehaniv C, Dautenhahn K. 2002. The correspondence problem. In *Imitation in Animals and Artifacts*, ed. K Dautenhahn, C Nehaniv, pp. 41–62. Cambridge, MA: MIT Press

Reviews not only the evidence on mirror neurons in macaques and humans, but also the evidence suggesting a mirror neuron deficit in autism.

This brain imaging study shows that human mirror neuron areas code differently the same action associated with different intentions.

Describes auditory responses in mirror neurons, demonstrating that mirror neurons also fire to the sound of action, even when the action is not seen.

Newman-Norlund RD, van Schie HT, van Zuijlen AM, Bekkering H. 2007. The mirror neuron system is more active during complementary compared with imitative action. *Nat. Neurosci.* 10:817–18

Niedenthal PM, Barsalou LW, Winkielman P, Krauth-Gruber S, Ric F. 2005. Embodiment in attitudes, social perception, and emotion. *Personal. Soc. Psychol. Rev.* 9:184–211

Nietzsche F. 1881. *Daybreak*. London: Cambridge Univ. Press

Passingham RE. 1993. *The Frontal Lobes and Voluntary Action*. New York: Oxford Univ. Press

Paukner A, Anderson JR, Borelli E, Visalberghi E, Ferrari PF. 2005. Macaques (*Macaca nemestrina*) recognize when they are being imitated. *Biol. Lett.* 1:219–22

Perrett DI, Harries MH, Bevan R, Thomas S, Benson PJ, et al. 1989. Frameworks of analysis for the neural representation of animate objects and actions. *J. Exp. Biol.* 146:87–113

Pfeifer JH, Iacoboni M, Mazziotta JC, Dapretto M. 2008. Mirroring others' emotions relates to empathy and interpersonal competence in children. *Neuroimage* 39:2076–85

Poe EA. 1982. *The Tell-Tale Heart and Other Writings*. New York: Bantam Books

Press C, Gillmeister H, Heyes C. 2007. Sensorimotor experience enhances automatic imitation of robotic action. *Proc. Biol. Sci.* 274:2639–44

Prinz W. 2005. An ideomotor approach to imitation. In *Perspectives on Imitation: From Neuroscience to Social Science*, ed. S Hurley, N Chater, pp. 141–56. Cambridge, MA: MIT Press

Proctor RW, Reeve TG. 1990. *Stimulus-Response Compatibility: An Integrated Perspective*. Amsterdam: Elsevier

Puce A, Allison T, Bentin S, Gore JC, McCarthy G. 1998. Temporal cortex activation in humans viewing eye and mouth movements. *J. Neurosci.* 18:2188–99

Puce A, Perrett D. 2003. Electrophysiology and brain imaging of biological motion. *Philos. Trans. R. Soc. Lond. B Biol. Sci.* 358:435–45

Rizzolatti G, Arbib MA. 1998. Language within our grasp. *Trends Neurosci.* 21:188–94

Rizzolatti G, Camarda R, Fogassi L, Gentilucci M, Luppino G, Matelli M. 1988. Functional organization of inferior area 6 in the macaque monkey. II. Area F5 and the control of distal movements. *Exp. Brain Res.* 71:491–507

Comprehensively reviews physiological properties and anatomical location of mirror neurons in macaques and putative mirror neuron areas in humans.

Rizzolatti G, Craighero L. 2004. The mirror-neuron system. *Annu. Rev. Neurosci.* 27:169–92

Rizzolatti G, Fadiga L, Gallese V, Fogassi L. 1996. Premotor cortex and the recognition of motor actions. *Brain Res. Cogn. Brain Res.* 3:131–41

Rizzolatti G, Fadiga L, Matelli M, Bettinardi V, Paulesu E, et al. 1996. Localization of grasp representations in humans by PET: 1. Observation versus execution. *Exp. Brain Res.* 111:246–52

Romanes GJ. 1883. *Mental Evolution in Animals*. London: Kegan Paul Trench

Smith A. 1759. *The Theory of Moral Sentiments*. Oxford, UK: Clarendon

Subiaul F, Cantlon JF, Holloway RL, Terrace HS. 2004. Cognitive imitation in rhesus macaques. *Science* 305:407–10

Tangney JP, Stuewig J, Mashek DJ. 2007. Moral emotions and moral behavior. *Annu. Rev. Psychol.* 58:345–72

Umiltà MA, Escola L, Intskirveli I, Grammont F, Rochat M, et al. 2008. When pliers become fingers in the monkey motor system. *Proc. Natl. Acad. Sci. USA* 105:2209–13

Describes mirror neurons responding to hidden actions.

Umiltà MA, Kohler E, Gallese V, Fogassi L, Fadiga L, et al. 2001. I know what you are doing. A neurophysiological study. *Neuron* 31:155–65

Voelkl B, Huber L. 2000. True imitation in marmosets. *Anim. Behav.* 60:195–202

Voelkl B, Huber L. 2007. Imitation as faithful copying of a novel technique in marmoset monkeys. *PLoS ONE* 2:e611

Wasserman EA, Miller RR. 1997. What's elementary about associative learning? *Annu. Rev. Psychol.* 48:573–607

Wittgenstein L. 1980. *Remarks on the Philosophy of Psychology*. Oxford, UK: Blackwell Sci.

Predicting Workplace Aggression and Violence

Julian Barling,[1] Kathryne E. Dupré,[2]
and E. Kevin Kelloway[3]

[1]School of Business, Queen's University, Kingston, Ontario, Canada K7L 3N6;
email: jbarling@business.queensu.ca

[2]Faculty of Business Administration, Memorial University of Newfoundland,
St. John's, Newfoundland, Canada A1B 3X5; email: kdupre@mun.ca

[3]Sobey School of Business, Saint Mary's University, Halifax, Nova Scotia,
Canada B3H 3C3; email: Kevin.kelloway@smu.ca

Annu. Rev. Psychol. 2009. 60:671–92

First published online as a Review in Advance on
September 15, 2008

The *Annual Review of Psychology* is online at
psych.annualreviews.org

This article's doi:
10.1146/annurev.psych.60.110707.163629

Key Words

myths, profiling, perceived injustice, displaced aggression, prevention

Abstract

Consistent with the relative recency of research on workplace aggression and the considerable media attention given to high-profile incidents, numerous myths about the nature of workplace aggression have emerged. In this review, we examine these myths from an evidence-based perspective, bringing greater clarity to our understanding of the predictors of workplace aggression. We conclude by pointing to the need for more research focusing on construct validity and prevention issues as well as for methodologies that minimize the likelihood of mono-method bias and that strengthen the ability to make causal inferences.

Contents

Workplace aggression: any behavior initiated by employees that is intended to harm another individual in their organization or the organization itself and that the target is motivated to avoid; sometimes differentiated from workplace violence in its emphasis on psychological aggression

INTRODUCTION

Just why employees might choose to engage in aggression is a question that has captured the public's imagination for many decades. As a result of media exposure given to dramatic workplace homicides, workplace aggression has received considerable public attention, and many myths surrounding this issue have emerged. Why people may choose to behave aggressively in organizations is an empirical question that has been confronted for only approximately 15 years (Barling 1996), and in this review, we use the results of this research to challenge widespread myths.

MYTH #1: WORKPLACE AGGRESSION AND VIOLENCE ARE INTERCHANGEABLE

Definitional Issues

Numerous reviewers have commented on the proliferation of conceptual and operational definitions of workplace aggression (e.g., Keashley & Jagatic 2003, Kelloway et al. 2006, Neuman & Baron 1998, Robinson & Greenberg 1998, Schat & Kelloway 2005, Snyder et al. 2005). Labels such as emotional abuse (Keashly 1998, 2001; Keashly & Harvey 2005), workplace incivility (Andersson & Pearson 1999), workplace violence (e.g., Rogers & Kelloway 1997; Schat & Kelloway 2000, 2003), antisocial work behavior (Giacalone & Greenberg 1997, O'Leary-Kelly et al. 2000), psychological abuse (Sheehan et al. 1990), bullying (Einarsen 1999, Hoel et al. 1999, Rayner & Cooper 2006, Zapf et al. 2003), and workplace harassment (e.g., Richman et al. 1999, Rospenda 2002, Rospenda & Richman 2005) are used to describe similar and often overlapping behavioral domains. These definitions vary along several dimensions, including the consideration given to perpetrators, actions, intentionality, targets, and outcomes (Snyder et al. 2005). In addition, differing degrees of severity ranging from physical assault (e.g., Kraus et al. 1995) to threats of assault (Jenkins 1996) and psychological aggression (e.g., being yelled at or cursed at; Baron & Neuman 1998, Rogers & Kelloway 1997, Schat & Kelloway 2000, 2003) are included in the realm of aggressive behaviors (Buss 1961).

Schat & Kelloway (2005, p. 191) offered a general definition of workplace aggression as "behavior by an individual or individuals within or outside an organization that is intended to physically or psychologically harm a worker or workers and occurs in a work-related context." They suggested that this definition (*a*) was consistent with definitions used in the general human aggression literature (e.g., Baron & Richardson 1994, Berkowitz 1993, Geen 2001), (*b*) was sufficiently general to include a wide range of physical and nonphysical behaviors that comprise workplace aggression, and (*c*) encompassed aggressive behaviors enacted by a variety of sources within (e.g., supervisors, coworkers) and outside of (e.g., clients, customers, patients) the organization (e.g., Greenberg & Barling 1999, LeBlanc & Kelloway 2002).

Although the terms "workplace aggression" and "workplace violence" are often used interchangeably, they are distinguishable. Conceptually, Schat & Kelloway (2005) suggested that workplace violence is a distinct form of workplace aggression that comprises behaviors that are intended to cause physical harm (e.g.,

physical assaults and/or the threat of assault). By definition, all violent behaviors are aggressive whereas not all aggressive behaviors are violent. This distinction is frequently made in research on both general (e.g., Anderson & Bushman 2002) and workplace (e.g., Greenberg & Barling 1999, Neuman & Baron 1998) aggression, and various authors (e.g., LeBlanc & Kelloway 2002, Schat & Kelloway 2003) provide factor-analytic evidence that physically and nonphysically aggressive behaviors are empirically related but distinct constructs (Barling et al. 1987). As is the case with romantic relationships (Cano et al. 1998, Murphy & O'Leary 1989), researchers have frequently noted the potential for aggressive behavior to escalate into a physical confrontation in both marital relationships (Murphy & O'Leary 1989) and workplace contexts (Barling 1996, Dupré & Barling 2006, Glomb 2002, Herschovis & Barling 2006), and victims of workplace physical violence are likely to have experienced prior nonphysical aggressive acts (Schat et al. 2006).

Prevalence Estimates

Prevalence estimates, invariably based on self-reports of victimization, also point to the need to distinguish between workplace aggression and violence. Prevalence estimates for physical violence range between just over 1% (Duhart 2001) to 5% of the workforce (U.S. Postal Serv. Comm. Safe Secure Workplace 2000) being assaulted over a 12-month span. In contrast, for nonphysical aggression, estimates range between 9% (Einarsen & Skogstad 1996) and 70% (Einarsen & Raknes 1997). In a study of Canadian public-sector employees, 69% responded that they had experienced some form of verbal workplace aggression (Pizzino 2002); in a study of public-sector employees in the United States, 71% indicated that within the past five years they had been victims of workplace incivility (Cortina et al. 2001).

In contrast, there are far fewer instances of workplace violence. One of the few datasets not based on self-reports of victimization indicates

Workplace violence: similar to workplace aggression, but the behavior enacted usually is more physical in nature

Individual differences: factors (e.g., trait anger) that differ across people and predispose some to respond in similar ways across situations

that there were 516 workplace homicides across all employees in the United States in 2006, a decrease of more than 50% from 1994 (Bur. Labor Stat. 2007). Between 1993 and 1999, the Bureau of Justice Statistics showed that aggression within workplaces assessed in the National Crime Victimization Survey (i.e., simple assault, aggravated assault, robbery, and rape/sexual assault) comprised 18% of all violent crime in the United States (Duhart 2001). However, during this same period, workplace aggression that fell into this category of violent crime decreased by approximately 44%, with each form of aggression reported as lower in 1999 than in 1993 (Duhart 2001).

Nonetheless, the widespread use of nonrepresentative samples, discrepancies in reporting time frames, variations in defining and operationalizing workplace aggression, as well as challenges associated with obtaining data on forms of aggression that are less visible than physical workplace aggression (such as psychological and verbal aggression; Barling 1996, Beale et al. 1996, Schat et al. 2006, VandenBos & Bulatao 1996) make it difficult to assess the actual prevalence of workplace aggression and violence. Accordingly, Schat et al. (2006) addressed these issues recently in their nationally representative probability sample of American workers. They reported that 6% of the workforce reported incidents of physical violence over a 12-month period. In contrast, 41.4% of the same respondents reported incidents of psychological aggression. Just over 13% of the sample reported experiencing workplace aggression on a weekly basis, while only 1.3% experienced violent acts on a weekly basis.

Thus, we conclude that although workplace aggression occurs relatively frequently, workplace violence is an infrequent occurrence. Indeed, as a point of comparison, more workers die each year because of occupational safety issues than by workplace violence. In turn, occupational diseases may claim more lives than do homicide and fatal accidents combined (Herbert & Landrigan 2000).

MYTH #2: PROFILING THE AGGRESSIVE EMPLOYEE

Consistent with the public attention focused on workplace aggression, stereotypes about the "typical" perpetrator have developed. In general, the resulting profile portrays the typical perpetrator as likely to be a young, male, white individual with poor self-esteem and an aggressive personality, with substance abuse issues and a fascination with weapons. Despite the questionable value of this approach (Day & Catano 2006), this profile may sometimes be used in personnel selection as a guide for excluding potentially aggressive individuals from the workplace (*N. Y. Times* 1993). Martinko et al. (2006) note, for example, that in at least some organizations, females are disproportionately employed in potentially stressful positions, presumably because they are less likely to respond to conflict and stress with aggression. Although the seeming simplicity of a profile makes it an attractive tool to practitioners (Gladwell 2006), understanding whether profiles have any predictive validity or utility is of considerable social importance from scientific, practical, and ethical or legal perspectives.

In this section, we examine existing data linking various demographic and individual-differences variables with workplace aggression. The possibility that such a link exists is reinforced by findings that individual differences may explain as much as 62% of the variance in workplace aggression in some studies (Douglas & Martinko 2001).

Gender

One of the most consistent findings in the social and behavioral sciences is that males tend to be more aggressive and violent than females (Eagly & Steffan 1986, Geen 2001, Martinko et al. 2006). As a result, it is not surprising that research focusing on workplace aggression investigates possible gender effects, providing a large database from which initial conclusions may be drawn. Most studies show that males engage in more workplace aggression than females (e.g., Baron et al. 1999, Dupré & Barling 2006, Haines et al. 2006, McFarlin et al. 2001). A few studies, however, show nonsignificant correlations between gender and workplace aggression (e.g., Douglas & Martinko 2001, Inness et al. 2005). Complicating the ability to derive any conclusions are data showing that, when workplace bullying is the outcome, females are more aggressive than men in some studies (Namie & Namie 2000) but are less aggressive in others (Parkins et al. 2006).

Age

A consistent finding within the social and behavioral sciences is that age is associated with the perpetration of aggression and violence (e.g., Feshbach 1997). One possible explanation for this is that with increasing age, people better understand the consequences of their behavior and are more capable of exerting control over any expression of anger. Studies on the link between age and workplace aggression yield mixed results. Whereas some studies yield a negative correlation between age and workplace aggression (e.g., Haines et al. 2006, Inness et al. 2005, McFarlin et al. 2001), others yield no significant correlation (e.g., Douglas & Martinko 2001, Dupré & Barling 2006, Greenberg & Barling 1999). Greenberg & Barling's (1999) data extend these findings by focusing on different targets, showing that there is no correlation between age and workplace aggression targeted against a supervisor, coworker, or subordinate.

Race

An integral part of the stereotypical profile of the violence-prone employee is that he is white; despite this, there are very few data examining this issue. McFarlin and colleagues' (2001) data support this assumption, but data on bullying (as opposed to workplace aggression) do not support this idea (Parkins et al. 2006). Last, while noting that her data suffer from "opportunity bias" (the sample was predominantly white and male), Glomb (2002) showed that beyond between-group differences, the perpetrator and victim were usually of the same race. This finding provides some support for Hershcovis & Barling's (2007) relational model of workplace aggression, which posits that the nature of the aggression is dependent on characteristics of the relationship between perpetrator and target.

Socioeconomic Status

Socioeconomic status is invariably reflected through three variables: education, income, and occupation (Gallo & Matthews 2003). McFarlin et al. (2001) showed a minimal but significant negative correlation between income (but not education) and verbal and physical aggression. Douglas & Martinko (2001) showed no significant link between workplace aggression and either education or profession, and Greenberg & Barling (1999) failed to find a link between either education or income and aggression against a supervisor, peer, or subordinate. Thus, there is minimal support for a link between socioeconomic status and workplace aggression in the few studies investigating this issue.

Colocation

Although not part of the stereotypical profile of the aggressive employee, one additional variable warrants consideration because it is associated with workplace aggression in several studies. Specifically, there is a positive correlation between the time the perpetrator and target spend together and workplace aggression, whether within subordinate-supervisor dyads (Dupré & Barling 2006, Glomb 2002, Harvey & Keashley 2003) or between coworkers (Glomb & Liao 2003). The additional likelihood that the time spent between perpetrator and target moderates the influence of subjective work experiences reinforces the importance of assessing the simultaneous influence of these predictor variables.

The individual differences described above all reflect demographic characteristics, broadly defined; what follows is a discussion of the possible relationship between personality attributes and workplace aggression.

Negative Affect

Negative affect reflects the individual predisposition to experience negative psychological states such as hostility, sadness, and anxiety; it is subclinical in nature and is differentiated from clinical experiences such as depression. Studies have investigated whether a link exists between negative affect and workplace aggression, consistent with its frequent focus within organizational behavior in general, and findings provide support for this link (Hepworth & Towler 2004, Hershcovis et al. 2007). This phenomenon extends beyond the supervisor-subordinate dyad to peers in workgroups (Glomb & Liao 2003); in addition, negative affect also moderates the effects of perceived injustice on retributive behaviors (Skarlicki et al. 1999).

Self-Esteem

Anderson & Bushman (2002) note that it has long been an article of faith that individuals low in self-esteem will be more susceptible to aggression in general, and there is some empirical support for a link between self-esteem and workplace aggression as well (Harvey & Keashly 2003, Inness et al. 2005). Nonetheless, the nature of the self-esteem must be accounted for, as an inflated or unstable self-esteem (which is akin to narcissism) is likely to predict aggression if self-esteem is threatened (Anderson & Bushman 2002). Because narcissism is associated with counterproductive workplace behaviors (which include psychologically aggressive behaviors; Judge et al. 2006, Penney & Spector 2002), the nature of the self-esteem needs to be addressed in future research.

Trait Anger and the Aggressive Personality

Some individuals are predisposed to respond to what they see as provocation with aggres-sion (Dill et al. 1997, Spielberger 1991), and research reveals consistent and strong correlations between trait anger and workplace aggression (e.g., Douglas & Martinko 2001, Glomb & Liao 2003, Hepworth & Towler 2004, Hershcovis et al. 2007, Parkins et al. 2006). Closely related to trait anger is the possible link between workplace aggression and an aggressive or hostile personality. Last, personal attitudes that sanction revenge as an acceptable behavior predict workplace aggression (Douglas & Martinko 2001, Hepworth & Towler 2004).

As noted above, one of the most consistent predictors of the enactment of aggression is perceived provocation. Closely aligned to this is the cognitive appraisal of, or causal reasoning about (Bing et al. 2007, Martinko et al. 2002), the precipitating interpersonal event. Several studies reveal a relationship between perceptions of hostile intent and aggression (e.g., Douglas & Martinko 2001, Epps & Kendall 1995).

As is the case in virtually all research focusing on the prediction of workplace aggression, all of these studies assume, and test, a linear explanation for the relationship between individual differences and workplace aggression. Geddes & Callister (2007) challenge this assumption, positing that higher levels of anger expression in some cases might have beneficial personal and organizational outcomes. Future research on trait anger (and other predictors) and workplace aggression may well benefit substantially from theorizing and research on possible nonlinear effects.

Personal History with Aggression

Social learning theory has long held that early exposure to aggression would have significant implications for subsequent enactment of aggression (e.g., Bandura 1973). Greenberg & Barling (1999) showed that a history of aggression predicts current aggression against coworkers and supervisors (Douglas & Martinko 2001, Inness et al. 2005). Given that other individual differences moderate the influence of negative workplace experiences on workplace aggression (e.g., Inness et al. 2005, Skarlicki et al. 1999), each of these person variables might well moderate the effects of perceived interpersonal provocation, an issue worthy of investigation in future research. In a study that reinforces the importance of separating the target of aggression (Hershcovis et al. 2007), Greenberg & Barling (1999) showed no effect of a history of aggression on current aggression against a coworker or subordinate.

Multivariate Analyses

There are ample data from which conclusions about workplace aggression might be drawn. However, doing so on the basis of zero-order correlations may capitalize on chance and perpetuate potentially erroneous stereotypes. In addition, as noted above, each of these person variables might moderate the effects of perceived interpersonal provocation (e.g., Inness et al. 2005, Skarlicki et al. 1999). Importantly, therefore, some studies provide a more nuanced multivariate perspective. In this respect, multivariate analyses such as Hershcovis and colleagues' (2007) meta-analysis of the predictors of workplace aggression and Inness and colleagues' (2005) within-person between-jobs analysis provide the basis from which appropriate conclusions about the relative importance of these demographic and individual difference variables might be drawn.

Beyond the ethical and legal concerns that would emerge from any attempt to base selection decisions on demographic profiles of potentially aggressive employees and to exclude them from potential employment during the selection process, the empirical data provide no support for such an approach (Day & Catano 2006). Even if such an approach were attempted, the resulting profile would likely be so broad as to be of little practical value (Paul & Townsend 1998), or as Gladwell (2006) concludes about attempts to profile aggressive dogs, successful profiling would require "... a more exacting set of generalizations to be more exactingly applied."

In contrast to the marginal findings with demographic variables, there are consistent relationships between personality variables (e.g., trait anger, negative affect) and workplace aggression, supporting claims that such information might be useful in the selection process. At the same time, however, Inness et al.'s (2005) observation from their within-subject between-jobs analyses suggests that workplace experiences explain substantially more variance in aggression than do personality variables, which calls into question the practical utility of pre-employment screening (Lanyon & Goodstein 2004) and reinforces the use of approaches that focus on enhancing the quality of work experiences and management behaviors (Litzky et al. 2006).

MYTH #3: MENTAL ILLNESS IS A FACTOR IN WORKPLACE VIOLENCE

One frequently held belief is that individuals who engage in acts of workplace violence suffer from some form of mental illness. Such beliefs are sustained in several ways. First, media stories about workplace violence incidents usually implicate mental illness (e.g., alcoholism, depression; Graham 1991, Halbfinger 2003, Stuart 1992). Second, from a scientific perspective, questions about the possible link between mental illness and violence or aggression in general are by no means new (Harris & Lurigo 2007), and there is a substantial body of research on this general topic. Surprisingly, therefore, there is much less empirical research assessing the possible link between different forms of mental illness and workplace aggression. The research that has been conducted has focused primarily on anxiety, depression, and substance abuse (specifically, alcohol).

A substantial body of research shows a link between alcohol use and general violence (Lipsey et al. 1997), and some research has been conducted addressing the link between alcohol use and workplace aggression. With few exceptions (e.g., Chen & Spector 1992), most studies

Profiling: the use of personal or demographic characteristics to determine whether an individual might be likely to become aggressive or violent in the workplace; often believed by proponents to be based on scientific evidence

support such a link. For example, McFarlin et al. (2001) showed substantial effects of the number of days of alcohol use in the past month as well as the number of days of heavy drinking on workplace aggression. Greenberg & Barling (1999) refined this, showing a link between quantity of alcohol consumed and aggression against a coworker. Moreover, the amount of alcohol consumed moderated the effects of employees' job insecurity and procedural injustice on aggression against subordinates and coworkers (Greenberg & Barling 1999).

Only one study investigated the link between anxiety and workplace bullying (Parkins et al. 2006), and this study showed no significant relationship.

Given the pervasive belief implicating mental illness in workplace aggression, the paucity of empirical research is somewhat surprising. One possible reason for this is the reluctance by behavioral scientists to straddle disciplinary boundaries (in this case, clinical and organizational psychology); however, generating a robust body of knowledge on the role of mental illness will require just such boundary spanning. The available data suggest that only modest links exist between some forms of mental illness (substance abuse) and workplace aggression, and mental illness plays no substantial role in the prediction of workplace aggression. Paraphrasing Friedman's (2006) observation about the link between mental illness and context-free aggression, then, we conclude by emphasizing that "most people who are violent are not mentally ill, and most people who are mentally ill are not violent."

MYTH #4: WORKPLACE AGGRESSION OCCURS BETWEEN SUBORDINATES AND SUPERVISORS

March 6, 1998: Before killing himself, a Connecticut Lottery Corporation Accountant searched for and then killed the Corporation's president and three of his supervisors (Springer 1998).

Typical media accounts of workplace aggression emphasize those instances in which an or-

ganizational member kills a workplace supervisor, perpetuating the myth that workplace aggression is a function of subordinate-supervisor relationships. However, situations such as the one described above are atypical (LeBlanc & Kelloway 2002). Although workplace aggression does tend to be target specific (Hershcovis et al. 2007, Inness et al. 2005), the perpetrator and victim within any instance of workplace aggression can vary considerably.

Sygnatur & Toscano (2000) found that 67% of workplace homicides occur during robberies and other crimes perpetrated by organizational outsiders, 15% were perpetrated by employees or former employees, 8% by customers or clients, 7% by acquaintances, and 4% by relatives. Peek-Asa et al. (1998) found that the perpetrators in more than 90% of nonfatal workplace assaults were not organizational insiders but rather were members of the public. Greenberg & Barling (1999) reported that 82%, 74%, and 76% of the 136 men who took part in their study admitted to some form of psychological aggression against coworkers, subordinates, and supervisors, respectively. Regarding insider aggression, Baron et al. (1999) found that although individuals were most likely to aggress against a coworker or their immediate supervisor, they also aggressed against subordinates and other supervisors (see sidebar Picket Line Violence).

Aggression in the workplace has been categorized into four types that are based on the perpetrator's relationship to the victim (Braverman 1999, Calif. Occup. Saf. Health Admin. 1995). Type I occurs when the perpetrator has no legitimate relationship with the targeted employees or organization and usually has entered the work environment to commit a criminal act (e.g., armed robbery, shoplifting). More than 65% of workplace homicides occur during a robbery (Sygnatur & Toscano 2000). For public servants, violence was most likely from clients, residents, or other members of the public (approximately 71% of those reporting workplace violence) rather than from coworkers (approximately 34% of those reporting workplace violence) (participants could report violence from both sources; Public Serv. Comm. 2002). Certain factors (e.g., contact with the public, handling money, working alone or in small numbers) increase the risk for this type of aggression (Castillo & Jenkins 1994, Davis 1987, Kraus 1987). Type II workplace aggression occurs when the offender has a legitimate relationship with the organization and commits an act of aggression while being served, cared for, or taught by members of the organization (e.g., customers, clients, inmates, students, or patients; LeBlanc & Kelloway 2002), and this type of aggression accounts for approximately 60% of nonfatal workplace assaults (Peek-Asa & Howard 1999). With regard to occupational context, employees who provide service, care, advice, or education are at greatest increased risk for assault (e.g., Amandus et al. 1996, Canad. Cent. Occup. Health Saf. 1999, LeBlanc & Kelloway 2002), especially if clients, customers, inmates, or patients are experiencing frustration, insecurity, or stress (Lamberg 1996, Nat. Inst. Occup. Saf. Health 2002, Painter 1987).

Type III aggression occurs when the perpetrator is an insider (e.g., a current or former employee of the organization who targets another past or present employee). Media accounts of workplace aggression typically focus on subordinate–supervisor aggression, and insider-initiated aggression has received significant research attention. When employees are the perpetrators, certain work experiences or situational factors consistently predict their aggression. Employees' workplace aggression has been linked to situational factors such as job stress (e.g., Chen & Spector 1992, Fox & Spector 1999, Glomb 2002), surveillance (Greenberg & Barling 1999), and supervision that is abusive (Inness et al. 2005), unfair (Baron et al. 1999), and overcontrolling (Dupré & Barling 2006). Role stressors such as role ambiguity and role conflict have been shown to be related to workplace bullying (Einarsen et al. 1994) and workplace aggression (e.g., Bedeian et al. 1980, Chen & Spector 1992). In their meta-analysis, Hershcovis et al. (2007) confirmed that role conflict significantly predicted

PICKET LINE VIOLENCE

Violence that occurs during the course of a labor dispute is frequently overlooked in discussions of workplace violence. In characterizing picket line violence, Thieblot et al. (1999) point out that labor disputes tend to involve two large categories of violent acts: confrontational and purposeful. Confrontational violence is that which breaks out at the spur of the moment during a conflict. In contrast, Thieblot et al. (1999) describe purposeful violence as planned and deliberate; in essence, violence can be used as a tool in a labor dispute.

The incidence of violence during a labor dispute appears to have diminished over time. Francis et al. (2006) report a marked decrease in incidence post 1995. However, violence remains a potent possibility during a labor dispute. Indeed, there is some speculation that picket line violence is "legitimated" by labor legislation and/or court rulings that do not discipline the participants in violent confrontations (Francis et al. 2006). A labor dispute is perhaps one of the few remaining aspects of a modern workplace in which violent confrontation is tolerated and even expected by the participants.

workplace aggression. Last, Type IV aggression occurs when the offender has a current or previous legitimate relationship with an employee of the organization (e.g., current or former spouse, relative, friend, or acquaintance). Lifetime prevalence rates of partner violence have been estimated at 25% for women and 8% for men (Tjaden & Thoennes 2000), and between 1% and 3% of all incidents of workplace violence are perpetrated by intimate acquaintances of the victim (Duhart 2001). Partner violence has considerable implications for both the individual and the workplace (Swanberg et al. 2006) (see sidebar Intimate Partner Violence).

Consequently, the belief that most workplace aggression occurs within the supervisor–subordinate relationship is incorrect, and there are both similar and unique predictors of aggression against different workplace targets (Inness et al. 2008). The search for a comprehensive understanding of the nature, prediction, and prevention of workplace aggression is a much more pervasive problem than this myth conveys, and future research needs to

INTIMATE PARTNER VIOLENCE

Although widely cited, the CAL/OSHA framework excludes other known sources of workplace violence. Swanberg et al. (2006), for example, note the possibility for family or intimate partner violence to spill over into the workplace, with adverse consequences for both the individual victims and their employing organizations.

For many individuals, work is a "social address," and partners or family members know where an individual works and, frequently, his/her schedule. Even when individuals separate from a partner, they often maintain their employment and, as a result, can be easily located. Lifetime prevalence rates of partner violence have been estimated at 25% for women and 8% for men (Tjaden & Thoennes 2000). Intimate partners are identified as the perpetrator in approximately 1% to 3% of all workplace violence incidents (Duhart 2001).

Intimate partner violence is exhibited in at least three predominant ways in the workplace: work disruption, stalking, and on-the-job harassment (Swanberg et al. 2006). Work disruption comprises activities that interfere with attendance or promptness at work. Stalking comprises unwanted and repeated threatening behaviors such as following someone, vandalizing property, or leaving unwanted messages. On-the-job harassment more typically includes the perpetrator appearing at the workplace and directly interfering with the victim's work.

focus on the many different relational contexts at work.

MYTH #5: WORKPLACE AGGRESSION IS RANDOM, UNPREDICTABLE, AND HENCE, NOT PREVENTABLE

The belief that workplace aggression occurs randomly is voiced frequently; fears that mental illness plays a major part in the perpetration of workplace aggression would exacerbate this. Yet the data suggest otherwise. As discussed above, some demographic factors and individual-difference variables are associated with workplace aggression. The consistency of these predictions alone belies the notion that workplace aggression is random and unpredictable.

Organizational injustice: the belief that one has been treated unfairly from a procedural, interpersonal, or distributive perspective

Much research has focused on situational or organizational predictors of aggression at work, with organizational injustice receiving considerable attention as a possible predictor of workplace aggression. Procedural and interpersonal justice are related to workplace aggression (e.g., Berry et al. 2007, Dupré & Barling 2006, Greenberg & Barling 1999, Hershcovis et al. 2007, Inness et al. 2005, Neuman & Baron 1998, Skarlicki & Folger 1997). In their meta-analysis, Hershcovis et al. (2007) found that interactional injustice was a stronger predictor of workplace aggression than was procedural injustice, and after controlling for interactional injustice, the effect of procedural injustice became nonsignificant. Abusive supervision (Inness et al. 2005) and other poor leadership behaviors (Hershcovis et al. 2007), along with stressors such as role conflict, role overload, role ambiguity, work constraints, and job autonomy (Bowling & Beehr 2006), also predict the enactment of workplace aggression.

Although research has focused on employees' perceived injustice, it may also play a salient role in client interactions (Smith et al. 1999). Clients who are denied service, for example, may be more likely to experience this denial as unjust and to commit acts of aggression.

As noted above, the role of individual differences has also been studied intensively, and there may be an interaction between situational and individual factors in the prediction of workplace aggression. Importantly, studies show that individual differences exacerbate the effects of workplace experiences (Aquino et al. 2004, Folger & Skarlicki 1998, Inness et al. 2005, Skarlicki et al. 1999).

Contextual factors outside of workplace experiences, such as societal influences, organizational climate, and organizational tolerance for workplace aggression (e.g., Aquino & Lamertz 2004), are also related to workplace aggression. Dietz et al. (2003) examined the effects of community-level violent crimes and plant-level procedural justice climate as predictors of workplace aggression. They showed that community violence level predicted workplace aggression whereas plant-level procedural justice did not. More recently, Spector et al. (2007) found that perceived violence climate was related to physical and verbal aggression experienced by nurses, along with injury from violence and perceptions of workplace danger.

Given the range of demographic, individual-difference, occupational, and situational predictors of workplace aggression identified over the past decade and evidence relating to the target-specific nature of the act (Hershcovis et al. 2007), the notion that acts of workplace aggression are random, and therefore unpredictable and not preventable, is not sustainable.

MYTH #6: LAYOFFS CAUSE WORKPLACE AGGRESSION

The "stress and potential violence triggered by the wave of corporate layoffs" is now the focus of employers in the prevention of violence at work. (Lombardi 1994, p. 16)

Contradicting the belief that workplace aggression is random, layoffs are often cited as major predictors of workplace aggression. Discussions about this possible link were frequent during the 1990s.

Research on workplace aggression was precipitated by a series of shootings in the U.S. post office (U. S. Post. Serv. Comm. Safe Secure Workpl. 2000) during the late 1980s and early 1990s (Kelloway et al. 2006). These well-publicized events focused public and research attention on workplace violence, resulting in the widely used phrase, "going postal," which typically denotes an employee losing control over his/her emotions and engaging in violent acts. The empirical status of this myth is important because it is so pervasive and persistent, suggesting that profiling may be a viable preventive strategy (*N. Y. Times* 1993) and extending the question of whether aggression is more likely to occur in some contexts.

Notions about the salience of layoffs per se was undoubtedly reinforced by the frequency of media reports linking acts of workplace aggression to downsizing and layoffs. Evidence-based conclusions about the role of layoffs and other workplace experiences are clearly needed.

Research evidence disputes any direct effect for the role of layoffs. Although layoffs are associated with anger, depression, and aggression among both victims and survivors, it is not the layoff per se that is implicated in subsequent acts of workplace aggression but rather the manner in which layoffs are conducted. If layoffs are not conducted appropriately, feelings of injustice and anger probably emerge (e.g., Catalano et al. 1997, Folger 1993, Vinokur et al. 1996), which are more likely to predict aggression than are the layoffs specifically (Brockner 2006).

Overall, therefore, there is no support for the notion that layoffs per se are associated with workplace aggression; indeed, it is more likely that most layoffs are not accompanied by workplace aggression, dispelling the myth that layoffs are a major predictor of workplace aggression. In contrast, the perceived fairness with which layoffs are implemented is critical, supporting the role of perceived injustice in workplace aggression.

Lastly, it is worth noting that the phrase "going postal" is somewhat of a misnomer: The prevalence rate of workplace violence, workplace aggression, and workplace homicide in the U.S. Postal Service is actually quite a bit lower than in the general workforce (U. S. Post. Serv. Comm. Safe Secure Workpl. 2000).

MYTH #7: WORKPLACE AGGRESSION WILL NOT BE REDUCED, IT WILL BE DISPLACED

"Work is, by its very nature, about violence—to the spirit as well as to the body. It is about ulcers as well as accidents, about shouting matches as well as fistfights, about nervous breakdowns as well as kicking the dog around. It is, above all (or beneath all) about daily humiliation." (Terkel 1974, p. xi)

Informed by his extensive interviews with working people, Terkel's (1974) observation

"Going postal": denotes the situation in which organizational members suddenly become extremely violent; derived after several incidents in the U.S. Postal Service in the late 1980s involving workplace homicides

Displaced aggression: the decision to direct one's aggression against a target other than the perceived provocateur, usually a target that is of lower power or status than oneself to limit the likelihood of retaliation

Situational specificity: factors inherent in a particular situation that make it likely that the same individuals will respond in unique ways within different situations or contexts

reinforces the notion that violence is embedded in the very fabric of work and that displaced aggression is an inherent part of this violence. Conceptually, displaced aggression is an idea that has its roots in classic psychodynamic theory, which initially represented an attempt to account for the unconscious motives underlying the behavior in question. This is markedly different from the way in which displaced aggression is typically dealt with in the literature on workplace aggression, where it is more about the target of aggression than the motives for the aggressive behavior. It occurs when an act of aggression is directed not toward the original source of the provocation, but instead toward a person or object that is targeted due to being in a particular place at a certain time and of a lower status than the instigator (Bushman & Baumeister 1998, Bushman et al. 2005, Marcus-Newhall et al. 2000, Miller et al. 2003, Pedersen 2006).

A few studies have examined displaced aggression. Even minor provocations may lead to displaced aggression. Bushman et al. (2005) found that individuals who ruminated about a previous experience that caused annoyance and frustration and then encountered a minor triggering event were more likely to engage in displaced aggression.

Although research findings are limited, they are mixed regarding the notion of displaced workplace aggression. Research and theory have suggested that workplace aggression is target specific (Barling 1996, Bennett & Robinson 2000, Greenberg & Barling 1999, Hershcovis et al. 2007, Inness et al. 2005, Robinson & Bennett 1995), and a target-specific response to a perceived provocation would be antithetical to the idea of displaced aggression. Yet there is some support for the displaced aggression (e.g., Mitchell & Ambrose 2007). Hoobler & Brass (2006) found that the family members of employees who were the target of abusive supervision reported greater undermining directed at family members. Hoobler & Brass (2006) asked subordinates about confronting their abusive supervisors, and found that the more abusive they perceived their supervisors

to be, the less likely subordinates were to confront them. Moreover, research shows that following perceived provocations, responses can be either person directed or organizational directed (Robinson & Bennett 1995).

Interpretations from prior research are difficult, however, because much of the research has explored the issue of aggression without specifying the target of the aggression (Hershcovis et al. 2007). Nonetheless, the most appropriate conclusion that is target-specific and displaced aggression need not be antithetical: Although considerable research supports the notion that target-specific aggression is a response to perceived provocations, under some conditions, individuals may choose to displace their aggression away from the provocateur. Rather than pursuing one or the other of these seemingly conflicting hypotheses, an investigation of the conditions under which aggression is likely to be target specific or displaced would best further the understanding of workplace aggression prediction.

MYTH #8: WORKPLACE AGGRESSION SPILLS OVER ACROSS CONTEXTS

Somewhat consistent with the idea of displaced aggression, one of the most enduring and intriguing questions concerning human aggression is whether people who are aggressive in one context or relationship are likely to be aggressive in other contexts or relationships because aggression is a function of the person. Or, conversely, is aggression a function of the situation, such that individuals will be aggressive in one relationship or context but not in another? In a sense, this question contrasts two different explanations for workplace aggression: situational specificity (which assumes that aggression is purposive and goal directed) and individual differences. As evident throughout this review, there is much research on individual and relational predictors of workplace aggression. Nonetheless, to be able to confront the questions posed by this myth, studies are required that focus on aggression across contexts and/or relationships while taking into account dispositional factors.

Greenberg & Barling (1999) reported significant correlations between aggression against supervisors, coworkers, and subordinates, providing initial support for individual-difference explanations. Nonetheless, the effects of perceived provocation did not spill over across contexts, suggesting the importance of situational specificity explanations. Inness and colleagues (2005) provided a more robust context in which this question could be examined. They focused on 105 employees who were moonlighting simultaneously in two separate jobs, each with a different supervisor. Personal factors (age, history of aggression) predicted a modest level of the variance in the primary and secondary jobs, although no significant correlation emerged in workplace aggression against the two different supervisors in the two jobs. Moreover, the situational predictors of supervisor-directed aggression (abusive supervision) were target specific. Inness et al. (2005) concluded by noting that situational factors, in comparison with personal factors, accounted for substantially more of the variance in workplace aggression.

CONCEPTUAL AND RESEARCH DIRECTIONS

Despite the fact that workplace aggression is by no means a recent phenomenon, research has addressed the issue of workplace aggression only over the past 15 years. Future research will lead to a better understanding of the predictors of workplace aggression if it focuses on several conceptual and methodological questions.

Perhaps most pressing are questions of construct validity. A critical first step is to discriminate between constructs that are frequently studied in isolation from each other, such as workplace aggression, bullying, abusive supervision, supervisory overcontrol, and workplace violence. Second, research might address the interrelationships of various forms of aggressive

PREDICTING TEENAGE WORKPLACE AGGRESSION

Evidence indicates that teenagers also enact workplace aggression. With more teenagers working now than in the past, understanding why they may engage in workplace aggression is both conceptually and practically important. Although research remains limited, perceptions of interpersonal injustice and abusive supervision are related to aggression directed at supervisors by teenage employees (Dupré et al. 2006). Dupré et al. also show that when teenagers work primarily for financial reasons, their perceptions of supervisor mistreatment are significantly related to aggression directed at workplace supervisors, but not when they work primarily for reasons of personal fulfillment. When financially dependent on their work, teenagers may feel tied to their jobs and use aggression to respond to perceived mistreatment. When less dependent on their jobs, teenagers may be more likely to exit a situation of perceived mistreatment. In terms of predicting workplace aggression, research should continue to focus on this cohort of employees, given that teenagers who learn to respond to situations in the workplace with aggression may continue to engage in aggression at work throughout their working lives.

behavior both within the workplace (supervisor, peer, and subordinate-targeted) and across domains (work, family and community). It is known that workplace aggression occurs among teenage employees (Dupré et al. 2006); thus, the question of whether aggression spans different roles might be extended (see sidebar Predicting Teenage Workplace Aggression). Specifically, research could focus on overlaps between school bullying (e.g., Raskauskas & Stoltz 2007, Veenstra et al. 2005), dating violence (O'Leary & Slep 2003), and workplace aggression (Dupré et al. 2006). Third, the nature of the relationship between workplace aggression and violence warrants attention. Given data from marital relationships (Murphy & O'Leary 1989), the suggestion that verbal or psychological aggression can escalate into physical aggression (Glomb 2002) warrants attention.

With few exceptions (e.g., Barling et al. 2001, Richman et al. 1999, Rospenda 2002), research on workplace aggression has developed in isolation from research on sexual harassment, thus extending questions about construct validity. Although recent factor analytic evidence suggests that sexual harassment and generalized workplace aggression are empirically distinct but related constructs (Fendrich et al. 2002), the predictive role of dominance and power in the enactment of sexual harassment (Berdahl 2007) reinforces the need for such research.

Knowledge that would facilitate the prevention of workplace aggression would be of substantive importance for organizational practitioners. A first step is to dispel myths that are of no validity or practical utility (e.g., notions pertaining to "going postal," profiling potentially aggressive employees, and the idea that workplace aggression is unpredictable). Isolating the organizational conditions that predict workplace aggression (e.g., perceived interpersonal injustice, poor leadership) would provide some indication of initiatives that organizations might choose to follow (e.g., leadership training). In this regard, research showing that workplace aggression and sexual harassment (Dekker & Barling 1998, Dupré & Barling 2006) are lower when employees perceive that the organization will impose sanctions is one possibility. However, because most workplace aggression occurs at the hands of organizational outsiders (e.g., customers, members of the public), any beneficial effects of organizational policies and sanctions against aggression would be limited to current employees. Given that most acts of workplace aggression will continue to be perpetrated by outsiders, training employees to anticipate and understand acts of workplace aggression (Schat & Kelloway 2000) and providing social support to individuals who experience aggressive acts (Schat & Kelloway 2003) are potential means of ameliorating the consequences of workplace aggression. Acknowledging that different individuals may choose to respond to acts of aggression in different ways (Adams-Roy & Barling 1998) and training them to respond effectively may also prevent future occurrences of workplace aggression.

Last, a methodological note is in order. To date, the study of workplace aggression has relied almost exclusively on self-reports, convenience samples, and self-reports of victimization or aggression typically collected as part of a cross-sectional organizational survey. Clearly required is research that excludes threats as a function of monomethod bias and is more conducive to causal inferences. The examination of specific incidents of aggression (Glomb 2002), perhaps in combination with an experience sampling methodology (e.g., Miner et al. 2005), and focusing on daily work experiences offer promising means of exploring the nature of this complex phenomenon. At the same time, moving beyond an individual focus to incorporate team-based experiences (Raver & Gelfand 2005) and multilevel perspectives might also enhance our understanding of workplace aggression.

CONCLUSION

We set out to provide an evidence-based examination of prevailing myths about the predictors of workplace aggression. Doing so shows that although acts of workplace aggression are frequent, workplace violence is infrequent, and there is little support for the notion of a profile of the typical violence-prone employee, although negative affect and trait anger do predict workplace aggression. Similarly, although perceived interpersonal provocation (whether in the form of injustice or poor leadership) predicts workplace aggression, neither mental illness nor layoffs per se do predict workplace aggression. Last, the notion of displaced aggression in the workplace has limited support. Focusing on several issues (e.g., construct validity, prevention) in future research while simultaneously minimizing the likelihood of monomethod bias and enhancing the ability to make causal inferences will advance our understanding of the predictors of workplace aggression.

SUMMARY POINTS

1. Attempts to profile potentially aggressive employees are not supported by the data. Perhaps because of the seeming simplicity in the notion of being able to exclude violent individuals from organizations, the notion of "profiling" potentially aggressive employees during the selection process is often touted as one way of limiting workplace aggression. However, the data do not support this approach: There are no single variables, or combinations of variables, that have sufficient predictive power to make this an empirically or ethically supportable process.

2. Most workplace aggression is not a function of "disgruntled" employees. Beliefs that workplace aggression is a function of "disgruntled employees" who "go postal" remain widespread. Recent data, including nationally representative probability samples of American workers, show that more employees experience aggression at the hands of organizational "outsiders" (e.g., customers) than at the hands of subordinates, and that experiencing aggression from peers and supervisors is by no means unusual.

3. Workplace aggression is not a function of layoffs per se (versus perceived provocation). The stereotypical view holds that layoffs are a major factor in the subsequent enactment of workplace aggression. Data, however, suggest otherwise: First, the overwhelming majority of layoffs take place without any aggression occurring as a result. Second, it is not the layoff per se that is implicated in subsequent aggression, but rather the way in which the layoff is implemented. To the extent that individuals perceive that the process was unfair, or that they were treated unjustly, target-specific aggression might ensue.

4. Workplace aggression is predictable. Despite lingering fears that workplace aggression is largely unpredictable (and the result of disgruntled employees), the data tend to suggest otherwise. Specifically, numerous studies now show that, like aggression in general, perceived provocation is a significant predictor of workplace aggression, and that this effect may be buffered (or exacerbated) by specific individual difference variables.

5. Workplace aggression is preventable. One possible implication emerging from the notion that workplace aggression is predictable is that it therefore might also be preventable. There are some studies showing that the perception that the organization will take some action against workplace aggression (or sexual harassment) may well be a significant factor in reducing workplace aggression.

6. Workplace aggression is not a function of mental illness. The notion that workplace aggression is committed by employees with some form of mental illness is widely held among the lay public, and frequently cited as a major causal factor in media reports following catastrophic incidents. While the possible role of mental illness in workplace aggression remains to be investigated in more depth, studies that have been conducted provide no compelling evidence for this notion at all. This is an important issue, because continuing to cling to this idea (*a*) will sustain the beliefs that workplace aggression is largely unpredictable and therefore not preventable, and (*b*) will continue to stigmatize employees who might already be vulnerable.

FUTURE ISSUES

We suggest that future research is most profitably directed at three general research needs: the need to address questions about the construct definition of workplace aggression, the need to address questions about prevention and harm reduction, and the need to incorporate more varied research methodologies.

1. Questions of construct definition. Noting the plethora of terms developed to label similar phenomenon, what is the relationship between behaviors such as aggression, bullying, abusive supervision, violence, harassment, and victimization? How do aggressive behaviors vary both within (i.e., directed at supervisors, coworkers, and clients) and across (i.e., work, family, and community) roles? How does aggressive behavior develop? Do school-yard bullies become workplace aggressors? What is the relationship between workplace violence and workplace aggression? Under what circumstances does aggressive behavior escalate into violence? What is the relationship between workplace aggression and sexual harassment?

2. Questions about prevention and mitigation. What is the role of organizational sanctions in preventing workplace violence? How can organizations intervene most effectively to both prevent and mitigate the effects of workplace aggression?

3. Questions of research methodology. To date, most research has been based on self-report and cross-sectional surveys. The next generation of studies will be based on longitudinal data, event-based methodologies, and multilevel analyses.

DISCLOSURE STATEMENT

The authors are not aware of any personal biases that might be perceived as affecting, or affect, the objectivity of this review.

ACKNOWLEDGMENTS

This work was supported by grants from the Social Sciences and Humanities Research Council of Canada.

LITERATURE CITED

Adams-Roy J, Barling J. 1998. Predicting the decision to confront or report sexual harassment. *J. Organ. Behav.* 19:329–36

Amandus HE, Zahm D, Friedmann R, Ruback RB, Block C, et al. 1996. Employee injuries and convenience store robberies in selected metropolitan areas. *J. Occup. Environ. Med.* 38:714–20

Anderson CA, Bushman BJ. 2002. Human aggression. *Annu. Rev. Psychol.* 53:27–51

Andersson LM, Pearson CM. 1999. Tit-for-tat? The spiralling effect of incivility in the workplace. *Acad. Manage. Rev.* 24:452–71

Aquino K, Galperin BL, Bennett RJ. 2004. Social status and aggressiveness as moderators of the relationship between interactional justice and workplace deviance. *J. Appl. Soc. Psychol.* 34:126–38

Aquino K, Lamertz K. 2004. A relational model of workplace victimization: social roles and patterns of victimization in dyadic relationships. *J. Appl. Psychol.* 89:1023–34

Bandura A. 1973. *Aggression: A Social Learning Analysis.* Englewood Cliffs, NJ: Prentice Hall

Barling J. 1996. The prediction, experience, and consequences of workplace violence. In *Violence on the Job: Identifying Risks and Developing Solutions*, ed. GR VandenBos, EQ Bulatao, pp. 29–49. Washington, DC: Am. Psychol. Assoc.

Comprehensive overview of theories of human aggression, including the roles of person and situational factors, cognition, affect, and arousal.

Proposes a relational model of workplace victimization predicated on dyadic roles and the organizational context in which they operate.

Barling J, O'Leary KD, Jouriles EN, Vivian D, MacEwen KE. 1987. Factor similarity of the Conflict Tactics Scales across samples, spouses and sites: issues and implications. *J. Fam. Violence* 2:37–53

Barling J, Rogers AG, Kelloway EK. 2001. Behind closed doors: in-home workers' experience of sexual harassment and workplace violence. *J. Occup. Health Psychol.* 6:255–69

Baron RA, Neuman JH. 1998. Workplace aggression—the iceberg beneath the tip of workplace violence: evidence on its forms, frequency, and targets. *Public Admin. Q.* 21:446–64

Baron RA, Neuman JH, Geddes D. 1999. Social and personal determinants of workplace aggression: evidence for the impact of perceived injustice and the type A behavior pattern. *Aggress. Behav.* 25:281–96

Baron RA, Richardson DR. 1994. *Human Aggression*. New York: Plenum. 2nd ed.

Beale D, Cox T, Leather P. 1996. Work-related violence—is national reporting good enough? *Work Stress* 10:99–103

Bedeian AG, Armenakis AA, Curran SM. 1980. Personality correlates of role stress. *Psychol. Rep.* 46:627–32

Bennett RJ, Robinson SL. 2000. Development of a measure of workplace deviance. *J. Appl. Psychol.* 85: 349–60

Berdahl JL. 2007. The sexual harassment of uppity women. *J. Appl. Psychol.* 93:425–37

Berkowitz L. 1993. *Aggression: Its Causes, Consequences, and Control*. Philadelphia, PA: Temple Univ. Press

Berry CM, Ones DS, Sackett PR. 2007. Interpersonal deviance, organizational deviance, and their common correlates: a review and meta-analysis. *J. Appl. Psychol.* 92:409–23

Bing MN, Stewart SM, Davison HK, Green PD, McIntyre MD, James LR. 2007. An integrative typology of personality assessment for aggression: implications for predicting counterproductive workplace behavior. *J. Appl. Psychol.* 92:722–44

Bowling NA, Beehr TA. 2006. Workplace harassment from the victim's perspective: a theoretical model and meta-analysis. *J. Appl. Psychol.* 91(5):998–1012

Braverman M. 1999. *Preventing Workplace Violence: A Guide for Employers and Practitioners*. Thousand Oaks, CA: Sage

Brockner J. 2006. Why it's so hard to be fair. *Harvard Bus. Rev.* 84(3):122–29

Bur. Labor Stat. 2007. *National Census of Fatal Occupational Injuries in 2006*. Washington, DC: Bur. Labor Stat.

Bushman BJ, Baumeister RF. 1998. Threatened egotism, narcissism, self-esteem, and direct and displaced aggression: Does self-love or self-hate lead to violence? *J. Personal. Soc. Psychol.* 75:219–29

Bushman BJ, Bonacci AM, Pedersen WC, Vasquez EA, Miller N. 2005. Chewing on it can chew you up: effects of rumination of triggered displaced aggression. *J. Personal. Soc. Psychol.* 88(6):969–83

Buss AH. 1961. *The Psychology of Aggression*. New York: Wiley

Calif. Occup. Saf. Health Admin. 1995. *Guidelines for Workplace Security*. Sacramento, CA: Calif. Occup. Saf. Health Admin.

Canad. Cent. Occup. Health Saf. 1999. *Violence in the workplace*. **http://www.ccohs.ca/oshanswers/psychosocial/violence.html**

Cano A, Avery-Leaf S, Cascardi M, O'Leary KD. 1998. Dating violence in two high school samples: discriminating variables. *J. Prim. Prev.* 18:431–46

Castillo DN, Jenkins EL. 1994. Industries and occupations at high risk for work-related homicide. *J. Occup. Med.* 36:125–32

Catalano R, Novaco R, McConnell W. 1997. A model of the net effect of job loss on violence. *J. Personal. Soc. Psychol.* 72:1440–47

Chen PY, Spector PE. 1992. Relationships of work stressors with aggression, withdrawal, theft and substance use: an exploratory study. *J. Occup. Organ. Psychol.* 65:177–84

Cortina LM, Magley VJ, Williams JH, Langhout RD. 2001. Incivility in the workplace: incidence and impact. *J. Occup. Health Psychol.* 6:64–80

Davis H. 1987. Workplace homicides of Texas males. *Am. J. Public Health* 77:1290–93

Day AL, Catano VM. 2006. Screening and selecting out violent employees. In *Handbook of Workplace Violence*, ed. EK Kelloway, J Barling, JJ Hurrell, pp. 549–77. Thousand Oaks, CA: Sage

Dekker I, Barling J. 1998. Personal and organizational predictors of workplace sexual harassment of women by men. *J. Occup. Health Psychol.* 3:7–18

Shows that interpersonal and organizational deviance are strongly correlated but have different relationships with personality and organizational citizenship behaviors, leading to the conclusion that these are separable constructs.

Addresses the incidence, targets, perpetrators, and consequences of workplace incivility (e.g., disrespect, degradation); shows that women experience incivility more than do men.

Dietz J, Robinson SL, Folger R, Baron RA, Schulz M. 2003. The impact of societal violence and organizational procedural justice climate on workplace aggression. *Acad. Manage. J.* 46:317–26

Dill KE, Anderson CA, Anderson KB, Deuser WE. 1997. Effects of aggressive personality on social expectations and social perceptions. *J. Personal. Soc. Psychol.* 31:272–92

Douglas SC, Martinko MJ. 2001. Exploring the role of individual differences in the prediction of workplace aggression. *J. Appl. Psychol.* 86:547–59

Duhart DT. 2001. *Bureau of Justice Statistics special report: violence in the workplace, 1993–1999.* NCJ 190076. Washington, DC: U.S. Bur. Justice Stat.

Dupré KE, Barling J. 2006. Predicting and preventing supervisory workplace aggression. *J. Occup. Health Psychol.* 11:13–26

Dupré KE, Inness M, Connelly CE, Barling J, Hoption C. 2006. Workplace aggression in teenage part-time employees. *J. Appl. Psychol.* 91(5):987–97

Eagly A, Steffan VJ. 1986. Gender and aggressive behavior: a meta-analytic review of the social psychological literature. *Psychol. Bull.* 100:309–30

Einarsen S. 1999. The nature and causes of bullying at work. *Int. J. Manpower* 20:16–27

Einarsen S, Raknes BI. 1997. Harassment at work and the victimization of men. *Violence Vict.* 12:247–63

Einarsen S, Raknes BI, Matthiesen SB. 1994. Bullying and harassment at work and their relationships to work environment quality: an exploratory study. *Eur. Work Organ. Psychol.* 4:381–401

Einarsen S, Skogstad A. 1996. Bullying at work: epidemiological findings in public and private organizations. *Eur. J. Work Organ. Psychol.* 5:185–201

Epps J, Kendall PC. 1995. Hostile attributional bias in adults. *Cogn. Ther. Res.* 19:159–78

Fendrich M, Woodward P, Richman JA. 2002. The structure of harassment and abuse in the workplace: a factorial comparison of two measures. *Violence Vict.* 17:491–505

Feshbach S. 1997. The psychology of aggression: insights and issues. In *Aggression: Biological, Developmental, and Social Perspectives*, ed. S Feshbach, J Zagrodzka, pp. 213–35. New York: Plenum

Folger R. 1993. Reactions to mistreatment at work. In *Social Psychology in Organizations: Advances in Theory and Research*, ed. K Murnighan, pp. 163–83. Englewood Cliffs, NJ: Prentice Hall

Folger R, Skarlicki DP. 1998. A popcorn metaphor for workplace violence. In *Dysfunctional Behaviour in Organizations: Violent and Deviant Behaviour*, Vol. 23, ed. RW Griffin, A O'Leary-Kelly, JM Collins, pp. 43–81. Greenwich, CT: JAI

Fox S, Spector PE. 1999. A model of work frustration-aggression. *J. Organ. Behav.* 20:915–31

Francis L, Cameron JE, Kelloway EK, 2006. Crossing the line: violence on the picket line. In *Handbook of Workplace Violence*, ed. EK Kelloway, J Barling, JJ Hurrell, pp. 231–60. Thousand Oaks, CA: Sage

Friedman RA. 2006. Violence and mental illness—how strong is the link? *N. Engl. J. Med.* 355(20):2062–64

Gallo LC, Matthews KA. 2003. Understanding the association between socioeconomic status and physical health: Do negative emotions play a role? *Psychol. Bull.* 129:10–51

Geddes D, Callister RR. 2007. Crossing the lines(s): a dual threshold model of anger in organizations. *Acad. Manage. Rev.* 32:721–46

Geen RG. 2001. *Human Aggression.* Buckingham, UK: Open Univ. Press. 2nd ed.

Giacalone RA, Greenberg J. 1997. *Antisocial Behavior in Organizations.* Thousand Oaks, CA: Sage

Gladwell M. 2006. Troublemakers: What pit bulls can teach us about profiling. *New Yorker*, Feb. 6

Glomb TM. 2002. Workplace anger and aggression: informing conceptual models with data from specific encounters. *J. Occup. Health Psychol.* 7:20–36

Glomb TM, Liao H. 2003. Interpersonal aggression in work groups: social influence, reciprocal and individual effects. *Acad. Manage. J.* 46:486–96

Graham JP. 1991 Disgruntled employees: ticking time bombs. *Secur. Manage.* 36:83,85

Greenberg L, Barling J. 1999. Predicting employee aggression against coworkers, subordinates and supervisors: the roles of person behaviors and perceived workplace factors. *J. Organ. Behav.* 2:897–913

Haines VY, Marchand A, Harvey S. 2006. Crossover of workplace aggression experiences in dual-earner couples. *J. Occup. Health Psychol.* 11:305–14

Halbfinger DM. 2003. Factory killer had a history of anger and racial taunts. *N. Y. Times*, July 10:A14

Harris A, Lurigo AJ. 2007. Mental illness and violence: a brief review of research and assessment strategies. *Aggress. Violent Behav.* 12:542–51

Shows that the rate of violent crime in the community is a better predictor of workplace aggression than is plant procedural justice; demonstrates the importance of considering extraorganizational predictors.

Investigates the role of six individual-difference variables, which together account for 62% of the variance in workplace aggression.

Shows the importance of injustice as a mediator between supervisors' controlling behavior and employee aggression and the moderating role of organizational sanctions.

Focuses on workplace aggression within teams; demonstrates that being the target of aggression predict one's own enactment of aggression.

Harvey S, Keashly L. 2003. Predicting the risk for aggression in the workplace: risk factors, self-esteem and time at work. *Soc. Behav. Personal.* 31:807–14

Hepworth W, Towler A. 2004. The effects of individual differences and charismatic leadership on workplace aggression. *J. Occup. Health Psychol.* 9:176–85

Herbert R, Landrigan PJ. 2000. Work-related death: a continuing epidemic. *Am. J. Public Health* 90(4):541–45

Herschcovis MS, Barling J. 2006. Preventing insider-initiated violence. In *Handbook of Workplace Violence*, ed. EK Kelloway, J Barling, JJ Hurrell, pp. 607–31. Thousand Oaks, CA: Sage

Hershcovis MS, Barling J. 2007. A relational perspective on workplace aggression: an examination of perpetrators and targets. In *Dysfunctional Workplace: Management Challenges and Symptoms*, ed. J Langan-Fox, CL Cooper, R Klimoski, pp. 268–84. Cheltenham, UK: Elgar

Hershcovis MS, Turner N, Barling J, Arnold KA, Dupré KE, et al. 2007. Predicting workplace aggression: a meta-analysis. *J. Appl. Psychol.* 92:228–38

Hoel H, Rayner C, Cooper CL. 1999. Workplace bullying. In *International Review of Industrial and Organizational Psychology*, ed. CL Cooper, IT Robertson, 14:195–230. Chichester, UK: Wiley

Hoobler JM, Brass DJ. 2006. Abusive supervision and family undermining as displaced aggression. *J. Appl. Psychol.* 91(5):1125–33

Inness M, Barling J, Turner N. 2005. Understanding supervisor-targeted aggression: a within-person, between-jobs design. *J. Appl. Psychol.* 90:731–39

Inness M, LeBlanc MM, Barling J. 2008. Psychosocial predictors of supervisor-, peer-, subordinate-, and service provider-targeted aggression. *J. Appl. Psychol.* In press

Jenkins EL. 1996. *Violence in the workplace: risk factors and prevention strategies.* DHHS (NIOSH) Publ. No. 96–100. Washington, DC: Gov. Print. Off.

Judge TA, LePine JA, Rich BL. 2006. Loving yourself abundantly: relationship of the narcissistic personality to self- and other perceptions of workplace deviance, leadership, and task and contextual performance. *J. Appl. Psychol.* 91:762–76

Keashly L. 1998. Emotional abuse in the workplace: conceptual and empirical issues. *J. Emot. Abuse* 1:85–115

Keashly L. 2001. Interpersonal and systemic aspects of emotional abuse at work: the target's perspective. *Violence Vict.* 16:233–68

Keashly L, Harvey S. 2005. Workplace emotional abuse. In *Handbook of Workplace Violence*, ed. EK Kelloway, J Barling, JJ Hurrell, pp. 95–121. Thousand Oaks, CA: Sage

Keashly L, Jagatic K. 2003. By any other name: American perspectives on workplace bullying. In *Bullying and Emotional Abuse in the Workplace: International Perspectives in Research and Practice*, ed. S Einarsen, H Hoel, D Zapf, CL Cooper, pp. 31–61. London: Taylor & Francis

Kelloway EK, Barling J, Hurrell JJ Jr. 2006. *Handbook of Workplace Violence*. Thousand Oaks, CA: Sage

Kraus JF. 1987. Homicide while at work: persons, industries, and occupations at high risk. *Am. J. Public Health* 77:1285–89

Kraus JF, Blander B, McArthur DL. 1995. Incidence, risk factors, and prevention strategies for work-related assault injuries: a review of what is known, what needs to be known, and countermeasures for intervention. *Annu. Rev. Public Health* 16:355–79

Lamberg L. 1996. Don't ignore patients' threats, psychiatrists told. *J. Am. Med. Assoc.* 275:1715–16

Lanyon RI, Goodstein LD. 2004. Validity and reliability of a pre-employment screening test: the counterproductive behaviour index (CBI). *J. Bus. Psychol.* 18:533–53

LeBlanc MM, Kelloway EK. 2002. Predictors and outcomes of workplace violence and aggression. *J. Appl. Psychol.* 87:444–53

Lipsey MW, Wilson DB, Cohen MA, Derzon JH. 1997. Is there a causal relationship between alcohol use and violence? In *Recent Developments in Alcoholism: Vol. XIII*, ed. M Galanter, pp. 245–82. New York: Plenum

Litzky BE, Eddleston KA, Kidder DL. 2006. The good, the bad and the misguided: how managers inadvertently encourage deviant behaviours. *Acad. Manag. Perspect.* 20:91–103

Lombardi KS. 1994. Efforts to stem violence in the workplace. *N. Y. Times*, Feb. 13. **http://query.nytimes.com/gst/fullpage.html?res=9B06E3DE1238F930A25751C0A962958260&scp=1&sq=efforts+to+stem+violence+in+the+workplace&st=nyt**

Analyzes the results of 57 empirical studies to identify the individual and organizational predictors of workplace aggression.

Comprehensive overview of the prevalence, contexts, sources, and forms of workplace aggression, and prevention and intervention initiatives.

Marcus-Newhall A, Pedersen WC, Carlson M, Miller N. 2000. Displaced aggression is alive and well: a meta-analytic review. *J. Personal. Soc. Psychol.* 78(4):670–89

Martinko MJ, Douglas SC, Harvey P. 2006. Understanding and managing workplace aggression. *Organ. Dyn.* 35:117–30

Martinko MJ, Grundlach MJ, Douglas SC. 2002. Toward an integrity theory of counterproductive workplace behaviour: a causal reasoning perspective. *Int. J. Select. Assess.* 10:36–50

McFarlin SK, Fals-Stewart W, Major DA, Justice EM. 2001. Alcohol use and workplace aggression: an examination of perpetration and victimization. *J. Subst. Abuse* 13:303–21

Miller N, Pedersen WC, Earleywine M, Pollock VE. 2003. A theoretical model of triggered displaced aggression. *Personal. Soc. Psychol. Rev.* 7:75–97

Miner AG, Glomb TM, Hulin C. 2005. Experience sampling mood and its correlates at work. *J. Occup. Organ. Psychol.* 78:171–93

Mitchell MS, Ambrose ML. 2007. Abusive supervision and workplace deviance and the moderating effects of negative reciprocity beliefs. *J. Appl. Psychol.* 92(4):1159–68

Murphy CM, O'Leary KD. 1989. Psychological aggression predicts physical aggression in early marriage. *J. Consult. Clin. Psychol.* 57:579–82

Namie G, Namie R. 2000. *The Bully at Work: What Can You Do to Stop the Hurt and Reclaim Your Dignity on the Job.* Naperville, IL: Sourcebooks

Nat. Inst. Occup. Saf. Health. 2002. *Violence: occupational hazards in hospitals.* DHHS Publ. No. 2002–101. **http://www.cdc.gov/niosh/2002-101.html#intro**

Neuman JH, Baron RA. 1998. Workplace violence and workplace aggression: evidence concerning specific forms, potential causes, and preferred targets. *J. Manage.* 24:391–411

N. Y. Times. 1993. Postal study aims to spot violence-prone workers. *N. Y. Times*, July 2:A9

O'Leary KD, Slep AM. 2003. A dyadic longitudinal model of adolescent dating aggression. *J. Child Adolesc. Psychol.* 32:314–27

O'Leary-Kelly AM, Duffy MK, Griffin RW. 2000. Construct confusion in the study of antisocial work behavior. In *Research in Personnel and Human Resource Management*, Vol. 18, ed. GR Ferris, pp. 275–303. Greenwich, CT: JAI

Painter K. 1987. "It's part of the job": violence at work. *Employ. Relat.* 9:30–40

Parkins IS, Fishbein HD, Ritchey PN. 2006. The influence of personality on workplace bullying and discrimination. *J. Appl. Soc. Psychol.* 36:2554–77

Paul RJ, Townsend JB. 1998. Violence in the workplace—a review with recommendations. *Employ. Rights Resp. J.* 11:1–14

Pedersen WC. 2006. The impact of attributional processes on triggered displaced aggression. *Motiv. Emot.* 30:75–87

Peek-Asa C, Howard J. 1999. Workplace-violence investigations by the California Division of Occupational Safety and Health, 1993–1996. *J. Occup. Environ. Med.* 41:647–53

Peek-Asa C, Schaffer KB, Kraus JF, Howard J. 1998. Surveillance of nonfatal workplace assault injuries, using police and employers' reports. *J. Occup. Environ. Med.* 40:707–13

Penney LM, Spector PE. 2002. Narcissism and counterproductive work behaviour: Do bigger egos mean bigger problems? *Int. J. Select. Assess.* 10:126–34

Pizzino A. 2002. Dealing with violence in the workplace: the experience of Canada unions. In *Violence at Work: Causes, Patterns and Prevention*, ed. M Gill, B Fisher, V Bowie, pp. 165–79. Cullompton, UK: Willan

Public Serv. Comm. 2002. *2002 Public Service Employment Survey.* **http://www.tbs-sct.gc.ca/media/nr-cp/2002/1202-eng.asp**

Raskauskas J, Stoltz AD. 2007. Involvement in traditional and electronic bullying among adolescents. *Dev. Psychol.* 43:564–75

Raver JL, Gelfand MJ. 2005. Beyond the individual victim: linking sexual harassment, team processes, and team performance. *Acad. Manage. J.* 48:387–400

Rayner C, Cooper CL. 2006. Workplace bullying. In *Handbook of Workplace Violence*, ed. EK Kelloway, J Barling, JJ Hurrell, pp. 121–46. Thousand Oaks, CA: Sage

Richman JA, Rospenda KM, Nawyn SJ, Flaherty JA, Fendrich M, et al. 1999. Sexual harassment and generalized workplace abuse among university employees: prevalence and mental health correlates. *Am. J. Public Health* 89:358–63

Robinson SL, Bennett RJ. 1995. A typology of deviant workplace behaviors: a multidimensional scaling study. *Acad. Manage. J.* 38:555–72

Robinson SL, Greenberg J. 1998. Employees behaving badly: dimension, determinants and dilemmas in the study of workplace deviance. In *Trends in Organizational Behavior*, Vol. 5, ed. CL Cooper, DM Rousseau, pp. 1–30. New York: Wiley

Rogers K, Kelloway EK. 1997. Violence at work: personal and organizational outcomes. *J. Occup. Health Psychol.* 2:63–71

Rospenda KM. 2002. Workplace harassment, services utilization, and drinking outcomes. *J. Occup. Health Psychol.* 7:141–55

Rospenda KM, Richman JA. 2005. Harassment and discrimination. In *Handbook of Work Stress*, ed. J Barling, EK Kelloway, MR Frone, pp. 149–88. Thousand Oaks, CA: Sage

Schat ACH, Frone M, Kelloway EK. 2006. Prevalence of workplace aggression in the U.S. workforce: findings from a national study. In *Handbook of Workplace Violence*, ed. EK Kelloway, J Barling, JJ Hurrell, pp. 47–90. Thousand Oaks, CA: Sage

Schat ACH, Kelloway EK. 2000. The effects of perceived control on the outcomes of workplace aggression and violence. *J. Occup. Health Psychol.* 4:386–402

Schat ACH, Kelloway EK. 2003. Reducing the adverse consequences of workplace aggression and violence: the buffering effects of organizational support. *J. Occup. Health Psychol.* 8:110–22

Schat ACH, Kelloway EK. 2005. Workplace violence. In *Handbook of Work Stress*, ed. J Barling, EK Kelloway, M Frone, pp. 189–218. Thousand Oaks, CA: Sage

Sheehan KH, Sheehan DV, White K, Leibowitz A, Baldwin DC. 1990. A pilot study of medical student "abuse": student perceptions of mistreatment and misconduct in medical school. *J. Am. Med. Assoc.* 263:533–37

Skarlicki DP, Folger R. 1997. Retaliation in the workplace: the roles of distributive, procedural and interactional justice. *J. Appl. Psychol.* 82:434–43

Skarlicki DP, Folger R, Tesluk P. 1999. Personality as a moderator in the relationship between fairness and retaliation. *Acad. Manage. J.* 42:100–8

Smith AK, Bolton RN, Wagner J. 1999. A model of customer satisfaction with service encounters involving failure and recovery. *J. Mark. Res.* 36(3):356–72

Snyder LA, Chen PY, Grubb PL, Roberts RK, Sauter SL, Swanson NG. 2005. Workplace aggression and violence against individuals and organizations: causes, consequences and interventions. In *Exploring Interpersonal Dynamics Research in Occupational Stress and Well Being*, Vol. 4, ed. P Perrewe, D Ganster, pp. 1–65. New York: Elsevier

Spector PE, Coulter ML, Stockwell HG, Matz MW. 2007. Relationships of workplace physical violence and verbal aggression with perceived safety, perceived violence climate, and strains in a healthcare setting. *Work Stress* 21:117–30

Spielberger CD. 1991. *State-Trait Anger Expression Inventory: Revised Research Edition*. Odessa, FL: Psychol. Assess. Resourc.

Springer J. 1998. Worker kills 4 at lottery headquarters. *Hartford Courant*, March 7. **http://www.pulitzer.org/archives/6203**

Stuart P. 1992. Murder on the job (killing of coworkers). *Personnel J.* 71:72–84

Swanberg JE, Logan TK, Marke C. 2006. The consequences of partner violence on employment and the workplace. In *Handbook of Workplace Violence*, ed. EK Kelloway, J. Barling, JJ Hurrell, pp. 351–80. Thousand Oaks, CA: Sage

Sygnatur EF, Toscano GA. 2000. Work-related homicides: the facts. *Compens. Work. Cond.* Spring:3–8

Terkel S. 1974. *Working: People Talk About What They Do All Day and How They Feel About What They Do All Day*. New York: Pantheon

Thieblot AJ, Haggard TR, Northrup HR. 1999. *Union Violence: The Record and the Response by the Courts, Legislatures, and the NLRB*. Fairfax, VA: George Mason Univ. Olin Inst. Employ. Pract. Policy. Rev. ed.

Tjaden P, Thoennes N. 2000. *Extent, nature, and consequences of intimate partner violence*. Washington, DC: U.S. Dep. Justice, Nat. Inst. Justice

U.S. Post. Serv. Comm. Safe Secure Workpl. 2000. *Report of the United States Postal Service Commission on a Safe and Secure Workplace*. New York: Nat. Cent. Addict. Subst. Abuse Columbia Univ.

VandenBos G, Bulatao EQ. 1996. Workplace violence: its scope and the issues. In *Violence on the Job: Identifying Risks and Developing Solutions*, ed. G VandenBos, EQ Bulatao, pp. 1–23. Washington, DC: Am. Psychol. Assoc.

Veenstra R, Lindenberg S, Oldehinkel AJ, De Winter AF, Verhulst FC, Ormel J. 2005. Bullying and victimization in elementary schools: a comparison of bullies, victims, bully/victims, and uninvolved preadolescents. *Dev. Psychol.* 41:672–82

Vinokur AD, Price RH, Caplan RD. 1996. Hard times and hurtful partners: how financial strain affects depression and relationship satisfaction of unemployed persons and their spouses. *J. Personal. Soc. Psychol.* 71:177–94

Zapf D, Einarsen S, Hoel H, Vartia M. 2003. Individual effects of exposure to bullying at work. In *Bullying and Emotional Abuse in the Workplace*, ed. S Einarsen, H Hoel, D Zapf, CL Cooper, pp. 103–26. New York: Taylor & Francis

The Social Brain: Neural Basis of Social Knowledge

Ralph Adolphs

California Institute of Technology (Caltech), Pasadena, California 91125;
email: radolphs@caltech.edu

Annu. Rev. Psychol. 2009. 60:693–716

First published online as a Review in Advance on
September 4, 2008

The *Annual Review of Psychology* is online at
psych.annualreviews.org

This article's doi:
10.1146/annurev.psych.60.110707.163514

Key Words

social cognition, social neuroscience, theory of mind, simulation,
empathy, amygdala, prefrontal cortex, modularity

Abstract

Social cognition in humans is distinguished by psychological processes
that allow us to make inferences about what is going on inside other
people—their intentions, feelings, and thoughts. Some of these processes likely account for aspects of human social behavior that are
unique, such as our culture and civilization. Most schemes divide social
information processing into those processes that are relatively automatic
and driven by the stimuli, versus those that are more deliberative and
controlled, and sensitive to context and strategy. These distinctions are
reflected in the neural structures that underlie social cognition, where
there is a recent wealth of data primarily from functional neuroimaging.
Here I provide a broad survey of the key abilities, processes, and ways
in which to relate these to data from cognitive neuroscience.

Contents

KNOWLEDGE OF MINDS

> The basic fact is thus that human beings are able to pool their cognitive resources in ways that other species are not ... made possible by a single very special form of social cognition, namely, the ability of individual organisms to understand conspecifics as beings *like themselves* who have intentional and mental lives like their own. (Tomasello 1999)

Comparative Studies

We are an essentially social species; no component of our civilization would be possible without large-scale collective behavior. Yet much of our social behavior arises from neurobiological and psychological mechanisms shared with other mammalian species, raising questions about why we are different. Part of this difference may arise from knowledge of our own minds and those of others, a type of knowledge different from that about the shared nonso-cial environment, and in degree if not in kind inaccessible and inconceivable to nonhuman animals.

There are three broad domains of knowledge that, taken together, seem to exhaust what it is that we can know or conceive of knowing. The first is the simplest to describe—it is knowledge of the nonsocial environment, the world we share with others. The common-sense view is that this domain of knowledge is shared, public, and hence objective in that sense. How we come to acquire this knowledge is also no mystery—through our senses and perception of the world (although the acquisition of such knowledge already depends on learning, selection, and categorization mechanisms that are in part innate). Although the kinds of inferences that we make about the world are certainly complex, it seems that much of this domain of knowledge is shared with other animals. Like us, mice, cats, dogs, and monkeys know about objects in the world, the properties they possess, and the events they transact; they know something about which objects are good and which are bad, and they direct their behavior accordingly.

The second and third domains of knowledge are more mysterious, and it is unclear to what extent, if at all, other animals have access to them. These are knowledge of other minds, and knowledge of our own mind. Although many biologists who study social behavior in animals treat their processing of social information as an issue in perception that is just a special instance of the first category discussed above, some, especially those working with primates, focus on knowledge of one's own and others' minds. Workhorse tasks have been devised to assess the abilities in question: deception as a test for knowledge of other minds, and mirror self-recognition as a test for self-knowledge.

Knowledge of the Minds of Others

One way of knowing about the social world, of course, is through the same processes by which we know about the nonsocial world.

There is overwhelming evidence that many animals are able to use social cues in sophisticated ways, and primates especially are able to track kinship and social rank over time (Cheney & Seyfarth 1990, Silk 2005)—abilities that make substantial demands on several cognitive domains, such as episodic memory. But it is also possible that the processes used for such social knowledge differ in important ways from those engaged in nonsocial knowledge: Many of these abilities look as if the animals were inferring mental states by them. For instance, dogs, unlike wolves, when faced with a problem that they cannot solve, know to look back to their owner in order to see what that person recommends they do (Miklosi et al. 2003). Thus, they know that the human "knows" something that can help them if they need additional information. Monkeys are able to distinguish human actions that are intentional: They fail to show any preference to eat from a bowl of food to which a human points with an elbow (because pointing with one's elbow doesn't make sense normally), but they do show a preference to eat from the bowl if a human points with an elbow while holding something else with both hands (because in that case the hands are not free to point and using the elbow makes sense) (Wood et al. 2007). However one wants to interpret these abilities, there is still doubt that they are sufficient to attribute a concept of "mind" or "subjective" or "consciousness" to animals (although, of course, higher animals do have minds together with subjective conscious experiences; it is just that they may not know that they do).

There is a large literature on experiments in our closest living relative, the chimpanzee, to attempt to demonstrate that they really do have a concept of other minds (although it is granted that the chimp's concept of mind would not be the same as the human's). The question was first posed explicitly in a famous article in the 1970s (Premack & Woodruff 1978) and was followed by a commentary in which philosopher Daniel Dennett recommended what has since become a common experimental strategy: To show that an animal can conceive of minds (has a "the-

ory of mind"), one must demonstrate a concept of false belief, which has been operationalized in animals as the ability to deceive. The reasoning here is that one must decouple the state of someone's mind (e.g., what they believe) from the state of the world (e.g., what they perceive). There are fairly detailed experiments of chimpanzee deception (Tomasello et al. 2003), and it certainly appears to be the case that chimpanzees are sensitive to what other chimps know and are able behaviorally to deceive them, although the interpretation of these findings remains debated (Povinelli & Vonk 2003). Daniel Povinelli has proposed an interesting experiment that joins knowledge of other minds with knowledge of one's own mind and that could be more decisive if it worked. Suppose we construct a helmet one can wear, that looks from the outside like a completely opaque bucket. Now, without any prior interaction with a person wearing one of these helmets, the chimp is given a red and a blue helmet to wear itself. It turns out that only the red helmet has a little monitor inside that is hooked up to a video camera, such that one can see what is in front of the helmet when one wears it. If the chimp, after having experienced "seeing" itself while wearing the red helmet, an experience completely novel and hence not subject to any prior associations, now begs for food from people wearing the red but not the blue helmet, this could count as unambiguous evidence that chimps can attribute mental states to others, with extrapolation from their own and unique conscious experience as the sole source of the inference. So far, there is no evidence that chimps can pass this test (Penn & Povinelli 2007), although this negative finding can be criticized on a number of grounds including the limited number of animals that have been tested on it and its highly artificial nature (compared to what chimps might be expected to encounter in nature). In fact, it has been pointed out that both the human samples often tested in such experiments (white, middle-class, Western humans) and the chimpanzee samples (captive chimpanzees) are highly atypical (Boesch 2007), making generalizations drawn from them unclear.

Knowledge of One's Own Mind

Demonstrating knowledge of one's own mind in animals is at an even more problematic stage. A classic test, mirror self-recognition, seems adequate to show recognition of one's own body but insufficient to show knowledge of one's own mind. Although it used to be thought that only great apes could recognize their own body in a mirror (Gallup 1970), such discrimination has now been shown for monkeys (de Waal et al. 2005), dolphins (Reiss & Marino 2001), and elephants (Plotnik et al. 2006). These tests, for their complete assessment, rely on the ability of the animal to behave on the basis of new self-relevant information it recognizes in a mirror, typically a colored mark of some kind on its skin that the animal then examines. A related set of tests are those for episodic memory, which are presumed to require projecting oneself into the past in order to re-experience it. Likewise related are tests for future episodic planning, which requires pre-experiencing something by projecting oneself into the future. As with deception and mirror self-identification, the evidence that animals can mentally travel outside of the present remains unclear (Emery & Clayton 2004, Roberts et al. 2008). What all these abilities share in common with the ability to know other minds is the flexible adoption of a point of view that is different (in space, time, or person) from the way one currently experiences the world. As such, they require the ability to make a distinction between world and mind, between objective and subjective. Although several animals can behave in very flexible ways that support some such ability, it remains unclear whether they truly are able to (*a*) experience a point of view that they deliberately imagine, (*b*) distinguish this experience from their own experience in the here and now, and (*c*) derive from this distinction a concept of "mind" of some sort.

Yet in typical adult humans there is no doubt whatsoever that we have knowledge of other minds and our own, and much of the research has focused on the detailed mechanisms that underlie these abilities rather than on demonstrations that we have them at all [although work in infants and children, not treated here, does focus on the age at which these abilities first emerge and how they develop (Blakemore 2008, Striano & Reid 2006); likewise, work in clinical populations such as autism focuses on whether and to what extent they are present (Baron-Cohen 1997, Frith 2001)]. The mechanisms are of great interest because they seem to require something different from, or additional to, the mechanisms that mediate our knowledge of the shared nonsocial environment. In the case of knowledge of other minds, we appear to begin with much the same information as for nonsocial objects—perception of a face, say—but then go on to make inferences that are unique: We infer emotions, intentions, and beliefs of the other person, none of which we can directly observe because they are internal, relational, or dispositional states in some way. This ability is referred to as "theory of mind" (Leslie 1987, Premack & Woodruff 1978). Our propensity to take this stance toward explaining intentional systems, whether human or not, is influenced by such factors as our motivation to understand a system and to connect with it socially (Epley et al. 2007).

Most puzzling of all is self-knowledge. Unlike the other two forms of knowledge, self-knowledge typically doesn't rely on perceptual observation at all, or at least not on teloreceptive perception. We know what we experience, believe, and think without relying on any observational inference, with the result that we are authoritative about our own minds in a way that other people, whose knowledge of our mind necessarily relies on observational evidence, could never be (which is not to say we are incorrigible on any particular occasion). So what is the source of input that constitutes the evidence on the basis of which we know what is going on in our own minds? One interesting idea is that the source is not sensory at all, but rather is motor in nature. We know what we feel, think, and believe because these are activities that we initiate and about which we can talk to others. This idea has been taken up by some philosophers who emphasize social communication and learning as an essential ingredient to giving content to mental states (Davidson 1987), by neuroscience theories of consciousness that argue sensory consciousness requires relay of information to the prefrontal cortex for action planning (Crick & Koch 1995), and by social neuroscientists who study intentional action and how our sense of agency allows us to understand others as responsible conscious beings (Frith 2007a).

The Consequences for Human Behavior

Although apes have group-specific repositories and transmission of social information that qualify as rudimentary cultures (Whiten et al. 1999), humans alone seem to have language and civilization, and no other mammal has come close to transforming the planet in the way we have. Yet the abilities that underlie this patent social difference remain unclear. Studies showing that great apes are worse than human children on tests of social cognition (Herrmann et al. 2007), especially social learning, even when they are equated with respect to nonsocial cognitive abilities, support the idea that human social cognition is special, perhaps in particular with regard to how we can learn through imitation. However, these studies, like all the others reviewed in the previous section, are heavily debated (for example, it is argued they may be too artificial to demonstrate the social cognitive skills that primates could exhibit in the wild, and solid evidence from field studies is incredibly difficult to obtain).

One set of behaviors that are being intensively investigated by anthropologists, economists, and biologists are those that produce cooperation (Gintis et al. 2003). Chimpanzees appear to have social cognitive abilities that are more adapted to competition than to cooperation (Hare & Tomasello 2004), and they show little spontaneous inclination to help others (Silk et al. 2005). There may be nonreciprocal altruistic behaviors and altruistic punishment (Fehr & Gaechter 2002) that occur only in humans. These abilities depend on a concept

of other minds, contribute to reputation and social status, and are critical to aspects of human society and its evolution. We both help and punish others, depending on the circumstances, even when these come at a cost to ourselves and even for unrelated people, when this is seen as fair, right, or for the greater good. One class of psychological processes that may mediate such behaviors is the moral emotions—strong motivational states, such as pity, pride, or guilt, that link perception of certain classes of social events to actions based on what we judge to be right or wrong.

SOCIAL PROCESSES AND SOCIAL BRAIN

Controlled and Automatic Processing

The currently dominant view among many cognitive psychologists and neuroscientists proposes two broad sets of processes: those that are controlled and those that are automatic. One could add a third category: those that mediate between controlled and automatic processes. The dichotomous scheme is summarized in a recent review (Lieberman 2007), which enumerates the various properties attributed to controlled and automatic processing. Controlled processes have long been assigned a host of other attributes: They are slow, effortful, reflective, arise late in evolution and development, and often involve language-based declarative reasoning and reflective thinking. Automatic processes are thought to be faster, spontaneous, reflexive, shared in common with a wide range of species and dominant early in development, and often involve emotions. The automatic nature of social cognition has often been stressed, since a large literature supports effects on social judgment and behavior that occur without deliberate reflection (Bargh & Ferguson 2000, Fiske & Taylor 2008). Yet sophisticated views of automaticity acknowledge that, although it is unintentional, automatic processing can be quite diverse and rich in nature (Bargh & Morsella 2008). Regardless of how one carves up the terrain, it seems apparent that both kinds of processes patently contribute to social cognition: Much of it is rapid and fraught with biases and stereotypes of which we may be unaware, consistent with automatic processing; at the same time, a hallmark of human social cognition is our ability to deploy behavior strategically—either to contribute toward the greater good of a society despite selfish inclinations to do otherwise, or to manipulate and deceive others who are trying to predict our behavior.

A large literature has examined the interaction between these two sets of processes. Cognitive control and regulation, abilities that develop relatively late throughout childhood and adolescence, appear to have evolved relatively recently (Braver & Barch 2006). One index of such control is the duration over which a stimulus can be decoupled from an action toward it, such as is seen in temporal discounting of rewards. Such discounting functions are relatively steep for most animals, longer for primates, and longest for humans, who can plan ahead over long time periods to delay obtaining an ultimate reward. Another example of cognitive control is emotion regulation, the ability to alter one's emotional response, expression, and indeed experience, volitionally—a process whose dysfunction in adults contributes to mood disorders (Ochsner & Gross 2005). There is also evidence for interaction in the opposite direction. Theories of decision-making, in particular, have recently argued that automatic, and often emotional, processing influences deliberate choices (Damasio 1994). In a similar vein, studies in the social psychology of stereotyping have shown that our opinions of, and behavior toward, other people are often influenced by covert attitudes that were triggered rapidly and automatically. For instance, social judgments such as trustworthiness can be made from very brief presentations of faces (Bar et al. 2006, Willis & Todorov 2006) that are thought to activate automatic schemas for the rapid, on-line evaluation of others. One very provocative study found that brief presentations of the faces of real, but unfamiliar, politicians could generate reliable judgments of how competent these politicians looked, without any additional information. Amazingly, such competence judgments based solely on the appearance of a face correlated (weakly but significantly) with real-world election outcomes for those politicians (Todorov et al. 2005).

Dimensions specific to social evaluation have also been proposed: Two universal dimensions of how we perceive and judge other people are competence and warmth (Fiske et al. 2007). These two dimensions capture much about how others might be disposed toward us and thus help us to predict their likely behavior. Perhaps one of the best examples of social cognition that demonstrates the rich interaction between seemingly opposite sets of processes is moral judgment. We judge actions to be right or wrong, and the people who carry them out to be good or bad, based on emotion, inference, automatic and reflective processing, and a host of processes that have evolved to subserve reciprocity, fairness, loyalty, respect, and other behavioral dispositions (Haidt 2007). Many of the distinctions between processes that have been made at the level of cognitive psychology are now being informed by data from neuroscience, which drives home the point of rich interaction even more.

A further consideration regarding the processes that subserve social behavior comes from anthropological and comparative data, which can be used to argue for those aspects of social behavior that may be disproportionate to humans, and to provide a corresponding link to those features of the brain that may be disproportionate to humans. We review some of these data in the next section and then turn to the neurobiology.

The Social Brain

The social brain hypothesis attempts to explain the extraordinary size and complexity of the human brain by appeal to particular pressures that a species adapted to social interaction would have had to face, ranging from deception to cooperation to ways of obtaining food and ensuring offspring (Allman 1999;

Barrett & Henzi 2005; Dunbar 1998; Dunbar & Schultz 2007a,b). In part, this is a chicken-and-egg question: Did greater general cognitive abilities and intelligence drive our social cognition, or did social cognition enable our intelligence in general (Roth & Dicke 2005)? The evolution of human brain size to its present 1.3 kg is notable for tremendous acceleration on an evolutionarily quite recent timescale, with major increases within less than a million years ago (Ruff et al. 1997). By comparison, the brain size of the great ape species closest in evolution to humans, such as chimpanzees and bonobos, is only 25%–35% of modern human brain size (about the size of the brain our hominid ancestors would likely have had about four million years ago), although body size is comparable. Given the increased maternal investment required to produce offspring with large brains, and the increased metabolic costs of maintaining a large brain (Isler & van Schaik 2006), the central puzzles of human brain evolution are: Why so large, and how could this possibly have taken place so recently?

Responses to these puzzles have often invoked presumptively special aspects of our social behavior. Byrne & Whiten (1988) were among the first to argue in favor of complex social environments as the primary selective pressure for human brain size and later included all aspects of social problem solving, both prosocial and deceitful, in their proposal, the "social brain hypothesis" (Dunbar 1998, Whiten & Byrne 1997). One class of empirical tests for this hypothesis seeks to determine whether those brain regions that differ most in size between humans and apes correspond to regions important for social cognition. Such analyses have pointed to the prefrontal cortex. Though the frontal cortex as a whole is not differentially enlarged in humans as compared to apes (Semendeferi et al. 2002), humans have a comparatively larger frontal polar cortex (Semendeferi et al. 2001) as well as more subtle increases in insular and temporal cortices (Semendeferi & Damasio 2000). Additional empirical tests of the social brain hypothesis focus on operationalizing social complexity in ways that include size of the over-

all group, size of an average grooming clique, size and frequency of temporally limited subgroups (e.g., coalitions), number and complexity of mating strategies, frequency and complexity of social play, frequency and complexity of deception, and the extent of social learning (Dunbar & Schultz 2007b). Some of these analyses suggest that prevalence of prosocial behaviors, specifically pair bonding behaviors, explain more variance in brain size than do other types of social complexity.

A final point of interest that brings together evolutionary and developmental aspects of human brain size is that humans are highly altricial: The brains of newborns are very immature, and our development, notably including social development, occurs over a protracted period of many years. One way of appreciating this fact is to note that human brains are only about 25% their adult volume at birth—constraints imposed in part by our bipedal nature and the evolution of the female pelvis, the shape of which limits the size of a newborn's head. By comparison, chimpanzee brains are nearly 50% their adult size at birth, and macaque monkey brains are about 70% of their adult size at birth. These differences in the size of the neonatal brain relative to the adult brain mirror the species' differences in the length of their development and their dependency on social support during this development. A recently found skull from a 1.8 million-year-old hominid child provided evidence that our ancestors had a cranial capacity at birth that is essentially like that of apes rather than like that of modern humans. This finding provides further evidence of a change in brain development that occurred relatively recently and that may be one of the features defining the evolution of our species (Coqueugnlot et al. 2004).

Social Modules?

Outlining the brain structures that participate in social cognition raises the question of whether these structures are in any sense specialized for processing social information or whether social cognition is just like cognition

FACE PROCESSING AND MODULARITY

One side of an argument about modularity has found responses with a region of the ventral temporal cortex in the fusiform gyrus, dubbed the fusiform face area (FFA), that are larger to faces than to any other visual object category (Kanwisher et al. 1997). The modularity of face processing is further supported by psychological effects unique to faces, such as disruption of processing with inversion, and by single neuron responses in the monkey brain selective to faces (Kanwisher & Yovel 2006, Tsao et al. 2006). However, the FFA also can be activated by nonface objects provided that subjects acquire substantial expertise with them, such as birds, cars, or butterflies in experts for those categories (Gauthier et al. 2000). Although the disproportionate activation by faces argues for a domain-specific module specialized to process a particular category of stimuli (faces) (Kanwisher 2000), the other data argue for a particular type of processing rather than processing for a particular stimulus category (Tarr & Gauthier 2000) (cf. **Figure 1**). Other imaging data have argued that faces are never represented in a single cortical region, but in a distributed region of cortex considerably more extensive than the FFA (Haxby et al. 2001). However, when competing stimuli are present, as would happen in naturally cluttered environments, the FFA indeed does seem to show a special selectivity for faces (Reddy & Kanwisher 2007).

in general, only applied to the domain of social behavior. There are some a priori reasons for thinking that we might have evolved specialized systems, because social behavior makes demands that are so unique. It requires rapid identification of social stimuli and signals (such as recognition of people and their dispositions toward us), vast integration of memory (to keep track of who is friend and foe based on past experience), anticipation of others' behavior in a reciprocal and often competitive setting (to generate the unique kind of knowledge outlined in the first section of this review), and the generation of normative evaluations (to motivate social behavior such as altruistic punishment). Each of these four examples has been proposed as a unique aspect of human cognition, and one might hypothesize that each is subserved by a specialized evolved

ability, or "module" (Barkow et al. 1992, Pinker 1997).

Modules have been proposed for how we process faces (see sidebar Face Processing and Modularity), for parametrically perceiving genetic relatedness (kinship) (Lieberman et al. 2007), and for detecting people who cheat on social contracts (Cosmides & Tooby 1992), an appealing idea from an evolutionary point of view, since such modules might be expected to facilitate human cooperation, altruistic punishment, and social norm compliance that regulate our ability to function in large groups. A common mechanism thought to mediate between perceptual detection and action is the motivation afforded by strong, often moral, emotions. One example is that the length of cohabitation with a member of the opposite sex calibrates perception of kinship, and correlates with the strength of moral opposition to incest (Lieberman et al. 2003). Moral judgments more generally show many of the features of automatic processing, often appear relatively modular in nature (Hauser 2006), and typically involve strong emotions (Greene & Haidt 2002, Haidt 2001), although it remains unclear whether the emotions are a cause or consequence of the judgment. In thinking about the extent to which social cognition might be special in some way, it is useful to distinguish such specialization at the level of the domain of information that is being processed (such as face perception) or at the level of the processes that are engaged (whether they are general purpose or special purpose) (Atkinson et al. 2008). This is schematized in **Figure 1**.

NEUROSCIENCE OF SOCIAL COGNITION

Perceiving Social Stimuli

The neural substrates of social cognition (see **Figure 2a**) are the topic of the rapidly growing field of social cognitive neuroscience (Ochsner 2007, Ochsner & Lieberman 2001), a subdomain of the broader field of social neuroscience (Cacioppo 1994, Cacioppo et al. 2001). One of the earliest reviews to summarize the components of a social brain proposed an initial set of structures thought to be involved in social behavior: the amygdala, the orbitofrontal cortex, and the temporal poles (Brothers 1990). More recent reviews have included additional structures and added putative roles for them (Adolphs 2003, Cacioppo et al. 2007, Fiske & Taylor 2008, Frith 2007b, Frith & Frith 2007, Lieberman 2007). In one scheme (**Figure 2b**; see color insert), early sensory cortices, as well as subcortical structures such as the amygdala, feed sensory information (in parallel routes) to a mosaic of cortical regions that analyze particular aspects of a stimulus or particular stimulus categories such as faces or bodies.

At the input end, we know by far the most about how socially relevant information is processed in the visual modality, although progress has been made for audition as well (Belin 2006). There is good evidence for conscious as well as nonconscious routes. The consciously accessible route is thought to depend on visual cortices in the temporal lobe that process object identity and that exhibit some interesting selectivity for social stimuli such as faces (see sidebar Face Processing and Modularity). A subcortical route through the superior colliculus, the mammalian homologue of the optic tectum (the primary visual pathway in amphibians, reptiles, and birds), is thought to be sufficient for visual processing whose results are not consciously accessible. For instance, when face stimuli are shown to one eye while a flickering checkerboard pattern is shown to the other eye, viewers are at chance in detecting the face stimulus even though it is present on one retina, and even though different emotional expressions shown on the invisible face stimulus result in differential activation of some brain regions (Jiang & He 2006). Two of these brain regions showing responses to unseen faces are the superior temporal sulcus, a region of visually responsive cortex, and the amygdala, a collection of nuclei in the medial temporal lobe, discussed further below.

Within the modality of touch, there are also distinct processing channels. Some of these,

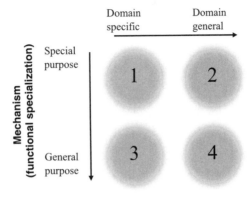

**Stimulus Information
(selectivity)**

Domain specific → Domain general

Mechanism (functional specialization)

Special purpose ↓ General purpose

1 2
3 4

Figure 1

Is social cognition special? Debates about the modularity of social information processing often revolve around the two dimensions shown in this schematic: Is the specialization at the level of processing algorithms (functional specialization) or at the level of the type of information being processed (stimulus selectivity)? A mechanism might be functionally monolithic and apply to a restricted set of stimuli (region 1) or applicable to a large domain of different kinds of stimuli (region 2). Alternatively, a mechanism might contribute to several distinct processes, but in the service of processing either a restricted stimulus class (region 3) or many (region 4). (Modified from Atkinson et al. 2008, Wheeler & Atkinson 2001.)

which signal interoceptive bodily information that subserves how we feel, are discussed further below. There also appears to be an exteroceptive channel that, unlike the main touch pathway, does not permit touch discrimination but is able to signal the social-emotional component of touch, such as a caress (Olausson et al. 2002). This pathway appears to rely on particular afferent channels that relay somatosensory information to the insula, a structure involved in affective processing and empathy, which we discuss below. Another sensory modality that may feature distinct channels, but about which relatively little is known in humans, is our sense of smell. In other mammals, there are two primary pathways—one through the olfactory bulb, the other through the vomeronasal system—both of which are involved in social and sexual behavior (Lin et al. 2005). There is some evidence in humans that aspects of our behavior can be influenced by odors without conscious awareness (Stern & McClintock 1998), and activation of brain regions involved in emotion has been

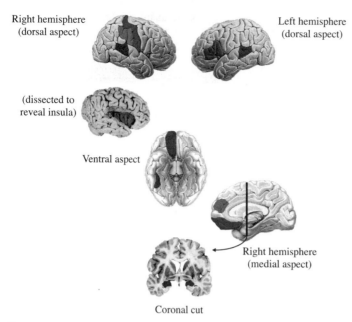

Right hemisphere
(dorsal aspect)

Left hemisphere
(dorsal aspect)

(dissected to
reveal insula)

Ventral aspect

Right hemisphere
(medial aspect)

Coronal cut

Figure 2a

Processes and brain structures involved in social cognition. Brain structures
involved in social cognition. This is, of course, an incomplete list and
emphasizes those structures discussed in the review and outlined in **Figure 2b**
(see color insert). (*Top left*) A right lateral view of a brain that shows
somatosensory cortices and superior temporal gyrus regions; roughly between
them and posterior would be the temporoparietal junction, which is not shaded
to preserve clarity of the figure. (*Top right*) Left prefrontal regions are also
involved in making personality attributions to others, and indicated again here
is the superior temporal gyrus, involved in processes such as biological motion.
Below these images are a picture of the insula, revealed when the frontal
operculum is removed, and below that, a ventral view of the brain showing
medial prefrontal cortex (in this ventral view, medial orbitofrontal cortex) and,
more posteriorly, the fusiform gyrus, involved in face processing. Below that, a
medial view of the right hemisphere shows the anterior cingulate and again the
medial prefrontal cortex. If one takes a coronal section along the line indicated,
this cut reveals the amygdala in the medial temporal lobe (very bottom image).

found in response to putative pheromone odors
(Savic et al. 2001), but the extent to which olfactory social cues play a role in everyday life
remains unclear.

Evaluating Social Stimuli

The amygdala. The observation (mentioned
in the previous section) that stimuli that cannot
be consciously perceived still result in discrim-
inative activation of the amygdala, has led to
the idea that the amygdala can provide rapid
and automatic processing that could bias so-

cial cognition. Indeed, its activation is correlated with racial stereotypes of which viewers
are unaware (Phelps et al. 2000). Its role in social
cognition has been studied most extensively in
regard to judgments we make about other people from their faces. Lesion studies found that
damage to the amygdala results in an impaired
ability to recognize emotional facial expressions
(Adolphs et al. 1994), an initial finding that has
been followed by a large literature documenting
the amygdala's involvement in both appetitive
and aversive emotional processing (Aggleton
2000). The amygdala has also been emphasized
historically as a structure important for that
emotional processing that contributes to social behavior (Kluver & Bucy 1939), another
strand in modern research on the amygdala.
Recently, at least some of this role has been
argued to be due to a more abstract function
for the amygdala in general arousal and vigilance (Whalen 1999): It appears to be important to evaluate stimuli as salient because they
are unpredictable, because they have been associated with reward or punishment, or because
they signal potentially important information.
For instance, the impaired recognition of facial
expressions of fear in a patient with amygdala
lesions (Adolphs et al. 1994) was found to result from an inability to guide one's gaze and
visual attention to features in faces normally
salient to recognize such expressions, notably
the eye region of the face (Adolphs et al. 2005)
(Figure 3). Another study found that sequences
of unpredictable tones elicited greater amygdala activation, compared with predictable
tones, even when no overt rewarding or punish-
ing outcomes were associated with those tones
(Herry et al. 2007). These recent findings support earlier ideas that the amygdala is involved
in vigilance for stimuli (in all sensory modalities) that are potentially salient because they are
ambiguous or unpredictable (Whalen 2007).
Other people may exemplify stimuli of that
sort.

The ventromedial prefrontal cortex. Ventral and medial regions of the prefrontal

cortex, which encompass a number of interconnected regions that process reward and punishment, regulate emotion, and maintain homeostasis (Öngür & Price 2000), have been linked to social behavior ever since the historical case of Phineas Gage, a nineteenth-century railroad worker who had an iron rod blasted through the front of his head in an accident (Damasio et al. 1994). Not only did Gage survive, but his personality also changed from shrewd, persistent, and respectable to profane, capricious, and unreliable after the accident [although the historical details of this account have been the topic of some debate (MacMillan 2000)]. The association of impairments in social behavior with ventromedial prefrontal cortex (VMPC) damage has since been investigated in much greater detail. Perhaps the most illustrative modern example is patient EVR (Damasio 1994, Eslinger & Damasio 1985). At age 35, EVR underwent resection of a bilateral orbitofrontal meningioma. Most of the VMPC, on both sides of the brain, was lesioned with the tumor resection. Following the surgery, EVR exhibited a remarkable decline in his personal and professional life, including two divorces, the loss of his job, and bankruptcy. Despite the gross alteration of his social conduct and decision-making, neuropsychological testing indicates EVR's intellectual abilities remained unchanged (Saver & Damasio 1991). Subsequent group studies of patients with damage to the VMPC have identified typical personality changes: blunted affect, poor frustration tolerance, impaired goal-directed behavior, inappropriate social conduct, and marked lack of insight into these changes (Barrash et al. 2000). Further experimental work has demonstrated that VMPC damage impairs autonomic responses to emotionally charged pictures (e.g., mutilated bodies, nudes) (Damasio et al. 1990) as well as to emotional memories. Studies involving gambling games indicate that VMPC patients experience diminished emotional arousal before making risky choices (Bechara et al. 1996), as well as diminished regret when considering alternate outcomes after making risky choices (Camille et al. 2004). In such games, patients with lesions to

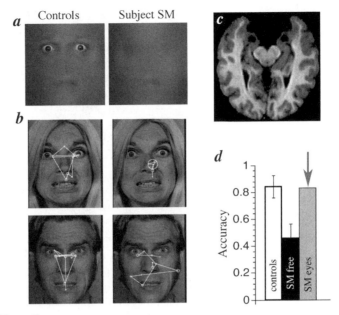

Figure 3

Abstract functions of the amygdala contribute to social perception. Bilateral amygdala lesions impair the use of the eyes and gaze to the eyes during emotion judgment. (*a*) A patient with bilateral damage to the amygdala made significantly less use of information from the eye region of faces when judging emotion. (*b*) While looking at whole faces, the patient (right column of images) exhibited abnormal face gaze, making far fewer fixations to the eyes than did controls (left column of images). This was observed across emotions (free viewing, emotion judgment, gender discrimination). (*c*) Magnetic resonance imaging scan of the patient's brain, whose lesion was relatively restricted to the entire amygdala, a very rare lesion in humans. The two round black regions near the top middle of the image are the lesioned amygdalae. (*d*) When the subject was instructed to look at the eyes ("SM eyes") in a whole face, she could do this, resulting in a remarkable recovery in ability to recognize the facial expression of fear. The findings show that an apparent role for the amygdala in processing fearful facial expressions is in fact more abstract and involves the detection of, and attentional direction onto, features that are socially informative. (Modified from Adolphs et al. 2005).

the VMPC persistently make disadvantageous choices. These results support an influential theory about the role of emotion in decision-making (including social decision-making), the so-called somatic marker hypothesis (Damasio 1994, 1996). The hypothesis argues that emotional signals, mediated in part by regions in the VMPC, can be elicited by the anticipation or consideration of the future outcomes of one's actions, and that this signal guides the decision that is made. There has been vigorous debate about whether these emotional signals are conscious or not (Bechara et al. 2005, Maia & McClelland 2004), with the current status being that they need not be conscious in order to influence behavior, although they can be brought into consciousness depending on the task in the experiment (Persaud et al. 2007).

Experimental tests that directly assess social knowledge provide further support for the role of VMPC in social cognition. Patients with VMPC damage have deficits in interpreting nonverbal social information such as facial expression, gestures, or body posture, even though they typically have preserved declarative knowledge of basic social and moral norms. Contextual interpretation of complex social information, such as judging faux pas and sarcasm, as well as aspects of moral judgment, is impaired as well (Beer et al. 2003, Hornak et al. 1996, Koenigs et al. 2007). In particular, damage to the VMPC appears to result in an inability to recognize social faux pas and reduces empathic concern for others (Shamay-Tsoory et al. 2003), an impairment that arises from the emotional contributions made by the VMPC to social cognition as opposed to other factors (such as perspective taking or theory of mind) (Shamay-Tsoory et al. 2005). Studies of moral cognition mentioned elsewhere in this review underscore the importance of VMPC in social decision-making (Koenigs et al. 2007, Moll et al. 2005).

Although the majority of studies have focused on, and the largest effects have been found for, patients who have bilateral damage to the VMPC, unilateral damage also causes the pattern of impairments described above, only milder. There appears to be an interesting asymmetry in that unilateral right-sided lesions seem to cause a more severe impairment than do unilateral left-sided lesions, an effect that was also seen in one of the studies cited above (Shamay-Tsoory et al. 2005). A further wrinkle on this story is that unilateral right lesions are more severe than left in males, whereas unilateral left lesions may be more severe than right in females (Tranel et al. 2005).

Patients with early-onset damage involving VMPC are a unique resource for investigating the development of social cognition. Like patients with adult-onset damage, individuals acquiring VMPC damage in infancy or early childhood manifest defects in social conduct and decision-making despite intact language, memory, and IQ. However, the social defects following early-onset VMPC damage appear more severe than in the adult-onset cases. Common features include apathy and unconcern; lack of guilt, empathy, or remorse; violent outbursts; lewd and irresponsible behavior; and petty criminal behavior together with a profound lack of awareness of these behavioral problems (Anderson et al. 2000). Unlike adult-onset cases, early-onset VMPC patients may have impaired knowledge of social and moral conventions (Anderson et al. 1999, 2000). These results indicate that the VMPC is critically involved in the acquisition of social and moral knowledge during development. Adult-onset VMPC patients, who presumably undergo normal social development, retain declarative access to social facts, but they appear to lose access to emotional signals that are necessary to guide appropriate on-line social and decision-making behavior in real-life situations. Early-onset VMPC patients seem to have never acquired appropriate levels of factual social knowledge in the first place, nor do they have access to normal online emotional processing, resulting in an even greater level of social impairment.

Empathy and simulation. One feature of human cognition is a rerepresentation of both sensory and motor information in order to permit more flexible behavior. For instance, a remapping of interoceptive information about the state of one's own body may allow humans and other primates to construct explicit representations of how they feel, and to know and consequently regulate how they feel in a flexible way. This remapping has been proposed to rely on relays of interoceptive processing into the insula, and a further remapping within the anterior insula is thought to consolidate body-state information about oneself with social and contextual information to provide a neural substrate of the conscious experience of emotions (Craig 2002, 2008). This region of the brain has been found to be activated in a large number of studies that involve other people, or information about other people, as the stimuli. For instance, observing the hand of a loved one receive a painful electric shock will activate the insula in the brain of the perceiver (Singer et al. 2004). This and other studies have tied the insula not only to the experience of one's own emotions, but also to the empathic feeling of others' emotions: one way in which we know what is going on inside other people is to simulate aspects of what is happening in their brain (Keysers & Gazzola 2007). Associating our observations of other people with representations of our own internal states, motivations, and intentions is hypothesized to be a general mechanism whereby we are able to generate knowledge of other minds (Keysers & Perrett 2004).

Mirroring other people can be entirely automatic, go unnoticed, and form one basis for learning about the world through others. For instance, the amygdala we discussed above has been classically shown to be necessary for acquiring Pavlovian fear conditioning, but it also turns out to be important for learning to fear a stimulus merely by observing another person experience its consequences (Olsson et al. 2007)—an effect that, like classical fear conditioning, can take place even when the stimuli cannot be consciously perceived (Olsson & Phelps 2004). In a study with rats, a naive observer rat that had not been subjected to aversive stimuli of any kind nonetheless showed discriminatory activation within the amygdala when it interacted with another rat, depending on whether or not that other rat had experienced electric shock (Knapska et al. 2006). These findings are in line with a large literature in social psychology confirming that we automatically and often nonconsciously pick up social signals from others. When we become aware that these signals are signals, more uniquely human forms of social cooperativity and deception may appear, and the knowingly shared conscious experience opens up forms of social learning on which culture can build (Frith & Frith 2007).

Empathy and emotion do not only include feelings, but they also motivate us to act, for instance when empathy causes sympathy (de Vignemont & Singer 2006). In its most schematic form, information would be expected to flow from high-level sensory representations that contribute to conscious experience of the world and our bodies, to high-level premotor representations that motivate action. The anterior cingulate cortex is one structure that is thought to receive high-level information about expected and actual sensory events, to monitor conflicts (Botvinick et al. 2004), and to integrate this with emotional information to motivate behavior (Craig 2008). It is activated in a number of experiments in which strong emotional information [such as pain (Vogt 2005) or social exclusion (Eisenberger et al. 2003)] lead to an interruption of ongoing processing and motivate a behavioral change (Devinsky et al. 1995). It appears to play a role at a high level of behavioral regulation in that it can adjust general learning about environmental contingencies when their reliability changes through time (Behrens et al. 2007)—presumably also an important role in updating our social information from other people.

Several other regions within the prefrontal cortex are routinely activated when people experience strong emotions and when they are motivated to take actions based on those emotions. These regions are all connected with the anterior cingulate cortex, include dorsolateral as well as ventromedial sectors of prefrontal cortex, and have been implicated in reward-based learning and instrumental behavior in both cooperative and competitive social interactions. They have also been highlighted as implementing one way in which emotions can motivate moral, altruistic, and socially regulatory behaviors (Damasio 1994, 2003). For instance, a network of orbitofrontal and dorsolateral prefrontal cortex is activated when punishment by others induces social norm compliance (Spitzer et al. 2007), and lesions to the ventromedial prefrontal cortex result in impaired social emotions, impaired social functioning in the real world, and an abnormal skew toward making utilitarian moral judgments when moral emotions and rational considerations are in conflict (Koenigs et al. 2007).

Emotions motivate behavior; thus, simulating other people's emotions provides us with one strategy for predicting what they are likely to do. A complementary strategy is to simulate aspects of the premotor representations that would normally accompany goal-directed behavior, a mechanism supported by finding representations, at the systems and cellular level (Gallese et al. 2004, Rizzolatti & Craighero 2004), that are engaged both when we plan to execute an action ourselves and when we observe another person carry out the same action. Although some of these "mirror" representations respond only to viewing a very specific action, the majority can abstract from the particulars of any specific action or even sensory modality to encode goal-directed intentions (Fogassi et al. 2005). Together, our ability to simulate motivational and premotor representations of other people may ground our ability to know about other minds (Gallese 2007), although deliberative reasoning (as formulated in classical theory-of-mind accounts) no doubt also plays a role. The extent to which these two processes, automatic simulation and more deliberately reflecting on mental states, come into play appears to depend on the demands of a task—their engagement is thus to some extent context-dependent (de Lange et al. 2008). It is also interesting to note that monkeys have such so-called "mirror neurons" but do not imitate or appear to know about other minds, indicating that additional enabling mechanisms, possibly including enculturation, are required for mere mirroring at the neural level to generate knowledge of other minds (Iriki 2006). Although historically it has been seen as distinct from simulation, theory-of-mind ability, broadly construed, encompasses several distinct strategies and several neural regions with a single goal: to understand the internal states that predict the behavior of other people. In fact, one may consider the outputs of a simulation/mirroring system as

the potential inputs to a mentalizing/theory-of-mind system: We may first generate motor representations of how another person is performing an action (via simulation and mirroring) and then use this representation in more flexible ways to infer the reasons and intentions behind the observed action (Keysers & Gazzola 2007).

Here we find another argument regarding modularity: the idea that our ability to reason about the minds of others, theory of mind, is an encapsulated, modular process of some kind (Leslie 1987). Theory-of-mind tasks, which ask subjects to reason about the intentions and beliefs of others, activate medial prefrontal cortex and the temporoparietal junction (TPJ). Complex biological motion that signals animacy activates high-level visual regions at the interface between processing streams for object identification (which includes the FFA; see sidebar Face Processing and Modularity) and visually guided action in the posterior superior temporal cortex (Schultz et al. 2005). This region is adjacent to, and one of the likely sources of input to, the TPJ, which in turn is involved in taking different spatial perspectives as well as the perspective of another person when we have to imagine their beliefs. The argument about the modularity of the TPJ arises from findings, on the one hand, that lesions within it impair the ability to attribute beliefs to others (Samson et al. 2004) and that it is activated selectively when we imagine the beliefs of somebody else (Saxe 2005), versus findings, on the other hand, that it is also activated when we redirect our attention in nonsocial tasks (Mitchell 2007).

There is less debate about the role of the medial prefrontal cortex in theory-of-mind abilities, as it is consistently activated when we think about other people's internal states (Amodio & Frith 2006, Saxe & Powell 2006). This region is activated when we need to infer the current beliefs of another person, evaluate their longer-term traits and dispositions, and when we think about our own minds. In fact, it is also activated when we think about the minds of animals (Mitchell et al. 2005). In short, it appears to come into play whenever we think about the mind at all, something that we may

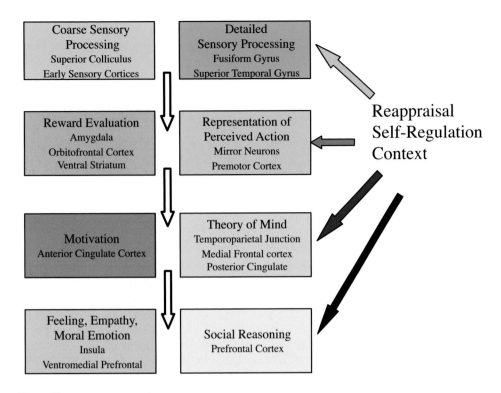

Figure 2b

The schematic outlines a set of processes related more to emotion and empathic simulation (*yellow* and *red boxes*, left), and a set of processes related to detailed perception of faces, biological motion, and theory of mind (*blue boxes*, right). Although there are many examples of processes from the list on the left being distinct from, or in opposition to, processes from the list on the right, the two often complement one another and come into play concurrently. All boxes can be modulated by controlled processing and context, although the extent of this is greatest for the more central processes (different shading of arrows, right). This schematic omits the substantial cross-talk between all of the boxes shown as well as the important role of feedback from "higher" to "lower" structures, part of which is encompassed by the self-regulation and reappraisal modulations (*black arrows*). (Modified from Adolphs 2003, Adolphs & Spezio 2008.)

do spontaneously when we are not engaged with the external world (Buckner & Carroll 2006, Mitchell et al. 2002). Another region activated in theory-of-mind tasks and likely involved in generating knowledge of both our own mind and the minds of others is the posterior cingulate cortex (Saxe & Powell 2006), a region that shows functional coupling with the medial prefrontal cortex at rest.

Modulating Social Cognition: Context and Regulation

It is likely that a similar story obtains for stimuli in all sensory modalities: There is processing that contributes to what we are conscious of, as well as processing that operates below the level of conscious reportability and discrimination; different properties of stimuli are processed in partly segregated but parallel processing streams; and this sensory processing is then associated with a variety of factors that determine its saliency and ultimately influence its deployment toward behavior. This largely feed-forward view of processing needs to be tempered by the fact that there is massive feedback everywhere in the brain, structurally often greater than the feed-forward projections. For instance, the amygdala projects back to all levels of cortical visual processing, those from which it receives input as well as earlier ones from which it does not, positioning it to influence visual information processing in a global fashion (Freese & Amaral 2005). Some of this feedback from "higher" to "lower" structures also implements aspects of controlled processing, such as emotion regulation (indicated by separate arrows in **Figure 2b**, although it in fact arises from some of the structures shown, notably the prefrontal cortex).

Social behavior depends critically on context and intention, a sensitivity that arises from the rich interplay between controlled and automatic processing of social information, and a modulation long emphasized within social psychology (Todorov et al. 2006). One way of viewing such modulations is to think of an initial feed-forward sweep of social information processing that is rapid and automatic, followed by cycles of additional processing that are biased by the first, but modulated by top-down effects that may incorporate controlled processing and conscious intent (Cunningham & Zelazo 2007). There are numerous examples at all levels of processing showing how contextual information modulates, or even gates, social information processing. At the sensory perceptual level, information about faces is processed differently depending on context. Thus, a surprised face can be interpreted as looking afraid or looking happy, depending on a preceding sentence (Kim et al. 2004). Afraid and angry faces are interpreted differently depending on whether their gaze is direct or averted (Adams & Kleck 2003). Some context modulates what we counterfactually expect might happen. Thus, in the example of social norm compliance, brain structures associated with strong emotions are activated only when the subject knows that punishment is possible, not when it is known to be impossible (Spitzer et al. 2007). An important and common finding (often utilized as a control condition in imaging studies) is that knowing that a particular event or outcome was intentionally caused by another person leads to a different interpretation than knowing that the event was unintentional or was caused by a computer. Thus, in the case of the negative emotions and anterior cingulate activation induced by social exclusion, this obtains only when the subject is convinced that other people are volitionally excluding him or her, not when the "exclusion" is explained as a technical malfunction of some sort (Eisenberger et al. 2003). What we know about people from their past behavior provides an important context that modulates our responses to, and actions toward, others. In studies of empathy, it was found that our perception of other people's fairness (from their behavior in an economic game) modulated how much empathy was felt when they were observed to be given painful electric shock, an effect that correlated with activation of the insula (Singer et al. 2006).

Emotional responses can be modulated not only by context, but also volitionally by reinterpreting a situation, or indeed solely by willful control. This is effortful, develops relatively late in childhood and adolescence, and depends on the prefrontal cortex (Ochsner & Gross 2005). Although it is somewhat simplistic, one useful heuristic is that more anterior regions within prefrontal cortex can exert cognitive control over successively posterior regions (Koechlin et al. 2003), an idea consistent with the role of frontal polar cortex (Brodmann's area 10, the most-anterior part of the brain) in overriding ongoing processing to explore new options in nonstationary environments (Daw et al. 2006). Interestingly, as we reviewed above, frontal polar cortex also appears to be a region that has expanded the most in human evolution (Semendeferi et al. 2001), and it is a region activated when we need to explicitly represent another person's mind as distinct from our own or the state of the world (Amodio & Frith 2006). Such a role may be critical to social communication, cooperation, and deception, and it may be unique to humans (Saxe 2006).

Another distinction that can be made is between sustained and volitional control on the one hand, and interruption of ongoing processing triggered by monitoring conflict on the other. These two functions have been argued to be subserved by dorsolateral regions of the prefrontal cortex and the anterior cingulate cortex, respectively (Miller & Cohen 2001). Cognitive control can extend to explicit regulation of one's own thoughts: One entertaining study found evidence for these two structures in sustained and transient suppression of forbidden thoughts (about a white bear in the experiment) (Mitchell et al. 2007). Other examples of the role of the dorsolateral prefrontal cortex in cognitive control abound. For instance, it is activated when shorter-term reward (which activates reward-related regions such as the ventral striatum and medial frontal cortex) must be foregone in lieu of longer-term reward (McClure et al. 2004). It is also activated in moral judgment tasks when an emotionally prepotent moral judgment must be overridden (in the fashion that Kant had in mind) to arrive at the decision that is best in terms of aggregate welfare (Greene et al. 2004). Moral dilemmas that pit strongly emotional outcomes against equally strong utilitarian considerations (e.g., smothering one's baby to prevent it from crying and giving away a group of people hiding in wartime) engage substantial cognitive conflict, and people do not give unanimous answers to such dilemmas. The proportion of cold utilitarian answers (e.g., smothering the baby) is increased by damage to regions that normally engage strong social emotions, such as the ventromedial prefrontal cortex (Koenigs et al. 2007), a finding we noted above. One could speculate that damage to the dorsolateral prefrontal cortex might result in the converse impairment: a larger proportion of emotional deontological answers (e.g., not smothering the baby, because this is felt to be too abhorrent and one cannot override the strong emotional aversion). The way in which our laws assign blame and dole out punishment also captures an important context effect: an interaction between the harmful consequences of an action, and the belief and intention of the person carrying it out. When examining good or bad consequences (e.g., somebody drank poison and died or drank water and lived) interacting with belief (e.g., the person offering the drink believed it was poison or did not), the results showed a strong interaction of the outcome with the belief. This interaction corresponded to activation of the TPJ (Young et al. 2007), a region discussed above in the representation of another mind's belief.

Interpretation of context and degree of control vary from person to person, and so it is perhaps not surprising that substantial individual differences exist in many of the processes and structures discussed above. In the case of empathy and the insula, individual differences exist on empathy questionnaires that correlate with the degree of insula activation. In the case of the amygdala, individual differences in anxiety correlate with amygdala activation to facial expressions, and there are now some intensively investigated genetic polymorphisms that are know to influence amygdala activation and may predispose to psychiatric illness

(Meyer-Lindenberg & Weinberger 2006, Skuse 2006). One particularly interesting story is a polymorphism in a gene that affects the level of the neurotransmitter serotonin in the brain (known to be involved in affiliative behaviors and influenced by drugs such as Prozac and ecstasy). The polymorphism (corresponding to two different but relatively common alleles) correlates with mood disorders and modulates the strength of cognitive control over amygdala processing by the anterior cingulate cortex, likely a substrate of emotion regulation (Pezawas et al. 2005).

CONCLUSION

Although many open questions remain, several of them linked to technical issues in measurement and analysis (see sidebar Future Challenges), it seems clear that human social cognition is both special and ubiquitous. It draws on many of the same brain structures involved in perception, cognition, and behavior more generally, but specialization may be evident at the level of neural processing as well (see sidebar Face Processing and Modularity). What then is it that distinguishes human social cognition from that of other species? Three prominent differences discussed above are: the ability to shift one's conscious experience to places and times outside the here-and-now, and into the viewpoint of another mind (Buckner & Carroll 2006, Suddendorf & Corballis 1997); the association of our evaluation of others with strong moral emotions that motivate particular aspects of social behavior, such as altruistic punishment (Fehr & Gaechter 2002); and the ability to use these abilities flexibly as a function of context, across considerable time intervals, and with the

FUTURE CHALLENGES

To understand the function of a neural structure, we need to know all its inputs and outputs, a description that is difficult to obtain in humans but becoming possible in some animal models. For instance, how olfactory information about a mate interacts with reward systems during mating to result in pair-bonding behavior of prairie voles has been worked out in spectacular detail (Insel & Young 2001, Young & Wang 2004). Two recent technical developments in magnetic resonance imaging are beginning to sketch such a picture also in humans: Diffusion imaging is providing information about the structural connectivity of the human brain, and functional connectivity modeling is providing estimates of information flow between structures; a currently hot area of development is integrating these two sources of connectivity information (Friston et al. 2003, Jbabdi et al. 2007). One functional network is the so-called default or resting-state network, first identified on the basis of positron emission tomography studies and thought to be active during rest, deactivated when we process external stimuli or engage in an externally directed task (Gusnard & Raichle 2001), and subserving processes that include perspective taking and self-reflection (Buckner & Carroll 2006). It may be one aspect of the automatic human propensity to think about what might happen, or what will happen in the future, in order to prepare ourselves and plan our behavior (Bar 2007). It is also intriguing to note that people with autism, who are impaired in social functioning, do not activate this same network at rest (Kennedy et al. 2006).

help of a prodigious episodic memory that helps us to keep track of a large number of other individuals and their past behavior (Stevens et al. 2005). When the demands on social cognition become severe, these three abilities taken together may define much of the nature of human conscious experience and indeed provide an argument for its emergence.

SUMMARY POINTS

1. Inferring what is going on inside other people's minds from their observed behavior may be a uniquely human ability, although other primates show precursors to this ability.

2. The ability to infer others' mental states is thought to be an important contributor to human culture and civilization.

3. Although many different psychological processes contribute to social cognition, they are often grouped into two broad categories: those related to automatic processing driven more by the stimuli and those related to controlled processing driven more by the person's goals and intentions.

4. Social information processing looks in many respects different from nonsocial information processing. This has provided support for some schemes that claim social information processing is modular.

5. The amygdala is a structure in the medial temporal lobe important to regulating social behavior and recognizing emotional facial expressions. However, recent work suggests its role is quite abstract and not specific to social cognition.

6. The orbitofrontal cortex is a region of cortex in the frontal lobes that is involved in reward processing. Lesions of this region in humans result in severe impairments in real-life social behavior despite cognition in other domains that is otherwise relatively intact.

7. The insula is a region of cortex buried underneath the frontal cortex that is involved in representing states of our own body, such as pain. It is also involved when we feel empathy for others, such as when we observe somebody else in pain.

8. Social cognition is sensitive to context, and the brain regions involved in social cognition are modulated in their activation by social context and volitional regulation.

9. Two hypotheses about how we infer other people's mental states are that we do so by simulation and empathy (abilities that involve regions such as the premotor cortex and the insula) or via more deliberate theory-of-mind abilities (which involve regions such as the medial prefrontal cortex and the temporoparietal junction).

DISCLOSURE STATEMENT

The author is not aware of any biases that might be perceived as affecting the objectivity of this review.

ACKNOWLEDGMENTS

This review was supported by grants from the National Institute of Mental Health, the Simons Foundation, and the Gordon and Betty Moore Foundation. I thank Phillipe Schyns, Joanne Silk, and Susan Fiske for helpful comments on the manuscript.

This study found that a patient with bilateral amygdala lesions was impaired in recognizing fear in facial expressions because patient failed to fixate the eyes in faces and thus failed to use facial information normally needed to recognize fear.

LITERATURE CITED

Adams RB, Kleck RE. 2003. Perceived gaze direction and the processing of facial displays of emotion. *Psychol. Sci.* 14:644–47

Adolphs R. 2003. Cognitive neuroscience of human social behavior. *Nat. Rev. Neurosci.* 4:165–78

Adolphs R. 2006. How do we know the minds of others? Domain-specificity, simulation, and enactive social cognition. *Brain Res.* 1079:25–35

Adolphs R, Gosselin F, Buchanan TW, Tranel D, Schyns P, Damasio AR. 2005. A mechanism for impaired fear recognition after amygdala damage. *Nature* 433:68–72

Adolphs R, Spezio M. 2008. The neuroscience of social cognition. In *Handbook of Neuroscience for the Behavioral Sciences*, ed. JT Cacioppo, G Berntson. New York: Wiley. In press

Adolphs R, Tranel D, Damasio H, Damasio A. 1994. Impaired recognition of emotion in facial expressions following bilateral damage to the human amygdala. *Nature* 372:669–72

Aggleton J, ed. 2000. *The Amygdala. A Functional Analysis*. New York: Oxford Univ. Press

Allman JM. 1999. *Evolving Brains*. New York: Sci. Am. Library

Amodio DM, Frith CD. 2006. Meeting of minds: the medial frontal cortex and social cognition. *Nat. Rev. Neurosci.* 7:268–77

Anderson SW, Bechara A, Damasio H, Tranel D, Damasio AR. 1999. Impairment of social and moral behavior related to early damage in human prefrontal cortex. *Nat. Neurosci.* 2:1032–37

Anderson SW, Damasio H, Tranel D, Damasio AR. 2000. Long-term sequelae of prefrontal cortex damage acquired in early childhood. *Dev. Neuropsychol.* 18:281–96

Atkinson AP, Heberlein AS, Adolphs R. 2008. Are people special? A brain's eye view. In *The Science of Social Vision*, ed. RB Adams, K Nakayama, S Shimojo. New York: Oxford Univ. Press. In press

Bar M. 2007. The proactive brain: using analogies and associations to generate predictions. *Trends Cogn. Sci.* 11:280–89

Bar M, Neta M, Linz H. 2006. Very first impressions. *Emotion* 6:269–78

Bargh JA, Ferguson MJ. 2000. Beyond behaviorism: on the automaticity of higher mental processes. *Psychol. Bull.* 126:925–45

Bargh JA, Morsella E. 2008. The unconscious mind. *Perspect. Psychol. Sci.* 3:73–79

Barkow JH, Cosmides L, Tooby J, eds. 1992. *The Adapted Mind: Evolutionary Psychology and the Generation of Culture*. New York: Oxford Univ. Press

Baron-Cohen S. 1997. *Mindblindness: An Essay on Autism and Theory of Mind*. Cambridge, MA: MIT Press. 200 pp.

Barrash J, Tranel D, Anderson SW. 2000. Acquired personality disturbances associated with bilateral damage to the ventromedial prefrontal region. *Dev. Neuropsychol.* 18:355–81

Barrett L, Henzi P. 2005. The social nature of primate cognition. *Proc. Biol. Sci.* 272:1865–75

Bechara A, Damasio H, Tranel D, Damasio A. 2005. The Iowa Gambling Task and the somatic marker hypothesis: some questions and answers. *Trends Cogn. Neurosci.* 9(4):159–62

Bechara A, Tranel D, Damasio H, Damasio AR. 1996. Failure to respond autonomically to anticipated future outcomes following damage to prefrontal cortex. *Cereb. Cortex* 6:215–25

Beer JS, Heerey EA, Keltner D, Scabini D, Knight RT. 2003. Regulatory functions of self-conscious emotion: insights from patients with orbitofrontal damage. *J. Personal. Soc. Psychol.* 85:594–604

Behrens TEJ, Woolrich MW, Walton ME, Rushworth MF. 2007. Learning the value of information in an uncertain world. *Nat. Neurosci.* 10:1214–21

Belin P. 2006. Voice processing in human and nonhuman primates. *Philos. Trans. R. Soc. Lond. B Biol. Sci.* 361:2091–107

Blakemore S-J. 2008. The social brain in adolescence. *Nat. Rev. Neurosci.* 9:267–77

Boesch C. 2007. What makes us human (*Homo sapiens*)? The challenge of cross-species comparison. *J. Comp. Psychol.* 121:227–40

Botvinick MM, Cohen JD, Carter CS. 2004. Conflict monitoring and anterior cingulate cortex: an update. *Trends Cogn. Sci.* 8:539–46

Braver TS, Barch DM. 2006. Extracting core components of cognitive control. *Trends Cogn. Sci.* 10:529–32

Brothers L. 1990. The social brain: a project for integrating primate behavior and neurophysiology in a new domain. *Concepts Neurosci.* 1:27–51

Buckner RL, Carroll DC. 2007. Self-projection and the brain. *Trends Cogn. Sci.* 11(2)49–57

Byrne R, Whiten A, eds. 1988. *Machiavellian Intelligence: Social Expertise and the Evolution of Intellect in Monkeys, Apes, and Humans*. Oxford: Clarendon

Cacioppo JT. 1994. Social neuroscience: autonomic, neuroendocrine, and immune responses to stress. *Psychophysiology* 31:113–28

Cacioppo JT, Amaral DG, Blanchard JJ, Cameron JL, Carter CS, et al. 2007. Social neuroscience: progress and implications for mental health. *Perspect. Psychol. Sci.* 2:99–123

Part of a debate about whether emotional biases in decision making are conscious.

Reviews common brain networks engaged when we daydream, recollect the past, imagine the future, and imagine other people's minds.

Cacioppo JT, Berntson GG, Adolphs R, Carter CS, Davidson RJ, et al., eds. 2001. *Foundations in Social Neuroscience*. Cambridge, MA: MIT Press

Camille N, Coricelli G, Sallet J, Pradat-Diehl P, Duhamel J-R, Sirigu A. 2004. The involvement of the orbitofrontal cortex in the experience of regret. *Science* 304:1167–70

Cheney DL, Seyfarth RM. 1990. *How Monkeys See the World*. Chicago, IL: Univ. Chicago Press

Coqueugnlot H, Hublin J-J, Vellon F, Houet F, Jacob T. 2004. Early brain growth in *Homo erectus* and implications for cognitive ability. *Nature* 431:299–332

Cosmides L, Tooby J. 1992. Cognitive adaptations for social exchange. In *The Adapted Mind: Evolutionary Psychology and the Generation of Culture*, ed. JH Barkow, L Cosmides, J Tooby, pp. 163–228. New York: Oxford Univ. Press

Craig AD. 2002. How do you feel? Interoception: the sense of the physiological condition of the body. *Nat. Rev. Neurosci.* 3:655–66

Craig AD. 2008. Interoception and emotion: a neuroanatomical perspective. In *Handbook of Emotions*, ed. M Lewis, L Feldman-Barrett, pp. 272–88. New York: Guilford. 3rd ed.

Crick F, Koch C. 1995. Are we aware of neural activity in primary visual cortex? *Nature* 375:121–23

Cunningham WA, Zelazo PD. 2007. Attitudes and evaluations: a social cognitive neuroscience perspective. *Trends Cogn. Sci.* 11:97–104

Damasio AR. 1994. *Descartes' Error: Emotion, Reason, and the Human Brain*. New York: Grosset/Putnam

Damasio AR. 1996. The somatic marker hypothesis and the possible functions of the prefrontal cortex. *Philos. Trans. R. Soc. Lond. B Biol. Sci.* 351:1413–20

Damasio AR. 2003. *Looking for Spinoza: Joy, Sorrow, and the Feeling Brain*. Orlando, FL: Harcourt

Damasio AR, Tranel D, Damasio H. 1990. Individuals with sociopathic behavior caused by frontal damage fail to respond autonomically to social stimuli. *Behav. Brain Res.* 41:81–94

Damasio H, Grabowski T, Frank R, Galaburda AM, Damasio AR. 1994. The return of Phineas Gage: clues about the brain from the skull of a famous patient. *Science* 264:1102–4

Davidson D. 1987. Knowing one's own mind. In *Proceedings and Addresses of the American Philosophical Association* 61:441–58. New York: Oxford Univ. Press

Daw N, O'Doherty JP, Dayan P, Seymour B, Dolan RJ. 2006. Polar exploration: cortical substrates for exploratory decisions in humans. *Nature* 441:876–79

de Lange FP, Spronk M, Willems RM, Toni I, Bekkering H. 2008. Complementary systems for understanding action intentions. *Curr. Biol.* 18:454–57

de Vignemont F, Singer T. 2006. The empathic brain: how, when and why? *Trends Cogn. Sci.* 10:436–41

de Waal F, Dindo M, Freeman CA, Hall MJ. 2005. The monkey in the mirror: hardly a stranger. *Proc. Natl. Acad. Sci. USA* 102:11140–47

Devinsky O, Morrell MJ, Vogt BA. 1995. Contributions of anterior cingulate cortex to behaviour. *Brain* 118(Pt. 1):279–306

Dunbar RI. 1998. The social brain hypothesis. *Evol. Anthropol.* 6:178–90

Dunbar RI, Schultz S. 2007a. Evolution in the social brain. *Science* 317:1344–47

Dunbar RI, Schultz S. 2007b. Understanding primate brain evolution. *Philos. Trans. R. Soc. Lond. B Biol. Sci.* 362:649–58

Eisenberger NI, Lieberman MD, Williams KD. 2003. Does rejection hurt? An fMRI study of social exclusion. *Science* 302:290–92

Emery NJ, Clayton NS. 2004. The mentality of crows: convergent evolution of intelligence in corvids and apes. *Science* 306:1903–7

Epley N, Waytz A, Cacioppo JT. 2007. On seeing human: a three-factor theory of anthropomorphism. *Psychol. Rev.* 114:864–86

Eslinger PJ, Damasio AR. 1985. Severe disturbance of higher cognition after bilateral frontal lobe ablation: patient EVR. *Neurology* 35:1731–41

Fehr E, Gaechter S. 2002. Altruistic punishment in humans. *Nature* 415:137–40

Fiske ST, Cuddy AJC, Glick P. 2007. Universal dimensions of social cognition: warmth and competence. *Trends Cogn. Sci.* 11:78–83

Fiske ST, Taylor SE. 2008. *Social Cognition: From Brains to Culture*. New York: McGraw-Hill. 3rd ed.

We punish others whose behavior we deem to be unfair, even when such punishment is at a cost to ourselves.

Fogassi L, Ferrari PF, Gesierich B, Rozzi S, Chersi F, Rizzolatti G. 2005. Parietal lobe: from action organization to intention understanding. *Science* 308:662–67

Freese JL, Amaral DG. 2005. The organization of projections from the amygdala to visual cortical areas TE and V1 in the macaque monkey. *J. Comp. Neurol.* 486:295–317

Friston KJ, Harrison L, Penny WD. 2003. Dynamic causal modeling. *Neuroimage* 19:1273–302

Frith CD. 2007a. *Making Up the Mind: How the Brain Creates Our Mental World.* New York: Blackwell Sci.

Frith CD. 2007b. The social brain? *Philos. Trans. R. Soc. Lond. B Biol. Sci.* 362:671–78

Frith CD, Frith U. 2007. Social cognition in humans. *Curr. Biol.* 17:R724–32

Frith U. 2001. Mind blindness and the brain in autism. *Neuron* 32:969–79

Gallese V. 2007. Before and below "theory of mind": embodied simulation and the neural correlates of social cognition. *Philos. Trans. R. Soc. Lond. B Biol. Sci.* 362:659–69

Gallese V, Keysers C, Rizzolatti G. 2004. A unifying view of the basis of social cognition. *Trends Cogn. Sci.* 8:396–403

Gallup GG. 1970. Chimpanzees: self-recognition. *Science* 167:86–87

Gauthier I, Skudlarski P, Gore JC, Anderson AW. 2000. Expertise for cars and birds recruits brain areas involved in face recognition. *Nat. Neurosci.* 3:191–97

Gintis H, Bowles S, Boyd R, Fehr E. 2003. Explaining altruistic behavior in humans. *Evol. Hum. Behav.* 24:153–72

Greene JD, Haidt J. 2002. How (and where) does moral judgment work? *Trends Cogn. Sci.* 6:517–23

Greene JD, Nystrom LE, Engell AD, Darley JM, Cohen JD. 2004. The neural bases of cognitive conflict and control in moral judgment. *Neuron* 44:389–400

Gusnard DA, Raichle MA. 2001. Searching for a baseline: functional imaging and the resting human brain. *Nat. Rev. Neurosci.* 2:685–94

Haidt J. 2001. The emotional dog and its rational tail: a social intuitionist approach to moral judgment. *Psychol. Rev.* 108:814–34

Haidt J. 2007. The new synthesis in moral psychology. *Science* 316:998–1002

Hare B, Tomasello M. 2004. Chimpanzees are more skillful in competitive than in cooperative cognitive tasks. *Anim. Behav.* 68:571–81

Hauser MD. 2006. *Moral Minds: How Nature Designed Our Universal Sense of Right and Wrong.* New York: HarperCollins

Haxby JV, Gobbini MI, Furey ML, Ishai A, Schouten JL, Pietrini P. 2001. Distributed and overlapping representation of faces and objects in ventral temporal cortex. *Science* 293:2425–29

Herrmann E, Call J, Hernandez-Lloreda MV, Hare B, Tomasello M. 2007. Humans have evolved specialized skills of social cognition: the cultural intelligence hypothesis. *Science* 317:1360–66

Herry C, Bach DR, Esposito F, DiSalle F, Perrig WJ, et al. 2007. Processing of temporal unpredictability in human and animal amygdala. *J. Neurosci.* 27:5958–66

Hornak J, Rolls ET, Wade D. 1996. Face and voice expression identification in patients with emotional and behavioral changes following ventral frontal lobe damage. *Neuropsychologia* 34:247–61

Insel TR, Young LJ. 2001. The neurobiology of attachment. *Nat. Rev. Neurosci.* 2:129–35

Iriki A. 2006. The neural origins and implications of imitation, mirror neurons and tool use. *Curr. Opin. Neurobiol.* 16:660–67

Isler K, van Schaik CP. 2006. Metabolic costs of brain size evolution. *Biol. Lett.* 2:557–60

Jbabdi S, Woolrich MW, Andersson JL, Behrens TE. 2007. A Bayesian framework for global tractography. *Neuroimage* 37:116–29

Jiang Y, He S. 2006. Cortical responses to invisible faces: dissociating subsystems for facial-information processing. *Curr. Biol.* 16:2023–29

Kanwisher N. 2000. Domain specificity in face perception. *Nat. Neurosci.* 3:759–63

Kanwisher N, McDermott J, Chun MM. 1997. The fusiform face area: a module in human extrastriate cortex specialized for face perception. *J. Neurosci.* 17:4302–11

Kanwisher N, Yovel G. 2006. The fusiform face area: a cortical region specialized for the perception of faces. *Philos. Trans. R. Soc. Lond. B Biol. Sci.* 361:2109–28

Kennedy DP, Redcay E, Courchesne E. 2006. Failing to deactivate: resting functional abnormalities in autism. *Proc. Natl. Acad. Sci. USA* 103:8275–80

The amygdala responds to temporally unpredictable (jittered) tones, even when these are not emotional.

A review of the best-understood model system for bonding and affiliative behaviors: the sexual behavior of voles.

Keysers C, Gazzola V. 2007. Integrating simulation and theory of mind: from self to social cognition. *Trends Cogn. Sci.* 11:194–96

Keysers C, Perrett DI. 2004. Demystifying social cognition: a Hebbian perspective. *Trends Cogn. Sci.* 8:501–7

Kim H, Somerville LH, Johnstone T, Polis S, Alexander AL, et al. 2004. Contextual modulation of amygdala responsivity to surprised faces. *J. Cogn. Neurosci.* 16:1730–45

Kluver H, Bucy PC. 1939. Preliminary analysis of functions of the temporal lobes in monkeys. *Arch. Neurol. Psychiatry* 42:979–97

Knapska E, Nikolaev E, Boguszewski P, Walasek G, Blaszczyk J, et al. 2006. Between-subject transfer of emotional information evokes specific pattern of amygdala activation. *Proc. Natl. Acad. Sci. USA* 103:3858–62

Koechlin E, Ody C, Kouneiher F. 2003. The architecture of cognitive control in the human prefrontal cortex. *Science* 302:1181–85

Koenigs M, Young L, Adolphs R, Tranel D, Cushman F, et al. 2007. Damage to the prefrontal cortex increases utilitarian moral judgments. *Nature* 446:908–11

Leslie A. 1987. Pretense and representation: the origins of "theory of mind." *Psychol. Rev.* 94:412–26

Lieberman D, Tooby J, Cosmides L. 2003. Does morality have a biological basis? An empirical test of the factors governing moral sentiments relating to incest. *Proc. R. Soc. Lond. B Biol. Sci.* 270:819–26

Lieberman D, Tooby J, Cosmides L. 2007. The architecture of human kin detection. *Nature* 445:727–31

Lieberman MD. 2007. Social cognitive neuroscience: a review of core processes. *Annu. Rev. Psychol.* 58:259–89

Lin DY, Zhang S-Z, Block E, Katz LC. 2005. Encoding social signals in the mouse main olfactory bulb. *Nature* 434:470–77

MacMillan M. 2000. *An Odd Kind of Fame: Stories of Phineas Gage*. Cambridge, MA: MIT Press

Maia TV, McClelland JE. 2004. A re-examination of the evidence for the somatic marker hypothesis: what participants really know in the Iowa gambling task. *Proc. Natl. Acad. Sci. USA* 101:16075–80

McClure SM, Laibson DI, Loewenstein G, Cohen JD. 2004. Separate neural systems value immediate and delayed monetary rewards. *Science* 306:503–7

Meyer-Lindenberg A, Weinberger DR. 2006. Intermediate phenotypes and genetic mechanisms of psychiatric disorders. *Nat. Rev. Neurosci.* 7:818–27

Miklosi A, Kubinyi E, Topal J, Gacsi M, Viranyi Z, Csanyi V. 2003. A simple reason for a big difference: Wolves do not look back at humans, but dogs do. *Curr. Biol.* 13:763–66

Miller EK, Cohen JD. 2001. An integrative theory of prefrontal cortex function. *Annu. Rev. Neurosci.* 24:167–202

Mitchell JP. 2007. Activity in right temporo-parietal junction is not selective for theory-of-mind. *Cereb. Cortex* 18(2):262–71

Mitchell JP, Banaji MR, Macrae CN. 2005. General and specific contributions of the medial prefrontal cortex to knowledge about mental states. *Neuroimage* 28:757–62

Mitchell JP, Heatherton TF, Kelley WM, Wyland CL, Wegner DM, Macrae CN. 2007. Separating sustained from transient aspects of cognitive control during thought suppression. *Psychol. Sci.* 18:292–97

Mitchell JP, Heatherton TF, Macrae CN. 2002. Distinct neural systems subserve person and object knowledge. *Proc. Natl. Acad. Sci. USA* 99:15238–43

Moll J, Zahn R, de Oliveira-Souza R, Krueger F, Grafman J. 2005. The neural basis of human moral cognition. *Nat. Rev. Neurosci.* 6:799–809

Ochsner KN. 2007. Social cognitive neuroscience: historical development, core principles, and future promise. In *Social Psychology: A Handbook of Basic Principles*, ed. A Kruglanski, ET Higgins, pp. 39–66. New York: Guilford. 2nd ed.

Ochsner KN, Gross JJ. 2005. The cognitive control of emotions. *Trends Cogn. Sci.* 9:242–49

Ochsner KN, Lieberman MD. 2001. The emergence of social cognitive neuroscience. *Am. Psychol.* 56:717–34

Olausson H, Lamarre Y, Backlund H, Morin C, Wallin BG, et al. 2002. Unmyelinated tactile afferents signal touch and project to insular cortex. *Nat. Neurosci.* 5:900–4

Olsson A, Nearing KI, Phelps EA. 2007. Learning fears by observing others: the neural systems of social fear transmission. *Soc. Cogn. Affect. Neurosci.* 2:3–11

Olsson A, Phelps EA. 2004. Learned fear of "unseen" faces after Pavlovian, observational, and instructed fear. *Psychol. Sci.* 15:822–28

Öngür D, Price JL. 2000. The organization of networks within the orbital and medial prefrontal cortex of rats, monkeys, and humans. *Cereb. Cortex* 10:206–19

Penn DC, Povinelli DJ. 2007. On the lack of evidence that nonhuman animals possess anything remotely resembling a "theory of mind." *Philos. Trans. R. Soc. Lond. B Biol. Sci.* 362:731–44

Persaud N, LcLeod P, Cowey A. 2007. Post-decision wagering objectively measures awareness. *Nat. Neurosci.* 10:257–61

Pezawas L, Meyer-Lindenberg A, Drabant EM, Verchinski BA, Munoz KE, et al. 2005. 5-HTTLPR polymorphism impacts human cingulate-amygdala interactions: a genetic susceptibility mechanism for depression. *Nat. Neurosci.* 8:828–34

Phelps EA, O'Connor KJ, Cunningham WA, Funayama ES, Gatenby JC, et al. 2000. Performance on indirect measures of race evaluation predicts amygdala activation. *J. Cogn. Neurosci.* 12:729–38

Pinker S. 1997. *How the Mind Works.* New York: Norton

Plotnik JM, de Waal F, Reiss D. 2006. Self-recognition in an Asian elephant. *Proc. Natl. Acad. Sci. USA* 103:17053–57

Povinelli DJ, Vonk J. 2003. Chimpanzee minds: suspiciously human? *Trends Cogn. Sci.* 7:157–60

Premack D, Woodruff G. 1978. Does the chimpanzee have a theory of mind? *Behav. Brain Sci.* 1:515–26

Reddy L, Kanwisher N. 2007. Category selectivity in the ventral visual pathway confers robustness to clutter and diverted attention. *Curr. Biol.* 17:2067–72

Reiss D, Marino L. 2001. Mirror self-recognition in the bottlenose dolphin: a case of cognitive convergence. *Proc. Natl. Acad. Sci. USA* 98:5937–42

Rizzolatti G, Craighero L. 2004. The mirror-neuron system. *Annu. Rev. Neurosci.* 27:169–92

Roberts WA, Feeney MC, MacPherson K, Petter M, McMillan N, Musolino E. 2008. Episodic-like memory in rats: Is it based on when or how long ago? *Science* 320:113–15

Roth G, Dicke U. 2005. Evolution of the brain and intelligence. *Trends Cogn. Sci.* 9:250–57

Ruff CB, Trinkaus E, Holliday TW. 1997. Body mass and encephalization in *Pleistocene Homo. Nature* 387:173–76

Samson D, Apperly I, Humphreys G. 2004. Left temporoparietal junction is necessary for representing someone else's belief. *Nat. Neurosci.* 7:499–500

Saver JL, Damasio AR. 1991. Preserved access and processing of social knowledge in a patient with acquired sociopathy due to ventromedial frontal damage. *Neuropsychologia* 29:1241–49

Savic I, Berglund H, Gulyas B, Roland P. 2001. Smelling of odorous sex hormone-like compounds causes sex-differentiated hypothalamic activation in humans. *Neuron* 31:661–68

Saxe R. 2005. Hybrid vigour: reply to Mitchell. *Trends Cogn. Sci.* 9:364

Saxe R. 2006. Uniquely human social cognition. *Curr. Opin. Neurobiol.* 16:235–39

Saxe R, Powell LJ. 2006. It's the thought that counts: specific brain regions for one component of theory of mind. *Psychol. Sci.* 17:692–99

Schultz J, Friston KJ, O'Doherty JP, Wolpert DM, Frith C. 2005. Activation in posterior superior temporal sulcus parallels parameters inducing the percept of animacy. *Neuron* 45:625–35

Semendeferi K, Armstrong E, Schleicher A, Zilles K, Van Hoesen GW. 2001. Prefrontal cortex in humans and apes: a comparative study of area 10. *Am. J. Phys. Anthropol.* 114:224–41

Semendeferi K, Damasio H. 2000. The brain and its main anatomical subdivisions in living hominoids using magnetic resonance imaging. *J. Hum. Evol.* 38:317–32

Semendeferi K, Lu A, Schenker N, Damasio H. 2002. Humans and great apes share a large frontal cortex. *Nat. Neurosci.* 5:272–77

Shamay-Tsoory SG, Tomer R, Berger BD, Aharon-Peretz J. 2003. Characterization of empathy deficits following prefrontal brain damage: the role of the right ventromedial prefrontal cortex. *J. Cogn. Neurosci.* 15:324–37

Shamay-Tsoory SG, Tomer R, Berger BD, Goldsher D, Aharon-Peretz J. 2005. Impaired "affective theory of mind" is associated with right ventromedial prefrontal damage. *Cogn. Behav. Neurol.* 18:55–67

Silk JB. 2005. Social components of fitness in primate groups. *Science* 317:1347–51

Shows that humans can learn to fear stimuli through direct experience (classical Pavlovian conditioning), through observation (social learning), and through instruction (unique to humans). However, only the first two can take place nonconsciously.

Silk JB, Brosnan SF, Vonk J, Henrich J, Povinelli D, et al. 2005. Chimpanzees are indifferent to the welfare of unrelated group members. *Nature* 437:1357–59

Singer T, Seymour B, O'Doherty J, Kaube H, Dolan RJ, Frith CD. 2004. Empathy for pain involves the affective but not sensory components of pain. *Science* 303:1157–62

Singer T, Seymour B, O'Doherty J, Stephan KE, Dolan RJ, Frith CD. 2006. Empathic neural responses are modulated by the perceived fairness of others. *Nature* 439:466–69

Skuse D. 2006. Genetic influences on the neural basis of social cognition. *Philos. Trans. R. Soc. Lond. B Biol. Sci.* 361:2129–41

Spitzer M, Fischbacher U, Hermberger B, Groen G, Fehr E. 2007. The neural signature of social norm compliance. *Neuron* 56:185–96

Stern K, McClintock MK. 1998. Regulation of ovulation by human pheromones. *Nature* 392:177–79

Stevens JA, Cushman F, Hauser M. 2005. Evolving the psychological mechanisms for cooperation. *Annu. Rev. Ecol. Evol. Syst.* 36:499–518

Striano T, Reid VM. 2006. Social cognition in the first year. *Trends Cogn. Sci.* 10:471–76

Suddendorf T, Corballis M. 1997. Mental time travel and the evolution of the human mind. *Genet. Soc. Gen. Psychol. Monogr.* 123:133–67

Tarr MJ, Gauthier I. 2000. FFA: a flexible fusiform area for subordinate-level visual processing automatized by expertise. *Nat. Neurosci.* 3:764–69

Todorov A, Harris LT, Fiske ST. 2006. Toward socially inspired social neuroscience. *Brain Res.* 1079:76–85

Todorov A, Mandisodza AN, Goren A, Hall CC. 2005. Inferences of competence from faces predict election outcomes. *Science* 308:1623–26

Tomasello M. 1999. *The Cultural Origins of Human Cognition*. Cambridge, MA: Harvard Univ. Press

Tomasello M, Call J, Hare B. 2003. Chimpanzees understand psychological states—the question is which ones and to what extent. *Trends Cogn. Sci.* 7:153–56

Tranel D, Damasio H, Denburg N, Bechara A. 2005. Does gender play a role in functional asymmetry of ventromedial prefrontal cortex? *Brain* 128:2872–81

Tsao DY, Freiwald WA, Tootell RBH, Livingstone MS. 2006. A cortical region consisting entirely of face-selective cells. *Science* 311:670–74

Vogt BA. 2005. Pain and emotion interactions in subregions of the cingulate gyrus. *Nat. Rev. Neurosci.* 6:533–44

Whalen PJ. 1999. Fear, vigilance, and ambiguity: initial neuroimaging studies of the human amygdala. *Curr. Dir. Psychol. Sci.* 7:177–87

Whalen PJ. 2007. The uncertainty of it all. *Trends Cogn. Sci.* 11:499–500

Wheeler M, Atkinson A. 2001. Domains, brains and evolution. In *Naturalism, Evolution and Mind*, ed. DM Walsh, pp. 239–66. Cambridge, UK: Cambridge Univ. Press

Whiten A, Byrne R, eds. 1997. *Machiavellian Intelligence II: Extensions and Evaluations*. Cambridge, UK: Cambridge Univ. Press

Whiten A, Goodall J, McGrew WC, Nishida T, Reynolds V, et al. 1999. Cultures in chimpanzees. *Nature* 399:682–85

Willis J, Todorov A. 2006. First impressions: making up your mind after a 100-ms exposure to a face. *Psychol. Sci.* 17:592–98

Wood JN, Glynn DD, Phillips BC, Hauser M. 2007. The perception of rational, goal-directed action in nonhuman primates. *Science* 317:1402–5

Young LJ, Cushman F, Hauser MD, Saxe R. 2007. The neural basis of the interaction between theory of mind and moral judgment. *Proc. Natl. Acad. Sci. USA* 104:8235–40

Young LJ, Wang Z. 2004. The neurobiology of pair bonding. *Nat. Neurosci.* 7:1048–54

Workplace Victimization: Aggression from the Target's Perspective

Karl Aquino[1] and Stefan Thau[2]

[1] Sauder School of Business, University of British Columbia, Vancouver, British Columbia V6T 1Z2; email: karl.aquino@sauder.ubc.ca

[2] Organizational Behavior Subject Area, London Business School, London, United Kingdom NW1 4SA; email: sthau@london.edu

Annu. Rev. Psychol. 2009. 60:717–41

The *Annual Review of Psychology* is online at psych.annualreviews.org

This article's doi: 10.1146/annurev.psych.60.110707.163703

Key Words

aggression, bullying, harassment, victimization, incivility

Abstract

This article reviews research on workplace victimization, which we define as acts of aggression perpetrated by one or more members of an organization that cause psychological, emotional, or physical harm to their intended target. We compare several types of victimizing behaviors that have been introduced into the organizational psychology literature to illustrate differences and similarities among them. We then review studies looking at who is likely to become a victim of aggression. Predictors include personality, demographic, behavioral, structural, and organizational variables. We also review research on coping strategies for victimization, which include problem-focused and emotion-focused strategies. We conclude with a summary of challenges for victimization research. These include addressing the proliferation of constructs and terms into the literature, attempting to clarify inconclusive findings, and using theory to guide the selection of study variables.

Contents

INTRODUCTION

Work organizations are like any other social setting where competition, scarce resources, time pressure, differences in goals and personalities, and other stresses of group life can sometimes lead people to aggress against coworkers, subordinates, and even authorities. Aggression has been defined as behavior directed toward another person or persons that is carried out with the intent to harm (Anderson & Bushman 2002, Buss 1961). For every perpetrator of workplace aggression, there is at least one victim. It is the victim's perspective that we examine in this review. By taking this perspective, we complement Anderson & Bushman's (2002) *Annual Review of Psychology* article that focused on the factors that motivate aggression and Barling et al.'s (2009) review of the predictors of workplace aggression appearing in this volume.

Previous reviews of aggression from a victim's perspective have been conducted (e.g., Einarsen 2000, Hoel et al. 1999, Hogh & Viitasara 2005, Salin 2003b, Tepper 2007); however, these reviews focused on specific types of aggressive behaviors such as bullying and abusive supervision. In contrast, we take a broader perspective by including studies examining other forms of aggressive behaviors along with studies of how employees cope with their victimization experiences. Our review extends a recent meta-analysis of workplace harassment (Bowling & Beehr 2006) by including studies examining antecedents (e.g., Big 5 traits and informal status) and outcomes of victimization (e.g., revenge, seeking social support). Also, we offer a critique of the current state of research on workplace aggression from the target's perspective and propose challenges for future research.

We refer to the experience of being a target of workplace aggression as "workplace victimization." Workplace victimization occurs when an employee's well-being is harmed by an act of aggression perpetrated by one or more members of the organization. An employee's well-being is harmed when fundamental psychological and physiological needs are unmet or thwarted. In general, these needs include a sense of belonging, a feeling that one is a worthy individual, believing that one has the ability to predict and to cognitively control one's environment, and being able to trust others (Stevens & Fiske 1995). The most basic physiological need is the avoidance of pain. We assume that being the target of workplace aggression can thwart the satisfaction of fundamental psychological needs and/or inflict psychological, emotional, and even physical pain upon its target.

We stated above that aggression has been defined as behavior directed toward another person or persons carried out with the intent to harm. Adopting this definition of aggression raises the epistemological challenge of determining whether an act was intentional and therefore aggressive. The position we adopt in our review is that there is no easy way to resolve this issue, but because we are interested in aggression from the target's perspective, we believe that for theoretical and practical purposes it is reasonable to classify a behavior is aggressive if the target perceives some possibility that it was performed with the intent to harm. Our position recognizes that the target's interpretation of another employee's behavior is likely to be most consequential from predicting his or her response. At the same time, we acknowledge that in some cases it is important to rely on more than just the target's interpretation; if, for example, he or she is seeking legal remedy or if internal disciplinary action is to be taken against the harm-doer.

As we document in our review, the costs of workplace victimization are high. Victims of aggressive actions suffer psychologically, become fatigued, stressed, sick, and sometimes traumatized. Consequently, individual, group, and organizational performance can suffer (Leymann 1990). Research on workplace aggression has increased over the past 20 years as these costs have become widely recognized by organizational psychologists, human resource practitioners, and the general public. Interestingly, North American scholars have generally studied the motives or characteristics of perpetrators of aggression, paying relatively less attention to understanding the experiences of victims, with the exception being studies of sexual harassment. In contrast, Northern European scholars have examined questions such as (a) Why do some employees but not others become victims of aggression? (b) What organizational conditions make victimization more likely? (c) What are the psychological and behavioral consequences of victimization? (d) What strategies do employees use to cope with victimization? In this review, we examine research on workplace victimization published from 1990 to the present to document the answers that past studies provide to these four questions.

Our review is necessarily selective. We chose articles that explicitly assess the target's experience, although some articles included in our review might have taken into account the role of the perpetrator if it was critical for understanding the target's response. We excluded from our review studies that focus primarily on sexual harassment. Other scholars have already conducted reviews on that topic (e.g., Cortina & Berdahl 2008, Fitzgerald 1993, O'Leary-Kelly et al. 2000), so rather than covering old ground we survey the literature on nonsexual forms of aggression. We also excluded from our review studies examining interactional justice, which has been defined as "the quality of interpersonal treatment received during the enactment of organizational procedures" (Bies & Moag 1986, p. 44). Interactional justice is a type of workplace behavior that arguably falls within the conceptual domain of workplace victimization. However, we chose not to review research on interactional justice for two reasons. First, reviews of this literature have already been conducted (Greenberg & Colquitt 2005), and second, we believe that the construct belongs in broader discussion of organizational justice that our review was not intended to address. We accessed the relevant literature by conducting a PsychInfo search of titles and abstracts covering the period from 1990 to 2005 and a manual search of more recent journals in applied psychology and organizational behavior. We chose for inclusion only empirical articles written in English and published in peer-reviewed journals. We cite theoretical papers if we deemed them relevant for clarifying construct definitions.

Our review begins by categorizing the types of victimizing behaviors researchers have studied. We then review studies examining the various factors that have been empirically related to perceptions of workplace victimization, looking first at individual factors such as personality, behavior, and demographics before turning to structural factors such as the target's formal or informal social position and to broader organizational-level factors such as the nature of the work being performed, job characteristics, and management styles. Next, we review studies documenting the consequences of victimization and how victimized employees cope with their experiences. We conclude with observations of what progress has been made in understanding workplace victimization and offer suggestions for advancing research in this area.

TYPES OF VICTIMIZING BEHAVIOR

Many kinds of aggressive behaviors can occur in the workplace, and researchers have introduced a myriad of terms into the literature to describe them. Among the ones appearing frequently in the literature are workplace harassment (Björkqvist et al. 1994, Bowling & Beehr 2006), mobbing (Leymann 1996, Zapf et al. 1996), petty tyranny (Ashforth 1997), bullying (e.g., Einarsen & Skogstad 1996, Salin 2003b, Vartia 1996), emotional abuse (Keashly 1998), abusive supervision (Tepper 2000), social undermining (Duffy et al. 2002), incivility (Andersson & Pearson 1999, Cortina et al. 2001), identity threats (Aquino & Douglas 2003), and victimization (Aquino et al. 1999). An underlying assumption of these descriptive terms is that the behavior being observed is aversive and potentially harmful to the intended target (see **Table 1**). Consequently, we believe all of them can be circumscribed within the broader construct space of workplace victimization as we have defined it.

There are obviously differences among the behaviors examined by various writers. But these differences are not substantial enough in our judgment to warrant exclusion from the larger "family" of workplace victimization behaviors that are the focus of this review. To take just one example, consider the definitions of workplace incivility and social undermining. Andersson & Pearson (1999) define workplace incivility as "low intensity deviant behavior with ambiguous intent to harm the target, in violation of workplace norms for mutual respect. Uncivil behaviors are characteristically rude and discourteous, displaying a lack of regard for others" (p. 457). In contrast, social undermining is defined as "behavior intended to hinder, over time, the ability to establish and maintain positive interpersonal relationships, work-related success, and favorable reputation" (Duffy et al. 2002, p. 332). The conceptual distinction between these two behaviors is that the intent to harm is less transparent to the victim of incivility than of social undermining. Yet both behaviors can thwart the satisfaction of fundamental psychological needs for self-esteem, a controllable and predictable environment, and sense of belonging. Both can also be construed by the victim as having been done intentionally. Consequently, for our purposes, they represent acts of workplace victimization.

The terms used in past studies to define and measure various forms of victimizations have some similarities and dissimilarities. We already mentioned that we can distinguish between behaviors that cause physiological and psychological harm. We can also distinguish between behaviors that cause direct and indirect harm (Buss 1961). Most of the studies we reviewed do not explicitly differentiate between direct and indirect forms of victimization, although some data suggest that indirect aggression is more frequent than direct aggression (Baron et al. 1999).

Table 1 summarizes the definitions of victimizing behaviors introduced by researchers. The table indicates whether the instruments used to measure these behaviors tap direct aggression, indirect aggression, or both.

A review of **Table 1** yields several insights into the current state of victimization research. First, most operationalizations emphasize psychological rather than physical harm, which makes sense because the latter are less common than the former (Barling et al. 2009). Physical acts of aggression such as hitting or pushing a fellow employee would likely result in serious punishment including criminal prosecution or dismissal from the job. Thus, we expect physical aggression to occur less frequently because the costs of engaging in such behavior are high. Second, some researchers are broadly interested in victimization by all organizational members without specific reference to the status of perpetrator (e.g., identity threat, Aquino & Douglas 2003; incivility, Andersson & Pearson 1999), whereas others make a distinction between whether the employee is victimized by higher- (e.g., supervisors, Tepper

Table 1 Constructs consistent with victimization definition by thwarted needs, direct/indirect behavior, and perpetrator status

Definition of construct	Thwarted needs are		Victimizing behaviors are		Perpetrator's status		
	Psychological	Physiological	Direct	Indirect	Higher	Coworker	Lower
Workplace harassment (Björkqvist et al. 1994, pp. 173–74): "Repeated activities, with the aim of bringing mental (but sometimes also physical) pain, and directed towards one or more individuals who, for one reason or another, are not able to defend themselves."	√	√	√	√	√	√	√
Bullying (Einarsen & Skogstad 1996, p. 191): "A situation where one or several individuals persistently over a period of time perceive themselves to be on the receiving end of negative actions from one or several persons, in a situation where the target of bullying has difficulty in defending him or herself against these actions."	√	√	√	√	√	√	√
Mobbing (Zapf et al. 1996, p. 215): "Severe form of harassing people in organizations."	√	√	√	√	√	√	√
A petty tyrant (Ashforth 1997, p. 126) is "someone who uses their power and authority oppressively, capriciously, and perhaps vindictively."	√	√	√	√	√		
Emotional abuse includes verbal and nonverbal modes of expression; repeated, or part of a pattern; unwelcome and unsolicited; violate a standard of appropriate conduct toward others; result in harm or injury; actor intended to harm; actor is in a more powerful position (Keashly 1998).	√	√	√	√	√	√	√
Workplace incivility (Andersson & Pearson 1999, p. 457; Cortina et al. 2001, p. 64): "Low-intensity deviant behavior with ambiguous intent to harm the target, in violation of workplace norms for mutual respect."	√		√	√	√	√	√

(Continued)

Table 1 *(Continued)*

Definition of construct	Thwarted needs are		Victimizing behaviors are		Perpetrator's status		
	Psychological	Physiological	Direct	Indirect	Higher	Coworker	Lower
Victimization (Aquino et al. 1999, p. 260): "Individual's perception of having been exposed, either momentarily or repeatedly, to the aggressive acts of one or more other persons."	✓	✓	✓	✓	✓	✓	✓
Abusive supervision (Tepper 2000, p. 178): "Extent to which supervisors engage in the sustained display of hostile verbal and nonverbal behaviors, excluding physical contact."	✓		✓	✓	✓		
Social undermining (Duffy et al. 2002, p. 332): "Behavior intended to hinder, over time, the ability to establish and maintain positive interpersonal relationships, work-related success, and favorable reputation."	✓		✓	✓	✓	✓	
Identity threat (Aquino & Douglas 2003, p. 196): "Overt action by another party that challenges, calls into question, or diminishes a person's sense of competence, dignity, or self-worth."	✓		✓		✓	✓	✓

2000) or same-status (coworkers, Aquino et al. 1999) organizational members. We found no studies that explicitly operationalized the victimization of higher-status by lower-status organizational members. Third, most of the Northern European operationalizations of victimization allow participants to indicate the status of the perpetrator separately, whereas most North American operationalizations make virtually no reference to the possibility of low-status perpetrators. Finally, **Table 1** shows that at some level all of the research using these different definitions deals with essentially the same phenomenon: victimization.

Our review of the victimization literature reveals three streams of research that attempt to answer the question of why someone is likely to become the target of aggression. The first investigates the role of the target's personality; the second investigates the target's behavior; and the third examines positional, structural, and social predictors of victimization.

WHO BECOMES A VICTIM?

Personality Characteristics

Among the many investigations into the role of personality as a predictor of victimization, the propensity to experience negative affect (trait NA, Watson & Clark 1984)—which includes emotions such as anger, fear, worry, anxiousness, sadness, and depression—shows the most consistent relationship to various victimization measures (e.g., Aquino et al. 1999, Aquino & Bradfield 2000, Coyne et al. 2000, Duffy et al. 2006b, Glasø et al. 2007, Matthiesen & Einarsen 1991, Tepper et al. 2006, Vartia 1996, Zellars et al. 2002).

Several explanations for the NA-victimization relationship have been proposed. According to some investigators, the relationship may be partly due to high-NA employees being perceived as hostile, demanding, or interpersonally difficult, making them more likely targets of aggression from other organizational members (Aquino et al. 1999, Aquino & Bradfield 2000, Tepper et al. 2006). This explanation is consistent with victim precipitation (Amir 1967), symbolic interactionist (Felson & Steadman 1983), and conflict escalation (Glomb 2002) models, which suggest that employees with certain personality characteristics tend to act in ways that violate social norms or threaten others' identities. As a result, they are targeted for aggression by those seeking to enforce norms prescribing cooperation, respect, or deference in interpersonal relations.

An alternative explanation for the NA-victimization relationship is that employees who have experienced aggression over a period of time developed high NA as a result (cf. Hansen et al. 2006, Mikkelsen & Einarsen 2002). Which of these explanations is more likely is difficult to determine without additional longitudinal studies, which are quite rare (for an exception, see Kivimaki et al. 2003).

A third possibility is that employees high in NA selectively recall (Blaney 1986) more negative events than do employees low in trait NA. This explanation needs to be tested with multisource designs that match employee and coworker reports to determine the level of agreement. A related explanation is that high-NA employees are more prone to make hostile attributions for ambiguous behaviors, and consequently they report more victimization than do employees low in NA. Supporting this possibility, Matthiesen & Einarsen (2004) found that some victims of bullying were extremely suspi-

MOTIVATION TO PERCEIVE VICTIMIZATION

Arguably, it is functional to know whether environments put one at risk of victimization. Knowing that one may be victimized can satisfy one's fundamental needs for uncertainty reduction and protecting self-esteem (Fiske 2004). However, the possibility of victimization may motivate employees to become hypervigilant to potential risks (Allen & Badcock 2003). Both situational and personality factors may contribute to some people being chronically overattuned to potential victimization (Kramer 1998). Some evidence in the close relationships literature suggests that people who are strongly motivated to acquire information that reveals harm will suffer from poor relationship quality (Ickes et al. 2003). If the risk of victimization is chronically salient, minor negative events will gain more importance in people's cognitive and emotional processes, and so events that would be unnoticed by others may be interpreted as victimization experiences.

cious of the outside world, which could make them more likely to interpret others' behavior as being more malevolent. Another study reported a positive relationship between a measure of hostile attribution bias and victimization (Aquino et al. 2004) (see sidebar Motivation to Perceive Victimization).

Research on the relationship between personality factors from the Big 5 reveals mixed findings. One study found that victimized employees tend to be more extraverted (Glasø et al. 2007), whereas other studies show that victims are more introverted than nonvictims (Coyne et al. 2000) or that victims and nonvictims do not differ on extraversion at all (Coyne et al. 2003, Vartia 1996). Some studies report that victimized employees tend to be more conscientious (Coyne et al. 2000), but other studies fail to support this relationship (Coyne et al. 2003). Coyne et al. (2003) found that victims of bullying tended to be lower in emotional stability in comparison with a control sample of nonvictims, which is consistent with the studies of NA reviewed above since people who lack emotional stability are more prone to experience negative emotions including anxiety, depression, and hostility (e.g., Costa et al. 1991).

Several studies have explored the role of self-esteem as a predictor of victimization. These studies show that employees with low self-esteem report more victimization (e.g., Einarsen et al. 1994, Harvey & Keashly 2003, Matthiesen & Einarsen 2001, Vartia 1996; see Bowling & Beehr 2006 for a meta-analytic review). A number of investigators have argued that victimization can undermine employees' self-esteem (Björkvist et al. 1994, Lee & Brotheridge 2006, Liefooghe & Davey 2001, Tepper 2000), but like the other personality variables reviewed, the causal direction of the self-esteem-victimization relationship is unclear. It could be that the relationship is due to previous victimization encounters and accumulated state self-esteem levels. It may also be that the emotional and behavioral tone of people with low self-esteem invites victimization because someone with low self-esteem is less able to assertively defend him or herself against others' aggression (Matthiesen & Einarsen 2001), deal constructively with conflict (Zapf 1999), or challenge those who try to exploit them. Supporting this latter view, Coyne et al. (2000) found that employee victims of aggression tended to score lower on personality measures of assertiveness, competitiveness, and extraversion than do nonvictims.

Demographics

Studies looking at the relationship between demographic variables including age, tenure, gender, and victimization do not show an obvious relationship between these variables. Zellars et al. (2002) report that employees' gender, age, and tenure were all unrelated to their perception of supervisor abuse. Vartia (1996) found no correlations between gender and bullying and only a small correlation between age and bullying. Einarsen & Skogstad (1996) found that older employees reported significantly more bullying than younger ones reported. However, Einarsen & Raknes (1997) found that among male workers, older ones reported significantly less exposure to potentially harassing behavior than did younger ones. In a number of stud-

ies, women report more victimization than men report (Aquino & Bradfield 2000; Björkqvist et al. 1994; Cortina et al. 2001; Salin 2001, 2003a; Tehrani 2004); in others, men report more victimization than do women (Jennifer et al. 2003). Finally, some studies find no or only marginal gender effects (Einarsen & Skogstad 1996, Hansen et al. 2006, Leymann 1996, Vartia & Hyyti 2002). Bowling & Beehr's (2006) meta-analysis found that some demographic variables are reliably related to victimization. Among these relationships were that females were less likely to be victimized than were men, employees with longer tenure were more likely to be victimized than were those with shorter tenure, and older employees were less likely to be victimized than were younger ones. However, Bowling & Beehr (2006) described all of these relationships as being relatively weak compared with the effects of work environment variables. One conclusion we draw from the studies we reviewed is that employee demographic variables are likely to explain relatively little variance in victimization, and so a more fruitful approach would be to examine possible mediators and moderators of the demographics-victimization relationship.

Behaviors

A handful of studies have directly examined how a target's behaviors might be associated with his or her perceptions of victimization. These studies show that low levels of citizenship behavior (Aquino & Bommer 2003), voicing discontent with previous mistreatment (Cortina & Magley 2003), and adopting an overly accommodating conflict management style (Aquino 2000, Zapf & Gross 2001) are associated with higher levels of victimization. However, Aquino (2000) also found that frequent victims used a dominant conflict style more so than did nonvictims. Aquino & Byron (2002) qualified the relationship between dominating behavior and victimization by showing a curvilinear pattern in student workgroups. The pattern was such that group members who were perceived as exhibiting either high or low levels of dominating behavior reported higher levels of victimization by group members than those who exhibited moderate levels of dominating behavior. However, this relationship was only found among men.

The studies discussed in previous sections of this review examined how characteristics of victims might predict whether they are likely to become targets of workplace aggression. Other studies have examined social structural predictors of victimization. By social structural predictors, we mean an employee's position within a larger social structure such as a formal hierarchy or an informal social network.

Structural Predictors of Victimization

Employees occupying lower positions in the organization's formal hierarchy have been shown in several studies to report higher levels of victimization (Aquino 2000, Aquino et al. 2004, Bjorkqvist et al. 1994, Hoel et al. 2001, Keashly et al. 1994, Salin 2001). But other studies show no significant, direct effects of formal hierarchical position on victimization (Aquino & Bradfield 2000, Aquino & Douglas 2003). One study reports that employees in managerial positions were more often victimized than those in nonmanagerial positions (Lamertz & Aquino 2004).

We reviewed two studies that looked at victimization as a function of employees' structural position within an informal social network. Using sociometric analysis, Coyne et al. (2004) studied 36 fire service teams in the United Kingdom and found that in contrast to the commonly held view that victims of bullying are usually social isolates (e.g., Salmivalli et al. 1996), fire service personnel who reported higher levels of bullying also tended to be considered preferred people to work with and to be placed within the main informal network. Self- and peer-reported victims were also more frequently nominated as stars in their team, although 24% of such victims were also rejected by the rest of the team. Lamertz & Aquino (2004) also used sociometric methods to study victimization among 32 employees in a single

bureau of a city government. They found that employees who maintained a balance in their dyadic friendship networks reported lower levels of victimization than did employees whose friendship networks were imbalanced. An example of an imbalanced friendship network would be one where one actor in a relationship chooses another actor as a friend, but the other actor does not make the same choice (i.e., the relationship is nonreciprocated). Such a pattern indicates a discrepancy in mutual esteem between two parties.

There do not appear to be consistent findings regarding the direct relationship between formal status and victimization. Studies looking at informal status by taking a social networks perspective are too few to draw firm conclusions. Based on our review of the existing literature, we believe the inconsistencies associated with the effect of formal status might be addressed by testing more complex models hypothesizing that status interacts with other factors to predict victimization. A few status studies have taken this approach and have found evidence supporting our argument.

Vartia & Hyyti (2002) found no differences in perceived victimization between men and women, but they did find that women were victimized more often by coworkers, whereas men were victimized equally across status groups. Salin (2003a) found that men were typically bullied by superiors, whereas women were typically bullied by superiors and colleagues in approximately equal proportions. In addition, none of the male victims, but one-fifth of female victims, reported being bullied by subordinates. Hoel et al. (2001) found an interaction between formal status and gender such that women in the highest organizational-status positions are more likely to be victimized than are men.

Another perspective suggests that possessing particular status characteristics in combination with behaving in certain ways can make employees more likely to be targets of aggression. Consistent with this perspective, one study found that low-organizational-status employees are more likely to be victimized when they also tend to use a highly accommodating style to resolve conflicts with coworkers (Aquino 2000). Another study showed that whites who exhibited higher levels of organizational citizenship behavior reported lower levels of victimization than did African Americans who exhibited similar levels of citizenship (Aquino & Bommer 2003).

Organizational Factors

A stream of empirical research on workplace aggression from the target's perspective has examined how organizational factors might affect employees' vulnerability to being victimized. One organizational factor that has been found to predict the likelihood of being victimized is the type of work the organization performs. Mikkelsen & Einarsen (2001) found that employees in a manufacturing company reported significantly more exposure to bullying than did employees in hospitals. A survey of 7787 employees from 14 Norwegian organizations found that respondents from public companies reported less bullying than those from private enterprises (Einarsen & Skogstad 1996). The investigators also reported that the highest prevalence rate of bullying over a six-month period was found among industrial workers, with 17.4% reporting having been bullied. The lowest prevalence rate was among psychologists and university employees. However, Salin (2001) surveyed 377 Finnish employees from various organizations and found that public sector employees reported higher levels of bullying than private sector employees reported, although this difference was statistically not significant. Hubert & van Veldhoven (2001) measured the prevalence of aggression in 11 different workforce sections in the Netherlands and found that aggression from colleagues or the boss was higher in sectors such as industry, education, (local) government, and public administration than in sectors such as business services and financial institutions.

Our review of studies comparing various forms of victimization as a function of occupation or work sector does not present a clear conclusion about what types of organizations or job sectors are likely to be associated with higher victimization. One logical prediction is that employees are more likely at risk of being victimized in organizations where they are required to interact frequently with others and to work interdependently. The ambiguity regarding occupation or work sector is to be expected given the multitude of other factors that are likely to vary across organizations even within the same industry. Consequently, researchers have examined specific attributes of the work environment.

Employees who report having less control over their jobs are more likely to report being mobbed (Zapf et al. 1996), bullied (Agervold & Mikkelsen 2004, Einarsen et al. 1994, Quine 2001), or directly and indirectly victimized by coworkers (Aquino et al. 1999). Bullying has been found to be higher when work is uninteresting and has low variability (Einarsen et al. 1994, Vartia 1996) or lacks meaning (Agervold & Mikkelsen 2004). Stressful and competitive work environments have been associated with higher levels of victimization (Coyne et al. 2003, Vartia 1996), as has role conflict (Einarsen et al. 1994, Skogstad et al. 2007a), role ambiguity (Agervold & Mikkelsen 2004, Jennifer et al. 2003, Quine 2001), the number of employees in the workplace (Einarsen & Skogstad 1996), high cooperation requirements (Zapf et al. 1996), greater workloads (Quine 2001), and being in a male- rather than female-dominated organization (Einarsen & Skogstad 1996). Liefooghe & Davey (2001) interviewed 113 employees and concluded that various organizational practices contribute to what the authors referred to as institutionalized bullying. These practices revolve around mechanisms of organizational control such as rules for monitoring and controlling time, the use of numerical performance measures, or the use of performance improvement mandates as a punishment for failure to perform. Their study is distinctive because it asserts that the organization rather than individuals within it is responsible for bullying. Finally, we found one study showing that organizational changes involving changes in technology, staff reductions, and wage cuts were positively related to what the researchers described as task-related bullying (e.g., "Being given tasks with unreasonable targets or deadlines," "Being exposed to an unmanageable workload") (Skogstad et al. 2007b). Skogstad and colleagues (2007b) speculated that one explanation for the relationship between organizational changes and bullying was that these changes led to reduced role clarity, higher workloads, and task fragmentation, which as the findings cited above show, are related to victimization.

Our review of studies examining workplace attributes as predictors of victimization reveals that the most consistent finding is the effect of role conflict or ambiguity. Our conclusions are supported by Bowling & Beehr's (2006) meta-analysis, which shows these two variables showed the strongest effect sizes among potential antecedents of various forms of victimizing behaviors, with $\rho = 0.44$ and $\rho = 0.30$ for the role conflict and role ambiguity, respectively. A lack of control over one's work environment was also found to be strongly associated with victimization in Bowling & Beehr's (2006) meta-analysis ($\rho = -0.25$), and this relationship is supported by our own review of published empirical studies.

A few studies have looked at the relationship between managerial or leadership styles and victimization. Ashforth (1997) found that subordinate ratings of petty tyranny were negatively correlated with managers' tolerance for ambiguity and Theory X beliefs and were positively correlated with managers having a bureaucratic orientation. Agervold & Mikkelsen (2004) found that bullied employees reported that they had received insufficient information from immediate superiors and had a serious conflict with their manager that was not satisfactorily resolved. Coyne et al. (2003) reported that victims of bullying perceived their work organizations to be characterized by more negative aspects, which included authoritarian management, and Einarsen et al. (1994) found that employees who were bullied reported being more dissatisfied with their organization's leadership. A study of bullying in public sector organizations concluded that weak and indistinct leadership contributed to workplace conflicts going unresolved and eventually escalating into bullying (Strandmark & Hallberg 2006). This qualitative study concluded that bullying results from unresolved value conflicts that are exacerbated by weak leadership. Skogstad et al. (2007a) showed that employees who described their superiors as adopting a laissez-faire leadership style, which is characterized by an absence of leadership, an unwillingness to intervene in employee affairs, a lack of transactions or agreements with followers, and a failure to meet the expectations of subordinates, reported higher levels of victimization. Moreover, Skogstad and colleagues (2007a) showed that the relationship between leadership style and victimization was partly mediated through role conflict and increased conflict with coworkers. Skogstad et al.'s (2007a) study is the only one we found that tested mediating mechanisms through which leader behavior might predict victimization. Our review of studies examining relationships between leadership and victimization suggests that leaders can potentially influence their subordinates' vulnerability to being victimized by failing to establish clear guidelines for what constitutes inappropriate conduct. It is also possible that certain types of management styles, such as those that are highly authoritarian or bureaucratic, result in subordinates being victimized by leaders.

CONSEQUENCES OF VICTIMIZATION

Not surprisingly, many studies have found consistent relationships between experiencing workplace victimization and a host of negative psychological, emotional, and physiological outcomes. Among the negative psychological consequences that have been reported are increased depression and anxiety (Björkqvist et al. 1994, Cortina et al. 2001, Haines et al. 2006, Hansen et al. 2006, Matthiesen & Einarsen 2001, Niedl 1996, Quine 2001, Tepper 2000, Zapf 1999), job stress (Agervold & Mikkelsen 2004, Budd et al. 1996,

Vartia & Hyyti 2002), posttraumatic stress (Fitzpatrick & Wilson 1999, Leymann & Gustavson 1996, Matthiesen & Einarsen 2004, Mikkelsen & Einarsen 2002), and decreased mental health (Hansen et al. 2006, Hoel et al. 2004, Hogh et al. 2005, Rogers & Kelloway 1997, Vartia & Hyyti 2002). Frequent victimization is also associated with negative somatic symptoms (LeBlanc & Kelloway 2002; Rogers & Kelloway 1997, Mikkelsen & Einarsen 2001, Schat & Kelloway 2000, Zapf et al. 1996), fatigue (Agervold & Mikkelsen 2004; Hogh et al. 2003, 2005), and sickness (Agervold & Mikkelsen 2004; Kivimäki et al. 2000). Affective responses to being victimized include diminished emotional well-being (LeBlanc & Kelloway 2002; Schat & Kelloway 2000), lower levels of job satisfaction (Budd et al. 1996, Keashly et al. 1997, Lapierre et al. 2005, Quine 2001, Tepper 2000, Vartia & Hyyti 2002) and life satisfaction (Tepper 2000), shame (Hallberg & Strandmark 2006, Lewis 2004), fear (Rogers & Kelloway 1997), and emotional exhaustion (Goldberg & Grandey 2007, Grandey et al. 2007, Tepper 2000, Winstanley & Whittington 2002). Bowling & Beehr's (2006) meta-analysis reports effect sizes associated with several of the psychological, physiological, and emotional consequences listed above, making their study a helpful guide for evaluating the effect sizes of victimization on a variety of individual outcomes. Bowling & Beehr (2006) found that the strongest effect sizes were between victimization and individual outcomes such as negative emotions at work, frustration, job satisfaction, and emotional exhaustion (burnout). Victimization showed weaker relationships (mean $\rho > 0.25$) to self-esteem and life satisfaction.

We reviewed three studies that show relationships between victimization and outcomes external to the organization. Tepper (2000) reported that abusive supervision was positively related to work and family life conflict. Lewis & Orford (2005) showed that victimized employees also negatively affected participants' nonwork relationships, and they suggested that victimization at work can produce a ripple effect

that compromises other potential sources of support. Haines et al. (2006) found that workplace aggression experienced by one partner in a dual-earner couple was related to the other partner's psychological distress. The investigators concluded that this relationship supported a crossover model in which one partner's work and family experiences affect the other partner's experiences.

Most of the studies we reviewed tested direct relationships between victimization and employee outcomes, but some looked at whether the relationship is moderated by other factors. Kaukiainen et al. (2001) found that victimization was more strongly related to negative physical and psychological symptoms for men than for women. Lapierre et al. (2005) showed that the negative relationship between victimization and job satisfaction was stronger for women than men. Hoel et al. (2004) reported that the relationship between victimization and mental health was stronger for older than for younger employees and for workers than for senior managers. Tepper (2000) found that the relationship between abusive supervision and outcomes such as depression, job satisfaction, and emotional exhaustion was stronger for subordinates who had low as compared to high job mobility. Duffy et al. (2006a) examined the consequences of social undermining and found that the relationship between undermining and outcomes such as job satisfaction, depression, and intention to quit was stronger when group-level supervisor undermining (the amount of supervisor or coworker undermining experienced by all group members) was low rather than high. The authors concluded that this pattern supported a "singled out" hypothesis in which the level of victimization within a group moderates the relationship between individual perceptions of victimization and outcomes.

STRATEGIES FOR COPING WITH VICTIMIZATION

We reviewed several studies that examined employee responses to victimization. We consider these responses to be examples of a broader set of strategies for coping with victimization. Lazarus & Folkman's (1984) transaction model of stress distinguishes between problem- and emotion-focused coping strategies. The goal of problem-focused strategies is to change the situation by eliminating the source of stress (e.g., by taking direct action against the perpetrator, seeking support from others) or one's view of the situation (e.g., positive reappraisal). Included in the category of problem-focused strategies are behaviors that could be considered aggressive, such as taking revenge against the perpetrator, but that are performed in response to an initial provocation. Also included are attempts to take advantage of social or organizational support systems that might act as a buffer against further victimization or provide protection or redress to the victim. The goal of emotion-focused strategies is to manage the emotional consequences of the stressor and could include attempts to escape psychologically (e.g., substance abuse) or to execute emotion-regulation strategies that minimize the negative impact of being victimized. We turn first to studies of problem-focused strategies.

Problem-Focused Coping Strategies

One problem-focused coping strategy is to retaliate against the perpetrator as a way of altering his or her behavior through punishment or by demonstrating one's willingness to defend against further mistreatment (Glomb 2002, Lee & Brotheridge 2006). An emerging empirical literature on revenge in organizations suggests that retaliatory aggression is considered by many people to be a morally legitimate response to being victimized (Tripp et al. 2002). Supporting this conclusion, Zapf & Gross (2001) reported that defending oneself was identified by 9% of their sample as a recommended strategy for coping with bullying, placing it somewhere between the most frequently recommended strategy of leaving the organization (22%) and the least-recommended strategy of protocol events (2%).

We reviewed three studies examining the possibility that victimization provokes retaliatory aggression against perpetrators. Dupré et al. (2006) found that teenage part-time employees who perceived high levels of abusive supervision reported more aggression against their supervisors when their financial reasons for working were high. Mitchell & Ambrose (2007) showed that subordinates who perceived high levels of abusive supervision reported engaging in more aggressive behavior directed toward their supervisors, and more so if the subordinate endorsed negative reciprocity beliefs. Tepper et al. (2001) found that victims of abusive supervision reported using dysfunctional resistance (e.g., ignoring one's supervisor or making a half-hearted effort on a task and letting the boss know that the employee could not do it) and constructive resistance (e.g., asking for additional clarification or explaining to the supervisor that the task could be done in a different way) against their supervisors more frequently than their nonabused counterparts reported. Tepper et al. (2001) interpreted the results involving dysfunctional resistance as indicating that victimizing behaviors can provoke behavioral coping responses that can potentially harm the perpetrator by threatening relationship quality and undermining the supervisor's authority to make a request. The findings involving constructive resistance were interpreted by Tepper et al. (2001) as indicating one possible way of breaking a cycle of hostility in interpersonal conflict by responding to abusive supervision in a nondestructive manner.

Most of the studies we reviewed show a relationship between victimization and aggressive behavioral responses that might be directed toward the perpetrator of aggression. Moreover, these responses were moderated by other factors. Aquino & Douglas (2003) found that employees who reported high levels of victimization and held favorable attitudes toward revenge reported engaging in more antisocial behavior directed toward other employees than those who held less-favorable attitudes toward revenge. Jockin et al. (2001) found that employees who reported high levels of victimization had more aggressive conflicts with coworkers if they were high in neuroticism. A third study found that perceived victimization was positively related to overt expressions of anger, but more so for employees who had a hostile attribution bias or who perceived the norms of their organization as encouraging oppositional behavior (Aquino et al. 2004). Zellars et al. (2002) found that employees who perceived higher levels of abusive supervision exhibited fewer organizational citizenship behaviors, but more so if they viewed citizenship behavior as an extrarole behavior. The investigators interpreted this pattern as suggesting that withholding extrarole behaviors might be one way for employees to take revenge against supervisors who victimize them. Lee & Brotheridge (2006) found that employees who reported being undermined were also more likely to report undermining others. Duffy et al. (2006a) showed that the group social context moderates the relationship between being the target of undermining and undermining others such that the relationship was stronger in groups where group-level undermining was low than in groups where it was high. Duffy et al. (2006a) interpreted this pattern as indicating that victimized employees are more likely to reciprocate negative behavior when they perceive themselves as being singled out for such treatment.

Demographic factors have been shown to moderate relationships between victimization and aggressive, problem-focused strategies. Ólafsson & Jóhannsdóttir (2004) found that males are more likely to confront bullies and less likely to seek help from organizational authorities than are females, and Aquino & Douglas (2003) found that interpersonally directed antisocial behavior against other employees was more strongly related to victimization among younger as compared to older employees.

A problem-focused strategy that does not involve an aggressive response by the victim is escaping the situation. Escape could include quitting or requesting a transfer within the organization (Niedl 1996, Tepper 2000, Zapf & Gross 2001), being frequently absent from work (Kivimäki et al. 2000, Zapf et al. 1996), or avoiding the perpetrator(s) and/or ignoring their behavior (Keashly et al. 1994). Another type of nonaggressive, problem-focused strategy is to seek support from the organization, family, friends, and fellow employees, or from professional services such as counselors. Rospenda et al. (2006) found that the experience of chronic, nonsexual harassment at work increased the likelihood that employees would use professional services (e.g., primary care physician, psychiatrist, clergy) to deal with work-related stress. However, their study failed to find evidence that these services ameliorated the negative effects of work harassment on mental health. Schat & Kelloway (2003) found that instrumental support, operationalized as support received from coworkers, managers, and supervisors following victimization, was associated with a reduction in negative psychological health consequences (i.e., low emotional well-being, poor somatic health, and negative job-related affect). They also found that informational support, operationalized as whether or not employees received training on how to deal with aggressive or threatening events at work, was associated with higher emotional well-being following victimization. Lewis & Orford (2005) interviewed 10 female victims of bullying and described how a lack of support from colleagues and the organization impaired these employees' ability to defend themselves against their perpetrators and led to increasing isolation, vulnerability, and diminished self-worth.

How effective are the various problem-focused strategies for coping with victimization? Zapf & Gross (2001) looked at 14 conflict-management coping strategies that victims of bullying used, including talking with the bullies, calling in the supervisor, taking long-term sick leave, and fighting back with similar means. The only strategy that was reported to have produced a significant improvement in their current situation was transferring to another job. Strategies that involved an active response to the bullies (i.e., fighting back with similar means, talking to the bullies) made the victim's situation significantly worse. Cortina & Magley (2003) found that employees who tried to cope with having been targets of aggressive action by confronting the perpetrator were more likely to report being recipients of work-retaliation victimization (e.g., discharge, involuntary transfer, demotion). Employees who used other voice strategies, such as seeking social support from others or whistle blowing, were more likely to be recipients of social-retaliation victimization (e.g., harassment, ostracism, threats) when dealing with powerful wrongdoers. Although Cortina & Magley (2003) found that retaliatory victimization has negative psychological and health consequences, worse consequences were experienced by employees who failed to speak out at all.

Studies of problem-focused strategies suggest that the more confrontational or aggressive the strategy, the more likely it is that the relationship between victim and perpetrator will escalate into a cycle of reciprocal aggression. Strategies such as expressing voice (Cortina & Magley 2003) or taking more of a constructive, problem-solving approach to conflict (Hogh & Dofradottir 2001) can be effective, perhaps because they help victims gain a sense of control over their situation. Perceiving control over the situation is important because these perceptions have been associated with reduced fear and enhanced emotional well-being for people who experience victimization (Schat & Kelloway 2000).

Based on our review, it appears that avoiding the perpetrator(s) or finding a way to leave the situation is the most effective coping strategy if effectiveness is defined in terms of reducing the frequency of being victimized, minimizing the cost of executing the strategy for the victim, and avoiding further conflict escalation. According to some studies (Keashly et al. 1994, Zapf & Gross 2001), it is also the preferred option for many victims. If leaving the situation is impractical or undesirable, then problem-solving strategies that allow the victim to gain a sense of control over his or her environment are likely to be most efficacious (see sidebar Self-Defeating Responses to Thwarted Needs).

SELF-DEFEATING RESPONSES TO THWARTED NEEDS

Some evidence suggests that employees who are victimized engage in a pattern of interpersonal work behaviors that might lead to further victimization. Thau et al. (2007) refer to these behaviors as self-defeating because they are inimical to the needs employees pursue (Baumeister & Scher 1988). In a study with employees and their supervisors in a clinical chemical laboratory, Thau et al. (2007) found that employees who feel that their belongingness needs are thwarted are more likely to engage in interpersonally harmful behaviors and less likely to engage in helping behaviors. Based on the norm of reciprocity (Gouldner 1960), coworkers will likely respond negatively and further thwart employees' belongingness needs. This may occur because employees who are victimized undergo self-regulation problems that make them focus on themselves and ignore the normative demands of their context (Blackhart et al. 2006). If this is true, then victimized employees may become locked into a vicious cycle in which the experience of victimization motivates them to engage in behaviors that invite further victimization.

Emotion-Focused Coping Strategies

We found some studies that examined the use of internal coping strategies to minimize the negative emotional and psychological consequences of victimization. One emotion-focused strategy is to use humor as a way to cope with victimization. Hogh & Dofradottir (2001) found that employees who were classified as being subjected to bullying (i.e., twice a month or daily over a 12-month period) used humor as a coping strategy more than those who reported being somewhat exposed to bullying (i.e., they reported being bullied between 1–23 times within the past 12 months) or not exposed at all. Keashly et al. (1994) reported that 40% of the 59 student participants in their sample said that they made a joke of the behavior as a way of coping with a hostile workplace event.

Studies of how employees respond to customers' verbal aggression show that they use either of two emotion-focused coping strategies: surface acting, which involves modifying behaviors by suppressing or faking expressions, and deep acting, which involves changing cognitions through perspective taking or focusing on positive things to regulate feelings (Grandey 2004). Grandey (2004) found that call center employees who experienced high stress as a result of an aggressive encounter with a customer performed more surface than deep acting compared to employees who experienced lower stress as a result of an aggressive customer encounter. Positive refocusing and perspective taking were more likely to be used by the low-stress than the high-stress employee group.

Another emotion-focused coping strategy is alcohol consumption. Although alcohol consumption is a behavior, we classify it as an emotion-focused strategy because in the context of workplace victimization, imbibing alcohol can reduce negative anxiety-related physiological and emotional effects of being victimized (Rospenda 2002). Supporting this possibility, nonsexual forms of victimization have been shown to be associated with increased drinking for men and women (Richman et al. 1992, 1996), suggesting that for some employees, drinking might be perceived as a legitimate way of managing the stress of being victimized.

Forgiveness is a third emotion-focused coping strategy that has begun to receive some attention in the literature. Forgiveness has been defined as an effort by the victim of harm-doing to overcome negative emotions and thoughts about the perpetrator and replace them with neutral or even positive ones (Aquino et al. 2006). Studies have shown that victimized employees are sometimes willing to forgive their transgressors (Aquino et al. 2006, Bradfield & Aquino 1999, Hallberg & Strandmark 2006, Struthers et al. 2005). However, despite evidence in the psychology literature that forgiveness can neutralize negative psychological consequences that result from being seriously victimized (Freedman & Enright 1996), we could not find one published empirical study that explicitly examined the consequences of forgiveness in the context of workplace victimization. The paucity of research on forgiveness as a coping strategy following victimization is an obvious gap in the literature we reviewed.

CONCLUSIONS

Our review of the literature identified three main challenges facing the study of workplace aggression from the target's perspective. First, the proliferation of constructs for describing the phenomenon poses a potential obstacle to achieving theoretical parsimony. Second, the causal direction of several relationships reported in the literature, particularly those regarding personality and victimization, is unclear. Third, a large number of studies that examine relationships between victimization and various individual and organizational factors were not theoretically motivated. We consider each of these challenges and offer suggestions for how the field might address them.

Proliferation of Constructs

Philosophers of science have argued that the introduction of multiple terms to describe a similar phenomenon can impede scientific parsimony and theoretical progress (e.g., Popper 1959/2002, Sober 1981). We do not advocate the use any particular measure of victimization in our review; however, we do believe it is worth exploring whether the conceptual overlap among the various measures used by researchers who claim to be tapping different constructs may actually be tapping into the same general construct that we have labeled workplace victimization. If this is true, then it implies that one measure may be as good as any other for examining the consequences of workplace victimization, so long as one makes clear what the relationship is between victim and perpetrator (i.e., is the perpetrator a coworker, supervisor, customer, etc.). Following the lead of the organizational citizenship literature (LePine et al. 2002), perhaps it is time for an empirical assessment to be conducted on the various measures of victimization most commonly used by researchers to determine whether they tap a common construct or whether there are in fact important distinctions between them that have implications for developing a theory of victimization. Alternatively, researchers who believe their particular construct, and the instrument used to measure it, does in fact capture a type of victimization that is distinct from other conceptualizations could support their claim empirically by showing that their construct predicts consequences that other constructs within the same victimization family (see **Table 1**) do not predict. For now, it seems important for investigators to acknowledge how related construct definitions used by other scholars working in the area can inform the state of the art of their own favored niche constructs.

Inconsistent Findings

We reported several inconsistent findings in the literature for variables that might indicate an employee's vulnerability to victimization, such as his or her gender or position within the organization's formal hierarchy or informal social network. We view these variables as possible indicators of vulnerability because they signify an employee's status and relative power within the organization. Perhaps one reason for the inconsistent findings is that markers of vulnerability may not always be salient to perpetrators (Fiske & Taylor 2007). If so, then situational factors that heighten the salience of such markers may also increase an employee's risk of victimization if the employee happens to possess them. A second reason why indicators of vulnerability have not been consistently related to victimization is that the perpetrator needs to be motivated to aggress. It follows that situational conditions that increase a would-be perpetrator's motivation to aggress, such as experiencing role conflict, working interdependently, or being in the presence of others who violate norms of social respect, can increase the likelihood that the would-be perpetrator will aggress against employees who possess markers of vulnerability.

Theoretical Development

Theoretical models of victimization have been proposed (e.g., Aquino & Lamertz 2004, Einarsen 2000, Keashly & Harvey 2005, Olson-Buchanan & Boswell 2008); however,

many of the studies we reviewed failed to provide a clear theoretical rationale for variable selection. We found theoretical underspecification to be particularly true of research on bullying and mobbing conducted in Northern Europe. Many of the Northern European studies we reviewed were more epidemiological, designed to assess frequencies of victimization among various groups rather than test theoretically derived hypotheses. One way to bring greater coherence to the literature would be for researchers to conduct more theory-guided meta-analyses similar to that of Bowling & Beehr (2006). We also note that both European and North American researchers often ignore well-established criminological literature on victimization (e.g., Hindelang et al. 1978, Schafer 1968). For example, Hindelang and colleagues (1978) proposed a model that explains victimization risk in terms of lifestyle exposure. Their model proposes that sociodemographic characteristics are associated with lifestyle differences that are expressed in the types of activities a person engages in, the time during which these activities occur, and the places they occur. With some modifications, their model could be applied to explain the risk of victimization in organizational settings since it is likely that factors that make people vulnerable to being victimized in one setting will do so in another.

We found numerous studies documenting consistent relationships between victimization and personality variables including negative affectivity and self-esteem. As we noted above, the causal direction of these relationships needs to be more firmly established. Theoretical arguments support the causal links from personality characteristics to victimization and vice versa. A case can also be made for bidirectional causality. What is clearly needed are studies using longitudinal or experimental designs to test which of these possibilities is best supported by data. Answering the causality question is important because it can help researchers understand whether the likelihood of being victimized may partly be a function of the victim's behavioral tendencies, which might be amenable to modification.

VICTIMIZATION IN DYADIC RELATIONSHIPS

Victimization often emerges in the context of dyadic relationships. Aquino & Lamertz (2004) proposed that employees sometimes enact certain relational roles within the organization's social system, leading them to experience either episodic or institutionalized forms of victimization. Aquino & Lamertz (2004) proposed four archetypal relational roles that can emerge in organizations: the dominating perpetrator, the reactive perpetrator, the submissive victim, and the provocative victim. Aquino & Lamertz (2004) theorized that the relationship between a given pair of employees who fit these role types will be characterized by certain behavioral styles, some of which can lead to interactions that are volatile and can lead one party to perceive that he or she has been victimized by the other. For example, a relational role composed of an employee who fits the provocative victim role type (i.e., he or she consistently behave in ways that violate social norms and threaten others' identities) and one who fits the reactive perpetrator role type (i.e., he or she responds very aggressively to perceived threats to his or her status or identity) is likely to be characterized by sporadic negative interactions over time that one or both parties can label as victimizing behavior.

Final Observations

We close with three final observations about the state of workplace victimization research. First, few studies make cross-cultural comparisons of victimization. For example, many of the bullying studies have been conducted in Scandinavian countries, which Hofstede (1980) has shown to be more egalitarian and feminine-oriented than the United States. In contrast, most studies of abusive supervision and incivility have been conducted in U.S. samples. It would be valuable to know whether the patterns of relationships found among these variables in existing studies would be replicated in another culture. Second, relatively few studies describe the process of victimization. Given the dynamic nature of social interaction and the possibility that victimization likely involves actions and reactions of would-be perpetrators and likely victims (Andersson & Pearson 1999, Aquino & Lamertz 2004, Glomb 2002), it seems important for researchers to conduct more studies documenting the complexity of this unfolding process, particularly in the context of ongoing relationships (see sidebar Victimization in Dyadic Relationships).

Finally, more work is needed examining the efficacy of prevention and intervention programs designed to help employees cope with being victimized. We reported some studies showing how institutional and social support might buffer the negative effects of victimization, but such studies are rare.

The aim of our review was to bring greater coherence to the study of what we have referred to as workplace victimization. We have tried to show that the many constructs that researchers have introduced into the literature to study aggression from the target's perspective share a common assumption about how these behaviors thwart the satisfaction of fundamental human needs. For this reason, we encouraged researchers to give due recognition to other constructs occupying the same conceptual space as their own. Another goal of our review was to document the parallel efforts of European and North American researchers. A number of findings reported by these scholars converge; others do not. What we noticed, though, is that researchers on one continent do not always acknowledge the work being done on the other. We hope that our review will help researchers bridge this continental divide so the study of workplace aggression from the target's perspective can become a truly international enterprise.

SUMMARY POINTS

1. An employee's well-being is harmed when fundamental psychological and physiological needs are unmet or thwarted. In general, psychological needs include a sense of belonging, a feeling that one is a worthy individual, believing that one has the ability to predict and

to cognitively control one's environment, and being able to trust others. The most basic physiological need is the avoidance of pain.

2. Many constructs that researchers have introduced into the literature share a common assumption about how the behaviors of interest thwart the satisfaction of fundamental human needs. Conceptual differences among these constructs are subtle, and research that focuses exclusively on constructs that are only marginally different from others within the family of victimizing behaviors impedes theoretical progress.

3. The costs of workplace victimization are high: Victims of aggressive actions suffer psychologically, become fatigued, stressed, sick, and sometimes traumatized. Consequently, group and organizational performance can suffer.

4. Among the many investigations into the role of personality as a predictor of victimization, the propensity to experience negative affect, which includes emotions such as anger, fear, worry, anxiousness, sadness, and depression, shows the most consistent relationship to various victimization measures.

5. Many studies have found reliable relationships between experiencing workplace victimization and a host of negative psychological, emotional, and physiological outcomes. Among the negative psychological consequences that have been reported are increased depression and anxiety, job stress, posttraumatic stress, and decreased mental health. Affective responses to being victimized include diminished emotional well-being, lower levels of job and life satisfaction, shame, fear, and emotional exhaustion.

6. Organizational factors such as role conflict and role ambiguity as well as management styles that do not provide clear guidelines for what constitutes inappropriate conduct can increase employees' risk of being victimized.

7. The coping strategy that appears to consistently produce a significant improvement in a victim's current circumstances is finding a way to avoid the perpetrator(s) or to leave the situation. Strategies that involve an active response to the bullies (e.g., fighting back with similar means, talking to the bullies) often make the situation significantly worse by escalating conflict. Coping strategies that allow victims to experience greater control over their situation, such as expressing voice or engaging in constructive problem solving, can also be effective.

FUTURE ISSUES

1. Past studies have focused on negative outcomes of victimization but have paid almost no attention to how victims may forgive or reconcile with perpetrators. The paucity of research on forgiveness as a coping strategy following victimization is an obvious gap in the literature.

2. It is time for an empirical assessment to be conducted on the various measures of victimization most commonly used by researchers to determine whether they tap a common construct or whether important distinctions exist between them that have implications for developing a theory of victimization.

3. The field could benefit from more cross-disciplinary applications of criminological theories to explain workplace victimization since many of the factors that make people vulnerable to being victimized in one setting are likely to do so in another.

4. Establishing causality for many of the relationships found in the literature among personality, behavior, and victimization is important because it can help researchers understand whether the likelihood of being victimized may partly be a function of the victim's behavioral tendencies, which might be amenable to modification.

5. Very few studies make cross-cultural comparisons of victimization.

6. It would be valuable to know whether the patterns of relationships found among these variables in existing studies would be replicated in another culture.

7. Like many phenomena in organizational behavior, causal tests of theories are scarce because longitudinal and experimental data are rare. More experimental and longitudinal studies are needed to triangulate cross-sectional field studies of victimization.

8. More work is needed examining the efficacy of prevention and intervention programs designed to help employees cope with being victimized.

DISCLOSURE STATEMENT

The authors are not aware of any biases that might be perceived as affecting the objectivity of this review.

ACKNOWLEDGMENTS

We thank Susan Fiske, Helge Hoel, Gregory Marr, Denise Salin, and Daniel Skarlicki for their comments on earlier versions of this paper. We also thank Marjorie Laven, Anne Pedersen, and Xiaozhou Hu for their assistance with the prepartion of the manuscript. This work was partially supported by a grant, awarded to Karl Aquino, from the Social Sciences and Humanities Research Council of Canada.

LITERATURE CITED

Agervold M, Mikkelsen EG. 2004. Relationships between bullying, psychosocial work environment and individual stress reactions. *Work Stress* 18:336–51

Allen NB, Badcock PBT. 2003. The social risk hypothesis of depressed mood: evolutionary, psychosocial, and neurobiological perspectives. *Psychol. Bull.* 129:887–913

Amir M. 1967. Victim precipitated forcible rape. *J. Crim. Law* 58(4):493–502

Anderson CA, Bushman BJ. 2002. Human aggression. *Annu. Rev. Psychol.* 53:27–51

Andersson LM, Pearson CM. 1999. Tit for tat? The spiraling effect of incivility in the workplace. *Acad. Manage. Rev.* 24:452–71

Aquino K. 2000. Structural and individual determinants of workplace victimization: the effects of hierarchical status and conflict management style. *J. Manage.* 26:171–93

Aquino K, Bommer WH. 2003. Preferential mistreatment: how victim status moderates the relationship between organizational citizenship behavior and workplace victimization. *Organ. Sci.* 14:374–85

Aquino K, Bradfield M. 2000. Perceived victimization in the workplace: the role of situational factors and victim characteristics. *Organ. Sci.* 11:525–37

Aquino K, Byron K. 2002. Dominating interpersonal behavior and perceived victimization in groups: evidence for a curvilinear relationship. *J. Manage.* 28:69–87

Aquino K, Douglas S. 2003. Identity threat and antisocial behavior in organizations: the moderating effects of individual differences, aggressive modeling, and hierarchical status. *Organ. Behav. Hum. Decis. Process.* 90:195–208

Aquino K, Douglas S, Martinko MJ. 2004. Overt anger in response to victimization: attributional style and organizational norms as moderators. *J. Occup. Health Psychol.* 9:152–64

Aquino K, Grover SL, Bradfield M, Allen D. 1999. The effects of negative affectivity, hierarchical status, and self-determination on workplace victimization. *Acad. Manage. J.* 42:260–72

Aquino K, Lamertz K. 2004. A relational model of workplace victimization: social roles and patterns of victimization in dyadic relationships. *J. Appl. Psychol.* 89:1023–34

Aquino K, Tripp TM, Bies RJ. 2006. Getting even or moving on? Power, procedural justice and types of offense as predictors of revenge, forgiveness, and avoidance in organizations. *J. Appl. Psychol.* 91:653–68

Ashforth BE. 1997. Petty tyranny in organizations: a preliminary examination of antecedents and consequences. *Can. J. Admin. Sci.* 14:126–40

Barling J, Dupré KE, Kelloway EK. 2009. Predicting workplace aggression and violence. *Annu. Rev. Psychol.* 60:671–92

Baron RA, Neuman JH, Geddes D. 1999. Social and personal determinants of workplace aggression: evidence for the impact of perceived injustice and the type A behavior pattern. *Aggress. Behav.* 25:281–96

Bies RJ, Moag JS. 1986. Interactional justice: communication criteria for fairness. In *Research on Negotiation in Organizations*, Vol. 1, ed. B Sheppard, pp. 43–55. Greenwich, CT: JAI Press

Björkqvist K, Österman K, Hjelt-Bäck M. 1994. Aggression among university employees. *Aggress. Behav.* 20:173–83

Blackhart GC, Baumeister RF, Twenge JM. 2006. Rejection's impact on self-defeating, prosocial, antisocial, and self-regulatory behaviors. In *Self and Relationships: Connecting Interpersonal and Intrapersonal Processes*, ed. KD Vohs, EJ Finkel, pp. 237–53. New York: Guilford

Blaney PH. 1986. Affect and memory: a review. *Psychol. Bull.* 99:229–46

Bowling NA, Beehr TA. 2006. Workplace harassment from the victim's perspective: a theoretical model and meta-analysis. *J. Appl. Psychol.* 91:998–1012

Bradfield M, Aquino K. 1999. The effects of blame attributions and offender likableness on forgiveness and revenge in the workplace. *J. Manage.* 25:607–31

Budd JW, Arvey RD, Lawless P. 1996. Correlates and consequences of workplace violence. *J. Occup. Health Psychol.* 1:197–210

Buss AH. 1961. *The Psychology of Aggression*. New York: Wiley

Cortina LM, Berdahl J. 2008. Sexual harassment in organizations: a decade of research in review. In *Handbook of Organizational Behavior*, ed. L Cooper, J Barling, pp. 469–97. Beverly Hills, CA: Sage

Cortina LM, Magley VJ. 2003. Raising voice, risking retaliation: events following interpersonal mistreatment in the workplace. *J. Occup. Health Psychol.* 8:247–65

Cortina LM, Magley VJ, Williams JH, Langhout RD. 2001. Incivility in the workplace: incidence and impact. *J. Occup. Health Psychol.* 6:64–80

Costa PT, McCrae RR, Dye DA. 1991. Facet scales for agreeableness and conscientiousness: a revision of the NEO personality inventory. *Personal. Individ. Differ.* 12: 887–98

Coyne I, Chong PSL, Seigne E, Randall P. 2003. Self and peer nominations of bullying: an analysis of incident rates, individual differences, and perceptions of the working environment. *Eur. J. Work Org. Psychol.* 12:209–28

Coyne I, Craig J, Chong PSL. 2004. Workplace bullying in a group context. *Br. J. Guid. Couns.* 32:301–17

Coyne I, Seigne E, Randall P. 2000. Predicting workplace victim status from personality. *Eur. J. Work Org. Psychol.* 9:335–49

Duffy MK, Ganster DC, Pagon M. 2002. Social undermining and social support in the workplace. *Acad. Manage. J.* 45:331–51

Duffy MK, Ganster DC, Shaw JD, Johnson JL, Pagon M. 2006a. The social context of undermining behavior at work. *Organ. Behav. Hum. Decis. Process.* 101:105–26

Duffy MK, Shaw JD, Scott KL, Tepper BJ. 2006b. The moderating roles of self-esteem and neuroticism. *J. Appl. Psychol.* 91:1066–77

Dupré KE, Inness M, Connelly CE, Barling J, Hoption C. 2006. Workplace aggression in teenage part-time employees. *J. Appl. Psychol.* 91:987–97

Einarsen S. 2000. Harassment and bullying at work: a review of the Scandinavian approach. *Aggress. Violent Behav.* 5:379–401

Einarsen S, Raknes BI. 1997. Harassment at work and the victimization of men. *Violence Vict.* 12:247–63

Einarsen S, Raknes BI, Matthiesen SB. 1994. Bullying and harassment at work and their relationship to work environment quality: an exploratory study. *Eur. J. Work Org. Psychol.* 4:381–401

Einarsen S, Skogstad A. 1996. Bullying at work: epidemiological findings in public and private organizations. *Eur. J. Work Org. Psychol.* 5:185–201

Felson RB, Steadman HJ. 1983. Situational factors in disputes leading to criminal violence. *Criminology* 21:59–74

Fiske ST. 2004. Intent and ordinary bias: unintended thought and social motivation create causal prejudice. *Soc. Just. Res.* 17:117–27

Fiske ST, Taylor SE. 2007. *Social Cognition: From Brains to Culture*. New York: McGraw-Hill

Fitzgerald LF. 1993. Sexual harassment—violence against women in the workplace. *Am. Psychol.* 48:1070–75

Fitzpatrick KM, Wilson M. 1999. Exposure to violence and posttraumatic stress symptomatology among abortion clinic workers. *J. Trauma. Stress* 12:227–42

Freedman SR, Enright RD. 1996. Forgiveness as an intervention goal with incest survivors. *J. Couns. Clin. Psychol.* 64:983–92

Glasø L, Matthiesen SB, Nielsen MB, Einarsen S. 2007. Do targets of workplace bullying portray a general victim personality profile? *Scand. J. Psychol.* 48:313–19

Glomb TM. 2002. Workplace anger and aggression: informing conceptual models with data from specific encounters. *J. Occup. Health Psychol.* 7:20–36

Goldberg LS, Grandey AA. 2007. Display rules versus display autonomy: emotion regulation, emotional exhaustion, and task performance in a call center simulation. *J. Occup. Health Psychol.* 12(3):301–18

Gouldner AW. 1960. The norm of reciprocity: a preliminary statement. *Am. Sociol. Rev.* 25:161–78

Grandey AA. 2004. The customer is not always right: customer aggression and emotional regulation of service employees. *J. Org. Behav.* 25:397–418

Grandey AA, Kern JH, Frone MR. 2007. Verbal abuse from outsiders versus insiders: comparing frequency, impact on emotional exhaustion, and the role of emotional labor. *J. Occup. Health Psychol.* 12(1):63–79

Greenberg J, Colquitt J. 2005. *Handbook of Organizational Justice*. Mahwah, NJ: Erlbaum

Haines VY, Marchand A, Harvey S. 2006. Crossover of workplace aggression experiences in dual-earner couples. *J. Occup. Health Psychol.* 11:305–14

Hallberg LRM, Strandmark M. 2006. Health consequences of workplace bullying: experiences from the perspective of employees in the public service sector. *Int. J. Qual. Studies Health Well.* 1:109–19

Hansen AM, Hogh A, Persson R, Karlson B, Garde AH, Orbaek P. 2006. Bullying at work, health outcomes, and physiological stress response. *J. Psychosom. Res.* 60:63–72

Harvey S, Keashly L. 2003. Predicting the risk for aggression in the workplace: risk factors, self-esteem and time at work. *Soc. Behav. Personal.* 31:807–14

Hindelang MJ, Gottfredson MR, Garofolo J. 1978. *Victims of Personal Crime: An Empirical Foundation for a Theory of Personal Victimization*. Cambridge, MA: Ballinger

Hoel H, Cooper CL, Faragher B. 2001. The experience of bullying in Great Britain: the impact of organizational status. *Eur. J. Work Org. Psychol.* 10:443–65

Hoel H, Rayner C, Cooper CL. 1999. Workplace bullying. *Int. Rev. Ind. Organ. Psychol.* 10:195–230

Hoel H, Faragher B, Cooper CL. 2004. Bullying is detrimental to health, but all bullying behaviors are not necessarily equally damaging. *Br. J. Guid. Couns.* 32:367–87

Hofstede G. 1980. *Culture's Consequences: Individual Differences in Work-Related Values*. Newbury Park, CA: Sage

Hogh A, Borg V, Mikkelsen KL. 2003. Work-related violence as a predictor of fatigue: a 5-year follow-up of the Danish work environment cohort study. *Work Stress* 17:182–94

Hogh A, Dofradottir A. 2001. Coping with bullying in the workplace. *Eur. J. Work Org. Psychol.* 10:485–95

Hogh A, Henriksson ME, Burr H. 2005. A 5-year follow-up study of aggression at work and psychological health. *Int. J. Behav. Med.* 12:256–65

Hogh A, Viitasara E. 2005. A systematic review of longitudinal studies of nonfatal workplace violence. *Eur. J. Work Org. Psychol.* 14:291–313

Hubert AB, van Veldhoven M. Risk sectors for undesirable behavior and mobbing. *Eur. J. Work Org. Psychol.* 10:415–24

Ickes W, Dugosh JW, Simpson JA, Wilson CL. 2003. Suspicious minds: the motivation to acquire relationship threatening information. *Pers. Relat.* 10:131–48

Jennifer D, Cowie H, Ananiadou K. 2003. Perceptions and experience of workplace bullying in five different working populations. *Aggress. Behav.* 29:489–96

Jockin V, Arvey RD, McGue M. 2001. Perceived victimization moderates self-reports of workplace aggression and conflict. *J. Appl. Psychol.* 86:1262–69

Kaukiainen A, Salmivalli C, Bjorkqvist K, Osterman K, Lahtinen A, et al. 2001. Overt and covert aggression in work settings in relation to the subjective well-being of employees. *Aggress. Behav.* 27:360–71

Keashly L. 1998. Emotional abuse in the workplace: conceptual and empirical issues. *J. Emot. Abuse* 1:85–117

Keashly L, Harvey S. 2005. Emotional abuse in the workplace. In *Counterproductive Work Behavior: Investigations of Actors and Targets*, ed. S Fox, PE Spector, pp. 201–35. Washington, DC: Am. Psychol. Assoc.

Keashly L, Hunter S, Harvey S. 1997. Abusive interaction and role state stressors: relative impact on student residence assistant stress and work attitudes. *Work Stress.* 11:175–85

Keashly L, Trott V, MacLean LM. 1994. Abusive behavior in the workplace: a preliminary investigation. *Violence Vict.* 9:341–57

Kivimäki M, Elovainio M, Vahtera J. 2000. Workplace bullying and sickness absence in hospital staff. *Occup. Environ. Med.* 57:656–60

Kivimaki M, Virtanen M, Vartia M, Elovainio M, Vahtera J, Keltikangas-Jarvinen L. 2003. Workplace bullying and the risk of cardiovascular disease and depression. *Occup. Environ. Med.* 60:779–83

Kramer RM. 1998. Paranoid cognition in social systems: thinking and acting in the shadow of doubt. *Personal. Soc. Psychol. Rev.* 2:251–75

Lamertz K, Aquino K. 2004. Social power, social status and perceptual similarity of workplace victimization: a social network analysis of stratification. *Hum. Relat.* 57:795–822

Lapierre LM, Spector PE, Leck JD. 2005. Sexual versus nonsexual workplace aggression and victims' overall job satisfaction: a meta-analysis. *J. Occup. Health Psychol.* 10:155–69

Lazarus RS, Folkman S. 1984. *Stress, Appraisal, and Coping*. New York: Springer

LeBlanc MM, Kelloway EK. 2002. Predictors and outcomes of workplace violence and aggression. *J. Appl. Psychol.* 87:444–53

Lee R, Brotheridge C. 2006. When prey turns predatory: workplace bullying as a predictor of counteraggression/bullying, coping, and well being. *Eur. J. Work Org. Psychol.* 15:352–77

LePine JA, Erez A, Johnson DE. 2002. A meta-analysis of the dimensionality of organizational citizenship behavior. *J. Appl. Psychol.* 87(1):52–65

Lewis D. 2004. Bullying at work: the impact of shame among university and college lecturers. *Br. J. Guid. Couns.* 32:281–99

Lewis SE, Orford JLM. 2005. Women's experiences of workplace bullying: changes in social relationships. *J. Comm. Appl. Soc.* 15:29–47

Leymann H. 1990. Mobbing and psychological terror at workplaces. *Violence Vict.* 5:119–26

Leymann H. 1996. The content and development of mobbing at work. *Eur. J. Work Org. Psychol.* 5:165–84

Leymann H, Gustavson A. 1996. Mobbing at work and the development of post-traumatic stress disorders. *Eur. J. Work Org. Psychol.* 5:251–75

Liefooghe APD, Davey KM. 2001. Accounts of workplace bullying: the role of the organization. *Eur. J. Work Org. Psychol.* 10:375–92

Matthiesen SB, Einarsen S. 2001. MMPI-2 configurations among victims of bullying at work. *Eur. J. Work Org. Psychol.* 10:467–84

Matthiesen SB, Einarsen S. 2004. Psychiatric distress and symptoms of PTSD among victims of bullying at work. *Br. J. Guid. Couns.* 32:335–56

Mikkelsen EG, Einarsen S. 2001. Bullying in Danish work-life: prevalence and health correlates. *Eur. J. Work Org. Psychol.* 10:393–413

Mikkelsen EG, Einarsen S. 2002. Basic assumptions and post-traumatic stress among victims of workplace bullying. *Eur. J. Work Org. Psychol.* 11:87–111

Mitchell MS, Ambrose ML. 2007. Abusive supervision and workplace deviance and the moderating effects of negative reciprocity beliefs. *J. Appl. Psychol.* 92:1159–68

Niedl K. 1996. Mobbing and well-being: economic and personnel development implications. *Eur. J. Work Org. Psychol.* 5:239–49

Ólafsson RF, Jóhannsdóttir HL. 2004. Coping with bullying in the workplace: the effect of gender, age and type of bullying. *Br. J. Guid. Couns.* 32:319–33

O'Leary-Kelly AM, Paetzold RL, Griffin RW. 2000. Sexual harassment as aggressive behavior: an actor-based perspective. *Acad. Manage. Rev.* 25:372–88

Olson-Buchanan JB, Boswell WR. 2008. An integrative model of experiencing and responding to mistreatment at work. *Acad. Manage. Rev.* 33:76–96

Popper K. 2002 (1959). *The Logic of Scientific Discovery*. New York: Routledge. 2nd Engl. ed.

Quine L. 2001. Workplace bullying in nurses. *J. Health Psychol.* 6:73–84

Richman JA, Flaherty A, Rospenda KM. 1996. Perceived workplace harassment experiences and problem drinking among physicians: broadening the stress/alienation paradigm. *Addiction* 91:391–403

Richman JA, Flaherty A, Rospenda KM, Christensen ML. 1992. Mental health consequences and correlates of reported medical student abuse. *J. Am. Med. Assoc.* 267:692–94

Rogers KA, Kelloway EK. 1997. Violence at work: personal and organizational outcomes. *J. Occup. Health Psychol.* 2:63–71

Rospenda KM. 2002. Workplace harassment, services utilization, and drinking outcomes. *J. Occup. Health Psychol.* 7:141–55

Rospenda KM, Richman JA, Shannon CA. 2006. Patterns of workplace harassment, gender, and use of services: an update. *J. Occup. Health Psychol.* 11:379–93

Salin D. 2001. Prevalence and forms of bullying among business professionals: a comparison of two different strategies for measuring bullying. *Eur. J. Work Org. Psychol.* 10:425–41

Salin D. 2003a. The significance of gender in the prevalence, forms and perceptions of workplace bullying. *Nord. Organ.* 5:30–50

Salin D. 2003b. Ways of explaining workplace bullying: a review of enabling, motivating and precipitating structures and processes in the work environment. *Hum. Relat.* 56:1213–32

Salmivalli C, Lagerspetz K, Björkqvist K, Österman K, Kauikianen A. 1996. Bullying as a group process: participant roles and their relations to social status within the group. *Aggress. Behav.* 22:1–15

Schafer S. 1968. *The Victim and His Criminal: A Study in Functional Responsibility*. New York: Random House

Schat ACH, Kelloway EK. 2000. Effects of perceived control on the outcomes of workplace aggression and violence. *J. Occup. Health Psychol.* 5:386–402

Schat ACH, Kelloway EK. 2003. Reducing the adverse consequences of workplace aggression and violence: the buffering effects of organizational support. *J. Occup. Health Psychol.* 8:110–22

Skogstad A, Einarsen S, Torsheim T, Aasland MS, Hetland H. 2007a. The destructiveness of laissez-faire leadership behavior. *J. Occup. Health Psychol.* 12:80–92

Skogstad A, Matthiesen SB, Einarsen S. 2007b. Organizational changes: a precursor of bullying at work. *Int. J. Org. Theory Behav.* 10:58–94

Sober E. 1981. The principle of parsimony. *Br. J. Philos. Sci.* 32(2):145–56

Stevens LE, Fiske ST. 1995. Motivation and cognition in social life: a social survival perspective. *Soc. Cogn.* 13:189–214

Strandmark MK, Hallberg LRM. 2006. The origin of workplace bullying: experiences from the perspective of bully victims in the public service sector. *J. Nurs. Manage.* 14:1–10

Struthers CW, Dupuis R, Eaton J. 2005. Promoting forgiveness among coworkers following a workplace transgression. The effects of social motivation training. *Can. J. Behav. Sci.* 37:299–308

Tehrani N. 2004. Bullying: a source of chronic post traumatic stress? *Br. J. Guid. Couns.* 32:357–466

Tepper BJ. 2000. Consequences of abusive supervision. *Acad. Manage. J.* 43:178–90

Tepper BJ. 2007. Abusive supervision in work organizations: review, synthesis, and research agenda. *J. Manage.* 33:261–89

Tepper BJ, Duffy MK, Shaw JD. 2001. Personality moderators of the relationship between abusive supervision and subordinates' resistance. *J. Appl. Psychol.* 86:974–83

Tepper BJ, Duffy MK, Henle CA, Lambert LS. 2006. Procedural injustice, victim precipitation, and abusive supervision. *Pers. Psychol.* 59:101–23

Thau S, Aquino K, Poortvliet PM. 2007. Self-defeating behaviors in organizations: the relationship between thwarted belonging and interpersonal work behaviors. *J. Appl. Psychol.* 92:840–47

Tripp TM, Bies RJ, Aquino K. 2002. Poetic justice or petty jealousy? The aesthetics of revenge. *Organ. Behav. Hum. Decis. Process.* 89:966–84

Vartia M. 1996. The sources of bullying—psychological work environment and organizational climate. *Eur. J. Work Org. Psychol.* 5:203–14

Vartia M, Hyyti J. 2002. Gender differences in workplace bullying among prison officers. *Eur. J. Work Org. Psychol.* 11:113–26

Watson D, Clark LA. 1984. Negative affectivity: the disposition to experience aversive emotional states. *Psychol. Bull.* 96:465–90

Winstanley S, Whittington R. 2002. Anxiety, burnout and coping styles in general hospital staff exposed to workplace aggression: a cyclical model of burnout and vulnerability to aggression. *Work Stress* 16:302–15

Zapf D. 1999. Organizational, work group related and personal causes of mobbing/bullying at work. *Int. J. Manpower* 20:70–85

Zapf D, Gross C. 2001. Conflict escalation and coping with workplace bullying: a replication and extension. *Eur. J. Work Org. Psychol.* 10:497–522

Zapf D, Knorz C, Kulla M. 1996. On the relationship between mobbing factors, and job content, social work environment, and health outcomes. *Eur. J. Work Org. Psychol.* 5:215–37

Zellars KL, Tepper BJ, Duffy MK. 2002. Abusive supervision and subordinate's organizational citizenship behavior. *J. Appl. Psychol.* 87:1068–76

Cumulative Indexes

Contributing Authors, Volumes 50–60

Pansky A, 51:481–537
Paradise R, 54:175–203
Park DC, 60:173–96
Parke RD, 55:365–99
Parks L, 56:571–600
Pashler H, 52:629–51
Pearce JM, 52:111–39
Peissig JJ, 58:75–96
Penn DC, 58:97–118
Pennebaker JW, 54:547–77
Penner LA, 56:365–92
Pennington BF, 60:283–306
Peplau LA, 58:405–24
Peretz I, 56:89–114
Phelps EA, 57:27–53
Phillips LA, 59:477–505
Piliavin JA, 56:365–92
Pinder CC, 56:485–516
Pittman TS, 59:361–85
Pizzagalli D, 53:545–74
Plomin R, 54:205–28
Polivy J, 53:187–213
Posluszny DM, 50:137–63
Posner MI, 58:1–23
Poulos AM, 56:207–34
Povinelli DJ, 58:97–118
Price DD, 59:565–90
Prislin R, 57:345–74
Putnam K, 53:545–74

Q

Quevedo K, 58:145–73
Quinn RE, 50:361–86

R

Rafaeli E, 54:579–616
Ratnam R, 51:699–725
Raudenbush SW, 52:501–25
Rausch JR, 59:537–63
Recanzone GH, 59:119–42
Rensink RA, 53:245–77
Reppucci ND, 50:387–418
Reuter-Lorenz P, 60:173–96
Revenson TA, 58:565–92
Rhodes G, 57:199–226
Rick S, 59:647–72
Roberts BW, 56:453–84
Roberts RD, 59:507–36
Robinson GE, 50:651–82
Robinson TE, 54:25–53
Robles TF, 53:83–107

Roediger HL III, 59:225–54
Rogoff B, 54:175–203
Rollman GB, 50:305–31
Rolls ET, 51:599–630
Rosenbaum DA, 52:453–70
Rosenthal R, 52:59–82
Rothbart MK, 58:1–23
Rourke BP, 53:309–39
Rubin KH, 60:141–71
Rubin M, 53:575–604
Runco MA, 55:657–87
Rusbult CE, 54:351–75
Russell JA, 54:329–49
Ruthruff E, 52:629–51
Rutter M, 53:463–90
Ryan RM, 52:141–66
Rynes SL, 56:571–600

S

Saab PG, 52:555–80
Sackett PR, 59:419–50
Salas E, 52:471–99
Salmon DP, 60:257–82
Sankis LM, 51:377–404
Sargis EG, 57:529–55
Saribay SA, 59:329–60
Saunders SM, 50:441–69
Saxe R, 55:87–124
Schall JD, 55:23–50
Schaller M, 55:689–714
Schaufeli WB, 52:397–422
Schippers MC, 58:515–41
Schneiderman N, 52:555–80
Schroeder DA, 56:365–92
Schultz W, 57:87–115
Schwartz MW, 51:255–77
Seeley RJ, 51:255–77
Serbin LA, 55:333–63
Seyfarth RM, 54:145–73
Shadish WR, 60:607–29
Shafir E, 53:491–517
Shaywitz BA, 59:451–75
Shaywitz SE, 59:451–75
Sherry DF, 57:167–97
Shevell SK, 59:143–66
Shiffrar M, 58:47–73
Shiner RL, 56:453–84
Shinn M, 54:427–59
Shors TJ, 57:55–85
Siegel JM, 55:125–48
Silberg J, 53:463–90

Simon AF, 51:149–69
Simonson I, 52:249–75
Simonton DK, 54:617–40
Sincharoen S, 57:585–611
Skinner EA, 58:119–44
Skitka LJ, 57:529–55
Smetana JG, 57:255–84
Snyder DK, 57:317–44
Snyder M, 50:273–303
Solomon KO, 51:121–47
Spears R, 53:161–86
Sporer AK, 60:229–55
Staddon JER, 54:115–44
Stanton AL, 58:565–92
Staudinger UM, 50:471–507
Steel GD, 51:227–53
Steinberg L, 52:83–110
Stewart AJ, 55:519–44
Stewart MO, 57:285–315
Stickgold R, 57:139–66
Strunk D, 57:285–315
Stuewig J, 58:345–72
Stukas AA Jr, 50:273–303
Stuss DT, 53:401–33
Sue S, 60:525–48
Suedfeld P, 51:227–53
Suh EM, 53:133–60
Sullivan JL, 50:625–50
Sutter ML, 59:119–42

T

Tangney JP, 58:345–72
Tarr MJ, 58:75–96
Tees RC, 50:509–35
Tennen H, 58:565–92
Thau S, 60:717–41
Thompson RF, 56:1–23
Tindale RS, 55:623–55
Tolan P, 57:557–83
Toohey SM, 54:427–59
Tourangeau R, 55:775–801
Transue JE, 50:625–50
Treat TA, 50:215–41
Triandis HC, 53:133–60
Trickett EJ, 60:395–419
Tulving E, 53:1–25
Tyler TR, 57:375–400

U

Uleman JS, 59:329–60

V

Valley KL, 51:279–314
van Knippenberg D, 58:515–41
Van Lange PAM, 54:351–75
Velleman PF, 52:305–35
Volkmar F, 56:315–36

W

Wahlsten D, 50:599–624
Wainer H, 52:305–35
Walker BM, 58:453–77
Walker E, 55:401–30
Walker MP, 57:139–66
Walumbwa FO, 60:421–49
Warriner EM, 53:309–39
Watkins LR, 51:29–57
Weber EU, 60:53–85

Weber TJ, 60:421–49
Wegner DM, 51:59–91
Weick KE, 50:361–86
Weinman J, 59:477–505
Weiss H, 53:279–307
Weisz JR, 56:337–63
Wells GL, 54:277–95
Welsh DP, 60:631–52
Wenzlaff RM, 51:59–91
Werker JF, 50:509–35
Whisman MA, 57:317–44
Widiger TA, 51:377–404
Wigfield A, 53:109–32
Williams KD, 58:425–52
Willis H, 53:575–604
Wilson TD, 55:493–518
Wingate LR, 56:287–314
Winter DA, 58:453–77

Wixted JT, 55:235–69
Wood JM, 53:519–43
Wood W, 51:539–70
Woods SC, 51:255–77
Woolard JL, 50:387–418
Wulfeck B, 52:369–96

Y

Yuille A, 55:271–304

Z

Zane N, 60:525–48
Zatorre RJ, 56:89–114
Zimmer-Gembeck MJ,
    58:119–44

Chapter Titles, Volumes 50–60

Marketing and Consumer Behavior

Consumer Research: In Search of Identity	I Simonson, Z Carmon, R Dhar, A Drolet, SM Nowlis	52:249–75
Consumer Psychology: Categorization, Inferences, Affect, and Persuasion	B Loken	57:453–85
Conceptual Consumption	D Ariely, MI Norton	60:475–99

Organizational Psychology or Organizational Behavior

Organizational Behavior: Affect in the Workplace	A Brief, H Weiss	53:279–307

Cognition in Organizations

Cognition in Organizations	GP Hodgkinson, MP Healey	59:387–417

Groups and Teams

Teams in Organizations: From Input-Process-Output Models to IMOI Models	DR Ilgen, JR Hollenbeck, M Johnson, D Jundt	56:517–43
Work Group Diversity	D van Knippenberg, MC Schippers	58:515–41

Leadership

Presidential Leadership	GR Goethals	56:545–70
Leadership: Current Theories, Research, and Future Directions	BJ Avolio, FO Walumbwa, TJ Weber	60:421–49

Work Motivation

Work Motivation Theory and Research at the Dawn of the Twenty-First Century	GP Latham, CC Pinder	56:485–516

Perception

High-Level Scene Perception	JM Henderson, A Hollingworth	50:243–71
Influences on Infant Speech Processing: Toward a New Synthesis	JF Werker, RC Tees	50:509–35

Personality

Scientific and Social Significance of Assessing Individual Differences: "Sinking Shafts at a Few Critical Points"	D Lubinski	51:405–44

Timely Topics

Vision

ANNUAL REVIEWS
Intelligent Synthesis of the Scientific Literature

Annual Reviews – Your Starting Point for Research Online
http://arjournals.annualreviews.org

- Over 1150 Annual Reviews volumes—more than 26,000 critical, authoritative review articles in 35 disciplines spanning the Biomedical, Physical, and Social sciences—available online, including all Annual Reviews back volumes, dating to 1932

- Current individual subscriptions include seamless online access to full-text articles, PDFs, Reviews in Advance (as much as 6 months ahead of print publication), bibliographies, and other supplementary material in the current volume and the prior 4 years' volumes

- All articles are fully supplemented, searchable, and downloadable—see http://psych.annualreviews.org

- Access links to the reviewed references (when available online)

- Site features include customized alerting services, citation tracking, and saved searches

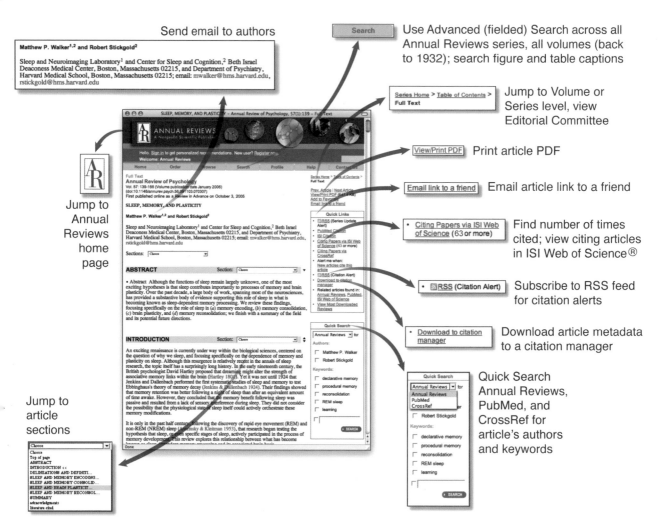

Send email to authors

Use Advanced (fielded) Search across all Annual Reviews series, all volumes (back to 1932); search figure and table captions

Jump to Volume or Series level, view Editorial Committee

Print article PDF

Email article link to a friend

Find number of times cited; view citing articles in ISI Web of Science®

Subscribe to RSS feed for citation alerts

Download article metadata to a citation manager

Quick Search Annual Reviews, PubMed, and CrossRef for article's authors and keywords

Jump to Annual Reviews home page

Jump to article sections